Introducing Philosophy Through Film

INTRODUCING PHILOSOPHY THROUGH FILM

KEY TEXTS, DISCUSSION, AND FILM SELECTIONS

Edited by

Richard Fumerton

and

Diane Jeske

WILEY-BLACKWELL

A John Wiley & Sons, Ltd., Publication

Registered Office
John Wiley & Sons Ltd, The Atrium, Southern Gate, Chichester, West Sussex, PO19 8SQ, United Kingdom

Editorial Offices
350 Main Street, Malden, MA 02148-5020, USA
9600 Garsington Road, Oxford, OX4 2DQ, UK
The Atrium, Southern Gate, Chichester, West Sussex, PO19 8SQ, UK

For details of our global editorial offices, for customer services, and for information about how to apply for permission to reuse the copyright material in this book please see our website at www.wiley.com/wiley-blackwell.

Library of Congress Cataloging-in-Publication Data
Introducing philosophy through film : key texts, discussion, and film selections / edited by Richard Fumerton and Diane Jeske.
        p. cm.
    Includes bibliographical references and index.
    ISBN 978-1-4051-7102-1 (hardcover : alk. paper) – ISBN 978-1-4051-7101-4 (pbk. : alk. paper)
1. Philosophy.   2. Film criticism.   I. Fumerton, Richard A., 1949–   II. Jeske, Diane, 1967–
    BD31.I58 2010
    190–dc22

                                                                                            2008045562

A catalogue record for this book is available from the British Library.

Set in 9.5/11.5pt Minion by Graphicraft Limited, Hong Kong
Printed in Singapore by Ho Printing Singapore Pte Ltd

06   2014

For Alexandra Rose (R.F.)
For Sara, Emma, and Kate (D.J.)

Contents

Part V: Philosophy of Time   469

Part VI: Free Will, Foreknowledge, and Determinism   503

Preface

In this book we try to combine all the virtues of a serious introductory anthology of classical and contemporary readings with a novel pedagogical tool that will engage and excite students who have never before been exposed to academic philosophy. Indeed, we think that the book will so captivate the imagination of the philosophically uninitiated that it may find an audience in high schools. As it is, a number of high schools already experiment with philosophy as an elective. The availability of a text like this might make the option even more attractive.

We have discussed this project with a great many philosophers at all stages of their careers. Without exception, they have been excited about this approach to teaching philosophy. Many indicated that they have thought about using films in their classes, or even have shown the occasional film, but are reluctant to put the time and effort into compiling a more extensive and manageable list of film clips. We recently co-taught a summer course in which we put together scenes from many of the films we outline in our table of contents. It was the most successful introductory course we have ever taught. In particular, we have never seen students so animated in discussion. Even those students who were clearly by nature shy quickly became active participants.

From the beginnings of analytic philosophy, thought experiments have been an indispensable tool in the evaluation of philosophical theories about the nature of knowledge, perception and its relation to the physical world, the self and its identity through time, justice and morality, space and time, free will and determinism, and the existence and nature of God. But we have found that our students sometimes find the philosopher's description of hypothetical situations incomplete, remote, and artificial. For many students, these descriptions lack a kind of context, detail, vivacity, intimacy, and realism that would make it easier to test "intuitions" about what we would or wouldn't say in describing the situation. More and more frequently we have found ourselves appealing to various films in order to breathe life into the less colorful philosophical appeals to possibilities. We have seen students get excited about old philosophical controversies when they can relate them to movies in which they have become completely engrossed and which they have already often discussed with friends. New technology now makes it feasible to combine a text of classical and contemporary philosophical discussions of fundamental problems in philosophy with introductions that include chapter-by-chapter discussion of clips of popular films, films that illustrate vividly some of the crucial possibilities that are critical to philosophical arguments and positions raised in the readings.

Part Introductions

There are introductions to each of the Parts contained in the anthology, and each Part ends with a list of study questions tying readings to film. In these introductions, we do not try to provide detailed summaries of either the articles or the films contained in these sections. Rather, we try to give the reader a feel for the philosophical landscape. We try to outline in an accessible way some of the main philosophical issues arising in each area, referring along the way to articles or films that seem relevant to those issues. In discussing the films (particularly in discussion questions), we often make reference by DVD chapter to specific scenes that seem to us philosophically interesting or thought-provoking. We sometimes give a sketch of the plot line, but given the widespread popularity of some of these films it didn't seem profitable to give anything other than a superficial overview. The showing of the film or the philosophically relevant parts of the film will, by itself, set the relevant stage.

About the Use of DVDs

Initially, our hope was that we could arrange for an instructor's copy of the book to come with a DVD containing philosophically relevant edited scenes from the movies listed in the table of contents. While some films are in the public domain, copyright issues concerning the use of more recent films (some of which might be of most interest to students) made the idea of an instructor's DVD impractical. It still might be possible to post onto a course website clips of films (and certainly links to sites such as YouTube that contain clips like *Mr Deity*). Instructors should thoroughly research copyright issues, however, before generating such sites.

All the relevant films referred to in this anthology can be obtained easily. Usually, they will be available to the instructor in the university's library, and, in any event, are easily accessed at any movie rental. When we taught our *Philosophy Through Film* course recently, we had no difficulty finding all the DVDs we wanted to use. In some cases, the film clips we recommend using will stand on their own. In others, students will rely on plot summaries provided in the introductions to various sections of the book to provide context for the clip. In still other cases, it may be important for students to see the entire film. This is particularly true of the films used in the section in the anthology on personal relationships and their implications for morality (Part IV, section B "Obligations to Intimates"). So, for example, the nuanced relationships in *The Third Man*, *Casablanca*, and *High Noon* can best be appreciated only by those who have seen the film in its entirety. This being so, the instructor can arrange for showings outside of class and can use relevant clips in class to emphasize points drawn from the films.

As indicated above, our introductions to various sections of the book will often include specific advice concerning the parts of films that we think should be used in class. DVDs are divided into "chapters" that are easily accessible on the DVD "menu." In the introduction to Part II, "The Problem of Perception," we discuss, for example, and suggest showing, chapter 23 of *Total Recall*, the scene in which the hero purports to have a refutation of the possibility that he is dreaming. These detailed suggestions about which chapters of DVDs seem particularly relevant to the philosophical issues at hand are intended to save instructors time in making decisions about how to use the DVDs in classroom presentations. But they are, of course, only suggestions. Again, our own experience suggests that one can most profitably use a variety of approaches in exposing students to the relevant films. Assignments outside of class (including arranged showings), the use of clips in class, and perhaps, occasionally, a long showing in a given class, vary presentation in ways that are both interesting and pedagogically desirable.

Acknowledgments

We would like to thank Jeff Dean for his support and enthusiasm for this project. We also received helpful comments from a number of anonymous reviewers for Blackwell. Special thanks are owed to Heather Libby and Chris Lammer-Heindel, who helped review and revise earlier drafts of introductions and who also helped select film chapters and design study questions. Allison Roggenburg was of great help finding and organizing the various readings we chose to include in the anthology. We have received (and continue to receive) countless suggestions of philosophically interesting films from colleagues and former students, and for that we thank them very much.

Source Acknowledgments

The editor and publisher gratefully acknowledge the permission granted to reproduce the copyright material in this book:

1 René Descartes, *Meditation I* and excerpt from *Meditation VI*, from *The Philosophical Works of Descartes*, vol. 1, trans. E. Haldane and G. Ross (Cambridge: Cambridge University Press, 1967). © 1967 by Cambridge University Press. Reproduced with permission from Cambridge University Press.

2 John Locke, "Some Further Considerations Concerning Our Simple Ideas of Sensation." Chapter VIII from *An Essay Concerning Human Understanding*. Available at http://ebooks.adelaide.edu/au/1/locke/john/181u/B2.8.html. Accessed 2/19/2008.

3 George Berkeley, *Three Dialogues Between Hylas and Philonous* (Chicago: The Open Court Publishing Co., 1906).

4 David Hume, "Of the Sceptical and Other Systems of Philosophy," from David Hume, *A Treatise on Human Nature*, ed. L. A. Selby-Bigge (Oxford: Clarendon Press, 1896).

5 A. J. Ayer, "The Self and the Common World," from *Language, Truth and Logic* (New York: Dover, 1952), pp. 120–32. © 1952 by Alfred Jules Ayer. Reprinted with permission from Victor Gollancz, an imprint of The Orion Publishing Group.

6 Hilary Putnam, "Brains in a Vat," from *Reason, Truth and History* (Cambridge: Cambridge University Press, 1981), pp. 1–21. © 1981 by Cambridge University Press. Reproduced with permission from the author and Cambridge University Press.

7 Richard Fumerton, "The Structure of Skeptical Arguments and its Metaepistemological Implications," from *Metaepistemology and Skepticism* (Lanham, MD: Rowman & Littlefield, 1995), pp. 29–54. © 1995 by Rowman & Littlefield Publishers, Inc. Reprinted with permission from Rowman & Littlefield.

8 Robert Nozick, "The Experience Machine," from *Anarchy, State and Utopia* (Oxford: Blackwell Publishing, 1980), pp. 42–5.

9 René Descartes, *Meditation II* from *The Philosophical Works of Descartes*, vol. 1, trans. E. Haldane and G. Ross (Cambridge: Cambridge University Press, 1967). © 1967 by Cambridge University Press. Reproduced with permission from Cambridge University Press.

10 Gilbert Ryle, "Descartes' Myth," from *The Concept of Mind* (Chicago: University of Chicago Press, 1984), pp. 11–24. © 1949 by Gilbert Ryle. Reprinted by permission of the Principal, Fellows and Scholars of Hertford College in the University of Oxford and Taylor & Francis Books UK.

11 J. J. C. Smart, "Sensations and Brain Processes." *The Philosophical Review* 68, no. 2 (April 1959), pp. 141–56. © 1959 by

Duke University Press. All rights reserved. Used by permission of the publisher.

12 Thomas Nagel, "What Is It Like to Be a Bat?" *The Philosophical Review* 83, no. 4 (October 1974), pp. 435–50. © 1974 by Thomas Nagel. Reprinted by permission of the author.

13 Frank Jackson, "What Mary Didn't Know." *The Journal of Philosophy* 83, no. 5 (May 1986), pp. 291–5. © 1986 by The Journal of Philosophy, Inc. Reprinted with permission from the author and The Journal of Philosophy.

14 John Searle, "Minds, Brains and Programs." *Behavioral and Brain Sciences* 3 (1980), pp. 417–57. © 1980 by Cambridge University Press. Reproduced with permission from the author and Cambridge University Press.

15 David Lewis, "Mad Pain and Martian Pain." *Philosophical Papers*, vol. 1. Oxford: Oxford Unviersity Press, 1983. Copyright © 1983 by David Lewis. Reprinted with permission from Oxford University Press.

16 Paul M. Churchland, "Eliminative Materialism," from *Matter and Consciousness: A Contemporary Introduction to the Philosophy of Mind*, rev. edn. (Cambridge, MA: MIT Press, 1994), pp. 43–9. © 1988 by Massachusetts Institute of Technology. Reprinted with permission from The MIT Press.

17 John Locke, "Of Identity and Diversity," from John Locke, *An Essay Concerning Human Understanding*, ed. Alexander Fraser (Oxford: Clarendon Press, 1894).

18 Bernard Williams, "The Self and the Future." *The Philosophical Review* LXXIX (1970), pp. 161–80. © 1970, the Sage School of Philosophy at Cornell University. All rights reserved. Used by permission of the publisher, Duke University Press.

19 Derek Parfit, *Reasons and Persons* (Oxford: Oxford University Press, 1984), pp. 82–91. © 1984 by Derek Parfit. Reprinted with permission from Oxford University Press.

20 John Perry, "The Second Night," from *A Dialogue on Personal Identity and Immortality* (Indianapolis: Hackett Publishing, 1978), pp. 1, 19–36. © 1978 by John Perry. Reprinted by permission of Hackett

Publishing Company, Inc. All rights reserved.

21 David Hume, "On the Immortality of the Soul," from *Essays on Suicide, and The Immortality of the Soul* (London, 1783).

22 John Stuart Mill, *Utilitarianism* (Garden City, NY: Dolphin Books, 1961), pp. 406–28, 438–45.

23 Immanuel Kant, *Groundwork for the Metaphysics of Morals*, trans. Arnulf Zweig, ed. Thomas E. Hill, Jr. and Arnulf Zweig (Oxford: Oxford University Press, 2002). © 2002 by Thomas E. Hill, Jr. and Arnulf Zweig. Reprinted with permission from Oxford University Press.

24 W. D. Ross, "What Makes Right Acts Right?" from *The Right and the Good* (Indianapolis: Hackett Publishing, 1930), pp. 16–34, 39–41. © 1930 by Oxford University Press. Reprinted with permission from Oxford University Press.

25 Bernard Williams, "A Critique of Utilitarianism," from J. J. C. Smart and Bernard Williams, *Utilitarianism: For and Against* (Cambridge: Cambridge University Press, 1973), pp. 82–117. © 1973 by Cambridge University Press. Reproduced with permission from Cambridge University Press.

26 J. J. C. Smart, "An Outline of a System of Utilitarian Ethics," from J. J. C. Smart and Bernard Williams, *Utilitarianism: For and Against* (Cambridge: Cambridge University Press, 1973), pp. 82–117. © 1973 by Cambridge University Press. Reproduced with permission from Cambridge University Press.

27 Shelly Kagan, "Intending Harm," from *The Limits of Morality* (Oxford: Oxford University Press, 1989), pp. 165–82. © 1989 by Shelly Kagan. Reprinted with permission from Oxford University Press.

28 *United States v. Holmes.* 26 F. Cas. 360 (1842).

29 *The Queen v. Dudley and Stephens* 14 Q.B.D. 273 (1884).

30 Thomas Nagel, "War and Massacre," from *Mortal Questions* (Cambridge: Cambridge University Press, 1979), pp. 53–74. © 1979 by Cambridge University Press. Reproduced with permission from the author and Cambridge University Press.

31 Aristotle, *Nicomachean Ethics*, trans. and ed. Roger Crisp (Cambridge: Cambridge University Press, 2000), pp. 143–53. © 2000 by Cambridge University Press. Reproduced with permission from the translator and Cambridge University Press.

32 C. D. Broad, "Self and Others" (1953), from *Broad's Critical Essays in Moral Philosophy* (1971), pp. 262–82.

33 Christina Hoff Sommers, "Filial Morality." *The Journal of Philosophy* 83, no. 8 (August 1986), pp. 439–56. © 1986 by The Journal of Philosophy, Inc. Reprinted with permission from the author and The Journal of Philosophy.

34 Peter Railton, "Alienation, Consequentialism, and the Demands of Morality." *Philosophy and Public Affairs* 13, no. 2 (Spring 1984), pp. 134–71. © 1984 by Philosophy and Public Affairs. Reprinted with permission from Blackwell Publishing.

35 Diane Jeske and Richard Fumerton, "Relatives and Relativism." *Philosophical Studies* 87 (1997), pp. 143–57. © 1997 by Springer Netherlands. Reprinted with permission from Springer.

36 Diane Jeske, "Families, Friends, and Special Obligations." *Canadian Journal of Philosophy* 28, no. 4 (December 1998), pp. 527–56. © 1997 by Philosophical Studies. Reprinted by permission of the University of Calgary Press.

37 Nel Noddings, "An Ethic of Caring," from *Caring: A Feminine Approach to Ethics and Moral Education*, 2nd edn. (Berkeley: University of California Press, 2003), pp. 79–103. © 2003 by The Regents of the University of California. Reprinted with permission from the author and The University of California Press.

38 Roderick M. Chisholm and Richard Taylor, "Making Things to Have Happened." *Analysis* 20, no. 4 (March 1960), pp. 73–8. © 1960 by Analysis. Reprinted with permission from Blackwell Publishing.

39 From Richard Taylor, *Metaphysics*, 4th edn. (Englewood Cliffs, NJ: Prentice Hall, 1992), pp. 68–74, 77–87. © 1992 by Prentice Hall, Inc. Reprinted by permission of Pearson Education, Inc., Upper Saddle River, NJ.

40 David Lewis, "The Paradoxes of Time Travel." *American Philosophical Quarterly* 13, no. 2 (April 1976), pp. 145–52. © 1976 by American Philosophical Quarterly. Reprinted with permission from American Philosophical Quarterly.

41 From *Aristotle's Categories and Propositions (De Interpretatione)*, trans. H. G. Apostle (Des Moines, IA: Peripatetic Press, 1980), pp. 34–7. © 1980 by H. G. Apostle. Reprinted by permission of Peripatetic Press.

42 David Hume, "Of Liberty and Necessity," from David Hume, *A Treatise on Human Nature*, ed. L. A. Selby-Bigge (Oxford: Clarendon Press, 1896).

43 John Hospers, "Meaning and Free Will." *Philosophy and Phenomenological Research* 10, no. 3 (March 1950), pp. 307–30. © 1950 by Philosophy and Phenomenological Research. Reprinted with permission from Blackwell Publishing.

44 J. R. Lucas, "Determinism," from *The Freedom of the Will* (Oxford: Oxford University Press, 1970), pp. 51–66. © 1970 by Oxford University Press. Reprinted with permission from Blackwell Publishing.

45 Harry G. Frankfurt, "Freedom of the Will and the Concept of a Person." *The Journal of Philosophy* 68, no. 1 (January 1971), pp. 5–20. © 1971 by The Journal of Philosophy, Inc. Reprinted with permission from the author and The Journal of Philosophy.

46 The M'Naghten Rules, House of Lords, 1843.

47 The Insanity Defense, The American Law Institute, 1956.

48 Joel Feinberg, "What Is So Special About Mental Illness?" from *Doing and Deserving* (Princeton: Princeton University Press, 1970), pp. 272–92. © 1970 by Joel Feinberg. Reprinted by kind permission of Betty Feinberg.

49 From Blaise Pascal, *Pensées*, ed. and trans. Roger Ariew (Indianapolis: Hackett Publishing Co, 2005), pp. 211–15. © 2005 by Hackett Publishing Company, Inc. Reprinted by permission of Hackett Publishing Company, Inc. All rights reserved.

50 Anselm, "The Ontological Argument," from *Proslogion: With the Replies of Gaunilo and Anselm*, trans. Thomas Williams

(Indianapolis: Hackett Publishing Co., 2001), pp. 7–9. Translation © 2001 by Hackett Publishing Company, Inc. Reprinted by permission of Hackett Publishing Company, Inc. All rights reserved.

51   From William L. Rowe, *Philosophy of Religion: An Introduction*, 4th edn. (Belmont, CA: Wadsworth Thomas Learning, 2007), pp. 19, 21–6, 36, 54–66, 68. © 2007 by Wadsworth, a part of Cengage Learning, Inc. Reproduced by permission. www.cengage.com/permissions.

52   J. L. Mackie, "Evil and Omnipotence." *Mind* 64, no. 254 (April 1955), pp. 200–12.

© 1955 by the Mind Association. Reprinted with permission from Oxford Unviersity Press.

53   Bertrand Russell, "Why I Am Not A Christian," from *Bertrand Russell on God and Religion*, ed. Al Seckel (Buffalo, NY: Prometheus Books, 1986), pp. 57–71. © 1957, 1985 by George Allen & Unwin Ltd. All rights reserved. Reprinted with the permission of Simon & Schuster Adult Publishing Group, Taylor & Francis Books UK, and The Bertrand Russell Peace Foundation Ltd, from "Why I Am Not A Christian", by Bertrand Russell.

Part I

Introduction: Philosophical Analysis, Argument, and the Relevance of Thought Experiments

Films:
Monty Python, "The Argument Skit"
Pulp Fiction
Seinfeld episode: *The Soup*

Introduction

Analytic Philosophy and the Importance of Imagination

If there is one uncontroversial claim one can make about the nature of philosophy, it is that almost every other philosophical issue is highly controversial. Philosophers don't agree with each other about much, and that includes what it is that they are doing when they do philosophy. The English-speaking world is dominated, to a large extent, by what goes under the label of analytic philosophy. And to the extent that philosophers are willing to describe themselves as analytic philosophers, it is safe to presume that they think analysis is an important part of what they do when they philosophize. But they don't agree with each other either about what analysis is, or even *what* it is that they are analyzing. Some talk about analyzing the meanings of words or sentences. Others think that they are analyzing concepts or ideas. Still others think of themselves as analyzing properties, states of affairs, or facts. On at least one classical view, whatever it is that one is analyzing, the process of analysis involves breaking the complex down into parts. So, for example, if one is trying to analyze knowledge, one will try to break down knowledge into its constituent "parts." The linguistic philosopher might think of this as breaking down the *meaning* of a sentence "S knows that P" into sentences each of which captures a part of the meaning of the sentence to be analyzed

and all of which together exhaust the meaning. Non-linguistic philosophers might insist that they are trying to break down the *idea* of someone's knowing a proposition into simpler ideas out of which the first is composed. Still others will insist that they are taking the *property* of knowing and breaking it down into its constitutive properties. But however analytic philosophers think of analysis and its objects, there has historically been rather widespread agreement that successful completion of the task requires finding conditions that are individually conceptually necessary, and jointly conceptually sufficient for the application of a concept. What does this mean?

As a first stab we might try the following: P is conceptually *necessary* for Q when it is absolutely impossible for Q to be true while P is false. P is conceptually *sufficient* for Q when it is absolutely impossible for P to be true while Q is false. This preliminary attempt to make clear the relevant senses of necessity and sufficiency is itself problematic in that it relies on an as yet unanalyzed concept of absolute impossibility. The impossibility in question is something very strong indeed. It may be impossible in some sense for an infant to lift a car, but historically most philosophers haven't thought that this kind of *causal* impossibility is the sort relevant to evaluating philosophical theses about necessary connections. Again, historically it has seemed that *conceivability* is at least one relevant test of the sort of possibility and impossibility we are claiming when we offer philosophical analyses. So if we think we can even *conceive* of, or *imagine*, a situation in which P is true while Q is false, then we won't be entitled to claim that Q is a conceptually necessary condition for P. The relevance of conceivability might be seen most clearly if we think of analysis as *conceptual* analysis. If someone tells us that the very idea of something being F just includes as a constituent the idea of being G, how would it be possible for us to form the thought that something is F without its being G? Thinking that it is F is just supposed to include thinking that it is G. One can get a somewhat comical take on the role of thought experiments in evaluating the meaning of a term or concept by looking at the discussion in *Pulp Fiction* over the nature of a sexual act (chapters 3–4) or by reviewing the disagreement over what constitutes a meal in the Seinfeld episode (*The Soup*).

Analytic philosophy today is more divided than ever over how to think of philosophical analysis. We have focused above on meaning or conceptual analysis. For a variety of reasons, many contemporary philosophers want to model philosophical analysis in such a way that there is a greater role to be played by empirical discovery. Just as one can discover through experience that water is H_2O, one might be able to rely on science, this philosopher argues, to help tell us, for example, what a person is, or what a person's survival consists in. Even these philosophers, however, are interested *as philosophers* in the *essential* properties of various kinds of things. An essential property of a *particular* thing is a property the thing can't lose without ceasing to exist. An essential property of a *kind* of thing is a property a thing must have to be of that kind. So most of the philosophers urging us to think of analysis this way will claim that having a certain molecular structure is an essential property of water. Its odor, its color, its taste – these are properties that water can lose without ceasing to be water. Conversely, there can be kinds of liquids that look, smell, and taste just like water without being water – they might have the "wrong" microstructure to be of that kind. So if (and this is a big "if") a correct philosophical analysis of water includes reference to its molecular structure then it would seem that at least some analyses can be discovered only through investigation of the world.

Now philosophers of this stripe owe us an account of how one goes about determining what is or is not an essential property (of either a thing or a kind of thing). Often, however, the essentialist (as we might call this philosopher) relies on our "intuitions" – intuitions that seem guided, once again, by thought experiments of the sort discussed in connection with conceptual analysis.

In any event, once one convinces oneself that analysis involves coming up with necessary and sufficient conditions for the truth of assertions employing certain fundamentally interesting philosophical concepts, and one convinces oneself that a relevant test for the plausibility of such claims involves considering what one can consistently conceive or imagine, one sees the relevance of thought experiments. In Aristophanes' *The Birds*, some philosophers were sitting around arguing about how to define or analyze being human. One came up with the idea that we could understand being human in terms of being a featherless biped. In response to this suggestion, a member of the group left, plucked a chicken, and threw it into the circle formed by the discussants. The wag offered what we call a *counterexample*. Plucked chickens may walk on two legs and be featherless, but they are certainly not humans. Being a featherless biped is not *sufficient* for being a human. Though it would have involved considerably more violence, the same critic might have lopped the legs off some human and displayed the poor creature as decisive evidence that walking on two legs is not *necessary* for being human either. The counterexample offered by the character in the play involved actual situations, but clearly one of them needn't have gone to the trouble of plucking a chicken to convince the others that there is more to being human than having no feathers and walking on two legs. It would have been enough to get the participants in the discussion to *imagine* a chicken without feathers to get them to realize that the proposed definition was inadequate.

Another example of the role of thought experiments might be helpful. We earlier noted that philosophers have tried to define or analyze knowledge. Many in the twentieth century supposed that we could analyze knowledge as true belief supported by strong evidence. A kind of counterexample presented by Edmund Gettier (and earlier by Bertrand Russell) seems to present a serious problem for such a view. Let us use Russell's thought experiment. Imagine that someone is looking at a clock that indicates that it is 3.00 p.m. when in fact it is. Unbeknownst to the person looking at the clock, however, the clock is broken and it is a happy coincidence, therefore, that the observer forms a true belief. What we seem to have is a true belief supported by perfectly good evidence which nevertheless doesn't constitute knowledge.

The above thought experiments are simple enough that they can be presented in a relatively straightforward manner. Other thought experiments, however, can become considerably more complicated and, interestingly enough, variations on them have often been central to the plots of films. By way of arguing that our sense experience never guarantees the truth of any belief we form about the external world, some philosophers have appealed to the possibility that we are always dreaming, the victims of demonic machination, or other forms of consistent hallucination. Episodes of *Star Trek*, and such well-known films as *Total Recall* and *The Matrix* have exploited just such possibilities. We have also discovered that the films themselves give rise to interestingly new philosophical issues. So, for example, in *The Matrix* the plot seems to presuppose that there is some sort of causal interaction between characters who are "sharing" a hallucinatory experience. Indeed, there is often violent conflict with winners and losers, and the skill of the participants in the conflict is supposed to determine the outcome. It is not at all clear just exactly how one is supposed to conceptualize these possibilities. Questioning the intelligibility of the plot leads to interesting discussions of perception, mind, and causation.

Philosophers trying to figure out the nature of persons have wondered whether we can "separate" a person into physical and mental components. They have wondered, indeed, whether it makes sense to suppose that a person could "leave" his or her body and continue to exist as the same person. If we decide that we can, in principle, separate our existence from the existence of our body, then we need to figure out what is necessary and sufficient for our continued existence. What role does memory play? Personality? Beliefs? In trying to answer some of these questions about mind and body, philosophers offer descriptions of all sorts of hypothetical situations, many of which have been entertainingly and, some would argue, convincingly depicted (as genuine possibilities) in film. The intelligibility of "movement" of a person from one body to another is a presupposition of the film *Heaven Can Wait* (a remake of *Here Comes Mister Jordan*). That movie ends with a decidedly Cartesian rather than a Lockean or Humean view about what is necessary for the survival of a person through time (see Part III). The central character is supposed to survive despite having a new body, no memory of his prior existence, and all the memories of the supposedly now dead person whose identity he has assumed. All, it seems, that could remain is a mysterious "soul" whose persistence, Locke thought, even if intelligible, seems unrelated to our ordinary concepts of and judgments about persistence of persons through time. For Locke, memory is the "glue" that joins temporal "stages" to form a single temporally extended person. While *Heaven Can Wait* challenges the *necessity* of the "thread" of memory for an individual's identity through time, *Multiplicity* and *The Sixth Day* make vivid the cloning thought experiments that are supposed to present difficulty for the idea that a continuity of memory is *sufficient* for the identity of an individual through time. Throughout most of *The Sixth Day*, the central character gave us every indication of being Adam Gibson. *He* had every reason to believe he was Adam Gibson. But in the surprising plot twist, his identity becomes highly problematic. Either he wasn't the person he had every reason to believe he was, or there was more than one Adam Gibson.

The field of ethics is particularly fertile ground for the use of film as a way of generating the kind of moral dilemmas about which philosophers worry in evaluating various ethical theories. One of the most influential sorts of objection to act consequentialist views of morality (crudely, views according to which what one ought to do is a function of what maximizes value) is argument by counterexample. Thus the act consequentialist is supposed to be committed to the view that apparently morally abominable actions would in fact be morally permissible. Given the act consequentialist's views, it seems that no kind of action (killing innocents, framing people for crimes, lying, adultery) is such that it is always wrong. The plots of many movies focus on just the sorts of controversies that are raised by consequentialist reasoning. The classic *Abandon Ship!* was based on a true story of the captain of a lifeboat who, on consequentialist grounds, made some highly controversial decisions about who would live and who would die. *Saving Private Ryan* centers around a "rescue" mission of highly dubious consequentialist value and would provide a wonderful opportunity to test intuitions about when consequentialist reasoning should prevail. In the movie *Fail Safe*, the President's decision to obliterate New York City in an effort to avoid global nuclear war is another example of a moral conclusion that might seem justified on utilitarian grounds, but that would no doubt strike many of our students as highly questionable. The debate over consequentialism is a centerpiece of much disagreement about the nature and morality of punishment. The film *Minority Report* makes vivid controversies over whether it is an individual's past actions that alone justify punishment or whether one can use the power of the state to pre-empt future misdeeds. Although the movie involves exotic possibilities of precognition, our own knowledge of the likelihood of recidivism on the part of, say, child molesters is not so very different from the psychics' ability to predict future crimes.

The debate over consequentialism is not, of course, the only issue in ethical theory. Many ethicists recently have become increasingly interested in the significance that intimate relations to others should play in ethical decision-making. Do we have special obligations to friends, lovers, family members, fellow citizens, etc., that can override other sorts of reasons we might have to act or refrain from acting in certain ways? Films like *Casablanca, The Music Box, Nick of Time*, and *The Third Man*, in addition to being wonderful films, are excellent vehicles for introducing a nuanced discussion of these sorts of issues.

Philosophy of space and time, though perhaps not one of the most central areas of philosophy, is one that raises fascinating questions about possibilities that have been explored repeatedly in highly entertaining films. The issues raised by these films are particularly intriguing and engaging. The possibility of time travel lies at the heart of *Planet of the Apes, Back to the Future, Frequency, Somewhere in Time*, and *A Sound of Thunder*. Such films provide a particularly good opportunity to question more carefully the extent to which we can rely on our initial impressions about what is or is not conceivable. While we seem to be able to follow the plots of such movies in a way that suggests that the stories they tell are at least consistent, there are notorious paradoxes that arise in connection with time travel (some of which actually come up in the films) that might lead one to doubt one's initial impression of coherence.

It is more difficult to find films that bear directly on issues in philosophy of religion. It hardly seems worthwhile to view films that depict evil, for example, when all we need to do is read a newspaper to convince ourselves that apparent evil exists. Nevertheless, there is an interesting and surprisingly underemphasized issue that needs to be addressed in considering the implications of the existence of evil for the plausibility of the hypothesis that God exists. The classic argument from the existence of evil against the existence of God presupposes that God is omniscient, omnipotent, and omnibenevolent. If such a being exists, the argument goes, how could He allow evil? Theists make several responses. Many presuppose the characterization of God as perfect. But one interesting way of escaping the objection involves positing a God or Gods who are not perfect, i.e. not omniscient, omnipotent, and omnibenevolent. Interestingly, it is not clear that two of the classic arguments for the existence of God, the cosmological (first cause) and the teleological (argument from design), even if sound, license a conclusion to the existence of a *perfect* being. Of course, once one allows that God might be something less than perfect, one faces additional problems trying to explain precisely what the difference is between a God and some very powerful alien. Movies like *Star Trek V: The Final Frontier, Jason and the Argonauts*, and *Dogma* portray Gods that may well be the sorts of "creators" who should satisfy proponents of the cosmological argument and the argument from design, but who fall far short of perfection.

Just as many philosophical problems in religion defy easy illustration with film, so also it is not easy to raise some of the more fundamental issues that underlie disputes involving freedom, determinism, and responsibility. Those who enter into these debates, perhaps not surprisingly, often do not distinguish the relevance of determinism, foreknowledge, and even simply there being truths about the future to the possibility of genuine freedom, freedom of a sort that is compatible with responsibility. There are a number of films in which the plot seems to presuppose that future events have already left their "imprint" on the past. In *The Omen*, for example, the photographer's pictures contain indications that their subjects will die in particular ways. If this influence on the past is possible only on the supposition that the future events are going to occur, were the characters *destined* to meet their unfortunate fates? More generally, does the fact that there are truths about our future lives imply that our future is beyond our control? Is a world in which we cannot control our future decisions, a world in which we can legitimately be held morally responsible for those decisions? In *Minority Report*, the central character is "seen" by the clairvoyants to commit a future killing (or at least a killing that will take place in the absence of intervention). That character, at the last moment before the killing is "meant" to take place, claims to have a "free" will that allows him to choose an alternative (despite the fact that the death actually does occur). Is the truth of his claim compatible with presuppositions of the plot? If the other "criminals" in the film who were apprehended on the basis of the seers' predictions were in some sense *predetermined* to commit crimes in the absence of intervention, was it appropriate for the state to hold them morally *responsible* and thus *deserving* of punishment?

There is considerable controversy over whether people are, in some sense, determined to act as they do. In the film *The Boys From Brazil*, there is an effort to replicate Hitler by taking his DNA and duplicating the environmental circumstances in which he was raised. Is the presupposition that such an effort would succeed plausible? The film *Compulsion* presents a classic attempt to offer a generic defense of reduced responsibility based on deterministic presuppositions. Whether or not determinism is true, the law does seem to recognize a relevant distinction between people who are not responsible for reasons of perhaps even "temporary" insanity. The *Law and Order* episode we include involves this sort of defense. Is there any principled way to make the distinction between "normal" behavior for which we hold people responsible and behavior we excuse for reasons of "mental disease or defect"? The issues of freedom most naturally come up when we are considering the question of whether to excuse people for acting badly. In *A Clockwork Orange*, the conditioning techniques were viewed by some as controversial because they were thought to preclude any genuine choice for good or evil on the part of the actor. Was there anything problematic about the revolutionary ideas for conditioning behavior? Was the state-ordered conditioning in principle any different from the conditioning employed by any responsible parent raising a child?

Philosophical Argument

Argument is (arguably) the essence of philosophy. To get good at philosophy, you must get good at giving and critically evaluating argument. As the philosopher conceives of argument, all arguments have (by definition) premises and a conclusion. The conclusion is some claim we are trying to establish; the premises are claims advanced in support of the conclusion. Philosophers distinguish two kinds of *standards* one can employ in evaluating arguments – *deductive* standards and *non-deductive* (sometimes called inductive) standards. (Instead of two kinds of standards for evaluating arguments, some philosophers talk of a distinction between two kinds of arguments – deductive arguments and non-deductive arguments. We strongly discourage this practice.) One and the same argument can be correctly judged good by one set of standards and bad by another, and if one asks whether the argument is "really" deductive or non-deductive it is not clear how to understand the question.

Deductive standards

Most of the arguments philosophers give are designed to satisfy deductive standards. To be good or sound by deductive standards, an argument must have true premises and the premises must *entail* the conclusion. The premises of an argument entail its conclusion (crudely put) when it is impossible for the premises to be true while the conclusion is false. When an argument's premises do entail its conclusion, we say that the argument is deductively valid. In a course on formal logic, one learns definitions, axioms, and rules, allowing one to determine which arguments are deductively valid and which are deductively invalid. So, for example, the arguments by counterexample we discussed earlier have the following form:

If P then Q. But not-Q. Therefore not-P.

(If being human were nothing more than being a featherless biped, then a plucked chicken would be a human. But a plucked chicken is obviously not a human. Therefore, it is not the case that being human is nothing more than being a featherless biped). The argument form even has a name (*modus tollens*). But there are a great many other deductively valid argument forms. You may have read in some high school "logic" texts that it is the mark of deductively valid reasoning that it always moves from the general to the particular. This is wrong. All the following are examples of deductively valid argument forms:

(1) All F's are G
(2) This is an F
Therefore,
(3) This is G
(where one can substitute for "F" and "G" any term picking out a property or characteristic)

(1) If P then Q
(2) P
Therefore,
(3) Q
(where one can substitute for the "P"'s and "Q"'s any claim that can be true or false)

(1) Either P or Q
(2) not-P
Therefore,
(3) Q

(1) P
Therefore,
(2) P or Q

(1) P
(2) not-Q

Therefore,
(3) It is not the case that if P then Q

Having true premises and being deductively valid are the two conditions that define the *technical* notion of being deductively sound. But one can legitimately *criticize* arguments that might be deductively sound. Often, for example, philosophers accuse each other of *begging the question* in advancing a given argument. It is not that easy to define this familiar charge. Roughly, we would suggest that one begs the question when one's premises *too obviously* presuppose the truth of one's conclusion (something that might vary from one context of debate to another). We need to use the expression "too obviously," for there is, of course, a sense in which all deductively valid arguments have premises that presuppose the truth of the conclusion – the argument wouldn't be valid if it were possible for the premises to be true while the conclusion is false. Monty Python's "The Argument Skit" provides an amusing guide to paradigmatic question-begging. Often the paid arguer seems to do nothing more than simply assert something incompatible with what is said by the poor person who paid good money for an argument. Arguments of the form "P, therefore P," or "P, therefore, not-not-P," are all deductively valid. And, of course, when P is true they are sound. But they are pathetic nevertheless. One can't convince someone of P's truth using an argument whose premise is P. The most interesting arguments take one to an often controversial conclusion relying on premises each of which by itself seems perfectly reasonable. To be sure, if the argument is deductively valid, the conjunction of premises will implicitly "contain" the conclusion. But even if one didn't already accept the conclusion one can find the premises individually plausible.

One can also criticize arguments that may be deductively sound for employing premises that themselves require justification – premises that are *too controversial* given the context of the discussion to stand alone. Again, the success of this charge might very well be context-sensitive. When two monks are debating some claim about what Moses did, they might be quite happy with an argument whose premises presuppose the veracity of the Bible. If an atheist joined the discussion, however, such premises might quickly be challenged as being sorely in need of further justification. In ordinary debates, we take for granted the legitimacy of perception as a way of gaining information about the world. But as we shall see, in the context of addressing skeptical challenges to our knowledge of the external world, the skeptic will almost certainly balk at your presupposing the reliability of perception in attempting to meet the skeptic's challenge.

Of course, one can always complain that the person putting forth an argument failed to offer evidence in support of the premises of that argument. Some philosophers, Descartes perhaps, would argue that an ideal argument begins with self-evident premises – premises that we know without having to infer them from some other different truth. In practice, however, we are often satisfied if an argument employs premises that seem much more obvious than the truth of its conclusion. Again, what one can get away with when one relies on a premise for which one did not argue might well vary from context to context.

Non-deductive standards

When one evaluates an argument employing non-deductive standards, one no longer insists that the argument be deductively valid in order to be good. Just as with deductive standards, one insists that for the argument to be good, the premises be true. But the argument can "pass" non-deductive standards if the premises merely make highly probable the truth of its conclusion. While there is a fair bit of agreement on which arguments are deductively valid, there is far more controversy concerning when an argument's premises make only very likely a conclusion. One kind of argument that might seem to satisfy non-deductive standards is enumerative induction. Enumerative induction employs premises describing an observed correlation between certain properties. Its conclusion either projects that correlation to all unobserved cases, or projects it in some particular case where one of the properties is known to be present. So both of the following are examples of enumerative induction:

(1) All observed metal has expanded when heated
Therefore,

(2) All metal (past, present, and future) expands when heated

(1) All observed metal has expanded when heated
(2) This piece of metal has been heated
Therefore,
(3) This piece of metal will expand

Neither argument is deductively valid. To paraphrase Russell, turkeys find out to their sorrow that they can find themselves fed every time they are called only to discover that this time the call portends a quite different fate.

The conclusion of an inductive argument is probable only relative to its premises. It is in the nature of probability that a given conclusion might be probable relative to one body of evidence and improbable relative to another. Relative to the fact that I hold a ticket in a fair lottery, it is usually very unlikely that I am a winner. Relative to the fact that I hold the ticket and that my friend has left a breathless message on my answering machine that I won the lottery, it is quite probable that I did win.

Enumerative induction can take one further than deductively valid reasoning, but it can't take one very far. One seems limited by such reasoning to reaching conclusions about the kind of phenomena one can directly observe. If, as Hume argued, one can only directly observe mental states, it is hard to say how one can get beyond knowledge of this kind of thing. It is not even clear how one can "certify" the reliability of memory using inductive reasoning. Inductive reasoning proceeds from observations about *past* correlations between certain properties. But how does one get justified beliefs about those past correlations? Arguably, we have no alternative but to rely on apparent memory. I have reason to believe that I've always found F's together with G's because I seem to remember always finding a G when I found an F. But why should we trust apparent memory? To offer an inductive argument for the reliability of memory, we would need to rely on the past reliability of apparent memory. But to get to that past we would again need to rely on memory.

At least some philosophers would argue that we need to expand the kinds of non-deductive inference that are legitimate. So, for example, some philosophers would argue that we should view reasoning from apparent memory as an independent and perfectly legitimate sort of non-deductive reasoning. Others would claim that reasoning from sense-experience to objective external reality is another independent and perfectly legitimate sort of non-deductive reasoning. Still others would emphasize the importance of reasoning to the best explanation – one observes some phenomenon and accepts some hypothesis because it would "best" explain the phenomenon in question. But, again, it is an understatement to suggest that there is no agreement on how to decide when a method of forming belief is, in fact, one that passes our non-deductive standards for evaluating arguments. There are literally no uncontroversial examples of legitimate non-deductive reasoning.

Part II

The Problem of Perception

Films:
Total Recall
The Matrix
Star Trek TV episode: *The Menagerie*

Introduction

The epistemological problem of perception concerns the question of how, if at all, we can know or justifiably believe truths about a world of objective, mind-independent objects when all we ever have ultimately to rely on as evidence is subjective, fleeting experience. Attempts to answer this epistemological question inevitably give rise to metaphysical questions about the very nature of external reality and its connection to subjective appearance. Fumerton's "The Structure of Skeptical Arguments and its Metaepistemological Implications" (see chapter 7) attempts to set forth the general structure of classical skeptical arguments.

The first step in developing the epistemological problem of perception involves driving a kind of logical wedge between the best evidence we have for commonplace beliefs about the physical world around us and the truth of those beliefs. Although he was ultimately interested in showing how knowledge was possible, Descartes famously began by attempting to cast doubt on all sorts of seemingly unproblematic beliefs. His method of doubt was designed to discover secure *foundations* for an ideal system of knowledge. The foundations of knowledge consist in those assertions whose truth cannot be doubted.

One candidate for foundational knowledge rejected by Descartes was knowledge of the physical world. He argued that the best evidence we could have for believing in the existence of physical objects was the "testimony" of our senses. Everything we know about the physical world can be traced eventually to something we know about that world through visual, tactile, auditory, gustatory, and olfactory sensations. Descartes argued that one cannot trust entirely that which sometimes deceives and called attention to the fact that our senses sometimes deceive us – square towers can look round at a distance; in the fog we can mistake a stranger for a friend. But surely the only lesson that can be learned from the above examples is that we must be wary of trusting the senses when the conditions of perception are less than ideal. When an object appears immediately before us under *optimum* conditions of perception, how could one reach a false conclusion about the existence of *that* object?

At this point Descartes introduces one of the most discussed arguments in epistemology, the famous dream argument.[1] He reminds us that we have all had vivid dreams and in the course of those dreams have taken for granted all sorts of purported truths about our surroundings. The evidence we have for believing what we do about our present surroundings is no better than the evidence we had when dreaming, and is, therefore, always perfectly compatible with the *possibility* that we are dreaming. Later in the *Meditations*, to make the same point not only about knowledge of the external world, but also to cast doubt on even elementary truths of arithmetic, Descartes invokes the possibility that there exists an all-powerful, evil demon. Restricting our attention to the evil demon argument and its application to the problem of perception, Descartes asks us to imagine that we are constantly and consistently being deceived by an evil demon with the power to plant in us sensations and ideas of a non-existent external world, thus inducing in us massively false beliefs. More contemporary variations on the dream and demon arguments appeal to the fascinating discoveries of cognitive science to make the same point. Can't we imagine that a "mad" neurophysiologist has stolen your brain in the middle of the night? That brain, now sitting in a vat in the scientist's laboratory, is hooked up to various electrodes while it is "played" so as to produce the enormous range of experience that you falsely take to be accurately representing your physical surroundings.

All these thought experiments are designed to convince you that no matter how good your evidence seems to be supporting commonplace beliefs about the external world, that evidence never entails (never guarantees) the truth of what you believe. But the legitimacy of the thought experiments and the claims about what is or is not genuinely imaginable have been called into question by many who fear the specter of radical skepticism once one allows a "veil" of perception to separate us from the objective world. In "Brains in a Vat," Hilary Putnam, for example, claims that it is itself a kind of illusion to suppose that we could be the victims of massive and consistent illusion. Our very ability to think of external reality, he seems to argue, requires that we interact with that reality in ways that are not *fundamentally* at odds with our beliefs.

While one can legitimately cast doubt on the intelligibility of thought experiments designed to establish certain possibilities, it is interesting to note that variations on the philosopher's abstract thought experiments have formed the plot lines of popular films and television programs. In the pilot episode of the original *Star Trek* series, the story centered around the inhabitants of a planet who had "demon-like" powers to induce in others massive hallucinatory experience. In a subsequent episode, *The Menagerie* (incorporating the pilot episode) the dilemma ultimately facing a badly disfigured and paralyzed former captain of the *Enterprise* was whether or not to return to that planet so as to live out the rest

of his life in a hallucinatory world provided by those with the special powers (in blissful co-existence with an equally disfigured, but soon to be through hallucination "beautiful" woman companion). The apparent intelligibility of the episode not only seems to reinforce the idea that massive deception is possible, it also provides a good opportunity to discuss a common question raised in connection with skeptical scenarios. What difference would it make if all of our experiences were hallucinatory? If the world of mere appearance would be indistinguishable from veridical experience, why should we care? In "Some Further Considerations Concerning Our Simple Ideas of Sensation," John Locke himself seems to offer this as a kind of frustrated rejoinder to Descartes's dream argument. Reflection on the kind of hallucinatory life the captain chose might be a profitable way to further explore this position.

The movie *Total Recall* is set in a future in which people are encouraged to take hallucinatory "vacations" (less expensive and less prone to disaster than the real thing, and far more exotic to boot). The plot develops in such a way as to provide fertile ground for philosophical speculation. As it turns out, it becomes entirely unclear whether the hero's fantastic adventures on Mars are part of the *Recall*-induced hallucination or whether he has actually escaped the machine only to discover that he is an actual secret agent destined to discover a great mystery about the Red Planet. There is an early scene in the movie (chapters 7–8), usually overlooked by most viewers, that, when combined with a later scene (chapter 40), might give one an important clue from the third-person perspective with respect to the question of whether what the character experiences is veridical or imaginary. And there is another scene in the movie (chapter 23) in which the central character purports to have a "proof," from the first-person perspective, that his experiences are indeed veridical and not hallucinatory. While the proof was probably not intended to satisfy Cartesian doubt, it would be interesting to discuss in connection with the more extreme skepticism advanced by Hume (see below).

The Matrix is perhaps the best illustration of a film based on the intelligibility of skeptical scenarios. In the film, the world has evolved in such a way that the vast majority of people lead apparently normal lives while in reality their bodies are floating in vats and are kept alive only as sources of energy provided by their brains that respond to computer-induced hallucinatory experience. In the film, Neo eventually "discovers" that he has been mistaking hallucination for reality. The film contains a dramatic scene in which (as a result of taking a pill?!!) he "awakens" to his envatted condition (chapter 10). Neo (and we as audience) seems to have no difficulty construing his new and, arguably, bizarre experiences as reflecting reality. But Descartes himself suggests a solution to his dream argument in *Meditation Six*. Descartes argues that if we can establish the existence of a non-deceiving God, we can be sure that we are not being consistently deceived by sensation. In particular, if we pay close attention to the way in which our experience "fits" with prior experience, we can distinguish veridical and non-veridical experience. But on Descartes's criterion, Neo should probably have concluded that his "post-pill" experiences were the hallucination. They surely represented a dramatic break with any prior experiences. On the other hand, perhaps one need do no more than reflect on the possibility of boring and mundane dreams to realize that Descartes's suggestion is highly problematic.

In addition to stressing the appearance/reality distinction that has so worried philosophers, the movie also raises interesting questions about the possibility (and intelligibility) of causal connections between hallucinatory events and the state of the hallucinator's body. Scenes of violent "physical conflict" (chapters 14–15, 33–4) between characters who are in some sense "sharing" a hallucinatory environment raise interesting questions about how, if at all, one can understand shared hallucination or the exercise of "skill" within the framework of a "program." Could an agent's knowledge of "control" over experience deflect certain skeptical possibilities? After all, if being in the *Matrix* involves having one's experiences (*all* of one's experiences) induced by a computer, then in what sense could a person in the *Matrix* causally affect the visual, tactile, and kinesthetic experiences associated with hallucinatory combat?

The scenes (chapters 7–12) in which the hero makes the transition from envatted hallucinator to the "real world" are excellent ways to integrate discussion of Putnam's arguments involving brains in a vat. Putnam will no doubt argue that our apparent ability to follow and understand the plot of the movie is perfectly compatible with his conclusion that the mind associated with the envatted body could never, even in principle, reach a correct conclusion about his condition, but it would be useful to discuss this alleged distinction between third-person and first-person perspectives through a closer examination of this film. (It is actually not clear that Putnam would deny that these "brains in a vat" could not entertain thoughts about a physical environment. Putnam's considered view is, or at least should be, that it makes no sense to suppose that a conscious being could entertain the possibility of being a brain in a vat if that conscious being exists in a universe that has *always* consisted only of brains in vats. Various indirect causal chains leading to brain states might be "good enough" to secure the possibility of reference to external objects. Putnam seems committed to the view that if the programmer of the brains in vats has the right sort of connection to a physical environment to allow thoughts about it, then the thoughts he induces can share that content.)

There is a later scene in the movie (chapter 25) in which one of the villains makes clear that he prefers to return to the hallucinatory world of the Matrix rather than continue to live the drab and dangerous existence of reality. Like Captain Pike's dilemma in *The Menagerie*, the reasons offered by the villain provide an excellent opportunity to focus on the question of precisely what one does or doesn't lose in a world in which appearance is caused in ways quite different from what we suppose to be the case. In "The Experience Machine," Robert Nozick suggests that most of us would never choose a hallucinatory existence (no matter how pleasurable that existence would be) over reality. Captain Pike and the villain of the Matrix clearly disagree with Nozick.

The apparent intelligibility of the plot lines in the above movies might seem to support strongly Descartes's claim that the evidence of the senses always leaves open the possibility of massive error. But interestingly enough, students can easily get used to the idea that we can't know with absolute certainty anything about the external world (the past, the future, other minds, etc.). It is a short step, however, from Cartesian skepticism about the possibility of getting absolute certainty of truth to a more drastic sort of skepticism put forth by the famous Scottish philosopher David Hume. In our selection here, Hume distinguishes the view of the "vulgar" – that we are directly aware of external reality, from the view of the "philosopher" – that we infer the existence of external reality from a world of appearance that in some sense accurately "pictures" that reality. Like Berkeley, who in his *Three Dialogues* has Philonous unrelentingly push Hylas away from the idea that we have "direct" awareness of anything mind-independent, Hume also argues that the vulgar view isn't compatible with familiar facts about perceptual relativity and the intelligibility of the skeptical scenarios discussed above. To save "commonsense," Berkeley heroically tries to construct a physical world out of ideas (*idealism*). In the same spirit, Ayer, in "The Self and the Common World," embraces a version of *phenomenalism* – the view that we can "translate" talk about external reality into complex talk about actual and "possible" sensations (*sense data*). Hume, however, was under no illusion that he could save common sense by "building" the world of enduring, external objects out of fleeting perceptions. Unfortunately, the philosophical view that we could only infer external reality from subjective appearance, Hume argued, inevitably leads either to the conclusion that we have no rational beliefs about external reality or the more extreme conclusion that we can't even form an intelligible idea of external reality. Consider the first position. Starting from the premise that sensations (perceptions) are not identical with and do not entail the existence of physical objects, Hume argued that we can never establish sensation as a reliable indicator of external reality. He argued as follows:

(1)   To justifiably believe in the existence of physical objects based on what we know about the occurrence of sensation, we would need to justifiably believe that sensations are a reliable indicator of external reality.

(2)   To justifiably believe that sensations are a reliable indicator of external reality, we would need to observe that in the past whenever (or at least usually) when we have certain kinds of sensations, certain objects were present causing them.

(3)   But there is no way of establishing a correlation between sensations and objects – all we ever have to rely on ultimately in reaching conclusions about the world around us is what we know about the nature of appearance.

Therefore,

(4)   While we might be able to justifiably believe that one sensation is a reliable indicator of another, we could never justifiably believe that a sensation is a reliable indicator of something other than a sensation, and we can never justifiably believe in the existence of physical objects based on what we know about sensation.

The above argument is enormously powerful and suggests that once we drop a veil of perception between the external world and us, we might have a terrible time gaining *any* sort of insight into what sort of world, if any, exists beyond that veil. The vast majority of the inhabitants of *The Matrix* world lived their lives oblivious to their actual circumstances. The world they took for granted didn't exist, but they had no way of rationally suspecting the truth. What reason do we have for believing that the world we take ourselves to live in has any more reality?

Note

1   Descartes was not the first to consider skeptical arguments of this sort – they can be traced at least to Sextus Empiricus. But his was one of the more poetic and influential discussions of the argument.

1

First Meditation and excerpt from Sixth Meditation

René Descartes

Meditation I

Of the things which may be brought within the sphere of the doubtful

It is now some years since I detected how many were the false beliefs that I had from my earliest youth admitted as true, and how doubtful was everything I had since constructed on this basis; and from that time I was convinced that I must once for all seriously undertake to rid myself of all the opinions which I had formerly accepted, and commence to build anew from the foundation, if I wanted to establish any firm and permanent structure in the sciences. But as this enterprise appeared to be a very great one, I waited until I had attained an age so mature that I could not hope that at any later date I should be better fitted to execute my design. This reason caused me to delay so long that I should feel that I was doing wrong were I to occupy in deliberation the time that yet remains to me for action. To-day, then, since very opportunely for the plan I have in view I have delivered my mind from every care [and am happily agitated by no passions] and since I have procured for myself an assured leisure in a peaceable retirement, I shall at last seriously and freely address myself to the general upheaval of all my former opinions.

Now for this object it is not necessary that I should show that all of these are false – I shall perhaps never arrive at this end. But inasmuch as reason already persuades me that I ought no less carefully to withhold my assent from matters which are not entirely certain and indubitable than from those which appear to me manifestly to be false, if I am able to find in each one some reason to doubt, this will suffice to justify my rejecting the whole. And for that end it will not be requisite that I should examine each in particular, which would be an endless undertaking; for owing to the fact that the destruction of the foundations of necessity brings with it the downfall of the rest of the edifice, I shall only in the first place attack those principles upon which all my former opinions rested.

All that up to the present time I have accepted as most true and certain I have learned either from the senses or through the senses; but it is sometimes proved to me that these senses are deceptive, and it is wiser not to trust entirely to any thing by which we have once been deceived.

But it may be that although the senses sometimes deceive us concerning things which are

René Descartes, *Meditation I* and excerpt from *Meditation VI*, from *The Philosophical Works of Descartes*, vol. 1, trans. E. Haldane and G. Ross (Cambridge: Cambridge University Press, 1967). © 1967 by Cambridge University Press. Reproduced with permission from Cambridge University Press.

hardly perceptible, or very far away, there are yet many others to be met with as to which we cannot reasonably have any doubt, although we recognise them by their means. For example, there is the fact that I am here, seated by the fire, attired in a dressing gown, having this paper in my hands and other similar matters. And how could I deny that these hands and this body are mine, were it not perhaps that I compare myself to certain persons, devoid of sense, whose cerebella are so troubled and clouded by the violent vapours of black bile, that they constantly assure us that they think they are kings when they are really quite poor, or that they are clothed in purple when they are really without covering, or who imagine that they have an earthenware head or are nothing but pumpkins or are made of glass. But they are mad, and I should not be any the less insane were I to follow examples so extravagant.

At the same time I must remember that I am a man, and that consequently I am in the habit of sleeping, and in my dreams representing to myself the same things or sometimes even less probable things, than do those who are insane in their waking moments. How often has it happened to me that in the night I dreamt that I found myself in this particular place, that I was dressed and seated near the fire, whilst in reality I was lying undressed in bed! At this moment it does indeed seem to me that it is with eyes awake that I am looking at this paper; that this head which I move is not asleep, that it is deliberately and of set purpose that I extend my hand and perceive it; what happens in sleep does not appear so clear nor so distinct as does all this. But in thinking over this I remind myself that on many occasions I have in sleep been deceived by similar illusions, and in dwelling carefully on this reflection I see so manifestly that there are no certain indications by which we may clearly distinguish wakefulness from sleep that I am lost in astonishment. And my astonishment is such that it is almost capable of persuading me that I now dream.

Now let us assume that we are asleep and that all these particulars, e.g. that we open our eyes, shake our head, extend our hands, and so on, are but false delusions; and let us reflect that possibly neither our hands nor our whole body are such as they appear to us to be. At the same time we must at least confess that the things which are represented to us in sleep are like painted representations which can only have been formed as the counterparts of something real and true, and that in this way those general things at least, i.e. eyes, a head, hands, and a whole body, are not imaginary things, but things really existent. For, as a matter of fact, painters, even when they study with the greatest skill to represent sirens and satyrs by forms the most strange and extraordinary, cannot give them natures which are entirely new, but merely make a certain medley of the members of different animals; or if their imagination is extravagant enough to invent something so novel that nothing similar has ever before been seen, and that then their work represents a thing purely fictitious and absolutely false, it is certain all the same that the colours of which this is composed are necessarily real. And for the same reason, although these general things, to wit, [a body], eyes, a head, hands, and such like, may be imaginary, we are bound at the same time to confess that there are at least some other objects yet more simple and more universal, which are real and true; and of these just in the same way as with certain real colours, all these images of things which dwell in our thoughts, whether true and real or false and fantastic, are formed.

To such a class of things pertains corporeal nature in general, and its extension, the figure of extended things, their quantity or magnitude and number, as also the place in which they are, the time which measures their duration, and so on.

That is possibly why our reasoning is not unjust when we conclude from this that Physics, Astronomy, Medicine and all other sciences which have as their end the consideration of composite things, are very dubious and uncertain; but that Arithmetic, Geometry and other sciences of that kind which only treat of things that are very simple and very general, without taking great trouble to ascertain whether they are actually existent or not, contain some measure of certainty and an element of the indubitable. For whether I am awake or asleep, two and three together always form five, and the square can never have more than four sides, and it does not seem possible that truths so clear and apparent can be suspected of any falsity [or uncertainty].

Nevertheless I have long had fixed in my mind the belief that an all-powerful God existed by whom I have been created such as I am. But how do I know that He has not brought it to pass that there is no earth, no heaven, no extended body, no magnitude, no place, and that nevertheless [I possess the perceptions of all these things and that] they seem to me to exist just exactly as I now see them? And, besides, as I sometimes imagine that others deceive themselves in the things which they think they know best, how do I know that I am not deceived every time that I add two and three, or count the sides of a square, or judge of things yet simpler, if anything simpler can be imagined? But possibly God has not desired that I should be thus deceived, for He is said to be supremely good. If, however, it is contrary to His goodness to have made me such that I constantly deceive myself, it would also appear to be contrary to His goodness to permit me to be sometimes deceived, and nevertheless I cannot doubt that He does permit this.

There may indeed be those who would prefer to deny the existence of a God so powerful, rather than believe that all other things are uncertain. But let us not oppose them for the present, and grant that all that is here said of a God is a fable; nevertheless in whatever way they suppose that I have arrived at the state of being that I have reached – whether they attribute it to fate or to accident, or make out that it is by a continual succession of antecedents, or by some other method – since to err and deceive oneself is a defect, it is clear that the greater will be the probability of my being so imperfect as to deceive myself ever, as is the Author to whom they assign my origin the less powerful. To these reasons I have certainly nothing to reply, but at the end I feel constrained to confess that there is nothing in all that I formerly believed to be true, of which I cannot in some measure doubt, and that not merely through want of thought or through levity, but for reasons which are very powerful and maturely considered; so that henceforth I ought not the less carefully to refrain from giving credence to these opinions than to that which is manifestly false, if I desire to arrive at any certainty [in the sciences].

But it is not sufficient to have made these remarks, we must also be careful to keep them in mind. For these ancient and commonly held opinions still revert frequently to my mind, long and familiar custom having given them the right to occupy my mind against my inclination and rendered them almost masters of my belief; nor

will I ever lose the habit of deferring to them or of placing my confidence in them, so long as I consider them as they really are, i.e. opinions in some measure doubtful, as I have just shown, and at the same time highly probable, so that there is much more reason to believe in than to deny them. That is why I consider that I shall not be acting amiss, if, taking of set purpose a contrary belief, I allow myself to be deceived, and for a certain time pretend that all these opinions are entirely false and imaginary, until at last, having thus balanced my former prejudices with my latter [so that they cannot divert my opinions more to one side than to the other], my judgment will no longer be dominated by bad usage or turned away from the right knowledge of the truth. For I am assured that there can be neither peril nor error in this course, and that I cannot at present yield too much to distrust, since I am not considering the question of action, but only of knowledge.

I shall then suppose, not that God who is supremely good and the fountain of truth, but some evil genius not less powerful than deceitful, has employed his whole energies in deceiving me; I shall consider that the heavens, the earth, colours, figures, sound, and all other external things are nought but the illusions and dreams of which this genius has availed himself in order to lay traps for my credulity; I shall consider myself as having no hands, no eyes, no flesh, no blood, nor any senses, yet falsely believing myself to possess all these things; I shall remain obstinately attached to this idea, and if by this means it is not in my power to arrive at the knowledge of any truth, I may at least do what is in my power [i.e. suspend my judgment], and with firm purpose avoid giving credence to any false thing, or being imposed upon by this arch deceiver, however powerful and deceptive he may be. But this task is a laborious one, and insensibly a certain lassitude leads me into the course of my ordinary life. And just as a captive who in sleep enjoys an imaginary liberty, when he begins to suspect that his liberty is but a dream, fears to awaken, and conspires with these agreeable illusions that the deception may be prolonged, so insensibly of my own accord I fall back into my former opinions, and I dread awakening from this slumber, lest the laborious wakefulness which would follow the tranquillity of this repose should have to be spent not in daylight, but in the excessive darkness of the difficulties which have just been discussed.

Meditation VI

Of the existence of material things, and of the real distinction between the soul and body of man

[. . .]

And certainly this consideration is of great service to me, not only in enabling me to recognise all the errors to which my nature is subject, but also in enabling me to avoid them or to correct them more easily. For knowing that all my senses more frequently indicate to me truth than falsehood respecting the things which concern that which is beneficial to the body, and being able almost always to avail myself of many of them in order to examine one particular thing, and, besides that, being able to make use of my memory in order to connect the present with the past, and of my understanding which already has discovered all the causes of my errors, I ought no longer to fear that falsity may be found in matters every day presented to me by my senses. And I ought to set aside all the doubts of these past days as hyperbolical and ridiculous, particularly that very common uncertainty respecting sleep, which I could not distinguish from the waking state; for at present I find a very notable difference between the two, inasmuch as our memory can never connect our dreams one with the other, or with the whole course of our lives, as it unites events which happen to us while we are awake. And, as a matter of fact, if someone, while I was awake, quite suddenly appeared to me and disappeared as fast as do the images which I see in sleep, so that I could not know from whence the form came nor whither it went, it would not be without reason that I should deem it a spectre or a phantom formed by my brain [and similar to those which I form in sleep], rather than a real man. But when I perceive things as to which I know distinctly both the place from which they proceed, and that in which they are, and the time at which they appeared to me; and when, without any interruption, I can connect the perceptions which I have of them with the whole course of my life, I am perfectly assured that these perceptions occur while I am waking and not during sleep. And I ought in no wise to doubt the truth of such matters, if, after having called up all my senses, my memory, and my understanding, to examine them, nothing is brought to evidence by any one of them which is repugnant to what is set forth by the others. For because God is in no wise a deceiver, it follows that I am not deceived in this. But because the exigencies of action often oblige us to make up our minds before having leisure to examine matters carefully, we must confess that the life of man is very frequently subject to error in respect to individual objects, and we must in the end acknowledge the infirmity of our nature.

2

Some Further Considerations Concerning Our Simple Ideas of Sensation

John Locke

1. Positive ideas from privative causes. Concerning the simple ideas of Sensation, it is to be considered, – that whatsoever is so constituted in nature as to be able, by affecting our senses, to cause any perception in the mind, doth thereby produce in the understanding a simple idea; which, whatever be the external cause of it, when it comes to be taken notice of by our discerning faculty, it is by the mind looked on and considered there to be a real positive idea in the understanding, as much as any other whatsoever; though, perhaps, the cause of it be but a privation of the subject.

2. Ideas in the mind distinguished from that in things which gives rise to them. Thus the ideas of heat and cold, light and darkness, white and black, motion and rest, are equally clear and positive ideas in the mind; though, perhaps, some of the causes which produce them are barely privations, in those subjects from whence our senses derive those ideas. These the understanding, in its view of them, considers all as distinct positive ideas, without taking notice of the causes that produce them: which is an inquiry not belonging to the idea, as it is in the understanding, but to the nature of the things existing without us. These are two very different things, and carefully to be distinguished; it being one thing to perceive and know the idea of white or black, and quite another to examine what kind of particles they must be, and how ranged in the superficies, to make any object appear white or black.

3. We may have the ideas when we are ignorant of their physical causes. A painter or dyer who never inquired into their causes hath the ideas of white and black, and other colours, as clearly, perfectly, and distinctly in his understanding, and perhaps more distinctly, than the philosopher who hath busied himself in considering their natures, and thinks he knows how far either of them is, in its cause, positive or privative; and the idea of black is no less positive in his mind than that of white, however the cause of that colour in the external object may be only a privation.

4. Why a privative cause in nature may occasion a positive idea. If it were the design of my present undertaking to inquire into the natural causes and manner of perception, I should offer this as a reason why a privative cause might, in some cases at least, produce a positive idea; viz. that all sensation being produced in us only by different degrees and modes of motion in our animal spirits, variously agitated by external objects, the abatement of any former motion must as necessarily produce a new sensation as the variation or increase of it; and so

John Locke, "Some Further Considerations Concerning Our Simple Ideas of Sensation." Chapter VIII from *An Essay Concerning Human Understanding*. Available at http://ebooks.adelaide.edu.au/1/locke/john/181u/B2.8.html. Accessed 2/19/2008.

introduce a new idea, which depends only on a different motion of the animal spirits in that organ.

5. Negative names need not be meaningless. But whether this be so or not I will not here determine, but appeal to every one's own experience, whether the shadow of a man, though it consists of nothing but the absence of light (and the more the absence of light is, the more discernible is the shadow) does not, when a man looks on it, cause as clear and positive idea in his mind as a man himself, though covered over with clear sunshine? And the picture of a shadow is a positive thing. Indeed, we have negative names, which stand not directly for positive ideas, but for their absence, such as insipid, silence, nihil, &c.; which words denote positive ideas, v.g. taste, sound, being, with a signification of their absence.

6. Whether any ideas are due to causes really privative. And thus one may truly be said to see darkness. For, supposing a hole perfectly dark, from whence no light is reflected, it is certain one may see the figure of it, or it may be painted; or whether the ink I write with makes any other idea, is a question. The privative causes I have here assigned of positive ideas are according to the common opinion; but, in truth, it will be hard to determine whether there be really any ideas from a privative cause, till it be determined, whether rest be any more a privation than motion.

7. Ideas in the mind, qualities in bodies. To discover the nature of our ideas the better, and to discourse of them intelligibly, it will be convenient to distinguish them as they are ideas or perceptions in our minds; and as they are modifications of matter in the bodies that cause such perceptions in us: that so we may not think (as perhaps usually is done) that they are exactly the images and resemblances of something inherent in the subject; most of those of sensation being in the mind no more the likeness of something existing without us, than the names that stand for them are the likeness of our ideas, which yet upon hearing they are apt to excite in us.

8. Our ideas and the qualities of bodies. Whatsoever the mind perceives in itself, or is the immediate object of perception, thought, or understanding, that I call idea; and the power to produce any idea in our mind, I call quality of

the subject wherein that power is. Thus a snowball having the power to produce in us the ideas of white, cold, and round, – the power to produce those ideas in us, as they are in the snowball, I call qualities; and as they are sensations or perceptions in our understandings, I call them ideas; which ideas, if I speak of sometimes as in the things themselves, I would be understood to mean those qualities in the objects which produce them in us.

9. Primary qualities of bodies. Qualities thus considered in bodies are, first, such as are utterly inseparable from the body, in what state soever it be; and such as in all the alterations and changes it suffers, all the force can be used upon it, it constantly keeps; and such as sense constantly finds in every particle of matter which has bulk enough to be perceived; and the mind finds inseparable from every particle of matter, though less than to make itself singly be perceived by our senses: v.g. Take a grain of wheat, divide it into two parts; each part has still solidity, extension, figure, and mobility: divide it again, and it retains still the same qualities; and so divide it on, till the parts become insensible; they must retain still each of them all those qualities. For division (which is all that a mill, or pestle, or any other body, does upon another, in reducing it to insensible parts) can never take away either solidity, extension, figure, or mobility from any body, but only makes two or more distinct separate masses of matter, of that which was but one before; all which distinct masses, reckoned as so many distinct bodies, after division, make a certain number. These I call original or primary qualities of body, which I think we may observe to produce simple ideas in us, viz. solidity, extension, figure, motion or rest, and number.

10. Secondary qualities of bodies. Secondly, such qualities which in truth are nothing in the objects themselves but power to produce various sensations in us by their primary qualities, i.e. by the bulk, figure, texture, and motion of their insensible parts, as colours, sounds, tastes, &c. These I call secondary qualities. To these might be added a third sort, which are allowed to be barely powers; though they are as much real qualities in the subject as those which I, to comply with the common way of speaking, call qualities, but for distinction, secondary qualities. For the power in fire to produce a new colour,

or consistency, in wax or clay, – by its primary qualities, is as much a quality in fire, as the power it has to produce in me a new idea or sensation of warmth or burning, which I felt not before, – by the same primary qualities, viz. the bulk, texture, and motion of its insensible parts.

11.   How bodies produce ideas in us. The next thing to be considered is, how bodies produce ideas in us; and that is manifestly by impulse, the only way which we can conceive bodies to operate in.

12.   By motions, external, and in our organism. If then external objects be not united to our minds when they produce ideas therein; and yet we perceive these original qualities in such of them as singly fall under our senses, it is evident that some motion must be thence continued by our nerves, or animal spirits, by some parts of our bodies, to the brains or the seat of sensation, there to produce in our minds the particular ideas we have of them. And since the extension, figure, number, and motion of bodies of an observable bigness, may be perceived at a distance by the sight, it is evident some singly imperceptible bodies must come from them to the eyes, and thereby convey to the brain some motion; which produces these ideas which we have of them in us.

13.   How secondary qualities produce their ideas. After the same manner, that the ideas of these original qualities are produced in us, we may conceive that the ideas of secondary qualities are also produced, viz. by the operation of insensible particles on our senses. For, it being manifest that there are bodies and good store of bodies, each whereof are so small, that we cannot by any of our senses discover either their bulk, figure, or motion, – as is evident in the particles of the air and water, and others extremely smaller than those; perhaps as much smaller than the particles of air and water, as the particles of air and water are smaller than peas or hail-stones; – let us suppose at present that the different motions and figures, bulk and number, of such particles, affecting the several organs of our senses, produce in us those different sensations which we have from the colours and smells of bodies; v.g. that a violet, by the impulse of such insensible particles of matter, of peculiar figures and bulks, and in different degrees and modifications of their motions, causes the ideas of the blue colour, and

sweet scent of that flower to be produced in our minds. It being no more impossible to conceive that God should annex such ideas to such motions, with which they have no similitude, than that he should annex the idea of pain to the motion of a piece of steel dividing our flesh, with which that idea hath no resemblance.

14.   They depend on the primary qualities. What I have said concerning colours and smells may be understood also of tastes and sounds, and other the like sensible qualities; which, whatever reality we by mistake attribute to them, are in truth nothing in the objects themselves, but powers to produce various sensations in us; and depend on those primary qualities, viz. bulk, figure, texture, and motion of parts as I have said.

15.   Ideas of primary qualities are resemblances; of secondary, not. From whence I think it easy to draw this observation, – that the ideas of primary qualities of bodies are resemblances of them, and their patterns do really exist in the bodies themselves, but the ideas produced in us by these secondary qualities have no resemblance of them at all. There is nothing like our ideas, existing in the bodies themselves. They are, in the bodies we denominate from them, only a power to produce those sensations in us: and what is sweet, blue, or warm in idea, is but the certain bulk, figure, and motion of the insensible parts, in the bodies themselves, which we call so.

16.   Examples. Flame is denominated hot and light; snow, white and cold; and manna, white and sweet, from the ideas they produce in us. Which qualities are commonly thought to be the same in those bodies that those ideas are in us, the one the perfect resemblance of the other, as they are in a mirror, and it would by most men be judged very extravagant if one should say otherwise. And yet he that will consider that the same fire that, at one distance produces in us the sensation of warmth, does, at a nearer approach, produce in us the far different sensation of pain, ought to bethink himself what reason he has to say – that this idea of warmth, which was produced in him by the fire, is actually in the fire; and his idea of pain, which the same fire produced in him the same way, is not in the fire. Why are whiteness and coldness in snow, and pain not, when it produces the one and the other idea in us; and can do neither, but by the bulk, figure, number, and motion of its solid parts?

17. The ideas of the primary alone really exist. The particular bulk, number, figure, and motion of the parts of fire or snow are really in them, – whether any one's senses perceive them or no: and therefore they may be called real qualities, because they really exist in those bodies. But light, heat, whiteness, or coldness, are no more really in them than sickness or pain is in manna. Take away the sensation of them; let not the eyes see light or colours, nor the ears hear sounds; let the palate not taste, nor the nose smell, and all colours, tastes, odours, and sounds, as they are such particular ideas, vanish and cease, and are reduced to their causes, i.e. bulk, figure, and motion of parts.

18. The secondary exist in things only as modes of the primary. A piece of manna of a sensible bulk is able to produce in us the idea of a round or square figure; and by being removed from one place to another, the idea of motion. This idea of motion represents it as it really is in manna moving: a circle or square are the same, whether in idea or existence, in the mind or in the manna. And this, both motion and figure, are really in the manna, whether we take notice of them or no: this everybody is ready to agree to. Besides, manna, by the bulk, figure, texture, and motion of its parts, has a power to produce the sensations of sickness, and sometimes of acute pains or gripings in us. That these ideas of sickness and pain are not in the manna, but effects of its operations on us, and are nowhere when we feel them not; this also every one readily agrees to. And yet men are hardly to be brought to think that sweetness and whiteness are not really in manna; which are but the effects of the operations of manna, by the motion, size, and figure of its particles, on the eyes and palate: as the pain and sickness caused by manna are confessedly nothing but the effects of its operations on the stomach and guts, by the size, motion, and figure of its insensible parts, (for by nothing else can a body operate, as has been proved): as if it could not operate on the eyes and palate, and thereby produce in the mind particular distinct ideas, which in itself it has not, as well as we allow it can operate on the guts and stomach, and thereby produce distinct ideas, which in itself it has not. These ideas, being all effects of the operations of manna on several parts of our bodies, by the size, figure number, and motion of its parts;

– why those produced by the eyes and palate should rather be thought to be really in the manna, than those produced by the stomach and guts; or why the pain and sickness, ideas that are the effect of manna, should be thought to be nowhere when they are not felt; and yet the sweetness and whiteness, effects of the same manna on other parts of the body, by ways equally as unknown, should be thought to exist in the manna, when they are not seen or tasted, would need some reason to explain.

19. Examples. Let us consider the red and white colours in porphyry. Hinder light from striking on it, and its colours vanish; it no longer produces any such ideas in us: upon the return of light it produces these appearances on us again. Can any one think any real alterations are made in the porphyry by the presence or absence of light; and that those ideas of whiteness and redness are really in porphyry in the light, when it is plain it has no colour in the dark? It has, indeed, such a configuration of particles, both night and day, as are apt, by the rays of light rebounding from some parts of that hard stone, to produce in us the idea of redness, and from others the idea of whiteness; but whiteness or redness are not in it at any time, but such a texture that hath the power to produce such a sensation in us.

20. Pound an almond, and the clear white colour will be altered into a dirty one, and the sweet taste into an oily one. What real alteration can the beating of the pestle make in any body, but an alteration of the texture of it?

21. Explains how water felt as cold by one hand may be warm to the other. Ideas being thus distinguished and understood, we may be able to give an account how the same water, at the same time, may produce the idea of cold by one hand and of heat by the other: whereas it is impossible that the same water, if those ideas were really in it, should at the same time be both hot and cold. For, if we imagine warmth, as it is in our hands, to be nothing but a certain sort and degree of motion in the minute particles of our nerves or animal spirits, we may understand how it is possible that the same water may, at the same time, produce the sensations of heat in one hand and cold in the other; which yet figure never does, that never producing – the idea of a square by one hand which has produced the idea of a globe by another. But if the sensation of heat and cold be

nothing but the increase or diminution of the motion of the minute parts of our bodies, caused by the corpuscles of any other body, it is easy to be understood, that if that motion be greater in one hand than in the other; if a body be applied to the two hands, which has in its minute particles a greater motion than in those of one of the hands, and a less than in those of the other, it will increase the motion of the one hand and lessen it in the other; and so cause the different sensations of heat and cold that depend thereon.

22.   An excursion into natural philosophy. I have in what just goes before been engaged in physical inquiries a little further than perhaps I intended. But, it being necessary to make the nature of sensation a little understood; and to make the difference between the qualities in bodies, and the ideas produced by them in the mind, to be distinctly conceived, without which it were impossible to discourse intelligibly of them; – I hope I shall be pardoned this little excursion into natural philosophy; it being necessary in our present inquiry to distinguish the primary and real qualities of bodies, which are always in them (viz. solidity, extension, figure, number, and motion, or rest, and are sometimes perceived by us, viz. when the bodies they are in are big enough singly to be discerned), from those secondary and imputed qualities, which are but the powers of several combinations of those primary ones, when they operate without being distinctly discerned; – whereby we may also come to know what ideas are, and what are not, resemblances of something really existing in the bodies we denominate from them.

23.   Three sorts of qualities in bodies. The qualities, then, that are in bodies, rightly considered, are of three sorts: –

First, The bulk, figure, number, situation, and motion or rest of their solid parts. Those are in them, whether we perceive them or not; and when they are of that size that we can discover them, we have by these an idea of the thing as it is in itself; as is plain in artificial things. These I call primary qualities.

Secondly, The power that is in any body, by reason of its insensible primary qualities, to operate after a peculiar manner on any of our senses, and thereby produce in us the different ideas of several colours, sounds, smells, tastes, &c. These are usually called sensible qualities.

Thirdly, The power that is in any body, by reason of the particular constitution of its primary qualities, to make such a change in the bulk, figure, texture, and motion of another body, as to make it operate on our senses differently from what it did before. Thus the sun has a power to make wax white, and fire to make lead fluid. These are usually called powers.

The first of these, as has been said, I think may be properly called real, original, or primary qualities; because they are in the things themselves, whether they are perceived or not: and upon their different modifications it is that the secondary qualities depend.

The other two are only powers to act differently upon other things: which powers result from the different modifications of those primary qualities.

24.   The first are resemblances; the second thought to be resemblances, but are not; the third neither are nor are thought so. But, though the two latter sorts of qualities are powers barely, and nothing but powers, relating to several other bodies, and resulting from the different modifications of the original qualities, yet they are generally otherwise thought of. For the second sort, viz, the powers to produce several ideas in us, by our senses, are looked upon as real qualities in the things thus affecting us: but the third sort are called and esteemed barely powers. v.g. The idea of heat or light, which we receive by our eyes, or touch, from the sun, are commonly thought real qualities existing in the sun, and something more than mere powers in it. But when we consider the sun in reference to wax, which it melts or blanches, we look on the whiteness and softness produced in the wax, not as qualities in the sun, but effects produced by powers in it. Whereas, if rightly considered, these qualities of light and warmth, which are perceptions in me when I am warmed or enlightened by the sun, are no otherwise in the sun, than the changes made in the wax, when it is blanched or melted, are in the sun. They are all of them equally powers in the sun, depending on its primary qualities; whereby it is able, in the one case, so to alter the bulk, figure, texture, or motion of some of the insensible parts of my eyes or hands, as thereby to produce in me the idea of light or heat; and in the other, it is able so to alter the bulk, figure, texture, or motion of the insensible parts of the

wax, as to make them fit to produce in me the distinct ideas of white and fluid.

25.   Why the secondary are ordinarily taken for real qualities, and not for bare powers. The reason why the one are ordinarily taken for real qualities, and the other only for bare powers, seems to be, because the ideas we have of distinct colours, sounds, &c., containing nothing at all in them of bulk, figure, or motion, we are not apt to think them the effects of these primary qualities; which appear not, to our senses, to operate in their production, and with which they have not any apparent congruity or conceivable connexion. Hence it is that we are so forward to imagine, that those ideas are the resemblances of something really existing in the objects themselves: since sensation discovers nothing of bulk, figure, or motion of parts in their production; nor can reason show how bodies, by their bulk, figure, and motion, should produce in the mind the ideas of blue or yellow, &c. But, in the other case, in the operations of bodies changing the qualities one of another, we plainly discover that the quality produced hath commonly no resemblance with anything in the thing producing it; wherefore we look on it as a bare effect of power. For, through receiving the idea of heat or light from the sun, we are apt to think it is a perception and resemblance of such a quality in the sun; yet when we see wax, or a fair face, receive change of colour from the sun, we cannot imagine that to be the reception or resemblance of anything in the sun, because we find not those different colours in the sun itself. For, our senses being able to observe a likeness or unlikeness of sensible qualities in two different external objects, we forwardly enough conclude the production of any sensible quality in any subject to be an effect of bare power, and not the communication of any quality which was really in the efficient, when we find no such sensible quality in the thing that produced it. But our senses, not being able to discover any unlikeness between the idea produced in us, and the quality of the object producing it, we are apt to imagine that our ideas are resemblances of something in the objects, and not the effects of certain powers placed in the modification of their primary qualities, with which primary qualities the ideas produced in us have no resemblance.

26.   Secondary qualities twofold; first, immediately perceivable; secondly, mediately perceivable. To conclude. Besides those before-mentioned primary qualities in bodies, viz. bulk, figure, extension, number, and motion of their solid parts; all the rest, whereby we take notice of bodies, and distinguish them one from another, are nothing else but several powers in them, depending on those primary qualities; whereby they are fitted, either by immediately operating on our bodies to produce several different ideas in us; or else, by operating on other bodies, so to change their primary qualities as to render them capable of producing ideas in us different from what before they did. The former of these, I think, may be called secondary qualities immediately perceivable: the latter, secondary qualities, mediately perceivable.

3

Three Dialogues Between Hylas and Philonous

George Berkeley

The First Dialogue

Philonous. Good morning, Hylas. I did not expect to find you abroad[1] so early.

Hylas. It is indeed something unusual, but my thoughts were so taken up with a subject I was discoursing of last night that, finding I could not sleep, I resolved to rise and take a turn in the garden.

Phil. It happened well, to let you see what innocent and agreeable pleasures you lose every morning. Can there be a pleasanter time of the day, or a more delightful season of the year? That purple sky, these wild but sweet notes of birds, the fragrant bloom upon the trees and flowers, the gentle influence of the rising sun – these and a thousand nameless beauties of nature inspire the soul with secret transports; its faculties, too, being at this time fresh and lively, are fit for those meditations which the solitude of a garden and tranquility of the morning naturally dispose us to. But I am afraid I interrupt your thoughts, for you seemed very intent on something.

Hyl. It is true, I was, and shall be obliged to you if you will permit me to go on in the same vein; not that I would by any means deprive myself of your company, for my thoughts always flow more easily in conversation with a friend than when I am alone; but my request is that you would suffer me to impart my reflections to you.

Phil. With all my heart, it is what I should have requested myself if you had not prevented me.

Hyl. I was considering the odd fate of those men who have in all ages, through an affectation of being distinguished from the vulgar,[2] or some unaccountable turn of thought, pretended either to believe nothing at all or to believe the most extravagant things in the world. This, however, might be borne, if their paradoxes and skepticism did not draw after them some consequences of general disadvantage to mankind. But the mischief lies here: that when men of less leisure see them who are supposed to have spent their whole time in the pursuits of knowledge professing an entire ignorance of all things or advancing such notions as are repugnant to plain and commonly received principles, they will be tempted to entertain suspicions concerning the most important truths, which they had hitherto held sacred and unquestionable.

Phil. I entirely agree with you as to the ill tendency of the affected doubts of some philosophers and fantastical conceits of others. I am even so far gone of late in this way of thinking that I have quitted several of the sublime notions I had got in their schools for vulgar opinions. And I give it you on my word, since this revolt from metaphysical notions to the plain dictates of nature and common sense, I find my understanding strangely enlightened, so that I can now easily

George Berkeley, *Three Dialogues Between Hylas and Philonous* (Chicago: The Open Court Publishing Co., 1906).

comprehend a great many things which before were all mystery and riddle.

Hyl. I am glad to find there was nothing in the accounts I heard of you.

Phil. Pray,[3] what were those?

Hyl. You were represented in last night's conversation as one who maintained the most extravagant opinion that ever entered into the mind of man, namely, that there is no such thing as material substance in the world.

Phil. That there is no such thing as what philosophers call "material substance," I am seriously persuaded; but if I were made to see anything absurd or skeptical in this, I should then have the same reason to renounce this, that I imagine I have now to reject the contrary opinion.

Hyl. What?! Can anything be more fantastic, more repugnant to common sense, or a more manifest piece of skepticism, than to believe there is no such thing as *matter*?

Phil. Softly, good Hylas. What if it should prove that you, who hold there is, are by virtue of that opinion a greater skeptic and maintain more paradoxes and repugnancies[4] to common sense than I who believe no such thing?

Hyl. You may as soon persuade me the part is greater than the whole, as that, in order to avoid absurdity and skepticism, I should ever be obliged to give up my opinion in this point.

Phil. Well then, are you content to admit that opinion for true which, upon examination, shall appear most agreeable to common sense and remote from skepticism?

Hyl. With all my heart. Since you are for raising disputes about the plainest things in nature, I am content for once to hear what you have to say.

Phil. Pray, Hylas, what do you mean by a "skeptic"?

Hyl. I mean what all men mean, one that doubts of everything.

Phil. He then who entertains no doubt concerning some particular point, with regard to that point cannot be thought a skeptic.

Hyl. I agree with you.

Phil. Of which does doubting consist in, embracing the affirmative or negative side of a question?

Hyl. In neither; for whoever understands English cannot but know that "doubting" signifies a suspense[5] between both.

Phil. He then that denies any point can no more be said to doubt of it, than he who affirms it with the same degree of assurance.

Hyl. True.

Phil. And, consequently, for such his denial is no more to be esteemed a skeptic than the other.

Hyl. I acknowledge it.

Phil. How comes it to pass then, Hylas, that you pronounce me a skeptic, because I deny what you affirm, namely, the existence of matter? Since, for all you can tell, I am as peremptory in my denial as you in your affirmation.

Hyl. Hold, Philonous, I have been a little out in my definition; but every false step a man makes in discourse is not to be insisted on. I said indeed that a "skeptic" was one who doubted of everything, but I should have added: or who denies the reality and truth of things.

Phil. What things? Do you mean the principles and theorems of sciences? But these you know are universal intellectual notions, and consequently independent of matter; the denial therefore of this does not imply denying them.

Hyl. I grant it. But are there no other things? What do you think of distrusting the senses, of denying the real existence of sensible things, or pretending to know nothing of them. Is not this sufficient to denominate a man a skeptic?

Phil. Shall we therefore examine which of us it is that denies the reality of sensible things or professes the greatest ignorance of them, since, if I take you rightly, he is to be esteemed the greatest skeptic?

Hyl. That is what I desire.

Phil. What mean you by "sensible things?"

Hyl. Those things which are perceived by the senses. Can you imagine that I mean anything else?

Phil. Pardon me, Hylas, if I am desirous clearly to apprehend your notions, since this may much shorten our inquiry. Suffer me then to ask you this further question: Are those things only perceived by the senses which are perceived immediately? Or may those things properly be said to be "sensible" which are perceived mediately, or not without the intervention of others?

Hyl. I do not sufficiently understand you.

Phil. In reading a book, what I immediately perceive are the letters, but mediately, or by means of these, are suggested to my mind the notions of God, virtue, truth, etc. Now, that the letters are truly sensible things, or perceived by sense, there is no doubt; but I would know whether you take the things suggested by them to be so too.

Hyl. No, certainly, it would be absurd to think God or virtue sensible things, though they may be signified and suggested to the mind by sensible marks with which they have an arbitrary connection.

Phil. It seems, then, that by "sensible things" you mean those only which can be perceived immediately by sense?

Hyl. Right.

Phil. Does it not follow from this that, though I see one part of the sky red, and another blue, and that my reason does then evidently conclude there must be some cause of that diversity of colors, yet that cause cannot be said to be a sensible thing or perceived by the sense of seeing?

Hyl. It does.

Phil. In like manner, though I hear variety of sounds, yet I cannot be said to hear the causes of those sounds.

Hyl. You cannot.

Phil. And when by my touch I perceive a thing to be hot and heavy, I cannot say, with any truth or propriety, that I feel the cause of its heat or weight.

Hyl. To prevent any more questions of this kind, I tell you once for all that by "sensible things" I mean those only which are perceived by sense, and that in truth the senses perceive nothing which they do not perceive immediately, for they make no inferences. The deducing therefore of causes or occasions from effects and appearances, which alone are perceived by sense, entirely relates to reason.

Phil. This point then is agreed between us – that *sensible things are those only which are immediately perceived by sense.* You will further inform me whether we immediately perceive by sight anything besides light, and colors, and figures; or by hearing anything but sounds; by the palate anything besides tastes; by the smell, besides odors; or by the touch, more than tangible qualities.

Hyl. We do not.

Phil. It seems, therefore, that if you take away all sensible qualities, there remains nothing sensible?

Hyl. I grant it.

Phil. Sensible things therefore are nothing else but so many sensible qualities or combinations of sensible qualities?

Hyl. Nothing else.

Phil. Heat then is a sensible thing?

Hyl. Certainly.

Phil. Does the reality of sensible things consist in being perceived? Or, is it something distinct from their being perceived, and that bears no relation to the mind?

Hyl. To *exist* is one thing, and to be *perceived* is another.

Phil. I speak with regard to sensible things only – and of these I ask, whether by their real existence you mean a subsistence exterior to the mind and distinct from their being perceived?

Hyl. I mean a real absolute being, distinct from and without any relation to their being perceived.

Phil. Heat, therefore, if it is allowed a real being, must exist without the mind?

Hyl. It must.

Phil. Tell me, Hylas, is this real existence equally compatible to all degrees of heat which we perceive, or is there any reason why we should attribute it to some and deny it to others? And if there is, pray let me know that reason.

Hyl. Whatever degree of heat we perceive by sense, we may be sure the same exists in the object that occasions it.

Phil. What?! The greatest as well as the least?

Hyl. I tell you, the reason is plainly the same in respect of both: they are both perceived by sense; no, the greater degree of heat is more sensibly perceived and, consequently, if there is any difference, we are more certain of its real existence than we can be of the reality of a lesser degree.

Phil. But is not the most vehement and intense degree of heat a very great pain?

Hyl. No one can deny it.

Phil. And is any unperceiving thing capable of pain or pleasure?

Hyl. No certainly.

Phil. Is your material substance a senseless being or a being endowed with sense and perception?

Hyl. It is senseless without doubt.

Phil. It cannot, therefore, be the subject of pain?

Hyl. By no means.

Phil. Nor consequently of the greatest heat perceived by sense, since you acknowledge this to be no small pain.

Hyl. I grant it.

Phil. What shall we say then of your external object – is it a material substance or not?

Hyl. It is a material substance with the sensible qualities inhering in it.

Phil. How then can a great heat exist in it, since you own[6] it cannot in a material substance? I desire you would clear this point.

Hyl. Hold, Philonous, I fear I was out in yielding intense heat to be a pain. It should seem rather that pain is something distinct from heat, and the consequence or effect of it.

Phil. Upon putting your hand near the fire, do you perceive one simple uniform sensation or two distinct sensations?

Hyl. But one simple sensation.

Phil. Is not the heat immediately perceived?

Hyl. It is.

Phil. And the pain?

Hyl. True.

Phil. Seeing therefore they are both immediately perceived at the same time, and the fire affects you only with one simple or uncompounded idea, it follows that this same simple idea is both the intense heat immediately perceived and the pain; and, consequently, that the intense heat immediately perceived is nothing distinct from a particular sort of pain.

Hyl. It seems so.

Phil. Again, try in your thoughts, Hylas, if you can conceive a vehement sensation to be without pain or pleasure.

Hyl. I cannot.

Phil. Qr can you frame to yourself an idea of sensible pain or pleasure in general, abstracted from every particular idea of heat, cold, tastes, smells, etc.?

Hyl. I do not find that I can.

Phil. Does it not therefore follow that sensible pain is nothing distinct from those sensations or ideas, in an intense degree?

Hyl. It is undeniable; and, to speak the truth, I begin to suspect a very great heat cannot exist but in a mind perceiving it.

Phil. What?! Are you then in that *skeptical* state of suspense, between affirming and denying?

Hyl. I think I may be positive in the point. A very violent and painful heat cannot exist without the mind.

Phil. It has not therefore, according to you, any real being?

Hyl. I own it.

Phil. Is it therefore certain that there is no body in nature really hot?

Hyl. I have not denied there is any real heat in bodies. I only say there is no such thing as an intense real heat.

Phil. But did you not say before that all degrees of heat were equally real – or, if there was any difference, that the greater would be more undoubtedly real than the lesser?

Hyl. True; but it was because I did not then consider the ground there is for distinguishing between them, which I now plainly see. And it is this: because intense heat is nothing else but a particular kind of painful sensation, and pain cannot exist but in a perceiving being, it follows that no intense heat can really exist in an unperceiving corporeal substance. But this is no reason why we should deny heat in an inferior degree to exist in such a substance.

Phil. But how shall we be able to discern those degrees of heat which exist only in the mind from those which exist without it?

Hyl. That is no difficult matter. You know the least pain cannot exist unperceived; whatever, therefore, degree of heat is a pain, exists only in the mind. But as for all other degrees of heat nothing obliges us to think the same of them.

Phil. I think you granted before that no unperceiving being was capable of pleasure any more than of pain.

Hyl. I did.

Phil. And is not warmth, or a more gentle degree of heat than what causes uneasiness, a pleasure?

Hyl. What then?

Phil. Consequently it cannot exist without the mind in an unperceiving substance or body.

Hyl. So it seems.

Phil. Since, therefore, as well those degrees of heat that are not painful, as those that are, can exist only in a thinking substance, may we not conclude that external bodies are absolutely incapable of any degree of heat whatsoever?

Hyl. On second thought, I do not think it so evident that warmth is a pleasure as that a great degree of heat is a pain.

Phil. I do not pretend that warmth is as great a pleasure as heat is a pain. But if you grant it to be even a small pleasure, it serves to make good my conclusion.

Hyl. I could rather call it an "indolence." It seems to be nothing more than a privation of both pain and pleasure. And that such a quality or state as this may agree to an unthinking substance, I hope you will not deny.

Phil. If you are resolved to maintain that warmth, or a gentle degree of heat, is no pleasure, I know not how to convince you otherwise than by appealing to your own sense. But what do you think of cold?

Hyl. The same that I do of heat. An intense degree of cold is a pain, for to feel a very great cold is to perceive a great uneasiness; it cannot, therefore, exist without the mind, but a lesser degree of cold may, as well as a lesser degree of heat.

Phil. Those bodies, therefore, upon whose application to our own we perceive a moderate degree of heat, must be concluded to have a moderate degree of heat or warmth in them; and those, upon whose application we feel a like degree of cold, must be thought to have cold in them.

Hyl. They must.

Phil. Can any doctrine be true that necessarily leads a man into an absurdity?

Hyl. Without doubt it cannot.

Phil. Is it not an absurdity to think that the same thing should be at the same time both cold and warm?

Hyl. It is.

Phil. Suppose now one of your hands hot, and the other cold, and that they are both at once put into the same vessel of water in an intermediate state; will not the water seem cold to one hand, and warm to the other?

Hyl. It will.

Phil. Ought we not therefore, by your principles, to conclude it is really both cold and warm at the same time – that is, according to your own concession, to believe an absurdity?

Hyl. I confess it seems so.

Phil. Consequently, the principles themselves are false, since you have granted that no true principle leads to an absurdity.

Hyl. But, after all, can anything be more absurd than to say *there is no heat in the fire*?

Phil. To make the point still clearer; tell me whether, in two cases exactly alike, we ought not to make the same judgment?

Hyl. We ought.

Phil. When a pin pricks your finger, does it not rend and divide the fibers of your flesh?

Hyl. It does.

Phil. And when a coal burns your finger, does it do any more?

Hyl. It does not.

Phil. Since, therefore, you neither judge the sensation itself occasioned by the pin, nor anything like it, to be in the pin, you should not, conformably to what you have now granted, judge the sensation occasioned by the fire, or anything like it, to be in the fire.

Hyl. Well, since it must be so, I am content to yield this point and acknowledge that heat and cold are only sensations existing in our minds. But there still remain qualities enough to secure the reality of external things.

Phil. But what will you say, Hylas, if it shall appear that the case is the same with regard to all other sensible qualities, and that they can no more be supposed to exist without the mind than heat and cold?

Hyl. Then, indeed, you will have done something to the purpose; but that is what I despair of seeing proved.

Phil. Let us examine them in order. What do you think of tastes – do they exist without the mind or not?

Hyl. Can any man in his senses doubt whether sugar is sweet or wormwood[7] bitter?

Phil. Inform me, Hylas. Is a sweet taste a particular kind of pleasure or pleasant sensation, or is it not?

Hyl. It is.

Phil. And is not bitterness some kind of uneasiness or pain?

Hyl. I grant it.

Phil. If, therefore, sugar and wormwood are unthinking corporeal substances existing without the mind, how can sweetness and bitterness, that is, pleasure and pain, agree to them?

Hyl. Hold on, Philonous, I now see what it was that deluded me all this time. You asked whether heat and cold, sweetness and bitterness, were not particular sorts of pleasure and pain – to which I answered simply that they were. Whereas I should have thus distinguished: Those qualities, as perceived by us, are pleasures or pains, but not as existing in the external objects. We must not therefore conclude absolutely that there is no heat in the fire or sweetness in the sugar, but only that heat or sweetness, as perceived by us, are not in the fire or sugar. What do you say to this?

Phil. I say it is nothing to the purpose. Our discourse proceeded altogether concerning sensible things, which you defined to be the things we "immediately perceive by our senses." Whatever other qualities, therefore, you speak of, as distinct from these, I know nothing of them, neither do they at all belong to the point in dispute. You may, indeed, pretend to have discovered certain qualities which you do not perceive and assert those insensible qualities exist in fire and sugar. But what use can be made of this to your present purpose, I am at a loss to conceive. Tell me then once more, do you acknowledge that heat and cold, sweetness and bitterness – meaning those qualities which are perceived by the senses – do not exist without the mind?

Hyl. I see it is to no purpose to hold out, so I give up the cause as to those mentioned qualities. Though I profess it sounds odd to say that sugar is not sweet.

Phil. But, for your further satisfaction, take this along with you: That which at other times seems sweet shall, to a distempered palate, appear bitter. And nothing can be plainer than that different persons perceive different tastes in the same food, since that which one man delights in, another abhors. And how could this be, if the taste was something really inherent in the food?

Hyl. I acknowledge I do not know how.

Phil. In the next place, odors are to be considered. And with regard to these, I would fain[8] know whether what has been said of tastes does not exactly agree to them? Are they not so many pleasing or displeasing sensations?

Hyl. They are.

Phil. Can you then conceive it possible that they should exist in an unperceiving thing?

Hyl. I cannot.

Phil. Or can you imagine that filth and ordure[9] affect those brute animals that feed on them out of choice with the same smells which we perceive in them?

Hyl. By no means.

Phil. May we not therefore conclude of smells, as of the other aforementioned qualities, that they cannot exist in any but a perceiving substance or mind?

Hyl. I think so.

Phil. Then as to sounds, what must we think of them – are they accidents really inherent in external bodies or not?

Hyl. That they inhere not in the sonorous bodies is plain from this: because a bell struck in the exhausted receiver of an air-pump sends forth no sound. The air, therefore, must be thought the subject of sound.

Phil. What reason is there for that, Hylas?

Hyl. Because, when any motion is raised in the air, we perceive a sound greater or lesser in proportion to the air's motion; but without some motion in the air we never hear any sound at all.

Phil. And granting that we never hear a sound but when some motion is produced in the air, yet I do not see how you can infer from this that the sound itself is in the air.

Hyl. It is this very motion in the external air that produces in the mind the sensation of sound. For, striking on the drum of the ear, it causes a vibration, which, by the auditory nerves being communicated to the brain, the soul is thereupon affected with the sensation called sound.

Phil. What?! Is sound then a sensation?

Hyl. I tell you, as perceived by us, it is a particular sensation in the mind.

Phil. And can any sensation exist without the mind?

Hyl. No, certainly.

Phil. How then can sound, being a sensation, exist in the air, if by the "air" you mean a senseless substance existing without the mind?

Hyl. You must distinguish, Philonous, between sound as it is perceived by us and as it is in itself; or – which is the same thing – between the sound we immediately perceive and that which exists without us. The former, indeed, is a particular kind of sensation, but the latter is merely a vibrating or undulating motion in the air.

Phil. I thought I had already obviated that distinction by the answer I gave when you were applying it in a like case before. But, to say no more of that, are you sure then that sound is really nothing but motion?

Hyl. I am.

Phil. Whatever, therefore, agrees to real sound may with truth be attributed to motion?

Hyl. It may.

Phil. It is then good sense to speak of "motion" as of a thing that is *loud*, *sweet*, *acute*, or *grave*.

Hyl. I see you are resolved not to understand me. Is it not evident those accidents or modes belong only to sensible sound, or sound in the common acceptation[10] of the word, but not to sound in the real and philosophic sense, which, as I just now told you, is nothing but a certain motion of the air?

Phil. It seems then there are two sorts of sound – the one vulgar, or that which is heard, the other philosophical and real?

Hyl. Even so.

Phil. And the latter consists in motion?

Hyl. I told you so before.

Phil. Tell me, Hylas, to which of the senses do you think the idea of motion belongs – to the hearing?

Hyl. No, certainly, but to the sight and touch.

Phil. It should follow then that, according to you, real sounds may possibly be *seen* or *felt*, but never *heard*.

Hyl. Look you, Philonous, you may, if you please, make a jest of my opinion, but that will not alter the truth of things. I own, indeed, the inferences you draw me into sound something oddly; but common language, you know, is framed by, and for the use of, the vulgar. We must not therefore wonder if expressions adapted to exact philosophic notions seem uncouth and out of the way.

Phil. Is it come to that? I assure you I imagine myself to have gained no small point, since you make so light of departing from common phrases and opinions, it being a main part of our inquiry to examine whose notions are widest of the common road and most repugnant to the general sense of the world. But can you think it no more than a philosophical paradox, to say that *real sounds are never heard* and that the idea of them is obtained by some other sense? And is there nothing in this contrary to nature and the truth of things?

Hyl. To deal ingenuously, I do not like it. And, after the concessions already made, I had as well grant that sounds too have no real being without the mind.

Phil. And I hope you will make no difficulty to acknowledge the same of colors.

Hyl. Pardon me; the case of colors is very different. Can anything be plainer than that we see them on the objects?

Phil. The objects you speak of are, I suppose, corporeal substances existing without the mind?

Hyl. They are.

Phil. And have true and real colors inhering in them?

Hyl. Each visible object has that color which we see in it.

Phil. How?! Is there anything visible but what we perceive by sight?

Hyl. There is not.

Phil. And do we perceive anything by sense which we do not perceive immediately?

Hyl. How often must I be obliged to repeat the same thing? I tell you, we do not.

Phil. Have patience, good Hylas, and tell me once more whether there is anything immediately perceived by the senses except sensible qualities. I know you asserted there was not; but I would now be informed whether you still persist in the same opinion.

Hyl. I do.

Phil. Pray, is your corporeal substance either a sensible quality or made up of sensible qualities?

Hyl. What a question that is! Who ever thought it was?

Phil. My reason for asking was, because in saying "each visible object has that color which we see in it," you make visible objects to be corporeal substances, which implies either that corporeal substances are sensible qualities or else that there is something besides sensible qualities perceived by sight; but as this point was formerly agreed between us, and is still maintained by you, it is a clear consequence that your corporeal substance is nothing distinct from sensible qualities.

Hyl. You may draw as many absurd consequences as you please and endeavor to perplex the plainest things, but you shall never persuade me out of my senses. I clearly understand my own meaning.

Phil. I wish you would make me understand it, too. But since you are unwilling to have your notion of corporeal substance examined, I shall urge that point no further. Only be pleased to let me know whether the same colors which we see exist in external bodies or some other.

Hyl. The very same.

Phil. What?! Are then the beautiful red and purple we see on yonder clouds really in them? Or do you imagine they have in themselves any other form than that of a dark mist or vapor?

Hyl. I must own, Philonous, those colors are not really in the clouds as they seem to be at this distance. They are only apparent colors.

Phil. "Apparent" you call them? How shall we distinguish these apparent colors from real?

Hyl. Very easily. Those are to be thought apparent which, appearing only at a distance, vanish upon a nearer approach.

Phil. And those, I suppose, are to be thought real which are discovered by the most near and exact survey.

Hyl. Right.

Phil. Is the nearest and exactest survey made by the help of a microscope or by the naked eye?

Hyl. By a microscope, doubtless.

Phil. But a microscope often discovers colors in an object different from those perceived by the unassisted sight. And, in case we had microscopes magnifying to any assigned degree, it is certain that no object whatsoever, viewed through them, would appear in the same color which it exhibits to the naked eye.

Hyl. And what will you conclude from all this? You cannot argue that there are really and naturally no colors on objects because by artificial managements they may be altered or made to vanish.

Phil. I think it may evidently be concluded from your own concessions that all the colors we see with our naked eyes are only apparent as those on the clouds, since they vanish upon a more close and accurate inspection which is afforded us by a microscope. Then, as to what you say by way of prevention: I ask you whether the real and natural state of an object is better discovered by a very sharp and piercing sight or by one which is less sharp?

Hyl. By the former without doubt.

Phil. Is it not plain from dioptrics[11] that microscopes make the sight more penetrating and represent objects as they would appear to the eye in case it were naturally endowed with a most exquisite sharpness?

Hyl. It is.

Phil. Consequently, the microscopic representation is to be thought that which best sets forth the real nature of the thing, or what it is in itself. The colors, therefore, perceived by it are more genuine and real than those perceived otherwise.

Hyl. I confess there is something in what you say.

Phil. Besides, it is not only possible but manifest that there actually are animals whose eyes are by nature framed to perceive those things which by reason of their minuteness escape our sight.

What do you think of those inconceivably small animals perceived by glasses? Must we suppose they are all stark blind? Or, in case they see, can it be imagined their sight has not the same use in preserving their bodies from injuries which appears in that of all other animals? And if it has, is it not evident they must see particles less than their own bodies, which will present them with a far different view in each object from that which strikes our senses? Even our own eyes do not always represent objects to us after the same manner. In the case of jaundice, everyone knows that all things seem yellow. Is it not therefore highly probable that those animals in whose eyes we discern a very different texture from that of ours, and whose bodies abound with different humors, do not see the same colors in every object that we do? From all this should it not seem to follow that all colors are equally apparent, and that none of those which we perceive are really inherent in any outward object?

Hyl. It should.

Phil. The point will be past all doubt if you consider that, in case colors were real properties or affections inherent in external bodies, they could admit of no alteration without some change wrought in the very bodies themselves. But is it not evident from what has been said that, upon the use of microscopes, upon a change happening in the humors of the eye, or a variation of distance, without any manner of real alteration in the thing itself, the colors of any object are either changed or totally disappear? No, all other circumstances remaining the same, change but the situation of some objects and they shall present different colors to the eye. The same thing happens upon viewing an object in various degrees of light. And what is more known than that the same bodies appear differently colored by candlelight from what they do in the open day? Add to these the experiment of a prism which, separating the heterogeneous rays of light, alters the color of any object and will cause the whitest to appear of a deep blue or red to the naked eye. And now tell me whether you are still of the opinion that every body has its true real color inhering in it; and if you think it has, I would fain know further from you what certain distance and position of the object, what peculiar texture and formation of the eye, what degree or kind of light is necessary for ascertaining that true color and distinguishing it from apparent ones.

Hyl. I own myself entirely satisfied that they are all equally apparent and that there is no such thing as color really inhering in external bodies, but that it is altogether in the light. And what confirms me in this opinion is that in proportion to the light, colors are still more or less vivid; and if there is no light, then there are no colors perceived. Besides, allowing there are colors on external objects, yet, how is it possible for us to perceive them? For no external body affects the mind unless it act first on our organs of sense. But the only action of bodies is motion, and motion cannot be communicated otherwise than by impulse. A distant object, therefore, cannot act on the eye, nor consequently make itself or its properties perceivable to the soul. From this it plainly follows that it is immediately some contiguous substance which, operating on the eye, occasions a perception of colors – and such is light.

Phil. How? Is light then a substance?

Hyl. I tell you, Philonous, external light is nothing but a thin fluid substance whose minute particles, being agitated with a brisk motion and in various manners reflected from the different surfaces of outward objects to the eyes, communicate different motions to the optic nerves, which, being propagated to the brain, cause therein various impressions – and these are attended with the sensations of red, blue, yellow, etc.

Phil. It seems, then, the light does no more than shake the optic nerves.

Hyl. Nothing else.

Phil. And consequent to each particular motion of the nerves the mind is affected with a sensation, which is some particular color.

Hyl. Right.

Phil. And these sensations have no existence without the mind.

Hyl. They have not.

Phil. How then do you affirm that colors are in the light, since by "light" you understand a corporeal substance external to the mind?

Hyl. Light and colors, as immediately perceived by us, I grant cannot exist without the mind. But in themselves they are only the motions and configurations of certain insensible particles of matter.

Phil. Colors, then, in the vulgar sense, or taken for the immediate objects of sight, cannot agree to any but a perceiving substance.

Hyl. That is what I say.

Phil. Well then, since you give up the point as to those sensible qualities which are alone thought colors by all mankind besides, you may hold what you please with regard to those invisible ones of the philosophers. It is not my business to dispute about them; only I would advise you to bethink yourself whether, considering the inquiry we are upon, it is prudent for you to affirm: *the red and blue which we see are not real colors, but certain unknown motions and figures which no man ever did or can see are truly so.* Are not these shocking notions, and are not they subject to as many ridiculous inferences as those you were obliged to renounce before in the case of sounds?

Hyl. I frankly own, Philonous, that it is in vain to stand out any longer. Colors, sounds, tastes, in a word, all those termed "secondary qualities," have certainly no existence without the mind. But by this acknowledgment I must not be supposed to derogate anything from the reality of matter or external objects, seeing it is no more than several philosophers maintain who nevertheless are the furthest imaginable from denying matter. For the clearer understanding of this you must know sensible qualities are by philosophers divided into *primary* and *secondary*. The former are extension, figure, solidity, gravity, motion, and rest. And these they hold exist really in bodies. The latter are those above enumerated, or, briefly, all sensible qualities besides the primary, which they assert are only so many sensations or ideas existing nowhere but in the mind. But all this, I doubt not, you are already apprised of. For my part, I have been a long time sensible there was such an opinion current among philosophers, but was never thoroughly convinced of its truth until now.

Phil. You are still then of the opinion that extension and figures are inherent in external unthinking substances?

Hyl. I am.

Phil. But what if the same arguments which are brought against secondary qualities will hold good against these also?

Hyl. Why then I shall be obliged to think they too exist only in the mind.

Phil. Is it your opinion the very figure and extension which you perceive by sense exist in the outward object or material substance?

Hyl. It is.

Phil. Have all other animals as good grounds to think the same of the figure and extension which they see and feel?

Hyl. Without doubt, if they have any thought at all.

Phil. Answer me, Hylas. Do you think the senses were bestowed upon all animals for their preservation and wellbeing in life? Or were they given to men alone for this end?

Hyl. I make no question but they have the same use in all other animals.

Phil. If so, is it not necessary they should be enabled by them to perceive their own limbs and those bodies which are capable of harming them?

Hyl. Certainly.

Phil. A mite therefore must be supposed to see his own foot, and things equal or even less than it, as bodies of some considerable dimension, though at the same time they appear to you scarce discernible or at best as so many visible points?

Hyl. I cannot deny it.

Phil. And to creatures less than the mite they will seem yet larger?

Hyl. They will.

Phil. To the extent that what you can hardly discern will to another extremely minute animal appear as some huge mountain?

Hyl. All this I grant.

Phil. Can one and the same thing be at the same time in itself of different dimensions?

Hyl. That would be absurd to imagine.

Phil. But from what you have laid down it follows, that both the extension perceived by you, and that perceived by the mite itself, as likewise all those perceived by lesser animals, are each of them the true extension of the mite's foot – that is to say, by your own principles you are led into an absurdity.

Hyl. There seems to be some difficulty in the point.

Phil. Again, have you not acknowledged that no real inherent property of any object can be changed, without some change in the thing itself?

Hyl. I have.

Phil. But, as we approach to or recede from an object, the visible extension varies, being at one distance ten or an hundred times greater than at another. Does it not therefore follow from this, likewise, that it is not really inherent in the object?

Hyl. I own I am at a loss what to think.

Phil. Your judgment will soon be determined if you will venture to think as freely concerning this quality as you have done concerning the rest. Was it not admitted as a good argument that neither heat nor cold was in the water because it seemed warm to one hand and cold to the other?

Hyl. It was.

Phil. Is it not the very same reasoning to conclude there is no extension or figure in an object because to one eye it shall seem little, smooth, and round, when at the same time it appears to the other, great, uneven, and angular?

Hyl. The very same. But does this latter fact ever happen?

Phil. You may at any time make the experiment by looking with one eye bare, and with the other through a microscope.

Hyl. I know not how to maintain it, and yet I am loath to give up *extension*; I see so many odd consequences following upon such a concession.

Phil. Odd, you say? After the concessions already made, I hope you will stick at nothing for its oddness. [But, on the other hand, should it not seem very odd if the general reasoning which includes all other sensible qualities did not also include extension? If it is allowed that no idea nor anything like an idea can exist in an unperceiving substance, then surely it follows that no figure or mode of extension, which we can either perceive or imagine or have any idea of, can be really inherent in matter – not to mention the peculiar difficulty there must be in conceiving a material substance, prior to and distinct from extension, to be the *substratum* of extension. Whatever the sensible quality may be – figure, or sound, or color – it seems alike impossible it should subsist in that which does not perceive it.]

Hyl. I give up the point for the present, reserving still a right to retract my opinion in case I shall hereafter discover any false step in my progress to it.

Phil. That is a right you cannot be denied. Figures and extension being dispatched, we proceed next to motion. Can a real motion in any external body be at the same time very swift and very slow?

Hyl. It cannot.

Phil. Is not the motion of a body swift in a reciprocal proportion to the time it takes up in describing[12] any given space? Thus a body that describes a mile in an hour moves three times faster than it would in case it described only a mile in three hours.

Hyl. I agree with you.

Phil. And is not time measured by the succession of ideas in our minds?

Hyl. It is.

Phil. And is it not possible ideas should succeed one another twice as fast in your mind as they do in mine, or in that of some spirit of another kind?

Hyl. I own it.

Phil. Consequently, the same body may to another seem to perform its motion over any space in half the time that it does to you. And the same reasoning will hold as to any other proportion – that is to say, according to your principles, since the motions perceived are both really in the object, it is possible one and the same body shall be really moved the same way at once, both very swift and very slow. How is this consistent either with common sense or with what you just now granted?

Hyl. I have nothing to say to it.

Phil. Then as for solidity; either you do not mean any sensible quality by that word, and so it is beside our inquiry, or, if you do, it must be either hardness or resistance. But both the one and the other are plainly relative to our senses – it being evident that what seems hard to one animal may appear soft to another who has greater force and firmness of limbs. Nor is it less plain that the resistance I feel is not in the body.

Hyl. I own the very sensation of resistance, which is all you immediately perceive, is not in the body, but the cause of that sensation is.

Phil. But the causes of our sensations are not things immediately perceived, and therefore are not sensible. This point I thought had been already determined.

Hyl. I own it was; but you will pardon me if I seem a little embarrassed. I do not know how to quit my old notions.

Phil. To help you out, do but consider that if extension is once acknowledged to have no existence without the mind, the same must necessarily be granted of motion, solidity, and gravity, since they all evidently suppose extension. It is therefore superfluous to inquire particularly concerning each of them. In denying extension, you have denied them all to have any real existence.

Hyl. I wonder, Philonous, if what you say is true, why those philosophers who deny the secondary qualities any real existence should yet attribute it to the primary. If there is no difference between them, how can this be accounted for?

Phil. It is not my business to account for every opinion of the philosophers. But, among other reasons which may be assigned for this, it seems probable that pleasure and pain being annexed to the former rather than the latter may be one. Heat and cold, tastes and smells have something more vividly pleasing or disagreeable than the ideas of extension, figure, and motion affect us with. And, it being too visibly absurd to hold that pain or pleasure can be in an unperceiving substance, men are more easily weaned from believing the external existence of the secondary than the primary qualities. You will be satisfied there is something in this if you recollect the difference you made between an intense and more moderate degree of heat, allowing the one a real existence while you denied it to the other. But, after all, there is no rational ground for that distinction, for surely an indifferent sensation is as truly a *sensation* as one more pleasing or painful, and consequently should not any more than they be supposed to exist in an unthinking subject.

Hyl. It is just come into my head, Philonous, that I have somewhere heard of a distinction between absolute and sensible extension. Now though it is acknowledged that *great* and *small*, consisting merely in the relation which other extended beings have to the parts of our own bodies, do not really inhere in the substances themselves, yet nothing obliges us to hold the same with regard to *absolute extension*, which is something abstracted from *great* and *small*, from this or that particular magnitude or figure. So likewise as to motion – *swift* and *slow* are altogether relative to the succession of ideas in our own minds. But it does not follow, because those modifications of motion do not exist without the mind, that therefore absolute motion abstracted from them does not.

Phil. Pray what is it that distinguishes one motion, or one part of extension, from another? Is it not something sensible, as some degree of swiftness or slowness, some certain magnitude or figure peculiar to each?

Hyl. I think so.

Phil. These qualities, therefore, stripped of all sensible properties, are without all specific and numerical differences, as the Schools[13] call them.

Hyl. They are.

Phil. That is to say, they are extension in general, and motion in general.

Hyl. Let it be so.

Phil. But it is a universally received maxim that *everything which exists is particular.*[14] How then can motion in general, or extension in general, exist in any corporeal substance?

Hyl. I will take time to solve your difficulty.

Phil. But I think the point may be speedily decided. Without doubt you can tell whether you are able to frame this or that idea. Now I am content to put our dispute on this issue. If you can frame in your thoughts a distinct abstract idea of motion or extension divested of all those sensible modes as swift and slow, great and small, round and square, and the like, which are acknowledged to exist only in the mind, I will then yield the point you contend for. But if you cannot, it will be unreasonable on your side to insist any longer upon what you have no notion of.

Hyl. To confess ingenuously, I cannot.

Phil. Can you even separate the ideas of extension and motion from the ideas of all those qualities which they who make the distinction term "secondary"?

Hyl. What?! Is it not an easy matter to consider extension and motion by themselves, abstracted from all other sensible qualities? Pray how do the mathematicians treat of them?

Phil. I acknowledge, Hylas, it is not difficult to form general propositions and reasonings about those qualities without mentioning any other, and, in this sense, to consider or treat of them abstractedly. But how does it follow that because I can pronounce the word "motion" by itself, I can form the idea of it in my mind exclusive of body? Or because theorems may be made of extension and figures, without any mention of *great* or *small*, or any other sensible mode or quality, that therefore it is possible such an abstract idea of extension, without any particular size or figure or sensible quality, should be distinctly formed and apprehended by the mind? Mathematicians treat of quantity without regarding what other sensible qualities it is attended with, as being altogether indifferent to their demonstrations. But when, laying aside the words, they contemplate the bare ideas, I believe you will find they are not the pure abstracted ideas of extension.

Hyl. But what do you say to *pure intellect*? May not abstracted ideas be framed by that faculty?

Phil. Since I cannot frame abstract ideas at all,[15] it is plain I cannot frame them by the help of "pure intellect," whatever faculty you understand by those words. Besides – not to inquire into the nature of pure intellect and its spiritual objects, as *virtue, reason, God,* or the like – this much seems manifest, that sensible things are only to be perceived by sense or represented by the imagination. Figures, therefore, and extension, being originally perceived by sense, do not belong to pure intellect. But, for your further satisfaction, try if you can to frame the idea of any figure abstracted from all particularities of size, or even from other sensible qualities.

Hyl. Let me think a little – I do not find that I can.

Phil. And can you think it possible that should really exist in nature which implies a repugnancy in its conception?

Hyl. By no means.

Phil. Since therefore it is impossible even for the mind to disunite the ideas of extension and motion from all other sensible qualities, does it not follow that where the one exists there necessarily the other exists likewise?

Hyl. It should seem so.

Phil. Consequently, the very same arguments which you admitted as conclusive against the secondary qualities are without any further application of force against the primary, too. Besides, if you will trust your senses, is it not plain all sensible qualities coexist, or to them appear as being in the same place? Do they ever represent a motion or figure as being divested of all other visible and tangible qualities?

Hyl. You need say no more on this head. I am free to own, if there is no secret error or oversight in our proceedings so far, that all sensible qualities are alike to be denied existence without the mind. But my fear is that I have been too liberal in my former concessions, or overlooked some fallacy or other. In short, I did not take time to think.

Phil. For that matter, Hylas, you may take what time you please in reviewing the progress of our inquiry. You are at liberty to recover any slips you might have made, or offer whatever you have omitted which makes for your first opinion.

Hyl. One great oversight I take to be this: that I did not sufficiently distinguish the *object* from the *sensation*. Now though this latter may not exist without the mind, yet it will not follow from this that the former cannot.

Phil. What object do you mean? The object of the senses?

Hyl. The same.

Phil. It is then immediately perceived.

Hyl. Right.

Phil. Make me to understand the difference between what is immediately perceived and a sensation.

Hyl. The sensation I take to be an act of the mind perceiving; besides which there is something perceived, and this I call the "object." For example, there is red and yellow on that tulip. But then the act of perceiving those colors is in me only, and not in the tulip.

Phil. What tulip do you speak of? Is it that which you see?

Hyl. The same.

Phil. And what do you see besides color, figure, and extension?

Hyl. Nothing.

Phil. What you would say then is that the red and yellow are coexistent with the extension – is it not?

Hyl. That is not all. I would say they have a real existence without the mind in some unthinking substance.

Phil. That the colors are really in the tulip which I see is manifest. Neither can it be denied that this tulip may exist independent of your mind or mine; but that any immediate object of the senses – that is, any idea, or combination of ideas – should exist in an unthinking substance, or exterior to all minds, is in itself an evident contradiction. Nor can I imagine how this follows from what you said just now, namely, that the red and yellow were on the tulip *you saw*, since you do not pretend to *see* that unthinking substance.

Hyl. You have an artful way, Philonous, of diverting our inquiry from the subject.

Phil. I see you have no mind to be pressed that way. To return then to your distinction between *sensation* and *object*; if I take you right, you distinguish in every perception two things, the one an action of the mind, the other not.

Hyl. True.

Phil. And this action cannot exist in, or belong to, any unthinking thing, but whatever besides is implied in a perception may?

Hyl. That is my meaning.

Phil. So that if there was a perception without any act of the mind, it would be possible such a perception should exist in an unthinking substance?

Hyl. I grant it. But it is impossible there should be such a perception.

Phil. When is the mind said to be active?

Hyl. When it produces, puts an end to, or changes anything.

Phil. Can the mind produce, discontinue, or change anything but by an act of the will?

Hyl. It cannot.

Phil. The mind therefore is to be accounted active in its perceptions insofar as volition is included in them?

Hyl. It is.

Phil. In plucking this flower I am active, because I do it by the motion of my hand, which was consequent upon my volition; so likewise in applying it to my nose. But is either of these smelling?

Hyl. No.

Phil. I act, too, in drawing the air through my nose, because my breathing so rather than otherwise is the effect of my volition. But neither can this be called "smelling," for if it were, I should smell every time I breathed in that manner.

Hyl. True.

Phil. Smelling then is somewhat consequent to all this?

Hyl. It is.

Phil. But I do not find my will concerned any further. Whatever more there is – as that I perceive such a particular smell or any smell at all – this is independent of my will, and in that I am altogether passive. Do you find it otherwise with you, Hylas?

Hyl. No, the very same.

Phil. Then, as to seeing, is it not in your power to open your eyes or keep them shut, to turn them this or that way?

Hyl. Without doubt.

Phil. But does it in like manner depend on your will that in looking on this flower you perceive *white* rather than any other color? Or directing your open eyes towards yonder part of the heaven, can you avoid seeing the sun? Or is light or darkness the effect of your volition?

Hyl. No, certainly.

Phil. You are then in these respects altogether passive?

Hyl. I am.

Phil. Tell me now whether *seeing* consists in perceiving light and colors or in opening and turning the eyes?

Hyl. Without doubt, in the former.

Phil. Since, therefore, you are in the very perception of light and colors altogether passive, what is become of that action you were speaking of as an ingredient in every sensation? And does it not follow from your own concessions that the perception of light and colors, including no action in it, may exist in an unperceiving substance? And is not this a plain contradiction?

Hyl. I do not know what to think of it.

Phil. Besides, since you distinguish the *active* and *passive* in every perception, you must do it in that of pain. But how is it possible that pain, be it as little active as you please, should exist in an unperceiving substance? In short, do but consider the point and then confess ingenuously whether light and colors, tastes, sounds, etc. are not all equally passions or sensations in the soul. You may indeed call them "external objects" and give them in words what subsistence you please. But examine your own thoughts and then tell me whether it is not as I say?

Hyl. I acknowledge, Philonous, that, upon a fair observation of what passes in my mind, I can discover nothing else but that I am a thinking being, affected with variety of sensations; neither is it possible to conceive how a sensation should exist in an unperceiving substance. But then, on the other hand, when I look on sensible things in a different view, considering them as so many modes and qualities, I find it necessary to suppose a material *substratum*, without which they cannot be conceived to exist.[16]

Phil. "Material substratum" you call it? Pray, by which of your senses did you become acquainted with that being?

Hyl. It is not itself sensible; its modes and qualities only being perceived by the senses.

Phil. I presume then it was by reflection and reason that you obtained the idea of it.

Hyl. I do not pretend to any proper positive idea of it. However, I conclude it exists because qualities cannot be conceived to exist without a support.

Phil. It seems then you have only a relative notion of it, or that you conceive it not otherwise than by conceiving the relation it bears to sensible qualities.

Hyl. Right.

Phil. Be pleased, therefore, to let me know in what that relation consists.

Hyl. Is it not sufficiently expressed in the term "substratum" or "substance"?

Phil. If so, the word "substratum" should import that it is spread under the sensible qualities or accidents?

Hyl. True.

Phil. And consequently under extension?

Hyl. I own it.

Phil. It is therefore somewhat in its own nature entirely distinct from extension?

Hyl. I tell you extension is only a mode, and matter is something that supports modes. And is it not evident the thing supported is different from the thing supporting?

Phil. So that something distinct from, and exclusive of, extension is supposed to be the *substratum* of extension?

Hyl. Just so.

Phil. Answer me, Hylas. Can a thing be spread without extension? Or is not the idea of extension necessarily included in *spreading*?

Hyl. It is.

Phil. Whatever therefore you suppose spread under anything must have in itself an extension distinct from the extension of that thing under which it is spread?

Hyl. It must.

Phil. Consequently, every corporeal substance being the *substratum* of extension must have in itself another extension by which it is qualified to be a *substratum* – and so on to infinity. And I ask whether this is not absurd in itself and repugnant to what you granted just now, namely, that the *substratum* was something distinct from and exclusive of extension?

Hyl. Yes, but, Philonous, you take me wrong. I do not mean that matter is *spread* in a gross literal sense under extension. The word "substratum" is used only to express in general the same thing with "substance."

Phil. Well then, let us examine the relation implied in the term "substance." Is it not that it stands under accidents?

Hyl. The very same.

Phil. But that one thing may stand under or support another, must it not be extended?

Hyl. It must.

Phil. Is not therefore this supposition liable to the same absurdity with the former?

Hyl. You still take things in a strict literal sense – that is not fair, Philonous.

Phil. I am not for imposing any sense on your words. You are at liberty to explain them as you please. Only, I beseech you, make me understand something by them. You tell me, matter supports or stands under accidents. How! Is it as your legs support your body?

Hyl. No; that is the literal sense.

Phil. Pray let me know any sense, literal or not literal, that you understand it in. – How long must I wait for an answer, Hylas?

Hyl. I declare I know not what to say. I once thought I understood well enough what was meant by matter's supporting accidents. But now, the more I think on it, the less can I comprehend it; in short, I find that I know nothing of it.

Phil. It seems then you have no idea at all, neither relative nor positive of matter; you know neither what it is in itself nor what relation it bears to accidents?

Hyl. I acknowledge it.

Phil. And yet you asserted that you could not conceive how qualities or accidents should really exist without conceiving at the same time a material support of them?

Hyl. I did.

Phil. That is to say, when you conceive the real existence of qualities, you do in addition conceive something which you cannot conceive.

Hyl. It was wrong I own. But still I fear there is some fallacy or other. Pray, what think you of this? It is just come into my head that the ground of all our mistake lies in your treating of each quality by itself. Now, I grant that each

quality cannot singly subsist without the mind. Color cannot without extension, neither can figure without some other sensible quality. But as the several qualities united or blended together form entire sensible things, nothing hinders why such things may not be supposed to exist without the mind.

Phil. Either, Hylas, you are jesting or have a very bad memory. Though, indeed, we went through all the qualities by name one after another, yet my arguments, or rather your concessions, nowhere tended to prove that the secondary qualities did not subsist each alone by itself, but that they were not *at all* without the mind. Indeed, in treating of figure and motion we concluded they could not exist without the mind, because it was impossible even in thought to separate them from all secondary qualities, so as to conceive them existing by themselves. But then this was not the only argument made use of upon that occasion. But – to pass by all that has been so far said and reckon it for nothing, if you will have it so – I am content to put the whole upon this issue. If you can conceive it possible for any mixture or combination of qualities, or any sensible object whatever, to exist without the mind, then I will grant it actually to be so.

Hyl. If it comes to that, the point will soon be decided. What is more easy than to conceive a tree or house existing by itself, independent of, and unperceived by, any mind whatsoever? I do at this present time conceive them existing after that manner.

Phil. What are you saying, Hylas – can you see a thing which is at the same time unseen?

Hyl. No, that would be a contradiction.

Phil. Is it not as great a contradiction to talk of *conceiving* a thing which is *unconceived*?

Hyl. It is.

Phil. The tree or house, therefore, which you think of is conceived by you?

Hyl. How should it be otherwise?

Phil. And what is conceived is surely in the mind?

Hyl. Without question, that which is conceived is in the mind.

Phil. How then did you come to say you conceived a house or tree existing independent and out of all minds whatsoever?

Hyl. That was, I own, an oversight, but stay, let me consider what led me into it. It is a pleasant mistake enough. As I was thinking of a tree in a solitary place, where no one was present to see it, I thought that was to conceive a tree as existing unperceived or unthought of, not considering that I myself conceived it all the while. But now I plainly see that all I can do is to frame ideas in my own mind. I may indeed conceive in my own thoughts the idea of a tree, or a house, or a mountain, but that is all. And this is far from proving that I can conceive them *existing out of the minds of all spirits.*

Phil. You acknowledge then that you cannot possibly conceive how any one corporeal sensible thing should exist otherwise than in the mind?

Hyl. I do.

Phil. And yet you will earnestly contend for the truth of that which you cannot so much as conceive?

Hyl. I profess I do not know what to think; but still there are some scruples[17] that remain with me. Is it not certain I see things at a distance? Do we not perceive the stars and moon, for example, to be a great way off? Is not this, I say, manifest to the senses?

Phil. Do you not in a dream, too, perceive those or the like objects?

Hyl. I do.

Phil. And have they not then the same appearance of being distant?

Hyl. They have.

Phil. But you do not conclude from this the apparitions in a dream to be without the mind?

Hyl. By no means.

Phil. You ought not therefore to conclude that sensible objects are without the mind, from their appearance or manner wherein they are perceived.

Hyl. I acknowledge it. But does not my sense deceive me in those cases?

Phil. By no means. The idea or thing which you immediately perceive, neither sense nor reason informs you that it actually exists without the mind. By sense you only know that you are affected with such certain sensations of light and colors, etc. And these you will not say are without the mind.

Hyl. True, but, besides all that, do you not think the sight suggests something of *outness* or *distance*?

Phil. Upon approaching a distant object, do the visible size and figure change perpetually or do they appear the same at all distances?

Hyl. They are in a continual change.

Phil. Sight, therefore, does not suggest or any way inform you, that the visible object you immediately perceive, exists at a distance, or will be perceived when you advance farther onward, there being a continued series of visible objects succeeding each other during the whole time of your approach.

Hyl. It does not; but still I know, upon seeing an object, what object I shall perceive after having passed over a certain distance. No matter whether it is exactly the same or not, there is still something of distance suggested in the case.

Phil. Good Hylas, do but reflect a little on the point, and then tell me whether there is any more in it than this. From the ideas you actually perceive by sight, you have by experience learned to collect what other ideas you will – according to the standing order of nature – be affected with, after such a certain succession of time and motion.

Hyl. Upon the whole, I take it to be nothing else.

Phil. Now is it not plain that if we suppose a man born blind, was on a sudden made to see, he could at first have no experience of what may be suggested by sight.[18]

Hyl. It is.

Phil. He would not then, according to you, have any notion of distance annexed to the things he saw, but would take them for a new set of sensations existing only in his mind?

Hyl. It is undeniable.

Phil. But to make it still more plain: is not *distance* a line turned endwise to the eye?

Hyl. It is.

Phil. And can a line so situated be perceived by sight?

Hyl. It cannot.

Phil. Does it not therefore follow that distance is not properly and immediately perceived by sight?

Hyl. It should seem so.

Phil. Again, is it your opinion that colors are at a distance?

Hyl. It must be acknowledged they are only in the mind.

Phil. But do not colors appear to the eye as coexisting in the same place with extension and figures?

Hyl. They do.

Phil. How can you then conclude from sight that figures exist without, when you acknowledge colors do not; the sensible appearance being the very same with regard to both?

Hyl. I do not know what to answer.

Phil. But allowing that distance was truly and immediately perceived by the mind, yet it would not follow from this that it existed out of the mind. For whatever is immediately perceived is an idea – and can any *idea* exist out of the mind?

Hyl. To suppose that would be absurd. But, inform me, Philonous, can we perceive or know nothing besides our ideas?

Phil. As for the rational deducing of causes from effects, that is beside our inquiry. And by the senses you can best tell whether you perceive anything which is not immediately perceived. And I ask you whether the things immediately perceived are other than your own sensations or ideas? You have indeed more than once, in the course of this conversation, declared yourself on those points, but you seem by this last question to have departed from what you then thought.

Hyl. To speak the truth, Philonous, I think there are two kinds of objects: the one perceived immediately, which are likewise called "ideas," the other are real things or external objects perceived by the mediation of ideas, which are their images and representations. Now I own ideas do not exist without the mind, but the latter sort of objects do. I am sorry I did not think of this distinction sooner; it would probably have cut short your discourse.

Phil. Are those external objects perceived by sense or by some other faculty?

Hyl. They are perceived by sense.

Phil. How? Is there anything perceived by sense which is not immediately perceived?

Hyl. Yes, Philonous, in some sort there is. For example, when I look on a picture or statue of Julius Caesar, I may be said, after a manner, to perceive him – though not immediately – by my senses.

Phil. It seems then you will have our ideas, which alone are immediately perceived, to be pictures of external things, and that these also are perceived by sense inasmuch as they have a conformity or resemblance to our ideas?

Hyl. That is my meaning.

Phil. And in the same way that Julius Caesar, in himself invisible, is nevertheless perceived by sight, real things, in themselves imperceptible, are perceived by sense.

Hyl. In the very same.

Phil. Tell me, Hylas, when you behold the picture of Julius Caesar, do you see with your eyes any more than some colors and figures with a certain symmetry and composition of the whole?

Hyl. Nothing else.

Phil. And would not a man who had never known anything of Julius Caesar see as much?

Hyl. He would.

Phil. Consequently, he has his sight and the use of it in as perfect a degree as you.

Hyl. I agree with you.

Phil. From where does it come then that your thoughts are directed to the Roman emperor, and his are not? This cannot proceed from the sensations or ideas of sense by you then perceived, since you acknowledge you have no advantage over him in that respect. It should seem therefore to proceed from reason and memory – should it not?

Hyl. It should.

Phil. Consequently, it will not follow from that instance that anything is perceived by sense which is not immediately perceived. Though I grant we may in one acceptation be said to perceive sensible things mediately by sense – that is, when, from a frequently perceived connection, the immediate perception of ideas by one sense suggests to the mind others perhaps belonging to another sense, which are accustomed to be connected with them. For instance, when I hear a coach drive along the streets, immediately I perceive only the sound; but from the experience I have had that such a sound is connected with a coach, I am said to hear the coach. It is nevertheless evident that, in truth and strictness, nothing can be *heard* but *sound*; and the coach is not then properly perceived by sense, but suggested from experience. So likewise when we are said to see a red-hot bar of iron; the solidity and heat of the iron are not the objects of sight, but suggested to the imagination by the color and figure, which are properly perceived by that sense. In short, those things alone are actually and strictly perceived by any sense which would have been perceived in case that same sense had then been first conferred on us. As for other things, it is plain they are only suggested to the mind by experience grounded on former perceptions. But to return to your comparison of Caesar's picture, it is plain, if you keep to that, you must hold the real things or archetypes of our ideas are not perceived by sense, but by some internal faculty of the soul, as reason or memory. I would therefore fain know what arguments you can draw from reason for the existence of what you call "real things" or "material objects," or whether you remember to have seen them formerly as they are in themselves, or if you have heard or read of any one that did.

Hyl. I see, Philonous, you are disposed to raillery;[19] but that will never convince me.

Phil. My aim is only to learn from you, the way to come at the knowledge of "material beings." Whatever we perceive is perceived either immediately or mediately – by sense, or by reason and reflection. But, as you have excluded sense, pray show me what reason you have to believe their existence, or what *medium* you can possibly make use of to prove it either to mine or your own understanding.

Hyl. To deal ingenuously, Philonous, now that I consider the point, I do not find I can give you any good reason for it. But this much seems pretty plain, that it is at least possible such things may really exist. And as long as there is no absurdity in supposing them, I am resolved to believe as I did, until you bring good reasons to the contrary.

Phil. What?! Is it come to this, that you only believe the existence of material objects, and that your belief is founded barely on the possibility of its being true? Then you will have me bring reasons against it, though another would think it reasonable the proof should lie on him who holds the affirmative. And, after all, this very point which you are now resolved to maintain without any reason is in effect what you have more than once during this discourse seen good reason to give up. But to pass over all this – if I understand you rightly, you say our ideas do not exist without the mind, but that they are copies, images, or representations of certain originals that do?

Hyl. You take me right.

Phil. They are then like external things?

Hyl. They are.

Phil. Have those things a stable and permanent nature, independent of our senses, or are they in a perpetual change, upon our producing any motions in our bodies, suspending, exerting, or altering our faculties or organs of sense?

Hyl. Real things, it is plain, have a fixed and real nature, which remains the same notwithstanding any change in our senses or in the posture and motion of our bodies, which indeed may affect the ideas in our minds, but it would be absurd to think they had the same effect on things existing without the mind.

Phil. How then is it possible that things perpetually fleeting and variable as our ideas should be copies or images of anything fixed and constant? Or, in other words, since all sensible qualities, as size, figure, color, etc. – that is, our ideas – are continually changing upon every alteration in the distance, medium, or instruments of sensation, how can any determinate material objects be properly represented or painted forth by several distinct things, each of which is so different from and unlike the rest? Or, if you say it resembles some one only of our ideas, how shall we be able to distinguish the true copy from all the false ones?

Hyl. I profess, Philonous, I am at a loss. I do not know what to say to this.

Phil. But neither is this all. Which are material objects in themselves – perceptible or imperceptible?

Hyl. Properly and immediately nothing can be perceived but ideas. All material things, therefore, are in themselves insensible and to be perceived only by our ideas.

Phil. Ideas then are sensible, and their archetypes or originals insensible?

Hyl. Right.

Phil. But how can that which is sensible be like that which is insensible? Can a real thing, in itself *invisible*, be like a *color*, or a real thing which is not *audible* be like a *sound*? In a word, can anything be like a sensation or idea, but another sensation or idea?

Hyl. I must own, I think not.

Phil. Is it possible there should be any doubt in the point? Do you not perfectly know your own ideas?

Hyl. I know them perfectly, since what I do not perceive or know can be no part of my idea.

Phil. Consider, therefore, and examine them, and then tell me if there is anything in them which can exist without the mind, or if you can conceive anything like them existing without the mind.

Hyl. Upon inquiry, I find it is impossible for me to conceive or understand how anything but an idea can be like an idea. And it is most evident that *no idea can exist without the mind.*

Phil. You are, therefore, by your principles forced to deny the reality of sensible things, since you made it to consist in an absolute existence exterior to the mind. That is to say, you are a downright *skeptic.* So I have gained my point, which was to show your principles led to skepticism.

Hyl. For the present I am, if not entirely convinced, at least silenced.

Phil. I would fain know what more you would require in order to have a perfect conviction. Have you not had the liberty of explaining yourself all manner of ways? Were any little slips in discourse laid hold and insisted on? Or were you not allowed to retract or reinforce anything you had offered as best served your purpose? Has not everything you could say been heard and examined with all the fairness imaginable? In a word, have you not in every point been convinced out of your own mouth? And, if you can at present discover any flaw in any of your former concessions, or think of any remaining subterfuge, any new distinction, color, or comment whatsoever, why do you not produce it?

Hyl. A little patience, Philonous. I am at present so amazed to see myself ensnared, and as it were imprisoned in the labyrinths you have drawn me into, that on the sudden it cannot be expected I should find my way out. You must give me time to look about me and recollect myself.

Phil. Listen – is not this the college bell?

Hyl. It rings for prayers.

Phil. We will go in then, if you please, and meet here again tomorrow morning. In the meantime, you may employ your thoughts on this morning's discourse and try if you can find any fallacy in it, or invent any new means to extricate yourself.

Hyl. Agreed.

The Second Dialogue

Hylas. I beg your pardon, Philonous, for not meeting you sooner. All this morning my head was so filled with our late conversation that I had not leisure to think of the time of the day, or indeed of anything else.

Philonous. I am glad you were so intent upon it, in hopes if there were any mistakes in your concessions, or fallacies in my reasonings from them, you will now discover[20] them to me.

Hyl. I assure you, I have done nothing ever since I saw you but search after mistakes and fallacies, and, with that in view have minutely examined the whole series of yesterday's discourse; but all in vain, for the notions it led me into, upon review, appear still more clear and evident, and the more I consider them, the more irresistibly do they force my assent.

Phil. And is this not, do you think, a sign that they are genuine, that they proceed from nature and are conformable to right reason? Truth and beauty are in this alike, that the strictest survey sets them both off to advantage, while the false luster of error and disguise cannot endure being reviewed or too nearly inspected.

Hyl. I own there is a great deal in what you say. Nor can anyone be more entirely satisfied of the truth of those odd consequences so long as I have in view the reasonings that lead to them. But when these are out of my thoughts, there seems, on the other hand, something so satisfactory, so natural and intelligible in the modern way of explaining things that I profess I know not how to reject it.

Phil. I do not know what way you mean.

Hyl. I mean the way of accounting for our sensations or ideas.

Phil. How is that?

Hyl. It is supposed the soul makes her residence in some part of the brain, from which the nerves take their rise, and are from there extended to all parts of the body; and that outward objects, by the different impressions they make on the organs of sense, communicate certain vibrating motions to the nerves, and these, being filled with spirits, propagate them to the brain or seat of the soul, which, according to the various impressions or traces thereby made in the brain, is variously affected with ideas.

Phil. And you call this an explication of the manner whereby we are affected with ideas?

Hyl. Why not, Philonous? Have you anything to object against it?

Phil. I would first know whether I rightly understand your hypothesis. You make certain traces in the brain to be the causes or occasions of our ideas. Pray tell me, whether by the "brain" you mean any sensible thing?

Hyl. What else do you think I could mean?

Phil. Sensible things are all immediately perceivable; and those things which are immediately perceivable are ideas; and these exist only in the mind. This much you have, if I am not mistaken, long since agreed to.

Hyl. I do not deny it.

Phil. The brain therefore you speak of, being a sensible thing, exists only in the mind. Now, I would fain know whether you think it reasonable to suppose that one idea or thing existing in the mind occasions all other ideas. And if you think so, pray how do you account for the origin of that primary idea or brain itself?

Hyl. I do not explain the origin of our ideas by that brain which is perceivable to sense, this being itself only a combination of sensible ideas, but by another which I imagine.

Phil. But are not things imagined as truly *in the mind* as things perceived?

Hyl. I must confess they are.

Phil. It comes, therefore, to the same thing; and you have been all this while accounting for ideas by certain motions or impressions of the brain – that is, by some alterations in an idea, whether sensible or imaginable, it matters not.

Hyl. I begin to suspect my hypothesis.

Phil. Beside spirits, all that we know or conceive are our own ideas. When, therefore, you say all ideas are occasioned by impressions in the brain, do you conceive this brain or not? If you do, then you talk of ideas imprinted in an idea causing that same idea, which is absurd. If you do not conceive it, you talk unintelligibly, instead of forming a reasonable hypothesis.

Hyl. I now clearly see it was a mere dream. There is nothing in it.

Phil. You need not be much concerned about it; for, after all, this way of explaining things, as you called it, could never have satisfied any reasonable man. What connection is there between a motion in the nerves and the sensations of sound or color in the mind? Or how is it possible these should be the effect of that?

Hyl. But I could never think it had so little in it as now it seems to have.

Phil. Well then, are you at length satisfied that no sensible things have a real existence, and that you are in truth an arrant *skeptic*?

Hyl. It is too plain to be denied.

Phil. Look! Are not the fields covered with a delightful verdure[21]? Is there not something in the woods and groves, in the rivers and clear springs, that soothes, that delights, that transports the soul? At the prospect of the wide and deep ocean, or some huge mountain whose top is lost in the clouds, or of an old gloomy forest, are not our minds filled with a pleasing horror? Even in rocks and deserts, is there not an agreeable wildness? How sincere a pleasure is it to behold the natural beauties of the earth! To preserve and renew our relish for them, is not the veil of night alternately drawn over her face, and does she not change her dress with the seasons? How aptly are the elements disposed! What variety and use in the meanest productions of nature! What delicacy, what beauty, what contrivance in animal and vegetable bodies? How exquisitely are all things suited as well to their particular ends as to constitute apposite[22] parts of the whole! And while they mutually aid and support, do they not also set off and illustrate each other? Raise now your thoughts from this ball of earth to all those glorious luminaries that adorn the high arch of heaven. The motion and situation of the planets, are they not admirable for use and order? Were those (miscalled "erratic"[23]) globes ever known to stray in their repeated journeys through the pathless void? Do they not measure areas round the sun ever proportioned to the times? So fixed, so immutable are the laws by which the unseen Author of nature actuates the universe. How vivid and radiant is the luster of the fixed stars! How magnificent and rich that negligent profusion with which they appear to be scattered throughout the whole azure vault! Yet, if you take the telescope, it brings into your sight a new host of stars that escape the naked eye. Here they seem contiguous and minute, but to a nearer view immense orbs of light at various distances, far sunk in the abyss of space. Now you must call imagination to your aid. The feeble narrow sense cannot descry[24] innumerable worlds revolving round the central fires, and in those worlds the energy of an all-perfect Mind displayed in endless forms. But neither sense nor imagination are big enough to comprehend the boundless extent with all its glittering furniture. Though the laboring mind exert and strain each power to its utmost reach, there still stands out ungrasped a surplus immeasurable. Yet all the vast bodies that compose this mighty frame, however distant and remote, are by some secret mechanism, some divine art and force linked in a mutual dependence and intercourse with each other, even with this earth, which was almost slipped from my thoughts and lost in the crowd of worlds. Is not the whole system immense, beautiful, glorious beyond expression and beyond thought? What treatment then do those philosophers deserve who would deprive these noble and delightful scenes of all reality? How should those principles be entertained that lead us to think all the visible beauty of the creation a false imaginary glare? To be plain, can you expect this skepticism of yours will not be thought extravagantly absurd by all men of sense?

Hyl. Other men may think as they please, but for your part you have nothing to reproach me with. My comfort is you are as much a skeptic as I am.

Phil. There, Hylas, I must beg leave to differ from you.

Hyl. What?! Have you all along agreed to the premises, and do you now deny the conclusion and leave me to maintain those paradoxes by myself which you led me into? This surely is not fair.

Phil. I deny that I agreed with you in those notions that led to skepticism. You indeed said the reality of sensible things consisted in *an absolute existence* out of the minds of spirits, or distinct from their being perceived. And, pursuant to this notion of reality, you are obliged to deny sensible things any real existence – that is, according to your own definition, you profess yourself a skeptic. But I neither said nor thought the reality of sensible things was to be defined after that manner. To me it is evident, for the reasons you allow of, that sensible things cannot exist otherwise than in a mind or spirit. From which I conclude, not that they have no real existence, but that, seeing they depend not on my thought and have an existence distinct from being perceived by me, *there must be some other mind in which they exist*. As sure, therefore, as the sensible world really exists, so sure is there an infinite omnipresent Spirit who contains and supports it.

Hyl. What?! This is no more than I and all Christians hold; no, and all others too who believe there is a God and that He knows and comprehends all things.

Phil. Yes, but here lies the difference. Men commonly believe that all things are known or perceived by God because they believe the being of a God; whereas I, on the other side, immediately and necessarily conclude the being of a God because all sensible things must be perceived by Him.

Hyl. But so long as we all believe the same thing, what does it matter how we come by that belief?

Phil. But neither do we agree in the same opinion. For philosophers, though they acknowledge all corporeal beings to be perceived by God, yet they attribute to them an absolute subsistence distinct from their being perceived by any mind whatever, which I do not. Besides, is there no difference between saying, *there is a God, therefore He perceives all things*, and saying, *sensible things do really exist; and if they really exist, they are necessarily perceived by an infinite mind; therefore, there is an infinite mind, or God*. This furnishes you with a direct and immediate demonstration, from a most evident principle, of the *being of a God*. Divines and philosophers had proved beyond all controversy, from the beauty and usefulness of the several parts of the creation, that it was the workmanship of God. But that – setting aside all help of astronomy and natural philosophy, all contemplation of the contrivance, order, and adjustment of things – an infinite Mind should be necessarily inferred from the bare existence of the sensible world is an advantage peculiar to them only who have made this easy reflection: that the sensible world is that which we perceive by our several senses; and that nothing is perceived by the senses besides ideas; and that no idea or archetype of an idea can exist otherwise than in a mind. You may now, without any laborious search into the sciences, without any subtlety of reason or tedious length of discourse, oppose and baffle the most strenuous advocate for atheism. Those miserable refuges, whether in an eternal succession of unthinking causes and effects or in a fortuitous concourse of atoms; those wild imaginations of Vanini, Hobbes, and Spinoza[25] – in a word, the whole system of atheism – is it not entirely overthrown by this single reflection on the repugnancy included in supposing the whole or any part, even the most rude and shapeless, of the visible world to exist without a mind? Let any one of those abettors of impiety but look into his own thoughts, and there try if he can conceive how so much as a rock, a desert, a chaos, or confused jumble of atoms, how anything at all, either sensible or imaginable, can exist independent of a mind, and he need go no further to be convinced of his folly. Can anything be fairer than to put a dispute on such an issue and leave it to a man himself to see if he can conceive, even in thought, what he holds to be true in fact, and from a notion to allow it a real existence?

Hyl. It cannot be denied there is something highly serviceable to religion in what you advance. But do you not think it looks very like a notion entertained by some eminent moderns, of *seeing all things in God?*[26]

Phil. I would gladly know that opinion; pray explain it to me.

Hyl. They conceive that the soul, being immaterial, is incapable of being united with material things so as to perceive them in themselves, but that she perceives them by her union with the substance of God, which, being spiritual is therefore purely intelligible, or capable of being the immediate object of a spirit's thought. Besides, the divine essence contains in it perfections correspondent to each created being, and which are, for that reason, proper to exhibit or represent them to the mind.

Phil. I do not understand how our ideas, which are things altogether passive and inert, can be the essence or any part – or like any part – of the essence or substance of God, who is an impassive, indivisible, purely active being. There are many more difficulties and objections which occur at first view against this hypothesis, but I shall only add that it is liable to all the absurdities of the common hypotheses in making a created world exist otherwise than in the mind of a spirit. Besides all which, it has this peculiar to itself that it makes that material world serve to no purpose. And if it passes for a good argument against other hypotheses in the sciences that they suppose nature or the divine wisdom to make something in vain, or do that by tedious roundabout methods which might have been performed in a much more easy and compendious way, what shall we think of that hypothesis which supposes the whole world made in vain?

Hyl. But what do you say, are not you too of the opinion that we see all things in God? If I am not mistaken, what you advance comes near it.

Phil. [Few men think, yet all will have opinions. Hence men's opinions are superficial and confused. It is nothing strange that tenets which in themselves are ever so different should nevertheless be confounded with each other by those who do not consider them attentively. I shall not therefore be surprised if some men imagine that I run into the enthusiasm of Malebranche, though in truth I am very remote from it. He builds on the most abstract general ideas, which I entirely disclaim. He asserts an absolute external world, which I deny. He maintains that we are deceived by our senses and know not the real natures or the true forms and figures of extended beings – to all of which I hold the direct contrary. So that, upon the whole, there are no principles more fundamentally opposite than his and mine. It must be owned] I entirely agree with what the Holy Scripture says, "That in God we live, and move, and have our being."[27] But that we see things in His essence, after the manner above set forth, I am far from believing. Take here in brief my meaning. It is evident that the things I perceive are my own ideas, and that no idea can exist unless it is in a mind. Nor is it less plain that these ideas, or things perceived by me, either themselves or their archetypes, exist independently of my mind, since I know myself not to be their author, it being out of my power to determine at pleasure, what particular ideas I shall be affected with upon opening my eyes or ears. They must therefore exist in some other mind, whose will it is they should be exhibited to me. The things, I say, immediately perceived, are ideas or sensations, call them whichever you will. But how can any idea or sensation exist in, or be produced by, anything but a mind or spirit? This indeed is inconceivable; and to assert that which is inconceivable is to talk nonsense, is it not?

Hyl. Without doubt.

Phil. But, on the other hand, it is very conceivable that they should exist in and be produced by a spirit, since this is no more than I daily experience in myself – inasmuch as I perceive numberless ideas, and, by an act of my will, can form a great variety of them and raise them up in my imagination – though, it must be confessed, these creatures of the fancy are not altogether so distinct, so strong, vivid, and permanent, as those perceived by my senses, which latter are called "real things." From all which I conclude, *there is a mind which affects me every moment with all the sensible impressions I perceive.* And from the variety, order, and manner of these I conclude the author of them to be *wise, powerful, and good beyond comprehension*. Mark it well: I do not say I see things by perceiving that which represents them in the intelligible substance of God. This I do not understand; but I say the things perceived by me are known by the understanding and produced by the will of an infinite Spirit. And is not all this most plain and evident? Is there any more in it than what a little observation in our own minds, and that which passes in them, not only enables us to conceive, but also obliges us to acknowledge?

Hyl. I think I understand you very clearly and own the proof you give of a Deity seems no less evident than it is surprising. But allowing that God is the supreme and universal cause of all things, yet may not there be still a third nature besides spirits and ideas? May we not admit a subordinate and limited cause of our ideas? In a word, may there not for all that be *matter*?

Phil. How often must I inculcate the same thing? You allow the things immediately perceived by sense to exist nowhere without the mind; but there is nothing perceived by sense which is not perceived immediately: therefore, there is nothing sensible that exists without the mind. The matter, therefore, which you still insist on is something intelligible, I suppose – something that may be discovered by reason and not by sense.

Hyl. You are in the right.

Phil. Pray let me know what reasoning your belief of matter is grounded on, and what this matter is in your present sense of it.

Hyl. I find myself affected with various ideas of which I know I am not the cause; neither are they the cause of themselves or of one another, or capable of subsisting by themselves, as being altogether inactive, fleeting, dependent beings. They have therefore some cause distinct from me and them, of which I pretend to know no more than that it is *the cause of my ideas*. And this thing, whatever it be, I call "matter."

Phil. Tell me, Hylas, has everyone a liberty to change the current proper signification annexed to a common name in any language? For example, suppose a traveler should tell you that in a certain country men pass unhurt through the fire; and, upon explaining himself, you found he meant by the word "fire" that which others call "water"; or, if he should assert there are trees that

walk upon two legs, meaning men by the term "trees." Would you think this reasonable?

Hyl. No, I should think it very absurd. Common custom is the standard of propriety in language. And for any man to affect speaking improperly is to pervert the use of speech, and can never serve to a better purpose than to protract and multiply disputes where there is no difference in opinion.

Phil. And does not "matter," in the common current acceptation of the word, signify an extended, solid, moveable, unthinking, inactive substance?

Hyl. It does.

Phil. And has it not been made evident that no such substance can possibly exist? And though it should be allowed to exist, yet how can that which is *inactive* be a *cause*, or that which is *unthinking* be a *cause of thought*? You may, indeed, if you please, annex to the word "matter" a contrary meaning to what is vulgarly received, and tell me you understand by it an unextended, thinking, active being which is the cause of our ideas. But what else is this than to play with words and run into that very fault you just now condemned with so much reason? I do by no means find fault with your reasoning, in that you collect a cause from the phenomena; but I deny that the cause deducible by reason can properly be termed "matter."

Hyl. There is indeed something in what you say. But I am afraid you do not thoroughly comprehend my meaning. I would by no means be thought to deny that God, or an infinite Spirit, is the supreme cause of all things. All I contend for is that, subordinate to the Supreme Agent there is a cause of a limited and inferior nature, which concurs in the production of our ideas, not by any act of will or spiritual efficiency, but by that kind of action which belongs to matter, namely, motion.

Phil. I find you are at every turn relapsing into your old exploded conceit of a moveable and consequently an extended substance existing without the mind. What?! Have you already forgotten you were convinced, or are you willing I should repeat what has been said on that head? In truth this is not fair dealing in you still to suppose the being of that which you have so often acknowledged to have no being. But, not to insist further on what has been so largely handled,

I ask whether all your ideas are not perfectly passive and inert, including nothing of action in them.

Hyl. They are.

Phil. And are sensible qualities anything else but ideas?

Hyl. How often have I acknowledged that they are not.

Phil. But is not motion a sensible quality?

Hyl. It is.

Phil. Consequently, it is no action?

Hyl. I agree with you. And indeed it is very plain that when I stir my finger it remains passive, but my will which produced the motion is active.

Phil. Now I desire to know, in the first place, whether, motion being allowed to be no action, you can conceive any action besides volition; and, in the second place, whether to say something and conceive nothing is not to talk nonsense; and, lastly, whether, having considered the premises, you do not perceive that to suppose any efficient or active cause of our ideas other than *spirit* is highly absurd and unreasonable?

Hyl. I give up the point entirely. But, though matter may not be a cause, yet what hinders its being an *instrument* subservient to the Supreme Agent in the production of our ideas?

Phil. An instrument, you say; pray what may be the figure, springs, wheels, and motions of that instrument?

Hyl. Those I pretend to determine nothing of, both the substance and its qualities being entirely unknown to me.

Phil. What?! You are then of opinion it is made up of unknown parts, that it has unknown motions, and an unknown shape?

Hyl. I do not believe that it has any figure or motion at all, being already convinced that no sensible qualities can exist in an unperceiving substance.

Phil. But what notion is it possible to frame of an instrument void of all sensible qualities, even extension itself?

Hyl. I do not pretend to have any notion of it.

Phil. And what reason do you have to think this unknown, this inconceivable something does exist? Is it that you imagine God cannot act as well without it, or that you find by experience the use of some such thing when you form ideas in your own mind?

Hyl. You are always teasing me for reasons of my belief. Pray what reasons have you not to believe it?

Phil. It is to me a sufficient reason not to believe the existence of anything if I see no reason for believing it. But, not to insist on reasons for believing, you will not so much as let me know what it is you would have me believe, since you say you have no manner of notion of it. After all, let me entreat you to consider whether it is like a philosopher, or even like a man of common sense, to pretend to believe you know not what, and you know not why.

Hyl. Hold, Philonous. When I tell you matter is an *instrument*, I do not mean altogether nothing. It is true, I know not the particular kind of instrument, but, however, I have some notion of *instrument in general*, which I apply to it.

Phil. But what if it should prove that there is something, even in the most general notion of *instrument*, as taken in a distinct sense from *cause*, which makes the use of it inconsistent with the divine attributes?

Hyl. Make that appear and I shall give up the point.

Phil. What do you mean by the general nature or notion of instrument?

Hyl. That which is common to all particular instruments composes the general notion.

Phil. Is it not common to all instruments that they are applied to doing those things only which cannot be performed by the mere act of our wills? Thus, for instance, I never use an instrument to move my finger, because it is done by a volition. But I should use one if I were to remove part of a rock or tear up a tree by the roots. Are you of the same mind? Or can you show any example where an instrument is made use of in producing an effect immediately depending on the will of the agent?

Hyl. I own I cannot.

Phil. How, therefore, can you suppose that an all-perfect Spirit, on whose will all things have an absolute and immediate dependence, should need an instrument in His operations or, not needing it, make use of it? Thus it seems to me that you are obliged to own the use of a lifeless inactive instrument to be incompatible with the infinite perfection of God – that is, by your own confession, to give up the point.

Hyl. It does not readily occur what I can answer you.

Phil. But I think you should be ready to own the truth when it has been fairly proved to you. We, indeed, who are beings of finite powers, are forced to make use of instruments. And the use of an instrument shows the agent to be limited by rules of another's prescription, and that he cannot obtain his end but in such a way and by such conditions. From which it seems a clear consequence that the Supreme Unlimited Agent uses no tool or instrument at all. The will of an Omnipotent Spirit is no sooner exerted than executed, without the application of means, which, if they are employed by inferior agents, it is not upon account of any real efficacy that is in them, or necessary aptitude to produce any effect, but merely in compliance with the laws of nature or those conditions prescribed to them by the First Cause, who is Himself above all limitation or prescription whatsoever.

Hyl. I will no longer maintain that matter is an instrument. However, I would not be understood to give up its existence neither, since, notwithstanding what has been said, it may still be an *occasion*.

Phil. How many shapes is your matter to take? Or how often must it be proved not to exist, before you are content to part with it? But to say no more of this – though by all the laws of disputation I may justly blame you for so frequently changing the signification of the principal term – I would fain know what you mean by affirming that matter is an occasion, having already denied it to be a cause. And when you have shown in what sense you understand "occasion," pray, in the next place, be pleased to show me what reason induces you to believe there is such an occasion of our ideas?

Hyl. As to the first point: by "occasion" I mean an inactive unthinking being, at the presence whereof God excites ideas in our minds.

Phil. And what may be the nature of that inactive, unthinking being?

Hyl. I know nothing of its nature.

Phil. Proceed then to the second point and assign some reason why we should allow an existence to this inactive, unthinking, unknown thing.

Hyl. When we see ideas produced in our minds after an orderly and constant manner, it is natural to think they have some fixed and regular occasions at the presence of which they are excited.

Phil. You acknowledge then God alone to be the cause of our ideas, and that He causes them at the presence of those occasions.

Hyl. That is my opinion.

Phil. Those things which you say are present to God, without doubt He perceives.

Hyl. Certainly – otherwise they could not be to Him an occasion of acting.

Phil. Not to insist now on your making sense of this hypothesis, or answering all the puzzling questions and difficulties it is liable to: I only ask whether the order and regularity observable in the series of our ideas, or the course of nature, is not sufficiently accounted for by the wisdom and power of God; and whether it does not derogate from those attributes to suppose He is influenced, directed, or put in mind, when and what He is to act, by any unthinking substance? And, lastly, whether, in case I granted all you contend for, it would make anything to your purpose, it not being easy to conceive how the external or absolute existence of an unthinking substance, distinct from its being perceived, can be inferred from my allowing that there are certain things perceived by the mind of God which are to Him the occasion of producing ideas in us?

Hyl. I am perfectly at a loss what to think, this notion of occasion seeming now altogether as groundless as the rest.

Phil. Do you not at length perceive that in all these different acceptations of matter you have been only supposing you know not what, for no manner of reason and to no kind of use?

Hyl. I freely own myself less fond of my notions, since they have been so accurately examined. But still, I think I have some confused perception that there is such a thing as matter.

Phil. Either you perceive the being of matter immediately or mediately. If immediately, pray inform me by which of the senses you perceive it. If mediately, let me know by what reasoning it is inferred from those things which you perceive immediately. So much for the perception. Then for the matter itself, I ask whether it is object, substratum, cause, instrument, or occasion? You have already pleaded for each of these, shifting your notions, and making matter to appear sometimes in one shape, then in another. And what you have offered has been disapproved and rejected by yourself. If you have anything new to advance I would gladly hear it.

Hyl. I think I have already offered all I had to say on those heads. I am at a loss what more to urge.

Phil. And yet you are loath to part with your old prejudice. But to make you quit it more easily, I desire that, besides what has been suggested up till now, you will further consider whether, upon supposition that matter exists, you can possibly conceive how you should be affected by it. Or, supposing it did not exist, whether it is not evident you might for all that be affected with the same ideas you now are, and consequently have the very same reasons to believe its existence that you now can have?

Hyl. I acknowledge it is possible we might perceive all things just as we do now, though there was no matter in the world; neither can I conceive, if there is matter, how it should produce any idea in our minds. And I do further grant you have entirely satisfied me that it is impossible there should be such a thing as matter in any of the foregoing acceptations. But still I cannot help supposing that there is matter in some sense or other. What that is I do not indeed pretend to determine.

Phil. I do not expect you should define exactly the nature of that unknown being. Only be pleased to tell me, whether it is a substance – and if so, whether you can suppose a substance without accidents; or in case you suppose it to have accidents or qualities, I desire you will let me know what those qualities are, at least what is meant by matter's supporting them?

Hyl. We have already argued on those points. I have no more to say to them. But, to prevent any further questions, let me tell you I at present understand by "matter" neither substance nor accident, thinking nor extended being, neither cause, instrument, nor occasion, but something entirely unknown, distinct from all these.

Phil. It seems then you include in your present notion of matter nothing but the general abstract idea of *entity*.

Hyl. Nothing else, save only that I superadd to this general idea the negation of all those particular things, qualities, or ideas that I perceive, imagine, or in any way apprehend.

Phil. Pray where do you suppose this unknown matter to exist?

Hyl. Oh Philonous! Now you think you have entangled me; for if I say it exists in place, then you will infer that it exists in the mind, since it is agreed that place or extension exists only in the mind. But I am not ashamed to own my ignorance. I know not where it exists; only I am sure it exists not in place. There is a negative answer for you – and you must expect no other to all the questions you put for the future about matter.

Phil. Since you will not tell me where it exists, be pleased to inform me after what manner you suppose it to exist, or what you mean by its existence?

Hyl. It neither thinks nor acts, neither perceives nor is perceived.

Phil. But what is there positive in your abstracted notion of its existence?

Hyl. Upon a nice observation, I do not find I have any positive notion or meaning at all. I tell you again, I am not ashamed to own my ignorance. I know not what is meant by its existence or how it exists.

Phil. Continue, good Hylas, to act the same ingenuous part and tell me sincerely whether you can frame a distinct idea of entity in general, prescinded[28] from and exclusive of all thinking and corporeal beings, all particular things whatsoever.

Hyl. Hold, let me think a little – I profess, Philonous, I do not find that I can. At first glance I thought I had some dilute and airy notion of pure entity in abstract, but upon closer attention it has quite vanished out of sight. The more I think on it, the more am I confirmed in my prudent resolution of giving none but negative answers and not pretending to the least degree of any positive knowledge or conception of matter, its *where*, its *how*, its *entity*, or anything belonging to it.

Phil. When, therefore, you speak of the existence of matter, you have not any notion in your mind?

Hyl. None at all.

Phil. Pray tell me if the case stands not thus: At first, from a belief of material substance, you would have it that the immediate objects existed without the mind; then, that their archetypes; then, causes; next, instruments; then, occasions; lastly, *something in general*, which being interpreted proves *nothing*. So matter comes to nothing. What do you think, Hylas, is not this a fair summary of your whole proceeding?

Hyl. Be that as it will, yet I still insist upon it, that our not being able to conceive a thing is no argument against its existence.

Phil. That from a cause, effect, operation, sign, or other circumstance there may reasonably be inferred the existence of a thing not immediately perceived, and that it would be absurd for any man to argue against the existence of that thing from his having no direct and positive notion of it, I freely own. But where there is nothing of all this; where neither reason nor revelation induce us to believe the existence of a thing; where we have not even a relative notion of it; where an abstraction is made from perceiving and being perceived, from spirit and idea; lastly, where there is not so much as the most inadequate or faint idea pretended to, I will not, indeed, then conclude against the reality of any notion or existence of anything; but my inference shall be that you mean nothing at all, that you employ words to no manner of purpose, without any design or signification whatsoever. And I leave it to you to consider how mere jargon should be treated.

Hyl. To deal frankly with you, Philonous, your arguments seem in themselves unanswerable, but they have not so great an effect on me as to produce that entire conviction, that hearty acquiescence which attends demonstration. I find myself relapsing into an obscure surmise of I know not what – *matter.*

Phil. But are you not sensible, Hylas, that two things must concur to take away all scruple and work a plenary assent in the mind? Let a visible object be set in never so clear a light, yet, if there is any imperfection in the sight, or if the eye is not directed towards it, it will not be distinctly seen. And though a demonstration be never so well grounded and fairly proposed, yet, if there is in addition a stain of prejudice or a wrong bias on the understanding, can it be expected on a sudden to perceive clearly and adhere firmly to the truth? No, there is need of time and pains: the attention must be awakened and detained by a frequent repetition of the same thing placed often in the same, often in different lights. I have said it already, and find I must still repeat and inculcate, that it is an unaccountable license you take in pretending to maintain you know not what, for you know not what reason, to you know not what purpose. Can this be paralleled in any art or science, any sect or profession of men? Or is there anything so barefacedly groundless and unreasonable to be met with even in the lowest of common conversation? But, perhaps, you will still say, matter may exist, though at the same time you neither know what is meant by "matter" nor by its "existence." This indeed is surprising, and the more so because it is altogether voluntary, you not being led to it by any one reason; for I challenge you to show me that thing in nature which needs matter to explain or account for it.

Hyl. The reality of things cannot be maintained without supposing the existence of matter. And is not this, you think, a good reason why I should be earnest in its defense?

Phil. The reality of things! What things, sensible or intelligible?

Hyl. Sensible things.

Phil. My glove, for example?

Hyl. That or any other thing perceived by the senses.

Phil. But to fix on some particular thing, is it not a sufficient evidence to me of the existence of this *glove* that I see it, and feel it, and wear it? Or, if this will not do, how is it possible I should be assured of the reality of this thing which I actually see in this place by supposing that some unknown thing, which I never did or can see, exists after an unknown manner, in an unknown place, or in no place at all? How can the supposed reality of that which is intangible be a proof that anything tangible really exists? Or of that which is invisible, that any visible thing, or, in general, of anything which is imperceptible, that a perceptible exists? Do but explain this, and I shall think nothing too hard for you.

Hyl. Upon the whole, I am content to own the existence of matter is highly improbable; but the direct and absolute impossibility of it does not appear to me.

Phil. But granting matter to be possible, yet, upon that account merely, it can have no more claim to existence than a golden mountain or a centaur.

Hyl. I acknowledge it, but still you do not deny it is possible; and that which is possible, for all you know, may actually exist.

Phil. I deny it to be possible, and have, if I am not mistake, evidently proved from your own concessions that it is not. In the common sense of the word "matter," is there any more implied, than an extended, solid, figured, moveable substance existing without the mind? And have not you acknowledged over and over that you have seen evident reason for denying the possibility of such a substance?

Hyl. True, but that is only one sense of the term "matter."

Phil. But is it not the only proper genuine received sense? And if matter in such a sense is proved impossible, may it not be thought with good grounds absolutely impossible? How else could anything be proved impossible? Or, indeed, how could there be any proof at all one way or other to a man who takes the liberty to unsettle and change the common signification of words?

Hyl. I thought philosophers might be allowed to speak more accurately than the vulgar and were not always confined to the common acceptation of a term.

Phil. But this now mentioned is the common received sense among philosophers themselves. But, not to insist on that, have you not been allowed to take matter in what sense you pleased? And have you not used this privilege in the utmost extent, sometimes entirely changing, at others leaving out or putting into the definition of it whatever for the present best served your design, contrary to all the known rules of reason and logic? And has not this shifting, unfair method of yours spun out our dispute to an unnecessary length, matter having been particularly examined and by your own confession refuted in each of those senses? And can any more be required to prove the absolute impossibility of a thing than proving it impossible in every particular sense that either you or anyone else understands it in?

Hyl. But I am not so thoroughly satisfied that you have proved the impossibility of matter in the last most obscure, abstracted, and indefinite sense.

Phil. When is a thing shown to be impossible?

Hyl. When a repugnancy is demonstrated between the ideas comprehended in its definition.

Phil. But where there are no ideas, there no repugnancy can be demonstrated between ideas?

Hyl. I agree with you.

Phil. Now, in that which you call the obscure, indefinite sense of the word "matter," it is plain, by your own confession, there was included no idea at all, no sense except an unknown sense, which is the same thing as none. You are not,

therefore, to expect I should prove a repugnancy between ideas where there are no ideas, or the impossibility of matter taken in an *unknown* sense – that is, no sense at all. My business was only to show you meant *nothing*, and this you were brought to own. So that, in all your various senses, you have been shown either to mean nothing at all or, if anything, an absurdity. And if this is not sufficient to prove the impossibility of a thing, I desire you will let me know what is.

Hyl. I acknowledge you have proved that matter is impossible; nor do I see what more can be said in defense of it. But, at the same time that I give up this, I suspect all my other notions. For surely none could be more seemingly evident than this once was, and yet it now seems as false and absurd as ever it did true before. But I think we have discussed the point sufficiently for the present. The remaining part of the day I would willingly spend in running over in my thoughts the several heads of this morning's conversation, and tomorrow shall be glad to meet you here again about the same time.

Phil. I will not fail to attend you.

The Third Dialogue

Philonous. Tell me, Hylas, what are the fruits of yesterday's meditation? Has it confirmed you in the same mind you were in at parting, or have you since seen cause to change your opinion?

Hylas. Truly my opinion is that all our opinions are alike vain and uncertain. What we approve today, we condemn tomorrow. We keep a stir about knowledge and spend our lives in the pursuit of it, when, alas, we know nothing all the while; nor do I think it possible for us ever to know anything in this life. Our faculties are too narrow and too few. Nature certainly never intended us for speculation.

Phil. What?! You say we can know nothing, Hylas?

Hyl. There is not that single thing in the world of which we can know the real nature, or what it is in itself.

Phil. Will you tell me I do not really know what fire or water is?

Hyl. You may indeed know that fire appears hot, and water fluid; but this is no more than knowing what sensations are produced in your own mind upon the application of fire and water to your organs of sense. Their internal constitution, their true and real nature, you are utterly in the dark as to *that*.

Phil. Do I not know this to be a real stone that I stand on, and that which I see before my eyes to be a real tree?

Hyl. Know? No, it is impossible you or any man alive should know it. All you know is that you have such a certain idea or appearance in your own mind. But what is this to the real tree or stone? I tell you that color, figure, and hardness, which you perceive, are not the real natures of those things, or in the least like them. The same may be said of all other real things or corporeal substances which compose the world. They have, none of them, anything in themselves, like those sensible qualities by us perceived. We should not, therefore, pretend to affirm or know anything of them, as they are in their own nature.

Phil. But surely, Hylas, I can distinguish gold, for example, from iron – and how could this be if I knew not what either truly was?

Hyl. Believe me, Philonous, you can only distinguish between your own ideas. That yellowness, that weight, and other sensible qualities, do you think they are really in the gold? They are only relative to the senses and have no absolute existence in nature. And in pretending to distinguish the species of real things by the appearances in your mind, you may perhaps act as wisely as he that should conclude two men were of a different species because their clothes were not of the same color.

Phil. It seems, then, we are altogether put off with the appearances of things, and those false ones, too. The very meat I eat, and the cloth I wear, have nothing in them like what I see and feel.

Hyl. Even so.

Phil. But is it not strange the whole world should be thus imposed on and so foolish as to believe their senses? And yet I do not know how it is, but men eat, and drink, and sleep, and perform all the offices of life as comfortably and conveniently as if they really knew the things they are conversant about.

Hyl. They do so; but you know ordinary practice does not require a nicety of speculative knowledge. Hence the vulgar retain their mistakes, and for all that make a shift to bustle through the affairs of life. But philosophers know better things.

Phil. You mean they know that they *know nothing*.

Hyl. That is the very top and perfection of human knowledge.

Phil. But are you all this while in earnest, Hylas; and are you seriously persuaded that you know nothing real in the world? Suppose you are going to write, would you not call for pen, ink, and paper, like another man; and do you not know what it is you call for?

Hyl. How often must I tell you that I do not know the real nature of any one thing in the universe? I may indeed upon occasion make use of pen, ink, and paper. But what any one of them is in its own true nature, I declare positively I do not know. And the same is true with regard to every other corporeal thing. And, what is more, we are not only ignorant of the true and real nature of things, but even of their existence. It cannot be denied that we perceive such certain appearances or ideas; but it cannot be concluded from this that bodies really exist. No, now that I think on it, I must, agreeably to my former concessions, further declare that it is impossible any real corporeal thing should exist in nature.

Phil. You amaze me. Was ever anything more wild and extravagant than the notions you now maintain? And is it not evident you are led into all these extravagances by the belief of *material substance?* This makes you dream of those unknown natures in everything. It is this that occasions your distinguishing between the reality and sensible appearances of things. It is to this you are indebted for being ignorant of what everybody else knows perfectly well. Nor is this all: you are not only ignorant of the true nature of everything, but you do not know whether anything really exists, or whether there are any true natures at all, inasmuch as you attribute to your material beings an absolute or external existence in which you suppose their reality consists. And as you are forced in the end to acknowledge such an existence means either a direct repugnancy or nothing at all, it follows that you are obliged to pull down your own hypothesis of material substance and positively to deny the real existence of any part of the universe. And so you are plunged into the deepest and most deplorable *skepticism* that ever man was. Tell me, Hylas, is it not as I say?

Hyl. I agree with you. Material substance was no more than a hypothesis, and a false and groundless one, too. I will no longer spend my breath in defense of it. But whatever hypothesis you advance, or whatever scheme of things you introduce in its stead, I do not doubt it will appear every bit as false; let me but be allowed to question you upon it. That is, suffer me to serve you in your own kind, and I warrant it shall conduct you through as many perplexities and contradictions to the very same state of skepticism that I myself am in at present.

Phil. I assure you, Hylas, I do not pretend to frame any hypothesis at all. I am of a vulgar cast, simple enough to believe my senses and leave things as I find them. To be plain, it is my opinion that the real things are those very things I see and feel, and perceive by my senses. These I know and, finding they answer all the necessities and purposes of life, have no reason to be solicitous about any other unknown beings. A piece of sensible bread, for instance, would stay my stomach better than ten thousand times as much of that insensible, unintelligible, real bread you speak of. It is likewise my opinion that colors and other sensible qualities are on the objects. I cannot for my life help thinking that snow is white, and fire hot. You, indeed, who by "snow" and "fire" mean certain external, unperceived, unperceiving substances are in the right to deny whiteness or heat to be affections inherent in them. But I, who understand by those words the things I see and feel, am obliged to think like other folks. And as I am no skeptic with regard to the nature of things, so neither am I as to their existence. That a thing should be really perceived by my senses and at the same time not really exist is to me a plain contradiction, since I cannot prescind or abstract, even in thought, the existence of a sensible thing from its being perceived. Wood, stones, fire, water, flesh, iron, and the like things which I name and discourse of are things that I know. And I should not have known them but that I perceived them by my senses; and things perceived by the senses are immediately perceived; and things immediately perceived are ideas; and ideas cannot exist without the mind; their existence therefore consists in being perceived; when, therefore, they are actually perceived, there can be no doubt of their existence. Away then with all that skepticism, all those ridiculous philosophical doubts. What a jest is it for a philosopher to question the existence of sensible

things until he has it proved to him from the veracity of god,[29] or to pretend our knowledge in this point falls short of intuition or demonstration![30] I might as well doubt of my own being as of the being of those things I actually see and feel.

Hyl. Not so fast, Philonous; you say you cannot conceive how sensible things should exist without the mind. Do you not?

Phil. I do.

Hyl. Supposing you were annihilated, cannot you conceive it possible that things perceivable by sense may still exist?

Phil. I can; but then it must be in another mind. When I deny sensible things an existence out of the mind, I do not mean my mind in particular, but all minds. Now it is plain they have an existence exterior to my mind, since I find them by experience to be independent of it. There is therefore some other mind in which they exist during the intervals between the times of my perceiving them – as likewise they did before my birth, and would do after my supposed annihilation. And as the same is true with regard to all other finite created spirits, it necessarily follows, there is an *omnipresent, eternal Mind* which knows and comprehends all things, and exhibits them to our view in such a manner and according to such rules as He Himself has ordained and are by us termed the "laws of nature."

Hyl. Answer me, Philonous. Are all our ideas perfectly inert beings? Or have they any agency included in them?

Phil. They are altogether passive and inert.

Hyl. And is not God an agent, a being purely active?

Phil. I acknowledge it.

Hyl. No idea, therefore, can be like unto or represent the nature of God?

Phil. It cannot.

Hyl. Since, therefore, you have no idea of the mind of God, how can you conceive it possible that things should exist in His mind? Or, if you can conceive the mind of God without having an idea of it, why may not I be allowed to conceive the existence of matter, notwithstanding that I have no idea of it?

Phil. As to your first question: I own I have properly no idea, either of God or any other spirit; for these, being active, cannot be represented by things perfectly inert, as our ideas are. I do nevertheless know that I, who am a spirit or thinking substance, exist as certainly as I know my ideas exist. Further, I know what I mean by the terms "I" and "myself"; and I know this immediately or intuitively, though I do not perceive it as I perceive a triangle, a color, or a sound. The mind, spirit, or soul is that indivisible, unextended thing which thinks, acts, and perceives. I say "indivisible," because unextended; and "unextended," because extended, figured, moveable things, are ideas; and that which perceives ideas, which thinks and wills, is plainly itself no idea, nor like an idea. Ideas are things inactive and perceived, and spirits a sort of beings altogether different from them. I do not therefore say my soul is an idea, or like an idea. However, taking the word "idea" in a large sense, my soul may be said to furnish me with an idea – that is, an image or likeness of God – though indeed extremely inadequate. For all the notion I have of God is obtained by reflecting on my own soul, heightening its powers, and removing its imperfections.[31] I have, therefore, though not an inactive idea, yet in myself some sort of an active thinking image of the Deity. And though I perceive Him not by sense, yet I have a notion of Him, or know Him by reflection and reasoning. My own mind and my own ideas I have an immediate knowledge of; and, by the help of these, do mediately apprehend the possibility of the existence of other spirits and ideas. Further, from my own being, and from the dependency I find in myself and my ideas, I do, by an act of reason, necessarily infer the existence of a God and of all created things in the mind of God. So much for your first question. For the second: I suppose by this time you can answer it yourself. For you neither perceive matter objectively, as you do an inactive being or idea, nor know it, as you do yourself by a reflective act. Neither do you mediately apprehend it by similitude[32] of the one or the other, nor yet collect it by reasoning from that which you know immediately. All of which makes the case of *matter* widely different from that of the Deity.

[*Hyl.* You say your own soul supplies you with some sort of an idea or image of God. But at the same time you acknowledge you have, properly speaking, no idea of your own soul. You even affirm that spirits are a sort of beings altogether different from ideas. Consequently, that no idea can be like a spirit. We have, therefore, no idea of any spirit. You admit nevertheless that there is spiritual substance, although you have no idea of it, while you deny there can be such a thing as material substance, because you have no notion or idea of it. Is this fair dealing? To act consistently, you must either admit matter or reject spirit. What do you say to this?

Phil. I say, in the first place, that I do not deny the existence of material substance merely because I have no notion of it, but because the notion of it is inconsistent, or, in other words, because it is repugnant that there should be a notion of it. Many things, for all I know, may exist, of which neither I nor any other man has or can have any idea or notion whatsoever. But then those things must be possible, that is, nothing inconsistent must be included in their definition. I say, secondly, that, although we believe things to exist which we do not perceive, yet we may not believe that any particular thing exists without some reason for such belief; but I have no reason for believing the existence of matter. I have no immediate intuition of it, neither can I mediately from my sensations, ideas, notions, actions, or passions infer an unthinking, unperceiving, inactive substance, either by probable deduction or necessary consequence. Whereas the being of myself, that is, my own soul, mind, or thinking principle, I evidently know by reflection. You will forgive me if I repeat the same things in answer to the same objections. In the very notion or definition of material substance there is included a manifest repugnance and inconsistency. But this cannot be said of the notion of spirit. That ideas should exist in what does not perceive, or be produced by what does not act, is repugnant. But it is no repugnancy to say that a perceiving thing should be the subject of ideas, or an active thing the cause of them. It is granted we have neither an immediate evidence nor a demonstrative knowledge of the existence of other finite spirits, but it will not then follow that such spirits are on a foot with material substances; if to suppose the one is inconsistent, and it is not inconsistent to suppose the other; if the one can be inferred by no argument, and there is a probability for the other; if we see signs and effects indicating distinct finite agents like ourselves, and see no sign or symptom whatever that leads to a rational belief of matter. I say, lastly, that I have a notion of spirit, though I have not, strictly speaking, an idea of it. I do not perceive it as an idea or by means of an idea, but know it by reflection.

Hyl. Notwithstanding all you have said, to me it seems that, according to your own way of thinking, and in consequence of your own principles, it should follow that you are only a system of floating ideas without any substance to support them.[33] Words are not to be used without a meaning. And as there is no more meaning in *spiritual* substance than in *material* substance, the one is to be exploded as well as the other.

Phil. How often must I repeat that I know or am conscious of my own being, and that I myself am not my ideas, but something else, a thinking active principle that perceives, knows, wills, and operates about ideas. I know that I, one and the same self, perceive both colors and sounds; that a color cannot perceive a sound, nor a sound a color; that I am therefore one individual principle, distinct from color and sound, and, for the same reason, from all other sensible things and inert ideas. But I am not in like manner conscious either of the existence or essence of matter. On the contrary, I know that nothing inconsistent can exist, and that the existence of matter implies an inconsistency. Further, I know what I mean when I affirm that there is a spiritual substance or support of ideas, that is, that a spirit knows and perceives ideas. But I do not know what is meant when it is said that an unperceiving substance has inherent in it and supports either ideas or the archetypes of ideas. There is, therefore, upon the whole no parity of case between spirit and matter.]

Hyl. I own myself satisfied in this point. But do you in earnest think the real existence of sensible things consists in their being actually perceived? If so, how does it come that all mankind distinguish between them? Ask the first man you meet, and he shall tell you, *to be perceived* is one thing and *to exist* is another.

Phil. I am content, Hylas, to appeal to the common sense of the world for the truth of my notion. Ask the gardener why he thinks yonder cherry tree exists in the garden, and he shall tell you, because he sees and feels it – in a word, because he perceives it by his senses. Ask him why he thinks an orange tree is not there, and he shall tell you, because he does not perceive it. What he perceives by sense, that he terms a real being, and says it *is* or *exists*; but that which is not perceivable, the same, he says, has no being.

Hyl. Yes, Philonous, I grant the existence of a sensible thing consists in being perceivable, but not in being actually perceived.

Phil. And what is perceivable but an idea? And can an idea exist without being actually perceived? These are points long since agreed between us.

Hyl. But be your opinion never so true, yet surely you will not deny it is shocking and contrary to the common sense of men. Ask the fellow whether yonder tree has an existence out of his mind – what answer do you think he would make?

Phil. The same that I should myself, namely, that it does exist out of his mind. But then to a Christian it cannot surely be shocking to say, the real tree existing without his mind, is truly known and comprehended by – that is *exists in* – the infinite mind of God. Probably he may not at first glance be aware of the direct and immediate proof there is of this, inasmuch as the very being of a tree, or any other sensible thing, implies a mind in which it is. But the point itself he cannot deny. The question between the materialists and me is not whether things have a real existence out of the mind of this or that person, but, whether they have an absolute existence, distinct from being perceived by God, and exterior to all minds. This, indeed, some heathens and philosophers have affirmed, but whoever entertains notions of the Deity suitable to the Holy Scriptures will be of another opinion.

Hyl. But according to your notions, what difference is there between real things and chimeras formed by the imagination, or the visions of a dream, since they are all equally in the mind?

Phil. The ideas formed by the imagination are faint and indistinct; they have besides an entire dependence on the will. But the ideas perceived by sense, that is, real things, are more vivid and clear, and, being imprinted on the mind by a spirit distinct from us, have not the like dependence on our will. There is, therefore, no danger of confounding these with the foregoing, and there is as little of confounding them with the visions of a dream, which are dim, irregular, and confused. And though they should happen to be never so lively and natural, yet by their not being connected and of a piece with the preceding and subsequent transactions of our lives, they might easily be distinguished from realities. In short, by whatever method you distinguish *things* from *chimeras* on your scheme, the same, it is evident, will hold also upon mine. For it must be, I presume, by some perceived difference, and I am not for depriving you of any one thing that you perceive.

Hyl. But still, Philonous, you hold, there is nothing in the world but spirits and ideas. And this, you must necessarily acknowledge, sounds very oddly.

Phil. I own the word "idea," not being commonly used for "thing," sounds something out of the way. My reason for using it was because a necessary relation to the mind is understood to be implied by that term; and it is now commonly used by philosophers to denote the immediate objects of the understanding. But however oddly the proposition may sound in words, yet it includes nothing so very strange or shocking in its sense, which in effect amounts to no more than this, namely, that there are only things perceiving and things perceived; or that every unthinking being is necessarily, and from the very nature of its existence, perceived by some mind, if not by any finite created mind, yet certainly by the infinite mind of God in whom "we live, and move, and have our being."[34] Is this as strange as to say the sensible qualities are not on the objects, or that we cannot be sure of the existence of things, or know anything of their real natures, though we both see and feel them and perceive them by all our senses?

Hyl. And, in consequence of this, must we not think there are no such things as physical or corporeal causes, but that a spirit is the immediate cause of all the *phenomena* in nature? Can there be anything more extravagant than this?

Phil. Yes, it is infinitely more extravagant to say a thing which is inert operates on the mind, and which is unperceiving is the cause of our perceptions. Besides, that which to you – I do not know for what reason – seems so extravagant is no more than the Holy Scriptures assert in a hundred places. In them God is represented as the sole and immediate author of all those effects which some heathens and philosophers are accustomed to ascribe to nature, matter, fate, or the like unthinking principle. This is so much the

constant language of Scripture that it would be needless to confirm it by citations.

Hyl. You are not aware, Philonous, that in making God the immediate author of all the motions in nature, you make Him the author of murder sacrilege, adultery, and the like heinous sins.

Phil. In answer to that I observe, first, that the imputation of guilt is the same whether a person commits an action with or without an instrument. In case, therefore, you suppose God to act by the mediation of an instrument or occasion called "matter," you as truly make Him the author of sin as I, who think Him the immediate agent in all those operations vulgarly ascribed to nature. I further observe that sin or moral turpitude does not consist in the outward physical action or motion, but in the internal deviation of the will from the laws of reason and religion. This is plain, in that the killing an enemy in a battle, or putting a criminal legally to death, is not thought sinful, though the outward act be the very same with that in the case of murder. Since, therefore, sin does not consist in the physical action, making God an immediate cause of all such actions is not making Him the author of sin. Lastly, I have nowhere said that God is the only agent who produces all the motions in bodies. It is true, I have denied there are any other agents besides spirits, but this is very consistent with allowing to thinking rational beings, in the production of motions, the use of limited powers ultimately, indeed, derived from God, but immediately under the direction of their own wills, which is sufficient to entitle them to all the guilt of their actions.

Hyl. But denying matter, Philonous, or corporeal substance – there is the point. You can never persuade me that this is not repugnant to the universal sense of mankind. Were our dispute to be determined by most voices, I am confident you would give up the point without gathering the votes.

Phil. I wish both our opinions were fairly stated and submitted to the judgment of men who had plain common sense, without the prejudices of a learned education. Let me be represented as one who trusts his senses, who thinks he knows the things he sees and feels, and entertains no doubts of their existence; and you fairly set forth with all your doubts, your paradoxes, and your

skepticism about you, and I shall willingly acquiesce in the determination of any indifferent
person. That there is no substance in which ideas
can exist besides spirit is to me evident. And that
the objects immediately perceived are ideas is on
all hands agreed. And that sensible qualities are
objects immediately perceived no one can deny.
It is therefore evident there can be no *substratum*
of those qualities but spirit, in which they exist,
not by way of mode or property, but as a thing
perceived in that which perceives it. I deny,
therefore, that there is any unthinking *substratum*
of the objects of sense, and in that acceptation that
there is any material substance. But if by "material substance" is meant only sensible body, that
which is seen and felt – and the unphilosophical
part of the world, I dare say, mean no more – then
I am more certain of matter's existence than you
or any other philosopher pretend to be. If there
is anything which makes the generality of mankind averse from the notions I espouse, it is a
misapprehension that I deny the reality of sensible things; but as it is you who are guilty of that
and not I, it follows that in truth their aversion
is against your notions and not mine. I do therefore assert that I am as certain as of my own being
that there are bodies or corporeal substances –
meaning the things I perceive by my senses – and
that, granting this, the bulk of mankind will take
no thought about, nor think themselves at all concerned in the fate of, those unknown natures
and philosophical quiddities[35] which some men
are so fond of.

Hyl. What do you say to this? Since, according
to you, men judge of the reality of things by their
senses, how can a man be mistaken in thinking
the moon a plain lucid surface, about a foot in
diameter; or a square tower, seen at a distance,
round; or an oar, with one end in the water,
crooked?

Phil. He is not mistaken with regard to the ideas
he actually perceives, but in the inferences he
makes from his present perceptions. Thus, in the
case of the oar, what he immediately perceives by
sight is certainly crooked, and so far he is in the
right. But if he then concludes that upon taking
the oar out of the water he shall perceive the same
crookedness, or that it would affect his touch as
crooked things are accustomed to do, in that he
is mistaken. In like manner, if he shall conclude
from what he perceives in one station, that, in case

he advances towards the moon or tower, he
should still be affected with the like ideas, he is
mistaken. But his mistake lies not in what he
perceives immediately and at present – it being a
manifest contradiction to suppose he should err
in respect of that – but in the wrong judgment
he makes concerning the ideas he apprehends to
be connected with those immediately perceived,
or concerning the ideas that, from what he perceives at present, he imagines would be perceived
in other circumstances. The case is the same
with regard to the Copernican system.[36] We do
not here perceive any motion of the earth; but it
would be erroneous to conclude from this that,
in case we were placed at as great a distance from
that as we are now from the other planets, we
should not then perceive its motion.

Hyl. I understand you and must necessarily
own you say things plausible enough, but give
me leave to put you in mind of one thing. Pray,
Philonous, were you not formerly as positive
that matter existed as you are now that it does
not?

Phil. I was. But here lies the difference. Before,
my positiveness was founded, without examination, upon prejudice; but now, after inquiry,
upon evidence.

Hyl. After all, it seems our dispute is rather
about words than things. We agree in the thing,
but differ in the name. That we are affected with
ideas from without is evident; and it is no less
evident, that there must be – I will not say
archetypes, but – powers without the mind,
corresponding to those ideas. And as these
powers cannot subsist by themselves, there is
some subject of them necessarily to be admitted,
which I call "matter," and you call "spirit." This
is all the difference.

Phil. Pray, Hylas, is that powerful being, or
subject of powers, extended?

Hyl. It does not have extension; but it has the
power to raise in you the idea of extension.

Phil. It is therefore itself unextended?

Hyl. I grant it.

Phil. Is it not also active?

Hyl. Without doubt; otherwise, how could we
attribute powers to it?

Phil. Now let me ask you two questions: *First,*
whether it is agreeable to the usage either of
philosophers or others to give the name "matter"
to an unextended active being? And, *secondly,*

whether it is not ridiculously absurd to misapply names contrary to the common use of language?

Hyl. Well then, let it not be called "matter," since you will have it so, but some "third nature" distinct from matter and spirit. For what reason is there why you should call it spirit? Does not the notion of spirit imply that it is thinking as well as active and unextended?

Phil. My reason is this: Because I have a mind to have some notion or meaning in what I say, but I have no notion of any action distinct from volition, neither can I conceive volition to be anywhere but in a spirit; therefore, when I speak of an active being, I am obliged to mean a spirit. Besides, what can be plainer than that a thing which has no ideas in itself cannot impart them to me; and, if it has ideas, surely it must be a spirit. To make you comprehend the point still more clearly if it is possible: I assert as well as you that, since we are affected from without, we must allow powers to be without in a being distinct from ourselves. So far we are agreed. But then we differ as to the kind of this powerful being. I will have it to be spirit, you matter or I know not what – I may add too, you know not what – third nature. Thus I prove it to be spirit. From the effects I see produced, I conclude there are actions; and because actions, volitions; and because there are volitions, there must be a will. Again, the things I perceive must have an existence, they or their archetypes, out of my mind; but, being ideas, neither they nor their archetypes can exist otherwise than in an understanding; there is therefore an understanding. But will and understanding constitute in the strictest sense a mind or spirit. The powerful cause, therefore, of my ideas is in strict propriety of speech a *spirit*.

Hyl. And now I warrant you think you have made the point very clear, little suspecting that what you advance leads directly to a contradiction. Is it not an absurdity to imagine any imperfection in God?

Phil. Without a doubt.

Hyl. To suffer pain is an imperfection?

Phil. It is.

Hyl. Are we not sometimes affected with pain and uneasiness by some other being?

Phil. We are.

Hyl. And have you not said that being is a spirit, and is not that spirit God?

Phil. I grant it.

Hyl. But you have asserted that whatever ideas we perceive from without are in the mind which affects us. The ideas, therefore, of pain and uneasiness are in God, or, in other words, God suffers pain – that is to say, there is an imperfection in the divine nature, which you acknowledged was absurd. So you are caught in a plain contradiction.

Phil. That God knows or understands all things, and that He knows among other things what pain is, even every sort of painful sensation, and what it is for His creatures to suffer pain, I make no question. But that God, though He knows and sometimes causes painful sensations in us, can Himself suffer pain, I positively deny. We, who are limited and dependent spirits, are liable to impressions of sense, the effects of an external agent, which, being produced against our wills, are sometimes painful and uneasy. But God, whom no external being can affect, who perceives nothing by sense as we do, whose will is absolute and independent, causing all things, and liable to be thwarted or resisted by nothing, it is evident such a being as this can suffer nothing, nor be affected with any painful sensation, or indeed any sensation at all. We are chained to a body, that is to say, our perceptions are connected with corporeal motions. By the law of our nature we are affected upon every alteration in the nervous parts of our sensible body – which sensible body, rightly considered, is nothing but a complexion of such qualities or ideas as have no existence distinct from being perceived by a mind – so that this connection of sensations with corporeal motions means no more than a correspondence in the order of nature between two sets of ideas, or things immediately perceivable. But God is a pure spirit, disengaged from all such sympathy or natural ties. No corporeal motions are attended with the sensations of pain or pleasure in His mind. To know everything knowable is certainly a perfection, but to endure, or suffer, or feel anything by sense is an imperfection. The former, I say, agrees to God, but not the latter. God knows or has ideas, but His ideas are not conveyed to Him by sense, as ours are. Your not distinguishing where there is so manifest a difference makes you fancy you see an absurdity where there is none.

Hyl. But all this while you have not considered that the quantity of matter has been demonstrated to be proportioned to the gravity of bodies.[37] And what can withstand demonstration?

Phil. Let me see how you demonstrate that point.

Hyl. I lay it down for a principle that the moments or quantities of motion in bodies are in a direct compounded reason of the velocities and quantities of matter contained in them. Hence, where the velocities are equal, it follows the moments are directly as the quantity of matter in each. But it is found by experience that all bodies – abating the small inequalities arising from the resistance of the air – descend with an equal velocity; the motion therefore of descending bodies, and consequently their gravity, which is the cause or principle of that motion, is proportional to the quantity of matter – which was to be demonstrated.

Phil. You lay it down as a self-evident principle that the quantity of motion in any body is proportional to the velocity and matter taken together; and this is made use of to prove a proposition from which the existence of matter is inferred. Pray is not this arguing in a circle?

Hyl. In the premise I only mean that the motion is proportional to the velocity, jointly with the extension and solidity.

Phil. But allowing this to be true, yet it will not then follow that gravity is proportional to matter in your philosophic sense of the word, except you take it for granted that unknown *substratum*, or whatever else you call it, is proportional to those sensible qualities, which to suppose is plainly begging the question. That there is magnitude and solidity, or resistance, perceived by sense, I readily grant, as likewise, that gravity may be proportional to those qualities I will not dispute. But that either these qualities as perceived by us, or the powers producing them, do exist in a *material substratum* – this is what I deny, and you, indeed, affirm but, notwithstanding your demonstration, have not yet proved.

Hyl. I shall insist no longer on that point. Do you think, however, you shall persuade me that the natural philosophers have been dreaming all this while? Pray what becomes of all their hypotheses and explications of the phenomena which suppose the existence of matter?

Phil. What do you mean, Hylas, by the "phenomena"?

Hyl. I mean the appearances which I perceive by my senses.

Phil. And the appearances perceived by sense, are they not ideas?

Hyl. I have told you so a hundred times.

Phil. Therefore, to explain the phenomena is to show how we come to be affected with ideas in that manner and order wherein they are imprinted on our senses. Is it not?

Hyl. It is.

Phil. Now if you can prove that any philosopher has explained the production of any one idea in our minds by the help of *matter*, I shall forever acquiesce and look on all that has been said against it as nothing; but if you cannot, it is vain to urge the explication of phenomena. That a being endowed with knowledge and will should produce or exhibit ideas is easily understood. But that a being which is utterly destitute of these faculties should be able to produce ideas, or in any sort to affect an intelligence, this I can never understand. This I say, though we had some positive conception of matter, though we knew its qualities and could comprehend its existence, would yet be so far from explaining things that it is it self the most inexplicable thing in the world. And yet, for all this, it will not follow that philosophers have been doing nothing; for by observing and reasoning upon the connection of ideas, they discover the laws and methods of nature, which is a part of knowledge both useful and entertaining.

Hyl. After all, can it be supposed God would deceive all mankind? Do you imagine He would have induced the whole world to believe the being of matter if there was no such thing?

Phil. That every epidemic[38] opinion arising from prejudice, or passion, or thoughtlessness may be imputed to God as the author of it, I believe you will not affirm. Whatever opinion we father on[39] Him, it must be either because He has discovered it to us by supernatural revelation or because it is so evident to our natural faculties, which were framed and given us by God, that it is impossible we should withhold our assent from it. But where is the revelation? Or where is the evidence that extorts the belief of matter? No, how does it appear that matter, taken for something distinct from what we perceive by our senses, is thought to exist by all mankind, or, indeed, by any except a few philosophers who do not know what they would be at? Your question supposes these points are clear; and, when you have cleared them, I shall think myself obliged to give you another answer. In the meantime let it suffice that I tell you I do not suppose God has deceived mankind at all.

Hyl. But the novelty, Philonous, the novelty! There lies the danger. New notions should always be discountenanced; they unsettle men's minds, and nobody knows where they will end.

Phil. Why rejecting a notion that has no foundation either in sense or in reason, or in Divine authority, should be thought to unsettle the belief of such opinions as are grounded on all or any of these, I cannot imagine. That innovations in government and religion are dangerous and ought to be discountenanced, I freely own. But is there the like reason why they should be discouraged in philosophy? Making anything known which was unknown before is an innovation in knowledge; and if all such innovations had been forbidden, men would [not]⁴⁰ have made a notable progress in the arts and sciences. But it is none of my business to plead for novelties and paradoxes. That the qualities we perceive are not on the objects; that we must not believe our senses; that we know nothing of the real nature of things and can never be assured even of their existence; that real colors and sounds are nothing but certain unknown figures and motions; that motions are in themselves neither swift nor slow; that there are in bodies absolute extensions without any particular magnitude or figure; that a thing stupid, thoughtless, and inactive operates on a spirit; that the least particle of a body contains innumerable extended parts – these are the novelties, these are the strange notions which shock the genuine uncorrupted judgment of all mankind, and, being once admitted, embarrass the mind with endless doubts and difficulties. And it is against these and the like innovations I endeavor to vindicate common sense. It is true, in doing this I may perhaps be obliged to use some ambages⁴¹ and ways of speech not common. But if my notions are once thoroughly understood, that which is most singular⁴² in them will in effect be found to amount to no more than this: that it is absolutely impossible and a plain contradiction to suppose any unthinking being should exist without being perceived by a mind. And if this notion is singular, it is a shame

it should be so at this time of day and in a Christian country.

Hyl. As for the difficulties other opinions may be liable to, those are out of the question. It is your business to defend your own opinion. Can anything be plainer than that you are for changing all things into ideas? You, I say, who are not ashamed to charge me with skepticism. This is so plain, there is no denying it.

Phil. You mistake me. I am not for changing things into ideas, but rather ideas into things, since those immediate objects of perception, which, according to you, are only appearances of things, I take to be the real things themselves.

Hyl. Things! You may pretend what you please; but it is certain you leave us nothing but the empty forms of things, the outside only which strikes the senses.

Phil. What you call the empty forms and outside of things seems to me the very things themselves. Nor are they empty or incomplete otherwise than upon your supposition that matter is an essential part of all corporeal things. We both, therefore, agree in this: that we perceive only sensible forms. But in this we differ: you will have them to be empty appearances, I real beings. In short, you do not trust your senses, I do.

Hyl. You say you believe your senses, and seem to applaud yourself that in this you agree with the vulgar. According to you, therefore, the true nature of a thing is discovered by the senses. If so, where does that disagreement from? Why is not the same figure, and other sensible qualities, perceived all manner of ways? And why should we use a microscope the better to discover the true nature of a body, if it were discoverable to the naked eye?

Phil. Strictly speaking, Hylas, we do not see the same object that we feel; neither is the same object perceived by the microscope which was by the naked eye. But in case every variation was thought sufficient to constitute a new kind or individual, the endless number of confusion of names would render language impracticable. Therefore, to avoid this as well as other inconveniences which are obvious upon a little thought, men combine together several ideas, apprehended by various senses, or by the same sense at different times or in different circumstances, but observed, however, to have some connection in nature, either with respect to coexistence or succession;

all which they refer to one name and consider as one thing. Hence it follows that when I examine by my other senses a thing I have seen, it is not in order to understand better the same object which I had perceived by sight, the object of one sense not being perceived by the other senses. And when I look through a microscope, it is not that I may perceive more clearly what I perceived already with my bare eyes, the object perceived by the glass being quite different from the former. But in both cases my aim is only to know what ideas are connected together; and the more a man knows of the connection of ideas, the more he is said to know of the nature of things. What, therefore, if our ideas are variable? What if our senses are not in all circumstances affected with the same appearances? It will not then follow they are not to be trusted or that they are inconsistent either with themselves or anything else, except with your preconceived notion of – I know not what – one single, unchanged, unperceivable, real nature, marked by each name: which prejudice seems to have taken its rise from not rightly understanding the common language of men speaking of several distinct ideas as united into one thing by the mind. And, indeed, there is cause to suspect several erroneous conceits of the philosophers are owing to the same origin: while they began to build their schemes, not so much on notions as on words which were framed by the vulgar merely for convenience and dispatch in the common actions of life, without any regard to speculation.

Hyl. I think I apprehend your meaning.

Phil. It is your opinion the ideas we perceive by our senses are not real things, but images or copies of them. Our knowledge, therefore, is no further real than as our ideas are the true representations of those originals. But as these supposed originals are in themselves unknown, it is impossible to know how far our ideas resemble them, or whether they resemble them at all. We cannot, therefore, be sure we have any real knowledge. Further, as our ideas are perpetually varied, without any change in the supposed real things, it necessarily follows they cannot all be true copies of them, or, if some are, and others are not, it is impossible to distinguish the former from the latter. And this plunges us yet deeper in uncertainty. Again, when we consider the point, we cannot conceive how any idea, or anything like

an idea, should have an absolute existence out of a mind, nor consequently, according to you, how there should be any real thing in nature. The result of all this is that we are thrown into the most hopeless and abandoned *skepticism*. Now give me leave to ask you, *first*, whether your referring ideas to certain absolutely existing unperceived substances, as their originals, is not the source of all this skepticism? *Secondly*, whether you are informed, either by sense or reason, of the existence of those unknown originals? And in case you are not, whether it is not absurd to suppose them? *Thirdly*, whether, upon inquiry, you find there is any thing distinctly conceived or meant by the "absolute or external existence of unperceiving substances"? *Lastly*, whether, the premises considered, it is not the wisest way to follow nature, trust your senses, and, laying aside all anxious thought about unknown natures or substances, admit with the vulgar those for real things which are perceived by the senses?

Hyl. For the present I have no inclination to the answering part. I would much rather see how you can get over what follows. Pray, are not the objects perceived by the senses of one likewise perceivable to others present? If there were a hundred more here, they would all see the garden, the trees, and flowers, as I see them. But they are not in the same manner affected with the ideas I frame in my imagination. Does not this make a difference between the former sort of objects and the latter?

Phil. I grant it does. Nor have I ever denied a difference between the objects of sense and those of imagination. But what would you infer from this? You cannot say that sensible objects exist unperceived because they are perceived by many.

Hyl. I own I can make nothing of that objection, but it has led me into another. Is it not your opinion that by our senses we perceive only the ideas existing in our minds?

Phil. It is.

Hyl. But the same idea which is in my mind cannot be in yours or in any other mind. Does it not, therefore, follow from your principles that no two can see the same thing? And is not this highly absurd?

Phil. If the term "same" be taken in the vulgar acceptation,[43] it is certain – and not at all repugnant to the principles I maintain – that different persons may perceive the same thing, or the same thing or idea exist in different minds. Words are of arbitrary imposition; and since men are used to apply the word "same" where no distinction or variety is perceived, and I do not pretend to alter their perceptions, it follows that, as men have said before, *several saw the same thing*, so they may, upon like occasions, still continue to use the same phrase without any deviation either from propriety of language or the truth of things. But if the term "same" is used in the acceptation of philosophers who pretend to an abstracted notion of identity, then, according to their sundry definitions of this notion – for it is not yet agreed wherein that philosophic identity consists – it may or may not be possible for different persons to perceive the same thing. But whether philosophers shall think fit to call a thing the "same" or not, is, I conceive, of small importance. Let us suppose several men together, all endued with the same faculties, and consequently affected in like sort by their senses, and who had yet never known the use of language; they would without question agree in their perceptions. Though perhaps, when they came to the use of speech, some regarding the uniformity of what was perceived might call it the "same" thing; others, especially regarding the diversity of persons who perceived, might choose the denomination of different things. But who does not see that all the dispute is about a word – namely, whether what is perceived by different persons may yet have the term "same" applied to it? Or suppose a house whose walls or outward shell remaining unaltered, the chambers are all pulled down, and new ones built in their place, and that you should call this the "same," and I should say it was not the "same" house – would we not for all this perfectly agree in our thoughts of the house considered in itself? And would not all the difference consist in a sound? If you should say we differed in our notions, for that you superadded to your idea of the house the simple abstracted idea of identity, whereas I did not, I would tell you I know not what you mean by that "abstracted idea of identity," and should desire you to look into your own thoughts and be sure you understood yourself. – Why so silent, Hylas? Are you not yet satisfied men may dispute about identity and diversity without any real difference in their thoughts and opinions abstracted from names? Take this further reflection with

you: that whether matter is allowed to exist or not, the case is exactly the same as to the point in hand. For the materialists themselves acknowledge what we immediately perceive by our senses to be our own ideas. Your difficulty, therefore, that no two see the same thing counts equally against the materialists and me.

Hyl. But they suppose an external archetype to which referring their several ideas they may truly be said to perceive the same thing.

Phil. And – not to mention your having discarded those archetypes – so may you suppose an external archetype on my principles; *external*, I mean, to your own mind, though, indeed, it must be supposed to exist in that mind which comprehends all things; but then this serves all the ends of identity as well as if it existed out of a mind. And I am sure you yourself will not say it is less intelligible.

Hyl. You have indeed clearly satisfied me either that there is no difficulty at bottom in this point or, if there is, that it counts equally against both opinions.

Phil. But that which counts equally against two contradictory opinions, can be a proof against neither.

Hyl. I acknowledge it. But, after all, Philonous, when I consider the substance of what you advance against skepticism, it amounts to no more than this: We are sure that we really see, hear, feel – in a word, that we are affected with sensible impressions.

Phil. And how are we concerned any further? I see this cherry, I feel it, I taste it – and I am sure *nothing* cannot be seen, or felt, or tasted – it is therefore *real*. Take away the sensations of softness, moisture, redness, tartness, and you take away the cherry. Since it is not a being distinct from sensations, a cherry, I say, is nothing but a congeries[44] of sensible impressions, or ideas perceived by various senses, which ideas are united into one thing – or have one name given them – by the mind because they are observed to attend each other. Thus, when the palate is affected with such a particular taste, the sight is affected with a red color, the touch with roundness, softness, etc. Hence, when I see and feel and taste in sundry certain manners, I am sure the cherry exists or is real, its reality being in my opinion nothing abstracted from those sensations. But if by the word "cherry" you mean an unknown nature distinct from all those sensible qualities, and by its "existence" something distinct from its being perceived, then, indeed, I own, neither you nor I, nor any one else, can be sure it exists.

Hyl. But what would you say, Philonous, if I should bring the very same reasons against the existence of sensible things in a mind which you have offered against their existing in a material *substratum*?

Phil. When I see your reasons, you shall hear what I have to say to them.

Hyl. Is the mind extended or unextended?

Phil. Unextended, without doubt.

Hyl. Do you say the things you perceive are in your mind?

Phil. They are.

Hyl. Again, have I not heard you speak of sensible impressions?

Phil. I believe you may.

Hyl. Explain to me now, O Philonous, how it is possible there should be room for all those trees and houses to exist in your mind. Can extended things be contained in that which is unextended? Or are we to imagine impressions made on a thing void of all solidity? You cannot say objects are in your mind, as books in your study, or that things are imprinted on it as the figure of a seal upon wax. In what sense, therefore, are we to understand those expressions? Explain this to me if you can, and I shall then be able to answer all those queries you formerly put to me about my *substratum*.

Phil. Look, Hylas, when I speak of objects as existing in the mind or imprinted on the senses, I would not be understood in the gross literal sense, as when bodies are said to exist in a place or a seal to make an impression upon wax. My meaning is only that the mind comprehends or perceives them, and that it is affected from without or by some being distinct from itself. This is my explication of your difficulty; and how it can serve to make your tenet of an unperceiving material *substratum* intelligible, I would fain know.

Hyl. No, if that is all, I confess I do not see what use can be made of it. But are you not guilty of some abuse of language in this?

Phil. None at all. It is no more than common custom, which you know is the rule of language, has authorized, nothing being more usual than for philosophers to speak of the immediate objects of the understanding as things existing in the mind. Nor is there anything in this but what is conformable to the general analogy of language; most part of the mental operations being signified by words borrowed from sensible things, as is plain in the terms "comprehend," "reflect," "discourse," etc., which, being applied to the mind, must not be taken in their gross original sense.

Hyl. You have, I own, satisfied me in this point. But there still remains one great difficulty, which I do not know how you will get over. And, indeed, it is of such importance that if you could solve all others without being able to find a solution for this, you must never expect to make me a proselyte to your principles.

Phil. Let me know this mighty difficulty.

Hyl. The Scripture account of the creation is what appears to me utterly irreconcilable with your notions. Moses tells us of a creation – a creation of what? of ideas? No, certainly, but of things, of real things, solid corporeal substances. Bring your principles to agree with this and I shall perhaps agree with you.

Phil. Moses mentions the sun, moon, and stars, earth and sea, plants and animals: That all these do really exist and were in the beginning created by God, I make no question. If by "ideas" you mean fictions and fancies of the mind, then these are no ideas. If by "ideas" you mean immediate objects of the understanding, or sensible things which cannot exist unperceived, or out of a mind, then these things are ideas. But whether you do or do not call them "ideas," it matters little. The difference is only about a name. And whether that name is retained or rejected, the sense, the truth, and reality of things continues the same. In common talk, the objects of our senses are not termed "ideas" but "things." Call them so still, provided you do not attribute to them any absolute external existence, and I shall never quarrel with you for a word. The creation, therefore, I allow to have been a creation of things, of *real* things. Neither is this in the least inconsistent with my principles, as is evident from what I have now said; and would have been evident to you without this if you had not forgotten what had been so often said before. But as for solid corporeal substances, I desire you to show where Moses makes any mention of them; and if they should be mentioned by him, or any other inspired writer, it would still be incumbent on you to show those words were not taken in the vulgar acceptation for things falling under our senses, but in the philosophic acceptation for matter or an unknown quiddity with an absolute existence. When you have proved these points, then – and not until then – may you bring the authority of Moses into our dispute.

Hyl. It is in vain to dispute about a point so clear. I am content to refer it to your own conscience. Are you not satisfied there is some peculiar repugnancy between the Mosaic account of the creation and your notions?

Phil. If all possible sense which can be put on the first chapter of Genesis may be conceived as consistently with my principles as any other, then it has no peculiar repugnancy with them. But there is no sense you may not as well conceive, believing as I do. Since, besides spirits, all you conceive are ideas, and the existence of these I do not deny. Neither do you pretend they exist without the mind.

Hyl. Pray let me see any sense you can understand it in.

Phil. Why, I imagine that if I had been present at the creation, I should have seen things produced into being – that is, become perceptible in the order described by the sacred historian. I ever before believed the Mosaic account of the creation, and now find no alteration in my manner of believing it. When things are said to begin or end their existence, we do not mean this with regard to God, but His Creatures. All objects are eternally known by God, or, which is the same thing, have an eternal existence in His mind; but when things before imperceptible to creatures are, by a decree of God, made perceptible to them, then are they said to begin a relative existence with respect to created minds. Upon reading therefore the Mosaic account of the creation, I understand that the several parts of the world became gradually perceivable to finite spirits endowed with proper faculties, so that, whoever such were present, they were in truth perceived by them. This is the literal obvious sense suggested to me by the words of the Holy Scripture, in which is included no mention or no thought either of *substratum*, instrument, occasion, or absolute existence. And, upon inquiry, I do not doubt, it will be found that most plain honest men who believe the creation never think of those things any more than I. What metaphysical sense you may understand it in, you only can tell.

Hyl. But, Philonous, you do not seem to be aware that you allow created things in the beginning only a relative and consequently hypothetical being – that is to say, upon supposition there were men to perceive them, without which they have no actuality of absolute existence wherein creation might terminate. Is it not, therefore, according to you, plainly impossible the creation of any inanimate creatures should precede that of man? And is not this directly contrary to the Mosaic account?

Phil. In answer to that I say, *first*, created beings might begin to exist in the mind of other created intelligences beside men. You will not, therefore, be able to prove any contradiction between Moses and my notions unless you first show there was no other order of finite created spirits in being before man. I say further – in case we conceive the creation as we should at this time a parcel of plants or vegetables of all sorts produced by an invisible power in a desert where nobody was present – that this way of explaining or conceiving it is consistent with my principles, since they deprive you of nothing, either sensible or imaginable; that it exactly suits with the common, natural, undebauched notions of mankind; that it manifests the dependence of all things on God, and consequently has all the good effect or influence, which it is possible that important article of our faith should have in making men humble, thankful, and resigned to their Creator. I say, moreover, that, in this naked conception of things, divested of words, there will not be found any notion of what you call the "actuality of absolute existence." You may indeed raise a dust with those terms, and so lengthen our dispute to no purpose. But I entreat you calmly to look into your own thoughts and then tell me if they are not a useless and unintelligible jargon.

Hyl. I own I have no very clear notion annexed to them. But what do you say to this? Do you not make the existence of sensible things consist in their being in a mind? And were not all things eternally in the mind of God? Did they not therefore exist from all eternity, according to you? And how could that which was eternal, be created in time? Can anything be clearer or better connected than this?

Phil. And are not you too of the opinion that God knew all things from eternity?

Hyl. I am.

Phil. Consequently, they always had a being in the Divine intellect.

Hyl. This I acknowledge.

Phil. By your own confession, therefore, nothing is new, or begins to be, in respect of the mind of God. So we are agreed in that point.

Hyl. What shall we make then of the creation?

Phil. May we not understand it to have been entirely in respect of finite spirits, so that things, with regard to us, may properly be said to begin their existence, or be created, when God decreed they should become perceptible to intelligent creatures, in that order and manner which He then established and we now call the laws of nature? You may call this a "relative" or "hypothetical" existence, if you please. But so long as it supplies us with the most natural, obvious, and literal sense of the Mosaic history of the creation; so long as it answers all the religious ends of that great article – in a word, so long as you can assign no other sense or meaning in its stead, why should we reject this? Is it to comply with a ridiculous skeptical humor of making everything nonsense and unintelligible? I am sure you cannot say it is for the glory of God. For allowing it to be a thing possible and conceivable that the corporeal world should have an absolute subsistence extrinsic to the mind of God, as well as to the minds of all created spirits, yet how could this set forth either the immensity or omniscience of the Deity or the necessary and immediate dependence of all things on Him? No, would it not rather seem to derogate from those attributes?

Hyl. Well, but as to this decree of God's for making things perceptible, what do you say, Philonous, is it not plain God did either execute that decree from all eternity or at some certain time began to will what He had not actually willed before, but only designed to will? If the former, then there could be no creation or beginning of existence in finite things. If the latter, then we must acknowledge something new to befall the Deity, which implies a sort of change; and all change argues imperfection.

Phil. Pray consider what you are doing. Is it not evident this objection concludes equally against a creation in any sense, no, against every other act of the Deity discoverable by the light of nature? None of which can we conceive otherwise than as performed in time and having a beginning. God is a being of transcendent and unlimited perfections; His nature, therefore, is incomprehensible to finite spirits. It is not, therefore, to be expected that any man, whether materialist or immaterialist, should have exactly just notions of the Deity, His attributes, and ways of operation. If then you would infer anything against me, your difficulty must not be drawn from the inadequateness of our conceptions of the Divine nature, which is unavoidable on any scheme, but from the denial of matter, of which there is not one word, directly or indirectly, in what you have now objected.

Hyl. I must acknowledge, the difficulties you are concerned to clear are such only as arise from the non-existence of matter and are peculiar to that notion. So far you are in the right. But I cannot by any means bring myself to think there is no such peculiar repugnancy between the creation and your opinion, though, indeed, where to fix it I do not distinctly know.

Phil. What would you have? Do I not acknowledge a twofold state of things, the one ectypal[45] or natural, the other archetypal and eternal? The former was created in time, the latter existed from everlasting in the mind of God. Is not this agreeable to the common notions of divines? Or is any more than this necessary in order to conceive the creation? But you suspect some peculiar repugnancy, though you know not where it lies. To take away all possibility of scruple in the case, do but consider this one point: either you are not able to conceive the creation on any hypothesis whatsoever, and if so, there is no ground for dislike or complaint against any particular opinion on that score; or you are able to conceive it, and if so, why not on my principles, since thereby nothing conceivable is taken away? You have all along been allowed the full scope of sense, imagination, and reason. Whatever, therefore, you could before apprehend, either immediately or mediately by your senses, or by ratiocination[46] from your senses, whatever you could perceive, imagine, or understand, remains still with you. If, therefore, the notion you have of the creation by other principles is intelligible, you have it still upon mine; if it is not intelligible, I conceive it to be no notion at all, and so there is no loss of it. And, indeed, it seems to me very plain that the supposition of matter, that is, a thing perfectly unknown and inconceivable, cannot serve to make us conceive anything. And I hope it need not be proved to you, that if the existence of matter does not make the creation conceivable, the creation's being without it inconceivable can be no objection against its nonexistence.

Hyl. I confess, Philonous, you have almost satisfied me in this point of the creation.

Phil. I would fain know why you are not quite satisfied. You tell me indeed of a repugnancy between the Mosaic history and immaterialism – but you know not where it lies. Is this reasonable, Hylas? Can you expect I should solve a difficulty without knowing what it is? But to pass by all that, would not a man think you were assured there is no repugnancy between the received notions of materialists and the inspired writings?

Hyl. And so I am.

Phil. Ought the historical part of Scripture to be understood in a plain obvious sense, or in a sense which is metaphysical and out of the way?

Hyl. In the plain sense, doubtless.

Phil. When Moses speaks of herbs, earth, water, etc. as having been created by God, do you not think the sensible things commonly signified by those words are suggested to every unphilosophical reader?

Hyl. I cannot help thinking so.

Phil. And are not all ideas, or things perceived by sense, to be denied a real existence by the doctrine of the materialist?

Hyl. This I have already acknowledged.

Phil. The creation, therefore, according to them, was not the creation of things sensible, which have only a relative being, but of certain unknown natures, which have an absolute being wherein creation might terminate.

Hyl. True.

Phil. Is it not, therefore, evident the asserters of matter destroy the plain obvious sense of Moses, with which their notions are *utterly* inconsistent, and instead of it obtrude[47] on us I know not what, something equally unintelligible to themselves and me?

Hyl. I cannot contradict you.

Phil. Moses tells us of a creation. A creation of what? of unknown quiddities, of occasions, or *substratums*? No, certainly, but of things obvious to the senses. You must first reconcile this with your notions if you expect I should be reconciled to them.

Hyl. I see you can assault me with my own weapons.

Phil. Then as to *absolute existence*, was there ever known a more jejune[48] notion than that? Something it is, so abstracted and unintelligible, that you have frankly owned you could not conceive it, much less explain anything by it. But allowing matter to exist, and the notion of absolute existence to be clear as light, yet was this ever known to make the creation more credible? No, has it not furnished the atheists and infidels of all ages with the most plausible argument against a creation? That a corporeal substance which has an absolute existence without the minds of spirits should be produced out of nothing by the mere will of a spirit, has been looked upon as a thing so contrary to all reason, so impossible and absurd, that not only the most celebrated among the ancients, but even various modern and Christian philosophers have thought matter coeternal with the Deity. Lay these things together and then judge you whether materialism disposes men to believe the creation of things.

Hyl. I own, Philonous, I think it does not. This of the creation is the last objection I can think of; and I must necessarily own it has been sufficiently answered as well as the rest. Nothing now remains to be overcome but a sort of unaccountable backwardness that I find in myself towards your notions.

Phil. When a man is swayed, he knows not why, to one side of a question, can this, do you think, be anything else but the effect of prejudice, which never fails to attend old and rooted notions? And, indeed, in this respect I cannot deny the belief of matter to have very much the advantage over the contrary opinion with men of a learned education.

Hyl. I confess it seems to be as you say.

Phil. As a balance, therefore, to this weight of prejudice, let us throw into the scale the great advantages that arise from the belief of immaterialism, both in regard to religion and human learning. The being of a God and incorruptibility of the soul, those great articles of religion, are they not proved with the clearest and most immediate evidence? When I say the being of a *God*, I do not mean an obscure general cause of things, of which we have no conception, but *God* in the strict and proper sense of the word. A being whose spirituality, omnipresence, providence, omniscience, infinite power and goodness are as conspicuous as the existence of sensible things, of which – notwithstanding the fallacious pretences and affected scruples of skeptics – there is no more reason to doubt than of our own being. Then, with relation to human sciences: In natural philosophy, what intricacies, what obscurities, what contradictions, has the belief of matter led men into! To say nothing of the numberless disputes about its extent, continuity, homogeneity, gravity, divisibility, etc. Do they not pretend to explain all things by bodies operating on bodies, according to the laws of motion? And yet, are they able to comprehend how one body should move another? No, admitting there was no difficulty in reconciling the notion of an inert being with a cause or in conceiving how an accident might pass from one body to another, yet, by all their strained thoughts and extravagant suppositions, have they been able to reach the mechanical production of any one animal or vegetable body? Can they account, by the laws of motion, for sounds, tastes, smells, or colors, or for the regular course of things? Have they accounted, by physical principles, for the aptitude and contrivance even of the most inconsiderable parts of the universe? But laying aside matter and corporeal causes and admitting only the efficiency of an All-perfect Mind, are not all the effects of nature easy and intelligible? If the *phenomena* are nothing else but *ideas*, God is a *spirit*, but matter an unintelligent, unperceiving being. If they demonstrate an unlimited power in their cause, God is active and omnipotent, but matter an inert mass. If the order, regularity, and usefulness of them can never be sufficiently admired, God is infinitely wise and provident, but matter destitute of all contrivance and design. These surely are great advantages in *physics*. Not to mention that the apprehension of a distant Deity naturally disposes men to a negligence in their *moral* actions, which they would be more cautious of in case they thought Him immediately present and acting on their minds without the interposition of matter or unthinking second causes. Then in *metaphysics*: what difficulties concerning entity in abstract, substantial forms, hylarchic principles, plastic natures, substance and accident, principle of individuation,[49] possibility of matter's thinking,[50] origin of ideas, the manner how two independent substances so widely different as *spirit* and *matter* should mutually operate on each other? What difficulties, I say, and endless disquisitions[51] concerning these and innumerable other like

points do we escape by supposing only spirits and ideas? Even the *mathematics* themselves, if we take away the absolute existence of extended things, become much more clear and easy, the most shocking paradoxes and intricate speculations in those sciences depending on the infinite divisibility of finite extension, which depends on that supposition. But what need is there to insist on the particular sciences? Is not that opposition to all science whatsoever, that frenzy of the ancient and modern skeptics, built on the same foundation? Or can you produce so much as one argument against the reality of corporeal things, or in behalf of that avowed utter ignorance of their natures, which does not suppose their reality to consist in an external absolute existence? Upon this supposition, indeed, the objections from the change of colors in a pigeon's neck, or the appearances of a broken oar in the water, must be allowed to have weight. But those and the like objections vanish if we do not maintain the being of absolute external originals, but place the reality of things in ideas, fleeting, indeed, and changeable; however, not changed at random, but according to the fixed order of nature. For herein consists that constancy and truth of things which secures all the concerns of life, and distinguishes that which is *real* from the irregular visions of the fancy.

Hyl. I agree to all you have now said and must own that nothing can incline me to embrace your opinion more than the advantages I see it is attended with. I am by nature lazy, and this would be a mighty abridgment in knowledge. What doubts, what hypotheses, what labyrinths of amusement, what fields of disputation, what an ocean of false learning may be avoided by that single notion of *immaterialism*!

Phil. After all, is there anything further remaining to be done? You may remember you promised to embrace that opinion which upon examination should appear most agreeable to common sense and remote from skepticism. This, by your own confession, is that which denies matter or the absolute existence of corporeal things. Nor is this all; the same notion has been proved several ways, viewed in different lights, pursued in its consequences, and all objections against it cleared. Can there be a greater evidence of its truth? Or is it possible it should have all the marks of a true opinion and yet be false?

Hyl. I own myself entirely satisfied for the present in all respects. But what security can I have that I shall still continue the same full assent to your opinion and that no unthought-of objection or difficulty will occur hereafter?

Phil. Pray, Hylas, do you in other cases, when a point is once evidently proved, withhold your assent on account of objections or difficulties it may be liable to? Are the difficulties that attend the doctrine of incommensurable quantities, of the angle of contact, of the asymptotes to curves, or the like, sufficient to make you hold out against mathematical demonstration?[52] Or will you disbelieve the providence of God because there may be some particular things which you do not know how to reconcile with it? If there are difficulties attending immaterialism, there are at the same time direct and evident proofs for it. But for the existence of matter there is not one proof, and far more numerous and insurmountable objections lie against it. But where are those mighty difficulties you insist on? Alas! You do not know where or what they are; something which may possibly occur hereafter. If this is a sufficient pretence for withholding your full assent, you should never yield it to any proposition, however free from exceptions, however clearly and solidly demonstrated.

Hyl. You have satisfied me, Philonous.

Phil. But to arm you against all future objections, do but consider that which bears equally hard on two contradictory opinions can be a proof against neither. Whenever, therefore, any difficulty occurs, try if you can find a solution for it on the hypothesis of the materialists. Do not be deceived by words, but sound your own thoughts. And in case you cannot conceive it easier by the help of *materialism*, it is plain it can be no objection against *immaterialism*. Had you proceeded all along by this rule, you would probably have spared yourself abundance of trouble in objecting, since of all your difficulties I challenge you to show one that is explained by matter, no, which is not more unintelligible with than without that supposition, and consequently makes rather *against* than *for* it. You should consider, in each particular, whether the difficulty arises from the *non-existence of matter*. If it does not, you might as well argue from the infinite divisibility of extension against the Divine prescience as from such a difficulty against immaterialism. And yet, upon recollection, I believe you

will find this to have been often, if not always, the case. You should likewise take heed not to argue on a *petitio principii*.[53] One is apt to say the unknown substances ought to be esteemed real things rather than the ideas in our minds; and who can tell but the unthinking external substance may concur as a cause or instrument in the production of our ideas? But is not this proceeding on a supposition that there are such external substances? And to suppose this, is it not begging the question? But above all things you should beware of imposing on yourself by that vulgar sophism which is called *ignoratio elenchi*.[54] You talked often as if you thought I maintained the non-existence of sensible things, whereas in truth no one can be more thoroughly assured of their existence than I am; and it is you who doubt – I should have said, positively deny it. Everything that is seen, felt, heard, or any way perceived by the senses is, on the principles I embrace, a real being, but not on yours. Remember, the matter you contend for is an unknown somewhat – if indeed it may be termed "somewhat" – which is quite stripped of all sensible qualities, and can neither be perceived by sense, nor apprehended by the mind. Remember, I say that it is not any object which is hard or soft, hot or cold, blue or white, round or square, etc. For all these things I affirm do exist. Though, indeed, I deny they have an existence distinct from being perceived, or that they exist out of all minds whatsoever. Think on these points; let them be attentively considered and still kept in view. Otherwise you will not comprehend the state of the question, without which your objections will always be wide of the mark, and, instead of mine, may possibly be directed – as more than once they have been – against your own notions.

Hyl. I must needs own, Philonous, nothing seems to have kept me from agreeing with you more than this same *mistaking the question*. In denying matter, at first glimpse I am tempted to imagine you deny the things we see and feel, but, upon reflection, find there is no ground for it. What do you think, therefore, of retaining the name "matter" and applying it to sensible things? This may be done without any change in your sentiments; and, believe me, it would be a means of reconciling them to some persons who may be more shocked at an innovation in words than in opinion.

Phil. With all my heart, retain the word "matter" and apply it to the objects of sense, if you please, provided you do not attribute to them any subsistence distinct from their being perceived. I shall never quarrel with you for an expression. "Matter" or "material substance" are terms introduced by philosophers, and, as used by them, imply a sort of independence, or a subsistence distinct from being perceived by a mind; but are never used by common people, or, if ever, it is to signify the immediate objects of sense. One would think, therefore, so long as the names of all particular things with the terms "sensible," "substance," "body,' "stuff," and the like, are retained, the word "matter" should be never missed in common talk. And in philosophical discourses it seems the best way to leave it quite out, since there is not perhaps any one thing that has more favored and strengthened the depraved bent of the mind toward atheism than the use of that general confused term.

Hyl. Well, but, Philonous, since I am content to give up the notion of an unthinking substance exterior to the mind, I think you ought not to deny me the privilege of using the word "matter" as I please, and annexing it to a collection of sensible qualities subsisting only in the mind. I freely own there is no other substance, in a strict sense, than *spirit.* But I have been so long accustomed to the term "matter" that I do not know how to part with it. To say there is no matter in the world is still shocking to me. Whereas to say there is no matter, if by that term is meant an unthinking substance existing without the mind, but if by "matter" is meant some sensible thing whose existence consists in being perceived, then there is matter – this distinction gives it quite another turn; and men will come into your notions with small difficulty when they are proposed in that manner. For, after all, the controversy about matter in the strict acceptation of it lies altogether between you and the philosophers, whose principles, I acknowledge, are not near so natural or so agreeable to the common sense of mankind and Holy Scripture as yours. There is nothing we either desire or shun but as it makes, or is apprehended to make, some part of our happiness or misery. But what has happiness or misery, joy or grief, pleasure or pain, to do with absolute existence, or with unknown entities abstracted from all relation to us? It is evident things regard us only as they are pleasing or displeasing; and they can please or displease only so far forth as they are perceived. Further, therefore, we are not concerned; and thus far you leave things as you found them. Yet still there is something new in this doctrine. It is plain, I do not now think with the philosophers, nor yet altogether with the vulgar. I would know how the case stands in that respect, precisely what you have added to or altered in my former notions.

Phil. I do not pretend to be a setter-up of new notions. My endeavors tend only to unite and place in a clearer light that truth which was before shared between the vulgar and the philosophers – the former being of opinion that *those things they immediately perceive are the real things*, and the latter that *the things immediately perceived are ideas which exist only in the mind* – which two notions put together do, in effect, constitute the substance of what I advance.

Hyl. I have been a long time distrusting my senses; I thought I saw things by a dim light and through false glasses. Now the glasses are removed and a new light breaks in upon my understanding. I am clearly convinced that I see things in their native forms and am no longer in pain about their unknown natures or absolute existence. This is the state I find myself in at present, though, indeed, the course that brought me to it I do not yet thoroughly comprehend. You set out upon the same principles that Academics,[55] Cartesians,[56] and the like sects usually do, and for a long time it looked as if you were advancing their philosophical skepticism; but, in the end, your conclusions are directly opposite to theirs.

Phil. You see, Hylas, the water of yonder fountain, how it is forced upwards, in a round column, to a certain height, at which it breaks and falls back into the basin from where it rose, its ascent as well as descent proceeding from the same uniform law or principle of gravitation. Just so, the same principles which at first view lead to skepticism, pursued to a certain point, bring men back to common sense.

Notes

1   *abroad:* outdoors.
2   *vulgar:* the common or ordinary class of people.
3   *Pray:* 'Please tell'.

4 *repugnancies*: contradictions or inconsistencies.

5 *a suspense*: suspension or uncertainty.

6 *own*: acknowledge, admit, or confess.

7 *wormwood*: the plant *Artemisia absinthium,* known for its bitter taste.

8 *fain*: gladly, willingly, or with pleasure.

9 *ordure*: excrement.

10 *common acceptation*: received meaning.

11 *dioptrics*: that part of the science of optics which treats of the refraction of light, as opposed to catoptics which treats of reflection.

12 *describing*: traveling.

13 *Schools*: The "philosophy of the Schools" or "Scholasticism" refers to the philosophical tradition that arose in the universities of medieval Europe and is associated with the methods and views of the major philosophers of the 13th and 14th centuries, including Aquinas, Scotus, and Ockham. Scholasticism dominated European philosophy into the 15th century.

14 This maxim reflects *nominalism* – the doctrine that abstract entities, or universals, conceived as the supposed referents of general terms such as 'blue' or 'triangle' do not really exist; hence, everything that exists is a particular. Nominalism is opposed to Platonism or realism, which maintains that abstract entities do really exist and that general terms do refer to these entities. The debate over the ontological status of universal was one of the primary topics of philosophical concern in the medieval period. Nominalists like Abelard and Ockham maintained that everything that exists is a particular. The classical empiricists – Hobbes, Locke, Berkeley, and Hume – followed these medieval predecessors in denying that general terms signify universals. Locke, for example, opened his discussion of general terms in *Essay* with, "All things that exist being particulars . . ." (3.3.1).

15 According to Locke, words refer to ideas, and general words refer to abstract ideas – ideas that are formed from our ideas of particular things by "leaving out . . . those particulars wherein they differ, and retaining only those wherein they agree" (*Essay* 3.3.9). The process of forming an abstract idea of a triangle, for example, consists in separating out all the features unique to this or that particular triangle and retaining only those features that all particular triangles share in common. The result of this process is the idea of a triangle that is "neither oblique nor rectangle, neither equilateral, equicrural, nor scalenon; but all and none of these at once" (*Essay* 4.7.9). Because he believes that our ideas are determinate in all their features and particular in their content, Berkeley believes that we do not possess an idea of a triangle corresponding to this characterization.

In the Introduction to his *Principles* (§6–21), Berkeley offered a thorough critique of Locke's account of abstract ideas, which purported to establish "the impossibility of abstract ideas."

16 Hylas' argument here mirrors Locke's at (*Essay* 2.23.1).

17 *scruples*: doubts or uncertainties.

18 William Molyneaux (1656–98), an Irish philosopher and scientist, posed the following problem in a letter to Locke (1688): "if a man born blind, and able to distinguish by touch between a globe and a cube, were made to see, could he now tell by sight which was the cube and which the globe, before he touched them?" The "Molyneaux problem" was widely discussed in the 18th and 19th centuries. Molyneaux, Locke (*Essay* 2.9.8) and Berkeley (*New Theory of Vision* §121–46) all answered the question in the negative. Leibniz, however, answered the question in the affirmative. See Morgan, M., *Molyneaux's Question.* (Cambridge: Cambridge University Press, 1977).

19 *raillery*: good-humored ridicule.

20 *discover*: reveal.

21 *verdure*: green vegetation.

22 *apposite*: appropriate or well-suited.

23 *"erratic"*: wandering or having no fixed course.

24 *descry*: perceive or observe.

25 Three philosophers believed by many early-modern thinkers to personify atheism. Giulio Cesare Vanini (1585–1619) was executed by the Parlement of Toulouse for atheism, blasphemy, and impiety. Vanini maintained the eternity of matter in his *De admirandis naturæ reginæ* (1616). In 1666 the English House of Commons passed a bill that included Thomas Hobbes' (1588–1679) *Leviathan* (1651) among other works to be investigated for atheistic tendencies. Hobbes was perhaps the most thoroughgoing materialist of the 17th century, and he maintained that God must be material. This, as well as his determinism, were taken to be wholly inconsistent with christian theology. Benedict de Spinoza (1632–77) was excommunicated from the Jewish synagogue in Amsterdam in 1656. He was taken to be an atheist because he identified God with nature and developed a thoroughly naturalistic and deterministic philosophy.

26 The reference is to Nicolas Malebranche (1638–1715).

27 Acts 17:28.

28 *prescinded*: detached or separated.

29 Descartes wrote in the Sixth Meditation of his *Meditations on First Philosophy*: "What of the other aspects of corporeal things which are either particular (for example that the sun is of such and such a size or shape), or less clearly understood, such as light or sound or pain, and so on? Despite

the high degree of doubt and uncertainty involved here, the very fact that God is not a deceiver, and the consequent impossibility of there being any falsity in my opinions which cannot be corrected by some other faculty supplied by God, offers me a sure hope that I can attain the truth even in these matters."

30 Locke wrote in his *Essay*, "The notice we have by our senses of the existing of things without us . . . [is] not altogether as certain as our intuitive knowledge, or the deductions of our reason employed about the clear abstract ideas of our own minds . . ." (4.11.3).

31 Berkeley's account of the origin of the idea of God parallels Locke's. See (*Essay* 2.23.33).

32 *similitude*: similarity.

33 Hylas here proposes a bundle theory of the self. Some commentators have argued that this passage inspired Hume to develop such a theory of self.

34 Acts 17:28.

35 'Quiddity' is a Scholastic term referring to the real essence of a thing – that which makes a thing what it is.

36 The astronomical theory propounded by Nicolaus Copernicus (1473–1543), according to which the planets move in orbits around the sun and the earth rotates once daily on its own axis.

37 The law of universal gravitation, formulated by Issac Newton (1642–1727) in *Philosophiae Naturalis Principia Mathematica* (*Mathematical Principles of Natural Philosophy*, 1687), states that every particle of matter in the universe attracts every other particle of matter with a force (F) that is proportional to the product of the masses of the particles (m1 and m2) and inversely proportional to the square of the distance between the particles (D). Summarized symbolically: $F = G(m1m2)/D2$, where G is the gravitational constant.

38 *epidemic*: widespread or prevalent.

39 *father on*: attribute to.

40 It would seem that either a 'not' has been omitted here – it is absent in all three editions – or perhaps Berkeley intended the claim to be sarcastic.

41 *ambages*: obscure ways of speaking.

42 *singular*: unusual or uncommon.

43 *vulgar acceptation*: ordinary or common meaning.

44 *congeries*: a collection of disparate items.

45 *ectypal*: pertaining to a copy or reproduction.

46 *ratiocination*: the process of reasoning.

47 *obtrude*: impose.

48 *jejune*: unsatisfying to the mind; wanting in substance.

49 These six scholastic (see First Dialogue, note 13 above) concepts have their origins in the philosophy of Plato and Aristotle. 'Entity in abstract' refers to the notion of existence or being in general. A substantial form is that which makes a substance be the kind of substance that it is, and which distinguishes it from other substances. 'Hylarchic principles' refers to principles governing matter. 'Plastic natures' signifies natural forces or principles causing growth or production. A principle of individuation expresses the haecceity of a thing – that is, the quality that makes a thing specifically or individually what it is.

50 In his *Essay* Locke wrote, "I see no contradiction in it, that the first Eternal thinking Being, or Omnipotent Spirit, should, if he pleased, give to certain systems of created senseless matter, put together as he sees fit, some degrees of sense, perception, and thought. . . ." (4.3.6).

51 *disquisitions*: subjects for investigation.

52 Two lengths are incommensurable (or incommensurate) if their ratio cannot be expressed as a ratio of whole numbers. For example, suppose *ABCD* is a square, the side of the square *AB* is incommensurable to the diagonal of the square *AC*. An angle of contact is the angle between a curve and its tangent at any point. An asymptote is a line or curve *A* related to another curve *B* such that as a point moves along one of the branches of *B* the distance between the point and *A* approaches zero. As Philonous's question here suggests, these concepts presented difficulties for mathematical reasoning at various points in its development. For example, in the early-5th century BCE, Pythagorean geometers assumed that any two lengths are commensurable. So, the discovery of incommensurables (now known as irrational numbers), led to an impasse in geometrical reasoning that persisted until later geometers, such as Theaetetus (c. 417–369 BCE), and Eudoxus (400–350 BCE), developed a theory of proportion that could account for incommensurables.

53 *petitio principii*: a fallacy in which the conclusion is taken for granted in a premise; begging the question.

54 *ignoratio elenchi*: a fallacy which consists in purportedly refuting an opponent's position while actually disproving a position that is not asserted.

55 The Academy was founded by Plato (c. 428–347 BCE) approximately in 387 BCE About 273 BCE, under the leadership of Arcesilaus of Pitane (c. 315–240 BCE), the so-called Middle Academy came to be dominated by skeptics.

56 Followers of René Descartes.

4

Of the Sceptical and
Other Systems of Philosophy

David Hume

Section I
Of Scepticism with Regard to Reason

In all demonstrative sciences the rules are certain
and infallible; but when we apply them, our
fallible and uncertain faculties are very apt to
depart from them, and fall into error. We must,
therefore, in every reasoning form a new judgment,
as a check or controul on our first judgment or
belief; and must enlarge our view to comprehend
a kind of history of all the instances, wherein our
understanding has deceiv'd us, compar'd with
those, wherein its testimony was just and true. Our
reason must be consider'd as a kind of cause, of
which truth is the natural effect; but such-a-one
as by the irruption of other causes, and by
the inconstancy of our mental powers, may
frequently be prevented. By this means all
knowledge degenerates into probability; and this
probability is greater or less, according to our
experience of the veracity or deceitfulness of our
understanding, and according to the simplicity or
intricacy of the question.

There is no Algebraist nor Mathematician so
expert in his science, as to place entire confidence in any truth immediately upon his discovery of it, or regard it as any thing, but a mere
probability. Every time he runs over his proofs,
his confidence encreases; but still more by the
approbation of his friends; and is rais'd to its
utmost perfection by the universal assent and
applauses of the learned world. Now 'tis evident,
that this gradual encrease of assurance is nothing
but the addition of new probabilities, and is deriv'd
from the constant union of causes and effects,
according to past experience and observation.

In accompts of any length or importance,
Merchants seldom trust to the infallible certainty
of numbers for their security; but by the artificial
structure of the accompts, produce a probability
beyond what is deriv'd from the skill and experience of the accomptant. For that is plainly of
itself some degree of probability; tho' uncertain
and variable, according to the degrees of his
experience and length of the accompt. Now as
none will maintain, that our assurance in a long
numeration exceeds probability, I may safely
affirm, that there scarce is any proposition
concerning numbers, of which we can have a
fuller security. For 'tis easily possible, by gradually diminishing the numbers, to reduce the
longest series of addition to the most simple
question, which can be form'd, to an addition of
two single numbers; and upon this supposition
we shall find it impracticable to shew the precise
limits of knowledge and of probability, or discover
that particular number, at which the one ends and
the other begins. But knowledge and probability

David Hume, "Of the Sceptical and Other Systems of Philosophy," from David Hume, *A Treatise on Human Nature*,
ed. L. A. Selby-Bigge (Oxford: Clarendon Press, 1896).

are of such contrary and disagreeing natures, that they cannot well run insensibly into each other, and that because they will not divide, but must be either entirely present, or entirely absent. Besides, if any single addition were certain, every one wou'd be so, and consequently the whole or total sum; unless the whole can be different from all its parts. I had almost said, that this was certain; but I reflect, that it must reduce *itself*, as well as every other reasoning, and from knowledge degenerate into probability.

Since therefore all knowledge resolves itself into probability, and becomes at last of the same nature with that evidence, which we employ in common life, we must now examine this latter species of reasoning, and see on what foundation it stands.

In every judgment, which we can form concerning probability, as well as concerning knowledge, we ought always to correct the first judgment, deriv'd from the nature of the object, by another judgment, deriv'd from the nature of the understanding. 'Tis certain a man of solid sense and long experience ought to have, and usually has, a greater assurance in his opinions, than one that is foolish and ignorant, and that our sentiments have different degrees of authority, even with ourselves, in proportion to the degrees of our reason and experience. In the man of the best sense and longest experience, this authority is never entire; since even such-a-one must be conscious of many errors in the past, and must still dread the like for the future. Here then arises a new species of probability to correct and regulate the first, and fix its just standard and proportion. As demonstration is subject to the controul of probability, so is probability liable to a new correction by a reflex act of the mind, wherein the nature of our understanding, and our reasoning from the first probability become our objects.

Having thus found in every probability, beside the original uncertainty inherent in the subject, a new uncertainty deriv'd from the weakness of that faculty, which judges, and having adjusted these two together, we are oblig'd by our reason to add a new doubt deriv'd from the possibility of error in the estimation we make of the truth and fidelity of our faculties. This is a doubt, which immediately occurs to us, and of which, if we wou'd closely pursue our reason, we cannot avoid giving a decision. But this decision,

tho' it shou'd be favourable to our preceeding judgment, being founded only on probability, must weaken still further our first evidence, and must itself be weaken'd by a fourth doubt of the same kind, and so on *in infinitum*; till at last there remain nothing of the original probability, however great we may suppose it to have been, and however small the diminution by every new uncertainty. No finite object can subsist under a decrease repeated *in infinitum*; and even the vastest quantity, which can enter into human imagination, must in this manner be reduc'd to nothing. Let our first belief be never so strong, it must infallibly perish by passing thro' so many new examinations, of which each diminishes somewhat of its force and vigour. When I reflect on the natural fallibility of my judgment, I have less confidence in my opinions, than when I only consider the objects concerning which I reason; and when I proceed still farther, to turn the scrutiny against every successive estimation I make of my faculties, all the rules of logic require a continual diminution, and at last a total extinction of belief and evidence.

Shou'd it here be ask'd me, whether I sincerely assent to this argument, which I seem to take such pains to inculcate, and whether I be really one of those sceptics, who hold that all is uncertain, and that our judgment is not in *any* thing possest of *any* measures of truth and falshood; I shou'd reply, that this question is entirely superfluous, and that neither I, nor any other person was ever sincerely and constantly of that opinion. Nature, by an absolute and uncontroulable necessity has determin'd us to judge as well as to breathe and feel; nor can we any more forbear viewing certain objects in a stronger and fuller light, upon account of their customary connexion with a present impression, than we can hinder ourselves from thinking as long as we are awake, or seeing the surrounding bodies, when we turn our eyes towards them in broad sunshine. Whoever has taken the pains to refute the cavils of this *total* scepticism, has really disputed without an antagonist, and endeavour'd by arguments to establish a faculty, which nature has antecedently implanted in the mind, and render'd unavoidable.

My intention then in displaying so carefully the arguments of that fantastic sect, is only to make the reader sensible of the truth of my hypothesis, *that all our reasonings concerning causes and effects are deriv'd from nothing but custom; and that belief is more properly an act of the sensitive, than of the cogitative part of our natures.* I have here prov'd, that the very same principles, which make us form a decision upon any subject, and correct that decision by the consideration of our genius and capacity, and of the situation of our mind, when we examin'd that subject; I say, I have prov'd, that these same principles, when carry'd farther, and apply'd to every new reflex judgment, must, by continually diminishing the original evidence, at last reduce it to nothing, and utterly subvert all belief and opinion. If belief, therefore, were a simple act of the thought, without any peculiar manner of conception, or the addition of a force and vivacity, it must infallibly destroy itself, and in every case terminate in a total suspense of judgment. But as experience will sufficiently convince any one, who thinks it worth while to try, that tho' he can find no error in the foregoing arguments, yet he still continues to believe, and think, and reason as usual, he may safely conclude, that his reasoning and belief is some sensation or peculiar manner of conception, which 'tis impossible for mere ideas and reflections to destroy.

But here, perhaps, it may be demanded, how it happens, even upon my hypothesis, that these arguments above-explain'd produce not a total suspense of judgment, and after what manner the mind ever retains a degree of assurance in any subject? [. . .]

I answer, that after the first and second decision; as the action of the mind becomes forc'd and unnatural, and the ideas faint and obscure; tho' the principles of judgment, and the ballancing of opposite causes be the same as at the very beginning; yet their influence on the imagination, and the vigour they add to, or diminish from the thought, is by no means equal. Where the mind reaches not its objects with easiness and facility, the same principles have not the same effect as in a more natural conception of the ideas; nor does the imagination feel a sensation, which holds any proportion with that which arises from its common judgments and opinions. The attention is on the stretch: The posture of the mind is uneasy; and the spirits being diverted from their natural course, are not govern'd in their movements by the same laws, at least not to the same

degree, as when they flow in their usual channel [. . .]

Section II
Of Scepticism with Regard to the Senses

Thus the sceptic still continues to reason and believe, even tho' he asserts, that he cannot defend his reason by reason; and by the same rule he must assent to the principle concerning the existence of body, tho' he cannot pretend by any arguments of philosophy to maintain its veracity. Nature has not left this to his choice, and has doubtless esteem'd it an affair of too great importance to be trusted to our uncertain reasonings and speculations. We may well ask, *What causes induce us to believe in the existence of body?* but 'tis in vain to ask, *Whether there be body or not?* That is a point, which we must take for granted in all our reasonings.

The subject, then, of our present enquiry is concerning the *causes* which induce us to believe in the existence of body: And my reasonings on this head I shall begin with a distinction, which at first sight may seem superfluous, but which will contribute very much to the perfect understanding of what follows. We ought to examine apart those two questions, which are commonly confounded together, *viz.* Why we attribute a CONTINU'D existence to objects, even when they are not present to the senses; and why we suppose them to have an existence DISTINCT from the mind and perception. Under this last head I comprehend their situation as well as relations, their *external* position as well as the *independence* of their existence and operation. These two questions concerning the continu'd and distinct existence of body are intimately connected together. For if the objects of our senses continue to exist, even when they are not perceiv'd, their existence is of course independent of and distinct from the perception; and *vice versa*, if their existence be independent of the perception and distinct from it, they must continue to exist, even tho' they be not perceiv'd. But tho' the decision of the one question decides the other; yet that we may the more easily discover the principles of human nature, from whence the decision arises, we shall carry along with us this distinction, and shall consider, whether it be the *senses, reason,* or the *imagination*, that produces the opinion of a *continu'd* or of a *distinct* existence. These are the only questions, that are intelligible on the present subject. For as to the notion of external existence, when taken for something specially different from our perceptions, we have already shewn its absurdity.

To begin with the SENSES, 'tis evident these faculties are incapable of giving rise to the notion of the *continu'd* existence of their objects, after they no longer appear to the senses. For that is a contradiction in terms, and supposes that the senses continue to operate, even after they have ceas'd all manner of operation. These faculties, therefore, if they have any influence in the present case, must produce the opinion of a distinct, not of a continu'd existence; and in order to that, must present their impressions either as images and representations, or as these very distinct and external existences.

That our senses offer not their impressions as the images of something *distinct*, or *independent*, and *external*, is evident; because they convey to us nothing but a single perception, and never give us the least intimation of any thing beyond. A single perception can never produce the idea of a double existence, but by some inference either of the reason or imagination. When the mind looks farther than what immediately appears to it, its conclusions can never be put to the account of the senses; and it certainly looks farther, when from a single perception it infers a double existence, and supposes the relations of resemblance and causation betwixt them.

If our senses, therefore, suggest any idea of distinct existences, they must convey the impressions as those very existences, by a kind of fallacy and illusion. Upon this head we may observe, that all sensations are felt by the mind, such as they really are, and that when we doubt, whether they present themselves as distinct objects, or as mere impressions, the difficulty is not concerning their nature, but concerning their relations and situation. Now if the senses presented our impressions as external to, and independent of ourselves, both the objects and ourselves must be obvious to our senses, otherwise they cou'd not be compar'd by these faculties. The difficulty, then, is how far we are *ourselves* the objects of our senses.

'Tis certain there is no question in philosophy more abstruse than that concerning identity, and the nature of the uniting principle, which constitutes a person. So far from being able by our senses merely to determine this question, we must have recourse to the most profound metaphysics to give a satisfactory answer to it; and in common life 'tis evident these ideas of self and person are never very fix'd nor determinate. 'Tis absurd, therefore, to imagine the senses can ever distinguish betwixt ourselves and external objects.

Add to this, that every impression, external and internal, passions, affections, sensations, pains and pleasures, are originally on the same footing; and that whatever other differences we may observe among them, they appear, all of them, in their true colours, as impressions or perceptions. And indeed, if we consider the matter aright, 'tis scarce possible it shou'd be otherwise, nor is it conceivable that our senses shou'd be more capable of deceiving us in the situation and relations, than in the nature of our impressions. For since all actions and sensations of the mind are known to us by consciousness, they must necessarily appear in every particular what they are, and be what they appear. Every thing that enters the mind, being in *reality* a perception, 'tis impossible any thing shou'd to *feeling* appear different. This were to suppose, that even where we are most intimately conscious, we might be mistaken.

But not to lose time in examining, whether 'tis possible for our senses to deceive us, and represent our perceptions as distinct from ourselves, that is as *external* to and *independent* of us; let us consider whether they really do so, and whether this error proceeds from an immediate sensation, or from some other causes.

To begin with the question concerning *external* existence, it may perhaps be said, that setting aside the metaphysical question of the identity of a thinking substance, our own body evidently belongs to us; and as several impressions appear exterior to the body, we suppose them also exterior to ourselves. The paper, on which I write at present, is beyond my hand. The table is beyond the paper. The walls of the chamber beyond the table. And in casting my eye towards the window, I perceive a great extent of fields and buildings beyond my chamber. From all this it may be infer'd, that no other faculty is requir'd, beside the senses, to convince us of the external existence of body. But to prevent this inference, we need only weigh the three following considerations. *First*,

That, properly speaking, 'tis not our body we perceive, when we regard our limbs and members, but certain impressions, which enter by the senses; so that the ascribing a real and corporeal existence to these impressions, or to their objects, is an act of the mind as difficult to explain, as that which we examine at present. *Secondly*, Sounds, and tastes, and smells, tho' commonly regarded by the mind as continu'd independent qualities, appear not to have any existence in extension, and consequently cannot appear to the senses as situated externally to the body. The reason, why we ascribe a place to them, shall be consider'd afterwards. *Thirdly*, Even our sight informs us not of distance or outness (so to speak) immediately and without a certain reasoning and experience, as is acknowledg'd by the most rational philosophers.

As to the *independency* of our perceptions on ourselves, this can never be an object of the senses; but any opinion we form concerning it, must be deriv'd from experience and observation: And we shall see afterwards, that our conclusions from experience are far from being favourable to the doctrine of the independency of our perceptions. Mean while we may observe that when we talk of real distinct existences, we have commonly more in our eye their independency than external situation in place, and think an object has a sufficient reality, when its Being is uninterrupted, and independent of the incessant revolutions, which we are conscious of in ourselves.

Thus to resume what I have said concerning the senses; they give us no notion of continu'd existence, because they cannot operate beyond the extent, in which they really operate. They as little produce the opinion of a distinct existence, because they neither can offer it to the mind as represented, nor as original. To offer it as represented, they must present both an object and an image. To make it appear as original, they must convey a falshood; and this falshood must lie in the relations and situation: In order to which they must be able to compare the object with ourselves; and even in that case they do not, nor is it possible they shou'd, deceive us. We may, therefore, conclude with certainty, that the opinion of a continu'd and of a distinct existence never arises from the senses.

To confirm this we may observe, that there are three different kinds of impressions convey'd by the senses. The first are those of the figure, bulk, motion and solidity of bodies. The second those of colours, tastes, smells, sounds, heat and cold. The third are the pains and pleasures, that arise from the application of objects to our bodies, as by the cutting of our flesh with steel, and such like. Both philosophers and the vulgar suppose the first of these to have a distinct continu'd existence. The vulgar only regard the second as on the same footing. Both philosophers and the vulgar, again, esteem the third to be merely perceptions; and consequently interrupted and dependent beings.

Now 'tis evident, that, whatever may be our philosophical opinion, colours, sounds, heat and cold, as far as appears to the senses, exist after the same manner with motion and solidity, and that the difference we make betwixt them in this respect, arises not from the mere perception. So strong is the prejudice for the distinct continu'd existence of the former qualities, that when the contrary opinion is advanc'd by modern philosophers, people imagine they can almost refute it from their feeling and experience, and that their very senses contradict this philosophy. 'Tis also evident, that colours, sounds, &c. are originally on the same footing with the pain that arises from steel, and pleasure that proceeds from a fire; and that the difference betwixt them is founded neither on perception nor reason, but on the imagination. For as they are confest to be, both of them, nothing but perceptions arising from the particular configurations and motions of the parts of body, wherein possibly can their difference consist? Upon the whole, then, we may conclude, that as far as the senses are judges, all perceptions are the same in the manner of their existence.

We may also observe in this instance of sounds and colours, that we can attribute a distinct continu'd existence to objects without ever consulting REASON, or weighing our opinions by any philosophical principles [. . .] For philosophy informs us, that every thing, which appears to the mind, is nothing but a perception, and is interrupted, and dependent on the mind; whereas the vulgar confound perceptions and objects, and attribute a distinct continu'd existence to the very things they feel or see. This sentiment, then, as it is entirely unreasonable, must proceed from some other faculty than the understanding. To which we may add, that as long as we take our perceptions and objects to be the same, we can never infer the existence of the one from that of the other, nor form any argument from the relation of cause and effect; which is the only one that can assure us of matter of fact. Even after we distinguish our perceptions from our objects, 'twill appear presently, that we are still incapable of reasoning from the existence of one to that of the other: So that upon the whole our reason neither does, nor is it possible it ever shou'd, upon any supposition, give us an assurance of the continu'd and distinct existence of body. That opinion must be entirely owing to the IMAGINATION: which must now be the subject of our enquiry.

Since all impressions are internal and perishing existences, and appear as such, the notion of their distinct and continu'd existence must arise from a concurrence of some of their qualities with the qualities of the imagination; and since this notion does not extend to all of them, it must arise from certain qualities peculiar to some impressions. 'Twill therefore be easy for us to discover these qualities by a comparison of the impressions, to which we attribute a distinct and continu'd existence, with those, which we regard as internal and perishing.

We may observe, then, that 'tis neither upon account of the involuntariness of certain impressions, as is commonly suppos'd, nor of their superior force and violence, that we attribute to them a reality, and continu'd existence, which we refuse to others, that are voluntary or feeble. For 'tis evident our pains and pleasures, our passions and affections, which we never suppose to have any existence beyond our perception, operate with greater violence, and are equally involuntary, as the impressions of figure and extension, colour and sound, which we suppose to be permanent beings. The heat of a fire, when moderate, is suppos'd to exist in the fire; but the pain, which it causes upon a near approach, is not taken to have any being except in the perception.

These vulgar opinions, then, being rejected, we must search for some other hypothesis, by which we may discover those peculiar qualities in our impressions, which makes us attribute to them a distinct and continu'd existence.

After a little examination, we shall find, that all those objects, to which we attribute a continu'd existence, have a peculiar *constancy*, which distinguishes them from the impressions, whose

existence depends upon our perception. Those mountains, and houses, and trees, which lie at present under my eye, have always appear'd to me in the same order; and when I lose sight of them by shutting my eyes or turning my head, I soon after find them return upon me without the least alteration. My bed and table, my books and papers, present themselves in the same uniform manner, and change not upon account of any interruption in my seeing or perceiving them. This is the case with all the impressions, whose objects are suppos'd to have an external existence; and is the case with no other impressions, whether gentle or violent, voluntary or involuntary.

This constancy, however, is not so perfect as not to admit of very considerable exceptions. Bodies often change their position and qualities, and after a little absence or interruption may become hardly knowable. But here 'tis observable, that even in these changes they preserve a *coherence*, and have a regular dependence on each other; which is the foundation of a kind of reasoning from causation, and produces the opinion of their continu'd existence. When I return to my chamber after an hour's absence, I find not my fire in the same situation, in which I left it: But then I am accustom'd in other instances to see a like alteration produc'd in a like time, whether I am present or absent, near or remote. This coherence, therefore, in their changes is one of the characteristics of external objects, as well as their constancy.

Having found that the opinion of the continu'd existence of body depends on the COHERENCE and CONSTANCY of certain impressions, I now proceed to examine after what manner these qualities give rise to so extraordinary an opinion. To begin with the coherence; we may observe, that tho' those internal impressions, which we regard as fleeting and perishing, have also a certain coherence or regularity in their appearances, yet 'tis of somewhat a different nature, from that which we discover in bodies. Our passions are found by experience to have a mutual connexion with and dependance on each other; but on no occasion is it necessary to suppose, that they have existed and operated, when they were not perceiv'd, in order to preserve the same dependence and connexion, of which we have had experience. The case is not the same with relation to external objects. Those require a continu'd existence, or otherwise lose, in a great measure, the regularity of their operation. I am here seated in my chamber with my face to the fire; and all the objects, that strike my senses, are contain'd in a few yards around me. My memory, indeed, informs me of the existence of many objects; but then this information extends not beyond their past existence, nor do either my senses or memory give any testimony to the continuance of their being. When therefore I am thus seated, and revolve over these thoughts, I hear on a sudden a noise as of a door turning upon its hinges; and a little after see a porter, who advances towards me. This gives occasion to many new reflexions and reasonings. First, I never have observ'd, that this noise cou'd proceed from any thing but the motion of a door; and therefore conclude, that the present is a contradiction to all past experience, unless the door, which I remember on t'other side the chamber, be still in being. Again, I have always found, that a human body was possest of a quality, which I call gravity, and which hinders it from mounting in the air, as this porter must have done to arrive at my chamber, unless the stairs I remember be not annihilated by my absence. But this is not all. I receive a letter, which upon opening it I perceive by the hand-writing and subscription to have come from a friend, who says he is two hundred leagues distant. 'Tis evident I can never account for this phænomenon, conformable to my experience in other instances, without spreading out in my mind the whole sea and continent between us, and supposing the effects and continu'd existence of posts and ferries, according to my memory and observation. To consider these phænomena of the porter and letter in a certain light, they are contradictions to common experience, and may be regarded as objections to those maxims, which we form concerning the connexions of causes and effects. I am accustom'd to hear such a sound, and see such an object in motion at the same time. I have not receiv'd in this particular instance both these perceptions. These observations are contrary, unless I suppose that the door still remains, and that it was open'd without my perceiving it: And this supposition, which was at first entirely arbitrary and hypothetical, acquires a force and evidence by its being the only one, upon which

I can reconcile these contradictions. There is scarce a moment of my life, wherein there is not a similar instance presented to me, and I have not occasion to suppose the continu'd existence of objects, in order to connect their past and present appearances, and give them such an union with each other, as I have found by experience to be suitable to their particular natures and circumstances. Here then I am naturally led to regard the world, as something real and durable, and as preserving its existence, even when it is no longer present to my perception.

But tho' this conclusion from the coherence of appearances may seem to be of the same nature with our reasonings concerning causes and effects; as being deriv'd from custom, and regulated by past experience; we shall find upon examination, that they are at the bottom considerably different from each other, and that this inference arises from the understanding, and from custom in an indirect and oblique manner. For 'twill readily be allow'd, that since nothing is ever really present to the mind, besides its own perceptions, 'tis not only impossible, that any habit shou'd ever be acquir'd otherwise than by the regular succession of these perceptions, but also that any habit shou'd ever exceed that degree of regularity. Any degree, therefore, of regularity in our perceptions, can never be a foundation for us to infer a greater degree of regularity in some objects, which are not perceiv'd; since this supposes a contradiction, viz. a habit acquir'd by what was never present to the mind. But 'tis evident, that whenever we infer the continu'd existence of the objects of sense from their coherence, and the frequency of their union, 'tis in order to bestow on the objects a greater regularity than what is observ'd in our mere perceptions. We remark a connexion betwixt two kinds of objects in their past appearance to the senses, but are not able to observe this connexion to be perfectly constant, since the turning about of our head, or the shutting of our eyes is able to break it. What then do we suppose in this case, but that these objects still continue their usual connexion, notwithstanding their apparent interruption, and that the irregular appearances are join'd by something, of which we are insensible? But as all reasoning concerning matters of fact arises only from custom, and custom can only be the effect of repeated perceptions, the extending of custom and reasoning beyond the perceptions can never be the direct and natural effect of the constant repetition and connexion, but must arise from the co-operation of some other principles.

[. . .] The imagination, when set into any train of thinking, is apt to continue, even when its object fails it, and like a galley put in motion by the oars, carries on its course without any new impulse [. . .] Objects have a certain coherence even as they appear to our senses; but this coherence is much greater and more uniform, if we suppose the objects to have a continu'd existence; and as the mind is once in the train of observing an uniformity among objects, it naturally continues, till it renders the uniformity as compleat as possible. The simple supposition of their continu'd existence suffices for this purpose, and gives us a notion of a much greater regularity among objects, than what they have when we look no farther than our senses.

But whatever force we may ascribe to this principle, I am afraid 'tis too weak to support alone so vast an edifice, as is that of the continu'd existence of all external bodies; and that we must join the *constancy* of their appearance to the *coherence*, in order to give a satisfactory account of that opinion. As the explication of this will lead me into a considerable compass of very profound reasoning; I think it proper, in order to avoid confusion, to give a short sketch or abridgment of my system, and afterwards draw out all its parts in their full compass. This inference from the constancy of our perceptions, like the precedent from their coherence, gives rise to the opinion of the *continu'd* existence of body, which is prior to that of its *distinct* existence, and produces that latter principle.

When we have been accustom'd to observe a constancy in certain impressions, and have found, that the perception of the sun or ocean, for instance, returns upon us after an absence or annihilation with like parts and in a like order, as at its first appearance, we are not apt to regard these interrupted perceptions as different, (which they really are) but on the contrary consider them as individually the same, upon account of their resemblance. But as this interruption of their existence is contrary to their perfect identity, and makes us regard the first impression as annihilated, and the second as newly created, we find ourselves somewhat at a loss, and are

involv'd in a kind of contradiction. In order to free ourselves from this difficulty, we disguise, as much as possible, the interruption, or rather remove it entirely, by supposing that these interrupted perceptions are connected by a real existence, of which we are insensible. This supposition, or idea of continu'd existence, acquires a force and vivacity from the memory of these broken impressions, and from that propensity, which they give us, to suppose them the same; and according to the precedent reasoning, the very essence of belief consists in the force and vivacity of the conception.

In order to justify this system, there are four things requisite. *First*, To explain the *principium individuationis*, or principle of identity. *Secondly*, Give a reason, why the resemblance of our broken and interrupted perceptions induces us to attribute an identity to them. *Thirdly*, Account for that propensity, which this illusion gives, to unite these broken appearances by a continu'd existence. *Fourthly* and lastly, Explain that force and vivacity of conception, which arises from the propensity.

First, As to the principle of individuation; we may observe, that the view of any one object is not sufficient to convey the idea of identity. For in that proposition, *an object is the same with itself*, if the idea express'd by the word, *object*, were no ways distinguish'd from that meant by *itself*, we really shou'd mean nothing, nor wou'd the proposition contain a predicate and a subject, which however are imply'd in this affirmation. One single object conveys the idea of unity, not that of identity.

On the other hand, a multiplicity of objects can never convey this idea, however resembling they may be suppos'd. The mind always pronounces the one not to be the other, and considers them as forming two, three, or any determinate number of objects, whose existences are entirely distinct and independent.

Since then both number and unity are incompatible with the relation of identity, it must lie in something that is neither of them. But to tell the truth, at first sight this seems utterly impossible. Betwixt unity and number there can be no medium; no more than betwixt existence and nonexistence. After one object is suppos'd to exist, we must either suppose another also to exist; in which case we have the idea of number:

Or we must suppose it not to exist; in which case the first object remains at unity.

To remove this difficulty, let us have recourse to the idea of time or duration. I have already observ'd, that time, in a strict sense, implies succession, and that when we apply its idea to any unchangeable object, 'tis only by a fiction of the imagination, by which the unchangeable object is suppos'd to participate of the changes of the co-existent objects, and in particular of that of our perceptions. This fiction of the imagination almost universally takes place; and 'tis by means of it, that a single object, plac'd before us, and survey'd for any time without our discovering in it any interruption or variation, is able to give us a notion of identity. For when we consider any two points of this time, we may place them in different lights: We may either survey them at the very same instant; in which case they give us the idea of number, both by themselves and by the object; which must be multiply'd, in order to be conceiv'd at once, as existent in these two different points of time: Or on the other hand, we may trace the succession of time by a like succession of ideas, and conceiving first one moment, along with the object then existent, imagine afterwards a change in the time without any *variation* or *interruption* in the object; in which case it gives us the idea of unity. Here then is an idea, which is a medium betwixt unity and number; or more properly speaking, is either of them, according to the view, in which we take it: And this idea we call that of identity. We cannot, in any propriety of speech, say, that an object is the same with itself, unless we mean, that the object existent at one time is the same with itself existent at another. By this means we make a difference, betwixt the idea meant by the word, *object*, and that meant by *itself*, without going the length of number, and at the same time without restraining ourselves to a strict and absolute unity.

Thus the principle of individuation is nothing but the *invariableness* and *uninterruptedness* of any object, thro' a suppos'd variation of time, by which the mind can trace it in the different periods of its existence, without any break of the view, and without being oblig'd to form the idea of multiplicity or number.

I now proceed to explain the *second* part of my system, and shew why the constancy of our perceptions makes us ascribe to them a perfect numerical identity, tho' there be very long intervals betwixt their appearance, and they have only one of the essential qualities of identity, *viz. invariableness*. That I may avoid all ambiguity and confusion on this head, I shall observe, that I here account for the opinions and belief of the vulgar with regard to the existence of body; and therefore must entirely conform myself to their manner of thinking and of expressing themselves. Now we have already observ'd, that however philosophers may distinguish betwixt the objects and perceptions of the senses; which they suppose co-existent and resembling; yet this is a distinction, which is not comprehended by the generality of mankind, who as they perceive only one being, can never assent to the opinion of a double existence and representation. Those very sensations, which enter by the eye or ear, are with them the true objects, nor can they readily conceive that this pen or paper, which is immediately perceiv'd, represents another, which is different from, but resembling it. In order, therefore, to accommodate myself to their notions, I shall at first suppose; that there is only a single existence, which I shall call indifferently *object* or *perception*, according as it shall seem best to suit my purpose, understanding by both of them what any common man means by a hat, or shoe, or stone, or any other impression, convey'd to him by his senses. I shall be sure to give warning, when I return to a more philosophical way of speaking and thinking.

To enter, therefore, upon the question concerning the source of the error and deception with regard to identity, when we attribute it to our resembling perceptions, notwithstanding their interruption; I must here recall an observation, which I have already prov'd and explain'd. Nothing is more apt to make us mistake one idea for another, than any relation betwixt them, which associates them together in the imagination, and makes it pass with facility from one to the other. Of all relations, that of resemblance is in this respect the most efficacious; and that because it not only causes an association of ideas, but also of dispositions, and makes us conceive the one idea by an act or operation of the mind, similar to that by which we conceive the other. This circumstance I have observ'd to be of great moment; and we may establish it for a general rule, that whatever ideas place the mind in the same disposition or in similar ones, are very apt to be confounded. The mind readily passes from one to the other, and perceives not the change without a strict attention, of which, generally speaking, 'tis wholly incapable.

In order to apply this general maxim, we must first examine the disposition of the mind in viewing any object which preserves a perfect identity, and then find some other object, that is confounded with it, by causing a similar disposition. When we fix our thought on any object, and suppose it to continue the same for some time; 'tis evident we suppose the change to lie only in the time, and never exert ourselves to produce any new image or idea of the object. The faculties of the mind repose themselves in a manner, and take no more exercise, than what is necessary to continue that idea, of which we were formerly possest, and which subsists without variation or interruption. The passage from one moment to another is scarce felt, and distinguishes not itself by a different perception or idea, which may require a different direction of the spirits, in order to its conception.

Now what other objects, beside identical ones, are capable of placing the mind in the same disposition, when it considers them, and of causing the same uninterrupted passage of the imagination from one idea to another? This question is of the last importance. For if we can find any such objects, we may certainly conclude, from the foregoing principle, that they are very naturally confounded with identical ones, and are taken for them in most of our reasonings. But tho' this question be very important, 'tis not very difficult nor doubtful. For I immediately reply, that a succession of related objects places the mind in this disposition, and is consider'd with the same smooth and uninterrupted progress of the imagination, as attends the view of the same invariable object. The very nature and essence of relation is to connect our ideas with each other, and upon the appearance of one, to facilitate the transition to its correlative. The passage betwixt related ideas is, therefore, so smooth and easy, that it produces little alteration on the mind, and seems like the continuation of the same action; and as the continuation of the same action is an effect of the continu'd view of the same object, 'tis for this reason we attribute sameness to every succession of related objects. The thought slides along the succession with equal facility, as if it consider'd only one object; and therefore confounds the succession with the identity.

We shall afterwards see many instances of this tendency of relation to make us ascribe an *identity* to *different* objects; but shall here confine ourselves to the present subject. We find by experience, that there is such a *constancy* in almost all the impressions of the senses, that their interruption produces no alteration on them, and hinders them not from returning the same in appearance and in situation as at their first existence. I survey the furniture of my chamber; I shut my eyes, and afterwards open them; and find the new perceptions to resemble perfectly those, which formerly struck my senses. This resemblance is observ'd in a thousand instances, and naturally connects together our ideas of these interrupted perceptions by the strongest relation, and conveys the mind with an easy transition from one to another. An easy transition or passage of the imagination, along the ideas of these different and interrupted perceptions, is almost the same disposition of mind with that in which we consider one constant and uninterrupted perception. 'Tis therefore very natural for us to mistake the one for the other.[1]

The persons, who entertain this opinion concerning the identity of our resembling perceptions, are in general all the unthinking and unphilosophical part of mankind, (that is, all of us, at one time or other) and consequently such as suppose their perceptions to be their only objects, and never think of a double existence internal and external, representing and represented. The very image, which is present to the senses, is with us the real body; and 'tis to these interrupted images we ascribe a perfect identity. But as the interruption of the appearance seems contrary to the identity, and naturally leads us to regard these resembling perceptions as different from each other, we here find ourselves at a loss how to reconcile such opposite opinions. The smooth passage of the imagination along the ideas of the resembling perceptions makes us ascribe to them a perfect identity. The interrupted manner of their appearance makes us consider them as so many resembling, but still distinct beings, which appear after certain intervals. The perplexity arising from this contradiction produces a propension to unite these broken appearances by the fiction of a continu'd existence, which is the *third* part of that hypothesis I propos'd to explain.

Nothing is more certain from experience, than that any contradiction either to the sentiments or passions gives a sensible uneasiness, whether it proceeds from without or from within; from the opposition of external objects, or from the combat of internal principles. On the contrary, whatever strikes in with the natural propensities, and either externally forwards their satisfaction, or internally concurs with their movements, is sure to give a sensible pleasure. Now there being here an opposition betwixt the notion of the identity of resembling perceptions, and the interruption of their appearance, the mind must be uneasy in that situation, and will naturally seek relief from the uneasiness. Since the uneasiness arises from the opposition of two contrary principles, it must look for relief by sacrificing the one to the other. But as the smooth passage of our thought along our resembling perceptions makes us ascribe to them an identity, we can never without reluctance yield up that opinion. We must, therefore, turn to the other side, and suppose that our perceptions are no longer interrupted, but preserve a continu'd as well as an invariable existence, and are by that means entirely the same. But here the interruptions in the appearance of these perceptions are so long and frequent, that 'tis impossible to overlook them; and as the *appearance* of a perception in the mind and its *existence* seem at first sight entirely the same, it may be doubted, whether we can ever assent to so palpable a contradiction, and suppose a perception to exist without being present to the mind. In order to clear up this matter, and learn how the interruption in the appearance of a perception implies not necessarily an interruption in its existence, 'twill be proper to touch upon some principles, which we shall have occasion to explain more fully afterwards.

We may begin with observing, that the difficulty in the present case is not concerning the matter of fact, or whether the mind forms such a conclusion concerning the continu'd existence of its perceptions, but only concerning the manner in which the conclusion is form'd, and principles from which it is deriv'd. 'Tis certain, that almost all mankind, and even philosophers themselves, for the greatest part of their lives, take their perceptions to be their only objects, and suppose, that the very being, which is intimately present to the mind, is the real body or material existence. 'Tis also certain, that this very perception or object is suppos'd to have a continu'd uninterrupted being, and neither to be annihilated by our absence, nor to be brought into existence by our presence. When we are absent from it, we say it still exists, but that we do not feel, we do not see it. When we are present, we say we feel, or see it. Here then may arise two questions; *First*, How we can satisfy ourselves in supposing a perception to be absent from the mind without being annihilated. *Secondly*, After what manner we conceive an object to become present to the mind, without some new creation of a perception or image; and what we mean by this *seeing*, and *feeling*, and *perceiving*.

As to the first question; we may observe, that what we call a *mind*, is nothing but a heap or collection of different perceptions, united together by certain relations, and suppos'd, tho' falsely, to be endow'd with a perfect simplicity and identity. Now as every perception is distinguishable from another, and may be consider'd as separately existent; it evidently follows, that there is no absurdity in separating any particular perception from the mind; that is, in breaking off all its relations, with that connected mass of perceptions, which constitute a thinking being.

The same reasoning affords us an answer to the second question. If the name of *perception* renders not this separation from a mind absurd and contradictory, the name of *object*, standing for the very same thing, can never render their conjunction impossible. External objects are seen, and felt, and become present to the mind; that is, they acquire such a relation to a connected heap of perceptions, as to influence them very considerably in augmenting their number by present reflexions and passions, and in storing the memory with ideas. The same continu'd and uninterrupted Being may, therefore, be sometimes present to the mind, and sometimes absent from it, without any real or essential change in the Being itself. An interrupted appearance to the senses implies not necessarily an interruption in the existence. The supposition of the continu'd existence of sensible objects or perceptions involves no contradiction. We may easily indulge our inclination to that supposition. When the exact resemblance of our perceptions makes us ascribe to them an identity, we may remove the seeming interruption by feigning a continu'd being, which may fill those intervals, and preserve a perfect and entire identity to our perceptions.

But as we here not only *feign* but *believe* this continu'd existence, the question is, *from whence arises such a belief*; and this question leads us to the *fourth* member of this system. It has been prov'd already, that belief in general consists in nothing, but the vivacity of an idea; and that an idea may acquire this vivacity by its relation to some present impression [...]

But suppose, that this propensity arises from some other principle, besides that of relation; 'tis evident it must still have the same effect, and convey the vivacity from the impression to the idea. Now this is exactly the present case. Our memory presents us with a vast number of instances of perceptions perfectly resembling each other, that return at different distances of time, and after considerable interruptions. This resemblance gives us a propension to consider these interrupted perceptions as the same; and also a propension to connect them by a continu'd existence, in order to justify this identity, and avoid the contradiction, in which the interrupted appearance of these perceptions seems necessarily to involve us. Here then we have a propensity to feign the continu'd existence of all sensible objects; and as this propensity arises from some lively impressions of the memory, it bestows a vivacity on that fiction; or in other words, makes us believe the continu'd existence of body. If sometimes we ascribe a continu'd existence to objects, which are perfectly new to us, and of whose constancy and coherence we have no experience, 'tis because the manner, in which they present themselves to our senses, resembles that of constant and coherent objects; and this resemblance is a source of reasoning and analogy, and leads us to attribute the same qualities to the similar objects.

I believe an intelligent reader will find less difficulty to assent to this system, than to comprehend it fully and distinctly, and will allow, after a little reflection, that every part carries its own proof along with it. 'Tis indeed evident, that as the vulgar *suppose* their perceptions to be their only objects, and at the same time *believe* the continu'd existence of matter, we must account for the origin of the belief upon that supposition.

Now upon that supposition, 'tis a false opinion that any of our objects, or perceptions, are identically the same after an interruption; and consequently the opinion of their identity can never arise from reason, but must arise from the imagination. The imagination is seduc'd into such an opinion only by means of the resemblance of certain perceptions; since we find they are only our resembling perceptions, which we have a propension to suppose the same. This propension to bestow an identity on our resembling perceptions, produces the fiction of a continu'd existence; since that fiction, as well as the identity, is really false, as is acknowledg'd by all philosophers, and has no other effect than to remedy the interruption of our perceptions, which is the only circumstance that is contrary to their identity. In the last place this propension causes belief by means of the present impressions of the memory; since without the remembrance of former sensations, 'tis plain we never shou'd have any belief of the continu'd existence of body. Thus in examining all these parts, we find that each of them is supported by the strongest proofs; and that all of them together form a consistent system, which is perfectly convincing. A strong propensity or inclination alone, without any present impression, will sometimes cause a belief or opinion. How much more when aided by that circumstance?

But tho' we are led after this manner, by the natural propensity of the imagination, to ascribe a continu'd existence to those sensible objects or perceptions, which we find to resemble each other in their interrupted appearance; yet a very little reflection and philosophy is sufficient to make us perceive the fallacy of that opinion. I have already observ'd, that there is an intimate connexion betwixt those two principles, of a *continu'd* and of a *distinct* or *independent* existence, and that we no sooner establish the one than the other follows, as a necessary consequence. 'Tis the opinion of a continu'd existence, which first takes place, and without much study or reflection draws the other along with it, wherever the mind follows its first and most natural tendency. But when we compare experiments, and reason a little upon them, we quickly perceive, that the doctrine of the independent existence of our sensible perceptions is contrary to the plainest experience. This leads us backward upon our footsteps to perceive our error in attributing a continu'd existence to our perceptions, and is the origin of many very curious opinions, which we shall here endeavour to account for.

'Twill first be proper to observe a few of those experiments, which convince us, that our perceptions are not possest of any independent existence. When we press one eye with a finger, we immediately perceive all the objects to become double, and one half of them to be remov'd from their common and natural position. But as we do not attribute a continu'd existence to both these perceptions, and as they are both of the same nature, we clearly perceive, that all our perceptions are dependent on our organs, and the disposition of our nerves and animal spirits. This opinion is confirm'd by the seeming encrease and diminution of objects, according to their distance; by the apparent alterations in their figure; by the changes in their colour and other qualities from our sickness and distempers; and by an infinite number of other experiments of the same kind; from all which we learn, that our sensible perceptions are not possest of any distinct or independent existence.

The natural consequence of this reasoning shou'd be, that our perceptions have no more a continu'd than an independent existence; and indeed philosophers have so far run into this opinion, that they change their system, and distinguish, (as we shall do for the future) betwixt perceptions and objects, of which the former are suppos'd to be interrupted, and perishing, and different at every different return; the latter to be uninterrupted, and to preserve a continu'd existence and identity. But however philosophical this new system may be esteem'd, I assert that 'tis only a palliative remedy, and that it contains all the difficulties of the vulgar system, with some others, that are peculiar to itself. There are no principles either of the understanding or fancy, which lead us directly to embrace this opinion of the double existence of perceptions and objects, nor can we arrive at it but by passing thro' the common hypothesis of the identity and continuance of our interrupted perceptions. Were we not first perswaded, that our perceptions are our only objects, and continue to exist even when they no longer make their appearance to the senses, we shou'd never be led to think, that our perceptions and objects are different, and that our objects alone preserve a continu'd existence. 'The latter

hypothesis has no primary recommendation either to reason or the imagination, but acquires all its influence on the imagination from the former.' This proposition contains two parts, which we shall endeavour to prove as distinctly and clearly, as such abstruse subjects will permit.

As to the first part of the proposition, *that this philosophical hypothesis has no primary recommendation, either to reason or the imagination*, we may soon satisfy ourselves with regard to *reason* by the following reflections. The only existences, of which we are certain, are perceptions, which being immediately present to us by consciousness, command our strongest assent, and are the first foundation of all our conclusions. The only conclusion we can draw from the existence of one thing to that of another, is by means of the relation of cause and effect, which shews, that there is a connexion betwixt them, and that the existence of one is dependent on that of the other. The idea of this relation is deriv'd from past experience, by which we find, that two beings are constantly conjoin'd together, and are always present at once to the mind. But as no beings are ever present to the mind but perceptions; it follows that we may observe a conjunction or a relation of cause and effect between different perceptions, but can never observe it between perceptions and objects. 'Tis impossible, therefore, that from the existence or any of the qualities of the former, we can ever form any conclusion concerning the existence of the latter, or ever satisfy our reason in this particular.

'Tis no less certain, that this philosophical system has no primary recommendation to the *imagination*, and that that faculty wou'd never, of itself, and by its original tendency, have fallen upon such a principle. I confess it will be somewhat difficult to prove this to the full satisfaction of the reader; because it implies a negative, which in many cases will not admit of any positive proof. If any one wou'd take the pains to examine this question, and wou'd invent a system, to account for the direct origin of this opinion from the imagination, we shou'd be able, by the examination of that system, to pronounce a certain judgment in the present subject. Let it be taken for granted, that our perceptions are broken, and interrupted, and however like, are still different from each other; and let any one upon this supposition shew why the fancy, directly and immediately, proceeds to the belief of another existence, resembling these perceptions in their nature, but yet continu'd, and uninterrupted, and identical; and after he has done this to my satisfaction, I promise to renounce my present opinion. Mean while I cannot forbear concluding, from the very abstractedness and difficulty of the first supposition, that 'tis an improper subject for the fancy to work upon. Whoever wou'd explain the origin of the *common* opinion concerning the continu'd and distinct existence of body, must take the mind in its *common* situation, and must proceed upon the supposition, that our perceptions are our only objects, and continue to exist even when they are not perceiv'd. Tho' this opinion be false, 'tis the most natural of any, and has alone any primary recommendation to the fancy.

As to the second part of the proposition, *that the philosophical system acquires all its influence on the imagination from the vulgar one*; we may observe, that this is a natural and unavoidable consequence of the foregoing conclusion, *that it has no primary recommendation to reason or the imagination*. For as the philosophical system is found by experience to take hold of many minds, and in particular of all those, who reflect ever so little on this subject, it must derive all its authority from the vulgar system; since it has no original authority of its own. The manner, in which these two systems, tho' directly contrary, are connected together, may be explain'd, as follows.

[...] As a little reflection destroys [the] conclusion, that our perceptions have a continu'd existence, by shewing that they have a dependent one, 'twou'd naturally be expected, that we must altogether reject the opinion, that there is such a thing in nature as a continu'd existence, which is preserv'd even when it no longer appears to the senses. The case, however, is otherwise. Philosophers are so far from rejecting the opinion of a continu'd existence upon rejecting that of the independence and continuance of our sensible perceptions, that tho' all sects agree in the latter sentiment, the former, which is, in a manner, its necessary consequence, has been peculiar to a few extravagant sceptics; who after all maintain'd that opinion in words only, and were never able to bring themselves sincerely to believe it.

There is a great difference betwixt such opinions as we form after a calm and profound reflection, and such as we embrace by a kind of instinct or natural impulse, on account of their suitableness and conformity to the mind. If these opinions become contrary, 'tis not difficult to foresee which of them will have the advantage. As long as our attention is bent upon the subject, the philosophical and study'd principle may prevail; but the moment we relax our thoughts, nature will display herself, and draw us back to our former opinion. Nay she has sometimes such an influence, that she can stop our progress, even in the midst of our most profound reflections, and keep us from running on with all the consequences of any philosophical opinion. Thus tho' we clearly perceive the dependence and interruption of our perceptions, we stop short in our career, and never upon that account reject the notion of an independent and continu'd existence. That opinion has taken such deep root in the imagination, that 'tis impossible ever to eradicate it, nor will any strain'd metaphysical conviction of the dependence of our perceptions be sufficient for that purpose.

But tho' our natural and obvious principles here prevail above our study'd reflections, 'tis certain there must be some struggle and opposition in the case; at least so long as these reflections retain any force or vivacity. In order to set ourselves at ease in this particular, we contrive a new hypothesis, which seems to comprehend both these principles of reason and imagination. This hypothesis is the philosophical one of the double existence of perceptions and objects; which pleases our reason, in allowing, that our dependent perceptions are interrupted and different; and at the same time is agreeable to the imagination, in attributing a continu'd existence to something else, which we call *objects*. This philosophical system, therefore, is the monstrous offspring of two principles, which are contrary to each other, which are both at once embrac'd by the mind, and which are unable mutually to destroy each other. The imagination tells us, that our resembling perceptions have a continu'd and uninterrupted existence, and are not annihilated by their absence. Reflection tells us, that even our resembling perceptions are interrupted in their existence, and different from each other. The contradiction betwixt these opinions we elude by a new fiction, which is conformable to the hypotheses both of reflection and fancy, by ascribing these contrary qualities to different existences; the *interruption* to perceptions, and the *continuance* to objects. Nature is obstinate, and will not quit the field, however strongly attack'd by reason; and at the same time reason is so clear in the point, that there is no possibility of disguising her. Not being able to reconcile these two enemies, we endeavour to set ourselves at ease as much as possible, by successively granting to each whatever it demands, and by feigning a double existence, where each may find something, that has all the conditions it desires [...]

There are other particulars of this system, wherein we may remark its dependence on the fancy, in a very conspicuous manner. Of these, I shall observe the two following. *First*, We suppose external objects to resemble internal perceptions. I have already shewn, that the relation of cause and effect can never afford us any just conclusion from the existence or qualities of our perceptions to the existence of external continu'd objects: And I shall farther add, that even tho' they cou'd afford such a conclusion, we shou'd never have any reason to infer, that our objects resemble our perceptions. That opinion, therefore, is deriv'd from nothing but the quality of the fancy above-explain'd, *that it borrows all its ideas from some precedent perception.* We never can conceive any thing but perceptions, and therefore must make every thing resemble them.

Secondly, As we suppose our objects in general to resemble our perceptions, so we take it for granted, that every particular object resembles that perception, which it causes. The relation of cause and effect determines us to join the other of resemblance; and the ideas of these existences being already united together in the fancy by the former relation, we naturally add the latter to compleat the union. We have a strong propensity to compleat every union by joining new relations to those which we have before observ'd betwixt any ideas, as we shall have occasion to observe presently.

Having thus given an account of all the systems both popular and philosophical, with regard to external existences, I cannot forbear giving vent to a certain sentiment, which arises upon reviewing those systems. I begun this subject with premising, that we ought to have an implicit faith in our senses, and that this wou'd be the conclusion, I shou'd draw from the whole of my reasoning. But to be ingenuous, I feel myself *at present* of a quite contrary sentiment, and am more inclin'd to repose no faith at all in my senses, or

rather imagination, than to place in it such an implicit confidence. I cannot conceive how such trivial qualities of the fancy, conducted by such false suppositions, can ever lead to any solid and rational system. They are the coherence and constancy of our perceptions, which produce the opinion of their continu'd existence; tho' these qualities of perceptions have no perceivable connexion with such an existence. The constancy of our perceptions has the most considerable effect, and yet is attended with the greatest difficulties. 'Tis a gross illusion to suppose, that our resembling perceptions are numerically the same; and 'tis this illusion, which leads us into the opinion, that these perceptions are uninterrupted, and are still existent, even when they are not present to the senses. This is the case with our popular system. And as to our philosophical one, 'tis liable to the same difficulties; and is over-and-above loaded with this absurdity, that it at once denies and establishes the vulgar supposition. Philosophers deny our resembling perceptions to be identically the same, and uninterrupted; and yet have so great a propensity to believe them such, that they arbitrarily invent a new set of perceptions, to which they attribute these qualities. I say, a new set of perceptions: For we may well suppose in general, but 'tis impossible for us distinctly to conceive, objects to be in their nature any thing but exactly the same with perceptions. What then can we look for from this confusion of groundless and extraordinary opinions but error and falshood? And how can we justify to ourselves any belief we repose in them?

This sceptical doubt, both with respect to reason and the senses, is a malady, which can never be radically cur'd, but must return upon us every moment, however we may chace it away, and sometimes may seem entirely free from it. 'Tis impossible upon any system to defend either our understanding or senses; and we but expose them farther when we endeavour to justify them in that manner. As the sceptical doubt arises naturally from a profound and intense reflection on those subjects, it always encreases, the farther we carry our reflections, whether in opposition or conformity to it. Carelessness and in-attention alone can afford us any remedy. For this reason I rely entirely upon them; and take it for granted, whatever may be the reader's opinion at this present moment, that an hour hence he will be persuaded there is both an external and internal world; and going upon that supposition, I intend to examine some general systems both ancient and modern, which have been propos'd of both, before I proceed to a more particular enquiry concerning our impressions. This will not, perhaps, in the end be found foreign to our present purpose.

Note

1   This reasoning, it must be confest, is somewhat abstruse, and difficult to be comprehended; but it is remarkable, that this very difficulty may be converted into a proof of the reasoning. We may observe, that there are two relations, and both of them resemblances, which contribute to our mistaking the succession of our interrupted perceptions for an identical object. The first is, the resemblance of perceptions: The second is the resemblance, which the act of the mind in surveying a succession of resembling objects bears to that in surveying an identical object. Now these resemblances we are apt to confound with each other; and 'tis natural we shou'd, according to this very reasoning. But let us keep them distinct, and we shall find no difficulty in conceiving the precedent argument.

5

The Self and the Common World

A. J. Ayer

It is customary for the authors of epistemological treatises to assume that our empirical knowledge must have a basis of certainty, and that there must therefore be objects whose existence is logically indubitable. And they believe, for the most part, that it is their business, not merely to describe these objects, which they regard as being immediately "given" to us, but also to provide a logical proof of the existence of objects which are not so "given." For they think that without such a proof the greater part of our so-called empirical knowledge will lack the certification which it logically requires.

To those who have followed the argument of this book it will, however, be clear that these familiar assumptions are mistaken. For we have seen that our claims to empirical knowledge are not susceptible of a logical, but only of a pragmatic, justification. It is futile, and therefore illegitimate, to demand an *a priori* proof of the existence of objects which are not immediately "given." For, unless they are metaphysical objects, the occurrence of certain sense-experiences will itself constitute the only proof of their existence which is requisite or obtainable; and the question whether the appropriate sense-experiences do or do not occur in the relevant circumstances is one that must be decided in actual practice, and not

by any *a priori* argumentation. We have already applied these considerations to the so-called problem of perception, and we shall shortly be applying them also to the traditional "problems" of our knowledge of our own existence, and of the existence of other people. In the case of the problem of perception, we found that in order to avoid metaphysics we were obliged to adopt a phenomenalist standpoint, and we shall find that the same treatment must be accorded to the other problems to which we have just now referred.

We have seen, furthermore, that there are no objects whose existence is indubitable. For, since existence is not a predicate, to assert that an object exists is always to assert a synthetic proposition; and it has been shown that no synthetic propositions are logically sacrosanct. All of them, including the propositions which describe the content of our sensations, are hypotheses which, however great their probability, we may eventually find it expedient to abandon. And this means that our empirical knowledge cannot have a basis of logical certainty. It follows, indeed, from the definition of a synthetic proposition that it cannot be either proved or disproved by formal logic. The man who denies such a proposition may be acting irrationally, by contemporary standards of rationality, but he is not necessarily contradicting himself. And we know that the only propositions that are certain are those which cannot be denied without self-contradiction, inasmuch as they are tautologies.

It must not be thought that in denying that our empirical knowledge has a basis of certainty we are denying that any objects are really "given." For to say that an object is immediately "given" is to say merely that it is the content of a sense-experience, and we are very far from maintaining that our sense-experiences have no real content, or even that their content is in any way indescribable. All that we are maintaining in this connection is that any description of the content of any sense-experience is an empirical hypothesis of whose validity there can be no guarantee. And this is by no means equivalent to maintaining that no such hypothesis can actually be valid. We shall not, indeed, attempt to formulate any such hypotheses ourselves, because the discussion of psychological questions is out of place in a philosophical enquiry; and we have already made it clear that our empiricism is not logically dependent on an atomistic psychology, such as Hume and Mach adopted, but is compatible with any theory whatsoever concerning the actual characteristics of our sensory fields. For the empiricist doctrine to which we are committed is a logical doctrine concerning the distinction between analytic propositions, synthetic propositions, and metaphysical verbiage; and as such it has no bearing on any psychological question of fact.

It is not possible, however, to set aside all the questions which philosophers have raised in connection with the "given" as being psychological in character, and so outside the scope of this enquiry. In particular, it is impossible to deal in this way with the question whether sense-contents are mental or physical, or with the question whether they are in any sense private to a single self, or with the question whether they can exist without being experienced. For none of these three questions is capable of being solved by an empirical test. They must, if they are soluble at all, be soluble *a priori*. And as they are all questions which have given rise to much dispute among philosophers, we shall in fact attempt to provide for each of them a definitive *a priori* solution.

To begin with, we must make it clear that we do not accept the realist analysis of our sensations in terms of subject, act, and object. For neither the existence of the substance which is supposed to perform the so-called act of sensing nor the existence of the act itself, as an entity distinct from the sense-contents on which it is supposed to be directed, is in the least capable of being verified. We do not deny, indeed, that a given sense-content can legitimately be said to be experienced by a particular subject; but we shall see that this relation of being experienced by a particular subject is to be analysed in terms of the relationship of sense-contents to one another, and not in terms of a substantival ego and its mysterious acts. Accordingly we define a sense-content not as the object, but as a part of a sense-experience. And from this it follows that the existence of a sense-content always entails the existence of a sense-experience.

It is necessary, at this point, to remark that when one says that a sense-experience, or a sense-content, exists, one is making a different type of statement from that which one makes when one says that a material thing exists. For the existence of a material thing is defined in terms of the actual and possible occurrence of the sense-contents which constitute it as a logical construction, and one cannot significantly speak of a sense-experience, which is a whole composed of sense-contents, or of a sense-content itself as if it were a logical construction out of sense-contents. And in fact when we say that a given sense-content or sense-experience exists, we are saying no more than that it occurs. And, accordingly, it seems advisable always to speak of the "occurrence" of sense-contents and sense-experiences in preference to speaking of their "existence," and so to avoid the danger of treating sense-contents as if they were material things.

The answer to the question whether sense-contents are mental or physical is that they are neither; or rather, that the distinction between what is mental and what is physical does not apply to sense-contents. It applies only to objects which are logical constructions out of them. But what differentiates one such logical construction from another is the fact that it is constituted by different sense-contents or by sense-contents differently related. So that when we distinguish a given mental object from a given physical object, or a mental object from another mental object, or a physical object from another physical object, we are in every case distinguishing between different logical constructions whose elements cannot themselves be said to be either mental or physical. It is, indeed, not impossible for a sense-content to be an element both of a mental and of a physical object; but it is necessary that some of the elements, or some of the relations, should be different in the two logical constructions. And it may be advisable here to repeat that, when we refer to an object as a logical construction out of certain sense-contents, we are not saying that it is actually constructed out of those sense-contents, or that the sense-contents are in any way parts of it, but are merely expressing, in a convenient, if somewhat misleading, fashion, the syntactical fact that all sentences referring to it are translatable into sentences referring to them.

The fact that the distinction between mind and matter applies only to logical constructions and that all distinctions between logical constructions are reducible to distinctions between sense-contents, proves that the difference between the entire class of mental objects and the entire class of physical objects is not in any sense more fundamental than the difference between any two subclasses of mental objects, or the difference between any two subclasses of physical objects. Actually, the distinguishing feature of the objects belonging to the category of "one's own mental states" is the fact that they are mainly constituted by "introspective" sense-contents and by sense-contents which are elements of one's own body; and the distinguishing feature of the objects belonging to the category of "the mental states of others" is the fact that they are mainly constituted by sense-contents which are elements of other living bodies; and what makes one unite these two classes of objects to form the single class of mental objects is the fact that there is a high degree of qualitative similarity between many of the sense-contents which are elements of other living bodies and many of the elements of one's own. But we are not now concerned with the provision of an exact definition of "mentality." We are interested only in making it plain that the distinction between mind and matter, applying as it does to logical constructions out of sense-contents, cannot apply to sense-contents themselves. For a distinction between logical constructions which is constituted by the fact that there are certain distinctions between their elements is clearly of a different type from any distinction that can obtain between the elements.

It should be clear, also, that there is no philosophical problem concerning the relationship of mind and matter, other than the linguistic problems of defining certain symbols which denote logical constructions in terms of symbols which denote sense-contents. The problems with which philosophers have vexed themselves in the past, concerning the possibility of bridging the "gulf" between mind and matter in knowledge or in action, are all fictitious problems arising out of the senseless metaphysical conception of mind and matter, or minds and material things, as "substances." Being freed from metaphysics, we see that there can be no *a priori* objections to the existence either of causal or of epistemological connections between minds and material things. For, roughly speaking, all that we are saying when we say that the mental state of a person A at a time t is a state of awareness of a material thing X, is that the sense-experience which is the element of A occurring at time t contains a sense-content which is an element of X, and also certain images which define A's expectation of the occurrence in suitable circumstances of certain further elements of X, and that this expectation is correct: and what we are saying when we assert that a mental object M and a physical object X are causally connected is that, in certain conditions, the occurrence of a certain sort of sense-content, which is an element of M, is a reliable sign of the occurrence of a certain sort of sense-content, which is an element of X, or vice versa, And the question whether any propositions of these kinds are true or not is clearly an empirical question. It cannot be decided, as metaphysicians have attempted to decide it, *a priori*.

We turn now to consider the question of the subjectivity of sense-contents – that is, to consider whether it is or is not logically possible for a sense-content to occur in the sense-history of more than a single self. And in order to decide this question we must proceed to give an analysis of the notion of a self.

The problem which now confronts us is analogous to the problem of perception with which we have already dealt. We know that a self, if it is not to be treated as a metaphysical entity, must be held to be a logical construction out of sense-experiences. It is, in fact, a logical construction out of the sense-experiences which constitute the actual and possible sense-history of a self. And, accordingly, if we ask what is the nature of the self, we are asking what is the relationship that must obtain between sense-experiences for them to belong to the sense-history of the same self. And the answer to this question is that for any two sense-experiences to belong to the sense-history of the same self it is necessary and sufficient that they should contain organic sense-contents which are elements of the same body.[1] But, as it is logically impossible for any organic sense-content to be an element of more than one body, the relation of "belonging to the sense-history of the same self" turns out to be a symmetrical and transitive relation. And, from the fact that the relation of belonging to the sense-history of the same self is symmetrical and transitive, it follows necessarily that the series of sense-experiences which constitute the sense-histories of different selves cannot have any members in common. And this is tantamount to saying that it is logically impossible for a sense-experience to belong to the sense-history of more than a single self. But if all sense-experiences are subjective, then, all sense-contents are subjective. For it is necessary by definition for a sense-content to be contained in a single sense-experience.

To many people, the account of the self, on which this conclusion depends, will no doubt appear paradoxical. For it is still fashionable to regard the self as a substance. But, when one comes to enquire into the nature of this substance, one finds that it is an entirely unobservable entity. It may be suggested that it is revealed in self-consciousness but this is not the case. For all that is involved in self-consciousness is the ability of a self to remember some of its earlier states. And to say that a self A is able to remember some of its earlier states is to say merely that some of the sense-experiences which constitute A contain memory images which correspond to sense-contents which have previously occurred in the sense-history of A.[2] And thus we find that the possibility of self-consciousness in no way involves the existence of a substantive ego. But if the substantive ego is not revealed in self-consciousness, it is not revealed anywhere. The existence of such an entity is completely unverifiable. And

accordingly, we must conclude that the assumption of its existence is no less metaphysical than Locke's discredited assumption of the existence of a material substratum. For it is clearly no more significant to assert that an "unobservable somewhat" underlies the sensations which are the sole empirical manifestations of the self than it is to assert that an "unobservable somewhat" underlies the sensations which are the sole empirical manifestations of a material thing. The considerations which make it necessary, as Berkeley saw, to give a phenomenalist account of material things, make it necessary also, as Berkeley did not see, to give a phenomenalist account of the self.

Our reasoning on this point, as on so many others, is in conformity with Hume's. He, too, rejected the notion of a substantive ego on the ground that no such entity was observable. For, he said, whenever he entered most intimately into what he called himself, he always stumbled on some particular perception or other – of heat or cold, light or shade, love or hatred, pain or pleasure. He never could catch himself at any time without a perception, and never could observe anything but the perception. And this led him to assert that a self was "nothing but a bundle or collection of different perceptions."[3] But, having asserted this, he found himself unable to discover the principle on which innumerable distinct perceptions among which it was impossible to perceive any "real connection" were united to form a single self. He saw that the memory must be regarded not as producing, but rather as discovering, personal identity – or, in other words, that, whereas self-consciousness has to be defined in terms of memory, self-identity cannot be; for the number of my perceptions which I can remember at any time always falls far short of the number of those which have actually occurred in my history, and those which I cannot remember are no less constitutive of my self than those which I can. But having, on this ground, rejected the claim of memory to be the unifying principle of the self, Hume was obliged to confess that he did not know what was the connection between perceptions in virtue of which they formed a single self.[4] And this confession has often been taken by rationalist authors as evidence that it is impossible for a consistent empiricist to give a satisfactory account of the self.

For our part, we have shown that this charge against empiricism is unfounded. For we have solved Hume's problem by defining personal identity in terms of bodily identity, and bodily identity is to be defined in terms of the resemblance and continuity of sense-contents. And this procedure is justified by the fact that whereas it is permissible, in our language, to speak of a man as surviving a complete loss of memory, or a complete change of character, it is self-contradictory to speak of a man as surviving the annihilation of his body.[5] For that which is supposed to survive by those who look forward to a "life after death" is not the empirical self, but a metaphysical entity – the soul. And this metaphysical entity, concerning which no genuine hypothesis can be formulated, has no logical connection whatsoever with the self.

It must, however, be remarked that, although we have vindicated Hume's contention that it is necessary to give a phenomenalist account of the nature of the self, our actual definition of the self is not a mere restatement of his. For we do not hold, as he apparently did, that the self is an aggregate of sense-experiences, or that the sense-experiences which constitute a particular self are in any sense parts of it. What we hold is that the self is reducible to sense-experiences, in the sense that to say anything about the self is always to say something about sense-experiences; and our definition of personal identity is intended to show how this reduction could be made.

In thus combining a thoroughgoing phenomenalism with the admission that all sense-experiences, and the sense-contents which form part of them, are private to a single self, we are pursuing a course to which the following objection is likely to be raised. It will be said that anyone who maintains both that all empirical knowledge resolves itself on analysis into knowledge of the relationships of sense-contents, and also that the whole of a man's sense-history is private to himself, is logically obliged to be a solipsist – that is, to hold that no other people besides himself exist, or at any rate that there is no good reason to suppose that any other people beside himself exist. For it follows from his premises, so it will be argued, that the sense-experiences of another person cannot possibly form part of his own experience, and consequently that he cannot have the slightest ground

for believing in their occurrence; and, in that case, if people are nothing but logical constructions out of their sense-experiences, he cannot have the slightest ground for believing in the existence of any other people. And it will be said that even if such a solipsistic doctrine cannot be shown to be self-contradictory, it is nevertheless known to be false.[6]

I propose to meet this objection, not by denying that solipsism is known to be false, but by denying that it is a necessary consequence of our epistemology. I am, indeed, prepared to admit that if the personality of others was something that I could not possibly observe, then I should have no reason to believe in the existence of anyone else. And in admitting this I am conceding a point which would not, I think, be conceded by the majority of those philosophers who hold, as we do, that a sense-content cannot belong to the sense-history of more than a single self. They would maintain, on the contrary, that, although one cannot in any sense observe the existence of other people, one can nevertheless infer their existence with a high degree of probability from one's own experiences. They would say that my observation of a body whose behaviour resembled the behaviour of my own body entitled me to think it probable that that body was related to a self which I could not observe, in the same way as my body was related to my own observable self. And in saying this, they would be attempting to answer not the psychological question, What causes me to believe in the existence of other people? but the logical question, What good reason have I for believing in the existence of other people? So that their view cannot be refuted, as is sometimes supposed, by an argument which shows that infants come by their belief in the existence of other people intuitively, and not through a process of inference. For although my belief in a certain proposition may in fact be causally dependent on my apprehension of the evidence which makes the belief rational, it is not necessary that it should be. It is not self contradictory to say that beliefs for which there are rational grounds are frequently arrived at by irrational means.

The correct way to refute this view that I can use an argument from analogy, based on the fact that there is a perceptible resemblance between the behaviour of other bodies and that of my own, to justify a belief in the existence of other people whose experiences I could not conceivably observe, is to point out that no argument can render probable a completely unverifiable hypothesis. I can legitimately use an argument from analogy to establish the probable existence of an object which has never in fact manifested itself in my experience, provided that the object is such that it could conceivably be manifested in my experience. If this condition is not fulfilled, then, as far as I am concerned, the object is a metaphysical object, and the assertion that it exists and has certain properties is a metaphysical assertion. And, since a metaphysical assertion is senseless, no argument can possibly render it probable. But, on the view which we are discussing, I must regard other people as metaphysical objects; for it is assumed that their experiences are completely inaccessible to my observation.

The conclusion to be drawn from this is not that the existence of other people is for me a metaphysical, and so fictitious, hypothesis, but that the assumption that other people's experiences are completely inaccessible to my observation is false; just as the conclusion to be drawn from the fact that Locke's notion of a material substratum is metaphysical is not that all the assertions which we make about material things are nonsensical, but that Locke's analysis of the concept of a material thing is false. And just as I must define material things and my own self in terms of their empirical manifestations, so I must define other people in terms of their empirical manifestations – that is, in terms of the behaviour of their bodies, and ultimately in terms of sense-contents. The assumption that "behind" these sense-contents there are entities which are not even in principle accessible to my observation can have no more significance for me than the admittedly metaphysical assumption that such entities "underlie" the sense-contents which constitute material things for me, or my own self. And thus I find that I have as good a reason to believe in the existence of other people as I have to believe in the existence of material things. For in each case my hypothesis is verified by the occurrence in my sense-history of the appropriate series of sense-contents.[7]

It must not be thought that this reduction of other people's experiences to one's own in any way involves a denial of their reality. Each of us must define the experiences of the others in terms of what he can at least in principle observe, but this does not mean that each of us must regard all the others as so many robots. On the contrary, the distinction between a conscious man and an unconscious machine resolves itself into a distinction between different types of perceptible behaviour. The only ground I can have for asserting that an object which appears to be a conscious being is not really a conscious being, but only a dummy or a machine, is that it fails to satisfy one of the empirical tests by which the presence or absence of consciousness is determined. If I know that an object behaves in every way as a conscious being must, by definition, behave, then I know that it is really conscious. And this is an analytical proposition. For when I assert that an object is conscious I am asserting no more than that it would, in response to any conceivable test, exhibit the empirical manifestations of consciousness. I am not making a metaphysical postulate concerning the occurrence of events which I could not, even in principle, observe.

It appears, then, that the fact that a man's sense-experiences are private to himself, inasmuch as each of them contains an organic sense-content which belongs to his body and to no other, is perfectly compatible with his having good reason to believe in the existence of other men. For, if he is to avoid metaphysics, he must define the existence of other men in terms of the actual and hypothetical occurrence of certain sense-contents, and then the fact that the requisite sense-contents do occur in his sense-history gives him a good reason for believing that there are other conscious beings besides himself. And thus we see that the philosophical problem of "our knowledge of other people" is not the insoluble, and, indeed, fictitious, problem of establishing by argument the existence of entities which are altogether unobservable, but is simply the problem of indicating the way in which a certain type of hypothesis is empirically verified.

It must be made clear, finally, that our phenomenalism is compatible not merely with the fact that each of us has good reason to believe that there exist a number of conscious beings of the same kind as himself, but also with the fact that each of us has good reason to believe that these beings communicate with one another and with him, and inhabit a common world. For it might appear, at first sight, as if the view that all synthetic propositions ultimately referred to sense-contents, coupled with the view that no sense-content could belong to the sense-history of more than one person, implied that no one could have any good reason to believe that a synthetic proposition ever had the same literal meaning for any other person as it had for himself. That is, it might be thought that if each person's experiences were private to himself, no one could have good reason to believe that any other person's experiences were qualitatively the same as his own, and consequently that no one could have good reason to believe that the propositions which he understood, referring as they did to the contents of his own sense-experiences, were ever understood in the same way by anybody else.[8] But this reasoning would be fallacious. It does not follow from the fact that each man's experiences are private to himself that no one ever has good reason to believe that another man's experiences are qualitatively the same as his own. For we define the qualitative identity and difference of two people's sense-experiences in terms of the similarity and dissimilarity of their reactions to empirical tests. To determine, for instance, whether two people have the same colour sense we observe whether they classify all the colour expanses with which they are confronted in the same way; and, when we say that a man is colour-blind, what we are asserting is that he classifies certain colour expanses in a different way from that in which they would be classified by the majority of people. It may be objected that the fact that two people classify colour expanses in the same way proves only that their colour worlds have the same structure, and not that they have the same content; that it is possible for another man to assent to every proposition which I make about colours on the basis of entirely different colour sensations, although, since the difference is systematic, neither of us is ever in a position to detect it. But the answer to this is that each of us has to define the content of another man's sense-experiences in terms of what he can himself observe. If he regards the experiences of others as essentially unobservable entities, whose nature has somehow to be inferred from the subjects' perceptible behaviour, then, as we have seen, even the proposition that there are other conscious

beings becomes for him a metaphysical hypothesis. Accordingly, it is a mistake to draw a distinction between the structure and the content of people's sensations – such as that the structure alone is accessible to the observation of others, the content inaccessible. For if the contents of other people's sensations really were inaccessible to my observation, then I could never say anything about them. But, in fact, I do make significant statements about them; and that is because I define them, and the relations between them, in terms of what I can myself observe.

In the same way, each of us has good reason to suppose that other people understand him, and that he understands them, because he observes that his utterances have the effect on their actions which he regards as appropriate, and that they also regard as appropriate the effect which their utterances have on his actions; and mutual understanding is defined in terms of such harmony of behaviour. And, since to assert that two people inhabit a common world is to assert that they are capable, at least in principle, of understanding one another, it follows that each of us, although his sense-experiences are private to himself, has good reason to believe that he and other conscious beings inhabit a common world. For each of us observes the behaviour, on the part of himself and others, which constitutes the requisite understanding. And there is nothing in our epistemology which involves a denial of this fact.

Notes

1 This is not the only criterion. Vide my *The Foundations of Empirical Knowledge* (London: Macmillan, 1940), pp. 142–4.

2 cf. Bertrand Russell, *Analysis of Mind*, Lecture IX.

3 *Treatise of Human Nature*, Book I, Part IV, section vi.

4 *Treatise of Human Nature*, Appendix.

5 This is not true if one adopts a psychological criterion of personal identity.

6 cf. L. S. Stebbing, *Logical Positivism and Analysis* (London: H. Milford, 1933).

7 cf. Rudolf Carnap, "Scheinprobleme in der Philosophie: das Fremdpsychische und der Realismusstreit," and "Psychologie in physikalische Sprache," *Erkenntnis*, Vol. III, 1932.

8 This argument is used by Professor L. S. Stebbing in her article on "Communication and Verification," *Supplementary Proceedings of the Aristotelian Society*, 1934.

6

Brains in a Vat

Hilary Putnam

An ant is crawling on a patch of sand. As it crawls, it traces a line in the sand. By pure chance the line that it traces curves and recrosses itself in such a way that it ends up looking like a recognizable caricature of Winston Churchill. Has the ant traced a picture of Winston Churchill, a picture that *depicts* Churchill?

Most people would say, on a little reflection, that it has not. The ant, after all, has never seen Churchill, or even a picture of Churchill, and it had no intention of depicting Churchill. It simply traced a line (and even *that* was unintentional), a line that *we* can "see as" a picture of Churchill.

We can express this by saying that the line is not "in itself" a representation[1] of anything rather than anything else. Similarity (of a certain very complicated sort) to the features of Winston Churchill is not sufficient to make something represent or refer to Churchill. Nor is it necessary: in our community the printed shape "Winston Churchill," the spoken words "Winston Churchill," and many other things are used to represent Churchill (though not pictorially), while not having the sort of similarity to Churchill that a picture – even a line drawing – has. If *similarity* is not necessary or sufficient to make something represent something else, how can *anything* be

necessary or sufficient for this purpose? How on earth can one thing represent (or "stand for," etc.) a different thing?

The answer may seem easy. Suppose the ant had seen Winston Churchill, and suppose that it had the intelligence and skill to draw a picture of him. Suppose it produced the caricature *intentionally*. Then the line would have represented Churchill.

On the other hand, suppose the line had the shape WINSTON CHURCHILL. And suppose this was just accident (ignoring the improbability involved). Then the "printed shape" WINSTON CHURCHILL would *not* have represented Churchill although that printed shape does represent Churchill when it occurs in almost any book today.

So it may seem that what is necessary for representation, or what is mainly necessary for representation, is *intention*.

But to have the intention that *anything*, even private language (even the words "Winston Churchill" spoken in my mind and not out loud), should *represent* Churchill, I must have been able to *think about* Churchill in the first place. If lines in the sand, noises, etc., cannot "in themselves" represent anything, then how is it that thought forms can "in themselves" represent

Hilary Putnam, "Brains in a Vat," from *Reason, Truth and History* (Cambridge: Cambridge University Press, 1981), pp 1–21. © 1981 by Cambridge University Press. Reproduced with permission from the author and Cambridge University Press.

anything? Or can they? How can thought reach out and "grasp" what is external?

Some philosophers have, in the past, leaped from this sort of consideration to what they take to be a proof that the mind is *essentially non-physical in nature*. The argument is simple; what we said about the ant's curve applies to any physical object. No physical object can, in itself, refer to one thing rather than to another; nevertheless, *thoughts in the mind* obviously do succeed in referring to one thing rather than another. So thoughts (and hence the mind) are of an essentially different nature than physical objects. Thoughts have the characteristic of *intentionality* – they can refer to something else; nothing physical has "intentionality," save as that intentionality is derivative from some employment of that physical thing by a mind. Or so it is claimed. This is too quick; just postulating mysterious powers of mind solves nothing. But the problem is very real. How is intentionality, reference, possible?

1.   Magical Theories of Reference

We saw that the ant's "picture" has no necessary connection with Winston Churchill. The mere fact that the "picture" bears a "resemblance" to Churchill does not make it into a real picture, nor does it make it a representation of Churchill. Unless the ant is an intelligent ant (which it isn't) and knows about Churchill (which it doesn't), the curve it traced is not a picture or even a representation of anything. Some primitive people believe that some representations (in particular, *names*) have a necessary connection with their bearers; that to know the "true name" of someone or something gives one power over it. This power comes from the *magical connection* between the name and the bearer of the name; once one realizes that a name *only* has a contextual, contingent, conventional connection with its bearer, it is hard to see why knowledge of the name should have any mystical significance.

What is important to realize is that what goes for physical pictures also goes for mental images, and for mental representations in general; mental representations no more have a necessary connection with what they represent than physical representations do. The contrary supposition is a survival of magical thinking.

Perhaps the point is easiest to grasp in the case of mental *images*. (Perhaps the first philosopher to grasp the enormous significance of this point, even if he was not the first to actually make it, was Wittgenstein.) Suppose there is a planet somewhere on which human beings have evolved (or been deposited by alien spacemen, or what have you). Suppose these humans, although otherwise like us, have never seen *trees*. Suppose they have never imagined trees (perhaps vegetable life exists on their planet only in the form of molds). Suppose one day a picture of a tree is accidentally dropped on their planet by a spaceship which passes on without having other contact with them. Imagine them puzzling over the picture. What in the world is this? All sorts of speculations occur to them: a building, a canopy, even an animal of some kind. But suppose they never come close to the truth.

For *us* the picture is a representation of a tree. For these humans the picture only represents a strange object, nature and function unknown. Suppose one of them has a mental image which is exactly like one of my mental images of a tree as a result of having seen the picture. His mental image is not a *representation of a tree*. It is only a representation of the strange object (whatever it is) that the mysterious picture represents.

Still, someone might argue that the mental image is *in fact* a representation of a tree, if only because the picture which caused this mental image was itself a representation of a tree to begin with. There is a causal chain from actual trees to the mental image even if it is a very strange one.

But even this causal chain can be imagined absent. Suppose the "picture of the tree" that the spaceship dropped was not really a picture of a tree, but the accidental result of some spilled paints. Even if it looked exactly like a picture of a tree, it was, in truth, no more a picture of a tree than the ant's "caricature" of Churchill was a picture of Churchill. We can even imagine that the spaceship which dropped the "picture" came from a planet which knew nothing of trees. Then the humans would still have mental images qualitatively identical with my image of a tree, but they would not be images which represented a tree any more than anything else.

The same thing is true of *words*. A discourse on paper might seem to be a perfect description of trees, but if it was produced by monkeys randomly hitting keys on a typewriter for millions of years, then the words do not refer to anything. If there were a person who memorized those words and said them in his mind without understanding them, then they would not refer to anything when thought in the mind, either.

Imagine the person who is saying those words in his mind has been hypnotized. Suppose the words are in Japanese, and the person has been told that he understands Japanese. Suppose that as he thinks those words he has a "feeling of understanding." (Although if someone broke into his train of thought and asked him what the words he was thinking *meant*, he would discover he couldn't say.) Perhaps the illusion would be so perfect that the person could even fool a Japanese telepath! But if he couldn't use the words in the right contexts, answer questions about what he "thought," etc., then he didn't understand them.

By combining these science fiction stories I have been telling, we can contrive a case in which someone thinks words which are in fact a description of trees in some language *and* simultaneously has appropriate mental images, but *neither* understands the words *nor* knows what a tree is. We can even imagine that the mental images were caused by paint-spills (although the person has been hypnotized to think that they are images of something appropriate to his thought – only, if he were asked, he wouldn't be able to say of what). And we can imagine that the language the person is thinking in is one neither the hypnotist nor the person hypnotized has ever heard of – perhaps it is just coincidence that these "nonsense sentences," as the hypnotist supposes them to be, are a description of trees in Japanese. In short, everything passing before the person's mind might be qualitatively identical with what was passing through the mind of a Japanese speaker who was *really* thinking about trees – but none of it would refer to trees.

All of this is really impossible, of course, in the way that it is really impossible that monkeys should by chance type out a copy of *Hamlet*. That is to say that the probabilities against it are so high as to mean it will never really happen (we think). But it is not logically impossible, or even physically impossible. It *could* happen (compatibly with physical law and, perhaps, compatibly with

actual conditions in the universe, if there are lots of intelligent beings on other planets). And if it did happen, it would be a striking demonstration of an important conceptual truth; that even a large and complex system of representations, both verbal and visual, still does not have an *intrinsic* built-in, magical connection with what it represents – a connection independent of how it was caused and what the dispositions of the speaker or thinker are. And this is true whether the system of representations (words and images, in the case of the example) is physically realized – the words are written or spoken, and the pictures are physical pictures – or only realized in the mind. Thought words and mental pictures do not *intrinsically* represent what they are about.

2.   The Case of the Brains in a Vat

Here is a science fiction possibility discussed by philosophers: imagine that a human being (you can imagine this to be yourself) has been subjected to an operation by an evil scientist. The person's brain (your brain) has been removed from the body and placed in a vat of nutrients which keep the brain alive. The nerve endings have been connected to a super-scientific computer which causes the person whose brain it is to have the illusion that everything is perfectly normal. There seem to be people, objects, the sky, etc; but really all the person (you) is experiencing is the result of electronic impulses travelling from the computer to the nerve endings. The computer is so clever that if the person tries to raise his hand, the feedback from the computer will cause him to "see" and "feel" the hand being raised. Moreover, by varying the program, the evil scientist can cause the victim to "experience" (or hallucinate) any situation or environment the evil scientist wishes. He can also obliterate the memory of the brain operation, so that the victim will seem to himself to have always been in this environment. It can even seem to the victim that he is sitting and reading these very words about the amusing but quite absurd supposition that there is an evil scientist who removes people's brains from their bodies and places them in a vat of nutrients which keep the brains alive. The nerve endings are supposed to be connected to a super-scientific computer which causes the person whose brain it is to have the illusion that . . .

When this sort of possibility is mentioned in a lecture on the Theory of Knowledge, the purpose, of course, is to raise the classical problem of scepticism with respect to the external world in a modern way. (*How do you know you aren't in this predicament?*) But this predicament is also a useful device for raising issues about the mind/world relationship.

Instead of having just one brain in a vat, we could imagine that all human beings (perhaps all sentient beings) are brains in a vat (or nervous systems in a vat in case some beings with just a minimal nervous system already count as "sentient"). Of course, the evil scientist would have to be outside – or would he? Perhaps there is no evil scientist, perhaps (though this is absurd) the universe just happens to consist of automatic machinery tending a vat full of brains and nervous systems.

This time let us suppose that the automatic machinery is programmed to give us all a *collective* hallucination, rather than a number of separate unrelated hallucinations. Thus, when I seem to myself to be talking to you, you seem to yourself to be hearing my words. Of course, it is not the case that my words actually reach your ears – for you don't have (real) ears, nor do I have a real mouth and tongue. Rather, when I produce my words, what happens is that the efferent impulses travel from my brain to the computer, which both causes me to "hear" my own voice uttering those words and "feel" my tongue moving, etc., and causes you to "hear" my words, "see" me speaking, etc. In this case, we are, in a sense, actually in communication. I am not mistaken about your real existence (only about the existence of your body and the "external world," apart from brains). From a certain point of view, it doesn't even matter that "the whole world" is a collective hallucination; for you do, after all, really hear my words when I speak to you, even if the mechanism isn't what we suppose it to be. (Of course, if we were two lovers making love, rather than just two people carrying on a conversation, then the suggestion that it was just two brains in a vat might be disturbing.)

I want now to ask a question which will seem very silly and obvious (at least to some people, including some very sophisticated philosophers),

but which will take us to real philosophical depths rather quickly. Suppose this whole story were actually true. Could we, if we were brains in a vat in this way, *say* or *think* that we were?

I am going to argue that the answer is "No, we couldn't." In fact, I am going to argue that the supposition that we are actually brains in a vat, although it violates no physical law, and is perfectly consistent with everything we have experienced, cannot possibly be true. It *cannot possibly be true*, because it is, in a certain way, self-refuting.

The argument I am going to present is an unusual one, and it took me several years to convince myself that it is really right. But it is a correct argument. What makes it seem so strange is that it is connected with some of the very deepest issues in philosophy. (It first occurred to me when I was thinking about a theorem in modern logic the "Skolem–Löwenheim Theorem" and I suddenly saw a connection between this theorem and some arguments in Wittgenstein's *Philosophical Investigations*.)

A "self-refuting supposition" is one whose truth implies its own falsity. For example, consider the thesis *that all general statements are false*. This is a general statement. So if it is true, then it must be false. Hence, it is false. Sometimes a thesis is called "self-refuting" if it is *the supposition that the thesis is entertained or enunciated* that implies its falsity. For example, "I do not exist" is self-refuting if thought by *me* (for any "*me*"). So one can be certain that one oneself exists, if one thinks about it (as Descartes argued).

What I shall show is that the supposition that we are brains in a vat has just this property. If we can consider whether it is true or false, then it is not true (I shall show). Hence it is not true.

Before I give the argument, let us consider why it seems so strange that such an argument can be given (at least to philosophers who subscribe to a "copy" conception of truth). We conceded that it is compatible with physical law that there should be a world in which all sentient beings are brains in a vat. As philosophers say, there is a "possible world" in which all sentient beings are brains in a vat. (This "possible world" talk makes it sound as if there is a *place* where any absurd supposition is true, which is why it can be very misleading in philosophy.) The humans in that possible world have exactly the same experiences that *we* do. They think the same thoughts we do (at least, the same words, images, thought-forms, etc., go through their minds). Yet, I am claiming that there is an argument we can give that shows we are not brains in a vat. How can there be? And why couldn't the people in the possible world who really are brains in a vat give it too?

The answer is going to be (basically) this: although the people in that possible world can think and "say" any words we can think and say, they cannot (I claim) *refer* to what we can refer to. In particular, they cannot think or say that they are brains in a vat (*even by thinking "we are brains in a vat"*).

3. Turing's Test

Suppose someone succeeds in inventing a computer which can actually carry on an intelligent conversation with one (on as many subjects as an intelligent person might). How can one decide if the computer is "conscious"?

The British logician Alan Turing proposed the following test:[2] let someone carry on a conversation with the computer and a conversation with a person whom he does not know. If he cannot tell which is the computer and which is the human being, then (assume the test to be repeated a sufficient number of times with different interlocutors) the computer is conscious. In short, a computing machine is conscious if it can pass the "Turing Test." (The conversations are not to be carried on face to face, of course, since the interlocutor is not to know the visual appearance of either of his two conversational partners. Nor is voice to be used, since the mechanical voice might simply sound different from a human voice. Imagine, rather, that the conversations are all carried on via electric typewriter. The interlocutor types in his statements, questions, etc., and the two partners – the machine and the person – respond via the electric keyboard. Also, the machine may *lie* – asked "Are you a machine" it might reply, "No, I'm an assistant in the lab here.")

The idea that this test is really a definitive test of consciousness has been criticized by a number of authors (who are by no means hostile in principle to the idea that a machine might be conscious). But this is not our topic at this time. I wish to use the general idea of the Turing test, the general idea of a *dialogic test of competence*, for a different purpose, the purpose of exploring the notion of *reference*.

Imagine a situation in which the problem is not to determine if the partner is really a person or a machine, but is rather to determine if the partner uses the words to refer as we do. The obvious test is, again, to carry on a conversation, and, if no problems arise, if the partner "passes" in the sense of being indistinguishable from someone who is certified in advance to be speaking the same language, referring to the usual sorts of objects, etc., to conclude that the partner does refer to objects as we do. When the purpose of the Turing test is as just described, that is, to determine the existence of (shared) reference, I shall refer to the test as the *Turing Test for Reference*. And, just as philosophers have discussed the question whether the original Turing test is a *definitive* test for consciousness, i.e., the question of whether a machine which "passes" the test not just once but regularly is *necessarily* conscious, so, in the same way, I wish to discuss the question of whether the Turing Test for Reference just suggested is a definitive test for shared reference.

The answer will turn out to be "No." The Turing Test for Reference is not definitive. It is certainly an excellent test in practice; but it is not logically impossible (though it is certainly highly improbable) that someone could pass the Turing Test for Reference and not be referring to anything. It follows from this, as we shall see, that we can extend our observation that words (and whole texts and discourses) do not have a necessary connection to their referents. Even if we consider not words by themselves but rules deciding what words may appropriately be produced in certain contexts – even if we consider, in computer jargon, *programs for using words* – unless those programs themselves *refer to something extra-linguistic* there is still no determinate reference that those words possess. This will be a crucial step in the process of reaching the conclusion that the Brain-in-a-Vat Worlders cannot refer to anything external at all (and hence cannot say that they are Brain-in-a-Vat Worlders).

Suppose, for example, that I am in the Turing situation (playing the "Imitation Game," in

Turing's terminology) and my partner is actually a machine. Suppose this machine is able to win the game ("passes" the test). Imagine the machine to be programmed to produce beautiful responses in English to statements, questions, remarks, etc. in English, but that it has no sense organs (other than the hookup to my electric typewriter), and no motor organs (other than the electric typewriter). (As far as I can make out, Turing does not assume that the possession of either sense organs or motor organs is necessary for consciousness or intelligence.) Assume that not only does the machine lack electronic eyes and ears, etc., but that there are no provisions in the machine's program, the program for playing the Imitation Game, for incorporating inputs from such sense organs, or for controlling a body. What should we say about such a machine?

To me, it seems evident that we cannot and should not attribute reference to such a device. It is true that the machine can discourse beautifully about, say, the scenery in New England. But it could not recognize an apple tree or an apple, a mountain or a cow, a field or a steeple, if it were in front of one.

What we have is a device for producing sentences in response to sentences. But none of these sentences is at all connected to the real world. *If one coupled two of these machines and let them play the Imitation Game with each other, then they would go on "fooling" each other forever, even if the rest of the world disappeared!* There is no more reason to regard the machine's talk of apples as referring to real world apples than there is to regard the ant's "drawing" as referring to Winston Churchill.

What produces the illusion of reference, meaning, intelligence, etc., here is the fact that there is a convention of representation which *we* have under which the machine's discourse refers to apples, steeples, New England, etc. Similarly, there is the *illusion* that the ant has caricatured Churchill, for the same reason. But we are able to perceive, handle, deal with apples and fields. Our talk of apples and fields is intimately connected with our *non-verbal* transactions with apples and fields. There are "language entry rules" which take us from experiences of apples to such utterances as "I see an apple," and "language exit rules" which take us from decisions expressed in linguistic form ("I am going to buy some apples") to actions other than speaking. Lacking either language entry rules or language exit rules, there is no reason to regard the conversation of the machine (or of the two machines, in the case we envisaged of two machines playing the Imitation Game with each other) as more than syntactic play. Syntactic play that *resembles* intelligent discourse, to be sure; but only as (and no more than) the ant's curve resembles a biting caricature.

In the case of the ant, we could have argued that the ant would have drawn the same curve even if Winston Churchill had never existed. In the case of the machine, we cannot quite make the parallel argument; if apples, trees, steeples and fields had not existed, then, presumably, the programmers would not have produced that same program. Although the machine does *not perceive* apples, fields, or steeples, its creator–designers did. There is *some* causal connection between the machine and the real world apples, etc., via the perceptual experience and knowledge of the creator–designers. But such a weak connection can hardly suffice for reference. Not only is it logically possible, though fantastically improbable, that the same machine *could* have existed even if apples, fields, and steeples had not existed; more important, the machine is utterly insensitive to the *continued* existence of apples, fields, steeples, etc. Even if all these things *ceased* to exist, the machine would still discourse just as happily in the same way. That is why the machine cannot be regarded as referring at all.

The point that is relevant for our discussion is that there is nothing in Turing's Test to rule out a machine which is programmed to do nothing *but* play the Imitation Game, and that a machine which can do nothing *but* play the Imitation Game is *clearly* not referring any more than a record player is.

4. Brains in a Vat (Again)

Let us compare the hypothetical "brains in a vat" with the machines just described. There are obviously important differences. The brains in a vat do not have sense organs, but they do have *provision* for sense organs; that is, there are afferent nerve endings, there are inputs from these afferent nerve endings, and these inputs figure in the "program" of the brains in the vat just as they do in the program of our brains. The brains in a vat are *brains*; moreover, they are *functioning* brains, and they function by the same rules as brains do in the actual world. For these reasons, it would seem absurd to deny consciousness or intelligence to them. But the fact that they are conscious and intelligent does not mean that their words refer to what our words refer. The question we are interested in is this: do their verbalizations containing, say, the word "tree" actually refer to *trees*? More generally: can they refer to *external* objects at all? (As opposed to, for example, objects in the image produced by the automatic machinery.)

To fix our ideas, let us specify that the automatic machinery is supposed to have come into existence by some kind of cosmic chance or coincidence (or, perhaps, to have always existed). In this hypothetical world, the automatic machinery itself is supposed to have no intelligent creator–designers. In fact, as we said at the beginning of this chapter, we may imagine that all sentient beings (however minimal their sentience) are inside the vat.

This assumption does not help. For there is no connection between the *word* "tree" as used by these brains and actual trees. They would still use the word "tree" just as they do, think just the thoughts they do, have just the images they have, even if there were no actual trees. Their images, words, etc., are qualitatively identical with images, words, etc., which do represent trees in *our* world; but we have already seen (the ant again!) that qualitative similarity to something which represents an object (Winston Churchill or a tree) does not make a thing a representation all by itself. In short, the brains in a vat are not thinking about real trees when they think "there is a tree in front of me" because there is nothing by virtue of which their thought "tree" represents actual trees.

If this seems hasty, reflect on the following: we have seen that the words do not necessarily refer to trees even if they are arranged in a sequence which is identical with a discourse which (were it to occur in one of our minds) would unquestionably *be about trees* in the actual world. Nor does the "program," in the sense of the rules, practices, dispositions of the brains to verbal behavior, necessarily refer to trees or bring about

reference to trees through the connections it establishes between words and words, or *linguistic* cues and *linguistic* responses. If these brains think about, refer to, represent trees (real trees, outside the vat), then it must be because of the way the "program" connects the system of language to *nonverbal* input and outputs. There are indeed such non-verbal inputs and outputs in the Brain-in-a-Vat world (those efferent and afferent nerve endings again!), but we also saw that the "sense-data" produced by the automatic machinery do not represent trees (or anything external) even when they resemble our tree-images exactly. Just as a splash of paint might resemble a tree picture without *being* a tree picture, so, we saw, a "sense datum" might be qualitatively identical with an "image of a tree" without being an image of a tree. How can the fact that, in the case of the brains in a vat, the language is connected by the program with sensory inputs which do not intrinsically or extrinsically represent trees (or anything external) possibly bring it about that the whole system of representations, the language-in-use, *does* refer to or represent trees or anything external?

The answer is that it cannot. The whole system of sense-data, motor signals to the efferent endings, and verbally or conceptually mediated thought connected by "language entry rules" to the sense-data (or whatever) as inputs and by "language exit rules" to the motor signals as outputs, has no more connection to *trees* than the ant's curve has to Winston Churchill. Once we see that the *qualitative similarity* (amounting, if you like, to qualitative identity) between the thoughts of the brains in a vat and the thoughts of someone in the actual world by no means implies sameness of reference, it is not hard to see that there is no basis at all for regarding the brain in a vat as referring to external things.

5. The Premisses of the Argument

I have now given the argument promised to show that the brains in a vat cannot think or say that they are brains in a vat. It remains only to make it explicit and to examine its structure.

By what was just said, when the brain in a vat (in the world where every sentient being is and always was a brain in a vat) thinks "There is a tree in front of me," his thought does not refer to actual trees. On some theories it might refer to trees in the image, or to the electronic impulses that cause tree experiences, or to the features of the program that are responsible for those electronic impulses. These theories are not ruled out by what was just said, for there is a close causal connection between the use of the word "tree" in vat-English and the presence of trees in the image, the presence of electronic impulses of a certain kind, and the presence of certain features in the machine's program. On these theories the brain is *right*, not *wrong* in thinking "There is a tree in front of me." Given what "tree" refers to in vat-English and what "in front of" refers to, assuming one of these theories is correct, then the truth-conditions for "There is a tree in front of me" when it occurs in vat-English are simply that a tree in the image be "in front of" the "me" in question – in the image – or, perhaps, that the kind of electronic impulse that normally produces this experience be coming from the automatic machinery, or, perhaps, that the feature of the machinery that is supposed to produce the "tree in front of one" experience be operating. And these truth-conditions are certainly fulfilled.

By the same argument, "vat" refers to vats in the image in vat-English, or something related (electronic impulses or program features), but certainly not to real vats, since the use of "vat" in vat-English has no causal connection to real vats (apart from the connection that the brains in a vat wouldn't be able to use the word "vat," if it were not for the presence of one particular vat – the vat they are in; but this connection obtains between the use of *every* word in vat-English and that one particular vat; it is not a special connection between the use of the *particular* word "vat" and

vats). Similarly, "nutrient fluid" refers to a liquid in the image in vat-English, or something related (electronic impulses or program features). It follows that if their "possible world" is really the actual one, and we are really the brains in a vat, then what we now mean by "we are brains in a vat" is that *we are brains in a vat in the image* or something of that kind (if we mean anything at all). But part of the hypothesis that we are brains in a vat is that we aren't brains in a vat in the image (i.e., what we are "hallucinating" isn't that we are brains in a vat). So, if we are brains in a vat, then the sentence "We are brains in a vat" says something false (if it says anything). In short, if we are brains in a vat, then "We are brains in a vat" is false. So it is (necessarily) false.

Notes

1 In this essay the terms "representation" and "reference" always refer to a relation between a word (or other sort of sign, symbol, or representation) and something that actually exists (i.e., not just an "object of thought"). There is a sense of "refer" in which I can "refer" to what does not exist; this is not the sense in which "refer" is used here. An older word for what I call "representation" or "reference" is *denotation*.

Secondly, I follow the custom of modern logicians and use "exist" to mean "exist in the past, present, or future." Thus Winston Churchill "exists," and we can "refer to" or "represent" Winston Churchill, even though he is no longer alive.

2 A. M. Turing, "Computing Machinery and Intelligence," *Mind* (1950), reprinted in A. R. Anderson (ed.), *Minds and Machines* (Englewood Cliffs: Prentice-Hall, 1964).

The Structure of Skeptical Arguments and Its Metaepistemological Implications

Richard Fumerton

Kinds of Skepticism

My primary concern in this chapter is to sketch what I take to be the most interesting form of skeptical argument and to examine in a preliminary way the metaepistemological presuppositions, if any, of skeptical arguments. I also attempt to address here some important challenges to the skeptic's method that do not explicitly rely on metaepistemological positions.

I hasten to emphasize that my concern in setting forth what I take to be the most interesting form of skeptical argument is not primarily historical. I do think that one can find the kind of skeptical argument I discuss developed in some detail by the Modern philosophers, and that its paradigm expression can be found in the writings of David Hume, but I will not defend this claim. Much of my view about the structure of skeptical argument also parallels the excellent discussion of this issue in chapter 2 of Ayer's classic book *The Problem of Knowledge*. I also remind the reader that the kind of skepticism in which I am primarily interested involves claims not about knowledge but about the epistemic rationality of belief. I have already observed that the historical discussion of skepticism is couched mostly in terms of what one

can or cannot know. I am interested in what one can or cannot rationally believe.

Perhaps we should begin by making some familiar distinctions between kinds of skepticism. One distinction we have just marked – the distinction between skeptical claims about knowledge and skeptical claims about epistemically justified or rational belief. Let us refer to these two kinds of skepticism as *weak* and *strong* skepticism, respectively. As we noted earlier, the claim that one cannot *know* something (particularly if one adds the appropriate dramatic emphasis to "know") is relatively weak from the philosophical perspective in that one can easily concede this sort of skepticism with a kind of resigned respect for the fallibility of human consciousness. The claim that one cannot even rationally believe that something is true is much stronger, much more extreme. It seems to give the person who wants to continue believing what common sense requires nothing on which to fall back.

In addition to distinguishing strong and weak skepticism, we can also distinguish global and local skepticism. The global skeptic makes a claim about our epistemic access to *all* truth. Specifically, weak global skepticism maintains that one has no knowledge of anything. Strong global skepticism

Richard Fumerton, "The Structure of Skeptical Arguments and its Metaepistemological Implications," from *Metaepistemology and Skepticism* (Lanham, MD: Rowman & Littlefield, 1995), pp. 29–54. © 1995 by Rowman & Littlefield Publishers, Inc. Reprinted with permission from Rowman & Littlefield.

maintains that one has no epistemically rational beliefs about anything. Local skepticism is skepticism (weak or strong) with respect to a given class of propositions. Thus, we can be a skeptic with respect to propositions about the physical world, the past, other minds, the future, theoretical entities in physics, the existence of God, or any other subclass of propositions.

Skeptical claims can be made with or without modal operators. Thus the skeptic can claim only that we do not have knowledge or rational belief or that we *cannot* have knowledge or rational belief. When we examine more closely the kinds of arguments skeptics advance in support of their claims, we shall see that they typically support the stronger modal claims.

One must also distinguish first-level skepticism from second-level skepticism, or skepticism from what we might call metaskepticism.[1] Second-level skepticism involves skeptical claims about whether or not we have knowledge or rational belief. It is argued by some (even some externalists) that if certain versions of externalism are true, it may make first-level knowledge or rational beliefs *possible* only to invite skepticism about whether or not one ever has such knowledge or rational belief. Some might hope to concede the externalists' claims at the first level but allow for the legitimacy of traditional skeptical concerns at the next level. I attempt to show later on that from the philosophical perspective, nothing of any interest should change when one moves up a level and that the widespread feeling that something *does* change when one is operating from within an externalist framework has enormously significant implications.

So again, the kind of skepticism with which I am primarily concerned is strong skepticism. Historically, I think there have been very few *global* strong skeptics. It is, of course, the most paradoxical of skepticisms because it entails that one has no epistemic justification for believing it. Whether we should conclude that it is therefore of no philosophical interest is something that we discuss toward the end of this chapter when we examine various charges of self-refutation leveled against the skeptic. The vast majority of skeptics, I argue, have actually presupposed knowledge or justified belief with respect to some class of propositions. Skeptics in the empiricist tradition almost all seemed to presuppose unproblematic access to occurrent mental states. Indeed, the presupposition was so complete that one rarely even finds the Modern philosophers *raising* the question of whether or not one can know that one is in a certain subjective mental state. Furthermore, almost all skeptics seemed to presuppose knowledge of at least logical relations. They seemed to presuppose that one can recognize or "see" contradiction, at least some simple necessary truths, and at least some simple entailments.[2] As we shall see, the question of whether or not skeptics can "contain" their local skepticism is a matter of some controversy.

The Structure of Skeptical Arguments for Strong Local Skepticism

If one examines classic arguments for strong local skepticism, one can discover, I think, a recurring pattern. First the skeptic indicates the class of propositions under skeptical attack. Then the skeptic attempts to exhaustively characterize the most plausible candidate for something that could conceivably justify, or make rational, belief in this kind of proposition. Next the skeptic attempts to drive a logical wedge between the available justification and the proposition it is supposed to justify. The wedge is logical. The claim at this point is only that the justification available for that belief does not logically guarantee the truth of the proposition believed. It is conceivable that someone has precisely that sort of justification even though the belief in question is false. At this point, the Cartesian skeptic might end the argument with the weak skeptical conclusion that it is not possible to know *with certainty* the proposition believed. But this conclusion does not get one strong skepticism. The strong skeptic goes on to argue that the logical gap cannot be bridged using any legitimate nondeductive reasoning.

Let us try to illustrate the kind of skeptical argument discussed above with a few examples, and let us begin with familiar epistemological problems concerning our access to the external world. Our strong skeptic with respect to the physical world argues that it is not epistemically rational for us to believe any proposition asserting the existence of a physical object. To what evidence might we appeal in trying to justify our belief in the existence of some object? The best evidence we could possibly get (according to common sense) is the testimony of our senses. The presumption is that if I cannot rationally believe that there is a table in front of me now when I seem to see and feel a table, there is no proposition describing a physical object that it would be epistemically rational for me to believe. But does any number of truths about the phenomenological character of my subjective and fleeting sensations ever logically guarantee the truth of any proposition describing the physical world? The answer, the skeptic argues, is clearly no.

To support this answer the skeptic will often appeal to the famous *skeptical scenarios*. A skeptical scenario is simply a description of a perfectly intelligible hypothetical situation in which someone has the best possible justification for believing a proposition about the physical world, even though that proposition is false. In the case of beliefs about physical objects, the skeptical scenarios describe hypothetical situations in which one has the best possible evidence in the form of sensation that, for instance, the table exists, even though it does not. The great fascination of skeptical arguments no doubt is owed in large part to their exotic appeals to the possibilities of dreams, hallucinations, malevolent demons, brains in a vat, telepathic powers, and the like. No matter how vivid my visual and tactile sensations may seem to me right now, who could deny that it is at least conceivable that I have these qualitatively same sensations in a vivid dream or in a drug-induced hallucination? And if I am dreaming or hallucinating, it would be mere chance that the table I take to be there exists.

Mad neurophysiologists with futuristic knowledge of the workings of the brain provide particularly useful grist for the skeptic's mill. Many of the antiskeptics have an almost slavish devotion to the dictates of science, and science seems to tell us that it is brain events that are the immediate causes of (or, on some views, are identical to) sensations. By stimulating the relevant part of the brain in the appropriate way, it seems in principle possible to produce the very electrical discharge that will cause me to seem to see a table. If we "tickle" another region of the brain in just the right way, we can get a tactile "table" sensation. Indeed, if our neurophysiologist of the future has enough skill, sophisticated instruments, and

knowledge of the brain, there is no reason to suppose that the brain could not be played like a piano to produce the extraordinarily complex set of sensations associated with visiting the Grand Canyon. And if it can be done, it can be done surreptitiously without the knowledge (or memory, if the knowledge once existed) of the subject. The intelligibility of the hypotheses seems hardly in question. It is the stuff of some extremely good and utterly *intelligible* literature and cinema.[3] To be sure, the skeptic's appeals to such possibilities are not considered unproblematic in the context of a skeptical argument, and we shall examine some of the complaints shortly. Still, it seems to be almost obvious that one can distinguish sensations from truths about the physical world and that no conjunction of truths about sensations will ever entail a truth about the physical world.

But so what? Epistemically justified or rational belief does not require the inconceivability of error, and even weaker concepts of knowledge defined in terms of justified true belief seem to make knowledge perfectly compatible with the conceivability of error. It is here that Hume took the skeptical concern to its natural conclusion. If sensations can occur in the absence of the physical objects we take them to indicate, what reason do we have for supposing that it is even likely that when we have certain sensations, certain physical objects exist? Well, how do we establish one thing as evidence for the existence of another? Perhaps the most familiar pattern of inference we employ to answer such questions is inductive argument. We take dark clouds to be a good indication of an imminent storm because in the past we have *observed* a correlation between the presence of such clouds and subsequent storms. We take the sound of barking to be a reliable (if not infallible) indicator of the presence of a dog because in the past we have *observed* a correlation between the occurrence of such sounds and the presence of a dog.

If we use this model to understand our reasons for relying on sensation as an indicator of physical objects, then to avoid strong skepticism we would need to make plausible the claim that we have in some sense *observed* a constant or near constant correlation between the occurrence of certain sensations and the existence of certain objects. But this, of course, we cannot do. We cannot step outside sensation to compare the sensation with the physical object it is supposed to represent. To use an inductive argument for the conclusion that sensation is a reliable indicator of the presence of physical objects, we would need access to physical objects that is independent of sensation. Without such access we could never discover the necessary constant conjunction of sensation and object. But we have no access to the physical world except through our sensations. Assuming we have unproblematic access to the past, we can perhaps correlate sensations. We can discover all sorts of interesting connections between visual, kinesthetic, tactile, auditory, gustatory, and olfactory sensations. But we can never step outside our mental states in order to correlate a mental state with something other than a mental state. And in the absence of our ability to discover correlations between the mental and the physical, we will never be able to rationally believe that there is a connection between the two.

In developing the above skeptical argument, one does need to establish the intelligibility of sensations occurring in the absence of the physical objects we take them to represent. Notice, however, that one can take the argument seriously and remain neutral on many of the controversies concerning the metaphysical analysis of sensation. One can think that the visual sensations that occur in the absence of physical objects involve our being related to another kind of object, a sense datum, or one can think that visual sensation should be understood as a nonrelational property of the mind or self (the so-called appearing or adverbial theory of sensation). All that one needs to take the skeptical challenge seriously is some understanding of sensation that allows us to speak meaningfully of the occurrence of sensations in the absence of physical objects.

Although epistemological problems of perception have occupied center stage in the history of skeptical challenges, epistemological problems concerning our access to the past through memory almost certainly have a more fundamental logical place in the ordering of skeptical issues to be resolved. The problem has received far less attention from philosophers partly because it is much less obvious how to characterize the nature of the available justification. If we suppose for a moment that there is such a thing as a memory

"experience," an experience that can be veridical or nonveridical with respect to the past, the skeptical argument involving the past will closely parallel the argument for strong skepticism with respect to the physical world. *Ultimately*, in reaching conclusions about the past one must rely on what one seems to remember. But one scarcely needs an argument (particularly when one gets to be my age) that memory is fallible. One can have a *vivid* apparent recollection that one did something even if one did not. If an argument is needed, we can return to the apparent causal dependency of experience on brain events. If one can in principle produce nonveridical sensations by stimulating the brain, one can presumably find that region of the brain responsible for memory "experiences" and produce them at will. But if the occurrence of memory experiences is logically compatible with the events we seem to remember not having occurred, then what reason do we have for thinking that such memory experiences are reliable indicators of past events? It is tempting to rely again on inductive reasoning, but it would seem that such reasoning is once more unavailable. An inductive justification for the reliability of memory would proceed from a premise describing correlations between *past* memory experiences and the events we took them to correctly represent. But the skeptic wants to know what your reason is for supposing that in the past memory has typically been reliable. And, of course, the skeptic wants you to answer that question without begging the question, that is, without relying on memory. But if one cannot rely on the fact that one remembers having veridical memory experiences to justify one's belief that a memory experience is a reliable indicator of a past event, how could one ever get away from the present to gain access to the past?

Notice how much more fundamental the problem of memory is than other epistemological problems. Almost all candidates for resolving the problem of perception minimally presuppose that we have access at least to past sensations. Discussion of the notorious problem of induction again almost always presupposes that we have access to past correlations between properties in order to ask how one can justifiably project these past correlations into the future. In the context of worrying about how we can justify our belief in other minds relying only on observational knowledge of physical behavior, epistemologists typically "give" one knowledge of past correlations between one's own behavior and one's own mental states, that is to say, they presuppose that there is some solution to both the epistemological problems of perception and of memory. And philosophers of science who worry about the possibility of justifying belief in hypotheses that deal with micro-phenomena that are in principle unobservable (compared with the way in which ordinary macro-objects are presumed to be observable) typically assume the legitimacy of our conclusions concerning the macro-sized objects of the physical world, the past, and projectibility of observed correlations.

I suggested that the relative lack of concern with epistemological problems concerning memory might be due in part to the difficulty one has formulating the problem. As long as one supposes that there are such things as memory experiences, the skeptical argument goes relatively straightforwardly. But the existence of memory experience is far from uncontroversial. To be sure, philosophers do not agree much on how to understand visual, kinesthetic, tactile, gustatory, and olfactory sensations, or even the intelligibility of talk about the occurrence of sensations without physical objects. But that something new and in some sense *occurrent* comes into existence when I open my eyes, and ceases to exist when I close them, seems hardly problematic. It is far less obvious that when I remember putting my car keys on the desk something came into existence at a certain time, which can be meaningfully described as an occurrent mental state of seeming to remember having done something. As we shall see, the problematic nature of the presupposition that there are memory experiences can contribute to the attraction that externalist analyses of knowledge and justification have for so many philosophers.

Metaepistemological Presuppositions of the Skeptical Arguments

It seems to me that reflection on the above examples of skeptical reasoning strongly suggests that the skeptic relies implicitly on a principle that I call the principle of inferential justification:

To be justified in believing one proposition *P* on the basis of another proposition *E*, one must be (1) justified in believing *E* and (2) justified in believing that *E* makes probable *P*.

Arguments for strong local skepticism typically invoke clause 2 of the principle first and then often counter proposed attempts to satisfy clause 2 by relying on clause 1. Thus the argument for strong skepticism with respect to the physical world relies on clause 2 by insisting that a belief in physical objects *inferred* from what we know about the character of our sensations is rational only if we have some reason to suppose that there is a connection between the occurrence of certain sensations and the existence of certain objects. When one attempts to inductively infer the existence of such a connection from a premise describing past correlations between sensations and objects, the skeptic invokes clause 1 of the principle to challenge our justification for believing the premise of that inductive argument. The argument for strong skepticism with respect to the past also relies on clause 2 insisting that any justified conclusion about the past inferred from what we seem to remember must include justification for believing that memory experiences are a reliable indicator of past events. Again, when an inductive justification of such reliability is attempted, clause 1 of the principle is invoked to challenge our ability to rationally believe the premise of the inductive argument, a premise that will describe past events and again require an inference based on memory.

It is tempting to think that the question of whether or not one accepts the principle of inferential justification determines whether or not one is an internalist or an externalist in epistemology. It is certainly true, as we shall see, that paradigm externalists reject at least clause 2 of the principle. It is *not* true, however, that paradigm externalists reject clause 1. Nevertheless, the above skeptical arguments do not get off the ground unless it is presumed that a reasonable conclusion based on premises requires a reasonable belief in the proposition that the premises make probable the conclusion. And on one reading, externalists avoid traditional skeptical problems by refusing to accept clause 2 of the principle of inferential justification.

The issue is, however, complicated. First, it is not clear that the principle of inferential justification constitutes a metaepistemological principle. On the face of it, one could accept the principle as a very general normative principle of epistemology. Second, it is not clear that one should simply define the internalism/externalism controversy in terms of whether one does or does not accept both clauses of the principle of inferential justification. [. . .] [B]efore we leave this preliminary discussion of skeptical arguments, I want to emphasize and clarify certain features of the arguments. I also want to reply to a number of objections that are leveled against skepticism, objections that do not explicitly focus on the principle of inferential justification and any metaepistemological implications that acceptance of that principle might be thought to have. My goal is to leave the skeptic in as strong a position as possible when we consider the question of whether the externalist revolution in epistemology is the only effective way to circumvent the skeptical challenge.

Clarification of the Skeptical Arguments and Charges of Self-Refutation

Inference and inferential justification

If the skeptic does rely on the principle of *inferential* justification in presenting skeptical arguments with respect to our epistemic access to the physical world, the past, other minds, the future, and so on, he is obviously committed to the conclusion that the only justification available in all of these cases is inferential in character. This is a feature of the classical skeptical argument that has understandably come under considerable attack. In what sense do I actually *infer* the existence of the familiar objects around me now? Is it not even more strained to talk as if my belief about what I had for breakfast this morning involved some inference from propositions describing the phenomenological character of my present memory states? Many philosophers would even suggest that our beliefs about the conscious states of those around us are misleadingly described as involving inference.[4] When someone is writhing on the ground before me, I "see" the suffering directly. I hardly notice first a pattern of behavior,

think about correlations between behavior and pain, and then reach the conclusion that the person before me is in pain. Of course, if we are relying on phenomenological evidence in order to determine whether it is plausible to maintain that an inference has taken place, it is equally problematic to suppose even that beliefs about the future typically involve inference. When I drink the water I expect it to quench my thirst. This expectation is probably (although not necessarily) *caused* by past associations of drinking water and subsequent diminution of thirst, but I can confidently assert that I never recall having attempted to list the occasions on which drinking water quenched my thirst in order to generate the premises of an inductive argument. My memory is so bad, I would be hard pressed to come up with more than a dozen such occasions, hardly enough to get me the kind of impressive correlation one should have for a strong inductive argument.

Whether or not the justification available for a given belief involves inference will be a difficult question to answer and will inevitably involve complex philosophical controversies. In characterizing a kind of justification as inferential, we seem to be implicitly contrasting that justification with some other kind of justification – noninferential justification. Obviously one needs an analysis of the distinction [. . .]. For now, let us make some relatively innocuous comments about ways of thinking about the distinction that bear on the reader's rather natural concern that the skeptic is talking about inference where there appears to be no inference.

The first distinction one might make when facing this sort of objection to talk about inference is the familiar distinction in philosophy of science between the context of discovery and the context of justification. It is not obvious that in order for one's justification to be inferential one must actually go through some process of conscious inference. It is one thing to arrive at a conclusion. It is another to justify that conclusion. It is almost certainly the case, it seems to me, that we do *not* usually formulate, and perhaps *never* have formulated, premises describing the phenomenological character of sensation as part of an attempt to gather evidence in support of our beliefs about the world around us. Indeed, it is probably seriously misleading to talk about my *belief* that there is a table before me and a wall behind me now. Philosophers have a tendency to oversimplify the range of intentional states that the conscious human mind can exemplify, and our language may even be inadequate to capture the subtle differences between them. There does seem to me to be a difference between belief and what one might call expectation. I do not so much believe that the wall is behind me as I expect it to be there. The expectation may consist in nothing more than the disposition to believe the proposition were I to entertain it, and the disposition to be extremely surprised if I were to turn around and not have the familiar range of experiences associated with there being a wall there. In any event, these beliefs (occurrent or dispositional) and expectations are still the kinds of things that can be justified or unjustified and we can still raise questions about the justification *available* to support such beliefs.

But surely, one might object, this is a little too slick. The skeptics and their opponents are raising questions about whether our *actual* beliefs are *actually* rational or not. And if we accept the framework within which the skeptics are asking this question, it would seem that their opponents run the risk of getting caught in the presupposition that if we are actually justified in thinking that there is a table before us, we must have actually gone through some process of inference. The *availability* of a legitimate inference that we might have engaged in seems neither here nor there when it comes to the question of whether a belief *is* justified. This is perhaps a point well taken, and I argue later that a complete answer to it requires that we distinguish a number of different senses in which we can talk about a belief's being inferentially justified. In particular, it will be useful to distinguish an *ideal* sort of justification from derivative concepts of justification. For now, let us be content with these observations. First, nearly everyone who talks about inferential justification wants to allow that the beliefs that are involved in inferentially justifying another belief might be merely dispositional. Second, engaging in conscious consideration of some set of premises on the way to reaching a conclusion that is consciously thought of as following from those premises is not a necessary condition for the justification supporting that belief to be inferential.

The role of skeptical scenarios

Although it is perhaps obvious already from the earlier discussion of the form of classical skeptical arguments, I want to emphasize the limited role that the familiar skeptical scenarios play in generating the skeptical conclusion.[5] As I presented those skeptical arguments, appeal to the possibility of dreams, hallucinations, artificially stimulated brains, and the like is primarily designed to support the conclusion that one has no *direct*, unproblematic access to the truth of the propositions under skeptical attack, and one cannot *deduce* the propositions under skeptical attack from the available evidence. The skeptic I am interested in is *not* presenting the following superficially similar argument for skepticism concerning the external world: The hypothesis that there is no table before you now but you are dreaming (hallucinating, having your brain artificially stimulated by a neurophysiologist, being deceived by an evil demon) contradicts your commonsense belief, and you do not know or have reason to believe that this alternative hypothesis is false. Therefore, you do not know or have reason to believe that you are really seeing a table. This argument simply invites the kind of response that Peter Klein developed so plausibly in his excellent book *Certainty*. That disarmingly straightforward response is to announce that we do have epistemic reason to reject the skeptical scenarios, a reason that consists in our being justified in accepting commonsense conclusions about the physical world. One might just as well argue, after all, that since the skeptical hypotheses are incompatible with the dictates of common sense and the dictates of common sense are epistemically rational, then the skeptical hypotheses are irrational. We can deduce their falsehood from the commonsense premises rationally believed. There is nothing wrong with Klein's *strategy* for defeating this form of skeptical argument, provided that he can establish the crucial conclusion that our commonplace beliefs are epistemically rational.

Again, however, as I construe the skeptic's appeal to the intelligibility of skeptical hypotheses, they are designed only to show something about the nature of our justification for believing propositions about the physical world, the past, other minds, and so on, namely that such justification involves nondeductive inference. If this conclusion can be reached, then one forgets about skeptical scenarios and invokes straightforwardly the principle of inferential justification. Once we have agreed, for example, that the occurrence of our sensations is perfectly compatible with there being no physical world, the skeptic can invoke the principle of inferential justification in order to request some positive reason to suppose that there is at least a *probabilistic* connection between the occurrence of certain sensations and the existence of certain objects.

Notice that here there is no burden of proof. Many discussions of skeptical challenges begin with a frantic jockeying for position. The antiskeptic wants the skeptic to give some positive reason for supposing that there is no physical world, and in the absence of such argument proposes that we continue with the beliefs that we are in any event disposed to have. The skeptic, however, armed with the principle of inferential justification, can adopt what seems to me the correct philosophical attitude that the principle of inferential justification plays no favorites, recognizes no special burdens of proof. The astrologer and the astronomer, the gypsy fortune-teller and the economic forecaster, the druid examining entrails and the physicist looking at tracks in cloud chambers are all expected to have reason to believe that their respective evidence makes probable their conclusions if the conclusions are to be rational. And you are expected to have reason to think that your sensations make probable the existence of the objects you take them to indicate if you are to be justified in believing the dictates of common sense.

Before leaving this preliminary discussion of the role played by appeals to skeptical scenarios, I should add that there is at least one attempt to satisfy the second condition of the principle of inferential justification that can give rise to a second purpose served by appeals to the intelligibility of such hypotheses. Whereas earlier in this century philosophers tended to emphasize the prominence of enumerative induction as the most obvious candidate for legitimate nondeductive reasoning, contemporary philosophers who realize the limitations of inductive reasoning as a means of regaining commonsense beliefs about the world have often turned to so-called reasoning to the best explanation.[6] The physical world,

the past, other minds, lawful regularities, and theoretical entities are posited, the argument goes, as the best explanation for the order in which sensations come and go, the existence of memory experiences, the behavior of other bodies, observed regularity, and phenomena in the macroworld. In response to this gambit the skeptic will often request criteria for "best explanation" and turn again to skeptical scenarios to argue that there are always alternative explanations that compete with our "commonsense" hypotheses and that satisfy equally well the criteria of good explanation.[7] [. . .]

Epistemological commonsensism

I have suggested that the skeptic who invokes the principle of inferential justification wants a level playing field. In particular, the skeptic will not give the mere fact that you are inclined to believe a hypothesis any particular weight. There are, however, many philosophers who would argue that one must simply rule out skeptical conclusions from the start. The most common form of argument in analytic philosophy is the reductio. One objects to a philosophical position by pointing out that it has absurd consequences and is therefore absurd. But strong skepticism with respect to commonsense beliefs is itself patently absurd, the argument continues, and is a sufficient reason to reject any view, including a metaepistemological view, that leads to it. We might call the view that rules out skepticism from the start and evaluates metaepistemological views in part by the way in which they allow one to avoid skepticism, epistemological commonsensism. I return later to the suggestion that skeptical conclusions are absurd, but for now I want to make at least a preliminary comment on one sort of argument for it. The most obvious question the skeptic will ask is *why* we should assume at the outset that the beliefs we take to be justified are justified. The answer that we must start somewhere will no doubt not please a skeptic who is disinclined to start a careful reexamination of all of our beliefs with the presupposition that most of those we take to be justified are justified.

A somewhat more sophisticated answer involves appeal to science and evolution. We can assume, the argument goes, that most of our beliefs are justified because it is obviously evolutionarily advantageous to have justified beliefs and science tells us that what is evolutionarily advantageous has a high probability of occurring, other things being equal. Such an argument will not impress traditional skeptics, of course, because they will correctly point out that the pronouncements of science can be used to refute skepticism only if they are themselves justified. Their justification, however, presupposes solutions to the various problems the skeptic presents.

Whether or not science can refute traditional skepticism will, as we shall see, depend itself on the plausibility of certain metaepistemological views. But for now I also want to remind the reader that even if we give ourselves full access to the pronouncements of science, it is not clear that science does tell us that it is evolutionarily advantageous to have justified or rational beliefs. Many of the empirical conclusions of science seem to suggest that much of what we expect or take for granted is "programmed" into us through evolution. If children had to reason deductively and nondeductively to the various conclusions they take for granted, their chances of survival would no doubt be rather slim. There is no reason to believe that we are not simply programmed to respond to certain stimuli with certain intentional states, just as lower life forms appear to be programmed to respond to certain stimuli with appropriate behavior. Now *given* certain metaepistemological views that we will discuss later, the causal origin of these spontaneous unreflective beliefs might be sufficient to make them justified, but one might also conclude that nature has simply no need to satisfy the *philosopher's* desire for having fully justified belief. One might, in other words, argue that if what science tells us is true, one might well expect that nature has probably not constructed us to believe only that which we have good reason to believe. Commonsense science might well tell us that through evolution nature has decided that it would be better for us to have true beliefs than justified beliefs.[8]

Of course, if we could *know* this we would again have reason to believe that most of our beliefs are true. My only concern here is to point out that our scientific *beliefs* are perfectly compatible with the conclusion that those beliefs are quite unjustified, and may well even suggest that con-

clusion, given certain metaepistemological views about what is required for justification. It is probably just this thought that led Hume to observe, with respect to the question of whether or not man should believe in a physical world, "Nature has not left this to his choice, and doubtless esteem'd it an affair of too great importance to be trusted to our uncertain reasonings and speculations."[9]

Charges of self-refutation

Epistemological commonsensism maintains that skepticism runs afoul of methodological constraints on epistemological investigation. The charge of self-refutation is a much more specific criticism of skepticism and must be treated very carefully. Let us begin by distinguishing two ways in which an argument might be charged with self-refutation. The first charge of self-refutation consists in the claim that the conclusion of a skeptical argument is inconsistent with the premises that are used to reach that conclusion, or in the claim that the very intelligibility of the skeptical conclusion requires that it be rejected. Let us say that an argument with this feature is formally self-refuting. If the conclusion of an argument really is inconsistent with its premises, then of course the argument either is formally invalid or has necessarily false premises. In either case an argument that is formally self-refuting in this way is always unsound. A more interesting and probably more commmon criticism of skeptical arguments is that they are *epistemically* self-refuting. Let us say that a skeptical argument is epistemically self-refuting if the truth of its conclusion implies that one has no justification for accepting its premises. But if one has no justification for accepting its premises, then the very principle of inferential justification upon which the skeptic relies implies that one cannot be justified in believing the conclusion by inferring it from the premises.

Of the two ways in which one might assert that skepticism is self-refuting, the charge of formal self-refutation is going to be the hardest to make stick. The most common allegations of formal self-refutation today involve claims about language and intentionality. Largely under the influence of the later Wittgenstein, a number of philosophers have explicitly or implicitly adopted what one might call a *contrast* theory of meaning. Roughly, the idea seems to be that a predicate expression "*X*" only has meaning if there are things that are both correctly and incorrectly described as being *X*. Thus, on my reading of Wittgenstein's private language argument, the fundamental objection to a private language has nothing much to do with memory. The problem is that a private linguist is the sole arbiter of how similar something must be to a paradigm member of a class to count as similar enough to be described in the same way. But as the sole judge it will not be possible to make a mistake, and where there is no possibility of error there is no possibility of getting it right. It is only meaningful to talk about the correct application of a rule if it can be contrasted with an incorrect application of the rule. If one applies this principle to dreams, hallucinations, and more generally, nonveridical experience, it will make sense to speak of nonveridical experience only if we are contrasting such experience with something else.

The contrast theory of meaning as stated is far too crude to evaluate. Suffice it to say, for our purposes, any remotely plausible version of the view would have to stress the modal operators. It will make sense to talk about dreams only if it is *possible* to have an experience that is not part of a dream. It will make sense to say of something that it is not a unicorn only if it is *possible* for something to be a unicorn. But to entertain the possibility that one is always dreaming, always hallucinating, or always being deceived by the senses is not to entertain the hypothesis that veridical experience is in any way *impossible*.

In response, the antiskeptic pushing this argument might appeal to a still more controversial verificationist theory of meaning. Roughly, the idea is that for *X* to be meaningful, not only must it be possible for both something to be *X* and something not to be *X*, but we must have *criteria* for distinguishing the *X*s from the not-*X*s. But for the more vague expression "criteria," this principle is, of course, familiar as at least a relative of the logical positivists' old verifiability criterion of empirical meaningfulness. On the face of it, however, the verifiability criterion of meaning, even in its very weak forms, has little to recommend it. As others have pointed out, we can entertain perfectly meaningful hypotheses that we could not in principle verify or disconfirm. Consider, for example, the proposition that there are things of

which no one has ever or will have ever thought. What are our criteria for picking out the things about which we have never thought? Far from being meaningless, the hypothesis is entirely plausible. But if we can entertain and even believe such a hypothesis, why should we be unable to suppose that the causes of our sensations are radically different from any of which we have thought, and different in a way that would make *all* of our ordinary beliefs about the causes of sensations false?

Without focusing as much on language alone as a means of representation, Putnam also seriously questions the intelligibility of the skeptical conclusion given its premises. In the now-famous discussion of "Brains in a Vat,"[10] Putnam argues that if we were brains in a vat we couldn't assert that we are brains in a vat. It will not be possible to do justice to the argument here because it rests on a highly sophisticated, controversial, and incomplete theory of what is involved in one thing representing another. Given the attention the argument has received, however, I should at least indicate how I would respond.

Crudely, Putnam's idea is that for a mental state, a thought, to be a thought of *X*, *X* must causally interact with the state that represents it. Like most theories of representation, the principle would be qualified to allow for complex thoughts of nonexistent things that are "constructed" by the mind out of simpler thoughts. Hume, for example, thought that all simple ideas had their source in experience but allowed that one could form the idea of a unicorn without seeing one by "putting together" the idea of a horse and a horn. So, too, Putnam could allow that one might form the idea of things that do not exist by putting together the ideas of things with which one has had causal interaction. Within the framework of such a view, for my talk or thought of physical objects to mean what it does, my language and mental states must have interacted in the appropriate way with the physical world. Brains in a vat, by hypothesis, do not interact with the physical world in the way that would be relevant to allowing such brains to represent physical objects. But if brains in a vat cannot represent physical objects, then they cannot coherently frame the hypothesis (as we understand it) that they might be *brains* in a *vat*. By the same reasoning, they cannot coherently frame the hypothesis (as we understand it) that there might be no *physical world*. For these hypotheses to be genuinely meaningful, they would have to be false.

I have argued elsewhere that the theories of representation on which the argument rests are false, and for that reason, and because an excursion into the metaphysics of intentionality would take us too far afield, perhaps we should content ourselves with the observation that even if something like Putnam's conception of representation were correct, he would not get much ammunition for use against the skeptic. By now I think that almost everyone agrees that Putnam's original argument involved rhetorical "stretch." For obvious reasons, even if we assume as true everything Putnam claimed about representation, it would still be possible for *me* to be a brain in a vat now, for *me* to have always been a brain in a vat, for *all* humans to be brains in a vat now, and for *all* humans to always have been brains in a vat. The reason all of these hypotheses are intelligible on Putnam's view is that our ability to represent can "piggyback" on prior representation. The relevant causal chains that allow us to represent an *X* can be extraordinarily convoluted. And the skeptic can surely get what is needed (particularly given the limited role skeptical scenarios play on my construal of the skeptical argument) from the intelligibility of the above skeptical scenarios.

The other observation I would make is that the ability to construct complex ideas of things that do not exist out of simpler ideas representing existents leaves enormous room for the skeptic to argue that hypotheses about the physical world might all be intelligible while at the same time being false. Put briefly, why should we not suppose that the concept of a physical object just is one of those innumerably many concepts of something that does not exist? On one historically prominent conception of the physical world, physical objects are *thought* of as the causes of certain sensations that stand in certain isomorphic relations with the sense data they cause. If one can construct the thought of phlogiston only to find out that there is nothing corresponding to it, why can one not construct the thought of a physical world only to realize that one has no reason to believe that there is such a thing? The ideas of sensation and causation might be traced to actual phenomena. But a complex idea formed out of these might not. I am not arguing for such

an analysis of the concept of a physical object. I am only pointing out that in the absence of considerable argument to the contrary, there is every reason to suppose that if one can have ideas of nonexistent things, one can have the idea of a nonexistent physical world.

A more whimsical argument still for the incoherence of skeptical challenges to common beliefs is suggested by Davidson's much discussed remarks concerning interpretation. Davidson (1981) argues, perhaps not too implausibly, that in interpreting another's language I must (methodologically) assume that most of what that person asserts and believes is true. He then argues that even an *omniscient* being would need to employ such a principle of charity when interpreting ordinary claims about the world. But if an *omnisicent* being would need to believe that most of what we believe is true, then most of what we believe is true! The argument seems too good to be true and, of course, it is. Foley and I have pointed out that Davidson's argument actually needs a premise asserting the existence of an omniscient being to secure its conclusion.[11] To fully understand how so many people could have taken seriously the argument, we would need to examine more fully the presuppositions of the counterfactual conditional about the omniscient being. As this would take us too far afield, I simply refer the reader to our article on Davidson's "theism."

It was obviously going to be an uphill battle to make good the claim that there is something formally self-refuting in the skeptic's position. It would be more than a little odd to be able to reach the conclusion that a position with which people have been fascinated for thousands of years was in some deep sense literally unintelligible. The charge of epistemic self-refutation, however, is likely to be more significant. A skeptic who is in the business of undermining presuppositions about the rationality of our beliefs must be careful that the foundations on which the skepticism gets built are not undermined in the process. In what ways might an argument be epistemically self-refuting?

Consider again classical skeptical arguments for strong local skepticism concerning propositions describing the physical world. You will recall that a crucial step in the skeptical argument is to establish the possibility of sensations occurring without the physical objects we take those sensations to represent. In arguing that this is a genuine possibility, the skeptic appeals to the possibility of dreams, hallucinations, or surreptitious manipulation of that part of the brain directly responsible for producing sensations. But if the skeptic appeals to facts about the causal dependency of sensations on brain events, or facts about the hallucinogenic character of certain drugs, or previous occasions on which dream experiences seemed indistinguishable from the experiences of waking life, then surely the skeptic must be justified in believing these truths about the physical world in order to generate the conclusion that one cannot be justified in believing any proposition about the physical world. The skeptical conclusion, however, entails that the skeptic has no justification for believing these commonplace truisms about the causal conditions surrounding sensation.

Is there any way for the skeptic to avoid the charge of epistemic self-refutation? I think there is, and that it involves careful use of modal operators. To be sure, many of the classic skeptics (or philosophers seriously advancing for consideration skeptical arguments) appeared to appeal to facts about the physical world in advancing their argument. Thus, in his refutation of epistemological direct realism, Hume certainly did start talking about what happens to your visual sensation when you press against the side of your eye.[12] And Descartes does sometimes describe actual dreams he remembers having.[13] But given the purpose that appeal to these skeptical hypotheses is designed to serve, these philosophers need not have made any claims about what actually happens. One need only appeal to the *intelligibility* of vivid dreams, hallucinations, or the causal dependency of sensations on a physical world to establish that there is no logical connection between the occurrence of sensations and the existence of physical objects. Claims about possibilities are not in any obvious sense contingent, and would not fall within the scope of the propositions under attack by the skeptic advancing local skepticism with respect to the physical world. It must be conceded that the most convincing proof of a possibility is an actuality. Descartes's dream argument would hardly have fascinated us so much were we never to have vivid dreams. Indeed, Descartes probably would not have

thought of the argument in the first place (nor would he even have been understood) were people not convinced that dreams do occur. And if people did not believe the scientific data on the brain, one would not get very far appealing to the possibility of producing sensation by manipulating the brain. But a clever enough philosopher could have formulated these hypotheses as possibilities even without the empirical evidence that the possibilities are actual and could have reached the appropriate conclusions about whether or not our access to the physical world was direct. Since the appeal to possibilities presupposes no knowledge or rational belief about the physical world, a skeptical conclusion based in part on such appeals involves no epistemic self-refutation.

Earlier, I argued that the problem of skepticism with respect to the physical world is not the most fundamental of the local skeptical challenges. Without rational beliefs about the past, one could not even learn anything about connections between sensations that one might hope to use in justifying belief about the physical world. But strong skeptical conclusions about the rationality of belief in past events is much more likely to end up involving epistemic self-refutation. The problem is more severe, of course, the stricter one's conception of what the past is. In the most extreme view, "now" refers to an instant in time, and the epistemological problem of access to the past is the problem of how one can reasonably infer the occurrence of *any* past events from data that is available to consciousness *now*, this instant. Reasoning itself, including skeptical reasoning, takes place over time. The skeptic moves step by step to a skeptical conclusion. If the skeptic implicitly accepts the principle of inferential justification, then to be justified in reaching a skeptical conclusion each step in the reasoning process must itself be justified. But if one has no justification for believing anything about the past, if one is an epistemic prisoner of present consciousness, how could the skeptic be justified in believing the premises of the skeptical argument?

One attempt to get around the problem is to expand "now" to include what is sometimes called a specious present. Consciousness is capable of grasping directly and immediately an expanse of time and a sequence of events that are included in that limited time. If the specious present is "large" enough and the skeptic's reasoning is quick enough, one might try to avoid the charge of epistemic self-refutation this way. Needless to say, it would not be easy to decide on the duration of a specious present. Unless it grows to an implausible size, the skeptic must think a lot faster than I can to escape epistemic self-refutation in this way.

Curley (1978) has argued that a skeptic can avoid charges of epistemic self-refutation by holding the premises of the skeptical argument to much lower epistemic standards than those challenged by the conclusion. This escape certainly would be in principle available to the philosopher arguing only for weak skepticism with respect to the past. One could easily reconcile the conclusion that we cannot know with absolute certainty anything about the past with the claims that one has some reason to believe some propositions about the past, and that those somewhat rational beliefs are sufficient to entitle one to accept rationally the skeptical conclusion. But this reply is clearly unavailable to the philosopher arguing for strong skepticism.

Ultimately, it may be that the charge of epistemic self-refutation will stick in the case of the most extreme skepticism about the past. The reason again is straightforward. As we already have had occasion to note, all strong global skepticism is epistemically self-refuting. If one concludes that one has no epistemic reason for believing anything at all, then it follows that one has no epistemic reason for believing that one has no epistemic reason for believing anything at all. Further, one has no epistemic reason for believing anything upon which one bases one's conclusion that one has no epistemic reason for believing anything at all. That is precisely why so few skeptics have been strong global skeptics. In particular, skeptics have almost always presupposed a kind of unproblematic access to some foundational empirical data and to the legitimacy of the reasoning on which their skeptical conclusions depend. But an extreme, strong skepticism with respect to the past challenges the unproblematic access to reasoning and seems to run the danger of spilling over into areas not under skeptical attack.

If the skeptic has difficulty denying the charge of epistemic self-refutation to this very fundamental sort of strong local skepticism, perhaps the next best move is to absorb it in a way that leaves the force of the skeptical argument intact. Is one in a position, after all, to dismiss an argument on the grounds that it is epistemically self-refuting? Well, if strong skepticism with respect to the past is epistemically self-refuting, then by definition, the skeptic is not epistemically rational in believing at least some of the premises of the argument. But if the argument is a valid argument and if the anti-skeptic *believes* the premises of the argument, the anti-skeptic is hardly out of the woods.

When I was a child I owned a "magic" eight ball whose function was to predict the future. You asked the eight ball a question that could be answered "Yes" or "No," shook the ball, and a "Yes" or "No" floated to a transparent opening in the ball. Now suppose we lived in a culture in which people took the eight ball to be a reliable guide to the future. If you asked the eight ball "Will it rain tomorrow?" and the eight ball answered "Yes," then, according to the members of our culture, you would be epistemically justified in believing that it will rain. Let us also suppose that our culture contains a few annoying skeptics who do not see what possible grounds one could have for supposing that the eight ball's answers are reliable predictors of the future, and who advocate strong skepticism toward conclusions reached via eight-ball reasoning. Finally, let us suppose that one day a skeptic gets the bright idea of asking the eight ball whether or not conclusions reached via eight-ball reasoning are rational, and the eight ball answers "No." To the chagrin of the supporters of commonsense eight-ball reasoning, the results of the experiment are duplicated again and again. In what position are eight-ball reasoners left?

I suppose die-hard proponents of eight-ball reasoning can argue that our skeptic who concludes that it is irrational to believe the dictates of the eight ball, is certainly in no position to use the eight ball's "answers" to reach that conclusion. This seems right, of course. The skeptical argument that proceeds from observations about what the eight ball indicates and reaches a conclusion about the illegitimacy of eight-ball reasoning is epistemically self-refuting. But should the eight-ball reasoners be celebrating? Can they go on as before, trusting the predictions of the eight ball? If it is obvious that the skeptic's eight-ball argument is epistemically self-refuting, it seems equally obvious that the anti-skeptic cannot continue to embrace the unproblematic legitimacy of eight-ball reasoning. The skeptical argument has revealed an internal problem for the anti-skeptic despite the fact that the argument is epistemically self-refuting. In the same way, I would suggest, a skeptical argument with the conclusion that beliefs about the past are epistemically irrational is not something one can dismiss just because one concludes that even the skeptic would have to rely on some beliefs about the past in order to reach the skeptical conclusion. As long as the anti-skeptic shares belief in the premises that the skeptic acknowledges one has no epistemic reason to accept, and as long as the anti-skeptic has no reason to reject the legitimacy of the skeptic's reasoning, the anti-skeptic cannot simply dismiss the import of the argument on the grounds that it is epistemically self-refuting.

It is perhaps worth emphasizing again that as I presented them, most skeptical arguments for strong local skepticism are not epistemically self-refuting. The premises that the skeptic would need to believe rationally in order to infer the skeptical conclusion fall outside the class of propositions under skeptical attack. A fundamental and extreme sort of local skepticism concerning belief about the past may encounter difficulties with epistemic self-refutation, but the argument will still be a thorn in the side of the anti-skeptic until the anti-skeptic can figure out which of the skeptic's premises should be abandoned.

In the preceding discussion we distinguished charges of formal and epistemic self-refutation that might be leveled against the skeptic's arguments. In addition to these relatively precise criticisms of skepticism there is a somewhat more nebulous charge that is related to criticisms associated both with epistemic commonsensism and charges of self-refutation. That criticism attempts to denigrate the importance of the skeptical challenge by observing that it is in some way impossible to take skepticism seriously. In fact, most philosophers have never treated skepticism as a viable option. Even those who are interested in the skeptical challenge are primarily interested in finding the correct way of refuting what is assumed to be an illegitimate conclusion. Everything the skeptic *does* belies the seriousness of the skeptical position. The famous philosophical skeptics, after all, have gone to great lengths to publish their skeptical treatises and in doing so have made clear that they assume that there are other minds (and so

implicitly other bodies). Skeptics who managed to survive made the same inductive inferences rejected as illegitimate in their skeptical "mode." They also argued with their fellow philosophers, past and present, and in doing so placed complete faith in the existence of a past revealed to them through memory. The very activity of philosophy, Butchvarov argues, is one that presupposes the existence of an external world, a past, and other minds, and the philosophers who realize this can take philosophy seriously only if they reject strong skepticism.[14] Reaching a skeptical conclusion is incompatible with taking oneself and one's work seriously. Philosophical skepticism is not then a serious philosophical position.

The charge invoked here is *not* the charge of formal epistemic self-refutation. The claim is not that the skeptic's conclusion entails that the skeptic has no reason to believe the conclusion. The alleged self-refutation is more subtle. It amounts to the claim that in embracing a skeptical conclusion as a serious philosophical position the skeptic is implicitly engaging in behavior that makes sense only against the backdrop of a set of beliefs that are incompatible with radical skepticism.

The first step in a skeptical response to this sort of criticism involves the obvious distinction between believing something and rationally believing something. Of course, there are no skeptics who withhold belief with respect to the questions of whether there is a past, a physical world (in some sense of "physical"), other minds, and regularities that can be safely projected into the future. But it is by no means obvious that to believe *P* one must believe that it is epistemically rational to believe *P*. I know all sorts of very religious people who seem to quite happily concede that their theism is epistemically irrational. Earlier, when discussing the question of whether the concept of justified belief is a normative concept, we very briefly raised the question of the extent to which belief is something we *control*. I sidestepped the issue of whether it was in principle possible to produce belief through an act of will, but it is difficult to deny that as a matter of empirical fact we simply find ourselves believing all sorts of things. It is not until our first philosophy class that many of us even raise the question of whether the things we take for granted are epistemically rational for us to accept. Indeed, it seems to me that philosophers too often forget that the questions raised by the skeptic *are philosophical* questions. They are questions raised by people who have a certain kind of philosophical curiosity that arises naturally from a very unnatural kind of activity. I argued earlier that there may well be different concepts of epistemic rationality and that some of these concepts might have particular relevance to *philosophy*. It may be that the philosopher is interested in and *wants* a kind of justification that ordinary people do not even think about in their day-to-day lives. The philosophical skeptic may best be construed as telling the philosopher that this kind of justification is unavailable. In every other walk of life people must get used to the idea that they cannot have everything they want, and the skeptic might maintain that it is a kind of perverted optimism to suppose that the *kind* of justification that would satisfy the *kind* of curiosity that afflicts the epistemologist is there to be found. This is a theme to which I return in the final chapter.

Notes

1 Klein (1981) calls this *iterative* skepticism.
2 Of course, when the necessary truths and falsehoods and the logical entailments get complex, the story may be different. In particular, if time is required to "see" the truth or entailment, then memory may be involved in the discovery of such truth or entailment. If memory is required to discover complex necessary truth or entailment, then any skepticism with respect to memory will infect all knowledge that explicitly or implicitly relies on it.
3 Although not neurophysiologists, the Martians in Bradbury's *The Martian Chronicles* caused the initial visitors from Earth no end of trouble through their telepathic ability to induce hallucinatory experiences. At the risk of exposing the shallowness of my aesthetic sensibilities, I would also mention the film *Total Recall*, whose plot centers on the question of whether the protagonist is really on a trip to Mars or is enjoying the experiences of an artificially induced fantasy.
4 Sartre (1966, part 4) would certainly reject the claim that our beliefs about others always involve inference if this is intended to be a phenomenological description of how our minds work. On the other hand, with philosophers in this tradition it is notoriously difficult to get an unambiguous statement of their views about the

epistemological significance of their phenomenological observations.
5 In contrast, for example, to the more pivotal role they play in, say, Stroud 1984.
6 Indeed, some – Gilbert Harman, for example – have argued that inductive reasoning is itself a species of reasoning to the best explanation. See Harman 1965, 1970.
7 For a detailed discussion of this move by the skeptic, see Alston 1993, chapt. 4.
8 Plantinga (1993b, chap. 12) appears to argue that it is difficult to see how natural selection would favor even true beliefs. The right false belief coupled with the right odd desires will do wonders for increasing the probability of my survival.
9 Hume 1888, p. 187.
10 Putnam 1981, chap. 1. [See also this vol., chapter 6.]
11 Fumerton and Foley 1985.
12 See Hume 1888, p. 210.
13 In his famous opening remarks in Meditation I.
14 See Butchvarov 1992.

References

Alston, W. (1993) *The Reliability of Sense Perception.* Ithaca: Cornell University Press.

Ayer, A. J. (1956) *The Problem of Knowledge.* Harmondsworth: Penguin.

Butchvarov, P. (1992) "Wittgenstein and Skepticism with Regard to the Senses," in S. Techrarian and A. Serafini, *Wittgenstein and Contemporary Philosophy.* Wakefield, NH: Lonwood Academic.

Curley, E. M. *Descartes Against the Skeptics.* Cambridge, MA: Harvard University Press.

Davidson, D. (1981) "A Coherence Theory of Truth and Knowledge," in Dieter Heibrich, ed., *Kant, Oder Hegel?* Stuttgart: Klett-Cotta Buchaudlang.

Fumerton, R. and Foley, R. (1985) "Davidson's Theism." *Philosophical Studies* 48: 83–9.

Harman, G. (1965) "The Inference to the Best Explanation." *Philosophical Review* 74: 88–95.

Harman, G. (1970) "Induction," in Marshall Swain, ed., *Induction, Acceptance and Rational Belief.* Dordrecht: Reidel.

Hume, D. (1888) *A Treatise of Human Nature,* ed. L. A. Selby-Bigge. Oxford: Oxford University Press.

Klein, P. *Certainty.* Minneapolis: University of Minnesota Press.

Plantinga, A. (1993) *Warrant and Proper Function.* Oxford: Oxford University Press.

Putnam, H. (1981) *Reason, Truth, and History.* Cambridge: Cambridge University Press.

Sartre, J.-P. (1996) *Being and Nothingness.* New York: Simon and Schuster.

Stroud, B. (1984) *The Significance of Philosophical Skepticism.* Oxford: Clarendon Press.

8

The Experience Machine

Robert Nozick

There are also substantial puzzles when we ask what matters other than how *people's* experiences feel "from the inside." Suppose there were an experience machine that would give you any experience you desired. Superduper neuropsychologists could stimulate your brain so that you would think and feel you were writing a great novel, or making a friend, or reading an interesting book. All the time you would be floating in a tank, with electrodes attached to your brain. Should you plug into this machine for life, preprogramming your life's experiences? If you are worried about missing out on desirable experiences, we can suppose that business enterprises have researched thoroughly the lives of many others. You can pick and choose from their large library or smorgasbord of such experiences, selecting your life's experiences for, say, the next two years. After two years have passed, you will have ten minutes or ten hours out of the tank, to select the experiences of your *next* two years. Of course, while in the tank you won't know that you're there; you'll think it's all actually happening. Others can also plug in to have the experiences they want, so there's no need to stay unplugged to serve them. (Ignore problems such as who will service the machines if everyone plugs in.) Would you plug in? *What else can matter to us, other than how our lives feel from the inside?* Nor should you refrain because of the

few moments of distress between the moment you've decided and the moment you're plugged. What's a few moments of distress compared to a lifetime of bliss (if that's what you choose), and why feel any distress at all if your decision *is* the best one?

What does matter to us in addition to our experiences? First, we want to *do* certain things, and not just have the experience of doing them. In the case of certain experiences, it is only because first we want to do the actions that we want the experiences of doing them or thinking we've done them. (But *why* do we want to do the activities rather than merely to experience them?) A second reason for not plugging in is that we want to *be* a certain way, to be a certain sort of person. Someone floating in a tank is an indeterminate blob. There is no answer to the question of what a person is like who has long been in the tank. Is he courageous, kind, intelligent, witty, loving? It's not merely that it's difficult to tell; there's no way he is. Plugging into the machine is a kind of suicide. It will seem to some, trapped by a picture, that nothing about what we are like can matter except as it gets reflected in our experiences. But should it be surprising that what *we are* is important to us? Why should we be concerned only with how our time is filled, but not with what we are?

Robert Nozick, "The Experience Machine," from *Anarchy, State and Utopia* (Oxford: Blackwell Publishing, 1980), pp. 42–5.

Thirdly, plugging into an experience machine limits us to a man-made reality, to a world no deeper or more important than that which people can construct. There is no *actual* contact with any deeper reality, though the experience of it can be simulated. Many persons desire to leave themselves open to such contact and to a plumbing of deeper significance.[1] This clarifies the intensity of the conflict over psychoactive drugs, which some view as mere local experience machines, and others view as avenues to a deeper reality; what some view as equivalent to surrender to the experience machine, others view as following one of the reasons *not* to surrender!

We learn that something matters to us in addition to experience by imagining an experience machine and then realizing that we would not use it. We can continue to imagine a sequence of machines each designed to fill lacks suggested for the earlier machines. For example, since the experience machine doesn't meet our desire to *be* a certain way, imagine a transformation machine which transforms us into whatever sort of person we'd like to be (compatible with our staying us). Surely one would not use the transformation machine to become as one would wish, and thereupon plug into the experience machine![2] So something matters in addition to one's experiences *and* what one is like. Nor is the reason merely that one's experiences are unconnected with what one is like. For the experience machine might be limited to provide only experiences possible to the sort of person plugged in. Is it that we want to make a difference in the world? Consider then the result machine, which produces in the world any result you would produce and injects your vector input into any joint activity. We shall not pursue here the fascinating details of these or other machines. What is most disturbing about them is their living of our lives for us. Is it misguided to search for *particular* additional functions beyond the competence of machines to do for us? Perhaps what we desire is to live (an active

web) ourselves, in contact with reality. (And this, machines cannot do *for* us.) Without elaborating on the implications of this, which I believe connect surprisingly with issues about free will and causal accounts of knowledge, we need merely note the intricacy of the question of what matters *for people* other than their experiences. Until one finds a satisfactory answer, and determines that this answer does not *also* apply to animals, one cannot reasonably claim that only the felt experiences of animals limit what we may do to them.

Notes

1 Traditional religious views differ on the *point* of contact with a transcendent reality. Some say that contact yields eternal bliss or Nirvana, but they have not distinguished this sufficiently from merely a *very* long run on the experience machine. Others think it is intrinsically desirable to do the will of a higher being which created us all, though presumably no one would think this if we discovered we had been created as an object of amusement by some superpowerful child from another galaxy or dimension. Still others imagine an eventual merging with a higher reality, leaving unclear its desirability, or where that merging leaves *us*.

2 Some wouldn't use the transformation machine at all; it seems like *cheating*. But the one-time use of the transformation machine would not remove all challenges; there would still be obstacles for the new us to overcome, a new plateau from which to strive even higher. And is this plateau any the less earned or deserved than that provided by genetic endowment and early childhood environment? But if the transformation machine could be used indefinitely often, so that we could accomplish anything by pushing a button to transform ourselves into someone who could do it easily, there would remain no limits we *need* to strain against or try to transcend. Would there be anything left *to do*? Do some theological views place God outside of time because an omniscient omnipotent being couldn't fill up his days?

Questions for Discussion

In thinking about the following questions try to connect your answers to the issues raised in the assigned readings.

1 Could Descartes just have easily appealed to the kind of possibilities exploited in *The Matrix*, *The Menagerie*, or *Total Recall* in order to cast doubt on the truth of beliefs about the external world? Are there advantages that the "Evil Demon" hypothesis has over the dream argument, the "*Matrix* possibility," or the "Menagerie"? In thinking about this question, you might keep in mind that many philosophers have argued that skeptical arguments are self-refuting. There are different ways in which an argument can be self-refuting. The most straightforward form of self-refutation involves an argument whose premises cannot be true if the conclusion is true. Another form of self-refutation, we might call it epistemic self-refutation, involves arguments whose premises cannot be known or justifiably believed if the conclusion is true.

2 In the last paragraph from the *Sixth Meditation*, Descartes claims that he can distinguish between his waking life and his dream life. How does he think that this distinction is possible? Imagine you are writing the script for a film that is meant to disprove Descartes's argument regarding this matter; how would you present evidence that he is mistaken in that he can so easily distinguish between the two sorts of experiences?

3 When the hero in *The Matrix* is supposed to become aware of his "real" situation (chapters 8–12), does he actually have any more reason to believe that this is reality than that his previous environment was "real?" Evaluate Descartes's proposed criterion (from the *Sixth Meditation*) for distinguishing between dreams and reality.

4 In all the films we have looked at in this section, the characters seem to have some sort of *control* over the sequence of experiences they have (even when they are supposed to be the victims of some sort of illusion or deception). Is this compatible with the idea that their experiences are caused in the way described?

5 At the end of *Total Recall*, the hero wonders whether the experiences portrayed in the film might be all hallucinatory (chapter 26). Was there a clue in the film clips shown that suggests an answer to that question (from the third-person perspective)?

6 In *Total Recall*, there is a scene (chapter 23) in which the hero is confronted by a character who claims to be part of a *Recall*-induced hallucination and who claims that he was inserted into the program in an effort to "shock" the hero out of a computer-generated program in which he is "trapped." The hero purports to have discovered that the person is real and that the claims about hallucination are false. What was the evidence appealed to and was it good evidence?

7   Were there any other clues to which the hero could have appealed in *Total Recall* in order to discover whether his experiences were veridical or not? Would the solution Descartes proposes in the *Sixth Meditation* to skeptical doubts be available to the hero?

8   Do any of the plots of the films we have seen undermine Descartes's answer to the skeptic as presented in his *Sixth Meditation*?

9   Is there some way of making sense of the early scene in *The Matrix* (chapters 6–7) in which the hero is "bugged" (while still in his hallucinatory state) to help the villains discover the whereabouts of the rebel movement? (Why would a "hallucinatory" bug help anyone trace anything?)

10 What are we supposed to believe about the progress the hero makes in *The Matrix* concerning his ability to deal with the hallucinatory reality he can be programmed to enter? What precisely is the skill he has learned?

11 Can we make sense of people entering a hallucinatory reality in which they *interact* with other hallucinators?

12 Would the hallucination-induced world that the disfigured Captain Pike enters at the end of *The Menagerie* be a world in which he could enjoy life the same way he could in a "normal" reality in which he was not physically disabled? Was the "traitor" Cypher in *The Matrix*, who opts for a life of hallucinatory bliss over a life outside the matrix (chapter 19), rational? Discuss in connection with Nozick's argument from "The Experience Machine."

13 Are there any relevant differences between the victims of hallucinatory experience in *The Matrix* and the brains in a vat discussed by Putnam? What would, or should, *Putnam* say in answering this question? Can the victims of Matrix-induced hallucination still have thoughts that are about an external world?

14 Does the plot of *The Matrix* present difficulties for Ayer's claim that a "phenomenalist standpoint" can allow us to understand talk of an external world in terms of sense data? Explain why or why not. Suppose Neo is a thoroughgoing phenomenalist of Ayer's variety; when he leaves the Matrix-world, what would he say of his past experience?

Part III
Philosophy of Mind

Films:
What Dreams May Come
Bicentennial Man
Heaven Can Wait
The Sixth Day
The Prestige
Multiplicity
Star Trek TV episode: *Turn About Intruder*

Introduction

When Gregor Samsa woke up one morning from unsettling dreams, he found himself changed in his bed into a monstrous vermin. He was lying on his back as hard as armor plate, and when he lifted his head a little, he saw his vaulted brown belly, sectioned by arch-shaped ribs, to whose dome the cover, about to slide off completely, could barely cling. His many legs, pitifully thin compared with the size of the rest of him, were waving helplessly before his eyes.

"What's happened to me?" he thought.

Thus begins Franz Kafka's famous novel *The Metamorphosis*. And thus also begins one of the most intriguing of philosophical questions: could a person such as Gregor Samsa get a new body? Kafka's opening paragraph certainly seems intelligible: our initial reaction, even if mixed with surprise, is likely to be: "How awful to have the grotesque body of some giant beetle!" We understand poor Gregor's lament as he wonders what has happened to *him*, i.e. to the very same person who went to bed the night before in a man's body.

Of course, none of us actually worries about finding ourselves having come to inhabit the body of a giant insect. But, as always in philosophy, we are not primarily concerned with whether body transfers do or even ever will happen. Rather, we are concerned to answer the question as to whether a person's getting a new body is a *conceptual* possibility. In order to answer this question, we need to ask whether there is a *necessary* connection between the existence of a particular person and the existence of a particular body. How are we as persons, or minds, related to our bodies? What is a mind? Is it a physical substance, some sort of mental substance, both, or neither? If we or our minds are distinct from our bodies, how do we interact with our bodies and with the physical world more generally?

As with the question of our previous unit about the relation between the evidence of our senses and our knowledge of the external world, here also we do well to begin with Descartes's *Meditations*. After presenting his hypothesis of an evil demon, Descartes, at the end of the *First Meditation*, leaves us in a state of extreme and all-encompassing doubt. What, if anything, can we know? In response, in his *Second Meditation*, reproduced here, Descartes offers us what has become perhaps the most famous of all philosophical arguments (suggesting, perhaps, that widespread acclaim and fame depend upon having very few premises), his so-called *Cogito*: "I think, therefore I am." Even if *I* am being deceived by an evil demon, there must be an *I* who is being deceived – my very doubt shows that I cannot reasonably doubt my own existence. But *I* can still doubt whether *I* have a body or whether my body is simply an illusion that I am dreaming or which has been cooked up by a demon. Conclusion? *I* must be something distinct from my body. Thus Descartes arrives at the classic statement of mind–body dualism: the mind is something wholly distinct from the body. The body is a physical substance, the mind a mental substance that occupies neither time nor space. Nonetheless, as Descartes vividly explains in the *Sixth Meditation*, the mind and the body interact in an intimate way: the mind is not to the body simply as a captain is to her ship. But how this purely mental substance that is not in space is supposed to causally interact with the spatially located physical body is certainly much less clear than how a captain guides her ship across the ocean.[1]

John Locke presents a thought experiment that, while initially seeming to reinforce the Cartesian conception of the self, does in fact, when considered further, serve to undermine that conception. Locke's thought experiment is not only one of the neatest and most compelling in the history of philosophy; it is also vividly illustrated by numerous popular films. We are to imagine that, one night, in their respective homes, a poor cobbler and a prince each fall asleep in their beds. When morning comes, however, we have a distinctly Kafkaesque scenario: the person in the cobbler's bed, who has the body of the cobbler, has all the memories and character traits of the prince. Similarly, the person in the prince's bed with the prince's body has all of the memories and character traits of the poor cobbler. So, for example, we can imagine that the cobbler-body person is now privy to state secrets that only the prince knows, while the prince-body person suddenly knows how to repair the heels on his shoes. Surely, Locke argues, the natural description of this case is that the prince wakes up in the cobbler's body and vice versa. But if two people could switch bodies, then persons must be, as Descartes argued, something distinct from their bodies.

Locke has no quarrel with that last claim, but he does think that Descartes is wrong to postulate that the survival of a person is to be equated with the survival of some purely mental substance that has memories, experiences, beliefs, doubts, hopes, imaginings, etc. Instead, Locke thinks that the survival of a person is a function of the continuation of a mental life *composed* of those memories. To show this, he asks you to imagine that you come to know that you, in fact, have the very same soul or mental substance (sometimes referred to, for obvious reasons, as a Cartesian ego) as Socrates.

But you have no memories of Socrates' life (nor do you have any other psychological similarity to Socrates). Is it plausible to suppose that you are, in fact, identical with Socrates? Similarly, suppose that the person in your body has all the memories and wisdom of Socrates, but does not have his soul – aren't you, nonetheless, identical with Socrates? Given that Descartes's mental substance is distinct not only from any physical body but also from any particular memories, etc., one and the same mental substance could underlie completely discontinuous mental lives. Locke concludes that it is the continuity of the mental life, in particular of memory, that constitutes the identity and persistence of a person through time, not the identity of some underlying mental substratum.

The possibility of body transfer is, as we have said, a popular film device. The ease with which we are able to follow such plots suggests that most of us hold, at least implicitly, either a Lockean or a Cartesian conception of our identities, both at a time and over time. For example, in a well-known episode of *Star Trek*, Captain Kirk finds himself in a woman's body, while the woman finds herself in Kirk's body. Such a body transfer could be understood as a case in which Kirk's ego, carrying all of his memories, etc., moves itself into the woman's body, and vice versa. But because the viewer can track only the bodies and the mental lives of the two persons involved, we cannot use this case to decide between the Cartesian and the Lockean conceptions of the person: did the souls stay put, providing the substratum for new mental lives, or did they act as the vehicles for the body transfer, carrying the mental lives to their new physical homes? Because this case is one of a male to female (and vice versa) body transfer, it also raises questions about whether a person's sex is essential to her identity. Is it harder to imagine ourselves getting the body of a member of the opposite sex than that of someone of the same sex? Similarly, is it harder to imagine getting a body very different from our own, such as that of a "monstrous vermin"?

This question seems to be answered in favor of the Cartesian in the film *Heaven Can Wait*. The end of the film suggests that the protagonist lives on in a new body, even though the person in that body has none of our protagonist's memories, etc. Worse still (for the Lockean), the person who is supposed to have survived in another body has all the apparent memories of the original "owner" of the body. Nevertheless, the movie suggests that there is a kind of "glint" in his eye (discernible to the girl "he" loved), indicating some underlying source of identity: some sort of soul or ego that is there in the new body, even though it has apparently had its former mental life washed off, as chalk is erased from a blackboard.

In the past 30 years, a new interest in the relationship between the self and its body has developed. The currency of these popular images of Cartesianism and/or Lockeanism has been mirrored in new and ingenious versions of Locke's classic thought experiments. Bernard Williams opens his now classic piece "The Self and the Future" with what seems like a standard Lockean body-transfer case. But then Williams turns this very thought experiment around on us, drawing out our intuition that the person goes where her body goes. Like Williams, John Perry also provides an extended argument in his dialogue for distrusting "intuitions" about the possibility of surviving the death of one's body. Together, Williams and Perry present interesting questions about our trust in thought experiments and the relevance of the expressions used to describe the cases. This issue, of course, ties directly to the question about the role that visual images in film can have in suggesting and/or offering support for philosophical theses. How much of a role should philosophers give such visual or verbal thought experiments? This question, an underlying theme of this text, is central to an understanding of the nature of the philosophical method and thereby of philosophy itself.

Derek Parfit, in his influential and widely discussed *Reasons and Persons*, describes versions of Locke – and Williams – like thought experiments in which a person is transformed gradually in such a way that either (1) he comes to have Greta Garbo's body, or (2) his body comes to exemplify Greta Garbo's mental life. But then Parfit presents his "Combined Spectrum" in which the physical and psychological are gradually changed *simultaneously*. At no point in the gradual change does it seem that we can pinpoint a place where our initial person ceases to exist, but he surely does not exist at the end of the spectrum where we have, in essence, a physical and psychological replica of Greta Garbo. This case provides the motivation for Parfit's radical claim that *there is no fact of the matter as to whether the original person has*

continued to exist or not, i.e. there is simply no true or false answer to the question, "Would I survive the sorts of changes that occur in the middle of the Combined Spectrum?"

Another question that is raised by Parfit's Combined Spectrum is how we are to regard the replica of Greta Garbo that exists at the end of the series of simultaneous changes. Is this really Greta Garbo? Would replication be a way of surviving? This sort of issue has become particularly gripping, given the cloning of Dolly the sheep and the resulting media concern about the impending possibility (here not just conceptual but also technological) of cloning human beings. Cloning, however, is not really replication, but, rather, the creation of a new person from some tissue of an already existing person. But suppose that actual replication could occur. This is the premise of the film *Multiplicity*, in which the protagonist undergoes a procedure which results in multiple copies of him being made. Each one of the copies has much of the same mental life as the original, and so, from the perspective of each copy, it appears that *he* is the original: from the inside, there is nothing to provide reason to suppose that one is a copy or an original (consider the scene in which the clone wakes up worrying the attempt at cloning was a failure: chapter 4). This same worry is echoed in the film *The Sixth Day*, in which Arnold Schwarzenegger is battling an enemy who is able to replicate persons: he keeps his hench people "alive" by making replicas whenever they "die" (chapter 12). This enemy also, as it turns out, replicates Arnold's character, and we are as mystified as the Arnold-being who appears on the screen – is he the original or not? Does the answer to the question of whether replication preserves identity turn at all on whether or not the "original" survives along with the replica? Is our view about whether the "survival" of the magician in *The Prestige* importantly influenced by the fact that the replica "pops" into existence as the original dies (chapters 21–3)? Further, should it matter to us (or to our loved ones), if we survive in conventional form or if we "die" and then are replicated? Is replication a type of survival? If not, should actual survival be of concern to us? Perhaps replication, even if not survival, is as good as survival.

Most of the philosophical works and the films that we have discussed so far in this section argue for, suggest, or motivate, some conception of the person and/or the mental as distinct from the body, i.e. from the physical. Many people, however, are convinced that such a conception of the mental is not in line with a modern "scientific" world-view. After all, such people claim, we know that fiddling with someone's brain, either through the aid of chemicals or through actual surgical intervention, can alter memories, personality, knowledge, beliefs, moods, etc. Now, clearly, such causal links do not undermine Descartes or Locke; after all, neither denied that the body affects the mind and vice versa. But problems about mind–body interaction, and metaphysical worries about "queer" and "spooky" things such as immaterial souls, have led some philosophers to propose physicalist conceptions of the mental, the simplest of which is behaviorism (see Gilbert Ryle's "Descartes' Myth"). According to the behaviorist, it is a misunderstanding to conceive of mental states as something distinct from and the cause of our behavior – mental states are just dispositions to behave in certain ways under certain kinds of circumstances. So, just as the fragility of glass is its disposition to break when dropped, etc., so to be in pain is a disposition to wince, to seek relief, etc.

There are obvious difficulties with the behaviorist conception of the mental. First, there seem to be obvious counterexamples to any proposed behavioristic analysis. Spartan children were conditioned not to exhibit pain behavior. Did successful elimination of the disposition to behave eliminate pain for Spartans? Can one even begin to formulate descriptions of plausible dispositions that define mental states in a purely physicalist language? Suppose that someone suggests, for example, that to be in pain is to be disposed to say certain things under certain conditions. It might be true that if I am in pain and I am asked whether I am, I will respond "Yes," but this is only true if I *want* to communicate with you truthfully. This behavioristic "translation" of the claim that I am in pain will now need to eliminate reference to the psychological state of wanting.

There is another fundamental difficulty with behaviorism that is suggested by the analogy to the disposition of glass to break when dropped. The glass is disposed to break upon hitting the floor *because* it has a certain structure. This structure provides the grounds for the disposition to break. Similarly, then, it seems natural to suppose

that there is some ground of a person's disposition to wince or to take an aspirin: they exhibit this behavior *because* they are in pain. So it seems more natural to equate pain with some internal structure of the person, just as we identified the ground of the fragility of the glass with some internal structure of the glass.

Many physicalists, then, adopt a version of what is sometimes called the mind–brain identity theory, a theory which identifies mental states with states of the brain (J. J. C. Smart) or a version of functionalism, which identifies mental states with so-called functional states *realized by* states of the central nervous system (David Lewis). The functionalist's view is not easy to define, and it is often not even clear what precisely the difference is between the mind–brain identity theorist, the behaviorist, and the functionalist. Crudely put, the functionalist wants to identify mental states in terms of their causal (functional) role. The functionalist typically wants to capture the point discussed above and allow that there is something actually occurring that is, for example, your pain. Being in pain, for the functionalist, might be thought of as being in that state caused by damage to the body and which in turn produces (normally) behavior that is conducive to the healing of that damage. Perhaps the easiest way to get a grasp on the functionalist's view is to consider an analogy. We might both have computers that are in the state of spell-checking a given document – spell-checking can be understood in terms of the state of the computer that is caused by giving it a certain command and that results in highlighted misspelled words. Of course, both the hardware of my computer, and even the software my computer uses, might be quite different from yours. On the functionalist view, the common state of spell-checking stands to the different underlying "mechanisms" the way a mental state stands to its underlying or realizing "mechanisms." The functionalists claim that it is an advantage of their physicalism that they can accommodate the obvious possibility that two creatures (humans and Lewis's Martians, for example) can both be in pain even if the physical realizations of the pain are radically different.

Resistance to physicalism in both its identity theory and functionalist incarnations has come from two opposing camps. First, both Thomas Nagel and Frank Jackson have argued that if physicalism were true, then we would know everything there is to know about the world if we knew all of the physical facts about the world. Both Nagel and Jackson present thought experiments that, they claim, support the thesis that knowledge of physical facts and only physical facts would not be complete knowledge of the world – there are some irreducibly mental features of the world (what it is like to be a bat, what it is like to see a red object). On the basis of these thought experiments, Nagel and Jackson support *property dualism*, the view that mental properties are *sui generis*, and, thus, not reducible to physical properties.

A very different kind of physicalism is offered by Paul Churchland, who defends *eliminative materialism*. Churchland argues that the term "mental property (or state)" does not refer to anything in the world. "Mental state" is like "unicorn:" neither term refers to any actually existing objects, properties, or facts in the world. Thus, according to Churchland, we ought to ditch our "folk psychological" language that invokes desires, pains, pleasures, hopes, and fears, and try to formulate a purely neurophysiological language of brain states, synapses, and neural networks. Churchland's view puzzles many philosophers: it is difficult to see how someone is lucky enough to get through life without occasionally experiencing the kind of searing pain that is difficult to "treat" with the right philosophical theory. Furthermore, how can someone who purports to *believe* the truth of eliminative materialism *believe* that there are no such things as beliefs?

Finally, issues about personal identity and the nature of the mental create puzzles and problems in two important areas, one of which drives highly funded scientific and technical research, and the other of which plagues all of us in our confrontations with our own deaths and those of our loved ones. The first issue is that of AI – artificial intelligence. Could we construct a "robot" that not only behaves as though "she" has an "inner" mental life, but that actually has such a mental life? In the film *Bicentennial Man*, Robin Williams plays a robot who becomes increasingly more complex and who eventually forces society to consider the question of whether he has become a person. The television series and related movies of *Star Trek: The Next Generation* have an intriguing character named Data, an "android" who is constructed as a computer

with human appearance and behavior. Data can have beliefs, apparently, but not emotions, unless he can find and get implanted in his "brain" the so-called "emotion chip." If collections of wires appropriately programmed could think and have emotions, does that undermine Cartesian dualism? Are we just naturally occurring computers with sophisticated programs? Is there any distinction between exhibiting certain behaviors and having a mental life? In other words, is there anything interior distinct from physical behaviors? John Searle, in his famous article "Minds, Brains, and Programs," uses a clever thought experiment to cast serious doubt on any hasty conclusion concerning the supposed thought processes of a computer. But, if Searle is right, what is essential to thought?

The existence of a soul has been the center of religious thought and hope for millennia. In Christian thought, influenced in some of its philosophical manifestations by Platonic and neo-Platonic thought, the body is imbued with a soul by God, and the soul lives after the body dies a physical death. The soul is non-corporeal and so occupies neither space nor time. (Descartes' Catholicism was one of his driving philosophical motivations.) In "Of the Immortality of the Soul," Hume tries to cast doubt on the rationality of belief in immortality. But we can also separate the question of whether such belief is rational from the question of whether we can even make sense of surviving the death of our bodies. Without a soul, the possibility of an afterlife is difficult to comprehend. In the film *What Dreams May Come*, we are presented with a fantastical cinematic version of an afterlife. How are we to understand the nature of persons, given the assumptions of an afterlife upon which the movie depends? (Questions about the nature of persons are also raised by the assumption of "visible" ghosts or apparitions, common to many films.)

Note

1   Descartes hypothesized that the point of contact between the mind and the body is the pineal gland. Whatever one thinks of the science of this hypothesis, it is quite clear that a physical intermediary, a part of the physical body itself, is not going to go very far in helping the philosopher to understand mind–body interaction.

9

Second Meditation

René Descartes

Meditation II

Of the nature of the human mind; and that it is
more easily known than the body

The Meditation of yesterday filled my mind with
so many doubts that it is no longer in my power
to forget them. And yet I do not see in what
manner I can resolve them; and, just as if I had
all of a sudden fallen into very deep water, I am
so disconcerted that I can neither make certain
of setting my feet on the bottom, nor can I swim
and so support myself on the surface. I shall
nevertheless make an effort and follow anew the
same path as that on which I yesterday entered,
i.e. I shall proceed by setting aside all that in which
the least doubt could be supposed to exist, just
as if I had discovered that it was absolutely false;
and I shall ever follow in this road until I have
met with something which is certain, or at least,
if I can do nothing else, until I have learned for
certain that there is nothing in the world that is
certain. Archimedes, in order that he might draw
the terrestrial globe out of its place, and transport
it elsewhere, demanded only that one point should
be fixed and immoveable; in the same way I shall
have the right to conceive high hopes if I am happy
enough to discover one thing only which is
certain and indubitable.

I suppose, then, that all the things that I see
are false; I persuade myself that nothing has ever
existed of all that my fallacious memory represents to me. I consider that I possess no senses;
I imagine that body, figure, extension, movement and place are but the fictions of my mind.
What, then, can be esteemed as true? Perhaps
nothing at all, unless that there is nothing in the
world that is certain.

But how can I know there is not something
different from those things that I have just considered, of which one cannot have the slightest
doubt? Is there not some God, or some other being
by whatever name we call it, who puts these
reflections into my mind? That is not necessary,
for is it not possible that I am capable of producing
them myself? I myself, am I not at least something?
But I have already denied that I had senses and
body. Yet I hesitate, for what follows from that?
Am I so dependent on body and senses that I
cannot exist without these? But I was persuaded
that there was nothing in all the world, that there
was no heaven, no earth, that there were no
minds, nor any bodies: was I not then likewise
persuaded that I did not exist? Not at all; of a

René Descartes, *Meditation II* from *The Philosophical Works of Descartes*, vol. 1, trans. E. Haldane and G. Ross
(Cambridge: Cambridge University Press, 1967). © 1967 by Cambridge University Press. Reproduced with permission
from Cambridge University Press.

surety I myself did exist since I persuaded myself of something [or merely because I thought of something]. But there is some deceiver or other, very powerful and very cunning, who ever employs his ingenuity in deceiving me. Then without doubt I exist also if he deceives me, and let him deceive me as much as he will, he can never cause me to be nothing so long as I think that I am something. So that after having reflected well and carefully examined all things, we must come to the definite conclusion that this proposition: I am, I exist, is necessarily true each time that I pronounce it, or that I mentally conceive it.

But I do not yet know clearly enough what I am, I who am certain that I am; and hence I must be careful to see that I do not imprudently take some other object in place of myself, and thus that I do not go astray in respect of this knowledge that I hold to be the most certain and most evident of all that I have formerly learned. That is why I shall now consider anew what I believed myself to be before I embarked upon these last reflections; and of my former opinions I shall withdraw all that might even in a small degree be invalidated by the reasons which I have just brought forward, in order that there may be nothing at all left beyond what is absolutely certain and indubitable.

What then did I formerly believe myself to be? Undoubtedly I believed myself to be a man. But what is a man? Shall I say a reasonable animal? Certainly not; for then I should have to inquire what an animal is, and what is reasonable; and thus from a single question I should insensibly fall into an infinitude of others more difficult; and I should not wish to waste the little time and leisure remaining to me in trying to unravel subtleties like these. But I shall rather stop here to consider the thoughts which of themselves spring up in my mind, and which were not inspired by anything beyond my own nature alone when I applied myself to the consideration of my being. In the first place, then, I considered myself as having a face, hands, arms, and all that system of members composed of bones and flesh as seen in a corpse which I designated by the name of body. In addition to this I considered that I was nourished, that I walked, that I felt, and that I thought, and I referred all these actions to the soul: but I did not stop to consider what the soul was, or if I did

stop, I imagined that it was something extremely rare and subtle like a wind, a flame, or an ether, which was spread throughout my grosser parts. As to body I had no manner of doubt about its nature, but thought I had a very clear knowledge of it; and if I had desired to explain it according to the notions that I had then formed of it, I should have described it thus: By the body I understand all that which can be defined by a certain figure: something which can be confined in a certain place, and which can fill a given space in such a way that every other body will be excluded from it; which can be perceived either by touch, or by sight, or by hearing, or by taste, or by smell: which can be moved in many ways not, in truth, by itself, but by something which is foreign to it, by which it is touched [and from which it receives impressions]: for to have the power of self-movement, as also of feeling or of thinking, I did not consider to appertain to the nature of body: on the contrary, I was rather astonished to find that faculties similar to them existed in some bodies.

But what am I, now that I suppose that there is a certain genius which is extremely powerful, and, if I may say so, malicious, who employs all his powers in deceiving me? Can I affirm that I possess the least of all those things which I have just said pertain to the nature of body? I pause to consider, I revolve all these things in my mind, and I find none of which I can say that it pertains to me. It would be tedious to stop to enumerate them. Let us pass to the attributes of soul and see if there is any one which is in me? What of nutrition or walking [the first mentioned]? But if it is so that I have no body it is also true that I can neither walk nor take nourishment. Another attribute is sensation. But one cannot feel without body, and besides I have thought I perceived many things during sleep that I recognized in my waking moments as not having been experienced at all. What of thinking? I find here that thought is an attribute that belongs to me; it alone cannot be separated from me. I am, I exist, that is certain. But how often? Just when I think; for it might possibly be the case if I ceased entirely to think, that I should likewise cease altogether to exist. I do not now admit anything which is not necessarily true: to speak accurately I am not more than a thing which thinks, that is to say a mind or a soul, or an understanding, or a reason, which are terms whose significance was formerly unknown to me. I am, however, a real thing and really exist; but what thing? I have answered: a thing which thinks.

And what more? I shall exercise my imagination [in order to see if I am not something more]. I am not a collection of members which we call the human body: I am not a subtle air distributed through these members, I am not a wind, a fire, a vapour, a breath, nor anything at all which I can imagine or conceive; because I have assumed that all these were nothing. Without changing that supposition I find that I only leave myself certain of the fact that I am somewhat. But perhaps it is true that these same things which I supposed were non-existent because they are unknown to me, are really not different from the self which I know. I am not sure about this, I shall not dispute about it now; I can only give judgment on things that are known to me. I know that I exist, and I inquire what I am, I whom I know to exist. But it is very certain that the knowledge of my existence taken in its precise significance does not depend on things whose existence is not yet known to me; consequently it does not depend on those which I can feign in imagination. And indeed the very term *feign* in imagination proves to me my error, for I really do this if I image myself a something, since to imagine is nothing else than to contemplate the figure or image of a corporeal thing. But I already know for certain that I am, and that it may be that all these images, and, speaking generally, all things that relate to the nature of body are nothing but dreams [and chimeras]. For this reason I see clearly that I have as little reason to say, "I shall stimulate my imagination in order to know more distinctly what I am," than if I were to say, "I am now awake, and I perceive somewhat that is real and true: but because I do not yet perceive it distinctly enough, I shall go to sleep of express purpose, so that my dreams may represent the perception with greatest truth and evidence." And, thus, I know for certain that nothing of all that I can understand by means of my imagination belongs to this knowledge which I have of myself, and that it is necessary to recall the mind from this mode of thought with the utmost diligence in order that it may be able to know its own nature with perfect distinctness.

But what then am I? A thing which thinks. What is a thing which thinks? It is a thing which doubts, understands, [conceives], affirms, denies, wills, refuses, which also imagines and feels.

Certainly it is no small matter if all these things pertain to my nature. But why should they not so pertain? Am I not that being who now doubts nearly everything, who nevertheless understands certain things, who affirms that one only is true, who denies all the others, who desires to know more, is averse from being deceived, who imagines many things, sometimes indeed despite his will, and who perceives many likewise, as by the intervention of the bodily organs? Is there nothing in all this which is as true as it is certain that I exist, even though I should always sleep and though he who has given me being employed all his ingenuity in deceiving me? Is there likewise any one of these attributes which can be distinguished from my thought, or which might be said to be separated from myself? For it is so evident of itself that it is I who doubts, who understands, and who desires, that there is no reason here to add anything to explain it. And I have certainly the power of imagining likewise; for although it may happen (as I formerly supposed) that none of the things which I imagine are true, nevertheless this power of imagining does not cease to be really in use, and it forms part of my thought. Finally, I am the same who feels, that is to say, who perceives certain things, as by the organs of sense, since in truth I see light, I hear noise, I feel heat. But it will be said that these phenomena are false and that I am dreaming. Let it be so; still it is at least quite certain that it seems to me that I see light, that I hear noise and that I feel heat. That cannot be false; properly speaking it is what is in me called feeling; and used in this precise sense that is no other thing than thinking.

From this time I begin to know what I am with a little more clearness and distinction than before; but nevertheless it still seems to me, and I cannot prevent myself from thinking, that corporeal things, whose images are framed by thought, which are tested by the senses, are much more distinctly known than that obscure part of me which does not come under the imagination. Although really it is very strange to say that I know and understand more distinctly these things whose existence seems to me dubious, which are unknown to me, and which do not belong to me, than others of the truth of which I am convinced, which are known to me and which pertain to my real nature, in a word, than myself. But I see clearly how the case stands: my mind loves to wander, and cannot yet suffer itself to be retained within the just limits of truth. Very good, let us once more give it the freest rein, so that, when afterwards we seize the proper occasion for pulling up, it may the more easily be regulated and controlled.

Let us begin by considering the commonest matters, those which we believe to be the most distinctly comprehended, to wit, the bodies which we touch and see; not indeed bodies in general, for these general ideas are usually a little more confused, but let us consider one body in particular. Let us take, for example, this piece of wax: it has been taken freshly from the hive, and it has not yet lost the sweetness of the honey which it contains; it still retains somewhat of the odour of the flowers from which it has been culled; its colour, its figure, its size are apparent; it is hard, cold, easily handled, and if you strike it with the finger, it will emit a sound. Finally all the things which are requisite to cause us distinctly to recognise a body, are met with in it. But notice that while I speak and approach the fire what remained of the taste is exhaled, the smell evaporates, the colour alters, the figure is destroyed, the size increases, it becomes liquid, it heats, scarcely can one handle it, and when one strikes it, no sound is emitted. Does the same wax remain after this change? We must confess that it remains; none would judge otherwise. What then did I know so distinctly in this piece of wax? It could certainly be nothing of all that the senses brought to my notice, since all these things which fall under taste, smell, sight, touch, and hearing, are found to be changed, and yet the same wax remains.

Perhaps it was what I now think, viz. that this wax was not that sweetness of honey, nor that agreeable scent of flowers, nor that particular whiteness, nor that figure, nor that sound, but simply a body which a little while before appeared to me as perceptible under these forms, and which is now perceptible under others. But what, precisely, is it that I imagine when I form such conceptions? Let us attentively consider this, and, abstracting from all that does not belong to the wax, let us see what remains. Certainly nothing remains excepting a certain extended thing which is flexible and movable. But what is the meaning of flexible and movable? Is it not that I imagine that this piece of wax being round is capable of becoming square and of passing from a square to a triangular figure? No, certainly it is not that, since I imagine it admits of an infinitude of similar changes, and I nevertheless do not know how to compass the infinitude by my imagination, and consequently this conception which I have of the wax is not brought about by the faculty of imagination. What now is this extension? Is it not also unknown? For it becomes greater when the wax is melted, greater when it is boiled, and greater still when the heat increases; and I should not conceive [clearly] according to truth what wax is, if I did not think that even this piece that we are considering is capable of receiving more variations in extension than I have ever imagined. We must then grant that I could not even understand through the imagination what this piece of wax is, and that it is my mind alone which perceives it. I say this piece of wax in particular, for as to wax in general it is yet clearer. But what is this piece of wax which cannot be understood excepting by the [understanding or] mind? It is certainly the same that I see, touch, imagine, and finally it is the same which I have always believed it to be from the beginning. But what must particularly be observed is that its perception is neither an act of vision, nor of touch, nor of imagination, and has never been such although it may have appeared formerly to be so, but only an intuition of the mind, which may be imperfect and confused as it was formerly, or clear and distinct as it is at present, according as my attention is more or less directed to the elements which are found in it and of which it is composed.

Yet in the meantime I am greatly astonished when I consider [the great feebleness of mind] and its proneness to fall [insensibly] into error; for although without giving expression to my thoughts I consider all this in my own mind, words often impede me and I am almost deceived by the terms of ordinary language. For we say that we see the same wax, if it is present, and not that we simply judge that it is the same from its having the same colour and figure. From this I should conclude that I knew the wax by means of vision and not simply by the intuition of the mind; unless by chance I remember that, when looking from a window and saying I see men who pass in the street, I really do not see them, but infer that what I see is men, just as I say that I see wax. And yet what do I see from the window but hats and coats which may cover automatic machines? Yet I judge these to be men. And similarly solely by the faculty of judgment which rests in my mind, I comprehend that which I believed I saw with my eyes.

A man who makes it his aim to raise his knowledge above the common should be ashamed to derive the occasion for doubting from the forms of speech invented by the vulgar; I prefer to pass on and consider whether I had a more evident and perfect conception of what the wax was when I first perceived it, and when I believed I knew it by means of the external senses or at least by the common sense as it is called, that is to say by the imaginative faculty, or whether my present conception is clearer now that I have most carefully examined what it is, and in what way it can be known. It would certainly be absurd to doubt as to this. For what was there in this first perception which was distinct? What was there which might not as well have been perceived by any of the animals? But when I distinguish the wax from its external forms, and when, just as if I had taken from it its vestments, I consider it quite naked, it is certain that although some error may still be found in my judgment, I can nevertheless not perceive it thus without a human mind.

But finally what shall I say of this mind, that is, of myself, for up to this point I do not admit in myself anything but mind? What then, I who seem to perceive this piece of wax so distinctly, do I not know myself, not only with much more truth and certainty, but also with much more distinctness and clearness? For if I judge that the wax is or exists from the fact that I see it, it certainly follows much more clearly that I am or that I exist myself from the fact that I see it. For it may be that what I see is not really wax, it may also be that I do not possess eyes with which to see anything; but it cannot be that when I see, or (for I no longer take account of the distinction) when I think I see, that I myself who think am nought. So if I judge that the wax exists from the fact that I touch it, the same thing will follow, to wit, that I am; and if I judge that my imagination, or some other cause, whatever it is, persuades me that the wax exists, I shall still conclude the same. And what I have here remarked of wax may be applied to all other things which are external to me [and which are met with outside of me]. And further, if the [notion or] perception of wax has seemed to me clearer and more distinct, not only after the sight or the touch, but also after many other causes have rendered it quite manifest to me, with how much more [evidence] and distinctness must it be said that I now know myself, since all the reasons which contribute to the knowledge of wax, or any other body whatever, are yet better proofs of the nature of my mind! And there are so many other things in the mind itself which may contribute to the elucidation of its nature, that those which depend on body such as these just mentioned, hardly merit being taken into account.

But finally here I am, having insensibly reverted to the point I desired, for, since it is now manifest to me that even bodies are not properly speaking known by the senses or by the faculty of imagination, but by the understanding only, and since they are not known from the fact that they are seen or touched, but only because they are understood, I see clearly that there is nothing which is easier for me to know than my mind. But because it is difficult to rid oneself so promptly of an opinion to which one was accustomed for so long, it will be well that I should halt a little at this point, so that by the length of my meditation I may more deeply imprint on my memory this new knowledge.

10

Descartes' Myth

Gilbert Ryle

(1) The Official Doctrine

There is a doctrine about the nature and place of minds which is so prevalent among theorists and even among laymen that it deserves to be described as the official theory. Most philosophers, psychologists and religious teachers subscribe, with minor reservations, to its main articles and, although they admit certain theoretical difficulties in it, they tend to assume that these can be overcome without serious modifications being made to the architecture of the theory. It will be argued here that the central principles of the doctrine are unsound and conflict with the whole body of what we know about minds when we are not speculating about them.

The official doctrine, which hails chiefly from Descartes, is something like this. With the doubtful exceptions of idiots and infants in arms every human being has both a body and a mind. Some would prefer to say that every human being is both a body and a mind. His body and his mind are ordinarily harnessed together, but after the death of the body his mind may continue to exist and function.

Human bodies are in space and are subject to the mechanical laws which govern all other bodies in space. Bodily processes and states can be inspected by external observers. So a man's bodily life is as much a public affair as are the lives of animals and reptiles and even as the careers of trees, crystals and planets.

But minds are not in space, nor are their operations subject to mechanical laws. The workings of one mind are not witnessable by other observers; its career is private. Only I can take direct cognisance of the states and processes of my own mind. A person therefore lives through two collateral histories, one consisting of what happens in and to his body, the other consisting of what happens in and to his mind. The first is public, the second private. The events in the first history are events in the physical world, those in the second are events in the mental world.

It has been disputed whether a person does or can directly monitor all or only some of the episodes of his own private history; but, according to the official doctrine, of at least some of these episodes he has direct and unchallengeable cognisance. In consciousness, self-consciousness and introspection he is directly and authentically apprised of the present states and operations of his mind. He may have great or small uncertainties about concurrent and adjacent episodes in the physical world, but he can have none about at least part of what is momentarily occupying his mind.

Gilbert Ryle, "Descartes' Myth," from *The Concept of Mind* (Chicago: University of Chicago Press, 1984), pp. 11–24.

It is customary to express this bifurcation of his two lives and of his two worlds by saying that the things and events which belong to the physical world, including his own body, are external, while the workings of his own mind are internal. This antithesis of outer and inner is of course meant to be construed as a metaphor, since minds, not being in space, could not be described as being spatially inside anything else, or as having things going on spatially inside themselves. But relapses from this good intention are common and theorists are found speculating how stimuli, the physical sources of which are yards or miles outside a person's skin, can generate mental responses inside his skull, or how decisions framed inside his cranium can set going movements of his extremities.

Even when 'inner' and 'outer' are construed as metaphors, the problem how a person's mind and body influence one another is notoriously charged with theoretical difficulties. What the mind wills, the legs, arms and the tongue execute; what affects the ear and the eye has something to do with what the mind perceives; grimaces and smiles betray the mind's moods and bodily castigations lead, it is hoped, to moral improvement. But the actual transactions between the episodes of the private history and those of the public history remain mysterious, since by definition they can belong to neither series. They could not be reported among the happenings described in a person's autobiography of his inner life, but nor could they be reported among those described in some one else's biography of that person's overt career. They can be inspected neither by introspection nor by laboratory experiment. They are theoretical shuttlecocks which are forever being bandied from the physiologist back to the psychologist and from the psychologist back to the physiologist.

Underlying this partly metaphorical representation of the bifurcation of a person's two lives there is a seemingly more profound and philosophical assumption. It is assumed that there are two different kinds of existence or status. What exists or happens may have the status of physical existence, or it may have the status of mental existence. Somewhat as the faces of coins are either heads or tails, or somewhat as living creatures are either male or female, so, it is supposed, some existing is physical existing, other existing is mental existing. It is a necessary feature of what has physical existence that it is in space and time; it is a necessary feature of what has mental existence that it is in time but not in space. What has physical existence is composed of matter, or else is a function of matter; what has mental existence consists of consciousness, or else is a function of consciousness.

There is thus a polar opposition between mind and matter, an opposition which is often brought out as follows. Material objects are situated in a common field, known as 'space', and what happens to one body in one part of space is mechanically connected with what happens to other bodies in other parts of space. But mental happenings occur in insulated fields, known as 'minds', and there is, apart maybe from telepathy, no direct causal connection between what happens in one mind and what happens in another. Only through the medium of the public physical world can the mind of one person make a difference to the mind of another. The mind is its own place and in his inner life each of us lives the life of a ghostly Robinson Crusoe. People can see, hear and jolt one another's bodies, but they are irremediably blind and deaf to the workings of one another's minds and inoperative upon them.

What sort of knowledge can be secured of the workings of a mind? On the one side, according to the official theory, a person has direct knowledge of the best imaginable kind of the workings of his own mind. Mental states and processes are (or are normally) conscious states and processes, and the consciousness which irradiates them can engender no illusions and leaves the door open for no doubts. A person's present thinkings, feelings and willings, his perceivings, rememberings and imaginings are intrinsically 'phosphorescent'; their existence and their nature are inevitably betrayed to their owner. The inner life is a stream of consciousness of such a sort that it would be absurd to suggest that the mind whose life is that stream might be unaware of what is passing down it.

True, the evidence adduced recently by Freud seems to show that there exist channels tributary to this stream, which run hidden from their owner. People are actuated by impulses the existence of which they vigorously disavow; some of their thoughts differ from the thoughts which they acknowledge; and some of the actions which they think they will to perform they do not really will. They are thoroughly gulled by some of their own hypocrisies and they successfully ignore facts about their mental lives which on the official theory ought to be patent to them. Holders of the official theory tend, however, to maintain that anyhow in normal circumstances a person must be directly and authentically seized of the present state and workings of his own mind.

Besides being currently supplied with these alleged immediate data of consciousness, a person is also generally supposed to be able to exercise from time to time a special kind of perception, namely inner perception, or intro-spection. He can take a (non-optical) 'look' at what is passing in his mind. Not only can he view and scrutinize a flower through his sense of sight and listen to and discriminate the notes of a bell through his sense of hearing; he can also reflectively or introspectively watch, without any bodily organ of sense, the current episodes of his inner life. This self-observation is also com-monly supposed to be immune from illusion, confusion or doubt. A mind's reports of its own affairs have a certainty superior to the best that is possessed by its reports of matters in the physical world. Sense-perceptions can, but con-sciousness and introspection cannot, be mistaken or confused.

On the other side, one person has no direct access of any sort to the events of the inner life of another. He cannot do better than make problematic inferences from the observed behaviour of the other person's body to the states of mind which, by analogy from his own conduct, he supposes to be signalised by that behaviour. Direct access to the workings of a mind is the privilege of that mind itself; in default of such privileged access, the workings of one mind are inevitably occult to everyone else. For the supposed arguments from bodily move-ments similar to their own to mental workings similar to their own would lack any possibility of observational corroboration. Not unnaturally, therefore, an adherent of the official theory finds it difficult to resist this consequence of his pre-misses, that he has no good reason to believe that there do exist minds other than his own. Even if he prefers to believe that to other human bodies there are harnessed minds not unlike his own, he cannot claim to be able to discover their individual characteristics, or the particular things that they undergo and do. Absolute solitude is on this showing the ineluctable destiny of the soul. Only our bodies can meet.

As a necessary corollary of this general scheme there is implicitly prescribed a special way of construing our ordinary concepts of mental powers and operations. The verbs, nouns and adjectives, with which in ordinary life we describe the wits, characters and higher-grade perform-ances of the people with whom we have do, are required to be construed as signifying special episodes in their secret histories, or else as signifying tendencies for such episodes to occur. When someone is described as knowing, believ-ing or guessing something, as hoping, dreading, intending or shirking something, as designing this or being amused at that, these verbs are supposed to denote the occurrence of specific modifications in his (to us) occult stream of consciousness. Only his own privileged access to this stream in direct awareness and introspection could provide authentic testimony that these mental-conduct verbs were correctly or incorrectly applied. The onlooker, be he teacher, critic, biographer or friend, can never assure himself that his comments have any vestige of truth. Yet it was just because we do in fact all know how to make such comments, make them with general correctness and correct them when they turn out to be confused or mistaken, that philosophers found it necessary to construct their theories of the nature and place of minds. Finding mental-conduct concepts being regularly and effectively used, they properly sought to fix their logical geography. But the logical geography officially recommended would entail that there could be no regular or effective use of these mental-conduct concepts in our descriptions of, and prescriptions for, other people's minds.

(2)   The Absurdity of the Official Doctrine

Such in outline is the official theory. I shall often speak of it, with deliberate abusiveness, as 'the dogma of the Ghost in the Machine'. I hope to prove that it is entirely false, and false not in detail but in principle. It is not merely an assemblage of particular mistakes. It is one big mistake and a mistake of a special kind. It is, namely, a category-mistake. It represents the facts of mental life as if they belonged to one logical type or category (or range of types or categories), when they actually belong to another. The dogma is therefore a philosopher's myth. In attempting to explode the myth I shall probably be taken to be denying well-known facts about the mental life of human beings, and my plea that I aim at doing nothing more than rectify the logic of mental-conduct concepts will probably be disallowed as mere subterfuge.

I must first indicate what is meant by the phrase 'Category-mistake'. This I do in a series of illustrations.

A foreigner visiting Oxford or Cambridge for the first time is shown a number of colleges, libraries, playing fields, museums, scientific departments and administrative offices. He then asks 'But where is the University? I have seen where the members of the Colleges live, where the Registrar works, where the scientists experiment and the rest. But I have not yet seen the University in which reside and work the members of your University.' It has then to be explained to him that the University is not another collateral institution, some ulterior counterpart to the colleges, laboratories and offices which he has seen. The University is just the way in which all that he has already seen is organized. When they are seen and when their co-ordination is understood, the University has been seen. His mistake lay in his innocent assumption that it was correct to speak of Christ Church, the Bodleian Library, the Ashmolean Museum *and* the University, to speak, that is, as if 'the University' stood for an extra member of the class of which these other units are members. He was mistakenly allocating the University to the same category as that to which the other institutions belong.

The same mistake would be made by a child witnessing the march-past of a division, who, having had pointed out to him such and such battalions, batteries, squadrons, etc., asked when the division was going to appear. He would be supposing that a division was a counterpart to the units already seen, partly similar to them and partly unlike them. He would be shown his mistake by being told that in watching the battalions, batteries and squadrons marching past he had

been watching the division marching past. The march-past was not a parade of battalions, batteries, squadrons *and* a division; it was a parade of the battalions, batteries and squadrons *of* a division.

One more illustration. A foreigner watching his first game of cricket learns what are the functions of the bowlers, the batsmen, the fielders, the umpires and the scorers. He then says 'But there is no one left on the field to contribute the famous element of team-spirit. I see who does the bowling, the batting and the wicket-keeping; but I do not see whose role it is to exercise *esprit de corps.*' Once more, it would have to be explained that he was looking for the wrong type of thing. Team-spirit is not another cricketing-operation supplementary to all of the other special tasks. It is, roughly, the keenness with which each of the special tasks is performed, and performing a task keenly is not performing two tasks. Certainly exhibiting team-spirit is not the same thing as bowling or catching, but nor is it a third thing such that we can say that the bowler first bowls *and* then exhibits team-spirit or that a fielder is at a given moment *either* catching *or* displaying *esprit de corps*.

These illustrations of category-mistakes have a common feature which must be noticed. The mistakes were made by people who did not know how to wield the concepts *University*, *division* and *team-spirit*. Their puzzles arose from inability to use certain items in the English vocabulary.

The theoretically interesting category-mistakes are those made by people who are perfectly competent to apply concepts, at least in the situations with which they are familiar, but are still liable in their abstract thinking to allocate those concepts to logical types to which they do not belong. An instance of a mistake of this sort would be the following story. A student of politics has learned the main differences between the British, the French and the American Constitutions, and has learned also the differences and connections between the Cabinet, Parliament, the various Ministries, the Judicature and the Church of England. But he still becomes embarrassed when asked questions about the connections between the Church of England, the Home Office and the British Constitution. For while the Church and the Home Office are institutions, the British

Constitution is not another institution in the same sense of that noun. So inter-institutional relations which can be asserted or denied to hold between the Church and the Home Office cannot be asserted or denied to hold between either of them and the British Constitution. 'The British Constitution' is not a term of the same logical type as 'the Home Office' and 'the Church of England'. In a partially similar way, John Doe may be a relative, a friend, an enemy or a stranger to Richard Roe; but he cannot be any of these things to the Average Taxpayer. He knows how to talk sense in certain sorts of discussions about the Average Taxpayer, but he is baffled to say why he could not come across him in the street as he can come across Richard Roe.

It is pertinent to our main subject to notice that, so long as the student of politics continues to think of the British Constitution as a counterpart to the other institutions, he will tend to describe it as a mysteriously occult institution; and so long as John Doe continues to think of the Average Taxpayer as a fellow-citizen, he will tend to think of him as an elusive insubstantial man, a ghost who is everywhere yet nowhere.

My destructive purpose is to show that a family of radical category-mistakes is the source of the double-life theory. The representation of a person as a ghost mysteriously ensconced in a machine derives from this argument. Because, as is true, a person's thinking, feeling and purposive doing cannot be described solely in the idioms of physics, chemistry and physiology, therefore they must be described in counterpart idioms. As the human body is a complex organised unit, so the human mind must be another complex organised unit, though one made of a different sort of stuff and with a different sort of structure. Or, again, as the human body, like any other parcel of matter, is a field of causes and effects, so the mind must be another field of causes and effects, though not (Heaven be praised) mechanical causes and effects.

(3)   The Origin of the Category-mistake

One of the chief intellectual origins of what I have yet to prove to be the Cartesian category-mistake seems to be this. When Galileo showed that his methods of scientific discovery were competent to provide a mechanical theory which should cover every occupant of space, Descartes found in himself two conflicting motives. As a man of scientific genius he could not but endorse the claims of mechanics, yet as a religious and moral man he could not accept, as Hobbes accepted, the discouraging rider to those claims, namely that human nature differs only in degree of complexity from clockwork. The mental could not be just a variety of the mechanical.

He and subsequent philosophers naturally but erroneously availed themselves of the following escape-route. Since mental-conduct words are not to be construed as signifying the occurrence of mechanical processes, they must be construed as signifying the occurrence of non-mechanical processes; since mechanical laws explain movements in space as the effects of other movements in space, other laws must explain some of the non-spatial workings of minds as the effects of other non-spatial workings of minds. The difference between the human behaviours which we describe as intelligent and those which we describe as unintelligent must be a difference in their causation; so, while some movements of human tongues and limbs are the effects of mechanical causes, others must be the effects of non-mechanical causes, i.e. some issue from movements of particles of matter, others from workings of the mind.

The differences between the physical and the mental were thus represented as differences inside the common framework of the categories of 'thing', 'stuff', 'attribute', 'state', 'process', 'change', 'cause' and 'effect'. Minds are things, but different sorts of things from bodies; mental processes are causes and effects, but different sorts of causes and effects from bodily movements. And so on. Somewhat as the foreigner expected the University to be an extra edifice, rather like a college but also considerably different, so the repudiators of mechanism represented minds as extra centres of causal processes, rather like machines but also considerably different from them. Their theory was a para-mechanical hypothesis.

That this assumption was at the heart of the doctrine is shown by the fact that there was from the beginning felt to be a major theoretical difficulty in explaining how minds can influence and be influenced by bodies. How can a mental process, such as willing, cause spatial movements like the movements of the tongue? How can a physical change in the optic nerve have among its effects a mind's perception of a flash of light? This notorious crux by itself shows the logical mould into which Descartes pressed his theory of the mind. It was the self-same mould into which he and Galileo set their mechanics. Still unwittingly adhering to the grammar of mechanics, he tried to avert disaster by describing minds in what was merely an obverse vocabulary. The workings of minds had to be described by the mere negatives of the specific descriptions given to bodies; they are not in space, they are not motions, they are not modifications of matter, they are not accessible to public observation. Minds are not bits of clockwork, they are just bits of not-clockwork.

As thus represented, minds are not merely ghosts harnessed to machines, they are themselves just spectral machines. Though the human body is an engine, it it not quite an ordinary engine, since some of its workings are governed by another engine inside it – this interior governor-engine being one of a very special sort. It is invisible, inaudible and it has no size or weight. It cannot be taken to bits and the laws it obeys are not those known to ordinary engineers. Nothing is known of how it governs the bodily engine.

A second major crux points the same moral. Since, according to the doctrine, minds belong to the same category as bodies and since bodies are rigidly governed by mechanical laws, it seemed to many theorists to follow that minds must be similarly governed by rigid non-mechanical laws. The physical world is a deterministic system, so the mental world must be a deterministic system. Bodies cannot help the modifications that they undergo, so minds cannot help pursuing the careers fixed for them. *Responsibility, choice, merit* and *demerit* are therefore inapplicable concepts – unless the compromise solution is adopted of saying that the laws governing mental processes, unlike those governing physical processes, have the congenial attribute of being only rather rigid. The problem of the Freedom of the Will was the problem how to reconcile the hypothesis that minds are to be described in terms drawn from the categories of mechanics with the knowledge that higher-grade human conduct is not of a piece with the behaviour of machines.

It is an historical curiosity that it was not noticed that the entire argument was broken-backed. Theorists correctly assumed that any sane man could already recognise the differences between, say, rational and non-rational utterances or between purposive and automatic behaviour. Else there would have been nothing requiring to be salved from mechanism. Yet the explanation given presupposed that one person could in principle never recognise the difference between the rational and the irrational utterances issuing from other human bodies, since he could never get access to the postulated immaterial causes of some of their utterances. Save for the doubtful exception of himself, he could never tell the difference between a man and a Robot. It would have to be conceded, for example, that, for all that we can tell, the inner lives of persons who are classed as idiots or lunatics are as rational as those of anyone else. Perhaps only their overt behaviour is disappointing; that is to say, perhaps 'idiots' are not really idiotic, or 'lunatics' lunatic. Perhaps, too, some of those who are classed as sane are really idiots. According to the theory, external observers could never know how the overt behaviour of others is correlated with their mental powers and processes and so they could never know or even plausibly conjecture whether their applications of mental-conduct concepts to these other people were correct or incorrect. It would then be hazardous or impossible for a man to claim sanity or logical consistency even for himself, since he would be debarred from comparing his own performances with those of others. In short, our characterisations of persons and their performances as intelligent, prudent and virtuous or as stupid, hypocritical and cowardly could never have been made, so the problem of providing a special causal hypothesis to serve as the basis of such diagnoses would never have arisen. The question, 'How do persons differ from machines?' arose just because everyone already knew how to apply mental-conduct concepts before the new causal hypothesis was introduced. This causal hypothesis could not therefore be the source of the criteria used in those applications. Nor, of course, has the causal hypothesis in any degree improved our handling of those criteria. We still distinguish good from bad arithmetic, politic from impolitic conduct and fertile from infertile imaginations in the ways in which Descartes himself distinguished them before and after he speculated how the applicability of these criteria was compatible with the principle of mechanical causation.

He had mistaken the logic of his problem. Instead of asking by what criteria intelligent behaviour is actually distinguished from non-intelligent behaviour, he asked 'Given that the principle of mechanical causation does not tell us the difference, what other causal principle will tell it us?' He realised that the problem was not one of mechanics and assumed that it must therefore be one of some counterpart to mechanics. Not unnaturally psychology is often cast for just this role.

When two terms belong to the same category, it is proper to construct conjunctive propositions embodying them. Thus a purchaser may say that he bought a left-hand glove and a right-hand glove, but not that he bought a left-hand glove, a right-hand glove and a pair of gloves. 'She came home in a flood of tears and a sedan-chair' is a well-known joke based on the absurdity of conjoining terms of different types. It would have been equally ridiculous to construct the disjunction 'She came home either in a flood of tears or else in a sedan-chair'. Now the dogma of the Ghost in the Machine does just this. It maintains that there exist both bodies and minds; that there occur physical processes and mental processes; that there are mechanical causes of corporeal movements and mental causes of corporeal movements. I shall argue that these and other analogous conjunctions are absurd; but, it must be noticed, the argument will not show that either of the illegitimately conjoined propositions is absurd in itself. I am not, for example, denying that there occur mental processes. Doing long division is a mental process and so is making a joke. But I am saying that the phrase 'there occur mental processes' does not mean the same sort of thing as 'there occur physical processes', and, therefore, that it makes no sense to conjoin or disjoin the two.

If my argument is successful, there will follow some interesting consequences. First, the hallowed contrast between Mind and Matter will be dissipated, but dissipated not by either of the equally hallowed absorptions of Mind by Matter or of Matter by Mind, but in quite a different way. For the seeming contrast of the two will be shown to be as illegitimate as would be the contrast of 'she

came home in a flood of tears' and 'she came home in a sedan-chair'. The belief that there is a polar opposition between Mind and Matter is the belief that they are terms of the same logical type.

It will also follow that both Idealism and Materialism are answers to an improper question. The 'reduction' of the material world to mental states and processes, as well as the 'reduction' of mental states and processes to physical states and processes, presuppose the legitimacy of the disjunction 'Either there exist minds or there exist bodies (but not both)'. It would be like saying, 'Either she bought a left-hand and a right-hand glove or she bought a pair of gloves (but not both)'.

It is perfectly proper to say, in one logical tone of voice, that there exist minds and to say, in another logical tone of voice, that there exist bodies. But these expressions do not indicate two different species of existence, for 'existence' is not a generic word like 'coloured' or 'sexed'. They indicate two different senses of 'exist', somewhat as 'rising' has different senses in 'the tide is rising', 'hopes are rising', and 'the average age of death is rising'. A man would be thought to be making a poor joke who said that three things are now rising, namely the tide, hopes and the average age of death. It would be just as good or bad a joke to say that there exist prime numbers and Wednesdays and public opinions and navies; or that there exist both minds and bodies. In the succeeding chapters I try to prove that the official theory does rest on a batch of category-mistakes by showing that logically absurd corollaries follow from it. The exhibition of these absurdities will have the constructive effect of bringing out part of the correct logic of mental-conduct concepts.

(4)   Historical Note

It would not be true to say that the official theory derives solely from Descartes' theories, or even from a more widespread anxiety about the implications of seventeenth century mechanics. Scholastic and Reformation theology had schooled the intellects of the scientists as well as of the laymen, philosophers and clerics of that age. Stoic-Augustinian theories of the will were embedded in the Calvinist doctrines of sin and grace; Platonic and Aristotelian theories of the intellect shaped the orthodox doctrines of the immortality of the soul. Descartes was reformulating already prevalent theological doctrines of the soul in the new syntax of Galileo. The theologian's privacy of conscience became the philosopher's privacy of consciousness, and what had been the bogy of Predestination reappeared as the bogy of Determinism.

It would also not be true to say that the two-worlds myth did no theoretical good. Myths often do a lot of theoretical good, while they are still new. One benefit bestowed by the para-mechanical myth was that it partly superannuated the then prevalent para-political myth. Minds and their Faculties had previously been described by analogies with political superiors and political subordinates. The idioms used were those of ruling, obeying, collaborating and rebelling. They survived and still survive in many ethical and some epistemological discussions. As, in physics, the new myth of occult Forces was a scientific improvement on the old myth of Final Causes, so, in anthropological and psychological theory, the new myth of hidden operations, impulses and agencies was an improvement on the old myth of dictations, deferences and disobediences.

11

Sensations and Brain Processes

J. J. C. Smart

Suppose that I report that I have at this moment a roundish, blurry-edged after-image which is yellowish towards its edge and is orange towards its centre. What is it that I am reporting?[1] One answer to this question might be that I am not reporting anything, that when I say that it looks to me as though there is a roundish yellowy orange patch of light on the wall I am expressing some sort of *temptation*, the temptation to say that there *is* a roundish yellowy orange patch on the wall (though I may know that there is not such a patch on the wall). This is perhaps Wittgenstein's view in the *Philosophical Investigations* (see paragraphs 367, 370). Similarly, when I "report" a pain, I am not really reporting anything (or, if you like, I am reporting in a queer sense of "reporting"), but am doing a sophisticated sort of wince. (See paragraph 244: "The verbal expression of pain replaces crying and does not describe it." Nor does it describe anything else?)[2] I prefer most of the time to discuss an after-image rather than a pain, because the word "pain" brings in something which is irrelevant to my purpose: the notion of "distress." I think that "he is in pain" entails "he is in distress," that is, that he is in a certain agitation-condition.[3] Similarly, to say "I am in pain" may be to do more than "replace pain behavior": it may be partly to report something, though this something is quite nonmysterious,

being an agitation-condition, and so susceptible of behavioristic analysis. The suggestion I wish if possible to avoid is a different one, namely that "I am in pain" is a genuine report, and that what it reports is an irreducibly psychical something. And similarly the suggestion I wish to resist is also that to say "I have a yellowish orange after-image" is to report something irreducibly psychical.

Why do I wish to resist this suggestion? Mainly because of Occam's razor. It seems to me that science is increasingly giving us a viewpoint whereby organisms are able to be seen as physico-chemical mechanisms:[4] it seems that even the behavior of man himself will one day be explicable in mechanistic terms. There does seem to be, so far as science is concerned, nothing in the world but increasingly complex arrangements of physical constituents. All except for one place: in consciousness. That is, for a full description of what is going on in a man you would have to mention not only the physical processes in his tissue, glands, nervous system, and so forth, but also his states of consciousness: his visual, auditory, and tactual sensations, his aches and pains. That these should be *correlated* with brain processes does not help, for to say that they are *correlated* is to say that they are something "over and above." You cannot correlate something with itself. You correlate footprints with

J. J. C. Smart, "Sensations and Brain Processes." *The Philosophical Review* 68, no. 2 (April 1959), pp. 141–56. © 1959 by Duke University Press. All rights reserved. Used by permission of the publisher.

burglars, but not Bill Sikes the burglar with Bill Sikes the burglar. So sensations, states of consciousness, do seem to be the one sort of thing left outside the physicalist picture, and for various reasons I just cannot believe that this can be so. That everything should be explicable in terms of physics (together of course with descriptions of the ways in which the parts are put together – roughly, biology is to physics as radio-engineering is to electro-magnetism) except the occurrence of sensations seems to me to be frankly unbelievable. Such sensations would be "nomological danglers," to use Feigl's expression.[5] It is not often realized how odd would be the laws whereby these nomological danglers would dangle. It is sometimes asked, "Why can't there be psycho-physical laws which are of a novel sort, just as the laws of electricity and magnetism were novelties from the standpoint of Newtonian mechanics?" Certainly we are pretty sure in the future to come across new ultimate laws of a novel type, but I expect them to relate simple constituents: for example, whatever ultimate particles are then in vogue. I cannot believe that ultimate laws of nature could relate simple constituents to configurations consisting of perhaps billions of neurons (and goodness knows how many billion billions of ultimate particles) all put together for all the world as though their main purpose in life was to be a negative feedback mechanism of a complicated sort. Such ultimate laws would be like nothing so far known in science. They have a queer "smell" to them. I am just unable to believe in the nomological danglers themselves, or in the laws whereby they would dangle. If any philosophical arguments seemed to compel us to believe in such things, I would suspect a catch in the argument. In any case it is the object of this paper to show that there are no philosophical arguments which compel us to be dualists.

The above is largely a confession of faith, but it explains why I find Wittgenstein's position (as I construe it) so congenial. For on this view there are, in a sense, no sensations. A man is a vast arrangement of physical particles, but there are not, over and above this, sensations or states of consciousness. There are just behavioral facts about this vast mechanism, such as that it expresses a temptation (behavior disposition) to say "there is a yellowish-red patch on the wall" or that it goes through a sophisticated sort of

wince, that is, says "I am in pain." Admittedly Wittgenstein says that though the sensation "is not a something," it is nevertheless "not a nothing either" (paragraph 304), but this need only mean that the word "ache" has a use. An ache is a thing, but only in the innocuous sense in which the plain man, in the first paragraph of Frege's *Foundations of Arithmetic*, answers the question "what is the number one?" by "a thing." It should be noted that when I assert that to say "I have a yellowish-orange after-image" is to express a temptation to assert the physical-object statement "there is a yellowish-orange patch on the wall," I mean that saying "I have a yellowish-orange after-image" is (partly) the exercise of the disposition[6] which is the temptation. It is not to *report* that I have the temptation, any more than is "I love you" normally a report that I love someone. Saying "I love you" is just part of the behavior which is the exercise of the disposition of loving someone.

Though, for the reasons given above, I am very receptive to the above "expressive" account of sensation statements, I do not feel that it will quite do the trick. Maybe this is because I have not thought it out sufficiently, but it does seem to me as though, when a person says "I have an after-image," he *is* making a genuine report, and that when he says "I have a pain," he *is* doing more than "replace pain-behavior," and that "this more" is not just to say that he is in distress. I am not so sure, however, that to admit this is to admit that there are nonphysical correlates of brain processes. Why should not sensations just be brain processes of a certain sort? There are, of course, well-known (as well as lesser-known) philosophical objections to the view that reports of sensations are reports of brain-processes, but I shall try to argue that these arguments are by no means as cogent as is commonly thought to be the case.

Let me first try to state more accurately the thesis that sensations are brain processes. It is not the thesis that, for example, "after-image" or "ache" means the same as "brain process of sort X" (where "X" is replaced by a description of a certain sort of brain process). It is that, in so far as "after-image" or "ache" is a report of a process, it is a report of a process that *happens to be* a brain process. It follows that the thesis does not claim that sensation statements can be *translated* into statements about brain processes.[7] Nor does it claim that the logic of a sensation statement is the same as that of a brain-process statement. All it claims is that in so far as a sensation statement is a report of something, that something is in fact a brain process. Sensations are nothing over and above brain processes. Nations are nothing "over and above" citizens, but this does not prevent the logic of nation statements being very different from the logic of citizen statements, nor does it insure the translatability of nation statements into citizen statements. (I do not, however, wish to assert that the relation of sensation statements to brain-process statements is very like that of nation statements to citizen statements. Nations do not just *happen to be* nothing over and above citizens, for example. I bring in the "nations" example merely to make a negative point: that the fact that the logic of A-statements is different from that of B-statements does not insure that A's are anything over and above B's.)

Remarks on identity. When I say that a sensation is a brain process or that lightning is an electric discharge, I am using "is" in the sense of strict identity. (Just as in the – in this case necessary – proposition "7 is identical with the smallest prime number greater than 5.") When I say that a sensation is a brain process or that lightning is an electric discharge I do not mean just that the sensation is somehow spatially or temporally continuous with the brain process or that the lightning is just spatially or temporally continuous with the discharge. When on the other hand I say that the successful general is the same person as the small boy who stole the apples I mean only that the successful general I see before me is a time slice[8] of the same four-dimensional object of which the small boy stealing apples is an earlier time slice. However, the four-dimensional object which has the general-I-see-before-me for its late time slice is identical in the strict sense with the four-dimensional object which has the small-boy-stealing-apples for an early time slice. I distinguish these two senses of "is identical with" because I wish to make it clear that the brain-process doctrine asserts identity in the *strict* sense.

I shall now discuss various possible objections to the view that the processes reported in sensation statements are in fact processes in the brain. Most of us have met some of these objections in our first year as philosophy students. All the more reason to take a good look at them. Others of the objections will be more recondite and subtle.

Objection 1. Any illiterate peasant can talk perfectly well about his after-images, or how things look or feel to him, or about his aches and pains, and yet he may know nothing whatever about neurophysiology. A man may, like Aristotle, believe that the brain is an organ for cooling the body without any impairment of his ability to make true statements about his sensations. Hence the things we are talking about when we describe our sensations cannot be processes in the brain.

Reply. You might as well say that a nation of slug-abeds, who never saw the morning star or knew of its existence, or who had never thought of the expression "the Morning Star," but who used the expression "the Evening Star" perfectly well, could not use this expression to refer to the same entity as we refer to (and describe as) "the Morning Star."[9]

You may object that the Morning Star is in a sense not the very same thing as the Evening Star, but only something spatio-temporally continuous with it. That is, you may say that the Morning Star is not the Evening Star in the strict sense of "identity" that I distinguished earlier. I can perhaps forestall this objection by considering the slug-abeds to be New Zealanders and the early risers to be Englishmen. Then the thing the New Zealanders describe as "the Morning Star" could be the very same thing (in the strict sense) as the Englishmen describe as "the Evening Star." And yet they could be ignorant of this fact.

There is, however, a more plausible example. Consider lightning.[10] Modern physical science tells us that lightning is a certain kind of electrical discharge due to ionization of clouds of water-vapor in the atmosphere. This, it is now believed, is what the true nature of lightning is. Note that there are not two things: a flash of lightning and an electrical discharge. There is one thing, a flash of lightning, which is described scientifically as an electrical discharge to the earth from a cloud of ionized water-molecules. The case is not at all like that of explaining a footprint by reference to a burglar. We say that what lightning really is, what its true nature as revealed by science is, is an electric discharge. (It is not the true nature of a footprint to be a burglar.)

To forestall irrelevant objections, I should like to make it clear that by "lightning" I mean the publicly observable physical object, lightning, not a visual sense-datum of lightning. I say that the publicly observable physical object lightning is in fact the electric discharge, not just a correlate of it. The sense-datum, or at least the having of the sense-datum, the "look" of lightning, may well in my view be a correlate of the electric discharge. For in my view it is a brain state *caused* by the lightning. But we should no more confuse sensations of lightning with lightning than we confuse sensations of a table with the table.

In short, the reply to Objection 1 is that there can be contingent statements of the form "A is identical with B," and a person may well know that something is an A without knowing that it is a B. An illiterate peasant might well be able to talk about his sensations without knowing about his brain processes, just as he can talk about lightning though he knows nothing of electricity.

Objection 2. It is only a contingent fact (if it is a fact) that when we have a certain kind of sensation there is a certain kind of process in our brain. Indeed it is possible, though perhaps in the highest degree unlikely, that our present physiological theories will be as out of date as the ancient theory connecting mental processes with goings on in the heart. It follows that when we report a sensation we are not reporting a brain-process.

Reply. The objection certainly proves that when we say "I have an after-image" we cannot *mean* something of the form "I have such and such a brain-process." But this does not show that what we report (having an after-image) is not *in fact* a brain process. "I see lightning" does not *mean* "I see an electric discharge." Indeed, it is logically possible (though highly unlikely) that the electrical discharge account of lightning might one day be given up. Again, "I see the Evening Star" does not *mean* the same as "I see the Morning Star," and yet "the Evening Star and the Morning Star are one and the same thing" is a contingent proposition. Possibly Objection 2 derives some of its apparent strength from a "Fido" – Fido theory of meaning. If the meaning of an expression were what the expression named, then of course it *would* follow from the fact that "sensation" and "brain-process" have different meanings that they cannot name one and the same thing.

Objection 3.[11] Even if Objections 1 and 2 do not prove that sensations are something over and above brain-processes, they do prove that the qualities of sensations are something over and above the qualities of brain-processes. That is, it may be possible to get out of asserting the existence of irreducibly psychic processes, but not out of asserting the existence of irreducibly psychic *properties*. For suppose we identify the Morning Star with the Evening Star. Then there must be some properties which logically imply that of being the Morning Star, and quite distinct properties which entail that of being the Evening Star. Again, there must be some properties (for example, that of being a yellow flash) which are logically distinct from those in the physicalist story.

Indeed, it might be thought that the objection succeeds at one jump. For consider the property of "being a yellow flash." It might seem that this property lies inevitably outside the physicalist framework within which I am trying to work (either by "yellow" being an objective emergent property of physical objects, or else by being a power to produce yellow sense-data, where "yellow," in this second instantiation of the word, refers to a purely phenomenal or introspectible quality). I must therefore digress for a moment and indicate how I deal with secondary qualities. I shall concentrate on color.

First of all, let me introduce the concept of a normal percipient. One person is more a normal percipient than another if he can make color discriminations that the other cannot. For example, if A can pick a lettuce leaf out of a heap of cabbage leaves, whereas B cannot though he can pick a lettuce leaf out of a heap of beetroot leaves, then A is more normal than B. (I am assuming that A and B are not given time to distinguish the leaves by their slight difference in shape, and so forth.) From the concept of "more normal than" it is easy to see how we can introduce the concept of "normal." Of course, Eskimos may make the finest discriminations at the blue end of the spectrum, Hottentots at the red end. In this case the concept of a normal percipient is a slightly idealized one, rather like that of "the mean sun" in astronomical chronology. There is no need to go into such subtleties now. I say that "This is red" means something roughly like "A normal percipient would not easily pick this out of a clump of geranium petals though he would pick it out of a clump of lettuce leaves." Of course it does not exactly mean this: a person might know the meaning of "red" without knowing anything about geraniums, or even about normal percipients. But the point is that a person can be *trained* to say "This is red" of objects which would not easily be picked out of geranium petals by a normal percipient, and so on. (Note that even a color-blind person can reasonably assert that something is red, though of course he needs to use another human being, not just himself, as his "color meter.") This account of secondary qualities explains their unimportance in physics. For obviously the discriminations and lack of discriminations made by a very complex neurophysiological mechanism are hardly likely to correspond to simple and nonarbitrary distinctions in nature.

I therefore elucidate colors as powers, in Locke's sense, to evoke certain sorts of discriminatory responses in human beings. They are also, of course, powers to cause sensations in human beings (an account still nearer Locke's). But these sensations, I am arguing, are identifiable with brain processes.

Now how do I get over the objection that a sensation can be identified with a brain process only if it has some phenomenal property, not possessed by brain processes, whereby one-half of the identification may be, so to speak, pinned down?

My suggestion is as follows. When a person says, "I see a yellowish-orange after-image," he is saying something like this: "*There is something going on which is like what is going on when* I have my eyes open, am awake, and there is an orange illuminated in good light in front of me, that is, when I really see an orange." (And there is no reason why a person should not say the same thing when he is having a veridical sense-datum, so long as we construe "like" in the last sentence in such a sense that something can be like itself.) Notice that the italicized words, namely "there is something going on which is like what is going on when," are all quasi-logical or topic-neutral words. This explains why the ancient Greek peasant's reports about his sensations can be neutral between dualistic metaphysics or my materialistic metaphysics. It explains how sensations can be brain-processes and yet how those

who report them need know nothing about brain-processes. For he reports them only very abstractly as "something going on which is like what is going on when . . ." Similarly, a person may say "someone is in the room," thus reporting truly that the doctor is in the room, even though he has never heard of doctors. (There are not two people in the room: "someone" *and* the doctor.) This account of sensation statements also explains the singular elusiveness of "raw feels" – why no one seems to be able to pin any properties on them.[12] Raw feels, in my view, are colorless for the very same reason that *something* is colorless. This does not mean that sensations do not have properties, for if they are brain-processes they certainly have properties. It only means that in speaking of them as being like or unlike one another we need not know or mention these properties.

This, then, is how I would reply to Objection 3. The strength of my reply depends on the possibility of our being able to report that one thing is like another without being able to state the respect in which it is like. I am not sure whether this is so or not, and that is why I regard Objection 3 as the strongest with which I have to deal.

Objection 4.   The after-image is not in physical space. The brain-process is. So the after-image is not a brain-process.

Reply.   This is an *ignoratio elenchi*. I am not arguing that the after-image is a brain-process, but that the experience of having an after-image is a brain-process. It is the *experience* which is reported in the introspective report. Similarly, if it is objected that the after-image is yellowy-orange but that a surgeon looking into your brain would see nothing yellowy-orange, my reply is that it is the experience of seeing yellowy-orange that is being described, and this experience is not a yellowy-orange something. So to say that a brain-process cannot be yellowy-orange is not to say that a brain-process cannot in fact be the experience of having a yellowy-orange after-image. There is, in a sense, no such thing as an after-image or a sense-datum, though there is such a thing as the experience of having an image, and this experience is described indirectly in material object language, not in phenomenal language, for there is no such thing.[13] We describe the experience by saying, in effect, that it is like the experience we have when, for example, we really see a yellowy-orange patch on the wall. Trees and wallpaper can be green, but not the experience of seeing or imagining a tree or wallpaper. (Or if they are described as green or yellow this can only be in a derived sense.)

Objection 5.   It would make sense to say of a molecular movement in the brain that it is swift or slow, straight or circular, but it makes no sense to say this of the experience of seeing something yellow.

Reply.   So far we have not given sense to talk of experiences as swift or slow, straight or circular. But I am not claiming that "experience" and "brain-process" mean the same or even that they have the same logic. "Somebody" and "the doctor" do not have the same logic, but this does not lead us to suppose that talking about somebody telephoning is talking about someone over and above, say, the doctor. The ordinary man when he reports an experience is reporting that something is going on, but he leaves it open as to what sort of thing is going on, whether in a material solid medium, or perhaps in some sort of gaseous medium, or even perhaps in some sort of nonspatial medium (if this makes sense). All that I am saying is that "experience" and "brain-process" may in fact refer to the same thing, and if so we may easily adopt a convention (which is not a change in our present rules for the use of experience words but an addition to them) whereby it would make sense to talk of an experience in terms appropriate to physical processes.

Objection 6.   Sensations are private, brain processes are *public*. If I sincerely say, "I see a yellowish-orange after-image" and I am not making a verbal mistake, then I cannot be wrong. But I can be wrong about a brain-process. The scientist looking into my brain might be having an illusion. Moreover, it makes sense to say that two or more people are observing the same brain-process but not that two or more people are reporting the same inner experience.

Reply.   This shows that the language of introspective reports has a different logic from the language of material processes. It is obvious that until the brain-process theory is much improved and widely accepted there will be no *criteria* for saying "Smith has an experience of such-and-such a sort" *except* Smith's introspective reports. So we have adopted a rule of language that (normally) what Smith says goes.

Objection 7.   I can imagine myself turned to stone and yet having images, aches, pains, and so on.

Reply.   I can imagine that the electrical theory of lightning is false, that lightning is some sort of purely optical phenomenon. I can imagine that lightning is not an electrical discharge. I can imagine that the Evening Star is not the Morning Star. But it is. All the objection shows is that "experience" and "brain-process" do not have the same meaning. It does not show that an experience is not in fact a brain process.

This objection is perhaps much the same as one which can be summed up by the slogan: "What can be composed of nothing cannot be composed of anything."[14] The argument goes as follows: on the brain-process thesis the identity between the brain-process and the experience is a contingent one. So it is logically possible that there should be no brain-process, and no process of any other sort, either (no heart process, no kidney process, no liver process). There would be the experience but no "corresponding" physiological process with which we might be able to identify it empirically.

I suspect that the objector is thinking of the experience as a ghostly entity. So it is composed of something, not of nothing, after all. On his view it is composed of ghost stuff, and on mine it is composed of brain stuff. Perhaps the counter-reply will be[15] that the experience is simple and uncompounded, and so it is not composed of anything after all. This seems to be a quibble, for, if it were taken seriously, the remark "What can be composed of nothing cannot be composed of anything" could be recast as an a priori argument against Democritus and atomism and for Descartes and infinite divisibility. And it seems odd that a question of this sort could be settled a priori. We must therefore construe the word "composed" in a very weak sense, which would allow us to say that even an indivisible atom is composed of something (namely, itself). The dualist cannot really say that an experience can be composed of nothing. For he holds that experiences are something over and above material processes, that is, that they are a sort of ghost stuff. (Or perhaps ripples in an underlying ghost stuff.) I say that the dualist's hypothesis is a perfectly intelligible one. But I say that experiences are not to be identified with ghost stuff but with brain stuff. This is another hypothesis, and in my view a very plausible one. The present argument cannot knock it down a priori.

Objection 8. The "beetle in the box" objection (see Wittgenstein, *Philosophical Investigations*, paragraph 293). How could descriptions of experiences, if these are genuine reports, get a foothold in language? For any rule of language must have public criteria for its correct application.

Reply. The change from describing how things are to describing how we feel is just a change from uninhibitedly saying "this is so" to saying "this looks so." That is, when the naive person might be tempted to say, "There is a patch of light on the wall which moves whenever I move my eyes" or "A pin is being stuck into me," we have learned how to resist this temptation and say "It *looks as though* there is a patch of light on the wallpaper" or "It *feels as though* someone were sticking a pin into me." The introspective account tells us about the individual's state of consciousness in the same way as does "I see a patch of light" or "I feel a pin being stuck into me": it differs from the corresponding perception statement in so far as (a) in the perception statement the individual "goes beyond the evidence of his senses" in describing his environment and (b) in the introspective report he withholds descriptive epithets he is inclined to ascribe to the environment, perhaps because he suspects that they may not be appropriate to the actual state of affairs. Psychologically speaking, the change from talking about the environment to talking about one's state of consciousness is simply a matter of inhibiting descriptive reactions not justified by appearances alone, and of disinhibiting descriptive reactions which are normally inhibited because the individual has learned that they are unlikely to provide a reliable guide to the state of the environment in the prevailing circumstances.[16] To say that something looks green to me is to say that my experience is like the experience I get when I see something that really is green. In my reply to Objection 3, I pointed out the extreme openness or generality of statements which report experiences. This explains why there is no language of private qualities. (Just as "someone," unlike "the doctor," is a colorless word.)[17]

If it is asked what is the difference between those brain processes which, in my view, are experiences

and those brain processes which are not, I can only reply that this is at present unknown. But it does not seem to me altogether fanciful to conjecture that the difference may in part be that between perception and reception (in Dr D. M. MacKay's terminology) and that the type of brain process which is an experience might be identifiable with MacKay's active "matching response."[18]

I have now considered a number of objections to the brain-process thesis. I wish now to conclude by some remarks on the logical status of the thesis itself. U. T. Place seems to hold that it is a straight-out scientific hypothesis.[19] If so, he is partly right and partly wrong. If the issue is between (say) a brain-process thesis and a heart thesis, or a liver thesis, or a kidney thesis, then the issue is a purely empirical one, and the verdict is overwhelmingly in favor of the brain. The right sorts of things don't go on in the heart, liver, or kidney, nor do these organs possess the right sort of complexity of structure. On the other hand, if the issue is between a brain-or-heart-or-liver-or-kidney thesis (that is, some form of materialism) on the one hand and epiphenomenalism on the other hand, then the issue is not an empirical one. For there is no conceivable experiment which could decide between materialism and epiphenomenalism. This latter issue is not like the average straight-out empirical issue in science, but like the issue between the nineteenth-century English naturalist Philip Gosse[20] and the orthodox geologists and paleontologists of his day. According to Gosse, the earth was created about 4000 B.C. exactly as described in *Genesis*, with twisted rock strata, "evidence" of erosion, and so forth, and all sorts of fossils, all in their appropriate strata, just as if the usual evolutionist story had been true. Clearly this theory is in a sense irrefutable: no evidence can possibly tell against it. Let us ignore the theological setting in which Philip Gosse's hypothesis had been placed, thus ruling out objections of a theological kind, such as "what a queer God who would go to such elaborate lengths to deceive us." Let us suppose that it is held that the universe just *began* in 4004 B.C. with the initial conditions just everywhere as they were in 4004 B.C., and in particular that our own planet began with sediment in the rivers, eroded cliffs, fossils in the rocks, and so on. No scientist would ever entertain this as a serious hypothesis, consistent though it is with all possible evidence. The hypothesis offends against the principles of parsimony and simplicity. There would be far too many brute and inexplicable facts. Why are pterodactyl bones just as they are ? No explanation in terms of the evolution of pterodactyls from earlier forms of life would any longer be possible. We would have millions of facts about the world as it was in 4004 B.C. that just have to be *accepted*.

The issue between the brain-process theory and epiphenomenalism seems to be of the above sort. (Assuming that a behavioristic reduction of introspective reports is not possible.) If it be agreed that there are no cogent philosophical arguments which force us into accepting dualism, and if the brain process theory and dualism are equally consistent with the facts, then the principles of parsimony and simplicity seem to me to decide overwhelmingly in favor of the brain-process theory. As I pointed out earlier, dualism involves a large number of irreducible psychophysical laws (whereby the "nomological danglers" dangle) of a queer sort, that just have to be taken on trust, and are just as difficult to swallow as the irreducible facts about the paleontology of the earth with which we are faced on Philip Gosse's theory.

Notes

1 This paper takes its departure from arguments to be found in U. T. Place's "Is Consciousness a Brain Process?" (*British Journal of Psychology*, XLVII, 1956, 44–50). I have had the benefit of discussing Place's thesis in a good many universities in the United States and Australia, and I hope that the present paper answers objections to his thesis which Place has not considered, and presents his thesis in a more nearly unobjectionable form. This paper is meant also to supplement "The 'Mental' and the 'Physical'," by H. Feigl (in *Minnesota Studies in the Philosophy of Science*, II, 370–497), which argues for much the same thesis as Place's.

2 Some philosophers of my acquaintance, who have the advantage over me in having known Wittgenstein, would say that this interpretation of him is too behavioristic. However, it seems to me a very natural interpretation of his printed words, and whether or not it is Wittgenstein's real view it is certainly an interesting and important one. I wish to consider it here as a possible rival both

to the "brain-process" thesis and to straight-out old-fashioned dualism.

3 See Ryle, *Concept of Mind* (New York, 1949), p. 93.

4 On this point see Paul Oppenheim and Hilary Putnam, "Unity of Science as a Working Hypothesis," in *Minnesota Studies in the Philosophy of Science*, II, 3–36; also my note "Plausible Reasoning in Philosophy," *Mind*, LXVI (1957), 75–8.

5 Feigl, *op. cit.*, p. 428.

6 Wittgenstein did not like the word "disposition." I am using it to put in a nutshell (and perhaps inaccurately) the view which I am attributing to Wittgenstein. I should like to repeat that I do not wish to claim that my interpretation of Wittgenstein is correct. Some of those who knew him do not interpret him in this way. It is merely a view which I find myself extracting from his printed words and which I think is important and worth discussing for its own sake.

7 See Place, *op. cit.*, p. 45, near top, and Feigl, *op. cit.*, p. 390, near top.

8 See J. H. Woodger, *Theory Construction* (Chicago, 1939), p. 38 (*International Encyclopedia of Unified Science*, Vol. 2, No. 5). I here permit myself to speak loosely. For warnings against possible ways of going wrong with this sort of talk, see my note "Spatialising Time," *Mind*, LXIV (1955), 239–41.

9 Cf. Feigl, *op. cit.*, p. 439.

10 See Place, *op. cit.*, p. 47; also Feigl, *op. cit.*, p. 438.

11 I think this objection was first put to me by Professor Max Black. I think it is the most subtle of any of those I have considered, and the one which I am least confident of having satisfactorily met.

12 See B. A. Farrell, "Experience," *Mind*, LIX (1950), especially 174.

13 Dr J. R. Smythies claims that a sense-datum language could be taught independently of the material object language ("A Note on the Fallacy of the 'Phenomenological Fallacy,'" *British Journal of Psychology*, XLVIII, 1957, 141–4). I am not so sure of this: there must be some public criteria for a person having got a rule wrong before we can teach him the rule. I suppose someone might *accidentally* learn color words by Dr Smythies' procedure. I am not, of course, denying that we can learn a sense-datum language in the sense that we can learn to report our experience. Nor would Place deny it.

14 I owe this objection to Mr C. B. Martin. I gather that he no longer wishes to maintain this objection, at any rate in its present form.

15 Martin did not make this reply, but one of his students did.

16 I owe this point to Place, in correspondence.

17 The "beetle in the box" objection is, *if it is sound,*
    an objection to *any* view, and in particular the
    Cartesian one, that introspective reports are gen-
    uine reports. So it is no objection to a weaker
    thesis that I would be concerned to uphold,
    namely, that if introspective reports of "experiences"
    are genuinely reports, then the things they are
    reports of are in fact brain processes.

18 See his article "Towards an Information-Flow
    model of Human Behaviour," *British Journal of
    Psychology,* XLVII (1956), 30–43.
19 *Op. cit.*
20 See the entertaining account of Gosse's book
    Omphalos by Martin Gardner in *Fads and
    Fallacies in the Name of Science* (2nd ed., New York,
    1957).

12

What Is It Like to Be a Bat?

Thomas Nagel

Consciousness is what makes the mind-body problem really intractable. Perhaps that is why current discussions of the problem give it little attention or get it obviously wrong. The recent wave of reductionist euphoria has produced several analyses of mental phenomena and mental concepts designed to explain the possibility of some variety of materialism, psychophysical identification, or reduction.[1] But the problems dealt with are those common to this type of reduction and other types, and what makes the mind-body problem unique, and unlike the water-H_2O problem or the Turing machine-IBM machine problem or the lightning-electrical discharge problem or the gene-DNA problem or the oak tree-hydrocarbon problem, is ignored.

Every reductionist has his favorite analogy from modern science. It is most unlikely that any of these unrelated examples of successful reduction will shed light on the relation of mind to brain. But philosophers share the general human weakness for explanations of what is incomprehensible in terms suited for what is familiar and well understood, though entirely different. This has led to the acceptance of implausible accounts of the mental largely because they would permit familiar kinds of reduction. I shall try to explain why the usual examples do not help us to understand the relation between mind and body – why, indeed, we have at present no conception of what an explanation of the physical nature of a mental phenomenon would be. Without consciousness the mind-body problem would be much less interesting. With consciousness it seems hopeless. The most important and characteristic feature of conscious mental phenomena is very poorly understood. Most reductionist theories do not even try to explain it. And careful examination will show that no currently available concept of reduction is applicable to it. Perhaps a new theoretical form can be devised for the purpose, but such a solution, if it exists, lies in the distant intellectual future.

Conscious experience is a widespread phenomenon. It occurs at many levels of animal life, though we cannot be sure of its presence in the simpler organisms, and it is very difficult to say in general what provides evidence of it. (Some extremists have been prepared to deny it even of mammals other than man.) No doubt it occurs in countless forms totally unimaginable to us, on other planets in other solar systems throughout the universe. But no matter how the form may vary, the fact that an organism has conscious experience *at all* means, basically, that there is something it is like to *be* that organism. There may be further implications about the form of the experience; there may even (though I doubt it)

Thomas Nagel, "What Is It Like to Be a Bat?" *The Philosophical Review* 83, no. 4 (October 1974), pp. 435–50. © 1974 by Thomas Nagel. Reprinted by permission of the author.

be implications about the behavior of the organism. But fundamentally an organism has conscious mental states if and only if there is something that it is like to *be* that organism – something it is like *for* the organism.

We may call this the subjective character of experience. It is not captured by any of the familiar, recently devised reductive analyses of the mental, for all of them are logically compatible with its absence. It is not analyzable in terms of any explanatory system of functional states, or intentional states, since these could be ascribed to robots or automata that behaved like people though they experienced nothing.[2] It is not analyzable in terms of the causal role of experiences in relation to typical human behavior – for similar reasons.[3] I do not deny that conscious mental states and events cause behavior, nor that they may be given functional characterizations. I deny only that this kind of thing exhausts their analysis. Any reductionist program has to to be based on an analysis of what is to be reduced. If the analysis leaves something out, the problem will be falsely posed. It is useless to base the defense of materialism on any analysis of mental phenomena that fails to deal explicitly with their subjective character. For there is no reason to suppose that a reduction which seems plausible when no attempt is made to account for consciousness can be extended to include consciousness. Without some idea, therefore, of what the subjective character of experience is, we cannot know what is required of a physicalist theory.

While an account of the physical basis of mind must explain many things, this appears to be the most difficult. It is impossible to exclude the phenomenological features of experience from a reduction in the same way that one excludes the phenomenal features of an ordinary substance from a physical or chemical reduction of it – namely, by explaining them as effects on the minds of human observers.[4] If physicalism is to be defended, the phenomenological features must themselves be given a physical account. But when we examine their subjective character it seems that such a result is impossible. The reason is that every subjective phenomenon is essentially connected with a single point of view, and it seems inevitable that an objective, physical theory will abandon that point of view.

Let me first try to state the issue somewhat more fully than by referring to the relation between the subjective and the objective, or between the *pour-soi* and the *en-soi*. This is far from easy. Facts about what it is like to be an *X* are very peculiar, so peculiar that some may be inclined to doubt their reality, or the significance of claims about them. To illustrate the connection between subjectivity and a point of view, and to make evident the importance of subjective features, it will help to explore the matter in relation to an example that brings out clearly the divergence between the two types of conception, subjective and objective.

I assume we all believe that bats have experience. After all, they are mammals, and there is no more doubt that they have experience than that mice or pigeons or whales have experience. I have chosen bats instead of wasps or flounders because if one travels too far down the phylogenetic tree, people gradually shed their faith that there is experience there at all. Bats, although more closely related to us than those other species, nevertheless present a range of activity and a sensory apparatus so different from ours that the problem I want to pose is exceptionally vivid (though it certainly could be raised with other species). Even without the benefit of philosophical reflection, anyone who has spent some time in an enclosed space with an excited bat knows what it is to encounter a fundamentally *alien* form of life.

I have said that the essence of the belief that bats have experience is that there is something that it is like to be a bat. Now we know that most bats (the microchiroptera, to be precise) perceive the external world primarily by sonar, or echolocation, detecting the reflections, from objects within range, of their own rapid, subtly modulated, high-frequency shrieks. Their brains are designed to correlate the outgoing impulses with the subsequent echoes, and the information thus acquired enables bats to make precise discriminations of distance, size, shape, motion, and texture comparable to those we make by vision. But bat sonar, though clearly a form of perception, is not similar in its operation to any sense that we possess, and there is no reason to suppose that it is subjectively like anything we can experience or imagine. This appears to create difficulties for the notion of what it is like to be a bat. We must consider whether any method will permit us to extrapolate to the inner life of the bat from our own case,[5] and if not, what alternative methods there may be for understanding the notion.

Our own experience provides the basic material for our imagination, whose range is therefore limited. It will not help to try to imagine that one has webbing on one's arms, which enables one to fly around at dusk and dawn catching insects in one's mouth; that one has very poor vision, and perceives the surrounding world by a system of reflected high-frequency sound signals; and that one spends the day hanging upside down by one's feet in an attic. In so far as I can imagine this (which is not very far), it tells me only what it would be like for *me* to behave as a bat behaves. But that is not the question. I want to know what it is like for a *bat* to be a bat. Yet if I try to imagine this, I am restricted to the resources of my own mind, and those resources are inadequate to the task. I cannot perform it either by imagining additions to my present experience, or by imagining segments gradually subtracted from it, or by imagining some combination of additions, subtractions, and modifications.

To the extent that I could look and behave like a wasp or a bat without changing my fundamental structure, my experiences would not be anything like the experiences of those animals. On the other hand, it is doubtful that any meaning can be attached to the supposition that I should possess the internal neurophysiological constitution of a bat. Even if I could by gradual degrees be transformed into a bat, nothing in my present constitution enables me to imagine what the experiences of such a future stage of myself thus metamorphosed would be like. The best evidence would come from the experiences of bats, if we only knew what they were like.

So if extrapolation from our own case is involved in the idea of what it is like to be a bat, the extrapolation must be incompletable. We cannot form more than a schematic conception of what it *is* like. For example, we may ascribe general *types* of experience on the basis of the animal's structure and behavior. Thus we describe bat sonar as a form of three-dimensional forward perception; we believe that bats feel some versions of pain, fear, hunger, and lust, and that they have other, more familiar types of perception besides sonar. But we believe that these experiences also have in each case a specific subjective character, which it is beyond our ability to conceive. And if there is conscious life elsewhere in the universe, it is likely that some of it will not be describable even in the most general experiential terms available to us.[6] (The problem is not confined to exotic cases, however, for it exists between one person and another. The subjective character of the experience of a person deaf and blind from birth is not accessible to me, for example, nor presumably is mine to him. This does not prevent us each from believing that the other's experience has such a subjective character.)

If anyone is inclined to deny that we can believe in the existence of facts like this whose exact nature we cannot possibly conceive, he should reflect that in contemplating the bats we are in much the same position that intelligent bats or Martians[7] would occupy if they tried to form a conception of what it was like to be us. The structure of their own minds might make it impossible for them to succeed, but we know they would be wrong to conclude that there is not anything precise that it is like to be us: that only certain general types of mental state could be ascribed to us (perhaps perception and appetite would be concepts common to us both; perhaps not). We know they would be wrong to draw such a skeptical conclusion because we know what it is like to be us. And we know that while it includes an enormous amount of variation and complexity, and while we do not possess the vocabulary to describe it adequately, its subjective charater is highly specific, and in some respects describable in terms that can be understood only by creatures like us. The fact that we cannot expect ever to accommodate in our language a detailed description of Martian or bat phenomenology should not lead us to dismiss as meaningless the claim that bats and Martians have experiences fully comparable in richness of detail to our own. It would be fine if someone were to develop concepts and a theory that enabled us to think about those things; but such an understanding may be permanently denied to us by the limits of our nature. And to deny the reality or logical significance of what we can never describe or understand is the crudest form of cognitive dissonance.

This brings us to the edge of a topic that requires much more discussion than I can give it here: namely, the relation between facts on the one hand and conceptual schemes or systems of representation on the other. My realism about the subjective domain in all its forms implies a belief in the existence of facts beyond the reach of human concepts. Certainly it is possible for a human being to believe that there are facts which humans never *will* possess the requisite concepts to represent or comprehend. Indeed, it would be foolish to doubt this, given the finiteness of humanity's expectations. After all, there would have been transfinite numbers even if everyone had been wiped out by the Black Death before Cantor discovered them. But one might also believe that there are facts which *could* not ever be represented or comprehended by human beings, even if the species lasted forever – simply because our structure does not permit us to operate with concepts of the requisite type. This impossibility might even be observed by other beings, but it is not clear that the existence of such beings, or the possibility of their existence, is a precondition of the significance of the hypothesis that there are humanly inaccessible facts. (After all, the nature of beings with access to humanly inaccessible facts is presumably itself a humanly inaccessible fact.) Reflection on what it is like to be a bat seems to lead us, therefore, to the conclusion that there are facts that do not consist in the truth of propositions expressible in a human language. We can be compelled to recognize the existence of such facts without being able to state or comprehend them.

I shall not pursue this subject, however. Its bearing on the topic before us (namely, the mind-body problem) is that it enables us to make a general observation about the subjective character of experience. Whatever may be the status of facts about what it is like to be a human being, or a bat, or a Martian, these appear to be facts that embody a particular point of view.

I am not adverting here to the alleged privacy of experience to its possessor. The point of view in question is not one accessible only to a single individual. Rather it is a *type*. It is often possible to take up a point of view other than one's own, so the comprehension of such facts is not limited to one's own case. There is a sense in which phenomenological facts are perfectly objective: one person can know or say of another what the quality of the other's experience is. They are

subjective, however, in the sense that even this objective ascription of experience is possible only for someone sufficiently similar to the object of ascription to be able to adopt his point of view – to understand the ascription in the first person as well as in the third, so to speak. The more different from oneself the other experiencer is, the less success one can expect with this enterprise. In our own case we occupy the relevant point of view, but we will have as much difficulty understanding our own experience properly if we approach it from another point of view as we would if we tried to understand the experience of another species without taking up *its* point of view.[8]

This bears directly on the mind-body problem. For if the facts of experience – facts about what it is like *for* the experiencing organism – are accessible only from one point of view, then it is a mystery how the true character of experiences could be revealed in the physical operation of that organism. The latter is a domain of objective facts *par excellence* – the kind that can be observed and understood from many points of view and by individuals with differing perceptual systems. There are no comparable imaginative obstacles to the acquisition of knowledge about bat neurophysiology by human scientists, and intelligent bats or Martians might learn more about the human brain than we ever will.

This is not by itself an argument against reduction. A Martian scientist with no understanding of visual perception could understand the rainbow, or lightning, or clouds as physical phenomena, though he would never be able to understand the human concepts of rainbow, lightning, or cloud, or the place these things occupy in our phenomenal world. The objective nature of the things picked out by these concepts could be apprehended by him because, although the concepts themselves are connected with a particular point of view and a particular visual phenomenology, the things apprehended from that point of view are not: they are observable from the point of view but external to it; hence they can be comprehended from other points of view also, either by the same organisms or by others. Lightning has an objective character that is not exhausted by its visual appearance, and this can be investigated by a Martian without vision. To be precise, it has a *more* objective character than is revealed in its visual appearance. In speaking of the move from subjective to objective characterization, I wish to remain noncommittal about the existence of an end point, the completely objective intrinsic nature of the thing, which one might or might not be able to reach. It may be more accurate to think of objectivity as a direction in which the understanding can travel. And in understanding a phenomenon like lightning, it is legitimate to go as far away as one can from a strictly human viewpoint.[9]

In the case of experience, on the other hand, the connection with a particular point of view seems much closer. It is difficult to understand what could be meant by the *objective* character of an experience, apart from the particular point of view from which its subject apprehends it. After all, what would be left of what it was like to be a bat if one removed the viewpoint of the bat? But if experience does not have, in addition to its subjective character, an objective nature that can be apprehended from many different points of view, then how can it be supposed that a Martian investigating my brain might be observing physical processes which were my mental processes (as he might observe physical processes which were bolts of lightning), only from a different point of view? How, for that matter, could a human physiologist observe them from another point of view?[10]

We appear to be faced with a general difficulty about psychophysical reduction. In other areas the process of reduction is a move in the direction of greater objectivity, toward a more accurate view of the real nature of things. This is accomplished by reducing our dependence on individual or species-specific points of view toward the object of investigation. We describe it not in terms of the impressions it makes on our senses, but in terms of its more general effects and of properties detectable by means other than the human senses. The less it depends on a specifically human viewpoint, the more objective is our description. It is possible to follow this path because although the concepts and ideas we employ in thinking about the external world are initially applied from a point of view that involves our perceptual apparatus, they are used by us to refer to things beyond themselves – toward which we *have* the phenomenal point of view. Therefore we can abandon it in favor of another, and still be thinking about the same things.

Experience itself, however, does not seem to fit the pattern. The idea of moving from appearance to reality seems to make no sense here. What is the analogue in this case to pursuing a more objective understanding of the same phenomena by abandoning the initial subjective viewpoint toward them in favor of another that is more objective but concerns the same thing? Certainly it *appears* unlikely that we will get closer to the real nature of human experience by leaving behind the particularity of our human point of view and striving for a description in terms accessible to beings that could not imagine what it was like to be us. If the subjective character of experience is fully comprehensible only from one point of view, then any shift to greater objectivity – that is, less attachment to a specific viewpoint – does not take us nearer to the real nature of the phenomenon: it takes us farther away from it.

In a sense, the seeds of this objection to the reducibility of experience are already detectable in successful cases of reduction; for in discovering sound to be, in reality, a wave phenomenon in air or other media, we leave behind one viewpoint to take up another, and the auditory, human or animal viewpoint that we leave behind remains unreduced. Members of radically different species may both understand the same physical events in objective terms, and this does not require that they understand the phenomenal forms in which those events appear to the senses of members of the other species. Thus it is a condition of their referring to a common reality that their more particular viewpoints are not part of the common reality that they both apprehend. The reduction can succeed only if the species-specific viewpoint is omitted from what is to be reduced.

But while we are right to leave this point of view aside in seeking a fuller understanding of the external world, we cannot ignore it permanently, since it is the essence of the internal world, and not merely a point of view on it. Most of the neobehaviorism of recent philosophical psychology results from the effort to substitute an objective concept of mind for the real thing, in order to have nothing left over which cannot be reduced. If we acknowledge that a physical theory of mind must account for the subjective character of experience, we must admit that no presently available conception gives us a clue how this could be done. The problem is unique. If mental processes are indeed physical processes, then there is something it is like, intrinsically,[11] to undergo certain physical processes. What it is for such a thing to be the case remains a mystery.

What moral should be drawn from these reflections, and what should be done next? It would be a mistake to conclude that physicalism must be false. Nothing is proved by the inadequacy of physicalist hypotheses that assume a faulty objective analysis of mind. It would be truer to say that physicalism is a position we cannot understand because we do not at present have any conception of how it might be true. Perhaps it will be thought unreasonable to require such a conception as a condition of understanding. After all, it might be said, the meaning of physicalism is clear enough: mental states are states of the body; mental events are physical events. We do not know *which* physical states and events they are, but that should not prevent us from understanding the hypothesis. What could be clearer than the words "is" and "are"?

But I believe it is precisely this apparent clarity of the word "is" that is deceptive. Usually, when we are told that *X* is *Y* we know *how* it is supposed to be true, but that depends on a conceptual or theoretical background and is not conveyed by the "is" alone. We know how both "*X*" and "*Y*" refer, and the kinds of things to which they refer, and we have a rough idea how the two referential paths might converge on a single thing, be it an object, a person, a process, an event, or whatever. But when the two terms of the identification are very disparate it may not be so clear how it could be true. We may not have even a rough idea of how the two referential paths could converge, or what kind of things they might converge on, and a theoretical framework may have to be supplied to enable us to understand this. Without the framework, an air of mysticism surrounds the identification.

This explains the magical flavor of popular presentations of fundamental scientific discoveries, given out as propositions to which one must subscribe without really understanding them. For example, people are now told at an early age that all matter is really energy. But despite the fact that they know what "is" means, most of them never form a conception of what makes this claim true, because they lack the theoretical background.

At the present time the status of physicalism is similar to that which the hypothesis that matter is energy would have had if uttered by a pre-Socratic philosopher. We do not have the beginnings of a conception of how it might be true. In order to understand the hypothesis that a mental event is a physical event, we require more than an understanding of the word "is." The idea of how a mental and a physical term might refer to the same thing is lacking, and the usual analogies with theoretical identification in other fields fail to supply it. They fail because if we construe the reference of mental terms to physical events on the usual model, we either get a reappearance of separate subjective events as the effects through which mental reference to physical events is secured, or else we get a false account of how mental terms refer (for example, a causal behaviorist one).

Strangely enough, we may have evidence for the truth of something we cannot really understand. Suppose a caterpillar is locked in a sterile safe by someone unfamiliar with insect metamorphosis, and weeks later the safe is reopened, revealing a butterfly. If the person knows that the safe has been shut the whole time, he has reason to believe that the butterfly is or was once the caterpillar, without having any idea in what sense this might be so. (One possibility is that the caterpillar contained a tiny winged parasite that devoured it and grew into the butterfly.)

It is conceivable that we are in such a position with regard to physicalism. Donald Davidson has argued that if mental events have physical causes and effects, they must have physical descriptions. He holds that we have reason to believe this even though we do not – and in fact *could* not – have a general psychophysical theory.[12] His argument applies to intentional mental events, but I think we also have some reason to believe that sensations are physical processes, without being in a position to understand how. Davidson's position is that certain physical events have irreducibly mental properties, and perhaps some view describable in this way is correct. But nothing of which we can now form a conception corresponds to it; nor have we any idea what a theory would be like that enabled us to conceive of it.[13]

Very little work has been done on the basic question (from which mention of the brain can be entirely omitted) whether any sense can be made of experiences' having an objective character at all. Does it make sense, in other words, to ask what my experiences are *really* like, as opposed to how they appear to me? We cannot genuinely understand the hypothesis that their nature is captured in a physical description unless we understand the more fundamental idea that they *have* an objective nature (or that objective processes can have a subjective nature).[14]

I should like to close with a speculative proposal. It may be possible to approach the gap between subjective and objective from another direction. Setting aside temporarily the relation between the mind and the brain, we can pursue a more objective understanding of the mental in its own right. At present we are completely unequipped to think about the subjective character of experience without relying on the imagination – without taking up the point of view of the experiential subject. This should be regarded as a challenge to form new concepts and devise a new method – an objective phenomenology not dependent on empathy or the imagination. Though presumably it would not capture everything, its goal would be to describe, at least in part, the subjective character of experiences in a form comprehensible to beings incapable of having those experiences.

We would have to develop such a phenomenology to describe the sonar experiences of bats; but it would also be possible to begin with humans. One might try, for example, to develop concepts that could be used to explain to a person blind from birth what it was like to see. One would reach a blank wall eventually, but it should be possible to devise a method of expressing in objective terms much more than we can at present, and with much greater precision. The loose intermodal analogies – for example, "Red is like the sound of a trumpet" – which crop up in discussions of this subject are of little use. That should be clear to anyone who has both heard a trumpet and seen red. But structural features of perception might be more accessible to objective description, even though something would be left out. And concepts alternative to those we learn in the first person may enable us to arrive at a kind of understanding even of our own experience which is denied us by the very ease of description and lack of distance that subjective concepts afford.

Apart from its own interest, a phenomenology that is in this sense objective may permit questions about the physical[15] basis of experience to assume a more intelligible form. Aspects of subjective experience that admitted this kind of objective description might be better candidates for objective explanations of a more familiar sort. But whether or not this guess is correct, it seems unlikely that any physical theory of mind can be contemplated until more thought has been given to the general problem of subjective and objective. Otherwise we cannot even pose the mind-body problem without sidestepping it.[16]

Notes

1   Examples are J. J. C. Smart, *Philosophy and Scientific Realism* (London, 1963); David K. Lewis, "An Argument for the Identity Theory," *Journal of Philosophy*, LXIII (1966), reprinted with addenda in David M. Rosenthal, *Materialism & the Mind-Body Problem* (Englewood Cliffs, NJ, 1971); Hilary Putnam, "Psychological Predicates" in Capitan and Merrill, *Art, Mind, & Religion* (Pittsburgh, 1967), reprinted in Rosenthal, *op. cit.*, as "The Nature of Mental States"; D. M. Armstrong, *A Materialist Theory of the Mind* (London, 1968); D. C. Dennett, *Content and Consciousness* (London, 1969). I have expressed earlier doubts in "Armstrong on the Mind," *Philosophical Review*, LXXIX (1970), 394–403; "Brain Bisection and the Unity of Consciousness," *Synthèse*, 22 (1971); and a review of Dennett, *Journal of Philosophy*, LXIX (1972). See also Saul Kripke, "Naming and Necessity" in Davidson and Harman, *Semantics of Natural Language* (Dordrecht, 1972), esp. pp. 334–42; and M. T. Thornton, "Ostensive Terms and Materialism," *The Monist*, 56 (1972).

2   Perhaps there could not actually be such robots. Perhaps anything complex enough to behave like a person would have experiences. But that, if true, is a fact which cannot be discovered merely by analyzing the concept of experience.

3   It is not equivalent to that about which we are incorrigible, both because we are not incorrigible about experience and because experience is present in animals lacking language and thought, who have no beliefs at all about their experiences.

4 Cf. Richard Rorty, "Mind-Body Identity, Privacy, and Categories," *The Review of Metaphysics*, XIX (1965), esp. 37–8.

5 By "our own case" I do not mean just "my own case," but rather the mentalistic ideas that we apply unproblematically to ourselves and other human beings.

6 Therefore the analogical form of the English expression "what it is *like*" is misleading. It does not mean "what (in our experience) it *resembles*," but rather "how it is for the subject himself."

7 Any intelligent extraterrestrial beings totally different from us.

8 It may be easier than I suppose to transcend inter-species barriers with the aid of the imagination. For example, blind people are able to detect objects near them by a form of sonar, using vocal clicks or taps of a cane. Perhaps if one knew what that was like, one could by extension imagine roughly what it was like to possess the much more refined sonar of a bat. The distance between oneself and other persons and other species can fall anywhere on a continuum. Even for other persons the understanding of what it is like to be them is only partial, and when one moves to species very different from oneself, a lesser degree of partial understanding may still be available. The imagination is remarkably flexible. My point, however, is not that we cannot *know* what it is like to be a bat. I am not raising that epistemological problem. My point is rather that even to form a *conception* of what it is like to be a bat (and a fortiori to know what it is like to be a bat) one must take up the bat's point of view. If one can take it up roughly, or partially, then one's conception will also be rough or partial. Or so it seems in our present state of understanding.

9 The problem I am going to raise can therefore be posed even if the distinction between more subjective and more objective descriptions or viewpoints can itself be made only within a larger human point of view. I do not accept this kind of conceptual relativism, but it need not be refuted to make the point that psychophysical reduction cannot be accommodated by the subjective-to-objective model familiar from other cases.

10 The problem is not just that when I look at the "Mona Lisa," my visual experience has a certain quality, no trace of which is to be found by someone looking into my brain. For even if he did observe there a tiny image of the "Mona Lisa," he would have no reason to identify it with the experience.

11 The relation would therefore not be a contingent one, like that of a cause and its distinct effect. It would be necessarily true that a certain physical state felt a certain way. Saul Kripke (*op. cit.*) argues that causal behaviorist and related analyses of the mental fail because they construe, e.g., "pain" as a merely contingent name of pains. The subjective character of an experience ("its immediate phenomenological quality" Kripke calls it [p. 340]) is the essential property left out by such analyses, and the one in virtue of which it is, necessarily, the experience it is. My view is closely related to his. Like Kripke, I find the hypothesis that a certain brain state should *necessarily* have a certain subjective character incomprehensible without further explanation. No such explanation emerges from theories which view the mind-brain relation as contingent, but perhaps there are other alternatives, not yet discovered.

A theory that explained how the mind-brain relation was necessary would still leave us with Kripke's problem of explaining why it nevertheless appears contingent. That difficulty seems to me surmountable, in the following way. We may imagine something by representing it to ourselves either perceptually, sympathetically, or symbolically. I shall not try to say how symbolic imagination works, but part of what happens in the other two cases is this. To imagine something perceptually, we put ourselves in a conscious state resembling the state we would be in if we perceived it. To imagine something sympathetically, we put ourselves in a conscious state resembling the thing itself. (This method can be used only to imagine mental events and states – our own or another's.) When we try to imagine a mental state occurring without its associated brain state, we first sympathetically imagine the occurrence of the mental state: that is, we put ourselves into a state that resembles it mentally. At the same time, we attempt to perceptually imagine the non-occurrence of the associated physical state, by putting ourselves into another state unconnected with the first: one resembling that which we would be in if we perceived the non-occurrence of the physical state. Where the imagination of physical features is perceptual and the imagination of mental features is sympathetic, it appears to us that we can imagine any experience occurring without its associated brain state, and vice versa. The relation between them will appear contingent even if it is necessary, because of the independence of the disparate types of imagination.

(Solipsism, incidentally, results if one misinterprets sympathetic imagination as if it worked like perceptual imagination: it then seems impossible to imagine any experience that is not one's own.)

12 See "Mental Events" in Foster and Swanson, *Experience and Theory* (Amherst, 1970); though

I don't understand the argument against psycho-physical laws.

13 Similar remarks apply to my paper "Physicalism," *Philosophical Review* LXXIV (1965), 339–56, reprinted with postscript in John O'Connor, *Modern Materialism* (New York, 1969).

14 This question also lies at the heart of the problem of other minds, whose close connection with the mind-body problem is often overlooked. If one understood how subjective experience could have an objective nature, one would understand the existence of subjects other than oneself.

15 I have not defined the term "physical." Obviously it does not apply just to what can be described by the concepts of contemporary physics, since we expect further developments. Some may think

there is nothing to prevent mental phenomena from eventually being recognized as physical in their own right. But whatever else may be said of the physical, it has to be objective. So if our idea of the physical ever expands to include mental phenomena, it will have to assign them an objective character – whether or not this is done by analyzing them in terms of other phenomena already regarded as physical. It seems to me more likely, however, that mental-physical relations will eventually be expressed in a theory whose fundamental terms cannot be placed clearly in either category.

16 I have read versions of this paper to a number of audiences, and am indebted to many people for their comments.

13

What Mary Didn't Know

Frank Jackson

Mary is confined to a black-and-white room, is educated through black-and-white books and through lectures relayed on black-and-white television. In this way she learns everything there is to know about the physical nature of the world. She knows all the physical facts about us and our environment, in a wide sense of 'physical' which includes everything in *completed* physics, chemistry, and neurophysiology, and all there is to know about the causal and relational facts consequent upon all this, including of course functional roles. If physicalism is true, she knows all there is to know. For to suppose otherwise is to suppose that there is more to know than every physical fact, and that is just what physicalism denies.

Physicalism is not the noncontroversial thesis that the actual world is largely physical, but the challenging thesis that it is entirely physical. This is why physicalists must hold that complete physical knowledge is complete knowledge simpliciter. For suppose it is not complete: then our world must differ from a world, *W(P)*, for which it is complete, and the difference must be in nonphysical facts; for our world and *W(P)* agree in all matters physical. Hence, physicalism would be false at our world (though contingently so, for it would be true at *W(P)*).[1]

It seems, however, that Mary does not know all there is to know. For when she is let out of the black-and-white room or given a color television, she will learn what it is like to see something red, say. This is rightly described as *learning* – she will not say "ho, hum." Hence, physicalism is false. This is the knowledge argument against physicalism in one of its manifestations.[2] This note is a reply to three objections to it mounted by Paul M. Churchland.[3]

I. Three Clarifications

The knowledge argument does not rest on the dubious claim that logically you cannot imagine what sensing red is like unless you have sensed red. Powers of imagination are not to the point. The contention about Mary is not that, despite her fantastic grasp of neurophysiology and everything else physical, she *could not imagine* what it is like to sense red; it is that, as a matter of fact, she *would not know*. But if physicalism is true, she would know; and no great powers of imagination would be called for. Imagination is a faculty that those who *lack* knowledge need to fall back on.

Frank Jackson, "What Mary Didn't Know." *The Journal of Philosophy* 83, no. 5 (May 1986), pp. 291–5. © 1986 by The Journal of Philosophy, Inc. Reprinted with permission from the author and The Journal of Philosophy.

Secondly, the intensionality of knowledge is not to the point. The argument does not rest on assuming falsely that, if S knows that a is F and if $a = b$, then S knows that b is F. It is concerned with the nature of Mary's total body of knowledge before she is released: is it complete, or do some facts escape it? What is to the point is that S may know that a is F and *know* that $a = b$, yet arguably not know that b is F, by virtue of not being sufficiently logically alert to follow the consequences through. If Mary's lack of knowledge were at all like this, there would be no threat to physicalism in it. But it is very hard to believe that her lack of knowledge could be remedied merely by her explicitly following through enough logical consequences of her vast physical knowledge. Endowing her with great logical acumen and persistence is not in itself enough to fill in the gaps in her knowledge. On being let out, she will not say "I could have worked all this out before by making some more purely logical inferences."

Thirdly, the knowledge Mary lacked which is of particular point for the knowledge argument against physicalism is *knowledge about the experiences of others*, not about her own. When she is let out, she has new experiences, color experiences she has never had before. It is not, therefore, an objection to physicalism that she learns *something* on being let out. Before she was let out, she could not have known facts about her experience of red, for there were no such facts to know. That physicalist and nonphysicalist alike can agree on. After she is let out, things change; and physicalism can happily admit that she learns this; after all, some physical things will change, for instance, her brain states and their functional roles. The trouble for physicalism is that, after Mary sees her first ripe tomato, she will realize how impoverished her conception of the mental life of *others* has been *all along*. She will realize that there was, all the time she was carrying out her laborious investigations into the neurophysiologies of others and into the functional roles of their internal states, something about these people she was quite unaware of. All along their experiences (or many of them, those got from tomatoes, the sky, ...) had a feature conspicuous to them but until now hidden from her (in fact, not in logic). But she knew all the physical facts about them all along; hence, what she did not know until her release is not a physical fact about their experiences. But it is a fact about them. That is the trouble for physicalism.

II. Churchland's Three Objections

(i) Churchland's first objection is that the knowledge argument contains a defect that "is simplicity itself" (23). The argument equivocates on the sense of 'knows about'. How so? Churchland suggests that the following is "a conveniently tightened version" of the knowledge argument:

(1) Mary knows everything there is to know about brain states and their properties.
(2) It is not the case that Mary knows everything there is to know about sensations and their properties.

Therefore, by Leibniz's law,

(3) Sensations and their properties $\neq$ brain states and their properties (23).

Churchland observes, plausibly enough, that the type or kind of knowledge involved in premise 1 is distinct from the kind of knowledge involved in premise 2. We might follow his lead and tag the first 'knowledge by description', and the second 'knowledge by acquaintance'; but, whatever the tags, he is right that the displayed argument involves a highly dubious use of Leibniz's law.

My reply is that the displayed argument may be convenient, but it is not accurate. It is not the knowledge argument. Take, for instance, premise 1. The whole thrust of the knowledge argument is that Mary (before her release) does *not* know everything there is to know about brain states and their properties, because she does not know about certain qualia associated with them. What is complete, according to the argument, is her knowledge of matters physical. A convenient and accurate way of displaying the argument is:

(1)′ Mary (before her release) knows everything physical there is to know about other people.
(2)′ Mary (before her release) does not know everything there is to know about other people (because she *learns* something about them on her release).

Therefore,

(3)′ There are truths about other people (and herself) which escape the physicalist story.

What is immediately to the point is not the kind, manner, or type of knowledge Mary has, but *what* she knows. What she knows beforehand is ex hypothesi everything physical there is to know, but is it everything there is to know? That is the crucial question.

There is, though, a relevant challenge involving questions about kinds of knowledge. It concerns the *support* for premise 2′. The case for premise 2′ is that Mary learns something on her release, she acquires knowledge, and that entails that her knowledge beforehand (*what* she knew, never mind whether by description, acquaintance, or whatever) was incomplete. The challenge, mounted by David Lewis and Laurence Nemirow, is that on her release Mary does *not* learn something or acquire knowledge in the relevant sense. What Mary acquires when she is released is a certain representational or imaginative ability; it is knowledge how rather than knowledge that. Hence, a physicalist can admit that Mary acquires something very significant of a knowledge kind – which can hardly be denied – without admitting that this shows that her earlier factual knowledge is defective. She knew all *that* there was to know about the experiences of others beforehand, but lacked an ability until after her release.[4]

Now it is certainly true that Mary will acquire abilities of various kinds after her release. She will, for instance, be able to imagine what seeing red is like, be able to remember what it is like, and be able to understand why her friends regarded her as so deprived (something which, until her release, had always mystified her). But is it plausible that that is *all* she will acquire? Suppose she received a lecture on skepticism about other minds while she was incarcerated. On her release she sees a ripe tomato in normal conditions, and so has a sensation of red. Her first reaction is to say that she now knows more about the kind of experiences others have when looking at ripe tomatoes. She then remembers the lecture and starts to worry. Does she really know more about what their experiences are like, or is she indulging in a wild generalization from one case?

In the end she decides she does know, and that skepticism is mistaken (even if, like so many of us, she is not sure how to demonstrate its errors). What was she to-ing and fro-ing about – her abilities? Surely not; her representational abilities were a known constant throughout. What else then was she agonizing about than whether or not she had gained factual knowledge of others? There would be nothing to agonize about if ability was *all* she acquired on her release.

I grant that I have no *proof* that Mary acquires on her release, as well as abilities, factual knowledge about the experiences of others – and not just because I have no disproof of skepticism. My claim is that the knowledge argument is a valid argument from highly plausible, though admittedly not demonstrable, premises to the conclusion that physicalism is false. And that, after all, is about as good an objection as one could expect in this area of philosophy.

(ii) Churchland's second objection (24/5) is that there must be something wrong with the argument, for it proves too much. Suppose Mary received a special series of lectures over her black-and-white television from a full-blown dualist, explaining the "laws" governing the behavior of "ectoplasm" and telling her about qualia. This would not affect the plausibility of the claim that on her release she learns something. So if the argument works against physicalism, it works against dualism too.

My reply is that lectures about qualia over black-and-white television do not tell Mary all there is to know about qualia. They may tell her some things about qualia, for instance, that they do not appear in the physicalist's story, and that the quale we use 'yellow' for is nearly as different from the one we use 'blue' for as is white from black. But why should it be supposed that they tell her everything about qualia? On the other hand, it is plausible that lectures over black-and-white television might in principle tell Mary everything in the physicalist's story. You do not need color television to learn physics or functionalist psychology. To obtain a good argument against dualism (attribute dualism; ectoplasm is a bit of fun), the premise in the knowledge argument that Mary has the full story according to physicalism before her release, has to be replaced by a premise that she has the full story according to dualism. The former is plausible; the latter is not. Hence, there is no "parity of reasons" trouble for dualists who use the knowledge argument.

(iii) Churchland's third objection is that the knowledge argument claims "that Mary could not even *imagine* what the relevant experience would be like, despite her exhaustive neuroscientific knowledge, and hence must still be missing certain crucial information" (25), a claim he goes on to argue against.

But, as we emphasized earlier, the knowledge argument claims that Mary would not know what the relevant experience is like. What she could imagine is another matter. If her knowledge is defective, despite being all there is to know according to physicalism, then physicalism is false, whatever her powers of imagination.

Notes

1 The claim here is not that, if physicalism is true, only what is expressed in explicitly physical language is an item of knowledge. It is that, if physicalism is true, then if you know everything expressed or expressible in explicitly physical language, you know everything. *Pace* Terence Horgan, "Jackson on Physical Information and Qualia," *Philosophical Quarterly*, XXXIV, 135 (April 1984): 147–52.

2 Namely, that in my "Epiphenomenal Qualia," *ibid.*, XXXII, 127 (April 1982): 127–36. See also Thomas Nagel, "What Is It Like to Be a Bat?", *Philosophical Review*, LXXXIII, 4 (October 1974): 435–50, and Howard Robinson, *Matter and Sense* (New York: Cambridge, 1982).

3 "Reduction, Qualia, and the Direct Introspection of Brain States," *Journal of Philosophy*, LXXXII, 1 (January 1985): 8–28. Unless otherwise stated, future page references are to this paper.

4 See Laurence Nemirow, review of Thomas Nagel, *Mortal Questions*, *Philosophical Review*, LXXXIX, 3 (July 1980): 473–7, and David Lewis, "Postscript to 'Mad Pain and Martian Pain'," *Philosophical Papers*, vol. I (New York: Oxford, 1983). Churchland mentions both Nemirow and Lewis, and it may be that he intended his objection to be essentially the one I have just given. However, he says quite explicitly (bottom of p. 23) that his objection does not need an "ability" analysis of the relevant knowledge.

14

Minds, Brains, and Programs

John R. Searle

What psychological and philosophical signific-ance should we attach to recent efforts at com-puter simulations of human cognitive capacities? In answering this question, I find it useful to distinguish what I will call "strong" AI from "weak" or "cautious" AI (artificial intelligence). According to weak AI, the principal value of the computer in the study of the mind is that it gives us a very powerful tool. For example, it enables us to formulate and test hypotheses in a more rigorous and precise fashion. But according to strong AI, the computer is not merely a tool in the study of the mind; rather, the appropriately programmed computer really *is* a mind, in the sense that computers given the right programs can be literally said to *understand* and have other cognitive states. In strong AI, because the pro-grammed computer has cognitive states, the programs are not mere tools that enable us to test psychological explanations; rather, the programs are themselves the explanations.

I have no objection to the claims of weak AI, at least as far as this article is concerned. My discussion here will be directed at the claims I have defined as those of strong AI, specifically the claim that the appropriately programmed com-puter literally has cognitive states and that the pro-grams thereby explain human cognition. When

I hereafter refer to AI, I have in mind the strong version, as expressed by these two claims.

I will consider the work of Roger Schank and his colleagues at Yale (Schank and Abelson 1977), because I am more familiar with it than I am with any other similar claims, and because it pro-vides a very clear example of the sort of work I wish to examine. But nothing that follows depends upon the details of Schank's programs. The same arguments would apply to Winograd's SHRDLU (Winograd 1973), Weizenbaum's ELIZA (Weizenbaum 1965), and indeed any Turing machine simulation of human mental phenomena. [. . .]

Very briefly, and leaving out the various details, one can describe Schank's program as follows: The aim of the program is to simulate the human ability to understand stories. It is characteristic of human beings' story-understanding capacity that they can answer questions about the story even though the information that they give was never explicitly stated in the story. Thus, for example, suppose you are given the following story: "A man went into a restaurant and ordered a hamburger. When the hamburger arrived it was burned to a crisp, and the man stormed out of the restaurant angrily, without paying for the burger or leaving a tip." Now, if you are asked "Did the man eat

John Searle, "Minds, Brains and Programs." *Behavioral and Brain Sciences* 3 (1980), pp. 417–57. © 1980 by Cambridge University Press. Reproduced with permission from the author and Cambridge University Press.

the hamburger?" you will presumably answer, "No, he did not." Similarly, if you are given the following story: "A man went into a restaurant and ordered a hamburger; when the hamburger came he was very pleased with it; and as he left the restaurant he gave the waitress a large tip before paying his bill," and you are asked the question, "Did the man eat the hamburger?" you will presumably answer, "Yes, he ate the hamburger." Now Schank's machines can similarly answer questions about restaurants in this fashion. To do this, they have a "representation" of the sort of information that human beings have about restaurants, which enables them to answer such questions as those above, given these sorts of stories. When the machine is given the story and then asked the question, the machine will print out answers of the sort that we would expect human beings to give if told similar stories. Partisans of strong AI claim that in this question and answer sequence the machine is not only simulating a human ability but also (1) that the machine can literally be said to *understand* the story and provide the answers to questions, and (2) that what the machine and its program do *explains* the human ability to understand the story and answer questions about it.

Both claims seem to me to be totally unsupported by Schank's work, as I will attempt to show in what follows.[1]

One way to test any theory of the mind is to ask oneself what it would be like if my mind actually worked on the principles that the theory says all minds work on. Let us apply this test to the Schank program with the following *Gedankenexperiment*. Suppose that I'm locked in a room and given a large batch of Chinese writing. Suppose furthermore (as is indeed the case) that I know no Chinese, either written or spoken, and that I'm not even confident that I could recognize Chinese writing as Chinese writing distinct from, say, Japanese writing or meaningless squiggles. To me, Chinese writing is just so many meaningless squiggles. Now suppose further that after this first batch of Chinese writing I am given a second batch of Chinese script together with a set of rules for correlating the second batch with the first batch. The rules are in English, and I understand these rules as well as any other native speaker of English. They enable me to correlate one set of formal symbols with another set of formal symbols, and all that "formal" means here is that I can identify the symbols entirely by their shapes. Now suppose also that I am given a third batch of Chinese symbols together with some instructions, again in English, that enable me to correlate elements of this third batch with the first two batches, and these rules instruct me how to give back certain Chinese symbols with certain sorts of shapes in response to certain sorts of shapes given me in the third batch. Unknown to me, the people who are giving me all of these symbols call the first batch a "script," they call the second batch a "story," and they call the third batch "questions." Furthermore, they call the symbols I give them back in response to the third batch "answers to the questions," and the set of rules in English that they gave me, they call the "program." Now just to complicate the story a little, imagine that these people also give me stories in English, which I understand, and they then ask me questions in English about these stories, and I give them back answers in English. Suppose also that after a while I got so good at following the instructions for manipulating the Chinese symbols and the programmers get so good at writing the programs that from the external point of view – that is, from the point of view of somebody outside the room in which I am locked – my answers to the questions are absolutely indistinguishable from those of native Chinese speakers. Nobody just looking at my answers can tell that I don't speak a word of Chinese. Let us also suppose that my answers to the English questions are, as they no doubt would be, indistinguishable from those of other native English speakers, for the simple reason that I am a native English speaker. From the external point of view – from the point of view of someone reading my "answers" – the answers to the Chinese questions and the English questions are equally good. But in the Chinese case, unlike the English case, I produce the answers by manipulating uninterpreted formal symbols. As far as the Chinese is concerned, I simply behave like a computer; I perform computational operations on formally specified elements. For the purposes of the Chinese, I am simply an instantiation of the computer program.

Now the claims made by strong AI are that the programmed computer understands the stories and that the program in some sense explains human understanding. But we are now in a position to examine these claims in light of our thought experiment.

1.   As regards the first claim, it seems to me quite obvious in the example that I do not understand a word of Chinese stories. I have inputs and outputs that are indistinguishable from those of the native Chinese speaker, and I can have any formal program you like, but I still understand nothing. For the same reasons, Schank's computer understands nothing of any stories, whether in Chinese, English, or whatever, since in the Chinese case the computer is me, and in cases where the computer is not me, the computer has nothing more than I have in the case where I understand nothing.

2.   As regards the second claim, that the program explains human understanding, we can see that the computer and its program do not provide sufficient conditions of understanding since the computer and the program are functioning, and there is no understanding. But does it even provide a necessary condition or a significant contribution to understanding? One of the claims made by the supporters of strong AI is that when I understand a story in English, what I am doing is exactly the same – or perhaps more of the same – as what I was doing in manipulating the Chinese symbols. It is simply more formal symbol manipulation that distinguishes the case in English, where I do understand, from the case in Chinese where I don't. I have not demonstrated that this claim is false, but it would certainly appear an incredible claim in the example. Such plausibility as the claim has derives from the supposition that we can construct a program that will have the same inputs and outputs as native speakers, and in addition we assume that speakers have some level of description where they are also instantiations of a program. On the basis of these two assumptions we assume that even if Schank's program isn't the whole story about understanding, it may be part of the story. Well, I suppose that is an empirical possibility, but not the slightest reason has so far been given to believe that it is true, since what is suggested – though certainly not demonstrated – by the example is that the computer program is simply irrelevant to my understanding of the story. In the Chinese case I have everything that artificial intelligence can put into me by way of a program, and I understand nothing; in the English case I understand everything, and there is so far no reason at all to suppose that my understanding has anything to do with computer programs, that is, with computational operations on purely formally specified elements. As long as the program is defined in terms of computational operations on purely formally defined elements, what the example suggests is that these by themselves have no interesting connection with understanding. They are certainly not sufficient conditions, and not the slightest reason has been given to suppose that they are necessary conditions or even that they make a significant contribution to understanding. Notice that the force of the argument is not simply that different machines can have the same input and output while operating on different formal principles – that is not the point at all. Rather, whatever purely formal principles you put into the computer, they will not be sufficient for understanding, since a human will be able to follow the formal principles without understanding anything. No reason whatever has been offered to suppose that such principles are necessary or even contributory, since no reason has been given to suppose that when I understand English I am operating with any formal program at all.

Well, then, what is it that I have in the case of the English sentences that I do not have in the case of the Chinese sentences? The obvious answer is that I know what the former mean, while I haven't the faintest idea what the latter mean. But in what does this consist and why couldn't we give it to a machine, whatever it is? I will return to this question later, but first I want to continue with the example.

I have had the occasions to present this example to several workers in artificial intelligence, and, interestingly, they do not seem to agree on what the proper reply to it is. I get a surprising variety of replies, and in what follows I will consider the most common of these (specified along with their geographic origins).

But first I want to block some common misunderstandings about "understanding": In many of these discussions one finds a lot of fancy footwork about the word "understanding." My critics point out that there are many different degrees of understanding; that "understanding" is not a simple two-place predicate; that there are even different kinds and levels of understanding, and often the law of excluded middle doesn't even apply in a straightforward way to statements of the form "*x* understands *y*"; that in many cases it is a matter for decision and not a simple matter of fact whether *x* understands *y*; and so on. To all of these points I want to say: of course, of course. But they have nothing to do with the points at issue. There are clear cases in which "understanding" literally applies and clear cases in which it does not apply; and these two sorts of cases are all I need for this argument.[2] I understand stories in English; to a lesser degree I can understand stories in French; to a still lesser degree, stories in German; and in Chinese, not at all. My car and my adding machine, on the other hand, understand nothing: they are not in that line of business. We often attribute "understanding" and other cognitive predicates by metaphor and analogy to cars, adding machines, and other artifacts, but nothing is proved by such attributions. We say, "The door *knows* when to open because of its photoelectric cell," "The adding machine *knows how* (*understands how*, is *able*) to do addition and subtraction but not division," and "The thermostat *perceives* changes in the temperature." The reason we make these attributions is quite interesting, and it has to do with the fact that in artifacts we extend our own intentionality;[3] our tools are extensions of our purposes, and so we find it natural to make metaphorical attributions of intentionality to them; but I take it no philosophical ice is cut by such examples. The sense in which an automatic door "understands instructions" from its photoelectric cell is not at all the sense in which I understand English. If the sense in which Schank's programmed computers understand stories is supposed to be the metaphorical sense in which the door understands, and not the sense in which I understand English, the issue would not be worth discussing. But Newell and Simon (1963) write that the kind of cognition they claim for computers is exactly the same as for human beings. I like the straightforwardness of this claim, and it is the sort of claim I will be considering. I will argue that in the literal sense the programmed computer understands what the car and the adding machine understand, namely, exactly nothing. The computer understanding is not just (like

my understanding of German) partial or incomplete; it is zero.

Now to the replies.

I.   The Systems Reply (Berkeley)

"While it is true that the individual person who is locked in the room does not understand the story, the fact is that he is merely part of a whole system, and the system does understand the story. The person has a large ledger in front of him in which are written the rules, he has a lot of scratch paper and pencils for doing calculations, he has 'data banks' of sets of Chinese symbols. Now, understanding is not being ascribed to the mere individual; rather it is being ascribed to this whole system of which he is a part."

My response to the systems theory is quite simple: Let the individual internalize all of these elements of the system. He memorizes the rules in the ledger and the data banks of Chinese symbols, and he does all the calculations in his head. The individual then incorporates the entire system. There isn't anything at all to the system that he does not encompass. We can even get rid of the room and suppose he works outdoors. All the same, he understands nothing of the Chinese, and a fortiori neither does the system, because there isn't anything in the system that isn't in him. If he doesn't understand, then there is no way the system could understand because the system is just a part of him.

Actually I feel somewhat embarrassed to give even this answer to the systems theory because the theory seems to me so implausible to start with. The idea is that while a person doesn't understand Chinese, somehow the *conjunction* of that person and bits of paper might understand Chinese. It is not easy for me to imagine how someone who was not in the grip of an ideology would find the idea at all plausible. Still, I think many people who are committed to the ideology of strong AI will in the end be inclined to say something very much like this; so let us pursue it a bit further. According to one version of this view, while the man in the internalized systems example doesn't understand Chinese in the sense that a native Chinese speaker does (because, for example, he doesn't know that the story refers to restaurants and hamburgers, etc.), still "the man as a formal symbol manipulation system" *really does understand Chinese*. The subsystem of the man that is the formal symbol manipulation system for Chinese should not be confused with the subsystem for English.

So there are really two subsystems in the man: one understands English, the other Chinese, and "it's just that the two systems have little to do with each other." But, I want to reply, not only do they have little to do with each other, they are not even remotely alike. The subsystem that understands English (assuming we allow ourselves to talk in this jargon of "subsystems" for a moment) knows that the stories are about restaurants and eating hamburgers, he knows that he is being asked questions about restaurants and that he is answering questions as best he can by making various inferences from the content of the story, and so on. But the Chinese system knows none of this. Whereas the English subsystem knows that "hamburgers" refers to hamburgers, the Chinese subsystem knows only that "squiggle squiggle" is followed by "squoggle squoggle." All he knows is that various formal symbols are being introduced at one end and manipulated according to rules written in English, and other symbols are going out at the other end. The whole point of the original example was to argue that such symbol manipulation by itself couldn't be sufficient for understanding Chinese in any literal sense because the man could write "squoggle squoggle" after "squiggle squiggle" without understanding anything in Chinese. And it doesn't meet that argument to postulate subsystems within the man, because the subsystems are no better off than the man was in the first place: they still don't have anything even remotely like what the English-speaking man (or subsystem) has. Indeed, in the case as described, the Chinese subsystem is simply a part of the English subsystem, a part that engages in meaningless symbol manipulation according to rules in English.

Let us ask ourselves what is supposed to motivate the systems reply in the first place; that is, what *independent* grounds are there supposed to be for saying that the agent must have a subsystem within him that literally understands stories in Chinese? As far as I can tell the only grounds are that in the example I have the same input and output as native Chinese speakers and a program that goes from one to the other. But the whole point

of the examples has been to try to show that that couldn't be sufficient for understanding, in the sense in which I understand stories in English, because a person, and hence the set of systems that go to make up a person, could have the right combination of input, output, and program and still not understand anything in the relevant literal sense in which I understand English. The only motivation for saying there *must* be a subsystem in me that understands Chinese is that I have a program and I can pass the Turing test; I can fool native Chinese speakers. But precisely one of the points at issue is the adequacy of the Turing test. The example shows that there could be two "systems," both of which pass the Turing test, but only one of which understands; and it is no argument against this point to say that since they both pass the Turing test they must both understand, since this claim fails to meet the argument that the system in me that understands English has a great deal more than the system that merely processes Chinese. In short, the systems reply simply begs the question by insisting without argument that the system must understand Chinese.

Furthermore, the systems reply would appear to lead to consequences that are independently absurd. If we are to conclude that there must be cognition in me on the grounds that I have a certain sort of input and output and a program in between, then it looks like all sorts of noncognitive subsystems are going to turn out to be cognitive. For example, there is a level of description at which my stomach does information processing, and it instantiates any number of computer programs, but I take it we do not want to say that it has any understanding (cf. Pylyshyn 1980). But if we accept the systems reply, then it is hard to see how we avoid saying that stomach, heart, liver, and so on are all understanding subsystems, since there is no principled way to distinguish the motivation for saying the Chinese subsystem understands from saying that the stomach understands. It is, by the way, not an answer to this point to say that the Chinese system has information as input and output and the stomach has food and food products as input and output, since from the point of view of the agent, from my point of view, there is no information in either the food or the Chinese – the Chinese is just so many meaningless squiggles. The information in the Chinese case is solely in the eyes of the programmers and the interpreters, and there is nothing to prevent them from treating the input and output of my digestive organs as information if they so desire.

This last point bears on some independent problems in strong AI, and it is worth digressing for a moment to explain it. If strong AI is to be a branch of psychology, then it must be able to distinguish those systems that are genuinely mental from those that are not. It must be able to distinguish the principles on which the mind works from those on which nonmental systems work; otherwise it will offer us no explanations of what is specifically mental about the mental. And the mental-nonmental distinction cannot be just in the eye of the beholder but it must be intrinsic to the systems; otherwise it would be up to any beholder to treat people as nonmental and, for example, hurricanes as mental if he likes. But quite often in the AI literature the distinction is blurred in ways that would in the long run prove disastrous to the claim that AI is a cognitive inquiry. McCarthy, for example, writes, "Machines as simple as thermostats can be said to have beliefs, and having beliefs seems to be a characteristic of most machines capable of problem solving performance" (McCarthy 1979). Anyone who thinks strong AI has a chance as a theory of the mind ought to ponder the implications of that remark. We are asked to accept it as a discovery of strong AI that the hunk of metal on the wall that we use to regulate the temperature has beliefs in exactly the same sense that we, our spouses, and our children have beliefs, and furthermore that "most" of the other machines in the room – telephone, tape recorder, adding machine, electric light switch – also have beliefs in this literal sense. It is not the aim of this article to argue against McCarthy's point, so I will simply assert the following without argument. The study of the mind starts with such facts as that humans have beliefs, while thermostats, telephones, and adding machines don't. If you get a theory that denies this point you have produced a counterexample to the theory and the theory is false. One gets the impression that people in the AI who write this sort of thing think they can get away with it because they don't really take it seriously, and they don't think anyone else will either. I propose, for a moment at least, to take it seriously. Think hard for one minute about what would be necessary to establish that the hunk of metal on the wall over there had real beliefs, beliefs with direction of fit, propositional content, and conditions of satisfaction; beliefs that had the possibility of being strong beliefs or weak beliefs; nervous, anxious, or secure beliefs; dogmatic, rational, or superstitious beliefs; blind faiths or hesitant cogitations; any kind of beliefs. The thermostat is not a candidate. Neither is stomach, liver, adding machine, or telephone. However, since we are taking the idea seriously, notice that its truth would be fatal to strong AI's claim to be a science of the mind. For now the mind is everywhere. What we wanted to know is what distinguishes the mind from thermostats and livers. And if McCarthy were right, strong AI wouldn't have a hope of telling us that.

II.   The Robot Reply (Yale)

"Suppose we wrote a different kind of program from Schank's program. Suppose we put a computer inside a robot, and this computer would not just take in formal symbols as input and give out formal symbols as output, but rather would actually operate the robot in such a way that the robot does something very much like perceiving, walking, moving about, hammering nails, eating, drinking – anything you like. The robot would, for example, have a television camera attached to it that enabled it to see, it would have arms and legs that enabled it to 'act,' and all of this would be controlled by its computer 'brain.' Such a robot would, unlike Schank's computer, have genuine understanding and other mental states."

The first thing to notice about the robot reply is that it tacitly concedes that cognition is not solely a matter of formal symbol manipulation, since this reply adds a set of causal relations with the outside world (cf. Fodor 1980). But the answer to the robot reply is that the addition of such "perceptual" and "motor" capacities adds nothing by way of understanding, in particular, or intentionality, in general, to Schank's original program. To see this, notice that the same thought experiment applies to the robot case. Suppose that instead of the computer inside the robot, you put me inside the room and, as in the original Chinese case, you give me more Chinese symbols with more instructions in English for matching Chinese symbols to Chinese symbols and feeding back

Chinese symbols to the outside. Suppose, unknown to me, some of the Chinese symbols that come to me come from a television camera attached to the robot and other Chinese symbols that I am giving out serve to make the motors inside the robot move the robot's legs or arms. It is important to emphasize that all I am doing is manipulating formal symbols: I know none of these other facts, I am receiving "information" from the robot's "perceptual" apparatus, and I am giving out "instructions" to its motor apparatus without knowing either of these facts. I am the robot's homunculus, but unlike the traditional homunculus, I don't know what's going on. I don't understand anything except the rules for symbol manipulation. Now in this case I want to say that the robot has no intentional states at all; it is simply moving about as a result of its electrical wiring and its program. And furthermore, by instantiating the program I have no intentional states of the relevant type. All I do is follow formal instructions about manipulating formal symbols.

III. The Brain Simulator Reply (Berkeley and MIT)

"Suppose we design a program that doesn't represent information that we have about the world, such as the information in Schank's scripts, but simulates the actual sequence of neuron firings at the synapses of the brain of a native Chinese speaker when he understands stories in Chinese and gives answers to them. The machine takes in Chinese stories and questions about them as input, it simulates the formal structure of actual Chinese brains in processing these stories, and it gives out Chinese answers as outputs. We can even imagine that the machine operates, not with a single serial program, but with a whole set of programs operating in parallel, in the manner that actual human brains presumably operate when they process natural language. Now surely in such a case we would have to say that the machine understood the stories: and if we refuse to say that, wouldn't we also have to deny that native Chinese speakers understood the stories? At the level of the synapses, what would or could be different about the program of the computer and the program of the Chinese brain?"

Before countering this reply I want to digress to note that it is an odd reply for any partisan of artificial intelligence (or functionalism, etc.) to make: I thought the whole idea of strong AI is that we don't need to know how the brain works to know how the mind works. The basic hypothesis, or so I had supposed, was that there is a level of mental operations consisting of computational processes over formal elements that constitute the essence of the mental and can be realized in all sorts of different brain processes, in the same way that any computer program can be realized in different computer hardwares: On the assumptions of strong AI, the mind is to the brain as the program is to the hardware, and thus we can understand the mind without doing neurophysiology. If we had to know how the brain worked to do AI, we wouldn't bother with AI. However, even getting this close to the operation of the brain is still not sufficient to produce understanding. To see this, image that instead of a monolingual man in a room shuffling symbols we have the man operate an elaborate set of water pipes with valves connecting them. When the man receives the Chinese symbols, he looks up in the program, written in English, which valves he has to turn on and off. Each water connection corresponds to a synapse in the Chinese brain, and the whole system is rigged up so that after doing all the right firings, that is after turning on all the right faucets, the Chinese answers pop out at the output end of the series of pipes.

Now where is the understanding in this system? It takes Chinese as input, it simulates the formal structure of the synapses of the Chinese brain, and it gives Chinese as output. But the man certainly doesn't understand Chinese, and neither do the water pipes, and if we are tempted to adopt what I think is the absurd view that somehow the *conjunction* of man *and* water pipes understands, remember that in principle the man can internalize the formal structure of the water pipes and do all the "neuron firings" in his imagination. The problem with the brain simulator is that it is simulating the wrong things about the brain. As long as it simulates only the formal structure of the sequence of neuron firings at the synapses, it won't have simulated what matters about the brain, namely its causal properties, its ability to produce intentional states. And that the formal properties are not sufficient for the causal properties is shown by the water pipe example: we can have all the formal properties carved off from the relevant neurobiological causal properties.

IV. The Combination Reply (Berkeley and Stanford)

"While each of the previous three replies might not be completely convincing by itself as a refutation of the Chinese room counter-example, if you take all three together they are collectively much more convincing and even decisive. Imagine a robot with a brain-shaped computer lodged in its cranial cavity, imagine the computer programmed with all the synapses of a human brain, imagine the whole behavior of the robot is indistinguishable from human behavior, and now think of the whole thing as a unified system and not just as a computer with inputs and outputs. Surely in such a case we would have to ascribe intentionality to the system."

I entirely agree that in such a case we would find it rational and indeed irresistible to accept the hypothesis that the robot had intentionality, as long as we knew nothing more about it. Indeed, besides appearance and behavior, the other elements of the combination are really irrelevant. If we could build a robot whose behavior was indistinguishable over a large range from human behavior, we would attribute intentionality to it, pending some reason not to. We wouldn't need to know in advance that its computer brain was a formal analogue of the human brain.

But I really don't see that this is any help to the claims of strong AI, and here's why: According to strong AI, instantiating a formal program with the right input and output is a sufficient condition of, indeed is constitutive of, intentionality. As Newell (1979) puts it, the essence of the mental is the operation of a physical symbol system. But the attributions of intentionality that we make to the robot in this example have nothing to do with formal programs. They are simply based on the assumption that if the robot looks and behaves sufficiently like us, then we would suppose, until proven otherwise, that it must have mental states like ours that cause and are expressed by its behavior and it must have an inner mechanism capable of producing such mental states. If we knew independently how to account for its behavior without such assumptions we would not attribute intentionality to it, especially if we knew it had a formal program. And this is precisely the point of my earlier reply to objection II.

Suppose we knew that the robot's behavior was entirely accounted for by the fact that a man inside it was receiving uninterpreted formal symbols from the robot's sensory receptors and sending out uninterpreted formal symbols to its motor mechanisms, and the man was doing the symbol manipulation in accordance with a bunch of rules. Furthermore, suppose the man knows none of these facts about the robot, all he knows is which operations to perform on which meaningless symbols. In such a case we would regard the robot as an ingenious mechanical dummy. The hypothesis that the dummy has a mind would now be unwarranted and unnecessary, for there is now no longer any reason to ascribe intentionality to the robot or to the system of which it is a part (except of course for the man's intentionality in manipulating the symbols). The formal symbol manipulations go on, the input and output are correctly matched, but the only real locus of intentionality is the man, and he doesn't know any of the relevant intentional states; he doesn't, for example, *see* what comes into the robot's eyes, he doesn't *intend* to move the robot's arm, and he doesn't *understand* any of the remarks made to or by the robot. Nor, for the reasons stated earlier, does the system of which man and robot are a part.

To see this point, contrast this case with cases in which we find it completely natural to ascribe intentionality to members of certain other primate species such as apes and monkeys and to domestic animals such as dogs. The reasons we find it natural are, roughly, two: We can't make sense of the animal's behavior without the ascription of intentionality, and we can see that the beasts are made of similar stuff to ourselves – that is an eye, that a nose, this is its skin, and so on. Given the coherence of the animal's behavior and the assumption of the same causal stuff underlying it, we assume both that the animal must have mental states underlying its behavior, and that the mental states must be produced by mechanisms made out of the stuff that is like our stuff. We would certainly make similar assumptions about the robot unless we had some reason not to, but as soon as we knew that the behavior was the result of a formal program, and that the actual causal properties of the physical substance were irrelevant we would abandon the assumption of intentionality.

There are two other responses to my example that come up frequently (and so are worth discussing) but really miss the point.

V.   The Other Minds Reply (Yale)

"How do you know that other people understand Chinese or anything else? Only by their behavior. Now the computer can pass the behavioral tests as well as they can (in principle), so if you are going to attribute cognition to other people you must in principle also attribute it to computers."

This objection really is only worth a short reply. The problem in this discussion is not about how I know that other people have cognitive states, but rather what it is that I am attributing to them when I attribute cognitive states to them. The thrust of the argument is that it couldn't be just computational processes and their output because the computational processes and their output can exist without the cognitive state. It is no answer to this argument to feign anesthesia. In "cognitive sciences" one presupposes the reality and knowability of the mental in the same way that in physical sciences one has to presuppose the reality and knowability of physical objects.

VI.   The Many Mansions Reply (Berkeley)

"Your whole argument presupposes that AI is only about analog and digital computers. But that just happens to be the present state of technology. Whatever these causal processes are that you say are essential for intentionality (assuming you are right), eventually we will be able to build devices that have these causal processes, and that will be artificial intelligence. So your arguments are in no way directed at the ability of artificial intelligence to produce and explain cognition."

I really have no objection to this reply save to say that it in effect trivializes the project of strong AI by redefining it as whatever artificially produces and explains cognition. The interest of the original claim made on behalf of artificial intelligence is that it was a precise, well defined thesis: mental processes are computational processes over formally defined elements. I have been concerned to challenge that thesis. If the claim is redefined so that it is no longer that thesis, my objections no longer apply because there is no longer a testable hypothesis for them to apply to.

Let us now return to the question I promised I would try to answer: Granted that in my original example I understand the English and I do not understand the Chinese, and granted therefore that the machine doesn't understand either English or Chinese, still there must be something about me that makes it the case that I understand English and a corresponding something lacking in me that makes it the case that I fail to understand Chinese. Now why couldn't we give those somethings, whatever they are, to a machine?

I see no reason in principle why we couldn't give a machine the capacity to understand English or Chinese, since in an important sense our bodies with our brains are precisely such machines. But I do see very strong arguments for saying that we could not give such a thing to a machine where the operation of the machine is defined solely in terms of computational processes over formally defined elements; that is, where the operational of the machine is defined as an instantiation of a computer program. It is not because I am the instantiation of a computer program that I am able to understand English and have other forms of intentionality (I am, I suppose, the instantiation of any number of computer programs), but as far as we know it is because I am a certain sort of organism with a certain biological (i.e., chemical and physical) structure, and this structure, under certain conditions, is causally capable of producing perception, action, understanding, learning, and other intentional phenomena. And part of the point of the present argument is that only something that had those causal powers could have that intentionality. Perhaps other physical and chemical processes could produce exactly these effects; perhaps, for example, Martians also have intentionality but their brains are made of different stuff. That is an empirical question, rather like the question whether photosynthesis can be done by something with a chemistry different from that of chlorophyll.

But the main point of the present argument is that no purely formal model will ever be sufficient by itself for intentionality because the formal properties are not by themselves constitutive of intentionality, and they have by themselves no causal powers except the power, when instantiated, to produce the next stage of the formalism when the machine is running. And any other causal properties that particular realizations of the formal model have, are irrelevant to the formal model because we can always put the same formal model in a different realization where those causal properties are obviously absent. Even if, by some miracle, Chinese speakers exactly realize Schank's program, we can put the same program in English speakers, water pipes, or computers, none of which understand Chinese, the program notwithstanding.

What matters about brain operations is not the formal shadow cast by the sequence of synapses but rather the actual properties of the sequences. All the arguments for the strong version of artificial intelligence that I have seen insist on drawing an outline around the shadows cast by cognition and then claiming that the shadows are the real thing.

By way of concluding I want to try to state some of the general philosophical points implicit in the argument. For clarity I will try to do it in a question-and-answer fashion, and I begin with that old chestnut of a question:

"Could a machine think?"

The answer is, obviously, yes. We are precisely such machines.

"Yes, but could an artifact, a man-made machine, think?"

Assuming it is possible to produce artificially a machine with a nervous system, neurons with axons and dendrites, and all the rest of it, sufficiently like ours, again the answer to the question seems to be obviously, yes. If you can exactly duplicate the causes, you could duplicate the effects. And indeed it might be possible to produce consciousness, intentionality, and all the rest of it using some other sorts of chemical principles than those that human beings use. It is, as I said, an empirical question.

"OK, but could a digital computer think?"

If by "digital computer" we mean anything at all that has a level of description where it can correctly be described as the instantiation of a computer program, then again the answer is, of course, yes, since we are the instantiations of any number of computer programs, and we can think.

"But could something think, understand, and so on *solely* in virtue of being a computer with a right sort of program? Could instantiating a program, the right program of course, by itself be a sufficient condition of understanding?"

This I think is the right question to ask, though it is usually confused with one or more of the earlier questions, and the answer to it is no.

"Why not?"

Because the formal symbol manipulations by themselves don't have any intentionality; they are quite meaningless; they aren't even *symbol* manipulations, since the symbols don't symbolize anything. In the linguistic jargon, they have only a syntax but no semantics. Such intentionality as computers appear to have is solely in the minds of those who program them and those who use them, those who send in the input and those who interpret the output.

The aim of the Chinese room example was to try to show this by showing that as soon as we put something into the system that really does have intentionality (a man), and we program him with the formal program, you can see that the formal program carries no additional intentionality. It adds nothing, for example, to a man's ability to understand Chinese.

Precisely that feature of AI that seemed so appealing – the distinction between the program and the realization – proves fatal to the claim that simulation could be duplication. The distinction between the program and its realization in the hardware seems to be parallel to the distinction between the level of mental operations and the level of brain operations. And if we could describe the level of mental operations as a formal program, then it seems we could describe what was essential about the mind without doing either introspective psychology or neurophysiology of the brain. But the equation "mind is to brain as program is to hardware" breaks down at several points, among them the following three:

First, the distinction between program and realization has the consequence that the same program could have all sorts of crazy realizations that had no form of intentionality. Weizenbaum (1976, Ch. 2), for example, shows in detail how to construct a computer using a roll of toilet paper and a pile of small stones. Similarly, the Chinese story understanding program can be programmed into a sequence of water pipes, a set of wind machines, or a monolingual English speaker, none of which thereby acquires an understanding of Chinese. Stones, toilet paper, wind, and water pipes are the wrong kind of stuff to have intentionality in the first place – only something that has the same causal powers as brains can have intentionality – and though the English speaker has the right kind of stuff for intentionality you can easily see that he doesn't get any extra intentionality by memorizing the program, since memorizing it won't teach him Chinese.

Second, the program is purely formal, but the intentional states are not in that way formal. They are defined in terms of their content, not their form. The belief that it is raining, for example, is not defined as a certain formal shape, but as a certain mental content with conditions of satisfaction, a direction of fit (see Searle 1979), and the like. Indeed the belief as such hasn't even got a formal shape in this syntactic sense, since one and the same belief can be given an indefinite number of different syntactic expressions in different linguistic systems.

Third, as I mentioned before, mental states and events are literally a product of the operation of the brain, but the program is not in that way a product of the computer.

"Well if programs are in no way constitutive of mental processes, why have so many people believed the converse? That at least needs some explanation."

I don't really know the answer to that one. The idea that computer simulations could be the real thing ought to have seemed suspicious in the first place because the computer isn't confined to simulating mental operations, by any means. No one supposes that computer simulations of a fire-alarm fire will burn the neighborhood down or that a computer simulation of a rainstorm will leave us all drenched. Why on earth would anyone suppose that a computer simulation of understanding actually understood anything? It is sometimes said that it would be frightfully hard to get computers to feel pain or fall in love, but

love and pain are neither harder nor easier than cognition or anything else. For simulation, all you need is the right input and output and a program in the middle that transforms the former into the latter. That is all the computer has for anything it does. To confuse simulation with duplication is the same mistake, whether it is pain, love, cognition, fires, or rainstorms.

Still, there are several reasons why AI must have seemed – and to many people perhaps still does seem – in some way to reproduce and thereby explain mental phenomena, and I believe we will not succeed in removing these illusions until we have fully exposed the reasons that give rise to them.

First, and perhaps the most important, is a confusion about the notion of "information processing": many people in cognitive science believe that the human brain, with its mind, does something called "information processing," and analogously the computer with its program does information processing; but fires and rainstorms, on the other hand, don't do information processing at all. Thus, though the computer can simulate the formal features of any process whatever, it stands in a special relation to the mind and brain because when the computer is properly programmed, ideally with the same program as the brain, the information processing is identical in the two cases, and this information processing is really the essence of the mental. But the trouble with this argument is that it rests on an ambiguity in the notion of "information." In the sense in which people "process information" when they reflect, say, on problems in arithmetic or when they read and answer questions about stories, the programmed computer does not do "information processing." Rather, what it does is manipulate formal symbols. The fact that the programmer and the interpreter of the computer output use the symbols to stand for objects in the world is totally beyond the scope of the computer. The computer, to repeat, has a syntax but no semantics. Thus, if you type into the computer "2 plus 2 equals?" it will type out "4." But it has no idea that "4" means 4 or that it means anything at all. And the point is not that it lacks some second-order information about the interpretation of its first-order symbols, but rather that its first-order symbols don't have any interpretations as far as the computer is concerned. All the computer has is more symbols. The introduction of the notion of "information processing" therefore produces a dilemma: either we construe the notion of "information processing" in such a way that it implies intentionality as part of the process or we don't. If the former, then the programmed computer does not do information processing, it only manipulates formal symbols. If the latter, then, though the computer does information processing, it is only doing so in the sense in which adding machines, typewriters, stomachs, thermostats, rainstorms, and hurricanes do information processing; namely, they have a level of description at which we can describe them as taking information in at one end, transforming it, and producing information as output. But in this case it is up to outside observers to interpret the input and output as information in the ordinary sense. And no similarity is established between the computer and the brain in terms of any similarity of information processing.

Second, in much of AI there is a residual behaviorism or operationalism. Since appropriately programmed computers can have input-output patterns similar to those of human beings, we are tempted to postulate mental states in the computer similar to human mental states. But once we see that it is both conceptually and empirically possible for a system to have human capacities in some realm without having any intentionality at all, we should be able to overcome this impulse. My desk adding machine has calculating capacities, but no intentionality, and in this paper I have tried to show that a system could have input and output capabilities that duplicated those of a native Chinese speaker and still not understand Chinese, regardless of how it was programmed. The Turing test is typical of the tradition in being unashamedly behavioristic and operationalistic, and I believe that if AI workers totally repudiated behaviorism and operationalism much of the confusion between simulation and duplication would be eliminated.

Third, this residual operationalism is joined to a residual form of dualism; indeed strong AI only makes sense given the dualistic assumption that, where the mind is concerned, the brain doesn't matter. In strong AI (and in functionalism, as well) what matters are programs, and programs are independent of their realization in machines; indeed, as far as AI is concerned, the same program could be realized by an electronic machine, a Cartesian mental substance, or a Hegelian world spirit. The single most surprising discovery that I have made in discussing these issues is that many AI workers are quite shocked by my idea that actual human mental phenomena might be dependent on actual physical-chemical properties of actual human brains. But if you think about it a minute you can see that I should not have been surprised; for unless you accept some form of dualism, the strong AI project hasn't got a chance. The project is to reproduce and explain the mental by designing programs, but unless the mind is not only conceptually but empirically independent of the brain you couldn't carry out the project, for the program is completely independent of any realization. Unless you believe that the mind is separable from the brain both conceptually and empirically – dualism in a strong form – you cannot hope to reproduce the mental by writing and running programs since programs must be independent of brains or any other particular forms of instantiation. If mental operations consist in computational operations on formal symbols, then it follows that they have no interesting connection with the brain; the only connection would be that the brain just happens to be one of the indefinitely many types of machines capable of instantiating the program. This form of dualism is not the traditional Cartesian variety that claims there are two sorts of *substances*, but it is Cartesian in the sense that it insists that what is specifically mental about the mind has no intrinsic connection with the actual properties of the brain. This underlying dualism is masked from us by the fact that AI literature contains frequent fulminations against "dualism"; what the authors seem to be unaware of is that their position presupposes a strong version of dualism.

"Could a machine think?" My own view is that *only* a machine could think, and indeed only very special kinds of machines, namely brains and machines that had the same causal powers as brains. And that is the main reason strong AI has had little to tell us about thinking, since it has nothing to tell us about machines. By its own definition, it is about programs, and programs are not machines. Whatever else intentionality is, it is a biological phenomenon, and it is as likely to be as causally dependent on the specific biochemistry of its origins as lactation, photosynthesis, or any other biological phenomena. No one would suppose that we could produce milk and sugar by running a computer simulation of the formal sequences in lactation and photosynthesis, but where the mind is concerned many people are willing to believe in such a miracle because of a deep and abiding dualism: the mind they suppose is a matter of formal processes and is independent of quite specific material causes in the way that milk and sugar are not.

In defense of this dualism the hope is often expressed that the brain is a digital computer (early computers, by the way, were often called "electronic brains"). But that is no help. Of course the brain is a digital computer. Since everything is a digital computer, brains are too. The point is that the brain's causal capacity to produce intentionality cannot consist in its instantiating a computer program, since for any program you like it is possible for something to instantiate that program and still not have any mental states. Whatever it is that the brain does to produce intentionality, it cannot consist in instantiating a program since no program, by itself, is sufficient for intentionality.

Notes

1 I am not, of course, saying that Schank himself is committed to these claims.
2 Also, "understanding" implies both the possession of mental (intentional) states and the truth (validity, success) of these states. For the purposes of this discussion we are concerned only with the possession of the states.
3 Intentionality is by definition that feature of certain mental states by which they are directed at or about objects and states of affairs in the world. Thus, beliefs, desires, and intentions are intentional states; undirected forms of anxiety and depression are not.

References

Fodor, J. A. 1968. The appeal to tacit knowledge in psychological explanation. *Journal of Philosophy* 65: 627–40.

Fodor, J. A. 1980. Methodological solipsism considered as a research strategy in cognitive psychology. *Behavioral and Brain Sciences* 3:1.

McCarthy, J. 1979. Ascribing mental qualities to machines. In: *Philosophical perceptives in artificial intelligence*, ed. M. Ringle. Atlantic Highlands, NJ: Humanities Press.

Newell, A. 1973. Physical symbol systems. Lecture at the La Jolla Conference on Cognitive Science.

Newell, A., and Simon, H. A. 1963. GPS, a program that simulates human thought. In: *Computers and thought*. ed. A. Feigenbaum & V. Feldman, pp. 279–93. New York: McGraw-Hill.

Pylyshyn, Z. W. 1980. Computation and cognition: issues in the foundations of cognitive science. *Behavioral and Brain Sciences* 3.

Schank, R. C., and Abelson, R. P. 1977. *Scripts, plans, goals, and understanding*. Hillsdale, NJ: Lawrence Erlbaum.

Searle, J. R. 1979. The intentionality of intention and action. *Inquiry* 22: 253–80.

Weizenbaum, J. 1965. Eliza – a computer program for the study of natural language communication between man and machine. *Communication of the Association for Computing Machinery* 9: 36–45.

Weizenbaum, J. 1976. *Computer power and human reason*. San Francisco: W. H. Freeman.

Winograd, T. 1973. A procedural model of language understanding. In: *Computer models of thought and language*, ed. R. Schank & K. Colby. San Franciso: W. H. Freeman.

15

Mad Pain and Martian Pain

David Lewis

I

There might be a strange man who sometimes feels pain, just as we do, but whose pain differs greatly from ours in its causes and effects. Our pain is typically caused by cuts, burns, pressure, and the like; his is caused by moderate exercise on an empty stomach. Our pain is generally distracting; his turns his mind to mathematics, facilitating concentration on that but distracting him from anything else. Intense pain has no tendency whatever to cause him to groan or writhe, but does cause him to cross his legs and snap his fingers. He is not in the least motivated to prevent pain or to get rid of it. In short, he feels pain but his pain does not at all occupy the typical causal role of pain. He would doubtless seem to us to be some sort of madman, and that is what I shall call him, though of course the sort of madness I have imagined may bear little resemblance to the real thing.

I said there might be such a madman. I don't know how to prove that something is possible, but my opinion that this is a possible case seems pretty firm. If I want a credible theory of mind, I need a theory that does not deny the possibility of mad pain. I needn't mind conceding that perhaps the madman is not in pain in *quite* the

same sense that the rest of us are, but there had better be some straightforward sense in which he and we are both in pain.

Also, there might be a Martian who sometimes feels pain, just as we do, but whose pain differs greatly from ours in its physical realization. His hydraulic mind contains nothing like our neurons. Rather, there are varying amounts of fluid in many inflatable cavities, and the inflation of any one of these cavities opens some valves and closes others. His mental plumbing pervades most of his body – in fact, all but the heat exchanger inside his head. When you pinch his skin you cause no firing of C-fibers – he has none – but, rather, you cause the inflation of many smallish cavities in his feet. When these cavities are inflated, he is in pain. And the effects of his pain are fitting: his thought and activity are disrupted, he groans and writhes, he is strongly motivated to stop you from pinching him and to see to it that you never do again. In short, he feels pain but lacks the bodily states that either are pain or else accompany it in us.

There might be such a Martian; this opinion too seems pretty firm. A credible theory of mind had better not deny the possibility of Martian pain. I needn't mind conceding that perhaps the Martian is not in pain in *quite* the same sense that

David Lewis, "Mad Pain and Martian Pain." *Philosophical Papers*, vol. 1. Oxford: Oxford University Press, 1983.

we Earthlings are, but there had better be some straightforward sense in which he and we are both in pain.

II

A credible theory of mind needs to make a place both for mad pain and for Martian pain. Prima facie, it seems hard for a materialist theory to pass this twofold test. As philosophers, we would like to characterize pain a priori. (We might settle for less, but let's start by asking for all we want.) As materialists, we want to characterize pain as a physical phenomenon. We can speak of the place of pain in the causal network from stimuli to inner states to behavior. And we can speak of the physical processes that go on when there is pain and that take their place in that causal network. We seem to have no other resources but these. But the lesson of mad pain is that pain is associated only contingently with its causal role, while the lesson of Martian pain is that pain is connected only contingently with its physical realization. How can we characterize pain a priori in terms of causal role and physical realization, and yet respect both kinds of contingency?

A simple identity theory straightforwardly solves the problem of mad pain. It goes just as straightforwardly wrong about Martian pain. A simple behaviorism or functionalism goes the other way: right about the Martian, wrong about the madman. The theories that fail our twofold test so decisively are altogether too simple. (Perhaps they are too simple ever to have had adherents.) It seems that a theory that can pass our test will have to be a mixed theory. It will have to be able to tell us that the madman and the Martian are both in pain, but for different reasons: the madman because he is in the right physical state, the Martian because he is in a state rightly situated in the causal network.

Certainly we can cook up a mixed theory. Here's an easy recipe: First, find a theory to take care of the common man and the madman, disregarding the Martian – presumably an identity theory. Second, find a theory to take care of the common man and the Martian, disregarding the madman – presumably some sort of behaviorism or functionalism. Then disjoin the two: say that to be in pain is to be in pain either according to the first theory or according to the second. Alternatively, claim ambiguity: say that to be in pain in one sense is to be in pain according to the first theory, to be in pain in another sense is to be in pain according to the second theory.

This strategy seems desperate. One wonders why we should have a disjunctive or ambiguous concept of pain, if common men who suffer pain are always in pain according to both disjuncts or both disambiguations. It detracts from the credibility of a theory that it posits a useless complexity in our concept of pain – useless in application to the common man, at least, and therefore useless almost always.

I don't object to the strategy of claiming ambiguity. As you'll see, I shall defend a version of it. But it's not plausible to cook up an ambiguity ad hoc to account for the compossibility of mad pain and Martian pain. It would be better to find a widespread sort of ambiguity, a sort we would believe in no matter what we thought about pain, and show that it will solve our problem. That is my plan.

III

A dozen years or so ago, D. M. Armstrong and I (independently) proposed a materialist theory of mind that joins claims of type-type psychophysical identity with a behaviorist or functionalist way of characterizing mental states such as pain.[1] I believe our theory passes the twofold test. Positing no ambiguity without independent reason, it provides natural senses in which both madman and Martian are in pain. It wriggles through between Syclla and Charybdis.

Our view is that the concept of pain, or indeed of any other experience or mental state, is the concept of a state that occupies a certain causal role, a state with certain typical causes and effects. It is the concept of a state apt for being caused by certain stimuli and apt for causing certain behavior. Or, better, of a state apt for being caused in certain ways by stimuli plus other mental states and apt for combining with certain other mental states to jointly cause certain behavior. It is the concept of a member of a system of states that together more or less realize the pattern of causal generalizations set forth in commonsense psychology. (That system may be characterized as a whole and its members characterized afterward by reference to their place in it.)

If the concept of pain is the concept of a state that occupies a certain causal role, then whatever state does occupy that role is pain. If the state of having neurons hooked up in a certain way and firing in a certain pattern is the state properly apt for causing and being caused, as we materialists think, then that neural state is pain. But the concept of pain is not the concept of that neural state. ("The concept of . . ." is an intensional functor.) The concept of pain, unlike the concept of that neural state which in fact is pain, would have applied to some different state if the relevant causal relations had been different. Pain might have not been pain. The occupant of the role might have not occupied it. Some other state might have occupied it instead. Something that is not pain might have been pain.

This is not to say, of course, that it might have been that pain was not pain and nonpain was pain; that is, that it might have been that the occupant of the role did not occupy it and some nonoccupant did. Compare: "The winner might have lost" (true) versus "It might have been that the winner lost" (false). No wording is entirely unambiguous, but I trust my meaning is clear.

In short, the concept of pain as Armstrong and I understand it is a *nonrigid* concept. Likewise the word "pain" is a nonrigid designator. It is a contingent matter what state the concept and the word apply to. It depends on what causes what. The same goes for the rest of our concepts and ordinary names of mental states.

Some need hear no more. The notion that mental concepts and names are nonrigid, wherefore what *is* pain might not have been, seems to them just self-evidently false.[2] I cannot tell why they think so. Bracketing my own theoretical commitments, I think I would have no opinion one way or the other. It's not that I don't care about shaping theory to respect naive opinion as well as can be, but in this case I have no naive opinion to respect. If I am not speaking to your condition, so be it.

If pain is identical to a certain neural state, the identity is contingent. Whether it holds is one of the things that varies from one possible world to another. But take care. I do not say that here we

have two states, pain and some neural state, that are contingently identical, identical at this world but different at another. Since I'm serious about the identity, we have not two states but one. This one state, this neural state which is pain, is not contingently identical to itself. It does not differ from itself at any world. Nothing does.[3] What's true is, rather, that the concept and name of pain contingently apply to some neural state at this world, but do not apply to it at another. Similarly, it is a contingent truth that Bruce is our cat, but it's wrong to say that Bruce and our cat are contingently identical. Our cat Bruce is necessarily self-identical. What is contingent is that the nonrigid concept of being our cat applies to Bruce rather than to some other cat, or none.

IV

Nonrigidity might begin at home. All actualities are possibilities, so the variety of possibilities includes the variety of actualities. Though some possibilities are thoroughly otherworldly, others may be found on planets within range of our telescopes. One such planet is Mars.

If a nonrigid concept or name applies to different states in different possible cases, it should be no surprise if it also applies to different states in different actual cases. Nonrigidity is to logical space as other relativities are to ordinary space. If the word "pain" designates one state at our actual world and another at a possible world where our counterparts have a different internal structure, then also it may designate one state on Earth and another on Mars. Or, better, since Martians may come here and we may go to Mars, it may designate one state for Earthlings and another for Martians.

We may say that some state *occupies a causal role for a population*. We may say this whether the population is situated entirely at our actual world, or partly at our actual world and partly at other worlds, or entirely at other worlds. If the concept of pain is the concept of a state that occupies that role, then we may say that a state *is pain for a population*. Then we may say that a certain pattern of firing of neurons is pain for the population of actual Earthlings and some but not all of our otherworldly counterparts, whereas the inflation of certain cavities in the feet is pain for the population of actual Martians and some of their otherworldly counterparts. Human pain is the state that occupies the role of pain for humans. Martian pain is the state that occupies the same role for Martians.

A state occupies a causal role for a population, and the concept of occupant of that role applies to it, if and only if, with few exceptions, whenever a member of that population is in that state, his being in that state has the sort of causes and effects given by the role.

The thing to say about Martian pain is that the Martian is in pain because he is in a state that occupies the causal role of pain for Martians, whereas we are in pain because we are in a state that occupies the role of pain for us.

V

Now, what of the madman? He is in pain, but he is not in a state that occupies the causal role of pain for him. He is in a state that occupies that role for most of us, but he is an exception. The causal role of a pattern of firing of neurons depends on one's circuit diagram, and he is hooked up wrong.

His state does not occupy the role of pain for a population comprising himself and his fellow madmen. But it does occupy that role for a more salient population – mankind at large. He is a man, albeit an exceptional one, and a member of that larger population.

We have allowed for exceptions. I spoke of the definitive syndrome of *typical* causes and effects. Armstrong spoke of a state *apt for* having certain causes and effects; that does not mean that it has them invariably. Again, I spoke of a system of states that *comes near* to realizing commonsense psychology. A state may therefore occupy a role for mankind even if it does not at all occupy that role for some mad minority of mankind.

The thing to say about mad pain is that the madman is in pain because he is in the state that occupies the causal role of pain for the population comprising all mankind. He is an exceptional member of that population. The state that occupies the role for the population does not occupy it for him.

VI

We may say that X is in pain simpliciter if and only if X is in the state that occupies the causal role of pain for the *appropriate* population. But what is the appropriate population? Perhaps (1) it should be *us*; after all, it's our concept and our word. On the other hand, if it's X we're talking about, perhaps (2) it should be a population that X himself belongs to, and (3) it should preferably be one in which X is not exceptional. Either way, (4) an appropriate population should be a natural kind – a species, perhaps.

If X is you and I – human and unexceptional – all four considerations pull together. The appropriate population consists of mankind as it actually is, extending into other worlds only to an extent that does not make the actual majority exceptional.

Since the four criteria agree in the case of the common man, which is the case we usually have in mind, there is no reason why we should have made up our minds about their relative importance in cases of conflict. It should be no surprise if ambiguity and uncertainty arise in such cases. Still, some cases do seem reasonably clear.

If X is our Martian, we are inclined to say that he is in pain when the cavities in his feet are inflated; and so says the theory, provided that criterion (1) is outweighed by the other three, so that the appropriate population is taken to be the species of Martians to which X belongs.

If X is our madman, we are inclined to say that he is in pain when he is in the state that occupies the role of pain for the rest of us; and so says the theory, provided that criterion (3) is outweighed by the other three, so that the appropriate population is taken to be mankind.

We might also consider the case of a mad Martian, related to other Martians as the madman is to the rest of us. If X is a mad Martian, I would be inclined to say that he in pain when the cavities in his feet are inflated; and so says our theory provided that criteria (2) and (4) together outweigh either (1) or (3) by itself.

Other cases are less clear-cut. Since the balance is less definitely in favor of one population or another, we may perceive the relativity to population by feeling genuinely undecided. Suppose the state that plays the role of pain for us plays instead the role of thirst for a certain small subpopulation of mankind, and vice versa. When one of them has the state that is pain for us and thirst for him, there may be genuine and irresolvable indecision about whether to call him pained or thirsty – that is, whether to think of him as a madman or as a Martian. Criterion (1) suggests calling his state pain and regarding him as an exception; criteria (2) and (3) suggest shifting to a subpopulation and calling his state thirst. Criterion (4) could go either way, since mankind and the exceptional subpopulation may both be natural kinds. (Perhaps it is relevant to ask whether membership in the subpopulation is hereditary.)

The interchange of pain and thirst parallels the traditional problem of inverted spectra. I have suggested that there is no determinate fact of the matter about whether the victim of interchange undergoes pain or thirst. I think this conclusion accords well with the fact that there seems to be no persuasive solution one way or the other to the old problem of inverted spectra. I would say that there is a good sense in which the alleged victim of inverted spectra sees red when he looks at grass: he is in a state that occupies the role of seeing red for mankind in general. And there is an equally good sense in which he sees green: he is in a state that occupies the role of seeing green for him, and for a small subpopulation of which he is an unexceptional member and which has some claim to be regarded as a natural kind. You are right to say either, though not in the same breath. Need more be said?

To sum up. Armstrong and I claim to give a schema that, if filled in, would characterize pain and other states a priori. If the causal facts are right, then also we characterize pain as a physical phenomenon. By allowing for exceptional members of a population, we associate pain only contingently with its causal role. Therefore we do not deny the possibility of mad pain, provided there is not too much of it. By allowing for variation from one population to another (actual or merely possible) we associate pain only contingently with its physical realization. Therefore we do not deny the possibility of Martian pain. If different ways of filling in the relativity to population may be said to yield different senses of the word "pain," then we plead ambiguity. The madman is in pain in one sense, or relative to one population. The Martian is in pain in another sense, or relative to another population. (So is the mad Martian.)

But we do not posit ambiguity ad hoc. The requisite flexibility is explained simply by supposing that we have not bothered to make up our minds about semantic niceties that would make no difference to any commonplace case. The ambiguity that arises in cases of inverted spectra and the like is simply one instance of a commonplace kind of ambiguity – a kind that may arise whenever we have tacit relativity and criteria of selection that sometimes fail to choose a definite relatum. It is the same kind of ambiguity that arises if someone speaks of relevant studies without making clear whether he means relevance to current affairs, to spiritual well-being, to understanding, or what.

VII

We have a place for commonplace pain, mad pain, Martian pain, and even mad Martian pain. But one case remains problematic. What about pain in a being who is mad, alien, and unique? Have we made a place for that? It seems not. Since he is mad, we may suppose that his alleged state of pain does not occupy the proper causal role for him. Since he is alien, we may also suppose that it does not occupy the proper role for us. And since he is unique, it does not occupy the proper role for others of his species. What is left?

(One thing that might be left is the population consisting of him and his unactualized counterparts at other worlds. If he went mad as a result of some improbable accident, perhaps we can say that he is in pain because he is in the state that occupies the role for most of his alternative possible selves; the state that would have occupied the role for him if he had developed in a more probable way. To make the problem as hard as possible, I must suppose that this solution is unavailable. He did *not* narrowly escape being so constituted that his present state would have occupied the role of pain.)

I think we cannot and need not solve this problem. Our only recourse is to deny that the case is possible. To stipulate that the being in this example is in pain was illegitimate. That seems credible enough. Admittedly, I might have thought offhand that the case was possible. No wonder; it merely combines elements of other cases that are possible. But I am willing to change my mind. Unlike my opinions about the possibility of mad pain and Martian pain, my naive opinions about this case are not firm enough to carry much weight.

VIII

Finally, I would like to try to preempt an objection. I can hear it said that I have been strangely silent about the very center of my topic. *What is it like* to be the madman, the Martian, the mad Martian, the victim of interchange of pain and thirst, or the being who is mad, alien, and unique? What is the *phenomenal character* of his state? If it *feels* to him like pain, then it *is* pain, whatever its causal role or physical nature. If not, it isn't. It's that simple!

Yes. It would indeed be a mistake to consider whether a state is pain while ignoring what it is like to have it. Fortunately, I have not made that mistake. Indeed, it is an impossible mistake to make. It is like the impossible mistake of considering whether a number is composite while ignoring the question of what factors it has.

Pain is a feeling.[4] Surely that is uncontroversial. To have pain and to feel pain are one and the same. For a state to be pain and for it to feel painful are likewise one and the same. A theory of what it is for a state to be pain is inescapably a theory of what it is like to be in that state, of how that state feels, of the phenomenal character of that state. Far from ignoring questions of how states feel in the odd cases we have been considering, I have been discussing nothing else!

Only if you believe on independent grounds that considerations of causal role and physical realization have no bearing on whether a state is pain should you say that they have no bearing on how that state feels.

Notes

1 D. M. Armstrong, *A Materialist Theory of the Mind* (London: Routledge, 1968); "The Nature of Mind," in C. V. Borst, ed., *The Mind/Brain Identity Theory* (London: Macmillan, 1970), pp. 67–97; "The Causal Theory of the Mind," *Neue Heft für Philosophie*, no. 11 (Vendenhoek & Ruprecht, 1977), pp. 82–95. David Lewis, "An Argument for the Identity Theory," in *Philosophical Papers*, vol. 1 (New York: Oxford University Press, 1983); review of *Art, Mind, and Religion, Journal of Philosophy* 66 (1969): 22–7, particularly pp. 23–5; "Psychophysical and Theoretical Identifications," *Australasian Journal of Philosophy* 50 (1972): 249–58; "Radical Interpretation," in *Philosophical Papers*, vol. 1.

2 For instance, see Saul A. Kripke, "Naming and Necessity," in Gilbert Harman and Donald Davidson, eds., *Semantics of Natural Language* (Dordrecht: Reidel, 1972), pp. 253–355, 763–9, particularly pp. 335–6. Note that the sort of identity theory that Kripke opposes by argument, rather than by appeal to self-evidence, is not the sort that Armstrong and I propose.

3 The closest we can come is to have something at one world with twin counterparts at another. See my "Counterpart Theory and Quantified Modal Logic," in *Philosophical Papers*, vol. 1. That possibility is irrelevant to the present case.

4 Occurrent pain, that is. Maybe a disposition that sometimes but not always causes occurrent pain might also be called "pain."

16

Eliminative Materialism

Paul M. Churchland

The identity theory was called into doubt not because the prospects for a materialist account of our mental capacities were thought to be poor, but because it seemed unlikely that the arrival of an adequate materialist theory would bring with it the nice one-to-one match-ups, between the concepts of folk psychology and the concepts of theoretical neuroscience, that intertheoretic reduction requires. The reason for that doubt was the great variety of quite different physical systems that could instantiate the required functional organization. *Eliminative materialism* also doubts that the correct neuroscientific account of human capacities will produce a neat reduction of our common-sense framework, but here the doubts arise from a quite different source.

As the eliminative materialists see it, the one-to-one match-ups will not be found, and our common-sense psychological framework will not enjoy an intertheoretic reduction, *because our common-sense psychological framework is a false and radically misleading conception of the causes of human behavior and the nature of cognitive activity*. On this view, folk psychology is not just an incomplete representation of our inner natures; it is an outright *mis*representation of our internal states and activities. Consequently, we cannot expect a truly adequate neuroscientific account of our inner lives to provide theoretical categories that match up nicely with the categories of our common-sense framework. Accordingly, we must expect that the older framework will simply be eliminated, rather than be reduced, by a matured neuroscience.

Historical Parallels

As the identity theorist can point to historical cases of successful intertheoretic reduction, so the eliminative materialist can point to historical cases of the outright elimination of the ontology of an older theory in favor of the ontology of a new and superior theory. For most of the eighteenth and nineteenth centuries, learned people believed that heat was a subtle *fluid* held in bodies, much in the way water is held in a sponge. A fair body of moderately successful theory described the way this fluid substance – called "caloric" – flowed within a body, or from one body to another, and how it produced thermal expansion, melting, boiling, and so forth. But by the end of the last century it had become abundantly clear that heat was not a substance at all, but just the energy of motion of the trillions of jostling molecules that make up the heated body

Paul M. Churchland, "Eliminative Materialism," from *Matter and Consciousness: A Contemporary Introduction to the Philosophy of Mind*, rev. edn. (Cambridge, MA: MIT Press, 1994), pp. 43–9. © 1988 by Massachusetts Institute of Technology. Reprinted with permission from The MIT Press.

itself. The new theory – the "corpuscular/kinetic theory of matter and heat" – was much more successful than the old in explaining and predicting the thermal behavior of bodies. And since we were unable to *identify* caloric fluid with kinetic energy (according to the old theory, caloric is a material *substance*; according to the new theory, kinetic energy is a form of *motion*), it was finally agreed that there is *no such thing* as caloric. Caloric was simply eliminated from our accepted ontology.

A second example. It used to be thought that when a piece of wood burns, or a piece of metal rusts, a spiritlike substance called "phlogiston" was being released: briskly, in the former case, slowly in the latter. Once gone, that 'noble' substance left only a base pile of ash or rust. It later came to be appreciated that both processes involve, not the loss of something, but the *gaining* of a substance taken from the atmosphere: oxygen. Phlogiston emerged, not as an incomplete description of what was going on, but as a radical misdescription. Phlogiston was therefore not suitable for reduction to or identification with some notion from within the new oxygen chemistry, and it was simply eliminated from science.

Admittedly, both of these examples concern the elimination of something nonobservable, but our history also includes the elimination of certain widely accepted 'observables'. Before Copernicus' views became available, almost any human who ventured out at night could look up at *the starry sphere of the heavens*, and if he stayed for more than a few minutes he could also see that it *turned*, around an axis through Polaris. What the sphere was made of (crystal?) and what made it turn (the gods?) were theoretical questions that exercised us for over two millennia. But hardly anyone doubted the existence of what everyone could observe with their own eyes. In the end, however, we learned to reinterpret our visual experience of the night sky within a very different conceptual framework, and the turning sphere evaporated.

Witches provide another example. Psychosis is a fairly common affliction among humans, and in earlier centuries its victims were standardly seen as cases of demonic possession, as instances of Satan's spirit itself, glaring malevolently out at us from behind the victims' eyes. That witches exist was not a matter of any controversy. One would

occasionally see them, in any city or hamlet, engaged in incoherent, paranoid, or even murderous behavior. But observable or not, we eventually decided that witches simply do not exist. We concluded that the concept of a witch is an element in a conceptual framework that misrepresents so badly the phenomena to which it was standardly applied that literal application of the notion should be permanently withdrawn. Modern theories of mental dysfunction led to the elimination of witches from our serious ontology.

The concepts of folk psychology – belief, desire, fear, sensation, pain, joy, and so on – await a similar fate, according to the view at issue. And when neuroscience has matured to the point where the poverty of our current conceptions is apparent to everyone, and the superiority of the new framework is established, we shall then be able to set about *re*conceiving our internal states and activities, within a truly adequate conceptual framework at last. Our explanations of one another's behavior will appeal to such things as our neuropharmacological states, the neural activity in specialized anatomical areas, and whatever other states are deemed relevant by the new theory. Our private introspection will also be transformed, and may be profoundly enhanced by reason of the more accurate and penetrating framework it will have to work with – just as the astronomer's perception of the night sky is much enhanced by the detailed knowledge of modern astronomical theory that he or she possesses.

The magnitude of the conceptual revolution here suggested should not be minimized: it would be enormous. And the benefits to humanity might be equally great. If each of us possessed an accurate neuroscientific understanding of (what we now conceive dimly as) the varieties and causes of mental illness, the factors involved in learning, the neural basis of emotions, intelligence, and socialization, then the sum total of human misery might be much reduced. The simple increase in mutual understanding that the new framework made possible could contribute substantially toward a more peaceful and humane society. Of course, there would be dangers as well: increased knowledge means increased power, and power can always be misused.

Arguments for Eliminative Materialism

The arguments for eliminative materialism are diffuse and less than decisive, but they are stronger than is widely supposed. The distinguishing feature of this position is its denial that a smooth intertheoretic reduction is to be expected – even a species-specific reduction – of the framework of folk psychology to the framework of a matured neuroscience. The reason for this denial is the eliminative materialist's conviction that folk psychology is a hopelessly primitive and deeply confused conception of our internal activities. But why this low opinion of our common-sense conceptions?

There are at least three reasons. First, the eliminative materialist will point to the widespread explanatory, predictive, and manipulative failures of folk psychology. So much of what is central and familiar to us remains a complete mystery from within folk psychology. We do not know what *sleep* is, or why we have to have it, despite spending a full third of our lives in that condition. (The answer, "For rest," is mistaken. Even if people are allowed to rest continuously, their need for sleep is undiminished. Apparently, sleep serves some deeper functions, but we do not yet know what they are.) We do not understand how *learning* transforms each of us from a gaping infant to a cunning adult, or how differences in *intelligence* are grounded. We have not the slightest idea how *memory* works, or how we manage to retrieve relevant bits of information instantly from the awesome mass we have stored. We do not know what *mental illness* is, nor how to cure it.

In sum, the most central things about us remain almost entirely mysterious from within folk psychology. And the defects noted cannot be blamed on inadequate time allowed for their correction, for folk psychology has enjoyed no significant changes or advances in well over 2,000 years, despite its manifest failures. Truly successful theories may be expected to reduce, but significantly unsuccessful theories merit no such expectation.

This argument from explanatory poverty has a further aspect. So long as one sticks to normal brains, the poverty of folk psychology is perhaps not strikingly evident. But as soon as one examines the many perplexing behavioral and cognitive deficits suffered by people with *damaged* brains, one's descriptive and explanatory resources start to claw the air [. . .]. As with other humble theories asked to operate successfully in unexplored extensions of their old domain (for example, Newtonian mechanics in the domain of velocities close to the velocity of light, and the classical gas law in the domain of high pressures or temperatures), the descriptive and explanatory inadequacies of folk psychology become starkly evident.

The second argument tries to draw an inductive lesson from our conceptual history. Our early folk theories of motion were profoundly confused, and were eventually displaced entirely by more sophisticated theories. Our early folk theories of the structure and activity of the heavens were wildly off the mark, and survive only as historical lessons in how wrong we can be. Our folk theories of the nature of fire, and the nature of life, were similarly cockeyed. And one could go on, since the vast majority of our past folk conceptions have been similarly exploded. All except folk psychology, which survives to this day and has only recently begun to feel pressure. But the phenomenon of conscious intelligence is surely a more complex and difficult phenomenon than any of those just listed. So far as accurate understanding is concerned, it would be a *miracle* if we had got *that* one right the very first time, when we fell down so badly on all the others. Folk psychology has survived for so very long, presumably, not because it is basically correct in its representations, but because the phenomena addressed are so surpassingly difficult that any useful handle on them, no matter how feeble, is unlikely to be displaced in a hurry.

A third argument attempts to find an a priori advantage for eliminative materialism over the identity theory and functionalism. It attempts to counter the common intuition that eliminative materialism is distantly possible, perhaps, but is much less probable than either the identity theory or functionalism. The focus again is on whether the concepts of folk psychology will find vindicating match-ups in a matured neuroscience. The eliminativist bets no; the other two bet yes. (Even the functionalist bets yes, but expects the match-ups to be only species-specific, or only person-specific. Functionalism, recall, denies the existence only of *universal* type/type identities.)

The eliminativist will point out that the requirements on a reduction are rather demanding. The new theory must entail a set of principles and embedded concepts that mirrors very closely the specific conceptual structure to be reduced. And the fact is, there are vastly many more ways of being an explanatorily successful neuroscience while *not* mirroring the structure of folk psychology, than there are ways of being an explanatorily successful neuroscience while also *mirroring* the very specific structure of folk psychology. Accordingly, the a priori probability of eliminative materialism is not lower, but substantially *higher* than that of either of its competitors. One's initial intuitions here are simply mistaken.

Granted, this initial a priori advantage could be reduced if there were a very strong presumption in favor of the truth of folk psychology – true theories are better bets to win reduction. But according to the first two arguments, the presumptions on this point should run in precisely the opposite direction.

Arguments against Eliminative Materialism

The initial plausibility of this rather radical view is low for almost everyone, since it denies deeply entrenched assumptions. That is at best a question-begging complaint, of course, since those assumptions are precisely what is at issue. But the following line of thought does attempt to mount a real argument.

Eliminative materialism is false, runs the argument, because one's introspection reveals directly the existence of pains, beliefs, desires, fears, and so forth. Their existence is as obvious as anything could be.

The eliminative materialist will reply that this argument makes the same mistake that an ancient or medieval person would be making if he insisted that he could just see with his own eyes that the heavens form a turning sphere, or that witches exist. The fact is, all observation occurs within some system of concepts, and our observation judgments are only as good as the conceptual framework in which they are expressed. In all three cases – the starry sphere, witches, and the familiar mental states – precisely what is

challenged is the integrity of the background conceptual frameworks in which the observation judgments are expressed. To insist on the validity of one's experiences, *traditionally interpreted*, is therefore to beg the very question at issue. For in all three cases, the question is whether we should *reconceive* the nature of some familiar observational domain.

A second criticism attempts to find an incoherence in the eliminative materialist's position. The bald statement of eliminative materialism is that the familiar mental states do not really exist. But that statement is meaningful, runs the argument, only if it is the expression of a certain *belief*, and an *intention* to communicate, and a *knowledge* of the language, and so forth. But if the statement is true, then no such mental states exist, and the statement is therefore a meaningless string of marks or noises, and cannot be true. Evidently, the assumption that eliminative materialism is true entails that it cannot be true.

The hole in this argument is the premise concerning the conditions necessary for a statement to be meaningful. It begs the question. If eliminative materialism is true, then meaningfulness must have some different source. To insist on the 'old' source is to insist on the validity of the very framework at issue. Again, an historical parallel may be helpful here. Consider the medieval theory that being biologically *alive* is a matter of being ensouled by an immaterial *vital spirit*. And consider the following response to someone who has expressed disbelief in that theory.

> My learned friend has stated that there is no such thing as vital spirit. But this statement is incoherent. For if it is true, then my friend does not have vital spirit, and must therefore be *dead*. But if he is dead, then his statement is just a string of noises, devoid of meaning or truth. Evidently, the assumption that antivitalism is true entails that it cannot be true! Q.E.D.

This second argument is now a joke, but the first argument begs the question in exactly the same way.

A final criticism draws a much weaker conclusion, but makes a rather stronger case. Eliminative materialism, it has been said, is making mountains out of molehills. It exaggerates the defects in folk psychology, and underplays its real successes. Perhaps the arrival of a matured neuroscience will require the elimination of the occasional folk-psychological concept, continues the criticism, and a minor adjustment in certain folk-psychological principles may have to be endured. But the large-scale elimination forecast by the eliminative materialist is just an alarmist worry or a romantic enthusiasm.

Perhaps this complaint is correct. And perhaps it is merely complacent. Whichever, it does bring out the important point that we do not confront two simple and mutually exclusive possibilities here: pure reduction versus pure elimination.

Rather, these are the end points of a smooth spectrum of possible outcomes, between which there are mixed cases of partial elimination and partial reduction. Only empirical research can tell us where on that spectrum our own case will fall. Perhaps we should speak here, more liberally, of "revisionary materialism", instead of concentrating on the more radical possibility of an across-the-board elimination. Perhaps we should. But it has been my aim in this section to make it at least intelligible to you that our collective conceptual destiny lies substantially toward the revolutionary end of the spectrum.

17

Of Identity and Diversity

John Locke

1. Another occasion, the mind often takes of comparing, is the very Being of things, when considering any thing as existing at any determin'd time and place, we compare it with it self existing at another time, and thereon form the *Ideas* of *Identity* and *Diversity*. When we see any thing to be in any place in any instant of time, we are sure, (be it what it will) that it is that very thing, and not another, which at that same time exists in another place, how like and undistinguishable soever it may be in all other respects: And in this consists *Identity*, when the *Ideas* it is attributed to vary not at all from what they were that moment, wherein we consider their former existence, and to which we compare the present. For we never finding, nor conceiving it possible, that two things of the same kind should exist in the same place at the same time, we rightly conclude, that whatever exists any where at any time, excludes all of the same kind, and is there it self alone. When therefore we demand, whether any thing be the same or no, it refers always to something that existed such a time in such a place, which 'twas certain, at that instant, was the same with it self and no other: From whence it follows, that one thing cannot have two beginnings of Existence, nor two things one beginning, it being impossible for two things of the same kind, to be or exist in the same instant, in the very same place; or one and the same thing in different places. That therefore that had one beginning is the same thing, and that which had a different beginning in time and place from that, is not the same but divers. That which has made the Difficulty about this Relation, has been the little care and attention used in having precise Notions of the things to which it is attributed.

2. We have the *Ideas* but of three sorts of Substances; 1. God. 2. Finite Intelligences. 3. *Bodies*. First, God is without beginning, eternal, unalterable, and every where; and therefore concerning his Identity, there can be no doubt. Secondly, Finite Spirits having had each its determinate time and place of beginning to exist, the relation to that time and place will always determine to each of them its Identity as long as it exists.

Thirdly, The same will hold of every Particle of Matter, to which no Addition or Substraction of Matter being made, it is the same. For though these three sorts of Substances, as we term them, do not exclude one another out of the same place; yet we cannot conceive but that they must necessarily each of them exclude any of the same kind out of the same place: Or else the Notions and Names of Identity and Diversity would be in vain, and there could be no such distinction of Substances, or any thing else one from another.

John Locke, "Of Identity and Diversity," from John Locke, *An Essay Concerning Human Understanding*, ed. Alexander Fraser (Oxford: Clarendon Press, 1894).

For Example, could two Bodies be in the same place at the same time; then those two parcels of Matter must be one and the same, take them great or little; nay, all Bodies must be one and the same. For by the same reason that two particles of Matter may be in one place, all Bodies may be in one place: Which, when it can be supposed, takes away the distinction of Identity and Diversity, of one and more, and renders it ridiculous. But it being a contradiction, that two or more should be one, Identity and Diversity are relations and ways of comparing well founded, and of use to the Understanding. All other things being but Modes or Relations ultimately terminated in Substances, the Identity and Diversity of each particular Existence of them too will be by the same way determined: Only as to things whose Existence is in succession, such as are the Actions of finite Beings, *v.g. Motion* and *Thought*, both which consist in a continued train of Succession, concerning their Diversity there can be no question: Because each perishing the moment it begins, they cannot exist in different times, or in different places, as permanent Beings can at different times exist in distant places; and therefore no motion or thought considered as at different times can be the same, each part thereof having a different beginning of Existence.

3. From what has been said, 'tis easy to discover, what is so much enquired after, the *principium Individuationis*, and that 'tis plain is Existence it self, which determines a Being of any sort to a particular time and place incommunicable to two Beings of the same kind. This though it seems easier to conceive in simple Substances or Modes; yet when reflected on, is not more difficult in compounded ones, if care be taken to what it is applied; *v.g.* Let us suppose an Atom, i.e. a continued body under one immutable Superficies, existing in a determined time and place: 'tis evident, that, considered in any instant of its Existence, it is, in that instant, the same with it self. For being, at that instant, what it is, and nothing else, it is the same, and so must continue, as long as its Existence is continued: for so long it will be the same, and no other. In like manner, if two or more Atoms be joined together into the same Mass, every one of those Atoms will be the same, by the foregoing Rule: And whilst they exist united together, the Mass, consisting of the same

Atoms, must be the same Mass, or the same Body, let the parts be never so differently jumbled: But if one of these Atoms be taken away, or one new one added, it is no longer the same Mass, or the same Body. In the state of living Creatures, their Identity depends not on a Mass of the same Particles; but on something else. For in them the variation of great parcels of Matter alters not the Identity: An Oak, growing from a Plant to a great Tree, and then lopp'd, is still the same Oak: And a Colt grown up to a Horse, sometimes fat, sometimes lean, is all the while the same Horse: though, in both these Cases, there may be a manifest change of the parts: So that truly they are not either of them the same Masses of Matter, though they be truly one of them the same Oak, and the other the same Horse. The reason whereof is, that in these two cases of a Mass of Matter, and a living Body, *Identity* is not applied to the same thing.

4. We must therefore consider wherein an Oak differs from a Mass of Matter, and that seems to me to be in this; that the one is only the Cohesion of Particles of Matter any how united, the other such a disposition of them as constitutes the parts of an Oak; and such an Organization of those parts, as is fit to receive, and distribute nourishment, so as to continue, and frame the Wood, Bark, and Leaves, *etc.* of an Oak, in which consists the vegetable Life. That being then one Plant, which has such an Organization of Parts in one coherent Body, partaking of one Common Life, it continues to be the same Plant, as long as it partakes of the same Life, though that Life be communicated to new Particles of Matter vitally united to the living Plant, in a like continued Organization, conformable to that sort of Plants. For this Organization being at any one instant in any one Collection of *Matter*, is in that particular concrete distinguished from all other, and is that individual Life, which existing constantly from that moment both forwards and backwards in the same continuity of insensibly succeeding Parts united to the living Body of the Plant, it has that Identity, which makes the same Plant, and all the parts of it, parts of the same Plant, during all the time that they exist united in that continued Organization, which is fit to convey that Common Life to all the Parts so united.

5. The Case is not so much different in *Brutes*, but that any one may hence see what

makes an Animal, and continues it the same. Something we have like this in Machines, and may serve to illustrate it. For Example, what is a Watch? 'Tis plain 'tis nothing but a fit Organization, or Construction of Parts, to a certain end, which, when a sufficient force is added to it, it is capable to attain. If we would suppose this Machine one continued Body, all whose organized Parts were repair'd, increas'd or diminish'd, by a constant Addition or Separation of insensible Parts, with one Common Life, we should have something very much like the Body of an Animal, with this difference, That in an Animal the fitness of the Organization, and the Motion wherein Life consists, begin together, the Motion coming from within; but in Machines the force, coming sensibly from without, is often away, when the Organ is in order, and well fitted to receive it.

6.   This also shews wherein the Identity of the same *Man* consists; *viz.* in nothing but a participation of the same continued Life, by constantly fleeting Particles of Matter, in succession vitally united to the same organized Body. He that shall place the *Identity* of Man in any thing else, but like that of other Animals in one fitly organized Body taken in any one instant, and from thence continued under one Organization of Life in several successively fleeting Particles of Matter, united to it, will find it hard, to make an *Embryo*, one of Years, mad, and sober, the same Man, by any Supposition, that will not make it possible for *Seth, Ismael, Socrates, Pilate,* St. *Austin,* and *Cæsar Borgia* to be the same Man. For if the *Identity* of Soul alone makes the same Man, and there be nothing in the Nature of Matter, why the same individual Spirit may not be united to different Bodies, it will be possible, that those Men, living in distant Ages, and of different Tempers, may have been the same Man: Which way of speaking must be from a very strange use of the is Word *Man,* applied to an *Idea,* out of which Body and Shape is excluded: And that way of speaking would agree yet worse with the Notions of those Philosophers, who allow of Transmigration, and are of Opinion that the Souls of Men may, for their Miscarriages, be detruded into the Bodies of Beasts, as fit Habitations with Organs suited to the satisfaction of their Brutal Inclinations. But yet I think no body, could he be sure that the Soul of *Heliogabalus* were in one of his Hogs, would yet say that Hog were a *Man* or *Heliogabalus.*

7.   'Tis not therefore Unity of Substance that comprehends all sorts of *Identity,* or will determine it in every Case: But to conceive, and judge of it aright, we must consider what *Idea* the Word it is applied to stands for: It being one thing to be the same *Substance,* another the same *Man,* and a third the same *Person,* if *Person, Man,* and *Substance,* are three Names standing for three different *Ideas;* for such as is the *Idea* belonging to that Name, such must be the *Identity:* Which if it had been a little more carefully attended to, would possibly have prevented a great deal of that Confusion, which often occurs about this Matter, with no small seeming Difficulties; especially concerning *Personal Identity,* which therefore we shall in the next place a little consider.

8.   An Animal is a living organized Body; and consequently, the same Animal, as we have observed, is the same continued Life communicated to different Particles of Matter, as they happen successively to be united to that organiz'd living Body. And whatever is talked of other definitions, ingenuous observation puts it past doubt, that the *Idea* in our Minds, of which the Sound *Man* in our Mouths is the Sign, is nothing else but of an Animal of such a certain Form: Since I think I may be confident, that whoever should see a Creature of his own Shape and Make, though it had no more reason all its Life, than a *Cat* or a *Parrot,* would call him still a *Man;* or whoever should hear a *Cat* or a *Parrot* discourse, reason, and philosophize, would call or think it nothing but a *Cat* or a *Parrot;* and say, the one was a dull irrational *Man,* and the other a very intelligent rational *Parrot.* A Relation we have in an Author of great note is sufficient to countenance the supposition of a rational *Parrot.* His Words are.

"I had a mind to know from *Prince Maurice*'s own Mouth, the account of a common, but much credited Story, that I had heard so often from many others, of an old *Parrot* he had in *Brasil,* during his Government there, that spoke, and asked, and answered common Questions like a reasonable Creature; so that those of his Train there, generally concluded it to be Witchery or Possession; and one of his Chaplains, who lived long afterwards in *Holland,* would never from that time endure a *Parrot*, but said, they all had a Devil in them. I had heard many particulars of this Story, and assevered by People hard to be discredited, which made me ask *Prince Maurice* what there was of it. He said, with his usual plainess, and dryness in talk, there was something true, but a great deal false, of what had been reported. I desired to know of him, what there was of the first; he told me short and coldly, that he had heard of such an old *Parrot* when he came to *Brasil*, and though he believed nothing of it, and 'twas a good way off, yet he had so much Curiosity as to send for it, that 'twas a very great and a very old one; and when it came first into the Room where the Prince was, with a great many *Dutch-men* about him, it said presently, *What a company of white Men are here?* They asked it what he thought that Man was, pointing at the Prince? It answered, *Some General or other*; when they brought it close to him, he asked it, *D'ou venes vous?* it answered, *De Marinnan*. The Prince, *A qui estes vous?* The Parrot, *A un Portugais*. Prince, *Que fais tu la?* Parrot, *Je garde les poulles*. The Prince laughed and said, *Vous gardez les poulles?* The Parrot answered, *Ouy, moy et je scay bien faire*; and made the Chuck four or five times that People use to make to Chickens when they call them.[1] I set down the Words of this worthy Dialogue in *French*, just as Prince *Maurice* said them to me. I asked him in what Language the *Parrot* spoke, and he said, in *Brasilian*; I asked whether he understood *Brasilian*; he said No, but he had taken care to have two Interpreters by him, the one a *Dutch-man*, that spoke *Brasilian*, and the other a *Brasilian*, that spoke *Dutch*; that he asked them separately and privately, and both of them agreed in telling him just the same thing that the *Parrot* said. I could not but tell this odd Story, because it is so much out of the way, and from the first hand, and what may pass for a good one; for I dare say this Prince, at least, believed himself in all he told me, having ever passed for a very honest and pious Man; I leave it to Naturalists to reason, and to other Men to believe as they please upon it; however, it is not, perhaps, amiss to relieve or enliven a busie Scene sometimes with such digressions, whether to the purpose or no."

I have taken care that the Reader should have the Story at large in the Authors own Words, because he seems to me not to have thought it incredible; for it cannot be imagined that so able a Man as he, who had sufficiency enough to warrant all the Testimonies he gives of himself, should take so much pains, in a place where it had nothing to do, to pin so close, not only on a Man whom he mentions as his Friend, but on a Prince in whom he acknowledges very great Honesty and Piety, a Story which if he himself thought incredible, he could not but also think ridiculous. The Prince, 'tis plain, who vouches this Story, and our Author who relates it from him, both of them call this Talker a *Parrot*; and I ask any one else who thinks such a Story fit to be told, whether if this *Parrot*, and all of its kind, had always talked as we have a Princes word for it, this one did, whether, I say, they would not have passed for a race of *rational Animals*, but yet whether for all that, they would have been allowed to be Men and not *Parrots*? For I presume 'tis not the *Idea* of a thinking or rational Being alone, that makes the *Idea* of a *Man* in most Peoples Sense; but of a Body so and so shaped joined to it; and if that be the *Idea* of a *Man*, the same successive Body not shifted all at once, must as well as the same immaterial Spirit go to the making of the same *Man*.

9. This being premised to find wherein *personal Identity* consists, we must consider what *Person* stands for; which, I think, is a thinking intelligent Being, that has reason and reflection, and can consider it self as it self, the same thinking thing in different times and places; which it does only by that consciousness, which is inseparable from thinking, and as it seems to me essential to it: It being impossible for any one to perceive, without perceiving, that he does perceive. When we see, hear, smell, taste, feel, meditate, or will any thing, we know that we do so. Thus it is always as to our present Sensations and Perceptions: And by this every one is to himself, that which he calls *self*: It not being considered in this case, whether the same *self* be continued in the same, or divers Substances. For since consciousness always accompanies thinking, and 'tis that, that makes every one to be, what he calls *self*; and thereby distinguishes himself from all other thinking things, in this alone consists *personal Identity*, i.e. the sameness of a rational Being: And as far as this consciousness can be extended backwards to any past Action or Thought, so far reaches the Identity of that *Person*; it is the same

self now it was then; and 'tis by the same *self* with this present one that now reflects on it, that that Action was done.

10.   But it is farther enquir'd whether it be the same Identical Substance. This few would think they had reason to doubt of, if these Perceptions, with their consciousness, always remain'd present in the Mind, whereby the same thinking thing would be always consciously present, and, as would be thought, evidently the same to it self. But that which seems to make the difficulty is this, that this consciousness, being interrupted always by forgetfulness, there being no moment of our Lives wherein we have the whole train of all our past Actions before our Eyes in one view: But even the best Memories losing the sight of one part whilst they are viewing another; and we some-times, and that the greatest part of our Lives, not reflecting on our past selves, being intent on our present Thoughts, and in sound sleep, having no Thoughts at all, or at least none with that consciousness, which remarks our waking Thoughts. I say, in all these cases, our con-sciousness being interrupted, and we losing the sight of our past *selves*, doubts are raised whether we are the same thinking thing; *i.e.* the same substance or no. Which however reasonable, or unreasonable, concerns not *personal Identity* at all. The Question being what makes the same *Person*, and not whether it be the same Identical Substance, which always thinks in the same *Person*, which in this case matters not at all. Different Substances, by the same consciousness (where they do is partake in it) being united into one Person; as well as different Bodies, by the same Life are united into one Animal, whose *Identity* is preserved, in that change of Substances, by the unity of one continued Life. For it being the same consciousness that makes a Man be himself to himself, *personal Identity* depends on that only, whether it be annexed only to one individual Substance, or can be continued in a succession of several Substances. For as far as any intelligent Being can repeat the *Idea* of any past Action with the same consciousness it had of it at first, and with the same consciousness it has of any present Action; so far it is the same *personal self*. For it is by the consciousness it has of its present Thoughts and Actions, that it is *self* to it *self* now, and so will be the same *self* as far as the same consciousness can extend to Actions past or to come; and would be by distance of Time, or change of Substance, no more two *Persons* than a Man be two Men, by wearing other Cloaths to Day than he did Yesterday, with a long or short sleep between: The same consciousness uniting those distant Actions into the same *Person*, what-ever Substances contributed to their Production.

11.   That this is so, we have some kind of Evidence in our very Bodies, all whose Particles, whilst vitally united to this same thinking conscious self, so that we feel when they are touch'd, and are affected by, and conscious of good or harm that happens to them, are a part of our *selves*: i.e. of our thinking conscious *self*. Thus the Limbs of his Body is to every one a part of *himself*: He sympathizes and is concerned for them. Cut off an hand, and thereby separate it from that con-sciousness, we had of its Heat, Cold, and other Affections; and it is then no longer a part of that which is *himself*, any more than the remotest part of Matter. Thus we see the *Substance*, whereof *personal self* consisted at one time, may be varied at another, without the change of per-sonal *Identity*: There being no Question about the same Person, though the Limbs, which but now were a part of it, be cut off.

12.   But the Question is, whether if the same Substance, which thinks, be changed, it can be the same Person, or remaining the same, it can be different Persons.

And to this I answer first, this can be no Question at all to those, who place Thought in a purely material, animal, Constitution, void of an immaterial Substance. For, whether their Supposition be true or no, 'tis plain they conceive personal Identity preserved in something else than Identity of Substance; as animal Identity is preserved in Identity of Life, and not of Sub-stance. And therefore those, who place thinking in an immaterial Substance only, before they can come to deal with these Men, must shew why personal Identity cannot be preserved in the change of immaterial Substances, or variety of par-ticular immaterial Substances, as well as animal Identity is preserved in the change of mater-ial Substances, or variety of particular Bodies: Unless they will say, 'tis one immaterial Spirit, that makes the same Life in Brutes; as it is one imma-terial Spirit that makes the same Person in Men, which the *Cartesians* at least will not admit, for fear of making Brutes thinking things too.

13.   But next, as to the first part of the Question, Whether if the same thinking Substance (supposing immaterial Substances only to think) be changed, it can be the same Person. I answer, that cannot be resolv'd, but by those, who know what kind of Substances they are, that do think; and whether the consciousness of past Actions can be transferr'd from one thinking Substance to another. I grant, were the same Consciousness the same individual Action, it could not: But it being but a present representation of a past Action, why it may not be possible, that that may be represented to the Mind to have been, which really never was, will remain to be shewn. And therefore how far the consciousness of past Actions is annexed to any individual Agent, so that another cannot possibly have it, will be hard for us to determine, till we know what kind of Action it is, that cannot be done without a reflex Act of Perception accompanying it, and how perform'd by thinking Substances, who cannot think without being conscious of it. But that which we call the *same consciousness*, not being the same individual Act, why one intellectual Substance may not have represented to it, as done by it self, what it never did, and was perhaps done by some other Agent, why I say such a representation may not possibly be without reality of Matter of Fact, as well as several representations in Dreams are, which yet, whilst dreaming, we take for true, will be difficult to conclude from the Nature of things. And that it never is so, will by us, till we have clearer views of the Nature of thinking Substances, be best resolv'd into the Goodness of God, who as far as the Happiness or Misery of any of his sensible Creatures is concerned in it, will not by a fatal Error of theirs transfer from one to another, that consciousness, which draws Reward or Punishment with it. How far this may be an Argument against those who would place Thinking in a System of fleeting animal Spirits, I leave to be considered. But yet to return to the Question before us, it must be allowed, That if the same consciousness (which, as has been shewn, is quite a different thing from the same numerical Figure or Motion in Body) can be transferr'd from one thinking Substance to another, it will be possible, that two thinking Substances may make but one Person. For the same consciousness being preserv'd, whether in the same or different Substances, the personal Identity is preserv'd.

14.   As to the second part of the Question, Whether the same immaterial Substance remaining, there may be two distinct Persons; which Question seems to me to be built on this, Whether the same immaterial Being, being conscious of the Actions of its past Duration, may be wholly stripp'd of all the consciousness of its past Existence, and lose it beyond the power of ever retrieving again: And so as it were beginning a new Account from a new Period, have a consciousness that cannot reach beyond this new State. All those who hold pre-existence, are evidently of this Mind, since they allow the Soul to have no remaining consciousness of what it did in that pre-existent State, either wholly separate from Body, or informing any other Body; and if they should not, 'tis plain Experience would be against them. So that personal Identity reaching no farther than consciousness reaches, a pre-existent Spirit not having continued so many Ages in a state of Silence, must needs make different Persons. Suppose a Christian *Platonist* or *Pythagorean*, should upon God's having ended all his Works of Creation the Seventh Day, think his Soul hath existed ever since; and should imagine it has revolved in several Humane Bodies, as I once met with one, who was perswaded his had been the Soul of *Socrates* (how reasonably I will not dispute. This I know, that in the Post he fill'd, which was no inconsiderable one, he passed for a very rational Man, and the Press has shewn, that he wanted not Parts or Learning) would any one say, that he, being not conscious of any of *Socrates's* Actions or Thoughts, could be the same Person with *Socrates*? Let any one reflect upon himself, and conclude, that he has in himself an immaterial Spirit, which is that which thinks in him, and in the constant change of his Body keeps him the same; and is that which he calls himself: Let him also suppose it to be the same Soul, that was in *Nestor* or *Thersites*, at the Siege of *Troy*, (For Souls being, as far as we know any thing of them in their Nature, indifferent to any parcel of Matter, the Supposition has no apparent absurdity in it) which it may have been, as well as it is now, the Soul of any other Man: But he, now having no consciousness of any of the Actions either of *Nestor* or *Thersites*, does, or can he, conceive himself the same Person with either of them? Can he be concerned in either of their Actions? Attribute them to himself, or think

them his own more than the Actions of any other Man, that ever existed? So that this consciousness not reaching to any of the Actions of either of those Men, he is no more one *self* with either of them, than if the Soul or immaterial Spirit, that now informs him, had been created, and began to exist, when it began to inform his present Body, though it were never so true, that the same Spirit that informed *Nestor's* or *Thersites's* Body, were numerically the same that now informs his. For this would no more make him the same Person with *Nestor*, than if some of the Particles of Matter, that were once a part of *Nestor*, were now a part of this Man, the same immaterial Substance without the same consciousness, no more making the same Person by being united to any Body, than the same Particle of Matter without consciousness united to any Body, makes the same Person. But let him once find himself conscious of any of the Actions of *Nestor*, he then finds himself the same Person with *Nestor*.

15.   And thus we may be able without any difficulty to conceive, the same Person at the Resurrection, though in a Body not exactly in make or parts the same which he had here, the same consciousness going along with the Soul that inhabits it. But yet the Soul alone in the change of Bodies, would scarce to any one, but to him that makes the Soul the *Man*, be enough to make the same *Man*. For should the Soul of a Prince, carrying with it the consciousness of the Prince's past Life, enter and inform the Body of a Cobler as soon as deserted by his own Soul, every one sees, he would be the same Person with the Prince, accountable only for the Prince's Actions: But who would say it was the same Man? The Body too goes to the making the Man, and would, I guess, to every Body determine the Man in this case, wherein the Soul, with all its Princely Thoughts about it, would not make another Man: But he would be the same Cobler to every one besides himself. I know that in the ordinary way of speaking, the same Person, and the same Man, stand for one and the same thing. And indeed every one will always have a liberty to speak, as he pleases, and to apply what articulate Sounds to what *Ideas* he thinks fit, and change them as often as he pleases. But yet when we will enquire, what makes the same *Spirit, Man,* or *Person,* we must fix the *Ideas* of *Spirit, Man,* or *Person,* in our

Minds; and having resolved with our selves what we mean by them, it will not be hard to determine, in either of them, or the like, when it is the *same*, and when not.

16.   But though the same immaterial Substance, or Soul does not alone, where-ever it be, and in whatsoever State, make the same Man; yet 'tis plain consciousness, as far as ever it can be extended, should it be to Ages past, unites Existences, and Actions, very remote in time, into the same Person, as well as it does the Existence and Actions of the immediately preceding moment: So that whatever has the consciousness of present and past Actions, is the same Person to whom they both belong. Had I the same consciousness, that I saw the Ark and *Noah's* Flood, as that I saw an overflowing of the *Thames* last Winter, or as that I write now, I could no more doubt that I, that write this now, that saw the *Thames* overflow'd last Winter, and that view'd the Flood at the general Deluge, was the same *self*, place that *self* in what Substance you please, than that I that write this am the same *my self* now whilst I write (whether I consist of all the same Substance, material or immaterial, or no) that I was Yesterday. For as to this point of being the same *self*, it matters not whether this present *self* be made up of the same or other Substances, I being as much concern'd, and as justly accountable for any Action was done a thousand Years since, appropriated to me now by this self-consciousness, as I am, for what I did the last moment.

17.   *Self* is that conscious thinking thing, (whatever Substance, made up of whether Spiritual, or Material, Simple, or Compounded, it matters not) which is sensible, or conscious of Pleasure and Pain, capable of Happiness or Misery, and so is concern'd for it *self*, as far as that consciousness extends. Thus every one finds, that whilst comprehended under that consciousness, the little Finger is as much a part of it *self*, as what is most so. Upon separation of this little Finger, should this consciousness go along with the little Finger, and leave the rest of the Body, 'tis evident the little Finger would be the *Person*, the *same Person*; and *self* then would have nothing to do with the rest of the Body. As in this case it is the consciousness that goes along with the Substance, when one part is separated from another, which makes the same *Person*, and

constitutes this inseparable *self*: so it is in reference to Substances remote in time. That with which the *consciousness* of this present thinking thing can join it self, makes the same *Person*, and is one *self* with it, and with nothing else; and so attributes to it *self*, and owns all the Actions of that thing, as its own, as far as that consciousness reaches, and no farther; as every one who reflects will perceive.

18.   In this *personal Identity* is founded all the Right and Justice of Reward and Punishment; Happiness and Misery, being that, for which every one is concerned for *himself*, not mattering what becomes of any Substance, not joined to, or affected with that consciousness. For as it is evident in the instance I gave but now, if the consciousness went along with the little Finger, when it was cut off, that would be the same *self* which was concerned for the whole Body Yesterday, as making a part of it *self*, whose Actions then it cannot but admit as its own now. Though if the same Body should still live, and immediately from the separation of the little Finger have its own peculiar consciousness, whereof the little Finger knew nothing, it would not at all be concerned for it, as a part of it *self*, or could own any of its Actions, or have any of them imputed to him.

19.   This may shew us wherein *personal Identity* consists, not in the Identity of Substance, but, as I have said, in the Identity of *consciousness*, wherein, *if Socrates* and the present Mayor of *Quinborough* agree, they are the same Person: If the same *Socrates* waking and sleeping do not partake of the same *consciousness, Socrates* waking and sleeping is not the same Person. And to punish *Socrates* waking, for what sleeping *Socrates* thought, and waking *Socrates* was never conscious of, would be no more of Right, than to punish one Twin for what his Brother-Twin did, whereof he knew nothing, because their outsides were so like, that they could not be distinguished; for such Twins have been seen.

20.   But yet possibly it will still be objected, suppose I wholly lose the memory of some parts of my Life, beyond a possibility of retrieving them, so that perhaps I shall never be conscious of them again; yet am I not the same Person, that did those Actions, had those Thoughts, that I was once conscious of, though I have now forgot them? To which I answer, that we must here take notice what the Word *I* is applied to, which in this case is the Man only. And the same Man being presumed to be the same Person, *I* is easily here supposed to stand also for the same Person. But if it be possible for the same Man to have distinct incommunicable consciousness at different times, it is past doubt the same Man would at different times make different Persons; which, we see, is the Sense of Mankind in the solemnest Declaration of their Opinions, Humane Laws not punishing the *Mad Man* for the *Sober Man*'s Actions, nor the *Sober Man* for what the *Mad Man* did, thereby making them two Persons; which is somewhat explained by our way of speaking in *English*, when we say such an one *is not himself*, or is *besides himself*; in which Phrases it is insinuated, as if those who now, or, at least, first used them, thought, that *self* was changed, the *self* same Person was no longer in that Man.

21.   But yet 'tis hard to conceive, that *Socrates* the same individual Man should be two Persons. To help us a little in this, we must consider what is meant by *Socrates*, or the same individual *Man*.

First, It must be either the same individual, immaterial, thinking Substance: In short, the same numerical Soul, and nothing else.

Secondly, Or the same Animal, without any regard to an immaterial Soul.

Thirdly, Or the same immaterial Spirit united to the same Animal.

Now take which of these Suppositions you please, it is impossible to make personal Identity to consist in any thing but consciousness; or reach any farther than that does.

For by the First of them, it must be allowed possible that a Man born of different Women, and in distant times, may be the same Man. A way of speaking, which whoever admits, must allow it possible, for the same Man to be two distinct Persons, as any two that have lived in different Ages without the knowledge of one anothers Thoughts.

By the Second and Third, *Socrates* in this Life, and after it, cannot be the same Man any way, but by the same consciousness; and so making *Humane Identity* to consist in the same thing wherein we place *Personal Identity*, there will be no difficulty to allow the same Man to be the same Person. But then they who place *Humane Identity* in consciousness only, and not in something else, must consider how they will make the

Infant *Socrates* the same Man with *Socrates* after the Resurrection. But whatsoever to some Men makes a *Man*, and consequently the same individual Man, wherein perhaps few are agreed, personal Identity can by us be placed in nothing but consciousness (which is that alone which makes what we call *self*) without involving us in great Absurdities.

22.   But is not a Man Drunk and Sober the same Person, why else is he punish'd for the Fact he commits when Drunk, though he be never afterwards conscious of it? Just as much the same Person, as a Man that walks, and does other things in his sleep, is the same Person, and is answerable for any mischief he shall do in it. Humane Laws punish both with a Justice suitable to their way of Knowledge: Because in these cases, they cannot distinguish certainly what is real, what counterfeit; and so the ignorance in Drunkenness or Sleep is not admitted as a plea. For though punishment be annexed to personality, and personality to consciousness, and the Drunkard perhaps be not conscious of what he did; yet Humane Judicatures justly punish him; because the Fact is proved against him, but want of consciousness cannot be proved for him. But in the great Day, wherein the Secrets of all Hearts shall be laid open, it may be reasonable to think, no one shall be made to answer for what he knows nothing of; but shall receive his Doom, his Conscience accusing or excusing him.

23.   Nothing but consciousness can unite remote Existences into the same Person, the Identity of Substance will not do it. For whatever Substance there is, however framed, without consciousness, there is no Person: And a Carcase may be a Person, as well as any sort of Substance be so without consciousness.

Could we suppose two distinct incommunicable consciousnesses acting the same Body, the one constantly by Day, the other by Night; and on the other side the same consciousness acting by Intervals two distinct Bodies: I ask in the first case, Whether the *Day* and the *Night-man* would not be two as distinct Persons, as *Socrates* and *Plato*; and whether in the second case, there would not be one Person in two distinct Bodies, as much as one Man is the same in two distinct clothings. Nor is it at all material to say, that this same, and this distinct *consciousness* in the cases above-mentioned, is owing to the same and distinct immaterial Substances, bringing it with them to those Bodies, which whether true or no, alters not the case: Since 'tis evident the *personal Identity* would equally be determined by the consciousness, whether that consciousness were annexed to some individual immaterial Substance or no. For granting that the thinking Substance in Man must be necessarily suppos'd immaterial, 'tis evident, that immaterial thinking thing may sometimes part with its past consciousness, and be restored to it again, as appears in the forgetfulness Men often have of their past Actions, and the Mind many times recovers the memory of a past consciousness, which it had lost for twenty Years together. Make these intervals of Memory and Forgetfulness to take their turns regularly by Day and Night, and you have two Persons with the same immaterial Spirit, as much as in the former instance two Persons with the same Body. So that *self* is not determined by Identity or Diversity of Substance, which it cannot be sure of, but only by Identity of consciousness.

24.   Indeed it may conceive the Substance whereof it is now made up, to have existed formerly, united in the same conscious Being: But consciousness removed, that Substance is no more it *self*, or makes no more a part of it, than any other Substance, as is evident in the instance, we have already given, of a Limb cut off, of whose Heat, or Cold, or other Affections, having no longer any consciousness, it is no more of a Man's self than any other Matter of the Universe. In like manner it will be in reference to any immaterial Substance, which is void of that consciousness whereby I am my *self* to my *self*: If there be any part of its Existence, which I cannot upon recollection join with that present consciousness, whereby I am now my *self*, it is in that part of its Existence no more my *self*, than any other immaterial Being. For whatsoever any Substance has thought or done, which I cannot recollect, and by my consciousness make my own Thought and Action, it will no more belong to me, whether a part of me thought or did it, than if it had been thought or done by any other immaterial Being any where existing.

25.   I agree the more probable Opinion is, that this consciousness is annexed to, and the Affection of one individual immaterial Substance.

But let Men according to their divers Hypotheses resolve of that as they please. This every intelligent Being, sensible of Happiness or Misery, must grant, that there is something that is *himself*, that he is concerned for, and would have happy; that this *self* has existed in a continued Duration more than one instant, and therefore 'tis possible may exist, as it has done, Months and Years to come, without any certain bounds to be set to its duration; and may be the same *self*, by the same consciousness, continued on for the future. And thus, by this consciousness, he finds himself to be the *same self* which did such or such an Action some Years since, by which he comes to be happy or miserable now. In all which account of *self*, the same numerical Substance is not considered, as making the same *self*: But the same continued consciousness, in which several Substances may have been united, and again separated from it, which, whilst they continued in a vital union with that, wherein this consciousness then resided, made a part of that same *self*. Thus any part of our Bodies vitally united to that, which is conscious in us, makes a part of our *selves*: But upon separation from the vital union, by which that consciousness is communicated, that, which a moment since was part of our *selves*, is now no more so, than a part of another Man's *self* is a part of me; and 'tis not impossible, but in a little time may become a real part of another Person. And so we have the same numerical Substance become a part of two different Persons; and the same Person preserved under the change of various is Substances. Could we suppose any Spirit wholly stripp'd of all its memory or consciousness of past Actions, as we find our Minds always are of a great part of ours, and sometimes of them all, the union or separation of such a Spiritual Substance would make no variation of personal Identity, any more than that of any Particle of Matter does. Any Substance vitally united to the present thinking Being, is a part of that very *same self* which now is: Any thing united to it by a consciousness of former Actions makes also a part of the *same self*, which is the same both then and now.

26.   *Person*, as I take it, is the name for this *self*. Where-ever a Man finds, what he calls *himself*, there I think another may say is the same *Person*. It is a Forensick Term appropriating Actions and their Merit; and so belongs only to intelligent Agents capable of a Law, and Happiness and Misery. This personality extends it *self* beyond present Existence to what is past, only by consciousness, whereby it becomes concerned and accountable, owns and imputes to it *self* past Actions, just upon the same ground, and for the same reason, that it does the present. All which is founded in a concern for Happiness the unavoidable concomitant of consciousness, that which is conscious of Pleasure and Pain, desiring, that that *self*, that is conscious, should be happy. And therefore whatever past Actions it cannot reconcile or appropriate to that present *self* by consciousness, it can be no more concerned in, than if they had never been done: And to receive Pleasure or Pain; *i.e.* Reward or Punishment, on the account of any such Action, is all one, as to be made happy or miserable in its first being, without any demerit at all. For supposing a Man punish'd now, for what he had done in another Life, whereof he could be made to have no consciousness at all, what difference is there between that Punishment, and being created miserable? And therefore conformable to this, the Apostle tells us, that at the Great Day, when every one shall *receive according to his doings, the secrets of all Hearts shall be laid open.*[2] The Sentence shall be justified by the consciousness all Persons shall have, that they *themselves* in what Bodies soever they appear, or what Substances soever that consciousness adheres to, are the *same*, that committed those Actions, and deserve that Punishment for them.

27.   I am apt enough to think I have in treating of this Subject made some Suppositions that will look strange to some Readers, and possibly they are so in themselves. But yet I think, they are such, as are pardonable in this ignorance we are in of the Nature of that thinking thing, that is in us, and which we look on as our *selves*. Did we know what it was, or how it was tied to a certain System of fleeting Animal Spirits; or whether it could, or could not perform its Operations of Thinking and Memory out of a Body organized as ours is; and whether it has pleased God, that no one such Spirit shall ever be united to any but one such Body, upon the right Constitution of whose Organs its Memory should depend, we might see the Absurdity of some of those Suppositions I have made. But taking, as we ordinarily now do, (in the dark concerning these Matters) the Soul of a Man, for an immaterial Substance, independent from Matter, and indifferent alike to it all, there can from the Nature of

things, be no Absurdity at all, to suppose, that the same Soul may, at different times be united to different Bodies, and with them make up, for that time, one Man; As well as we suppose a part of a Sheep's Body yesterday should be a part of a Man's Body tomorrow, and in that union make a vital part of *Melibœus* himself as well as it did of his Ram.

28.   To conclude, whatever Substance begins to exist, it must, during its Existence, necessarily be the same: Whatever Compositions of Substances begin to exist, during the union of those Substances, the concrete must be the same: Whatsoever Mode begins to exist, during its Existence, it is the same: And so if the Composition be of distinct Substances, and different Modes, the same Rule holds. Whereby it will appear, that the difficulty or obscurity, that has been about this Matter, rather rises from the Names ill used, than from any obscurity in things themselves. For whatever makes the specifick *Idea*, to which the name is applied, if that *Idea* be steadily kept to, the distinction of any thing into the same, and divers will easily be conceived, and there can arise no doubt about it.

29.   For supposing a rational Spirit be the *Idea* of a *Man*, 'tis easie to know, what is the *same Man, viz.* the *same Spirit*, whether separate or in a Body will be the *same Man*. Supposing a rational Spirit vitally united to a Body of a certain conformation of Parts to make a *Man*, whilst that rational Spirit, with that vital conformation of Parts, though continued in a fleeting successive Body, remains, it will be the *same Man*. But if to any one the *Idea* of a *Man* be, but the vital union of Parts in a certain shape; as long as that vital union and shape remains, in a concrete no otherwise the same, but by a continued succession of fleeting Particles, it will be the same *Man*. For whatever be the composition whereof the complex *Idea* is made, whenever Existence makes it one particular thing under any denomination, the same Existence continued, preserves it the same individual under the same denomination.

Notes

1   *Whence come ye? It answered, From* Marinnan, *The* Prince, *To whom do you belong? The* Parrot, *To a* Portugeze. Prince, *What do you there?* Parrot, *I look after the Chickens. The* Prince laughed and said, *You look after the Chickens? The* Parrot answered, *Yes I, and I know well enough how to do it.*

2   *Cf.* 1 Cor. 14: 25 *and* 2 Cor. 5: 10.

18

The Self and the Future

Bernard Williams

Suppose that there were some process to which two persons, *A* and *B*, could be subjected as a result of which they might be said – question-beggingly – to have *exchanged bodies*. That is to say – less question-beggingly – there is a certain human body which is such that when previously we were confronted with it, we were confronted with person *A*, certain utterances coming from it were expressive of memories of the past experiences of *A*, certain movements of it partly constituted the actions of *A* and were taken as expressive of the character of *A*, and so forth; but now, after the process is completed, utterances coming from this body are expressive of what seem to be just those memories which previously we identified as memories of the past experiences of *B*, its movements partly constitute actions expressive of the character of *B*, and so forth; and conversely with the other body.

There are certain important philosophical limitations on how such imaginary cases are to be constructed, and how they are to be taken when constructed in various ways. I shall mention two principal limitations, not in order to pursue them further here, but precisely in order to get them out of the way.

There are certain limitations, particularly with regard to character and mannerisms, to our ability to imagine such cases even in the most restricted sense of our being disposed to take the later performances of that body which was previously *A*'s as expressive of *B*'s character; if the previous *A* and *B* were extremely unlike one another both physically and psychologically, and if, say, in addition, they were of different sex, there might be grave difficulties in reading *B*'s dispositions in any possible performances of *A*'s body. Let us forget this, and for the present purpose just take *A* and *B* as being sufficiently alike (however alike that has to be) for the difficulty not to arise; after the experiment, persons familiar with *A* and *B* are just *overwhelmingly struck* by the *B*-ish character of the doings associated with what was previously *A*'s body, and conversely. Thus the feat of imagining an exchange of bodies is supposed possible in the most restricted sense. But now there is a further limitation which has to be overcome if the feat is to be not merely possible in the most restricted sense but also is to have an outcome which, on serious reflection, we are prepared to describe as *A* and *B* having changed bodies – that is, an outcome where, confronted with what was previously *A*'s body, we are prepared seriously to say that we are now confronted with *B*.

It would seem a necessary condition of so doing that the utterances coming from that body

Bernard Williams, "The Self and the Future." *The Philosophical Review* LXXIX (1970), pp. 161–80. © 1970, the Sage School of Philosophy at Cornell University. All rights reserved. Used by permission of the publisher, Duke University Press.

be taken as genuinely expressive of memories of B's past. But memory is a causal notion; and as we actually use it, it seems a necessary condition of x's present knowledge of x's earlier experiences constituting memory of those experiences that the causal chain linking the experiences and the knowledge should not run outside x's body. Hence if utterances coming from a given body are to be taken as expressive of memories of the experiences of B, there should be some suitable causal link between the appropriate state of that body and the original happening of those experiences to B. One radical way of securing that condition in the imagined exchange case is to suppose, with Shoemaker,[1] that the brains of A and of B are transposed. We may not need so radical a condition. Thus suppose it were possible to extract information from a man's brain and store it in a device while his brain was repaired, or even renewed, the information then being replaced: it would seem exaggerated to insist that the resultant man could not possibly have the memories he had before the operation. With regard to our knowledge of our own past, we draw distinctions between merely recalling, being reminded, and learning again, and those distinctions correspond (roughly) to distinctions between no new input, partial new input, and total new input with regard to the information in question; and it seems clear that the information-parking case just imagined would not count as new input in the sense necessary and sufficient for 'learning again'. Hence we can imagine the case we are concerned with in terms of information extracted into such devices from A's and B's brains and replaced in the other brain; this is the sort of model which, I think not unfairly for the present argument, I shall have in mind.

We imagine the following. The process considered above exists; two persons can enter some machine, let us say, and emerge changed in the appropriate ways. If A and B are the persons who enter, let us call the persons who emerge the A-body-person and the B-body-person: the A-body-person is that person (whoever it is) with whom I am confronted when, after the experiment, I am confronted with that body which previously was A's body – that is to say, that person who would naturally be taken for A by someone who just saw this person, was familiar with A's appearance before the experiment, and did not know

about the happening of the experiment. A non-question-begging description of the experiment will leave it open which (if either) of the persons A and B the A-body-person is; the description of the experiment as 'persons changing bodies' of course implies that the A-body-person is actually B.

We take two persons A and B who are going to have the process carried out on them. (We can suppose, rather hazily, that they are willing for this to happen; to investigate at all closely at this stage why they might be willing or unwilling, what they would fear, and so forth, would anticipate some later issues.) We further announce that one of the two resultant persons, the A-body-person and the B-body-person, is going after the experiment to be given $100,000, while the other is going to be tortured. We then ask each of A and B to choose which treatment should be dealt out to which of the persons who will emerge from the experiment, the choice to be made (if it can be) on selfish grounds.

Suppose that A chooses that the B-body-person should get the pleasant treatment and the A-body-person the unpleasant treatment; and B chooses conversely (this might indicate that they thought that 'changing bodies' was indeed a good description of the outcome). The experimenter cannot act in accordance with both these sets of preferences, those expressed by A and those expressed by B. Hence there is one clear sense in which A and B cannot both get what they want: namely, that if the experimenter, before the experiment, announces to A and B that he intends to carry out the alternative (for example), of treating the B-body-person unpleasantly and the A-body-person pleasantly – then A can say rightly, 'That's not the outcome I chose to happen', and B can say rightly, 'That's just the outcome I chose to happen'. So, evidently, A and B before the experiment can each come to know either that the outcome he chose will be that which will happen, or that the one he chose will not happen, and in that sense they can get or fail to get what they wanted. But is it also true that when the experimenter proceeds after the experiment to act in accordance with one of the preferences and not the other, *then* one of A and B will have got what he wanted, and the other not?

There seems very good ground for saying so. For suppose the experimenter, having elicited

A's and *B*'s preference, says nothing to *A* and *B* about what he will do; conducts the experiment; and then, for example, gives the unpleasant treatment to the *B*-body-person and the pleasant treatment to the *A*-body-person. Then the *B*-body-person will not only complain of the unpleasant treatment as such, but will complain (since he has *A*'s memories) that that was not the outcome he chose, since he chose that the *B*-body-person should be well treated; and since *A* made his choice in selfish spirit, he may add that he precisely chose in that way because he did not want the unpleasant things to happen to *him*. The *A*-body-person meanwhile will express satisfaction both at the receipt of the $100,000, and also at the fact that the experimenter has chosen to act in the way that he, *B*, so wisely chose. These facts make a strong case for saying that the experimenter has brought it about that *B* did in the outcome get what he wanted and *A* did not. It is therefore a strong case for saying that the *B*-body-person really is *A*, and the *A*-body-person really is *B*; and therefore for saying that the process of the experiment really is that of changing bodies. For the same reasons it would seem that *A* and *B* in our example really did choose wisely, and that it was *A*'s bad luck that the choice he correctly made was not carried out, *B*'s good luck that the choice he correctly made was carried out. This seems to show that to care about what happens to me in the future is not necessarily to care about what happens to *this* body (the one I now have); and this in turn might be taken to show that in some sense of Descartes's obscure phrase, I and my body are 'really distinct' (though, of course, nothing in these considerations could support the idea that I could exist without a body at all).

These suggestions seem to be reinforced if we consider the cases where *A* and *B* make other choices with regard to the experiment. Suppose that *A* chooses that the *A*-body-person should get the money, and the *B*-body-person get the pain, and *B* chooses conversely. Here again there can be no outcome which matches the expressed preferences of both of them: they cannot both get what they want. The experimenter announces, before the experiment, that the *A*-body-person will in fact get the money, and the *B*-body-person will get the pain. So *A* at this stage gets what he wants (the announced outcome matches his expressed preference). After the experiment, the distribution is carried out as announced. Both the *A*-body-person and the *B*-body-person will have to agree that what is happening is in accordance with the preference that *A* originally expressed. The *B*-body-person will naturally express this acknowledgement (since he has *A*'s memories) by saying that this is the distribution he chose; he will recall, among other things, the experimenter announcing this outcome, his approving it as what he chose, and so forth. However, he (the *B*-body-person) certainly does not like what is now happening to him, and would much prefer to be receiving what the *A*-body-person is receiving – namely, $100,000. The *A*-body-person will on the other hand recall choosing an outcome other than this one, but will reckon it good luck that the experimenter did not do what he recalls choosing. It looks, then, as though the *A*-body-person has got what he wanted, but not what he chose, while the *B*-body-person has got what he chose, but not what he wanted. So once more it looks as though they are, respectively, *B* and *A*; and that in this case the original choices of both *A* and *B* were unwise.

Suppose, lastly, that in the original choice *A* takes the line of the first case and *B* of the second: that is, *A* chooses that the *B*-body-person should get the money and the *A*-body-person the pain, and *B* chooses exactly the same thing. In this case, the experimenter would seem to be in the happy situation of giving both persons what they want – or at least, like God, what they have chosen. In this case, the *B*-body-person likes what he is receiving, recalls choosing it, and congratulates himself on the wisdom of (as he puts it) his choice; while the *A*-body-person does not like what he is receiving, recalls choosing it, and is forced to acknowledge that (as he puts it) his choice was unwise. So once more we seem to get results to support the suggestions drawn from the first case.

Let us now consider the question, not of *A* and *B* choosing certain outcomes to take place after the experiment, but of their willingness to engage in the experiment at all. If they were initially inclined to accept the description of the experiment as 'changing bodies' then one thing that would interest them would be the character of the other person's body. In this respect also what would happen after the experiment would seem to suggest that 'changing bodies' was a good description of the experiment. If *A* and *B* agreed to the experiment, being each not displeased with the appearance, physique, and so forth of the other person's body; after the experiment the *B*-body-person might well be found saying such things as: 'When I agreed to this experiment, I thought that *B*'s face was quite attractive, but now I look at it in the mirror, I am not so sure'; or the *A*-body-person might say 'When I agreed to this experiment I did not know that *A* had a wooden leg; but now, after it is over, I find that I have this wooden leg, and I want the experiment reversed.' It is possible that he might say further that he finds the leg very uncomfortable, and that the *B*-body-person should say, for instance, that he recalls that he found it very uncomfortable at first, but one gets used to it: but perhaps one would need to know more than at least I do about the physiology of habituation to artificial limbs to know whether the *A*-body-person would find the leg uncomfortable: that body, after all, has had the leg on it for some time. But apart from this sort of detail, the general line of the outcome regarded from this point of view seems to confirm our previous conclusions about the experiment.

Now let us suppose that when the experiment is proposed (in non-question-begging terms) *A* and *B* think rather of their psychological advantages and disadvantages. *A*'s thoughts turn primarily to certain sorts of anxiety to which he is very prone, while *B* is concerned with the frightful memories he has of past experiences which still distress him. They each hope that the experiment will in some way result in their being able to get away from these things. They may even have been impressed by philosophical arguments to the effect that bodily continuity is at least a necessary condition of personal identity: *A*, for example, reasons that, granted the experiment comes off, then the person who is bodily continuous with him will not have this anxiety, and while the other person will no doubt have some anxiety – perhaps in some sense his anxiety – at least that person will not be he. The experiment is performed and the experimenter (to whom *A* and *B* previously revealed privately their several difficulties and hopes) asks the *A*-body-person whether he has got rid of his anxiety. This person presumably replies that he does not know what the man is talking about; he never had such anxiety, but he did have some very disagreeable memories, and

recalls engaging in the experiment to get rid of them, and is disappointed to discover that he still has them. The *B*-body-person will react in a similar way to questions about his painful memories, pointing out that he still has his anxiety. These results seem to confirm still further the description of the experiment as 'changing bodies'. And all the results suggest that the only rational thing to do, confronted with such an experiment, would be to identify oneself with one's memories, and so forth, and not with one's body. The philosophical arguments designed to show that bodily continuity was at least a necessary condition of personal identity would seem to be just mistaken.

Let us now consider something apparently different. Someone in whose power I am tells me that I am going to be tortured tomorrow. I am frightened, and look forward to tomorrow in great apprehension. He adds that when the time comes, I shall not remember being told that this was going to happen to me, since shortly before the torture something else will be done to me which will make me forget the announcement. This certainly will not cheer me up, since I know perfectly well that I can forget things, and that there is such a thing as indeed being tortured unexpectedly because I had forgotten or been made to forget a prediction of the torture: that will still be a torture which, so long as I do know about the prediction, I look forward to in fear. He then adds that my forgetting the announcement will be only part of a larger process: when the moment of torture comes, I shall not remember any of the things I am now in a position to remember. This does not cheer me up, either, since I can readily conceive of being involved in an accident, for instance, as a result of which I wake up in a completely amnesiac state and also in great pain; that could certainly happen to me, I should not like it to happen to me, nor to know that it was going to happen to me. He now further adds that at the moment of torture I shall not only not remember the things I am now in a position to remember, but will have a different set of impressions of my past, quite different from the memories I now have. I do not think that this would cheer me up, either. For I can at least conceive the possibility, if not the concrete reality, of going completely mad, and thinking perhaps that I am George IV or somebody; and being told that something like that was going to happen to me would have no tendency to reduce the terror of being told authoritatively that I was going to be tortured, but would merely compound the horror. Nor do I see why I should be put into any better frame of mind by the person in charge adding lastly that the impressions of my past with which I shall be equipped on the eve of torture will exactly fit the past of another person now living, and that indeed I shall acquire these impressions by (for instance) information now in his brain being copied into mine. Fear, surely, would still be the proper reaction: and not because one did not know what was going to happen, but because in one vital respect at least one did know what was going to happen – torture, which one can indeed expect to happen to oneself, and to be preceded by certain mental derangements as well.

If this is right, the whole question seems now to be totally mysterious. For what we have just been through is of course merely one side, differently represented, of the transaction which we considered before; and it represents it as a perfectly hateful prospect, while the previous considerations represented it as something one should rationally, perhaps even cheerfully, choose out of the options there presented. It is differently presented, of course, and in two notable respects; but when we look at these two differences of presentation, can we really convince ourselves that the second presentation is wrong or misleading, thus leaving the road open to the first version which at the time seemed so convincing? Surely not.

The first difference is that in the second version the torture is throughout represented as going to happen to *me*: 'you', the man in charge persistently says. Thus he is not very neutral. But should he have been neutral? Or, to put it another way, does his use of the second person have a merely emotional and rhetorical effect on me, making me afraid when further reflection would have shown that I had no reason to be? It is certainly not obviously so. The problem just is that through every step of his predictions I seem to be able to follow him successfully. And if I reflect on whether what he has said gives me grounds for fearing that I shall be tortured, I could consider that behind my fears lies some principle such as this: that my undergoing physical pain in the future is not excluded by any psychological state I may be in at the time, with the platitudinous exception of those psychological states which in themselves exclude experiencing pain, notably (if it is a psychological state) unconsciousness. In particular, what impressions I have about the past will not have any effect on whether I undergo the pain or not. This principle seems sound enough.

It is an important fact that not everything I would, as things are, regard as an evil would be something that I should rationally fear as an evil if it were predicted that it would happen to me in the future and also predicted that I should undergo significant psychological changes in the meantime. For the fact that I regard that happening, things being as they are, as an evil can be dependent on factors of belief or character which might themselves be modified by the psychological changes in question. Thus if I am appallingly subject to acrophobia, and am told that I shall find myself on top of a steep mountain in the near future, I shall to that extent be afraid; but if I am told that I shall be psychologically changed in the meantime in such a way as to rid me of my acrophobia (and as with the other prediction, I believe it), then I have no reason to be afraid of the predicted happening, or at least not the same reason. Again, I might look forward to meeting a certain person again with either alarm or excitement because of my memories of our past relations. In some part, these memories operate in connexion with my emotion, not only on the present time, but projectively forward: for it is to a meeting itself affected by the presence of those memories that I look forward. If I am convinced that when the time comes I shall not have those memories, then I shall not have just the same reasons as before for looking forward to that meeting with the one emotion or the other. (Spiritualism, incidentally, appears to involve the belief that I have just the same reasons for a given attitude toward encountering people again after I am dead, as I did before: with the one modification that I can be sure it will all be very nice.)

Physical pain, however, the example which for simplicity (and not for any obsessional reason) I have taken, is absolutely minimally dependent on character or belief. No amount of change in my character or my beliefs would seem to affect substantially the nastiness of tortures applied to me; correspondingly, no degree of predicted change in my character and beliefs can unseat the fear of torture which, together with those changes, is predicted for me.

I am not at all suggesting that the *only* basis, or indeed the only rational basis, for fear in the face of these various predictions is how things will be relative to my psychological state in the eventual outcome. I am merely pointing out that this is one component; it is not the only one. For certainly one will fear and otherwise reject the changes themselves, or in very many cases one would. Thus one of the old paradoxes of hedonistic utilitarianism; if one had assurances that undergoing certain operations and being attached to a machine would provide one for the rest of one's existence with an unending sequence of delicious and varied experiences, one might very well reject the option, and react with fear if someone proposed to apply it compulsorily; and that fear and horror would seem appropriate reactions in the second case may help to discredit the interpretation (if anyone has the nerve to propose it) that one's reason for rejecting the option voluntarily would be a consciousness of duties to others which one in one's hedonic state would leave undone. The prospect of contented madness or vegetableness is found by many (not perhaps by all) appalling in ways which are obviously not a function of how things would then be for them, for things would then be for them not appalling. In the case we are at present discussing, these sorts of considerations seem merely to make it clearer that the predictions of the man in charge provide a double ground of horror: at the prospect of torture, and at the prospect of the change in character and in impressions of the past that will precede it. And certainly, to repeat what has already been said, the prospect of the second certainly seems to provide no ground for rejecting or not fearing the prospect of the first.

I said that there were two notable differences between the second presentation of our situation and the first. The first difference, which we have just said something about, was that the man predicted the torture for *me*, a psychologically very changed 'me'. We have yet to find a reason for saying that he should not have done this, or that I really should be unable to follow him if he does; I seem to be able to follow him only too well.

The second difference is that in this presentation he does not mention the other man, except in the somewhat incidental rôle of being the provenance of the impressions of the past I end up with. He does not mention him at all as someone who will end up with impressions of the past derived from me (and, incidentally, with $100,000 as well – a consideration which, in the frame of mind appropriate to this version, will merely make me jealous).

But why *should* he mention this man and what is going to happen to him? My selfish concern is to be told what is going to happen to me, and now I know: torture, preceded by changes of character, brain operations, changes in impressions of the past. The knowledge that one other person, or none, or many will be similarly mistreated may affect me in other ways, of sympathy, greater horror at the power of this tyrant, and so forth; but surely it cannot affect my expectations of torture? But – someone will say – this is to leave out exactly the feature which, as the first presentation of the case showed, makes all the difference: for it is to leave out the person who, as the first presentation showed, will be you. It is to leave out not merely a feature which should fundamentally affect your fears, it is to leave out the very person for whom you are fearful. So of course, the objector will say, this makes all the difference.

But can it? Consider the following series of cases. In each case we are to suppose that after what is described, A is, as before, to be tortured; we are also to suppose the person A is informed beforehand that just these things followed by the torture will happen to him:

(i)   A is subjected to an operation which produces total amnesia;

(ii)   amnesia is produced in A, and other interference leads to certain changes in his character;

(iii)   changes in his character are produced, and at the same time certain illusory 'memory' beliefs are induced in him: these are of a quite fictitious kind and do not fit the life of any actual person;

(iv)   the same as (iii), except that both the character traits and the 'memory' impressions are designed to be appropriate to another actual person, B;

(v) the same as (iv), except that the result is produced by putting the information into A from the brain of B, by a method which leaves B the same as he was before;

(vi) the same happens to A as in (v), but B is not left the same, since a similar operation is conducted in the reverse direction.

I take it that no-one is going to dispute that A has reasons, and fairly straightforward reasons, for fear of pain when the prospect is that of situation (i); there seems no conceivable reason why this should not extend to situation (ii), and the situation (iii) can surely introduce no difference of principle – it just seems a situation which for more than one reason we should have grounds for fearing, as suggested above. Situation (iv) at least introduces the person B, who was the focus of the objection we are now discussing. But it does not seem to introduce him in any way which makes a material difference; if I can expect pain through a transformation which involves new 'memory'-impressions, it would seem a purely external fact, relative to that, that the 'memory'-impressions had a model. Nor, in (iv), do we satisfy a causal condition which I mentioned at the beginning for the 'memories' actually being memories; though notice that if the job were done thoroughly, I might well be able to elicit from the A-body-person the kinds of remarks about his previous expectations of the experiment – remarks appropriate to the original B – which so impressed us in the first version of the story. I shall have a similar assurance of this being so in situation (v), where, moreover, a plausible application of the causal condition is available.

But two things are to be noticed about this situation. First, if we concentrate on A and the A-body-person, we do not seem to have added anything which from the point of view of his fears makes any material difference; just as, in the move from (iii) to (iv), it made no relevant difference that the new 'memory'-impressions which precede the pain had, as it happened, a model, so in the move from (iv) to (v) all we have added is that they have a model which is also their cause: and it is still difficult to see why that, to him looking forward, could possibly make the difference between expecting pain and not expecting pain. To illustrate that point from the case of character: if A is capable of expecting pain, he is capable of expecting pain preceded by a change in his dispositions – and to that expectation it can make no difference, whether that change in his dispositions is modelled on, or indeed indirectly caused by, the dispositions of some other person. If his fears can, as it were, reach through the change, it seems a mere trimming how the change is in fact induced. The second point about situation (v) is that if the crucial question for A's fears with regard to what befalls the A-body-person is whether the A-body-person is or is not the person B,[2] then that condition has not yet been satisfied in situation (v): for there we have an undisputed B in addition to the A-body-person, and certainly those two are not the same person.

But in situation (vi), we seemed to think, that is finally what he is. But if A's original fears could reach through the expected changes in (v), as they did in (iv) and (iii), then certainly they can reach through in (vi). Indeed, from the point of view of A's expectations and fears, there is less difference between (vi) and (v) than there is between (v) and (iv) or between (iv) and (iii). In those transitions, there were at least differences – though we could not see that they were really relevant differences – in the content or cause of what happened to him; in the present case there is absolutely no difference at all in what happens to him, the only difference being in what happens to someone else. If he can fear pain when (v) is predicted, why should he cease to when (vi) is?

I can see only one way of relevantly laying great weight on the transition from (v) to (vi); and this involves a considerable difficulty. This is to deny that, as I put it, the transition from (v) to (vi) involves merely the addition of something happening to *somebody else*; what rather it does, it will be said, is to involve the reintroduction of A himself, as the B-body-person; since he has reappeared in this form, it is for this person, and not for the unfortunate A-body-person, that A will have his expectations. This is to reassert, in effect, the viewpoint emphasised in our first presentation of the experiment. But this surely has the consequence that A should not have fears for the A-body-person who appeared in situation (v). For by the present argument, the A-body-person in (vi) is not A; the B-body-person is. But the A-body-person in (v) is, in character, history, everything, exactly the same as the A-body-person in (vi); so if the latter is not A, then neither is the former. (It is this point, no doubt, that encourages one to speak of the difference that goes with (vi) as being, on the present view, the *reintroduction* of *A*.) But no-one else in (v) has any better claim to be *A*. So in (v), it seems, *A* just does not exist. This would certainly explain why *A* should have no fears for the state of things in (v) – though he might well have fears for the path to it. But it rather looked earlier as though he could well have fears for the state of things in (v). Let us grant, however, that that was an illusion, and that *A* really does not exist in (v); then does he exist in (iv), (iii), (ii), or (i)? It seems very difficult to deny it for (i) and (ii); are we perhaps to draw the line between (iii) and (iv)?

Here someone will say: you must not insist on drawing a line – borderline cases are borderline cases, and you must not push our concepts beyond their limits. But this well-known piece of advice, sensible as it is in many cases, seems in the present case to involve an extraordinary difficulty. It may intellectually comfort observers of *A*'s situation; but what is *A* supposed to make of it? To be told that a future situation is a borderline one for its being myself that is hurt, that it is conceptually undecidable whether it will be me or not, is something which, it seems, I can do nothing with; because, in particular, it seems to have no comprehensible representation in my expectations and the emotions that go with them.

If I expect that a certain situation, *S*, will come about in the future, there is of course a wide range of emotions and concerns, directed on *S*, which I may experience now in relation to my expectation. Unless I am exceptionally egoistic, it is not a condition on my being concerned in relation to this expectation, that I myself will be involved in *S* – where my being 'involved' in *S* means that I figure in *S* as someone doing something at that time or having something done to me, or, again, that *S* will have consequences affecting me at that or some subsequent time. There are some emotions, however, which I will feel only if I will be involved in *S*, and fear is an obvious example.

Now the description of *S* under which it figures in my expectations will necessarily be, in various ways, indeterminate; and one way in which it may be indeterminate is that it leaves open whether I shall be involved in *S* or not. Thus I may have good reason to expect that one of us five is going to get hurt, but no reason to expect it to be me rather than one of the others. My present emotions will be correspondingly affected by this indeterminacy. Thus, sticking to the egoistic concern involved in fear, I shall presumably be somewhat more cheerful than if I knew it was going to be me, somewhat less cheerful than if I had been left out altogether. Fear will be mixed with, and qualified by, apprehension; and so forth. These emotions revolve around the thought of the eventual determination of the indeterminacy; moments of straight fear focus on its really turning out to be me, of hope on its turning out not to be me. All the emotions are related to the coming about of what I expect: and what I expect in such a case just cannot come about save by coming about in one of the ways or another.

There are other ways in which indeterminate expectations can be related to fear. Thus I may expect (perhaps neurotically) that something nasty is going to happen to me, indeed expect that when it happens it will take some determinate form, but have no range, or no closed range, of candidates for the determinate form to rehearse in my present thought. Different from this would be the fear of something radically indeterminate – the fear (one might say) of a nameless horror. If somebody had such a fear, one could even say that he had, in a sense, a perfectly determinate expectation: if what he expects indeed comes about, there will be nothing more determinate to be said about it after the event than was said in the expectation. Both these cases of course are cases of *fear* because one thing that is fixed amid the indeterminacy is the belief that it is me to whom the things will happen.

Central to the expectation of *S* is the thought of what it will be like when it happens – thought which may be indeterminate, range over alternatives, and so forth. When *S* involves me, there can be the possibility of a special form of such thought: the thought of how it will be for me, the imaginative projection of myself as participant in *S*.[3] I do not have to think about *S* in this way, when it involves me; but I may be able to. (It might be suggested that this possibility was even mirrored in the language, in the distinction between 'expecting to be hurt' and 'expecting that I shall be hurt'; but I am very doubtful about this point, which is in any case of no importance.)

Suppose now that there is an S with regard to which it is for conceptual reasons undecidable whether it involves me or not, as is proposed for the experimental situation by the line we are discussing. It is important that the expectation of S is not *indeterminate* in any of the ways we have just been considering. It is not like the nameless horror, since the fixed point of that case was that it was going to happen to the subject, and that made his state unequivocally fear. Nor is it like the expectation of the man who expects one of the five to be hurt; his fear was indeed equivocal, but its focus, and that of the expectation, was that when S came about, it would certainly come about in one way or the other. In the present case, fear (of the torture, that is to say, not of the initial experiment) seems neither appropriate, nor inappropriate, nor appropriately equivocal. Relatedly, the subject has an incurable difficulty about how he may think about S. If he engages in projective imaginative thinking (about how it will be for him), he implicitly answers the necessarily unanswerable question; if he thinks that he cannot engage in such thinking, it looks very much as if he also answers it, though in the opposite direction. Perhaps he must just refrain from such thinking; but is he just refraining from it, if it is incurably undecidable whether he can or cannot engage in it?

It may be said that all that these considerations can show is that fear, at any rate, does not get its proper footing in this case; but that there could be some other, more ambivalent, form of concern which would indeed be appropriate to this particular expectation, the expectation of the conceptually undecidable situation. There are, perhaps, analogous feelings that actually occur in actual situations. Thus material objects do occasionally undergo puzzling transformations which leave a conceptual shadow over their identity. Suppose I were sentimentally attached to an object to which this sort of thing then happened; it might be that I could neither feel about it quite as I did originally, nor be totally indifferent to it, but would have some other and rather ambivalent feeling towards it. Similarly, it may be said, toward the prospective sufferer of pain, my identity relations with whom are conceptually

shadowed, I can feel neither as I would if he were certainly me, nor as I would if he were certainly not, but rather some such ambivalent concern.

But this analogy does little to remove the most baffling aspect of the present case – an aspect which has already turned up in what was said about the subject's difficulty in thinking either projectively or non-projectively about the situation. For to regard the prospective pain-sufferer *just* like the transmogrified object of sentiment, and to conceive of my ambivalent distress about his future pain as just like ambivalent distress about some future damage to such an object, is of course to leave him and me clearly distinct from one another, and thus to displace the conceptual shadow from its proper place. I have to get nearer to him than that. But is there any nearer that I can get to him without expecting his pain? If there is, the analogy has not shown us it. We can certainly not get nearer by expecting, as it were, *ambivalent* pain; there is no place at all for that. There seems to be an obstinate bafflement to mirroring in my expectations a situation in which it is conceptually undecidable whether I occur.

The bafflement seems, moreover, to turn to plain absurdity if we move from conceptual undecidability to its close friend and neighbour, conventionalist decision. This comes out if we consider another description, overtly conventionalist, of the series of cases which occasioned the present discussion. This description would reject a point I relied on in an earlier argument – namely, that if we deny that the A-body-person in (vi) is A (because the B-body-person is), then we must deny that the A-body-person in (v) is A, since they are exactly similar. 'No', it may be said, 'this is just to assume that we say the same in different sorts of situation. No doubt when we have the very good candidate for being A – namely, the B-body-person – we call him A; but this does not mean that we should not call the A-body-person A in that other situation when we have no better candidate around. Different situations call for different descriptions.' This line of talk is the sort of thing indeed appropriate to lawyers deciding the ownership of some property which has undergone some bewildering set of transformations; they just have to decide, and in each situation, let us suppose, it has got to go to somebody, on as reasonable grounds as the facts and the law admit. But as a line to deal with a person's fears or expectations about his own future, it seems to have no sense at all. If A's fears can extend to what will happen to the A-body-person in (v), I do not see how they can be rationally diverted from the fate of the exactly similar person in (vi) by his being told that someone would have a reason in the latter situation which he would not have in the former for deciding to call another person A.

Thus, to sum up, it looks as though there are two presentations of the imagined experiment and the choice associated with it, each of which carries conviction, and which lead to contrary conclusions. The idea, moreover, that the situation after the experiment is conceptually undecidable in the relevant respect seems not to assist, but rather to increase, the puzzlement; while the idea (so often appealed to in these matters) that it is conventionally decidable is even worse. Following from all that, I am not in the least clear which option it would be wise to take if one were presented with them before the experiment. I find that rather disturbing.

Whatever the puzzlement, there is one feature of the arguments which have led to it which is worth picking out, since it runs counter to something which is, I think, often rather vaguely supposed. It is often recognised that there are 'first-personal' and 'third-personal' aspects of questions about persons, and that there are difficulties about the relations between them. It is also recognised that 'mentalistic' considerations (as we may vaguely call them) and considerations of bodily continuity are involved in questions of personal identity (which is not to say that there are mentalistic and bodily criteria of personal identity). It is tempting to think that the two distinctions run in parallel: roughly, that a first-person approach concentrates attention on mentalistic considerations, while a third-personal approach emphasises considerations of bodily continuity. The present discussion is an illustration of exactly the opposite. The first argument, which led to the 'mentalistic' conclusion that A and B would change bodies and that each person should identify himself with the destination of his memories and character, was an argument entirely conducted in third-personal terms. The second argument, which suggested the bodily continuity identification, concerned itself with the first-personal issue of what A could expect. That this is so seems to me (though I will not discuss it further here) of some significance.

I will end by suggesting one rather shaky way in which one might approach a resolution of the problem, using only the limited materials already available.

The apparently decisive arguments of the first presentation, which suggested that A should identify himself with the B-body-person, turned on the extreme neatness of the situation in satisfying, if any could, the description of 'changing bodies'. But this neatness is basically artificial; it is the product of the will of the experimenter to produce a situation which would naturally elicit, with minimum hesitation, that description. By the sorts of methods he employed, he could easily have left off earlier or gone on further. He could have stopped at situation (v), leaving B as he was; or he could have gone on and produced two persons each with A-like character and memories, as well as one or two with B-like characteristics. If he had done either of those, we should have been in yet greater difficulty about what to say; he just chose to make it as easy as possible for us to find something to say. Now if we had some model of ghostly persons in bodies, which were in some sense actually moved around by certain procedures, we could regard the neat experiment just as the *effective* experiment: the one method that really did result in the ghostly persons' changing places without being destroyed, dispersed, or whatever. But we cannot seriously use such a model. The experimenter has not in the sense of that model *induced* a change of bodies; he has rather produced the one situation out of a range of equally possible situations which we should be most disposed to call a change of bodies. As against this, the principle that one's fears can extend to future pain whatever psychological changes precede it seems positively straightforward. Perhaps, indeed, it is not; but we need to be shown what is wrong with it. Until we are shown what is wrong with it, we should perhaps decide that if we were the person A then, if we were to decide selfishly, we should pass the pain to the B-body-person. It would be risky: that there is room for the notion of a *risk* here is itself a major feature of the problem.

Notes

1 *Self-Knowledge and Self-Identity* (Ithaca, NY, 1963), pp. 23 seq.

2 This of course does not have to be the crucial question, but it seems one fair way of taking up the present objection.

3 For a more detailed treatment of issues related to this, see Williams, *Problems of the Self* (Cambridge, 1973), pp. 38 *seq.*

19

From *Reasons and Persons*

Derek Parfit

Overdetermination

Return now to the pints of water and the wounded men. Let us add some features to this case. Suppose that, before the water-cart is driven to these men, you arrive, with another pint. The wounded men need more than a single pint. After drinking this pint their intensely painful thirst would not be fully relieved. But the water-cart can hold only one thousand pints. It is now full. If you add your pint, this will merely cause one pint to overflow down some drain.

You have no moral reason to add your pint, since this would merely cause a pint to be wasted. According to (C10), you ought to add your pint if this would make you a member of a group who together benefit other people. We may think that, if you add your pint, you are *not* a member of the group who together benefit the wounded men. Some of your pint may be drunk by these wounded men. And you are acting in the same way as the other altruists did. But we might claim, 'Unlike the other altruists, you do not give to each of the wounded men an extra thousandth of a pint of water. Your act has no effect on the amount of water that these men receive.'

Things are not so simple. If you add your pint, this will be a case involving overdetermination.

It is true of you that, if you had not contributed, this would have made no difference to the amount of water that the men drink. But, since you have contributed, the same is true of each of the other altruists. It is true that, if any one of these altruists had not contributed, this would have made no difference to the amount of water that the men drink. The water-cart would not have been full when you arrive, and your pint would have made it full. What is true of you is true of each of the other altruists. It is therefore true that you *are* a member of the group who together benefit the wounded men.

We must again appeal to what the agents know, or have reason to believe. Suppose that the other altruists had no reason to believe that you would arrive, with your extra pint. Each ought to have poured in his pint. This is because each had good reason to believe that he would be a member of a group of whom it is true both (1) that they together benefit the wounded men, and (2) that they benefit these men *most* if they *all* pour in their pints. When you arrive, you know that the water-cart is full. You have no reason to contribute, since you know that you would *not* be a member of such a group. If you contribute, you will instead be a member of a group *which is too large*. We should claim

Derek Parfit, *Reasons and Persons* (Oxford: Oxford University Press, 1984), pp. 82–91. © 1984 by Derek Parfit. Reprinted with permission from Oxford University Press.

(C13) Suppose that there is some group who, by acting in a certain way, will together benefit other people. If someone believes that this group either is, or would be if he joined, *too large*, he has no moral reason to join this group. A group is *too large* if it is true that, if one or more of its members had not acted, this would not have reduced the benefit that this group gives to other people.

If you add your pint, this will make this group of altruists too large. If you do *not* add your pint, this group will *not* be too large. This is a special borderline case. (C13) also covers the more common cases where some group is already too large.

Rational Altruism

The Fifth Mistake in moral mathematics is the belief that imperceptible effects cannot be morally significant. This is a very serious mistake. When all the Harmless Torturers act, each is acting *very* wrongly. This is true even though each makes no one perceptibly worse off. The same could be true of us. We should cease to think that an act cannot be wrong, *because* of its effects on other people, if this act makes no one perceptibly worse off. Each of our acts may be *very* wrong, because of its effects on other people, even if none of these people could ever notice any of these effects. Our acts may *together* make these people very much worse off.

The Fourth Mistake is equally serious. If we believe that trivial effects can be morally ignored, we may often make people very much worse off. Remember the Fisherman's Dilemma. Where there is overfishing, or declining stocks, it can be better for each if he tries to catch more, worse for each if all do. Consider

How the Fishermen Cause a Disaster. There are many fishermen, who earn their living by fishing separately on some large lake. If each fisherman does not restrict his catch, he will catch within the next few seasons more fish. But he will thereby lower the total catch by a much larger number. Since there are many fishermen, if each does not restrict his catch, he will only trivially affect the number caught by each of the others.

The fishermen believe that such trivial effects can be morally ignored. Because they believe this, even though they never do what they believe to be wrong, they do not restrict their catches. Each thereby increases his own catch, but causes a much greater lowering in the total catch. Because they all act in this way, the result is a disaster. After a few seasons, all catch very many fewer fish. They cannot feed themselves or their children.

If these fisherman knew the facts, had sufficient altruism, and avoided the Fourth Mistake, they would escape this disaster. Each knows that, if he does not restrict his catch, this will be somewhat better for himself, whatever others do. And each knows that, if he acts in this way, the effects on each of the others will be trivial. But the fishermen should not believe that these trivial effects can be morally ignored. They should believe that acting in this way is wrong.

As before, there are two ways in which we could explain why these acts are wrong. We could appeal to the total effect of each person's act. Each fisherman knows that, if he does not restrict his catch, he will catch more fish, but he will reduce the total catch by a much larger number. For the sake of a small gain to himself, he imposes on others a much greater total loss. We could claim that such acts are wrong. This claim does not assume that there can be imperceptible harms and benefits. It is therefore less controversial than the corresponding claim about what each of the Harmless Torturers does.

Our alternative is to appeal to what these fishermen together do. Each fisherman knows that, if he and all the others do not restrict their catches, they will together impose upon themselves a great total loss. Rational altruists would believe these acts to be wrong. They would avoid this disaster.

It may be said: 'So would rational egoists. Each knows that, if he does not restrict his catch, he is a member of a group who impose upon themselves a great loss. It is irrational to act in this way, even in self-interested terms.' As I shall argue in the next chapter, this claim is not justified. Each knows that, if he does not restrict his catch, this will be *better* for himself. This is so whatever others do. When someone does what he knows will be better for himself, it cannot be claimed that his act is irrational in self-interested terms.

Remember next

The Commuter's Dilemma. Suppose that we live in the suburbs of a large city. We can get to and return from work either by car or by bus. Since there are no bus-lanes, extra traffic slows buses just as much as it slows cars. We could therefore know the following to be true. When most of us are going by car, if any one of us goes by car rather than by bus, he will thereby save himself some time, but he will impose on others a much greater total loss of time. This effect would be dispersed. Each might cause a hundred others to be delayed for twenty seconds, or cause a thousand others to be delayed for two seconds. Most of us would regard such effects as so trivial that they can be morally ignored. We would then believe that, in this Commuter's Dilemma, even a rational altruist can justifiably choose to go by car rather than by bus. But if most of us make this choice we shall all be delayed for a long time every day.

Rational altruists would avoid this result. As before, they could appeal either to the effects of what each person does, or to the effects of what all together do. Each saves himself some time, at the cost of imposing on others a much greater total loss of time. We could claim that it is wrong to act in this way, even though the effects on each of the others would be trivial. We could instead claim that this act is wrong, because those who act in this way together impose on everyone a great loss of time. If we accept either of these claims, and have sufficient altruism, we would solve the Commuter's Dilemma, saving ourselves much time every day.

Similar reasoning applies to countless other cases. For one more example, consider the devices that purify the gases that our cars emit. We would think it wrong to save ourselves the cost of repairing this device, if in consequence we imposed great air-pollution on some other single person. But many of us would not think this wrong if it merely trivially or imperceptibly increased the air-pollution suffered by each of very many people. This would be the actual effect in many large cities. It might be much better for all of us if none of us caused such pollution. But, to believe that we are acting wrongly, many of us need to change our view. We must cease to believe that an act cannot be wrong, because of its effects on other people, if these effects are either trivial or imperceptible.

As conditions change, we may need to make some changes in the way we think about morality. I have been arguing for one such change. Common-Sense Morality works best in small communities. When there are few of us, if we give to or impose on others great total benefits or harms, we must be affecting other people in significant ways, that would be grounds either for gratitude, or resentment. In small communities, it is a plausible claim that we cannot have harmed others if there is no one with an obvious complaint, or ground for resenting what we have done.

Until this century, most of mankind lived in small communities. What each did could affect only a few others. But conditions have now changed. Each of us can now, in countless ways, affect countless other people. We can have real though small effects on thousands or millions of people. When these effects are widely dispersed, they may be either trivial, or imperceptible. It now makes a great difference whether we continue to believe that we cannot have greatly harmed or benefited others unless there are people with obvious grounds for resentment or gratitude. While we continue to believe this, even if we care about effects on others, we may fail to solve many serious Prisoner's Dilemmas. For the sake of small benefits to ourselves, or our families, each of us may deny others much greater total benefits, or impose on others much greater total harms. We may think this permissible because the effects on each of the others will be either trivial or imperceptible. If this is what we think, what we do will often be much worse for all of us.

If we cared sufficiently about effects on others, and changed our moral view, we would solve such problems. It is not enough to ask, 'Will my act harm other people?' Even if the answer is No, my act may still be wrong, because of its effects. The effects that it will have when it is considered on its own may not be its only relevant effects. I should ask, 'Will my act be one of a set of acts that will *together* harm other people?' The answer may be Yes. And the harm to others may be great. If this is so, I may be acting *very* wrongly, like the Harmless Torturers. We must accept this view if our concern for others is to yield solutions to most of the many Prisoner's Dilemmas that we face: most of the many cases where, if each of us rather than none of us does what will be better for himself – or for his family, or those he loves – this will be worse, and often *much* worse, for everyone.

Theories that are Directly Self-defeating

We often face Many-Person Prisoner's Dilemmas. It is often true that, if each rather than none of us does what will be better for himself, or his family, or those he loves, this will be worse for all of us. If each of us is disposed to act in this way, these cases raise a practical problem. Unless something changes, the outcome will be worse for all of us.

This problem has two kinds of solution: political and psychological. Of the psychological solutions, the most important are the moral solutions. As I argued, there are many cases where we need a moral solution.

I described four of these solutions. These are provided by four motives: trustworthiness, reluctance to be a free-rider, wanting to satisfy the Kantian Test, and sufficient altruism. There are two forms of each moral solution. When one of these motives leads someone to make the altruistic choice, what this person does may either be, or not be, worse for him. This distinction raises deep questions. I shall simply state what my arguments assume. On all plausible theories about self-interest, what is in our interests partly depends on what our motives or desires are. If we have moral motives, it may therefore not be true that the altruistic choice will be worse for us. But this might be true. Even if it is, we might still make this choice.

I am here dismissing four claims. Some say that no one does what he believes will be worse for him. This has been often refuted. Others say that what each does is, by definition, best for him. In the economist's phrase, it will 'maximize his utility'. Since this is merely a definition, it cannot be false. But it is here irrelevant. It is simply not about what is in a person's own long-term self-interest. Others say that virtue is always rewarded. Unless there is an after-life, this has also been refuted. Others say that virtue is its own reward. On the Objective List Theory, being moral and acting morally may be one of the things that make our lives go better. But, on the plausible versions of this theory, there could be cases where acting morally would be, on the whole, worse for someone. Acting morally might deprive this person of too many of the other things that make our lives go better.

To return to my own claims. Many Prisoner's Dilemmas need moral solutions. To achieve these solutions, we must be directly disposed to make the altruistic choice. There are two forms of each moral solution. One form abolishes the Dilemma. In these cases, because we have some moral motive, it is not true that it will be worse for each if he makes the altruistic choice. But in other cases this is still true. Even in such cases, we might make this choice. Each might do, for moral reasons, what he knows will be worse for him.

We often need moral solutions of this second form. Call them *self-denying*. They solve the practical problem. The outcome is better for everyone. But they do not abolish the Dilemma. A theoretical problem remains.

The problem is this. We may have moral reasons to make the altruistic choice. But it will be better for each if he makes the self-benefiting choice. Morality conflicts with self-interest. When these conflict, what is it rational to do?

On the Self-interest Theory, it is the self-benefiting choice which is rational. If we believe S, we shall be ambivalent about self-denying moral solutions. We shall believe that, to achieve such solutions, we must all act irrationally.

Many writers resist this conclusion. Some claim that moral reasons are not weaker than self-interested reasons. Others claim, more boldly, that they are stronger. On their view, it is the self-benefiting choice which is irrational.

This debate may seem unresolvable. How can these two kinds of reason be weighed against each other? Moral reasons are, of course, morally supreme. But self-interested reasons are, in self-interested terms, supreme. Where can we find a neutral scale?

In Prisoner's Dilemmas, Does S Fail in its Own Terms?

It has been claimed that we do not need a neutral scale. There is a sense in which, in Prisoner's

Dilemmas, the Self-interest Theory is self-defeating. It has been claimed that, since this is true, moral reasons are superior to self-interested reasons, even in self-interested terms.

As we have seen, S might be individually indirectly self-defeating. It might be worse for someone if he was never self-denying. But this is not true in Prisoner's Dilemmas. The bad effects are here produced by acts, not dispositions. And it is clear which choice will be better for each person. It is true of each that, if he makes the altruistic choice, this will certainly be worse for him. S tells each to make the self-benefiting choice. And, whatever others do, it will be better for each if he himself makes this choice. S is not here individually self-defeating. But, in the sense defined in Section 22, S is *directly collectively* self-defeating. If all successfully follow S, this will be worse for each than if none do.

Does this show that, if we all follow S, we are irrational? We can start with a smaller question. If we believe S, would our theory be failing even in its own terms?

We could answer: 'No. The pursuit by each of self-interest is better for him. It succeeds. Why is S collectively self-defeating? Only because the pursuit of self-interest is worse for others. This does not make it unsuccessful. It is not benevolence.'

If we are self-interested, we shall of course deplore Prisoner's Dilemmas. These are not the cases loved by classical economists, where each gains if everyone pursues self-interest. We might say: 'In those cases, S both works and approves the situation. In Prisoner's Dilemmas, S still works. Each still gains from his own pursuit of self-interest. But since each loses even more from the self-interested acts of others, S here condemns the situation.'

This may seem an evasion. When it would be worse for each if we all pursued self-interest, it may seem that the Self-interest Theory *should* condemn itself. Suppose that in some other group, facing the same Dilemmas, all make the altruistic choice. They might say to us: 'You think us irrational. But we are better off than you. We do better even in self-interested terms.'

We could answer: 'That is just a play on words. You "do better" only in the sense that you are better off. Each of you is *doing* worse in self-interested terms. Each is doing what he knows will be worse for him.' We might add: 'What is worse

for each of us is that, in our group, there are no fools. Each of you has better luck. Though your irrationality is bad for you, you gain even more from the irrationality of others.'

They might answer: 'You are partly right. Each of us *is* doing worse in self-interested terms. But, though *each* is doing worse, *we* are doing better. This is not a play on words. Each of us is better off because of what we *do*.'

This suggestion is more promising. Return to the simpler Two-Person Case. Each could either benefit himself (E) or give to the other some greater benefit (A). The outcomes would be as shown below.

		You	
		do E	do A
I	do E	Third-best for each	Best for me, worst for you
	do A	Worst for me, best for you	Second-best for both

To ensure that neither's choice can affect the other's – which might produce reciprocity – suppose that we cannot communicate. If I do A rather than E, that will then be worse for me. This is so whatever you do. And the same holds for you. If we both do A rather than E, each is therefore doing worse in self-interested terms. The suggestion is that *we* are doing better.

What makes this promising is that it contrasts *each* with *we*. As we have seen, what is false of each may be true of us. It can be true for example that, though *each* harms no one, *we together* harm other people. If we both do A rather than E, is it true that, though each is doing worse in self-interested terms, we together are doing better?

We can use this test. The Self-interest Theory gives to each a certain aim. Each does better in S's terms if, of the acts that are possible for him, he does what causes his S-given aim to be better achieved. *We* do better in S's terms if, of the acts that are possible for us, we do what causes the S-given aims *of each* to be better achieved. This test seems fair. It might show that, if each does the best he can in S's terms, we together could not do better.

When we are measuring success, only *ultimate* aims count. Suppose that we are trying to scratch our own backs. The ultimate aim of each might be that he cease to itch. We would then do better if we scratched each other's backs. But we might be contortionists: the ultimate aim of each might be that his back be scratched *by himself*. If we scratched each other's backs, we would then do worse.

What is the ultimate aim that the Self-interest Theory gives to each? Is it that his interests be advanced, or that his interests be advanced *by himself*? On the Self-interest Theory, if someone's interests are advanced by himself, this person is acting rationally. I can therefore restate my question. What is the ultimate aim given to each by S? Is it that his interests be advanced, or that he act rationally?

In Section 3 I defended the following answer. Like all theories about rationality, S gives to each the formal aim that he act rationally. But, according to S, this formal aim is not, as such, a substantive aim. S gives to each person one ultimate substantive aim: that his life goes, for him, as well as possible. On the Hedonistic Theory about self-interest, being rational and acting rationally are not part of this aim. They are both mere means. On some other theories about self-interest, being rational and acting rationally are not mere means. They are both, whatever their effects may be, parts of the ultimate substantive aim that S gives to each person. But this would not be true

when they would be, on the whole, worse for someone.

We can imagine a theory that gives to each person this substantive aim: that his interests be advanced *by himself*. Someone who believes this theory might crudely misinterpret Nietzsche, and value 'the fiercest self-reliance'. If we both did A rather than E, we would be doing worse in these sub-Nietzschean terms. The interests of each would be better advanced. But neither's interests would be advanced by himself, so the sub-Nietzschean aim would be worse achieved.

If we both do A rather than E, are we doing better in S's terms? We cause the interests of each to be better advanced. In this respect, we are doing better in S's terms, causing the S-given aim of each to be better achieved. On the Hedonistic Theory about self-interest, this completely answers my question. On this theory, S claims any act to be a mere means. The aim is always the effect on one's conscious life. (Nietzsche's 'blond beasts' were, it is said, lions. But, for them too, acting is a means. They prefer to eat what others kill.)

On some other theories about self-interest, more must be said. According to S, if we both do A rather than E, we are both acting irrationally. Each is doing what he knows will be worse for himself. On some theories about self-interest, being rational and acting rationally are parts of the aim that S gives to each. On these theories, some apparent Prisoner's Dilemmas are not true Dilemmas.

20

A Dialogue on Personal Identity and Immortality

John Perry

This is a record of conversations of Gretchen Weirob, a teacher of philosophy at a small mid-western college, and two of her friends. The conversations took place in her hospital room on the three nights before she died from injuries sustained in a motorcycle accident. Sam Miller is a chaplain and a long-time friend of Weirob's; Dave Cohen is a former student of hers.

[Editor's Note: In Perry's three dialogues, Gretchen Weirob's friends try to convince her that she is wrong to deny even the possibility of surviving the death of her physical body. In the First Dialogue (The First Night), Miller turns to the idea of an immaterial soul that could survive the physical body to which it is connected. Weirob complains about the intelligibility of identifying and re-identifying these souls that are distinct from "their" bodies. In the following Second Dialogue (The Second Night), reprinted here, Miller tries again to convince Weirob that we can make sense of a person's surviving the loss of a physical body through relying on our understanding of psychological states and connections between them.]

The Second Night

WEIROB: Well, Sam, have you figured out a way to make sense of the identity of immaterial souls?

MILLER: No, I have decided it was a mistake to build my argument on such a dubious notion.

WEIROB: Have you then given up on survival? I think such a position would be a hard one for a clergyman to live with, and would feel bad about having pushed you so far.

MILLER: Don't worry. I'm more convinced than ever. I stayed up late last night thinking and reading, and I'm sure I can convince you now.

WEIROB: Get with it, time is running out.

MILLER: First, let me explain why, independently of my desire to defend survival after death, I am dissatisfied with your view that personal identity is just bodily identity. My argument will be very similar to the one you used to convince me that personal identity could not be identified with identity of an immaterial soul.

Consider a person waking up tomorrow morning, conscious, but not yet ready to open her eyes and look around and, so to speak, let the new day officially begin.

WEIROB: Such a state is familiar enough, I admit.

MILLER: Now couldn't such a person tell who she was? That is, even before opening her eyes and looking around, and in particular before looking at her body or making any judgments about it, wouldn't she be able to say who she was? Surely most of us, in the morning, know who we are before opening our eyes and recognizing our own bodies, do we not?

WEIROB: You seem to be right about that.

MILLER: But such a judgment as this person makes – we shall suppose she judges "I am Gretchen Weirob" – is a judgment of personal identity. Suppose she says to herself, "I am the very person who was arguing with Sam Miller last night." This is clearly a statement about her identity with someone who was alive the night before. And she could make this judgment without examining her body at all. You could have made just this judgment this morning, before opening your eyes.

WEIROB: Well, in fact I did so. I remembered our conversation of last night and said to myself, "Could I be the rude person who was so hard on Sam Miller's attempts to comfort me?" And, of course, my answer was that I not only could be but was that very rude person.

MILLER: But then by the same principle you used last night personal identity cannot be bodily identity. For you said that it could not be identity of immaterial soul because we were not judging as to identity of immaterial soul when we judge as to personal identity. But by the same token, as my example shows, we are not judging as to bodily identity when we judge as to personal identity. For we can judge who we are, and that

we are the very person who did such and such and so and so, without having to make any judgments at all about the body. So, personal identity, while it may not consist of identity of an immaterial soul, does not consist in identity of material body either.

WEIROB: I did argue as you remember. But I also said that the notion of the identity of an immaterial unobservable unextended soul seemed to make no sense at all. This is one reason that cannot be what we are judging about, when we judge as to personal identity. Bodily identity at least makes sense. Perhaps we are assuming sameness of body, without looking.

MILLER: Granted. But you do admit that we do not in our own cases actually need to make a judgment of bodily identity in order to make a judgment of personal identity?

WEIROB: I don't think I will admit it. I will let it pass, so that we may proceed.

MILLER: Okay. Now it seems to me we are even able to imagine awakening and finding ourselves to have a *different* body than the one we had before. Suppose yourself just as I have described you. And now suppose you finally open your eyes and see, not the body you have grown so familiar with over the years, but one of a fundamentally different shape and size.

WEIROB: Well, I should suppose I had been asleep for a very long time and lost a lot of weight – perhaps I was in a coma for a year or so.

MILLER: But isn't it at least conceivable that it should not be your old body at all? I seem to be able to imagine awakening with a totally new body.

WEIROB: And how would you suppose that this came about?

MILLER: That's beside the point. I'm not saying I can imagine a procedure that would bring this about. I'm saying I can imagine it happening to me. In Kafka's *Metamorphosis*, someone awakens as a cockroach. I can't imagine what would make this happen to me or anyone else, but I can imagine awakening with the body of a cockroach. It is incredible that it should happen – that I do not deny. I simply mean I can imagine experiencing it. It doesn't seem contradictory or incoherent, simply unlikely and inexplicable.

WEIROB: So, if I admit this can be imagined, what follows then?

MILLER: Well, I think it follows that personal identity does not just amount to bodily identity. For I would not, finding that I had a new body, conclude that I was not the very same person I was before. I would be the same *person*, though I did not have the same *body*. So we would have identity of person but not identity of body. So personal identity cannot just amount to bodily identity.

WEIROB: Well suppose – and I emphasize *suppose* – I grant you all of this. Where does it leave you? What do you claim I have recognized as the same, if not my body and not my immaterial soul?

MILLER: I don't claim that you have recognized anything as the same, except the person involved, that is, you yourself.

WEIROB: I'm not sure what you mean.

MILLER: Let me appeal as you did to the Blue River. Suppose I take a visitor to the stretch of river by the old Mill, and then drive him toward Manhattan. After an hour-or-so drive we see another stretch of river, and I say, "That's the same river we saw this morning." As you pointed out yesterday, I don't thereby imply that the very same molecules of water are seen both times. And the places are different, perhaps a hundred miles apart. And the shape and color and level of pollution might all be different. What do I see later in the day that is identical with what I saw earlier in the day?

WEIROB: Nothing except the river itself.

MILLER: Exactly. But now notice that what I see, strictly speaking, is not the whole river but only a part of it. I see different parts of the same river at the two different times. So really, if we restrict ourselves to what I literally see, I do not judge identity at all, but something else.

WEIROB: And what might that be?

MILLER: In saying that the river seen earlier, and the river seen later, are one and the same river, do I mean any more than that the stretch of water seen later and that stretch of water seen earlier are connected by other stretches of water?

WEIROB: That's about right. If the stretches of water are so connected there is but one river of which they are both parts.

MILLER: Yes, that's what I mean. The statement of identity, "This river is the same one we saw this morning," is in a sense about rivers. But in a way it is also about stretches of water or river parts.

WEIROB: So is all of this something special about rivers?

MILLER: Not at all. It is a recurring pattern. After all, we constantly deal with objects extended in space and time. But we are seldom aware of the objects' wholes, but only of their parts or stretches of their histories. When a statement of identity is not just something trivial, like "This bed is this bed," it is usually because we are really judging that different parts fit together, in some appropriate pattern, into a certain kind of whole.

WEIROB: I'm not sure I see just what you mean yet.

MILLER: Let me give you another example. Suppose we are sitting together watching the first game of a double-header. You ask me, "Is this game identical with this game?" This is a perfectly stupid question, though, of course, strictly speaking it makes sense and the answer is "yes."

But now suppose you leave in the sixth inning to go for hot dogs. You are delayed, and return after about forty-five minutes or so. You ask, "Is this the same game I was watching?" Now your question is not stupid, but perfectly appropriate.

WEIROB: Because the first game might still be going on or it might have ended, and the second game begun, by the time I return.

MILLER: Exactly. Which is to say somehow different parts of the game – different innings, or at least different plays – were somehow involved in your question. That's why it wasn't stupid or trivial but significant.

WEIROB: So, you think that judgments as to the identity of an object of a certain kind – rivers or baseball games or whatever – involve judgments as to the *parts* of those things being connected in a certain way, and are significant only when different parts are involved. Is that your point?

MILLER: Yes, and I think it is an important one. How foolish it would be, when we ask a question about the identity of baseball games, to look for something *else*, other than the game as a whole, which had to be the same. It could be the same game, even if different players were involved. It could be the same game, even if it had been moved to a different field. These other things, the innings, the plays, the players, the field, don't have to be the same at the different times for the game to be the same, they just have to be related in certain ways so as to make that complex whole we call a single game.

WEIROB: You think we were going off on a kind of a wild-goose chase when we asked whether it was the identity of soul or body that was involved in the identity of persons?

MILLER: Yes. The answer I should now give is neither. We are wondering about the identity of the person. Of course, if by "soul" we just mean "person," there is no problem. But if we mean, as I did yesterday, some other thing whose identity is already understood, which has to be the same when persons are the same, we are just fooling ourselves with words.

WEIROB: With rivers and baseball games, I can see that they are made up of parts connected in a certain way. The connection is, of course, different in the two cases, as is the sort of

"part" involved. River parts must be connected physically with other river parts to form a continuous whole. Baseball innings must be connected so that the score, batting order, and the like are carried over from the earlier inning to the later one according to the rules. Is there something analogous we are to say about persons?

MILLER: Writers who concern themselves with this speak of "person-stages." That is just a stretch of consciousness, such as you and I are aware of now. I am aware of a flow of thoughts and feelings that are mine, you are aware of yours. A person is just a whole composed of such stretches as parts, not some substance that underlies them, as I thought yesterday, and not the body in which they occur, as you seem to think. That is the conception of a person I wish to defend today.

WEIROB: So when I awoke and said to myself, "I am the one who was so rude to Sam Miller last night," I was judging that a certain stretch of consciousness I was then aware of, and an earlier one I remembered having been aware of, form a single whole of the appropriate sort – a single stream of consciousness, we might say.

MILLER: Yes, that's it exactly. You need not worry about whether the same immaterial soul is involved, or even whether that makes sense. Nor need you worry about whether the same body is involved, as indeed you do not since you don't even have to open your eyes and look. Identity is not, so to speak, something under the person-stages, nor in something they are attached to, but something you build from them.

Now survival, you can plainly see, is no problem at all once we have this conception of personal identity. All you need suppose is that there is, in Heaven, a conscious being, and that the person-stages that make her up are in the appropriate relation to those that now make you up, so that they are parts of the same whole – namely, you. If so, you have survived. So will you admit now that survival is at least possible?

WEIROB: Hold on, hold on. Comforting me is not that easy. You will have to show that it is possible that these person-stages or stretches of consciousness be related in the appropriate way. And to do that, won't you have to tell me what that way is?

MILLER: Yes, of course. I was getting ahead of myself. It is right at this point that my reading was particularly helpful. In a chapter of his *Essay On Human Understanding* Locke discusses this very question. He suggests that the relation between two person-stages or stretches of consciousness that makes them stages of a single person is just that the later one contains memories of the earlier one. He doesn't say this in so many words – he talks of "extending our consciousness back in time." But he seems to be thinking of memory.

WEIROB: So, any past thought or feeling or intention or desire that I can remember having is mine?

MILLER: That's right. I can remember only my own past thoughts and feelings, and you only yours. Of course, everyone would readily admit that. Locke's insight is to take this relation as the source of identity and not just its consequence. To remember – or more plausibly, to be able to remember – the thoughts and feelings of a person who was conscious in the past is just what it is to be that person.

Now you can easily see that this solves the problem of the possibility of survival. As I was saying, all you need to do is imagine someone at some future time, not on this earth and not with your present thoughts and feelings, remembering the very conversation we are having now. This does not require sameness of anything else, but it amounts to sameness of person. So, now will you admit it?

WEIROB: No, I don't.

MILLER: Well, what's the problem now?

WEIROB: I admit that if I remember having a certain thought or feeling had by some person in the past, then I must indeed be that person. Though I can remember watching others think, I cannot remember their thinking, any more than I can experience it at the time it occurs if it is theirs and not mine. This is the kernel of Locke's idea, and I don't see that I could deny it.

But we must distinguish – as I'm sure you will agree – between *actually* remembering and merely *seeming* to remember. Many men who think that they are Napoleon claim to remember losing the battle of Waterloo. We may suppose them to be sincere, and to really seem to remember it. But they do not actually remember because they were not at the battle and are not Napoleon.

MILLER: Of course I admit that we must distinguish between actually remembering and only seeming to.

WEIROB: And you will admit too, I trust, that the thought of some person at some far place and some distant time seeming to remember this conversation I am having with you would not give me the sort of comfort that the prospect of survival is supposed to provide. I would have no reason to anticipate future experiences of this person, simply because she is to *seem* to remember my experiences. The experiences of such a deluded imposter are not ones I can look forward to having.

MILLER: I agree.

WEIROB: So the mere possibility of someone in the future seeming to remember this conversation does not show the possibility of my surviving. Only the possibility of someone actually remembering this conversation – or, to be precise, the experiences I am having – would show that.

MILLER: Of course. But what are you driving at? Where is the problem? I can imagine someone being deluded, but also someone actually being you and remembering your present thoughts.

WEIROB: But, what's the difference? How do you know *which* of the two you are imagining, and *what* you have shown possible?

MILLER: Well, I just imagine the one and not the other. I don't see the force of your argument.

WEIROB: Let me try to make it clear with another example. Imagine two persons. One is talking to you, saying certain words, having certain thoughts, and so forth. The other is not talking to you at all, but is in the next room being hypnotized. The hypnotist gives to this person a post-hypnotic suggestion that upon awakening he will remember having had certain thoughts and having uttered certain words to you. The thoughts and words he mentions happen to be just the thoughts and words which the first person actually thinks and says. Do you understand the situation?

MILLER: Yes, continue.

WEIROB: Now, in a while, both of the people are saying sentences which begin, "I remember saying to Sam Miller –" and "I remember thinking as I talked to Sam Miller." And they both report remembering just the same thoughts and utterances. One of these will be remembering and the other only seeming to remember, right?

MILLER: Of course.

WEIROB: Now which one is *actually* remembering?

MILLER: Why, the very one who was in the room talking to me, of course. The other one is just under the influence of the suggestion made by the hypnotist and not remembering talking to me at all.

WEIROB: Now you agree that the difference between them does not consist in the content of what they are now thinking or saying.

MILLER: Agreed. The difference is in the relation to the past thinking and speaking. In the one case the relation of memory obtains. In the other, it does not.

WEIROB: But they both satisfy part of the conditions of remembering, for they both *seem to remember*. So there must be some further condition that the one satisfies and the other does not. I am trying to get you to say what that further condition is.

MILLER: Well, I said that the one who had been in this room talking would be remembering.

WEIROB: In other words, given two putative rememberers of some past thought or action, the real rememberer is the one who, in addition to seeming to remember the past thought or action, actually thought it or did it.

MILLER: Yes.

WEIROB: That is to say, the one who is identical with the person who did the past thinking and uttering.

MILLER: Yes, I admit it.

WEIROB: So, your argument just amounts to this. Survival is possible, because imaginable. It is imaginable, because my identity with some Heavenly person is imaginable. To imagine it, we imagine a person in Heaven who, First, seems to remember my thoughts and actions, and Second, is me.

Surely, there could hardly be a tighter circle. If I have doubts that the Heavenly person is me, I will have doubts as to whether she is really remembering or only seeming to. No one could doubt the possibility of some future person who, after death, seemed to remember the things he thought and did. But that possibility does not resolve the issue about the possibility of survival. Only the possibility of someone *actually* remembering could do that – for that, as we agree, is sufficient for identity. But doubts about survival and identity simply go over without remainder into doubts about whether the memories would be actual or merely apparent. You guarantee me no more than the possibility of a deluded Heavenly imposter.

COHEN: But wait, Gretchen. I think Sam was less than fair to his own idea just now.

WEIROB: You think you can break out of the circle of using real memory to explain identity, and identity to mark the difference between real and apparent memory? Feel free to try.

COHEN: Let us return to your case of the hypnotist. You point out that we have two putative rememberers. You ask what marks the difference, and claim the answer must be the circular one – that the real rememberer is the person who actually had the experiences both seem to remember.

But that is not the only possible answer. The experiences themselves cause the later apparent memories in the one case, while the hypnotist causes them in the other. We can say that the rememberer is the one of the two whose memories were *caused in the right way* by the earlier experiences. We thus distinguish between the rememberer and the hypnotic subject, without appeal to identity.

The idea that real memory amounts to apparent memory plus identity is misleading anyway. I seem to remember, as a small child, knocking over the Menorah so the candles fell into and spoiled a tureen of soup. And I did actually perform such a feat. So we have apparent memory and identity. But I do *not* actually remember; I was much too young when I did this to remember it now. I have simply been told the story so often I seem to remember.

Here the suggestion that real memory is apparent memory that was caused in the appropriate way by the past events fares better. Not my experience of pulling over the Menorah, but hearing my parents talk about it later, caused my memory-like impressions.

WEIROB: You analyze personal identity into memory, and memory into apparent memory which is caused in the right way. A person is a certain sort of causal process.

COHEN: Right.

WEIROB: Suppose now for the sake of argument I accept this. How does it help Sam in his defense of the possibility of survival? In ordinary memory, the causal chain from remembered event to memory of it never leads us outside the confines of a single body. Indeed, the normal process of which you speak surely involves storage of information somehow in the brain. How can the states of my brain, when I die, influence in the appropriate way the apparent memories of the Heavenly person Sam takes to be me?

COHEN: Well, I didn't intend to be defending the possibility of survival. That is Sam's problem. I just like the idea that personal identity can be explained in terms of memory, and not just in terms of identity of the body.

MILLER: But surely, this does provide me with the basis for further defense. Your challenge, Gretchen, was to explain the difference between two persons in Heaven, one who actually remembers your experience – and so is you – and one who simply seems to remember it. But can I not just say that the one who is you is the one whose states were caused in the appropriate way? I do not mean the way they would be in a normal case of earthly memory. But in the case of the Heavenly being who is you, God would have created her with the brain states (or whatever) she has *because* you had the ones you had at death. Surely it is not the exact form of the dependence of my later memories on my earlier perceptions that makes them really memories, but the fact that the process involved has preserved information.

WEIROB: So if God creates a Heavenly person, designing her brain to duplicate the brain I have upon death, that person is me. If, on the other hand, a Heavenly being should come to be with those very same memory-like states by accident (if there are accidents in Heaven) it would not be me.

MILLER: Exactly. Are you satisfied now that survival makes perfectly good sense?

WEIROB: No, I'm still quite unconvinced.

The problem I see is this. If God could create one person in Heaven, and by designing her after me, make her me, why could he not make two such bodies, and cause this transfer of information into both of them? Would both of these Heavenly persons then be me? It seems as clear as anything in philosophy that from

A is B

and

C is B

where by "is" we mean identity, we can infer,

A is C.

So, if each of these Heavenly persons is me, they must be each other. But then they are not two but one. But my assumption was that God creates two, not one. He could create them physically distinct, capable of independent movement, perhaps in widely separated Heavenly locations, each with her own duties to perform, her own circle of Heavenly friends, and the like.

So either God, by creating a Heavenly person with a brain modeled after mine, does not really create someone identical with me but merely someone similar to me, or God is somehow limited to making only one such being. I can see no reason why, if there were a God, He should be so limited. So I take the first option. He could create someone similar to me, but not someone who would *be* me. Either your analysis of memory is wrong, and such a being does not, after all, remember what I am doing or saying, or memory is not sufficient for personal identity. Your theory has gone wrong somewhere, for it leads to absurdity.

COHEN: But wait. Why can't Sam simply say that if God makes one such creature, she is you, while if he makes more, none of them is you? It's possible that he makes only one. So it's possible that you survive. Sam always meant to allow that it's *possible* that you won't survive. He had in mind the case in which there is no God to make the appropriate Heavenly persons, or God exists, but doesn't make even one. You have simply shown that there is another way of not surviving. Instead of making too few Heavenly rememberers, He makes too many. So what? He might make the right number, and then you would survive.

WEIROB: Your remarks really amount to a change in your position. Now you are not claiming that memory alone is enough for personal identity. Now, it is memory *plus* lack of competition, the absence of other rememberers, that is needed for personal identity.

COHEN: It does amount to a change of position. But what of it? Is there anything untenable about the position as changed?

WEIROB: Let's look at this from the point of view of the Heavenly person. She says to herself, "Oh, I must be Gretchen Weirob, for I remember doing what she did and saying what she said." But now that's a pretty tenuous conclusion, isn't it? She is really only entitled to say, "Oh, either I'm Gretchen Weirob, or God has created more than one being like me, and none of us is." Identity has become something dependent on things wholly extrinsic to her. Who she is now turns on not just her states of mind and their relation to my states of mind, but on the existence or nonexistence of other people. Is this really what you want to maintain?

Or look at it from my point of view. God creates one of me in Heaven. Surely I should be glad if convinced this was to happen. Now he creates another, and I should despair again, for this means I won't survive after all.

How can doubling a good deed make it worthless?

COHEN: Are you saying that there is some contradiction in my suggestion that only creation of a unique Heavenly Gretchen counts as your survival?

WEIROB: No, it's not contradictory, as far as I can see. But it seems odd in a way that shows that something somewhere is wrong with your theory. Here is a certain relationship I have with a Heavenly person. There being such a person, to whom I am related in this way, is something that is of great importance to me, a source of comfort. It makes it appropriate for me to anticipate having her experiences, since she is just me. Why should my having that relation to another being destroy my relation to this one? You say because then I will not be identical with either of them. But since you have provided a theory about what that identity consists in, we can look and see what it amounts to for me to be or not to be identical. If she is to remember my experience, I can rightly anticipate hers. But then it seems the doubling makes no difference. And yet it must, for one cannot be identical with two. So you add, in a purely *ad hoc* manner, that her memory of me isn't enough to make my anticipation of her experiences appropriate, if there are two rather than one so linked. Isn't it more reasonable to conclude, since memory does not secure identity when there are two Heavenly Gretchens, it also doesn't when there is only one?

COHEN: There is something *ad hoc* about it, I admit. But perhaps that's just the way our concept works. You have not elicited a contradiction –

WEIROB: An infinite pile of absurdities has the same weight as a contradiction. And absurdities can be generated without limit from your account. Suppose God created this Heavenly person before I died. Then He in effect kills me; if He has already created her, then you really are not talking to whom you think, but someone new, created by Gretchen Weirob's strange death moments ago. Or suppose He first creates one being in Heaven, who is me. Then He creates another. Does the first cease to be me? If God can create such beings in Heaven, surely He can do so in Albuquerque. And there is nothing on your theory to favor this body before you as Gretchen Weirob's, over the one belonging to the person created in Albuquerque. So I am to suppose that if God were to do this, I would suddenly cease to be. I'm tempted to say I would cease to be Gretchen Weirob. But that would be a confused way of putting it. There would be here, in my place, a new person with false memories of having been Gretchen Weirob, who has just died of competition – a strange death if ever there was one. She would have no right to my name, my bank account, or the services of my doctor, who is paid from insurance premiums paid for by deductions from Gretchen Weirob's past salary. Surely this is nonsense; however carefully God should choose to duplicate me, in Heaven or in Albuquerque, I would not cease to be, or cease to be who I am. You may reply that God, being benevolent, would never create an extra Gretchen Weirob. But I do not say that he would, but only that if he did this would not, as your theory implies, mean that I cease to exist. Your theory gives the wrong answer in this possible circumstance, so it must be wrong. I think I have been given no motivation to abandon the most obvious and straightforward view on these matters. I am a live body, and when that body dies, my existence will be at an end.

21

On the Immortality of the Soul

David Hume

By the mere light of reason it seems difficult to prove the *Immortality* of the *Soul*; the arguments for it are commonly derived either from *metaphysical* topics, or moral or physical. But in reality 'tis the Gospel, and the Gospel alone, that has brought *life and immortality to light*.

I.   *Metaphysical* topics suppose that the soul is immaterial, and that 'tis impossible for thought to belong to a material substance. — But just metaphysics teach us that the notion of substance is wholly confused and imperfect, and that we have no other idea of any substance, than as an aggregate of particular qualities, inhering in an unknown something. Matter, therefore, and spirit, are at bottom equally unknown, and we cannot determine what qualities inhere in the one or in the other. They likewise teach us that nothing can be decided *a priori* concerning any cause or effect, and that experience being the only source of our judgments of this nature, we cannot know from any other principle, whether matter, by its structure or arrangement, may not be the cause of thought. Abstract reasonings cannot decide any question of fact or existence. — But admitting a spiritual substance to be dispersed throughout the universe, like the ethereal fire of the *Stoics*, and to be the only inherent subject of thought, we have reason to conclude from *analogy* that nature uses it after the manner she does the other substance, *matter*. She employs it as a kind of paste or clay; modifies it into a variety of forms and existences; dissolves after a time each modification, and from its substance erects a new form. As the same material substance may successively compose the bodies of all animals, the same spiritual substance may compose their minds: Their consciousness, or that system of thought which they formed during life, may be continually dissolved by death. And nothing interests them in the new modification. The most positive asserters of the mortality of the soul, never denied the immortality of its substance. And that an immaterial substance, as well as a material, may lose its memory or consciousness, appears in part from experience, if the soul be immaterial. — Reasoning from the common course of nature, and without supposing any new interposition of the supreme cause, which ought always to be excluded from philosophy, what is incorruptible must also be ingenerable. The Soul therefore if immortal, existed before our birth; and if the former existence no ways concerned us, neither will the latter. — Animals undoubtedly feel, think, love, hate, will, and even reason, tho' in a more imperfect manner than men; are their souls also immaterial and immortal?

II.   Let us now consider the *moral* arguments, chiefly those derived from the justice of God,

David Hume, "On the Immortality of the Soul," from *Essays on Suicide, and The Immortality of the Soul* (London, 1783).

which is supposed to be farther interested in the farther punishment of the vicious and reward of the virtuous. — But these arguments are grounded on the supposition that God has attributes beyond what he has exerted in this universe, with which alone we are acquainted. Whence do we infer the existence of these attributes? — 'tis very safe for us to affirm, that whatever we know the Deity to have actually done, is best; but 'tis very dangerous to affirm, that he must always do what to us seems best. In how many instances would this reasoning fail us with regard to the present world? — But if any purpose of nature be clear, we may affirm, that the whole scope and intention of man's creation, so far as we can judge by natural reason, is limited to the present life. With how weak a concern from the original inherent structure of the mind and passions, does he ever look farther? What comparison either for steadiness or efficacy, betwixt so floating an idea, and the most doubtful persuasion of any matter of fact that occurs in common life. There arise indeed in some minds some unaccountable terrors with regard to futurity; but these would quickly vanish were they not artificially fostered by precept and education. And those who foster them, what is their motive? Only to gain a livelihood, and to acquire power and riches in this world. Their very zeal and industry therefore is an argument against them.

What cruelty, what iniquity, what injustice in nature, to confine all our concern, as well as all our knowledge, to the present life, if there be another scene still waiting us, of infinitely greater consequence? Ought this barbarous deceit to be ascribed to a beneficent and wise being? — Observe with what exact proportion the task to be performed and the performing powers are adjusted throughout all nature. If the reason of man gives him great superiority above other animals, his necessities are proportionably multiplied upon him; his whole time, his whole capacity, activity, courage, and passion, find sufficient employment in fencing against the miseries of his present condition, and frequently, nay almost always are too slender for the business assigned them. — A pair of shoes perhaps was never yet wrought to the highest degree of perfection which that commodity is capable of attaining. Yet it is necessary, at least very useful, that there should be some politicians

and moralists, even some geometers, poets, and philosophers among mankind. The powers of men are no more superior to their wants, considered merely in this life, than those of foxes and hares are, compared to *their* wants and to their period of existence. The inference from parity of reason is therefore obvious. —

On the theory of the Soul's mortality, the inferiority of women's capacity is easily accounted for. Their domestic life requires no higher faculties, either of mind or body. This circumstance vanishes and becomes absolutely insignificant, on the religious theory: the one sex has an equal task to perform as the other; their powers of reason and resolution ought also to have been equal, and both of them infinitely greater than at present. As every effect implies a cause, and that another, till we reach the first cause of all, which is the Deity; every thing that happens is ordained by him, and nothing can be the object of his punishment or vengeance. — By what rule are punishments and rewards distributed? What is the divine standard of merit and demerit? shall we suppose that human sentiments have place in the Deity? How bold that hypothesis. We have no conception of any other sentiments. — According to human sentiments, sense, courage, good manners, industry, prudence, genius, &c. are essential parts of personal merits. Shall we therefore erect an elysium for poets and heroes like that of the ancient mythology? Why confine all rewards to one species of virtue? Punishment, without any proper end or purpose, is inconsistent with *our* ideas of goodness and justice, and no end can be served by it after the whole scene is closed. Punishment, according to our conception, should bear some proportion to the offence. Why then eternal punishment for the temporary offences of so frail a creature as man? Can any one approve of *Alexander*'s rage, who intended to exterminate a whole nation because they had seized his favorite horse Bucephalus?

Heaven and Hell suppose two distinct species of men, the good and the bad; but the greatest part of mankind float betwixt vice and virtue. — Were one to go round the world with an intention of giving a good supper to the righteous, and a sound drubbing to the wicked, he would frequently be embarrassed in his choice, and would find that the merits and the demerits of most men and women scarcely amount to the value of either. — To suppose measures of approbation and blame different from the human confounds every thing. Whence do we learn that there is such a thing as moral distinctions, but from our own sentiments? — What man who has not *met* with personal provocation (or what good-natured man who has) could inflict on crimes, from the sense of blame alone, even the common, legal, frivolous punishments? And does any thing steel the breast of judges and juries against the sentiments of humanity but reflection on necessity and public interest? By the Roman law those who had been guilty of parricide and confessed their crime, were put into a sack alone with an ape, a dog, and a serpent, and thrown into the river. Death alone was the punishment of those who denied their guilt, however fully proved. A criminal was tried before Augustus, and condemned after a full conviction, but the humane emperor, when he put the last interrogatory, gave it such a turn as to lead the wretch into a denial of his guilt. "You surely (said the prince) did not kill your father." This lenity suits our natural ideas of *right* even towards the greatest of all criminals, and even though it prevents so inconsiderable a sufference. Nay even the most bigotted priest would naturally without reflection approve of it, provided the crime was not heresy or infidelity; for as these crimes hurt himself in his *temporal* interest and advantages, perhaps he may not be altogether so indulgent to them. The chief source of moral ideas is the reflection on the interest of human society. Ought these interests, so short, so frivolous, to be guarded by punishments eternal and infinite? The damnation of one man is an infinitely greater evil in the universe, than the subversion of a thousand millions of kingdoms. Nature has rendered human infancy peculiarly frail and mortal, as it were on purpose to refute the notion of a probationary state; the half of mankind die before they are rational creatures.

III. The *Physical* arguments from the analogy of nature are strong for the mortality of the soul, and are really the only philosophical arguments which ought to be admitted with regard to this question, or indeed any question of fact. — Where any two objects are so closely connected that all alterations which we have ever seen in the one, are attended with proportionable alterations in the other; we ought to conclude by all rules of analogy, that, when there are still greater alterations produced in the former, and it is totally dissolved, there follows a total dissolution of the latter. — Sleep, a very small effect on the body, is attended with a temporary extinction, at least a great confusion in the soul. — The weakness of the body and that of the mind in infancy are exactly proportioned, their vigour in manhood, their sympathetic disorder in sickness; their common gradual decay in old age. The step further seems unavoidable; their common dissolution in death. The last symptoms which the mind discovers are disorder, weakness, insensibility, and stupidity, the fore-runners of its annihilation. The farther progress of the same causes increasing, the same effects totally extinguish it. Judging by the usual analogy of nature, no form can continue when transferred to a condition of life very different from the original one, in which it was placed. Trees perish in the water, fishes in the air, animals in the earth. Even so small a difference as that of climate is often fatal. What reason then to imagine, that an immense alteration, such as is made on the soul by the dissolution of its body and all its organs of thought and sensation, can be effected without the dissolution of the whole? Every thing is in common betwixt soul and body. The organs of the one are all of them the organs of the other. The existence therefore of the one must be dependant on that of the other. — The souls of animals are allowed to be mortal; and these bear so near a resemblance to the souls of men, that the analogy from one to the other forms a very strong argument. Their bodies are not more resembling; yet no one rejects the argument drawn from comparative anatomy. The *Metempsychosis* is therefore the only system of this kind that philosophy can harken to.

Nothing in this world is perpetual, every thing however seemingly firm is in continual flux and change, the world itself gives symptoms of frailty and dissolution. How contrary to analogy, therefore, to imagine that one single form, seemingly the frailest of any, and subject to the greatest disorders, is immortal and indissoluble? What daring theory is that! how lightly, not to say how rashly entertained! How to dispose of the infinite number of posthumous existences ought also to embarrass the religious theory. Every planet in every solar system we are at liberty to imagine peopled with intelligent mortal beings, at least we can fix on no other supposition. For these then a new universe must every generation be created beyond the bounds of the present universe, or one must have been created at first so prodigiously wise as to admit of this continual influx of beings. Ought such bold suppositions to be received by any philosophy, and that merely on the pretext of a bare possibility? When it is asked whether *Agamemnon Thersites, Hannibal, Varro,* and every stupid clown that ever existed in Italy, Scythia, Bactria or Guinea, are now alive; can any man think, that a scrutiny of nature will furnish arguments strong enough to answer so strange a question in the affirmative? The want of argument without revelation sufficiently establishes the negative. — "*Quanto facilius*" (says Pliny) "*certius que sibi quemque credere, ac specimen securitatis antigene tali sumere experimento.*" Our insensibility before the composition of the body, seems to natural reason a proof of a like state after dissolution. Were our horrors of annihilation an original passion, not the effect of our general love of happiness, it would rather prove the mortality of the soul. For as nature does nothing in vain, she would never give us a horror against an impossible event. She may give us a horror against an unavoidable; yet the human species could not be preserved had not nature inspired us with an aversion toward it. All doctrines are to be suspected which are favored by our passions, and the hopes and fears which gave rise to this doctrine are very obvious.

'Tis an infinite advantage in every controversy to defend the negative. If the question be out of the common experienced course of nature, this circumstance is almost if not altogether decisive. By what arguments or analogies can we prove any state of existence, which no one ever saw, and which no way resembles any that ever was seen? Who will repose such trust in any pretended philosophy as to admit upon its testimony the reality of so marvelous a scene? Some new species of logic is requisite for that purpose, and some new faculties of the mind, that may enable us to comprehend that logic.

Nothing could set in a fuller light the infinite obligations which mankind have to divine revelation, since we find that no other medium could ascertain this great and important truth.

Questions for Discussion

1 (a) Describe the final scene of *Heaven Can Wait*. How do you think the filmmakers intended us to understand the relationship between the Warren Beatty character and the person presented to us on the screen? What theories of the nature of the person can make sense of this scene? Are any incompatible with it? Explain.

   (b) Upon discovering that "glint" in his eye, the Julie Christie character seems content that she has not lost her love (final scenes). Is her reaction rational? Why or why not?

2 (a) Imagine that you are the character in *The Sixth Day* with Arnold Schwarzenegger's body. Can you have knowledge that you are the protagonist of the film as opposed to a replica of him? If so, how? If not, why not?

   (b) Should it matter to you whether you are the original person or merely a replica? Should it matter to you, if you are Arnold's wife, whether the person in front of you is a replica or your original husband? If you were the Adam Gibson clone, would you be content to "leave the scene" at the end of the movie despite the fact that you are, presumably, still in love with your "wife" and "child"? Would the possibility of replication open the door to immortality? Explain and discuss with reference to Descartes's arguments for thinking that the mind is distinct from the body.

3 (a) Describe the premise of *Multiplicity*. Suppose someone were to claim that each one of the replicas is identical with the original Michael Keaton character. Should we accept such a claim? Why or why not?

   (b) Would Descartes have the same response to the situation in *Multiplicity* that Locke and/or Parfit would have? Why, or why not?

4 Describe what happens in the *Star Trek* episode – without presupposing any view about who the resultant persons are. How would Locke describe this case? How would Williams respond to Locke's description of the case? Do you think that Williams has an effective response to Locke? Why, or why not?

5 Do the films that you have seen from this section undermine a physicalist conception of the mind? Why or why not?

6 (a) Describe the premise of *What Dreams May Come*. What theory of the person and/or the mental seems required by that premise? Explain.

   (b) Does the notion of a life after the death of the physical body require the rejection of physicalism? Why or why not?

7 (a) Explain how Searle would use his example of the Chinese room to respond to the claim that Andrew (the Robin Williams character) in *Bicentennial Man* has a mind. Do you think that Searle's response is effective? Why or why not?

   (b) Do you think that it is more problematic to suppose that such robots have emotions than to suppose that they have beliefs? Why or why not?

8   Would Ryle be committed to saying that the gleefulness apparently exhibited by Galatea (chapter 16) in *Bicentennial Man* is "mental" in the same sense that the gleefulness you exhibit at times is mental?

9   As Andrew in *Bicentennial Man* gets new programming that allows him to have new experiences (chapter 21, for example), is he, in effect, in the same position as Mary in Jackson's "What Mary Didn't Know?" Does Andrew come to know something he was utterly incapable of knowing before he had these experiences?

10 In his dialogue, Perry makes a great deal of the difference between actually remembering and merely seeming to remember when it comes to the survival of a person. What guarantees that one actually remembers? What would Perry say about the question of whether the clones in *The Sixth Day* survive the cloning process?

11 Who would Parfit say has the best claim to being Adam Gibson after his cloning – the person with the original body or the clone? What attitude would/should Adam's wife have to the clone? Does it matter whether or not the "original" still survives? (One can ask the same question about the wife's relation to the various clones in *Multiplicity*.)

12 Does Angier survive the final version of "the transported man" illusion? Should he care before performing the illusion whether *he* will survive as "The Prestige?" Does his ability to survive the illusion depend in any way on the fact that after the illusion is complete there is only one candidate for the surviving Angier?

Part IV
Ethics

A. Act Consequentialism and its Critics

Films:
Abandon Ship!
Fail Safe
Dirty Harry
Sophie's Choice
Saving Private Ryan
Judgment at Nuremberg
Minority Report
24 (Season 3: 6.00–7.00 a.m.)
Titanic
Vertical Limit

Introduction

There is an ancient and fundamental debate in ethics between consequentialists and deontologists. The rich and textured plots of many films give us a way of bringing that debate to life. Before attempting to illustrate this claim, we should try to define more clearly the terms of the debate.

Consequentialism

A great many philosophers take the most fundamental concept in ethical theory to be that of intrinsic value (intrinsic goodness and badness). If we think about most of the things we take to be good (bad), a little reflection might convince us that we only view these things as good (bad) because they produce something else that is good (bad). So to take an example used by Plato in *The Republic*, we may regard regular exercise as good, but not many of us regard that exercise as good *for its own sake*. We think it is good to exercise only because we think that we will live a happier life through the health we enjoy as a product of that exercise. Or consider your annual trips to the dentist. It is obviously good to get your regular check-ups, but you don't think of having a sharp metal instrument dragged over your teeth as something that is good just for its own sake – you don't think of it as *intrinsically* good.

While this distinction between being good in itself (being intrinsically good), and being good

as a means (being instrumentally good) might at one level seem to be just plain common sense, there is no agreement among philosophers on which things are intrinsically good (bad), or on what it is that makes something intrinsically good (bad). Consider the latter question. *Strong objectivists* think that there is a property of being intrinsically good that some things have (and that most things lack). Furthermore, they believe that if X is intrinsically good, its being intrinsically good is a state of affairs that cannot be identified with anyone's attitude toward X. Our society might degenerate in such a way that most, or even all, people take no interest in knowledge, but the strong objectivist will argue that that psychological fact about people does not entail that knowledge comes to lack intrinsic value. Crudely put, *subjectivists* embrace the thesis that there is value in the world only because there are conscious beings who value things. One relativistic version of that view might hold that something X has intrinsic value *for someone S* if and only if S values X for its own sake. That which has intrinsic value for me might have no intrinsic value for you. Other versions of subjectivism might take the value of X to depend on the attitudes *most* people have toward X, or the attitudes most people with an appropriate range of experience have toward X.

Controversies over these metaethical issues must be distinguished from controversies over the substantive ethical question of what has intrinsic value, *however* that claim is understood. So some philosophers (hedonists) have held that there is one and only one thing that is intrinsically good, and that thing is pleasure; there is one and only one thing that is intrinsically bad, and that thing is pain. Sophisticated hedonists, like Mill, will quickly insist on distinguishing a wide range of different sorts of pleasures and pain. Humans are capable of experiencing not only physical pleasures (the pleasures associated with sex, food, drink, for example), but also intellectual pleasures (the pleasures associated with knowledge, aesthetic appreciation of works of art, deep and abiding friendship). Mill, like Plato before him, argued that while all pleasures are intrinsically good, the intellectual pleasures are far superior both in terms of quantity and quality than the physical pleasures (though it remains a matter of some controversy over just how precisely Mill understands what it *is* for one pleasure to be qualitatively superior to another).

While the hedonists embrace a "monism" with respect to what has intrinsic goodness, a great many other philosophers would insist on a pluralistic approach. So, for example, the objectivist, G. E. Moore, argued that knowledge and friendship also are intrinsically good. Indeed, whether one is an objectivist or a subjectivist with respect to value, it seems that there is nothing in either view that places any limits on the kinds of things that one could *consistently* (if not plausibly) take to have intrinsic value.

Let us suppose that we have answered to our satisfaction the question of what makes something intrinsically valuable and the question of which things are intrinsically valuable. It is tempting to think that we can now fairly straightforwardly understand the other ethical concepts in which we are interested in terms of this fundamental ethical notion. It is tempting to think that we can embrace some version of act consequentialism – the view that the rightness or wrongness of actions depends on the intrinsic value that attaches to the consequences of the alternatives open to us. More specifically, it seems plausible to suggest that what we ought to do, the right thing for us to do, is simply whatever yields the greatest net gain in terms of what has value. If we are subjectivists and relativists about value, the view might get somewhat more complicated. One obvious subjectivist/relativist version of consequentialism is

that each person ought to do what maximizes that which has value *for him*.

The above statements of the view are still crude. We will need a careful account of what constitutes alternative actions and we will also need a more careful discussion of what counts as a relevant consequence. Among act consequentialisms, we can distinguish what we might call actual consequence, probable consequence, and value-adjusted possible consequence act consequentialism. The actual consequence act consequentialist identifies an action X as right if the sum of the positive and negative intrinsic value that attaches to the consequences that would *actually* occur as a result of doing X is greater than the sum of the positive and negative intrinsic value that attaches to the consequences that would actually occur as a result of choosing any alternative to X. The probable consequence act consequentialist suggests instead that the rightness or wrongness of an action depends on the sum of the values that attach to probable consequences of alternatives. The possible consequence act consequentialist insists that we need to take into account not only probable consequences but possible consequences, even those that are highly unlikely. If the President of the United States is considering taking action that has a 1/1000 chance of causing World War III, it is surely plausible to suppose that that possible consequence should be at least relevant to whether or not the action should be taken. To counter obvious objections, however, the possible consequence act consequentialist will concede that we need some device to take into account how likely a consequence is and *to adjust* the value that attaches to that possible consequence accordingly. On one standard view, one adjusts the value of a possible consequence by multiplying that value by the probability of its occurring. So if there is some consequence Y of my doing X that is very valuable, but Y has only a 1/100 chance of occurring, I adjust the value of Y for its probability by multiplying the number representing the value by 1/100. X will be the right action to take if the sum of the *adjusted* value that attaches to the possible consequences of doing X is greater than the sum of the adjusted value of the possible consequences of taking any alternative to X.

Act consequentialism is, at least initially, an enormously attractive view. Who could quarrel with the idea that we are behaving as we should when we make the world the best place we can? The view, has, however, come under unrelenting attack. The most common objections take the form of *reductio ad absurdum* – act consequentialism is supposed to entail obviously unacceptable propositions.

One obvious kind of problem is epistemological. Consider actual consequence act consequentialism. The actual consequences of an action continue into the indefinite future and usually the long-term consequences are unforeseeable. Suppose that you are contemplating having a child. That child may have children who have children who have children, and so on for generations to come. Among those descendants may be another Mother Teresa, another Adolf Hitler, the person who finds the cure for cancer, or the person who murders the person who would have found the cure for cancer. What chance does a finite being have of summing accurately the positive and negative value of consequences, most of which disappear into a dark and unknowable future? What chance does a finite being have, therefore, of calculating rationally the right course of action to take? The problem seems significantly less serious for the probable consequence act consequentialist, for one gets to ignore all those consequences that are unlikely (relative to one's evidence). Ironically, the less one knows, the easier one's consequentialist calculations get. Unfortunately, as we saw with the example of the President discussed above, it doesn't seem plausible to discount entirely the relevance of even very unlikely, but still possible, consequences. And once one allows into the picture possible consequences, the epistemological problem raises its ugly head again. There are more possible consequences than actual consequences and the task of identifying both their value and the probability of their occurring goes beyond daunting.

The epistemological objection presupposes that to be useful an ethical theory must allow one at least the possibility of reaching justified conclusions about what is right and wrong. Without that possibility the theory is useless. One might go some way to countering the epistemological problem by rejecting this presupposition and by making a clear distinction between reaching the conclusion that an alternative has the best

chance of being the right action to take and reaching the conclusion that it is the right action to take. Consider a simple analogy. Suppose you are forced to bet on the outcome of a rather silly contest. Five people (A, B, C, D, and E) are each to toss a coin 20 times. The winner of the contest will be the person who gets the most heads. You are given the opportunity to place your bet after three tosses have already been completed. After those three tosses, A has two heads and the rest each have had at most one head come up. Upon whom should you place your bet? The answer seems obvious. At this point A has the best chance of being the winner. Notice that the chance isn't very good. It is still much more likely than not that A will lose. But all you need in order to place a rational bet is the rational conclusion that A has the best chance of winning.

Perhaps life is a bit like the coin-tossing contest. Act consequentialism may rarely, if ever, allow us to conclude rationally that an alternative is the correct choice. But if the theory allows us to conclude, after some deliberation, that an alternative has the *best* chance of being the right course of action to take, the theory has left room for rational choice.

Aside from epistemological objections to act consequentialism, the view faces a host of other objections by counterexample. The view's critics appeal to a host of exotic hypothetical situations to draw out allegedly absurd consequences of the theory. Paraphrasing an example from Gilbert Harman, a surgeon has on his hands three important people, each of whom is about to make significant contributions to the betterment of our world, and each of whom is in dire need of a transplant. One needs a heart, another needs kidneys, and a third needs a liver. Fred, a bit of a klutz, walks into the surgery unit while looking for a dermatologist to cure a bad case of poison ivy. The surgeon sees in Fred a bounty of fresh organs, secretly and effectively dispatches him, and uses the organs to save the three lives. Superficial consequentialist calculations would seem to suggest that the surgeon did the right thing, but many react in horror to the suggestion that such an act would be not only morally permissible, but morally required.

Fred's cousin Sam lives in a town paralyzed by a particularly vicious string of violent murders.

Psychologists assure the town sheriff that if only he could arrest and successfully prosecute and punish a perpetrator of this sort of crime it would stop the crimes from occurring. The sheriff, frustrated by his inability to find a criminal, frames Sam for one of the crimes, arrests and punishes him, thus ending the wave of crime. On consequentialist considerations, the sheriff might seem to have done the right thing. But once again our moral sensibilities seem to be outraged at the suggestion that such behavior might be morally permissible.

In "A Critique of Utilitarianism," Bernard Williams graphically adds to the thought experiments with his examples of Jim and the Indians, and George and his job opportunity. Each example is designed to convince the reader that act consequentialism radically oversimplifies the kinds of calculations that moral agents are required and/or permitted to make. Williams makes a vague allusion to the legitimacy of personal projects taking precedence over utilitarian calculations, but it is far from clear what the status of a personal project is or what sort of limitations one might place on the *kinds* of personal projects that can legitimately take precedence over consequentialist calculations. The problem is particularly acute, for even those who are suspicious of the claim that there is no more to ethical judgment than consequentialist calculations are surely willing to admit that when the consequences of an action become significant enough, they constitute overwhelming moral considerations in favor of, or against, acting in a certain way. We might not cut up Fred to save five people, but if the fate of the entire world rests on our sacrificing Fred, it might seem that it is only the fanatic who resists the moral permissibility of the sacrifice.

R. M. Hare has argued that one should be highly suspicious of the kinds of thought experiments designed to cast doubt on the plausibility of act consequentialism. He claims, in effect, that our moral conditioning was designed to enable us to handle the kind of mundane moral dilemmas that we are likely to meet. If effective, this conditioning might lead us to respond with moral repulsion to lying, killing the innocent, breaking promises, framing innocent people, and the like, but given the fantastic nature of the hypothetical situations, typical moral responses are not to be trusted. There is a concern that the thought experiments that critics rely upon are too caricatured to enable one to clearly think through the implications of the situation. The characters have no flesh; the alternatives are left unspecified; the subtle emotional aspects of the situation are left underdescribed.

Fortunately, many of the kinds of thought experiments that philosophers rely upon are described in much more vivid detail in the context of film. In the movie *Abandon Ship!* the Williams example of trading the few for the many is brought to life. It is especially nice that the plot of the movie corresponds to a real-life situation that found its way into the courts (*US vs. Holmes*). In *Fail Safe*, the President of the United States faces nuclear Armageddon head on. Through an inexplicable accident, a squadron of bombers has been ordered to drop nuclear weapons on the Soviet Union. All efforts to recall the mission fail and one of the planes gets through to Moscow. In an effort to prevent a full-scale retaliation by the Soviet Union, the President offers the Soviet leader a more limited exchange of horror – he will destroy New York as a kind of good-faith apology for the destruction of Moscow (chapter 22). The Soviet leader agrees and World War III is avoided. Did the President do the right thing? Is what he did significantly different from what Truman did in dropping the A-bomb on Hiroshima and Nagasaki?

It is, perhaps, a long way from the President's lofty attempts to avoid World War III to Dirty Harry's attempts to discover the whereabouts of a girl buried alive by a sadistic kidnapper. In abstract discussions, most of us react with horror to the idea of torture as a legitimate tool to gain information – even when that information is vital to the well-being of others and the victim of the torture has behaved in morally reprehensible ways. When Harry Callaghan corners the kidnapper of the little girl, however, few viewers react with anything but encouragement as he deliberately inflicts more and more pain on the already injured kidnapper. Whatever initial reluctance the viewer might have had to approve of the torture is likely to disappear as a long overhead shot of the scene (chapter 20) pulls back farther and farther until the camera zooms in on the buried girl who will slowly suffocate unless Harry uncovers the child's whereabouts from the kidnapper.

If the right answer to the moral dilemma seems clear in some of the situations depicted on film, there is a decidedly mixed message sent by others. In *Saving Private Ryan*, a squad is asked to risk their lives to save the last remaining child of a mother whose family has been ravaged by war. Sent behind enemy lines, the members of the squad wonder, naturally enough, why it makes sense to risk the lives of many to save one – they all have mothers, fathers, brothers, and sisters, and it is unclear to them why the additional grief of one mother is worth risking that grief multiplied many times (chapters 5–6). The question the soldiers asked is never answered explicitly in the film, but the viewer will no doubt find a wealth of consequentialist and non-consequentialist intuitions to consult.

It strikes some that the mistake, almost the evil, of act consequentialism lies with the way in which it reduces ethical dilemmas to matters of cold calculation. Perhaps there are some moral problems that simply have no solution – there are situations in which one is faced with choices *all* of which are truly wrong. *Sophie's Choice* presents the heroine with a decision so shocking, so almost unimaginable, that one might wonder whether it even makes sense to describe her as having done the right thing. She is forced by a brutal Nazi to choose the death of one of her children in order to save the other (chapter 32–4). Rather than have both children die, she makes the horrible choice. It might somehow seem to trivialize the decision to describe her as having made the right choice, as having done what she ought to do. On the other hand, the frightening dilemma of life is that one cannot escape choice. There is really no such thing as doing nothing. One can fail to act in a number of different ways, but that failure to act is a choice just like other choices, with its own potentially terrible consequences. Sophie *had* to make a choice – saying nothing is a choice – and a plausible ethical theory must surely provide us with the tools to evaluate that choice.

Alternatives to Act Consequentialism

It seems to many that act consequentialism gives us the wrong answer in many hypothetical situations, including those portrayed in the films discussed above. Dissatisfaction with act consequentialism leads to a search for alternative theories. One such theory – rule consequentialism – is often described, as the name might suggest, as a *modification* of consequentialism. The view is so different, however, it is at best misleading to describe it as a version of consequentialism at all. The rule consequentialist rejects the act consequentialist's view that one must compare the (actual, probable, or possible) consequences of alternative acts. Rather, one must always assess the rightness or wrongness of an act by reference to the correct *rules* of morality. These rules have no exceptions and literally *define* what is permissible, obligatory, and forbidden. They are rules that are *constitutive* of morality, in the way in which the rules of baseball define the game of baseball. As Mill did, most act utilitarians will invariably recognize the importance of "secondary" rules to guide one in situations in which one doesn't have time to carefully evaluate the consequences of individual actions. Emphasizing the importance of rough-and-ready guidelines to use in making decisions does not, however, make one a rule consequentialist. If the rules are thought of as simply useful lessons learned from past evaluations of individual acts, these "rules of thumb" are not what the rule consequentialist uses to *define* rightness and wrongness.

Rule consequentialists owe us an account of what makes a given rule the correct rule governing a certain kind of action, and this is where the view does bring in consequences. The view that we might call "actual consequence rule consequentialism" defines a rule governing, for example, making a promise as correct, if the sum of the value of the actual consequences of people in general following that rule is greater than the sum of the value of the actual consequences of people in general following any alternative rule. Just as with act consequentialism, the rule consequentialist might turn to probable, or value-adjusted possible, consequences instead. The rule consequentialist thinks that the emphasis on rules allows the view to skirt some of the problems facing act consequentialism, but the claim is hardly uncontroversial. In "An Outline of a System of Utilitarian ethics," J. J. C. Smart claims that rule consequentialism (he calls it restricted utilitarianism) creates only the illusion of an advantage over act consequentialism (he calls it extreme consequentialism). Furthermore, rule consequentialism might seem to face a dilemma. If the rules stay general (always tell the truth, always keep a promise, always be loyal to friends), they will inevitably conflict. We will find situations in which we can't be loyal to a friend without breaking a promise, or without lying to another. The rule consequentialist must now give us instructions on how to weigh the relative importance of these rules when they do conflict. Alternatively, the rule consequentialist might try modifying the rules so as to avoid even the possibility of conflict. The correct rule for promising might be something very complicated: Always keep a promise unless by breaking it you can save a life or prevent an armed robbery or help a lost child or visit a dying relative or help in a crucial experiment that might yield a medical breakthrough, or. . . . Or what? The list seems endless. What you really want to suggest, argues the act consequentialist, is that one should keep a promise unless by breaking it you can do more good than by keeping it. But that's what act consequentialism maintained all along.

W. D. Ross rejects any attempt to define obligation in terms of the goodness and badness of consequences. He embraces the deontological view that we cannot define rightness and wrongness in terms of the goodness and badness of consequences. According to Ross, certain action kinds are simply *prima facie* obligatory or forbidden. The *prima facie* qualification, though, is critical, for Ross wants to acknowledge the commonsense intuition that even if it is always *prima facie* wrong, say, to break a promise, circumstances can arise in which, all things being considered, it would be the right thing to do. Ross, then, faces a problem analogous to one discussed in connection with rule consequentialism. He needs to give us instructions on how to weigh *prima facie* rightness and wrongness in order to get an all things considered assessment of what we ought to do – and he needs to do this without implicitly slipping back into some form of consequentialism.

Kant probably held a more extreme version of deontology. He seems to think that certain kinds of actions are categorically forbidden. One is never permitted to act in a certain way unless one could consistently will that everyone act in that way. On Kant's view, one's being able consistently to will a maxim (an action guiding rule) seems to have something to do with one's being able actually to accomplish one's goals in a world in which the maxim is universally followed. Kant's famous test of wrongness is, however, at least similar to another with which many of us are familiar. Most of us grew up with angry parents occasionally asking us how we would like it if everyone did what we just did. But the "what if everyone were to do it?" test of wrongness is hardly unproblematic. A great deal hinges on how we identify action kinds. Kant, for example, presumably wants his test to rule out an extreme egoistic approach to decision-making. But there is at least one form of universalizing that will give the egoist no problem at all. Just as I act so as to maximize benefits to myself, so I can consistently want everyone to adopt my well-being as their ultimate goal. This move is presumably not in the spirit of the test Kant proposes, but we need a specific understanding of the test that rules it out.

22

Utilitarianism

John Stuart Mill

What Utilitarianism Is

A passing remark is all that needs be given to the ignorant blunder of supposing that those who stand up for utility as the test of right and wrong, use the term in that restricted and merely colloquial sense in which utility is opposed to pleasure. An apology is due to the philosophical opponents of utilitarianism, for even the momentary appearance of confounding them with anyone capable of so absurd a misconception; which is the more extraordinary, inasmuch as the contrary accusation, of referring everything to pleasure, and that too in its grossest form, is another of the common charges against utilitarianism: and, as has been pointedly remarked by an able writer, the same sort of persons, and often the very same persons, denounce the theory "as impracticably dry when the word utility precedes the word pleasure, and as too practicably voluptuous when the word pleasure precedes the word utility." Those who know anything about the matter are aware that every writer, from Epicurus to Bentham, who maintained the theory of utility, meant by it, not something to be contradistinguished from pleasure, but pleasure itself, together with exemption from pain; and instead of opposing the useful to the agreeable or the ornamental, have always declared that the useful means these, among

other things. Yet the common herd, including the herd of writers, not only in newspapers, and periodicals, but in books of weight and pretension, are perpetually falling into this shallow mistake. Having caught up the word 'utilitarian,' while knowing nothing whatever about it but its sound, they habitually express by it the rejection, or the neglect, of pleasure in some of its forms: of beauty, of ornament, or of amusement. Nor is the term thus ignorantly misapplied solely in disparagement, but occasionally in compliment; as though it implied superiority to frivolity and the mere pleasures of the moment. And this perverted use is the only one in which the word is popularly known, and the one from which the new generation are acquiring their sole notion of its meaning. Those who introduced the word, but who had for many years discontinued it as a distinctive appellation, may well feel themselves called upon to resume it, if by doing so they can hope to contribute anything towards rescuing it from this utter degradation.

The creed which accepts as the foundation of morals *utility*, or the *greatest happiness principle*, holds that actions are right in proportion as they tend to promote happiness, wrong as they tend to produce the reverse of happiness. By 'happiness' is intended pleasure, and the absence of pain; by 'unhappiness,' pain, and the privation of pleasure. To give a clear view of the moral

John Stuart Mill, *Utilitarianism* (Garden City, NY: Dolphin Books, 1961), pp. 406–28, 438–45.

standard set up by the theory, much more requires to be said; in particular, what things it includes in the ideas of pain and pleasure; and to what extent this is left an open question. But these supplementary explanations do not affect the theory of life on which this theory of morality is grounded – namely, that pleasure, and freedom from pain, are the only things desirable as ends; and that all desirable things (which are as numerous in the utilitarian as in any other scheme) are desirable either for the pleasure inherent in themselves, or as means to the promotion of pleasure and the prevention of pain.

Now such a theory of life excites in many minds, and among them in some of the most estimable in feeling and purpose, inveterate dislike. To suppose that life has (as they express it) no higher end than pleasure – no better and nobler object of desire and pursuit – they designate as utterly mean and groveling; as a doctrine worthy only of swine, to whom the followers of Epicurus were, at a very early period, contemptuously likened; and modern holders of the doctrine are occasionally made the subject of equally polite comparisons by its German, French, and English assailants.

When thus attacked, the Epicureans have always answered that it is not they but their accusers who represent human nature in a degrading light; since the accusation supposes human beings to be capable of no pleasures except those of which swine are capable. If this supposition were true, the charge could not be gainsaid, but would then be no longer an imputation; for if the sources of pleasure were precisely the same to human beings and to swine, the rule of life which is good enough for the one would be good enough for the other. The comparison of the Epicurean life to that of beasts is felt as degrading, precisely because a beast's pleasures do not satisfy a human being's conceptions of happiness. Human beings have faculties more elevated than the animal appetites, and when once made conscious of them, do not regard anything as happiness which does not include their gratification. I do not, indeed, consider the Epicureans to have been by any means faultless in drawing out their scheme of consequences from the utilitarian principle. To do this in any sufficient manner, many Stoic, as well as Christian elements require to be included. But there is no known Epicurean

theory of life which does not assign to the pleasures of the intellect, of the feelings and imagination, and of the moral sentiments, a much higher value as pleasures than to those of mere sensation. It must be admitted, however, that utilitarian writers in general have placed the superiority of mental over bodily pleasures chiefly in the greater permanency, safety, uncostliness, etc., of the former – that is, in their circumstantial advantages rather than in their intrinsic nature. And on all these points utilitarians have fully proved their case; but they might have taken the other, and, as it may be called, higher ground, with entire consistency. It is quite compatible with the principle of utility to recognize the fact, that some *kinds* of pleasure are more desirable and more valuable than others. It would be absurd that while, in estimating all other things, quality is considered as well as quantity, the estimation of pleasures should be supposed to depend on quantity alone.

If I am asked what I mean by difference of quality in pleasures, or what makes one pleasure more valuable than another merely as a pleasure, except its being greater in amount, there is but one possible answer. Of two pleasures, if there be one to which all or almost all who have experience of both give a decided preference, irrespective of any feeling of moral obligation to prefer it, that is the more desirable pleasure. If one of the two is, by those who are competently acquainted with both, placed so far above the other that they prefer it, even though knowing it to be attended with a greater amount of discontent, and would not resign it for any quantity of the other pleasure which their nature is capable of, we are justified in ascribing to the preferred enjoyment a superiority in quality, so far outweighing quantity as to render it, in comparison, of small account.

Now it is an unquestionable fact that those who are equally acquainted with, and equally capable of appreciating and enjoying, both, do give a most marked preference to the manner of existence which employs their higher faculties. Few human creatures would consent to be changed into any of the lower animals, for a promise of the fullest allowance of a beast's pleasures; no intelligent human being would consent to be a fool, no instructed person would be an ignoramus, no person of feeling and conscience would be selfish and base, even though they should be persuaded that the fool, the dunce, or the rascal is better satisfied with his lot than they are with theirs. They would not resign what they possess more than he for the most complete satisfaction of all the desires which they have in common with him. If they ever fancy they would, it is only in cases of unhappiness so extreme, that to escape from it they would exchange their lot for almost any other, however undesirable in their own eyes. A being of higher faculties requires more to make him happy, is capable probably of more acute suffering, and certainly accessible to it at more points, than one of an inferior type; but in spite of these liabilities, he can never really wish to sink into what he feels to be a lower grade of existence. We may give what explanation we please of this unwillingness: we may attribute it to pride, a name which is given indiscriminately to some of the most and to some of the least estimable feelings of which mankind are capable; we may refer it to the love of liberty and personal independence, an appeal to which was with the Stoics one of the most effective means for the inculcation of it; to the love of power, or to the love of excitement, both of which do really enter into and contribute to it: but its most appropriate appellation is a sense of dignity, which all human beings possess in one form or other, and in some, though by no means in exact, proportion to their higher faculties, and which is so essential a part of the happiness of those in whom it is strong, that nothing which conflicts with it could be, otherwise than momentarily, an object of desire to them. Whoever supposes that this preference takes place at a sacrifice of happiness – that the superior being, in anything like equal circumstances, is not happier than the inferior – confounds the two very different ideas, of *happiness* and *content*. It is indisputable that the being whose capacities of enjoyment are low, has the greatest chance of having them fully satisfied; and a highly endowed being will always feel that any happiness which he can look for, as the world is constituted, is imperfect. But he can learn to bear its imperfections, if they are at all bearable; and they will not make him envy the being who is indeed unconscious of the imperfections, but only because he feels not at all the good which those imperfections qualify. It is better to be a human being dissatisfied than a pig

satisfied; better to be Socrates dissatisfied than a fool satisfied. And if the fool, or the pig, are of a different opinion, it is because they only know their own side of the question. The other party to the comparison knows both sides.

It may be objected that many who are capable of the higher pleasures, occasionally, under the influence of temptation, postpone them to the lower. But this is quite compatible with a full appreciation of the intrinsic superiority of the higher. Men often, from infirmity of character, make their election for the nearer good, though they know it to be the less valuable; and this no less when the choice is between two bodily pleasures, than when it is between bodily and mental. They pursue sensual indulgences to the injury of health, though perfectly aware that health is the greater good. It may be further objected that many who begin with youthful enthusiasm for everything noble, as they advance in years sink into indolence and selfishness. But I do not believe that those who undergo this very common change, voluntarily choose the lower description of pleasures in preference to the higher. I believe that before they devote themselves exclusively to the one, they have already become incapable of the other. Capacity for the nobler feelings is in most natures a very tender plant, easily killed, not only by hostile influences, but by mere want of sustenance; and in the majority of young persons it speedily dies away if the occupations to which their position in life has devoted them, and the society into which it has thrown them, are not favorable to keeping that higher capacity in exercise. Men lose their high aspirations as they lose their intellectual tastes, because they have not time or opportunity for indulging them; and they addict themselves to inferior pleasures not because they deliberately prefer them, but because they are either the only ones to which they have access or the only ones which they are any longer capable of enjoying. It may be questioned whether anyone who has remained equally susceptible to both classes of pleasures, ever knowingly and calmly preferred the lower; though many, in all ages, have broken down in an ineffectual attempt to combine both.

From this verdict of the only competent judges I apprehend there can be no appeal. On a question which is the best worth having of two pleasures, or which of two modes of existence is the most grateful to the feelings, apart from its moral attributes and from its consequences, the judgment of those who are qualified by knowledge of both, or, if they differ, that of the majority among them, must be admitted as final. And there need be the less hesitation to accept this judgment respecting the quality of pleasures, since there is no other tribunal to be referred to even on the question of quantity. What means are there of determining which is the acutest of two pains, or the intensest of two pleasurable sensations, except the general suffrage of those who are familiar with both? Neither pains nor pleasures are homogeneous, and pain is always heterogeneous with pleasure. What is there to decide whether a particular pleasure is worth purchasing at the cost of a particular pain, except the feelings and judgment of the experienced? When, therefore, those feelings and judgment declare the pleasures derived from the higher faculties to be preferable *in kind*, apart from the question of intensity, to those of which the animal nature, disjoined from the higher faculties, is susceptible, they are entitled on this subject to the same regard.

I have dwelt on this point, as being a necessary part of a perfectly just conception of utility, or happiness, considered as the directive rule of human conduct. But it is by no means an indispensable condition to the acceptance of the utilitarian standard; for that standard is not the agent's own greatest happiness, but the greatest amount of happiness altogether; and if it may possibly be doubted whether a noble character is always the happier for its nobleness, there can be no doubt that it makes other people happier, and that the world in general is immensely a gainer by it. Utilitarianism, therefore, could only attain its end by the general cultivation of nobleness of character, even if each individual were only benefited by the nobleness of others, and his own, so far as happiness is concerned, were a sheer deduction from the benefit. But the bare enunciation of such an absurdity as this last renders refutation superfluous.

According to the 'greatest happiness principle,' as above explained, the ultimate end, with reference to and for the sake of which all other things are desirable (whether we are considering our own good or that of other people), is an existence exempt as far as possible from pain, and as rich as possible in enjoyments, both in point of quantity and quality; the test of quality, and the rule for measuring it against quantity, being the preference felt by those who in their opportunities of experience, to which must be added their habits of self-consciousness and self-observation, are best furnished with the means of comparison. This, being, according to the utilitarian opinion, the end of human action, is necessarily also the standard of morality; which may accordingly be defined, the rules and precepts for human conduct, by the observance of which an existence such as has been described might be, to the greatest extent possible, secured to all mankind; and not to them only, but, so far as the nature of things admits, to the whole sentient creation.

Against this doctrine, however, arises another class of objectors, who say that happiness, in any form, cannot be the rational purpose of human life and action; because, in the first place, it is unattainable: and they contemptuously ask, what right hast thou to be happy? – a question which Mr Carlyle clenches by the addition, What right, a short time ago, hadst thou even *to be*? Next, they say that men can do *without* happiness; that all noble human beings have felt this, and could not have become noble but by learning the lesson of *Entsagen*, or renunciation; which lesson, thoroughly learnt and submitted to, they affirm to be the beginning and necessary condition of all virtue.

The first of these objections would go to the root of the matter were it well founded; for if no happiness is to be had at all by human beings, the attainment of it cannot be the end of morality, or of any rational conduct. Though, even in that case, something might still be said for the utilitarian theory; since utility includes not solely the pursuit of happiness, but the prevention or mitigation of unhappiness; and if the former aim be chimerical, there will be all the greater scope and more imperative need for the latter, so long at least as mankind think fit to live, and do not take refuge in the simultaneous act of suicide recommended under certain conditions by Novalis. When, however, it is thus positively asserted to be impossible that human life should be happy, the assertion, if not something like a verbal quibble, is at least an exaggeration. If by happiness be meant a continuity of highly pleasurable excitement, it is evident enough that this is impossible. A state of exalted pleasure lasts only moments, or in some cases, and with some intermissions, hours or days, and is the occasional brilliant flash of enjoyment, not its permanent and steady flame. Of this the philosophers who have taught that happiness is the end of life were as fully aware as those who taunt them. The happiness which they meant was not a life of rapture; but moments of such, in an existence made up of few and transitory pains, many and various pleasures, with a decided predominance of the active over the passive, and having as the foundation of the whole, not to expect more from life than it is capable of bestowing. A life thus composed to those who have been fortunate enough to obtain it, has always appeared worthy of the name of happiness. And such an existence is even now the lot of many, during some considerable portion of their lives. The present wretched education, and wretched social arrangements, are the only real hindrance to its being attainable by almost all.

The objectors perhaps may doubt whether human beings, if taught to consider happiness as the end of life, would be satisfied with such a moderate share of it. But great numbers of mankind have been satisfied with much less. The main constituents of a satisfied life appear to be two, either of which by itself is often found sufficient for the purpose: tranquillity and excitement. With much tranquillity, many find that they can be content with very little pleasure; with much excitement, many can reconcile themselves to a considerable quantity of pain. There is assuredly no inherent impossibility in enabling even the mass of mankind to unite both; since the two are so far from being incompatible that they are in natural alliance, the prolongation of either being a preparation for, and exciting a wish for, the other. It is only those in whom indolence amounts to a vice, that do not desire excitement after an interval of repose; it is only those in whom the need of excitement is a disease, that feel the tranquillity which follows excitement dull and insipid, instead of pleasurable in direct proportion to the excitement which preceded it. When people who are tolerably fortunate in their outward lot do not find in life sufficient enjoyment to make it valuable to them, the cause generally is, caring for nobody but themselves. To those who

have neither public nor private affections, the excitements of life are much curtailed, and in any case dwindle in value as the time approaches when all selfish interests must be terminated by death; while those who leave after them objects of personal affection, and especially those who have also cultivated a fellow-feeling with the collective interests of mankind, retain as lively an interest in life on the eve of death as in the vigor of youth and health. Next to selfishness, the principal cause which makes life unsatisfactory is want of mental cultivation. A cultivated mind (I do not mean that of a philosopher, but any mind to which the fountains of knowledge have been opened, and which has been taught, in any tolerable degree, to exercise its faculties) finds sources of inexhaustible interest in all that surrounds it; in the objects of nature, the achievements of art, the imaginations of poetry, the incidents of history, the ways of mankind, past and present, and their prospects in the future. It is possible, indeed, to become indifferent to all this, and that too without having exhausted a thousandth part of it; but only when one has had from the beginning no moral or human interest in these things, and has sought in them only the gratification of curiosity.

Now there is absolutely no reason in the nature of things why an amount of mental culture sufficient to give an intelligent interest in these objects of contemplation, should not be the inheritance of everyone born in a civilized country. As little is there an inherent necessity that any human being should be a selfish egotist, devoid of every feeling or care but those which center in his own miserable individuality. Something far superior to this is sufficiently common even now, to give ample earnest of what the human species may be made. Genuine private affections, and a sincere interest in the public good, are possible, though in unequal degrees, to every rightly brought up human being. In a world in which there is so much to interest, so much to enjoy, and so much also to correct and improve, everyone who has this moderate amount of moral and intellectual requisites is capable of an existence which may be called enviable; and unless such a person, through bad laws, or subjection to the will of others, is denied the liberty to use the sources of happiness within his reach, he will not fail to find this enviable existence, if he escape the positive evils of life, the great sources of physical and mental suffering – such as indigence, disease, and the unkindness, worthlessness, or premature loss of objects of affection. The main stress of the problem lies, therefore, in the contest with these calamities, from which it is a rare good fortune entirely to escape; which, as things now are, cannot be obviated, and often cannot be in any material degree mitigated. Yet no one whose opinion deserves a moment's consideration can doubt that most of the great positive evils of the world are in themselves removable, and will, if human affairs continue to improve, be in the end reduced within narrow limits. Poverty, in any sense implying suffering, may be completely extinguished by the wisdom of society, combined with the good sense and providence of individuals. Even that most intractable of enemies, disease, may be indefinitely reduced in dimensions by good physical and moral education, and proper control of noxious influences; while the progress of science holds out a promise for the future of still more direct conquests over this detestable foe. And every advance in that direction relieves us from some, not only of the chances which cut short our own lives, but, what concerns us still more, which deprive us of those in whom our happiness is wrapt up. As for vicissitudes of fortune, and other disappointments connected with worldly circumstances, these are principally the effect either of gross imprudence, of ill-regulated desires, or of bad or imperfect social institutions. All the grand sources, in short, of human suffering are in a great degree, many of them almost entirely, conquerable by human care and effort; and though their removal is grievously slow – though a long succession of generations will perish in the breach before the conquest is completed, and this world becomes all that, if will and knowledge were not wanting, it might easily be made – yet every mind sufficiently intelligent and generous to bear a part, however small and unconspicuous, in the endeavor, will draw a noble enjoyment from the contest itself, which he would not for any bribe in the form of selfish indulgence consent to be without.

And this leads to the true estimation of what is said by the objectors concerning the possibility, and the obligation, of learning to do without happiness. Unquestionably it is possible to do without happiness; it is done involuntarily by nineteen-twentieths of mankind, even in those parts of our present world which are least deep in barbarism; and it often has to be done voluntarily by the hero or the martyr, for the sake of something which he prizes more than his individual happiness. But this something, what is it, unless the happiness of others, or some of the requisites of happiness? It is noble to be capable of resigning entirely one's own portion of happiness, or chances of it: but, after all, this self-sacrifice must be for some end; it is not its own end; and if we are told that its end is not happiness, but virtue, which is better than happiness, I ask, would the sacrifice be made if the hero or martyr did not believe that it would earn for others immunity from similar sacrifices? Would it be made if he thought that his renunciation of happiness for himself would produce no fruit for any of his fellow creatures, but to make their lot like his, and place them also in the condition of persons who have renounced happiness? All honor to those who can abnegate for themselves the personal enjoyment of life, when by such renunciation they contribute worthily to increase the amount of happiness in the world; but he who does it, or professes to do it, for any other purpose, is no more deserving of admiration from the ascetic mounted on his pillar. He may be an inspiriting proof of what men *can* do, but assuredly not an example of what they *should*.

Though it is only in a very imperfect state of the world's arrangements that anyone can best serve the happiness of others by the absolute sacrifice of his own, yet so long as the world is in that imperfect state, I fully acknowledge that the readiness to make such a sacrifice is the highest virtue which can be found in man. I will add that in this condition of the world, paradoxical as the assertion may be, the conscious ability to do without happiness gives the best prospect of realizing such happiness as is attainable. For nothing except that consciousness can raise a person above the chances of life, by making him feel that, let fate and fortune do their worst, they have not power to subdue him; which, once felt, frees him from excess of anxiety concerning the evils of life, and enables him, like many a Stoic in the worst times of the Roman Empire, to cultivate in tranquillity the sources of satisfaction accessible to him, without concerning himself about the uncertainty of their duration, any more than about their inevitable end.

Meanwhile, let utilitarians never cease to claim the morality of self-devotion as a possession which belongs by as good a right to them, as either to the Stoic or to the Transcendentalist. The utilitarian morality does recognize in human beings the power of sacrificing their own greatest good for the good of others. It only refuses to admit that the sacrifice is itself a good. A sacrifice which does not increase, or tend to increase, the sum total of happiness, it considers as wasted. The only self-renunciation which it applauds, is devotion to the happiness, or to some of the means of happiness, of others; either of mankind collectively, or of individuals within the limits imposed by the collective interests of mankind.

I must again repeat, what the assailants of utilitarianism seldom have the justice to acknowledge, that the happiness which forms the utilitarian standard of what is right in conduct, is not the agent's own happiness, but that of all concerned. As between his own happiness and that of others, utilitarianism requires him to be as strictly impartial as a disinterested and benevolent spectator. In the golden rule of Jesus of Nazareth, we read the complete spirit of the ethics of utility. To do as you would be done by, and to love your neighbor as yourself, constitute the ideal perfection of utilitarian morality. As the means of making the nearest approach to this ideal, utility would enjoin, first, that laws and social arrangements should place the happiness, or (as speaking practically it may be called) the interest, of every individual, as nearly as possible in harmony with the interest of the whole; and secondly, that education and opinion, which have so vast a power over human character, should so use that power as to establish in the mind of every individual an indissoluble association between his own happiness and the good of the whole – especially between his own happiness and the practice of such modes of conduct, negative and positive, as regard for the universal happiness prescribes; so that not only he may be unable to conceive the possibility of happiness to himself, consistently with conduct opposed to the general good, but also that a direct impulse to promote the general good may be in every individual one of the habitual motives of action, and the sentiments connected therewith may fill a large and prominent place in every human being's sentient existence. If the impugners of the utilitarian morality represented it to their own minds in this its true character, I know not what recommendation possessed by any other morality they could possibly affirm to be wanting to it; what more beautiful or more exalted developments of human nature any other ethical system can be supposed to foster, or what springs of action, not accessible to the utilitarian, such systems rely on for giving effect to their mandates.

The objectors to utilitarianism cannot always be charged with representing it in a discreditable light. On the contrary, those among them who entertain anything like a just idea of its disinterested character sometimes find fault with its standard as being too high for humanity. They say it is exacting too much to require that people shall always act from the inducement of promoting the general interests of society. But this is to mistake the very meaning of a standard of morals, and confound the rule of action with the motive of it. It is the business of ethics to tell us what are our duties, or by what test we may know them; but no system of ethics requires that the sole motive of all we do shall be a feeling of duty; on the contrary, ninety-nine hundredths of all our actions are done from other motives, and rightly so done, if the rule of duty does not condemn them. It is the more unjust to utilitarianism that this particular misapprehension should be made a ground of objection to it, inasmuch as utilitarian moralists have gone beyond almost all others in affirming that the motive has nothing to do with the morality of the action, though much with the worth of the agent. He who saves a fellow creature from drowning does what is morally right, whether his motive be duty, or the hope of being paid for his trouble; he who betrays the friend that trusts him, is guilty of a crime, even if his object be to serve another friend to whom he is under greater obligations. But to speak only of actions done from the motive of duty, and in direct obedience to principle: it is a misapprehension of the utilitarian mode of thought, to conceive it as implying that people should fix their minds upon so wide a generality as the world, or society at large. The great majority of good actions are intended not for the benefit of the world, but for that of individuals, of which the good of the world is made up; and the thoughts of the most virtuous man need not on these occasions travel beyond the particular persons concerned, except so far as is necessary to assure himself that in benefiting them he is not violating the rights, that is, the legitimate and authorized expectations, of anyone else. The multiplication of happiness is, according to the utilitarian ethics, the object of virtue: the occasions on which any person (except one in a thousand) has it in his power to do this on an extended scale, in other words to be a public benefactor, are but exceptional, and on these occasions alone is he called on to consider public utility; in every other case, private utility, the interest or happiness of some few persons, is all he has to attend to. Those alone the influence of whose actions extends to society in general, need concern themselves habitually about so large an object. In the case of abstinences indeed – of things which people forbear to do from moral considerations, though the consequences in the particular case might be beneficial – it would be unworthy of an intelligent agent not to be consciously aware that the action is of a class which, if practiced generally, would be generally injurious, and that this is the ground of the obligation to abstain from it. The amount of regard for the public interest implied in this recognition is no greater than is demanded by every system of morals, for they all enjoin to abstain from whatever is manifestly pernicious to society.

The same considerations dispose of another reproach against the doctrine of utility, founded on a still grosser misconception of the purpose of a standard of morality, and of the very meaning of the words right and wrong. It is often affirmed that utilitarianism renders men cold and unsympathizing; that it chills their moral feelings towards individuals; that it makes them regard only the dry and hard consideration of the consequences of actions, not taking into their moral estimate the qualities from which those actions emanate. If the assertion means that they do not allow their judgment respecting the rightness or wrongness of an action to be influenced by their opinion of the qualities of the person who does it, this is a complaint not against utilitarianism, but against having any standard of morality at all; for certainly no known ethical standard decides an action to be good or bad because it is done by a good or a bad man, still less because done by an amiable, a brave, or a benevolent man, or the contrary. These considerations are relevant, not to the estimation of actions, but of persons; and there is nothing in the utilitarian theory inconsistent with the fact that there are other things which interest us in persons besides the rightness and wrongness of their actions. The Stoics, indeed, with the paradoxical misuse of language which was part of their system, and by which they strove to raise themselves above all concern about anything but virtue, were fond of saying that he who has that has everything; that he, and only he, is rich, is beautiful, is a king. But no claim of this description is made for the virtuous man by the utilitarian doctrine. Utilitarians are quite aware that there are other desirable possessions and qualities besides virtue, and are perfectly willing to allow to all of them their full worth. They are also aware that a right action does not necessarily indicate a virtuous character, and that actions which are blamable, often proceed from qualities entitled to praise. When this is apparent in any particular case, it modifies their estimation, not certainly of the act, but of the agent. I grant that they are, notwithstanding, of opinion that in the long run the best proof of a good character is good actions; and resolutely refuse to consider any mental disposition as good, of which the predominant tendency is to produce bad conduct. This makes them unpopular with many people; but it is an unpopularity which they must share with everyone who regards the distinction between right and wrong in a serious light; and the reproach is not one which a conscientious utilitarian need be anxious to repel.

If no more be meant by the objection than that many utilitarians look on the morality of actions, as measured by the utilitarian standard, with too exclusive a regard, and do not lay sufficient stress upon the other beauties of character which go towards making a human being lovable or admirable, this may be admitted. Utilitarians who have cultivated their moral feelings, but not their sympathies nor their artistic perceptions, do fall into this mistake; and so do all other moralists under the same conditions. What can be said in excuse for other moralists is equally available for them, namely, that if there is to be any error, it is better that it should be on that side. As a matter of fact, we may affirm that among utilitarians as among adherents of other systems, there is every imaginable degree of rigidity and of laxity in the application of their standard: some are even puritanically rigorous, while others are as indulgent as can possibly be desired by sinner or by sentimentalist. But on the whole, a doctrine which brings prominently forward the interest that mankind have in the repression and prevention of conduct which violates the moral law, is likely to be inferior to no other in turning the sanctions of opinion against such violations. It is true, the question, "What does violate the moral law?" is one on which those who recognize different standards of morality are likely now and then to differ. But difference of opinion on moral questions was not first introduced into the world by utilitarianism, while that doctrine does supply, if not always an easy, at all events a tangible and intelligible mode of deciding such differences.

It may not be superfluous to notice a few more of the common misapprehensions of utilitarian ethics, even those which are so obvious and gross that it might appear impossible for any person of candor and intelligence to fall into them; since persons, even of considerable mental endowments, often give themselves so little trouble to understand the bearings of any opinion against which they entertain a prejudice, and men are in general so little conscious of this voluntary ignorance as a defect, that the vulgarest misunderstandings of ethical doctrines are continually met with in the deliberate writings of persons of the greatest pretensions both to high principle and to philosophy. We not uncommonly hear the doctrine of utility inveighed against as a *godless* doctrine. If it be necessary to say anything at all against so mere an assumption, we may say that the question depends upon what idea we have formed of the moral character of the Deity. If it be a true belief that God desires, above all things, the happiness of his creatures, and that this was his purpose in their creation, utility is not only not a godless doctrine, but more profoundly religious than any other. If it be meant that utilitarianism does not recognize the revealed will of God as the supreme law of morals, I answer that a utilitarian who believes in the perfect goodness and wisdom of God, necessarily believes that whatever God has thought fit to reveal on the subject of morals, must fulfil the requirements of utility in a supreme degree. But others besides utilitarians have been of opinion that the Christian revelation was intended, and is fitted, to inform the hearts and minds of mankind with a spirit which should enable them to find for themselves what is right, and incline them to do it when found, rather than to tell them, except in a very general way, what it is; and that we need a doctrine of ethics, carefully followed out, to *interpret* to us the will of God. Whether this opinion is correct or not, it is superfluous here to discuss; since whatever aid religion, either natural or revealed, can afford to ethical investigation, is as open to the utilitarian moralist as to any other. He can use it as the testimony of God to the usefulness or hurtfulness of any given course of action, by as good a right as others can use it for the indication of a transcendental law, having no connection with usefulness or with happiness.

Again, utility is often summarily stigmatized as an immoral doctrine by giving it the name of *expediency*, and taking advantage of the popular use of that term to contrast it with *principle*. But the *expedient*, in the sense in which it is opposed to the *right*, generally means that which is expedient for the particular interest of the agent himself; as when a minister sacrifices the interests of his country to keep himself in place. When it means anything better than this, it means that which is expedient for some immediate object, some temporary purpose, but which violates a rule whose observance is expedient in a much higher degree. The expedient, in this sense, instead of being the same thing with the useful, is a branch of the hurtful. Thus, it would often be expedient, for the purpose of getting over some momentary embarrassment, or attaining some object immediately useful to ourselves or others, to tell a lie. But inasmuch as the cultivation in ourselves of a sensitive feeling on the subject of veracity, is one of the most useful, and the enfeeblement of that feeling one of the most hurtful, things to which our conduct can be instrumental; and inasmuch as any, even unintentional, deviation from truth, does that much towards weakening the trustworthiness of human assertion, which is not only the principal support of all present social well-being, but the insufficiency of which does more than any one thing that can be named to keep back civilization, virtue, everything on which human happiness on the largest scale depends; we feel that the violation, for a present advantage, of a rule of such transcendenant expediency, is not expedient, and that he who, for the sake of a convenience to himself or to some other individual, does what depends on him to deprive mankind of the good, and inflict upon them the evil, involved in the greater or less reliance which they can place in each other's word, acts the part of one of their worst enemies. Yet that even this rule, sacred as it is, admits of possible exceptions, is acknowledged by all moralists; the chief of which is when the withholding of some fact (as of information from a malefactor, or of bad news from a person dangerously ill) would save an individual (especially an individual other than oneself) from great and unmerited evil, and when the withholding can only be effected by denial. But in order that the exception may not extend itself beyond the need, and may have the least possible effect in weakening reliance on veracity, it ought to be recognized, and, if possible, its limits defined; and if the principle of utility is good for anything, it must be good for weighing these conflicting utilities against one another, and marking out the region within which one or the other preponderates.

Again, defenders of utility often find themselves called upon to reply to such objections as this – that there is not time, previous to action, for calculating and weighing the effects of any line of conduct on the general happiness. This is exactly as if anyone were to say that it is impossible to guide our conduct by Christianity, because there is not time, on every occasion on which anything has to be done, to read through the Old and New Testaments. The answer to the objection is that there has been ample time, namely, the whole past duration of the human species. During all that time, mankind have been learning by experience the tendencies of actions; on which experience all the prudence, as well as all the morality of life, are dependent. People talk as if the commencement of this course of experience had hitherto been put off, and as if, at the moment when some man feels tempted to meddle with the property or life of another, he had to begin considering for the first time whether murder and theft are injurious to human happiness. Even then I do not think that he would find the question very puzzling; but, at all events, the matter is now done to his hand. It is truly a whimsical supposition that, if mankind were agreed in considering utility to be the test of morality, they would remain without any agreement as to what *is* useful, and would take no measures for having their notions on the subject taught to the young, and enforced by law and opinion. There is no difficulty in proving any ethical standard whatever to work ill, if we suppose universal idiocy to be conjoined with it; but on any hypothesis short of that, mankind must by this time have acquired positive beliefs as to the effects of some actions on their happiness; and the beliefs which have thus come down are the rules of morality for the multitude, and for the philosopher until he has succeeded in finding better. That philosophers might easily do this, even now, on many subjects; that the received code of ethics is by no means of divine right; and that mankind have still much to learn as to the effects of actions on the general happiness, I admit, or rather, earnestly maintain. The corollaries from the principle of utility, like the precepts of every practical art, admit of indefinite improvement, and, in a progressive state of the human mind, their improvement is perpetually going on. But to consider the rules of morality as improvable, is one thing; to pass over the intermediate generalizations entirely, and endeavor to test each individual action directly by the first principle, is another. It is a strange notion that the acknowledgment of a first principle is inconsistent with the admission of secondary ones. To inform a traveler respecting the place of his ultimate destination, is not to forbid the use of landmarks and direction-posts on the way. The proposition that happiness is the end and aim of morality, does not mean that no road ought to be laid down to that goal, or that persons going thither should not be advised to take one direction rather than another. Men really ought to leave off talking a kind of nonsense on this subject, which they would neither talk nor listen to on other matters of practical concernment. Nobody argues that the art of navigation is not founded on astronomy, because sailors cannot wait to calculate the Nautical Almanac. Being rational creatures, they go to sea with it ready calculated; and all rational creatures go out upon the sea of life with their minds made up on the common questions of right and wrong, as well as on many of the far more difficult questions of wise and foolish. And this, as long as foresight is a human quality, it is to be presumed they will continue to do. Whatever we adopt as the fundamental principle of morality, we require subordinate principles to apply it by; the impossibility of doing without them, being common to all systems, can afford no argument against anyone in particular; but gravely to argue as if no such secondary principles could be had, and as if mankind had remained till now, and always must remain, without drawing any general conclusions from the experience of human life, is as high a pitch, I think, as absurdity has ever reached in philosophical controversy.

The remainder of the stock arguments against utilitarianism mostly consist in laying to its charge the common infirmities of human nature, and the general difficulties which embarrass conscientious persons in shaping their course through life. We are told that a utilitarian will be apt to make his own particular case an exception to moral rules, and when under temptation will see a utility in the breach of a rule greater than he will see in its observance. But is utility the only creed which is able to furnish us with excuses for evil-doing, and means of cheating our own conscience? They are afforded in abundance by all doctrines which recognize as a fact in morals the existence of conflicting considerations; which all doctrines do, that have been believed by sane persons. It is not the fault of any creed, but of the complicated nature of human affairs, that rules of conduct cannot be so framed as to require no exceptions, and that hardly any kind of action can safely be laid down as either always obligatory or always condemnable. There is no ethical creed which does not temper the rigidity of its laws by giving a certain latitude, under the moral responsibility of the agent, for accommodation to peculiarities of circumstances; and under every creed, at the opening thus made, self-deception and dishonest casuistry get in. There exists no moral system under which there do not arise unequivocal cases of conflicting obligation. These are the real difficulties, the knotty points both in the theory of ethics, and in the conscientious guidance of personal conduct. They are overcome practically, with greater or with less success,

according to the intellect and virtue of the individual; but it can hardly be pretended that anyone will be the less qualified for dealing with them, from possessing an ultimate standard to which conflicting rights and duties can be referred. If utility is the ultimate source of moral obligations, utility may be invoked to decide between them when their demands are incompatible. Though the application of the standard may be difficult, it is better than none at all; while in other systems, the moral laws all claiming independent authority, there is no common umpire entitled to interfere between them: their claims to precedence one over another rest on little better than sophistry, and unless determined, as they generally are, by the unacknowledged influence of considerations of utility, afford a free scope for the action of personal desires and partialities. We must remember that only in these cases of conflict between secondary principles is it requisite that first principles should be appealed to. There is no case of moral obligation in which some secondary principle is not involved; and if only one, there can seldom be any real doubt which one it is, in the mind of any person by whom the principle itself is recognized.

Of What Sort of Proof the Principle of Utility is Susceptible

It has already been remarked that questions of ultimate ends do not admit of proof, in the ordinary acceptation of the term. To be incapable of proof by reasoning is common to all first principles: to the first premises of our knowledge as well as to those of our conduct. But the former, being matters of fact, may be the subject of a direct appeal to the faculties which judge of fact – namely, our senses, and our internal consciousness. Can an appeal be made to the same faculties on questions of practical ends? Or by what other faculty is cognizance taken of them?

Questions about ends are, in other words, questions what things are desirable. The utilitarian doctrine is that happiness is desirable, and the only thing desirable, as an end; all other things being only desirable as means to that end. What ought to be required of this doctrine – what conditions is it requisite that the doctrine should fulfil – to make good its claim to be believed?

The only proof capable of being given that an object is visible, is that people actually see it. The only proof that a sound is audible, is that people hear it: and so of the other sources of our experience. In like manner, I apprehend, the sole evidence it is possible to produce that anything is desirable, is that people do actually desire it. If the end which the utilitarian doctrine proposes to itself were not, in theory and in practice, acknowledged to be an end, nothing could ever convince any person that it was so. No reason can be given why the general happiness is desirable except that each person, so far as he believes it to be attainable, desires his own happiness. This, however, being a fact, we have not only all the proof which the case admits of, but all which it is possible to require, that happiness is a good: that each person's happiness is a good to that person, and the general happiness, therefore, a good to the aggregate of all persons. Happiness has made out its title as one of the ends of conduct, and consequently one of the criteria of morality.

But it has not, by this alone, proved itself to be the sole criterion. To do that, it would seem, by the same rule, necessary to show, not only that people desire happiness, but that they never desire anything else. Now it is palpable that they do desire things which, in common language, are decidedly distinguished from happiness. They desire, for example, virtue, and the absence of vice, no less really than pleasure and the absence of pain. The desire of virtue is not as universal, but it is as authentic a fact, as the desire of happiness. And hence the opponents of the utilitarian standard deem that they have a right to infer that there are other ends of human action besides happiness, and that happiness is not the standard of approbation and disapprobation.

But does the utilitarian doctrine deny that people desire virtue, or maintain that virtue is not a thing to be desired? The very reverse. It maintains not only that virtue is to be desired, but that it is to be desired disinterestedly, for itself. Whatever may be the opinion of utilitarian moralists as to the original conditions by which virtue is made virtue; however they may believe (as they do) that actions and dispositions are only virtuous because they promote another end than virtue: yet this being granted, and it having been decided, from considerations of this description, what is virtuous, they not only place virtue at the very head of the things which are good as means to the ultimate end, but they also recognize as a psychological fact the possibility of its being, to the individual, a good in itself, without looking to any end beyond it; and hold that the mind is not in a right state, not in a state conformable to utility, not in the state most conducive to the general happiness, unless it does love virtue in this manner – as a thing desirable in itself, even although, in the individual instance, it should not produce those other desirable consequences which it tends to produce, and on account of which it is held to be virtue. This opinion is not, in the smallest degree, a departure from the happiness principle. The ingredients of happiness are very various, and each of them is desirable in itself, and not merely when considered as swelling an aggregate. The principle of utility does not mean that any given pleasure, as music, for instance, or any given exemption from pain, as for example health, is to be looked upon as means to a collective something termed happiness, and to be desired on that account. They are desired and desirable in and for themselves; besides being means, they are a part of the end. Virtue, according to the utilitarian doctrine, is not naturally and originally part of the end, but it is capable of becoming so; and in those who love it disinterestedly it has become so, and is desired and cherished, not as a means to happiness, but as a part of their happiness.

To illustrate this farther, we may remember that virtue is not the only thing, originally a means, and which if it were not a means to anything else, would be and remain indifferent, but which by association with what it is a means to, comes to be desired for itself, and that too with the utmost intensity. What, for example, shall we say of the love of money? There is nothing originally more desirable about money than about any heap of glittering pebbles. Its worth is solely that of the things which it will buy; the desires for other things than itself, which it is a means of gratifying. Yet the love of money is not only one of the strongest moving forces of human life, but money is, in many cases, desired in and for itself; the desire to possess it is often stronger than the desire to use it, and goes on increasing when all the desires which point to ends beyond it, to be compassed by it, are falling off. It may, then, be said truly, that money is desired not for the sake of an end, but as part of the end. From being a means to happiness, it has come to be itself a principal ingredient of the individual's conception of happiness. The same may be said of the majority of the great objects of human life – power, for example, or fame; except that to each of these there is a certain amount of immediate pleasure annexed, which has at least the semblance of being naturally inherent in them; a thing which cannot be said of money. Still, however, the strongest natural attraction, both of power and of fame, is the immense aid they give to the attainment of our other wishes; and it is the strong association thus generated between them and all our objects of desire, which gives to the direct desire of them the intensity it often assumes, so as in some characters to surpass in strength all other desires. In these cases the means have become a part of the end, and a more important part of it than any of the things which they are means to. What was once desired as an instrument for the attainment of happiness, has come to be desired for its own sake. In being desired for its own sake it is, however, desired as *part* of happiness. The person is made, or thinks he would be made, happy by its mere possession; and is made unhappy by failure to obtain it. The desire of it is not a different thing from the desire of happiness, any more than the love of music, or the desire of health. They are included in happiness. They are some of the elements of which the desire of happiness is made up. Happiness is not an abstract idea, but a concrete whole; and these are some of its parts. And the utilitarian standard sanctions and approves their being so. Life would be a poor thing, very ill provided with sources of happiness, if there were not this provision of nature, by which things originally indifferent, but conducive to, or otherwise associated with, the satisfaction of our primitive desires, become in themselves sources of pleasure more valuable than the primitive pleasures, both in permanency, in the space of human existence that they are capable of covering, and even in intensity.

Virtue, according to the utilitarian conception, is a good of this description. There was no original desire of it, or motive to it, save its conduciveness to pleasure, and especially to protection from pain. But through the association thus formed, it may be felt a good in itself, and

desired as such with as great intensity as any other good; and with this difference between it and the love of money, of power, or of fame, that all of these may, and often do, render the individual noxious to the other members of the society to which he belongs, whereas there is nothing which makes him so much a blessing to them as the cultivation of the disinterested love of virtue. And consequently, the utilitarian standard, while it tolerates and approves those other acquired desires, up to the point beyond which they would be more injurious to the general happiness than promotive of it, enjoins and requires the cultivation of the love of virtue up to the greatest strength possible, as being above all things important to the general happiness.

It results from the preceding considerations, that there is in reality nothing desired except happiness. Whatever is desired otherwise than *as a means* to some end beyond itself, and ultimately to happiness, is desired as itself a part of happiness, and is not desired for itself until it has become so. Those who desire virtue for its own sake, desire it either because the consciousness of it is a pleasure, or because the consciousness of being without it is a pain, or for both reasons united; as in truth the pleasure and pain seldom exist separately, but almost always together, the same person feeling pleasure in the degree of virtue attained, and pain in not having attained more. If one of these gave him no pleasure, and the other no pain, he would not love or desire virtue, or would desire it only for the other benefits which it might produce to himself or to persons whom he cared for.

We have now, then, an answer to the question, of what sort of proof the principle of utility is susceptible. If the opinion which I have now stated is psychologically true – if human nature is so constituted as to desire nothing which is not either a part of happiness or a means of happiness, we can have no other proof, and we require no other, that these are the only things desirable. If so, happiness is the sole end of human action, and the promotion of it the test by which to judge of all human conduct; from whence it necessarily follows that it must be the criterion of morality, since a part is included in the whole.

And now to decide whether this is really so; whether mankind do desire nothing for itself but that which is a pleasure to them, or of which the absence is a pain: we have evidently arrived at a question of fact and experience, dependent, like all similar questions, upon evidence. It can only be determined by practiced self-consciousness and self-observation, assisted by observation of others. I believe that these sources of evidence, impartially consulted, will declare that desiring a thing and finding it pleasant, aversion to it and thinking of it as painful, are phenomena entirely inseparable, or rather two parts of the same phenomenon; in strictness of language, two different modes of naming the same psychological fact: that to think of an object as desirable (*unless for the sake of its consequences*), and to think of it as pleasant, are one and the same thing; and that to desire anything, except in proportion as the idea of it is pleasant, is a physical and metaphysical impossibility.

So obvious does this appear to me that I expect it will hardly be disputed; and the objection made will be, not that desire can possibly be directed to anything ultimately except pleasure and exemption from pain, but that the will is a different thing from desire: that a person of confirmed virtue, or any other person whose purposes are fixed, carries out his purposes without any thought of the pleasure he has in contemplating them, or expects to derive from their fulfilment; and persists in acting on them, even though these pleasures are much diminished, by changes in his character or decay of his passive sensibilities, or are outweighed by the pains which the pursuit of the purposes may bring upon him. All this I fully admit, and have stated it elsewhere, as positively and emphatically as anyone. Will, the active phenomenon, is a different thing from desire, the state of passive sensibility, and though originally an offshoot from it, may in time take root and detach itself from the parent stock; so much so, that in the case of an habitual purpose, instead of willing the thing because we desire it, we often desire it only because we will it. This, however, is but an instance of that familiar fact, the power of habit, and is nowise confined to the case of virtuous actions. Many indifferent things which men originally did from a motive of some sort, they continue to do from habit. Sometimes this is done unconsciously, the consciousness coming only after the action; at other times with conscious volition, but volition which has become habitual,

and is put in operation by the force of habit, in opposition perhaps to the deliberate preference, as often happens with those who have contracted habits of vicious or hurtful indulgence. Third and last comes the case in which the habitual act of will in the individual instance is not in contradiction to the general intention prevailing at other times, but in fulfilment of it; as in the case of the person of confirmed virtue, and of all who pursue deliberately and consistently any determinate end. The distinction between will and desire thus understood is an authentic and highly important psychological fact; but the fact consists solely in this – that will, like all other parts of our constitution, is amenable to habit, and that we may will from habit what we no longer desire for itself, or desire only because we will it. It is not the less true that will, in the beginning, is entirely produced by desire; including in that term the repelling influence of pain as well as the attractive one of pleasure. Let us take into consideration, no longer the person who has a confirmed will to do right, but him in whom that virtuous will is still feeble, conquerable by temptation, and not to be fully relied on; by what means can it be strengthened? How can the will to be virtuous, where it does not exist in sufficient force, be implanted or awakened? Only by making the person *desire* virtue – by making him think of it in a pleasurable light, or of its absence in a painful one. It is by associating the doing right with pleasure, or the doing wrong with pain, or by eliciting and impressing and bringing home to the person's experience the pleasure naturally involved in the one or the pain in the other, that it is possible to call forth that will to be virtuous, which, when confirmed, acts without any thought of either pleasure or pain. Will is the child of desire, and passes out of the dominion of its parent only to come under that of habit. That which is the result of habit affords no presumption of being intrinsically good; and there would be no reason for wishing that the purpose of virtue should become independent of pleasure and pain, were it not that the influence of the pleasurable and painful associations which prompt to virtue is not sufficiently to be depended on for unerring constancy of action until it has acquired the support of habit. Both in feeling and in conduct, habit is the only thing which imparts certainty; and it is because of the importance to others of being able to rely absolutely on one's feelings and conduct, and to oneself of being able to rely on one's own, that the will to do right ought to be cultivated into this habitual independence. In other words, this state of the will is a means to good, not intrinsically a good; and does not contradict the doctrine that nothing is a good to human beings but in so far as it is either itself pleasurable, or a means of attaining pleasure or averting pain.

But, if this doctrine be true, the principle of utility is proved. Whether it is so or not, must now be left to the consideration of the thoughtful reader.

23

Groundwork for the Metaphysics of Morals

Immanuel Kant

Passage from the Common Rational Knowledge of Morality to the Philosophical

[The unqualified value of a good will]

It is impossible to imagine anything at all in the world, or even beyond it, that can be called good without qualification – except a *good will*. Intelligence, wit, judgement, and the other mental talents, whatever we may call them, or courage, decisiveness, and perseverance, are, as qualities of *temperament*, certainly good and desirable in many respects; but they can also be extremely bad and harmful when the will which makes use of these *gifts of nature* and whose specific quality we refer to as *character*, is not good. It is exactly the same with *gifts of fortune*. Power, wealth, honour, even health and that total well-being and contentment with one's condition which we call '*happiness*', can make a person bold but consequently often reckless as well, unless a good will is present to correct their influence on the mind, thus adjusting the whole principle of one's action to render it conformable to universal ends. It goes without saying that the sight of a creature enjoying uninterrupted prosperity, but never feeling the slightest pull of a pure and good will, cannot excite approval in a rational and impartial spectator. Consequently, a good will seems to constitute the indispensable condition even of our worthiness to be happy.

Some qualities, even though they are helpful to this good will and can make its task very much easier, nevertheless have no intrinsic unconditional worth. Rather, they presuppose a good will which puts limits on the esteem in which they are rightly held and forbids us to regard them as absolutely good. Moderation in emotions and passions, self-control, and sober reflection are not only good in many respects: they may even seem to constitute part of the inner worth of a person. Yet they are far from being properly described as good without qualification (however unconditionally they were prized by the ancients). For without the principles of a good will those qualities may become exceedingly bad; the passionless composure of a villain makes him not merely more dangerous but also directly more detestable in our eyes than we would have taken him to be without it.

A good will is not good because of its effects or accomplishments, and not because of its adequacy to achieve any proposed end: it is good only by virtue of its willing – that is, it is good in

Immanuel Kant, *Groundwork for the Metaphysics of Morals*, trans. Arnulf Zweig, ed. Thomas E. Hill, Jr. and Arnulf Zweig (Oxford: Oxford University Press, 2002). © 2002 by Thomas E. Hill, Jr. and Arnulf Zweig. Reprinted with permission from Oxford University Press.

itself. Considered in itself it is to be treasured as incomparably higher than anything it could ever bring about merely in order to satisfy some inclination or, if you like, the sum total of all inclinations. Even if it were to happen that, because of some particularly unfortunate fate or the miserly bequest of a step-motherly nature, this will were completely powerless to carry out its aims; if with even its utmost effort it still accomplished nothing, so that only good will itself remained (not, of course, as a mere wish, but as the summoning of every means in our power), even then it would still, like a jewel, glisten in its own right, as something that has its full worth in itself. Its utility or ineffectuality can neither add to nor subtract from this worth. Utility would be merely, as it were, its setting, enabling us to handle it better in our ordinary dealings or to attract to it the attention of those who are not yet experts, but not why we recommend it to experts and determine its worth.

[*Good will, not happiness, is the natural end of reason*]

Yet there is something so strange in this idea of the absolute worth of a mere will, all utility being left out of account, that, in spite of all the agreement this idea receives even from common reason, the suspicion must arise that perhaps its hidden basis is merely some high-flown fantasy, and that we may have misunderstood the purpose of nature in appointing reason as ruler of our will. Let us therefore examine this idea from this perspective.

In the natural constitution of an organized being – that is, a being properly equipped for life – we take it as a principle that no instrument for any purpose will be found in that being unless it is also the most appropriate and best adapted for that purpose. Now if nature's real purpose for a being possessed of reason and a will were its *preservation*, its *welfare*, or in a word its *happiness*, then nature would have hit on a very bad arrangement if it assigned the creature's reason the job of carrying out this purpose. For all the actions this creature has to perform with this end in view, and the whole rule of its conduct, would have been disclosed to it far more precisely by instinct; and the end in question could have been attained far more surely by instinct than it

ever could be by reason. If, in that case, reason had been given to this favoured creature additionally, its service would have been only to contemplate the fortunate constitution of the creature's nature, to admire it, enjoy it, and be grateful to its beneficent Cause. But reason would not have been given in order that this creature would subject its faculty of desire to such feeble and defective guidance or to meddle incompetently with nature's purpose. In a word, nature would have prevented reason from striking out into a practical use and from presuming, with its feeble insights, to think out for itself a plan for happiness and for the means of attaining it. Nature would herself have taken over not only the choice of ends but also that of means, and would with wise foresight have entrusted both to instinct alone.

And in fact we do find that the more one devotes one's cultivated reason to the enjoyment of life and happiness, the further away does one get from true contentment. This is why a certain degree of *misology*, i.e., hatred of reason, arises in many people, including those who have been most tempted by this use of reason, if only they are candid enough to admit it. For, according to their calculation of all the benefits they draw – I will not say from the invention of all the arts of common luxury, but even from the sciences (which in the final analysis seem to them to be only a luxury of the understanding) – they find that instead of gaining in happiness they have in fact only brought more trouble on their heads. They therefore come to envy, rather than despise, more ordinary people, who are closer to being guided by mere natural instinct and who do not let their reason have much influence on conduct. To this extent we must admit that the judgement of those who seek to moderate – and even to reduce below zero – the boasting glorification of benefits that reason is supposed to provide in the way of happiness and contentment with life, is by no means morose or ungrateful for the kindness of the world's ruler. That judgement rather is based on the idea that our existence has another and much worthier purpose, for which, and not for happiness, our reason is properly intended, an end which, therefore, is the supreme condition to which our private ends must for the most part be subordinated.

For since reason is not sufficiently competent to guide the will safely with regard to its objects and the satisfaction of all our needs (which it in part even multiplies) – a goal to which an implanted natural instinct would have led us much more certainly – and since reason is nevertheless given to us as a practical faculty – that is, as one which is supposed to influence the *will*; since, finally, reason was absolutely necessary for this purpose, as nature has everywhere distributed her abilities so as to fit the functions they are to perform; reason's true vocation must therefore be to produce a *will* which is *good in itself*, not just *good as a means* to some further end. Such a will must not be the sole and complete good, but it must be the highest good and the condition of all the rest, even of all our longing for happiness. In that case it is entirely compatible with the wisdom of nature that the cultivation of reason, which is required for the former unconditional purpose, may in many ways, at least in this life, restrict the attainment of the second, conditional purpose – happiness – and indeed that it can even reduce it to less than nothing. Nor does nature here violate its own purpose, for reason, which recognizes as its highest practical vocation the establishment of a good will, is capable only of its own peculiar kind of satisfaction – satisfaction from fulfilling a purpose which reason alone determines, even if this fulfilment damages the ends of inclination.

[*The concept of duty includes the concept of a good will*]

We must thus develop the concept of a will estimable in itself and good apart from any further aim. This concept is already present in the natural, healthy mind, which requires not so much instruction as merely clarification. It is this concept that always holds the highest place in estimating the total worth of our actions and it constitutes the condition of all the rest. Let us then take up the concept of *duty*, which includes that of a good will, the latter however being here under certain subjective limitations and obstacles. These, so far from hiding a good will or disguising it, rather bring it out by contrast and make it shine forth more brightly.

[*A good will is manifested when we act out of duty rather than inclination; only such acts have moral worth*]

I will here omit all actions already recognized as opposed to duty, even if they may be useful from this or that perspective; for about these it makes no sense even to ask the question whether they might have been done *out of duty* since they are directly opposed to it. I will also set aside actions that in fact accord with duty, yet for one has no *direct inclination*, but which one performs because impelled to do so by some other inclination. For in such a case it is easy to decide whether the action [which accords with duty] was done *out of duty* or for some self-interested goal. This distinction is far more difficult to perceive when the action accords with duty but the agent has in addition a *direct* inclination to do it. For example, it is certainly in accord with duty that a shopkeeper should not overcharge an inexperienced customer; and, where there is much business, a prudent merchant refrains from doing this and maintains a fixed general price for everybody, so that a child can buy from him just as well as anyone else. People thus get *honest* treatment. But this is not nearly enough to justify our believing that the shopkeeper acted in this way out of duty or from principles of honesty; his interests required him to act as he did. We cannot assume him to have in addition a direct inclination towards his customers, leading him, as it were out of love, to give no one preferential treatment over another person in the matter of price. Thus the action was done neither out of duty nor from immediate inclination, but solely out of self-interest.

On the other hand, it is a duty to preserve one's life, and every one also has a direct inclination to do it. But for that reason the often-fearful care that most people take for their lives has no intrinsic worth, and the maxim of their action has no moral merit. They do protect their lives *in conformity with duty*, but not *out of duty*. If, by contrast, disappointments and hopeless misery have entirely taken away someone's taste for life; if that wretched person, strong in soul and more angered at fate than fainthearted or cast down, longs for death and still preserves life without loving it – not out of inclination or fear but out of duty – then indeed that person's maxim has moral worth.

It is a duty to help others where one can, and besides this many souls are so compassionately disposed that, without any further motive of vanity or self-interest, they find an inner pleasure in spreading joy around them, taking delight in the contentment of others, so far as they have brought it about. Yet I maintain that, however dutiful and kind an action of this sort may be, it still has no genuinely moral worth. It is on a level with other inclinations – for example, the inclination to pursue honour, which if fortunate enough to aim at something generally useful and consistent with duty, something consequently honourable, deserves praise and encouragement but not esteem. For its maxim lacks the moral merit of such actions done not out of inclination but out of *duty*. Suppose then that the mind of this humanitarian were overclouded by sorrows of his own which extinguished all compassion for the fate of others, but that he still had the power to assist others in distress; suppose though that their adversity no longer stirred him, because he is preoccupied with his own; and now imagine that, though no longer moved by any inclination, he nevertheless tears himself out of this deadly apathy and does the action without any inclination, solely out of duty. Then for the first time his action has its genuine moral worth. Furthermore, if nature had put little sympathy into this or that person's heart; if he, though an honest man, were cold in temperament and indifferent to the sufferings of others – perhaps because he has the special gifts of patience and fortitude in his own sufferings and he assumes or even demands the same of others; if such a man (who would in truth not be the worst product of nature) were not exactly fashioned by nature to be a humanitarian, would he not still find in himself a source from which he might give himself a worth far higher than that of a good-natured temperament? Assuredly he would. It is precisely in this that the worth of character begins to show – a moral worth, and incomparably the highest – namely, that he does good, not out of inclination, but out of duty.

To secure one's own happiness is a duty (at least indirectly); for discontent with one's condition when pressed by many cares and amidst unsatisfied needs might easily become a *great temptation to transgress one's duties*. But even apart from duty, all human beings already have by their own nature the strongest and deepest inclination towards happiness, because it is precisely in this idea that all the inclinations come together. The prescription for happiness is, how-

ever, often so constituted that it greatly interferes with some inclinations, and yet we cannot form a precise conception of the satisfaction of all inclinations as a sum, the conception to which we give the name "happiness". Hence it is not surprising that a single inclination, well defined as to what it promises and as to the time at which it can be satisfied, may outweigh a fluctuating idea; so, for example, a man who suffers from gout, may choose to enjoy whatever he likes and put up with what he must – because according to his calculations he has at least not sacrificed the enjoyment of the present moment to some possibly groundless expectations of happiness allegedly attached to health. But even in this case, if the universal inclination to happiness has failed to determine his will, and if good health, at least for him, did not enter into his calculations, what would remain, as in other cases, is a law – the law that he ought to promote his happiness, not out of inclination, but out of duty. And only from this law would his conduct begin to have real moral worth.

It is doubtless in this sense that we should understand too the passages from Scripture in which we are commanded to love our neighbour and even our enemy. For love as inclination cannot be commanded; but kindness done out of duty – although no inclination impels us, and even although natural and unconquerable aversion stands in our way – is *practical love*, not *pathological love*. It resides in the will and not in the partiality of feeling, in principles of action and not in melting compassion; and it is this practical love alone that can be commanded.

[*What makes acts out of duty morally worthy is not their actual or intended results, but the underlying principle on which they are based*]

The second proposition is this: The moral worth of an action done out of duty has its moral worth, not *in the objective* to be reached by that action, but in the maxim in accordance with which the action is decided upon; it depends, therefore, not on actualizing the object of the action, but solely on the *principle of volition* in accordance with which the action was done, without any regard for objects of the faculty of desire. It is clear from our previous discussion that the objectives we may have in acting, and also our actions' effects considered as ends and as what motivates our volition, can give to actions no unconditional or moral worth. Where then can this worth be found if not in the willing of the action's hoped for effect? It can be found nowhere but *in the principle of the will*, irrespective of the ends that can be brought about by such action. For the will stands, so to speak, at the crossroads between its a priori principle, which is formal, and its a posteriori motivation, which is material; and since it must be determined by something, it will have to be determined by the formal principle of volition, since every material principle is ruled out when an action is done out of duty.

[Duty and respect for law]

The third proposition, which follows from the two preceding, I would express in this way: *Duty is the necessity of an act done out of respect for the law.* While I can certainly have an *inclination* for an object that results from my proposed action, I can never *respect it*, precisely because it is nothing but an effect of a will and not its activity. Similarly I cannot respect any inclination whatsoever, whether it be my own inclination or that of another. At most I can approve of that towards which I feel an inclination, and occasionally I can like the object of somebody else's inclination myself – that is, see it as conducive to my own advantage. But the only thing that could be an object of respect (and thus a commandment) for me is something that is conjoined with my will purely as a ground and never as a consequence, something that does not serve my inclination but overpowers it or at least excludes it entirely from my decision-making – consequently, nothing but the law itself. Now if an action done out of duty is supposed to exclude totally the influence of inclination, and, along with inclination, every object of volition, then nothing remains that could determine the will except objectively *the law* and subjectively *pure respect* for this practical law. What is left therefore is the maxim,[1] to obey this sort of law even when doing so is prejudicial to all my inclinations.

[Identification of the principle of a good will: the formula of universal law]

Thus the moral worth of an action depends neither on the result expected from that action nor on any principle of action that has to borrow its motive from this expected result. For all these results (such as one's own pleasurable condition or even the promotion of the happiness of others) could have been brought about by other causes as well. It would not require the will of a rational being to produce them, but it is only in such a will that the highest and unconditional good can be found. That pre-eminent good which we call "moral" consists therefore in nothing but *the idea of the law* in itself, which certainly *is present only in a rational being* – so far as that idea, and not an expected result, is the determining ground of the will. And this pre-eminent good is already present in the person who acts in accordance with this idea; we need not await the result of the action in order to find it.[2]

But what kind of law can it be, the idea of which must determine the will, even without considering the expected result, if that will is to be called good absolutely and without qualification? Since I have robbed the will of every inducement that might arise for it from its obeying any particular law, the only thing remaining that could serve the will as a principle is the universal conformity of actions to law as such. That is, I ought never to act in such a way *that I could not also will that my maxim should become a universal law.* Here it is the mere conformity to law as such (without presupposing any law prescribing particular actions) that serves the will as its principle, and must so serve it if duty is not to be a totally empty delusion and a chimerical concept. Common human reason, when engaged in making practical judgements, also agrees with this completely and has that principle constantly in view.

[Example: the wrongness of a lying promise]

Suppose, for example, the question is this: May I, when in distress, make a promise with the intention not to keep it? Here I easily distinguish the different meanings this question can have, whether it is prudent to make a false promise, or whether it is in accord with duty. The first no doubt can often be the case. Of course I see that [even for prudence] it is not enough just to extricate myself from my present predicament by means of this deception; I need to consider whether this lie might give rise to even greater troubles than those from which I am escaping, since, for all my supposed *cunning*, it is not so easy to foresee all the consequences, e.g., the loss of trust may cost me more than all the misfortune I am now trying to avoid. I must consider therefore whether it might be *more* prudent for me to act on a general maxim and make it a habit to issue a promise only when I intend to keep it. But it is soon clear to me that such a maxim is always based solely on fear of consequences. To tell the truth out of duty is something entirely different from telling the truth out of fear of troublesome consequences; for in the first case the concept of the action itself already contains a law for me, while in the second case I must first look around to see how I am likely to be affected by the action. For deviating from the principle of duty is quite certainly bad; but deserting my prudential maxim can often be greatly to my advantage, though it is admittedly safer to stick to it. If, on the other hand, I want to find out most quickly but unerringly the answer to a different question – whether a deceitful promise accords with duty – I must ask myself 'Would I really be content if my maxim (the maxim of getting out of a difficulty by making a false promise) were to hold as a universal law (one valid both for myself and for others)'? And could I really say to myself, 'Let everyone be allowed to make a false promise if they find themselves in difficulties from which there is otherwise no escape'? I immediately see that I can indeed will the lie, but I cannot will a universal law to lie. For with such a law, there would actually be no promising at all, since it would be futile for me to allege my intentions with regard to some future actions to others who would not believe me, or who, if they did so over-hastily, would pay me back in the same coin. Consequently my maxim, as soon as it became a universal law, would necessarily subvert itself.

Thus I need no far-reaching acuteness to know what I have to do in order that my volition can be morally good. Inexperienced in the ways of the world and incapable of anticipating all its actual events, I ask myself only, 'Can you will that your maxim become a universal law?' If not, that maxim must be repudiated, and not because of any impending disadvantage to you or even to others, but because it cannot fit as a principle into a possible universal legislation, and reason forces me to offer my immediate respect to such legislation. As yet I have no *insight* into the grounds of that respect (something the philosopher may investigate), but I do at least understand this much: it is the appreciation of something whose worth far exceeds all the worth of anything favoured by inclination. I understand too that the necessity that I act out of *pure* respect for the practical law is what constitutes duty. To duty every other motive must give way, because it is the condition of a will good *in itself*, whose worth transcends all else.

[*The general competence of ordinary human reason and judgement*]

Considering the moral knowledge of common human reason we have thus arrived at its principle, a principle it admittedly does not think about abstractly in such a universal formulation; but which it really does always have in view and employs as the standard in its judging. It would be easy to show here how common human reason, with this compass in hand, knows very well how to distinguish what is good or evil, consistent or inconsistent with duty, in all cases that present themselves. Without attempting to teach it anything new, one merely has to make reason attend, as Socrates did, to its own principle. Therefore neither science nor philosophy is needed in order for us to know what one has to do to be honest and good, and even to be wise and virtuous. This is something that we could have suspected from the start: that knowledge of what it is incumbent upon everyone to do, and so also to know, would be attainable by everyone, even the most ordinary human being. Here we cannot help but be impressed when we notice the great advantage that the power of practical judgement has over theoretical judgement, in the minds of ordinary people. In theoretical judgements, if common reason dares to go beyond the laws of experience and the perceptions of the senses, it falls into sheer inconceivabilities and self-contradictions, or at least into a chaos of uncertainty, obscurity, and vacillation. On the practical side, however, the power of judgement first begins to look its best when the ordinary mind excludes all sensuous motives from its practical laws. The ordinary mind then becomes even subtle – perhaps vexing itself with its con-science or with other claims regarding what is to be called "right", or trying to determine honestly for its own instruction the worth of various actions. But what is most important, the common understanding has, in the latter case, as good a chance of hitting the mark as any philosopher has. Indeed its chances are almost better than a philosopher's, since the latter's judgement has no principle different from that of ordinary intelligence, and a philosopher's judgement may easily be confused by a mass of strange and irrelevant considerations and caused to turn from the right path. Would it not be wise there-fore to accept the judgement of common reason in moral matters, or to bring in philosophy at most to make the system of morals more complete and comprehensible and to present its rules in formulations more convenient to use (especially in disputation) – but not to lead the common human understanding away from its happy sim-plicity in matters of action and set it on a new path of inquiry and instruction?

[Why moral philosophy is needed]

A wonderful thing about innocence – but also something very bad – is that it cannot defend itself very well and is easily led astray. For this reason even wisdom – which otherwise is more a matter of acting than knowing – also needs science, not in order to learn from it, but in order to gain access and durability for what it prescribes. Human beings feel within themselves a powerful coun-terweight opposed to all the commandments of duty, which reason portrays as so worthy of esteem: the counterweight of needs and inclina-tions, whose total satisfaction people sum up under the name 'happiness'. But reason, without promising anything to inclination, dictates its prescriptions relentlessly, thus treating with neglect and contempt those blustering and seemingly legitimate claims (which refuse to be suppressed by any commandment). From this there arises a *natural dialectic* – that is, a tendency to quibble with these strict laws of duty, to cast doubt on their validity or at least on their purity and strictness, and, if possible, to make them conform better to our wishes and inclinations. This means corrupting their very foundations and destroying their dignity – a result that even com-mon practical reason cannot ultimately endorse.

In this way *common human reason* is driven, not by any cognitive need (which never touches it so long as it is content to be mere sound reason), but on practical grounds, driven to leave its own sphere and take a step into the field of *practical philosophy*. There it seeks instruction and precise direction as to the source of its own principle and about the correct function of this principle in con-trast with maxims based on need and inclination. It ventures into philosophy so as to escape from the perplexity caused by conflicting claims and so as to avoid the risk of losing all genuine moral principles through the obscurity into which it eas-ily falls. Thus, just as happens in its theoretical use, a *dialectic* arises unnoticed when practical common reason is cultivated, and it is forced to seek help in philosophy. As with the theoretical use of reason, the conflict will be resolved only by a thorough critical examination of our reason.

Transition from Popular Moral Philosophy to a Metaphysics of Morals

[The need for a priori method in ethics]

Although we have drawn our previous concept of duty from the common use of our practical reason, this by no means implies that we have treated it as a concept derived from experience. On the contrary, if we pay attention to our experience of what human beings do and fail to do, we encounter frequent and, I must admit, justified complaints that one cannot in fact point to any sure examples of the disposition to act out of pure duty. Thus we hear the charge that, although many things may be done that are in accord with what duty commands, it still remains doubtful whether those actions are really done out of duty, and doubtful therefore whether they have moral worth. That is why there have always been philosophers who abso-lutely denied the reality of this disposition in human conduct and ascribed everything we do to more or less refined self-love. But those philo-sophers have not denied the correctness of the concept of morality. Rather, they have spoken with sincere regret of the frailty and corruption of human nature, noble enough to take as its rule an Idea so worthy of respect, but at the same time too weak to follow it, so that reason, which should serve as the law-giver to human nature, is used only to serve the interests of our inclinations, either singly or, at most, to maximize their compatibility. It is in fact absolutely impossible to identify by experience, with complete certainty, a single case in which the maxim of an action – an action that accords with duty – was based exclusively on moral reasons and the thought of one's duty. There are cases when the most searching self-examination comes up with nothing but duty as the moral reason that could have been strong enough to move us to this or that good action or to some great sacrifice. But we cannot conclude from this with certainty that the real determining cause of our will was not some secret impulse of self-love, disguising itself as that Idea of duty. So we like to flatter ourselves with the false claim to a nobler motive but in fact we can never, even with the most rigorous self-examination, completely uncover our hidden motivations. For when moral worth is the issue, what counts is not the actions which one sees, but their inner principles, which one does not see.

Furthermore, there is no better way to serve the interests of those who mock all morality as a mere phantom of the brain, an illusion with which, out of vanity, the human imagination puffs itself up, than to concede that concepts of duty must be drawn solely from experience (as people find it only too easy to believe about all other concepts). For by conceding this we prepare an assured victory for those scoffers. Out of charity I am willing to grant that most of our actions are in accord with duty; but if we look more closely at the devising and striving that lies behind them, then everywhere we run into the dear self which is always there; and it is this and not the strict command of duty (which would often require self-denial) that underlies our intentions. One need not be an enemy of virtue but only a dispassionate observer who does not immediately confuse even the liveliest wish for goodness with its reality, to become doubtful at certain moments whether any genuine virtue can really be found in the world. (Such doubts occur particularly as one grows older and experience renders one's power of judgement and observation shrewder and more discerning.) And at that point only one thing can protect us against a complete abandonment of our Ideas of duty, or can preserve in us a well-founded respect for its law: the clear conviction that even if there never were any actions springing from such pure sources, the question at issue here is not whether this or that actually occurs. The question is rather whether reason, by itself and independently of all appearances, commands what ought to be done, actions of which the world has perhaps never until now provided an example – actions whose feasibility might well be doubted by those who rest everything on experience – which are nevertheless commanded inexorably by reason. For example, the duty to be totally sincere in one's friendships can be demanded of everyone even if up to now there may never have existed a totally sincere friend. For this duty, as duty in general, lies prior to all experience in the Idea of a power of reason which determines the will by a priori grounds.

Unless we wish to deny to the concept of morality all truth and all application to a possible object, we must grant that its law is so broad in meaning that it must be valid not merely for human beings, but for all rational beings as such, and valid not merely under contingent conditions and subject to exceptions, but with absolute necessity. It is therefore clear that no experience could warrant even the possibility of such absolutely certain and necessary laws. For by what right can we make something that is perhaps valid only under the contingent human conditions into an object of unlimited respect and view it as universally prescribed for every rational creature? And how could laws for determining our will be taken as laws for determining the will of rational beings in general – and only on that account laws for determining our will – if these laws were merely empirical and did not have their source completely a priori in pure, but practical, reason?

[Moral principles not derivable from examples]

Nor could one give morality worse advice than by trying to derive it from examples. For every example of morality presented to me must itself first be assessed with moral principles to see whether it deserves to be used as an original example, i.e., as a model. By no means can it have the authority to give us the concept of morality. Even the Holy One of the Gospels must first be compared with our ideal of moral perfection before we can acknowledge Him to be such. Even He says of Himself: 'Why do you call Me (whom you see) good? There is none good (the archetype of the good) but the one God alone (whom you do not see).' But where do we get the concept of God as the highest good? Only from the *Idea* of moral perfection which reason designs a priori and connects inseparably with the concept of a free will. Imitation has no place in moral matters, and examples serve us only for encouragement – that is, they set beyond doubt the feasibility of doing what the law commands and they make perceptible what the law prescribing conduct expresses in more general terms; but examples can never justify our guiding ourselves by examples and setting aside their true origin which resides in reason.

[*The inadequacy of popular practical philosophy*]

If, then, there is no genuine supreme principle of morality that is not grounded on pure reason alone, independently of all experience, I think it should be unnecessary even to ask whether it is desirable to exhibit these concepts in general (abstractly) – these concepts which, together with their corresponding principles, hold a priori, in so far as knowledge which establishes this is to be distinguished from common knowledge and described as philosophical. But nowadays it may well be necessary to raise this question. For if we took a vote on which is to be preferred, pure rational knowledge detached from everything empirical – that is to say, a metaphysic of morals – or popular practical philosophy, we can easily guess on which side the majority would stand.

It is certainly most commendable to descend to the level of folk concepts once the ascent to the principles of pure reason has been satisfactorily completed. This ascent could be described as first *grounding* moral philosophy on metaphysics and subsequently, when moral philosophy has been established, winning *acceptance* for it by giving it a popular character. But it is utterly absurd to aim at popularity in our first investigation, on which the whole correctness of our principles depends. Not only can such a procedure never lay claim to the extremely rare merit of *truly philosophical popularity*, since it takes no skill to be generally understandable once one renounces all thorough probing: what that popularizing produces is a disgusting mishmash of second-hand observations and half-reasoned principles. Empty-headed people regale themselves with this, because it is something useful in everyday chitchat. More insightful people, on the other hand, are confused by it and avert their eyes, dissatisfied but not knowing how to help themselves. They turn away, but philosophers who see through this deception get little hearing if they urge those moralists to postpone this so-called popularizing for a while until the achievement of some definite insight earns them the right to be popular.

We need only look at essays on morality written in this fashionable style. What we run into is a marvellous medley – now the talk is of the particular vocation of human nature (but along with this also the Idea of a rational nature as such), now they talk of perfection, now of happiness, here moral feeling and there the fear of God; a little of this and a little of that. But it never occurs to anyone to ask whether the principles of morality are to be sought at all in our knowledge of human nature (which we can get only from experience); nor does it occur to them that if this is not so – if these principles are to be found completely a priori and free from empirical elements in concepts of pure reason and absolutely nowhere else, even to the slightest extent – they had better pursue the latter investigation altogether separately, as pure practical philosophy, or (if one may use a word so much vilified) as a metaphysics[3] of morals. They do not see that this investigation must be completed entirely by itself and that the public, which demands popularity, should be put off until the outcome of this undertaking is at hand.

Nevertheless, such a completely isolated metaphysics of morals, mixed with no anthropology, no theology, no physics or hyperphysics, still less with occult qualities (which one might call 'hypophysical'), is not only an indispensable underlying support for all theoretical and precisely defined knowledge of duties; it is also something to be desired and of the utmost importance for the actual fulfilment of moral precepts. For the pure thought of duty and of the moral law generally, unmixed with any additional empirical inducements, has an influence on the human heart much more powerful than all other motivations[4] that may arise from the field of experience, so much so that reason, conscious of its own dignity, despises these and is able gradually to become their master. The thought of duty and the moral law has this influence through reason alone (and reason first learns from this that by itself it is able to be practical [as well as theoretical]). A mixed moral theory, on the other hand, compounded of motives derived from feeling or inclination and also of rational concepts, must make the mind vacillate between [different] sources of motivation that cannot be brought under any single principle and that can guide us only by sheer accident to the good, and often to the evil.

[*Conclusions about method in basic moral philosophy*]

From what has been said, it is clear that all moral concepts have their seat and origin in reason completely a priori, and this is just as true of the most ordinary human intellect as of the most highly theoretical. Moral principles cannot be abstracted from any empirical, and therefore merely contingent, cognition. Their worthiness to serve as supreme practical principles lies precisely in this purity of their origin. Everything empirical added to them subtracts just that much from their genuine influence and from the unqualified worth of the corresponding actions. It is of the utmost necessity – and not only from a cognitive point of view, where our concern is exclusively with theory, but it is also of the utmost importance for action, that we derive these concepts and laws from pure reason, enunciating them pure and unmixed, and indeed determine the scope of this whole practical but pure sphere of rational cognition – that is, of this whole faculty of pure practical reason. But in doing this, we must not make its principles depend on the particular nature of human reason – as speculative philosophy allows and even at times requires. Since moral laws must hold for every rational being as such, our principles must instead be derived from the universal concept of a rational being as such. In this way the whole of ethics, which does require anthropology for its *application* to human beings, should at first be expounded independently of this and fully, as pure philosophy, that is, as metaphysics (which is quite possible to do in a totally separate branch of knowledge such as this). We are well aware that without possessing such a metaphysics it is not only futile to try to determine precisely, for purposes of speculative judgement, the moral element of duty in all actions which

accord with duty; it is impossible to establish morality on genuine principles even for merely ordinary practical purposes and particularly for moral instruction, if we lack such a metaphysics. Only in this way can we produce pure moral dispositions and engraft them onto the minds of human beings for the sake of the world's highest good.

In this study we must not go merely from common moral judgement (which is here worthy of great respect) to philosophical judgement, as has already been done, but advance by natural steps from a popular philosophy which goes no further than it can grope by means of examples, to metaphysics (which is not restricted by anything empirical, and – since it must survey the totality of this kind of rational knowledge – extends itself even to Ideas, where examples themselves forsake us). We must pursue and portray in detail the faculty of practical reason, from its general ordinances right up to the point where the concept of duty arises from it.

[*Practical reason, imperfect wills, and the idea of imperatives*]

Everything in nature works in accordance with laws. Only a rational being has the power to act in accordance with the idea of laws – that is, in accordance with principles – and thus has a will. Since reason is required if we are to derive actions from laws, the will is nothing else than practical reason. If reason were inevitably to determine the will, then, in a being of this kind, actions which are recognized as objectively necessary would also be subjectively necessary – that is to say, the will would be a power to choose only that which reason independently of inclination recognizes to be practically necessary, that is, sees to be good. But if reason by itself alone is not sufficient to determine the will; if the will is exposed also to subjective conditions (certain incentives) which do not always harmonize with the objective ones; if, in a word, (as is actually the case with human beings) the will is not of itself completely in accord with reason; then actions which are recognized to be objectively necessary are subjectively contingent, and the determining of such a will in accordance with objective laws is constraint; that is, the relation between objective laws and an incompletely good will can be represented as the determining of a rational being's will by principles that are indeed principles of reason, but principles to which this will by its own nature is not necessarily obedient.

The idea of an objective principle, in so far as it constrains a will, is called a commandment (of reason), and the formulation of this commandment is a called an Imperative.

[Types of imperative]

All imperatives are expressed by a 'must'. Thereby they mark a constraint, that is to say, the relation of an objective law of reason to a will that in its subjective constitution is not necessarily determined by this law. Imperatives say that something would be good to do or to leave undone; but they say this to a will that does not always do something simply because it has been informed that it is a good thing to do. Practical good however is something that determines the will by means of what reason presents to it, and therefore not by means of subjective causes but objectively – that is, by reasons that are valid for every rational being as such. The practical good is distinguished from the pleasant, which influences the will solely through the medium of sensation as a result of purely subjective causes, effective only for the senses of this person or that, not as a principle of reason valid for everyone.[5]

A perfectly good will would thus be just as much subject to objective laws (laws of the Good), but it could not for that reason be thought to be constrained to act lawfully, since by its own subjective constitution, it can be moved only by the concept of the Good. Hence no imperatives hold for the divine will or, more generally, for a holy will. The "must" is here out of place, because the "willing" is already of itself necessarily in agreement with the law. For this reason imperatives are only formulas for expressing the relation of objective laws of willing in general to the subjective imperfection of the will of this or that rational being – for example, the human will.

All imperatives command either hypothetically or categorically. Hypothetical imperatives declare a possible action to be practically necessary as a means to the attainment of something else that one wants (or that one may want). A categorical imperative would be one that represented an action as itself objectively necessary, without regard to any further end.

Since every practical law presents a possible action as good and therefore as necessary for a subject whose actions are determined by reason, all imperatives are therefore formulae for determining an action which is necessary according to the principle of a will in some way good. If the action would be good only as a means to something else, the imperative is hypothetical; if the action is thought of as good in itself and therefore as necessary for a will which of itself conforms to reason as its principle, then the imperative is categorical.

An imperative therefore states which of my possible actions would be good. The imperative formulates a practical rule for a will that does not perform an action immediately just because that action is good, partly because the subject does not always know that a good action is good, partly because, even if he did know this, his maxims might still be contrary to the objective principles of practical reason.

A hypothetical imperative thus says only that an action is good for some purpose or other, either possible or actual. In the first case it is a problematic practical principle; in the second case an assertoric practical principle. A categorical imperative, which declares an action to be objectively necessary of itself without reference to any purpose – that is, even without any further end – ranks as an apodictic practical principle.

What is possible only through the powers of some rational being can also be thought of as a possible purpose of some will. Consequently, if we think of principles of action as stating what is necessary in order to achieve some possible purpose, there are in fact infinitely many principles of action. All sciences have a practical part consisting of projects, which suppose that some end is possible for us, and imperatives, which tell us how that end is to be reached. These imperatives can in general be called imperatives of *skill*. Here there is no question at all as to whether the end is reasonable and good, but only about what one would have to do to attain it. The prescriptions required by a doctor in order to cure a patient and those that a poisoner needs in order to bring about certain death are of equal value so far as each will accomplish its purpose perfectly. Since young people do not know what ends may occur to them in the course of life, parents try to make their children learn *many kinds* of things. They try carefully to teach *skill* in the use of means to *various* desired ends, not knowing with certainty which possible end may in the future become an actual goal adopted by their pupil. Their anxiety in this matter is so great that they commonly neglect to form and correct their children's judgements about the worth of things that they might possibly adopt as ends.

There is, however, *one* end that we may pre-suppose as actual in all rational beings (so far as they are dependent beings to whom imperatives apply); and thus there is one aim which they not only *might* have, but which we can assume with certainty that they all *do* have by a necessity of nature and that aim is *perfect happiness*. The hypothetical imperative which affirms the prac-tical necessity of an action as a means to the promotion of perfect happiness is an assertoric imperative. We must not characterize it as neces-sary merely for some uncertain, merely possible purpose, but as necessary for a purpose that we can presuppose a priori and with certainty to be present in everyone because it belongs to the essence of human beings. Now we can call skill in the choice of the means to one's own greatest well-being "prudence"[6] in the narrowest sense of the word. So the imperative concerning the choice of means to one's own happiness – that is, the precept of prudence – still remains hypo-thetical; the action is commanded not absolutely but only as a means to a further end.

Finally, there is one imperative which com-mands a certain line of conduct directly, without assuming or being conditional on any further goal to be reached by that conduct. This imper-ative is categorical. It is concerned not with the material of the action and its anticipated result, but with its form and with the principle from which the action itself results. And what is essen-tially good in the action consists in the [agent's] disposition, whatever the result may be. This imperative may be called the imperative of morality.

Volition in accordance with these three kinds of principles is also sharply distinguished by the dissimilarity in how they constrain the will. To make this dissimilarity obvious, I think we would name them most appropriately if we called them rules of skill, counsels of prudence, or com-mandments (laws) of morality, respectively. For only law carries with it the concept of necessity, an unconditional and objective and therefore universally valid necessity; and commandments are laws that must be obeyed, even against in-clination. Counsels do indeed involve necessity, but a necessity valid only under a subjective and contingent condition – namely, depending on whether this or that human being counts this or that as essential to his happiness. As against this, a categorical imperative is limited by no condi-tion and can actually be called a commandment in the strict sense, being absolutely, although practically, necessary. We could also call imper-atives of the first kind technical (concerned with art), imperatives of the second kind pragmatic[7] (concerned with well-being), and imperatives of the third kind moral (concerned with free conduct as such – that is, with morals).

[How are hypothetical imperatives possible?]

The question now arises 'How are all these imperatives possible?' This question does not ask how an action commanded by the imperative can be performed, but merely how we can understand the constraining of the will, which imperatives express in setting us a task. How an imperative of skill is possible requires no special discussion. Whoever wills the end also wills (so far as reason has decisive influence on his actions) the means which are indispensably necessary and in his power. This proposition is analytic as far as willing is concerned. For when I will an object as an effect of my action I already conceive of my causality as an acting cause – that is, the use of means is included in the concept of the end; and the imperative merely extracts the concept of actions necessary to this end from the concept of willing an end. (Of course synthetic propositions are required in determining the means to a proposed end, but these propositions are concerned, not with the ground, the act of will, but with how to actualize the object.) Mathematics teaches, and certainly by synthetic propositions alone, that in order to bisect a line according to a reliable principle I must make two intersecting arcs from each of its extremities. But if I know that the aforesaid effect can be produced only by such an action, then the proposition 'If I fully will the effect, I must also will the action required to produce it' is analytic. For it is one and the same thing to think of something as an effect that is in a certain way possible through me and to think of myself as acting in this same way.

If it were only that easy to provide a definite concept of perfect happiness the imperatives of prudence would coincide entirely with those of skill and would be equally analytic. For then it could be said in this case as in the former case, 'Whoever wills the end, also (necessarily, according to reason) wills the sole means which are in his power.' Unfortunately, however, the concept of perfect happiness is such a vague concept that although everyone wants it, they can never say definitely and self-consistently what it really is that they wish and will. The reason for this is that all the elements that belong to the concept of happiness are empirical – that is, they must be borrowed from experience; but the Idea of perfect happiness requires an absolute whole, a maximum, of well-being in my present and in every future state. Now it is impossible for even the most insightful and most capable but finite being to form here a definite concept of what he really wants. Is it riches that he wants? How much anxiety, envy, and intrigue might he not bring on his own head in this way! Is it knowledge and insight? This might just give him an eye even sharper in seeing evils at present hidden from him and yet unavoidable, making those evils all the more frightful, or it might add a load of still further needs to the desires which already give him trouble enough. Is it long life? Who will guarantee that it would not be a life of long misery? Is it at least health? How often has not physical infirmity kept someone from excesses into which perfect health would have let him fall! – and so on. In short, he has no principle by which he is able to decide with complete certainty what would make him truly happy, since for this he would require omniscience. Thus we cannot act on definite principles in order to be happy, but only on empirical counsels, for example, of diet, frugality, politeness, reserve, and so on – things which experience shows contribute most to well-being on the average. Hence the imperatives of prudence, strictly speaking, do not command at all – that is, they cannot exhibit actions objectively as practically necessary. They should be taken as pieces of advice (consilia), rather than as commandments (praecepta), of reason. The problem of determining certainly and universally what action will promote the perfect happiness of a rational being is completely insoluble; and consequently in regard to this there is no imperative possible which in the strictest sense could command us to do what will make us happy, since perfect happiness is an ideal, not of reason, but of imagination – an ideal resting merely on empirical grounds, of which it is vain to expect that they should determine an action by which we could attain the totality of a series of consequences which is in fact infinite. Nevertheless, if we were to assume that the means to happiness could be discovered with certainty, this imperative of prudence would be an analytic practical proposition; for it differs from the imperative of skill only in this – that in the latter the end is merely possible, while in the former the end is given. In spite of this difference, since both command solely the means to something assumed to be willed as an end, the imperative that commands him who wills the end to will the means is in both cases analytic. Thus, the possibility of an imperative of prudence also poses no difficulty.

[How is a categorical imperative possible?]

By contrast, 'How is the imperative of morality possible?' is beyond all doubt the one question in need of solution. For the moral imperative is in no way hypothetical, and consequently the objective necessity, which it affirms, cannot be supported by any presupposition, as was the case with hypothetical imperatives. But we must never forget that it is impossible to settle by any example, i.e., empirically, whether there is any imperative of this kind at all; we should rather worry that all imperatives that seem to be categorical may yet be hypothetical in some hidden way. For example, when it is said, 'You must abstain from making deceitful promises,' one assumes that the necessity for this abstention is not mere advice so as to avoid some further evil – as though the meaning of what was said was, You ought not to make a deceitful promise lest, when it comes to light, you destroy your credit. On the contrary, an action of this kind would have to be considered as bad in itself, and the imperative of the prohibition would be therefore categorical. Even so, no example can show with certainty that the will would be determined here solely by the law without any further motivation, although it may appear to be so; for it is always possible that fear of disgrace, perhaps also hidden dread of other risks, may unconsciously influence the will. Who can prove by experience the non-existence of a cause? For experience shows only that we do not perceive it. In such a case, however, the so-called moral imperative, which as such appears to be categorical and unconditional, would in fact be only a pragmatic prescription calling attention to our own advantage and merely instructing us to take this into account.

We shall thus have to investigate entirely a priori the possibility of a categorical imperative, since here we do not enjoy the advantage of having its reality given in experience so that the discussion of its possibility would be needed merely to explain, and not to establish it. However, we can see the following at least provisionally: that the categorical imperative alone purports to be a practical law, while all the rest may be called principles of the will but not laws; for an action that is necessary merely to achieve some arbitrary purpose can be considered as in itself contingent, and we can always escape from the prescription if we abandon the purpose; whereas an unconditional commandment does not leave it open to the will to do the opposite at its discretion and therefore alone carries with it that necessity which we demand from a law.

In the second place, with this categorical imperative or law of morality the reason for our difficulty (in comprehending its possibility) is a very serious one. We have here a synthetic a priori practical proposition;[8] and since in theoretical knowledge there is so much difficulty in comprehending the possibility of propositions of this kind, we may well assume that the difficulty will be no less in the practical sphere.

[*The universal law formulation of the categorical imperative and its derivation*]

The first part of our task is to see whether perhaps the mere concept of a categorical imperative might also give us the formula containing the only proposition that can be a categorical imperative. Showing how such an absolute commandment is possible will still require special and difficult effort, even when we know what the commandment asserts. But we postpone this to the last section.

If I think of a *hypothetical* imperative as such, I do not know beforehand what it will contain – not until I am given its condition. But if I think of a *categorical imperative*, I know right away what it contains. For since this imperative contains, besides the law, only the necessity that the maxim[9] conform to this law, while the law, as we have seen, contains no condition limiting it, there is nothing left over to which the maxim of action should conform except the universality of a law as such; and it is only this conformity that the imperative asserts to be necessary.

There is therefore only one categorical imperative and it is this: 'Act only on that maxim by which you can at the same time will that it should become a universal law.'

Now if all imperatives of duty can be derived from this one imperative as their principle, then even though we leave it unsettled whether what we call duty is or is not an empty concept, we shall still be able to indicate at least what we understand by it and what the concept means.

[*A variation: the universal law of nature formulation*]

Because the universality of law according to which effects occur constitutes what is properly called nature in its most general sense (nature as regards its form) – that is, the existence of things so far as this is determined by universal laws – the universal imperative of duty could also be formulated as follows: 'Act as though the maxim of your action were to become by your will a universal law of nature.'

[*Four examples*]

We shall now enumerate some duties, dividing them in the usual way into duties towards ourselves and duties towards others and into perfect and imperfect duties.[10]

1. A man feels sick of life as the result of a mounting series of misfortunes that has reduced him to hopelessness, but he still possesses enough of his reason to ask himself whether it

would not be contrary to his duty to himself to take his own life. Now he tests whether the maxim of his action could really become a universal law of nature. His maxim, however, is: 'I make it my principle out of self-love to shorten my life if its continuance threatens more evil than it promises advantage.' The only further question is whether this principle of self-love can become a universal law of nature. But one sees at once that a nature whose law was that the very same feeling meant to promote life should actually destroy life would contradict itself, and hence would not endure as nature. The maxim therefore could not possibly be a general law of nature and thus it wholly contradicts the supreme principle of all duty.

2.   Another finds himself driven by need to borrow money. He knows very well that he will not be able to pay it back, but he sees too that nobody will lend him anything unless he firmly promises to pay it back within a fixed time. He wants to make such a promise, but he still has enough conscience to ask himself, 'Isn't it impermissible and contrary to duty to get out of one's difficulties this way?' Suppose, however, that he did decide to do it. The maxim of his action would run thus: 'When I believe myself short of money, I will borrow money and promise to pay it back, even though I know that this will never be done.' Now this principle of self-love or personal advantage is perhaps quite compatible with my own entire future welfare; only there remains the question 'Is it right?' I therefore transform the unfair demand of self-love into a universal law and frame my question thus: 'How would things stand if my maxim became a universal law?' I then see immediately that this maxim can never qualify as a self-consistent universal law of nature, but must necessarily contradict itself. For the universality of a law that permits anyone who believes himself to be in need to make any promise he pleases with the intention of not keeping it would make promising, and the very purpose one has in promising, itself impossible. For no one would believe he was being promised anything, but would laugh at any such utterance as hollow pretence.

3.   A third finds in himself a talent that, with a certain amount of cultivation, could make him a useful man for all sorts of purposes. But he sees himself in comfortable circumstances, and he prefers to give himself up to pleasure rather than to bother about increasing and improving his fortunate natural aptitudes. Yet he asks himself further 'Does my maxim of neglecting my natural gifts, besides agreeing with my taste for amusement, agree also with what is called duty?' He then sees that a nature could indeed endure under such a universal law, even if (like the South Sea Islanders) every man should let his talents rust and should be bent on devoting his life solely to idleness, amusement, procreation – in a word, to enjoyment. Only he cannot possibly *will* that this should become a universal law of nature or should be implanted in us as such a law by a natural instinct. For as a rational being he necessarily wills that all his powers should be developed, since they are after all useful to him and given to him for all sorts of possible purposes.

4.   A fourth man, who is himself flourishing but sees others who have to struggle with great hardships (and whom he could easily help) thinks to himself: 'What do I care? Let every one be as happy as Heaven intends or as he can make himself; I won't deprive him of anything; I won't even envy him; but I don't feel like contributing anything to his well-being or to helping him in his distress!' Now admittedly if such an attitude were a universal law of nature, the human race could survive perfectly well and doubtless even better than when everybody chatters about sympathy and good will, and even makes an effort, now and then, to practise them, but, when one can get away with it, swindles, traffics in human rights, or violates them in other ways. But although it is possible that a universal law of nature in accord with this maxim could exist, it is impossible to *will* that such a principle should hold everywhere as a law of nature. For a will that intended this would be in conflict with itself, since many situations might arise in which the man needs love and sympathy from others, and in which, by such a law of nature generated by his own will, he would rob himself of all hope of the help he wants.

[*The two kinds of maxims that fail the test*]

These are some of the many actual duties – or at least of what we take to be actual – whose derivation from the single principle cited above is perspicuous. We must be able to will that a maxim of our action should become a universal law – this is the authoritative model for moral judging of action generally. Some actions are so constituted that we cannot even *conceive* without contradiction that their maxim be a universal law of nature, let alone that we could *will* that it *ought* to become one. In the case of other actions, we do not find this inner impossibility, but it is still impossible to *will* that their maxim should be raised to the universality of a law of nature, because such a will would contradict itself. We see readily that the first kind of action is opposed to strict or narrow duty, the second opposed only to wide (meritorious) duty; Thus all duties – so far as the type of obligation (not the object of its action) is concerned – are fully set out in these examples as dependent on our single principle.

[*The typical problem: making exceptions for ourselves*]

If we now look at ourselves whenever we transgress a duty, we find that we in fact do not intend that our maxim should become a universal law. For this is impossible for us. What we really intend is rather that its opposite should remain a law generally; we only take the liberty of making an *exception* to it, for ourselves or (of course just this once) to satisfy our inclination. Consequently if we weighed it all up from one and the same perspective – that of reason – we should find a contradiction in our own will, the contradiction that a certain principle should be objectively necessary as a universal law and yet subjectively should not hold universally but should admit of exceptions. But there is actually no contradiction here, since we are first considering our action from the perspective of a will wholly in accord with reason, and then considering exactly the same action from the point of view of a will affected by inclination. What we have is rather an opposition (antagonism) of inclination to the precept of reason whereby the universality of the principle (*universalitas*) is transformed into a mere generality (*generalitas*) in order that the practical principle of reason can meet the maxim halfway. This procedure, though unjustifiable in our own impartial judgement, proves nevertheless that we in fact recognize the validity of the categorical imperative and (with all respect to it) merely allow ourselves a few exceptions that are, as we pretend, unimportant and apparently forced upon us.

[*The proof still missing and why it must be a priori*]

We have thus at least shown this much – that if duty is a concept that is to have meaning and actual legislative authority for our actions, it can be expressed only in categorical imperatives and not at all in hypothetical ones. At the same time – and this is already a great deal – we have set forth clearly, and defined for every use, the content of the categorical imperative, which must contain the principle of all duty (if there is to be such a thing at all). But we are still not so far advanced as to prove a priori that there actually is an imperative of this kind – that there is a practical law which by itself commands absolutely and without any further motivation, and that it is our duty to follow this law.

If we really intend to arrive at this proof it is extremely important to remember that we should not let ourselves think for a moment that the reality of this principle can be derived from *the particular characteristics of human nature*. For duty has to be a practical, unconditional necessity of action; it must therefore hold for all rational beings (to whom alone an imperative can apply at all), and *only for that reason* a law that holds also for all human wills. Whatever, on the other hand, is derived from the special predisposition of humanity, from certain feelings and propensities, and even, if this were possible, from some special bent peculiar to human reason and not holding necessarily for the will of every rational being – all this can indeed supply a personal maxim, but not a law: it can give us a subjective principle – one on which we have a natural disposition and inclination to act – but not an objective principle on which we should be directed to act even though our every propensity, inclination, and natural bent were opposed to it. This is so much the case that the sublimity and inner dignity of the commandment is even more manifest in a duty, the fewer subjective causes there are for obeying it and the more there are against it, but without this weakening in the slightest the constraint exercised by the law or diminishing its validity.

Here we see philosophy placed in what is actually a precarious position, a position that is supposed to be firm though it is neither suspended from heaven nor supported by the earth. Here she must show her purity as the sustainer of her own laws – not as the herald of laws that some implanted sense or who knows what guardian-like nature has whispered to her. Such laws, though perhaps always better than nothing, can never furnish us with fundamental principles dictated by reason, principles whose origin must be completely a priori and, because of this, have commanding authority. Such fundamental principles expect nothing from human inclinations but everything from the supremacy of the law and the respect owed it. Without this they condemn human beings to self-contempt and inner disgust.

Everything empirical is thus not only wholly unfit to contribute to the principle of morality; it is highly damaging to the purity of moral practices themselves. For, in morality, the proper worth of an absolutely good will, a worth exalted above all price, lies precisely in the freedom of its principle of action from any influence by contingent reasons that only experience can provide. We cannot warn too strongly or too often against the slack, or indeed vulgar, attitude which searches among empirical motives and laws for the principle; for human reason in its weariness is glad to rest on this cushion, and in a dream of sweet illusions (which allow it to embrace a cloud instead of Juno) to substitute for morality a bastard patched up from limbs of very diverse parentage, looking like anything one wishes to see in it, only not resembling virtue to anyone who has once beheld her in her true form.[11]

Our question then is this: 'Is it a necessary law *for all rational beings* to judge their actions always in accordance with those maxims which they can themselves will that they should serve as universal laws?' If it is a necessary law, it must already be connected (entirely a priori) with the concept of the will of a rational being as such. But in order to discover this connection we must, however reluctantly, venture into metaphysics, although into a region of metaphysics different from that of speculative philosophy, namely, the metaphysics of morals. In a practical philosophy we are not concerned with assuming reasons for what happens, but with acknowledging laws for what ought to happen, even if it may never happen – that is, objective practical laws. And here we have no need to investigate the reasons why anything pleases or displeases, how the pleasure of mere sensation differs from taste, and whether the latter is distinct from general satisfaction of reason. We need not inquire on what the feelings of pleasure and displeasure are based, or how from these feelings there arise desires and inclinations; and how from these, with the co-operation of reason, there arise maxims. For all this belongs to empirical psychology, which would constitute the second part of the study of nature, if we regard the latter as the *philosophy of nature* to the extent to which it rests on *empirical laws*. Here, however, we are discussing objective practical laws, and consequently the relation of a will to itself insofar as it determines itself solely by reason. Everything related to the empirical then falls away of itself; for if *reason all by itself* determines conduct (and the possibility of this is what we now wish to investigate), it must necessarily do so a priori.

[*Objective and relative ends*]

We think of the will as a power of determining oneself to act *in conformity with the idea of certain laws*. And such a power can be found only in rational beings. Now, what serves the will as the objective ground of its self-determining is an *end*; and this end, if it is given by reason alone, must be equally valid for all rational beings. On the other hand, something that contains merely the ground of the possibility of an action, where the result of that action is the end, is called a *means*. The subjective ground of desiring is a *driving-spring*; the objective ground of willing is *a motivating reason*. Hence the difference between subjective ends, which depend on driving-springs, and objective ends, which depend on motivating reasons that are valid for every rational being. Practical principles are *formal* if they abstract from all subjective ends; they are *material*, on the other hand, if they are based on subjective ends and consequently on certain driving-springs. Those ends that a rational being at his own discretion sets for himself as *what he intends to accomplish* through his action (material ends) are in every case only relative; for what gives them worth is only their relation to some subject's particularly constituted faculty of desire. Such worth can therefore provide no universal principles, no principles valid and necessary for all rational beings and for every act of will – that is, it can provide no practical laws. Consequently all these relative ends are only the ground of hypothetical imperatives.

Suppose, however, there were something *whose existence in itself* had an absolute worth, something that, as an end *in itself*, could be a ground of definite laws. Then in it and in it alone, would the ground of a possible categorical imperative, that is, of a practical law, reside.

[*The humanity as an end formulation*]

Now, I say, a human being, and in general every rational being, *does exist* as an end in himself, *not merely as a means* to be used by this or that will as it pleases. In all his actions, whether they are directed to himself or to other rational beings, a human being must always be viewed *at the same time as an end*. All the objects of inclination have only a conditional worth; for if these inclinations and the needs based on them did not exist, their object would be worthless. But inclinations themselves, as sources of needs, are so far from having absolute value to make them desirable for their own sake that it must rather be the universal wish of every rational being to be wholly free of them. Thus the value of any object *that is to be acquired* by our action is always conditional. Beings whose existence depends not on our will but on nature still have only a relative value as means and are therefore called *things*, if they lack reason. Rational beings, on the other hand, are called *persons* because, their nature already marks them out as ends in themselves – that is, as something which ought not to be used *merely as a means* – and consequently imposes restrictions on all choice making (and is an object of respect). Persons, therefore, are not merely subjective ends whose existence as an effect of our actions has a value *for us*. They are *objective ends* – that is, things whose existence is in itself an end, and indeed an end such that no other end can be substituted for it, no end to which they should serve *merely* as a means. For if this were not so, there would be nothing at all having *absolute value* anywhere. But if all value were conditional,

and thus contingent, then no supreme principle could be found for reason at all.

If then there is to be a supreme practical principle and a categorical imperative for the human will, it must be such that it forms an objective principle of the will from the idea of something which is necessarily an end for everyone because *it is an end in itself*, a principle that can therefore serve as a universal practical law. The ground of this principle is: *Rational nature exists as an end in itself*. This is the way in which a human being necessarily conceives his own existence, and it is therefore a *subjective* principle of human actions. But it is also the way in which every other rational being conceives his existence, on the same rational ground which holds also for me;[12] hence it is at the same time an *objective* principle from which, since it is a supreme practical ground, it must be possible to derive all laws of the will. The practical imperative will therefore be the following: *Act in such a way that you treat humanity, whether in your own person or in any other person, always at the same time as an end, never merely as a means.* We will now see whether this can be carried out in practice.

[*Examples*]

Let us keep to our previous examples.

First, as regards the concept of necessary duty to oneself, the man who contemplates suicide will ask himself whether his action could be compatible with the Idea of humanity as *an end in itself*. If he damages himself in order to escape from a painful situation, he is making use of a person *merely as a means* to maintain a tolerable state of affairs till the end of his life. But a human being is not a thing – not something to be used *merely* as a means: he must always in all his actions be regarded as an end in himself. Hence I cannot dispose of a human being in my own person, by maiming, corrupting, or killing him. (I must here forgo a more precise definition of this principle that would forestall any misunderstanding – for example, as to having limbs amputated to save myself or exposing my life to danger in order to preserve it, and so on – this discussion belongs to ethics proper.)

Secondly, as regards necessary or strict duty owed to others, the man who has in mind making a false promise to others will see at once that he is intending to make use of another person *merely as a means* to an end which that person does not share. For the person whom I seek to use for my own purposes by such a promise cannot possibly agree with my way of treating him, and so cannot himself share the end of the action. This incompatibility with the principle of duty to others can be seen more distinctly when we bring in examples of attacks on the freedom and property of others. For then it is manifest that a violator of the rights of human beings intends to use the person of others merely as a means without taking into consideration that, as rational beings, they must always at the same time be valued as ends – that is, treated only as beings who must themselves be able to share in the end of the very same action.[13]

Thirdly, as regards contingent (meritorious) duty to oneself, it is not enough that an action not conflict with humanity in our own person as an end in itself: it must also *harmonize with this end*. Now there are in humanity capacities for greater perfection that form part of nature's purpose for humanity in our own person. To neglect these can perhaps be compatible with the *survival* of humanity as an end in itself, but not with the *promotion* of that end.

Fourthly, as regards meritorious duties to others, the natural end that all human beings seek is their own perfect happiness. Now the human race might indeed exist if everybody contributed nothing to the happiness of others but at the same time refrained from deliberately impairing it. This harmonizing with humanity *as an end in itself* would, however, be merely negative and not positive, unless everyone also endeavours, as far as he can, to further the ends of others. For the ends of any person who is an end in himself must, if this idea is to have its full effect in me, be also, as far as possible, *my* ends.

[*The autonomy formulation*]

This principle of humanity, and in general of every rational agent, *as an end in itself* (a principle which is the supreme limiting condition on every person's freedom of action) is not borrowed from experience: first, because it is universal, applying to all rational beings generally, and no experience is sufficient to determine anything about all such beings; secondly, because in this principle we conceive of humanity not as an end that one happens to have (a subjective end) – that is, as an object which people, as a matter of fact, happen to make their end. We conceive of it rather as an objective end – one that, as a law, should constitute the supreme limiting condition on all subjective ends, whatever those ends may be. This principle must therefore spring from pure reason.

That is to say, the ground of every practical legislating lies *objectively in the rule* and in the form of universality that (according to our first principle) makes the rule fit to be a law (and possibly a law of nature); *subjectively*, however, the ground of practical legislating lies in the *end*. But, according to our second principle, the *subject* of all ends is every rational being as an end in itself. From this there follows our third practical principle of the will: the supreme condition of the will's harmony with universal practical reason is the Idea of *the will of every rational being as a will that legislates universal law*.

By this principle all maxims are rejected which are inconsistent with the will's own universal lawgiving. The will is therefore not merely subject to the law, but subject in such a way that it must be considered as also *giving the law to itself* and only for this reason as first of all subject to the law (of which it can regard itself as the author).

Imperatives as formulated above excluded from their legislative authority every admixture of interest as a motivation. They either commanded a conformity of actions to universal law, a conformity analogous to a *natural order*, or they asserted the prerogative of rational beings to be regarded universally as *supreme ends* in themselves. (This followed from the mere fact that these imperatives were conceived as categorical.) But the imperatives were only *assumed* to be categorical because we had to make this assumption if we wished to explain the concept of duty. That there were practical propositions that command categorically could not itself be proved, any more than it can be proved here in this chapter. But one thing might have been done – namely, to show that in willing something just out of duty the renunciation of all interest is the specific mark distinguishing a categorical from a hypothetical imperative. This is what we are doing in the present third formulation of the principle –

namely, in the Idea of the will of every rational being as *a will that legislates universal law*.

For once we think of a will of this kind, it becomes clear that while a will *that is subject to laws* may be bound to this law by some interest, a will that is itself a supreme lawgiver cannot possibly depend on any interest; for such a dependent will would itself require yet another law in order to restrict the interest of self-love by the condition that this interest must be valid as a universal law.

Thus the *principle* that every human will is *a will that enacts universal laws in all its maxims*[14] *would be well adapted* to be a categorical imperative, provided only that this principle is correct in other ways. Because of the Idea of giving universal law, it is *based on no interest*, and consequently, of all possible imperatives it alone can be *unconditional*. Or better still, let us take the converse of this proposition: if there is a categorical imperative (a law that applies to the will of every rational being), it can command us only to act always on the maxim of its will as one which could at the same time look upon itself as giving universal laws. For only then is the practical principle, and the imperative that the will obeys, unconditional, because the imperative cannot be based on any interest.

If we look back on all the previous efforts to discover the principle of morality, it is no wonder that they have all had to fail. One saw that human beings are bound to laws by their duty, but it never occurred to anyone that they are subject only to *laws which they themselves have given* but which are nevertheless *universal*, and that people are bound only to act in conformity with a will that is their own but that is, according to nature's purpose, a will that gives universal law. For when one thought of human beings merely as subject to a law (whatever it might be), the law had to carry with it some interest, as stimulus or compulsion to obedience, because it did not spring as law from their *own* will: in order to conform to the law, their will had to be compelled by *something else* to act in a certain way. But this strictly necessary consequence meant that all the labour spent in trying to find a supreme foundation for duty was irrevocably lost. For what one discovered was never duty, but only the necessity of acting from a certain interest. This interest might be one's own or another's. But the resulting imperative was bound to be always a conditional one and could not at all serve as a moral commandment. I therefore want to call my principle the principle of the *Autonomy* of the will in contrast with all others, which I therefore count as *Heteronomy*.

[*The kingdom of ends formulation*]

The concept of every rational being as a being who must regard itself as making universal law by all the maxims of its will, and must seek to judge itself and its actions from this standpoint, leads to a closely connected and very fruitful concept – namely, that of *a kingdom of ends*.

I understand by a 'kingdom' the systematic union of different rational beings under common laws. Now since laws determine ends as regards their universal validity, we can – if we abstract from the personal differences between rational beings, and also from the content of their private ends – conceive a whole of all ends systematically united (a whole composed of rational beings as ends in themselves and also of the personal ends which each may set for himself); that is, we can conceive of a kingdom of ends which is possible in accordance with the aforesaid principles.

For rational beings all stand under the *law* that each of them should treat himself and all others *never merely as a means* but always *at the same time as an end in himself*. But from this there arises a systematic union of rational beings through shared objective laws – that is, a kingdom. Since these laws aim precisely at the relation of such beings to one another as ends and means, this kingdom may be called a kingdom of ends (admittedly only an ideal).

A rational being, however, belongs to the kingdom of ends as a *member*, if, while legislating its universal laws, he is also subject to these laws. He belongs to the kingdom as its *head*, if, as legislating, he is not subject to the will of any other being.

A rational being must always regard himself as lawgiving in a kingdom of ends made possible through freedom of the will – whether as member or as head. But he cannot maintain the position of head merely through the maxim of his will, but only if he is a completely independent being, without needs and with an unlimited power adequate to his will.

Thus morality consists in the relation of all action to just that lawgiving through which a kingdom of ends is made possible. But this lawgiving must be found in every rational being itself and must be capable of arising from the will of that being. The principle of its will is therefore this: never to perform any action except one whose maxim could also be a universal law, and thus to act only on a maxim *through which the will could regard itself at the same time as enacting universal law*. If maxims are not already by their very nature in harmony with this objective principle of rational beings as legislating universal law, the necessity of acting on this principle is called a constraint on the choice of actions, i.e., *duty*. Duty does not apply to the head in a kingdom of ends, but it does apply to every member and to all of them in equal measure.

The practical necessity of acting on this principle – that is, duty – is not based at all on feelings, impulses, and inclinations, but only on the relation of rational beings to one another, a relation in which the will of a rational being must always be regarded as *lawgiving*, because otherwise it could not be thought of as *an end in itself*. Reason thus relates every maxim of a universally legislating will to every other will and also to every action towards oneself: it does so, not because of any further motive or future advantage, but from the Idea of the *dignity* of a rational being who obeys no law other than one which he himself also enacts.

[Dignity and price]

In the kingdom of ends everything has either a *price* or a *dignity*. Whatever has a price can be replaced by something else as *equivalent*. Whatever by contrast is exalted above all price and so admits of no equivalent has a dignity.

Whatever is relative to universal human inclinations and needs has a *market price*. Whatever, even without presupposing a need, accords with a certain taste – that is, with satisfaction in the mere random play of our mental powers – has an *attachment price*. But that which constitutes the sole condition under which anything can be an end in itself has not mere relative worth, i.e., a price, but an inner worth – i.e., *dignity*.

Now morality is the only condition under which a rational being can be an end in itself; for only through this is it possible to be a lawgiving member in the kingdom of ends. Therefore morality, and humanity so far as it is capable of morality, is the only thing that has dignity. Skill and diligence in work have a market price; wit, lively imagination, and humour have an attachment price but fidelity to promises and benevolence out of basic principles (not out of instinct) have an inner worth. Nature and art alike offer nothing that could replace their lack; for their worth consists not in the effects which result from them, not in the advantage of profit they produce, but in the intentions – that is, in the maxims of the will – which are ready in this way to reveal themselves in action even if they are not favoured by success. Such actions too need no recommendation from any subjective disposition or taste in order to be regarded with immediate favour and approval; they need no direct predilection or feeling for them. They exhibit as an object of immediate respect the will that performs them; since nothing but reason is required in order to *impose* them on the will. Nor is the will to be *coaxed* into them, which would anyhow be a contradiction in the case of duties. This assessment lets us recognize the value of such a mental attitude as dignity and puts it infinitely above all price, with which it cannot be brought into comparison or computation without, as it were, violating its holiness.

And what is it then that justifies a morally good disposition, or virtue, in making such lofty claims? It is nothing less than the *sharing* which it allows to a rational being in *giving universal laws*, which therefore renders him fit to be a member in a possible kingdom of ends. His own nature as an end in himself already marked out this fitness and therefore his status as lawgiver in a kingdom of ends and as free from all laws of nature, obedient only to those laws which he himself prescribes, laws according to which his maxims can participate in the making of universal law (to which he at the same time subjects himself). For nothing can have worth other than that determined for it by the law. But the lawgiving that determines all worth must therefore have a dignity, i.e., an unconditional and incomparable worth. The word 'respect' is the only suitable expression for the esteem that a rational being must necessarily feel for such lawgiving. *Autonomy* is thus the basis of the dignity of human nature and of every rational nature.

Notes

1 A *maxim* is the subjective principle of volition: an objective principle (that is, one which would also serve subjectively as a practical principle for all rational beings if reason had full control over the faculty of desire) is a practical *law*.

2 It might be objected that instead of clearly resolving the question by means of a concept of reason I have tried to take refuge in an obscure feeling, under the cover of the word '*respect*' [*Achtung*]. However, though respect is a feeling, it is not a feeling that we are caused to *receive* by some (external) influence; rather, it is a feeling that is *self-generated* by a rational concept, and it is therefore different in kind from feelings of the first sort, all of which can be reduced to inclination or fear. What I recognize directly as a law for myself, I recognize with respect, which means nothing more than the consciousness of my will's *submission* to the law, without the mediation of any other influences on my mind. The direct determination of the will by the law, and the awareness of that determination, is called '*respect*', so we should see respect as the *effect* of the law on a person rather than as what *produces* the law. Actually, respect is the thought of something of such worth that it breaches my self-love. It is neither an object of inclination nor an object of fear, though it is somewhat analogous to both. The sole *object* of respect is the [moral] *law* – that law which we impose *on ourselves* and yet recognize as necessary in itself. As a law, we must submit to it without any consulting of self-love; as self-imposed it is nevertheless a consequence of our will. Considered in the first way, it is analogous to fear; considered in the second way, analogous to inclination. All respect for a person is actually only respect for the law (of righteousness, etc.) that that person exemplifies. Because we regard the development of our talents as a duty, we see a talented person also as a sort of *example of a law* (to strive to resemble that person), and this is what constitutes our respect. Any moral so-called *interest* consists solely in *respect* for the law.

3 We can, if we wish, distinguish pure moral philosophy (metaphysics) from applied (applied, that is, to human nature – just as pure mathematics is distinguished from applied mathematics and pure logic from applied logic). Using this terminology immediately reminds us that moral principles are not grounded on the peculiarities of human nature, but must be established a priori by themselves, though it must be possible to derive practical rules for human beings from them as well, just as it is for every kind of rational being.

4 I have a letter from the late, distinguished Professor Sulzer, in which he asks me why moral teachings are so ineffective, even though they contain much that is convincing to reason. My answer was delayed because I wanted it to be complete. Yet it is just this: the teachers themselves fail to make their concepts clear, and they overdo their job by looking for all sorts of inducements to moral goodness, spoiling their medicine altogether by their very attempt to make it really powerful. For the most ordinary observation shows that when a righteous act is represented as being done with a steadfast mind in complete disregard of any advantage in this world or another, and even under the greatest temptations of need or enticement, it far surpasses and eclipses any similar act that was affected even in the slightest by an extraneous incentive; it uplifts the soul and arouses the wish that we too could act in this way. Even children of moderate age feel this impression, and one should never present duties to them in any other way. [Editor's note: Johann Georg Sulzer (1720–79) was a prominent aesthetician and so-called 'popular philosopher', important in Berlin intellectual circles. The only extant letter from Sulzer to Kant does not in fact raise the particular question Kant here ascribes to him.]

5 The dependence of the faculty of desire on sensations is called an inclination, and thus an inclination always indicates a *need*. The dependence of a contingently determinable will on principles of reason is called an *interest*. Hence an interest is found only where there is a dependent will which of itself is not always in accord with reason; to God's will we cannot ascribe any interest. But even the human will can *take an interest* in something without therefore *acting out of interest*. The first expression signifies *practical* interest in the action; the second signifies *pathological* interest in the object of the action. The first indicates only dependence of the will on principles of reason in themselves; the second its dependence on principles of reason at the service of inclination – that is to say, where reason merely supplies a practical rule for meeting the needs of inclination. In the first case what interests me is the action; in the second case what interests me is the object of the action (so far as this object is pleasant to me). We have seen in [the first section] that in an action done out of duty one must consider not the interest in the object, but the interest in the action itself and its rational principle (namely, the law).

6 The word 'prudence' (*Klugheit*) is used in two senses; in one sense it can be called 'worldly wisdom' (*Weltklugheit*); in a second sense, 'personal

wisdom' (*Privatklugheit*). The first is a person's skill in influencing others in order to use them for his own ends. The second is the ability to combine all of these ends to his own lasting advantage. The latter is properly that to which the value of the former can itself be traced; and if a person is prudent in the first sense, but not in the second, we might better say that he is clever and astute, but on the whole imprudent.

7   It seems to me that the proper meaning of the word 'pragmatic' can be defined most accurately in this way. For *sanctions* that do not properly speaking spring from the law of states as necessary statutes, but arise from *provision* for the general welfare are called pragmatic. We say that a *history* is written pragmatically when it teaches *prudence* – that is, when it instructs the world how to provide for its interests better than, or at least as well as, the world of other times has done.

8   I connect the deed with the will a priori and thus necessarily, without supposing as a condition that there is any inclination for this deed (although I make this connection only objectively – that is to say, under the Idea of a power of reason that would have complete control over all subjective motives). Hence we have here a practical proposition in which the willing of an action is not derived analytically from some other volition already presupposed (for we do not possess any such perfect will); rather, the willing of the action is connected directly with the concept of the will of a rational being [but] as something that is not contained in this concept.

9   A *maxim* is a subjective principle of action and must be distinguished from an *objective principle* – namely, a practical law. The former contains a practical rule determined by reason in accordance with the conditions of the subject (often his ignorance or his inclinations); it is thus a principle on which the subject *acts*. A law, on the other hand, is an objective principle, valid for every rational being; and it is a principle on which he *ought to act* – that is, an imperative.

10   It should be noted that I reserve the division of duties entirely for a future *Metaphysic of Morals* and that my present division is put forward as an arbitrary one (merely for the purpose of arranging my examples). Further, I understand here by a perfect duty one that allows no exception in the interests of inclination, and so I recognize among *perfect duties*, both outer and inner duties. This runs contrary to the standard usage in the schools, but I do not intend to justify it here, since for my purpose it makes no difference whether this point is conceded or not.

11   To behold virtue in her true form means nothing other than to show morality stripped of any admixture with what is sensuous and of all the inauthentic adornments of reward or self-love. How much she then casts into the shade all else that appears enticing to the inclinations can be readily perceived by anyone willing to exert his reason in the slightest, if it is not entirely spoiled for all abstract thinking.

12   This proposition I put forward here as a postulate. [. . .]

13   Let no one think that the trivial '*quod tibi non vis fieri*, etc.' could here serve as a guide or principle. For it is merely a derivation from our principle, and subject to various qualifications: it cannot be a universal law since it contains the ground neither of duties to oneself nor of duties of kindness to others (for many a man would gladly consent that others should not benefit him if only he could be excused from showing benevolence to them). Nor, finally, does this rule contain the ground of strict duties owed to others; for the criminal would be able to argue on this basis against the judge who sentences him, and so on. [Ed. note: This refers to a negative version of the Golden Rule: Do not do to others what you do not want done to you.]

14   I may be excused from citing examples to illustrate this principle, since those that were already used to illustrate the categorical imperative and its formula can all serve the same purpose here.

24

What Makes Right Acts Right?

W. D. Ross

The real point at issue between hedonism and utilitarianism on the one hand and their opponents on the other is not whether 'right' means 'productive of so and so'; for it cannot with any plausibility be maintained that it does. The point at issue is that to which we now pass, viz. whether there is any general character which makes right acts right, and if so, what it is. Among the main historical attempts to state a single characteristic of all right actions which is the foundation of their rightness are those made by egoism and utilitarianism. But I do not propose to discuss these, not because the subject is unimportant, but because it has been dealt with so often and so well already, and because there has come to be so much agreement among moral philosophers that neither of these theories is satisfactory. A much more attractive theory has been put forward by Professor Moore: that what makes actions right is that they are productive of more *good* than could have been produced by any other action open to the agent.[1]

This theory is in fact the culmination of all the attempts to base rightness on productivity of some sort of result. The first form this attempt takes is the attempt to base rightness on conduciveness to the advantage or pleasure of the agent. This theory comes to grief over the fact, which stares us in the face, that a great part of duty consists in an observance of the rights and a furtherance of the interests of others, whatever the cost to ourselves may be. Plato and others may be right in holding that a regard for the rights of others never in the long run involves a loss of happiness for the agent, that 'the just life profits a man'. But this, even if true, is irrelevant to the rightness of the act. As soon as a man does an action *because* he thinks he will promote his own interests thereby, he is acting not from a sense of its rightness but from self-interest.

To the egoistic theory hedonistic utilitarianism supplies a much-needed amendment. It points out correctly that the fact that a certain pleasure will be enjoyed by the agent is no reason why he *ought* to bring it into being rather than an equal or greater pleasure to be enjoyed by another, though, human nature being what it is, it makes it not unlikely that he *will* try to bring it into being. But hedonistic utilitarianism in its turn needs a correction. On reflection it seems clear that pleasure is not the only thing in life that we think good in itself, that for instance we think the possession of a good character, or an intelligent understanding of the world, as good or better. A great advance is made by the substitution of 'productive of the greatest good' for 'productive of the greatest pleasure'.

W. D. Ross, "What Makes Right Acts Right?" from *The Right and the Good* (Indianapolis: Hackett Publishing, 1930), pp. 16–34, 39–41. © 1930 by Oxford University Press. Reprinted with permission from Oxford University Press.

Not only is this theory more attractive than hedonistic utilitarianism, but its logical relation to that theory is such that the latter could not be true unless *it* were true, while it might be true though hedonistic utilitarianism were not. It is in fact one of the logical bases of hedonistic utilitarianism. For the view that what produces the maximum pleasure is right has for its bases the views (1) that what produces the maximum good is right, and (2) that pleasure is the only thing good in itself. If they were not assuming that what produces the maximum *good* is right, the utilitarians' attempt to show that pleasure is the only thing good in itself, which is in fact the point they take most pains to establish, would have been quite irrelevant to their attempt to prove that only what produces the maximum *pleasure* is right. If, therefore, it can be shown that productivity of the maximum good is not what makes all right actions right, we shall *a fortiori* have refuted hedonistic utilitarianism.

When a plain man fulfils a promise because he thinks he ought to do so, it seems clear that he does so with no thought of its total consequences, still less with any opinion that these are likely to be the best possible. He thinks in fact much more of the past than of the future. What makes him think it right to act in a certain way is the fact that he has promised to do so – that and, usually, nothing more. That his act will produce the best possible consequences is not his reason for calling it right. What lends colour to the theory we are examining, then, is not the actions (which form probably a great majority of our actions) in which some such reflection as 'I have promised' is the only reason we give ourselves for thinking a certain action right, but the exceptional cases in which the consequences of fulfilling a promise (for instance) would be so disastrous to others that we judge it right not to do so. It must of course be admitted that such cases exist. If I have promised to meet a friend at a particular time for some trivial purpose, I should certainly think myself justified in breaking my engagement if by doing so I could prevent a serious accident or bring relief to the victims of one. And the supporters of the view we are examining hold that my thinking so is due to my thinking that I shall bring more good into existence by the one action than by the other. A different account may, however, be given of the matter, an account which will, I believe, show itself to be the true one. It may be said that besides the duty of fulfilling promises I have and recognize a duty of relieving distress,[2] and that when I think it right to do the latter at the cost of not doing the former, it is not because I think I shall produce more good thereby but because I think it the duty which is in the circumstances more of a duty. This account surely corresponds much more closely with what we really think in such a situation. If, so far as I can see, I could bring equal amounts of good into being by fulfilling my promise and by helping some one to whom I had made no promise, I should not hesitate to regard the former as my duty. Yet on the view that what is right is right because it is productive of the most good I should not so regard it.

There are two theories, each in its way simple, that offer a solution of such cases of conscience. One is the view of Kant, that there are certain duties of perfect obligation, such as those of fulfilling promises, of paying debts, of telling the truth, which admit of no exception whatever in favour of duties of imperfect obligation, such as that of relieving distress. The other is the view of, for instance, Professor Moore and Dr Rashdall, that there is only the duty of producing good, and that all 'conflicts of duties' should be resolved by asking 'by which action will most good be produced?' But it is more important that our theory fit the facts than that it be simple, and the account we have given above corresponds (it seems to me) better than either of the simpler theories with what we really think, viz. that normally promise-keeping, for example, should come before benevolence, but that when and only when the good to be produced by the benevolent act is very great and the promise comparatively trivial, the act of benevolence becomes our duty.

In fact the theory of 'ideal utilitarianism', if I may for brevity refer so to the theory of Professor Moore, seems to simplify unduly our relations to our fellows. It says, in effect, that the only morally significant relation in which my neighbours stand to me is that of being possible beneficiaries by my action.[3] They do stand in this relation to me, and this relation is morally significant. But they may also stand to me in the relation of promisee to promiser, of creditor to debtor, of wife to husband, of child to parent, of friend to friend, of fellow countryman to fellow countryman, and the like; and each of these relations is the foundation of a *prima facie* duty, which is more or less incumbent on me according to the circumstances of the case. When I am in a situation, as perhaps I always am, in which more than one of these *prima facie* duties is incumbent on me, what I have to do is to study the situation as fully as I can until I form the considered opinion (it is never more) that in the circumstances one of them is more incumbent than any other; then I am bound to think that to do this *prima facie* duty is my duty *sans phrase* in the situation.

I suggest '*prima facie* duty' or 'conditional duty' as a brief way of referring to the characteristic (quite distinct from that of being a duty proper) which an act has, in virtue of being of a certain kind (e.g. the keeping of a promise), of being an act which would be a duty proper if it were not at the same time of another kind which is morally significant. Whether an act is a duty proper or actual duty depends on *all* the morally significant kinds it is an instance of. The phrase '*prima facie* duty' must be apologized for, since (1) it suggests that what we are speaking of is a certain kind of duty, whereas it is in fact not a duty, but something related in a special way to duty. Strictly speaking, we want not a phrase in which duty is qualified by an adjective, but a separate noun. (2) '*Prima*' *facie* suggests that one is speaking only of an appearance which a moral situation presents at first sight, and which may turn out to be illusory; whereas what I am speaking of is an objective fact involved in the nature of the situation, or more strictly in an element of its nature, though not, as duty proper does, arising from its *whole* nature. I can, however, think of no term which fully meets the case. 'Claim' has been suggested by Professor Prichard. The word 'claim' has the advantage of being quite a familiar one in this connexion, and it seems to cover much of the ground. It would be quite natural to say, 'a person to whom I have made a promise has a claim on me', and also, 'a person whose distress I could relieve (at the cost of breaking the promise) has a claim on me'. But (1) while 'claim' is appropriate from *their* point of view, we want a word to express the corresponding fact from the agent's point of view – the fact of his being subject to claims that can be made against him; and ordinary language provides us with no

such correlative to 'claim'. And (2) (what is more important) 'claim' seems inevitably to suggest two persons, one of whom might make a claim on the other; and while this covers the ground of social duty, it is inappropriate in the case of that important part of duty which is the duty of cultivating a certain kind of character in oneself. It would be artificial, I think, and at any rate metaphorical, to say that one's character has a claim on oneself.

There is nothing arbitrary about these *prima facie* duties. Each rests on a definite circumstance which cannot seriously be held to be without moral significance. Of *prima facie* duties I suggest, without claiming completeness or finality for it, the following division.[4]

(1) Some duties rest on previous acts of my own. These duties seem to include two kinds, (*a*) those resting on a promise or what may fairly be called an implicit promise, such as the implicit undertaking not to tell lies which seems to be implied in the act of entering into conversation (at any rate by civilized men), or of writing books that purport to be history and not fiction. These may be called the duties of fidelity. (*b*) Those resting on a previous wrongful act. These may be called the duties of reparation. (2) Some rest on previous acts of other men, i.e. services done by them to me. These may be loosely described as the duties of gratitude. (3) Some rest on the fact or possibility of a distribution of pleasure or happiness (or of the means thereto) which is not in accordance with the merit of the persons concerned; in such cases there arises a duty to upset or prevent such a distribution. These are the duties of justice. (4) Some rest on the mere fact that there are other beings in the world whose condition we can make better in respect of virtue, or of intelligence, or of pleasure. These are the duties of beneficence. (5) Some rest on the fact that we can improve our own condition in respect of virtue or of intelligence. These are the duties of self-improvement. (6) I think that we should distinguish from (4) the duties that may be summed up under the title of 'not injuring others'. No doubt to injure others is incidentally to fail to do them good; but it seems to me clear that non-maleficence is apprehended as a duty distinct from that of beneficence, and as a duty of a more stringent character. It will be noticed that this alone among the types of duty has been

stated in a negative way. An attempt might no doubt be made to state this duty, like the others, in a positive way. It might be said that it is really the duty to prevent ourselves from acting either from an inclination to harm others or from an inclination to seek our own pleasure, in doing which we should incidentally harm them. But on reflection it seems clear that the primary duty here is the duty not to harm others, this being a duty whether or not we have an inclination that if followed would lead to our harming them; and that when we have such an inclination the primary duty not to harm others gives rise to a consequential duty to resist the inclination. The recognition of this duty of non-maleficence is the first step on the way to the recognition of the duty of beneficence; and that accounts for the prominence of the commands 'thou shalt not kill', 'thou shalt not commit adultery', 'thou shalt not steal', 'thou shalt not bear false witness', in so early a code as the Decalogue. But even when we have come to recognize the duty of beneficence, it appears to me that the duty of non-maleficence is recognized as a distinct one, and as *prima facie* more binding. We should not in general consider it justifiable to kill one person in order to keep another alive, or to steal from one in order to give alms to another.

The essential defect of the 'ideal utilitarian' theory is that it ignores, or at least does not do full justice to, the highly personal character of duty. If the only duty is to produce the maximum of good, the question who is to have the good – whether it is myself, or my benefactor, or a person to whom I have made a promise to confer that good on him, or a mere fellow man to whom I stand in no such special relation – should make no difference to my having a duty to produce that good. But we are all in fact sure that it makes a vast difference.

One or two other comments must be made on this provisional list of the divisions of duty. (1) The nomenclature is not strictly correct. For by 'fidelity' or 'gratitude' we mean, strictly, certain states of motivation; and, as I have urged, it is not our duty to have certain motives, but to do certain acts. By 'fidelity', for instance, is meant, strictly, the disposition to fulfil promises and implicit promises *because we have made them*. We have no general word to cover the actual fulfilment of promises and implicit promises

irrespective of motive; and I use 'fidelity', loosely but perhaps conveniently, to fill this gap. So too I use 'gratitude' for the returning of services, irrespective of motive. The term 'justice' is not so much confined, in ordinary usage, to a certain state of motivation, for we should often talk of a man as acting justly even when we did not think his motive was the wish to do what was just simply for the sake of doing so. Less apology is therefore needed for our use of 'justice' in this sense. And I have used the word 'beneficence' rather than 'benevolence', in order to emphasize the fact that it is our duty to do certain things, and not to do them from certain motives.

(2) If the objection be made, that this catalogue of the main types of duty is an unsystematic one resting on no logical principle, it may be replied, first, that it makes no claim to being ultimate. It is a *prima facie* classification of the duties which reflection on our moral convictions seems actually to reveal. And if these convictions are, as I would claim that they are, of the nature of knowledge, and if I have not misstated them, the list will be a list of authentic conditional duties, correct as far as it goes though not necessarily complete. The list of *goods* put forward by the rival theory is reached by exactly the same method – the only sound one in the circumstances – viz. that of direct reflection on what we really think. Loyalty to the facts is worth more than a symmetrical architectonic or a hastily reached simplicity. If further reflection discovers a perfect logical basis for this or for a better classification, so much the better.

(3) It may, again, be objected that our theory that there are these various and often conflicting types of *prima facie* duty leaves us with no principle upon which to discern what is our actual duty in particular circumstances. But this objection is not one which the rival theory is in a position to bring forward. For when we have to choose between the production of two heterogeneous goods, say knowledge and pleasure, the 'ideal utilitarian' theory can only fall back on an opinion, for which no logical basis can be offered, that one of the goods is the greater; and this is no better than a similar opinion that one of two duties is the more urgent. And again, when we consider the infinite variety of the effects of our actions in the way of pleasure, it must surely be admitted that the claim which *hedonism* sometimes makes,

that it offers a readily applicable criterion of right conduct, is quite illusory.

I am unwilling, however, to content myself with an *argumentum ad hominem*, and I would contend that in principle there is no reason to anticipate that every act that is our duty is so for one and the same reason. Why should two sets of circumstances, or one set of circumstances, *not* possess different characteristics, any one of which makes a certain act our *prima facie* duty? When I ask what it is that makes me in certain cases sure that I have a *prima facie* duty to do so and so, I find that it lies in the fact that I have made a promise; when I ask the same question in another case, I find the answer lies in the fact that I have done a wrong. And if on reflection I find (as I think I do) that neither of these reasons is reducible to the other, I must not on any *a priori* ground assume that such a reduction is possible.

An attempt may be made to arrange in a more systematic way the main types of duty which we have indicated. In the first place it seems self-evident that if there are things that are intrinsically good, it is *prima facie* a duty to bring them into existence rather than not to do so, and to bring as much of them into existence as possible. It will be argued in our fifth chapter that there are three main things that are intrinsically good – virtue, knowledge, and, with certain limitations, pleasure. And since a given virtuous disposition, for instance, is equally good whether it is realized in myself or in another, it seems to be my duty to bring it into existence whether in myself or in another. So too with a given piece of knowledge.

The case of pleasure is difficult; for while we clearly recognize a duty to produce pleasure for others, it is by no means so clear that we recognize a duty to produce pleasure for ourselves. This appears to arise from the following facts. The thought of an act as our duty is one that presupposes a certain amount of reflection about the act; and for that reason does not normally arise in connexion with acts towards which we are already impelled by another strong impulse. So far, the cause of our not thinking of the promotion of our own pleasure as a duty is analogous to the cause which usually prevents a highly sympathetic person from thinking of the promotion of the pleasure of others as a duty. He

is impelled so strongly by direct interest in the well-being of others towards promoting their pleasure that he does not stop to ask whether it is his duty to promote it; and we are all impelled so strongly towards the promotion of our own pleasure that we do not stop to ask whether it is a duty or not. But there is a further reason why even when we stop to think about the matter it does not usually present itself as a duty: viz. that, since the performance of most of our duties involves the giving up of some pleasure that we desire, the doing of duty and the getting of pleasure for ourselves come by a natural association of ideas to be thought of as incompatible things. This association of ideas is in the main salutary in its operation, since it puts a check on what but for it would be much too strong, the tendency to pursue one's own pleasure without thought of other considerations. Yet if pleasure is good, it seems in the long run clear that it is right to get it for ourselves as well as to produce it for others, when this does not involve the failure to discharge some more stringent *prima facie* duty. The question is a very difficult one, but it seems that this conclusion can be denied only on one or other of three grounds: (1) that pleasure is not *prima facie* good (i.e. good when it is neither the actualization of a bad disposition nor undeserved), (2) that there is no *prima facie* duty to produce as much that is good as we can, or (3) that though there is a *prima facie* duty to produce other things that are good, there is no *prima facie* duty to produce pleasure which will be enjoyed by ourselves. I give reasons later for not accepting the first contention. The second hardly admits of argument but seems to me plainly false. The third seems plausible only if we hold that an act that is pleasant or brings pleasure to ourselves must for that reason not be a duty; and this would lead to paradoxical consequences, such as that if a man enjoys giving pleasure to others or working for their moral improvement, it cannot be his duty to do so. Yet it seems to be a very stubborn fact, that in our ordinary consciousness we are not aware of a duty to get pleasure for ourselves; and by way of partial explanation of this I may add that though, as I think, one's own pleasure is a good and there is a duty to produce it, it is only if we *think* of our own pleasure not as simply our own pleasure, but as an objective good, something that an impartial spectator would approve, that we can think of the getting it as a duty; and we do not habitually think of it in this way.

If these contentions are right, what we have called the duty of beneficence and the duty of self-improvement rest on the same ground. No different principles of duty are involved in the two cases. If we feel a special responsibility for improving our own character rather than that of others, it is not because a special principle is involved, but because we are aware that the one is more under our control than the other. It was on this ground that Kant expressed the practical law of duty in the form 'seek to make yourself good and other people happy'. He was so persuaded of the internality of virtue that he regarded any attempt by one person to produce virtue in another as bound to produce, at most, only a counterfeit of virtue, the doing of externally right acts not from the true principle of virtuous action but out of regard to another person. It must be admitted that one man cannot compel another to be virtuous; compulsory virtue would just not be virtue. But experience clearly shows that Kant overshoots the mark when he contends that one man cannot do anything to *promote* virtue in another, to bring such influences to bear upon him that his own response to them is more likely to be virtuous than his response to other influences would have been. And our duty to do this is not different in kind from our duty to improve our own characters.

It is equally clear, and clear at an earlier stage of moral development, that if there are things that are bad in themselves we ought, *prima facie*, not to bring them upon others; and on this fact rests the duty of non-maleficence.

The duty of justice is particularly complicated, and the word is used to cover things which are really very different – things such as the payment of debts, the reparation of injuries done by oneself to another, and the bringing about of a distribution of happiness between other people in proportion to merit. I use the word to denote only the last of these three. In the fifth chapter I shall try to show that besides the three (comparatively) simple goods, virtue, knowledge, and pleasure, there is a more complex good, not reducible to these, consisting in the proportionment of happiness to virtue. The bringing of this about is a duty which we owe to all men

alike, though it may be reinforced by special responsibilities that we have undertaken to particular men. This, therefore, with beneficence and self-improvement, comes under the general principle that we should produce as much good as possible, though the good here involved is different in kind from any other.

But besides this general obligation, there are special obligations. These may arise, in the first place, incidentally, from acts which were not essentially meant to create such an obligation, but which nevertheless create it. From the nature of the case such acts may be of two kinds – the infliction of injuries on others, and the acceptance of benefits from them. It seems clear that these put us under a special obligation to other men, and that only these acts can do so incidentally. From these arise the twin duties of reparation and gratitude.

And finally there are special obligations arising from acts the very intention of which, when they were done, was to put us under such an obligation. The name for such acts is 'promises'; the name is wide enough if we are willing to include under it implicit promises, i.e. modes of behaviour in which without explicit verbal promise we intentionally create an expectation that we can be counted on to behave in a certain way in the interest of another person.

These seem to be, in principle, all the ways in which *prima facie* duties arise. In actual experience they are compounded together in highly complex ways. Thus, for example, the duty of obeying the laws of one's country arises partly (as Socrates contends in the *Crito*) from the duty of gratitude for the benefits one has received from it; partly from the implicit promise to obey which seems to be involved in permanent residence in a country whose laws we know we are *expected* to obey, and still more clearly involved when we ourselves invoke the protection of its laws (this is the truth underlying the doctrine of the social contract); and partly (if we are fortunate in our country) from the fact that its laws are potent instruments for the general good.

Or again, the sense of a general obligation to bring about (so far as we can) a just apportionment of happiness to merit is often greatly reinforced by the fact that many of the existing injustices are due to a social and economic system which we have, not indeed created, but taken part in and assented to; the duty of justice is then reinforced by the duty of reparation.

It is necessary to say something by way of clearing up the relation between *prima facie* duties and the actual or absolute duty to do one particular act in particular circumstances. If, as almost all moralists except Kant are agreed, and as most plain men think, it is sometimes right to tell a lie or to break a promise, it must be maintained that there is a difference between *prima facie* duty and actual or absolute duty. When we think ourselves justified in breaking, and indeed morally obliged to break, a promise in order to relieve some one's distress, we do not for a moment cease to recognize a *prima facie* duty to keep our promise, and this leads us to feel, not indeed shame or repentance, but certainly compunction, for behaving as we do; we recognize, further, that it is our duty to make up somehow to the promisee for the breaking of the promise. We have to distinguish from the characteristic of being our duty that of tending to be our duty. Any act that we do contains various elements in virtue of which it falls under various categories. In virtue of being the breaking of a promise, for instance, it tends to be wrong; in virtue of being an instance of relieving distress it tends to be right. Tendency to be one's duty may be called a parti-resultant attribute, i.e. one which belongs to an act in virtue of some one component in its nature. *Being* one's duty is a toti-resultant attribute, one which belongs to an act in virtue of its whole nature and of nothing less than this.[5] [. . .]

Another instance of the same distinction may be found in the operation of natural laws. *Qua* subject to the force of gravitation towards some other body, each body tends to move in a particular direction with a particular velocity; but its actual movement depends on *all* the forces to which it is subject. It is only by recognizing this distinction that we can preserve the absoluteness of laws of nature, and only by recognizing a corresponding distinction that we can preserve the absoluteness of the general principles of morality. But an important difference between the two cases must be pointed out. When we say that in virtue of gravitation a body tends to move in a certain way, we are referring to a causal influence actually exercised on it by another body or other bodies. When we say that in virtue of being deliberately untrue a certain remark

tends to be wrong, we are referring to no causal relation, to no relation that involves succession in time, but to such a relation as connects the various attributes of a mathematical figure. And if the word 'tendency' is thought to suggest too much a causal relation, it is better to talk of certain types of act as being *prima facie* right or wrong (or of different persons as having different and possibly conflicting claims upon us), than of their tending to be right or wrong.

Something should be said of the relation between our apprehension of the *prima facie* rightness of certain types of act and our mental attitude towards particular acts. It is proper to use the word 'apprehension' in the former case and not in the latter. That an act, *qua* fulfilling a promise, or *qua* effecting a just distribution of good, or *qua* returning services rendered, or *qua* promoting the good of others, or *qua* promoting the virtue or insight of the agent, is *prima facie* right, is self-evident; not in the sense that it is evident from the beginning of our lives, or as soon as we attend to the proposition for the first time, but in the sense that when we have reached sufficient mental maturity and have given sufficient attention to the proposition it is evident without any need of proof, or of evidence beyond itself. It is self-evident just as a mathematical axiom, or the validity of a form of inference, is evident. The moral order expressed in these propositions is just as much part of the fundamental nature of the universe (and, we may add, of any possible universe in which there were moral agents at all) as is the spatial or numerical structure expressed in the axioms of geometry or arithmetic. In our confidence that these propositions are true there is involved the same trust in our reason that is involved in our confidence in mathematics; and we should have no justification for trusting it in the latter sphere and distrusting it in the former. In both cases we are dealing with propositions that cannot be proved, but that just as certainly need no proof.

Some of these general principles of *prima facie* duty may appear to be open to criticism. It may be thought, for example, that the principle of returning good for good is a falling off from the Christian principle, generally and rightly recognized as expressing the highest morality, of returning good for evil. To this it may be replied that I do not suggest that there is a principle commanding us to return good for good and forbidding us to return good for evil, and that I do suggest that there is a positive duty to seek the good of all men. What I maintain is that an act in which good is returned for good is recognized as *specially* binding on us just because it is of that character, and that *ceteris paribus* any one would think it his duty to help his benefactors rather than his enemies, if he could not do both; just as it is generally recognized that *ceteris paribus* we should pay our debts rather than give our money in charity, when we cannot do both. A benefactor is not only a man, calling for our effort on his behalf on that ground, but also our benefactor, calling for our *special* effort on *that* ground.

Our judgements about our actual duty in concrete situations have none of the certainty that attaches to our recognition of the general principles of duty. A statement is certain, i.e. is an expression of knowledge, only in one or other of two cases: when it is either self-evident, or a valid conclusion from self-evident premises. And our judgements about our particular duties have neither of these characters. (1) They are not self-evident. Where a possible act is seen to have two characteristics, in virtue of one of which it is *prima facie* right, and in virtue of the other *prima facie* wrong, we are (I think) well aware that we are not certain whether we ought or ought not to do it; that whether we do it or not, we are taking a moral risk. We come in the long run, after consideration, to think one duty more pressing than the other, but we do not feel certain that it is so. And though we do not always recognize that a possible act has two such characteristics, and though there *may* be cases in which it has not, we are never certain that any particular possible act has not, and therefore never certain that it is right, nor certain that it is wrong. For, to go no further in the analysis, it is enough to point out that any particular act will in all probability in the course of time contribute to the bringing about of good or of evil for many human beings, and thus have a *prima facie* rightness or wrongness of which we know nothing. (2) Again, our judgements about our particular duties are not logical conclusions from self-evident premises. The only possible premises would be the general principles stating their *prima facie* rightness or wrongness *qua* having the different characteristics they do have;

and even if we could (as we cannot) apprehend the extent to which an act will tend on the one hand, for example, to bring about advantages for our benefactors, and on the other hand to bring about disadvantages for fellow men who are not our benefactors, there is no principle by which we can draw the conclusion that it is on the whole right or on the whole wrong. In this respect the judgement as to the rightness of a particular act is just like the judgement as to the beauty of a particular natural object or work of art. A poem is, for instance, in respect of certain qualities beautiful and in respect of certain others not beautiful; and our judgement as to the degree of beauty it possesses on the whole is never reached by logical reasoning from the apprehension of its particular beauties or particular defects. Both in this and in the moral case we have more or less probable opinions which are not logically justified conclusions from the general principles that are recognized as self-evident.

There is therefore much truth in the description of the right act as a fortunate act. If we cannot be certain that it is right, it is our good fortune if the act we do is the right act. This consideration does not, however, make the doing of our duty a mere matter of chance. There is a parallel here between the doing of duty and the doing of what will be to our personal advantage. We never *know* what act will in the long run be to our advantage. Yet it is certain that we are more likely in general to secure our advantage if we estimate to the best of our ability the probable tendencies of our actions in this respect, than if we act on caprice. And similarly we are more likely to do our duty if we reflect to the best of our ability on the *prima facie* rightness or wrongness of various possible acts in virtue of the characteristics we perceive them to have, than if we act without reflection. With this greater likelihood we must be content.

Many people would be inclined to say that the right act for me is not that whose general nature I have been describing, viz. that which if I were omniscient I should see to be my duty, but that which on all the evidence available to me I should think to be my duty. But suppose that from the state of partial knowledge in which I think act A to be my duty, I could pass to a state of perfect knowledge in which I saw act B to be my duty, should I not say 'act B was the right act for me to do'? I should no doubt add 'though I am not to be blamed for doing act *A*'. But in adding this, am I not passing from the question 'what is right' to the question 'what is morally good'? At the same time I am not making the *full* passage from the one notion to the other; for in order that the act should be morally good, or an act I am not to be blamed for doing, it must not merely be the act which it is reasonable for me to think my duty; it must also be done for that reason, or from some other morally good motive. Thus the conception of the right act as the act which it is reasonable for me to think my duty is an unsatisfactory compromise between the true notion of the right act and the notion of the morally good action.

The general principles of duty are obviously not self-evident from the beginning of our lives. How do they come to be so? The answer is, that they come to be self-evident to us just as mathematical axioms do. We find by experience that this couple of matches and that couple make four matches, that this couple of balls on a wire and that couple make four balls: and by reflection on these and similar discoveries we come to see that it is of the nature of two and two to make four. In a precisely similar way, we see the *prima facie* rightness of an act which would be the fulfilment of a particular promise, and of another which would be the fulfilment of another promise, and when we have reached sufficient maturity to think in general terms, we apprehend *prima facie* rightness to belong to the nature of any fulfilment of promise. What comes first in time is the apprehension of the self-evident *prima facie* rightness of an individual act of a particular type. From this we come by reflection to apprehend the self-evident general principle of *prima facie* duty. From this, too, perhaps along with the apprehension of the self-evident *prima facie* rightness of the same act in virtue of its having another characteristic as well, and perhaps in spite of the apprehension of its *prima facie* wrongness in virtue of its having some third characteristic, we come to believe something not self-evident at all, but an object of probable opinion, viz. that this particular act is (not *prima facie* but) actually right.

In this respect there is an important difference between rightness and mathematical properties. A triangle which is isosceles necessarily has two

of its angles equal, whatever other characteristics the triangle may have – whatever, for instance, be its area, or the size of its third angle. The equality of the two angles is a parti-resultant attribute. And the same is true of all mathematical attributes. It is true, I may add, of *prima facie* rightness. But no act is ever, in virtue of falling under some general description, necessarily actually right; its rightness depends on its whole nature[6] and not on any element in it. The reason is that no mathematical object (no figure, for instance, or angle) ever has two characteristics that tend to give it opposite resultant characteristics, while moral acts often (as every one knows) and indeed always (as on reflection we must admit) have different characteristics that tend to make them at the same time *prima facie* right and *prima facie* wrong; there is probably no act, for instance, which does good to any one without doing harm to some one else, and *vice versa*.

Supposing it to be agreed, as I think on reflection it must, that no one *means* by 'right' just 'productive of the best possible consequences', or 'optimific', the attributes 'right' and 'optimific' might stand in either of two kinds of relation to each other. (1) They might be so related that we could apprehend *a priori*, either immediately or deductively, that any act that is optimific is right and any act that is right is optimific, as we can apprehend that any triangle that is equilateral is equiangular and *vice versa*. Professor Moore's view is, I think, that the coextensiveness of 'right' and 'optimific' is apprehended immediately.[7] He rejects the possibility of any proof of it. Or (2) the two attributes might be such that the question whether they are invariably connected had to be answered by means of an inductive inquiry. Now at first sight it might seem as if the constant connexion of the two attributes could be immediately apprehended. It might seem absurd to suggest that it could be right for any one to do an act which would produce consequences less good than those which would be produced by some other act in his power. Yet a little thought will convince us that this is not absurd. The type of case in which it is easiest to see that this is so is, perhaps, that in which one has made a promise. In such a case we all think that *prima facie* it is our duty to fulfil the promise irrespective of the precise goodness of the total consequences. And though we do not think it is necessarily our actual or absolute duty to do so, we are far from thinking that any, even the slightest, gain in the value of the total consequences will necessarily justify us in doing something else instead. Suppose, to simplify the case by abstraction, that the fulfilment of a promise to A would produce 1,000 units of good[8] for him, but that by doing some other act I could produce 1,001 units of good for B, to whom I have made no promise, the other consequences of the two acts being of equal value; should we really think it self-evident that it was our duty to do the second act and not the first? I think not. We should, I fancy, hold that only a much greater disparity of value between the total consequences would justify us in failing to discharge our *prima facie* duty to A. After all, a promise is a promise, and is not to be treated so lightly as the theory we are examining would imply. What, exactly, a promise is, is not so easy to determine, but we are surely agreed that it constitutes a serious moral limitation to our freedom of action. To produce the 1,001 units of good for B rather than fulfil our promise to A would be to take, not perhaps our duty as philanthropists too seriously, but certainly our duty as makers of promises too lightly.

Or consider another phase of the same problem. If I have promised to confer on A a particular benefit containing 1,000 units of good, is it self-evident that if by doing some different act I could produce 1,001 units of good for A himself (the other consequences of the two acts being supposed equal in value), it would be right for me to do so? Again, I think not. Apart from my general *prima facie* duty to do A what good I can, I have another *prima facie* duty to do him the particular service I have promised to do him, and this is not to be set aside in consequence of a disparity of good of the order of 1,001 to 1,000, though a much greater disparity might justify me in so doing.

Or again, suppose that A is a very good and B a very bad man, should I then, even when I have made no promise, think it self-evidently right to produce 1,001 units of good for B rather than 1,000 for A? Surely not. I should be sensible of a *prima facie* duty of justice, i.e. of producing a distribution of goods in proportion to merit, which is not outweighed by such a slight disparity in the total goods to be produced.

Such instances – and they might easily be added to – make it clear that there is no self-evident connexion between the attributes 'right' and 'optimific'. The theory we are examining has a certain attractiveness when applied to our decision that a particular act is our duty (though I have tried to show that it does not agree with our actual moral judgements even here). But it is not even plausible when applied to our recognition of *prima facie* duty. For if it were self-evident that the right coincides with the optimific, it should be self-evident that what is *prima facie* right is *prima facie* optimific. But whereas we are certain that keeping a promise is *prima facie* right, we are not certain that it is *prima facie* optimific (though we are perhaps certain that it is *prima facie* bonific). Our certainty that it is *prima facie* right depends not on its consequences but on its being the fulfilment of a promise. The theory we are examining involves too much difference between the evident ground of our conviction about *prima facie* duty and the alleged ground of our conviction about actual duty.

The coextensiveness of the right and the optimific is, then, not self-evident. And I can see no way of proving it deductively; nor, so far as I know, has any one tried to do so. There remains the question whether it can be established inductively. Such an inquiry, to be conclusive, would have to be very thorough and extensive. We should have to take a large variety of the acts which we, to the best of our ability, judge to be right. We should have to trace as far as possible their consequences, not only for the persons directly affected but also for those indirectly affected, and to these no limit can be set. To make our inquiry thoroughly conclusive, we should have to do what we cannot do, viz. trace these consequences into an unending future. And even to make it reasonably conclusive, we should have to trace them far into the future. It is clear that the most we could possibly say is that a large variety of typical acts that are judged right appear, so far as we can trace their consequences, to produce more good than any other acts possible to the agents in the circumstances. And such a result falls far short of proving the constant connexion of the two attributes. But it is surely clear that no inductive inquiry justifying even this result has ever been carried through. The advocates of utilitarian systems have been so much persuaded either of the identity or of the self-evident connexion of the attributes 'right' and 'optimific' (or 'felicific') that they have not attempted even such an inductive inquiry as is possible. And in view of the enormous complexity of the task and the inevitable inconclusiveness of the result, it is worth no one's while to make the attempt. What, after all, would be gained by it? If, as I have tried to show, for an act to be right and to be optimific are not the same thing, and an act's being optimific is not even the ground of its being right, then if we could ask ourselves (though the question is really unmeaning) which we ought to do, right acts because they are right or optimific acts because they are optimific, our answer must be 'the former'. If they are optimific as well as right, that is interesting but not morally important; if not, we still ought to do them (which is only another way of saying that they *are* the right acts), and the question whether they are optimific has no importance for moral theory.

There is one direction in which a fairly serious attempt has been made to show the connexion of the attributes 'right' and 'optimific'. One of the most evident facts of our moral consciousness is the sense which we have of the sanctity of promises, a sense which does not, on the face of it, involve the thought that one will be bringing more good into existence by fulfilling the promise than by breaking it. It is plain, I think, that in our normal thought we consider that the fact that we have made a promise is in itself sufficient to create a duty of keeping it, the sense of duty resting on remembrance of the past promise and not on thoughts of the future consequences of its fulfilment. Utilitarianism tries to show that this is not so, that the sanctity of promises rests on the good consequences of the fulfilment of them and the bad consequences of their non-fulfilment. It does so in this way: it points out that when you break a promise you not only fail to confer a certain advantage on your promisee but you diminish his confidence, and indirectly the confidence of others, in the fulfilment of promises. You thus strike a blow at one of the devices that have been found most useful in the relations between man and man – the device on which, for example, the whole system of commercial credit rests – and you tend to bring about a state of things wherein each man, being entirely unable to rely on the keeping of promises by others, will have to do everything for himself, to the enormous impoverishment of human well-being.

To put the matter otherwise, utilitarians say that when a promise ought to be kept it is because the total good to be produced by keeping it is greater than the total good to be produced by breaking it, the former including as its main element the maintenance and strengthening of general mutual confidence, and the latter being greatly diminished by a weakening of this confidence. They say, in fact, that the case I put some pages back[9] never arises – the case in which by fulfilling a promise I shall bring into being 1,000 units of good for my promisee, and by breaking it 1,001 units of good for some one else, the other effects of the two acts being of equal value. The other effects, they say, never are of equal value. By keeping my promise I am helping to strengthen the system of mutual confidence; by breaking it I am helping to weaken this; so that really the first act produces $1,000 + x$ units of good, and the second $1,001 - y$ units, and the difference between $+x$ and $-y$ is enough to outweigh the slight superiority in the *immediate* effects of the second act. In answer to this it may be pointed out that there must be *some* amount of good that exceeds the difference between $+x$ and $-y$ (i.e. exceeds $x + y$); say, $x + y + z$. Let us suppose the *immediate* good effects of the second act to be assessed not at 1,001 but at $1,000 + x + y + z$. Then its *net* good effects are $1,000 + x + z$, i.e. greater than those of the fulfilment of the promise; and the utilitarian is bound to say forthwith that the promise should be broken. Now, we may ask whether that is really the way we think about promises? Do we really think that the production of the slightest balance of good, no matter who will enjoy it, by the breach of a promise frees us from the obligation to keep our promise? We need not doubt that a system by which promises are made and kept is one that has great advantages for the general well-being. But that is not the whole truth. To make a promise is not merely to adapt an ingenious device for promoting the general well-being; it is to put oneself in a new relation to one person in particular, a relation which creates a specifically new *prima facie* duty to him, not reducible to the duty of promoting the general well-being of society. By all means let us try to foresee the net good effects of keeping one's promise and the net good effects of breaking it, but even if we assess the first at $1,000 + x$ and the second at $1,000 + x + z$, the question still remains whether it is not our duty to fulfil the promise. It may be suspected, too, that the effect of a single keeping or breaking of a promise in strengthening or weakening the fabric of mutual confidence is greatly exaggerated by the theory we are examining. And if we suppose two men dying together alone, do we think that the duty of one to fulfil before he dies a promise he has made to the other would be extinguished by the fact that neither act would have any effect on the general confidence? Any one who holds this may be suspected of not having reflected on what a promise is.

I conclude that the attributes 'right' and 'optimific' are not identical, and that we do not know either by intuition, by deduction, or by induction that they coincide in their application, still less that the latter is the foundation of the former. It must be added, however, that if we are ever under no special obligation such as that of fidelity to a promisee or of gratitude to a bene-factor, we ought to do what will produce most good; and that even when we are under a special obligation the tendency of acts to promote gen-eral good is one of the main factors in determining whether they are right.

In what has preceded, a good deal of use has been made of 'what we really think' about moral questions; a certain theory has been rejected because it does not agree with what we really think. It might be said that this is in principle wrong; that we should not be content to expound what our present moral consciousness tells us but should aim at a criticism of our existing moral con-sciousness in the light of theory. Now I do not doubt that the moral consciousness of men has in detail undergone a good deal of modification as regards the things we think right, at the hands of moral theory. But if we are told, for instance, that we should give up our view that there is a special obligatoriness attaching to the keeping of promises because it is self-evident that the only duty is to produce as much good as possible, we have to ask ourselves whether we really, when we reflect, *are* convinced that this is self-evident, and whether we really *can* get rid of our view that promise-keeping has a bindingness independent of productiveness of maximum good. In my own experience I find that I cannot, in spite of a very genuine attempt to do so; and I venture to think that most people will find the same, and that just because they cannot lose the sense of special obligation, they cannot accept as self-evident, or even as true, the theory which would require them to do so. In fact it seems, on reflection, self-evident that a promise, simply as such, is something that *prima facie* ought to be kept, and it does *not*, on reflection, seem self-evident that production of maximum good is the only thing that makes an act obligatory. And to ask us to give up at the bidding of a theory our actual appre-hension of what is right and what is wrong seems like asking people to repudiate their actual experience of beauty, at the bidding of a theory which says 'only that which satisfies such and such conditions can be beautiful'. If what I have called our actual apprehension is (as I would maintain that it is) truly an apprehension, i.e. an instance of knowledge, the request is nothing less than absurd.

I would maintain, in fact, that what we are apt to describe as 'what we think' about moral questions contains a considerable amount that we do not think but know, and that this forms the standard by reference to which the truth of any moral theory has to be tested, instead of having itself to be tested by reference to any theory. I hope that I have in what precedes indicated what in my view these elements of knowledge are that are involved in our ordinary moral consciousness.

It would be a mistake to found a natural science on 'what we really think', i.e. on what reasonably thoughtful and well-educated people think about the subjects of the science before they have studied them scientifically. For such opinions are interpretations, and often misinter-pretations, of sense-experience; and the man of science must appeal from these to sense-experience itself, which furnishes his real data. In ethics no such appeal is possible. We have no more direct way of access to the facts about rightness and good-ness and about what things are right or good, than by thinking about them; the moral convictions of thoughtful and well-educated people are the data of ethics just as sense-perceptions are the data of a natural science. Just as some of the latter have to be rejected as illusory, so have some of the former; but as the latter are rejected only when they are in conflict with other more accurate sense-perceptions, the former are rejected only when they are in conflict with other convictions which stand better the test of reflection. The existing body of moral convictions of the best people is the cumulative product of the moral reflection of many generations, which has developed an extremely delicate power of appreciation of moral distinctions; and this the theorist cannot afford to treat with anything other than the greatest respect. The verdicts of the moral consciousness of the best people are the foundation on which he must build; though he must first compare them with one another and eliminate any contradictions they may contain.

It is worth while to try to state more definitely the nature of the acts that are right. We may try to state first what (if anything) is the universal nature of *all* acts that are right. It is obvious that any of the acts that we do has countless effects, directly or indirectly, on countless people, and the probability is that any act, however right it be, will have adverse effects (though these may be very trivial) on some innocent people. Similarly, any wrong act will probably have beneficial effects on some deserving people. Every act therefore, viewed in some aspects, will be *prima facie* right, and viewed in others, *prima facie* wrong, and right acts can be distinguished from wrong acts only as being those which, of all those possible for the agent in the circumstances, have the greatest balance of *prima facie* rightness, in those respects in which they *are prima facie* right, over their *prima facie* wrongness, in those respects in which they are *prima facie* wrong – *prima facie* rightness and wrongness being understood in the sense previously explained. For the estimation of the comparative stringency of these *prima facie* obligations no general rules can, so far as I can see, be laid down. We can only say that a great deal of stringency belongs to the duties of 'perfect obligation' – the duties of keeping our promises, of repairing wrongs we have done, and of returning the equivalent of services we have received. For the rest, ἐν τῇ αἰσθήσει ἡ κρίσις.[10] This sense of our particular duty in particular circumstances, preceded and informed by the fullest reflection we can bestow on the act in all its bearings, is highly fallible, but it is the only guide we have to our duty.

When we turn to consider the nature of individual right acts, the first point to which attention should be called is that any act may be correctly described in an indefinite, and in principle infinite, number of ways. An act is the production of a change in the state of affairs (if we ignore, for simplicity's sake, the comparatively few cases in which it is the maintenance of an existing state of affairs; cases which, I think, raise no special difficulty). Now the only changes we can *directly* produce are changes in our own bodies or in our own minds. But these are not, as such, what as a rule we think it our duty to produce. Consider some comparatively simple act, such as telling the truth or fulfilling a promise. In the first case what I produce directly is movements of my vocal organs. But what I think it my duty to produce is a true view in some one else's mind about some fact, and between my movement of my vocal organs and this result there intervenes a series of physical events and events in his mind. Again, in the second case, I may have promised, for instance, to return a book to a friend. I may be able, by a series of movements of my legs and hands, to place it in his hands. But what I am just as likely to do, and to think I have done my duty in doing, is to send it by a messenger or to hand it to his servant or to send it by post; and in each of these cases what I *do* directly is worthless in itself and is connected by a series of intermediate links with what I do think it is my duty to bring about, viz. his receiving what I have promised to return to him. This being so, it *seems* as if what I *do* has no obligatoriness in itself and as if one or other of three accounts should be given of the matter, each of which makes rightness not belong to what I do, considered in its own nature.

(1) One of them would be that what is obligatory is not *doing* anything in the natural sense of producing any change in the state of affairs, but *aiming at* something – at, for instance, my friend's reception of the book. But this account will not do. For (*a*) to aim at something is to act from a motive consisting of the wish to bring that thing about. But we have seen that motive never forms part of the content of our duty; if anything is certain about morals, that, I think, is certain. And (*b*) if I have promised to return the book to my friend, I obviously do not fulfil my promise and do my duty merely by aiming at his

receiving the book; I must see that he actually receives it. (2) A more plausible account is that which says I must do that which is likely to produce the result. But this account is open to the second of these objections, and probably also to the first. For in the first place, however likely my act may seem, even on careful consideration, and even however likely it may in fact be, to produce the result, if it does not produce it I have not done what I promised to do, i.e. have not done my duty. And secondly, when it is said that I ought to do what is likely to produce the result, what is *probably* meant is that I ought to do a certain thing as a result of the wish to produce a certain result, and of the thought that my act is likely to produce it; and this again introduces motive into the content of duty. (3) Much the most plausible of the three accounts is that which says, 'I ought to do that which will actually produce a certain result.' This escapes objection (*b*). Whether it escapes objection (*a*) or not depends on what exactly is meant. If it is meant that I ought to do a certain thing from the wish to produce a certain result and the thought that it will do so, the account is still open to objection (*a*). But if it is meant simply that I ought to do a certain thing, and that the reason why I ought to do it is that it will produce a certain result, objection (*a*) is avoided. Now this account in its second form is that which utilitarianism gives. It says what is right is certain acts, not certain acts motivated in a certain way; and it says that acts are never right by their own nature but by virtue of the goodness of their actual results. And this account is, I think, clearly nearer the truth than one which makes the rightness of an act depend on the goodness of either the *intended* or the *likely* results.

Nevertheless, this account appears not to be the true one. For it implies that what we consider right or our duty is what we do *directly*. It is this, e.g. the packing up and posting of the book, that derives its moral significance not from its own nature but from its consequences. But this is *not* what we should describe, strictly, as our duty; our duty is to fulfil our promise, i.e. to put the book into our friend's possession. This we consider obligatory in its own nature, just because it is a fulfilment of promise, and not because of *its* consequences. But, it might be replied by the utilitarian, I do not do this; I only do something that leads up to this, and what I do has no moral

significance in itself but only because of its consequences. In answer to this, however, we may point out that a cause produces not only its immediate, but also its remote consequences, and the latter no less than the former. I, therefore, not only produce the immediate movements of parts of my body but also my friend's reception of the book, which results from these. Or, if this be objected to on the grounds that I can hardly be said to have produced my friend's reception of the book when I have packed and posted it, owing to the time that has still to elapse before he receives it, and that to say I have produced the result hardly does justice to the part played by the Post Office, we may at least say that I have *secured* my friend's reception of the book. What I do is as truly describable in this way as by saying that it is the packing and posting of a book. (It is equally truly describable in many other ways; e.g. I have provided a few moments' employment for Post Office officials. But this is irrelevant to the argument.) And if we ask ourselves whether it is *qua* the packing and posting of a book, or *qua* the securing of my friend's getting what I have promised to return to him, that my action is right, it is clear that it is in the second capacity that it is right; and in this capacity, the only capacity in which it is right, it is right by its own nature and not because of its consequences.

This account may no doubt be objected to, on the ground that we are ignoring the freedom of will of the other agents – the sorter and the postman, for instance – who are equally responsible for the result. Society, it may be said, is not like a machine, in which event follows event by rigorous necessity. Some one may, for instance, in the exercise of his freedom of will, steal the book on the way. But it is to be observed that I have excluded that case, and any similar case. I am dealing with the case in which I secure my friend's receiving the book; and if he does not receive it I have not secured his receiving it. If on the other hand the book reaches its destination, that alone shows that, the system of things being what it is, the trains by which the book travels and the railway lines along which it travels being such as they are and subject to the laws they are subject to, the postal officials who handle it being such as they are, having the motives they have and being subject to the psychological laws they are subject to, my posting the book was the one further thing which was sufficient to procure my friend's receiving it. If it had not been sufficient, the result would not have followed. The attainment of the result proves the sufficiency of the means. The objection in fact rests on the supposition that there can be unmotived action, i.e. an event without a cause, and may be refuted by reflection on the universality of the law of causation.

It is equally true that non-attainment of the result proves the insufficiency of the means. If the book had been destroyed in a railway accident or stolen by a dishonest postman, that would prove that my immediate act was not sufficient to produce the desired result. We get the curious consequence that however carelessly I pack or dispatch the book, if it comes to hand I have done my duty, and however carefully I have acted, if the book does not come to hand I have not done my duty. Success and failure are the only test, and a sufficient test, of the performance of duty. Of course, I should deserve more praise in the second case than in the first; but that is an entirely different question; we must not mix up the question of right and wrong with that of the morally good and the morally bad. And that our conclusion is not as strange as at first sight it might seem is shown by the fact that if the carelessly dispatched book comes to hand, it is not my duty to send another copy, while if the carefully dispatched book does not come to hand I must send another copy to replace it. In the first case I have not my duty still to do, which shows that I have done it; in the second I have it still to do, which shows that I have not done it.

We have reached the result that my act is right *qua* being an ensuring of one of the particular states of affairs of which it is an ensuring, viz., in the case we have taken, of my friend's receiving the book I have promised to return to him. But this answer requires some correction; for it refers only to the *prima facie* rightness of my act. If to be a fulfilment of promise were a sufficient ground of the rightness of an act, all fulfilments of promises would be right, whereas it seems clear that there are cases in which some other *prima facie* duty overrides the *prima facie* duty of fulfilling a promise. The more correct answer would be that the ground of the actual rightness of the act is that, of all acts possible for the agent

in the circumstances, it is that whose *prima facie* rightness in the respects in which it is *prima facie* right most outweighs its *prima facie* wrongness in any respects in which it is *prima facie* wrong. But since its *prima facie* rightness is mainly due to its being a fulfilment of promise, we may call its being so the salient element in the ground of its rightness.

Subject to this qualification, then, it is as being the production (or if we prefer the word, the securing or ensuring) of the reception by my friend of what I have promised him (or in other words as the fulfilment of my promise) that my act is right. It is not right as a packing and posting of a book. The packing and posting of the book is only incidentally right, right only because it is a fulfilment of promise, which is what is directly or essentially right.

Our duty, then, is not to do certain things which will produce certain results. Our acts, at any rate our acts of special obligation, are not right because they will produce certain results – which is the view common to all forms of utilitarianism. To say that is to say that in the case in question what is essentially right is to pack and post a book, whereas what is essentially right is to secure the possession by my friend of what I have promised to return to him. An act is not right because it, being one thing, produces good results different from itself; it is right because it is itself the production of a certain state of affairs. Such production is right in itself, apart from any consequence.

But, it might be said, this analysis applies only to acts of special obligation; the utilitarian account still holds good for the acts in which we are not under a special obligation to any person or set of persons but only under that of augmenting the general good. Now merely to have established that there *are* special obligations to do certain things irrespective of their consequences would be already to have made a considerable breach in the utilitarian walls; for according to utilitarianism there is no such thing, there is only the single obligation to promote the general good. But, further, on reflection it is clear that just as (in the case we have taken) my act is not only the packing and posting of a book but the fulfilling of a promise, and just as it is in the latter capacity and not in the former that it is my duty, so an act whereby I augment the general good is not only, let us say, the writing of a begging letter on behalf of a hospital, but the producing (or ensuring) of whatever good ensues therefrom, and it is in the latter capacity and not in the former that it is right, if it *is* right. That which is right is right not because it is an act, one thing, which will produce another thing, an increase of the general welfare, but because it is itself the producing of an increase in the general welfare. Or, to qualify this in the necessary way, its being the production of an increase in the general welfare is the salient element in the ground of its rightness. Just as before we were led to recognize the *prima facie* rightness of the fulfilment of promises, we are now led to recognize the *prima facie* rightness of promoting the general welfare. In both cases we have to recognize the *intrinsic* rightness of a certain type of act, not depending on its consequences but on its own nature.

Notes

1 I take the theory which, as I have tried to show, seems to be put forward in *Ethics* rather than the earlier and less plausible theory put forward in *Principia Ethica*. [. . .]
2 These are not strictly speaking duties, but things that tend to be our duty, or *prima facie* duties. [. . .]
3 Some will think it, apart from other considerations, a sufficient refutation of this view to point out that I also stand in that relation to myself, so that for this view the distinction of oneself from others is morally insignificant.
4 I should make it plain at this stage that I am *assuming* the correctness of some of our main convictions as to *prima facie* duties, or, more strictly, am claiming that we *know* them to be true. To me it seems as self-evident as anything could be, that to make a promise, for instance, is to create a moral claim on us in someone else. Many readers will perhaps say that they do *not* know this to be true. If so, I certainly cannot prove it to them; I can only ask them to reflect again, in the hope that they will ultimately agree that they also know it to be true. The main moral convictions of the plain man seem to me to be, not opinions which it is for philosophy to prove or disprove, but knowledge from the start; and in my own case I seem to find little difficulty in distinguishing these essential convictions from other moral convictions which I also have, which are merely fallible opinions based on an imperfect study of the working for good or evil of certain institutions or types of action.
5 But cf. the qualification in n. 6.
6 To avoid complicating unduly the statement of the general view I am putting forward, I have here rather overstated it. Any act is the origination of a great variety of things many of which make no difference to its rightness or wrongness. But there are always many elements in its nature (i.e. in what it is the origination of) that make a difference to its rightness or wrongness, and no element in its nature can be dismissed without consideration as indifferent.
7 *Ethics*, 181.
8 I am assuming that good is objectively quantitative, but not that we can accurately assign an exact quantitative measure to it. Since it is of a definite amount, we can make the *supposition* that its amount is so-and-so, though we cannot with any confidence *assert* that it is.
9 p. 290.
10 'The decision rests with perception'. Arist. *Nic. Eth.* 1109 b 23, 1126 b 4.

25

A Critique of Utilitarianism

Bernard Williams

The Structure of Consequentialism

No one can hold that everything, of whatever category, that has value, has it in virtue of its consequences. If that were so, one would just go on for ever, and there would be an obviously hopeless regress. That regress would be hopeless even if one takes the view, which is not an absurd view, that although men set themselves ends and work towards them, it is very often not really the supposed end, but the effort towards it on which they set value – that they travel, not really in order to arrive (for as soon as they have arrived they set out for somewhere else), but rather they choose somewhere to arrive, in order to travel. Even on that view, not everything would have consequential value; what would have non-consequential value would in fact be travelling, even though people had to think of travelling as having the consequential value, and something else – the destination – the non-consequential value.

If not everything that has value has it in virtue of consequences, then presumably there are some types of thing which have non-consequential value, and also some particular things that have such value because they are instances of those types. Let us say, using a traditional term, that anything that has that sort of value, has *intrinsic* value.[1] I take it to be the central idea of consequentialism that the only kind of thing that has intrinsic value is states of affairs, and that anything else that has value has it because it conduces to some intrinsically valuable state of affairs.

How much, however, does this say? Does it succeed in distinguishing consequentialism from anything else? The trouble is that the term 'state of affairs' seems altogether too permissive to exclude anything: may not the obtaining of absolutely anything be represented formally as a state of affairs? A Kantian view of morality, for instance, is usually thought to be opposed to consequentialism, if any is; at the very least, if someone were going to show that Kantianism collapsed into consequentialism, it should be the product of a long and unobvious argument, and not just happen at the drop of a definition. But on the present account it looks as though Kantianism can be made instantly into a kind of consequentialism – a kind which identifies the states of affairs that have intrinsic value (or at least intrinsic moral value) as those that consist of actions being performed for duty's sake.[2] We need something more to our specification if it is to be the specification of anything distinctly consequentialist.

Bernard Williams, "A Critique of Utilitarianism," from J. J. C. Smart and Bernard Williams, *Utilitarianism: For and Against* (Cambridge: Cambridge University Press, 1973), pp. 82–117. © 1973 by Cambridge University Press. Reproduced with permission from Cambridge University Press.

The point of saying that consequentialism ascribes intrinsic value to states of affairs is rather to *contrast* states of affairs with other candidates for having such value: in particular, perhaps, actions. A distinctive mark of consequentialism might rather be this, that it regards the value of actions as always consequential (or, as we may more generally say, derivative), and not intrinsic. The value of actions would then lie in their causal properties, of producing valuable states of affairs; or if they did not derive their value in this simple way, they would derive it in some more roundabout way, as for instance by being expressive of some motive, or in accordance with some rule, whose operation in society conduced to desirable states of affairs. (The lengths to which such indirect derivations can be taken without wrecking the point of consequentialism is something we shall be considering later.)

To insist that what has intrinsic value are states of affairs and not actions seems to come near an important feature of consequentialism. Yet it may be that we have still not hit exactly what we want, and that the restriction is now too severe. Surely *some* actions, compatibly with consequentialism, might have intrinsic value? This is a question which has a special interest for utilitarianism, that is to say, the form of consequentialism concerned particularly with happiness. Traditionally utilitarians have tended to regard happiness or, again, pleasure, as experiences or sensations which were related to actions and activity as effect to cause; and, granted that view, utilitarianism will indeed see the value of all action as derivative, intrinsic value being reserved for the experiences of happiness. But that view of the relations between action and either pleasure or happiness is widely recognized to be inadequate. To say that a man finds certain actions or activity pleasant, or that they make him happy, or that he finds his happiness in them, is certainly not always to say that they induce certain sensations in him, and in the case of happiness, it is doubtful whether that is ever what is meant. Rather it means such things (among others) as that he enjoys doing these things for their own sake. It would trivialize the discussion of utilitarianism to tie it by definition to inadequate conceptions of happiness or pleasure, and we must be able to recognize as versions of utilitarianism those which, as most modern versions do, take as

central some notion such as *satisfaction*, and connect that criterially with such matters as the activities which a man will freely choose to engage in. But the activities which a man engages in for their own sake are activities in which he finds intrinsic value. So any specification of consequentialism which logically debars action or activity from having intrinsic value will be too restrictive even to admit the central case, utilitarianism, so soon as that takes on a more sophisticated and adequate conception of its basic value of happiness.

So far then, we seem to have one specification of consequentialism which is too generous to exclude anything, and another one which is too restrictive to admit even the central case. These difficulties arise from either admitting without question actions among desirable states of affairs, or blankly excluding all actions from the state of affairs category. This suggests that we shall do better by looking at the interrelations between states of affairs and actions.

It will be helpful, in doing this, to introduce the notion of the *right* action for an agent in given circumstances. I take it that in any form of direct consequentialism, and certainly in act-utilitarianism, the notion of the right action in given circumstances is a maximizing notion:[3] the right action is that which out of the actions available to the agent brings about or represents the highest degree of whatever it is the system in question regards as intrinsically valuable – in the central case, utilitarianism, this is of course happiness. In this argument, I shall confine myself to direct consequentialism, for which 'right action' is unqualifiedly a maximizing notion.

The notion of the right action as that which, of the possible alternatives, maximizes the good (where this embraces, in unfavourable circumstances, minimizing the bad), is an objective notion in this sense, that it is perfectly possible for an agent to be ignorant or mistaken, and non-culpably ignorant or mistaken, about what is the right action in the circumstances. Thus the assessment by others of whether the agent did, in this sense, do the right thing, is not bounded by the agent's state of knowledge at the time, and the claim that he did the wrong thing is compatible with recognizing that he did as well as anyone in his state of knowledge could have done.[4] It might be suggested that, contrary to this, we have already imported the subjective conditions of action in speaking of the best of the actions *available to him*: if he is ignorant or misinformed, then the actions which might seem to us available to him were not in any real sense available. But this would be an exaggeration; the notion of availability imports some, but not all, kinds of subjective condition. Over and above the question of actions which, granted his situation and powers, were physically not available to him, we might perhaps add that a course of action was not really available to an agent if his historical, cultural or psychological situation was such that it could not possibly occur to him. But it is scarcely reasonable to extend the notion of unavailability to actions which merely did not occur to him; and surely absurd to extend it to actions which did occur to him, but where he was misinformed about their consequences.

If then an agent does the right thing, he does the best of the alternatives available to him (where that, again, embraces the least bad: we shall omit this rider from now on). Standardly, the action will be right in virtue of its causal properties, of maximally conducing to good states of affairs. Sometimes, however, the relation of the action to the good state of affairs may not be that of cause to effect – the good state of affairs may be constituted, or partly constituted, by the agent's doing that act (as when under utilitarianism he just enjoys doing it, and there is no project available to him more productive of happiness for him or anyone else).

Although this may be so under consequentialism, there seems to be an important difference between this situation and a situation of an action's being right for some non-consequentialist reason, as for instance under a Kantian morality. This difference might be brought out intuitively by saying that for the consequentialist, even a situation of this kind in which the action itself possesses intrinsic value is one in which the rightness of the act is derived from the goodness of a certain state of affairs – the act is right *because* the state of affairs which consists in its being done is better than any other state of affairs accessible to the agent; whereas for the non-consequentialist it is sometimes, at least, the other way round, and a state of affairs which is better than the alternatives is so because it consists of the right act being done. This intuitive description of the difference has something in it, but it needs to be made more precise.

We can take a step towards making it more precise, perhaps, in the following way. Suppose S is some particular concrete situation. Consider the statement, made about some particular agent

(1) In S, he did the right thing in doing A.
     For consequentialists, (1) implies a statement of the form

(2) The state of affairs P is better than any other state of affairs accessible to him; where a state of affairs being 'accessible' to an agent means that it is a state of affairs which is the consequence of, or is constituted by, his doing an act available to him (for that, see above); and P is a state of affairs accessible to him only in virtue of his doing A.[5]
     Now in the exceptional case where it is just his doing A which carries the intrinsic value, we get for (2)

(3) The state of affairs which consists in his doing A is better than any other state of affairs accessible to him.
     It was just the possibility of this sort of case which raised the difficulty of not being able to distinguish between a sophisticated consequentialism and non-consequentialism. The question thus is: if (3) is what we get for consequentialism in this sort of case, is it what a non-consequentialist would regard as implied by (1)? If so, we still cannot tell the difference between them. But the answer in fact seems to be 'no'.

There are two reasons for this. One reason is that a non-consequentialist, though he must inevitably be able to attach a sense to (1), does not have to be able to attach a sense to (3) at all, while the consequentialist, of course, attaches a sense to (1) only because he attaches a sense to (3). Although the non-consequentialist is concerned with right actions – such as the carrying out of promises – he may have no general way of comparing states of affairs from a moral point of view at all. Indeed, we shall see later and in greater depth than these schematic arguments allow, that the emphasis on the necessary comparability of situations is a peculiar feature of consequentialism in general, and of utilitarianism in particular.

A different kind of reason emerges if we suppose that the non-consequentialist does admit, in general, comparison between states of affairs. Thus, we might suppose that some non-consequentialist would consider it a better state of things in which more, rather than fewer, people kept their promises, and kept them for non-consequentialist reasons. Yet consistently with that he could accept, in a particular case, all of the following: that X would do the right thing only if he kept his promise; that keeping his promise would involve (or consist in) doing A; that several other people would, as a matter of fact, keep their promises (and for the right reasons) if and only if X did not do A. There are all sorts of situations in which this sort of thing would be true: thus it might be the case that an effect of X's doing A would be to provide some inducement to these others which would lead them to break promises which otherwise they would have kept. Thus a non-consequentialist can hold both that it is a better state of affairs in which more people keep their promises, and that the right thing for X to do is something which brings it about that fewer promises are kept. Moreover, it is very obvious what view of things goes with holding that. It is one in which, even though from some abstract point of view one state of affairs is better than another, it does not follow that a given agent should regard it as his business to bring it about, even though it is open to him to do so. More than that, it might be that he could not properly regard it as his business. If the goodness of the world were to consist in people's fulfilling their obligations, it would by no means follow that one of my obligations was to bring it about that other people kept their obligations.

Of course, no sane person could really believe that the goodness of the world just consisted in people keeping their obligations. But that is just an example, to illustrate the point that under non-consequentialism (3) does not, as one might expect, follow from (1). Thus even allowing some actions to have intrinsic value, we can still distinguish consequentialism. A consequentialist view, then, is one in which a statement of the form (2) follows from a statement of the form (1). A non-consequentialist view is one in which this

is not so – not even when the (2)-statement takes the special form of (3).

This is not at all to say that the alternative to consequentialism is that one has to accept that there are some actions which one should always do, or again some which one should never do, *whatever the consequences*: this is a much stronger position than any involved, as I have defined the issues, in the denial of consequentialism. All that is involved, on the present account, in the denial of consequentialism, is that with respect to some type of action, there are some situations in which that would be the right thing to do, even though the state of affairs produced by one's doing that would be worse than some other state of affairs accessible to one. The claim that there is a type of action which is right *whatever the consequences* can be put by saying that with respect to some type of action, assumed as being adequately specified, then *whatever* the situation may (otherwise) be, that will be the right thing to do, *whatever* other state of affairs might be accessible to one, however much better it might be than the state of affairs produced by one's doing this action.

If that somewhat Moorean formulation has not hopelessly concealed the point, it will be seen that this second position – the *whatever the consequences* position – is very much stronger than the first, the mere rejection of consequentialism. It is perfectly consistent, and it might be thought a mark of sense, to believe, while not being a consequentialist, that there was no type of action which satisfied this second condition: that if an adequate (and non-question-begging) specification of a type of action has been given in advance, it is always possible to think of some situation in which the consequences of doing the action so specified would be so awful that it would be right to do something else.

Of course, one might think that there just *were* some types of action which satisfied this condition; though it seems to me obscure how one could have much faith in a list of such actions unless one supposed that it had supernatural warrant. Alternatively, one might think that while logically there was a difference between the two positions, in social and psychological fact they came to much the same thing, since so soon (it might be claimed) as people give up thinking in terms of certain things being right or wrong whatever the consequences, they turn to thinking in purely consequential terms. This might be offered as a very general proposition about human thought, or (more plausibly) as a sociological proposition about certain situations of social change, in which utilitarianism (in particular) looks the only coherent alternative to a dilapidated set of values. At the level of language, it is worth noting that the use of the word '*absolute*' mirrors, and perhaps also assists, this association: the claim that no type of action is 'absolutely right' – leaving aside the sense in which it means that the tightness of anything depends on the value-system of a society (the confused doctrine of relativism) – can mean either that no type of action is right-whatever-its-consequences, or, alternatively, that 'it all depends on the consequences', that is, in each case the decision whether an action is right is determined by its consequences.

A particular sort of psychological connexion – or in an old-fashioned use of the term, a 'moral' connexion – between the two positions might be found in this. If people do not regard certain things as 'absolutely out', then they are prepared to start thinking about extreme situations in which what would otherwise be out might, exceptionally, be justified. They will, if they are to get clear about what they believe, be prepared to compare different extreme situations and ask what action would be justified in them. But once they have got used to that, their inhibitions about thinking of everything in consequential terms disappear: the difference between the extreme situations and the less extreme, presents itself no longer as a difference between the exceptional and the usual, but between the greater and the less – and the consequential thoughts one was prepared to deploy in the greater it may seem quite irrational not to deploy in the less. A *fortiori*, someone might say: but he would have already had to complete this process to see it as a case of *a fortiori*.

One could regard this process of adaptation to consequentialism, moreover, not merely as a blank piece of psychological association, but as concealing a more elaborate structure of thought. One might have the idea that the *unthinkable* was itself a moral category; and in more than one way. It would be a feature of a man's moral outlook that he regarded certain courses of action as

unthinkable, in the sense that he would not entertain the idea of doing them: and the witness to that might, in many cases, be that they simply would not come into his head. Entertaining certain alternatives, regarding them indeed as *alternatives*, is itself something that he regards as dishonourable or morally absurd. But, further, he might equally find it unacceptable to consider what to do in certain conceivable situations. Logically, or indeed empirically conceivable they may be, but they are not to him morally conceivable, meaning by that that their occurrence as situations presenting him with a choice would represent not a special problem in his moral world, but something that lay beyond its limits. For him, there are certain situations so monstrous that the idea that the processes of moral rationality could yield an answer in them is insane: they are situations which so transcend in enormity the human business of moral deliberation that from a moral point of view it cannot matter any more what happens. Equally, for him, to spend time thinking what one would decide if one were in such a situation is also insane, if not merely frivolous.

For such a man, and indeed for anyone who is prepared to take him seriously, the demand, in Herman Kahn's words, to *think the unthinkable* is not an unquestionable demand of rationality, set against a cowardly or inert refusal to follow out one's moral thoughts. Rationality he sees as a demand not merely on him, but on the situations in, and about, which he has to think; unless the environment reveals minimum sanity, it is insanity to carry the decorum of sanity into it. Consequentialist rationality, however, and in particular utilitarian rationality, has no such limitations: making the best of a bad job is one of its maxims, and it will have something to say even on the difference between massacring seven million, and massacring seven million and one.

There are other important questions about the idea of the morally unthinkable, which we cannot pursue here. Here we have been concerned with the role it might play in someone's connecting, by more than a mistake, the idea that there was nothing which was right whatever the consequences, and the different idea that everything depends on consequences. While someone might, in this way or another, move from one of those ideas to the other, it is very important that the two ideas are different: especially important in a world where we have lost traditional reasons for resisting the first idea, but have more than enough reasons for fearing the second.

Negative Responsibility: and Two Examples

Although I have defined a state of affairs being *accessible* to an agent in terms of the actions which are *available* to him,[6] nevertheless it is the former notion which is really more important for consequentialism. Consequentialism is basically indifferent to whether a state of affairs consists in what I do, or is produced by what I do, where that notion is itself wide enough to include, for instance, situations in which other people do things which I have made them do, or allowed them to do, or encouraged them to do, or given them a chance to do. All that consequentialism is interested in is the idea of these doings being *consequences* of what I do, and that is a relation broad enough to include the relations just mentioned, and many others.

Just what the relation is, is a different question, and at least as obscure as the nature of its relative, cause and effect. It is not a question I shall try to pursue; I will rely on cases where I suppose that any consequentialist would be bound to regard the situations in question as consequences of what the agent does. There are cases where the supposed consequences stand in a rather remote relation to the action, which are sometimes difficult to assess from a practical point of view, but which raise no very interesting question for the present enquiry. The more interesting points about consequentialism lie rather elsewhere. There are certain situations in which the causation of the situation, the relation it has to what I do, is in no way remote or problematic in itself, and entirely justifies the claim that the situation is a consequence of what I do: for instance, it is quite clear, or reasonably clear, that if I do a certain thing, this situation will come about, and if I do not, it will not. So from a consequentialist point of view it goes into the calculation of consequences along with any other state of affairs accessible to me. Yet from some, at least, non-consequentialist points of view, there is a vital

difference between some such situations and others: namely, that in some a vital link in the production of the eventual outcome is provided by *someone else's* doing something. But for consequentialism, all causal connexions are on the same level, and it makes no difference, so far as that goes, whether the causation of a given state of affairs lies through another agent, or not.

Correspondingly, there is no relevant difference which consists *just* in one state of affairs being brought about by me, without intervention of other agents, and another being brought about through the intervention of other agents; although some genuinely causal differences involving a difference of value may correspond to that (as when, for instance, the other agents derive pleasure or pain from the transaction), that kind of difference will already be included in the specification of the state of affairs to be produced. Granted that the states of affairs have been adequately described in causally and evaluatively relevant terms, it makes no further comprehensible difference who produces them. It is because consequentialism attaches value ultimately to states of affairs, and its concern is with what states of affairs the world contains, that it essentially involves the notion of *negative responsibility*: that if I am ever responsible for anything, then I must be just as much responsible for things that I allow or fail to prevent, as I am for things that I myself, in the more everyday restricted sense, bring about.[7] Those things also must enter my deliberations, as a responsible moral agent, on the same footing. What matters is what states of affairs the world contains, and so what matters with respect to a given action is what comes about if it is done, and what comes about if it is not done, and those are questions not intrinsically affected by the nature of the causal linkage, in particular by whether the outcome is partly produced by other agents.

The strong doctrine of negative responsibility flows directly from consequentialism's assignment of ultimate value to states of affairs. Looked at from another point of view, it can be seen also as a special application of something that is favoured in many moral outlooks not themselves consequentialist – something which, indeed, some thinkers have been disposed to regard as the essence of morality itself: a principle of impartiality. Such a principle will claim that there can be no relevant difference from a moral point of view which consists just in the fact, not further explicable in general terms, that benefits or harms accrue to one person rather than to another – 'it's me' can never in itself be a morally comprehensible reason.[8] This principle, familiar with regard to the reception of harms and benefits, we can see consequentialism as extending to their production: from the moral point of view, there is no comprehensible difference which consists just in my bringing about a certain outcome rather than someone else's producing it. That the doctrine of negative responsibility represents in this way the extreme of impartiality, and abstracts from the identity of the agent, leaving just a locus of causal intervention in the world – that fact is not merely a surface paradox. It helps to explain why consequentialism can seem to some to express a more serious attitude than non-consequentialist views, why part of its appeal is to a certain kind of high-mindedness. Indeed, that is part of what is wrong with it.

For a lot of the time so far we have been operating at an exceedingly abstract level. This has been necessary in order to get clearer in general terms about the differences between consequentialist and other outlooks, an aim which is important if we want to know what features of them lead to what results for our thought. Now, however, let us look more concretely at two examples, to see what utilitarianism might say about them, what we might say about utilitarianism and, most importantly of all, what would be implied by certain ways of thinking about the situations. The examples are inevitably schematized, and they are open to the objection that they beg as many questions as they illuminate. There are two ways in particular in which examples in moral philosophy tend to beg important questions. One is that, as presented, they arbitrarily cut off and restrict the range of alternative courses of action – this objection might particularly be made against the first of my two examples. The second is that they inevitably present one with the situation as a going concern, and cut off questions about how the agent got into it, and correspondingly about moral considerations which might flow from that: this objection might perhaps specially arise with regard to the second of my two situations. These difficulties, however, just

have to be accepted, and if anyone finds these examples cripplingly defective in this sort of respect, then he must in his own thought rework them in richer and less question-begging form. If he feels that no presentation of any imagined situation can ever be other than misleading in morality, and that there can never be any substitute for the concrete experienced complexity of actual moral situations, then this discussion, with him, must certainly grind to a halt: but then one may legitimately wonder whether every discussion with him about conduct will not grind to a halt, including any discussion about the actual situations, since discussion about how one would think and feel about situations somewhat different from the actual (that is to say, situations to that extent imaginary) plays an important role in discussion of the actual.

(1)   George, who has just taken his Ph.D. in chemistry, finds it extremely difficult to get a job. He is not very robust in health, which cuts down the number of jobs he might be able to do satisfactorily. His wife has to go out to work to keep them, which itself causes a great deal of strain, since they have small children and there are severe problems about looking after them. The results of all this, especially on the children, are damaging. An older chemist, who knows about this situation, says that he can get George a decently paid job in a certain laboratory, which pursues research into chemical and biological warfare. George says that he cannot accept this, since he is opposed to chemical and biological warfare. The older man replies that he is not too keen on it himself, come to that, but after all George's refusal is not going to make the job or the laboratory go away; what is more, he happens to know that if George refuses the job, it will certainly go to a contemporary of George's who is not inhibited by any such scruples and is likely if appointed to push along the research with greater zeal than George would. Indeed, it is not merely concern for George and his family, but (to speak frankly and in confidence) some alarm about this other man's excess of zeal, which has led the older man to offer to use his influence to get George the job [. . .] George's wife, to whom he is deeply attached, has views (the details of which need not concern us) from which it follows that at least there is nothing particularly wrong with research into CBW. What should he do?

(2)   Jim finds himself in the central square of a small South American town. Tied up against the wall are a row of twenty Indians, most terrified, a few defiant, in front of them several armed men in uniform. A heavy man in a sweat-stained khaki shirt turns out to be the captain in charge and, after a good deal of questioning of Jim which establishes that he got there by accident while on a botanical expedition, explains that the Indians are a random group of the inhabitants who, after recent acts of protest against the government, are just about to be killed to remind other possible protestors of the advantages of not protesting. However, since Jim is an honoured visitor from another land, the captain is happy to offer him a guest's privilege of killing one of the Indians himself. If Jim accepts, then as a special mark of the occasion, the other Indians will be let off. Of course, if Jim refuses, then there is no special occasion, and Pedro here will do what he was about to do when Jim arrived, and kill them all. Jim, with some desperate recollection of schoolboy fiction, wonders whether if he got hold of a gun, he could hold the captain, Pedro and the rest of the soldiers to threat, but it is quite clear from the set-up that nothing of that kind is going to work: any attempt at that sort of thing will mean that all the Indians will be killed, and himself. The men against the wall, and the other villagers, understand the situation, and are obviously begging him to accept. What should he do?

To these dilemmas, it seems to me that utilitarianism replies, in the first case, that George should accept the job, and in the second, that Jim should kill the Indian. Not only does utilitarianism give these answers but, if the situations are essentially as described and there are no further special factors, it regards them, it seems to me, as *obviously* the right answers. But many of us would certainly wonder whether, in (1), that could possibly be the right answer at all; and in the case of (2), even one who came to think that perhaps that was the answer, might well wonder whether it was obviously the answer. Nor is it just a question of the rightness or obviousness of these answers. It is also a question of what sort of considerations come into finding the answer. A feature of utilitarianism is that it cuts out a kind of consideration which for some others makes a difference to what they feel about such cases: a consideration involving the idea, as we might first and very simply put it, that each of us is specially responsible for what *he* does, rather than for what other people do. This is an idea closely connected with the value of integrity. It is often suspected that utilitarianism, at least in its direct forms, makes integrity as a value more or less unintelligible. I shall try to show that this suspicion is correct. Of course, even if that is correct, it would not necessarily follow that we should reject utilitarianism; perhaps, as utilitarians sometimes suggest, we should just forget about integrity, in favour of such things as a concern for the general good. However, if I am right, we cannot merely do that, since the reason why utilitarianism cannot understand integrity is that it cannot coherently describe the relations between a man's projects and his actions.

Two Kinds of Remoter Effect

A lot of what we have to say about this question will be about the relations between my projects and other people's projects, But before we get on to that, we should first ask whether we are assuming too hastily what the utilitarian answers to the dilemmas will be. In terms of more direct effect of the possible decisions, there does not indeed seem much doubt about the answer in either case; but it might be said that in terms of more remote or less evident effects counterweights might be found to enter the utilitarian scales. Thus the effect on George of a decision to take the job might be invoked, or its effect on others who might know of his decision. The possibility of there being more beneficent labours in the future from which he might be barred or disqualified, might be mentioned; and so forth. Such effects – in particular, possible effects on the agent's character, and effects on the public at large – are often invoked by utilitarian writers dealing with problems about lying or promise-breaking, and some similar considerations might be invoked here.

There is one very general remark that is worth making about arguments of this sort. The certainty that attaches to these hypotheses about possible effects is usually pretty low; in some cases, indeed, the hypothesis invoked is so implausible that it would scarcely pass if it were not being used to deliver the respectable moral answer, as in the standard fantasy that one of the effects of one's telling a particular lie is to weaken the disposition of the world at large to tell the truth. The demands on the certainty or probability of these beliefs as beliefs about particular actions are much milder than they would be on beliefs favouring the unconventional course. It may be said that this is as it should be, since the presumption must be in favour of the conventional course: but that scarcely seems a *utilitarian* answer, unless utilitarianism has already taken off in the direction of not applying the consequences to the particular act at all.

Leaving aside that very general point, I want to consider now two types of effect that are often invoked by utilitarians, and which might be invoked in connexion with these imaginary cases. The attitude or tone involved in invoking these effects may sometimes seem peculiar; but that sort of peculiarity soon becomes familiar in utilitarian discussions, and indeed it can be something of an achievement to retain a sense of it.

First, there is the psychological effect on the agent. Our descriptions of these situations have not so far taken account of how George or Jim will be after they have taken the one course or the other; and it might be said that if they take the course which seemed at first the utilitarian one, the effects on them will be in fact bad enough and extensive enough to cancel out the initial utilitarian advantages of that course. Now there is one version of this effect in which, for a utilitarian, some confusion must be involved, namely that in which the agent feels bad, his subsequent conduct and relations are crippled and so on, *because he thinks that he has done the wrong thing* – for if the balance of outcomes was as it appeared to be *before* invoking this effect, then he has not (from the utilitarian point of view) done the wrong thing. So that version of the effect, for a rational and utilitarian agent, could not possibly make any difference to the assessment of right and wrong. However, perhaps he is not a thoroughly rational agent, and is disposed to have bad feelings, whichever he decided to do. Now such feelings, which are from a strictly utilitarian point of view irrational – nothing, a utilitarian can point out, is advanced by having them – cannot, consistently, have any great weight in a utilitarian calculation. I shall consider in a moment an argument to suggest that they should have no weight at all in it. But short of that, the utilitarian could reasonably say that such feelings should not be encouraged,

even if we accept their existence, and that to give them a lot of weight is to encourage them. Or, at the very best, even if they are straightforwardly and without any discount to be put into the calculation, their weight must be small: they are after all (and at best) one man's feelings.

That consideration might seem to have particular force in Jim's case. In George's case, his feelings represent a larger proportion of what is to be weighed, and are more commensurate in character with other items in the calculation. In Jim's case, however, his feelings might seem to be of very little weight compared with other things that are at stake. There is a powerful and recognizable appeal that can be made on this point: as that a refusal by Jim to do what he has been invited to do would be a kind of self-indulgent squeamishness. That is an appeal which can be made by other than utilitarians – indeed, there are some uses of it which cannot be consistently made by utilitarians, as when it essentially involves the idea that there is something dishonourable about such self-indulgence. But in some versions it is a familiar, and it must be said a powerful, weapon of utilitarianism. One must be clear, though, about what it can and cannot accomplish. The most it can do, so far as I can see, is to invite one to consider how seriously, and for what reasons, one feels that what one is invited to do is (in these circumstances) wrong, and in particular, to consider that question from the utilitarian point of view. When the agent is not seeing the situation from a utilitarian point of view, the appeal cannot force him to do so; and if he does come round to seeing it from a utilitarian point of view, there is virtually nothing left for the appeal to do. If he does not see it from a utilitarian point of view, he will not see his resistance to the invitation, and the unpleasant feelings he associates with accepting it, *just* as disagreeable experiences of his; they figure rather as emotional expressions of a thought that to accept would be wrong. He may be asked, as by the appeal, to consider whether he is right, and indeed whether he is fully serious, in thinking that. But the assertion of the appeal, that he is being self-indulgently squeamish, will not itself answer that question, or even help to answer it, since it essentially tells him to regard his feelings just as unpleasant experiences of his, and he cannot, by doing that, answer the question they pose when they are precisely not so regarded, but are regarded as indications[9] of what he thinks is right and wrong. If he does come round fully to the utilitarian point of view then of course he will regard these feelings just as unpleasant experiences of his. And once Jim – at least – has come to see them in that light, there is nothing left for the appeal to do, since *of course* his feelings, so regarded, are of virtually no weight at all in relation to the other things at stake. The 'squeamishness' appeal is not an argument which adds in a hitherto neglected consideration. Rather, it is an invitation to consider the situation, and one's own feelings, from a utilitarian point of view.

The reason why the squeamishness appeal can be very unsettling, and one can be unnerved by the suggestion of self-indulgence in going against utilitarian considerations, is not that we are utilitarians who are uncertain what utilitarian value to attach to our moral feelings, but that we are partially at least not utilitarians, and cannot regard our moral feelings merely as objects of utilitarian value. Because our moral relation to the world is partly given by such feelings, and by a sense of what we can or cannot 'live with', to come to regard those feelings from a purely utilitarian point of view, that is to say, as happenings outside one's moral self, is to lose a sense of one's moral identity; to lose, in the most literal way, one's integrity. At this point utilitarianism alienates one from one's moral feelings; we shall see a little later how, more basically, it alienates one from one's actions as well.

If, then, one is really going to regard one's feelings from a strictly utilitarian point of view, Jim should give very little weight at all to his; it seems almost indecent, in fact, once one has taken that point of view, to suppose that he should give any at all. In George's case one might feel that things were slightly different. It is interesting, though, that one reason why one might think that – namely that one person principally affected is his wife – is very dubiously available to a utilitarian. George's wife has some reason to be interested in George's integrity and his sense of it; the Indians, quite properly, have no interest in Jim's. But it is not at all clear how utilitarianism would describe that difference.

There is an argument, and a strong one, that a strict utilitarian should give not merely small extra weight, in calculations of right and wrong, to feelings of this kind, but that he should give absolutely no weight to them at all. This is based on the point, which we have already seen, that if a course of action is, before taking these sorts of feelings into account, utilitarianly preferable, then bad feelings about that kind of action will be from a utilitarian point of view irrational. Now it might be thought that even if that is so, it would not mean that in a utilitarian calculation such feelings should not be taken into account; it is after all a well-known boast of utilitarianism that it is a realistic outlook which seeks the best in the world as it is, and takes any form of happiness or unhappiness into account. While a utilitarian will no doubt seek to diminish the incidence of feelings which are utilitarianly irrational – or at least of disagreeable feelings which are so – he might be expected to take them into account while they exist. This is without doubt classical utilitarian doctrine, but there is good reason to think that utilitarianism cannot stick to it without embracing results which are startlingly unacceptable and perhaps self-defeating.

Suppose that there is in a certain society a racial minority. Considering merely the ordinary interests of the other citizens, as opposed to their sentiments, this minority does no particular harm; we may suppose that it does not confer any very great benefits either. Its presence is in those terms neutral or mildly beneficial. However, the other citizens have such prejudices that they find the sight of this group, even the knowledge of its presence, very disagreeable. Proposals are made for removing in some way this minority. If we assume various quite plausible things (as that programmes to change the majority sentiment are likely to be protracted and ineffective) then even if the removal would be unpleasant for the minority, a utilitarian calculation might well end up favouring this step, especially if the minority were a rather small minority and the majority were very severely prejudiced, that is to say, were made very severely uncomfortable by the presence of the minority.

A utilitarian might find that conclusion embarrassing; and not merely because of its nature, but because of the grounds on which it is reached. While a utilitarian might be expected to take into account certain other sorts of consequences of the prejudice, as that a majority prejudice is likely to be displayed in conduct disagreeable to the minority, and so forth, he might be made to wonder whether the unpleasant experiences of the prejudiced people should be allowed, *merely as such*, to count. If he does count them, merely as such, then he has once more separated himself from a body of ordinary moral thought which he might have hoped to accommodate; he may also have started on the path of defeating his own view of things. For one feature of these sentiments is that they are from the utilitarian point of view itself irrational, and a thoroughly utilitarian person would either not have them, or if he found that he did tend to have them, would himself seek to discount them. Since the sentiments in question are such that a rational utilitarian would discount them in himself, it is reasonable to suppose that he should discount them in his calculations about society; it does seem quite unreasonable for him to give just as much weight to feelings – considered just in themselves, one must recall, as experiences of those that have them – which are essentially based on views which are from a utilitarian point of view irrational, as to those which accord with utilitarian principles. Granted this idea, it seems reasonable for him to rejoin a body of moral thought in other respects congenial to him, and discount those sentiments, just considered in themselves, totally, on the principle that no pains or discomforts are to count in the utilitarian sum which their subjects have just because they hold views which are by utilitarian standards irrational. But if he accepts that, then in the cases we are at present considering no extra weight at all can be put in for bad feelings of George or Jim about their choices, if those choices are, leaving out those feelings, on the first round utilitarianly rational.

The psychological effect on the agent was the first of two general effects considered by utilitarians, which had to be discussed. The second is in general a more substantial item, but it need not take so long, since it is both clearer and has little application to the present cases. This is the *precedent effect*. As Burke rightly emphasized, this effect can be important: that one morally *can* do what someone has actually done, is a psychologically effective principle, if not a deontically valid one. For the effect to operate, obviously some conditions must hold on the publicity of the act and on such things as the status of the agent

(such considerations weighed importantly with Sir Thomas More); what these may be will vary evidently with circumstances.

In order for the precedent effect to make a difference to a utilitarian calculation, it must be based upon a confusion. For suppose that there is an act which would be the best in the circumstances, except that doing it will encourage by precedent other people to do things which will not be the best things to do. Then the situation of those other people must be relevantly different from that of the original agent; if it were not, then in doing the same as what would be the best course for the original agent, they would necessarily do the best thing themselves. But if the situations are in this way relevantly different, it must be a confused perception which takes the first situation, and the agent's course in it, as an adequate precedent for the second.

However, the fact that the precedent effect, if it really makes a difference, is in this sense based on a confusion, does not mean that it is not perfectly real, nor that it is to be discounted: social effects are by their nature confused in this sort of way. What it does emphasize is that calculations of the precedent effect have got to be realistic, involving considerations of how people are actually likely to be influenced. In the present examples, however, it is very implausible to think that the precedent effect could be invoked to make any difference to the calculation. Jim's case is extraordinary enough, and it is hard to imagine who the recipients of the effect might be supposed to be; while George is not in a sufficiently public situation or role for the question to arise in that form, and in any case one might suppose that the motivations of others on such an issue were quite likely to be fixed one way or another already.

No appeal, then, to these other effects is going to make a difference to what the utilitarian will decide about our examples. Let us now look more closely at the structure of those decisions.

Integrity

The situations have in common that if the agent does not do a certain disagreeable thing, someone else will, and in Jim's situation at least the result, the state of affairs after the other man has acted, if he does, will be worse than after Jim has acted, if Jim does. The same, on a smaller scale, is true of George's case. I have already suggested that it is inherent in consequentialism that it offers a strong doctrine of negative responsibility: if I know that if I do X, O_1 will eventuate, and if I refrain from doing X, O_2 will, and that O_2 is worse than O_1, then I am responsible for O_2 if I refrain voluntarily from doing X. 'You could have prevented it', as will be said, and truly, to Jim, if he refuses, by the relatives of the other Indians. (I shall leave the important question, which is to the side of the present issue, of the obligations, if any, that nest round the word 'know': how far does one, under utilitarianism, have to research into the possibilities of maximally beneficent action, including prevention?)

In the present cases, the situation of O_2 includes another agent bringing about results worse than O_1. So far as O_2 has been identified up to this point – merely as the worse outcome which will eventuate if I refrain from doing X – we might equally have said that what that other brings about is O_2; but that would be to under-describe the situation. For what occurs if Jim refrains from action is not solely twenty Indians dead, but *Pedro's killing twenty Indians*, and that is not a result which Pedro brings about, though the death of the Indians is. We can say: what one does is not included in the outcome of what one does, while what another does can be included in the outcome of what one does. For that to be so, as the terms are now being used, only a very weak condition has to be satisfied: for Pedro's killing the Indians to be the outcome of Jim's refusal, it only has to be causally true that if Jim had not refused, Pedro would not have done it.

That may be enough for us to speak, in some sense, of Jim's responsibility for that outcome, if it occurs; but it is certainly not enough, it is worth noticing, for us to speak of Jim's *making* those things happen. For granted this way of their coming about, he could have made them happen only by making Pedro shoot, and there is no acceptable sense in which his refusal makes Pedro shoot. If the captain had said on Jim's refusal, 'you leave me with no alternative', he would have been lying, like most who use that phrase. While the deaths, and the killing, may be the outcome of Jim's refusal, it is misleading to think, in such a case, of Jim having an *effect* on

the world through the medium (as it happens) of Pedro's acts; for this is to leave Pedro out of the picture in his essential role of one who has intentions and projects, projects for realizing which Jim's refusal would leave an opportunity. Instead of thinking in terms of supposed effects of Jim's projects on Pedro, it is more revealing to think in terms of the effects of Pedro's projects on Jim's decision. This is the direction from which I want to criticize the notion of negative responsibility.

There are of course other ways in which this notion can be criticized. Many have hoped to discredit it by insisting on the basic moral relevance of the distinction between action and inaction, between intervening and letting things take their course. The distinction is certainly of great moral significance, and indeed it is not easy to think of any moral outlook which could get along without making some use of it. But it is unclear, both in itself and in its moral applications, and the unclarities are of a kind which precisely cause it to give way when, in very difficult cases, weight has to be put on it. There is much to be said in this area, but I doubt whether the sort of dilemma we are considering is going to be resolved by a simple use of this distinction. Again, the issue of negative responsibility can be pressed on the question of how limits are to be placed on one's apparently boundless obligation, implied by utilitarianism, to improve the world. Some answers are needed to that, too – and answers which stop short of relapsing into the bad faith of supposing that one's responsibilities could be adequately characterized just by appeal to one's roles.[10] But, once again, while that is a real question, it cannot be brought to bear directly on the present kind of case, since it is hard to think of anyone supposing that in Jim's case it would be an adequate response for him to say that it was none of his business.

What projects does a utilitarian agent have? As a utilitarian, he has the general project of bringing about maximally desirable outcomes; how he is to do this at any given moment is a question of what causal levers, so to speak, are at that moment within reach. The desirable outcomes, however, do not just consist of agents carrying out *that* project; there must be other more basic or lower-order projects which he and other agents have, and the desirable outcomes are going to consist, in part, of the maximally harmonious realization of those projects ('in part', because one component of a utilitarianly desirable outcome may be the occurrence of agreeable experiences which are not the satisfaction of anybody's projects). Unless there were first-order projects, the general utilitarian project would have nothing to work on, and would be vacuous. What do the more basic or lower-order projects comprise? Many will be the obvious kinds of desires for things for oneself, one's family, one's friends, including basic necessities of life, and in more relaxed circumstances, objects of taste. Or there may be pursuits and interests of an intellectual, cultural or creative character. I introduce those as a separate class not because the objects of them lie in a separate class, and provide – as some utilitarians, in their churchy way, are fond of saying – 'higher' pleasures. I introduce them separately because the agent's identification with them may be of a different order. It does not have to be: cultural and aesthetic interests just belong, for many, along with any other taste; but some people's commitment to these kinds of interests just is at once more thoroughgoing and serious than their pursuit of various objects of taste, while it is more individual and permeated with character than the desire for the necessities of life.

Beyond these, someone may have projects connected with his support of some cause: Zionism, for instance, or the abolition of chemical and biological warfare. Or there may be projects which flow from some more general disposition towards human conduct and character, such as a hatred of injustice, or of cruelty, or of killing.

It may be said that this last sort of disposition and its associated project do not count as (logically) 'lower-order' relative to the higher-order project of maximizing desirable outcomes; rather, it may be said, it is itself a 'higher-order' project. The vital question is not, however, how it is to be classified, but whether it and similar projects are to count among the projects whose satisfaction is to be included in the maximizing sum, and, correspondingly, as contributing to the agent's happiness. If the utilitarian says 'no' to that, then he is almost certainly committed to a version of utilitarianism as absurdly superficial and shallow as Benthamite versions have often been accused of being. For this project will be discounted, presumably, on the ground that it involves, in the specification of its object, the mention of other people's happiness or interests: thus it is the kind of project which (unlike the pursuit of food for myself) presupposes a reference to other people's projects. But that criterion would eliminate any desire at all which was not blankly and in the most straightforward sense egoistic.[11] Thus we should be reduced to frankly egoistic first-order projects, and – for all essential purposes – the one second-order utilitarian project of maximally satisfying first-order projects. Utilitarianism has a tendency to slide in this direction, and to leave a vast hole in the range of human desires, between egoistic inclinations and necessities at one end, and impersonally benevolent happiness-management at the other. But the utilitarianism which has to leave this hole is the most primitive form, which offers a quite rudimentary account of desire. Modern versions of the theory are supposed to be neutral with regard to what sorts of things make people happy or what their projects are. Utilitarianism would do well then to acknowledge the evident fact that among the things that make people happy is not only making other people happy, but being taken up or involved in any of a vast range of projects, or – if we waive the evangelical and moralizing associations of the word – commitments. One can be committed to such things as a person, a cause, an institution, a career, one's own genius, or the pursuit of danger.

Now none of these is itself the *pursuit of happiness*: by an exceedingly ancient platitude, it is not at all clear that there could be anything which was just that, or at least anything that had the slightest chance of being successful. Happiness, rather, requires being involved in, or at least content with, something else.[12] It is not impossible for utilitarianism to accept that point: it does not have to be saddled with a naïve and absurd philosophy of mind about the relation between desire and happiness. What it does have to say is that if such commitments are worth while, then pursuing the projects that flow from them, and realizing some of those projects, will make the person for whom they are worth while, happy. It may be that to claim that is still wrong: it may well be that a commitment can make sense to a man (can make sense to his life) without his supposing that it will make him *happy.*[13] But that is not the present point; let us grant to utilitarianism that all worthwhile human projects must conduce, one way or another, to happiness. The point is that even if that is true, it does not follow, nor could it possibly be true, that those projects are themselves projects of pursuing happiness. One has to believe in, or at least want, or quite minimally, be content with, other things, for there to be anywhere that happiness can come from.

Utilitarianism, then, should be willing to agree that its general aim of maximizing happiness does not imply that what everyone is doing is just pursuing happiness. On the contrary, people have to be pursuing other things. What those other things may be, utilitarianism, sticking to its professed empirical stance, should be prepared just to find out. No doubt some possible projects it will want to discourage, on the grounds that their being pursued involves a negative balance of happiness to others: though even there, the unblinking accountant's eye of the strict utilitarian will have something to put in the positive column, the satisfactions of the destructive agent. Beyond that, there will be a vast variety of generally beneficent or at least harmless projects; and some no doubt, will take the form not just of tastes or fancies, but of what I have called 'commitments'. It may even be that the utilitarian researcher will find that many of those with commitments, who have really identified themselves with objects outside themselves, who are thoroughly involved with other persons, or institutions, or activities or causes, are actually happier than those whose projects and wants are not like that. If so, that is an important piece of utilitarian empirical lore.

When I say 'happier' here, I have in mind the sort of consideration which any utilitarian would be committed to accepting: as for instance that such people are less likely to have a break-down or commit suicide. Of course that is not all that is actually involved, but the point in this argument is to use to the maximum degree utilitarian notions, in order to locate a breaking point in utilitarian thought. In appealing to this strictly utilitarian notion, I am being more consistent with utilitarianism than Smart is. In his struggles with the problem of the brain-electrode man, Smart (p. 22) commends the idea that 'happy' is a partly evaluative term, in the sense that we call

'happiness' those kinds of satisfaction which, as things are, we approve of. But *by what standard* is this surplus element of approval supposed, from a utilitarian point of view, to be allocated? There is no source for it, on a strictly utilitarian view, except further degrees of satisfaction, but there are none of those available, or the problem would not arise. Nor does it help to appeal to the fact that we dislike in prospect things which we like when we get there, for from a utilitarian point of view it would seem that the original dislike was merely irrational or based on an error. Smart's argument at this point seems to be embarrassed by a well-known utilitarian uneasiness, which comes from a feeling that it is not respectable to ignore the 'deep', while, not having anywhere left in human life to locate it.[14]

Let us now go back to the agent as utilitarian, and his higher-order project of maximizing desirable outcomes. At this level, he is committed only to that: what the outcome will actually consist of will depend entirely on the facts, on what persons with what projects and what potential satisfactions there are within calculable reach of the causal levers near which he finds himself. His own substantial projects and commitments come into it, but only as one lot among others – they potentially provide one set of satisfactions among those which he may be able to assist from where he happens to be. He is the agent of the satisfaction system who happens to be at a particular point at a particular time: in Jim's case, our man in South America. His own decisions as a utilitarian agent are a function of all the satisfactions which he can affect from where he is: and this means that the projects of others, to an indeterminately great extent, determine his decision.

This may be so either positively or negatively. It will be so positively if agents within the causal field of his decision have projects which are at any rate harmless, and so should be assisted. It will equally be so, but negatively, if there is an agent within the causal field whose projects are harmful, and have to be frustrated to maximize desirable outcomes. So it is with Jim and the soldier Pedro. On the utilitarian view, the undesirable projects of other people as much determine, in this negative way, one's decisions as the desirable ones do positively: if those people were not there, or had different projects, the causal nexus would be different, and it is the actual state of the causal nexus which determines the decision. The determination to an indefinite degree of my decisions by other people's projects is just another aspect of my unlimited responsibility to act for the best in a causal framework formed to a considerable extent by their projects.

The decision so determined is, for utilitarianism, the right decision. But what if it conflicts with some project of mine? This, the utilitarian will say, has already been dealt with: the satisfaction to you of fulfilling your project, and any satisfactions to others of your so doing, have already been through the calculating device and have been found inadequate. Now in the case of many sorts of projects, that is a perfectly reasonable sort of answer. But in the case of projects of the sort I have called 'commitments', those with which one is more deeply and extensively involved and identified, this cannot just by itself be an adequate answer, and there may be no adequate answer at all. For, to take the extreme sort of case, how can a man, as a utilitarian agent, come to regard as one satisfaction among others, and a dispensable one, a project or attitude round which he has built his life, just because someone else's projects have so structured the causal scene that that is how the utilitarian sum comes out?

The point here is not, as utilitarians may hasten to say, that if the project or attitude is that central to his life, then to abandon it will be very disagreeable to him and great loss of utility will be involved. I have already argued in [the previous] section that it is not like that; on the contrary, once he is prepared to look at it like that, the argument in any serious case is over anyway. The point is that he is identified with his actions as flowing from projects and attitudes which in some cases he takes seriously at the deepest level, as what his life is about (or, in some cases, this section of his life – seriousness is not necessarily the same as persistence). It is absurd to demand of such a man, when the sums come in from the utility network which the projects of others have in part determined, that he should just step aside from his own project and decision and acknowledge the decision which utilitarian calculation requires. It is to alienate him in a real sense from his actions and the source of his action in his own convictions. It is to make him into a channel between the input of everyone's projects, including his own, and an output of optimific decision; but this is to neglect the extent to which *his* actions and *his* decisions have to be seen as the actions and decisions which flow from the projects and attitudes with which he is most closely identified. It is thus, in the most literal sense, an attack on his integrity.[15]

These sorts of considerations do not in themselves give solutions to practical dilemmas such as those provided by our examples; but I hope they help to provide other ways of thinking about them. In fact, it is not hard to see that in George's case, viewed from this perspective, the utilitarian solution would be wrong. Jim's case is different, and harder. But if (as I suppose) the utilitarian is probably right in this case, that is not to be found out just by asking the utilitarian's questions. Discussions of it – and I am not going to try to carry it further here – will have to take seriously the distinction between my killing someone, and its coming about because of what I do that someone else kills them: a distinction based, not so much on the distinction between action and inaction, as on the distinction between my projects and someone else's projects. At least it will have to start by taking that seriously, as utilitarianism does not; but then it will have to build out from there by asking why that distinction seems to have less, or a different, force in this case than it has in George's. One question here would be how far one's powerful objection to killing people just is, in fact, an application of a powerful objection to their being killed. Another dimension of that is the issue of how much it matters that the people at risk are actual, and there, as opposed to hypothetical, or future, or merely elsewhere.[16]

Notes

1 The terminology of things 'being valuable', 'having intrinsic value', etc., is not meant to beg any questions in general value-theory. Non-cognitive theories, such as Smart's, should be able to recognize the distinctions made here. [Williams is referring to Smart's essay, in Smart and Williams, eds., *Utilitarianism: For and Against* (Cambridge University Press, 1973).]
2 A point noted by Smart, p. 13.
3 Cf. Smart's definition, p. 45.

4 In Smart's terminology, the 'rational thing':
   pp. 46–7.

5 'Only' here may seem a bit strong: but I take it that
   it is not an unreasonable demand on an account
   of his doing *the* right thing in *S* that his action
   is uniquely singled out from the alternatives.
   A further detail: one should strictly say, not that
   (1) implies a statement of the form (2), but that
   (1) implies *that there is* a true statement of
   that form.

6 See last section.

7 This is a fairly modest sense of 'responsibility',
   introduced merely by one's ability to reflect on, and
   decide, what one ought to do. This presumably
   escapes Smart's ban on the notion of 'the responsibility' as 'a piece of metaphysical nonsense' – his
   remarks seem to be concerned solely with situations of inter-personal blame.

8 There is a tendency in some writers to suggest that
   it is not a comprehensible reason at all. But this,
   I suspect, is due to the overwhelming importance
   those writers ascribe to the moral point of view.

9 On the non-cognitivist meta-ethic in terms of
   which Smart presents his utilitarianism, the
   term 'indications' here would represent an
   understatement.

10 For some remarks bearing on this, see *Morality*,
   the section on 'Goodness and roles', and Cohen's
   article there cited. [Williams, *Morality: An
   Introduction to Ethics* (Harper and Row, New
   York, 1972).]

11 On the subject of egoistic and non-egoistic
   desires, see 'Egoism and altruism', in *Problems of*

   the Self (Cambridge University Press, London,
   1973).

12 This does not imply that there is no such thing
   as the project of pursuing pleasure. Some writers
   who have correctly resisted the view that all
   desires are desires for pleasure, have given an
   account of pleasure so thoroughly adverbial as
   to leave it quite unclear how there could be a
   distinctively hedonist way of life at all. Some
   room has to be left for that, though there are
   important difficulties both in defining it and
   living it. Thus (particularly in the case of the very
   rich) it often has highly ritual aspects, apparently
   part of a strategy to counter boredom.

13 For some remarks on this possibility, see
   Morality, section on 'What is morality about?'

14 One of many resemblances in spirit between
   utilitarianism and high-minded evangelical
   Christianity.

15 Interestingly related to these notions is the
   Socratic idea that courage is a virtue particularly
   connected with keeping a clear sense of what
   one regards as most important. They also centrally
   raise questions about the value of pride. Humility,
   as something beyond the real demand of correct
   self-appraisal, was specially a Christian virtue
   because it involved subservience to God. In a
   secular context it can only represent subservience
   to other men and their projects.

16 For a more general discussion of this issue see
   Charles Fried, *An Anatomy of Values* (Harvard
   University Press, Cambridge, Mass., 1970), Part
   Three.

26

An Outline of a System of Utilitarian Ethics

J. J. C. Smart

[. . .]

2. Act-utilitarianism and Rule-utilitarianism

The system of normative ethics which I am here concerned to defend is, as I have said earlier, *act-utilitarianism*. Act-utilitarianism is to be contrasted with rule-utilitarianism. Act-utilitarianism is the view that the rightness or wrongness of an action is to be judged by the consequences, good or bad, of the action itself. Rule-utilitarianism is the view that the rightness or wrongness of an action is to be judged by the goodness and badness of the consequences of a rule that everyone should perform the action in like circumstances. There are two sub-varieties of rule-utilitarianism according to whether one construes 'rule' here as 'actual rule' or 'possible rule'. With the former, one gets a view like that of S. E. Toulmin[1] and with the latter, one like Kant's.[2] That is, if it is permissible to interpret Kant's principle 'Act only on that maxim through which you can at the same time will that it should become a universal law' as 'Act only on that maxim which you as a humane and benevolent person would like to see established as a universal law.' Of course Kant would resist this appeal to human feeling, but it seems necessary in order to interpret his doctrine in a plausible way. A subtle version of the Kantian type of rule-utilitarianism is given by R. F. Harrod in his 'Utilitarianism Revised'.[3]

I have argued elsewhere[4] the objections to rule-utilitarianism as compared with act-utilitarianism.[5] Briefly they boil down to the accusation of rule worship:[6] the rule-utilitarian presumably advocates his principle because he is ultimately concerned with human happiness: why then should he advocate abiding by a rule when he knows that it will not in the present case be most beneficial to abide by it? The reply that in most cases it is most beneficial to abide by the rule seems irrelevant. And so is the reply that it would be better that everybody should abide by the rule than that nobody should. This is to suppose that the only alternative to 'everybody does *A*' is 'no one does *A*'. But clearly we have the possibility 'some people do *A* and some don't'. Hence to refuse to break a generally beneficial rule in those cases in which it is not most beneficial to obey it seems irrational and to be a case of rule worship.

The type of utilitarianism which I shall advocate will, then, be act-utilitarianism, not rule-utilitarianism.

J. J. C. Smart, "An Outline of a System of Utilitarian Ethics," from J. J. C. Smart and Bernard Williams, *Utilitarianism: For and Against* (Cambridge: Cambridge University Press, 1973), pp. 82–117. © 1973 by Cambridge University Press. Reproduced with permission from Cambridge University Press.

David Lyons has recently argued that rule-utilitarianism (by which, I think, he means the sort of rule-utilitarianism which I have called the Kantian one) collapses into act-utilitarianism.[7] His reasons are briefly as follows. Suppose that an exception to a rule R produces the best possible consequences. Then this is evidence that the rule R should be modified so as to allow this exception. Thus we get a new rule of the form 'do R except in circumstances of the sort C'. That is, whatever would lead the act-utilitarian to break a rule would lead the Kantian rule-utilitarian to modify the rule. Thus an adequate rule-utilitarianism would be extensionally equivalent to act-utilitarianism.

Lyons is particularly interested in what he calls 'threshold effects'. A difficulty for rule-utilitarianism has often appeared to be that of rules like 'do not walk on the grass' or 'do not fail to vote at an election'. In these cases it would seem that it is beneficial if some people, though not too many, break the rule. Lyons points out that we can distinguish the action of doing something (say, walking on the grass) after some largish number n other people have done it from the action of doing it when few or no people have done it. When these extra circumstances are written into the rule, Lyons holds that the rule will come to enjoin the same actions as would the act-utilitarian principle. However there seems to be one interesting sort of case which requires slightly different treatment. This is the sort of case in which not too many people must do action X, but each person must plan his action in ignorance of what the other person does. That is, what A does depends on what B does, and what B does depends on what A does. [. . .]

I am inclined to think that an adequate rule-utilitarianism would not only be extensionally equivalent to the act-utilitarian principle (i.e. would enjoin the same set of actions as it) but would in fact consist of one rule only, the act-utilitarian one: 'maximize probable benefit'. This is because any rule which can be formulated must be able to deal with an indefinite number of unforeseen types of contingency. No rule, short of the act-utilitarian one, can therefore be safely regarded as extensionally equivalent to the act-utilitarian principle unless it is that very principle itself. I therefore suggest that Lyons' type of consideration can be taken even further, and

that rule-utilitarianism of the Kantian sort must collapse into act-utilitarianism in an even stronger way: it must become a 'one-rule' rule-utilitarianism which is identical to act-utilitarianism. In any case, whether this is correct or not, it is with the defence of act-utilitarianism, and not with rule-utilitarianism (supposing that there are viable forms of rule-utilitarianism which may be distinguished from act-utilitarianism) that this monograph is concerned. (Lyons himself rejects utilitarianism.)

3. Hedonistic and Non-hedonistic Utilitarianism

An act-utilitarian judges the rightness or wrongness of actions by the goodness and badness of their consequences. But is he to judge the goodness and badness of the consequences of an action solely by their pleasantness and unpleasantness? Bentham,[8] who thought that quantity of pleasure being equal, the experience of playing pushpin was as good as that of reading poetry, could be classified as a hedonistic act-utilitarian. Moore,[9] who believed that some states of mind, such as those of acquiring knowledge, had intrinsic value quite independent of their pleasantness, can be called an ideal utilitarian. Mill seemed to occupy an intermediate position.[10] He held that there are higher and lower pleasures. This seems to imply that pleasure is a necessary condition for goodness but that goodness depends on other qualities of experience than pleasantness and unpleasantness. I propose to call Mill a quasi-ideal utilitarian. For Mill, pleasantness functions like x in the algebraic product, $x \times y \times z$. If $x = 0$ the product is zero. For Moore pleasantness functions more like x in $(x + 1) \times y \times z$. If $x = 0$ the product need not be zero. Of course this is only a very rough analogy.

What Bentham, Mill and Moore are all agreed on is that the rightness of an action is to be judged solely by consequences, states of affairs brought about by the action. Of course we shall have to be careful here not to construe 'state of affairs' so widely that any ethical doctrine becomes utilitarian. For if we did so we would not be saying anything at all in advocating utilitarianism. If, for example, we allowed 'the state of having just kept a promise', then a deontologist who said we should keep promises simply because they are promises would be a utilitarian. And we do not wish to allow this.

According to the type of non-cognitivist (or subjectivist) ethics that I am assuming, the function of the words 'ought' and 'good' is primarily to express approval, or in other words, to commend. With 'ought' we commend actions. With 'good' we may commend all sorts of things, but here I am concerned with 'good' as used to commend states of affairs or consequences of actions. Suppose we could know with certainty the total consequences of two alternative actions A and B, and suppose that A and B are the only possible actions open to us. Then in deciding whether we ought to do A or B, the act-utilitarian would ask whether the total consequences of A are better than those of B, or vice versa, or whether the total consequences are equal. That is, he commends A rather than B if he thinks that the total consequences of A are better than those of B. But to say 'better' is itself to commend. So the act-utilitarian has to do a double evaluation or piece of commending. First of all he has to evaluate consequences. Then on the basis of his evaluation of consequences he has to evaluate the actions A and B which would lead to these two sets of consequences. It is easy to fail to notice that this second evaluation is needed, but we can see that it is necessary if we remind ourselves of the following fact. This is that a non-utilitarian, say a philosopher of the type of Sir David Ross, might agree with us in the evaluation of the relative merits of the total sets of consequences of the actions A and B and yet disagree with us about whether we ought to do A or B. He might agree with us in the evaluation of total consequences but disagree with us in the evaluation of possible actions. He might say: "The total consequences of A are better than the total consequences of B, but it would be *unjust* to do A, for you *promised* to do B."

My chief concern in this study is with the *second* type of evaluation: the evaluation of actions. The utilitarian addresses himself to people who very likely agree with him as to what consequences are good ones, but who disagree with him about the principle that what we ought to do is to produce the best consequences. For a reason, which will appear presently, the difference between ideal and hedonistic utilitarianism in

most cases will not usually lead to a serious disagreement about what ought to be done in practice. In this section, however, I wish to clear the ground by saying something about the *first* type of evaluation, the evaluation of consequences. It is with respect to this evaluation that Bentham, Mill and Moore differ from one another. Let us consider Mill's contention that it is 'better to be Socrates dissatisfied than a fool satisfied'.[11] Mill holds that pleasure is not to be our sole criterion for evaluating consequences: the state of mind of Socrates might be less pleasurable than that of the fool, but, according to Mill, Socrates would be happier than the fool.

It is necessary to observe, first of all, that a purely hedonistic utilitarian, like Bentham, might agree with Mill in preferring the experiences of discontented philosophers to those of contented fools. His preference for the philosopher's state of mind, however, would not be an *intrinsic* one. He would say that the discontented philosopher is a useful agent in society and that the existence of Socrates is responsible for an improvement in the lot of humanity generally. Consider two brothers. One may be of a docile and easy temperament: he may lead a supremely contented and unambitious life, enjoying himself hugely. The other brother may be ambitious, may stretch his talents to the full, may strive for scientific success and academic honours, and may discover some invention or some remedy for disease or improvement in agriculture which will enable innumerable men of easy temperament to lead a contented life, whereas otherwise they would have been thwarted by poverty, disease or hunger. Or he may make some advance in pure science which will later have beneficial practical applications. Or, again, he may write poetry which will solace the leisure hours and stimulate the brains of practical men or scientists, thus indirectly leading to an improvement in society. That is, the pleasures of poetry or mathematics may be *extrinsically* valuable in a way in which those of pushpin or sun-bathing may not be. Though the poet or mathematician may be discontented, society as a whole may be the more contented for his presence.

Again, a man who enjoys pushpin is likely eventually to become bored with it, whereas the man who enjoys poetry is likely to retain this interest throughout his life. Moreover the reading of poetry may develop imagination and sensitivity, and so as a result of his interest in poetry a man may be able to do more for the happiness of others than if he had played pushpin and let his brain deteriorate. In short, both for the man immediately concerned and for others, the pleasures of poetry are, to use Bentham's word, more *fecund* than those of pushpin.

Perhaps, then, our preference for poetry over pushpin is not one of intrinsic value, but is merely one of extrinsic value. Perhaps strictly in itself and at a particular moment, a contented sheep is as good as a contented philosopher. However it is hard to agree to this. If we did we should have to agree that the human population ought ideally to be reduced by contraceptive methods and the sheep population more than correspondingly increased. Perhaps just so many humans should be left as could keep innumerable millions of placid sheep in contented idleness and immunity from depredations by ferocious animals. Indeed if a contented idiot is as good as a contented philosopher, and if a contented sheep is as good as a contented idiot, then a contented fish is as good as a contented sheep, and a contented beetle is as good as a contented fish. Where shall we stop?

Maybe we have gone wrong in talking of pleasure as though it were no more than contentment. Contentment consists roughly in relative absence of unsatisfied desires; pleasure is perhaps something more positive and consists in a balance between absence of unsatisfied desires and presence of satisfied desires. We might put the difference in this way: pure unconsciousness would be a limiting case of contentment, but not of pleasure. A stone has no unsatisfied desires, but then it just has no desires. Nevertheless, this consideration will not resolve the disagreement between Bentham and Mill. No doubt a dog has as intense a desire to discover rats as the philosopher has to discover the mysteries of the universe. Mill would wish to say that the pleasures of the philosopher were more valuable intrinsically than those of the dog, however intense these last might be.

It appears, then, that many of us may well have a preference not only for enjoyment as such but for certain sorts of enjoyment. And this goes for many of the humane and beneficent readers whom I am addressing. I suspect that they too have

an intrinsic preference for the more complex and intellectual pleasures. This is not surprising. We must not underrate the mere brute strength of a hard and fit human being: by any standards man is a large and strong animal. Nevertheless above all else man owes his survival to his superior intelligence. If man were not a species which was inclined above all else to think and strive, we should not be where we are now. No wonder that men have a liking for intelligence and complexity, and this may become increasingly so in future. Perhaps some people may feel that my remarks here are somewhat too complacent, in view of the liking of so many people for low-grade entertainments, such as certain popular television programmes. But even the most avid television addict probably enjoys solving practical problems connected with his car, his furniture, or his garden. However unintellectual he might be, he would certainly resent the suggestion that he should, if it were possible, change places with a contented sheep, or even a lively and happy dog. Nevertheless, when all is said and done, we must not disguise the fact that disagreements in ultimate attitude are possible between those who like Mill have, and those who like Bentham have not, an intrinsic preference for the 'higher' pleasures. However it is possible for two people to disagree about ultimate ends and yet agree in practice about what ought to be done. It is worth while enquiring how much practical ethics is likely to be affected by the possibility of disagreement over the question of Socrates dissatisfied versus the fool satisfied.

'Not very much', one feels like saying at first. We noted that the most complex and intellectual pleasures are also the most fecund. Poetry elevates the mind, makes one more sensitive, and so harmonizes with various intellectual pursuits, some of which are of practical value. Delight in mathematics is even more obviously, on Benthamite views, a pleasure worth encouraging, for on the progress of mathematics depends the progress of mankind. Even the most hedonistic schoolmaster would prefer to see his boys enjoying poetry and mathematics rather than neglecting these arts for the pleasures of marbles or the tuckshop. Indeed many of the brutish pleasures not only lack fecundity but are actually the reverse of fecund. To enjoy food too much is to end up fat, unhealthy and without zest or vigour.

To enjoy drink too much is even worse. In most circumstances of ordinary life the pure hedonist will agree in his practical recommendations with the quasi-ideal utilitarian.

This need not always be so. Some years ago two psychologists, Olds and Milner, carried out some experiments with rats.[12] Through the skull of each rat they inserted an electrode. These electrodes penetrated to various regions of the brain. In the case of some of these regions the rat showed behaviour characteristics of pleasure when a current was passed from the electrode, in others they seemed to show pain, and in others the stimulus seemed neutral. That a stimulus was pleasure-giving was shown by the fact that the rat would learn to pass the current himself by pressing a lever. He would neglect food and make straight for this lever and start stimulating himself. In some cases he would sit there pressing the lever every few seconds for hours on end. This calls up a pleasant picture of the voluptuary of the future, a bald-headed man with a number of electrodes protruding from his skull, one to give the physical pleasure of sex, one for that of eating, one for that of drinking, and so on. Now is this the sort of life that all our ethical planning should culminate in? A few hours' work a week, automatic factories, comfort and security from disease, and hours spent at a switch, continually electrifying various regions of one's brain? Surely not. Men were made for higher things, one can't help wanting to say, even though one knows that men weren't made for anything, but are the product of evolution by natural selection.

It might be said that the objection to continual sensual stimulation of the above sort is that though it would be pleasant in itself it would be infecund of future pleasures. This is often so with the ordinary sensual pleasures. Excessive indulgence in the physical pleasures of sex may possibly have a debilitating effect and may perhaps interfere with the deeper feelings of romantic love. But whether stimulation by the electrode method would have this weakening effect and whether it would impair the possibility of future pleasures of the same sort is another matter. For example, there would be no excessive secretion of hormones. The whole biochemical mechanism would, almost literally, be short-circuited. Maybe, however, a person who stimulated himself by the electrode method would find it so enjoyable that he would neglect all other pursuits. Maybe if everyone became an electrode operator people would lose interest in everything else and the human race would die out.

Suppose, however, that the facts turned out otherwise: that a man could (and would) do his full share of work in the office or the factory and come back in the evening to a few hours contented electrode work, without bad after-effects. This would be his greatest pleasure, and the pleasure would be so great intrinsically and so easily repeatable that its lack of fecundity would not matter. Indeed perhaps by this time human arts, such as medicine, engineering, agriculture and architecture will have been brought to a pitch of perfection sufficient to enable most of the human race to spend most of its time electrode operating, without compensating pains of starvation, disease and squalor. Would this be a satisfactory state of society? Would this be the millennium towards which we have been striving? Surely the pure hedonist would have to say that it was.

It is time, therefore, that we had another look at the concept of happiness. Should we say that the electrode operator was really happy? This is a difficult question to be clear about, because the concept of happiness is a tricky one. But whether we should call the electrode operator 'happy' or not, there is no doubt (a) that he would be *contented* and (b) that he would be *enjoying himself*.

Perhaps a possible reluctance to call the electrode operator 'happy' might come from the following circumstance. The electrode operator might be perfectly contented, might perfectly enjoy his electrode operating, and might not be willing to exchange his lot for any other. And we ourselves, perhaps, once we became electrode operators too, could become perfectly contented and satisfied. But nevertheless, as we are now, we just do not want to become electrode operators. We want other things, perhaps to write a book or get into a cricket team. If someone said 'from tomorrow onwards you are going to be forced to be an electrode operator' we should not be pleased. Maybe from tomorrow onwards, once the electrode work had started, we should be perfectly contented, but we are not contented now at the prospect. We are not satisfied at being told that we would be in a certain state from tomorrow onwards, even though we may know that from tomorrow onwards we should be perfectly satisfied. All this is psychologically possible. It is just the obverse of a situation which we often find. I remember an occasion on which I was suspended by cable car half-way up a precipitous mountain. As the cable car creaked upwards, apparently so flimsily held above the yawning chasm below, I fervently wished that I had never come in it. When I bought the ticket for the cable car I knew that I should shortly be wishing that I had never bought it. And yet I should have been annoyed if I had been refused it. Again, a man may be very anxious to catch a bus, so as to be in time for a dental appointment, and yet a few minutes later, while the drill is boring into his tooth, may wish that he had missed that bus. It is, contrariwise, perfectly possible that I should be annoyed today if told that from tomorrow onwards I should be an electrode addict, even though I knew that from tomorrow onwards I should be perfectly contented.

This, I think, explains part of our hesitancy about whether to call the electrode operator 'happy'. The notion of happiness ties up with that of contentment: to be fairly happy at least involves being fairly contented, though it involves something more as well. Though we should be contented when we became electrode operators, we are not contented now with the prospect that we should become electrode operators. Similarly if Socrates had become a fool he might thereafter have been perfectly contented. Nevertheless if beforehand he had been told that he would in the future become a fool he would have been even more dissatisfied than in fact he was. This is part of the trouble about the dispute between Bentham and Mill. The case involves the possibility of (a) our being contented if we are in a certain state, and (b) our being contented at the prospect of being so contented. Normally situations in which we should be contented go along with our being contented at the prospect of our getting into such situations. In the case of the electrode operator and in that of Socrates and the fool we are pulled two ways at once.

Now to call a person 'happy' is to say more than that he is contented for most of the time, or even that he frequently enjoys himself and is rarely discontented or in pain. It is, I think, in part to express a favourable attitude to the idea of such a form of contentment and enjoyment. That is,

for A to call B 'happy', A must be contented at the prospect of B being in his present state of mind and at the prospect of A himself, should the opportunity arise, enjoying that sort of state of mind. That is, 'happy' is a word which is mainly descriptive (tied to the concepts of contentment and enjoyment) but which is also partly evaluative. It is because Mill approves of the 'higher' pleasures, e.g. intellectual pleasures, so much more than he approves of the more simple and brutish pleasures, that, quite apart from consequences and side effects, he can pronounce the man who enjoys the pleasures of philosophical discourse as 'more happy' than the man who gets enjoyment from pushpin or beer drinking.

The word 'happy' is not wholly evaluative, for there would be something absurd, as opposed to merely unusual, in calling a man who was in pain, or who was not enjoying himself, or who hardly ever enjoyed himself, or who was in a more or less permanent state of intense dissatisfaction, a 'happy' man. For a man to be happy he must, as a minimal condition, be fairly contented and moderately enjoying himself for much of the time. Once this minimal condition is satisfied we can go on to evaluate various types of contentment and enjoyment and to grade them in terms of happiness. Happiness is, of course, a long-term concept in a way that enjoyment is not. We can talk of a man enjoying himself at a quarter past two precisely, but hardly of a man being happy at a quarter past two precisely. Similarly we can talk of it raining at a quarter past two precisely, but hardly about it being a wet climate at a quarter past two precisely. But happiness involves enjoyment at various times, just as a wet climate involves rain at various times.

To be enjoying oneself, Ryle once suggested, is to be doing what you want to be doing and not to be wanting to do anything else,[13] or, more accurately, we might say that one enjoys oneself the more one wants to be doing what one is in fact doing and the less one wants to be doing anything else. A man will not enjoy a round of golf if (a) he does not particularly want to play golf, or (b) though he wants to play golf there is something else he wishes he were doing at the same time, such as buying the vegetables for his wife, filling in his income tax forms, or listening to a lecture on philosophy. Even sensual pleasures come under the same description. For example the pleasure of eating an ice-cream involves having a certain physical sensation, in a way in which the pleasure of golf or of symbolic logic does not, but the man who is enjoying an ice-cream can still be said to be doing what he wants to do (have a certain physical sensation) and not to be wanting to do anything else. If his mind is preoccupied with work or if he is conscious of a pressing engagement somewhere else, he will not enjoy the physical sensation, however intense it be, or will not enjoy it very much.

The hedonistic ideal would then appear to reduce to a state of affairs in which each person is enjoying himself. Since, as we noted, a dog may, as far as we can tell, enjoy chasing a rat as much as a philosopher or a mathematician may enjoy solving a problem, we must, if we adopt the purely hedonistic position, defend the higher pleasures on account of their fecundity. And that might not turn out to be a workable defence in a world made safe for electrode operators.

To sum up so far, happiness is partly an evaluative concept, and so the utilitarian maxim 'You ought to maximize happiness' is doubly evaluative. There is the possibility of an ultimate disagreement between two utilitarians who differ over the question of pushpin versus poetry, or Socrates dissatisfied versus the fool satisfied. The case of the electrode operator shows that two utilitarians might come to advocate very different courses of actions if they differed about what constituted happiness, and this difference between them would be simply an ultimate difference in attitude. [. . .] So I do not wish to say that the difference in ultimate valuation between a hedonistic and a non-hedonistic utilitarian will *never* lead to difference in practice.

Leaving these more remote possibilities out of account, however, and considering the decisions we have to make at present, the question of whether the 'higher' pleasures should be preferred to the 'lower' ones does seem to be of slight practical importance. There are already perfectly good hedonistic arguments for poetry as against pushpin. As has been pointed out, the more complex pleasures are incomparably more fecund than the less complex ones: not only are they enjoyable in themselves but they are a means to further enjoyment. Still less, on the whole, do they lead to disillusionment, physical

deterioration or social disharmony. The connoisseur of poetry may enjoy himself no more than the connoisseur of whisky, but he runs no danger of a headache on the following morning. Moreover the question of whether the general happiness would be increased by replacing most of the human population by a bigger population of contented sheep and pigs is not one which by any stretch of the imagination could become a live issue. Even if we thought, on abstract grounds, that such a replacement would be desirable, we should not have the slightest chance of having our ideas generally adopted.

So much for the issue between Bentham and Mill. What about that between Mill and Moore? Could a pleasurable state of mind have no intrinsic value at all, or perhaps even a *negative* intrinsic value?[14] Are there pleasurable states of mind towards which we have an unfavourable attitude, even though we disregard their consequences? In order to decide this question let us imagine a universe consisting of one sentient being only, who falsely believes that there are other sentient beings and that they are undergoing exquisite torment. So far from being distressed by the thought, he takes a great delight in these imagined sufferings. Is this better or worse than a universe containing no sentient being at all? Is it worse, again, than a universe containing only one sentient being with the same beliefs as before but who sorrows at the imagined tortures of his fellow creatures? I suggest, as against Moore, that the universe containing the deluded sadist is the preferable one. After all he is happy, and since there is no other sentient being, what harm can he do? Moore would nevertheless agree that the sadist was happy, and this shows how happiness, though partly an evaluative concept, is also partly not an evaluative concept.

It is difficult, I admit, not to feel an immediate repugnance at the thought of the deluded sadist. If throughout our childhood we have been given an electric shock whenever we had tasted cheese, then cheese would have become immediately distasteful to us. Our repugnance to the sadist arises, naturally enough, because in our universe sadists invariably do harm. If we lived in a universe in which by some extraordinary laws of psychology a sadist was always confounded by his own knavish tricks and invariably did a great deal of good, then we should feel better disposed towards the sadistic mentality. Even if we could de-condition ourselves from feeling an immediate repugnance to a sadist (as we could de-condition ourselves from a repugnance to cheese by going through a course in which the taste of cheese was invariably associated with a pleasurable stimulus) language might make it difficult for us to distinguish an extrinsic distaste for sadism, founded on our distaste for the consequences of sadism, from an immediate distaste for sadism as such. Normally when we call a thing 'bad' we mean indifferently to express a dislike for it in itself or to express a dislike for what it leads to. When a state of mind is sometimes extrinsically good and sometimes extrinsically bad, we find it easy to distinguish between our intrinsic and extrinsic preferences for instances of it, but when a state of mind is always, or almost always, extrinsically bad, it is easy for us to confuse an extrinsic distaste for it with an intrinsic one. If we allow for this, it does not seem so absurd to hold that there are no pleasures which are intrinsically bad. Pleasures are bad only because they cause harm to the person who has them or to other people. But if anyone likes to disagree with me about this I do not feel very moved to argue the point. Such a disagreement about ultimate ends is not likely to lead to any disagreement in practice. For in all actual cases there are sufficient extrinsic reasons for abhorring sadism and similar states of mind. *Approximate* agreement about ultimate ends is often quite enough for rational and co-operative moral discourse. In practical cases the possibility of factual disagreement about what causes produce what effects is likely to be overwhelmingly more important than disagreement in ultimate ends between hedonistic and ideal utilitarians.

There are of course many valuations other than that of the intrinsic goodness of sadistic pleasures which divide the ideal from the hedonistic utilitarian. For example the ideal utilitarian would hold that an intellectual experience, even though not pleasurable, would be intrinsically good. Once more, however, I think we can convince ourselves that in most cases this disagreement about ends will not lead to disagreement about means. Intellectual experiences are in the hedonistic view extrinsically good. Of course there may be wider issues dividing the hedonistic from the ideal utilitarian, if Moore is the ideal utilitarian.

I would argue that Moore's principle of organic unities destroys the essential utilitarianism of his doctrine. He need never disagree in practice as a utilitarian ought to, with Sir David Ross. Every trick that Ross can play with his *prima facie* duties, Moore can play, in a different way, with his organic unities.[15]

[. . .]

7.   The Place of Rules in Act-utilitarianism

According to the act-utilitarian, then, the rational way to decide what to do is to decide to perform that one of those alternative actions open to us (including the null-action, the doing of nothing) which is likely to maximize the probable happiness or well-being of humanity as a whole, or more accurately, of all sentient beings.[16] The utilitarian position is here put forward as a criterion of rational choice. It is true that we may choose to habituate ourselves to behave in accordance with certain rules, such as to keep promises, in the belief that behaving in accordance with these rules is generally optimific, and in the knowledge that we most often just do not have time to work out individual pros and cons. When we act in such an habitual fashion we do not of course deliberate or make a choice. The act-utilitarian will, however, regard these rules as mere rules of thumb, and will use them only as rough guides. Normally he will act in accordance with them when he has no time for considering probable consequences or when the advantages of such a consideration of consequences are likely to be outweighed by the disadvantage of the waste of time involved. He acts in accordance with rules, in short, when there is no time to think, and since he does not think, the actions which he does habitually are not the outcome of moral thinking. When he has to think what to do, then there is a question of deliberation or choice, and it is precisely for such situations that the utilitarian criterion is intended.

It is, moreover, important to realize that there is no inconsistency whatever in an act-utilitarian's schooling himself to act, in normal circumstances, habitually and in accordance with stereotyped rules. He knows that a man about to save a drowning person has no time to consider various possibilities, such as that the drowning person is a dangerous criminal who will cause death and destruction, or that he is suffering from a painful and incapacitating disease from which death would be a merciful release, or that various timid people, watching from the bank, will suffer a heart attack if they see anyone else in the water. No, he knows that it is almost always right to save a drowning man, and in he goes. Again, he knows that we would go mad if we went in detail into the probable consequences of keeping or not keeping every trivial promise: we will do most good and reserve our mental energies for more important matters if we simply habituate ourselves to keep promises in all normal situations. Moreover he may suspect that on some occasions personal bias may prevent him from reasoning in a correct utilitarian fashion. Suppose he is trying to decide between two jobs, one of which is more highly paid than the other, though he has given an informal promise that he will take the lesser paid one. He may well deceive himself by underestimating the effects of breaking the promise (in causing loss of confidence) and by overestimating the good he can do in the highly paid job. He may well feel that if he trusts to the accepted rules he is more likely to act in the way that an unbiased act-utilitarian would recommend than he would be if he tried to evaluate the consequences of his possible actions himself. Indeed Moore argued on act-utilitarian grounds that one should never in concrete cases think as an act-utilitarian.[17]

This, however, is surely to exaggerate both the usefulness of rules and the human mind's propensity to unconscious bias. Nevertheless, right or wrong, this attitude of Moore's has a rational basis and (though his argument from probability considerations is faulty in detail) is not the law worship of the rule-utilitarian, who would say that we ought to keep to a rule that is the most generally optimific, even though we *knew* that obeying it in this particular instance would have bad consequences.

Nor is this utilitarian doctrine incompatible, as M. A. Kaplan[18] has suggested it is, with a recognition of the importance of warm and spontaneous expressions of emotion. Consider a case in which a man sees that his wife is tired, and simply from a spontaneous feeling of affection for her he

offers to wash the dishes. Does utilitarianism imply that he should have stopped to calculate the various consequences of his different possible courses of action? Certainly not. This would make married life a misery and the utilitarian knows very well as a rule of thumb that on occasions of this sort it is best to act spontaneously and without calculation. Moreover I have said that act-utilitarianism is meant to give a method of deciding what to do in those cases in which we do indeed decide what to do. On these occasions when we do not act as a result of deliberation and choice, that is, when we act spontaneously, no method of decision, whether utilitarian or non-utilitarian, comes into the matter. What does arise for the utilitarian is the question of whether or not he should consciously encourage in himself the tendency to certain types of spontaneous feeling. There are in fact very good utilitarian reasons why we should by all means cultivate in ourselves the tendency to certain types of warm and spontaneous feeling.

Though even the act-utilitarian may on occasion act habitually and in accordance with particular rules, his criterion is, as we have said, *applied* in cases in which he does not act habitually but in which he deliberates and chooses what to do. Now the right action for an agent in given circumstances is, we have said, that action which produces better results than any alternative action. If two or more actions produce equally good results, and if these results are better than the results of any other action open to the agent, then there is no such thing as *the* right action: there are two or more actions which are *a* right action. However this is a very exceptional state of affairs, which may well never in fact occur, and so usually I will speak loosely of the action which is *the* right one. We are now able to specify more clearly what is meant by 'alternative action' here. The fact that the utilitarian criterion is meant to apply in situations of deliberation and choice enables us to say that the class of alternative actions which we have in mind when we talk about an action having the best possible results is the class of actions which the agent could have performed if he had tried. For example, it would be better to bring a man back to life than to offer financial assistance to his dependants, but because it is technologically impossible to bring a man back to life, bringing the man back to life is not something we could do if we tried. On the other hand it may well be possible for us to give financial assistance to the dependants, and this then may be the right action. The right action is the action among those which we could do, i.e. those which we *would* do if we chose to, which has the best possible results.

It is true that the general concept of action is wider than that of deliberate choice. Many actions are performed habitually and without deliberation. But the actions for whose rightness we as agents want a criterion are, in the nature of the case, those done thinkingly and deliberately. An action is at any rate that sort of human performance which it is appropriate to praise, blame, punish or reward, and since it is often appropriate to praise, blame, punish, or reward habitual performances, the concept of action cannot be identified with that of the outcome of deliberation and choice. With habitual actions the only question that arises for an agent is that of whether or not he should strengthen the habit or break himself of it. And individual acts of habit-strengthening or habit-breaking can themselves be deliberate.

The utilitarian criterion, then, is designed to help a person, who could do various things if he chose to do them, to decide which of these things he should do. His utilitarian deliberation is one of the causal antecedents of his action, and it would be pointless if it were not. The utilitarian view is therefore perfectly compatible with determinism. The only sense of 'he could have done otherwise' that we require is the sense 'he would have done otherwise if he had chosen'. Whether the utilitarian view necessitates complete metaphysical determinism is another matter. All that it requires is that deliberation should determine actions in the way that everyone knows it does anyway. If it is argued that any indeterminism in the universe entails that we can never know the outcome of our actions, we can reply that in normal cases these indeterminacies will be so numerous as approximately to cancel one another out, and anyway all that we require for rational action is that some consequences of our actions should be *more probable* than others, and this is something which no indeterminist is likely to deny.

The utilitarian may now conveniently make a terminological recommendation. Let us use the word 'rational' as a term of commendation for that action which is, on the evidence available to the agent, *likely* to produce the best results, and to reserve the word 'right' as a term of commendation for the action which does *in fact* produce the best results. That is, let us say that what is rational is to try to perform the right action, to try to produce the best results. Or at least this formulation will do where there is an equal probability of achieving each possible set of results. If there is a very low probability of producing very good results, then it is natural to say that the rational agent would perhaps go for other more probable though not quite so good results. For a more accurate formulation we should have to weight the goodness of the results with their probabilities. However, neglecting this complication, we can say, roughly, that it is rational to perform the action which is on the available evidence the one which will produce the best results. This allows us to say, for example, that the agent did the right thing but irrationally (he was trying to do something else, or was trying to do this very thing but went about it unscientifically) and that he acted rationally but by bad luck did the wrong thing, because the things that seemed probable to him, for the best reasons, just did not happen.

Roughly, then: we shall use 'right' and 'wrong' to appraise choices on account of their actual success in promoting the general happiness, and we shall use 'rational' and 'irrational' to appraise them on account of their likely success. As was noted above (p. 320) 'likely success' must be interpreted in terms of maximizing the probable benefit, not in terms of probably maximizing the benefit. In effect, it is rational to do what you reasonably think to be right, and what will be right is what will maximize the probable benefit. We need, however, to make one qualification to this. A person may unreasonably believe what it would in fact be reasonable to believe. We shall still call such a person's action irrational. If the agent has been unscientific in his calculation of means–ends relationships he may decide that a certain course of action is probably best for human happiness, and it may indeed be so. When he performs this action we may still call his action irrational, because it was pure luck, not sound reasoning, that brought him to his conclusion.

'Rational' and 'irrational' and 'right' and 'wrong' so far have been introduced as terms of appraisal for chosen or deliberate actions only. There is no reason why we should not use the pair of terms 'right' and 'wrong' more widely so as to appraise even habitual actions. Nevertheless we shall not have much occasion to appraise actions that are not the outcome of choice. What we do need is a pair of terms of appraisal for *agents* and *motives*. I suggest that we use the terms 'good' and 'bad' for these purposes. A good agent is one who acts more nearly in a generally optimific way than does the average one. A bad agent is one who acts in a less optimific way than the average. A good motive is one which generally results in beneficent actions, and a bad motive is one which generally ends in maleficent actions. Clearly there is no inconsistency in saying that on a particular occasion a good man did a wrong action, that a bad man did a right action, that a right action was done from a bad motive, or that a wrong action was done from a good motive. Many specious arguments against utilitarianism come from obscuring these distinctions. Thus one may be got to admit that an action is 'right', meaning no more than that it is done from a good motive and is praiseworthy, and then it is pointed out that the action is not 'right' in the sense of being optimific. I do not wish to legislate as to how other people (particularly non-utilitarians) should use words like 'right' and 'wrong', but in the interests of clarity it is important for me to state how I propose to use them myself, and to try to keep the various distinctions clear.

It should be noted that in making this terminological recommendation I am not trying to smuggle in valuations under the guise of definitions, as Ardon Lyon, in a review of the first edition of this monograph,[19] has suggested that I have done. It is merely a recommendation to pre-empt the already evaluative words 'rational' and 'irrational' for one lot of commendatory or discommendatory jobs, the already evaluative words 'right' and 'wrong' for another lot of commendatory or discommendatory jobs, and the already evaluative words 'good' and 'bad' for yet another lot of commendatory or discommendatory jobs.

We can also use 'good' and 'bad' as terms of commendation or discommendation of actions themselves. In this case to commend or discommend an action is to commend or discommend the motive from which it sprang. This allows us to say that a man performed a bad action but that it was the right one, or that he performed a good action but that it was wrong. For example, a man near Berchtesgaden in 1938 might have jumped into a river and rescued a drowning man, only to find that it was Hitler. He would have done the wrong thing, for he would have saved the world a lot of trouble if he had left Hitler below the surface. On the other hand his motive, the desire to save life, would have been one which we approve of people having: in general, though not in this case, the desire to save life leads to acting rightly. It is worth our while to strengthen such a desire. Not only should we praise the action (thus expressing our approval of it) but we should perhaps even give the man a medal, thus encouraging others to emulate it. Indeed praise itself comes to have some of the social functions of medal giving: we come to like praise for its own sake, and are thus influenced by the possibility of being given it. Praising a person is thus an important action in itself – it has significant effects. A utilitarian must therefore learn to control his acts of praise and dispraise, thus perhaps concealing his approval of an action when he thinks that the expression of such approval might have bad effects, and perhaps even praising actions of which he does not really approve. Consider, for example, the case of an act-utilitarian, fighting in a war, who succeeds in capturing the commander of an enemy submarine. Assuming that it is a just war and that the act-utilitarian is fighting on the right side, the very courage and ability of the submarine commander has a tendency which is the reverse of optimific. Everything that the submarine commander has been doing was (in my proposed sense of the word) wrong. (I do not of course mean that he did anything wrong in the technological sense: presumably he knew how to manoeuvre his ship in the right way.) He has kept his boat cunningly concealed, when it would have been better for humanity if it had been a sitting duck, he has kept the morale of his crew high when it would have been better if they had been cowardly and inefficient, and has aimed his torpedoes with deadly effect so as to do the maximum harm. Nevertheless, once the enemy commander is captured, or even perhaps before he is captured, our act-utilitarian sailor does the right thing in praising the enemy commander, behaving chivalrously towards him, giving him honour and so on, for he is powerfully influencing his own men to aspire to similar professional courage and efficiency, to the ultimate benefit of mankind.

What I have said in the last paragraph about the occasional utility of praising harmful actions applies, I think, even when the utilitarian is speaking to other utilitarians. It applies even more when, as is more usually the case, the utilitarian is speaking to a predominantly non-utilitarian audience. To take an extreme case, suppose that the utilitarian is speaking to people who live in a society governed by a form of magical taboo ethics. He may consider that though on occasion keeping to the taboos does harm, on the whole the tendency of the taboo ethics is more beneficial than the sort of moral anarchy into which these people might fall if their reverence for their taboos was weakened. While, therefore, he would recognize that the system of taboos which governed these people's conduct was markedly inferior to a utilitarian ethic, nevertheless he might also recognize that these people's cultural background was such that they could not easily be persuaded to adopt a utilitarian ethic. He will, therefore, on act-utilitarian grounds, distribute his praise and blame in such a way as to strengthen, not to weaken, the system of taboo.

In an ordinary society we do not find such an extreme situation. Many people can be got to adopt a utilitarian, or almost utilitarian, way of thought, but many cannot. We may consider whether it may not be better to throw our weight on the side of the prevailing traditional morality, rather than on the side of trying to improve it with the risk of weakening respect for morality altogether. Sometimes the answer to this question will be 'yes', and sometimes 'no'. As Sidgwick said:[20]

> The doctrine that Universal Happiness is the ultimate *standard* must not be understood to imply that Universal Benevolence is . . . always the best *motive* of action. For . . . it is not necessary that the end which gives the criterion of rightness should always be the end at which we consciously aim: and if experience shows that the general happiness will be more satisfactorily attained if men frequently act from other motives than pure universal philanthropy, it is obvious that these other motives are to be preferred on Utilitarian principles.

In general, we may note, it is always dangerous to influence a person contrary to his conviction of what is right. More harm may be done in weakening his regard for duty than would be saved by preventing the particular action in question. Furthermore, to quote Sidgwick again, "any particular existing moral rule, though not the ideally best even for such beings, as existing men under the existing circumstances, may yet be the best that they can be got to obey".[21] We must also remember that some motives are likely to be present in excess rather than defect: in which case, however necessary they may be, it is not expedient to praise them. It is obviously useful to praise altruism, even though this is not pure generalized benevolence, the treating of oneself as neither more nor less important than anyone else, simply because most people err on the opposite side, from too much self-love and not enough altruism. It is, similarly, inexpedient to praise self-love, important though this is when it is kept in due proportion. In short, to quote Sidgwick once more, "in distributing our praise of human qualities, on utilitarian principles, we have to consider not primarily the usefulness of the quality, but the usefulness of the praise".[22]

Most men, we must never forget, are not act-utilitarians, and do not use the words 'good' and 'bad', when applied to agents or to motives, quite in the way which has here been recommended. When a man says that another is wicked he may even be saying something of a partly metaphysical or superstitious connotation. He may be saying that there is something like a yellow stain on the other man's soul. Of course he would not think this quite literally. If you asked him whether souls could be coloured, or whether yellow was a particularly abhorrent colour, he would of course laugh at you. His views about sin and wickedness may be left in comfortable obscurity. Nevertheless the things he *does* say may indeed entail something *like* the yellow stain view. 'Wicked' has thus come to have much more force than the utilitarian 'likely to be very harmful' or 'probably a menace'. To stigmatize a man as wicked is not, as things are, just to make men wary of him, but to make him the object of a peculiar and very powerful abhorrence, over and above the natural abhorrence one has from a dangerous natural object such as a typhoon or an octopus. And it may well be to the act-utilitarian's advantage, *qua* act-utilitarian, to acquiesce in this way of talking when he is in the company of non-utilitarians. He himself will not believe in yellow stains in souls, or anything like it. *Tout comprendre c'est tout pardonner*; a man is the result of heredity and environment. Nevertheless the utilitarian may influence behaviour in the way he desires by using 'wicked' in a quasi-superstitious way. Similarly a man about to be boiled alive by cannibals may usefully say that an imminent eclipse is a sign of the gods' displeasure at the proposed culinary activities. We have seen that in a completely utilitarian society the utility of praise of an agent's motives does not always go along with the utility of the action. Still more may this be so in a non-utilitarian society.

I cannot stress too often the importance of Sidgwick's distinction between the utility of an action and the utility of praise or blame of it, for many fallacious 'refutations' of utilitarianism depend for their plausibility on confusing the two things.

Thus A. N. Prior[23] quotes the nursery rhyme:

> For want of a nail
> The shoe was lost;
> For want of a shoe
> The horse was lost;
> For want of a horse
> The rider was lost;
> For want of a rider
> The battle was lost;
> For want of a battle
> The kingdom was lost;
> And all for the want
> Of a horse-shoe nail.

So it was all the blacksmith's fault! But, says Prior, it is surely hard to place on the smith's shoulders the responsibility for the loss of the kingdom. This is no objection, however, to act-utilitarianism. The utilitarian could quite consistently say that it would be useless to blame the blacksmith, or at any rate to blame him more than for any other more or less trivial case of 'bad maintenance'. The blacksmith had no reason to believe that the fate of the kingdom would depend on one nail. If you blame him you may make him neurotic and in future even more horses may be badly shod.

Moreover, says Prior, the loss of the kingdom was just as much the fault of someone whose negligence led to there being one fewer cannon in the field. If it had not been for this other piece of negligence the blacksmith's negligence would not have mattered. Whose was *the* responsibility? The act-utilitarian will quite consistently reply that the notion of *the* responsibility is a piece of metaphysical nonsense and should be replaced by 'Whom would it be useful to blame?' And in the case of such a close battle, no doubt it would be useful to blame quite a lot of people though no one very much. Unlike, for example, the case where a battle was lost on account of the general getting drunk, where considerable blame of one particular person would clearly be useful.

"But wouldn't a man go mad if he really tried to take the whole responsibility of everything upon himself in this way?" asks Prior. Clearly he would. The blacksmith must not mortify himself with morbid thoughts about his carelessness. He must remember that his carelessness was of the sort that is usually trivial, and that a lot of other people were equally careless. The battle was just a very close thing. But this refusal to blame himself, or blame himself very much, is surely consistent with the recognition that his action was *in fact* very wrong, that much harm would have been prevented if he had acted otherwise. Though if other people, e.g. the man whose fault it was that the extra cannon did not turn up, had acted differently, then the blacksmith's action would have in fact not been very wrong, though it would have been no more and no less blameworthy. A very wrong action is usually very blameworthy, but on some occasions, like the present one, a very wrong action can be hardly blameworthy at all. This seems paradoxical at first, but paradox disappears when we remember Sidgwick's distinction between the utility of an action and utility of praise of it.

The idea that a consistent utilitarian would go mad with worry about the various effects of his actions is perhaps closely connected with a curious argument against utilitarianism to be found in Baier's book *The Moral Point of View*.[24] Baier holds that (act-) utilitarianism must be rejected because it entails that we should never relax, that we should use up every available minute in good works, and we do not ordinarily think that this is so. The utilitarian has two effective replies.

The first is that perhaps what we ordinarily think is false. Perhaps a rational investigation would lead us to the conclusion that we should relax much less than we do. The second reply is that act-utilitarian premises do not entail that we should never relax. Maybe relaxing and doing few good works today increases threefold our capacity to do good works tomorrow. So relaxation and play can be defended even if we ignore, as we should not, their intrinsic pleasures.

I beg the reader, therefore, if ever he is impressed by any alleged refutation of act-utilitarianism, to bear in mind the distinction between the rightness or wrongness of an action and the goodness or badness of the agent, and Sidgwick's correlative and most important distinction between the utility of an action and the utility of praise or blame of it. The neglect of this distinction is one of the commonest causes of fallacious refutations of act-utilitarianism.

It is also necessary to remember that we are here considering utilitarianism as a *normative* system. The fact that it has consequences which conflict with some of our particular moral judgements need not be decisive against it. In science general principles must be tested by reference to particular facts of observation. In ethics we may well take the opposite attitude, and test our particular moral attitudes by reference to more general ones. The utilitarian can contend that since his principle rests on something so simple and natural as generalized benevolence it is more securely founded than our particular feelings, which may be subtly distorted by analogies with similar looking (but in reality totally different) types of case, and by all sorts of hangovers from traditional and uncritical ethical thinking.

If, of course, act-utilitarianism were put forward as a descriptive systematization of how ordinary men, or even we ourselves in our unreflective and uncritical moments, actually think about ethics, then of course it is easy to refute and I have no wish to defend it. Similarly again if it is put forward not as a *descriptive* theory but as an *explanatory* one.

John Plamenatz, in his *English Utilitarians*, seems to hold that utilitarianism "is destroyed and no part of it left standing".[25] This is apparently on the ground that the utilitarian *explanation* of social institutions will not work: that we cannot *explain* various institutions as having come

about because they lead to the maximum happiness. In this monograph I am not concerned with what our moral customs and institutions in fact are, and still less am I concerned with the question of *why* they are as they in fact are. I am concerned with a certain view about what they *ought* to be. The correctness of an ethical doctrine, when it is interpreted as recommendatory, is quite independent of its truth when it is interpreted as descriptive and of its truth when it is interpreted as explanatory. In fact it is precisely because a doctrine is false as description and as explanation that it becomes important as a possible recommendation.

[...]

10.   Utilitarianism and Justice

So far, I have done my best to state utilitarianism in a way which is conceptually clear and to rebut many common objections to it. At the time I wrote the earlier edition of this monograph I did so as a pretty single-minded utilitarian myself. It seemed to me then that since the utilitarian principle expressed the attitude of generalized benevolence, anyone who rejected utilitarianism would have to be hard hearted, i.e. to some extent non-benevolent, or else would have to be the prey of conceptual confusion or an unthinking adherent of traditional ways of thought, or perhaps be an adherent of some religious system of ethics, which could be undermined by metaphysical criticism. Admittedly utilitarianism does have consequences which are incompatible with the common moral consciousness, but I tended to take the view "so much the worse for the common moral consciousness". That is, I was inclined to reject the common methodology of testing general ethical principles by seeing how they square with our feelings in particular instances.

After all, one may feel somewhat as follows. What is the purpose of morality? (Answering this question is to make a moral judgement. To think that one could answer the question "What is the purpose of morality?" without making a moral judgement would be to condone the naturalistic fallacy, the fallacy of deducing an 'ought' from an 'is'.) Suppose that we say, as it is surely at least tempting to do, that the purpose of morality is to subserve the general happiness. Then it immediately seems to follow that we ought to reject any putative moral rule, or any particular moral feeling, which conflicts with the utilitarian principle. It is undeniable that we do have anti-utilitarian moral feelings in particular cases, but perhaps they should be discounted as far as possible, as due to our moral conditioning in childhood. (The weakness of this line of thought is that approval of the general principle of utilitarianism may be due to moral conditioning too. And even if benevolence were in some way a 'natural', not an 'artificial', attitude, this consideration could at best have persuasive force, without any clear rationale. To argue from the naturalness to the correctness of a moral attitude would be to commit the naturalistic fallacy.) Nevertheless in some moods the general principle of utilitarianism may recommend itself to us so much the more than do particular moral precepts, precisely because it *is* so general. We may therefore feel inclined to reject an ethical methodology which implies that we should test our general principles by our reactions in particular cases. Rather, we may come to feel, we should test our reactions in particular cases by reference to the most general principles. The analogy with science is not a good one, since it is not far off the truth to say that observation statements are more firmly based than the theories they test.[26] But why should our more particular moral feelings be more worthy of notice than our more generalized ones? That there should be a disanalogy between ethics and science is quite plausible if we accept a non-cognitivist theory of meta-ethics.

The utilitarian, then, will test his particular feelings by reference to his general principle, and not the general principle by reference to his particular feelings. Now while I have some tendency to take this point of view (and if I had not I would not have been impelled to state and defend utilitarianism as a system of normative ethics) I have also some tendency to feel the opposite, that we should sometimes test our general principles by how we feel about particular applications of them. (I am a bit like G. E. Moore in his reply to C. L. Stevenson,[27] where he feels both that he is right and Stevenson wrong and that he is wrong and Stevenson right. My own indecisiveness may be harder to resolve, since in my case

it is a matter of feeling, rather than intellect, which is involved.)

It is not difficult to show that utilitarianism could, in certain exceptional circumstances, have some very horrible consequences. In a very lucid and concise discussion note,[28] H. J. McCloskey has considered such a case. Suppose that the sheriff of a small town can prevent serious riots (in which hundreds of people will be killed) only by 'framing' and executing (as a scapegoat) an innocent man. In actual cases of this sort the utilitarian will usually be able to agree with our normal moral feelings about such matters. He will be able to point out that there would be some possibility of the sheriff's dishonesty being found out, with consequent weakening of confidence and respect for law and order in the community, the consequences of which would be far worse even than the painful deaths of hundreds of citizens. But as McCloskey is ready to point out, the case can be presented in such a way that these objections do not apply. For example, it can be imagined that the sheriff could have first-rate empirical evidence that he will not be found out. So the objection that the sheriff *knows* that the man he 'frames' will be killed, whereas he has only probable belief that the riot will occur unless he frames the man, is not a sound one. Someone like McCloskey can always strengthen his story to the point that we would just have to admit that if utilitarianism is correct, then the sheriff must frame the innocent man. (McCloskey also has cogently argued that similar objectionable consequences are also implied by rule-utilitarianism. That is, an unjust *system* of punishment might be more *useful* than a just one. Hence even if rule-utilitarianism can clearly be distinguished from act-utilitarianism, a utilitarian will not be able to avoid offensive consequences of his theory by retreating from the 'act' form to the 'rule' form.) Now though a utilitarian might argue that it is empirically unlikely that some such situation as McCloskey envisages would ever occur, McCloskey will point out that it is *logically* possible that such a situation will arise. If the utilitarian rejects the unjust act (or system) he is clearly giving up his utilitarianism. McCloskey then remarks: "But as far as I know, only J. J. C. Smart among the contemporary utilitarians, is happy to adopt this 'solution'." Here I must lodge a mild protest. McCloskey's use of the word 'happy' surely makes me look a most reprehensible person. Even in my most utilitarian moods I am not *happy* about this consequence of utilitarianism. Nevertheless, however unhappy about it he may be, the utilitarian must admit that he draws the consequence that he might find himself in circumstances where he ought to be unjust. Let us hope that this is a logical possibility and not a factual one. In hoping thus I am not being inconsistent with utilitarianism, since any injustice causes misery and so can be justified only as the lesser of two evils. The fewer the situations in which the utilitarian is forced to choose the lesser of two evils, the better he will be pleased. One must not think of the utilitarian as the sort of person who you would not trust further than you could kick him. As a matter of untutored sociological observation, I should say that in general utilitarians are more than usually trustworthy people, and that the sort of people who might do you down are rarely utilitarians.

It is also true that we should probably dislike and fear a man who could bring himself to do the right utilitarian act in a case of the sort envisaged by McCloskey. Though the man in this case might have done the right utilitarian act, his act would betoken a toughness and lack of squeamishness which would make him a dangerous person. We must remember that people have egoistic tendencies as well as beneficent ones, and should such a person be tempted to act wrongly he could act very wrongly indeed. A utilitarian who remembers the possible moral weakness of men might quite consistently prefer to be the sort of person who would not always be able to bring himself to do the right utilitarian act and to surround himself by people who would be too squeamish to act in a utilitarian manner in such extreme cases.

No, I am not happy to draw the conclusion that McCloskey quite rightly says that the utilitarian must draw. But neither am I happy with the anti-utilitarian conclusion. For if a case really *did* arise in which injustice was the lesser of two evils (in terms of human happiness and misery), then the anti-utilitarian conclusion is a very unpalatable one too, namely that in some circumstances one must choose the greater misery, perhaps the *very much* greater misery, such as that of hundreds of people suffering painful deaths.

Still, to be consistent, the utilitarian must accept McCloskey's challenge. Let us hope that the sort of possibility which he envisages will always be no more than a logical possibility and will never become an actuality. At any rate, even though I have suggested that in ethics we should test particular feelings by general attitudes, McCloskey's example makes me somewhat sympathetic to the opposite point of view. Perhaps indeed it is too much to hope that there is *any* possible ethical system which will appeal to all sides of our nature and to all our moods.[29] It is perfectly possible to have conflicting attitudes within oneself. It is quite conceivable that there is *no* possible ethical theory which will be conformable with all our attitudes. If the theory is utilitarian, then the possibility that sometimes it would be right to commit injustice will be felt to be acutely unsatisfactory by someone with a normal civilized upbringing. If on the other hand it is not utilitarian but has deontological elements, then it will have the unsatisfactory implication that sometimes avoidable misery (perhaps very great avoidable misery) ought not to be avoided. It might be thought that some compromise theory, on the lines of Sir David Ross's, in which there is some 'balancing up' between considerations of utility and those of deontology, might provide an acceptable compromise. The trouble with this, however, is that such a 'balancing' may not be possible: one can easily feel pulled sometimes one way and sometimes the other. How can one 'balance' a serious injustice, on the one hand, and hundreds of painful deaths, on the other hand? Even if we disregard our purely self-interested attitudes, for the sake of interpersonal discussions, so as to treat ourselves neither more nor less favourably than other people, it is still possible that there is no ethical system which would be satisfactory to all men, or even to one man at different times. It is possible that something similar is the case with science, that no scientific theory (known or unknown) is correct. If so, the world is more chaotic than we believe and hope that it is. But even though the world is not chaotic, men's moral feelings may be. On anthropological grounds it is only too likely that these feelings are to some extent chaotic. Both as children and as adults, we have probably had many different moral conditionings, which can easily be incompatible with one another.

Meanwhile, among possible options, utilitarianism does have its appeal. With its empirical attitude to questions of means and ends it is congenial to the scientific temper and it has flexibility to deal with a changing world. This last consideration is, however, more self-recommendation than justification. For if flexibility is a recommendation, this is because of the utility of flexibility.

Notes

1 *An Examination of the Place of Reason in Ethics* (Cambridge University Press, London, 1950).

2 Immanuel Kant, *Groundwork of the Metaphysic of Morals.* Translated from the German in *The Moral Law,* by H. J. Paton (Hutchinson, London, 1948).

3 *Mind* 45 (1936) 137–56.

4 In my article 'Extreme and restricted utilitarianism', *Philosophical Quarterly* 6 (1956) 344–54. This contains bad errors and a better version of the article will be found in Philippa Foot (ed.), *Theories of Ethics* (Oxford University Press, London, 1967), or Michael D. Bayles (ed.), *Contemporary Utilitarianism* (Doubleday, New York, 1968). In this article I used the terms 'extreme' and 'restricted' instead of Brandt's more felicitous 'act' and 'rule' which I now prefer.

5 For another discussion of what in effect is the same problem see A. K. Stout's excellent paper, 'But suppose everyone did the same', *Australasian Journal of Philosophy* 32 (1954) 1–29.

6 On rule worship see I. M. Crombie, 'Social clockwork and utilitarian morality', in D. M. Mackinnon (ed.), *Christian Faith and Communist Faith* (Macmillan, London, 1953). See p. 109.

7 David Lyons, *The Forms and Limits of Utilitarianism* (Oxford University Press, London, 1965). Rather similar considerations have been put forward by R. M. Hare, *Freedom and Reason* (Oxford University Press, London, 1963), pp. 131–6, and R. B. Brandt, 'Toward a credible form of utilitarianism', in H. N. Castañeda and G. Nakhnikian, *Morality and the Language of Conduct* (Wayne State University Press, Detroit, 1963), esp. pp. 119–23.

8 Jeremy Bentham's most important ethical work is 'An Introduction to the Principles of Morals and Legislation', in *A Fragment on Government and an Introduction to the Principles of Morals and Legislation,* ed. Wilfrid Harrison (Blackwell, Oxford, 1948). For the remark on poetry and pushpin see Bentham's *Works* (Tait, Edinburgh, 1843), vol. 2, pp. 253–4.

9 G. E. Moore, *Principia Ethica* (Cambridge University Press, London, 1962).

10 J. S. Mill, *Utilitarianism,* ed. Mary Warnock (Collins, London, 1962).

11 *Utilitarianism,* p. 9. The problem of the unhappy sage and the happy fool is cleverly stated in Voltaire's 'Histoire d'un bon Bramin', *Choix de Contes,* edited with an introduction and notes by F. C. Green (Cambridge University Press, London, 1951), pp. 245–7.

12 James Olds and Peter Milner, 'Positive reinforcement produced by electrical stimulation of the septal area and other regions of the rat brain', *Journal of Comparative and Physiological Psychology* 47 (1954) 419–27. James Olds, 'A preliminary mapping of electrical reinforcing effect in the rat brain', *ibid.* 49 (1956) 281–5. I. J. Good has also used these results of Olds and Milner in order to discuss ethical hedonism. See his 'A problem for the hedonist', in I. J. Good (ed.), *The Scientist Speculates* (Heinemann London, 1962). Good takes the possibility of this sort of thing to provide a *reductio ad absurdum* of hedonism.

13 Gilbert Ryle, *The Concept of Mind* (Hutchison, London, 1949). p. 108.

14 Cf. G. E. Moore, *Principia Ethica,* pp. 209–10.

15 A similar point is made by A. C. Ewing in his article 'Recent developments in British ethical thought', in C. A. Mace (ed.), *British Philosophy in the Mid-Century* (Allen and Unwin, London, 1957; second edition 1966). Ewing sees it not as I have done as showing that the principle of organic unities destroys the utilitarian character of a theory, but as a way of reconciling utilitarianism with Rossian principles.

16 In the first edition of this monograph I said 'which is likely to bring about the total situation now and in the future which is the best for the happiness or well-being of humanity as a whole, or more accurately, of all sentient beings'. This is inaccurate. To probably maximize the benefit is not the same as to maximize the probable benefit. This has been pointed out by David Braybrooke. See p. 35 of his article 'The choice between utilitarianisms', *American Philosophical Quarterly* 4 (1967) 28–38.

17 *Principia Ethica,* p. 162.

18 Morton A. Kaplan, 'Some problems of the extreme utilitarian position', *Ethics* 70 (1959–60) 228–32. This is a critique of my earlier article 'Extreme and restricted utilitarianism', *Philosophical Quarterly* 6 (1956) 344–54. He also puts forward a game theoretic argument against me, but this seems cogent only against an egoistic utilitarian. Kaplan continued the discussion in his interesting note 'Restricted utilitarianism', *Ethics* 71 (1960–1) 301–2.

19 *Durham University Journal* 55 (1963) 86–7.

20 *Methods of Ethics,* p. 413.

21 *Ibid.* p. 469.

22 *Ibid.* p. 428.

23 'The consequences of actions', *Aristotelian Society Supplementary Volume* 30 (1956) 91–9. See p. 95.

24 K. E. M. Baier, *The Moral Point of View* (Cornell University Press, Ithaca, New York, 1958), pp. 203–4.

25 *The English Utilitarians*, 2nd edn (Blackwell, Oxford, 1966), p. 145.

26 I say, 'not far off the truth' because observation statements are to some extent theory laden, and if they are laden with a bad theory we may have to reject them.

27 See P. A. Schilpp (ed.), *The Philosophy of G. E. Moore* (Northwestern University Press, Evanston, Illinois, 1942), p. 554.

28 H. J. McCloskey, 'A note on utilitarian punishment', *Mind* 72 (1963) 599.

29 J. W. N. Watkins considers this matter in his 'Negative utilitarianism', *Aristotelian Society Supp. Vol.* 67 (1963) 95–114. It is now apparent to me that my paper 'The methods of ethics and the methods of science', *Journal of Philosophy* 62 (1965) 344–9, on which the present section of this monograph is based, gives a misleading impression of Watkins's position in this respect.

27

Intending Harm

Shelly Kagan

Relevance Again

In the previous section I argued that the constraint against harm excuses too much, unless it can be supplemented with a requirement of due proportion – but that no satisfactory account of due proportion can be provided. In earlier sections I argued that the constraint also *condemns* too much, unless it can be modified in certain ways – but that the two suggested accounts of the constraint may be incapable of incorporating these modifications. For the most part, then, in our examination of the constraint against intending harm we have so far largely confined ourselves simply to considering the unpalatable implications of the constraint. But it is time to turn directly to the problem of justification, so let us bracket the previous objections, and pretend that the constraint against intending harm can be appropriately modified and supplemented, so that it neither condemns nor excuses too much.

As we have seen, the defense of a constraint against a given type of reaction can be understood as involving a series of three tasks. Therefore, to defend a constraint against intending harm, the moderate must do all of the following. First, he must establish (in a broad range of cases) the existence of a reason that particularly opposes intending harm. Second, the moderate must show that this reason is (typically) sufficiently powerful to override the countervailing reasons – in particular, the pro tanto reason to promote the good. Third, if there are any further conditions necessary for moral decisiveness, the moderate will have to show that the given reason meets these extra conditions as well. As with the discussion of the constraint against doing harm, however, I want to focus our attention on the first of these tasks. Let us assume that *if* the moderate can demonstrate the existence of a reason that particularly opposes intending harm, such a reason will be able to ground a constraint. Can the existence of the necessary reason be defended?

In Chapter 3 [of *The Limits of Morality*], when we considered the justification of the constraint against doing harm, I noted three mysteries that the moderate is unable to dispel: why should doing be morally more significant than allowing; why should doing harm be more significant than doing good; and why should harm-doing generate agent-relative rather than agent-neutral reasons? As we shall see, similar mysteries shroud the constraint against intending harm.

The first question, of course, is why the distinction between intending and merely foreseeing should be thought to be morally relevant. Obviously enough, belief in the relevance of the distinction underlies the constraint. For if the

Shelly Kagan, "Intending Harm," from *The Limits of Morality* (Oxford: Oxford University Press, 1989), pp. 165–82. © 1989 by Shelly Kagan. Reprinted with permission from Oxford University Press.

moderate is to hold that intending harm is opposed by a morally decisive reason, there must be something especially offensive about it – something distinguishing it from merely foreseeing harm. Countenancing harm where this is merely a foreseen side-effect of one's reaction may well be a serious matter; but intending harm is a more serious matter. Presumably, this view is at the heart of the moderate's attempt to defend a constraint against intending harm: I cannot intend harm even in order to prevent some greater harm, for in such a situation I have to choose between actually *intending* harm and merely *foreseeing* harm – and the former is more significant than the latter. As with the distinction between doing and allowing, I conceded at the start of the last chapter that the moral relevance of the distinction between what is intended and what is merely foreseen probably has some intuitive support. Once again, however, the question is whether the moderate can *justify* this position.

I have briefly indicated two plausible suggestions for locating the moral offensiveness of intending harm: in the first, the thought is that the agent is *aiming* at evil; in the second the idea is that such an agent *uses* the person whose harm he intends. Let's consider each suggestion in turn.

If an agent intends a state of affairs, then that state of affairs is a *goal* of his – even if it is only a derivative goal, taken on only because it is a necessary means to achieving some intrinsically desired goal. The agent shapes his reaction so as to promote the goal. He reacts in such a way as to nurture it: he does what he can to bring it about; he takes steps to avoid eliminating it; he deliberately refrains from hindering it. If the state of affairs is only intended as a means, then the agent might gladly use other, better means were any available. But if they are not, he turns his mind to pursuing the necessary means – and his behavior is *guided* by the need to countenance the (possibly subsidiary) goal. We might say that the agent *aims* at the goal.

Therefore – the moderate may argue – when an agent intends harm as a means, he has a subsidiary goal of *harm*. The agent shapes his reaction so as to promote that goal – that evil. His mind is turned (even if only in part) to nurturing evil. It does not matter that he acts with a heavy heart; the agent's reaction is still *guided* by the need to countenance evil. He *aims* at evil. But it is the

nature of evil that we should be *repelled* by it. It is of the essence of evil that it is not to be *aimed* at. Evil is not something we should be nurturing. Intending harm involves aiming at evil – and thus standing in a fundamentally incorrect relation to the essence of evil. When harm is merely a foreseen side-effect, however, one is not *aiming* at it – and so one does not stand in the essentially inappropriate relation. According to the first suggestion, this is the ground of the moral relevance of the distinction.[1]

We can grant the moderate the claim that to intend some state of affairs as a means is to have that state of affairs as a goal – to aim at it. Since harm is evil, it follows that to intend harm – even if only as a means – is to aim at evil, to have it as a goal. We can further grant that it is the nature of evil that we should be repelled by it. But it does not follow that it is always incorrect – let alone fundamentally incorrect – to intend evil; it does not follow that we should never aim at evil. This can be seen more clearly if we consider an example involving pain.

It is the nature of pain that we should attempt to repel it. Pain, after all, is not something that we want to nurture. Yet it does not follow from this that we should never aim at inflicting pain upon someone – that we should never have another's being in pain as our goal. For there could be cases in which causing someone to be in pain is a necessary means to preventing that person from undergoing even greater pain. Imagine a disease which has no painful symptoms for an initial period, but which – if left untreated – eventually erupts, regularly causing the patient excruciating pain, with no chance of remission or treatment. Luckily the disease can be cured, if treated during the initial, dormant stage. Treatment, however, requires inflicting a significant amount of pain upon the unfortunate patient: causing pain to the patient's body stimulates it to release certain hormones and antibodies (which cannot be otherwise produced) that destroy the disease-causing virus. Since the pain necessary for treatment, although significant, is far less than that caused by the disease itself, we may have good reason to deliberately induce pain in one who has recently contracted the disease.[2]

Note that the infliction of pain is no mere side-effect of providing the treatment; it is an essential means to curing the disease. If this is aiming at pain, having it as a goal, nurturing it – so be it. Arguably, it is the very fact that it is the essence of pain that it is not to be desired which justifies our decision to deliberately intend pain. At the very least, it does not follow from the essence of pain that it is fundamentally incorrect to aim at it. And this should help us to see, more generally, that it does not follow from the essence of *evil* that it is fundamentally incorrect to aim at it.

Of course, it may be objected that it was inappropriate to say that it is the *essence* of pain that we should repel it – given that pain can properly be used as a means to avoid pain. Depending on what we want to pack into the notion of essence, this may be so. But then it would be question-begging for the moderate to assume that it is the essence of *evil* that we should be repelled by it. All that could be uncontroversially claimed is that evil (like pain) is an intrinsically undesirable state of affairs; nothing would follow about its desirability in any given case, all things considered.

The negative nature of something does not entail that it is always incorrect to have some of it as a subsidiary goal. Intrinsic disvalue does not rule out the possibility of extrinsic value. Thus the realization that it is the nature of evil that it should repel us does not *entail* that evil should never be intended. And this means that the moderate has given us no reason to think that intending harm necessarily involves standing in a fundamentally incorrect relation to evil. Indeed, the example of the painful disease shows that such a claim is incorrect. This first suggestion, therefore, fails to ground the moral relevance of the distinction between intending and merely foreseeing harm.

The moderate might try to salvage this first argument by suggesting that the pain that is inflicted upon the diseased patient is not *evil*, in which case he may be able to retain his claim that aiming at evil is always morally offensive. But how is this suggestion to be defended? The moderate might note that the painful treatment is presumably given with the permission of the patient; but as was observed in the discussion of the permission principle, permission does not turn harm into non-harm. The patient's pain is still intrinsically evil, despite the patient's permission. The moderate may reply, of course, that although the patient's pain is still intrinsically evil, it is on balance a good –

for it has tremendous instrumental value as a means of avoiding much future pain. But if the moderate retreats in this manner to the claim that it is not aiming at intrinsic evil that is morally offensive, but rather aiming at what is evil on balance (i.e., including instrumental value) – then he has retreated too far. For if I kill the one to save the two, the death of the one – although intrinsically evil – is on balance a good (for it is a means of saving the lives of the two), and so the moderate would no longer have an explanation of what was morally offensive about intending the death of the one.

Presumably the moderate will want to emphasize the fact that when we inflict pain upon the patient, this is done for the sake of the patient's own greater good. In contrast, killing the one intends harm to the one for the sake of *others*. This difference between the two cases is certainly undeniable, but how does it help the moderate defend the relevance of the distinction between intending and merely foreseeing harm? Perhaps, armed with some version of the permission principle, the moderate will suggest that what is actually morally offensive is aiming at (an intrinsic) evil to one (without that one's permission) for the sake of others. No doubt something like this claim captures the moderate's intuitions reasonably well. But it seems clear that the notion that there is something fundamentally inappropriate about aiming at evil is no longer doing any real work here. The work is being done instead by the assumption that there is something especially offensive about evil to one serving as a means to the good of others. In effect, the first account of the moral offensiveness of intending harm has given way to the second account: intending harm is morally offensive because it involves *using* someone as a mere means.

It seems, then, that the attempt to defend the relevance of the distinction between intending and foreseeing harm in terms of the first account is ineffective. But before turning to see whether the second account fares any better, there is a further possibility that must be considered. For although the first account is inadequate taken by itself, perhaps it can be used to buttress a defense of the constraint which is based on respect. We have already considered attempts to ground constraints on the need to respect persons; and they have proved unsuccessful. But the feeling that respect for persons lies behind constraints is a persistent one, and so it is worth considering a new twist on the old argument.

There is certainly a strong temptation to insist that to intend the harm of another is to fail to accord that individual the respect which is his due. We are inclined to accept that intending harm is more disrespectful of the victim than merely foreseeing that harm. As before, the obvious reply is that to countenance harm which I could prevent – as when I fail to throw Maude the life preserver, and idly watch her drown – is to reveal straightforward lack of respect. (Such lack of respect seems even more in evidence when the harm is something I bring about, albeit as a side-effect.) Once again the moderate may note that cases of merely foreseeing harm are frequently motivated more from indifference than from contempt; and this will again prompt the reply that indifference to the fate of a person seems a sure sign of disrespect (or, at least, the absence of respect).

So far we have merely retraced familiar steps. But now the path changes. For previously – in the discussion of the constraint against *doing* harm – the extremist was able to continue with the observation that if indifference is *not* to be construed as a sign of disrespect, then the moderate will have to admit that many cases of violating the constraint against doing harm do not reveal disrespect for persons, for the harm is done out of indifference to the victim. This was a telling objection to the attempt to defend that constraint on the basis of respect. But no such objection can be leveled against the moderate now. For when an agent *intends* harm there can be no pretense that he is *indifferent* to it. This is what we learned from the claim that to intend is to aim, to have as a goal. An agent cannot be indifferent to what he intends: he necessarily has some sort of positive attitude to the obtaining of the intended state of affairs.

Thus if an agent intends the harm of another (even if only as a means), he has a positive attitude to that other's being harmed. And this – the moderate might argue – surely is a mark of greater disrespect than when the harm is merely foreseen, for in the latter case the attitude is at *worst* one of indifference. Even if such indifference reveals disrespect, a positive attitude to another's harm is a more significant type of

disrespect – and so the distinction between intending harm and merely foreseeing it is morally relevant.

This new version of the argument from respect, however, is no more successful than the others. We might start by noting that the argument is incorrect in suggesting that an agent's attitude toward harm that is merely foreseen will at worst be one of indifference. As I pointed out at the start of this chapter, an agent may favor some harm without intending it, provided that the agent's *reason* for countenancing the outcome is something other than the fact that it will promote some end of the agent's. Thus the agent is not necessarily indifferent to harm that is merely foreseen: he may have a positive attitude toward it. So – it might be argued – even if having a positive attitude toward the harm of another is a sign of disrespect, the moderate will not have shown that the intend/foresee distinction is morally relevant; the offensive attitude can be found on both sides of the line.

The moderate might insist, however, that these remarks do not undercut his claim to have established the moral relevance of the distinction. So long as it is granted that all cases of intending harm display the morally offensive positive attitude to the harm of others, the moderate can concede that some cases where harm is merely foreseen display the offensive feature as well. After all, the moderate never claimed that it is *only* the intending of harm that is forbidden. The claim was simply that the intend/foresee distinction is significant, since cases of intending harm are necessarily morally offensive, in a way that cases of foreseeing harm need not be. Given that a positive attitude toward the harm of another is always present when the harm is intended, but it cannot be argued that the positive attitude is always present when the harm is merely foreseen, the moderate may still claim to have established the relevance of the distinction.

The question to be asked of the moderate's argument, therefore, is whether it has established that cases of intending harm always involve a morally offensive attitude – in particular, always reveal disrespect. Now I think it must be conceded that there is a sense in which intending the harm of another always involves having a certain kind of positive attitude to that harm. But this, of course, does not yet establish the moderate's conclusion. For the argument also presupposes the claim that having a positive attitude to the harm of another is necessarily a mark of disrespect; yet the moderate has given us no reason to think that this is so.

Obviously there *are* cases where having a positive attitude toward another's harm is disrespectful: after all, it is disrespectful to mistreat a person, and it is disrespectful to have a positive attitude toward his mistreatment. But the moderate simply assumes without argument that there are no cases where the agent shows *no* disrespect even though he has a positive attitude toward another's harm – and this is the very point in question.

Now the example of the painful disease has already shown us that it needn't be disrespectful to intend harm to another person. So having a positive attitude toward the harm of another is not necessarily a sign of disrespect. Of course we can assume that the moderate means to restrict his claim to cases of intending harm to one for the sake of another. But the example of the painful disease still establishes an important point: having a positive attitude toward another's harm will *not* be a sign of disrespect if there is an adequate justification for intending harm to that person, and that is the agent's reason for intending the harm. It is because the moderate agrees that there is an adequate justification for intending harm to the diseased patient, that he admits that intending harm in this case does not reveal disrespect.

Thus, if the moderate assumes – as his argument requires – that intending harm to one for the sake of another always reveals disrespect for the one, he must be presupposing that there is no adequate justification for intending harm in such cases. But this is the very point of contention here between the extremist and the moderate – i.e., whether there is ever adequate justification for intending harm to one for the sake of others. The extremist holds that it is permissible to kill the one in order to save the two. The moderate thinks not. But it simply begs the question for the moderate to *presuppose* that there is no adequate justification for killing the one, for this is the conclusion that his argument is trying to *support*. Given the assumption that intending harm to one for the sake of others is unjustifiable, it no doubt follows that intending

that harm, and having a positive attitude toward that harm, reveal disrespect for the person being harmed. But the moderate cannot *use* the premise that intending harm to one for the sake of others reveals disrespect, in an attempt to demonstrate that intending harm in such cases is always morally offensive: there is no reason to believe the premise unless we already believe the conclusion.

For all that the moderate has shown, there may be cases in which intending harm to one as a means of saving others from harm is justified – and if there are such cases there is no reason to think that a positive attitude to the harm of the one must be a mark of disrespect. Thus the moderate has not actually supported the claim that intending harm necessarily reveals disrespect; and so the moral relevance of the distinction between what is intended and what is merely foreseen remains undemonstrated.

The first account of the constraint – which stresses that intending harm is aiming at harm – thus seems incapable of grounding the moral relevance of the distinction. Does the second account do any better? Recall that what is stressed here is that intending harm *uses* a person. When I intend harm to another as a means to some end of my own, I gain at the expense of the other. I profit from his misfortune; he is reduced to the status of a tool for furthering my goals. In contrast, it might be argued, when the harm to another is merely a foreseen side-effect, I do not use the other to further my ends. I do not profit from his misfortune, and he does not function as a mere tool. Thus the distinction between what is intended and what is merely foreseen marks a morally relevant line.

The suggested considerations, however, do not really point to the distinction between what is intended and what is merely foreseen. Talk of foreseen side-effects should not beguile us into thinking that what is merely foreseen must be causally irrelevant (at best) to promoting my ends. Recall once more a point made at the start of this chapter: it may be improper to call a harm a *means* to a given end unless the agent intends the harm; but that harm clearly can be a *vehicle* to that very end independently of what the agent intends. (For example, I may stand to profit from my rival's death, even though that fact is not my *reason* for countenancing her death. In such a case I do not intend her death as a means, but it is nonetheless a vehicle to my goal.) The mere fact that a countenanced harm is not intended does not mean that the harm cannot further my goals. Similarly, it may be improper to speak of 'using' a person unless the profiting from another's harm is intended; but the profiting itself can obviously occur even if it is unintended. And so there will be cases of unintended harm which nonetheless possess the morally offensive feature suggested by the second account. One can gain at the expense of another, and profit from the misfortunes of a person who may be effectively reduced to functioning as a mere machine which furthers one's goals – even when the harm is merely foreseen. If the morally offensive feature is the one suggested, then the distinction between what is intended and what is foreseen is not the morally relevant one. Instead, it seems that the relevant distinction will be between countenanced harms which are vehicles to the agent's ends, and countenanced harms which are not.

This distinction, however, will not suit the moderate's purposes. For as I noted at the beginning of the chapter, a constraint which simply forbids countenancing harms which are vehicles to one's ends – whether intended or not – will be unacceptably strong (indeed, it may be incoherent). The moderate must claim, therefore, that there is an important distinction *within* the class of countenanced harms which are vehicles. He must hold that there is something *particularly* significant about those cases where the harm is countenanced *because* of the fact that it is a vehicle. Only in this way can the moral relevance of the distinction between what is *intended* and what is merely *foreseen* be maintained. Nothing in the second account, however, suggests how this view might be defended.

The moderate might try to resurrect the argument from respect once again. Building on the previous attempt, he might suggest that when harm is intended the agent has a positive attitude toward it. Thus, even though it is true that there is always something morally offensive about profiting from the misfortune of another – whether the harm is intended or not – when the harm *is* intended the agent's reaction is particularly offensive. When an agent (merely) foresees that harm to another will be a vehicle to his ends, and he does not try to prevent this, his attitude may reveal a certain amount of disrespect.

But having a *positive* attitude to the fact that one is gaining from another's misfortune is a far greater mark of disrespect – and this is what intending harm involves. Thus the distinction between what is intended and what is foreseen is morally relevant after all.

I recognized earlier that there are cases where having a positive attitude toward another's harm is a mark of disrespect. It seems plausible to suggest that having a positive attitude toward someone's mistreatment reveals such a lack of respect. Thus, if the moderate is right that there is always something morally offensive about harm to a person serving as a vehicle to goals other than her own, then the moderate may also be right to conclude that intending such harm may be particularly disrespectful. But in fact the moderate has offered no support for as bold a claim as this. The argument fails for the same reasons that the earlier argument failed. There are, obviously, all too many cases where an agent unjustifiedly harms another so as to make his own illegitimate gains. But it does not follow that there are never cases where the harm is justified and the gain legitimate. If there are such cases then the mere fact that a person's harm serves as a vehicle – or even a means – will not entail that the person has been mistreated; and a positive attitude to such harm will not necessarily be a sign of disrespect. The moderate, of course, thinks that all cases of intending harm constitute mistreatment[3] – but he has given no reason to think so, and thus no reason to think that intending harm will always be especially disrespectful.

Perhaps I should indicate why I think that all such attempts to buttress the argument from respect must fail. For most cases, I believe, an act is only disrespectful *because* of the fact that it involves mistreatment: by mistreating another, the agent reveals that he lacks due regard for that other – thus, that he does not respect him. The treatment's being unjustified is the *ground* of its being an expression of disrespect. In effect, disrespect is normally something of an epiphenomenon: an act's being disrespectful cannot typically be the ground of its being mistreatment – for generally it is the fact that an act is unjustified which *makes* its performance disrespectful. In typical cases, then, an act can only be shown to be disrespectful if one *first* shows that it is unjustified.

Now this is not always the case: sometimes an act is meant as an *expression* of disrespect; it is intended to communicate to the receiver of the act (or to others) that the agent regards him with disdain or contempt. Such expressive acts may be conventional gestures of disrespect, or they may take on their communicative aspect in the given context. Other than the fact that the act is being done to communicate an attitude of disrespect, there need not be anything *else* about the content of the act that constitutes mistreatment. So in such cases it is (wholly or in part) the fact that the act expresses disrespect that makes the act unjustified. (Note that it need not always be improper to communicate disrespect; some scoundrels may deserve it. But for simplicity, let us assume that we are not dealing with such people.)

Now if, in a given situation, there were an adequate justification for performing a certain act, and that is why the agent does perform the act, then this intentionally communicative aspect does not come into play. In such cases an agent does not have, and is not trying to communicate, an attitude of disrespect. Of course, the agent's act may be *misinterpreted* as such an expression; but any act is open to misinterpretation. Except in extremely rare cases, the possibility of such misinterpretation will not be sufficient reason to forbid an act that there is otherwise good reason to perform.

Cases in which an act is meant to communicate an attitude of disrespect are unusual. In the typical case, as I have suggested, a reaction involves disrespect only *because* of the fact that it is unjustified. If there is good reason to perform an act, then the performance of the act will not reveal disrespect. It is *by virtue* of the justifiability or unjustifiability of a given act that performance of that act reveals or does not reveal disrespect. That is why the argument from respect must fail: it tries to claim that a certain kind of act's being disrespectful is the basis of its being unjustified. But I believe that the reverse is closer to the truth, that disrespect is typically epiphenomenal: the moderate must first show that harming is always unjustified; only then does it follow that it is always disrespectful. And what this means, of course, is that the moderate cannot hope to point to disrespect as the basis for harming having an especially morally offensive character.

Thus neither of the two accounts of the constraint is able to adequately defend the relevance of the distinction between what is intended and what is merely foreseen. Why the distinction should be thought relevant is, thus, a mystery. It corresponds to the first mystery surrounding the constraint against doing harm.

More Mysteries

The second mystery which shrouded the constraint against doing harm was the question why – even if we grant that doing is more significant than allowing – doing harm should be thought more significant than doing good. The corresponding question arises for the constraint against intending harm. It is, after all, possible to intend good as well as to intend harm. How does this affect the moderate's ability to defend the constraint?

If I kill the one as a means of saving the two, there is no denying that I intend harm to the one. But we must not overlook the fact that my *goal* is the saving of the two. That is, I intend good as well as intending harm. And there is no reason to think that the latter should be more significant than the former. If intending harm is especially morally offensive, then intending good should be especially morally pleasing; if there are powerful reasons that particularly oppose intending harm, there should be similarly powerful reasons that particularly support intending good. But if this is right, then the constraint against intending harm cannot get off the ground. When I kill the one to save the two, I intend both harm and good, and the magnification due to *intending* can simply be factored out: the situation seems to reduce to a choice between two lives and one – and the moderate has no reason to forbid killing the one.

After all, a constraint against intending harm requires the existence of a morally decisive reason. Thus it is not sufficient for the moderate merely to establish the existence of a reason that opposes intending harm. If that reason is to be morally decisive, it must outweigh the countervailing reasons – including any reasons there may be which support intending good. Now the moderate claims that the special character of intending (as opposed to merely foreseeing) generates a reason that particularly opposes intending harm. But unless the moderate can also show why the special character of intending should not equally generate a reason that particularly supports intending good, there will be no morally decisive reason not to intend harm.

This difficulty is most easily seen for the first account of the constraint – which argues that an agent who intends harm is aiming at evil. For a similar line of reasoning notes that an agent who intends good is aiming at good. Aiming at evil may cut against the normative grain, and therefore take on a special moral importance for the agent. But aiming at good cuts precisely *with* the normative grain, and should therefore take on a corresponding moral importance. If it is true that it is the essence of evil that it should not be aimed at, then it seems equally true that it is the essence of good that it *should* be aimed at. The notion of aiming is clearly incapable of discriminating between cases of aiming at evil and cases of aiming at good. And nothing that the first account offers suggests any reason for recognizing an asymmetry. But without an asymmetry between the importance of intending evil and the importance of intending good, the moderate is unable to defend the constraint.

Does the second account of the constraint fare any better? At first glance, at least, it seems as though this account may be able to escape the objection. Now the first account focused on the notion of aiming, and this prompted the recognition that one could aim at good as well as aiming at evil. But the second account suggests locating the moral offensiveness of intending harm in the fact that when I intend harm I am *using* another as a means; and this directs our attention to a different pair of corresponding relations. When I harm someone as a means I am using him. We must not, however, overlook the fact that it is also possible to use someone by *benefiting* him as a means. Of course, it may sound a bit odd to say that benefiting a person as a means is *using* that person, so let us adopt a more neutral sounding expression. Let us say that an agent *utilizes* a person when she benefits or harms him as a means. The relation that corresponds to harmfully utilizing someone, then, is beneficially utilizing someone.

The symmetry argument I used against the first account urges that when I kill the one to save the two, the positive relation in which I stand to the two corresponds to the negative relation in which I stand to the one – and that the very reasons which might support the claim that the negative relation is important equally support the claim that the positive relation is important. The notion which corresponds to aiming at evil, e.g., is aiming at good, and the moderate has to recognize that in killing the one to save the two I aim at good as well as at evil. This is why the first account is unable to justify the constraint.

But now the second account may appear to dodge the symmetry argument. For when I kill the one to save the two, although I *am* harming the one as a means, I am *not* benefiting the two as a means. That is, I harmfully utilize one, but I do not utilize the two at all. Consequently, even if the moderate concedes that both harming and benefiting as means take on special moral importance, it seems he needn't thereby abandon the defense of the constraint. Since the benefit to the two is not intended as a *means*, symmetry does not commit him to admitting that the magnification due to intending factors out. In killing the one to save the two I *use* the one; but I do not utilize the two. So a defense of the constraint which locates the moral offensiveness of violations in the fact that people are *used* does not seem undercut.

The symmetry argument fails to undermine the second account of the constraint, for that account is essentially limited to explaining what is wrong with intending harm as a *means*. As a result, that account cannot be forced by the symmetry argument into providing reasons for recognizing the significance of intending good as an *end*. But seeing why the symmetry argument fails in this way provides an indication of how the second account should be attacked. For as it stands, that account is fundamentally incomplete – offering no explanation of the moral offensiveness of intending harm as an end. The account will have to be supplemented. But once it *is* supplemented, the symmetry argument gains a footing once more: if intending harm as an end is morally significant, then intending good as an end must be equally significant. It is true that when I kill the one to save the two I intend harm (as a means). But I also intend good (as an end). The moderate will have no grounds for holding the former more significant than the latter – and so the defense of the constraint will collapse.

Thus, even if we grant that intending harm is a more significant category than merely foreseeing, the moderate has no reason to think that intending harm is morally more significant than intending good.[4] But without the latter assumption the constraint against intending harm cannot be maintained. As before, the moderate is left with the brute assertion that morality is more concerned with evil than with good. But the moderate has given us no reason at all to think that this is so. It is a second mystery.

Before turning to the third mystery, I want to indicate an extra embarrassment that greets the moderate. As just noted, the defense of the constraint is undercut by the fact that when I kill the one to save the two, I intend good as an end – and there is no reason to think that intending good (as an end) is less significant than intending harm (as a means). But as I also noted, it is not only intending good as an end which is possible: one can also intend good as a means. Now as we know, the moderate believes that there is an unusually weighty reason to avoid harming someone as a means. But by symmetry, then, shouldn't he also believe that there is an unusually weighty reason to attempt to benefit someone as a means? Obviously, however, the moderate believes in no such weighty reasons. Yet if harmfully utilizing a person is morally significant, then beneficially utilizing a person should be equally significant. Nothing that the moderate has said justifies the asymmetry – and it seems that the concept of intention is incapable of making the discrimination.

Consider, in this regard, the first account once more: if the moderate locates the moral offensiveness of intending harm (even if only as a means) in the fact that the agent is *aiming* at evil, then he will have to admit that even if an agent benefits another only as a means to achieving some end, that agent *aims* at the recipient's well-being (even if only derivatively). With the first account of the constraint, therefore, the moderate has no ground for holding beneficial utilization to be less significant than harmful utilization.

Thus the first account suffers from a double failure. On the one hand, it fails as a defense of the constraint (since it cannot explain why intending good to the two should not be as significant as intending harm to the one). And on the other hand, it cannot avoid the implausible view that

there are unusually weighty reasons favoring benefiting a person as a means (corresponding to the weighty reasons opposing harming someone as a means).

What about the second account of the constraint? Can this account justify the asymmetrical treatment of the two forms of utilization? It is actually rather unclear what implications this account should have for the case of benefiting another as a means. It might be suggested, first, that if there is an especially weighty reason which opposes using a person to his detriment – as the second account claims – then it would seem that there should be an equally weighty reason which *supports* 'using' a person to his advantage – i.e., benefiting him as means. However, it might be stressed instead that what is especially offensive about using another person is his being treated as a tool, as a means. Thus it might be suggested that a person is still being treated as a tool even when he is being *benefited* as a means. On this view, the second account can avoid the implausible claim that there is an especially weighty reason to benefit people as means. Yet the account now seems to be saddled with the equally implausible claim that there are especially weighty reasons that *oppose* benefiting people as means. (Perhaps the implausibility of this claim could be mitigated somewhat with the help of the permission principle. Presumably people typically don't mind being benefited as a means, and so perhaps their permission may be assumed. Yet if someone withholds her permission, is it really as morally offensive to benefit her as a means as it is to harm her as a means?) Other suggestions might be made as well. Fortunately, we need not settle the question of how the second account will handle cases of benefiting as a means; for our purposes, it is sufficient to bear in mind its failure with regard to the second mystery. Like the first account, the second account cannot explain why – when I kill the one to save the two – my intending good should be any less morally significant than my intending harm.

Unless the moderate can point to a morally decisive reason not to intend harm, there will be no justification for a constraint against my killing the one to save the two. But the moderate's failure to dispel the second mystery undermines the claim that there is such a morally decisive reason. For unless intending harm generates weightier reasons than those generated by intending good, there will be no reason to believe that the reason that opposes killing the one will be significant enough to outweigh the reason that supports saving the two. And as we have seen, the moderate has given us no reason to believe that intending harm is more significant than intending good.

The third mystery can be quickly recalled: even if we grant that intending harm is morally more significant than intending good – the moderate is still far from justifying a constraint against intending harm. For he still needs to offer an explanation of why the importance of intending harm should be embedded in an agent-relative structure. Embedded in an agent-neutral structure there will be no constraint – for I will be permitted to kill the one, even though this is intending harm, in order to prevent the two would-be murderers from harming their victims as means. As I noted in Chapter 2 [of *The Limits of Morality*], if a reason is to ground a constraint, that reason must be an agent-relative one; thus the moderate needs to argue that the reasons generated by intending harm are agent-relative rather than (only) agent-neutral. Yet nothing at all that the moderate has told us gives us reason to think that an agent's intending harm takes on a special moral importance for that agent alone, rather than being (what should be) the subject of equal concern for all agents who are in a position to do something about it.

The defense of a constraint against intending harm requires that the moderate establish the existence of a reason that opposes intending harm – a reason of exactly the right sort. This the moderate seems incapable of doing. Indeed, the same three mysteries which accompanied the constraint against doing harm haunt the constraint against intending harm: the moderate has not explained why intending is more significant than merely foreseeing; why intending harm is

more significant than intending good; and why the intending of harm generates agent-relative rather than agent-neutral reasons. To these three we can add several more. For we have seen that without a requirement of due proportion, the constraint against intending harm excuses too much. Yet any attempt to justify the requirement of due proportion (a chore which moderates in general have simply overlooked) would be plagued by mysteries similar to the ones which plague the constraint itself. From start to finish, then, the constraint against intending harm is in desperate need of justification – justification which is never provided. Coupled with the realization that the constraint probably has unpalatable implications, this provides the moderate with excellent reasons for abandoning it.

Notes

1 This account is borrowed from Nagel; his most recent statement of it is in *The View from Nowhere* (Oxford University Press, 1986), pp. 181–2.

2 I owe this example to Derek Parfit.

3 This is, of course, an overstatement. The moderate may well recognize cases in which someone has a special obligation to make some contribution to others (e.g., as a result of past promises, or through a principle of fair play). Should that contribution not be forthcoming, it may sometimes be permissible to coerce it – in effect, imposing a sacrifice as a means of aiding others. The existence of such cases obviously does not show that it is permissible to intend harm to one for the sake of others in the *absence* of such a special obligation. It is the latter sort of case that the moderate thinks always constitutes mistreatment, though he has not yet given reason to believe this.

4 The moderate might offer a dischargeability argument, similar to the one given in Chapter 3 concerning doing harm and doing good; but it would be subject to objections analogous to the ones given there.

28

United States v. Holmes (1842)

Opinion

The American ship William Brown, left Liverpool on the 13th of March, 1841, bound for Philadelphia in the United States. She had on board (besides a heavy cargo) 17 of a crew, and 65 passengers, Scotch and Irish emigrants. About 10 o'clock on the night of the 19th of April, when distant 250 miles southeast of Cape Race, Newfoundland, the vessel struck an iceberg, and began to fill so rapidly that it was evident she must soon go down. The long-boat and jolly-boat were cleared away and lowered. The captain, the second mate, 7 of the crew, and 1 passenger got into the jolly-boat. The first mate, 8 seamen, of whom the prisoner was one (these 9 being the entire remainder of the crew), and 22 passengers. In all 41 persons, got indiscriminately into the long-boat.[1] The remainder of the passengers, 31 persons, were obliged to remain on board the ship. In an hour and a half from the time when the ship struck, she went down, carrying with her every person who had not escaped to one or the other of the small boats. Thirty-one passengers thus perished.[2] On the following morning (Tuesday) the captain, being about to part company with the long-boat, gave its crew several directions, and, among other counsel, advised them to obey all the orders of the mate, as they would obey his, the captain's. This the crew promised that they would do. The long-boat was believed to be in general good condition; but she had not been in the water since leaving Liverpool, not thirty-five days; and as soon as she was launched, began to leak. She continued to leak the whole time; but the passengers had buckets, and tins, and, by bailing, were able to reduce the water, so as to make her hold her own. The plug was about an inch and a half in diameter. It came out more than once, and finally got lost; but its place was supplied by different expedients.

It appeared by the deposition of the captain, and of the second mate,[3] (the latter of whom had followed the sea twenty-one years; the former being, likewise, well-experienced), that on Tuesday morning when the two boats parted company, the long-boat and all on board were in great jeopardy. The gunwale was within from 5 to 12 inches of the water. "From the experience" which they had had, they thought "the long-boat was too unmanageable to be saved." If she had been what in marine phrase, is called a "leaky boat," she must have gone down. Even without a leak she would not have supported one-half her company, had there been "a moderate blow," "she would have swamped very quickly. The people were half naked and were "all crowded up together like sheep in a pen." "A very little irregularity in the stowage would have capsized the long-boat." If she had struck any piece of ice she would inevitably have gone down. There was great peril of ice for any boat." (Captain's and second mate's depositions.) Without going into more detail, the evidence of both these officers went to show that loaded as the long-boat was on Tuesday morning, the chances of living were much against her. But the captain thought, that even if lightened to the extent to which she afterwards was, "it would have been impossible to row her to land; and that the chances of her being picked up, were ninety-nine to one against her." It appeared, further, that on Monday night when the passengers on the ship (then settling towards her head and clearly going down) were shrieking, and calling on the captain to take them off on his boat, the mate on the long-boat said to them: "Poor souls! you're only going down a short time before we do." And, further, that on the following morning, before the boats parted company, the mate, in the long-boat, told the captain, in the jolly-boat, that the long-boat was unmanageable, and, that unless the captain would take some of the long-boat's passengers, it would be necessary to cast lots and throw some overboard. "I know what you mean," or, as stated by one witness, "I know what you'll have to do," said the captain. "Don't speak of that now. Let it be the last resort." There was little or no wind at this time, but pieces of ice were floating about.

Notwithstanding all this, the long-boat, loaded as she is above described to have been, did survive throughout the night of Monday, the day of Tuesday, and until 10 o'clock of Tuesday night, – full twenty-four hours after the ship struck the iceberg. The crew rowed, turn about, at intervals, and the passengers bailed. On Tuesday morning, after the long-boat and jolly-boat parted, it began to rain and continued to rain throughout the day and night of Tuesday. At night the wind began to freshen, the sea grew heavier, and once, or oftener, the waves splashed over the boat's bow so as to wet, all over, the passengers who were seated there. Pieces of ice were still floating around, and, during the day, icebergs had been seen. About 10 o'clock of Tuesday night, the prisoner and the rest of the crew began to throw over some of the passengers, and did not cease until they had thrown over 14 male passengers. These, with the exception of two married men and a small boy, constituted all the male passengers

aboard. Not one of the crew was cast over. One of them, the cook, was a negro.

It was among the facts of this case that, during these solemn and distressful hours, scarce a remark appeared to have been made in regard to what was going to be done, nor, while it was being done, as to the necessity for doing it. None of the crew of the long-boat were present at the trial, to testify, and, with the exception of one small boy, all the witnesses from the long-boat were women, – mostly quite young. It is probable that, by Tuesday night (the weather being cold, the persons on the boat partially naked, and the rain falling heavily, the witnesses had become considerably over-powered by exhaustion and cold, having been 24 hours in the boat. None of them spoke in a manner entirely explicit and satisfactory in regard to the most important point, viz the degree and imminence of the jeopardy at 10 o'clock on Tuesday night, when the throwing over began. As has been stated, few words were spoken. It appeared, only, that, about 10 o'clock of Tuesday night, it being then dark, the rain falling rather heavily, the sea somewhat freshening, and the boat having considerable water in it, the mate, who had been bailing for some time, gave it up, exclaiming: "This work won't do. Help me, God. Men, go to work." Some of the passengers cried out, about the same time: "The boat is sinking. The plug's out. God have mercy on our poor souls." Holmes and the crew did not proceed upon this order; and after a little while, the mate exclaimed again: "Men, you must go to work, or we shall all perish." They then went to work; and, as has been already stated, threw out, before they ended, 14 male passengers, and also 2 women.[4] The mate directed the crew "not to part man and wife, and not to throw over any women." There was no other principle of selection. There was no evidence of combination among the crew. No lots were cast, nor had the passengers, at any time, been either informed or consulted as to what was not done. Holmes was one of the persons who assisted in throwing the passengers over. The first man thrown over was one Riley, whom Holmes and the others told to stand up, which he did. They then threw him over, and afterwards Duffy, who, in vain besought them to spare him, for the sake of his wife and children who were on shore. They then seized a third man, but, his wife being aboard, he was spared. Coming to Charles Conlin, the man exclaimed: "Holmes, dear, sure you won't put me out?" "Yes, Charley," said Holmes, "you must go, too." And so he was thrown over. Next was Francis Askin, for the manslaughter of whom the prisoner was indicted. When laid hold of, he offered Holmes five sovereigns to spare his life till morning, "when," said he, "if God don't send us some help, we'll draw lots, and if the lot falls on me, I'll go over like a man." Holmes said, "I don't want your money, Frank," and put him overboard.

When one McAvoy was seized, he asked for five minutes to say his prayers, and, at the interposition of a negro, the cook, was allowed time to say them before he was cast overboard. It appeared also, that when Askin was put out, he had struggled violently, yet the boat had not sunk. Two men, very stiff with cold, who had hidden themselves, were thrown over after daylight on Wednesday morning when, clearly, there was no necessity for it.[5] On Wednesday morning, while yet in the boat, some of the witnesses had told the crew that they (i.e. the crew) should be made to die the death they had given to the others. The boat had provisions for six or seven days, close allowance; that is to say, 75 pounds of bread, 6 gallons of water, 8 or 10 pounds of meat, and a small bag of oatmeal. The mate had a chart, quadrant and compass. The weather was cold, and the passengers being half clothed, much benumbed. On Wednesday morning the weather cleared and early in the morning the long-boat was picked up by the ship "Crescent." All the persons who had not been thrown overboard were thus saved.

On the other hand the character of the prisoner stood forth, in many points in manly and interesting relief. A Finn by birth, he had followed the sea from youth and his frame and countenance would have made an artists's model for decision and strength. He had been the last man of the crew to leave the sinking ship. His efforts to save the passengers, at the time the ship struck, had been conspicuous, and, but that they were in discharge of duty, would have been called self-forget and most generous.[6] As a sailor, his captain and the second mate testified that he had ever been obedient to orders faithful to his duty, and efficient in the performance of it, – "remarkable so," said the second mate. "He was kind and obliging in every respect," said the captain, "to the passengers, to his shipmates, and to everybody.

Never heard one speak against him. He was always obedient to officers. I never had a better man on board ship. He was a first rate man." (Captain's deposition.) While on the long-boat, in order to protect the women, he had parted with all his clothes, except his shirt and pantaloons; and his conduct and language to the women were kind. After Askin had been thrown out, someone asked if any more were to be thrown over. "No," said Holmes, "no more shall be thrown over. If any more are lost, we will all be lost together." Of both passengers and crew, he finally became the only one whose energies and whose hopes did not sink into prostration. He was the first to descry the vessel which took them up, and by his exertions the ship was made to see, and, finally, to save them.[7]

The prisoner was indicted under the act of April 30, 1790, "for the punishment of certain crimes against the United States" (1 Story's Laws 83 [1 Stat, 115]), an act which ordains (section 12) that if any seaman &c., shall commit manslaughter upon the high seas, &c., on conviction, he shall be imprisoned not exceeding three years, and fined not exceeding one thousand dollars. The indictment charged that Holmes – First, with force, &c., "unlawfully and feloniously" did make an assult, &c., and cast and throw Askin from a vessel, belonging, &c., whose name was unknown, into the high seas by means of which, &c., Askin, in and with the waters thereof then and then was suffocated and drowned; second, in the same way, on board the long-boat of the ship William Brown, belonging, &c., did make an assault, &c., and cast, &c. The trial of the prisoner came on upon the 13th of April, 1842 a few days before the anniversary of the calamitous events referred to. The case was replete with incidents of deep romance and of pathetic interest. These, not being connected with the law of the case, of course do not appear in this report; but they had become known in a general way, to the public, before the trial; and on the day assigned for trial at the opening of the court, several stenographers connected with the newspaper press appeared within the bar, ready to report the evidence for their expectant readers.

BALDWIN, Circuit Justice, charging jury, alluded to the touching character of the case; and, after stating to the jury what was the offence laid in the indictment, his honour explained, with particularity, the distinction between murder and manslaughter. He said that malice was of the essence of murder, while want of criminal intention was consistent with the nature of manslaughter. He impressed strongly upon the jury, that the mere absence of malice did not render homicide excusable; that the act might be unlawful, as well as the union of the act and intention, in which union consisted the crime of murder. After giving several familiar instances of manslaughter, it explained that, although homicide was committed, there was yet an absence of bad motive, his honour proceeded with his charge nearly as follows:

In such cases the law neither excuses the act nor permits it to be justified as innocent; but, although inflicting some punishment, she yet looks with a benignant eye, through the thing done, to the mind and to the heart; and when, on a view of all the circumstances connected with the act, no evil spirit is discerned, her humanity forbids the exaction of life for life. But though, said the court, cases of this kind are viewed with tenderness, and punished in mercy, we must yet bear in mind that man, in taking away the life of a fellow being, assumes an awful responsibility to God, and to society; and that the administrators of public justice do themselves assume that responsibility if, when called on to pass judicially upon the act, they yield to the indulgence of misapplied humanity. It is one thing to give a favourable interpretation to evidence in order to mitigate an offence. It is a different thing, when we are asked, not to extenuate, but to justify, the act. In the former case, as I have said, our decision may in some degree be swayed by feelings of humanity; while, in the latter, it is the law of necessity alone which can disarm the vindicatory justice of the country. Where, indeed, a case does arise, embraced by this "law of necessity," the penal laws pass over such case in silence; for law is made to meet but the ordinary exigencies of life. But the case does not become "a case of necessity," unless all ordinary means of self preservation have been exhausted. The peril must be instant, overwhelming, leaving no alternative but to lose our own life, or to take the life of another person. An illustration of this principle occurs in the ordinary case of self-defense against lawless violence, aiming at

the destruction of life, or designing to inflict grievous injury to the person; and within this range may fall the taking of life under other circumstances where the act is indispensably requisite to self-existence. For example, suppose that two persons who owe no duty to one another that is not mutual, should, by accident, not attributable to either, be placed in a situation where both cannot survive. Neither is bound to save the other's life by sacrificing his own, nor would either commit a crime in saving his own life in a struggle for the only means of safety. Of this description of cases are those which have been cited to you by counsel, from writers on natural law – cases which we rather leave to your imagination than attempt minutely to describe. And I again state that when this great "law of necessity" does apply, and is not improperly exercised, the taking of life is devested of unlawfulness.

But in applying this law, we must look, not only to the jeopardy in which the parties are, but also to the relations in which they stand. The slayer must be under no obligation to make his own safety secondary to the safety of others. A familiar application of this principle presents itself in the obligations which rest upon the owners of stages, steamboats, and other vehicles of transportation. In consideration of the payment of fare, the owners of the vehicle are bound to transport the passengers to the place of contemplated destination. Having, in all emergencies, the conduct of the journey, and the control of the passengers, the owners rest under every obligation for care, skill, and general capacity; and if, from defect of any of these requisites, grievous injury is done to the passenger, the persons employed are liable. The passenger owes no duty but submission. He is under no obligation to protect and keep the conductor in safety, nor is the passenger bound to labour, except in cases of emergency, where his services are required by unanticipated and uncommon danger. Such, said the court, is the relation which exists on shipboard. The passenger stands in a position different from that of the officers and seamen. It is the sailor who must encounter the hardships and perils of the voyage. Nor can this relation be changed when the ship is lost by tempest or other danger of the sea, and all on board have betaken themselves, for safety, to the small boats; for imminence of danger can not absolve from duty. The sailor is bound, as before, to undergo whatever hazard is necessary to preserve the boat and the passengers. Should the emergency become so extreme as to call for the sacrifice of life, there can be no reason why the law does not still remain the same. The passenger, not being bound either to labour or to incur the risk of life, cannot be bound to sacrifice his existence to preserve the sailor's. The captain, indeed, and a sufficient number of seamen to navigate the boat, must be preserved; for, except these abide in the ship, all will perish. But if there be more seamen than are necessary to manage the boat, the supernumerary sailors have no right, for their safety, to sacrifice the passengers. The sailors and passengers, in fact, cannot be regarded as in equal positions. The sailor (to use the language of a distinguished writer) owes more benevolence to another than to himself. He is bound to set a greater value on the life of others than on his own. And while we admit that sailor and sailor may lawfully struggle with each other for the plank which can save but one, we think that, if the passenger is on the plank, even "the law of necessity" justifies not the sailor who takes it from him. This rule may be deemed a harsh one towards the sailor, who may have thus far done his duty, but when the danger is so extreme, that the only hope is in sacrificing either a sailor or a passenger, any alternative is hard; and would it not be the hardest of any to sacrifice a passenger in order to save a supernumerary sailor?

But, in addition, if the source of the danger have been obvious, and destruction ascertained to be certainly about to arrive, though at a future time, there should be consultation, and some mode of selection fixed, by which those in equal relations may have equal chance for their life. By what mode, then, should selection be made? The question is not without difficulty; nor do we know of any rule prescribed, either by statute or by common law, or even by speculative writers on the law of nature. In fact, no rule of general application can be prescribed for contingencies which are wholly unforeseen. There is, however, one condition of extremity for which all writers have prescribed the same rule. When the ship is in no danger of sinking, but all sustenance is exhausted, and a sacrifice of one person is necessary to appease the hunger of others, the selection is by lot. This mode is resorted to as the fairest

mode, and, in some sort, as an appeal to God, for selection of the victim. This manner, obviously, was regarded by the mate, in parting with the captain, as the one which it was proper to adopt, in case the long-boat could not live with all who were on board on Tuesday morning. The same manner, as would appear from the response given to the mate, had already suggested itself to the captain. For ourselves, we can conceive of no mode so consonant both to humanity and to justice; and the occasion, we think, must be peculiar which will dispense with its exercise. If, indeed, the peril be instant and overwhelming, leaving no chance of means, and no moment for deliberation, then, of course, there is no power to consult, to cast lots, or in any such way to decide; but even where the final disaster is thus sudden, if it have been foreseen as certainly about to arrive, if no new cause of danger have arisen to bring on the closing catastrophe, if time have existed to cast lots, and to select the victims, then, as we have said, sortition should be adopted. In no other than this or some like way are those having equal rights put upon an equal footing, and in no other way is it possible to guard against partiality and oppression, violence and conflict. What scene, indeed, more horrible, can imagination draw than a struggle between sailor and sailor, passenger and passenger, or, it may be, a mixed affray, in which, promiscuously, all destroy one another? This, too, in circumstances which have allowed time to decide, with justice, whose life should be calmly surrendered.

When the selection has been made by lots, the victim yields of course to his fate, or, if he resist, force may be employed to coerce submission. Whether or not "a case of necessity" has arisen, or whether the law under which death has been inflicted have been so exercised as to hold the executioner harmless, cannot depend on his own opinion; for no man may pass upon his own conduct when it concerns the rights, and especially, when it affects the lives, of others. We have already stated to you that, by the law of the land, homicide is sometimes justifiable; and the law defines the occasions in which it is so. The transaction must, therefore, be justified to the law; and the person accused rests under obligation to satisfy those who judicially scrutinize his case that it really transcended ordinary rules. In fact, any other principle would be followed by pernicious results, and, moreover, would not be practicable in application. Opinion or belief may be assumed, whether it exist or not; and if this mere opinion of the sailors will justify them in making a sacrifice of the passengers, of course, the mere opinion of the passengers would, in turn, justify these in making a sacrifice of the sailors. The passengers may have confidence in their own capacity to manage and preserve the boat, or the effort of either sailors or passengers to save the boat, may be clearly unavailing; and what, then, in a struggle against force and numbers, becomes of the safety of the seamen? Hard as is a seaman's life, would it not become yet more perilous if the passengers, who may outnumber them tenfold, should be allowed to judge when the dangers of the sea will justify a sacrifice of life? We are, therefore, satisfied, that, in requiring proof, which shall be satisfactory to you, of the existence of the necessity, we are fixing the rule which is, not merely the only one which is practicable, but, moreover, the only one which will secure the safety of the sailors themselves.

The court said, briefly, that the principles which had been laid down by them, as applicable to the crew, applied to the mate likewise, and that his order (on which much stress had been laid), if an unlawful order, would be no justification to the seamen, for that even seamen are not justified, in law, by obedience to commands which are unlawful. The court added that the case was one which involved questions of gravest consideration, and, as the facts, in some sort, were without precedent, that the court preferred to state the law, in the shape of such general principles as would comprehend the case, under any view which the jury might take of the evidence.

After a few remarks upon the evidence, the case was given to the jury, who, about 16 hours afterwards, and after having once returned to the bar, unable to agree, with some difficulty, found a verdict of guilty. The prisoner was, however, recommended to the mercy of the court. On the same day a rule was obtained to show cause why judgment should not be arrested and a new trial granted. The following ground was relied on for a new trial: Because the court, instead of telling the jury that, in a state of imminent and deadly peril, all men are reduced to a state of nature, and that there is, then, no distinction between the rights of sailor and passenger, adopted a contrary doctrine, and charged the jury accordingly.

Mr. Brown subsequently showed cause. He insisted largely upon the existence of the state of nature, as distinguished from the social state, and contended that to this state of nature the persons in the long-boat had become reduced on Tuesday night, at 10 o'clock, when Askin was thrown overboard. He iterated, illustrated, and enforced the argument contained in the closing part of the defence. For the arrest of judgment he argued that the indictment was defective in not stating the name of the boat on which the homicide was alleged to have been committed; that the counts in this respect wanted certainty. The United States did not reply.

THE COURT held the application for some days under advisement, and, at a subsequent day, discharged the rule. They said that, during the trial (aware that no similar case was recorded in juridical annals), they had given to the subject studious and deliberate consideration, and they had paid like regard to what was now urged, but that, notwithstanding all that had been said (and the arguments, it was admitted, were powerful), no error had been perceived by the court in its instructions to the jury. It is true, said the court, as is known by every one, that we do find in the text writers, and sometimes in judicial opinions, the phrases, "the law of nature," "the principles of natural right," and other expressions of a like signification; but, as applied to civilized men, nothing more can be meant by those expressions than that there are certain great and fundamental principles of justice which, in the constitution of nature, lie at the foundation and make part of all civil law, independently of express adoption or enactment. And to give to the expressions any other signification, to claim them as shewing an independent code, and one contrariant to those settled principles, which, however modified, make a part of civil law in all Christian nations, would be to make the writers who use the expressions law down as rules of action, principles which, in their nature, admit of no practical ascertainment or application. The law of nature forms part of the municipal law; and, in a proper case (as of self-defence), homicide is justifiable, not because the municipal law is subverted by the law of nature, but because no rule of the municipal law makes homicide, in such cases, criminal. It is, said the court, the municipal or civil law, as thus comprehensive, as founded in moral and social justice – the law of the land, in short, as existing and administered amongst us and all enlightened nations – that regulates the social duties of men, the duties of man towards his neighbour, everywhere. Everywhere are civilized men under its protection; everywhere, subject to its authority. It is part of the universal law. We cannot escape it in a case where it is applicable; and if, for the decision of any question, the proper rule is to be found in the municipal law, no code can be referred to as annulling its authority. Varying however, or however modified, the laws of all civilized nations, and, indeed, the very nature of the social constitution, place sailors and passengers in different relations. And, without stopping to speculate upon overnice questions not before us, or to involve ourselves in the labyrinth of ethical subtleties, we may safely say that the sailor's duty is the protection of the persons intrusted to his care, not their sacrifice – a duty we must again declare our opinion, that rests on him in every emergency of his calling, and from which it would be senseless, indeed, to absolve him exactly at those times when the obligation is most needed.

Respecting the form of the counts, the court said that the locality of the offence was sufficiently expressed, and that, in a case so peculiar, it was impossible to express the place with more precision.

When the prisoner was brought up for sentence, the learned judge said to him, that many circumstances in the affair were of a character to commend him to regard, yet, that the case was one in which some punishment was demanded; that it was in the power of the court to inflict the penalty of an imprisonment for a term of three years, and a fine of $1,000, but, in view of all the circumstances, and especially as the prisoner had been already confined in gaol several months, that the court would make the punishment more lenient. The convict was then sentenced to undergo an imprisonment in the Eastern Penitentiary of Pennsylvania, (solitary confinement) at hard labour, for the term of six months, and to pay a fine of $20.

Notes

1   The first mate and some of the crew of the long-boat were originally in the jolly-boat with the captain; but the mate, understanding navigation, was transferred, with a chart, quadrant, and compass, to the long-boat; and some of the crew were exchanged. The long-boat was 22¹/₂ feet long, 6 feet in the beam, and from 2¹/₂ feet long, 6 feet in the beam, and from 2¹/₂ to 3 feet deep.

2   One passenger had died after leaving Liverpool, and before the catastrophe of the 19th.

3   The captain and second mate, with the other persons in the jolly-boat, after having been out at sea six days, were picked up by a French fishing lugger. They afterwards came to Philadelphia, where by consent of the United States, the deposition of the captain and mate were taken, and the testimony was now read in evidence.

4   It was a matter of doubt whether these women (two sisters of Frank Askin, an Irish youth, spoken of further on) had been thrown over, or whether their sacrifice was an act of self-devotion and affection to their brother. When Holmes seized him, his sisters entreated for his life, and said that if he was thrown over they wished to be thrown over too; that "they wished to die the death of their brother." "Give me only a dress to put around me," said one of the sisters, after her brother had been thrown out, "and I care not now to live longer."

5   The exact condition of these two men did not appear. Some of the witnesses thought that they were too much frozen to recover. Others swore differently.

6   On board the long-boat, a widowed mother, a Scotswoman and her three daughters had escaped; but, just as the boat was about veering astern, and when there was great danger of being drawn into the vortex of the sinking ship, it was discovered that one of the family, a sick sister, had been left behind in the ship. Her mother was calling, "Isabel, Isabel, come, come!" But the girl was too sick to hear or to mind. Holmes, hearing the mother's cry, climbed up the ship's side (at great peril of his life, as was testified) ran astern, and, hoisting the sick girl upon his shoulders, swung himself and her over by the tackle by one arm, into the long-boat below. "O, mother, I am coming, I am coming!" responded the girl, as Holmes was lowering himself and her along the ship's side. On the trial, Holmes' counsel after describing with effect, the earlier circumstances of the catastrophe, thus opened his defence: "But hark, gentlemen. On that dreadful night, the crew and half the passengers having taken to the boats, the agonized voice of a mother is heard, even beyond the tumult and the outcry, calling for the preservation of her daughter who, in the consternation of the moment, had been forgotten, and remained on board the fated ship. In an instant you see an athletic sailor passing hand over hand, by means of a slender rope, until he regains the vessel. Behold him now on the

quarter-deck with one arm entwined around a sickly and half naked girl, in the depth of the night, surrounded by icebergs and the ocean, while, with the other, he swings himself and his almost lifeless burthen from the stern of the sinking ship into the boat below, and restores the child at once to the open arms and yearning of her mother. Yet, today, gentlemen, there, before you sits that selfsame heroic sailor, arraigned upon the charge of having voluntarily and feloniously deprived a fellow creature of his life: and that gentlemen, is the charge which you are summoned here to determine.

7   "The passengers, on Wednesday morning" said one of the witnesses, "looked very distressed: and Holmes told them to keep their hearts up." "The mate," said another witness "asked the men what he should do. Holmes said we ought not to steer for Newfoundland as we would never reach it, but to go south, as it would be warmer, and we might meet a vessel. The mate said he would do as Holmes wanted. He would give up all to Holmes. [. . .] I saw Holmes with a quilt. He tried to raise it to make a sail, but the wind was too strong. He then stood up and said he saw the mast of a vessel and afterwards got to work to raise a shawl on the end of an oar." In fact, as appeared by other parts of the testimony, Holmes' long-trained labouring eye descried the Crescent's main-mast, in the distant, several minutes before it was at all visable to anybody on board: and, while most of the boat's assemblage lay yet exhausted or despairing he had raised the signal of distress. His coolness and deep knowledge of sea life were not less manifested now, than his physical superiority had been before. The great distance of the Crescent rendered it almost impossible that Holmes' signal should be seen. The second mate of the vessel happened, however, to be aloft, watching for ice: and as soon as the ship responding to the signal, put about the voice of exultant joy and gratitude burst forth from the wretched assemblage on the long-boat. Some were crawling up the side of the boat to see the approaching vessel and others who had seemed congealed, now stood erect; "Lie down," said Holmes, "every soul of you and be still." "If they make so many of us on board, they will steer off another way and pretend they have not seen us."

29

The Queen v. Dudley and Stephens

Life-and-death decisions in extreme circumstances make for hard cases, morally and legally. This famous English case concerns four sailors adrift in a lifeboat. After twenty days with little food or water, two of them – Dudley and Stephens – killed the youngest member of their party, a boy seventeen or eighteen years old, and ate him. Four days later, the sailors were rescued. It is unlikely that they would have survived otherwise, and it is probable that the boy would have died before them.

Indictment for the murder of Richard Parker on the high seas within the jurisdiction of the Admiralty.

At the trial before Huddleston, B., at the Devon and Cornwall Winter Assizes, November 7, 1884, the jury, at the suggestion of the learned judge, found the facts of the case in a special verdict which stated "that on July 5, 1884, the prisoners, Thomas Dudley and Edward Stephens, with one Brooks, all able-bodied English seamen, and the deceased also an English boy, between seventeen and eighteen years of age, the crew of an English yacht, a registered English vessel, were cast away in a storm on the high seas 1,600 miles from the Cape of Good Hope, and were compelled to put into an open boat belonging to the said yacht. That in this boat they had no supply of water and no supply of food, except two 1 lb. tins of turnips, and for three days they had nothing else to subsist upon. That on the fourth day they caught a small turtle, upon which they subsisted for a few days, and this was the only food they had up to the twentieth day when the act now in question was committed. That on the twelfth day the remains of the turtle were entirely consumed, and for the next eight days they had nothing to eat. That they had no fresh water, except such rain as they from time to time caught in their oilskin capes. That the boat was drifting on the ocean, and was probably more than 1,000 miles away from land. That on the eighteenth day, when they had been seven days without food and five without water, the prisoners spoke to Brooks as to what should be done if no succour came, and suggested that some one should be sacrificed to save the rest, but Brooks dissented, and the boy, to whom they were understood to refer, was not consulted. That on the 24th of July, the day before the act now in question, the prisoner Dudley proposed to Stephens and Brooks that lots should be cast who should be put to death to save the rest, but Brooks refused to consent, and it was not put to the boy, and in point of fact there was no drawing of lots. That on that day the prisoners spoke of their having families, and suggested it would be better to kill the boy that their lives should be saved, and Dudley proposed that if there was no vessel in sight by the morrow morning the boy should be killed.

The Queen v. Dudley and Stephens 14 Q.B.D. 273 (1884).

That next day, the 25th of July, no vessel appearing, Dudley told Brooks that he had better go and have a sleep, and made signs to Stephens and Brooks that the boy had better be killed. The prisoner Stephens agreed to the act, but Brooks dissented from it. That the boy was then lying at the bottom of the boat quite helpless, and extremely weakened by famine and by drinking sea water, and unable to make any resistance, nor did he ever assent to his being killed. The prisoner Dudley offered a prayer asking forgiveness for them all if either of them should be tempted to commit a rash act, and that their souls might be saved. That Dudley, with the assent of Stephens, went to the boy, and telling him that his time was come, put a knife into his throat and killed him then and there; that the three men fed upon the body and blood of the boy for four days; that on the fourth day after the act had been committed the boat was picked up by a passing vessel, and the prisoners were rescued, still alive, but in the lowest state of prostration. That they were carried to the port of Falmouth, and committed for trial at Exeter. That if the men had not fed upon the body of the boy they would probably not have survived to be so picked up and rescued, but would within the four days have died of famine. That the boy, being in a much weaker condition, was likely to have died before them. That at the time of the act in question there was no sail in sight, nor any reasonable prospect of relief. That under these circumstances there appeared to the prisoners every probability that unless they then fed or very soon fed upon the boy or one of themselves they would die of starvation. That there was no appreciable chance of saving life except by killing some one for the others to eat. That assuming any necessity to kill anybody, there was no greater necessity for killing the boy than any of the other three men." But whether upon the whole matter by the jurors found the killing of Richard Parker by Dudley and Stephens be felony and murder the jurors are ignorant, and pray the advice of the Court thereupon, and if upon the whole matter the Court shall be of opinion that the killing of Richard Parker be felony and murder, then the jurors say that Dudley and Stephens were each guilty of felony and murder as alleged in the indictment.

The learned judge then adjourned the assizes until the 25th of November at the Royal Courts of Justice. On the application of the Crown they were again adjourned to the 4th of December, and the case ordered to be argued before a Court consisting of five judges.

Dec. 4. Sir H. James, A.G. (A. Charles, Q.C., C. Mathews, and Danckwerts, with him), appeared for the Crown [and] A. Collins, Q.C. (H. Clark, and Pyke, with him), for the prisoners . . .

Sir H. James, A.G., for the Crown:
. . . With regard to the substantial question in the case – whether the prisoners in killing Parker were guilty of murder – the law is that where a private person acting upon his own judgment takes the life of a fellow creature, his act can only be justified on the ground of self-defence – self-defence against the acts of the person whose life is taken. This principle has been extended to include the case of a man killing another to prevent him from committing some great crime upon a third person. But the principle has no application to this case, for the prisoners were not protecting themselves against any act of Parker. If he had had food in his possession and they had taken it from him, they would have been guilty of theft; and if they killed him to obtain this food, they would have been guilty of murder. [. . .]

A. Collins, Q.C., for the prisoners:
The facts found on the special verdict shew that the prisoners were not guilty of murder, at the time when they killed Parker, but killed him under the pressure of necessity. Necessity will excuse an act which would otherwise be a crime. Stephen, Digest of Criminal Law, art. 32, Necessity. The law as to compulsion by necessity is further explained in Stephen's History of the Criminal Law, vol. ii., p. 108, and an opinion is expressed that in the case often put by casuists, of two drowning men on a plank large enough to support one only, and one thrusting the other off, the survivor could not be subjected to legal punishment. In the American case of *The United States v. Holmes*, the proposition that a passenger on board a vessel may be thrown overboard to save the others is sanctioned. The law as to inevitable necessity is fully considered in Russell on Crimes, vol. i. p. 847. [. . .] Lord Bacon [. . .] gives the instance of two shipwrecked persons clinging to the same plank and one of them thrusting the other from it, finding that it will not support both,

and says that this homicide is excusable through unavoidable necessity and upon the great universal principle of self-preservation, which prompts every man to save his own life in preference to that of another, where one of them must inevitably perish. It is true that Hale's Pleas of the Crown, p. 54, states distinctly that hunger is no excuse for theft, but that is on the ground that there can be no such extreme necessity in this country. In the present case the prisoners were in circumstances where no assistance could be given. The essence of the crime of murder is intention, and here the intention of the prisoners was only to preserve their lives. [. . .]

Dec. 9. The judgment of the Court (Lord Coleridge, C.J., Grove and Denman, JJ., Pollock and Huddleston, BB.) was delivered by Lord Coleridge, C.J.:

The two prisoners, Thomas Dudley and Edwin Stephens, were indicted for the murder of Richard Parker on the high seas on the 25th of July in the present year. They were tried before my Brother Huddleston at Exeter on the 6th of November, and, under the direction of my learned Brother, the jury returned a special verdict, the legal effect of which has been argued before us, and on which we are now to pronounce judgment.

The special verdict as, after certain objections by Mr. Collins to which the Attorney General yielded, it is finally settled before us is as follows. [His Lordship read the special verdict as above set out.] From these facts, stated with the cold precision of a special verdict, it appears sufficiently that the prisoners were subject to terrible temptation, to sufferings which might break down the bodily power of the strongest man, and try the conscience of the best. Other details yet more harrowing, facts still more loathsome and appalling, were presented to the jury, and are to be found recorded in my learned Brother's notes. But nevertheless this is clear, that the prisoners put to death a weak and unoffending boy upon the chance of preserving their own lives by feeding upon his flesh and blood after he was killed, and with the certainty of depriving *him* of any possible chance of survival. The verdict finds in terms that "if the men had not fed upon the body of the boy they would *probably* not have survived," and that "the boy being in a much weaker condition was *likely* to have died before them." They might possibly have been picked up next day by a passing ship; they might possibly not have been picked up at all; in either case it is obvious that the killing of the boy would have been an unnecessary and profitless act. It is found by the verdict that the boy was incapable of resistance, and, in fact, made none; and it is not even suggested that his death was due to any violence on his part attempted against, or even so much as feared by, those who killed him. Under these circumstances the jury say that they are ignorant whether those who killed him were guilty of murder, and have referred it to this Court to determine what is the legal consequence which follows from the facts which they have found. [. . .]

There remains to be considered the real question in the case – whether killing under the circumstances set forth in the verdict be or be not murder. The contention that it could be anything else was, to the minds of us all, both new and strange, and we stopped the Attorney General in his negative argument in order that we might hear what could be said in support of a proposition which appeared to us to be at once dangerous, immoral, and opposed to all legal principle and analogy. All, no doubt, that can be said has been urged before us, and we are now to consider and determine what it amounts to. First it is said that it follows from various definitions of murder in books of authority, which definitions imply, if they do not state, the doctrine, that in order to save your own life you may lawfully take away the life of another, when that other is neither attempting nor threatening yours, nor is guilty of any illegal act whatever towards you or any one else. But if these definitions be looked at they will not be found to sustain this contention. [. . .]

Is there, then, any authority for the proposition which has been presented to us? Decided cases there are none. [. . .] The American case cited by my Brother Stephen in his Digest, from Wharton on Homicide, in which it was decided, correctly indeed, that sailors had no right to throw passengers overboard to save themselves, but on the somewhat strange ground that the proper mode of determining who was to be sacrificed was to vote upon the subject by ballot, can hardly, as my Brother Stephen says, be an authority satisfactory to [this court]. [. . .]

The one real authority of former time is Lord Bacon, who [. . .] lays down the law as follows: – "Necessity carrieth a privilege in itself. Necessity is of three sorts – necessity of conservation of life, necessity of obedience, and necessity of the act of God or of a stranger. First of conservation of life; if a man steal viands to satisfy his present hunger, this is no felony nor larceny. So if divers be in danger of drowning by the casting away of some boat or barge, and one of them get to some plank, or on the boat's side to keep himself above water, and another to save his life thrust him from it, whereby he is drowned, this is neither se defendendo nor by misadventure, but justifiable." On this it is to be observed that Lord Bacon's proposition that stealing to satisfy hunger is no larceny is hardly supported by Staundforde, whom he cites for it, and is expressly contradicted by Lord Hale. [. . .] And for the proposition as to the plank or boat, it is said to be derived from the canonists. At any rate he cites no authority for it, and it must stand upon his own. Lord Bacon was great even as a lawyer; but it is permissible to much smaller men, relying upon principle and on the authority of others, the equals and even the superiors of Lord Bacon as lawyers, to question the soundness of his dictum. There are many conceivable states of things in which it might possibly be true, but if Lord Bacon meant to lay down the broad proposition that a man may save his life by killing, if necessary, an innocent and unoffending neighbour, it certainly is not law at the present day.

There remains the authority of my Brother Stephen, who, both in his Digest and in his History of the Criminal Law, uses language perhaps wide enough to cover this case. The language is somewhat vague in both places, but it does not in either place cover this case of necessity, and we have the best authority for saying that it was not meant to cover it.

[. . .] We are dealing with a case of private homicide, not one imposed upon men in the service of their Sovereign and in the defence of their country. Now it is admitted that the deliberate killing of this unoffending and unresisting boy was clearly murder, unless the killing can be justified by some well-recognised excuse admitted by the law. It is further admitted that there was in this case no such excuse, unless the killing was justified by what has been called "necessity." But the temptation to the act which existed here was not what the law has ever called necessity. Nor is this to be regretted. Though law

and morality are not the same, and many things may be immoral which are not necessarily illegal, yet the absolute divorce of law from morality would be of fatal consequence; and such divorce would follow if the temptation to murder in this case were to be held by law an absolute defence of it. It is not so. To preserve one's life is generally speaking a duty, but it may be the plainest and the highest duty to sacrifice it. War is full of instances in which it is a man's duty not to live, but to die. The duty, in case of shipwreck, of a captain to his crew, of the crew to the passengers, of soldiers to women and children, as in the noble case of the *Birkenhead*; these duties impose on men the moral necessity, not of the preservation, but of the sacrifice of their lives for others, from which in no country, least of all, it is to be hoped, in England, will men ever shrink, as indeed, they have not shrunk. It is not correct, therefore, to say that there is any absolute or unqualified necessity to preserve one's life. [. . .] It is not needful to point out the awful danger of admitting the principle which has been contended for. Who is to be the judge of this sort of necessity? By what measure is the comparative value of lives to be measured? Is it to be strength, or intellect, or what? It is plain that the principle leaves to him who is to profit by it to determine the necessity which will justify him in deliberately taking another's life to save his own. In this case the weakest, the youngest, the most unresisting, was chosen. Was it more necessary to kill him than one of the grown men? The answer must be "No." [. . .] [I]t is quite plain that such a principle once admitted might be made the legal cloak for unbridled passion and atrocious crime. There is no safe path for judges to tread but to ascertain the law to the best of their ability and to declare it according to their judgment; and if in any case the law appears to be too severe on individuals, to leave it to the Sovereign to exercise that prerogative of mercy which the Constitution has intrusted to the hands fittest to dispense it.

It must not be supposed that in refusing to admit temptation to be an excuse for crime it is forgotten how terrible the temptation was; how awful the suffering; how hard in such trials to keep the judgment straight and the conduct pure. We are often compelled to set up standards we cannot reach ourselves, and to lay down rules which we could not ourselves satisfy. But a man has no right to declare temptation to be an excuse, though he might himself have yielded to it, nor allow compassion for the criminal to change or weaken in any manner the legal definition of the crime. It is therefore our duty to declare that the prisoners' act in this case was wilful murder, that the facts as stated in the verdict are no legal justification of the homicide; and to say that in our unanimous opinion the prisoners are upon this special verdict guilty of murder.[1]

The Court then proceeded to pass sentence of death upon the prisoners.[2]

Notes

1 My brother Grove has furnished me with the following suggestion, too late to be embodied in the judgment but well worth preserving: "If the two accused men were justified in killing Parker, then if not rescued in time, two of the three survivors would be justified in killing the third, and of the two who remained the stronger would be justified in killing the weaker, so that three men might be justifiably killed to give the fourth a chance of surviving." [Note by Lord Coleridge.]

2 This sentence was afterwards commuted by the Crown to six months' imprisonment.

30

War and Massacre

Thomas Nagel

From the apathetic reaction to atrocities committed in Vietnam by the United States and its allies, one may conclude that moral restrictions on the conduct of war command almost as little sympathy among the general public as they do among those charged with the formation of US military policy.[1] Even when restrictions on the conduct of warfare are defended, it is usually on legal grounds alone: their moral basis is often poorly understood. I wish to argue that certain restrictions are neither arbitrary nor merely conventional, and that their validity does not depend simply on their usefulness. There is, in other words, a moral basis for the rules of war, even though the conventions now officially in force are far from giving it perfect expression.

I

No elaborate moral theory is required to account for what is wrong in cases like the Mylai massacre, since it did not serve, and was not intended to serve, any strategic purpose. Moreover, if the participation of the United States in the Indo-Chinese war is entirely wrong to begin with, then that engagement is incapable of providing a justification for *any* measures taken in its pursuit

– not only for the measures which are atrocities in every war, however just its aims.

But this war has revealed attitudes of a more general kind, which influenced the conduct of earlier wars as well. After it has ended, we shall still be faced with the problem of how warfare may be conducted, and the attitudes that have resulted in the specific conduct of this war will not have disappeared. Moreover, similar problems can arise in wars or rebellions fought for very different reasons, and against very different opponents. It is not easy to keep a firm grip on the idea of what is not permissible in warfare, because while some military actions are obvious atrocities, other cases are more difficult to assess, and the general principles underlying these judgments remain obscure. Such obscurity can lead to the abandonment of sound intuitions in favor of criteria whose rationale may be more obvious. If such a tendency is to be resisted, it will require a better understanding of the restrictions than we now have.

I propose to discuss the most general moral problem raised by the conduct of warfare: the problem of means and ends. In one view, there are limits on what may be done even in the service of an end worth pursuing – and even when adherence to the restriction may be very

Thomas Nagel, "War and Massacre," from *Mortal Questions* (Cambridge: Cambridge University Press, 1979), pp. 53–74.
© 1979 by Cambridge University Press. Reproduced with permission from the author and Cambridge University Press.

costly. A person who acknowledges the force of such restrictions can find himself in acute moral dilemmas. He may believe, for example, that by torturing a prisoner he can obtain information necessary to prevent a disaster, or that by obliterating one village with bombs he can halt a campaign of terrorism. If he believes that the gains from a certain measure will clearly outweigh its costs, yet still supects that he ought not to adopt it, then he is in a dilemma produced by the conflict between two disparate categories of moral reason: categories that may be called *utilitarian* and *absolutist*.

Utilitarianism gives primacy to a concern with what will *happen*. Absolutism gives primacy to a concern with what one is *doing*. The conflict between them arises because the alternatives we face are rarely just choices between *total outcomes*: they are also choices between alternative pathways or measures to be taken. When one of the choices is to do terrible things to another person, the problem is altered fundamentally; it is no longer merely a question of which outcome would be worse.

Few of us are completely immune to either of these types of moral intuition, though in some people, either naturally or for doctrinal reasons, one type will be dominant and the other suppressed or weak. But it is perfectly possible to feel the force of both types of reason very strongly; in that case the moral dilemma in certain situations of crisis will be acute, and it may appear that every possible course of action or inaction is unacceptable for one reason or another.

II

Although it is this dilemma that I propose to explore, most of the discussion will be devoted to its absolutist component. The utilitarian component is straightforward by comparison, and has a natural appeal to anyone who is not a complete skeptic about ethics. Utilitarianism says that one should try, either individually or through institutions, to maximize good and minimize evil (the definition of these categories need not enter into the schematic formulation of the view), and that if faced with the possibility of preventing a great evil by producing a lesser, one should choose the lesser evil. There are certainly problems about the formulation of utilitarianism, and much has been written about it, but its intent is morally transparent. Nevertheless, despite the additions and refinements, it continues to leave large portions of ethics unaccounted for. I do not suggest that some form of absolutism can account for them all, only that an examination of absolutism will lead us to see the complexity, and perhaps the incoherence, of our moral ideas.

Utilitarianism certainly justifies *some* restrictions on the conduct of warfare. There are strong utilitarian reasons for adhering to any limitation which seems natural to most people – particularly if the limitation is widely accepted already. An exceptional measure which seems to be justified by its results in a particular conflict may create a precedent with disastrous long-term effects.[2] It may even be argued that war involves violence on such a scale that it is never justified on utilitarian grounds – the consequences of refusing to go to war will never be as bad as the war itself would be, even if atrocities were not committed. Or in a more sophisticated vein it might be claimed that a uniform policy of never resorting to military force would do less harm in the long run, if followed consistently, than a policy of deciding each case on utilitarian grounds (even though on occasion particular applications of the pacifist policy might have worse results than a specific utilitarian decision). But I shall not consider these arguments, for my concern is with reasons of a different kind, which may remain when reasons of utility and interest fail.[3]

In the final analysis, I believe that the dilemma cannot always be resolved. While not every conflict between absolutism and utilitarianism creates an insoluble dilemma, and while it seems to me certainly right to adhere to absolutist restrictions unless the utilitarian considerations favoring violation are overpoweringly weighty and extremely certain – nevertheless, when that special condition is met, it may become impossible to adhere to an absolutist position. What I shall offer, therefore, is a somewhat qualified defense of absolutism. I believe it underlies a valid and fundamental type of moral judgment – which cannot be reduced to or overridden by other principles. And while there may be other principles just as fundamental, it is particularly important not to lose confidence in our absolutist intuitions, for they are often the only barrier before the abyss of utilitarian apologetics for large-scale murder.

III

One absolutist position that creates no problems of interpretation is pacifism: the view that one may not kill another person under any circumstances, no matter what good would be achieved or evil averted thereby. The type of absolutist position that I am going to discuss is different. Pacifism draws the conflict with utilitarian considerations very starkly. But there are other views according to which violence may be undertaken, even on a large scale, in a clearly just cause, so long as certain absolute restrictions on the character and direction of that violence are observed. The line is drawn somewhat closer to the bone, but it exists.

The philosopher who has done most to advance contemporary philosophical discussion of such a view, and to explain it to those unfamiliar with its extensive treatment in Roman Catholic moral theology, is G. E. M. Anscombe. In 1958 Miss Anscombe published a pamphlet entitled *Mr Truman's Degree*,[4] on the occasion of the award by Oxford University of an honorary doctorate to Harry Truman. The pamphlet explained why she had opposed the decision to award that degree, recounted the story of her unsuccessful opposition, and offered some reflections on the history of Truman's decision to drop atom bombs on Hiroshima and Nagasaki, and on the difference between murder and allowable killing in warfare. She pointed out that the policy of deliberately killing large numbers of civilians either as a means or as an end in itself did not originate with Truman, and was common practice among all parties during World War II for some time before Hiroshima. The Allied area bombings of German cities by conventional explosives included raids which killed more civilians than did the atomic attacks; the same is true of certain fire-bomb raids on Japan.

The policy of attacking the civilian population in order to induce an enemy to surrender, or to damage his morale, seems to have been widely accepted in the civilized world, and seems to be accepted still, at least if the stakes are high enough. It gives evidence of a moral conviction that the deliberate killing of noncombatants – women, children, old people – is permissible if enough can be gained by it. This follows from the more general position that any means can in principle be justified if it leads to a sufficiently worthy end. Such an attitude is evident not only in the more spectacular current weapons systems but also in the day-to-day conduct of the non-global war in Indo-China: the indiscriminate destructiveness of antipersonnel weapons, napalm, and aerial bombardment; cruelty to prisoners; massive relocation of civilians; destruction of crops; and so forth. An absolutist position opposes to this the view that certain acts cannot be justified no matter what the consequences. Among those acts is murder – the deliberate killing of the harmless: civilians, prisoners of war, and medical personnel.

In the present war such measures are sometimes said to be regrettable, but they are generally defended by reference to military necessity and the importance of the long-term consequences of success or failure in the war. I shall pass over the inadequacy of this consequentialist defense in its own terms. (That is the dominant form of moral criticism of the war, for it is part of what people mean when they ask, 'Is it worth it?') I am concerned rather to account for the inappropriateness of offering any defense of that kind for such actions.

Many people feel, without being able to say much more about it, that something has gone seriously wrong when certain measures are admitted into consideration in the first place. The fundamental mistake is made there, rather than at the point where the overall benefit of some monstrous measure is judged to outweigh its disadvantages, and it is adopted. An account of absolutism might help us to understand this. If it is not allowable to *do* certain things, such as killing unarmed prisoners or civilians, then no argument about what will happen if one does not do them can show that doing them would be all right.

Absolutism does not, of course, require one to ignore the consequences of one's acts. It operates as a limitation on utilitarian reasoning, not as a substitute for it. An absolutist can be expected to try to maximize good and minimize evil, so long as this does not require him to transgress an absolute prohibition like that against murder. But when such a conflict occurs, the prohibition takes complete precedence over any consideration of consequences. Some of the results of this view are clear enough. It requires us to forgo certain potentially useful military measures, such as the slaughter of hostages and prisoners or indiscriminate attempts to reduce the enemy civilian population by starvation, epidemic infectious diseases like anthrax and bubonic plague, or mass incineration. It means that we cannot deliberate on whether such measures are justified by the fact that they will avert still greater evils, for as intentional measures they cannot be justified in terms of any consequences whatever.

Someone unfamiliar with the events of this century might imagine that utilitarian arguments, or arguments of national interest, would suffice to deter measures of this sort. But it has become evident that such considerations are insufficient to prevent the adoption and employment of enormous antipopulation weapons once their use is considered a serious moral possibility. The same is true of the piecemeal wiping out of rural civilian populations in airborne antiguerrilla warfare. Once the door is opened to calculations of utility and national interest, the usual speculations about the future of freedom, peace, and economic prosperity can be brought to bear to ease the consciences of those responsible for a certain number of charred babies.

For this reason alone it is important to decide what is wrong with the frame of mind which allows such arguments to begin. But it is also important to understand absolutism in the cases where it genuinely conflicts with utility. Despite its appeal, it is a paradoxical position, for it can require that one refrain from choosing the lesser of two evils when that is the only choice one has. And it is additionally paradoxical because, unlike pacifism, it permits one to do horrible things to people in some circumstances but not in others.

IV

Before going on to say what, if anything, lies behind the position, there remain a few relatively technical matters which are best discussed at this point.

First, it is important to specify as clearly as possible the kind of thing to which absolutist prohibitions can apply. We must take seriously the proviso that they concern what we deliberately do to people. There could not, for example, without incoherence, be an absolute prohibition against *bringing about* the death of an innocent person. For one may find oneself in a situation in which, no matter what one does, some innocent people will die as a result. I do not mean just that there are cases in which someone will die no matter what one does, because one is not in a position to affect the outcome one way or the other. That, it is to be hoped, is one's relation to the deaths of most innocent people. I have in mind, rather, a case in which someone is bound to die, but who it is will depend on what one does. Sometimes these situations have natural causes, as when too few resources (medicine, lifeboats) are available to rescue everyone threatened with a certain catastrophe. Sometimes the situations are man-made, as when the only way to control a campaign of terrorism is to to employ terrorist tactics against the community from which it has arisen. Whatever one does in cases such as these, some innocent people will die as a result. If the absolutist prohibition forbade doing what would result in the deaths of innocent people, it would have the consequence that in such cases nothing one could do would be morally permissible.

This problem is avoided, however, because what absolutism forbids is *doing* certain things to people, rather than bringing about certain *results*. Not everything that happens to others as a result of what one does is something that one has *done* to them. Catholic moral theology seeks to make this distinction precise in a doctrine known as the law of double effect, which asserts that there is a morally relevant distinction between bringing about or permitting the death of an innocent person deliberately, either as an end in itself or as a means, and bringing it about or permitting it as a side effect of something else one does deliberately. In the latter case, even if the outcome is foreseen, it is not murder, and does not fall under the absolute prohibition, though of course it may still be wrong for other reasons (reasons of utility, for example). Briefly, the principle states that one is sometimes permitted knowingly to bring about or permit as a side-effect of one's actions something which it would be absolutely impermissible to bring about or permit deliberately as an end or as a means. In application to war or revolution, the law of double effect permits a certain amount of civilian carnage as a side-effect of bombing munitions plants or attacking enemy soldiers. And even this is permissible only if the cost is not too great to be justified by one's objectives.

However, despite its importance and its usefulness in accounting for certain plausible moral judgments, I do not believe that the law of double effect is a generally applicable test for the consequences of an absolutist position. Its own application is not always clear, so that it introduces uncertainty where there need not be uncertainty.

In Indo-China, for example, there is a great deal of aerial bombardment, strafing, spraying of napalm, and employment of pellet- or needle-spraying antipersonnel weapons against rural villages in which guerrillas are suspected to be hiding, or from which small-arms fire has been received. The majority of those killed and wounded in these aerial attacks are reported to be women and children, even when some combatants are caught as well. However, the government regards these civilian casualties as a regrettable side-effect of what is a legitimate attack against an armed enemy.

It might be thought easy to dismiss this as sophistry: if one bombs, burns, or strafes a village containing a hundred people, twenty of whom one believes to be guerrillas, so that by killing most of them one will be statistically likely to kill most of the guerrillas, then is not one's attack on the group of one hundred a *means* of destroying the guerrillas, pure and simple? If one makes no attempt to discriminate between guerrillas and civilians, as is impossible in an aerial attack on a small village, then one cannot regard as a mere side-effect the deaths of those in the group that one would not have bothered to kill if more selective means had been available.

The difficulty is that this argument depends on one particular description of the act, and the reply might be that the means used against the guerrillas is not: killing everybody in the village – but rather: obliteration bombing of the *area* in which the twenty guerrillas are known to be located. If there are civilians in the area as well, they will be killed as a side-effect of such action.[5]

Because of casuistical problems like this, I prefer to stay with the original, unanalyzed distinction between what one does to people and what merely happens to them as a result of what

one does. The law of double effect provides an approximation to that distinction in many cases, and perhaps it can be sharpened to the point where it does better than that. Certainly the original distinction itself needs clarification, particularly since some of the things we do to people involve things happening to them as a result of other things we do. In a case like the one discussed, however, it is clear that by bombing the village one slaughters and maims the civilians in it. Whereas by giving the only available medicine to one of two sufferers from a disease, one does not kill the other or deliberately allow him to die, even if he dies as a result.

The second technical point is this. The absolutist focus on actions rather than outcomes does not merely introduce a new, outstanding item into the catalogue of evils. That is, it does not say that the worst thing in the world is the deliberate murder of an innocent person. For if that were all, then one could presumably justify one such murder on the ground that it would prevent several others, or ten thousand on the ground that they would prevent a hundred thousand more. That is a familiar argument. But if this is allowable, then there is no absolute prohibition against murder after all. Absolutism requires that we *avoid* murder at all costs, not that we *prevent* it at all costs.

It would also be possible to adopt a deontological position less stringent than absolutism, without falling into utilitarianism. There are two ways in which someone might acknowledge the moral relevance of the distinction between deliberate and nondeliberate killing, without being an absolutist. One would be to count murder as a specially bad item in the catalogue of evils, much worse than accidental death or nondeliberate killing. But the other would be to say that deliberately killing an innocent is impermissible unless it is the only way to prevent some very large evil (say the deaths of fifty innocent people). Call this the *threshold* at which the prohibition against murder is overridden. The position is not absolutist, obviously, but it is also not equivalent to an assignment of utilitarian disvalue to murder equal to the disvalue of the threshold. This is easily seen. If a murder had the disvalue of fifty accidental deaths, it would still be permissible on utilitarian grounds to commit a murder to prevent one other murder, plus some lesser evil like a broken arm. Worse still, we would be required on utilitarian grounds to prevent one murder even at the cost of forty-nine accidental deaths that we could otherwise have prevented. These are not in fact consequences of a deontological prohibition against murder with a threshold, because it does not say that the occurrence of a certain kind of act is a bad thing, and therefore to be prevented, but rather tells everyone to *refrain* from such acts, except under certain conditions. In fact, it is perfectly compatible with a deontological prohibition against murder to hold that, considered as an outcome, a murder has *no* more disvalue than an accidental death. While the admission of thresholds would reduce the starkness of the conflicts discussed here, I do not think it would make them disappear, or change their basic character. They would persist in the clash between any deontological requirement and utilitarian values somewhat lower than its threshold.

Finally, let me remark on a frequent criticism of absolutism that depends on a misunderstanding. It is sometimes suggested that such prohibitions depend on a kind of moral self-interest, a primary obligation to preserve one's own moral purity, to keep one's hands clean no matter what happens to the rest of the world. If this were the position, it might be exposed to the charge of self-indulgence. After all, what gives one man a right to put the purity of his soul or the cleanness of his hands above the lives or welfare of large numbers of other people? It might be argued that a public servant like Truman has no right to put himself first in that way; therefore if he is convinced that the alternatives would be worse, he must give the order to drop the bombs, and take the burden of those deaths on himself, as he must do other distasteful things for the general good.

But there are two confusions behind the view that moral self-interest underlies moral absolutism. First, it is a confusion to suggest that the need to preserve one's moral purity might be the *source* of an obligation. For if by committing murder one sacrifices one's moral purity or integrity, that can only be because there is *already* something wrong with murder. The general reason against committing murder cannot therefore be merely that it makes one an immoral person. Secondly, the notion that one might sacrifice one's moral integrity justifiably, in the service of a sufficiently worthy end, is an incoherent notion. For if one were justified in making such a sacrifice (or even morally required to make it), then one would not be sacrificing one's moral integrity by adopting that course: one would be preserving it.

Moral absolutism is not unique among moral theories in requiring each person to do what will preserve his own moral purity in all circumstances. This is equally true of utilitarianism, or of any other theory which distinguishes between right and wrong. Any theory which defines the right course of action in various circumstances and asserts that one should adopt that course, *ipso facto* asserts that one should do what will preserve one's moral purity, simply because the right course of action *is* what will preserve one's moral purity in those circumstances. Of course utilitarianism does not assert that this is *why* one should adopt that course, but we have seen that the same is true of absolutism.

V

It is easier to dispose of false explanations of absolutism than to produce a true one. A positive account of the matter must begin with the observation that war, conflict, and aggression are relations between persons. The view that it can be wrong to consider merely the overall effect of one's action on the general welfare comes into prominence when those actions involve relations with others. A man's acts usually affect more people than he deals with directly, and those effects must naturally be considered in his decisions. But if there are special principles governing the manner in which he should *treat* people, that will require special attention to the particular persons toward whom the act is directed, rather than just to its total effect.

Absolutist restrictions in warfare appear to be of two types: restrictions on the class of persons at whom aggression or violence may be directed and restrictions on the manner of attack, given that the object falls within that class. These can be combined, however, under the principle that hostile treatment of any person must be justified in terms of something *about that person* which makes the treatment appropriate. Hostility is a personal relation, and it must be suited to its

target. One consequence of this condition will
be that certain persons may not be subjected
to hostile treatment in war at all, since nothing
about them justifies such treatment. Others will
be proper objects of hostility only in certain
circumstances, or when they are engaged in certain pursuits. And the appropriate manner and
extent of hostile treatment will depend on what
is justified by the particular case.

A coherent view of this type will hold that
extremely hostile behavior toward another is
compatible with treating him as a person – even
perhaps as an end in himself. This is possible only
if one has not automatically stopped treating him
as a person as soon as one starts to fight with him.
If hostile, aggressive, or combative treatment of
others always violated the condition that they be
treated as human beings, it would be difficult to
make further distinctions on that score *within* the
class of hostile actions. That point of view, on the
level of international relations, leads to the position that if complete pacifism is not accepted, no
holds need be barred at all, and we may slaughter
and massacre to our hearts' content, if it seems
advisable. Such a position is often expressed in
discussions of war crimes.

But the fact is that ordinary people do not
believe this about conflicts, physical or otherwise, between individuals, and there is no more
reason why it should be true of conflicts between
nations. There seems to be a perfectly natural
conception of the distinction between fighting
clean and fighting dirty. To fight dirty is to direct
one's hostility or aggression not at its proper
object, but at a peripheral target which may be
more vulnerable, and through which the proper
object can be attacked indirectly. This applies
in a fist fight, an election campaign, a duel, or a
philosophical argument. If the concept is general
enough to apply to all these matters, it should apply
to war – both to the conduct of individual soldiers
and to the conduct of nations.

Suppose that you are a candidate for public
office, convinced that the election of your
opponent would be a disaster, that he is an
unscrupulous demagogue who will serve a narrow range of interests and seriously infringe the
rights of those who disagree with him; and suppose you are convinced that you cannot defeat
him by conventional means. Now imagine that
various unconventional means present themselves

as possibilities: you possess information about
his sex life which would scandalize the electorate
if made public; or you learn that his wife is an
alcoholic or that in his youth he was associated
for a brief period with a proscribed political party,
and you believe that this information could be
used to blackmail him into withdrawing his
candidacy; or you can have a team of your supporters flatten the tires of a crucial subset of his
supporters on election day; or you are in a position to stuff the ballot boxes; or, more simply, you
can have him assassinated. What is wrong with
these methods, given that they will achieve an
overwhelmingly desirable result?

There are, of course, many things wrong with
them: some are against the law; some infringe the
procedures of an electoral process to which you
are presumably committed by taking part in it;
very importantly, some may backfire, and it is in
the interest of all political candidates to adhere
to an unspoken agreement not to allow certain
personal matters to intrude into a campaign. But
that is not all. We have in addition the feeling
that these measures, these methods of attack, are
irrelevant to the issue between you and your
opponent, that in taking them up you would not
be directing yourself to that which makes him
an object of your opposition. You would be
directing your attack not at the true target of your
hostility, but at peripheral targets that happen to
be vulnerable.

The same is true of a fight or argument outside the framework of any system of regulations
or law. In an altercation with a taxi driver over
an excessive fare, it is inappropriate to taunt
him about his accent, flatten one of his tires, or
smear chewing gum on his windshield; and it
remains inappropriate even if he casts aspersions
on your race, politics, or religion, or dumps the
contents of your suitcase into the street.[6]

The importance of such restrictions may vary
with the seriousness of the case; and what is
unjustifiable in one case may be justified in a more
extreme one. But they all derive from a single
principle: that hostility or aggression should be
directed at its true object. This means both that
it should be directed at the person or persons
who provoke it and that it should aim more
specifically at what is provocative about them.
The second condition will determine what form
the hostility may appropriately take.

It is evident that some idea of the relation in which one should stand to other people underlies this principle, but the idea is difficult to state. I believe it is roughly this: whatever one does to another person intentionally must be aimed at him as a subject, with the intention that he receive it as a subject. It should manifest an attitude to *him* rather than just to the situation, and he should be able to recognize it and identify himself as its object. The procedures by which such an attitude is manifested need not be addressed to the person directly. Surgery, for example, is not a form of personal confrontation but part of a medical treatment that can be offered to a patient face to face and received by him as a response to his needs and the natural outcome of an attitude toward *him*.

Hostile treatment, unlike surgery, is already addressed *to* a person, and does not take its interpersonal meaning from a wider context. But hostile acts can serve as the expression or implementation of only a limited range of attitudes to the person who is attacked. Those attitudes in turn have as objects certain real or presumed characteristics or activities of the person which are thought to justify them. When this background is absent, hostile or aggressive behavior can no longer be intended for the reception of the victim as a subject. Instead it takes on the character of a purely bureaucratic operation. This occurs when one attacks someone who is not the true object of one's hostility – the true object may be someone else, who can be attacked through the victim; or one may not be manifesting a hostile attitude toward anyone, but merely using the easiest available path to some desired goal. One finds oneself not facing or addressing the victim at all, but operating on him – without the larger context of personal interaction that surrounds a surgical operation.

If absolutism is to defend its claim to priority over considerations of utility, it must hold that the maintenance of a direct interpersonal response to the people one deals with is a requirement which no advantages can justify one in abandoning. The requirement is absolute only if it rules out any calculation of what would justify its violation. I have said earlier that there may be circumstances so extreme that they render an absolutist position untenable. One may find then that one has no choice but to do something terrible.

Nevertheless, even in such cases absolutism retains its force in that one cannot claim *justification* for the violation. It does not become *all right*.

As a tentative effort to explain this, let me try to connect absolutist limitations with the possibility of justifying *to the victim* what is being done to him. If one abandons a person in the course of rescuing several others from a fire or a sinking ship, one *could* say to him, 'You understand, I have to leave you to save the others.' Similarly, if one subjects an unwilling child to a painful surgical procedure, one can say to him, 'If you could understand, you would realize that I am doing this to help you.' One could *even* say, as one bayonets an enemy soldier, 'It's either you or me.' But one cannot really say while torturing a prisoner, 'You understand, I have to pull out your finger-nails because it is absolutely essential that we have the names of your confederates'; nor can one say to the victims of Hiroshima, 'You understand, we have to incinerate you to provide the Japanese government with an incentive to surrender.'

This does not take us very far, of course, since a utilitarian would presumably be willing to offer justifications of the latter sort to his victims, in cases where he thought they were sufficient. They are really justifications to the world at large, which the victim, as a reasonable man, would be expected to appreciate. However, there seems to me something wrong with this view, for it ignores the possibility that to treat someone else horribly puts you in a special relation to him, which may have to be defended in terms of other features of your relation to him. The suggestion needs much more development; but it may help us to understand how there may be requirements which are absolute in the sense that there can be no justification for violating them. If the justification for what one did to another person had to be such that it could be offered to him specifically, rather than just to the world at large, that would be a significant source of restraint.

If the account is to be deepened, I would hope for some results along the following lines. Absolutism is associated with a view of oneself as a small being interacting with others in a large world. The justifications it requires are primarily interpersonal. Utilitarianism is associated with a view of oneself as a benevolent bureaucrat distributing such benefits as one can control to countless other beings, with whom one may have various relations or none. The justifications it requires are primarily administrative. The argument between the two moral attitudes may depend on the relative priority of these two conceptions.[7]

VI

Some of the restrictions on methods of warfare which have been adhered to from time to time are to be explained by the mutual interests of the involved parties: restrictions on weaponry, treatment of prisoners, etc. But that is not all there is to it. The conditions of directness and relevance which I have argued apply to relations of conflict and aggression apply to war as well. I have said that there are two types of absolutist restrictions on the conduct of war: those that limit the legitimate targets of hostility and those that limit its character, even when the target is acceptable. I shall say something about each of these. As will become clear, the principle I have sketched does not yield an unambiguous answer in every case.

First let us see how it implies that attacks on some people are allowed, but not attacks on others. It may seem paradoxical to assert that to fire a machine gun at someone who is throwing hand grenades at your emplacement is to treat him as a human being. Yet the relation with him is direct and straightforward.[8] The attack is aimed specifically against the threat presented by a dangerous adversary, and not against a peripheral target through which he happens to be vulnerable but which has nothing to do with that threat. For example, you might stop him by machine-gunning his wife and children, who are standing nearby, thus distracting him from his aim of blowing you up and enabling you to capture him. But if his wife and children are not threatening your life, that would be to treat them as means with a vengeance.

This, however, is just Hiroshima on a smaller scale. One objection to weapons of mass annihilation – nuclear, thermonuclear, biological, or chemical – is that their indiscriminateness disqualifies them as direct instruments for the expression of hostile relations. In attacking the civilian population, one treats neither the military enemy nor the civilians with that minimal respect which is owed to them as human beings. This is clearly true of the direct attack on people who present no threat at all. But it is also true of the character of the attack on those who *are* threatening you, i.e., the government and military forces of the enemy. Your aggression is directed against an area of vulnerability quite distinct from any threat presented by them which you may be justified in meeting. You are taking aim at them through the mundane life and survival of their countrymen, instead of aiming at the destruction of their military capacity. And of course it does not require hydrogen bombs to commit such crimes.

This way of looking at the matter also helps us to understand the importance of the distinction between combatants and noncombatants, and the irrelevance of much of the criticism offered against its intelligibility and moral significance. According to an absolutist position, deliberate killing of the innocent is murder, and in warfare the role of the innocent is filled by noncombatants. This has been thought to raise two sorts of problems: first, the widely imagined difficulty of making a division, in modern warfare, between combatants and noncombatants; second, problems deriving from the connotation of the word 'innocence'.

Let me take up the latter question first.[9] In the absolutist position, the operative notion of innocence is not moral innocence, and it is not opposed to moral guilt. If it were, then we would be justified in killing a wicked but noncombatant hairdresser in an enemy city who supported the evil policies of his government, and unjustified in killing a morally pure conscript who was driving a tank toward us with the profoundest regrets and nothing but love in his heart. But moral innocence has very little to do with it, for in the definition of murder 'innocent' means 'currently harmless', and it is opposed not to 'guilty' but to 'doing harm'. It should be noted that such an analysis has the consequence that in war we may often be justified in killing people who do not deserve to die, and unjustified in killing people who do deserve to die, if anyone does.

So we must distinguish combatants from noncombatants on the basis of their immediate threat or harmfulness. I do not claim that the line is a sharp one, but it is not so difficult as is often supposed to place individuals on one side of it or the other. Children are not combatants even though they may join the armed forces if they are allowed to grow up. Women are not combatants just because they bear children or offer comfort to the soldiers. More problematic are the supporting personnel, whether in or out of uniform, from drivers of munitions trucks and army cooks to civilian munitions workers and farmers. I believe they can be plausibly classified by applying the condition that the prosecution of conflict must direct itself to the cause of danger, and not to what is peripheral. The threat presented by an army and its members does not consist merely in the fact that they are men, but in the fact that they are armed and are using their arms in the pursuit of certain objectives. Contributions to their arms and logistics are contributions to this threat; contributions to their mere existence as men are not. It is therefore wrong to direct an attack against those who merely serve the combatants' needs as human beings, such as farmers and food suppliers, even though survival as a human being is a necessary condition of efficient functioning as a soldier.

This brings us to the second group of restrictions: those that limit what may be done even to combatants. These limits are harder to explain clearly. Some of them may be arbitrary or conventional, and some may have to be derived from other sources; but I believe that the condition of directness and relevance in hostile relations accounts for them to a considerable extent.

Consider first a case which involves both a protected class of noncombatants and a restriction on the measures that may be used against combatants. One provision of the rules of war which is universally recognized, though it seems to be turning into a dead letter in Vietnam, is the special status of medical personnel and the wounded in warfare. It might be more efficient to shoot medical officers on sight and to let the enemy wounded die rather than be patched up to fight another day. But someone with medical insignia is supposed to be left alone and permitted to tend and retrieve the wounded. I believe this is because medical attention is a species of attention to completely general human needs, not specifically the needs of a combat soldier, and our conflict with the soldier is not with his existence as a human being.

By extending the application of this idea, one can justify prohibitions against certain particularly cruel weapons: starvation, poisoning, infectious diseases (supposing they could be inflicted on combatants only), weapons designed to maim or disfigure or torture the opponent rather than merely to stop him. It is not, I think, mere casuistry to claim that such weapons attack the men, not the soldiers. The effect of dum-dum bullets. for example, is much more extended than necessary to cope with the combat situation in which they are used. They abandon any attempt to discriminate in their effects between the combatant and the human being. For this reason the use of flamethrowers and napalm is an atrocity in all circumstances that I can imagine, whoever the target may be. Burns are both extremely painful and extremely disfiguring – far more than any other category of wound. That this well-known fact plays no (inhibiting) part in the determination of US weapons policy suggests that moral sensitivity among public officials has not increased markedly since the Spanish Inquisition.[10]

Finally, the same condition of appropriateness to the true object of hostility should limit the scope of attacks on an enemy country: its economy, agriculture, transportation system, and so forth. Even if the parties to a military conflict are considered to be not armies or governments but entire nations (which is usually a grave error), that does not justify one nation in warring against every aspect or element of another nation. That is not justified in a conflict between individuals, and nations are even more complex than individuals, so the same reasons apply. Like a human being, a nation is engaged in countless other pursuits while waging war, and it is not in those respects that it is an enemy.

The burden of the argument has been that absolutism about murder has a foundation in principles governing all one's relations to other persons, whether aggressive or amiable, and that these principles and that absolutism, apply to warfare as well, with the result that certain measures are impermissible no matter what the consequences.[11] I do not mean to romanticize war. It is sufficiently utopian to suggest that when nations conflict they might rise to the level of limited barbarity that typically characterizes violent conflict between individuals, rather than wallowing in the moral pit where they appear to have settled, surrounded by enormous arsenals.

VI

Having described the elements of the absolutist position, we must now return to the conflict between it and utilitarianism. Even if certain types of dirty tactics become acceptable when the stakes are high enough, the most serious of the prohibited acts, like murder and torture, are not just supposed to require unusually strong justification. They are supposed *never* to be done, because no quantity of resulting benefit is thought capable of *justifying* such treatment of a person.

The fact remains that when an absolutist knows or believes that the utilitarian cost of refusing to adopt a prohibited course will be very high, he may hold to his refusal to adopt it, but he will find it difficult to feel that a moral dilemma has been satisfactorily resolved. The same may be true of someone who rejects an absolutist requirement and adopts instead the course yielding the most acceptable consequences. In either case, it is possible to feel that one has acted for reasons insufficient to justify violation of the opposing principle. In situations of deadly conflict, particularly where a weaker party is threatened with annihilation or enslavement by a stronger one, the argument for resorting to atrocities can be powerful, and the dilemma acute.

There may exist principles, not yet codified, which would enable us to resolve such dilemmas. But then again there may not. We must face the pessimistic alternative that these two forms of moral intuition are not capable of being brought together into a single, coherent moral system, and that the world can present us with situations in which there is no honorable or moral course for a man to take, no course free of guilt and responsibility for evil.[12]

The idea of a moral blind alley is a perfectly intelligible one. It is possible to get into such a situation by one's own fault, and people do it all the time. If, for example, one makes two incompatible promises or commitments – becomes engaged to two people, for example – then there is no course one can take which is not wrong, for one must break one's promise to at least one of them. Making a clean breast of the whole thing will not be enough to remove one's reprehensibility. The existence of such cases is not morally disturbing, however, because we feel that the situation was not unavoidable: one had to do something wrong in the first place to get into it. But what if the world itself, or someone else's actions, could face a previously innocent person with a choice between morally abominable courses of action, and leave him no way to escape with his honor? Our intuitions rebel at the idea, for we feel that the constructibility of such a case must show a contradiction in our moral views. But it is not in itself a contradiction to say that someone can do X or not do X, and that for him to take either course would be wrong. It merely contradicts the supposition that *ought* implies *can* – since presumably one ought to refrain from what is wrong, and in such a case it is impossible to do so.[13] Given the limitations on human action, it is naive to suppose that there is a solution to every moral problem with which the world can face us. We have always known that the world is a bad place. It appears that it may be an evil place as well.

Notes

1 This essay was completed in 1971. Direct US military involvement in the Vietnam War lasted from 1961 to 1973. Hence the present tense.

2 Straightforward considerations of national interest often tend in the same direction: the inadvisability of using nuclear weapons seems to be overdetermined in this way.

3 These reasons, moreover, have special importance in that they are available even to one who denies the appropriateness of utilitarian considerations in international matters. He may acknowledge limitations on what may be done to the soldiers and civilians of other countries in pursuit of his nation's military objectives, while denying that one country should in general consider the interests of nationals of other countries in determining its policies.

4 (Privately printed.) See also her essay 'War and Murder', in *Nuclear Weapons and Christian Conscience*, ed. Walter Stein (London: The Merlin Press, 1961). The present paper is much indebted to these two essays throughout. These and related subjects are extensively treated by Paul Ramsey

in *The Just War* (New York: Scribners, 1968). Among recent writings that bear on the moral problem are Jonathan Bennett, 'Whatever the Consequences', *Analysis*, XXVI, no. 3 (1966), 83–102; and Philippa Foot, 'The Problem of Abortion and the Doctrine of the Double Effect', *Oxford Review*, V (1967), 5–15. Miss Anscombe's replies are 'A Note on Mr. Bennett', *Analysis*, XXVI, no. 3 (1966), 208 and 'Who is Wronged?', *Oxford Review*, V (1967), 16–17.

5   This counter-argument was suggested by Rogers Albritton.

6   Why, on the other hand, does it seem appropriate, rather than irrelevant, to punch someone in the mouth if he insults you? The answer is that in our culture it is an insult to punch someone in the mouth, and not just an injury. This reveals, by the way, a perfectly unobjectionable sense in which convention may play a part in determining exactly what falls under an absolutist restriction and what does not. I am indebted to Robert Fogelin for this point.

7   Finally, I should mention a different possibility, suggested by Robert Nozick: that there is a strong general presumption against benefiting from the calamity of another, whether or not it has been deliberately inflicted for that or any other reason. This broader principle may well lend its force to the absolutist position.

8   Marshall Cohen once remarked that, according to my view, shooting at someone establishes an I–thou relationship.

9   What I say on this subject derives from Anscombe.

10   Beyond this I feel uncertain. Ordinary bullets, after all, can cause death, and nothing is more permanent than that. I am not at all sure why we are justified in trying to kill those who are trying to kill us (rather than merely in trying to stop them with force which may also result in their deaths). It is often argued that incapacitating gases are a

relatively humane weapon (when not used, as in Vietnam, merely to make people easier to shoot). Perhaps the legitimacy of restrictions against them must depend on the dangers of escalation, and the great utility of maintaining *any* conventional category of restriction so long as nations are willing to adhere to it.

Let me make clear that I do not regard my argument as a defense of the moral immutability of the Hague and Geneva Conventions. Rather, I believe that they rest partly on a moral foundation, and that modifications of them should also be assessed on moral grounds.

11   It is possible to draw a more radical conclusion, which I shall not pursue here. Perhaps the technology and organization of modern war are such as to make it impossible to wage as an acceptable form of interpersonal or even international hostility. Perhaps it is too impersonal and large-scale for that. If so, then absolutism would in practice imply pacifism, given the present state of things. On the other hand, I am skeptical about the unstated assumption that a technology dictates its own use.

12   In his reply to this essay ('Rules of War and Moral Reasoning', *Philosophy & Public Affairs*, 1, no. 2 (Winter, 1972), 167), R. M. Hare pointed out the apparent discrepancy between my acceptance of such a possibility here and my earlier claim in section IV that absolutism must be formulated so as to avoid the consequence that in certain cases nothing one could do would be morally permissible. The difference is that in those cases the moral incoherence would result from the application of a single principle, whereas the dilemmas described here result from a conflict between two fundamentally different types of principle.

13   This was first pointed out to me by Christopher Boorse. The point is also made in E. J. Lemmon's 'Moral Dilemmas', *Philosophical Review*, LXXI (April, 1962), 150.

Questions for Discussion

1 What would you do if you were in charge of the lifeboat in *Abandon Ship!*? Does consequentialism clearly entail that you should choose who will live and who will die? Would any of the other ethical theories contained in the readings dictate a different course of action from consequentialism? Explain.

2 Did the President do the right thing in the movie *Fail Safe* when he offered to sacrifice New York to avoid World War III (chapters 22–8)? Of the ethical theories you have read, which, if any, would allow the President to reach the conclusion that he was acting as he should? Was the decision he faced different in kind (as opposed to degree) from the one facing Jim in the Williams article?

3 In *Dirty Harry*, was Harry right to torture the kidnapper until he revealed the whereabouts of the child (chapters 19–21)? Should Harry have been worried more about the "rights" of the accused? Can such rights "trump" the kind of concerns Harry had about the well-being of the kidnapped victim? Should we torture captured terrorists until they reveal information we seek? In general, can one legitimately violate the law in order to achieve good enough results? If the answer is yes, does this suggest that act consequentialism may be the correct ethical theory and that people who worry about so-called rights deserve all of Harry's contempt?

4 Torture was used against an evil person in the movie *Dirty Harry*. Can you imagine a situation in which it might be legitimate to torture even innocent people? Does the answer depend on which of the ethical theories presented is correct?

5 If Harry Callahan were a rule consequentialist would he be forced to reject the conclusion that he should torture the kidnapper? What would Ross say about a situation like this? What would Kant say?

6 Did Sophie do the right thing in *Sophie's Choice* when she agreed to make the decision over which child to save (chapters 32–4)? Is the dilemma she faced significantly different from the one faced by Jim in the Williams article?

7 Would Kant claim that Sophie failed to respect her daughter as a rational creature when she "chooses" to sacrifice her in order to save her son? How would Kagan respond to the claim that Sophie was wrongly treating her child as a means rather than an end in herself?

8 Can one morally "trade" one life to save many more? Discuss with respect to any relevant readings or films.

9 In the movie *Saving Private Ryan*, Private Reiben asks the following: "Where's the sense in risking the lives of the eight of us to save one guy?" (chapters 5–6). What answer – if any – do the soldiers come to accept? What do you think Mill would say about the mission to rescue Private Ryan?

10   In the film *Saving Private Ryan*, Corporal Upham quotes the following line: "Their's not to wonder why; their's but to do and die" (chapters 5–6), in reference to a soldier's obligation to obey orders. How do you think that an act utilitarian might attempt to justify adherence to such a "rule" for soldiers? Do you think that an act utilitarian could defend the soldiers' adherence to the principle to follow orders within the context of their particular mission to save Private Ryan?

11   Williams describes the chemist George who is torn between taking a job at a firm that violates many of his deeply held principles, and providing for his family. As a consequentialist, George can reason that someone is going to take the job whether he does or not, and it is better to have someone who will fight to change the firm than to have someone who is utterly callous. Is this sort of reasoning legitimate? Could Nazis in World War II justify their participation in genocide by arguing that it was going to happen in any event, and they could at least mitigate the suffering of people condemned to death by being kinder than the people who would have replaced them? Is George's position significantly different from that of the character portrayed by Burt Lancaster in *Judgment at Nuremberg*? Discuss in connection with Burt Lancaster's impassioned criticism of the defense lawyer (chapter 28).

12   Would a rule utilitarian be committed to the view that the judges on trial in *Judgment at Nuremberg* were justified in adhering to Nazi law?

13   Are there other films you have seen which might be used to criticize or support any of the ethical theories presented in the readings?

14   Were the police acting in morally responsible ways when they arrested people whom the psychics predicted would commit violent crime (*Minority Report*)? Does it make a difference if the psychics are only highly reliable but not infallible? If we have reason to believe that a certain sort of criminal will almost certainly commit the same kind of crime if released into society, should we make that criminal's sentence indefinite?

15   In the series *24* (Season 3, 6.00–7.00 a.m.) Jack Bauer faces the dilemma of killing his superior Chappelle at the directive of the terrorist Saunder. Saunder is threatening to release a vial of a deadly virus if Jack fails to shoot the innocent Chappelle. How do you think Mill would assess the moral dilemma? What action would he identify as being the right action for Jack to take? What would Kant say?

16   Explain Kant's categorical imperative. What action do you think the categorical imperative would prescribe in the dilemma faced by Sophie in the movie *Sophie's Choice*? Similarly, what action would be prescribed for Harry when he is considering torturing Scorpio (*Dirty Harry*), the President while debating whether to sacrifice New York (*Fail Safe*), or the officers deciding whether to arrest persons who have not yet committed crimes (*Minority Report*). Should one pay any attention to what a categorical imperative prescribes?

17 In the case of *US v. Holmes*, the defense argued that the seaman Holmes's actions were justified on the grounds of self-defense. Outline the argument for this claim and evaluate it. Do you believe that the survivors of *Titanic* who chose not to row back for those in the water could have offered a similar defense?

18 In the case of *The Queen v. Dudley and Stephens*, the defense argued that the killing of the boy Parker was justified on the grounds of necessity. What is your evaluation of this defense? Do you believe that a similar defense could have been offered by the officers who chose to hold the second- and third-class passengers of *Titanic* below deck (chapter 20)?

19 Nagel claims that the deliberate killing of noncombatants in war is wrong. How does he distinguish combatants from noncombatants? How does he justify his claim that killing noncombatants is wrong? Apply Nagel's argument to the President's decision to bomb New York City in *Fail Safe*.

20 At the beginning of *Vertical Limit* (chapters 1–2), the son is faced with the decision to cut the rope and kill his father or let the whole family die as a result of inaction. Did the son do the right thing?

Part IV
Ethics

B. Obligations to Intimates

Films:
The English Patient
Casablanca
The Third Man
The Music Box
High Noon
Nick of Time
24 (Season 1: 7.00–8.00 a.m.)

Introduction

Consider the following claim: we are morally justified and, in fact, *required* to exhibit concern for our friends and family members beyond that which we exhibit for complete strangers. Most of us are convinced that the betrayal or neglect of a friend or other loved one is one of the worst forms of moral wrongdoing. If we consider any wrong action, such as some particular act of lying, we will regard it as worse if we find out that the person lied to is the friend or lover of the person doing the lying. So it looks as though the intuition that we have obligations of a special sort to loved ones, or, as we will call them, "intimates," is one of the firmest in ethics, if not in all of philosophy. Thus, it can appear to provide a litmus test of the plausibility of an ethical theory, i.e. any theory that cannot accommodate the intuition that we have special obligations to intimates requires either revision or rejection.

But, as the reader will probably have realized by now, nothing is ever that easy in philosophy. For, as we do moral theory, we find that it is very difficult to find an otherwise plausible theory that accommodates our intuitions about special obligations to intimates. What could justify us in using more of our resources (our time, money, talents, emotional support, psychological acuity, etc.) to promote the good of certain persons than we devote to others who are perhaps much needier? Could the mere fact that we love these people have *moral* significance? The harder that we push on these sorts of questions, the more we will find ourselves wondering if the strength of our intuitions about special obligations to intimates is not really just self-serving parochialism. Is an appeal to the fact that I love someone any more relevant to what I ought, morally, to do than is an appeal to the fact that someone has the same color skin, belongs to the same religious denomination, or is of the same sex as me? In other words, can we offer a justification of special obligations to intimates that shows them to be something over and above the systematizing of our psychological prejudices?

The reason why the question about special obligations is so central to moral theory has to do with the peculiar nature of ethics as compared to other branches of philosophy. Epistemology, metaphysics, etc., are all purely theoretical endeavors. But ethics, as Socrates so eloquently pointed out, takes as its fundamental question, "How are we to live?" This is a question that everyone must be concerned with, whether or not they are a student of philosophy. We all do live as though we are justified and even required to show partiality to an extraordinarily small group of people, our intimates. Just think how radical an alteration of your life would be required in order to eliminate any partiality to your friends or family members. So the readings and films in this unit force us to consider whether the pattern of our lives and of others whom we think of as good people are really morally justified.

Intimates, Consequentialism, and Kantian Deontology

In order to see how philosophically vexing the issue of special obligations to intimates is, we can begin by considering how consequentialists and Kantians can try to accommodate them within their theories. Let us begin with consequentialism. Roughly, the consequentialist holds that we ought to maximize intrinsic value. (For the purposes of what follows, we can set aside the careful distinctions that we needed in the previous section, i.e. distinctions about various types of consequentialism.) Let us suppose that we are dealing with a version of consequentialism that regards all and only the well-being of persons (or other sentient beings) as having intrinsic value, where well-being could be understood in any number of ways, including as pleasure, as desire-satisfaction, as informed desire-satisfaction (satisfaction of desires where one has full and vivid knowledge of the nature of that which one desires), as higher-quality pleasures, etc. When we are working with this consequentialist criterion of right action, we are not allowed to give any extra weight to any person's well-being – all that we are allowed to consider is the sum total of well-being for all persons, considered impartially, that would be produced by alternative actions. So it seems that consequentialism would forbid any partiality to ourselves or to our intimates.

Consequentialists have been very aware of this apparent implication of their view. For most consequentialists, the intuitions regarding special obligations to intimates have been strong enough to induce them to try to show that the consequences of their view would not, contrary to initial appearances, include the sort of radical revision of our lives that complete impartiality to persons seems to dictate. We can understand their responses by considering three lines of response – one focusing on the actions of an agent, another focusing on the motives or character of the agent, and a third focusing on claims about what has intrinsic value.

One standard consequentialist response to this worry is to claim that each agent giving special attention to her intimates will, in the long run, produce the best overall consequences. Why would the consequentialist suppose that to be the case? There are two relevant factors here:

an agent's causal position, and her epistemic position. It is usually the case that we live in closer proximity to our intimates than we do to other persons. In addition, we know our intimates (this is part of what makes someone our intimate) and so know how to benefit them better than we know how to benefit some stranger. These two factors combined suggested to some consequentialists that well-being would best be promoted if each agent were to focus on the limited circle of people whom she knows best. Thus, we can understand the consequentialist as offering a justification behind the old saying, "Charity begins at home."

Contemporary consequentialists such as Peter Railton have modified the above consequentialist approach only by moving the focus from patterns of action to patterns of motivation and character. In his "Alienation, Consequentialism, and the Demands of Morality," Railton argues that even if particular actions of showing greater concern for intimates do not produce the best consequences, agents who act in those ways will, in the long run, maximize intrinsic value. Given that agents must have dispositions either to favor intimates or not to favor intimates, we ought to raise agents who do favor intimates even if their doing so on some particular occasion is not value maximizing. Thus, Railton claims that the best utilitarian agent may be one who performs certain wrong actions as a result of a disposition which will have better consequences in the long run than any other possible disposition that she could have.

Both of the above consequentialist lines of argument depend upon appeals to empirical claims about certain patterns of action or certain dispositions having the best long-run consequences. So, according to these views, it is a purely empirical matter as to whether we are justified or required to be partial to our intimates. It might seem that a consequentialist could place obligations to intimates on a firmer footing if she claimed that intimate relationships and the special caring that they involve are themselves intrinsically valuable. Thus, in showing partiality for my intimates, I would thereby be promoting an intrinsically valuable relationship. The difficulty that remains for the consequentialist is that each agent must weigh the value of her own relationships against the value of other peoples' relationships. So this strategy for accommodating special obligations to intimates within a consequentialist theory also depends on the truth of certain empirical claims about what sorts of actions or characters will have the best consequences. Will I best promote value by focusing on my own intimate relationships or by focusing on helping to develop and maintain the intimate relationships of other persons?

Does Kantian deontology fare any better than consequentialism? This is a difficult question to answer because of all the difficulties inherent in interpretation of the categorical imperative. Would one be violating the requirement that one ought always to treat persons as ends and never as mere means if one did not show differential concern for intimates? Even if one can universalize a maxim (a rule for action) according to which one will show special concern for intimates, this only shows that doing so is morally permissible, not that it is morally required. Most people think that taking special care of their loved ones is one of the demands of morality, not an optional way of behaving.

Many have concluded that the difficulty with these moral theories is their commitment to an ideal of impartiality that precludes granting moral significance to the sorts of personal relationships that most people place centrally in their moral lives. Before we commit to one of the above theories, we need to ask whether we find their accounts of the moral significance of intimate relationships plausible and also whether there are any alternatives to consequentialism and Kantian deontology that fare any better.

Some Alternatives

In order to accommodate our sense that intimate relationships are central to the moral life, moral theorists have developed some alternatives to the theories discussed above. The first alternative, however, is not a recent development in moral theory, but was, in fact, first defended by Aristotle. While consequentialists take the notion of goodness as fundamental and deontologists take right action as fundamental, virtue theorists take the virtue of moral agents as the fundamental term in their theories. According to such theorists, the primary object of moral evaluation is an agent's character. In his *Nicomachean Ethics*, Aristotle argues that the best life for a human being is determined by the nature of human beings. The virtues represent the excellences of character that satisfy the function of a human being. Virtuous persons can then enter friendships with other virtuous persons, and these relationships will express their characters and be central to a good life. Given that, for Aristotle, proper friendship is between two virtuous people, and virtue or goodness is worthy of love, friends are justified in loving one another. The possibility of virtue theory's providing a richer and more realistic picture of the moral life than its consequentialist and Kantian rivals has motivated many contemporary moral theorists to offer new versions of the ancient Aristotelian option.

Of course, such a theory of friendship and care for friends does not accommodate our intuitions about special concern for all our intimates, given that it applies only to virtuous persons, and either we or our intimates may not be fully virtuous people. Can we develop a theory that is more accommodating of such intuitions? In "Self and Others," C. D. Broad presents what he takes to be a version of commonsense morality according to which all our duties are proportional to the strength of our relationships to various persons. On this view – what he calls "self-referential altruism" – our strongest obligations are to the persons with whom we are intimate. But, it might be objected, isn't this just a description of our actual moral practices? Aren't we looking for some justification of those practices? If so, can a mere restatement of commonsense morality as "self-referential altruism" really count as justification?

A reading included in the last section can be seen as attempting to provide some justification for a moral theory that incorporates some version of Broad's self-referential altruism. W. D. Ross argues that we have various competing *prima facie* duties. Unlike in the Kantian theory, these principles do not all follow from some one fundamental principle such as the categorical imperative. So in each situation, we need to use judgment to weigh our *prima facie* duties against one another in order to determine which is our all-things-considered duty. Just as the relationship of promisor to promisee and the relationship of benefactor to recipient generate duties, so does the relationship between one friend and the other (or between two lovers). These sorts of special relationships have, by their very nature, certain moral properties, and their having such moral properties is not reducible to maximization of value, or promotion of virtue, or the treating of persons as ends.

In "Relatives and Relativism," Diane Jeske and Richard Fumerton clearly present the difficulty of incorporating special obligations to intimates within traditional consequentialist theories. They suggest both that some Rossian account of competing *prima facie* duties fares better than standard Kantian theories, and also that consequentialists face the problems they face because they accept a non-relative conception of intrinsic value. In the final analysis, Fumerton and Jeske argue that to accommodate intuitions about intimates, the consequentialist must inevitably accept a conception of value which is essentially relative, i.e. to say that x is intrinsically valuable for some given individual y is to say no more than that y values x intrinsically. On such a view nothing is valuable per se – things are only valuable for individuals or groups. Thus, given that most people greatly value their intimates, what they ought to do will involve benefiting their loved ones, certainly to a greater degree than they benefit complete strangers whom they may not value at all. The alternative is to introduce into one's theories non-consequentialist reasons generated by special relationships.

Of course, a relativistic version of consequentialism will seem unappealing to many people because of its denial that another person's welfare has intrinsic value *objectively*, i.e. independently of the agent's contingent psychological attitudes. Many moral philosophers would regard such a theory as too egoistic, whereas the very nature of caring demands a certain form of attention to the other person regardless of one's own subjective valuings. In some recent feminist ethics – a branch that has come to be known as ethics of care – theorists such as Nel Noddings have attempted to supplant the impartial focus of traditional ethics and to make personal caring relationships the cornerstone of ethics. While doing so certainly places personal loving relationships at the center of the moral life, we might wonder whether, in so doing, they thereby fail to take seriously our duties to strangers. We seem to

need a moral theory that appropriately balances personal and impersonal relationships, giving each their proper place in the moral life.

Morality, Intimacy, and the Movies

Films provide a great medium for discussing and focusing our intuitions and commitments about morality and personal relationships. Films about personal relationships often presuppose some moral commitments even if those commitments are not explicitly voiced by any of the characters in the film. We find ourselves rooting for the characters to take certain actions rather than others, or we admire certain choices that they make as opposed to other alternatives that were available. These spontaneous reactions on our part are often expressions of unspoken moral views about the appropriate weight to be given to impartial moral commitments or principles as opposed to moral duties arising from intimate relationships. In examining certain film situations, we can come to understand our potentially conflicting reactions to various moral choices that human beings must make.

We can see the conflict between personal and impersonal moral demands and compare two opposing resolutions to that conflict by contrasting two very popular films: *The English Patient* and the classic *Casablanca*. In the latter, Rick and Ilsa are reunited after they had been torn apart by war and occupation. These former lovers are still very much in love with one another, but Ilsa has in the meantime married Victor Laszlo, an important figure in the French Resistance to the Nazis. Laszlo depends on Ilsa for support in his fight, so she seems essential to his effectiveness. Rick must decide whether to help Laszlo and Ilsa escape in order to continue their work. Or should he keep Ilsa with him? Rick lets Ilsa and Laszlo go, because, he says, in light of the Nazi menace, the "problems of two people don't amount to a hill of beans" (chapters 32–4, but the central issue surfaces throughout the film).

The more recent film *The English Patient* is also set just before and during World War II. Almásy and Katharine meet and fall in love in pre-war Africa. They become lovers in spite of the fact that Katharine is married. On a flight over the desert, their plane crashes and Katharine is injured.

Almásy leaves her in a cave so that he can seek help. He promises his lover that he will return for her. But, given that the war has started, the British will not provide aid to Almásy who is from a country now allied with the Germans. So Almásy gains what he needs to return to Katherine by providing secret information about the British to the Germans, information that allows the Germans to round up and either torture or kill important British agents in North Africa (chapters 28–9). Unlike Rick, Almásy chooses his lover over supporting the fight against the Nazi evil. So Rick and Almásy represent different responses to the conflict between love and the best overall consequences or adherence to Kant's categorical imperative. Comparison of these two films provides fertile ground for understanding our own commitments and discussing the adequacy of those commitments.

Conflict of this sort is also the substance of the plot of the great film *The Third Man*. However, this film adds an extra layer of complexity to the moral issue by showing that not only may personal and impersonal demands conflict, but so may various personal demands. Holly Martins discovers that his charming and beloved friend Harry Lime has engaged in highly immoral activities that have harmed many children. While Martins decides that he cannot support his friend in the light of the evil that he has done (particularly, chapters 15 and 20), Anna makes the opposite decision, remaining loyal to Harry Lime to the end. In explaining her attitude, Anna claims that people don't change because you find out more about them (chapter 16). This might have been her way of saying that her relationship with Lime, the person, trumps any sort of knowledge she gains about the morality of his actions. How should we weigh impersonal and personal demands? Martins and Anna in *The Third Man* provide opposing visions of both friendship and of the moral life.

At first glance the classic *High Noon* may appear to be simply a Western suspense film. While it is certainly gripping and exciting, it actually provides a wonderful exercise in moral choice. Marshall Will Kane has just married Quaker Amy Fowler. Will is on his way out of town to start a new life as a shopkeeper when he gets word that a murderer that he sent to prison has just been released and is going to seek out Kane

to kill him. Kane decides to stay to confront this killer. All the town people desert him, and Amy, on the basis of her pacifist moral principles, initially decides to leave town, in light of Will's decision to stay, fight, and either kill or be killed. Should Amy abandon principle and support her husband? Or should she stick to her reasoned moral principle and abandon Will in light of his, by her light, immoral decision? She explains the reasons for her ethical stance to Will's ex-lover in a dramatic scene (chapter 16) but obviously rejects that stance when she finally comes to the aid of her husband (chapters 22–3). Our reactions to Amy's ultimate decision in the film reflect our own views about both her stated principles and the proper weighting of any such principle against personal commitments of love and marriage.

Morality and the Family

One type of obligation deserves special consideration. The institution of the family plays a central role in the moral thinking of individuals in our culture and in most other cultures. Most importantly, the relationship between parents and children seems to be of particular moral significance. Stories of parents abusing, neglecting, or abandoning their children arouse our strongest moral condemnation: we find such parents to be among the most morally abhorrent people that we can imagine. On the other side, stories of adult children failing to care for elderly parents or taking advantage of their parents' love also arouse moral indignation. Not only do parents owe care and love to their children, but, as a result of such care and love received, children owe the same to their parents in return (at least after they have become adults or have reached the age of responsible moral agency).

In "Filial Morality," Christina Hoff Sommers offers an account of why grown children have special obligations to their parents, based on the claim that the nurturing done by parents raises expectations of a reciprocal caring response. On the basis of such expectations, parents acquire special rights against their children, rights correlated with special obligations on the part of the children. In "Families, Friends, and Special Obligations," Diane Jeske argues that familial bonds create special obligations only if they are instances of a more general type of intimate relationship – i.e. that there is nothing morally special about familial ties considered in and of themselves. She then attempts to show that accounts of familial obligations based on genetic inheritance or social institutions and their associated roles are unacceptable.

For most of us, given the love and care that we and our parents have for one another, certain hard choices are avoided. Not so for Ann Talbot in the film *The Music Box*. Ann, a lawyer, must defend her father against charges of war crimes during the Nazi regime. Ann is convinced that her father, with whom she has a loving relationship, could not have committed the atrocities with which he is charged. What if he did do these things? What are her obligations toward him then? What are, then, her obligations to her young son, who is very close to his elderly grandfather? Does the care and love that her

father has shown her morally bind her to him? Is the biological tie at all morally significant? Ann's tragic choice reveals how the moral life can force us to make choices between impersonal morality and various familial ties (see particularly the scene in which she finally discovers the truth – chapters 24–5).

There may be no stronger sense of moral connection than that felt between a parent and his or her child. In *Nick of Time* a father must choose between saving his child and carrying out instructions to kill the President of the United States (chapter 3). While the movie never requires the hero to get to that point, it is interesting to ask ourselves whether there are any limits we would place on actions required to save our children. It is interesting to compare the father's dilemma in *Nick of Time* with Jack Bauer's dilemma in *24* (where he must choose between helping terrorists and saving his wife and child).

31

Nicomachean Ethics

Aristotle

Book VIII

Chapter 1

After this, the next step would be a discussion of friendship, since it is a virtue or involves virtue, and is an absolute necessity in life. No one would choose to live without friends, even if he had all the other goods. Indeed, rich people and those who have attained high office and power seem to stand in special need of friends. For what use is such prosperity if there is no opportunity for beneficence, which is exercised mainly and in its most commendable form towards friends? Or how could their prosperity be watched over and kept safe without friends? The greater it is, the greater the danger it is in. In poverty, too, and in other misfortunes, people think friends are the only resort.

Friendship benefits the young by keeping them from making mistakes, and the old by caring for them and helping them to finish jobs they are unable to finish themselves because of their weakness. And it benefits those in their prime by helping them to do noble actions – 'two going together' – since with friends they are more capable of thinking and acting.

And there seems to be a natural friendship of a parent for a child, and of a child for a parent,

and this occurs not only among human beings, but among birds and most animals. It also seems to exist naturally among members of the same species in relation to one another, particularly among human beings, which is why we praise people who are lovers of humanity. And one can see in one's travels how akin and friendly every human being is to every other.

Friendship seems also to hold cities together, and lawgivers to care more about it than about justice; for concord seems to be something like friendship, and this is what they aim at most of all, while taking special pains to eliminate civil conflict as something hostile. And when people are friends, they have no need of justice, while when they are just, they need friendship as well; and the highest form of justice seems to be a matter of friendship.

It is not only a necessary thing, but a noble one as well. We praise those who love their friends, and having many friends seems to be something noble. Again, we think that the same people are good and are friends.

There is a great deal of disagreement about friendship. Some people assume that it is a kind of likeness, that people who are alike are friends. Hence the sayings, 'Like to like', and 'Birds of a feather', and so on. Others claim, on the contrary, that people who are alike are 'like potters to one

Aristotle, *Nicomachean Ethics*, trans. and ed. Roger Crisp (Cambridge: Cambridge University Press, 2000), pp. 143–53.
© 2000 by Cambridge University Press. Reproduced with permission from the translator and Cambridge University Press.

another'. Some people inquire into these questions more deeply and in a way that is more proper to natural science. Euripides claims that:

> Parched earth loves the rain,
> And the revered heaven, when filled with rain,
> loves to fall to earth.

And Heraclitus says, 'Opposition is a helper', and, 'From discord comes the noblest harmony,' and, 'Everything comes to be through strife.' Others, such as Empedocles, say that, on the contrary, like seeks like.

The problems proper to natural science we can put to one side, since they are not germane to the present inquiry; let us consider those that are human and relate to character and feeling. For instance, can friendship arise between all kinds of people, or is it impossible for wicked people to be friends? Is there one species of friendship or several? Some think there is only one, because it admits of degrees, but their conviction is based on insufficient evidence; for things of different species also admit of variations of degree.

Chapter 2

Perhaps the matter will be clarified if we can understand what it is that is worthy of love. It seems that not everything is loved, but only what is worthy of love, and this is what is good, pleasant or useful. What is useful, however, would seem to be what is instrumental to some good or pleasure, so that what are worthy of love as ends are the good and the pleasant.

So do people love what is good, or what is good for them, since these are occasionally at variance (as happens also with what is pleasant)? Each person, it seems, loves what is good for him, and while what is good is unqualifiedly worthy of love, what is worthy of love for each individual is what is good for him. In fact, each person loves not what is good for him, but what seems good; this, however, will make no difference, since we shall say that this is what seems worthy of love. There are three reasons, then, for loving something.

Affection for soulless objects is not called friendship, since the affection is not mutual, nor is there any wishing good to the object (it would presumably be absurd to wish good to one's wine – if anything, one wishes that it keep, so that one may have it oneself). But people say that we ought to wish good things to a friend for his own sake. People describe those who do wish good things in this way, when the wish is not reciprocated, as having goodwill. For goodwill is said to count as friendship only when it is reciprocated.

Perhaps we should add 'and when it does not go unrecognized', since many have goodwill towards people they have not seen, but suppose to be good or useful; and the same feeling may exist in the other direction. They appear, then, to have goodwill to each other, but how could anyone call them friends when they are unaware of their attitude to one another? So they must have goodwill to each other, wish good things to each other for one of the reasons given, and not be unaware of it.

Chapter 3

Since these reasons differ from one another in species, so do the forms of affection and friendship. There are, then, three species of friendship, equal in number to the objects worthy of it. In the case of each object there is a corresponding mutual affection that does not go unrecognized, and those who love each other wish good things to each other in that respect in which they love one another.

Those who love one another for utility love the other not in himself, but only in so far as they will obtain some good for themselves from him. The same goes for those who love for pleasure; they do not like a witty person because of his character, but because they find him pleasing to themselves. So those who love for utility are fond of the other because of what is good for themselves, and those who love for pleasure because of what is pleasant for themselves, not in so far as the person they love is who he is, but in so far as he is useful or pleasant.

These friendships, then, are also incidental, since the person is loved not in so far as he is who he is, but in so far as he provides some good or pleasure. Such friendships are thus easily dissolved, when the parties to them do not remain unchanged; for if one party is no longer pleasant or useful, the other stops loving him.

What is useful does not remain the same, but differs according to different circumstances. So when the reason for their being friends has gone, the friendship is dissolved as well, since it existed only for that reason. This kind of friendship seems to come about among older people in particular, because at that age they are pursuing what is useful, not what is pleasant, and also among those in their prime or their youth who are pursuing their own advantage.

Nor do such people live in each other's company very much; for sometimes they do not even find each other pleasant. They have no further need of such association, unless they are useful to each other, because each finds the other pleasant only to the extent that he hopes for some good from him. In this class people also put the friendship between host and guest.

Friendship between the young seems to be for pleasure, since they live in accordance with their feelings, and pursue in particular what is pleasant for themselves and what is immediate. As they get older, however, what they find pleasant begins to change. This is why they are quick to become friends and quick to stop; their friendship fluctuates along with what they find pleasant, and this sort of pleasure is subject to rapid change. The young are also prone to erotic friendship, since it is generally a matter of following one's feelings, and aims at pleasure; they therefore quickly fall in love and quickly stop, often changing in one day. But they do wish to spend their days together and to live in one another's company, since this is how they attain what accords with their friendship.

Complete friendship is that of good people, those who are alike in their virtue: they each alike wish good things to each other in so far as they are good, and they are good in themselves. Those who wish good things to a friend for his own sake are friends most of all, since they are disposed in this way towards each other because of what they are, not for any incidental reason. So their friendship lasts as long as they are good, and virtue is an enduring thing. Each of them is good without qualification and good for his friend, since good people are both good without qualification and beneficial to each other. They are similarly pleasant as well, since good people are pleasant both without qualification and to each other; for each person finds his own actions and others like them pleasant, and the actions of good people are the same or alike.

Such friendship is, as one might expect, lasting, since in it are combined all the qualities that friends should have: every friendship is for a good or for pleasure, either without qualification or for the person who loves, and is based on some similarity. To this kind of friendship belong all the qualities we have mentioned, in virtue of the participants themselves; for they are alike in this way, and their friendship has the other qualities – what is unqualifiedly good and what is unqualifiedly pleasant – and these are most of all worthy of love. Love and friendship, then, are found most of all among people like this, and in their best form.

Naturally, such friendships are rare, because people of this kind are few. Besides, they require time and familiarity. As the saying goes, they cannot know each other until they have eaten the proverbial salt together; nor can they accept each other or be friends until each has shown himself to be worthy of love and gained the other's confidence. Those who are quick to show the signs of friendship to one another wish to be friends, but are not, unless they are worthy of friendship and know it. For though the wish for friendship arises quickly, friendship does not.

Chapter 4

This kind of friendship, then, is complete both in respect of its duration and in the other respects. Each gets from each the same or similar benefits, in every way, as ought to happen among friends. Friendship for pleasure bears a resemblance to this kind, since good people are pleasing to each other. The same sort of thing applies in the case of friendship for utility, since good people are useful to each other.

These lesser friendships, too, are especially lasting when each receives the same benefit – such as pleasure – from the other, and not merely that, but from the same source, as happens with witty people, and not with lover and beloved. For lover and beloved do not take pleasure in the same things, but the one in seeing the beloved, the other in the attentions of the lover. And sometimes, as the bloom of youth fades, the friendship fades too, since the lover does not find the sight of his beloved pleasing, while the beloved does not receive his attentions. But many do remain friends, if they are alike in character and have come to be fond of each other's characters through familiarity with them. But those lovers who exchange not pleasure but utility are friends to a lesser degree and less constant. Friends for utility part when the advantage disappears, because they were friends not of each other, but of gain.

For pleasure or for utility, then, even bad people can be friends with each other, or good people with bad, or one who is neither good nor bad with a person of any sort. But clearly only good people can be friends for the sake of the other person himself, because bad people do not enjoy each other's company unless there is some benefit in it for them.

Also, it is only the friendship of good people that provides protection against slander. For it is not easy to trust criticism of a person whom one has proved oneself over a long period of time; between good people there is trust, the feeling that the other would never do an injustice to one, and all the other things that are expected in true friendship. In the other kinds of friendship, however, there is nothing to prevent bad things like this happening.

People do describe as friends also those whose motive is utility, as cities are said to be friendly (since it seems to be for their own advantage that cities form alliances), and those who are fond of each other for pleasure, as children are. So presumably we ought also to say that such people are friends, but that there are several kinds of friendship. Friendship in the primary and real sense will be the friendship of good people in so far as they are good, while the rest will be friendships by being like it; it is in virtue of something good and something like what is found in true friendship that they are friends, because what is pleasant is good to lovers of pleasure. These friendships, however, are not very likely to coincide, and the same people do not become friends for both utility and pleasure; for things that are incidental are not often combined.

Friendship being divided into these species, then, it is bad people who will tend to be friends for pleasure or utility, since this is the respect in which they are alike. But good people will be friends for each other's sake, because they are friends in so far as they are good. These people, therefore, are friends without qualification, while the others are friends incidentally and through being like them.

Chapter 5

Just as with virtues some are called good in respect of a state of character, others in respect of an activity, so it is with friendship. For some people find their enjoyment in living in each other's company, and bestow good things on each other. Others, however, are asleep or separated by distance, and so do not engage in these activities of friendship, but nevertheless have a disposition to do so; for distance does not dissolve friendship without qualification, but it does dissolve its activity. But if the absence is a long one, it seems to make people forget their friendship. Hence the proverb: 'Many friendships has lack of conversation dissolved.'

Neither old nor ill-tempered people seem inclined to friendship. For little pleasure is to be found in them, and nobody can spend his days with someone he finds painful, or even not pleasing, since nature seems above all to avoid what is painful and aim at what is pleasant.

People who approve of each other but do not live in each other's company seem to have goodwill rather than friendship. For there is nothing so characteristic of friends as living in each other's company (because while people in need desire benefit, even the blessed desire to spend their days together, since solitude suits them least of all). But people cannot spend time together if they are not pleasing to each other and do not enjoy the same things, as comrades seem to.

Friendship in the fullest sense, then, is that between good people, as we have said a number of times already. For what is worthy of love and of choice seems to be what is good or pleasant without qualification, and what is worthy of love and of choice for each person seems to be what is good or pleasant for him; and a good person is worthy of love and of choice for another good person on both these grounds.

Affection seems to be a feeling, but friendship a state. For affection occurs no less towards soulless things, while mutual friendship involves rational choice, and rational choice comes from a state; and it is a state, not a feeling, that makes people wish good things to those they love, for their sake. And in loving their friend they love what is good for themselves; for the good person, in coming to be a friend, comes to be a good for his friend. Each, then, both loves what is good for himself, and returns like for like in what he wishes and in giving pleasure: friendship, people say, is equality, and both of these are found most of all in the friendship of the good.

Chapter 6

Friendship arises to a lesser degree between sour or elderly people, in so far as they are less good-tempered and find less enjoyment in mixing with others; and it is these qualities that seem to be especially characteristic and productive of friendship. This is why young people become friends quickly, but old people do not, since they do not become friends with those whose company they do not enjoy; likewise, nor do sour people. But they can have goodwill to each other, since they wish good to one another and meet one another's needs; but they are not really friends, because they do not spend their days together or enjoy each other's company, and these seem especially characteristic of friendship.

One cannot be a friend – in the sense of complete friendship – to many people, just as one cannot be in love with many people at the same time (love is like an excess, and such a thing arises naturally towards one individual). And it is not easy for the same person at the same time to please many people a great deal, or, presumably, to be good in relations with them. He must have experience of them as well, and become familiar with them, which is very difficult. But when the friendship is for utility or pleasure, it is possible to please many people, since many people can be pleased like this, and the services do not take long.

Of these two kinds, that for pleasure is more like friendship, when both parties make the same contribution and enjoy each other's company or the same things. The friendships of the young are like this, since one finds more of a generosity of spirit in these friendships. Friendship for utility, on the other hand, is for common tradesmen.

The blessed, too, though they have no need of useful friends, do need pleasant ones. For they wish to spend their lives in the company of others, and while they can bear what is painful for a short time, nobody could endure it continuously – not even the Good Itself, if it were painful to him. This

is why they seek friends who are pleasant. But presumably they ought to seek friends who are good as well, and also good for them, because they will then have what friends should have.

People in high office seem to have friends of different types; some people are useful to them, and others pleasant, but it is rare for the same people to be both. For they are not looking for people whose pleasantness is accompanied by virtue as well, or those who are useful for noble actions, but witty individuals if it is pleasure they seek, or people clever at doing what they are told; and rarely do these qualities occur in the same person.

Though we have indeed said that the good person is both pleasant and useful at the same time, he does not become a friend to a superior unless the latter is superior in virtue as well; otherwise he does not attain equality by being proportionately inferior. But superiors like this are rare.

The friendships we have discussed, then, are based on equality, since both sides get the same and wish the same to each other, or exchange one thing for another, such as pleasure for benefit. As we have said, however, these are lesser friendships and less lasting. But it is because of their similarity and dissimilarity to the same thing that they seem both to be and not to be friendships. It is because of their similarity to friendship based on virtue that they appear to be friendships (one of them involves pleasure and the other utility, and these are characteristics of friendship based on virtue as well); while it is because friendship based on virtue involves a refusal to listen to slander and is lasting, but these friendships change quickly and differ in many other ways as well, that they do not appear to be friendships – that is, because of their dissimilarity to friendship based on virtue.

Chapter 7

There is another species of friendship, that involving superiority – for example, that of father to son, and of older to younger in general, of man to woman, and of any ruler to his subject.

These friendships also differ from one another. That of parents to children is not the same as that of rulers to ruled; nor is that of father to son the same as that of son to father, or that of man to woman the same as that of woman to man.

For the virtue of each of these is different, the characteristic activity is different, and so are the reasons for their becoming friends; and therefore the affection and the friendship differ as well. Each, then, does not get the same from the other, nor should they seek it; but when children give to parents what they ought to give to those who brought them into being, and parents give what they ought to their children, the friendship between them will be lasting and good.

In all friendships involving superiority, the affection must be proportional as well. The better, that is to say, must be loved more than he loves, and so must the more useful, and each of the others likewise; when the affection is in accordance with merit, then a kind of equality results, which is of course thought to be a mark of friendship.

But what is equal does not seem to be the same in friendship as it is in just actions. For in just actions what is equal in the primary sense is what is in accordance with merit, while quantitative equality is secondary, whereas in friendship quantitative equality is primary and that in accordance with merit secondary. This becomes clear if a large gap develops in respect of virtue, vice, wealth or something else: then they are no longer friends, nor do they even expect to be. This is most obvious in the case of the gods, since they are the most superior to us in all good things. But it is clear also in the case of kings, since people who are much inferior do not expect to be friends with them, nor do worthless people expect to be friends with the best or the wisest.

In cases like this there is no precise point at which people cannot remain friends. For friendship can survive many losses, but when one side is removed at a great distance – as god is – then it is no longer possible. This is the source of the puzzle whether friends really wish one another the greatest good – to be gods – because they will no longer have them as friends, nor as goods (friends being goods). If, then, we were right to say that one friend wishes goods to the other for the other's sake, the latter must remain as he is, whatever that may be. So it is to the other as a human being that a friend will wish the greatest goods, though presumably not all of them, since it is for himself most of all that each person wishes what is good.

32

Self and Others

C. D. Broad

It seems fitting that the subject of a Herbert Spencer Lecture should be one that looks slightly old-fashioned, and it is desirable that it should not in fact be quite obsolete. I have therefore decided to discuss certain ethical questions which interested Spencer and his contemporaries, such as Sidgwick; which are of perennial interest; but which have now for many years been out of the limelight. I have lumped these questions together under the head of 'Self and Others', which was as adequate a short title as I could think of.

It will be convenient to start by considering two closely connected principles, formulated by Sidgwick, which lead, as we shall see, to what I am going to call 'Ethical Neutralism'. One of them is about good and evil, and the other about obligation. I will state them in Sidgwick's own words. (1) 'The good of any individual is of no more importance, from the point of view of the universe, than the good of any other'. (2) 'It is my duty to aim at good generally, so far as I can bring it about, and not merely at any particular part of it'. Sidgwick claimed that these principles are self-evident, and compared them to mathematical axioms.

It cannot be said that, as stated, they are as clear and unambiguous as one could wish. Let us us begin with the phrase 'the good of an individual'. It seems clear that we must distinguish between being a valuable or disvaluable *person*, on the one hand, and having a valuable or disvaluable *life-history*, on the other. The value or disvalue of a person depends primarily on the nature, the relative strength, and the organization or disorganization of his cognitive, conative, and emotional dispositions. The value or disvalue of his life history depends primarily on the nature, order, and interrelations of his experiences and actions, simultaneous and successive. No doubt the two are intimately inter-connected, but they remain fundamentally different. Cases might arise where one would have to choose between making a person better at the cost of making his life-history worse, or conversely. So 'the good of an individual' must be taken to cover both the value which resides in his personality and that which resides in his life-history.

Let us next consider the phrase 'from the point of view of the universe'. Sidgwick certainly did not believe that the universe literally has a point of view. And, *if* he had, one might well ask why it should be proper for any of us to adopt it. I think that the meaning of the principle can be expressed without using this phrase. Suppose that A and B are two individuals. They will always be unlike in many respects. They will have started with more or less dissimilar innate dispositions; they will have had more or less dissimilar experiences, and will thus have acquired dissimilar dispositional modifications; and they will stand

C. D. Broad, "Self and Others" (1953), from *Broad's Critical Essays in Moral Philosophy* (1971), pp. 262–82.

in dissimiliar relationships to other persons and things. In consequence of these qualitative and relational unlikenesses, the balance of good and evil in the world might be changed to a very different extent according to whether an experience of the same perfectly determinate kind were now to be produced in A and not in B, or in B and not in A. Sidgwick certainly did not wish to deny this perfectly obvious fact. I suggest that what he wanted to assert is this. Suppose that the balance of good and evil in the world *would* be changed to a different extent according to whether a precisely similar experience were to be produced in A and not in B or in B and not in A. Then this difference in value could not be due to the mere *numerical otherness* of A and B. It must always depend on some specific unlikeness in their qualities or dispositions or in their past history or present relationships. This is the only interpretation which I can suggest which makes the principle intelligible and obviously true. And, on that interpretation, it seems to me completely trivial.

Let us now consider the second principle. This alleges that 'it is my duty to aim at good generally, so far as I can bring it about, and not merely at any particular part of it'.

We must begin by calling to mind that Sidgwick was a Utilitarian about right and wrong and an Ethical Hedonist about good and evil. It seems to me, however, that we can deal with this principle without presupposing either of these two doctrines. For, on any view, *one* important *prima facie* duty is to produce and conserve good and to avert and diminish evil. And, on any view, we must distinguish between making a *person* better or worse and making his *life-history* better or worse, and we must include both under the head of doing good to him or harm to him. For the present purpose it does not matter whether we do or do not believe that the value or disvalue of a person can be defined in terms of that of his experiences, and it does not matter whether the value or disvalue of an experience does or does not depend solely on its pleasantness or unpleasantness respectively. We can take the principle to be concerned with the way in which an agent is obliged or permitted or forbidden to distribute his beneficent activities as between the various persons whose characters or life-histories he can effect for good or for ill.

On this understanding Sidgwick's second principle can be formulated as follows. The *only* legitimate ground for devoting more of one's beneficent activities to one person or group of persons rather than to another, among those whose characters or life-histories one can effect, is that by so doing one will produce more good or avert more evil *on the whole* than by making no selection or a different selection among one's possible beneficiaries.

What it comes to is this. A person may be, and in fact generally is, justified in limiting the range of his beneficent efforts, and in distributing them unequally within that limited range. But such limitation in range, and such inequality of distribution, *always* need justification, and they can be justified *only* on the following ground. It must be able to be shown that, owing to the agent's limited powers and resources, to the limitations of his knowledge and his natural sympathies, to the natural affection which only certain persons feel for him, and so on, he can produce most good or avert most evil *on the whole* by confining his beneficent activities to *a certain restricted part*.

Now this principle is by no means trivial, for I suppose that most people would be inclined *prima facie* to reject it as soon as they realised its implications, even if they were inclined to accept it as self-evident when they contemplated it in abstraction. For the common opinion certainly is that a person has a more urgent duty to benefit those who stand in certain relations to him, e.g. his children or his parents, than to benefit others who do not; and that this special urgency depends *directly* on those special relationships.

Whether Sidgwick's second principle be true or false, it has an important corollary, which we must now consider. Among those whose lives or personalities a man can effect for good or for ill is *himself*. Obviously each of us stands in a unique relation to himself, viz. that of personal identity. It is equally obvious that each of us stands to all other persons in a unique relation of an opposite kind, viz. personal diversity. Now it might be thought that either or both of these relationships impose special claims or special limitations on a person's beneficence.

The doctrine that each of us has a special obligation to benefit *himself*, as such, may be called *Ethical Egoism*; and the doctrine that each of us has a special obligation to benefit *others*, as such, may be called *Ethical Altruism*.

Now a plain consequence of Sidgwick's second principle is that both these doctrines are false, and that what may be called *Ethical Neutralism* is true. Suppose that, on a certain occasion, a person would increase the balance of good over evil in the world more by benefiting another, at the cost of forgoing a benefit or inflicting an injury on himself, than by any other action then open to him. Then it would be his duty to do this. Suppose that, on a certain other occasion, a person could increase that balance more by benefiting himself, at the cost of withholding a benefit from another or inflicting an injury on him, than by any other action then open to him. Then it would be his duty to do that.

I will now consider in some detail these three alternative doctrines about self and others. The first point which I will make is that neither Ethical Egoism nor Ethical Altruism can be rejected *in limine* as involving an internal inconsistency. Each of these doctrines might be held in milder or more extreme forms. It will suffice if I take the most extreme form of each, and show that it is internally coherent.

The extreme form of Ethical Egoism might be stated as follows. Each person is under a direct obligation to benefit him self as such. He is under no *direct* obligation to benefit any other person, though he will be under an indirect obligation to do this so far and only so far as that is the most efficient means available to him for benefiting himself. He is forbidden to benefit another person, if doing so will in in the long run be detrimental to himself.

Now suppose that A is an Ethical Egoist of this extreme kind. He can admit that, if a certain experience or a certain disposition of *his own* would be intrinsically good, a precisely similar experience or disposition of B's would *caeteris paribus* be also and equally good, i.e. he can admit Sidgwick's first principle. But he will assert that his duty is not to produce good experiences and good dispositions as such, without regard to the question of who will have them. A has an obligation to produce good experiences and good dispositions in A, and no direct obligation to produce them in B or in anyone else. Similarly, B has an obligation to produce good experiences and good dispositions in B, and no direct

obligation to produce then in A or anyone else. A can admit this about B, and B can admit it about A. Plainly there is no *internal inconsistency* in this doctrine. What it is inconsistent with is Sidgwick's principle that each of us has an unqualified obligation to maximize the balance of good over evil in the lives and personalities of all whom he can affect, and to pay no regard to the question which particular individuals or classes of individuals these goods and evils will occur in, except in so far as that may affect the balance.

In a similar way it could be shown that there is no internal inconsistency in Ethical Altruism, even in its most extreme form. It would be waste of time to give the argument in detail. But it will be worth while to state in passing what would be the extreme form of Ethical Altruism. It would come to this. Each person is under a direct obligation to benefit others as such. He is under no direct obligation to benefit himself as such, though he is under an indirect obligation to do this so far and only so far as that may be the most efficient means available to him for benefiting others. He is forbidden to benefit himself, if so doing will in the long run be detrimental to others.

A useful way of putting the difference between Neutralism, on the one hand, and the two rival doctrines, on the other, is this. Neutralism assumes that there is a certain *one* state of affairs, viz. the maximum balance of good over evil in the lives and personalities of the contemporary and future inhabitants of the world, at which *every-one* ought to aim as his *ultimate* end. Differences in the proximate ends of different persons are justified only in so far as the realization of the one ultimate end is best secured in practice by each person aiming, not directly at it, but at a prox-imate end of a more limited kind. The other two doctrines, at any rate in their extreme forms, deny that there is any *one* state of affairs at which *everyone* ought to aim as his ultimate end. There are, in fact, as many different ultimate ends as there are agents. On the egoistic theory, the ultimate end at which A should aim is the maximum balance of good over evil in A's life and personality. The same holds *mutatis mutandis* for B, C, etc. On the altruistic theory the ultimate end at which A should aim is the maximum balance of good over evil in the lives and personalities of all *others-than*-A. The same holds *mutatis mutandis* for B, C, etc. From this point of view the main difference between Egoism and Altruism is the following. For Egoism the various ultimate ends are mutually exclusive, whilst for Altruism the ultimate ends of any two persons have a very large field in common.

Before leaving this topic I would call attention to the following point. Suppose that an act will affect a certain person B and him alone. Then there will be a characteristic dissimilarity in the act according to whether it is done by B himself or by any other person. If it is done by B, it will be a *self-affecting act*; if it is done by any other person, it will be an *other-affecting act*. Now this kind of dissimilarity between acts, though it depends merely on the numerical identity or the numerical otherness of the agent-self and the patient-self, may be ethically relevant. If the agent-self and the patient-self be the same, the act may be right; if they are different, it may be indifferent or positively wrong. And the converse may be equally true. It is misleading to compare an act which is only self-affecting with one which would be other-affecting, however alike they may be in their consequences and in all other respects. For this dissimilarity may be ethically relevant. Undoubtedly common sense thinks that it is often highly relevant. To give to oneself an innocent pleasure is generally regarded as morally indifferent. To give to another a similar pleasure may be regarded as praiseworthy or even as obligatory. When we bear these facts in mind we see that Ethical Egoism and Ethical Altruism, even in their extreme form, are not merely free from internal inconsistency. They are also completely general and symmetrical as regards all individuals. It cannot be fairly objected to either of them that it gives an irrational preference to any individual, as such, over any other.

Let us now consider the three rival principles on their merits. I will begin with Ethical Neutralism. The first thing to be said about it is this. Suppose we define the phrase 'optimific act' as follows. An act is *optimific* if and only if its consequences in the long run would be *no worse* on balance than those of any other act open to the agent at the time. Then Neutralism is the only one of the three principles which could be combined with the doctrine that the right act in any situation *necessarily* coincides with an act which is optimific in that situation. Now many persons

have found the latter doctrine, viz. Utilitarianism, self-evident. Anyone who does so is committed to Neutralism, whether he finds the the latter self-evident on inspection or not. But such logical entailments always cut both ways. Anyone who feels doubts about Neutralism ought, to that extent, to feel doubts about Utilitarianism, even if on other grounds he were inclined to accept it.

The second comment to be made is this. The implications of Neutralism certainly do not commend themselves *prima facie* to common sense. It seems to be in some directions immorally selfish and in others immorally indiscriminate. It seems to ignore altogether the ethical relevance of the distinction between acts which are only self-affecting and those which are other-affecting. And among acts which are primarily other-affecting it denies any *direct* ethical relevance to the difference between more and less intimate relationships between an agent and his possible beneficiaries. Yet *prima facie* the special urgency of the claims of certain others upon one's beneficence seems to be founded *directly* on certain special relationships of those others to oneself. I shall return to this point at the end of the lecture; in the meanwhile I will consider Ethical Egoism and Ethical Altruism on their respective merits.

Ethical Egoism, unlike Neutralism, could take many forms. In its extreme form I think it may be rejected at once. I doubt whether anyone would seriously consider it unless, like Spinoza, he had already accepted *Psychological* Egoism. If a person is persuaded that it is psychologically impossible for anyone to act non-egoistically, he will have to hold that each man's duties are confined within the sphere which that psychological impossibility marks out. But, it seems to me, there is no valid reason for accepting psychological egoism. I propose, therefore, to consider a milder form of Ethical Egoism, viz. that which Bishop Butler enunciated in the following famous sentence: 'Though virtue . . . does indeed consist in affection to and pursuit of what is right and good as such, yet . . . when we sit down in a cool hour we can neither justify to ourselves this or any other pursuit till we are satisfied that it will be for our happiness or at least not contrary to it.'

Before considering this dictum critically I will make two historical remarks about it. The first is that Butler states it as a concession which he is willing to make for the sake of argument, and does not explicitly commit himself to it. The second is that Sidgwick, who was an exceptionally clear-headed and honest thinker, found *both* this principle *and* Neutralism self-evident when he contemplated each separately, and saw that they are incompatible with each other.

I find Butler's principle far from easy to interpret. The main difficulty is in the phrase 'justify to ourselves'. I think we may fairly assume that Butler held it to be *psychologically possible* for a person to undertake a course of action simply because he believes it to be right in the circumstances. For, otherwise, 'virtue' as defined by him would be a psychological impossibility. It is surely incredible that he should have held that. So what he must be saying would seem to be this. Although a person *can* undertake a certain course of action simply because he believes it to be right, and although he is acting *virtuously* only if he does so from that motive, his action still in some sense needs justification. It will not be justified in this sense, whatever that may be, unless it will be for the agent's happiness or at least not contrary to it.

Now does 'justification' here mean *moral* justification, or justification in some other sense which is not specifically moral? To justify an act *morally* it is surely necessary and sufficient to show that it is *morally right* for the agent to undertake it in the actual circumstances. I suspect that Butler must have had some kind of not specifically moral justification in mind. I suspect that he must have had the feeling that, however *right* an act may be, it must be condemned in a certain non-moral sense, e.g. as 'silly' or 'quixotic', unless it will confer some advantage on the agent personally or at least not be to his detriment. If so, it is difficult to see how specifically moral justification and this kind of non-moral *desideratum* can be weighed against each other, and why the latter should apparently be held to be in the last resort preponderant.

Let us, therefore, try to interpret 'justifiable' as meaning *morally* justifiable, and let us discuss the principle for ourselves on that interpretation, without regard to what Butler may have meant by it. On that view the principle would come to this. A person may believe a certain action to be right without considering whether it will make for his happiness or not. And he may undertake it simply because he believes it to be right and desires to do what is right as such. But, unless it makes for his happiness or is at least not contrary to it, it will not in fact *be* right.

In order to see what this comes to let us contrast it with ordinary Hedonistic Utilitarianism and with the Neutralism which is the corollary of the latter. Let us imagine a person who started as an ordinary hedonistic Utilitarian, and then came to accept this principle. What is the minimum change that he would have to make in his original position?

Even when he was an ordinary Hedonistic Utilitarian he would have had to consider *inter alia* the effects on his own happiness of each alternative possible course of action. But at that stage he would not attach either more or less weight to its effects on his own happiness as such than to its effects on the happiness of any other person. But, when he came to accept the Butler principle, he would have to reject as wrong, without regard to its effects on the welfare or illfare of others, every alternative which would not make for his own happiness or at any rate every alternative which would be contrary to his own happiness. It is only to the alternatives which remain after this preliminary process of elimination that he would apply the principles of ordinary Hedonistic Utilitarianism.

So far I have left unanalysed Butler's phrase 'being for one's own happiness or at least not contrary to it'. It remains to consider this. Let us suppose that the agent has open to him some alternatives which would *worsen* his hedonic state, some which would *leave it unchanged* on balance, and some which would *improve* it to various degrees. It seems clear that the principle would require him, under these circumstances, to reject any alternative which would *worsen* his hedonic state. But it is not clear that it would require him to reject *in limine* an alternative which would leave his hedonic state unchanged, in favour of one which would positively improve it. Nor is it clear that it would require him to reject, among those alternatives which would positively improve his hedonic state, any alternative which would improve it *less than* some other. What force is to be attached to the concessive phrase 'or at least not contrary to it'? Is egoistic honour satisfied by the minimal interpretation, or does it demand the maximal interpretation in the circumstances supposed?

In order to give the principle every chance I will put the *minimal* interpretation on it. On that interpretation it comes to this. Suppose that a person has alternatives open to him, some of which would worsen his hedonic state, some of which would leave it unchanged, and some of which would improve it to various degrees. Then, *before* considering the effects of these alternatives on the welfare or illfare of others, he must reject as wrong all alternatives which would *worsen* his hedonic state. But among the alternatives which are then left he need not reject as wrong those which would leave his hedonic state unchanged, in favour of those which would improve it. Among the latter he need not reject as wrong those which would improve it less than some others would do.

Now I do not find the least trace of self-evidence in the principle, even when thus minimally interpreted. Moreover, it is plainly in conflict with many of the moral judgments of common sense, for what that may be worth. It is often, e.g., held to be highly praiseworthy to choose an alternative which will positively worsen one's own hedonic state, if this is the only or the best means of securing some end which is valuable in itself, or if it is done for the sake of persons to whom the agent stands in certain special relationships. Even when we are not prepared to say that such an act of self-sacrifice is a duty, this is often not because we think it wrong, but because we think that the agent is doing something which is highly creditable to him but is more than the minimum which duty demands. But there are many cases in which we should be inclined to say that such an act is neither more nor less than a duty. This might be said, e.g., of certain acts of this kind done by a mother for her child, or by a son or daughter for an aged and infirm parent.

The principle would be more plausible if it were stated, not in terms of the agent's happiness or even of other forms of valuable experience, but in terms of improvement or injury to his personality. Let us then restate the principle as follows: Before an agent considers the effects of the various alternatives open to him on the welfare or illfare of others, he must reject as wrong any alternative which will *worsen his own*

personality. There are two remarks to be made about this.

In the first place, it is commonly held to be permissible or even obligatory for a person who stands in certain relations to others deliberately to sacrifice his *life*, if certain very valuable results can be secured for them in that way and in no other. One example is that of an officer deciding to blow up a certain bridge, where he will undoubtedly perish in the explosion but may save his country from invasion. Another is that of the captain of a sinking ship deliberately remaining on board in order that the passengers may have the best chance of being saved. Such cases might perhaps be covered by restating the principle in the following more restricted form: Among the alternatives which are *compatible with his own survival* an agent must reject as wrong any which will worsen his own character and personality.

The second point to note is an ambiguity in the phrase 'to improve or to worsen a man's personality'. This may be used in a specifically moral sense, or in a wider sense which may refer to other than specifically moral excellences and defects. In this wider sense one's personality is improved if one's table-manners or one's golf-handicap or one's powers of appreciating classical music are bettered. Now I do not think that any-one would find the amended principle plausible if 'worsening the agent's personality' were taken to include producing ill-effects on his *non-moral* powers and dispositions. We regard it as always regrettable, but often permissible and sometimes obligatory, for an agent to do an act which involves cramping his personality and forgoing many possible and desirable developments of it. Any intelligent and sensitive person who decides to devote his or her life to working among the sick or the insane inevitably does this, and we do not regard all such decisions as *ipso facto* morally wrong.

The case for the principle is at its strongest if it is put in the following highly restricted form: Among the alternatives open to him, which involve his own survival, an agent must reject as wrong any which will worsen his *moral* character. I think that common sense *would* feel rather uncomfortable in enjoining any such act on a person as a *duty*. But I doubt whether it would be prepared to say that every such act is *ipso facto* wrong. A daughter who gives up her life to tending a peevish invalid mother, instead of marrying and having children, certainly forgoes many possibilities of *moral* development and is likely to develop certain *moral* defects. Possibly her moral character may be improved in some directions, but it seems very doubtful whether the moral gain generally outweighs the moral loss and damage. Yet common sense hesitates to say that such a course of action is wrong. It just feels uncomfortable, and turns its attention as quickly as possible to more cheerful subjects.

The upshot of the discussion is that I am unable to suggest any form of Ethical Egoism, however qualified and attenuated, which appears to be self-evident and which is not plainly at variance with the moral judgments which ordinary people would make in certain particular cases. I pass therefore to the claims of Ethical Altruism.

This, like Ethical Egoism, can take many different forms. Unlike Ethical Egoism, even the most extreme form of it would hardly be rejected off-hand as plainly immoral, at any rate in countries where there is a Christian tradition. It might be described as quixotic or impracticable, but hardly as immoral. No doubt there is a sound practical motive for this more favourable attitude. We realize that most people are far more liable to err on the egoistic than on the altruistic side, and that in a world where so many people are too egoistic it would be unwise to do or say anything to discourage altruism. We also feel that there is something morally admirable in the will and the power to sacrifice one's own well-being – even one's own *moral* development – for the good of others. We therefore hesitate to condemn publicly even those instances of altruistic behaviour which we privately regard as excessive; and we console ourselves with the thought that there is no great risk of their becoming unduly frequent.

But, when this has been said, it must be admitted that there is no trace of self-evidence in the extreme forms of Ethical Altruism, and that they conflict in particular cases with the moral judgments of common sense. It is true that we might hesitate to say that a person has a direct *prima facie* obligation to seek his own happiness. But we certainly condemn morally a person who acts highly imprudently, i.e. one who unreasonably discounts his own probably future pleasures

and unpleasures in comparison with those which are immediately within his reach. It seems plausible to hold that such condemnation is at least in part *direct*, and that it is not wholly based on one's awareness of the fact that such a person is likely to become a burden to others. And when we turn from the good and bad experiences which a person may have in the course of his life to the goodness or badness which resides in his personality, we notice the following fact. Common sense appears to hold that each of us is under a fairly strong obligation to develop his own physical and intellectual powers, to organize his character into a coherent system, and not to allow himself to rust or to run to seed. No doubt one important ground for regarding self-culture and self-development as a duty is that they are necessary conditions for being *useful to others*. But I do not think it is plausible to hold that this is *merely* an indirect obligation, wholly subordinate to the direct obligation to be useful to others.

Let us, then, ignore the extremer forms of Ethical Altruism, and consider for a moment a principle which might be regarded as an altruistic counterpart to Butler's egoistic principle. This is Kant's famous maxim that it is always wrong to treat a person as a mere means, and a duty to treat him as an end. It is true that Kant held that this maxim should govern a person's dealings with himself as well as his dealings with others. But, if we confine our attention to the latter application of it, we might regard Kant's principle as setting a limit to the sacrifices which a person may legitimately impose on others, just as Butler's principle sets a limit to those which he may legitimately impose on himself.

I think that the terminology of 'means' and 'end' is unfortunate here, and that the word 'end' fails to express what Kant may have had in mind. The word 'end', when used in its ordinary sense, signifies primarily a possible state of affairs which someone desires to be realized, and towards the realization of which he can contribute by appropriate action. Now this possible state of affairs may be the future existence of an object of a certain kind, which does not at present exist, e.g. of a certain building which a person has planned and desires to have built. In that case this proposed object itself may be called an 'end' in a derivative sense in relation to that person.

I believe that these two inter-related senses are the only ones in which the word 'end' is commonly used, and the only ones in which it is correlative to the word 'means'. A 'means' is any object which a person uses as an instrument in carrying out a course of action undertaken in order to realize a possible state of affairs which is an end to him.

Now it is obvious enough that a person can be and often is treated as a *means*. A miner is so treated in so far as he is used for hewing coal, and a criminal is so treated when he is publicly punished in order to deter himself or others from similar criminal actions in future. But it is not at all clear that a person can be treated as an *end*, in the ordinary sense in which the terms 'end' and 'means' are correlatives. It is plain that a person *cannot* be an end in the first sense which I have mentioned. For a person is not a possible state of affairs. A person might be an end in the second sense, viz. an object whose existence someone desired to be realized and which will come into being through the deliberate action of that someone. In this sense a person might be an end to a eugenist or to an educator who had deliberately had him generated or subsequently moulded in accordance with his plans. In this sense a person may even be an end to himself, in perfectly intelligible phraseology. A man may, e.g., in early life form the desire to become a yogi, and by a long course of appropriate training and self-discipline he may eventually effect the transformation in his character and powers which he has sought. Such a person, in his later state, is an end in relation to himself as he was in his earlier states. Moreover, in such a case he has also continually used himself, in respect of certain of his powers and dispositions, as the means or instrument whereby he has eventually realized himself as an end.

When Kant talked of treating a person as a *means* I see no reason to doubt that he was using the word in its ordinary familiar sense. But when he talked of treating a person as an *end* I very much doubt whether he was using that word in any sense which is familiar and correlative to *means*. From the context I should judge that he meant treating a person as an entity which can significantly be said to have legal and moral *rights*, to be morally *responsible* for its actions, to *deserve* pleasure as a reward and pain as a punishment

for certain of his actions, and so on. To treat a person as a mere instrument is certainly to ignore such facts about him. But on the other hand, to treat him as a bearer of rights and duties, merits and demerits, is not appropriately described as treating him as an end.

The minimal interpretation which we might put on Kant's principal is this. It is always wrong to treat a *person* as if he were a mere animal, and still more wrong to treat him as if he were a mere inanimate object. For a person is a being who not only has sensations which may be painful and desires which may be thwarted, like an animal. He has also the power of rational and of reflective cognition; ideas of right and wrong, good and evil; and all those conative and emotional peculiarities, such as a sense of duty, feelings of remorse, etc., which depend on the former properties. In considering how to treat a person it can never be right simply to ignore those features which distinguish him from a mere animal and still more from an inanimate object.

When thus interpreted the principle is no doubt true and highly important. But it does not follow that, when one *has* taken account of the features which distinguish a person from a brute or an inanimate thing, and *has* endeavoured to give due weight to them, it is never right to treat him in certain respects as if he were the one or the other. It is not clear, e.g., that it is never right to compel a person to do what he believes to be wrong, e.g., to have his children vaccinated; or to restrain him from doing what he believes to be his duty, e.g., from sacrificing his first-born to Moloch. For, although he is a person, he is not the only one; and there may be situations in which, unless you treat a certain person as if he were a dangerous animal, he will infringe the rights and liberties and consciences of many other persons.

The sentiments of common sense at the present time in Western countries on such issues are highly complex and very mixed. The following remarks will serve to illustrate this.

(1) It is generally held to be permissible for an individual or a community to take the *life* of a person under certain circumstances. Any individual may do this if he is attacked and has serious reason to believe that he cannot save himself or those dependent on him from death

or serious injury at any less cost. When a country is at war those of its citizens who are members of its armed forces, not only *may* do this, but are under an *obligation* to do it to a member of an opposing force who refuses to surrender. A community may do it, through its authorized agent, to a citizen who has been convicted of murder and sentenced to death by due process of law; and it is the duty of the executioner to carry out the sentence. All this would have been accepted by Kant. Yet it is surely difficult to hold, without a great deal of palpable sophistication, that the attacker, the enemy soldier, and the condemned murderer are being treated as *ends* in any ordinarily accepted sense of that word. I think it is true that the attacker and the enemy soldier are also not being treated as *mere means*. The murder *is* being treated as a means in so far as the execution is intended to deter or to reform others.

(2) It is commonly held that there are circumstances in which it is right for A to take B's life, but it would be wrong for B to take his own life. Thus it is right and dutiful for the executioner to take the life of the condemned murderer, but wrong for the latter to anticipate him by committing suicide. (This furnishes a good example of the ethical relevance which common sense ascribes to the distinction between self-affecting and other-affecting acts.)

(3) On the other hand, common-sense holds that it may be right and praiseworthy for a person voluntarily to make sacrifices which it would be wrong for anyone else to impose on him. Thus, e.g., a medical research worker with no one dependent on him would be admired if he were to subject himself voluntarily to some process of treatment which might injure him permanently or kill him but which might lead to a valuable discovery. But it would be thought monstrously wrong to subject anyone against his will to such a process of treatment, or even, I think, to try to persuade him to subject himself to it.

(4) Common sense in contemporary Western societies holds very strongly that it is unconditionally wrong to subject an *innocent* person to loss or suffering in respect of a crime committed by another, even where there is good reason to believe that this would be more effective as a deterrent than any punishment that could be inflicted on the criminal himself. There is perhaps no other point at which pure Utilitarianism is in such complete and obvious conflict with common-sense morality as here. Even if a convincing case could be made out on Utilitarian grounds for the principle that only the guilty should suffer in respect of a crime – and it is very doubtful whether this could be done – common sense would feel that this line of argument is wholly irrelevant.

In view of such facts as I have stated above, it would be extremely hard to formulate any unconditional general principle about the limitation of the sacrifices which can be legitimately imposed on others. I suspect that any such formulation would have to contain so many qualifications that it could make no claim to embody a self-evident principle.

In considering Neutralism, Ethical Egoism, and Ethical Altruism I have in each case indicated some important points in which the doctrine seems to conflict with the morality of common sense. I will now consider briefly what seems to be the attitude of common sense towards the issue of self and others. I think that this position may be best described as *Self-referential Altruism*.

Common sense considers that the question whether an act is only self-affecting or is also other-affecting is often highly relevant to whether it is permissible or omissible, morally admirable or morally indifferent or morally culpable.

Its attitude is *altruistic* in the following respects. It considers that each of us is often under an obligation to sacrifice his own happiness, and sometimes to sacrifice the development of his own personality and even to give up his life, for the benefit of certain other persons and institutions, when it is quite uncertain whether on the whole more good will be produced or more evil averted by so doing than by acting otherwise. It tends to admire such acts, even when it regrets the necessity for them, and even when it thinks that on the whole they had better not have been done. It has no admiration, as such, for acts directed towards making one's own life happy, even when they do no harm to others. It does indeed admire acts directed to the development and improvement of the agent's own personality, whether in moral or in non-moral respects. But I think that its admiration is not very strong unless they are done against exceptionally great external obstacles (e.g. poverty or a criminal environment) or exceptionally great internal handicaps (e.g. ill-health or disablement or unusually violent passions).

On the other hand, the altruism which common sense approves is always *limited in scope*. It holds that each of us has specially urgent obligations to benefit certain individuals and groups which stand in certain special relations to *himself*, e.g. his parents, his children, his fellow-countrymen, etc. And it holds that these special relationships are the ultimate and sufficient ground for these specially urgent claims on one's beneficence.

The above paragraphs express what I mean by saying that the altruism which common sense accepts is self-referential. In conclusion I wish to raise this question. Could this common-sense position be circumvented by a person who found Neutralism self-evident, or by one who found the Utilitarian principle self-evident and was thus committed to Neutralism at the next move?

Such a person would, I think, have to do the following two things:

(1) He would have to show that all those special obligations which common-sense takes to be founded *directly* upon special relations of others to the agent, are *derivable* (so far as they are valid at all) from the one fundamental obligation to maximize the balance of good over evil in the lives and personalities of all contemporary and subsequent inhabitants of the world, taken as a whole. He would try to do this by reference to the obvious facts that each of us is limited in his powers and resources, in his knowledge of the needs of others, and in the range of his natural sympathies; and that each of us is an object of interest, affection, and natural expectation only to a limited class of his fellow-men. The best that the Neutralist could hope to achieve on these lines would be to reach a system of *derived* obligations, which agreed roughly in scope and in relative urgency with that set of obligations which common sense (mistakenly, on his view) takes to be founded *directly* upon various special relationships. In so far as this result was reached, the Neutralist might claim to accept in outline the same set of obligations which common sense does; to correct common-sense morality in matters of detail; and to substitute a single coherent system of obligations, deduced from a single self-evident moral principle and a number of admitted psychological facts, for a mere heap of unrelated and separately

grounded obligations. To have tried to carry this out in great detail and with much plausibility is one of the solid achievements of Sidgwick in his *Methods of Ethics*.

(2) To complete his case, the Neutralist would have to try to explain how common sense comes to make the fundamental mistake which, according to him, it does make. It seems to me that he might attempt this with some plausibility on the following lines. And here we make that concluding bow to the theory of evolution, without which a Herbert Spencer Lecture would surely be incomplete.

(i) Any society in which each member was prepared to make sacrifices for the benefit of the group as a whole and of certain smaller groups within it would be more likely to flourish and persist than one whose members were not prepared to make such sacrifices. Now egoistic and anti-social motives are extremely strong in everyone. Suppose, then, that there had been a society in which, no matter how, there had arisen a strong additional motive (no matter how absurd or superstitious) in support of self-sacrifice, on appropriate occasions, by a member of the group for the sake of the group as a whole or for that of certain smaller groups within it. Suppose that this motive was thereafter conveyed from one generation to another by example and by precept, and that it was supported by the sanctions of social praise and blame. Such a society would be likely to flourish, and to overcome other societies in which no such additional motive for limited self-sacrifice had arisen and been propagated. So its ways of thinking in these matters, and its sentiments of approval and disapproval concerning them, would tend to spread. They would spread directly through conquest, and indirectly by the prestige which the success of this society would give to it in the eyes of others.

(ii) Suppose, next, that there had been a society in which, no matter how, a strong additional motive for *unlimited* self-sacrifice had arisen and had been propagated from one generation to another. A society in which each member was as ready to sacrifice himself for other societies and their members as for his own society and its members, would be most unlikely to persist and flourish. Therefore such a society would be very likely to succumb in conflict with one of the former kind.

(iii)   Now suppose a long period of conflict between societies of the various types which I have imagined. It seems likely that the societies which would still be existing and would be predominant at the latter part of such a period would be those in which there had somehow arisen in the remote past a strong pro-emotion towards self-sacrifice confined within the society, and a strong anti-emotion towards extending it beyond those limits. Now these are exactly the kinds of society which we do find existing and flourishing in historical times.

The Neutralist might therefore argue as follows. Even if Neutralism be true, and even if it be self-evident to a philosopher who contemplates it in a cool hour in his study, there are powerful historical causes which would tend to make certain forms of restricted Altruism or qualified Egoism *seem* to be true to most unreflective persons at all times and even to many reflective ones at most times. Therefore the fact that common-sense rejects Neutralism, and tends to accept this other type of doctrine, is not a conclusive objection to the *truth*, or even to the *necessary* truth, of Neutralism.

33

Filial Morality

Christina Hoff Sommers

We not only find it hard to say exactly how much a son owes his parents, but we are even reluctant to investigate this.

Henry Sidgwick[1]

What rights do parents have to the special attentions of their adult children? Before this century there was no question that a filial relationship defined a natural obligation; philosophers might argue about the nature of filial obligation, but not about its reality. Today, not a few moralists dismiss it as an illusion, or give it secondary derivative status. A. John Simmons[2] expresses "doubts . . . concerning the existence of 'filial' debts," and Michael Slote[3] seeks to show that the idea of filial obedience is an illusion whose source is the false idea that one owes obedience to a divine being. Jeffrey Blustein[4] argues that parents who have done no more than their duty may be owed nothing, and Jane English[5] denies outright that there are any filial obligations not grounded in mutual friendship.

The current tendency to deny or reconstrue filial obligation is related to the more general difficulty that contemporary philosophers have when dealing with the special duties. An account of the special obligations to one's kin, friends, community or country puts considerable strain on moral theories such as Kantianism and utilitarianism, theories that seem better designed for telling us what we should be doing for everyone

impartially than for explaining something like filial obligation. The moral philosopher of a utilitarian or Kantian persuasion who is concerned to show that it is permissible to give some biased vent to family feeling *may* go on to become concerned with the more serious question of accounting for what appears to be a special obligation to care for and respect one's parents – but only as an afterthought. On the whole, the question of special agent-relative duties has not seemed pressing. In what follows I shall be arguing for a strong notion of filial obligation, and more generally I shall be making a case for the special moral relations. I first present some anecdotal materials that illustrate the thesis that a filial duty to respect one's parents is not an illusion.

I. The Concrete Dilemmas

I shall be concerned with the filial duties of adult children and more particularly with the duty to honor and respect. I have chosen almost randomly three situations each illustrating what seems to be censurable failure on the part of adult children

Christina Hoff Sommers, "Filial Morality." *The Journal of Philosophy* 83, no. 8 (August 1986), pp. 439–56. © 1986 by The Journal of Philosophy, Inc. Reprinted with permission from the author and The Journal of Philosophy.

to respect their parents or nurturers. It would not be hard to add to these cases and real life is continually adding to them.

1. An elderly man was interviewed on National Public Radio for a program on old age. This is what he said about his daughter.

> I live in a rooming house. I lost my wife about two years ago and I miss her very much . . . My little pleasure was to go to my daughter's house in Anaheim and have a Friday night meal. . . . She would make a meal that I would enjoy. . . . So my son-in-law got angry at me one time for a little nothing and ordered me out of the house. That was about eight months ago. . . . I was back once during the day when he was working. That was about two and a half or three months ago. I stayed for about two hours and left before he came home from work. But I did not enjoy the visit very much. That was the last time I was there to see my daughter.

2. An eighty-two year old woman (call her Miss Tate) spent thirty years working as a live-in housekeeper and baby-sitter for a judge's family in Massachusetts. The judge and his wife left her a small pension which inflation rendered inadequate. After her employers died, she lost contact with the children whom she had virtually brought up. One day Miss Tate arranged for a friend of hers to write to the children (by then middle-aged) telling them that she was sick and would like to see them. They never got around to visiting her or helping her in any way. She died last year without having heard from them.

3. The anthropologist Barbara Meyerhoff did a study of an elderly community in Venice, California.[6] She tells about the disappointment of a group of elders whose children failed to show up at their graduation from an adult education program:

> The graduates, 26 in all, were arranged in rows flanking the head table. They wore their finest clothing bearing blue and white satin ribbons that crossed the breast from shoulder to waist. Most were solemn and flushed with excitement. . . . No one talked openly about the conspicuous absence of the elders' children. (87, 104)

I believe it may be granted that the father who had dined once a week with his daughter has a legitimate complaint. And although Miss Tate was duly salaried throughout her long service with the judge's family, it seems clear that the children of that family owe her some special attention and regard for having brought them up. The graduation ceremony is yet another example of wrongful disregard and neglect. Some recent criticisms of traditional conceptions of filial duty (e.g., by Jane English and John Simmons) make much of examples involving unworthy parents. One may agree that exceptional parents can forfeit their moral claims on their children. (What, given his behavior, remains of Fyodor Karamazov's right to filial regard?) But I am here concerned with what is owed to the average parent who is neglected or whose wishes are disregarded when they could at some reasonable cost be respected. I assume that such filial disregard is wrong. Although the assumption is dogmatic, it can be defended – though not by any quick maneuver. Filial morality is but one topic in the morality of special relations. The attempt to understand filial morality will lead us to a synoptic look at the moral community as a whole and to an examination of the nature of the rights and obligations that bind its members.

II.   Shifting Conceptions

Jeffrey Blustein's *Parents and Children (op. cit.)* contains an excellent historical survey of the moral issues in the child-parent relationship. For Aristotle the obligation to serve and obey one's parents is like an obligation to repay a debt. Aquinas too explains the commandment to honor one's parents as "making a return for benefits received."[7] Both Aristotle and Aquinas count life itself as the first and most important gift that the child is given.

With Locke[8] the topic of filial morality changes: the discussion shifts from a concern with the authority and power of the parent to concern with the less formal, less enforceable, right to respect. Hume[9] was emphatic on the subject of filial ingratitude, saying, "Of all the crimes that human creatures are capable, the most horrid and unnatural is ingratitude, especially when it is committed against parents." By Sidgwick's time the special duties are beginning to be seen as problematic: "The question is on what principles ... we are to determine the nature and extent of the special claims of affection and kind services which arise out of ... particular relations of human beings" (242). Nevertheless, Sidgwick is still traditional in maintaining that "all are agreed that there are such duties, the non-performance of which is ground for censure," and he is himself concerned to show how "our common notion of Justice [is] applicable to these no less than to other duties" (243).

If we look at the writings of a contemporary utilitarian such as Peter Singer,[10] we find no talk of justice or duty or rights, and a fortiori, no talk of special duties or parental rights. Consider how Singer, applying a version of R. M. Hare's utilitarianism, approaches a case involving filial respect. He imagines himself about to dine with three friends when his father calls saying he is ill and asking him to visit. What shall he do?

> To decide impartially I must sum up the preferences for and against going to dinner with my friends, and those for and against visiting my father. Whatever action satisfies more preferences, adjusted according to the strength of the preferences, that is the action I ought to take. (101)

Note that the idea of a special obligation does not enter here. Nor is any weight given to the history of the filial relationship which typically includes some two decades of parental care and nurture. According to Singer, "adding and subtracting preferences in this manner" is the only rational way of reaching ethical judgment.

Utilitarian theory is not very accommodating to the special relations. And it would appear that Bernard Williams is right in finding the same true of Kantianism. According to Williams,[11] Kant's "moral point of view is specially characterized by its impartiality and its indifference to any particular relations to particular persons." In my opinion, giving no special consideration to one's kin commits what might be called the *Jellyby fallacy*. Mrs. Jellyby, a character in Charles Dickens' *Bleak House*,[12] devotes all of her considerable energies to the foreign poor to the complete neglect of her family. She is described as a "pretty diminutive woman with handsome eyes, though they had a curious habit of seeming to look a long way off. As if they could see

nothing nearer than Africa" (52). Dickens clearly intends her as someone whose moral priorities are ludicrously disordered. Yet by some modern lights Mrs. Jellyby could be viewed as a paragon of impartial rectitude. In the next two sections I will try to show what is wrong with an impartialist point of view and suggest a way to repair it.

III.   The Moral Domain

By a *moral domain* I mean a domain consisting of what G. J. Warnock[13] calls "moral patients." Equivalently, it consists of beings that have what Robert Nozick[14] calls "ethical pull." A being has *ethical pull* if it is ethically "considerable"; minimally, it is a being that should not be ill treated by a moral agent and whose ill treatment directly wrongs it. The extent of the moral domain is one area of contention (Mill includes animals; Kant does not). The nature of the moral domain is another. But here we find more uniformity. Utilitarians and deontologists are in agreement in conceiving of the moral domain as constituted by beings whose ethical pull is equal on all moral agents. To simplify matters, let us consider a domain consisting only of moral patients that are also moral agents. (For Kant, this is no special stipulation.) Then it is as if we have a gravitational field in which the force of gravitation is not affected by distance and all pairs of objects have the same attraction to one another. Or, if this sort of gravitational field is odd, consider a mutual admiration society no member of which is, intrinsically, more attractive than any other member. In this group, the pull of all is the same. Suppose that Buridan's ass was not standing in the exact middle of the bridge but was closer to one of the bags of feed at either end. We should still say that he was equally attracted to both bags, but also that he naturally would choose the closer one. So too does the utilitarian or Kantian say that the ethical pull of a needy East African and that of a needy relative are the same, but we can more easily act to help the relative. This theory of equal pull but unequal response saves the appearances for impartiality while acknowledging that, in practice, charity often begins and sometimes ends at home.

This is how the principle of impartiality appears in the moral theories of Kant and Mill.

Of course their conceptions of ethical pull differ. For the Kantian any being in the kingdom of ends is an embodiment of moral law whose force is uniform and unconditional. For the utilitarian, any being's desires are morally considerable, exerting equal attraction on all moral agents. Thus Kant and Mill, in their different ways, have a common view of the moral domain as a domain of moral patients exerting uniform pull on all moral agents. I shall refer to this as the *equal-pull (EP) thesis*. It is worth commenting on the underlying assumptions that led Kant and Mill to adopt this view of the moral domain.

It is a commonplace that Kant was concerned to free moral agency from its psychological or "anthropological" determinations. In doing so he offered us a conception of moral agents as rational beings which abstracts considerably from human and animal nature. It is less of a commonplace that utilitarian theory, in its modern development, tends also to be antithetical to important empirical aspects of human nature. For the Kantian, the empirical demon to be combatted and exorcized lies within the individual. For the utilitarian it is located within society and its customs, including practices that are the sociobiological inheritance of the species. According to an act utilitarian like Singer, reason frees ethical thought from the earlier moralities of kin and reciprocal altruism and opens it to the wider morality of disinterestedness and universal concern: "The principle of impartial consideration of interests . . . alone remains a rational basis for ethics" (*op. cit.*, 109). The equal-pull thesis is thus seen to be entailed by a principle of impartiality, common to Kantian and utilitarian ethics, which is seen as liberating us from the biased dictates of our psychological, biological, and socially conventional natures.[15]

IV.   Differential Pull

The doctrine of equal ethical pull is a modern development in the history of ethics. It is certainly not attributable to Aristotle or Aquinas, nor, arguably, to Locke. Kant's authority gave it common currency and made it, so to speak, foundational. It is, therefore, important to state that EP is a dogma. Why should it be assumed that ethical pull is constant regardless of circumstance, familiarity, kinship and other special

relations? The accepted answer is that EP makes sense of impartiality. The proponent of the special duties must accept this as a challenge: alternative suggestions for moral ontology must show how impartiality can be consistent with differential ethical forces.

I will refer to the rival thesis as the *thesis of differential pull (DP)*. According to the DP thesis, the ethical pull of a moral patient will always partly depend on how the moral patient is related to the moral agent on whom the pull is exerted. Moreover, the "how" of relatedness will be determined in part by the social practices and institutions in which the agent and patient play their roles. This does not mean that every moral agent will be differently affected, since it may be that different moral agents stand in the same relation to different moral patients. But where the relations differ in certain relevant ways, there the pull will differ. The relevant factors that determine ethical pull are in a broad sense circumstantial, including the particular social arrangements that determine what is expected from the moral agent. How particular circumstances and conventions shape the special duties is a complex question to which we cannot here do justice. We shall, however, approach it from a foundational standpoint which rejects EP and recognizes the crucial role of conventional practice, relationships, and roles in determining the nature and force of moral obligation. The gravitational metaphor may again be suggestive. In DP morality the community of agents and patients is analogous to a gravitational field where distance counts and forces vary in accordance with local conditions.

V.   Filial Duty

Filial duty, unlike the duty to keep a promise, is not self-imposed. But keeping the particular promise one has made is also a special duty, and the interplay of impartiality and specific obligation is more clearly seen in the case of a promise. We do well, therefore, to look at the way special circumstances shape obligations by examining more carefully the case of promise making.

A. I. Melden[16] has gone into the morality of promise keeping rather thoroughly, and I believe that some features of his analysis apply to the more general description of the way particular circumstances determine the degree of ethical pull on a moral agent. Following Locke, Melden assumes the natural right of noninterference with one's liberty to pursue one's interests (including one's interest in the well-being of others) where such pursuit does not interfere with a like liberty for others. Let an interest be called *invasive* if it is an interest in interfering with the pursuit of someone else's interests. Then the right that every moral patient possesses is the right not to be interfered with in the pursuit of his or her non-invasive interests. (In what follows 'interest' will mean noninvasive interest.)

According to Melden, a promiser "gives the promisee the action as his own." The promise-breaking failure to perform is then "tantamount to interfering with or subverting endeavours he [the promisee] has a right to pursue" (47). The promisee is "as entitled to [the action] as he is, as a responsible agent, to conduct his own affairs." What is special about this analysis is the formal grounding of the special positive duty of promise keeping in the minimalist negative obligation of noninterference. The negative, general, and indiscriminate obligation not to interfere is determined by the practice of promise making as a positive, specific, and discriminate obligation to act. Note how context here shapes and directs the initial obligation of noninterference and enhances its force. Given the conventions of the practice of promise making, the moral patient has novel and legitimate expectations of performances caused by the explicit assurances given by the promiser, who, in effect, has made over these performances to the promisee. And given these legitimate expectations, the agent's nonperformance of the promised act is invasive and tantamount to active interference with the patient's rights to its performance.

It is in the spirit of this approach to make the attempt to analyze other special obligations in the same manner. We assume a DP framework and a minimal universal deontological principle (the duty to refrain from interfering in the lives of others). This negative duty is refracted by the parochial situation as a special duty which may be positive in character, calling on the moral agent to act or refrain from acting in specific ways toward specific moral patients. This view of the special obligations needs to be justified. But for the present I merely seek to state it more fully.

The presumption of a special positive obligation arises for a moral agent when two conditions obtain: (1) In a given social arrangement (or practice) there is a specific interaction or transaction between moral agent and patient, such as promising and being promised, nurturing and being nurtured, befriending and being befriended. (2) The interaction in that context gives rise to certain conventional expectations (e.g., that a promise will be kept, that a marital partner will be faithful, that a child will respect the parent). In promising, the content of the obligation is verbally explicit. But this feature is not essential to the formation of other specific duties. In the filial situation, the basic relationship is that of nurtured to nurturer, a type of relationship which is very concrete, intimate, and long-lasting and which is considered to be more morally determining than any other in shaping a variety of rights and obligations.

Here is one of Alasdair MacIntyre's descriptions of the denizens of the moral domain:

> I am brother, cousin, and grandson, member of this household, that village, this tribe. These are not characteristics that belong to human beings accidentally, to be stripped away in order to discover "the real me". They are part of my substance, defining partially at least and sometimes wholly my obligations and my duties. (32)

MacIntyre's description takes Aristotle's dictum that man is a social animal in a sociological direction. A social animal has a specific social role whose prerogatives and obligations characterize a particular kind of person. Being a father or mother is socially as well as biologically descriptive: it not only defines what one is; it also defines who one is and what one owes.

Because it does violence to a social role, a filial breach is more serious than a breach of promise. In the promise the performance is legitimately expected, being, as it were, explicitly made over to the promisee as "his." In the filial situation the expected behavior is implicit, and the failure to perform affects the parent in a direct and personal way. To lose one's entitlements diminishes one as a person. Literature abounds with examples of such diminishment; King Lear is perhaps the paradigm. When Lear first becomes aware of Goneril's defection, he asks his companion:

"Who am I?" to which the reply is "A shadow." Causing humiliation is a prime reason why filial neglect is tantamount to active interference. One's sense of dignity varies with temperament. But dignity itself – in the context of an institution like the family – is objective, being inseparable from one's status and role in that context.

The filial duties of adult children include such things as being grateful, loyal, attentive, respectful and deferential to parents (more so than to strangers). Many adult children, of course, are respectful and attentive to their parents out of love, not duty. But, as Melden says: "The fact that, normally, there is love and affection that unites the members of the family . . . in no way undercuts the fact that there is a characteristic distribution of rights and obligations within the family circle" (67).

The mutual understanding created by a promise is simplicity itself when compared with the range of expected behavior that filial respect comprises. What is expected in the case of a promise is clearly specified by the moral agent, but with respect to most other special duties there is little that is verbally explicit. Filial obligation is thus essentially underdetermined, although there are clear cases of what counts as disrespect – as we have seen in our three cases. The complexity and nonspecificity of expected behavior which is written into the domestic arrangements do not affect what the promissory and the filial situation have in common: both may be viewed as particular contexts in which the moral agent must refrain from behavior that interferes with the normal prerogatives of the moral patient.[17]

By taking promising as a starting point in a discussion of special duties, one runs the risk of giving the impression that DP is generally to be understood as a form of social-contract theory. But a more balanced perspective considers the acts required by any of the special duties as naturally and implicitly "made over" within the practices and institutions that define the moral agent in his particular role as a "social animal." Within this perspective promising and other forms of contracting are themselves special cases and not paradigmatic. Indeed, the binding force of the obligation to fulfill an explicit contract is itself to be explained by the general account to be given of special duties in a DP theory.

VI. Grateful Duty

One group of contemporary moral philosophers, whom I shall tendentiously dub *sentimentalists*, has been vocal in pointing out the shortcomings of the mainstream theories in accounting for the morality of the special relations. But they would find my formal and traditional approach equally inadequate. The sentimentalists oppose deontological approaches to the morality of the parent-child relationship, arguing that *duties* of gratitude are paradoxical, that the "owing idiom" distorts the moral ideal of the parent-child relationship which should be characterized by love and mutual respect. For them, each family relationship is unique, its moral character determined by the idiosyncratic ties of its members. Carol Gilligan[18] has recently distinguished between an "ethic of care" and an "ethic of rights." The philosophers I have in mind are objecting to the aridity of the "rights perspective" and are urging moral philosophers to attend to the morality of special relations from a "care perspective." The distinction is suggestive, but the two perspectives are not necessarily exclusive. One may recognize one's duty in what one does spontaneously and generously. And just as a Kantian caricature holds one in greater esteem when one does what is right against one's inclination, so the idea of care, responsibility and personal commitment, without formal obligation, is an equally dangerous caricature.

Approaches that oppose care and friendship to rights and obligations can be shown to be sadly inadequate when applied to real-life cases. The following situation described in this letter to Ann Landers is not atypical:

Dear Ann Landers:
We have five children, all overachievers who have studied hard and done well. Two are medical doctors and one is a banker. . . . We are broke from paying off debts for their wedding and their education. . . . We rarely hear from our children. . . . Last week my husband asked our eldest son for some financial help. He was told 'File bankruptcy and move into a small apartment.' Ann, personal feelings are no longer a factor: it is a matter of survival. Is there any law that says our children must help out?[19]

There are laws in some states that would require that these children provide some minimal support for their indigent parents. But not a few contemporary philosophers could be aptly cited by those who would advocate their repeal. A. John Simmons, Jeffrey Blustein, and Michael Slote, for example, doubt that filial duty is to be understood in terms of special moral debts *owed* to parents. Simmons offers "reasons to believe that [the] particular duty meeting conduct [of parents to children] does not generate an obligation of gratitude on the child" (*op. cit.*, 182). And Blustein opposes what he and Jane English call the "owing idiom" for services parents were obligated to perform. "If parents have any right to repayment from their children, it can only be for that which was either above and beyond the call of parental duty, or not required by parental duty at all"[20] (The "overachievers" could not agree more.) Slote finds it "difficult to believe that one has a *duty* to show gratitude for benefits one has not requested" (320). Jane English characterizes filial duty in terms of the duties one good friend owes another. "[A]fter a friendship ends, the duties of friendship end" (354, 356).

Taking a sentimentalist view of gratitude, these philosophers are concerned to remove the taint of onerous duty from what should be a spontaneous and free desire to be considerate of one's parents. One may agree with the sentimentalists that there is something morally unsatisfactory in being considerate of one's parents *merely* out of duty. The mistake lies in thinking that duty and inclination are necessarily at odds. Moreover, the *having* of certain feelings and attitudes may be necessary for carrying out one's duty. Persons who lack feeling for their parents may be morally culpable for that very lack. The sentimentalist objection that this amounts to a paradoxical duty to *feel* (grateful, loyal, etc.) ignores the extent to which people are responsible for their characters; to have failed to develop in oneself the capacity to be considerate of others is to have failed morally, if only because many duties simply cannot be carried out by a cold and unfeeling moral agent.[21] Kant himself speaks of "the universal duty which devolves upon man of so ordering his life as to be fit for the performance of all moral duties."[22] And MacIntyre, who is no Kantian, makes the same point when he says, "moral education is an 'education sentimentale'" (151).

Sentimentalism is not harmlessly false. Its moral perspective on family relationships as spontaneous, voluntary, and duty-free is simply unrealistic. Anthropological observations provide a sounder perspective on filial obligation. Thus Corinne Nydegger[23] warns of the dangers of weakening the formal constraints that ensure that obligations are met: "No society, including our own, relies solely on . . . affection, good will and enlightened self-interest." She notes that the aged in particular "have a vested interest in the social control of obligations" (30).

It should be noted that the sentimentalist is arguing for a morality that is sensitive to special relations and personal commitment; this is in its own way a critique of EP morality. But sentimentalism ignores the extent to which the "care perspective" is itself dependent on a formal sense of what is fitting and morally proper. The ideal relationship cannot be "duty-free," if only because sentimental ties may come unraveled, often leaving one of the parties at a material disadvantage. Sentimentalism then places in a precarious position those who are not (or no longer) the fortunate beneficiaries of sincere personal commitments. If the EP moralist tends to be implausibly abstract and therefore inattentive to the morality of the special relations, the sentimentalist tends to err on the side of excessive narrowness by neglecting the impersonal "institutional" expectations and norms that qualify all special relations.

VII.   DP Morality: Some Qualifications

It might be thought that the difference between EP and DP tends to disappear when either theory is applied to concrete cases, since one must in any case look at the circumstances to determine the practical response. But this is to underestimate how what one *initially* takes to be the responsibility of moral agents to patients affects the procedure one uses in making practical decisions in particular circumstances. Recall again how Peter Singer's EP procedure pits the preferences of the three friends against the preferences of the father, and contrast this with a differential-pull approach that assumes discriminate and focused obligations to the father. Similarly, the adult children of the graduating elders and the children raised by Miss Tate gave no special weight to filial obligation in planning their day's activities.

There are, then, significant practical differences between a DP and an EP approach to concrete cases. The EP moralist is a respecter of the person whom he sees as an autonomous individual but no respector of the person as a social animal within its parochial preserve. Moreover, a DP theory that grounds duty in the minimal principle of noninterference is sensitive to the distinction between strict duty and benevolence. Behaving as one is dutybound to behave is not the whole of moral life. But duty (in the narrow sense) and benevolence are not commensurate. If I am right, the Anaheim woman is culpably disrespectful. But it would be absurd if (in the manner of Mrs Jellyby) she were to try to compensate for excluding her father by inviting several indigent gentlemen to dine in his stead.

I am arguing for a DP approach to the morality of the special relations. Williams, Nozick, MacIntyre, and others criticize utilitarianism and Kantianism for implausible consequences in this area. I believe that their objections to much of contemporary ethics are symptomatic of a growing discontent with the EP character of the current theories. It may be possible to revise the theories to avoid some of the implausible consequences. Rule utilitarianism seems to be a move in this direction. But, as they stand, their EP character leaves them open to criticism. EP is a dogma. But so is DP. My contention is that DP moral theories more plausibly account for our preanalytic moral judgments concerning what is right and wrong in a wide variety of real cases. Having said this, I will acknowledge that the proper antidote to the malaise Williams and others are pointing to will not be effectively available until DP moral theories are given a theoretical foundation as well worked out as those of the mainstream theories. Alasdair MacIntyre is a contemporary DP moralist who has perhaps gone furthest in this direction. Nozick and Williams are at least cognizant that a "particularistic" approach is needed.[24]

The DP moral theory is in any case better able to account for the discriminate duties that correspond to specific social roles and expectations. But of course not all duties are discriminate: there are requirements that devolve on everyone. This not only includes the negative requirement to refrain from harming one's fellowman, but also, in certain circumstances, to help him when one is singularly situated to do so. I am, for example, expected to help a lost child find its parent or to feed a starving stranger at my doorstep. Failure to do so violates an understanding that characterizes the loosest social ties binding us as fellow human beings. The "solitariness" that Hobbes speaks of is a myth; we are never in a totally unrelated "state of nature." The DP moralist recognizes degrees of relatedness and graded expectations. The most general types of positive behavior expected of anyone as a moral agent obey some minimal principle of Good Samaritanism applicable to "the stranger in thy midst."

Perhaps the most serious difficulty facing the DP approach is that it appears to leave the door wide open to ethical relativism. We turn now to this problem.

VIII. DP and Ethical Relativism

A theory is nonrelativistic if it has the resources to pass moral judgments on whole societies. My version of DP moral theory avoids ethical relativism by adopting a deontological principle (noninterference) which may be deployed in assessing and criticizing the moral legitimacy of the traditional arrangements within which purportedly moral interactions take place. We distinguish between unjust and merely imperfect arrangements. Arrangements that are essentially invasive are unjust and do not confer moral legitimacy on what is expected of those who are party to them. To correct the abuses of an unjust institution like slavery or a practice like suttee is to destroy the institution or practice. By contrast, an institution like marriage or the family will often contain some unjust features, but these are usually corrigible, and the institution itself is legitimate and morally determining in a straightforward sense.

In any case the DP moralist is in a position to hold that not all social arrangements impose moral imperatives. It is not clear to me that DP can avoid relativism without *some* deontological minimal ground. But conceivably a principle other than noninterference might better serve as universal ground of the special duties. What is essential to any deontologically grounded DP morality is the recognition that the universal deontological principle is differentiated and specified by local arrangements that determine what is legitimately expected of the moral agent.

It may now be clear in what sense I believe DP theories to be plausible. A moral theory is plausible to the extent that it accounts for our pretheoretical moral judgments. Such intuitive judgments are admittedly idiosyncratic and pre-judicial, being conditioned by our upbringing and the traditions we live by. The EP moralist nobly courts implausibility by jettisoning pre-judice and confronting moral decisions anew. By contrast, the DP moralist jettisons only those prejudices which are exposed as rooted in and conditioned by an unjust social arrangement. But for those institutions which are not unjust, our common-sense judgments of "what is expected" (from parents, from citizens, from adult children) are generally held to be reliable guides to the moral facts of life.

The version of DP that I favor accepts the Enlightenment doctrine of natural rights in the minimal form of a universal right to noninter-ference and the correlative duty of moral agents to respect that right. MacIntyre's version of DP is hostile to Enlightenment "modernism," abjuring all talk of universal rights or deontic principles of a universal character. It is in this sense more classical. An adequate version of DP must never-theless avoid the kind of ethical relativism that affords the moral philosopher no way to reject some social arrangements as immoral. MacIntyre appears to suggest that this can be achieved by accepting certain teleological constraints on good societies. Pending more detail, I am not con-vinced that a teleological approach can by itself do the critical job that needs to be done if we are to avoid an unacceptable ethical relativism. But other nondeontic approaches are possible. David Wong[25] has argued for a Confucian condi-tion of adequacy that grades societies as better or worse depending on how well they foster human flourishing. My own deontic approach is not opposed to teleological or Confucianist ways of judging the acceptability of social arrangements. If a given arrangement is degen-erate, then that is in itself a good reason to discount its norms as morally binding. But conceivably even a flourishing society could be unjust; nevertheless its civic norms should count as morally vacuous and illegitimate. It seems to me, therefore, that MacIntyre's version of DP

morality probably goes too far in its rejection of all liberal deontic principles.

I have argued that DP best explains what we intuitively accept as our moral obligations to parents and other persons who stand to us in special relations. And though my version of DP allows for criticizing unjust social arrangements, it may still seem unacceptably relativistic. For does it not allow that what is right for a daughter or son in one society is wrong for them in another? And does this not run afoul of the con-dition that what is right and wrong must be so universally? It should, I think, be acknowledged that the conservatism that is a feature of the doc-trine of differential pull is somewhat hospitable to ethical relativism. Put another way: differen-tial pull makes sense of ethical relativism's large grain of truth, but it does so without losing claim to its ability to evaluate morally the norms of dif-ferent societies and institutions. Institutions that allow or encourage interference with noninvasive interests are unjust, and we have noted that the adherent of differential pull is in as good a posi-tion to apply a universal principle in evaluating an institution as anyone of an EP persuasion. But application of DP will rule out some institutions while allowing *diverse* others to count as legitimate and just. Only a just institution can assign and shape a moral obligation for those who play their roles within it. However, there are many varieties of just institutions, and so, in particu-lar, are there many ways in which filial obligations are determined within different social and cultural contexts. What counts as filial respect in one context may not count as filial respect in another context. It is a virtue of our account that it not only tolerates but shows the way to justify different moral norms.

IX. Common Sense

The sociologist Edward Shils[26] warns about the consequences of the modern hostility to tradition in ways reminiscent of ecologists warning us about tampering with delicate natural systems that have taken millennia to evolve. The EP char-acter of much of modern philosophy encourages a hasty style of playing fast and loose with practices and institutions that define the tradi-tional ties binding the members of a family or community. And a duty-free sentimentalism is no kinder to traditional mores.

The appeal to common sense is often a way of paying proper attention to the way that particular circumstance and social practice enter into the shaping of obligations. This, to my mind, is Sidgwick's peculiar and saving grace. But many a moral philosopher lacks Sidgwick's firm appreciation of the role of accepted practice or common sense. I shall illustrate this by way of a final example.

Richard Wasserstrom in "Is Adultery Immoral?"[27] raises the question of whether the (alleged) obligation not to commit adultery might be explained by reasons that would apply to any two persons generally. It is, for example, wrong for any person to deceive another. And he discusses the destructive effects adultery has on the love that the marital partners bear to one another. What is missing from Wasserstrom's account is any hint that the obligations of marriage are shaped by the institution as it exists and that being "faithful" is a legitimate institutional expectation informing the way that the partners may treat each other. Wasserstrom does say that "we ought to have reasons for believing that marriage is a morally desirable and just social institution" (300). But what follows if it is? Wasserstrom does not say. What we want here is an account of how and why a married person who commits adultery may be wronging the partner. How, in particular, might an act of adultery be construed as unwarranted interference? The shift from the examination of an obligation that has its locus and form within a given institution to evaluating the institution itself is legitimate; but it is all too often a way of avoiding the more concrete and immediate investigation which is the bread and butter of normative ethics.

EP is ethics without ethos. So too is sentimentalism. Both have a disintegrative effect on tradition. Where EP and sentimentalism sit in judgment on ethos, DP respects it and seeks to rationalize it. The EP moralist is reformist in spirit, tending to look upon traditional arrangements as obstacles to social justice. John Rawls,[28] for example, is led to wonder whether the family is ethically justifiable:

It seems that even when fair opportunity (as it has been defined) is satisfied, the family will lead to unequal chances between individuals. Is the family to be abolished then? Taken by itself and given a certain primacy, the idea of equal opportunity inclines in this direction. But within the context of the theory of justice as a whole, there is less urgency to take this course. (511)

Not urgent perhaps, but not unreasonable either. A defender of filial morality cannot with equanimity entertain the idea of abolishing the family. Here Sidgwick is the welcome antidote. For him the suggestion that ethical principles might require the elimination of something so central to "established morality" betrays a misconception of the job of ethics. Instead, Sidgwick demands of philosophers that they "repudiate altogether that temper of rebellion . . . into which the reflective mind is always apt to fall when it is first convinced that the established rules are not intrinsically reasonable" (475).[29]

Reporting on how he arrived at his way of doing moral philosophy, Sidgwick tells of his rereading of Aristotle:

[A] light seemed to dawn upon me as to the meaning and drift of [Aristotle's] procedure. . . . What he gave us there was the Common Sense Morality of Greece, reduced to consistency by careful comparison: given not as something external to him but as what "we" – he and others – think, ascertained by reflection . . . Might I not imitate this: do the same for *our* morality here and now, in the same manner of impartial reflection on current opinion? (xx)

Notes

1 *The Methods of Ethics* (New York: Dover, 1966), p. 243.
2 *Moral Principles and Political Obligations* (Princeton, NJ: University Press, 1979), p. 162.
3 "Obedience and Illusion," in Onora O'Neill and William Ruddick, eds., *Having Children* (New York: Oxford, 1979), pp. 319–25.
4 *Parents and Children: The Ethics of the Family* (New York: Oxford, 1982).
5 "What Do Grown Children Owe Their Parents?", in O'Neill and Ruddick, *op. cit.*, pp. 351–6.
6 *Number Our Days* (New York: Simon & Schuster, 1978).
7 *Summa Theologiae*, vol. 34, R. J. Batten, trans. (New York: Blackfriars, 1975), 2a2ae.

8   John Locke, *Two Treatises of Government*, P. Laslett, ed. (New York: New American Library, 1965), Treatise 1, sec. 100.

9   David Hume, *A Treatise on Human Nature*, Bk. III, p. 1, sec. 1.

10 *The Expanding Circle: Ethics and Sociobiology* (New York: Farrar, Straus & Giroux, 1981).

11 "Persons, Character and Morality," in *Moral Luck* (New York: Cambridge, 1982), p. 2.

12 New York: New American Library, 1964.

13 *The Object of Morality* (London: Methuen, 1971), p. 152.

14 *Philosophical Explanations* (Cambridge, Mass.: Harvard, 1981), p. 451.

15 See Alasdair MacIntyre, *After Virtue* (Notre Dame, Ind.: University Press, 1981). When one contrasts this modern approach to morality with classical approaches that give full play to the social and biological natures of moral agents in determining the range of moral behavior, one may come to see the history of ethics in terms of a MacIntyrean Fall; MacIntyre speaks of the "crucial moral opposition between liberal individualism in some version or other and the Aristotelian tradition in some version or other" (241). For MacIntyre, the Enlightenment is a new Dark Age both because of its abstract conception of the autonomous individual and because of the neglect of parochial contexts in determining the special obligations that were once naturally understood in terms of social roles.

16 *Rights and Persons* (Los Angeles: California UP, 1977).

17 Our account of the special moral relations is concentrating on the way the universal duty to refrain from invasive interference is refracted through circumstance into a variety of positive and discriminate duties. But a particular arrangement may produce the opposite effect: it may qualify the universal obligation to refrain from invasive interference by allowing the moral agent liberties normally forbidden. A fair amount of invasive behavior is the norm in certain private and voluntary arrangements where there is an understanding that exceptional demands may be made. My particular concern with the positive (filial) obligations has led me to confine discussion to the way context obligates moral agents to perform and not with how or to what extent it may license them.

18 *In a Different Voice* (Cambridge, Mass.: Harvard, 1983).

19 *The Boston Globe*, Thursday, March 21, 1985.

20 Blustein, p. 182. According to Blustein, parents who are financially able are *obligated* to provide educational opportunities for children who are able to benefit from them.

21 See Marcia Baron, "The Alleged Moral Repugnance of Acting from Duty," *Journal of Philosophy*, LXXXI, 4 (April 1984): 197–220, especially pp. 204–5. She speaks of "the importance of the attitudes and dispositions one has when one performs certain acts, especially those which are intended to express affection or concern" and suggests that these attitudes constitute "certain parameters within which satisfactory ways of acting from duty must be located."

22 Immanuel Kant, "Proper Self-respect," from *Lectures on Ethics*, Louis Enfield, trans. (New York: Harper & Row, 1963).

23 "Family Ties of the Aged in Cross-cultural Perspective," *The Gerontologist*, XXIII, 1 (1983): 30.

24 Unfortunately, Nozick's particularism is "sentimentalist": "[Some] views will countenance particularism on one level by deriving it from 'universalistic' principles that hold at some deeper level. This misconstrues the moral weight of particularistic ties it seems to me; it is a worthwhile task, one I cannot undertake explicitly here, to investigate the nature of a more consistently particularistic theory – particularistic all the way down the line," *Philosophical Explanations* (New York: Cambridge, 1981), 456/7. The particularistic ties Nozick has in mind are not objectively institutional but subjectively interpersonal ("valuing the particularity of the other").

25 *Moral Relativity* (Berkeley: California UP, 1984).

26 Edward Shils, *Tradition* (Chicago: University of Chicago Press, 1981).

27 In Wasserstrom, ed., *Today's Moral Problems*, pp. 288–300. Michael Tooley's arguments for the moral legitimacy of infanticide provide another example of the consequences of uninhibited EP zeal. See his book *Abortion and Infanticide* (New York: Oxford, 1984), and my critical review "Tooley's Immodest Proposal," *Hastings Center Report*, XV, 5 (June 1985): 39–42.

28 *A Theory of Justice* (Cambridge, Mass.: Harvard, 1971).

29 C. D. Broad especially cautions utilitarian readers of Sidgwick to take this side of him seriously. "When all the relevant facts are taken into consideration it will scarcely ever be right for the utilitarian to break the rules of morality commonly accepted in his society," *Five Types of Ethical Theory* (New York: Humanities, 1951), p. 157.

34

Alienation, Consequentialism, and the Demands of Morality

Peter Railton

Introduction

Living up to the demands of morality may bring with it alienation – from one's personal commitments, from one's feelings or sentiments, from other people, or even from morality itself. In this article I will discuss several apparent instances of such alienation, and attempt a preliminary assessment of their bearing on questions about the acceptability of certain moral theories. Of special concern will be the question whether problems about alienation show consequentialist moral theories to be self-defeating.

I will not attempt a full or general characterization of alienation. Indeed, at a perfectly general level alienation can be characterized only very roughly as a kind of estrangement, distancing, or separateness (not necessarily consciously attended to) resulting in some sort of loss (not necessarily consciously noticed).[1] Rather than seek a general analysis I will rely upon examples to convey a sense of what is involved in the sorts of alienation with which I am concerned. There is nothing in a word, and the phenomena to be discussed below could all be considered while avoiding the controversial term 'alienation.' My sense, however, is that there is some point in using this formidable term, if only to draw attention to commonalities among problems not always noticed. For example,

in the final section of this article I will suggest that one important form of alienation in moral practice, the sense that morality confronts us as an alien set of demands, distant and disconnected from our actual concerns, can be mitigated by dealing with other sorts of alienation morality may induce. Finally, there are historical reasons, which will not be entered into here, for bringing these phenomena under a single label; part of the explanation of their existence lies in the conditions of modern "civil society," and in the philosophical traditions of empiricism and rationalism – which include a certain picture of the self's relation to the world – that have flourished in it.

Let us begin with two examples.

I. John and Anne and Lisa and Helen

To many, John has always seemed a model husband. He almost invariably shows great sensitivity to his wife's needs, and he willingly goes out of his way to meet them. He plainly feels great affection for her. When a friend remarks upon the extraordinary quality of John's concern for his wife, John responds without any self-indulgence or self-congratulation. "I've always thought that people should help each other when they're in a specially good position to do so. I know Anne better than

Peter Railton, "Alienation, Consequentialism, and the Demands of Morality." *Philosophy and Public Affairs* 13, no. 2 (Spring 1984), pp. 134–71. © 1984 by Philosophy and Public Affairs. Reprinted with permission from Blackwell Publishing.

anyone else does, so I know better what she wants and needs. Besides, I have such affection for her that it's no great burden – instead, I get a lot of satisfaction out of it. Just think how awful marriage would be, or life itself, if people didn't take special care of the ones they love." His friend accuses John of being unduly modest, but John's manner convinces him that he is telling the truth: this is really how he feels.

Lisa has gone through a series of disappointments over a short period, and has been profoundly depressed. In the end, however, with the help of others she has emerged from the long night of anxiety and melancholy. Only now is she able to talk openly with friends about her state of mind, and she turns to her oldest friend, Helen, who was a mainstay throughout. She'd like to find a way to thank Helen, since she's only too aware of how much of a burden she's been over these months, how much of a drag and a bore, as she puts it. "You don't have to thank me, Lisa," Helen replies, "you deserved it. It was the least I could do after all you've done for me. We're friends, remember? And we said a long time ago that we'd stick together no matter what. Some day I'll probably ask the same thing of you, and I know you'll come through. What else are friends for?" Lisa wonders whether Helen is saying this simply to avoid creating feelings of guilt, but Helen replies that she means every word – she couldn't bring herself to lie to Lisa if she tried.

II.   What's Missing?

What is troubling about the words of John and Helen? Both show stout character and moral awareness. John's remarks have a benevolent, consequentialist cast, while Helen reasons in a deontological language of duties, reciprocity, and respect. They are not self-centered or without feeling. Yet something seems wrong.

The place to look is not so much at what they say as what they don't say. Think, for example, of how John's remarks might sound to his wife. Anne might have hoped that it was, in some ultimate sense, in part for *her* sake and the sake of their love as such that John pays such special attention to her. That he devotes himself to her because of the characteristically good consequences of doing so seems to leave her, and their

relationship as such, too far out of the picture – this despite the fact that these characteristically good consequences depend in important ways on his special relation to her. She is being taken into account by John, but it might seem she is justified in being hurt by the way she is being taken into account. It is as if John viewed her, their relationship, and even his own affection for her from a distant, objective point of view – a moral point of view where reasons must be reasons for any rational agent and so must have an impersonal character even when they deal with personal matters. His wife might think a more personal point of view would also be appropriate, a point of view from which "It's my wife" or "It's Anne" would have direct and special relevance, and play an unmediated role in his answer to the question "*Why* do you attend to her so?"

Something similar is missing from Helen's account of why she stood by Lisa. While we understand that the specific duties she feels toward Lisa depend upon particular features of their relationship, still we would not be surprised if Lisa finds Helen's response to her expression of gratitude quite distant, even chilling. We need not question whether she has strong feeling for Lisa, but we may wonder at how that feeling finds expression in Helen's thinking.[2]

John and Helen both show alienation: there would seem to be an estrangement between their affections and their rational, deliberative selves; an abstract and universalizing point of view mediates their reponses to others and to their own sentiments. We should not assume that they have been caught in an uncharacteristic moment of moral reflection or after-the-fact rationalization; it is a settled part of their characters to think and act from a moral point of view. It is as if the world were for them a fabric of obligations and permissions in which personal considerations deserve recognition only to the extent that, and in the way that, such considerations find a place in this fabric.

To call John and Helen alienated from their affections or their intimates is not of itself to condemn them, nor is it to say that they are experiencing any sort of distress. One may be alienated from something without recognizing this as such or suffering in any conscious way from it, much as one may simply be uninterested in something without awareness or conscious suffering. But alienation is not mere lack of interest: John and Helen are not *uninterested* in their affections or in their intimates; rather, their interest takes a certain alienated form. While this alienation may not itself be a psychological affliction, it may be the basis of such afflictions – such as a sense of loneliness or emptiness – or of the loss of certain things of value – such as a sense of belonging or the pleasures of spontaneity. Moreover, their alienation may cause psychological distress in others, and make certain valuable sorts of relationships impossible.

However, we must be on guard lest oversimple categories distort our diagnosis. It seems to me wrong to picture the self as ordinarily divided into cognitive and affective halves, with deliberation and rationality belonging to the first, and sentiments belonging to the second. John's alienation is not a problem on the boundary of naturally given cognitive and affective selves, but a problem partially constituted by the bifurcation of his psyche into these separate spheres. *John's* deliberative self seems remarkably divorced from his affections, but not all psyches need be so divided. That there is a cognitive element in affection – that affection is not a mere "feeling" that is a given for the deliberative self but rather involves as well certain characteristic modes of thought and perception – is suggested by the difficulty some may have in believing that John really does love Anne if he persistently thinks about her in the way suggested by his remarks. Indeed, his affection for Anne does seem to have been demoted to a mere "feeling." For this reason among others, we should not think of John's alienation from his affections and his alienation from Anne as wholly independent phenomena, the one the cause of the other.[3] Of course, similar remarks apply to Helen.

III.   The Moral Point of View

Perhaps the lives of John and Anne or Helen and Lisa would be happier or fuller if none of the alienation mentioned were present. But is this a problem for *morality*? If, as some have contended, to have a morality is to make normative judgments from a moral point of view and be guided by them, and if by its nature a moral point of view must exclude considerations that lack universality, then any genuinely moral way of going about life would seem liable to produce the sorts of alienation mentioned above.[4] Thus it would be a conceptual confusion to ask that we never be required by morality to go beyond a personal point of view, since to fail ever to look at things from an impersonal (or nonpersonal) point of view would be to fail ever to *be* distinctively moral – not immoralism, perhaps, but amoralism. This would not be to say that there are not other points of view on life worthy of our attention,[5] or that taking a moral point of view is always appropriate – one could say that John and Helen show no moral defect in thinking so impersonally, although they do moralize to excess. But the fact that a particular morality requires us to take an impersonal point of view could not sensibly be held against it, for that would be what makes it a morality at all.

This sort of position strikes me as entirely too complacent. First, we must somehow give an account of practical reasoning that does not merely multiply points of view and divide the self – a more unified account is needed. Second, we must recognize that loving relationships, friendships, group loyalties, and spontaneous actions are among the most important contributors to whatever it is that makes life worthwhile; any moral theory deserving serious consideration must itself give them serious consideration. As William K. Frankena has written, "Morality is made for man, not man for morality."[6] Moral considerations are often supposed to be overriding in practical reasoning. If we were to find that adopting a particular morality led to irreconcilable conflict with central types of human well-being – as cases akin to John's and Helen's have led some to suspect – then this surely would give us good reason to doubt its claims.[7]

For example, in the closing sentences of *A Theory of Justice* John Rawls considers the "perspective of eternity," which is impartial across all individuals and times, and writes that this is a "form of *thought and feeling* that rational persons can adopt in the world." "Purity of heart," he concludes, "would be to see clearly and act with grace and self-command from this point of view."[8] This may or may not be purity of heart, but it could not be the standpoint of actual life without radically detaching the individual from a range of personal concerns and commitments. Presumably we should not read Rawls as recommending that we adopt this point of view in the bulk of our actions in daily life, but the fact that so purely abstracted a perspective is portrayed as a kind of moral ideal should at least start us wondering.[9] If to be more perfectly moral is to ascend ever higher toward *sub specie aeternitatis* abstraction, perhaps we made a mistake in boarding the moral escalator in the first place. Some of the very "weaknesses" that prevent us from achieving this moral ideal – strong attachments to persons or projects – seem to be part of a considerably more compelling human ideal.

Should we say at this point that the lesson is that we should give a more prominent role to the value of non-alienation in our moral reasoning? That would be too little too late: the problem seems to be the way in which morality asks us to look at things, not just the things it asks us to look at.

IV.   The "Paradox of Hedonism"

Rather than enter directly into the question whether being moral is a matter of taking a moral point of view and whether there is thus some sort of necessary connection between being moral and being alienated in a way detrimental to human flourishing, I will consider a related problem the solution to which may suggest a way of steering around obstacles to a more direct approach.

One version of the so-called "paradox of hedonism" is that adopting as one's exclusive ultimate end in life the pursuit of maximum happiness may well prevent one from having certain experiences or engaging in certain sorts of relationships or commitments that are among the greatest sources of happiness.[10] The hedonist, looking around him, may discover that some of those who are less concerned with their own happiness than he is, and who view people and projects less instrumentally than he does, actually manage to live happier lives than he despite his dogged pursuit of happiness. The "paradox" is pragmatic, not logical, but it looks deep nonetheless: the hedonist, it would appear, ought not to be a hedonist. It seems, then, as if we have come across a second case in which mediating one's

relations to people or projects by a particular point of view – in this case, a hedonistic point of view – may prevent one from attaining the fullest possible realization of sought-after values.

However, it is important to notice that even though adopting a hedonistic life project may tend to interfere with realizing that very project, there is no such natural exclusion between acting for the sake of another or a cause as such and recognizing how important this is to one's happiness. A spouse who acts for the sake of his mate may know full well that this is a source of deep satisfaction for him – in addition to providing him with reasons for acting internal to it, the relationship may also promote the external goal of achieving happiness. Moreover, while the pursuit of happiness may not be the reason he entered or sustains the relationship, he may also recognize that if it had not seemed likely to make him happy he would not have entered it, and that if it proved over time to be inconsistent with his happiness he would consider ending it.

It might be objected that one cannot really regard a person or a project as an end as such if one's commitment is in this way contingent or overridable. But were this so, we would be able to have very few commitments to ends as such. For example, one could not be committed to both one's spouse and one's child as ends as such, since at most one of these commitments could be overriding in cases of conflict. It is easy to confuse the notion of a commitment to an end *as such* (or *for its own sake*) with that of an *overriding* commitment, but strength is not the same as structure. To be committed to an end as such is a matter of (among other things) whether it furnishes one with reasons for acting that are not mediated by other concerns. It does not follow that these reasons must always outweigh whatever opposing reasons one may have, or that one may not at the same time have other, mediating reasons that also incline one to act on behalf of that end.

Actual commitments to ends as such, even when very strong, are subject to various qualifications and contingencies.[11] If a friend grows too predictable or moves off to a different part of the world, or if a planned life project proves less engaging or practical than one had imagined, commitments and affections naturally change. If a relationship were highly vulnerable to the least change, it would be strained to speak of genuine affection rather than, say, infatuation. But if members of a relationship came to believe that they would be better off without it, this ordinarily would be a non-trivial change, and it is not difficult to imagine that their commitment to the relationship might be contingent in this way but nonetheless real. Of course, a relationship involves a shared history and shared expectations as well as momentary experiences, and it is unusual that affection or concern can be changed overnight, or relationships begun or ended at will. Moreover, the sorts of affections and commitments that can play a decisive role in shaping one's life and in making possible the deeper sorts of satisfactions are not those that are easily overridden or subject to constant reassessment or second-guessing. Thus a sensible hedonist would not forever be subjecting his affections or commitments to egoistic calculation, nor would he attempt to break off a relationship or commitment merely because it might seem to him at a given moment that some other arrangement would make him happier. Commitments to others or to causes as such may be very closely linked to the self, and a hedonist who knows what he's about will not be one who turns on his self at the slightest provocation. Contingency is not expendability, and while some commitments are remarkably non-contingent – such as those of parent to child or patriot to country – it cannot be said that commitments of a more contingent sort are never genuine, or never conduce to the profounder sorts of happiness.[12]

Following these observations, we may reduce the force of the "paradox of hedonism" if we distinguish two forms of hedonism. *Subjective hedonism* is the view that one should adopt the hedonistic point of view in action, that is, that one should whenever possible attempt to determine which act seems most likely to contribute optimally to one's happiness, and behave accordingly. *Objective hedonism* is the view that one should follow that course of action which would in fact most contribute to one's happiness, even when this would involve *not* adopting the hedonistic point of view in action. An act will be called *subjectively hedonistic* if it is done from a hedonistic point of view; an act is *objectively hedonistic* if it is that act, of those available to the agent, which would most contribute to his happiness.[13] Let us call

someone a *sophisticated hedonist* if he aims to lead an objectively hedonistic life (that is, the happiest life available to him in the circumstances) and yet is not committed to subjective hedonism. Thus, within the limits of what is psychologically possible, a sophisticated hedonist is prepared to eschew the hedonistic point of view whenever taking this point of view conflicts with following an objectively hedonistic course of action. The so-called paradox of hedonism shows that there will be such conflicts: certain acts or courses of action may be objectively hedonistic only if not subjectively hedonistic. When things are put this way, it seems that the sophisticated hedonist faces a problem rather than a paradox: how to act in order to achieve maximum possible happiness if this is at times – or even often – *not* a matter of carrying out hedonistic deliberations.

The answer in any particular case will be complex and contextual – it seems unlikely that any one method of decision making would always promote thought and action most conducive to one's happiness. A sophisticated hedonist might proceed precisely by looking at the complex and contextual: observing the actual modes of thought and action of those people who are in some ways like himself and who seem most happy. If our assumptions are right, he will find that few such individuals are subjective hedonists; instead, they act for the sake of a variety of ends as such. He may then set out to develop in himself the traits of character, ways of thought, types of commitment, and so on, that seem common in happy lives. For example, if he notes that the happiest people often have strong loyalties to friends, he must ask how he can become a more loyal friend – not merely how he can seem to be a loyal friend (since those he has observed are not happy because they merely seem loyal) – but how he can in fact be one.

Could one really make such changes if one had as a goal leading an optimally happy life? The answer seems to me a qualified *yes*, but let us first look at a simpler case. A highly competitive tennis player comes to realize that his obsession with winning is keeping him from playing his best. A pro tells him that if he wants to win he must devote himself more to the game and its play as such and think less about his performance. In the commitment and concentration made possible by this devotion, he is told, lies the secret of successful tennis. So he spends a good deal of time developing an enduring devotion to many aspects of the activity, and finds it peculiarly satisfying to become so absorbed in it. He plays better, and would have given up the program of change if he did not, but he now finds that he plays tennis more for its own sake, enjoying greater internal as well as external rewards from the sport. Such a person would not keep thinking – on or off the court – "No matter how I play, the only thing I really care about is whether I win!" He would recognize such thoughts as self-defeating, as evidence that his old, unhelpful way of looking at things was returning. Nor would such a person be self-deceiving. He need not hide from himself his goal of winning, for this goal is consistent with his increased devotion to the game. His commitment to the activity is not eclipsed by, but made more vivid by, his desire to succeed at it.

The same sort of story might be told about a sophisticated hedonist and friendship. An individual could realize that his instrumental attitude toward his friends prevents him from achieving the fullest happiness friendship affords. He could then attempt to focus more on his friends as such, doing this somewhat deliberately, perhaps, until it comes more naturally. He might then find his friendships improved and himself happier. If he found instead that his relationships were deteriorating or his happiness declining, he would reconsider the idea. None of this need be hidden from himself: the external goal of happiness reinforces the internal goals of his relationships. The sophisticated hedonist's motivational structure should therefore meet a *counterfactual condition*: he need not always act for the sake of happiness, since he may do various things for their own sake or for the sake of others, but he would not act as he does if it were not compatible with his leading an objectively hedonistic life. Of course, a sophisticated hedonist cannot guarantee that he will meet this counterfactual condition, but only attempt to meet it as fully as possible.

Success at tennis is a relatively circumscribed goal, leaving much else about one's life undefined. Maximizing one's happiness, by contrast, seems all-consuming. Could commitments to other ends survive alongside it? Consider an analogy. Ned needs to make a living. More than that, he needs to make as much money as he can – he has

expensive tastes, a second marriage, and children reaching college age, and he does not have extensive means. He sets out to invest his money and his labor in ways he thinks will maximize return. Yet it does not follow that he acts as he does solely for the sake of earning as much as possible.[14] Although it is obviously true that he does what he does because he believes that it will maximize return, this does not preclude his doing it for other reasons as well, for example, for the sake of living well or taking care of his children. This may continue to be the case even if Ned comes to want money for its own sake, that is, if he comes to see the accumulation of wealth as intrinsically as well as extrinsically attractive.[15] Similarly, the stricture that one seek the objectively hedonistic life certainly provides one with considerable guidance, but it does not supply the whole of one's motives and goals in action.

My claim that the sophisticated hedonist can escape the paradox of hedonism was, however, qualified. It still seems possible that the happiest sorts of lives ordinarily attainable are those led by people who would reject even sophisticated hedonism, people whose character is such that if they were presented with a choice between two entire lives, one of which contains less total happiness but nonetheless realizes some other values more fully, they might well knowingly choose against maximal happiness. If this were so, it would show that a sophisticated hedonist might have reason for changing his beliefs so that he no longer accepts hedonism in any form. This still would not refute objective hedonism as an account of the (rational, prudential, or moral) *criterion* one's acts should meet, for it would be precisely in order to meet this criterion that the sophisticated hedonist would change his beliefs.[16]

V. The Place of Non-Alienation Among Human Values

Before discussing the applicability of what has been said about hedonism to morality, we should notice that alienation is not always a bad thing, that we may not want to overcome all forms of alienation, and that other values, which may conflict with non-alienation in particular cases, may at times have a greater claim on us. Let us look at a few such cases.

It has often been argued that a morality of duties and obligations may appropriately come into play in familial or friendly relationships when the relevant sentiments have given out, for instance, when one is exasperated with a friend, when love is tried, and so on.[17] 'Ought' implies 'can' (or, at least, 'could'), and while it may be better in human terms when we do what we ought to do at least in part out of feelings of love, friendship, or sympathy, there are times when we simply cannot muster these sentiments, and the right thing to do is to act as love or friendship or sympathy would have directed rather than refuse to perform any act done merely from a sense of duty.

But we should add a further role for unspontaneous, morally motivated action: even when love or concern is strong, it is often desirable that people achieve some distance from their sentiments or one another. A spouse may act toward his mate in a grossly overprotective way; a friend may indulge another's ultimately destructive tendencies; a parent may favor one child inordinately. Strong and immediate affection may overwhelm one's ability to see what another person actually needs or deserves. In such cases a certain distance between people or between an individual and his sentiments, and an intrusion of moral considerations into the gap thus created, may be a good thing, and part of genuine affection or commitment. The opposite view, that no such mediation is desirable as long as affection is strong, seems to me a piece of romanticism. Concern over alienation therefore ought not to take the form of a cult of "authenticity at any price."

Moreover, there will occur regular conflicts between avoiding alienation and achieving other important individual goals. One such goal is autonomy. Bernard Williams has emphasized that many of us have developed certain "ground projects" that give shape and meaning to our lives, and has drawn attention to the damage an individual may suffer if he is alienated from his ground projects by being forced to look at them as potentially overridable by moral considerations.[18] But against this it may be urged that it is crucial for autonomy that one hold one's commitments up for inspection – even one's ground projects. Our ground projects are often formed in our youth, in a particular family, class, or cultural background. It may be alienating and even disorienting to call these into question, but to fail to do so is to lose autonomy. Of course, autonomy could not sensibly require that we question all of our values and commitments at once, nor need it require us to be forever detached from what we are doing. It is quite possible to submit basic aspects of one's life to scrutiny and arrive at a set of autonomously chosen commitments that form the basis of an integrated life. Indeed, psychological conflicts and practical obstacles give us occasion for reexamining our basic commitments rather more often than we'd like.

At the same time, the tension between autonomy and non-alienation should not be exaggerated. Part of avoiding exaggeration is giving up the Kantian notion that autonomy is a matter of escaping determination by any contingency whatsoever. Part, too, is refusing to conflate autonomy with sheer independence from others. Both Rousseau and Marx emphasized that achieving control over one's own life requires participation in certain sorts of social relations – in fact, relations in which various kinds of alienation have been minimized.

Autonomy is but one value that may enter into complex trade-offs with non-alienation. Alienation and inauthenticity do have their uses. The alienation of some individuals or groups from their milieu may at times be necessary for fundamental social criticism or cultural innovation. And without some degree of inauthenticity, it is doubtful whether civil relations among people could long be maintained. It would take little ingenuity, but too much of the reader's patience, to construct here examples involving troubling conflicts between non-alienation and virtually any other worthy goal.

VI.   Reducing Alienation in Morality

Let us now move to morality proper. To do this with any definiteness, we must have a particular morality in mind. For various reasons, I think that the most plausible sort of morality is consequentialist in form, assessing rightness in terms of contribution to the good. In attempting to sketch how we might reduce alienation in moral theory and practice, therefore, I will work within a consequentialist framework (although a number of the arguments I will make could be made, *mutatis mutandis*, by a deontologist).

Of course, one has adopted no morality in particular even in adopting consequentialism unless one says what the good is. Let us, then, dwell briefly on axiology. One mistake of dominant consequentialist theories, I believe, is their failure to see that things other than subjective states can have intrinsic value. Allied to this is a tendency to reduce all intrinsic values to one – happiness. Both of these features of classical utilitarianism reflect forms of alienation. First, in divorcing subjective states from their objective counterparts, and claiming that we seek the latter exclusively for the sake of the former, utilitarianism cuts us off from the world in a way made graphic by examples such as that of the experience machine, a hypothetical device that can be programmed to provide one with whatever subjective states he may desire. The experience machine affords us decisive subjective advantages over actual life: few, if any, in actual life think they have achieved all that they could want, but the machine makes possible for each an existence that he cannot distinguish from such a happy state of affairs.[19] Despite this striking advantage, most rebel at the notion of the experience machine. As Robert Nozick and others have pointed out, it seems to matter to us what we actually *do* and *are* as well as how life *appears* to us.[20] We see the point of our lives as bound up with the world and other people in ways not captured by subjectivism, and our sense of loss in contemplating a life tied to an experience machine, quite literally alienated from the surrounding world, suggests where subjectivism has gone astray. Second, the reduction of all goals to the purely abstract goal of happiness or pleasure, as in hedonistic utilitarianism, treats all other goals instrumentally. Knowledge or friendship may promote happiness, but is it a fair characterization of our commitment to these goals to say that this is the only sense in which they are ultimately valuable? Doesn't the insistence that there is an abstract and uniform goal lying behind all of our ends bespeak an alienation from these particular ends?

Rather than pursue these questions further here, let me suggest an approach to the good that seems to me less hopeless as a way of capturing human value: a pluralistic approach in which several goods are viewed as intrinsically, non-morally valuable – such as happiness, knowledge, purposeful activity, autonomy, solidarity,

respect, and beauty.[21] These goods need not be ranked lexically, but may be attributed weights, and the criterion of rightness for an act would be that it must contribute to the weighted sum of these values in the long run. This creates the possibility of trade-offs among values of the kinds discussed in the previous section. However, I will not stop here to develop or defend such an account of the good and the right, since our task is to show how certain problems of alienation that arise in moral contexts might be dealt with if morality is assumed to have such a basis.

Consider, then, Juan, who, like John, has always seemed a model husband. When a friend remarks on the extraordinary concern he shows for his wife, Juan characteristically responds: "I love Linda. I even *like* her. So it means a lot to me to do things for her. After all we've been through, it's almost a part of me to do it." But his friend knows that Juan is a principled individual, and asks Juan how his marriage fits into that larger scheme. After all, he asks, it's fine for Juan and his wife to have such a close relationship, but what about all the other, needier people Juan could help if he broadened his horizon still further? Juan replies, "Look, it's a better world when people can have a relationship like ours – and nobody could if everyone were always asking themselves who's got the most need. It's not easy to make things work in this world, and one of the best things that happens to people is to have a close relationship like ours. You'd make things worse in a hurry if you broke up those close relationships for the sake of some higher goal. Anyhow, I know that you can't always put family first. The world isn't such a wonderful place that it's OK just to retreat into your own little circle. But still, you need that little circle. People get burned out, or lose touch, if they try to save the world by themselves. The ones who can stick with it and do a good job of making things better are usually the ones who can make that fit into a life that does not make them miserable. I haven't met any real saints lately, and I don't trust people who think they *are* saints."

If we contrast Juan with John, we do not find that the one allows moral considerations to enter his personal life while the other does not. Nor do we find that one is less serious in his moral concern. Rather, what Juan recognizes to be morally required is not by its nature incompatible with acting directly for the sake of another. It is important to Juan to subject his life to moral scrutiny – he is not merely stumped when asked for a defense of his acts above a personal level, he does not *just* say "Of course I take care of her, she's my wife!" or "It's Linda" and refuse to listen to the more impersonal considerations raised by his friend. It is consistent with what he says to imagine that his motivational structure has a form akin to that of the sophisticated hedonist, that is, his motivational structure meets a counterfactual condition: while he ordinarily does not do what he does simply for the sake of doing what's right, he would seek to lead a different sort of life if he did not think his were morally defensible. His love is not a romantic submersion in the other to the exclusion of worldly responsibilities, and to that extent it may be said to involve a degree of alienation from Linda. But this does not seem to drain human value from their relationship. Nor need one imagine that Linda would be saddened to hear Juan's words the way Anne might have been saddened to overhear the remarks of John.[22]

Moreover, because of his very willingness to question his life morally, Juan avoids a sort of alienation not sufficiently discussed – alienation from others, beyond one's intimate ties. Individuals who will not or cannot allow questions to arise about what they are doing from a broader perspective are in an important way cut off from their society and the larger world. They may not be troubled by this in any very direct way, but even so they may fail to experience that powerful sense of purpose and meaning that comes from seeing oneself as part of something larger and more enduring than oneself or one's intimate circle. The search for such a sense of purpose and meaning seems to me ubiquitous – surely much of the impulse to religion, to ethnic or regional identification (most strikingly, in the "rediscovery" of such identities), or to institutional loyalty stems from this desire to see ourselves as part of a more general, lasting, and worthwhile scheme of things.[23] This presumably is part of what is meant by saying that secularization has led to a sense of meaninglessness, or that the decline of traditional communities and societies has meant an increase in anomie. (The sophisticated hedonist, too, should take note: one way to gain a firmer sense that one's life is worthwhile, a sense that may

be important to realizing various values in one's own life, is to overcome alienation from others.)

Drawing upon our earlier discussion of two kinds of hedonism, let us now distinguish two kinds of consequentialism. *Subjective consequentialism* is the view that whenever one faces a choice of actions, one should attempt to determine which act of those available would most promote the good, and should then try to act accordingly. One is behaving as subjective consequentialism requires – that is, leading a *subjectively consequentialist life* – to the extent that one uses and follows a distinctively consequentialist mode of decision making, consciously aiming at the overall good and conscientiously using the best available information with the greatest possible rigor. *Objective consequentialism* is the view that the criterion of the rightness of an act or course of action is whether it in fact would most promote the good of those acts available to the agent. Subjective consequentialism, like subjective hedonism, is a view that prescribes following a particular mode of deliberation in action; objective consequentialism, like objective hedonism, concerns the outcomes actually brought about, and thus deals with the question of deliberation only in terms of the tendencies of certain forms of decision making to promote appropriate outcomes. Let us reserve the expression *objectively consequentialist act* (*or life*) for those acts (or that life) of those available to the agent that would bring about the best outcomes.[24] To complete the parallel, let us say that a *sophisticated consequentialist* is someone who has a standing commitment to leading an objectively consequentialist life, but who need not set special stock in any particular form of decision making and therefore does not necessarily seek to lead a subjectively consequentialist life. Juan, it might be argued (if the details were filled in), is a sophisticated consequentialist, since he seems to believe he should act for the best but does not seem to feel it appropriate to bring a consequentialist calculus to bear on his every act.

Is it bizarre, or contradictory, that being a sophisticated consequentialist may involve rejecting subjective consequentialism? After all, doesn't an adherent of subjective consequentialism also seek to lead an objectively consequentialist life? He may, but then he is mistaken in thinking that this means he should always undertake a distinctively consequentialist deliberation when faced with a choice. To see his mistake, we need only consider some examples.

It is well known that in certain emergencies, the best outcome requires action so swift as to preclude consequentialist deliberation. Thus a sophisticated consequentialist has reason to inculcate in himself certain dispositions to act rapidly in obvious emergencies. The disposition is not a mere reflex, but a developed pattern of action deliberately acquired. A simple example, but it should dispel the air of paradox.

Many decisions are too insignificant to warrant consequentialist deliberation ("Which shoelace should I do up first?") or too predictable in outcome ("Should I meet my morning class today as scheduled or should I linger over the newspaper?"). A famous old conundrum for consequentialism falls into a similar category: before I deliberate about an act, it seems I must decide how much time would be optimal to allocate for this deliberation; but then I must first decide how much time would be optimal to allocate for this time-allocation decision; but before that I must decide how much time would be optimal to allocate for *that* decision; and so on. The sophisticated consequentialist can block this paralyzing regress by noting that often the best thing to do is not to ask questions about time allocation at all; instead, he may develop standing dispositions to give more or less time to decisions depending upon their perceived importance, the amount of information available, the predictability of his choice, and so on. I think we all have dispositions of this sort, which account for our patience with some prolonged deliberations but not others.

There are somewhat more intriguing examples that have more to do with psychological interference than mere time efficiency: the timid, put-upon employee who knows that if he deliberates about whether to ask for a raise he will succumb to his timidity and fail to demand what he actually deserves; the self-conscious man who knows that if, at social gatherings, he is forever wondering how he should act, his behavior will be awkward and unnatural, contrary to his goal of acting naturally and appropriately; the tightrope walker who knows he must not reflect on the value of keeping his concentration; and so on. People can learn to avoid certain characteristically self-defeating lines of thought –

just as the tennis player in an earlier example learned to avoid thinking constantly about winning – and the sophisticated consequentialist may learn that consequentialist deliberation is in a variety of cases self-defeating, so that other habits of thought should be cultivated.

The sophisticated consequentialist need not be deceiving himself or acting in bad faith when he avoids consequentialist reasoning. He can fully recognize that he is developing the dispositions he does because they are necessary for promoting the good. Of course, he cannot be preoccupied with this fact all the while, but then one cannot be *preoccupied* with anything without this interfering with normal or appropriate patterns of thought and action.

To the list of cases of interference we may add John, whose all-purpose willingness to look at things by subjective consequentialist lights prevents the realization in him and in his relationships with others of values that he would recognize to be crucially important.

Bernard Williams has said that it shows consequentialism to be in grave trouble that it may have to usher itself from the scene as a mode of decision making in a number of important areas of life.[25] Though I think he has exaggerated the extent to which we would have to exclude consequentialist considerations from our lives in order to avoid disastrous results, it is fair to ask: If maximizing the good were in fact to require that consequentialist reasoning be *wholly* excluded, would this refute consequentialism? Imagine an all-knowing demon who controls the fate of the world and who visits unspeakable punishment upon man to the extent that he does not employ a Kantian morality. (Obviously, the demon is not himself a Kantian.) If such a demon existed, sophisticated consequentialists would have reason to convert to Kantianism, perhaps even to make whatever provisions could be made to erase consequentialism from the human memory and prevent any resurgence of it.

Does this possibility show that objective consequentialism is self-defeating? On the contrary, it shows that objective consequentialism has the virtue of not blurring the distinction between the *truth-conditions* of an ethical theory and its *acceptance-conditions* in particular contexts, a distinction philosophers have generally recognized for theories concerning other subject matters.

It might be objected that, unlike other theories, ethical theories must meet a condition of publicity, roughly to the effect that it must be possible under all circumstances for us to recognize a true ethical theory as such and to promulgate it publicly without thereby violating that theory itself.[26] Such a condition might be thought to follow from the social nature of morality. But any such condition would be question-begging against consequentialist theories, since it would require that one class of actions – acts of adopting or promulgating an ethical theory – *not* be assessed in terms of their consequences. Moreover, I fail to see how such a condition could emanate from the social character of morality. To prescribe the adoption and promulgation of a mode of decision making regardless of its consequences seems to me radically detached from human concerns, social or otherwise. If it is argued that an ethical theory that fails to meet the publicity requirement could under certain conditions endorse a course of action leading to the abuse and manipulation of man by man, we need only reflect that no psychologically possible decision procedure can guarantee that its widespread adoption could never have such a result. A "consequentialist demon" might increase the amount of abuse and manipulation in the world in direct proportion to the extent that people act according to the categorical imperative. Objective consequentialism (unlike certain deontological theories) has valuable flexibility in permitting us to take consequences into account in assessing the appropriateness of certain modes of decision making, thereby avoiding any sort of self-defeating decision procedure worship.

A further objection is that the lack of any direct link between objective consequentialism and a particular mode of decision making leaves the view too vague to provide adequate guidance in practice. On the contrary, objective consequentialism sets a definite and distinctive criterion of right action, and it becomes an empirical question (though not an easy one) which modes of decision making should be employed and when. It would be a mistake for an objective consequentialist to attempt to tighten the connection between his criterion of rightness and any particular mode of decision making: someone who recommended a particular mode of decision making regardless of consequences would not be a hard-nosed, non-evasive objective consequentialist, but a self-contradicting one.

VII.   Contrasting Approaches

The seeming "indirectness" of objective consequentialism may invite its confusion with familiar indirect consequentialist theories, such as rule-consequentialism. In fact, the subjective/objective distinction cuts across the rule/act distinction, and there are subjective and objective forms of both rule- and act-based theories. Thus far, we have dealt only with subjective and objective forms of act-consequentialism. By contrast, a *subjective rule*-consequentialist holds (roughly) that in deliberation we should always attempt to determine which act, of those available, conforms to that set of rules general acceptance of which would most promote the good; we then should attempt to perform this act. An *objective rule*-consequentialist sets actual conformity to the rules with the highest acceptance value as his criterion of right action, recognizing the possibility that the best set of rules might in some cases – or even always – recommend that one not perform rule-consequentialist deliberation.

Because I believe this last possibility must be taken seriously, I find the objective form of rule-consequentialism more plausible. Ultimately, however, I suspect that rule-consequentialism is untenable in either form, for it could recommend acts that (subjectively or objectively) accord with the best set of rules even when these rules are *not* in fact generally accepted, and when as a result these acts would have devastatingly bad consequences. "Let the rules with greatest acceptance utility be followed, though the heavens fall!" is no more plausible than "*Fiat justitia, ruat coelum!*" – and a good bit less ringing. Hence, the arguments in this article are based entirely upon act-consequentialism.

Indeed, once the subjective/objective distinction has been drawn, an act-consequentialist can capture some of the intuitions that have made rule- or trait-consequentialism appealing.[27] Surely part of the attraction of these indirect consequentialisms is the idea that one should have certain traits of character, or commitments to persons or principles, that are sturdy enough that one would at least sometimes refuse to forsake them even when this refusal is known to conflict with making some gain – perhaps small – in total utility. Unlike his subjective counterpart, the objective act-consequentialist is able to endorse characters and commitments that are sturdy in just this sense.

To see why, let us first return briefly to one of the simple examples of Section VI. A sophisticated act-consequentialist may recognize that if he were to develop a standing disposition to render prompt assistance in emergencies without going through elaborate act-consequentialist deliberation, there would almost certainly be cases in which he would perform acts worse than those he would have performed had he stopped to deliberate, for example, when his prompt action is misguided in a way he would have noticed had he thought the matter through. It may still be right for him to develop this disposition, for without it he would act rightly in emergencies still less often – a quick response is appropriate much more often than not, and it is not practically possible to develop a disposition that would lead one to respond promptly in exactly those cases where this would have the best results. While one can attempt to cultivate dispositions that are responsive to various factors which might indicate whether promptness is of greater importance than further thought, such refinements have their own costs and, given the limits of human resources, even the best cultivated dispositions will sometimes lead one astray. The objective act-consequentialist would thus recommend cultivating dispositions that will sometimes lead him to violate his own criterion of right action. Still, he will not, as a trait-consequentialist would, shift his criterion and say that an act is right if it stems from the traits it would be best overall to have (given the limits of what is humanly achievable, the balance of costs and benefits, and so on). Instead, he continues to believe that an act may stem from the dispositions it would be best to have, and yet be wrong (because it would produce worse consequences than other acts available to the agent in the circumstances).[28]

This line of argument can be extended to patterns of motivation, traits of character, and rules. A sophisticated act-consequentialist should realize that certain goods are reliably attainable – or attainable at all – only if people have well-developed characters; that the human psyche is capable of only so much self-regulation and refinement; and that human perception and reasoning are liable to a host of biases and errors. Therefore, individuals may be more likely to act rightly if they possess certain enduring motivational patterns, character traits, or *prima facie* commitments to rules in addition to whatever commitment they have to act for the best. Because such individuals would not consider consequences in all cases, they would miss a number of opportunities to maximize the good; but if they were instead always to attempt to assess outcomes, the overall result would be worse, for they would act correctly less often.[29]

We may now strengthen the argument to show that the objective act-consequentialist can approve of dispositions, characters, or commitments to rules that are sturdy in the sense mentioned above, that is, that do not merely supplement a commitment to act for the best, but sometimes override it, so that one knowingly does what is contrary to maximizing the good. Consider again Juan and Linda, whom we imagine to have a commuting marriage. They normally get together only every other week, but one week she seems a bit depressed and harried, and so he decides to take an extra trip in order to be with her. If he did not travel, he would save a fairly large sum that he could send OXFAM to dig a well in a drought-stricken village. Even reckoning in Linda's uninterrupted malaise, Juan's guilt, and any ill effects on their relationship, it may be that for Juan to contribute the fare to OXFAM would produce better consequences overall than the unscheduled trip. Let us suppose that Juan knows this, and that he could stay home and write the check if he tried. Still, given Juan's character, he in fact will not try to perform this more beneficial act but will travel to see Linda instead. The objective act-consequentialist will say that Juan performed the wrong act on this occasion. Yet he may also say that if Juan had had a character that would have led him to perform the better act (or made him more inclined to do so), he would have had to have been less devoted to Linda. Given the ways Juan can affect the world, it may be that if he were less devoted to Linda his overall contribution to human well-being would be less in the end, perhaps because he would become more cynical and self-centered. Thus it may be that Juan should have (should develop, encourage, and so on) a character such that he sometimes knowingly and deliberately acts contrary to his objective consequentialist duty. Any other character, of those actually available to him, would lead him to depart still further from an objectively consequentialist life. The issue is not whether staying home would *change* Juan's character – for we may suppose that it would not – but whether he would in fact decide to stay home if he had that character, of those available, that would lead him to perform the most beneficial overall sequence of acts. In some cases, then, there will exist an objective act-consequentialist argument for developing and sustaining characters of a kind Sidgwick and others have thought an act-consequentialist must condemn.[30]

VIII.   Demands and Disruptions

Before ending this discussion of consequentialism, let me mention one other large problem involving alienation that has seemed uniquely troubling for consequentialist theories and that shows how coming to terms with problems of alienation may be a social matter as well as a matter of individual psychology. Because consequentialist criteria of rightness are linked to maximal contribution to the good, whenever one does not perform the very best act one can, one is "negatively responsible" for any shortfall in total well-being that results. Bernard Williams has argued that to accept such a burden of responsibility would force most of us to abandon or be prepared to abandon many of our most basic individual commitments, alienating ourselves from the very things that mean the most to us.[31]

To be sure, objective act-consequentialism of the sort considered here is a demanding and potentially disruptive morality, even after allowances have been made for the psychological phenomena thus far discussed and for the difference between saying an act is wrong and saying that the agent ought to be blamed for it. But just *how* demanding or disruptive it would be for an individual is a function – as it arguably should be – of how bad the state of the world is, how others typically act, what institutions exist, and how much that individual is capable of doing. If wealth were more equitably distributed, if political systems were less repressive and more

responsive to the needs of their citizens, and if people were more generally prepared to accept certain responsibilities, then individuals' everyday lives would not have to be constantly disrupted for the sake of the good.

For example, in a society where there are no organized forms of disaster relief, it may be the case that if disaster were to strike a particular region, people all over the country would be obliged to make a special effort to provide aid. If, on the other hand, an adequate system of publicly financed disaster relief existed, then it probably would be a very poor idea for people to interrupt their normal lives and attempt to help – their efforts would probably be uncoordinated, ill-informed, an interference with skilled relief work, and economically disruptive (perhaps even damaging to the society's ability to pay for the relief effort).

By altering social and political arrangements we can lessen the disruptiveness of moral demands on our lives, and in the long run achieve better results than free-lance good-doing. A consequentialist theory is therefore likely to recommend that accepting negative responsibility is more a matter of supporting certain social and political arrangements (or rearrangements) than of setting out individually to save the world. Moreover, it is clear that such social and political changes cannot be made unless the lives of individuals are psychologically supportable in the meanwhile, and this provides substantial reason for rejecting the notion that we should abandon all that matters to us as individuals and devote ourselves solely to net social welfare. Finally, in many cases what matters most is *perceived* rather than actual demandingness or disruptiveness, and this will be a relative matter, depending upon normal expectations. If certain social or political arrangements encourage higher contribution as a matter of course, individuals may not sense these moral demands as excessively intrusive.

To speak of social and political changes is, of course, to suggest eliminating the social and political preconditions for a number of existing projects and relationships, and such changes are likely to produce some degree of alienation in those whose lives have been disrupted. To an extent such people may be able to find new projects and relationships as well as maintain a number of old projects and relationships, and thereby avoid intolerable alienation. But not all will escape serious alienation. We thus have a case in which alienation will exist whichever course of action we follow – either the alienation of those who find the loss of the old order disorienting, or the continuing alienation of those who under the present order cannot lead lives expressive of their individuality or goals. It would seem that to follow the logic of Williams' position would have the unduly conservative result of favoring those less alienated in the present state of affairs over those who might lead more satisfactory lives if certain changes were to occur. Such conservativism could hardly be warranted by a concern about alienation if the changes in question would bring about social and political preconditions for a more widespread enjoyment of meaningful lives. For example, it is disruptive of the ground projects of many men that women have begun to demand and receive greater equality in social and personal spheres, but such disruption may be offset by the opening of more avenues of self-development to a greater number of people.

In responding to Williams' objection regarding negative responsibility, I have focused more on the problem of disruptiveness than the problem of demandingness, and more on the social than the personal level. More would need to be said than I am able to say here to come fully to terms with his objection, although some very general remarks may be in order. The consequentialist starts out from the relatively simple idea that certain things seem to matter to people above all else. His root conception of moral rightness is therefore that it should matter above all else whether people, insofar as possible, actually realize these ends.[32] Consequentialist moralities of the sort considered here undeniably set a demanding standard, calling upon us to do more for one another than is now the practice. But this standard plainly does not require that most people lead intolerable lives for the sake of some greater good: the greater good is empirically equivalent to the best possible lives for the largest possible number of people.[33] Objective consequentialism gives full expression to this root intuition by setting as the criterion of rightness actual contribution to the realization of human value, allowing practices and forms of reasoning to take whatever shape this requires. It is thus not equivalent to requiring a certain, alienated way of

thinking about ourselves, our commitments, or how to act.

Samuel Scheffler has recently suggested that one response to the problems Williams raises about the impersonality and demandingness of consequentialism could be to depart from consequentialism at least far enough to recognize as a fundamental moral principle an agent-centered prerogative, roughly to the effect that one is not always obliged to maximize the good, although one is always permitted to do so if one wishes. This prerogative would make room for agents to give special attention to personal projects and commitments. However, the argument of this article, if successful, shows there to be a firm place in moral practice for prerogatives that afford such room even if one accepts a fully consequentialist fundamental moral theory.[34]

IX.   Alienation from Morality

By way of conclusion, I would like to turn to alienation from morality itself, the experience (conscious or unconscious) of morality as an external set of demands not rooted in our lives or accommodating to our perspectives. Giving a convincing answer to the question "Why should I be moral?" must involve diminishing the extent that morality appears alien.

Part of constructing such an answer is a matter of showing that abiding by morality need not alienate us from the particular commitments that make life worthwhile, and in the previous sections we have begun to see how this might be possible within an objective act-consequentialist account of what morality requires. We saw how in general various sorts of projects or relationships can continue to be a source of intrinsic value even though one recognizes that they might have to undergo changes if they could not be defended in their present form on moral grounds. And again, knowing that a commitment is morally defensible may well deepen its value for us, and may also make it possible for us to feel part of a larger world in a way that is itself of great value. If our commitments are regarded by others as responsible and valuable (or if we have reason to think that others should so regard them), this may enhance the meaning or value they have for ourselves, while if they are regarded by others as irresponsible or worthless (especially, if we suspect that others regard them so justly), this may make it more difficult for us to identify with them or find purpose or value in them. Our almost universal urge to rationalize our acts and lives attests our wish to see what we do as defensible from a more general point of view. I do not deny that bringing a more general perspective to bear on one's life may be costly to the self – it may cause reevaluations that lower self-esteem, produce guilt, alienation, and even problems of identity. But I do want to challenge the simple story often told in which there is a personal point of view from which we glimpse meanings which then vanish into insignificance when we adopt a more general perspective. In thought and action we shuttle back and forth from more personal to less personal standpoints, and both play an important role in the process whereby purpose, meaning, and identity are generated and sustained.[35] Moreover, it may be part of mature commitments, even of the most intimate sort, that a measure of perspective beyond the personal be maintained.

These remarks about the role of general perspectives in individual lives lead us to what I think is an equally important part of answering the question "Why should I be moral?": reconceptualization of the terms of the discussion to avoid starting off in an alienated fashion and ending up with the result that morality still seems alien. Before pursuing this idea, let us quickly glance at two existing approaches to the question.

Morality may be conceived of as in essence selfless, impartial, impersonal. To act morally is to subordinate the self and all contingencies concerning the self's relations with others or the world to a set of imperatives binding on us solely as rational beings. We should be moral, in this view, because it is ideally rational. However, morality thus conceived seems bound to appear as alien in daily life. "Purity of heart" in Rawls' sense would be essential to acting morally, and the moral way of life would appear well removed from our actual existence, enmeshed as we are in a web of "particularistic" commitments – which happen to supply our *raisons d'être*.

A common alternative conception of morality is not as an elevated purity of heart but as a good strategy for the self. Hobbesian atomic individuals are posited and appeal is made to game theory to show that pay-offs to such individuals may be

greater in certain conflict situations – such as reiterated prisoners' dilemmas – if they abide by certain constraints of a moral kind (at least, with regard to those who may reciprocate) rather than act merely prudentially. Behaving morally, then, may be an advantageous policy in certain social settings. However, it is not likely to be the *most* advantageous policy in general, when compared to a strategy that cunningly mixes some compliance with norms and some non-compliance; and presumably the Hobbesian individual is interested only in maximal self-advantage. Yet even if we leave aside worries about how far such arguments might be pushed, it needs to be said that morality as such would confront such an entrepreneurial self as an alien set of demands, for central to morality is the idea that others' interests must sometimes be given weight for reasons unrelated to one's own advantage.

Whatever their differences, these two apparently antithetical approaches to the question "Why should I be moral?" have remarkably similar underlying pictures of the problem. In these pictures, a presocial, rational, abstract individual is the starting point, and the task is to construct proper interpersonal relations out of such individuals. Of course, this conceit inverts reality: the rational individual of these approaches is a social and historical *product*. But that is old hat. We are not supposed to see this as any sort of history, we are told, but rather as a way of conceptualizing the questions of morality. Yet why when conceptualizing are we drawn to such asocial and ahistorical images? My modest proposal is that we should keep our attention fixed on society and history at least long enough to try recasting the problem in more naturalistic terms.[36]

As a start, let us begin with individuals situated in society, complete with identities, commitments, and social relations. What are the ingredients of such identities, commitments, and relations? When one studies relationships of deep commitment – of parent to child, or wife to husband – at close range, it becomes artificial to impose a dichotomy between what is done for the self and what is done for the other. We cannot decompose such relationships into a vector of self-concern and a vector of other-concern, even though concern for the self and the other are both present. The other has come to figure in the self in a fundamental way – or, perhaps a better way of putting it, the other has become a reference point of the self. If it is part of one's identity to be the parent of Jill or the husband of Linda, then the self has reference points beyond the ego, and that which affects these reference points may affect the self in an unmediated way.[37] These reference points do not all fall within the circle of intimate relationships, either. Among the most important constituents of identities are social, cultural, or religious ties – one is a Jew, a Southerner, a farmer, or an alumnus of Old Ivy. Our identities exist in relational, not absolute space, and except as they are fixed by reference points in others, in society, in culture, or in some larger constellation still, they are not fixed at all.[38]

There is a worthwhile analogy between meaning in lives and meaning in language. It has been a while since philosophers have thought it helpful to imagine that language is the arrangement resulting when we hook our private meanings up to a system of shared symbols. Meaning, we are told, resides to a crucial degree in use, in public contexts, in referential systems – it is possible for the self to use a language with meanings because the self is embedded in a set of social and historical practices. But ethical philosophers have continued to speak of the meaning of life in surprisingly private terms. Among recent attempts to give a foundation for morality, Nozick's perhaps places greatest weight on the idea of the meaning of life, which he sees as a matter of an individual's "ability to regulate and guide [his] life in accordance with some overall conception [he] chooses to accept," emphasizing the idea that an individual creates meaning through choice of a life plan; clearly, however, in order for choice to play a self-defining role, the options among which one chooses must already have some meaning independent of one's decisions.[39]

It is not only "the meaning of life" that carries such presuppositions. Consider, for example, another notion that has played a central role in moral discourse: respect. If the esteem of others is to matter to an individual those others must themselves have some significance to the individual; in order for their esteem to constitute the sought-after respect, the individual must himself have some degree of respect for them and their judgment.[40] If the self loses significance for others, this threatens its significance even for itself; if

others lose significance for the self, this threatens to remove the basis for self-significance. It is a commonplace of psychology and sociology that bereaved or deracinated individuals suffer not only a sense of loss owing to broken connections with others, but also a loss in the solidity of the self, and may therefore come to lose interest in the self or even a clear sense of identity. Reconstructing the self and self-interest in such cases is as much a matter of constructing new relations to others and the world as it is a feat of self-supporting self-reconstruction. Distracted by the picture of a hypothetical, presocial individual, philosophers have found it very easy to assume, wrongly, that in the actual world concern for oneself and one's goals is quite automatic, needing no outside support, while a direct concern for others is inevitably problematic, needing some further rationale.

It does not follow that there is any sort of categorical imperative to care about others or the world beyond the self as such. It is quite possible to have few external reference points and go through life in an alienated way. Life need not have much meaning in order to go on, and one does not even have to care whether life goes on. We cannot show that moral skepticism is necessarily irrational by pointing to facts about meaning, but a naturalistic approach to morality need no more refute radical skepticism than does a naturalistic approach to epistemology. For actual people, there may be surprisingly little distance between asking in earnest "Why should I take any interest in anyone else?" and asking "Why should I take any interest in myself?"[41] The proper response to the former is not merely to point out the indirect benefits of caring about things beyond the self, although this surely should be done, but to show how denying the significance of anything beyond the self may undercut the basis of significance for the self. There is again a close, but not exact parallel in language: people can get along without a language, although certainly not as well as they can with it; if someone were to ask "Why should I use my words the same way as others?" the proper response would not only be to point out the obvious benefits of using his words in this way, but also to point out that by refusing to use words the way others do he is undermining the basis of meaning in his own use of language.

These remarks need not lead us to a conservative traditionalism. We must share and preserve meanings in order to have a language at all, but we may use a common language to disagree and innovate. Contemporary philosophy of language makes us distrust any strict dichotomy between meaning, on the one hand, and belief and value, on the other; but there is obviously room within a system of meanings for divergence and change on empirical and normative matters. Language itself has undergone considerable change over the course of history, coevolving with beliefs and norms without in general violating the essential conditions of meaningfulness. Similarly, moral values and social practices may undergo change without obliterating the basis of meaningful lives, so long as certain essential conditions are fulfilled. (History does record some changes, such as the uprooting of tribal peoples, where these conditions were not met, with devastating results.)

A system of available, shared meanings would seem to be a precondition for sustaining the meaningfulness of individual lives in familiar sorts of social arrangements. Moreover, in such arrangements identity and self-significance seem to depend in part upon the significance of others to the self. If we are prepared to say that a sense of meaningfulness is a precondition for much else in life, then we may be on the way to answering the question "Why should I be moral?" for we have gone beyond pure egocentrism precisely by appealing to facts about the self.[42] Our earlier discussions have yielded two considerations that make the rest of the task of answering this question more tractable. First, we noted in discussing hedonism that individual lives seem most enjoyable when they involve commitments to causes beyond the self or to others as such. Further, we remarked that it is plausible that the happiest sorts of lives do not involve a commitment to hedonism even of a sophisticated sort. If a firm sense of meaningfulness is a precondition of the fullest happiness, this speculation becomes still more plausible. Second, we sketched a morality that began by taking seriously the various forms of human non-moral value, and then made room for morality in our lives by showing that we can raise moral questions without thereby destroying the possibility of realizing various intrinsic values from particular relationships and activities. That is, we saw how being moral might be compatible

(at least in these respects) with living a desirable life. It would take another article, and a long one, to show how these various pieces of the answer to "Why should I be moral?" might be made less rough and fitted together into a more solid structure. But by adopting a non-alienated starting point – that of situated rather than pre-social individuals – and by showing how some of the alienation associated with bringing morality to bear on our lives might be avoided, perhaps we have reduced the extent to which morality seems alien to us by its nature.

Notes

1   The loss in question need not be a loss of something of value, and *a fortiori* need not be a bad thing overall: there are some people, institutions, or cultures alienation from which would be a boon. Alienation is a more or less troubling phenomenon depending upon what is lost; and in the cases to be considered, what is lost is for the most part of substantial value. It does not follow, as we will see in Section V, that in all such cases alienation is a bad thing on balance. Moreover, I do not assume that the loss in question represents an actual *decline* in some value as the result of a separation coming into being where once there was none. It seems reasonable to say that an individual can experience a loss in being alienated from nature, for example, without assuming that he was ever in communion with it, much as we say it is a loss for someone never to receive an education or never to appreciate music. Regrettably, various relevant kinds and sources of alienation cannot be discussed here. A general, historical discussion of alienation may be found in Richard Schacht, *Alienation* (Garden City, NY: Doubleday, 1971).

2   This is not to say that no questions arise about whether Helen's (or John's) feelings and attitudes constitute the fullest sort of affection, as will be seen shortly.

3   Moreover, there is a sense in which someone whose responses to his affections or feelings are characteristically mediated by a calculating point of view may fail to know himself fully, or may seem in a way unknowable to others, and this "cognitive distance" may itself be part of his alienation. I am indebted here to Allan Gibbard.

4   There is a wide range of views about the nature of the moral point of view and its proper role in moral life. Is it necessary that one actually act on universal

principles, or merely that one be willing to universalize the principles upon which one acts? Does the moral point of view by its nature require us to consider everyone alike? Here I am using a rather strong reading of the moral point of view, according to which taking the moral point of view involves universalization and the equal consideration of all.

5 A moral point of view theorist might make use of the three points of view distinguished by Mill: the moral, the aesthetic, and the sympathetic. "The first addresses itself to our reason and conscience; the second to our imagination; the third to our human fellow-feeling," from "Bentham," reprinted in *John Stuart Mill: Utilitarianism and Other Writings*, ed. Mary Warnock (New York: New American Library, 1962), p. 121. What is morally right, in his view, may fail to be "loveable" (e.g., a parent strictly disciplining a child) or "beautiful" (e.g., an inauthentic gesture). Thus, the three points of view need not concur in their positive or negative assessments. Notice, however, that Mill has divided the self into three realms, of "reason and conscience," of "imagination," and of "human fellow-feeling"; notice, too, that he has chosen the word 'feeling' to characterize human affections.

6 William K. Frankena, *Ethics*, 2d ed. (Englewood Cliffs, NJ: Prentice-Hall, 1973), p. 116. Moralities that do not accord with this dictum – or a modified version of it that includes all sentient beings – might be deemed alienated in a Feuerbachian sense.

7 Mill, for instance, calls the moral point of view "unquestionably the first and most important," and while he thinks it the error of the moralizer (such as Bentham) to elevate the moral point of view and "sink the [aesthetic and sympathetic] entirely," he does not explain how to avoid such a result if the moral point of view is to be, as he says it ought, "paramount." See his "Bentham," pp. 121f.

Philosophers who have recently raised doubts about moralities for such reasons include Bernard Williams, in "A Critique of Utilitarianism," in J. J. C. Smart and B. Williams, *Utilitarianism: For and Against* (Cambridge: Cambridge University Press, 1973), and Michael Stocker, in "The Schizophrenia of Modern Ethical Theories," *Journal of Philosophy* 73 (1976): 453–66.

8 John Rawls, *A Theory of Justice* (Cambridge: Harvard University Press, 1971), p. 587, emphasis added.

9 I am not claiming that we should interpret all of Rawls' intricate moral theory in light of these few remarks. They are cited here merely to illustrate a certain tendency in moral thought, especially that of a Kantian inspiration.

10 This is a "paradox" for individual, egoistic hedonists. Other forms the "paradox of hedonism" may take are social in character: a society of egoistic hedonists might arguably achieve less total happiness than a society of more benevolent beings; or, taking happiness as the sole social goal might lead to a less happy society overall than could exist if a wider range of goals were pursued.

11 This is not to deny that there are indexical components to commitments.

12 It does seem likely to matter just what the commitment is contingent upon as well as just how contingent it is. I think it is an open question whether commitments contingent upon the satisfaction of egoistic hedonist criteria are of the sort that might figure in the happiest sorts of lives ordinarily available. We will return to this problem presently.

Those who have had close relationships often develop a sense of *duty* to one another that may outlast affection or emotional commitment, that is, they may have a sense of obligation to one another that is less contingent than affection or emotional commitment, and that should not simply be confused with them. If such a sense of obligation is in conflict with self-interest, and if it is a normal part of the most satisfying sorts of close relationships, then this may pose a problem for the egoistic hedonist.

13 A few remarks are needed. First, I will say that an act is available to an agent if he would succeed in performing it if he tried. Second, here and elsewhere in this article I mean to include quite "thick" descriptions of actions, so that it may be part of an action that one perform it with a certain intention or goal. In the short run (but not so much the long run) intentions, goals, motives, and the like are usually less subject to our deliberate control than overt behavior – it is easier to say "I'm sorry" than to say it and mean it. This, however, is a fact about the relative availability of acts to the agent at a given time, and should not dictate what is to count as an act. Third, here and elsewhere I ignore for simplicity's sake the possibility that more than one course of action may be maximally valuable. And fourth, for reasons I will not enter into here, I have formulated objective hedonism in terms of actual outcomes rather than expected values (relative to the information available to the agent). One could make virtually the same argument using an expected value formulation.

14 Michael Stocker considers related cases in "Morally Good Intentions," *The Monist* 54 (1970): 124–41. I am much indebted to his discussion.

15   There may be a parallelism of sorts between Ned's coming to seek money for its own sake and a certain pattern of moral development: what is originally sought in order to live up to familial or social expectations may come to be an end in itself.

It might be objected that the goal of earning as much money as possible is quite unlike the goal of being as happy as possible, since money is plainly instrumentally valuable even when it is sought for its own sake. But happiness, too, is instrumentally valuable, for it may contribute to realizing such goals as being a likeable or successful person.

16   An important objection to the claim that objective hedonism may serve as the *moral* criterion one's acts should meet, even if this means not believing in hedonism, is that moral principles must meet a *publicity* condition. I will discuss this objection in Section VI.

17   See, for example, Stocker, "The Schizophrenia of Modern Ethical Theories."

18   Williams, "Critique."

19   At least one qualification is needed: the subjective states must be psychologically possible. Perhaps some of us desire what are, in effect, psychologically impossible states.

20   Robert Nozick, *Anarchy, State, and Utopia* (New York: Basic Books, 1974), pp. 42ff.

21   To my knowledge, the best-developed method for justifying claims about intrinsic value involves thought-experiments of a familiar sort, in which, for example, we imagine two lives, or two worlds, alike in all but one respect, and then attempt to determine whether rational, well-informed, widely-experienced individuals would (when vividly aware of both alternatives) be indifferent between the two or have a settled preference for one over the other. Since no one is ideally rational, fully informed, or infinitely experienced, the best we can do is to take more seriously the judgments of those who come nearer to approximating these conditions. Worse yet: the best we can do is to take more seriously the judgments of those we *think* better approximate these conditions. (I am not supposing that facts or experience somehow entail values, but that in rational agents, beliefs and values show a marked mutual influence and coherence.) We may overcome some narrowness if we look at behavior and preferences in other societies and other epochs, but even here we must rely upon interpretations colored by our own beliefs and values. Within the confines of this article I must leave unanswered a host of deep and troubling questions about the nature of values and value judgments. Suffice it to say that there is

no reason to think that we are in a position to give anything but a tentative list of intrinsic goods.

It becomes a complex matter to describe the psychology of intrinsic value. For example, should we say that one values a relationship of solidarity, say, a friendship, *because it is* a friendship? That makes it sound as if it were somehow instrumental to the realization of some abstract value, friendship. Surely this is a misdescription. We may be able to get a clearer idea of what is involved by considering the case of happiness. We certainly do not value a particular bit of experienced happiness because it is instrumental in the realization of the abstract goal, happiness – we value the experience for its own sake because it is a happy experience. Similarly, a friendship is itself the valued thing, the thing of a valued kind. Of course, one can say that one values friendship and therefore seeks friends, just as one can say one values happiness and therefore seeks happy experiences. But this locution must be contrasted with what is being said when, for example, one talks of seeking *things that make one happy*. Friends are not "things that make one achieve friendship" – they partially constitute friendships, just as particular happy experience partially constitute happiness for an individual. Thus taking friendship as an intrinsic value does not entail viewing particular friendships instrumentally.

22   If one objects that Juan's commitment to Linda is lacking because it is contingent in some ways, the objector must show that the *kinds* of contingencies involved would destroy his relationship with Linda, especially since moral character often figures in commitments – the character of the other, or the compatibility of a commitment with one's having the sort of character one values – and the contingencies in Juan's case are due to his moral character.

23   I do not mean to suggest that such identities are always matters of choice for individuals. Quite the reverse, identities often arise through socialization, prejudice, and similar influences. The point rather is that there is a very general phenomenon of identification, badly in need of explanation, that to an important extent underlies such phenomena as socialization and prejudice, and that suggests the existence of certain needs in virtually all members of society – needs to which identification with entities beyond the self answers.

Many of us who resist raising questions about our lives from broader perspectives do so, I fear, not out of a sense that it would be difficult or impossible to lead a meaningful life if one entertained such perspectives, but rather out of a sense that our lives would not stand up to much scrutiny therefrom, so that leading a life that *would* seem meaningful from such perspectives would require us to change in some significant way.

24 Although the language here is causal – 'promoting' and 'bringing about' – it should be said that the relation of an act to the good need not always be causal. An act of learning may non-causally involve coming to have knowledge (an intrinsic good by my reckoning) as well as contributing causally to later realizations of intrinsic value. Causal consequences as such do not have a privileged status. As in the case of objective hedonism, I have formulated objective consequentialism in terms of actual outcomes (so-called "objective duty") rather than expected values relative to what is rational for the agent to believe ("subjective duty"). The main arguments of this article could be made using expected value, since the course of action with highest expected value need not in general be the subjectively consequentialist one. See also notes 13 and 21.

Are there any subjective consequentialists? Well, various theorists have claimed that a consequentialist must be a subjective consequentialist in order to be genuine – see Williams, "Critique," p. 135, and Rawls, *Theory of Justice*, p. 182.

25 Williams, "Critique," p. 135.

26 For discussion of a publicity condition, see Rawls, *Theory of Justice*, pp. 133, 177–82, 582. The question whether a publicity condition can be justified is a difficult one, deserving fuller discussion than I am able to give it here.

27 For an example of trait-consequentialism, see Robert M. Adams, "Motive Utilitarianism," *Journal of Philosophy* 73 (1976): 467–81.

28 By way of contrast, when Robert Adams considers application of a motive-utilitarian view to the ethics of actions, he suggests "conscience utilitarianism," the view that "we have a *moral duty* to do an act, if and only if it would be demanded of us by the most useful kind of conscience we could have," "Motive Utilitarianism," p. 479. Presumably, this means that it would be morally wrong to perform an act contrary to the demands of the most useful sort of conscience. I have resisted this sort of redefinition of rightness for actions, since I believe that the most useful sort of conscience may on occasion demand of us an act that does not have the best overall consequences of those available, and that performing this act would be wrong.

Of course, some difficulties attend the interpretation of this last sentence. I have assumed throughout that an act is available to an agent if he would succeed in performing it if he tried. I have

also taken a rather simple view of the complex matter of attaching outcomes to specific acts. In those rare cases in which the performance of even one exceptional (purportedly optimizing) act would completely undermine the agent's standing (optimal) disposition, it might not be possible after all to say that the exceptional act would be the right one to perform in the circumstances. (This question will arise again shortly.)

29 One conclusion of this discussion is that we cannot realistically expect people's behavior to be in strict compliance with the counterfactual condition even if they are committed sophisticated consequentialists. At best, a sophisticated consequentialist tries to meet this condition. But it should be no surprise that in practice we are unlikely to be morally ideal. Imperfections in information alone are enough to make it very improbable that individuals will lead objectively consequentialist lives. Whether or when to *blame* people for real or apparent failures to behave ideally is, of course, another matter.

Note that we must take into account not just the frequency with which right acts are performed, but the actual balance of gains and losses to overall well-being that results. Relative frequency of right action will settle the matter only in the (unusual) case where the amount of good at stake in each act of a given kind – for example, each emergency one comes across – is the same.

30 In *The Methods of Ethics*, bk. IV, chap, v, sec. 4, Sidgwick discusses "the Ideal of character and conduct" that a utilitarian should recognize as "the sum of excellences or Perfections," and writes that "a Utilitarian must hold that it is always wrong for a man knowingly to do anything other than what he believes to be most conducive to Universal Happiness" (p. 492). Here Sidgwick is uncharacteristically confused – and in two ways. First, considering act-by-act evaluation, an objective utilitarian can hold that an agent may simply be wrong in believing that a given course of action is most conducive to universal happiness, and therefore it may be right for him knowingly to do something other than this. Second, following Sidgwick's concern in this passage and looking at enduring traits of character rather than isolated acts, and even assuming the agent's belief to be correct, an objective utilitarian can hold that the ideal character for an individual, or for people in general, may involve a willingness knowingly to act contrary to maximal happiness when this is done for the sake of certain deep personal commitments. See Henry Sidgwick, *The Methods of Ethics*, 7th ed. (New York: Dover, 1966), p. 492.

It might be thought counterintuitive to say, in the example given, that it is not right for Juan to travel to see Linda. But it must be kept in mind that for an act-consequentialist to say that an action is not right is not to say that it is without merit, only that it is not the very best act available to the agent. And an intuitive sense of the rightness of visiting Linda may be due less to an evaluation of the act itself than to a reaction to the sort of character a person would have to have in order to stay home and write a check to OXFAM under the circumstances. Perhaps he would have to be too distant or righteous to have much appeal to us – especially in view of the fact that it is his spouse's anguish that is at stake. We have already seen how an act-consequentialist may share this sort of character assessment.

31 Williams, "Critique," sec. 3.

32 I appealed to this "root conception" in rejecting rule-consequentialism in Section VII. Although consequentialism is often condemned for failing to provide an account of morality consistent with respect for persons, this root conception provides the basis for a highly plausible notion of such respect. I doubt, however, that any fundamental ethical dispute between consequentialists and deontologists can be resolved by appeal to the idea of respect for persons. The deontologist has his notion of respect – e.g., that we not use people in certain ways – and the consequentialist has *his* – e.g., that the good of every person has an equal claim upon us, a claim unmediated by any notion of right or contract, so that we should do the most possible to bring about outcomes that actually advance the good of persons. For every consequentially justified act of manipulation to which the deontologist can point with alarm there is a deontologically justified act that fails to promote the well-being of some person(s) as fully as possible to which the consequentialist can point, appalled. Which notion takes "respect for persons" more seriously? There may be no non-question-begging answer, especially once the consequentialist has recognized such things as autonomy or respect as intrinsically valuable.

33 The qualification 'empirically equivalent to' is needed because in certain empirically unrealistic cases, such as utility monsters, the injunction "Maximize overall realization of human value" cannot be met by improving the lives of as large a proportion of the population as possible. However, under plausible assumptions about this world (including diminishing marginal value) the equivalence holds.

34 For Scheffler's view, see *The Rejection of Consequentialism: A Philosophical Investigation*

of the Considerations Underlying Rival Moral Conceptions (Oxford: Clarendon Press, 1982). The consequentialist may also argue that at least some of the debate set in motion by Williams is more properly concerned with the question of the relation between moral imperatives and imperatives of rationality than with the content of moral imperatives as such. (See note 42.)

35 For example, posterity may figure in our thinking in ways we seldom articulate. Thus, nihilism has seemed to some an appropriate response to the idea that mankind will soon destroy itself. "Everything would lose its point" is a reaction quite distinct from "Then we should enjoy ourselves as much as possible in the meantime," and perhaps equally comprehensible.

36 I do not deny that considerations about pay-offs of strategies in conflict situations may play a role in cultural or biological evolutionary explanations of certain moral sentiments or norms. Rather, I mean to suggest that there are characteristic sorts of abstractions and simplifications involved in game-theoretic analysis that may render it blind to certain phenomena crucial for understanding morality and its history, and for answering the question "Why should I be moral?" when posed by actual individuals.

37 Again we see the inadequacy of subjectivism about values. If, for example, part of one's identity is to be Jill's parent, then should Jill cease to exist, one's life could be said to have lost some of its purpose even if one were not aware of her death. As the example of the experience machine suggested earlier, there is an objective side to talk about purpose.

38 Here I do not have in mind identity in the sense usually at stake in discussions of personal identity. The issue is not identity as principle of individuation, but as *experienced*, as a sense of self – the stuff actual identity crises are made of.

39 Nozick, *Anarchy*, p. 49. (I ignore here Nozick's more recent remarks about the meaning of life in his *Philosophical Explanations* [Cambridge: Harvard University Press, 1981].) The notion of a "rationally chosen life plan" has figured prominently in the literature recently, in part due to Rawls' use of it in characterizing the good (see Rawls, *Theory of Justice*, ch. VII, "Goodness as Rationality"). Rawls' theory of the good is a complex matter, and it is difficult to connect his claims in any direct way to a view about the meaning of life. However, see T. M. Scanlon, "Rawls' Theory of Justice," *University of Pennsylvania Law Review* 121 (1973): 1020–69, for an interpretation of Rawls in which the notion of an individual as above all a rational chooser – more committed to

maintaining his status as a rational agent able to adopt and modify his goals than to any particular set of goals – functions as the ideal of a person implicit in Rawls' theory. On such a reading, we might interpolate into the original text the idea that meaning derives from autonomous individual choice, but this is highly speculative. In any event, recent discussions of rationally chosen life plans as the bearers of ultimate significance or value do not appear to me to do full justice to the ways in which lives actually come to be invested with meaning, especially since some meanings would have to be presupposed by any rational choice of a plan of life.

40 To be sure, this is but one of the forms of respect that are of importance to moral psychology. But as we see, self-respect has a number of interesting connections with respect for, and from, others.

41 This may be most evident in extreme cases. Survivors of Nazi death camps speak of the effort it sometimes took to sustain a will to survive, and of the importance of others, and of the sense of others, to this. A survivor of Treblinka recalls, "In our group we shared everything; and at the moment one of the group ate something without sharing it, we knew it was the beginning of the end for him." (Quoted in Terrence Des Pres, *The Survivor: An Anatomy of Life in the Death Camps* [New York: Oxford University Press, 1976], p. 96.) Many survivors say that the idea of staying alive to "bear witness," in order that the deaths of so many would not escape the world's notice, was decisive in sustaining their own commitment to survival.

42 One need not be a skeptic about morality or alienated from it in any general sense in order for the question "Why should I be moral?" to arise with great urgency. If in a given instance doing what is right or having the best sort of character were to conflict head-on with acting on behalf of a person or a project that one simply could not go against without devastating the self, then it may fail to be reasonable from the agent's standpoint to do what is right. It is always *morally* wrong (though not always morally blameworthy) to fail to perform morally required acts, but in certain circumstances that may be the most reasonable thing to do – not because of some larger moral scheme, but because of what matters to particular individuals. Therefore, in seeking an answer to "Why should I be moral?" I do not assume that it must always be possible to show that the moral course of action is ideally rational or otherwise optimal from the standpoint of the agent. (I could be more specific here if I had a clearer idea of what rationality is.) It would seem ambitious enough to attempt to show that, in general, there are highly desirable lives available to individuals consistent with their being moral. While we might hope for something stronger, this could be enough – given what can also be said on behalf of morality from more general viewpoints – to make morality a worthy candidate for our allegiance as individuals.

It should perhaps be said that on an objective consequentialist account, being moral need not be a matter of consciously following distinctively moral imperatives, so that what is at stake in asking "Why should I be moral?" in connection with such a theory is whether one has good reason to lead one's life in such a way that an objective consequentialist criterion of rightness is met as nearly as possible. In a given instance, this criterion might be met by acting out of a deeply felt emotion or an entrenched trait of character, without consulting morality or even directly in the face of it. This, once more, is an indication of objective consequentialism's flexibility: the idea is to *be* and *do* good, not necessarily to *pursue* goodness.

35

Relatives and Relativism

Diane Jeske and Richard Fumerton

Opposition to consequentialism has taken a variety of forms. Many critics, however, would claim that the most compelling objection to consequentialist moral theories is the "special obligations" objection, i.e. the claim that consequentialism is unable to accommodate the special obligations that we have to intimates and loved ones, obligations that play a central role in commonsense morality. Despite the attention that it has received, we do not think that the implications of the objection regarding special obligations have been appreciated or fully understood.[1] We will show that considerations about special obligations are decisive against certain historically dominant versions of consequentialism. In fact, we will argue, one must either abandon consequentialism in favor of a deontological view or, if one retains consequentialism, adopt a radical, relativistic version of the view based on a radically relativistic conception of value.

1. Consequentialism and Conceptions of Value

Before we consider the objection arising from considerations about special obligations, we need to define some key terms and make important distinctions.

We will use the term "consequentialist" to refer to those ethical theories in which the rightness or wrongness of actions is defined solely in terms of the act's maximizing (or not) the intrinsic value of actual, probable, or possible consequences.[2] If the theory's definition of right action makes reference to probable or possible consequences, the values of consequences will no doubt be adjusted for probability in one of the standard ways.[3] We will understand the consequences of an action to include not only its causal effects but also its logical implications.[4] Thus, a consequentialist can hold that if an act itself has intrinsic value, then that value must be added to the value of other consequences of the act in assessing its rightness or wrongness.

We will understand consequentialism such that it is compatible with any account of what has intrinsic value and with any analysis of what it is to have intrinsic value. Species of consequentialism can be differentiated according to the answers that they give to the following questions: (i) "What has (intrinsic) value?", and (ii) "What is it to have (intrinsic) value?" One of the most prominent forms of consequentialism is utilitarianism. For the purposes of this discussion we will say that utilitarians hold (i) that all and only human well-being has intrinsic value. So, for example, hedonistic utilitarians identify

Diane Jeske and Richard Fumerton, "Relatives and Relativism." *Philosophical Studies* 87 (1997), pp. 143–57. © 1997 by Springer Netherlands. Reprinted with permission from Springer.

well-being with pleasure and thus take all and only pleasure to have intrinsic value, whereas desire-satisfaction utilitarians identify well-being with the satisfaction of desires and thus take all and only the satisfaction of desire to have intrinsic value.[5]

Answers to question (ii), "What is it to have value?", can take either a relativist or a non-relativist form. (We will take as a defining feature of utilitarianism its adoption of a nonrelativist answer to (ii).) A relativist with respect to intrinsic value holds that a statement ascribing intrinsic value to some x is incomplete if it fails to indicate *for whom* x is valuable. The logically perspicuous statement ascribing intrinsic value always has the following form: "X is intrinsically valuable for or to S", where S can be either an individual or a group. Perhaps the most common version of relativism, and the version with which we will primarily be concerned, is what we will call "subjective relativism". A subjective relativist identifies x's being intrinsically valuable for S with the psychological fact that S does in fact value x intrinsically. The subjective relativist need not regard this psychological state of valuing x as an occurrent mental state but could instead regard it as a relatively stable disposition with regards to x. The subjective relativist could further restrict the subjective values relevant to moral judgments as those that would, for example, survive full exposure to relevant facts or vivid imagining of such facts.[6]

Subjective relativism needs to be carefully distinguished from another historically important view which we will call "subjective descriptivism". A subjective descriptivist holds that all ethical statements describe the subjective attitudes of the person making the statement. Thus, suppose that I say that it would be good for you to protect your child from harm. According to the subjective descriptivist, I am asserting that I approve of or value the state of affairs in which you protect your child from harm. However, according to the subjective relativist, my statement that x has value for you is to be understood as asserting a fact about *your* subjective relation to x. So, if I say that it would be good for you to protect your child from harm, I am asserting that *you* approve of or value the state of affairs in which you protect your child from harm.

Having defined relativism with respect to intrinsic value, we could say, straightforwardly, that a version of consequentialism is relativistic when the conception of intrinsic value it employs is relativistic. If we define relativistic consequentialism this way, however, it will be important to distinguish at least two different versions of the view. If one is a relativist about intrinsic value, the most natural and common view is that x's having value for S implies only that S has a reason to bring x about. We might say, then, that the reasons that relativistic values create are agent *relative*. The proponent of such a view would hold a *radically* relativistic version of consequentialism: the right action for an agent to perform is the action that maximizes that which has value *for the agent*.

It is at least formally possible to think of relativistic values as creating agent-neutral moral reasons for acting. One could hold that the fact that x is valued by S provides *anyone* in a position to promote x a reason to do so. Thus one could argue that within the framework of relativistic values the right action is the action that maximizes that which has value for any and all of those individuals affected by the action. Such a view would be analogous to the desire-satisfaction version of utilitarianism discussed above, but it would differ formally by denying objective value to the existence of a state of affairs that someone subjectively values. For many of us, the concept of an agent-neutral reason is inextricably tied to the concept of objective value, and, consequently, the above view will strike us as incongruous. In any event, in this paper we are concerned only with the radically relativistic consequentialism defined in the previous paragraph. We will argue that only it will survive the special obligations objection and that if one cannot embrace a radically relativistic conception of intrinsic value embedded in a radically relativistic consequentialism, one must abandon consequentialism entirely.

2. The "Special Obligations" Objection

The objection has most often been raised against the most historically prominent version of consequentialism, utilitarianism. But with appropriate modifications it can be raised against any version of consequentialism with a nonrelativistic conception of value. It will be easiest to explain the objection by looking at a specific example.

Consider a situation in which your child is in grave danger but the only way you can aid your child is at the expense of other children. Suppose, for example, you took your child canoeing. After taking the wrong fork in the river, your canoe overturns in the rapids. As it turns out, another canoe with two children has been caught in the same rapids and has suffered the same fate. You judge (correctly) that you can either save your child or save the two strangers but you cannot do both. (The two other children are relatively close to you but you will be unable to save your child who has drifted further away if you first save those other children.) What should you do? A great many of us will conclude that it would certainly be morally permissible for you to put your child's life first and some of us would conclude that you are *obligated* to give your child priority. How can a consequentialist accommodate this intuition?

It is difficult to see how any consequentialist with a nonrelativistic conception of value can agree that the parent is permitted to save her child at the expense of *two* other lives. If your child's life has intrinsic value then those other lives also have intrinsic value, twice as much. How can the fact that it is *your* child be morally relevant?

We have presented the objection as it relates to an obligation that seems to stem from a particularly intimate relationship, the parent/child relationship. But we can generate similar intuitions concerning a wide range of special relationships we bear to other individuals, relationships that, in turn, generate special obligations. So, for example, we would have no moral qualms about helping a friend or a colleague even if by doing so we forfeit the chance to help several other people whom we don't know. Some would even claim that helping people in our community, state, or country is preferable to helping "outsiders" even if we could help vastly many more by being less "provincial".

Radically relativistic consequentialism has no difficulty accommodating all of these intuitions. What one ought to do is always in part a function of what one values intrinsically.[7] It is a brute psychological fact that most parents value their children's well-being more than they value the well-being of other children. Similarly, we care more about our friends' happiness than the happiness of most of the people reading this paper. It is even plausible to claim that we care more

about our fellow citizens than we do about strangers in other countries. These psychological facts will often make it the case that the sum of the value of fulfilling "special obligations" is greater than the value that would be achieved by helping even many more people with whom we have no special connections. Note that it is only radically relativistic consequentialism combined with relativistic values that will accommodate the intuition. The version of consequentialism discussed above which identifies right action with action that maximizes that which has relativistic value for any persons affected by that action will not sanction your saving your child. After all, we may presume that the parents of the other children value their children's well-being as much as you value your own child's well-being.

For now let us set aside the relativistic consequentialist response to the objection and ask whether allowances can be made for special obligations from within the framework of nonrelativistic consequentialism.

3. Nonrelativistic Consequentialist Responses to the Objection

3.1. The contingent significance of special relations

Both Sidgwick and Mill are concerned with accommodating the intuitions underlying the claim that we have special obligations to people who stand in certain intimate relations with us but attempt to do so without abandoning utilitarianism (a form of nonrelativistic consequentialism).[8] They appealed to the contingent fact that benefiting intimates will in most situations maximize value. A parent is, after all, typically in the best position (epistemically and causally) to benefit her child. We know more about our own community that we do about others and if we are trying to increase the general happiness we might do best by concentrating our efforts where we are in the best position to judge their effects. Furthermore, a utilitarian concerned with maximizing happiness needs to consider all of the subtle effects that actions have on the agent herself. Most parents enjoy their own child's happiness more than the happiness of other children. Conversely, most parents would feel far more pain at causing their child unhappiness than they would at causing other children to be unhappy. If you let your child die in order to save two other children, then the agony of that decision would no doubt live with you forever. The psychological guilt you would feel might well outweigh whatever extra benefits would accrue to the families of the other children. To be sure, their parents would feel great pain at the loss of their children, but that pain might pale in comparison to the pain a parent would feel upon losing a child whose life she could have saved. Moreover, in calculating the effects of one's action one must include its effects on one's *character*, one's dispositions to act in certain ways. Dispositions to benefit one's own child before one benefits others' children may, if we consider a particular case in isolation, seem not to maximize value. However, if we consider the long-term consequences of a parent's having such a disposition, then our calculations might yield a different result.

The difficulty with appealing to contingent facts is that they are *contingent* facts. We can easily alter the hypothetical situation such that the consequences are different than those imagined by Sidgwick and Mill. Suppose that you know that the parents of the other two children are extraordinarily unstable and that they will have a much harder time coping with their own children's loss than you would have dealing with the loss of your child even given the fact that you have to live with your role in your child's death. Are we any more inclined to think that it would be morally illegitimate for you to save your own child?

The consequentialist will be right in insisting upon the importance of long-term consequences. Our actions affect our characters and dispositions in ways which will affect our future behavior. If I fail to save my child rather than the other two children, I may become hardened to the needs of my other intimates and even incapable of forming intimate relationships that allow me to promote value. But even if we allow that the parent suffers these effects upon her character, we need only suppose that she knows that the other parents will suffer equally devastating effects upon their characters in order to defuse the objection.

We have considered only briefly one strategy designed to accommodate special obligations within a nonrelativistic framework. But the moral

should be obvious: whenever the consequentialist appeals to further contingent consequences to accommodate special obligations, the critic can simply redescribe a case in which those consequences do not occur or are themselves outweighed by further similar consequences without affecting our intuitions about special obligations.

3.2.   Rule consequentialism and more contingencies

Our primary concern in this paper is to explore the implications of the special obligations objection for act consequentialism, the version of consequentialism that we take to be most plausible. There are, of course, a number of philosophers who would be happy to abandon act consequentialism in favor of the view known as rule consequentialism. It might, therefore, be worth very briefly exploring the question of whether rule consequentialists have any better prospects for dealing with the special obligations created by our relations with intimates.

The difficulties with rule consequentialism are notorious – it is even difficult to formulate a version of the view that will not collapse back into act consequentialism and can still be distinguished from a deontological view.[9] There are many different versions of rule consequentialism and it is obviously beyond the scope of this discussion to review the ways in which they differ. For our purposes we will work with the at least initially straightforward version of rule consequentialism according to which a right action is an action that is in accord with a rule such that everyone's (or most people's) following that rule maximizes value.[10] Thus, it may be that the act of my saving my child has worse consequences than the act of my saving the other two children. However, my saving my own child is in accord with a moral rule (parents ought to save their own children before they save other children), and the consequences of everyone's or most everyone's following that rule has better consequences than their following some alternative rule. But the rule consequentialist faces the same difficulty we posed for the act consequentialist. We simply imagine a world in which the consequences of people's following the rule "save your own children first" does not maximize value. The fact that most people following a given rule maximizes value is itself a contingent fact about the world. As with all contingent facts, we can imagine that the world is other than the way it is. If the facts about the consequences of a rule's being generally followed change, will our intuitions about the moral legitimacy of giving priority to one's children? If not, then the rule consequentialist fares no better than does the act consequentialist.

Now the rule consequentialist might complain at this point that we have far too glibly supposed the ease with which one could imagine a world in which parents acting without bias toward their children might have better consequences. Such a world, they might argue, would have to be drastically different from our own world and when one engages in such fantastic thought experiments, one can no longer trust one's "moral intuitions". We might think that we would still feel entitled to help our child at the expense of other children in the world we have asked the reader to imagine but that's only because we really haven't succeeded in imagining a world as different as that one would have to be. If it were really true that people in general giving priority to their children did not maximize well-being, and we knew that it was true, we wouldn't conclude that it was morally permissible to continue doing so.

But is it so difficult to imagine a world in which people following a rule requiring them to be specially concerned about, for example, their own children would be counterproductive? Suppose that some variation of Plato's utopian society is actually the best, a variation in which parents raise their own children but show them no preference. Of course, given human nature as it is, such a supposition might seem obviously false. But human nature could change. Suppose that as a result of generations of intense conflict between family units fighting over scarce resources, *most* people came to realize that the preferences that they showed their own children were counterproductive to society as a whole and, over several generations, eventually managed to eradicate such preferences. The evolution, however, was not universal, and there were still a few pockets of parents who continued to feel about their own children the way we feel about ours. In such a world, it is not implausible to suppose that the rule consequentialist's correct *rule* governing parent/child relationships is "show your child

no preference". But if you were one of the few "traditional" parents surviving, would you, if you could save only your own child or you could save two others, think that you ought to follow that rule and save the two children? For such parents, the special relationships that they have with their own children seem to generate special obligations regardless of the fact that, in their world, the rule that, generally followed, leads to the best consequences is a rule that requires parents not to favor their own children.

The rule consequentialist might reply that, in our hypothetical case, the rule would need to be refined. Perhaps the most beneficial rule would be one that differentiated between parents with special relationships to their children and parents without such relationships, for example, "show your child no preference if and only if you are not a 'traditional' parent". At this point, however, all we have to do is to imagine that the pockets of "traditional" parents are not isolated, that the behavior of the "evolved" parents is not independent of the behavior of the "traditional" parents; in other words, imagine that the situation in which the two sets of parents acted differently in similar situations is not stable. The behavior of the traditional parents would have an effect on that of the evolved parents, so that society would begin to deteriorate back to its former warlike condition. Knowing the consequences of not following the rule "show your child no preference", if you were a "traditional" parent, should you follow that rule, or should you save your own child rather than two others? Given the special relationship between you and your child, it seems that you should save your child.

The rule consequentialist could attempt to refine the rule even further. However, as the rule consequentialist begins refining rules more and more she must confront the worry that we mentioned above, the worry that her view will simply collapse back into a version of act consequentialism. Whether or not the view literally collapses into act consequentialism, the more complex the rule consequentialist's rules must be, the more often rule consequentialism will prescribe the same action as does act consequentialism. The closer rule consequentialism comes to act consequentialism, the more likely it is that considerations that lead us to reject the act consequentialist account of right action in certain cases will also lead us to reject the revised rule consequentialist account of right action in similar cases.

Of course, at this point, some might have different intuitions than we have. It is always difficult to know how to respond to a stalemate of moral intuitions.[11] Nonetheless, the difficulty now facing the rule consequentialist parallels the one that faced the act consequentialist. If you were inclined to agree that a parent ought to save her own child rather than two others even though such an action does not maximize value, why would you nonetheless hold that a parent should not save her own child rather than two others when such an action is not in accord with a rule which is such that, generally followed, would have the best consequences? This question raises a general worry about rule consequentialist theories, asking for a justification of such theories' focus upon the consequences of certain rules being generally followed rather than upon the consequences of specific actions.

We do not want to pursue a discussion of rule consequentialism as such, so we will leave the issue here. However, it does seem that, for many of us, our intuitions about how parents ought to behave do not vary in accord with changes with regard to what behavior will maximize consequences, either in the particular situation or as dictated by a rule that is generally followed. If one feels the force of the initial special obligations objection, if one agrees that there are obligations that *derive* from special relations that trump maximizing considerations with respect to the consequences of an individual act, then it is difficult to see how one would reach a different conclusion when one focuses on maximizing considerations with respect to the consequences of people in general acting in a certain way.

3.3. Actions and intrinsic value

As we define consequentialism, a consequentialist can assign intrinsic value to an act in virtue of its being of a certain type. So a consequentialist who wants to accommodate special obligations might try assigning great intrinsic value to a parent's saving her own child. In addition, then, to the positive value of my child's life, I must add the value of my saving my child's life, a value greater than that which attaches to my saving the other children's lives. If the value of saving my child's life is great enough, it might outweigh the suffering of many other people.[12]

Such a move will force a redescription of the hypothetical situation but will not save consequentialism. We need only describe a situation in which by saving your child's life you prevent two other parents from saving their children's lives. Suppose that you are on shore, and in order to save your drowning child, you must take a boat that two other parents were about to use to rescue their drowning children. We must now add to the relevant consequences of your action, the failure of two other parents to save their children. But these additional consequences do not affect our intuitions about your special obligations to save your own child.

A consequentialist can assign value to actions that derives from the fact of special relationships that hold between the actor and persons affected. However, as a nonrelativist, she must assign the same value to any action involving similar intimate relationships. Because the consequences of actions can affect the ability of others to fulfill *their* special obligations, we will always be able to describe hypothetical cases in which consequentialism yields implausible conclusions.

It must be emphasized, of course, that the argument here rests on an appeal to intuitions and one might again wonder whether it is so obvious that our intuitions about special obligations will not be affected by the added hypothesis that our fulfilling those obligations prevents others from fulfilling theirs. To be sure, intuitions might vary somewhat depending on the case. Certainly, if a father had to shoot two other parents to prevent them from getting to that boat first, most of us will probably have serious qualms about the moral permissibility of his doing so. If the boat was owned by one of the other parents and the parent we are imagining had to steal it in order to save his child's life (at the expense of those other parents saving their children), that might again affect our intuitions. But there is no mystery as to what the source of the conflicting intuitions might be. The radical relativist will no doubt value other things besides his children's well-being and as a consequentialist these values will enter into his calculations as to what would be morally right to do. The deontologist who acknowledges *prima facie* duties will no doubt recognize that there are *prima facie* duties other than saving one's own children and that these must be weighed against the obligation to save one's child. It is enough for our purposes, however, that we can force the non-relativistic consequentialist into admitting that there are at least *some* situations in which it would be morally permissible to favor one's intimates and relatives even at the expense of forfeiting a chance to maximize value. And that we think we can do. Again let us suppose that in the situation we described above it is a simple case of my being able to outrun the two other parents for a public boat which we are all entitled to use. I still realize that as a result of my winning this "competition" two children will lose their lives so that my child will live, and two parents will lose their ability to save their children's lives so that I will be able to save my child. We still have no hesitation in concluding that in this situation I would be behaving precisely as a parent should in taking the boat to save my child's life.

4.   Conclusions

Unless the consequentialist is willing to trace special obligations to agent-relative values, unless, for example, your special obligation to your child can be traced to the fact that your child's well-being has more value for you than the well-being of other children, then the consequentialist is committed to denying commonsense conclusions. So if one wants to accommodate special obligations and retain consequentialism, one must adopt a radically relativistic conception of value. Such relativism is not, of course, without its own critics. By making what one ought to do in part a function of brute psychological facts about what one values intrinsically, the relativistic consequentialist must allow that a person with odd enough intrinsic values should radically violate conventional morality. Just ask yourself what sort of life a masochistic sadist should live, according to the relativistic consequentialist.[13]

If one rejects relativistic consequentialism as the way to accommodate special obligations, what alternatives does one have? One can adopt a deontological view in which special relationships, in and of themselves, ground special obligations.[14]

To save one's child is *prima facie* right.[15] The *prima facie* rightness of such an action is not due to the value of one's child or the value of one's saving one's child. The rightness of the action supervenes on the nature of the parent/child relationship, but cannot be reduced to some fact about the value of consequences.[16]

There is considerable irony in the fact that two such radically different views about what makes an act right can appeal to the same intuitions as support. The relativistic consequentialist takes special relationships to create, in most cases, special obligations, but these obligations derive from the *contingent* fact that special relationships generate special concern, concern that will be reflected in the assignment of intrinsic value to certain consequences. The deontologist, on the other hand, agrees that special relationships create special obligations, but holds that these special obligations are generated by the relationships, in and of themselves, independently of contingent facts about psychological states.[17] What the two views have in common is that they give a prominent place to agent-relative reasons, either by denying that there are agent-neutral reasons or by holding that agent-relative reasons are not necessarily subordinate to agent-neutral reasons. When one sees the advantages of these two views over their competitors, one can see that the special obligations objection brings into stark relief a fundamental philosophical choice with respect to moral theory. The choice of a theory of right action seems to hinge on the acceptability or plausibility of a radically relativistic conception of intrinsic value.

Notes

1   See, for example, Bernard Williams' rather cryptic suggestions about the implications of the objection at the end of his "Persons, Character, and Morality", in *Moral Luck* (Cambridge: Cambridge University Press, 1981), pp. 18–19.

2   This is, of course, a definition that limits consequentialism to act consequentialism. Act consequentialism is our primary focus; however, we will briefly consider rule consequentialism in section 3.2 below.

3   See, for example, the discussion in Richard Fumerton, *Reason and Morality* (Ithaca: Cornell University Press, 1990).

4 So, for example, some causal effects of Jane's running 26.2 miles are Jane's getting tired and thirsty, Jane's friends being impressed, etc. But, a logical implication of Jane's running 26.2 miles is Jane's running of a marathon, because to run 26.2 miles just is to run a marathon.

5 So G. E. Moore's view would not, given our definition, be a utilitarian view, although it is, of course, a consequentialist view. See *Principia Ethica* (Cambridge: Cambridge University Press, 1903), esp. chapters 5 and 6.

6 For discussions that attempt to flesh out what exposure to relevant facts and vivid imagining consist in, see Richard Brandt, *A Theory of the Right and the Good* (Oxford: Clarendon Press, 1979), and Stephen Darwall, *Impartial Reason* (Ithaca: Cornell University Press, 1983).

It is unlikely that a subjective relativist will straightforwardly identify x's being instrumentally valuable for S with S's valuing x. From now on, whenever we speak of "value", we mean "intrinsic value", unless we indicate otherwise.

7 We say "in part" to allow for the effects of adjusting for probability. See note 3 above.

8 See Henry Sidgwick, *The Methods of Ethics* (Indianapolis: Hackett Publishing Co, 1981), pp. 241ff., and John Stuart Mill, *Utilitarianism* (Indianapolis: Hackett Publishing Co, 1979), p. 59.

9 See David Lyons, *Forms and Limits of Utilitarianism* (Oxford: Clarendon Press, 1965), chapter 4, and J. J. C. Smart, "An Outline of a System of Utilitarian Ethics", in *Utilitarianism: For and Against* with Bernard Williams (Cambridge: Cambridge University Press, 1973), pp. 9–12.

10 As we have said, there are more complex alternatives. As with act utilitarianism, the relevant consequences can be actual, probable, or possible, and if one moves from actual consequences one will again need some mechanism for adjusting the values assigned to consequences. Following a rule can be construed as succeeding or as trying to succeed in following that rule.

11 Of course, a consequentialist might warn against taking *any* intuitions very seriously, particularly intuitions about unrealistic hypothetical cases.

See, for example, R. M. Hare, "Ethical Theory and Utilitarianism", in *Utilitarianism and Beyond* ed. by A. K. Sen and Bernard Williams (Cambridge: Cambridge University Press, 1982), and J. J. C. Smart, "An Outline of a System of Utilitarian Ethics", in *Utilitarianism: For and Against* with Bernard Williams (Cambridge: Cambridge University Press, 1973), pp. 67ff. We leave aside such worries.

12 For examples of attempts to deal with the special obligations objection by adjustments in the theory of value, see David Brink, *Moral Realism and the Foundations of Ethics* (Cambridge: Cambridge University Press, 1989), pp. 264ff., and Peter Railton, "Alienation, Consequentialism, and the Demands of Morality", in *Ethical Theory* ed. Louis Pojman (Belmont, CA: Wadsworth Publishing Co., 1995), pp. 209–26.

13 For a defense of relativistic consequentialism, see Fumerton, *Reason and Morality*.

14 Not all deontological views will avoid some version of the "special obligations" objection. For example, there are obvious worries about how Kant could accommodate such obligations.

15 One may have a *prima facie* obligation to save one's own child, but such obligations will not always be one's all-things-considered obligation. If the consequences of not saving one's child are valuable enough, one's *Prima facie* obligation may be outweighed by competing considerations.

16 For a discussion of how such a deontological view can be motivated by a psychological reductionist conception of personal identity, see Diane Jeske, "Persons, Compensation, and Utilitarianism" *The Philosophical Review* October 1993: pp. 541–75. The view developed there shares some structural features with that developed by Thomas Nagel in *The View From Nowhere* (Oxford: Oxford University Press, 1986).

17 So the deontologist can hold that we ought to have, as one of our ends, the formation of special relationships, whereas the relativistic consequentialist will not be able to make any claims about what our final ends ought to be. Adopting a deontological view allows one the option of retaining a non-relativistic conception of intrinsic value.

36

Families, Friends, and Special Obligations

Diane Jeske

Most of us accept that we have special obligations to our family members: to, e.g., our parents, our siblings, and our grandparents. But it is extremely difficult to offer a plausible grounding for such obligations, given the apparent fact that (at least most) familial relationships are not voluntarily entered.[1] I did not choose to be my mother's daughter or my brother's sister, so why suppose that such facts about me are morally significant? Why suppose that I owe more to my mother or to my brother than natural duty requires that I do for all and any persons? Special obligations appear more problematic the less the relationships that supposedly generate them are akin to the relationship between promiser and promisee, a voluntarily assumed relationship. Thus, for example, special obligations to friends might appear less problematic than do those to family members, because it seems that we voluntarily choose our friends, and, thus, voluntarily choose to bear more for them than natural duty requires.

In light of these considerations, it seems that there are two options: given that familial relationships do not fit the model of the voluntary relation between promisee and promiser, we can deny that we have special obligations to family members (or claim that such apparently special obligations are really derived from our natural obligations are really derived from our natural duties[2]), or we can claim that familial relationships, in virtue of their unique character, generate obligations even though they are not voluntarily entered. While the first option, given the strength of our intuitions about familial obligations, should only be adopted as a last resort, the second, I will argue, has highly unattractive implications that we would do well to avoid.

I will argue that we do have special obligations to family members, but that such special obligations are not grounded by anything distinctive about familial relationships as such. Once we see the underlying rationale for taking the relation between promisee and promiser as the model of a special obligation-generating relationship, we will see that familial relations can, and often do, fit that model. Although we cannot reduce familial obligations to instances of promise-keeping, we can assimilate the former to the latter: relationships between family members are often relevantly similar to, although far more complex than the relationship between promisee and promiser, and, in both cases, it is the special relationship between the obligee and the obligor that grounds the special obligations. But, I will argue, the facts about familial relationships that ground special obligations have nothing to do with the biological relationship between the parties to the relationship or with cultural or social expectations or

Diane Jeske, "Families, Friends, and Special Obligations." *Canadian Journal of Philosophy* 28, no. 4 (December 1998), pp. 527–56. © 1997 by Philosophical Studies. Reprinted by permission of the University of Calgary Press.

traditions. The facts about relationships to family members that ground special obligations are facts that also characterize friendships or other intimate relationships.

I. Special Obligations and Special Relationships

First, we need to give a characterization of special obligations as opposed to natural duties, where natural duties are understood to be 'moral requirements which apply to all men irrespective of status or of acts performed . . . These duties are owed by all persons to all others.'[3] Because some of the philosophers that I will discuss use 'role obligation,' or 'special obligation' when referring to moral requirements that are acquired in a non-voluntary manner, I do not want to contrast special obligations with natural duties by defining the former as moral requirements acquired through some voluntary action of the obligor – whether they are so acquired is precisely what is at issue.[4] So I want to define 'special obligation' in a way that contrasts such obligations with natural duties while still leaving open whether such moral requirements are voluntarily acquired.[5]

We can understand special obligations as obligations that are owed not to all persons, but to some limited class of persons, where the fundamental justification for the having of such obligations is not the intrinsic nature of the obligee as such, or, at least, not only the intrinsic nature of the obligee. So, for example, consider my duty to throw a life preserver to a drowning person. I am morally required to throw the life preserver to a limited class of persons, namely the class consisting of the person in the river, but the fundamental justification for my having that duty is the nature of the person to whom the duty is owed – she is a rational being – and her nature is sufficient to ground the duty. My proximity to the drowning person *facilitates* my being able to fulfill my duty of mutual aid, but it is not part of the fundamental explanation of why I have such a duty in the first place. So it is the nature of the action, i.e. saving a rational being, that renders that action morally required.

Consider, on the other hand, my obligation to pay you the ten dollars that I promised to give to you. The fundamental explanation of why I have

an obligation to pay you ten dollars is not solely in terms of your rational nature and does not involve the intrinsic character of the action of giving ten dollars to rational beings.[6] My relation to you, i.e., the fact that I made a promise to you, does not simply facilitate my fulfilling some more general duty, but, rather, provides part of the constitutive explanation of why I have that obligation. Your nature and the nature of the action of giving you ten dollars are not sufficient to explain why I have the obligation to give you ten dollars.[7]

Special obligations of promise-keeping, then, are grounded by the special relationship between promiser and promisee. Another important class of special obligations, those that we have to our intimates, are also, I will argue, grounded by the special relationships in which we stand to our intimates.[8] Of course, the content of such obligations is less determinate than the content of those special obligations that result from the making of a promise.[9] But, like obligations of promise-keeping, our special obligations to care for our intimates result from the special character of our relationships to the obligees, not simply from the character of our intimates and the character of the actions involved in caring for them. Relations between friends and relations between family members are partly constituted by various forms of interaction, mutual attitudes, and intimacy, and, once we stand in such relations to other persons, we are obligated to promote their interests in ways and degrees in which we are not obligated to promote the interests of persons who are not intimately related to us. (My task in section III, where I present my own account of obligations to family members, will be to show why such relationships generate obligations.)

A defense of this view of the nature and source of familial obligations faces two obstacles. First, as I will point out in the next section, grounding special obligations on relationships of intimacy can appear much more problematic than grounding special obligations on relationships such as that between promisee and promiser. This worry about familial obligations as arising from relations of intimacy is what I will call the voluntarist challenge.[10] Second, the view that I have very briefly sketched assimilates familial obligations to obligations of friendship: both arise as a result of relationships of intimacy. Even if special obligations do supervene upon relationships of intimacy, some philosophers want to argue that special familial obligations, in particular those between parent and child, have a different source than do special obligations of friendship (although there can also, they grant, be obligations of friendship between parents and, at least adult, children).[11] And, in so arguing, such philosophers are following commonsense moral thinking, which seems to regard familial bonds as creating, by their nature as *familial*, special obligations, whereas my account finds something common to friendships and familial relations which generates special obligations. So there are two important challenges to the view that special familial obligations supervene on relationships of intimacy, one a general worry about the possibility of special obligations being grounded by such relations, the other a more specific worry about the nature of familial obligations.

II. The Voluntarist Challenge and the Deflationary Response

Promise-keeping appears to many to be an unproblematic type of special obligation. The making of a promise is a voluntary action: the relation of promiser to promisee is one that is freely entered. When the promise is not voluntary, it is not a genuine promise, or, it fails to generate obligations. So obligations of promise-keeping are ones that we assume explicitly and voluntarily. If we did not assume such obligations voluntarily, why should we suppose that we have greater obligations to our promisees than we have to others, given that our promisees do not have greater moral significance? The appeal of *voluntarism*, the thesis that the only way that we can acquire special obligations is through some voluntary action (or actions), a voluntary action (or actions) which we know or ought to know signals the assumption of special obligations, is revealed when we consider worries about, for example, obligations of fair play or gratitude. If someone thrusts benefits upon me, do I have special obligations to play a certain part in a cooperative scheme or to repay my benefactor in some way? Many would say: only if there was a possibility of my refusing the benefits; in other words, only if we can construe my acceptance of

the benefits as voluntary, and I could or should have known the implications of my acceptance of those benefits.[12]

Given the appeal of the voluntarist thesis, we can see why special obligations other than promise-keeping (and other sorts of clearly contractual obligations) appear difficult to justify, and why the difficulty of justifying them appears proportional to the extent to which the relations that allegedly generate them differ from the relation of promise-making. Thus, justifying special obligations of friendship seems more straightforward than does justifying special familial obligations. After all, it seems that persons choose their friends in ways that they do not choose their parents or siblings. And it seems that persons, when they are benefited by friends, are in positions to refuse the benefits, whereas this is not the case in many instances of benefits received from family members, in particular in the case of benefits conferred by parents upon their children. Thus, although special obligations of friendship seem able to satisfy the voluntarist – if we construe friendship as involving the voluntary generating of expectations, the making of promises, implicit or explicit, and the voluntary receipt of benefits – special obligations to family members, given the apparently nonvoluntary nature of such relations, remain highly suspect if we accept voluntarism.

One possible response to the voluntarist thesis is what I will call the deflationary response concerning special familial obligations. The deflationist argues that since special familial obligations do not straightforwardly satisfy the voluntarist thesis (i.e. they do not result from 'morally obligating voluntary acts (or series of acts),' such as promises or the signing of contracts), then, if they are genuine moral requirements it must be because they represent 'the way that we can most fully discharge a natural moral duty.'[13] Given that it is difficult to construe family obligations as resulting from an act or series of acts that constitute promises, contracts, or the voluntary acceptance of benefits, according to the deflationist view familial obligations are only justified if acting in accord with such obligations is the best way for persons to fulfill other, more general duties, such as, for example, their imperfect duties of charity.[14]

We can notice that according to the deflationary account our relationships to our family

members no longer provide part of the fundamental or constitutive explanation of why we
have the obligations to them that we do have.
Rather, our relationships to our family members
simply facilitate our capacity to fulfill our duties
to persons more generally. So, according to the
deflationary account, familial relationships provide what we can think of as *extrinsic* rather
than *intrinsic* grounds for special obligations.
The relationships, in and of themselves, provide
no grounds for the obligations. Rather, we have
the same duties to our family members as we have
to all persons, and the relationships we have to
family are instrumental in our being best able to
fulfill certain imperfect duties to persons generally. A utilitarian account of special obligations
to family members is a paradigm deflationary
account which reveals the worry about such
accounts: if obligations to family members are
really just instances of duties to promote the
good, then such obligations are always overridden when we can promote more good by failing
to act on such obligations. But it seems that we
are justified in acting to benefit family members
even if, by acting otherwise, we could have promoted more overall good (the same, of course,
seems to hold for the keeping of promises, as
has been pointed out by many philosophers).
Of course, rule- and motive-utilitarians make
concerted attempts to deal with these sorts of
difficulties, but the problems with such accounts
are well-known.[15]

Thus, the deflationary account should, I think,
only be accepted if we can find no plausible
account of familial obligations which renders
relations between family members intrinsic to
their justification; in other words, we should
not so quickly abandon the claim that special
familial obligations are genuinely special obligations. We can avoid the deflationary reduction
of apparently special familial obligations to
instances of natural duty by either (i) showing
how familial relations can meet the voluntarist
requirement, or (ii) rejecting the voluntarist
requirement. I will begin by presenting my own
account which, I will argue, satisfies the voluntarist thesis without reducing familial obligations
to instances of contractual obligations or of
natural duty. My account, however, does not
accommodate various commonsense intuitions
about familial obligations. Thus, I will, finally,

consider and reject various attempts to defend
familial obligations through a rejection of the
voluntarist thesis, attempts that seem to offer
better hopes of accommodating a wider range
of intuitions. The accounts that I will consider
attempt to ground such obligations on something
distinctive about familial relations as opposed to
other sorts of relationships.

III. Familial Obligations and Voluntarism

Although reducing obligations of friendship to
instances of contractual obligations can, given
the voluntary nature of friendships, appear, at least
initially, to be a plausible enterprise, the hopes
of any such reduction of familial obligations are
slim. As I have already pointed out, familial relationships seem to stand in sharp contrast to both
contractual relations and friendship relations in
so far as we do not choose our parents or siblings.
So, if we are to accommodate the voluntarist
thesis while avoiding a deflationary account, we
need to show that familial obligations, while not
instances of promise-keeping, nonetheless have the
same underlying grounds as do the latter sorts
of obligations, and thereby meet the voluntarist
requirement. Before offering my own account,
I will briefly consider an attempt to assimilate
familial obligations to obligations to keep promises
that fails, but which reveals, in its failure, what
must be done to meet the voluntarist challenge.

1. The appeal to expectations

One way to proceed is to show that both the institutions of promise-making and the institutions
of the family (and interactions between friends)
create expectations between the various participants in such institutions. As Christina Hoff
Sommers argues,

> Given the conventions of the practice of promise
> making, the moral patient has novel and legit-
> imate expectations of performances caused by the
> explicit assurances given by the promiser, who,
> in effect, has made over these performances to the
> promisee. And given these legitimate expectations,
> the agent's nonperformance of the promised act
> is invasive and tantamount to active interference
> with the patient's rights to its performance.[16]

So special obligations are generated by certain types of interaction (promising/being promised, befriending/being befriended, nurturing/being nurtured) that, given the social context 'give rise to certain conventional expectations (e.g. that a promise will be kept, that a marital partner will be faithful, that a child will respect the parent)' (Sommers 446).

Even if the account of promising offered by Sommers (and borrowed from Melden) were correct, it would still falter when extended to familial relationships. If I promise to give you ten dollars, it is *I, the obligor*, who have raised the expectations in you, the obligee, through my voluntary action. It is true that parents, for example, expect certain things from their adult children. The children, however, might respond: it is not *I, the alleged obligor*, who raised the expectations of my parents; rather, my parents expected something from me because of certain societal conventions in which I was not free to avoid implication. In the case of promising, it is some action of the *obligor* (against the background of a social custom regulating the utterance of 'I promise such-and-such') which raises the expectation. But in the case of parenting, it seems that we are supposed to think that expectations are raised through the actions of the *obligee* or through the mere existence of some societal conventions absent the voluntary participation of the alleged obligor.

Sommers's account is instructive in so far as it shows that any attempt to propitiate the voluntarist must focus on the *obligor*. Any appeal to expectations or roles that are beyond the control of the agent is a rejection of voluntarism (I will consider such accounts in section IV below). This throws us back to the problem that familial relations do not appear voluntary. But, I will suggest, appearances are misleading: while familial relations as such are unchosen, relationships of intimacy between family members are not, and it is these relations which ground special obligations between family members.

2. The appeal to autonomy

Recall the voluntarist thesis: the only way that we can acquire special obligations is through some voluntary action which we know or ought to know signals the assumption of such obligations.

I suggest that the voluntarist is motivated by a worry about the autonomy of the agents who are supposedly bound by special obligations. If I have not voluntarily committed myself to doing more for you than natural duty requires, then why suppose that I am obligated to do so just because I have landed in practices or institutions over which I have no control? The individual should be free to develop projects and plans, to mold her own life in whatever ways she chooses, within the bounds of what is required of her by natural duty, i.e. within the bounds set by the fundamental nature of other moral agents. Just because something is expected of me does not imply that I am obligated to comply. Familial institutions, however, do seem to be constraints placed upon us without our choice, and, therefore, familial demands appear to be paradigm instances of unjustified restrictions of the individual's autonomy.

Friendship, on the other hand, seems to be an instance of a relationship that individuals choose to enter and to maintain. Thus, obligations of friendship seem to be able to meet the voluntarist challenge because they are not infringements of but, rather, expressions of the individual's autonomy: friendships are part of freely chosen life plans and projects. But this dichotomy between the character of friendships and the character of familial relationships is too simplistic: both types of relationships are far more complex than they seem at first glance. Once we see that although obligations of friendship can meet the voluntarist challenge, but that they do so in a far more complex way than the above account suggests, we will be in a better position to see how familial obligations can meet the voluntarist challenge.[17] So, before we can address familial obligations, we need to spend some time examining the nature of friendship.

First, we need to notice that persons do not enter friendships in single discrete acts such as those involved in making a promise or a contract. It is even difficult to construe friendships as entered in a clearly identifiable series of such actions. Persons become friends after a certain amount of interaction of a particular sort, interaction that involves expressed concern, self-revelation, and, more simply, shared activities. But the sorts of interactions which, taken together, constitute a friendship are not such that any one of them need be morally significant in itself; for example, one or two expressions of concern will not constitute a friendship, nor will one or two revealing conversations. And it is not always an easy matter to determine whether two persons are friends. For example, at what point does a collegial relation develop into a friendship? Is the person whom one plays tennis with twice a week a friend? In trying to answer these types of questions, persons reflect on the nature of their interactions and the sort of intimacy that exists between them. Friendships are constituted by complex clusters of actions and attitudes, they are relationships of intimacy and expressed concern.

Now return to the voluntarist worry, which, I have suggested, is a worry about leaving persons space to develop projects and plans and to sustain their personal commitments. What the example of friendship shows is that commitments and projects are not always explicitly adopted in the way that promises are made. It is misleading to speak of making a friend, as though the making of a friendship is as simple as making a promise. I can find myself deeply committed to someone's well-being without ever having made any specific indication or expression of that commitment, either to that person or to myself. Friendships are different from marriages in not involving any specific vows or statements of commitment that clearly delineate to the persons involved the nature of their relationship and of their mutual expectations. (Of course, some friends may make such explicit statements, but they are usually made in order to state already existent facts about the relationship, as when friends say, 'You know that you can always come to me for help,' or 'I'll always be behind you.')

The voluntarist, however, will press in the following way: if the commitment was not voluntarily developed, then resultant obligations will reflect an infringement of the individual's autonomy. Further, if friendships are developed in the ways that I have suggested, can we really suppose that persons know that their actions signal the assumption of special obligations? First, let us ask, are friendships entered voluntarily? It is true that we are often thrust into the situations that lead to the formation of friendships: think of colleagues, college roommates, etc. But we can control what happens once we are thrust into those situations; after all, many colleagues or roommates never become friends. Friendship demands intimacy, where the intimacy involved cannot be forced.[18] A captor or someone observing my behavior for scientific purposes might come to know a great deal about me. But genuine intimacy demands, besides a history of causal interaction, a revealing of a person's self-understanding, and it demands a mutuality of such revelations. Thus, given that friendships are partly constituted by genuine intimacy, they are relationships that are voluntary.

Nonetheless, since the revelations and interactions that make an intimate relationship require time and many interactions – one conversation cannot a friendship make – the type of choice involved in friendship is not simple: choosing to make friends with someone is not like choosing to say 'I promise.' But notice that such complex choice is involved in most of the projects that are central to our lives: my choice to be a philosopher was not a simple one, made when I chose my college major or graduate school program – it is a choice involving self-definition, a choice the content and implications of which may only have become clear after many years. Similarly, consider a commitment to a social cause: such commitments often arise over time, as the result of series of reflections and various encounters. If the voluntarist is worried about leaving space to develop projects and commitments, she needs to look at how actual commitments and projects are developed. Since major life plans or commitments are not chosen in the straightforward way that promises are made, we need to cease to view the type of choice involved in promises and contracts as paradigmatic of the type that is expressive of autonomy. Relationships between promisees and promisers are the objects of simple choices, and, thus, the resultant obligations do not violate the promiser's autonomy. Intimate relationships are the objects of complex choices, and for that reason, resultant obligations do not violate the autonomy of the persons involved.

Thus, once we understand the underlying concern of the voluntarist, we can cease to focus on simple choice as always creating the special relationships that ground special obligations. Genuine intimacy cannot be coerced but neither can it be chosen in a single discrete act, comparable to saying 'I promise.' Intimacy is an achievement requiring effort and long interaction. But why suppose that once such intimacy exists, persons have special obligations to one another? Also, how do we determine the content of such obligations? In promising it is easy to answer the latter question, because, in choosing my relation with my promisee, I thereby also choose the content of my obligation. Given the complex choice involved in friendship, what do friends owe one another? This question leads us back also to a previous question: can persons be expected to know that the actions that ultimately constitute a friendship signal the assumption of special obligations?

In order to see why friendship relations ground obligations, it is important to recognize the peculiar character of the project or commitment that friendship is. It is a project that, unlike, for example, my project to be a philosopher, necessarily or essentially involves a specific other person. In fact, for me to be successful in fulfilling my project, it must be the case that that other person has a project involving me.[19] Friendship is, thus, what we can call a 'mutual project.' And, after a certain amount of time, it can be said to be *our* project rather than simply each of our projects individually.[20] Genuine intimacy demands such mutuality and reciprocity. So after a friendship is established, each friend has a project that essentially involves the other and demands her continued participation.[21] Whereas other projects sometimes create moral permissions, but not moral requirements, for agents to pursue the projects at the cost of the general interest, friendship creates obligations, types of moral requirements, to continue to care and to sustain intimacy,[22] because of its essentially shared character. Of course, in order to realize such facts, agents must reflect on the nature of friendship, or they will fail to recognize their obligations. But the shared character of friendship does not take much reflection to discern: persons can be expected to know that, when they develop an intimate relationship with another person, they have developed a shared project. Thus, while the voluntary nature of the friendship renders the demands placed on the parties in conformity with the requirement of voluntarism, it is the shared character of the project of an intimate relationship that creates the demands to continue to care and to sustain the project.[23]

To summarize: the voluntarist is worried about voluntary choice of commitments because she is concerned to protect a sphere of autonomous action wherein an agent can develop projects and plans. But when we look at friendship, a project that is central to many persons' lives and one of the most valuable that persons can develop, we see that the type of choice involved is far from straightforward. Intimacy, the core of friendships, cannot be chosen in a single, discrete act. But intimacy can ground obligations in so far as it is a mutual project that is expressive of the parties' autonomy: its mutual character is what generates obligations rather than permissions and the fact that genuine intimacy cannot be coerced is what undermines the voluntarist worry about special obligations of friendship.

It is clear why such an account of friendship opens the way to a parallel account of familial relationships. The difficulty with assimilating the two types of relationships arises when we try to assimilate both straightforwardly to the model of promises and contracts and try to see familial relationships *as such* as chosen. What is chosen, in a complex way, is a particular sort of relationship with a family member. Through biological chance or other circumstances we find ourselves involved in myriad causal interactions with family members. For many of us, these interactions are mutually caring and intimate. Often, just as in friendships, we have to reflect before we become aware of the nature of the intimacy that exists between ourselves and our family members, and we have little if any choice about the circumstances that lead to or are likely to result in the development of the relationship. Nonetheless, as we noticed with respect to friendship, these facts do not preclude the actions that constitute the relationship being themselves a matter of choice. Again, the type of choice involved is not simple as in promises and contracts, but there is no reason to take such instances of choice as the only genuine instances.[24]

But there are important differences between many familial relationships and friendships that seem to threaten my attempt to assimilate the two. With respect to siblings, parents, and, often, grandparents, we find ourselves in circumstances which necessitate interaction and, with respect to parents and grandparents, we are dependent upon them for care. As adults, we can, even in close quarters, simply refuse to do what is necessary for the development of a friendship: we can keep our emotional distance from colleagues or even roommates. But, as children, it might seem that we are forced, through our dependency, into intimate relationships with certain other persons, and we are not free to change our circumstances so as to avoid this dependency. Further, intimacy between, for example, parents and children, seems far from mutual: even when children do confide in their parents, it is rare for parents to reveal themselves to their children. So the intimacy between parents and children seems to be one of mutual interaction without any mutual self-revelations. Parental obligations to children, of course, can be construed as voluntarily assumed (but see note 1 above). But what about children's obligations to parents? These facts about dependency and lack of mutuality seem to undermine the assimilation to friendship.

It is true that the nature of intimacy that develops between, for example, siblings, is often based on knowledge about one another that could not be avoided given the conditions under which the siblings were raised. Similarly, the intimate knowledge that parents have of children is something which is necessitated by the dependence of the children. These facts create reasons to develop genuinely intimate relationships with both siblings and parents: relationships between adult children and parents and between adult siblings can realize forms of value that cannot be realized in any other way. The type of unconditional love that we can receive from parents ought not to be lightly disposed of.[25] And the type of history that we share with siblings can form the basis of peculiarly understanding interactions – the ability to deal with the foibles and eccentricities of others can be greatly enhanced by knowing how they were raised. Often such facts naturally lead persons to develop such relationships, so familial roles are often correlated with the types of relationships that generate special obligations. But they are not always so correlated. If genuine intimacy does not develop between adult children and parents or between adult siblings,[26] then adults do not have special obligations to parents or to siblings. Of course, there may be utilitarian reasons to care for those biologically related to us, but, as I pointed out above, such utilitarian reasons do not constitute genuinely special obligations, and can be overridden by competing utilitarian concerns, whereas genuinely special obligations can (but do not always) override utilitarian reasons. Thus, the mere fact of a biological relationship does not ground any special obligations.

This is the place at which many will balk at my account. I have not tied familial obligations to anything distinctive about familial relations, so there is always a real possibility that siblings will have no special obligations to one another, and, perhaps even more worrisome, that adult children will have no special obligations to parents, even if those parents have faithfully cared for them throughout their years of dependency. So, even if I have offered an account of special obligations to family members, I have not offered an account of distinctively *familial* obligations.

But, as I indicated above, special features of familial roles make intimacy and shared concern achievable in unique and peculiarly valuable forms. With no one but our siblings can we achieve the sort of understanding based on sharing the same upbringing. From no one but our parents can we receive unconditional love and support. These are facts, however, that hold only for certain familial relationships. Even in less than abusive situations, parents often are unable to let go of their roles of authority, thereby precluding any intimacy between them and their adult children. Thus, in order to live their own lives, such adult children begin to distance themselves from their parents. Similarly, siblings often become simply too different to be able to interact or communicate in any sort of effective manner. In such relationships, there are no mutual projects, and, thus, no special obligations. Such situations are usually highly unfortunate, but they do arise. In the next section, I will show the sorts of unattractive results we get if we attempt to ground familial obligations on something distinctive about biology or familial roles as such. As I said above, my account is counterintuitive in certain ways, but I will show why intuitions can be dangerous if we allow them to lead us blindly.

Also, we need to be wary of trying to find in relationships with family members the type of intimacy that we have with friends made in our adulthood. We often share common interests with the latter, and these interests form the basis of the friendship. Intimacy with parents is very different from that sort of intimacy: it is an intimacy often based on the longest shared history that we could possibly have with anyone. So in assimilating friendships with familial relations I do not want to obscure the differences between them: doing so could only cause confusion in trying to sort out what we owe to our various intimates. The nature of the relationship is what will determine the content of our obligations: what we must do in each case is to care for our intimates, because caring for them and promoting their interests is necessary for the sustaining of the project of friendship, but, in order to care for them, we must be attentive to their needs and interests and the context of the friendship.

Many people, however, will be uncomfortable with a view that denies that children have obligations to parents simply in virtue of the goods that parents typically bestow on their children. One popular account (see note 12 above) of obligations of adult children to parents is an appeal to obligations of gratitude for benefits received. More generally, however, one could claim that interactions between persons create obligations when such interactions involve the realization or conferring of goods of various sorts, or the shared endurance of harms. So, for example, adult children have obligations to parents because of their interactions which involved the parents conferring large benefits upon the children. Siblings have a history of helping one another, or, in abusive contexts, have a shared history of enduring harms from their parents. Of course, many non-familial relationships also then generate obligations as a result of a history of realizing or conferring goods or sharing harms. But familial relationships, given precisely the features that seem to create difficulties for my account, namely the forced dependency of children and enforced interaction of siblings, create unique opportunities for the realization or conferring of goods, and so will generate obligations in a reliable way. Such a view has the virtue of appealing to actual interactions between family members, and also has the virtue of appealing to a feature that many commonly associate with familial relations, namely, the realization of goods. According to such a view, it is irrelevant that we do not choose our family circumstances; rather, the fact that such circumstances create unique opportunities for sharing or realizing goods is sufficient to render

them circumstances which tend to give rise to special obligations.

While the realization of goods or sharing of harms can be important factors in developing and sustaining an intimate, loving relationship, and thus have a role to play in my account, I want to deny that a one-sided conferring of goods, as in the parent-young child relationship, is sufficient to generate special obligations, whether we appeal to gratitude or to some other account. Further, I want to deny that the realization or conferring of goods is necessary for the generation of special obligations. To begin with the latter point, consider friendships that begin as a result of the parties to the friendship being involved in immoral or trivial activities. Such persons can become very close and very committed to one another's well-being. As their relationship develops, then, they develop obligations to care for one another. Such concern may demand, whether they realize it or not, an attempt to change the nature of their shared and/or individual activities. They must be open to each other's needs and interests and such needs and interests may be at variance with actual subjective ends. Similarly, families are not always successful in realizing or conferring goods, particularly in difficult circumstances, or the members of a family may not realize what is necessary to promote each other's well-being. But as intimate, committed relationships develop between the members of such a family, they have special obligations to promote each other's well-being, no matter how inept or unsuccessful they have been at doing so in the past.

But what about the case where parents *are* successful in conferring large benefits (education, nourishment, moral training, etc.) upon their children? Shouldn't that be sufficient to generate special obligations for the children to care for their parents later in life? Of course, benefits that are voluntarily accepted, such as a college education, can create obligations. But what about the benefits conferred upon children at an age when they are unable to refuse the benefits or to know the implications of accepting such benefits? The difficulty with considering such cases is that parents who bestow such benefits usually love their children in ways that naturally lead to close and loving relationships later in life, and in such cases we think that children owe their parents a great deal. But consider a case where material benefits are bestowed on a child throughout her dependency, and then, when she reaches her adulthood, her parents focus all of their energy upon other pursuits, indicating that they think that they have done their duty by their offspring and can now focus on other endeavors. The child naturally develops other relationships, focusing her energies on persons with whom she is intimate. Does she have special obligations to care for her parents, given the benefits that they bestowed on her? I am inclined to think that she does not, given that she could not refuse the benefits and given that the benefits did not contribute to an intimate relationship. Again, utilitarian considerations may demand that we reciprocate with respect to good done to us, in order to insure that persons have motivation to do good, but the receipt of such goods does not generate genuinely special obligations.

Of course, more could be said concerning accounts that appeal to the realization of goods within relationships.[27] Such accounts, however, provide alternative models of obligations within both friendship and familial contexts; thus, they are in agreement with my account with respect to the claim that special obligations to family members, including parents, are not based on anything distinctive about familial relationships as such. But commonsense seems to regard us as having special *familial* obligations, where the very nature of familial bonds is the source of the obligations. So I want to now turn to consider views that are in agreement with commonsense on this point.

IV. Biology and Roles: Some Rejections of Voluntarism

When attempting to ground familial obligations on something distinctive about familial bonds as such, two routes immediately present themselves: one can appeal to biology or one can appeal to social roles and the nature of the social institution of the family.

1. The appeal to biology

I will not consider in any detail evolutionary ethics. One project that we can understand the evolutionary ethicist as pursuing is the determination of the genesis of our moral beliefs and practices.[28] Evolutionary ethicist Michael Ruse, for example, denies that there is any 'reasoned justification for ethics in the sense of foundations to which one can appeal in reasoned argument. All one can offer is a causal argument to show why we hold ethical beliefs.'[29] But showing how or why human beings may have developed the feeling of obligation to relatives neither supports nor undermines the claim that family members do have special obligations to one another, and it certainly cannot undermine attempts to offer 'reasoned justifications' of our ethical beliefs. However, rather than pursuing this issue, I want to consider the possibility of taking biology as a starting point for a reasoned ethical argument concerning obligations to family members.

Recall that I characterized natural duties as duties owed to all persons, where the fundamental justification or grounds for the having of such obligations is the intrinsic nature of persons, such as, perhaps, their rational nature. The difficulty with special obligations, I suggested, arises, in part, from the fact that they cannot be justified solely by reference to the nature of persons; rather, we must appeal to some contingent relationship holding between the obligee and the obligor. And, if that relationship is not voluntary in the way that contractual relationships are, then we run right into the voluntarist worry about individual autonomy.

A response to the way that I have set up this issue, a response that has become familiar in recent years, is to suggest that certain sorts of relationships are not contingent, that they, in fact, are at least partly constitutive of the self. Thus, the conception of a person's essential moral nature as involving only, say, rationality, is, it is said, far too thin a conception of the nature of persons. The voluntarist appears to deny the possibility or moral significance of what Michael Sandel has called 'constitutive attachments':

> But we cannot regard ourselves as independent in this way without great cost to those loyalties and convictions whose moral force consists partly in the fact that living by them is inseparable from understanding ourselves as the particular persons we are – as members of this family or community or nation or people. . . . Allegiances

such as these ... go beyond the obligations I voluntarily incur and the "natural duties" I owe to human beings as such ... [because] taken together [they] partly define the person I am.[30]

Raymond A. Belliotti follows Sandel in arguing that 'we have moral requirements of a special sort to those who contribute to and help nurture our identities, and those whose attachment is essential for our self-understanding.'[31] Belliotti claims that since the genetic contribution of parents plays a large part in constituting the identities of children, adult children have moral requirements to care for parents, even if parents and their adult children have not developed a relationship of intimacy. In fact, even abusive or absentee parents are owed at least prima facie obligations by their biological offspring.[32] Belliotti argues that 'if the acts of the self can create moral requirements (as is universally accepted), then the (other) constituents of self can also. Thus, as my biological parents' genetic [contribution] provides a most enduring aspect of who "I" am, I owe them certain moral requirements' (153).

Belliotti seems to be trying to show that if we accept the voluntarist thesis, then we must also accept that factors that contribute to our identity generate moral requirements:[33] 'if the *acts* of self create moral requirements, why cannot the self *itself* create moral requirements by its very nature' (153). So he rejects the voluntarist's claim that only voluntary acts of the agent can generate special obligations: facts that help to constitute the self can also generate moral requirements.

As Belliotti points out, such an appeal to biology has the implication that 'we owe more to those who are both biological and rearing parents than we do to parents who "only" rear us' (153). But we need to notice some of the implications of such a view. Suppose that a woman thought that she had been raised by her biological parents, and that she has developed an intimate relationship with those parents. She understands herself to have obligations to care for her parents, and she, thus, helps them when they need assistance, supports them in times of trouble, etc. On her thirtieth birthday, however, her 'parents' reveal to her that she was adopted as an infant, after being abandoned by her biological parents. Would this woman be justified in reassessing her obligations to her adoptive parents? Suppose

that she concludes that she owes them less than she had supposed, because they contributed nothing to her genetic make-up. This conclusion seems wrong. On the other hand, suppose that this woman decides that the lack of biological relationship matters not at all, and simply continues as before. According to Belliotti, it seems that we would have to criticize this woman for not attempting to find her biological parents (assuming that such could be done without extremely costly and time-consuming efforts). After all, she has moral requirements to those unknown biological parents, and so she must locate them in order to fulfill those requirements. Again, however, this just seems wrong. Even if the parents's genetic contribution was given with complete indifference to the resulting person, the adult child owes these strangers obligations.

Why should we accept all of these unattractive conclusions? I think that those who, like Belliotti, appeal to biology, are worried about the apparent implications of a view such as mine. Belliotti, for example, offers the following case:[34]

> Parent P sacrifices much in rearing child C. A relationship of love exists between them until C becomes 35 years old, at which point P and C become radically estranged. English [the Argument from Friendship – see note 17 above] maintains that C has no obligations (based on the parent-child relationship) to care for P when at age 70 P requires a variety of medical and other assistance. (151)

The force of this counterexample derives from its lack of detail. We are not told why 'P and C become radically estranged': was C angry about P's unwillingness to give her money for a vacation, or did P refuse to attend C's wedding because C was marrying a man of a different race? Just as with friendships, we are not always justified in ending intimate relationships with family members; thus, in the former case, C acts wrongly and does not thereby rid herself of her obligations to care for P later in life. In the latter case, however, if P, after reasonable efforts by C, cannot be brought to accept C's decision and C's new husband, then C is justified in ending her relationship with P. And why should the fact of genetic contribution generate any reasons for C to care for P later in life?

An even starker example is offered in the film *The Music Box*, in which an American woman, Ann, learns that her Hungarian immigrant father committed unthinkable acts of atrocity during the final months of World War II. When she confronts him with irrefutable evidence, he continues to deny his participation in the commission of war crimes, exhibiting a character with which she is completely unfamiliar. Ann turns her evidence over to the Justice Department. Suppose her father serves a prison term and later contacts her, asking for aid. My account yields that Ann has no special obligations to aid her father, not even prima facie ones based on biological connection. Do we really want to suppose that she does? Coming to grips with her biological connection to a man who tortured and killed hundreds of innocent people and who apparently enjoyed doing so would be a painful experience full of guilt, shame, and humiliation. Ann's father's lies and concealing of his actual character and past reveal his relationship to his daughter as a sham, and once that intimacy is destroyed or unmasked as unreal, she should cease to view herself as having any special obligations to him. Although this case is certainly extreme and uncommon, it serves to reveal why voluntarism is appealing: because Ann did not choose her biology, she is not morally constrained by it. Commonsense appeals to the moral import of the mere fact of the biological father/daughter relationship could only serve to cause Ann needless torment.

I do not want to deny that biology has some role to play in the story about the grounds of special obligations to parents (and to other family members). Genetics does influence who we become and intimacy is fostered when circumstances help us to understand ourselves. Reflecting on the ways that we are like our parents can contribute to our intimacy with them, and those likenesses might be the result of genetic predispositions. So it may be that such biology could help to form the basis of intimacy with unknown biological parents. But there are many people out there with whom we might become intimate, but we are not obligated to seek them all out and to acquire special obligations to them. Also, as the case of Ann shows, sometimes we need to distance ourselves from our biological relations and to forge identities for ourselves independent of such relations: Ann

would need to understand herself as not responsible for past acts simply in virtue of an unchosen biological relationship. The fact that we are the people we are in part because of biology is undeniable, but the voluntarist is right to focus upon the unchosen nature of biology: just because we cannot escape certain facts does not render such facts morally important.

2.   The appeal to roles

The mere fact of biological relationship seems insufficient to generate obligations, given that genetic contribution can occur in the absence of any interaction. But family seems to have, beyond its biological dimension, a social dimension. Social conventions generate particular understandings of social roles. But any appeal to such roles as the source of special familial obligations must overcome two challenges: (i) Why suppose that such roles generate obligations, given their unchosen character? and (ii) How do we deal with cases in which the circumstances of family are abusive, destructive, or stultifying?

Michael Hardimon, in his 'Role Obligations,'[35] offers an account of obligations attached to certain institutionally defined roles, namely 'political, familial, and occupational roles' (334), where a role is a '[constellation] of institutionally specified rights and duties organized around an institutionally specified social function' (334). He defines a role obligation as 'a moral requirement, which attaches to an institutional role, whose content is fixed by the function of the role, and whose normative force flows from the role' (334). Familial obligations, like political obligations, are what Hardimon calls noncontractual role obligations, and, as such, are

> in stark opposition to the familiar idea that the only way in which we can acquire role obligations – or, in any case, role obligations with genuine moral force – is by signing on for the roles to which they are attached. (343)

In other words, noncontractual role obligations violate the voluntarist thesis (what Hardimon calls the volunteer principle).

Hardimon claims that we ought to jettison the voluntarist thesis, the attractiveness of which stems, he claims, from 'the assumption that the alternatives of choice and impressment are exhaustive' (347). To be impressed into a social role would be to be forced into it against one's will, as sailors used to be impressed into service and were then expected to fulfill the obligations of their 'role.' Hardimon argues that for social roles such as daughter or sister, one is not impressed into the role, one is born into it, and, thus, one has not acquired it against one's will. We need not choose a social role for it to be true that we do not occupy it against our will. I did not choose to be my mother's daughter, but it is not the case that I am my mother's daughter against my will.

So which unchosen social roles into which we are born are such that they generate morally binding obligations? Hardimon's answer: social roles that are *reflectively acceptable*:

> To say that a social role is *reflectively acceptable* is to say that one would accept it upon reflection. Determining whether a given social role is reflectively acceptable involves stepping back from that role in thought and asking whether it is a role people ought to occupy and play. Determining that a given social role is reflectively acceptable involves judging that it is (in some sense) meaningful, rational, or good. (348)

Social roles can be reflectively acceptable even if people have never judged them to be so, so long as they would so judge them under relevant circumstances: 'in contrast to the volunteer principle [the voluntarist thesis], which calls for a form of *choice* that is actual, the ideal of reflective acceptability calls for a form of acceptance that is *hypothetical*' (348). Hardimon concludes that we should accept the *principle of reflective acceptability*: 'noncontractual role obligations are not morally binding unless the roles to which they attach are reflectively acceptable' (350).

Hardimon responds to both of the questions that I posed for views of the type he offers: (i) With respect to the question as to why we should suppose that unchosen roles can generate obligations, Hardimon responds by attempting to deflate the worries that seem to generate the voluntarist thesis, and he does this by contrasting birth with impressment. (ii) Hardimon's principle of reflective acceptability is his response to the worry about destructive or stultifying roles.

Hardimon's view, like the appeal to biology, has the advantage of appealing to something distinctive about family as generating familial obligations: Hardimon appeals to social roles as defined by the institution of the family.

But can we make sense of the family as an institution? Hardimon admits the difficulty here, but claims that whether or not we can understand families as institutions, 'we can speak of individual families as institutionally defined groups' (336) with 'institutionally defined' roles (336). With respect to certain familial roles such as that of parent of a minor, laws specify the obligations attached to the role (and, thus, perhaps, the rights attached to the role of child). But are the roles of, e.g., grandfather or sister institutionally defined, even in the sense of having legally specified rights or obligations? It seems not.

Now Hardimon could understand institutional roles as defined by the 'shared understandings' of a culture or society.[36] The capacity or function of a daughter or a sister would, then, be relative to one's culture. If this is what Hardimon has in mind, then it becomes clear why the worries of the voluntarist are pressing: why suppose that I have certain obligations simply because I am born into a certain social structure which regards me as having those obligations, given that the social structure into which I am born is completely beyond my control?[37]

At this point Hardimon has his principle of reflective acceptability to fall back on. He might say that the voluntarist worry seems pressing because of the worry about destructive or stultifying roles. But Hardimon holds that social roles generate obligations only within the limits set by the principle of reflective acceptability. One needs to ask about any social role, is it one that 'people ought to occupy and play'? Is it '(in some sense) meaningful, rational, or good'? In answering these questions, persons are to reflect first on the role as an 'abstract structure' and then reflect on the particular instantiation of the role which is their own (350).

This claim about abstract structures of familial roles reveals, I think, the problem with Hardimon's account of familial obligations or of any account that appeals to roles or shared understandings. What is the abstract structure of the role of daughter? Suppose that it involves the conception of a daughter as performing certain services for her parents, i.e. of fulfilling obligations of care. Now we ask, is it good that daughters do so? It looks as though the account has reduced to a utilitarian account of some sort, perhaps a rule-utilitarian account. But then it does not offer us any account of genuinely special obligations.

But, more importantly, any such abstract structure is an idealization, and any given individual's particular instantiation of the role is likely to be very different from the idealization. The individual's particular instantiation of the role is, in effect, the relationship she has with her family member. Why suppose that obligations are determined by the abstract idealization at all, rather than by the character of the particular realization of it? If I have an intimate relationship with my mother, does it matter what conception of mother/daughter relationships are current in or have a long tradition in my society? When Ann discovers that her father is a Nazi war criminal, should she reflect on abstract ideals of father/daughter relationships before making her decision as to what to do with the evidence? Of course, such abstract conceptions do affect our reflections on familial relationships, but that is a causal, not a normative claim, about how such relationships actually do proceed. Focus on stereotyped views of social roles diverts our attention away from the realities of actual relationships.

Furthermore, such focus can lead to a narrow vision of the family. Many people in non-traditional family structures, cases of adoptive parents, step parents, gay or lesbian couples with children, etc., have no abstract structures to which to appeal to try to understand their 'roles': society has not defined these roles and in some cases actively seeks to prevent the 'institutional definition' of such roles by legal or social norms.[38] It is the fact that relationships in such non-traditional families can be as caring and intimate as those in more traditional families that creates the same sorts of obligations in both types of family structures (when such obligations exist). It might be true that persons in non-biologically based families, while having special obligations to one another, have such obligations for different sorts of reasons than do persons in biologically-based families. Given, however, the implausibility of granting any moral significance to biology, we have no reason to suppose that such is the case. Hardimon says that in cases of 'novel or

transitional roles' (340), we may have difficulty in discerning the nature of our role and its attendant duties. But in trying to discern that nature, isn't the character of our relationship what we ought to look to? And why suppose that we should look to certain societal ideals or expectations when we are thinking about what we owe persons to whom we are biologically related?

The appeals to biology and to roles are the two clearest ways to try to find a distinctive basis for familial obligations: appeal to either the biological nature of family or to the societal definition of the institution of family. Both appeals seem motivated by the worry that persons ought not to be allowed, as the voluntarist seems to allow them, to just throw off their pasts and make radical choices. But we don't need roles or biology to see that this is wrong – all we need is some reflection on the nature of intimate relationships. It is not always morally permissible to abandon people with whom one has a history of intimacy and caring. We can accept that claim and accommodate the voluntarist as well.

V.   Conclusions

I have presented an account of obligations to family members that, I have argued, is able to meet the voluntarist challenge. My account, however, denies that there is anything distinctive about familial relationships as such that grounds those special obligations; rather, familial relationships are often relationships of intimacy, and intimate relationships, whether between family members or others, generate obligations. Further support for my view, I have suggested, arises from the inadequacies of those views that reject voluntarism and attempt to ground familial obligations on something distinctive about familial relationships, either their biological character or their institutional or social functions. Of course, even if we reject the claim that familial obligations are grounded on something distinctive about familial relationships as such, the plausibility of my account depends upon the plausibility of my account of friendship as opposed to an account based on, perhaps, the realization of goods or an Aristotelian appeal to the character of the loved one. But my account has the appeal of allowing us to accommodate voluntarism and a wide range of intimate relationships, thereby preserving the importance of individual autonomy and the moral significance of intimate, caring relationships.

Notes

1 The obvious exceptions are spousal relationships and parental relationships to children (but not vice versa). The former are easily accounted for by reference to the marriage contract or some similar explicit exchange of vows. The latter cannot always be seen as clear examples of the voluntary entering of a relationship, especially when abortion and/or contraceptive devices are not readily available. My primary concern is with those familial relationships that do not appear, in any cases, to be voluntarily entered.

2 I will briefly consider this option in section II below.

3 A. John Simmons, *Moral Principles and Political Obligations* (Princeton, NJ: Princeton University Press 1979), 13.

4 Also, I am not using the term 'obligation' to refer to a moral requirement with greater weight than a duty. In fact, some obligations, such as certain obligations of gratitude (if we have such obligations), may be fairly weak, while some duties, such as certain duties of mutual aid, are extremely stringent.

5 Simmons, in *Moral Principles and Political Obligations*, takes an obligation to be 'a moral requirement generated by the performance of some voluntary act (or omission)' (14). Thus my terminology is not in any sense standard, but, I suggest, it is useful for the discussion of obligations to family members. However, in my discussion of Belliotti in section IV below, I will deviate from my own terminology, which is specifically rejected by Belliotti (see note 33 below).

6 See also Simmons, *Moral Principles and Political Obligations*, 15.

7 Of course it might be said that your nature and the nature of the act of throwing a life preserver to you are not sufficient to explain why I have the duty to throw that life preserver to you: we also need to state that I happened to be standing on the bank of the river. But notice that once I am in a position to throw that life preserver to you, your nature and the nature of the action provide sufficient explanation of my duty. On the other hand, even when I am in a position to give you ten dollars (I have the money and you are standing in front of me with your hand out), appeal to your nature and the nature of the action are not

sufficient to explain or ground an obligation, unless we can appeal to a promise that I made to you. It might be responded that if we redescribe the action as an act of promise-keeping, then appeal to the nature of the act is sufficient to ground an obligation. However, this is not a normatively neutral redescription of the act: to say that it is an act of promise-keeping is to say that it is obligatory in so far as genuine promises generate obligations. However, there are difficulties here that I cannot address, and that need not be resolved for my purposes.

8 I have characterized natural duties as grounded by the nature of the persons to whom the duties are owed, while special obligations are not so grounded. Promise-keeping and, as I will argue, obligations to intimates are grounded by the character of the relationship between obligor and obligee. I have left it open that other types of special obligations may be grounded on some fact other than the relationship between obligor and obligee, although all special obligations will be grounded by something other than or more than the intrinsic nature of the obligee and the intrinsic character of the required action.

9 This fact about special obligations to intimates raises difficulties for my account that I will discuss in section III, 2 below.

10 For a discussion of the voluntarist objection to associative or special obligations more generally, see Samuel Scheffler, 'Families, Nations, and Strangers,' The Lindley Lecture at the University of Kansas (October 17, 1994). For my response to Scheffler, see my 'Associative Obligations, Voluntarism, and Equality,' *Pacific Philosophical Quarterly* 77 (1996) 289–309.

11 Of course, children may be required to care for older parents for any number of reasons, including utilitarian reasons. But such utilitarian reasons do not constitute special obligations: we have a general duty to promote or maximize well-being, and caring for parents may be a good or even the best way to fulfill such a duty. (If one is willing to view utilitarian duties as owed to other persons, then utilitarian duties are natural duties.) As I indicate in the next section, however, I am concerned to find the source of genuinely special obligations between family members.

12 See, for example, the discussion of obligations of fair play in Robert Nozick, *Anarchy, State, and Utopia* (New York: Basic Books 1974), 90ff. See also Simmons, *Moral Principles and Political Obligations*, chap. 5. Obligations of gratitude are often appealed to in order to explain what adult children owe to their parents. See, for example, Nancy S. Jecker, 'Are Filial Duties Unfounded?'

American Philosophical Quarterly 26 (1989) 73–80; and Terrance McConnell, *Gratitude* (Philadelphia: Temple University Press 1993), chap. 7.

13 A. John Simmons, 'External Justifications and Institutional Roles,' *The Journal of Philosophy* 93 (1996), 30.

14 If one is unhappy with my earlier attempt to distinguish special obligations from natural duties (where obligations of promise-keeping are included under the former heading), one can, for the purposes of my discussion, simply take as a starting point the claim that we have certain duties and obligations, including duties of mutual aid and obligations to keep the promises that we make. We can then see the deflationary account as holding that any obligations that we have to family members must be reducible (in a straightforward way) to some type or types of obligation or duty that were included in our initial set. If we understand the deflationary view in this way, then my view presented in section III will still not be deflationary, because I *assimilate* familial obligations to obligations of promise-keeping but I do not *reduce* the former to the latter.

15 For a more complete discussion of special obligations and utilitarianism, see my 'Relatives and Relativism,' with Richard Fumerton, *Philosophical Studies* 87 (1997) 143–57.

16 'Filial Morality,' *The Journal of Philosophy* 83 (1986), 446.

17 In her well-known paper 'What Do Grown Children Owe Their Parents?' (in *Having Children: Philosophical and Legal Reflections on Parenthood*, Onora O'Neill and William Ruddick, eds. [New York: Oxford University Press 1979] 351–6), Jane English argues that 'the duties of grown children are those of friends and result from love between them and their parents' (351). My account of familial obligations accepts, in some form, that claim of English's; however, my account is an attempt to explain *why* the features shared by friendships and certain familial relationships do in fact generate obligations, a question upon which English's paper is silent. By offering such an account, we will be in a far better position to respond to the views that I discuss in the next section.

18 I am grateful to Thomas Hurka for pointing out to me the need to differentiate between forced intimacy and genuine intimacy.

19 I am not, of course, talking about a project of having friends, or of making friends. I am speaking of a friendship with a certain person as a project. The latter but not the former essentially involves a specific other.

20 I do not mean my language of mutual projects and our projects to be taken as a rejection of individualism or of what has come to be known as 'atomism': I am not postulating some metaphysical 'us' distinct from the individual parties to the friendship. Rather, I am pointing out a fact about the character of the project of friendship and of the sorts of attitudes of the parties to a friendship. For a discussion of such projects that does reject individualism, see Charles Taylor, 'Cross-Purposes: The Liberal Communitarian Debate,' *Liberalism and the Moral Life*, N. Rosenblum, ed. (Cambridge, MA: Harvard University Press 1989) 159–82.

21 The having of such a project can be more or less explicitly articulated in the minds of the parties to the friendship; often, such articulation only occurs in times of crisis.

22 So, unlike with respect to most promises, there is an open-endedness about the content of duties to friends: they are required to care about one another and to maintain the friendship (of course, these are prima facie requirements that can be overridden). If Tracy is my friend, then, there are no specific acts, perhaps, that I am required to perform, unless certain specific acts are necessary conditions of my caring for Tracy and for sustaining our friendship. But, as with promising, what I owe is correlated with what I have chosen: in one case, I have chosen the content of my promise, in the other I have chosen the character of the shared project. I will return to this point below.

23 With respect to promising, it is the voluntary character of a promise that renders the resultant obligations in conformity with the voluntarist requirement. An account of promising would need to answer the second question: why do promises create such demands?

24 An analogous confusion sometimes arises in discussions of emotions. It is often said that we cannot choose to feel a particular emotion at a particular time. That is true, if we mean that we cannot choose to be, for example, angry, in the way that we can choose to say 'I promise.' But, over the course of time, we can make choices and perform actions that will influence the types of persons we become, such as whether we are people who get angry in certain types of circumstances. So the feeling of a particular emotion may not be voluntary in any straightforward way, but that does not mean that emotions are beyond our control.

25 See also Joseph Kupfer, 'Can Parents and Children Be Friends?' *American Philosophical Quarterly* 27 (1990) 15–26, for an interesting discussion of the relationships that can be realized between parents

and children, although I disagree with his claim that parents and adult children cannot be friends.

26 When I use the term 'adult,' I do not have any specific age in mind. So I do not mean to exclude teenagers. The ages at which persons can begin to develop friendships with parents can vary a great deal.

27 See note 12 above for references to works that develop accounts based on gratitude. One way to develop a more general account based on the realization of goods is to take an Aristotelian approach to special obligations; for example, see Thomas Hurka, *Perfectionism* (New York: Oxford University Press 1993), 134–6.

28 For an interesting critique of the various sociobiological enterprises in the context of E. O. Wilson's work, see Philip Kitcher, 'The Hypothalamic Imperative,' from *Vaulting Ambition* (Cambridge, MA: The MIT Press 1985) 417–34; reprinted in *Issues in Evolutionary Ethics*, Paul Thompson, ed. (Albany: State University of New York Press 1995) 203–23.

29 'Evolutionary Ethics: A Phoenix Arisen,' in *Issues in Evolutionary Ethics* 225–47.

30 *Liberalism and the Limits of Justice* (Cambridge, UK: Cambridge University Press 1982), 179.

31 'Honor Thy Father and Thy Mother and to Thine Own Self Be True,' *The Southern Journal of Philosophy* 24 (1986), 152.

32 Actually, Belliotti's view on this point is unclear. He seems to think that it does not matter whether we hold that children owe abusive parents prima facie obligations or we hold that such abusive parents 'fall outside the realm of consideration' (157). But, in order to be consistent, he (or anyone who thinks that biology generates moral requirements) has to hold the former: if genetic contribution generates moral requirements, then, even if such requirements can be overridden by other moral considerations, they still exist in abusive contexts. At least, such is the case, if one accepts what has come to be known as generalism,

as opposed to particularism. For a defense of particularism, see Jonathan Daily, *Moral Reasons* (Oxford: Blackwell 1993), chaps. 4–7.

33 Belliotti uses the term 'moral requirement' in order to avoid the debate about the distinctions between obligations, duties, and 'ought' judgments, so, in my discussion of his view, I will adhere to his terminology. See Belliotti, n. 10 (161).

34 Belliotti actually suggests another argument: just as we are permitted to pursue our own interests to a greater extent than we pursue those of persons generally, so we are required to pursue those of persons who are metaphysically closer to us to a greater extent (154). But the move from permissions to requirements in this argument is completely unwarranted. I think that the worry about a reliable source of obligations to parents is the primary motivation for the appeal to biology and so I focus on such an argument in the text.

35 *The Journal of Philosophy* 91 (1994) 333–63.

36 See Michael Walzer, *Spheres of Justice* (New York: Basic Books 1983).

37 The voluntarist worry is not, of course, the only worry about such a view. How can we determine which cultural understandings, if any, are shared? What is the relevant culture to which to appeal to understand the role of daughter or sister? I cannot here discuss all of the difficulties that face such a view.

38 These cases also reveal why Hardimon's appeal to birth as being different from impressment is useful, if at all, only in the case of biological familial relations. The more important worry about his contrast is that we can imagine many roles altered so that persons are born into them. Suppose that persons were born into the role of sailor in the navy as a result of having a parent in the navy and being born on board a naval vessel. And it might be 'meaningful, rational, or good' that persons play the role of sailor in the navy. See also Simmons, 'External Justifications and Institutional Roles,' 34–5.

37

An Ethic of Caring

Nel Noddings

From Natural to Ethical Caring

David Hume long ago contended that morality is founded upon and rooted in feeling – that the "final sentence" on matters of morality, "that which renders morality an active virtue" – ". . . this final sentence depends on some internal sense or feeling, which nature has made universal in the whole species. For what else can have an influence of this nature?"[1]

What is the nature of this feeling that is "universal in the whole species"? I want to suggest that morality as an "active virtue" requires two feelings and not just one. The first is the sentiment of natural caring. There can be no ethical sentiment without the initial, enabling sentiment. In situations where we act on behalf of the other because we want to do so, we are acting in accord with natural caring. A mother's caretaking efforts in behalf of her child are not usually considered ethical but natural. Even maternal animals take care of their offspring, and we do not credit them with ethical behavior.

The second sentiment occurs in response to a remembrance of the first. Nietzsche speaks of love and memory in the context of Christian love and Eros, but what he says may safely be taken out of context to illustrate the point I wish to make here:

There is something so ambiguous and suggestive about the word love, something that speaks to memory and to hope, that even the lowest intelligence and the coldest heart still feel something of the glimmer of this word. The cleverest woman and the most vulgar man recall the relatively least selfish moments of their whole life, even if Eros has taken only a low flight with them.[2]

This memory of our own best moments of caring and being cared for sweeps over us as a feeling – as an "I must" – in response to the plight of the other and our conflicting desire to serve our own interests. There is a transfer of feeling analogous to transfer of learning. In the intellectual domain, when I read a certain kind of mathematical puzzle, I may react by thinking, "That is like the sailors, monkey, and coconuts problem," and then, "Diophantine equations" or "modulo arithmetic" or "congruences." Similarly, when I encounter an other and feel the natural pang conflicted with my own desires – "I must – I do not want to" – I recognize the feeling and remember what has followed it in my own best moments. I have a picture of those moments in which I was cared for and in which I cared, and I may reach toward this memory and guide my conduct by it if I wish to do so.

Nel Noddings, "An Ethic of Caring," from *Caring: A Feminine Approach to Ethics and Moral Education*, 2nd edn. (Berkeley: University of California Press, 2003), pp. 79–103. © 2003 by The Regents of the University of California. Reprinted with permission from the author and The University of California Press.

Recognizing that ethical caring requires an effort that is not needed in natural caring does not commit us to a position that elevates ethical caring over natural caring. Kant has identified the ethical with that which is done out of duty and not out of love, and that distinction in itself seems right. But an ethic built on caring strives to maintain the caring attitude and is thus dependent upon, and not superior to, natural caring. The source of ethical behavior is, then, in twin sentiments – one that feels directly for the other and one that feels for and with that best self, who may accept and sustain the initial feeling rather than reject it.

We shall discuss the ethical ideal, that vision of best self, in some depth. When we commit ourselves to obey the "I must" even at its weakest and most fleeting, we are under the guidance of this ideal. It is not just any picture. Rather, it is our best picture of ourselves caring and being cared for. It may even be colored by acquaintance with one superior to us in caring, but, as I shall describe it, it is both constrained and attainable. It is limited by what we have already done and by what we are capable of, and it does not idealize the impossible so that we may escape into ideal abstraction.

Now, clearly, in pointing to Hume's "active virtue" and to an ethical ideal as the source of ethical behavior, I seem to be advocating an ethic of virtue. This is certainly true in part. Many philosophers recognize the need for a discussion of virtue as the energizing factor in moral behavior, even when they have given their best intellectual effort to a careful explication of their positions on obligation and justification.[3] When we discuss the ethical ideal, we shall be talking about "virtue," but we shall not let "virtue" dissipate into "the virtues" described in abstract categories. The holy man living abstemiously on top of the mountain, praying thrice daily, and denying himself human intercourse may display "virtues," but they are not the virtues of one-caring. The virtue described by the ethical ideal of one-caring is built up in relation. It reaches out to the other and grows in response to the other.

Since our discussion of virtue will be embedded in an exploration of moral activity we might do well to start by asking whether or under what circumstances we are obliged to respond to the initial "I must." Does it make sense to say that I am obliged to heed that which comes to me as obligation?

Obligation

There are moments for all of us when we care quite naturally. We just do care; no ethical effort is required. "Want" and "ought" are indistinguishable in such cases. I want to do what I or others might judge I ought to do. But can there be a "demand" to care? There can be, surely, no demand for the initial impulse that arises as a feeling, an inner voice saying "I must do something," in response to the need of the cared-for. This impulse arises naturally, at least occasionally, in the absence of pathology. We cannot demand that one have this impulse, but we shrink from one who never has it. One who never feels the pain of another, who never confesses the internal "I must" that is so familiar to most of us, is beyond our normal pattern of understanding. Her case is pathological, and we avoid her.

But even if I feel the initial "I must," I may reject it. I may reject it instantaneously by shifting from "I must do something" to "Something must be done," and removing myself from the set of possible agents through whom the action should be accomplished. I may reject it because I feel that there is nothing I can do. If I do either of these things without reflection upon what I might do in behalf of the cared-for, then I do not care. Caring requires me to respond to the initial impulse with an act of commitment: I commit myself either to overt action on behalf of the cared-for (I pick up my crying infant) or I commit myself to thinking about what I might do. In the latter case, as we have seen, I may or may not act overtly in behalf of the cared-for. I may abstain from action if I believe that anything I might do would tend to work against the best interests of the cared-for. But the test of my caring is not wholly in how things turn out; the primary test lies in an examination of what I considered, how fully I received the other, and whether the free pursuit of his projects is partly a result of the completion of my caring in him.

But am I obliged to embrace the "I must"? In this form, the question is a bit odd, for the "I must" carries obligation with it. It comes to us as obligation. But accepting and affirming the "I must" are different from feeling it, and these responses are what I am pointing to when I ask whether I am obliged to embrace the "I must." The question nags at us; it is a question that has been asked, in a variety of forms, over and over by moralists and moral theorists. Usually, the question arises as part of the broader question of justification. We ask something of the sort: Why must I (or should I) do what suggests itself to reason as "right" or as needing to be done for the sake of some other? We might prefer to supplement "reason" with "and/or feeling." This question is, of course, not the only thorny question in moral theory, but it is one that has plagued theorists who see clearly that there is no way to derive an "I ought" statement from a chain of facts. I may agree readily that "things would be better" – that is, that a certain state of affairs commonly agreed to be desirable might be attained – if a certain chain of events were to take place. But there is still nothing in this intellectual chain that can produce the "I ought." I may choose to remain an observer on the scene.

Now I am suggesting that the "I must" arises directly and prior to consideration of what it is that I might do. The initial feeling is the "I must." When it comes to me indistinguishable from the "I want," I proceed easily as one-caring. But often it comes to me conflicted. It may be barely perceptible, and it may be followed almost simultaneously by resistance. When someone asks me to get something for him or merely asks for my attention, the "I must" may be lost in a clamor of resistance. Now a second sentiment is required if I am to behave as one-caring. I care about myself as one-caring and, although I do not care naturally for the person who has asked something of me – at least not at this moment – I feel the genuine moral sentiment, the "I ought," that sensibility to which I have committed myself.

Let me try to make plausible my contention that the moral imperative arises directly.[4] And, of course, I must try to explain how caring and what I am calling the "moral imperative" are related. When my infant cries in the night, I not only feel that I must do something but I want to do something. Because I love this child, because I am bonded to him, I want to remove his pain as I would want to remove my own. The "I must" is not a dutiful imperative but one that accompanies the "I want." If I were tied to a chair, for

example, and wanted desperately to get free, I might say as I struggled, "I must do something; I must get out of these bonds." But this "must" is not yet the moral or ethical "ought." It is a "must" born of desire.

The most intimate situations of caring are, thus, natural. I do not feel that taking care of my own child is "moral" but, rather, natural. A woman who allows her own child to die of neglect is often considered sick rather than immoral; that is, we feel that either she or the situation into which she has been thrust must be pathological. Otherwise, the impulse to respond, to nurture the living infant, is overwhelming. We share the impulse with other creatures in the animal kingdom. Whether we want to consider this response as "instinctive" is problematic, because certain patterns of response may be implied by the term and because suspension of reflective consciousness seems also to be implied (and I am not suggesting that we have no choice), but I have no difficulty in considering it as innate. Indeed, I am claiming that the impulse to act in behalf of the present other is itself innate. It lies latent in each of us, awaiting gradual development in a succession of caring relations. I am suggesting that our inclination toward and interest in morality derives from caring. In caring, we accept the natural impulse to act on behalf of the present other. We are engrossed in the other. We have received him and feel his pain or happiness, but we are not compelled by this impulse. We have a choice; we may accept what we feel, or we may reject it. If we have a strong desire to be moral, we will not reject it, and this strong desire to be moral is derived, reflectively, from the more fundamental and natural desire to be and to remain related. To reject the feeling when it arises is either to be in an internal state of imbalance or to contribute willfully to the diminution of the ethical ideal.

But suppose in a particular case that the "I must" does not arise, or that it whispers faintly and disappears, leaving distrust, repugnance, or hate. Why, then, should I behave morally toward the object of my dislike? Why should I not accept feelings other than those characteristic of caring and, thus, achieve an internal state of balance through hate, anger, or malice?

The answer to this is, I think, that the genuine moral sentiment (our second sentiment) arises from an evaluation of the caring relation as good, as better than, superior to, other forms of relatedness. I feel the moral "I must" when I recognize that my response will either enhance or diminish my ethical ideal. It will serve either to increase or decrease the likelihood of genuine caring. My response affects me as one-caring. In a given situation with someone I am not fond of, I may be able to find all sorts of reasons why I should not respond to his need. I may be too busy. He may be undiscerning. The matter may be, on objective analysis, unimportant. But, before I decide, I must turn away from this analytic chain of thought and back to the concrete situation. Here is this person with this perceived need to which is attached this importance. I must put justification aside temporarily. Shall I respond? How do I feel as a duality about the "I" who will not respond?

I am obliged, then, to accept the initial "I must" when it occurs and even to fetch it out of recalcitrant slumber when it fails to awake spontaneously.[5] The source of my obligation is the value I place on the relatedness of caring. This value itself arises as a product of actual caring and being cared-for and my reflection on the goodness of these concrete caring situations.

Now, what sort of "goodness" is it that attaches to the caring relation? It cannot be a fully moral goodness, for we have already described forms of caring that are natural and require no moral effort. But it cannot be a fully nonmoral goodness either, for it would then join a class of goods many of which are widely separated from the moral good. It is, perhaps, properly described as a "premoral good," one that lies in a region with the moral good and shades over into it. We cannot always decide with certainty whether our caring response is natural or ethical. Indeed, the decision to respond ethically as one-caring may cause the lowering of barriers that previously prevented reception of the other, and natural caring may follow.

I have identified the source of our obligation and have said that we are obligated to accept, and even to call forth, the feeling "I must." But what exactly must I do? Can my obligation be set forth in a list or hierarchy of principles? So far, it seems that I am obligated to maintain an attitude and, thus, to meet the other as one-caring and, at the same time, to increase my own virtue

as one-caring. If I am advocating an ethic of virtue, do not all the usual dangers lie in wait: hypocrisy, self-righteousness, withdrawal from the public domain? We shall discuss these dangers as the idea of an ethical ideal is developed more fully.

Let me say here, however, why it seems preferable to place an ethical ideal above principle as a guide to moral action. It has been traditional in moral philosophy to insist that moral principles must be, by their very nature as moral principles, universifiable. If I am obligated to do X under certain conditions, then under sufficiently similar conditions you also are obligated to do X. But the principle of universifiability seems to depend, as Nietzsche pointed out, on a concept of "sameness."[6] In order to accept the principle, we should have to establish that human predicaments exhibit sufficient sameness, and this we cannot do without abstracting away from concrete situations those qualities that seem to reveal the sameness. In doing this, we often lose the very qualities or factors that gave rise to the moral question in the situation. That condition which makes the situation different and thereby induces genuine moral puzzlement cannot be satisfied by the application of principles developed in situations of sameness.

This does not mean that we cannot receive any guidance from an attempt to discover principles that seem to be universifiable. We can, under this sort of plan, arrive at the doctrine of "prima facie duty" described by W. D. Ross.[7] Ross himself, however, admits that this doctrine yields no real guidance for moral conduct in concrete situations. It guides us in abstract moral thinking; it tells us, theoretically, what to do, "all other things being equal." But other things are rarely if ever equal. A and B, struggling with a moral decision, are two different persons with different factual histories, different projects and aspirations, and different ideals. It may indeed be right, morally right, for A to do X and B to do not-X. We may, that is, connect "right" and "wrong" to faithfulness to the ethical ideal. This does not cast us into relativism, because the ideal contains at its heart a component that is universal: Maintenance of the caring relation.

Before turning to a discussion of "right" and "wrong" and their usefulness in an ethic of caring, we might try to clear up the problem earlier mentioned as a danger in any ethic of virtue: the temptation to withdraw from the public domain. It is a real danger. Even though we rejected the sort of virtue exhibited by the hermit-monk on the mountaintop, that rejection may have been one of personal choice. It still remains possible that an ethic of caring is compatible with the monk's choice, and that such an ethic even induces withdrawal. We are not going to be able to divide cases clearly. The monk who withdraws only to serve God is clearly under the guidance of an ethic that differs fundamentally from the ethic of caring. The source of his ethic is not the source of ours, and he might deny that any form of human relatedness could be a source for moral behavior. But if, when another intrudes upon his privacy, he receives the other as one-caring, we cannot charge him with violating our ethic. Further, as we saw in our discussion of the one-caring, there is a legitimate dread of the proximate stranger – of that person who may ask more than we feel able to give. We saw there that we cannot care for everyone. Caring itself is reduced to mere talk about caring when we attempt to do so. We must acknowledge, then, that an ethic of caring implies a limit on our obligation.

Our obligation is limited and delimited by relation. We are never free, in the human domain, to abandon our preparedness to care; but, practically, if we are meeting those in our inner circles adequately as ones-caring and receiving those linked to our inner circles by formal chains of relation, we shall limit the calls upon our obligation quite naturally. We are not obliged to summon the "I must" if there is no possibility of completion in the other. I am not obliged to care for starving children in Africa, because there is no way for this caring to be completed in the other unless I abandon the caring to which I am obligated. I may still choose to do something in the direction of caring, but I am not obliged to do so. When we discuss our obligation to animals, we shall see that this is even more sharply limited by relation. We cannot refuse obligation in human affairs by merely refusing to enter relation; we are, by virtue of our mutual humanity, already and perpetually in potential relation. Instead, we limit our obligation by examining the possibility of completion. In connection with animals, however, we may find it possible to refuse relation itself on the grounds of a species-specific impossibility of any form of reciprocity in caring.

Now, this is very important, and we should try to say clearly what governs our obligation. On the basis of what has been developed so far, there seem to be two criteria: the existence of or potential for present relation, and the dynamic potential for growth in relation, including the potential for increased reciprocity and, perhaps, mutuality. The first criterion establishes an absolute obligation and the second serves to put our obligations into an order of priority.

If the other toward whom we shall act is capable of responding as cared-for and there are no objective conditions that prevent our receiving this response – if, that is, our caring can be completed in the other – then we must meet that other as one-caring. If we do not care naturally, we must call upon our capacity for ethical caring. When we are in relation or when the other has addressed us, we must respond as one-caring. The imperative in relation is categorical. When relation has not yet been established, or when it may properly be refused (when no formal chain or natural circle is present), the imperative is more like that of the hypothetical: I must if I wish to (or am able to) move into relation.

The second criterion asks us to look at the nature of potential relation and, especially, at the capacity of the cared-for to respond. The potential for response in animals, for example, is nearly static; they cannot respond in mutuality, nor can the nature of their response change substantially. But a child's potential for increased response is enormous. If the possibility of relation is dynamic – if the relation may clearly grow with respect to reciprocity – then the possibility and degree of my obligation also grows. If response is imminent, so also is my obligation. This criterion will help us to distinguish between our obligation to members of the nonhuman animal world and, say, the human fetus. We must keep in mind, however, that the second criterion binds us in proportion to the probability of increased response and to the imminence of that response. Relation itself is fundamental in obligation.

I shall give an example of thinking guided by these criteria, but let us pause for a moment and ask what it is we are trying to accomplish.

I am working deliberately toward criteria that will preserve our deepest and most tender human feelings. The caring of mother for child, of human adult for human infant, elicits the tenderest feelings in most of us. Indeed, for many women, this feeling of nurturance lies at the very heart of what we assess as good. A philosophical position that has difficulty distinguishing between our obligation to human infants and, say, pigs is in some difficulty straight off. It violates our most deeply cherished feeling about human goodness. This violation does not, of course, make the position logically wrong, but it suggests that especially strong grounds will be needed to support it. In the absence of such strong grounds – and I shall argue in a later chapter that they are absent – we might prefer to establish a position that captures rather than denies our basic feelings. We might observe that man (in contrast to woman) has continually turned away from his inner self and feeling in pursuit of both science and ethics. With respect to strict science, this turning outward may be defensible; with respect to ethics, it has been disastrous.

Now, let's consider an example: the problem of abortion. Operating under the guidance of an ethic of caring, we are not likely to find abortion in general either right or wrong. We shall have to inquire into individual cases. An incipient embryo is an information speck – a set of controlling instructions for a future human being. Many of these specks are created and flushed away without their creators' awareness. From the view developed here, the information speck is an information speck; it has no given sanctity. There should be no concern over the waste of "human tissue," since nature herself is wildly prolific, even profligate.[8] The one-caring is concerned not with human tissue but with human consciousness – with pain, delight, hope, fear, entreaty, and response.

But suppose the information speck is mine, and I am aware of it. This child-to-be is the product of love between a man deeply cared-for and me. Will the child have his eyes or mine? His stature or mine? Our joint love of mathematics or his love of mechanics or my love of language? This is not just an information speck; it is endowed with prior love and current knowledge. It is sacred, but I – humbly, not presumptuously – confer sacredness upon it. I cannot, will not destroy it. It is

joined to loved others through formal chains of caring. It is linked to the inner circle in a clearly defined way. I might wish that I were not pregnant, but I cannot destroy this known and potentially loved person-to-be. There is already relation albeit indirect and formal. My decision is an ethical one born of natural caring.

But suppose, now, that my beloved child has grown up; it is she who is pregnant and considering abortion. She is not sure of the love between herself and the man. She is miserably worried about her economic and emotional future. I might like to convey sanctity on this information speck; but I am not God – only mother to this suffering cared-for. It is she who is conscious and in pain, and I as one-caring move to relieve the pain. This information speck is an information speck and that is all. There is no formal relation, given the breakdown between husband and wife, and with the embryo, there is no present relation; the possibility of future relation – while not absent, surely – is uncertain. But what of this possibility for growing response? Must we not consider it? We must indeed. As the embryo becomes a fetus and, growing daily, becomes more nearly capable of response as cared-for, our obligation grows from a nagging uncertainty – an "I must if I wish" – to an utter conviction that we must meet this small other as one-caring.

If we try to formalize what has been expressed in the concrete situations described so far, we arrive at a legal approach to abortion very like that of the Supreme Court: abortions should be freely available in the first trimester, subject to medical determination in the second trimester, and banned in the third, when the fetus is viable. A woman under the guidance of our ethic would be likely to recognize the growing possibility of relation; the potential is clearly dynamic. Further, many women recognize the relation as established when the fetus begins to move about. It is not a question of when life begins but of when relation begins.

But what if relation is never established? Suppose the child is born and the mother admits no sense of relatedness. May she commit infanticide? One who asks such questions misinterprets the concept of relatedness that I have been struggling to describe. Since the infant, even the near-natal fetus, is capable of relation – of the sweetest and most unselfconscious reciprocity – one who encounters the infant is obligated to meet it as one-caring. Both parts of this claim are essential; it is not only the child's capability to respond but also the encounter that induces obligation. There must exist the possibility for our caring to be completed in the other. If the mother does not care naturally, then she must summon ethical caring to support her as one-caring. She may not ethically ignore the child's cry to live.

The one-caring, in considering abortion as in all other matters, cares first for the one in immediate pain or peril. She might suggest a brief and direct form of counseling in which a young expectant mother could come to grips with her feelings. If the incipient child has been sanctified by its mother, every effort must be made to help the two to achieve a stable and hopeful life together; if it has not, it should be removed swiftly and mercifully with all loving attention to the woman, the conscious patient. Between these two clear reactions is a possible confused one: the young woman is not sure how she feels. The one-caring probes gently to see what has been considered, raising questions and retreating when the questions obviously have been considered and are now causing great pain. Is such a view "unprincipled"? If it is, it is boldly so; it is at least connected with the world as it is, at its best and at its worst, and it requires that we – in espousing a "best" – stand ready to actualize that preferred condition. The decision for or against abortion must be made by those directly involved in the concrete situation, but it need not be made alone. The one-caring cannot require everyone to behave as she would in a particular situation. Rather, when she dares to say, "I think you should do X," she adds, also, "Can I help you?" The one under her gaze is under her support and not her judgment.

One under the guidance of an ethic of caring is tempted to retreat to a manageable world. Her public life is limited by her insistence upon meeting the other as one-caring. So long as this is possible, she may reach outward and enlarge her circles of caring. When this reaching out destroys or drastically reduces her actual caring, she retreats and renews her contact with those who address her. If the retreat becomes a flight, an avoidance of the call to care, her ethical ideal is diminished. Similarly, if the retreat is away from human beings and toward other objects of caring – ideas, animals, humanity-at-large, God – her ethical ideal is virtually shattered. This is not a judgment, for we can understand and sympathize with one who makes such a choice. It is more in the nature of a perception: we see clearly what has been lost in the choice.

Our ethic of caring – which we might have called a "feminine ethic" – begins to look a bit mean in contrast to the masculine ethics of universal love or universal justice. But universal love is illusion. Under the illusion, some young people retreat to the church to worship that which they cannot actualize; some write lovely poetry extolling universal love; and some, in terrible disillusion, kill to establish the very principles which should have entreated them not to kill. Thus are lost both principles and persons.

Right and Wrong

How are we to make judgments of right and wrong under this ethic? First, it is important to understand that we are not primarily interested in judging but, rather, in heightening moral perception and sensitivity. But "right" and "wrong" can be useful.

Suppose a mother observes her young child pulling the kitten's tail or picking it up by the ears. She may exclaim, "Oh, no, it is not nice to hurt the kitty," or, "You must not hurt the kitty." Or she may simply say, "Stop. See – you are hurting the kitty," and she may then take the kitten in her own hands and show the child how to handle it. She holds the kitten gently, stroking it, and saying, "See? Ah, ah, kitty, nice kitty. . . ." What the mother is supposing in this interaction is that the realization that his act is hurting the kitten, supplemented by the knowledge of how to avoid inflicting hurt, will suffice to change the child's behavior. If she believes this, she has no need for the statement, "It is wrong to hurt the kitty." She is not threatening sanctions but drawing dual attention to a matter of fact (the hurting) and her own commitment (I will not hurt). Beyond this, she is supposing that her child, well-cared-for himself, does not want to inflict pain.

Now, I am not claiming through use of this illustration that moral statements are mere expressions of approval or disapproval, although they do serve an expressive function. A. J. Ayer, who did make a claim of this sort before modifying his position somewhat, uses an illustration very like the one just given to support an emotivist position.[9] But even if it were possible to take a purely analytic stance with respect to moral theory, as Ayer suggests he has done, that is certainly not what I intend to do. One who labels moral statements as expressions of approval or disapproval, and takes the matter to be finished with that, misses the very heart of morality. He misses the commitment to behave in a fashion compatible with caring. Thus he misses both feeling and content. I may, after all, express my approval or disapproval on matters that are not moral. Thus it is clear that when I make a moral judgment I am doing more than simply expressing approval or disapproval. I am both expressing my own commitment to behave in a way compatible with caring and appealing to the hearer to consider what he is doing. I may say first to a child, "Oh! Don't hurt the kitty!" And I may then add, "It is wrong to hurt the kitty." The word is not necessary, strictly speaking, but I may find it useful.

What do I mean by this? I certainly mean to express my own commitment, and I show this best by daily example. But I may mean to say more than this. I may explain to the child that not only do I feel this way but that our family does, that our community does, that our culture does. Here I must be very careful. Our community may say one thing and do quite another. Such contradiction is even more likely at the level of "our culture." But I express myself doubly in words and in acts, and I may search out examples in the larger culture to convince the child that significant others do feel this way. The one-caring is careful to distinguish between acts that violate caring, acts that she herself holds wrong, and those acts that "some people" hold to be wrong. She need not be condescending in this instruction. She is herself so reluctant to universalize beyond the demands of caring that she cannot say, "It is wrong," to everything that is illegal, church-forbidden, or contrary to a prevailing etiquette. But she can raise the question, attempt to justify the alien view, express her own objections, and support the child in his own exploration.

Emotivists are partly right, I think, when they suggest that we might effectively substitute a statement describing the fact or event that triggers our feeling or attitude for statements such as "It is wrong to do X." When I say to my child, "It is wrong to hurt the kitty," I mean (if I am not threatening sanctions) to inform him that he is hurting the kitten and, further, that I believe that if he perceives he is doing so, he will stop. I am counting on his gradually developing ability to feel pain in the other to induce a decision to stop. To say, "It is wrong to cause pain needlessly," contributes nothing by way of knowledge and can hardly be thought likely to change the attitude or behavior of one who might ask, "Why is it wrong?" If I say to someone, "You are hurting the cat," and he replies, "I know it – so what? I like hurting cats," I feel "zero at the bone." Saying to him, "It is wrong to hurt cats," adds little unless I intend to threaten sanctions. If I mean to equate "It is wrong to hurt cats" with "There will be a sure and specific punishment for hurting cats," then it would be more honest to say this. One either feels a sort of pain in response to the pain of others, or one does not feel it. If he does feel it, he does not need to be told that causing pain is wrong. If he does not feel it in a particular case, he may remember the feeling – as one remembers the sweetness of love on hearing a certain piece of music – and allow himself to be moved by this remembrance of feeling. For one who feels nothing, directly or by remembrance, we must prescribe reeducation or exile. Thus, at the foundation of moral behavior – as we have already pointed out – is feeling or sentiment. But, further, there is commitment to remain open to that feeling, to remember it, and to put one's thinking in its service. It is the particular commitment underlying genuine expressions of moral judgment – as well as the special content – that the emotivist misses.

The one-caring, clearly, applies "right" and "wrong" most confidently to her own decisions. This does not, as we have insisted before, make her a relativist. The caring attitude that lies at the heart of all ethical behavior is universal. As the mother in chapter two, who had to decide whether or not to leave her sick child, decided on the basis of a caring evaluation of the conditions and feelings of those involved, so in general the one-caring evaluates her own acts with respect to how faithfully they conform to what is known and felt through the receptivity of caring. But she also uses "right" and "wrong" instructively and respectfully to refer to the judgments of significant others. If she agrees because the matter at hand can be assessed in light of caring, she adds her personal commitment and example; if she has doubts – because the rule appealed to seems irrelevant or ambiguous in the light of caring – she still acknowledges the judgment but adds her own dissent or demurrer. Her eye is on the ethical development of the cared-for and, as she herself withholds judgment until she has heard the "whole story," she wants the cared-for to encounter others, receive them, and reflect on what he has received. Principles and rules are among the beliefs he will receive, and she wants him to consider these in the light of caring.

But is this all we can say about right and wrong? Is there not a firm foundation in morality for our legal judgments? Surely, we must be allowed to say, for example, that stealing is wrong and is, therefore, properly forbidden by law. Because it is so often wrong – and so easily demonstrated to be wrong – under an ethic of caring, we may accede that such a law has its roots *partly* in morality. We may legally punish one who has stolen, but we may not pass moral judgment on him until we know why he stole. An ethic of caring is likely to be stricter in its judgment, but more supportive and corrective in following up its judgment, than ethics otherwise grounded. For the one-caring, stealing is almost always wrong:

Ms. A talks with her young son. *But, Mother,* the boy pleads, *suppose I want to make you happy and I steal something you want from a big chain store. I haven't hurt anyone, have I? Yes, you have,* responds his mother, and she points to the predicament of the store managers who may be accused of poor stewardship and to the higher prices suffered by their neighbors. *Well, suppose I steal from a rich, rich person? He can replace what I take easily, and . . . Wait,* says Ms. A. *Is someone suffering? Are you stealing to relieve that suffering, and will you make certain that what you steal is used to relieve it?. . . But can't I steal to make someone happy?* her son persists. Slowly, patiently, Ms. A explains the position of one-caring. *Each one who comes under our gaze must be met as one-caring. When I want to please X and I turn toward Y as a means for satisfying my desire to please X, I must now meet Y as one-caring. I do not judge him for being rich – for treasuring

what I, perhaps, regard with indifference. I may not cause him pain by taking or destroying what he possesses. But what if I steal from a bad guy – someone who stole to get what he has? Ms. A smiles at her young son, struggling to avoid his ethical responsibility: Unless he is an immediate threat to you or someone else, you must meet him, too, as one-caring.*

The lessons in "right" and "wrong" are hard lessons – not swiftly accomplished by setting up as an objective the learning of some principle. We do not say: It is wrong to steal. Rather, we consider why it was wrong or may be wrong in this case to steal. We do not say: It is wrong to kill. By setting up such a principle, we also imply its exceptions, and then we may too easily act on authorized exceptions. The one-caring wants to consider, and wants her child to consider, the act itself in full context. She will send him into the world skeptical, vulnerable, courageous, disobedient, and tenderly receptive. The "world" may not depend upon him to obey its rules or fulfill its wishes, but you, the individual he encounters, may depend upon him to meet you as one-caring.

The Problem of Justification

Since I have chided the emotivist for not digging beneath the expressive layer of moral sentiment to the nature of the feeling itself and the commitment to act in accord with the feeling, one might ask whether I should not dig beneath the commitment. Why should I be committed to not causing pain? Now, clearly, in one sense, I cannot answer this better than we already have. When the "Why?" refers to motivation, we have seen that the one-caring receives the other and acts in the other's behalf as she would for herself; that is, she acts with a similar motive energy. Further, I have claimed that, when natural caring fails, the motive energy in behalf of the other can be summoned out of caring for the ethical self. We have discussed both natural caring and ethical caring. Ethical caring, as I have described it, depends not upon rule or principle but upon the development of an ideal self. It does not depend upon just any ideal of self, but the ideal developed in congruence with one's best remembrance of caring and being cared-for.

So far, in recommending the ethical ideal as a guide to ethical conduct, I have suggested that traditional approaches to the problem of justification are mistaken. When the ethical theorist asks, "Why should I behave thus-and-so?" his question is likely to be aimed at justification rather than motivation and at a logic that resides outside the person. He is asking for reasons of the sort we expect to find in logical demonstration. He may expect us to claim that moral judgments can be tested as claims to facts can be tested, or that moral judgments are derived from divine commandment, or that moral truths are intuitively apprehended. Once started on this line of discussion, we may find ourselves arguing abstractly about the status of relativism and absolutism, egoism and altruism, and a host of other positions that, I shall claim, are largely irrelevant to moral conduct. They are matters of considerable intellectual interest, but they are distractions if our primary interest is in ethical conduct.

Moral statements cannot be justified in the way that statements of fact can be justified. They are not truths. They are derived not from facts or principles but from the caring attitude. Indeed, we might say that moral statements come out of the moral view or attitude, which, as I have described it, is the rational attitude built upon natural caring. When we put it this way, we see that there can be no justification for taking the moral viewpoint – that in truth, the moral viewpoint is prior to any notion of justification.

But there is another difficulty in answering the request for justification. Consideration of problems of justification requires us to concentrate on moral judgments, on moral statements. Hence we are led to an exploration of the language and reasoning used to discuss moral conduct and away from an assessment of the concrete events in which we must choose whether and how to behave morally. Indeed, we are often led far beyond what we feel and intuitively judge to be right in a search for some simple and absolute guide to moral goodness.

For an ethic of caring, the problem of justification is not concentrated upon justified action in general. We are not "justified" – we are *obligated* – to do what is required to maintain and enhance caring. We must "justify" not-caring; that is, we must explain why, in the interest of caring for ourselves as ethical selves or in the interest of others for whom we care, we may

behave as ones-not-caring toward this particular other. In a related problem, we must justify doing what this other would not have us do to him as part of our genuine effort to care for him. But even in these cases, an ethic of caring does not emphasize justification. As one-caring, I am not seeking justification for my action; I am not standing alone before some tribunal. What I seek is completion in the other – the sense of being cared-for and, I hope, the renewed commitment of the cared-for to turn about and act as one-caring in the circles and chains within which he is defined. Thus, I am not justified but somehow fulfilled and completed in my own life and in the lives of those I have thus influenced.

It sounds all very nice, says my male colleague, but can you claim to be doing "ethics"? After all, ethics is the study of justified action. . . . Ah, yes. But, after "after-all," I am a woman, and I was not party to that definition. Shall we say then that I am talking about "how to meet the other morally"? Is this part of ethics? Is ethics part of this?

Women and Morality: Virtue

Many of us in education are keenly aware of the distortion that results from undue emphasis on moral judgments and justification. Lawrence Kohlberg's theory, for example, is widely held to be a model for moral education, but it is actually only a hierarchical description of moral reasoning.[10] It is well known, further, that the description may not be accurate. In particular, the fact that women seem often to be "stuck" at stage three might call the accuracy of the description into question. But perhaps the description is accurate within the domain of morality conceived as moral justification. If it is, we might well explore the possibility that feminine nonconformity to the Kohlberg model counts against the justification/judgment paradigm and not against women as moral thinkers.

Women, perhaps the majority of women, prefer to discuss moral problems in terms of concrete situations. They approach moral problems not as intellectual problems to be solved by abstract reasoning but as concrete human problems to be lived and to be solved in living. Their approach is founded in caring. Carol Gilligan describes the approach:

...women not only define themselves in a context of human relationship but also judge themselves in terms of their ability to care. Woman's place in man's life cycle has been that of nurturer, caretaker, and helpmate, the weaver of those networks of relationships on which she in turn relies.[11]

Faced with a hypothetical moral dilemma, women often ask for more information. It is not the case, certainly, that women cannot arrange principles hierarchically and derive conclusions logically. It is more likely that they see this process as peripheral to or even irrelevant to moral conduct. They want more information, I think, in order to form a picture. Ideally, they need to talk to the participants, to see their eyes and facial expressions, to size up the whole situation. Moral decisions are, after all, made in situations; they are qualitatively different from the solution of geometry problems. Women, like act-deontologists in general, give reasons for their acts, but the reasons point to feelings, needs, situational conditions, and their sense of personal ideal rather than universal principles and their application.

As we have seen, caring is not in itself a virtue. The genuine ethical commitment to maintain oneself as caring gives rise to the development and exercise of virtues, but these must be assessed in the context of caring situations. It is not, for example, patience itself that is a virtue but patience with respect to some infirmity of a particular cared-for or patience in instructing a concrete cared-for that is virtuous. We must not reify virtues and turn our caring toward them. If we do this, our ethic turns inward and is even less useful than an ethic of principles, which at least remains indirectly in contact with the acts we are assessing. The fulfillment of virtue is both in me and in the other.

A consideration of caring and an ethic built upon it give new meaning to what Kohlberg assesses as "stage three" morality. At this stage, persons behave morally in order to be thought of – or to think of themselves as – "good boys" or "good girls." Clearly, it makes a difference whether one chooses to be good or to be thought of as good. One who chooses to be good may not be "stuck," as Kohlberg suggests, in a stage of moral reasoning. Rather, she may have chosen an alternative route to moral conduct.

It should be clear that my description of an ethic of caring as a feminine ethic does not imply a claim to speak for all women nor to exclude men. As we shall see in the next chapter, there is reason to believe that women are somewhat better equipped for caring than men are. This is partly a result of the construction of psychological deep structures in the mother–child relationship. A girl can identify with the one caring for her and thus maintain relation while establishing identity. A boy must, however, find his identity with the absent one – the father – and thus disengage himself from the intimate relation of caring.[12]

There are many women who will deplore my insistence on locating the source of caring in human relations. The longing for something beyond is lovely – alluring – and it persists. It seems to me quite natural that men, many of whom are separated from the intimacy of caring, should create gods and seek security and love in worship. But what ethical need have women for God? I do not mean to suggest that women can brush aside an actually existing God but, if there is such a God, the human role in Its maintenance must be trivial. We can only contemplate the universe in awe and wonder, study it conscientiously, and live in it conservatively. Women, it seems to me, can accept the God of Spinoza and Einstein. What I mean to suggest is that women have no need of a conceptualized God, one wrought in the image of man. All the love and goodness commanded by such a God can be generated from the love and goodness found in the warmest and best human relations.

Let me say a little more here, because I know the position is a hard one for many – even for many I love. In our earlier discussion of Abraham, we saw a fundamental and deeply cut chasm between male and female views. We see this difference illustrated again in the New Testament. In Luke 16, we hear the story of a rich man who ignored the suffering of Lazarus, a beggar. After death, Lazarus finds peace and glory, but the rich man finds eternal torment. He cries to Abraham for mercy:

> Father Abraham, have mercy on me, and send Lazarus, that he may dip the tip of his finger in water, and cool my tongue; for I am tormented in this flame.

But Abraham said, Son, remember that thou in thy lifetime receivedst thy good things, and likewise Lazarus evil things: but now he is comforted and thou art tormented.

And beside all this, between us and you there is a great gulf fixed: so that they which would pass from hence to you cannot; neither can they pass to us, that would come from thence.[13]

But what prevents their passage? The judgmental love of the harsh father establishes the chasm. This is not the love of the mother, for even in despair she would cast herself across the chasm to relieve the suffering of her child. If he calls her, she will respond. Even the wickedest, if he calls, she must meet as one-caring. Now, I ask again, what ethical need has woman for God?

In the stories of Abraham, we hear the tragedy induced by the traditional, masculine approach to ethics. When Kierkegaard defends him in an agonized and obsessive search for "something beyond" to which he can repeatedly declare his devotion, he reveals the emptiness at the heart of his own concrete existence. If Abraham is lost, he, Kierkegaard, is lost. He observes: "So either there is a paradox, that the individual as the individual stands in an absolute relation to the absolute/or Abraham is lost."[14]

Woman, as one-caring, pities and fears both Abraham and Kierkegaard. Not only are they lost, but they would take all of us with them into the lonely wilderness of abstraction.

The Toughness of Caring

An ethic built on caring is thought by some to be tenderminded. It does involve construction of an ideal from the fact and memory of tenderness. The ethical sentiment itself requires a prior natural sentiment of caring and a willingness to sustain tenderness. But there is no assumption of innate human goodness and, when we move to the construction of a philosophy of education, we shall find enormous differences between the view developed here and that of those who find the child innately good. I shall not claim that the child is "innately wise and good," or that the aim of life is happiness, or that all will be well with the child if we resist interfering in its intellectual and moral life.[15] We have memories of caring,

of tenderness, and these lead us to a vision of what is good – a state that is good-in-itself and a commitment to sustain and enhance that good (the desire and commitment to be moral). But we have other memories as well, and we have other desires. An ethic of caring takes into account these other tendencies and desires; it is precisely because the tendency to treat each other well is so fragile that we must strive so consistently to care.

Far from being romantic, an ethic of caring is practical, made for this earth. Its toughness is disclosed in a variety of features, the most important of which I shall try to describe briefly here.

First, since caring is a relation, an ethic built on it is naturally other regarding. Since I am defined in relation, I do not sacrifice myself when I move toward the other as one-caring. Caring is, thus, both self-serving and other-serving. Willard Gaylin describes it as necessary to the survival of the species: "If one's frame of reference focuses on the individual, caring seems self-sacrificing. But if the focus is on the group, on the species, it is the ultimate self-serving device – the sine qua non of survival."[16]

Clearly, this is so. But while I am drawn to the other, while I am instinctively called to nurture and protect, I am also the initiator and chooser of my acts. I may act in accordance with that which is good in my deepest nature, or I may seek to avoid it – either by forsaking relation or by trying to transform that which is feeling and action into that which is all propositional talk and principle. If I suppose, for example, that I am somehow alone and totally responsible for either the apprehension or creation of moral principles, I may find myself in some difficulty when it comes to caring for myself. If moral principles govern my conduct with respect to others, if I must always regard the other in order to be moral, how can I properly meet my own needs and desires? How can I, morally, care for myself?

An ethic of caring is a tough ethic. It does not separate self and other in caring, although, of course, it identifies the special contribution of the one-caring and the cared-for in caring. In contrast to some forms of agapism, for example, it has no problem in advocating a deep and steady caring for self. In a discussion of other-regarding forms of agapism, Gene Outka considers the case of a woman tied to a demanding parent. He explores the possibility of her finding justification for leaving in an assessment of the greatest good for all concerned, and he properly recommends that her own interests be included. In discussing the insistence of some agapists on entirely other-regarding justification, he explores the possibility of her breaking away "to become a medical doctor," thereby satisfying the need for multilateral other-interests.[17] The one-caring throws up her hands at such casting about for reasons. She needs no special justification to care for herself for, if she is not supported and cared-for, she may be entirely lost as one-caring. If caring is to be maintained, clearly, the one-caring must be maintained. She must be strong, courageous, and capable of joy.

When we looked at the one-caring in conflict (e.g., Mr. Jones and his mother), we saw that he or she can be overwhelmed by cares and burdens. The ethical responsibility of the one-caring is to look clear-eyed on what is happening to her ideal and how well she is meeting it. She sees herself, perhaps, as caring lovingly for her parent. But perhaps he is cantankerous, ungrateful, rude, and even dirty. She sees herself becoming impatient, grouchy, tired, and filled with self-pity. She can stay and live by an honestly diminished ideal – "I am a tired, grouchy, pitiful caretaker of my old father" – or she can free herself to whatever degree she must to remain minimally but actually caring. The ethical self does not live partitioned off from the rest of the person. Thinking guided by caring does not seek to justify a way out by means of a litany of predicted "goods," but it seeks a way to remain one-caring and, if at all possible, to enhance the ethical ideal. In such a quest, there is no way to disregard the self, or to remain impartial, or to adopt the stance of a disinterested observer. Pursuit of the ethical ideal demands impassioned and realistic commitment.

We see still another reason for accepting constraints on our ethical ideals. When we accept honestly our loves, our innate ferocity, our capacity for hate, we may use all this as information in building the safeguards and alarms that must be part of the ideal. We know better what we must work toward, what we must prevent, and the conditions under which we are lost as ones-caring. Instead of hiding from our natural impulses and pretending that we can achieve goodness through lofty abstractions, we accept what is there – all of it – and use what we have already assessed as good to control that which is not-good.

Caring preserves both the group and the individual and, as we have already seen, it limits our obligation so that it may realistically be met. It will not allow us to be distracted by visions of universal love, perfect justice, or a world unified under principle. It does not say, "Thou shalt not kill," and then seek other principles under which killing is, after all, justified. If the other is a clear and immediate danger to me or to my cared-fors, I must stop him, and I might need to kill him. But I cannot kill in the name of principle or justice. I must meet this other – even this evil other – as one-caring so long as caring itself is not endangered by my doing so. I must, for example, oppose capital punishment. I do not begin by saying, "Capital punishment is wrong." Thus I do not fall into the trap of having to supply reasons for its wrongness that will be endlessly disputed at a logical level. I do not say, "Life is sacred," for I cannot name a source of sacredness. I may point to the irrevocability of the decision, but this is not in itself decisive, even for me, because in many cases the decision would be just and I could not regret the demise of the condemned. (I have, after all, confessed my own ferocity; in the heat of emotion, I might have torn him to shreds if I had caught him molesting my child.)

My concern is for the ethical ideal, for my own ethical ideal and for whatever part of it others in my community may share. Ideally, another human being should be able to request, with expectation of positive response, my help and comfort. If I am not blinded by fear, or rage, or hatred, I should reach out as one-caring to the proximate stranger who entreats my help. This is the ideal one-caring creates. I should be able to respond to the condemned man's entreaty, "Help me." We must ask, then, after the effects of capital punishment on jurors, on judges, on jailers, on wardens, on newspersons "covering" the execution, on ministers visiting the condemned, on citizens affirming the sentence, on doctors certifying first that the condemned is well enough to be executed and second that he is dead. What effects have capital punishment on the ethical ideals of the participants? For me, if I had to participate, the ethical ideal would be diminished. Diminished. The ideal itself would be diminished. My act would either be wrong or barely right – right in a depleted sense. I might, indeed, participate ethically – rightly – in an execution but only at the cost of revising my ethical ideal downward. If I do not revise it and still participate, then my act is wrong, and I am a hypocrite and unethical. It is the difference between "I don't believe in killing, but . . ." and "I did not believe in killing cold-bloodedly, but now I see that I must and for these reasons." In the latter case, I may retain my ethicality, but at considerable cost. My ideal must forever carry with it not only what I would be but what I am and have been. There is no unbridgeable chasm between what I am and what I will be. I build the bridge to my future self, and this is why I oppose capital punishment. I do not want to kill if other options are open to me, and I do not want to ask others in the community to do what may diminish their own ethical ideals.

While I must not kill in obedience to law or principle, I may not, either, refuse to kill in obedience to principle. To remain one-caring, I might have to kill. Consider the case of a woman who kills her sleeping husband. Under most circumstances, the one-caring would judge such an act wrong. It violates the very possibility of caring for the husband. But as she hears how the husband abused his wife and children, about the fear with which the woman lived, about the past efforts to solve the problem legally, the one-caring revises her judgment. The jury finds the woman not guilty by reason of an extenuated self-defense. The one-caring finds her ethical, but under the guidance of a sadly diminished ethical ideal. The woman has behaved in the only way she found open to protect herself and her children and, thus, she has behaved in accord with the current vision of herself as one-caring. But what a horrible vision! She is now one-who-has-killed once and who would not kill again, and never again simply one who would not kill. The test of ultimate blame or blamelessness, under an ethic of caring, lies in how the ethical ideal was diminished. Did the agent choose the degraded vision out of greed, cruelty, or personal interest? Or was she driven to it by unscrupulous others who made caring impossible to sustain?

We see that our own ethicality is not entirely "up to us." Like Winston in *Nineteen Eighty-Four*, we are fragile; we depend upon each other

even for our own goodness. This recognition casts some doubt on Immanuel Kant's position:

> It is contradictory to say that I make another person's *perfection* my end and consider myself obliged to promote this. For the *perfection* of another man, as a person, consists precisely of *his own* power to adopt his end in accordance with his own concept of duty; and it is self-contradictory to demand that I do (make it my duty to do) what only the other person himself can do.[18]

In one sense, we agree fully with Kant. We cannot define another's perfection; we, as ones-caring, will not even define the principles by which he should live, nor can we prescribe the particular acts he should perform to meet that perfection. But we must be exquisitely sensitive to that ideal of perfection and, in the absence of a repugnance overwhelming to one-caring, we must as ones-caring act to promote that ideal. As parents and educators, we have perhaps no single greater or higher duty than this.

The duty to enhance the ethical ideal, the commitment to caring, invokes a duty to promote skepticism and noninstitutional affiliation. In a deep sense, no institution or nation can be ethical. It cannot meet the other as one-caring or as one trying to care. It can only capture in general terms what particular ones-caring would like to have done in well-described situations. Laws, manifestos, and proclamations are not, on this account, either empty or useless; but they are limited, and they may support immoral as well as moral actions. Only the individual can be truly called to ethical behavior, and the individual can never give way to encapsulated moral guides, although she may safely accept them in ordinary, untroubled times.

Everything depends, then, upon the will to be good, to remain in caring relation to the other. How may we help ourselves and each other to sustain this will?

Notes

1   David Hume, "An Enquiry Concerning the Principles of Morals," in *Ethical Theories*, ed. A. I. Melden (Englewood Cliffs, N.J.: Prentice-Hall, Inc., 1967), p. 275.

2 Friedrich Nietzsche, "Mixed Opinions and Maxims," in *The Portable Nietzsche*, ed. Walter Kaufmann (New York: The Viking Press, Inc., 1954), p. 65.

3 See, for example, William F. Frankena, *Ethics* (Englewood Cliffs, N.J.: Prentice-Hall, Inc., 1973), pp. 63–71.

4 The argument here is, I think, compatible with that of Philippa Foot, "Reasons for Action and Desires," in *Virtues and Vices*, ed. Philippa Foot (Berkeley, Los Angeles, London: University of California Press, 1978), pp. 148–56. My argument, however, relies on a basic desire, universal in all human beings, to be in relation – to care and be cared for.

5 The question of "summonability" is a vital one for ethicists who rely on good or altruistic feelings for moral motivation. Note treatment of this problem in Lawrence R. Blum, *Friendship, Altruism, and Morality* (London: Routledge & Kegan Paul, 1980), pp. 20–3 and pp. 194–203. See, also, Henry Sidgwick, *The Methods of Ethics* (Indianapolis: Hackett, 1981), and Philip Mercer, *Sympathy and Ethics* (Oxford: Clarendon Press, 1962).

6 Friedrich Nietzsche, *The Will to Power*, trans. Walter Kaufmann (New York: Random House, 1967), pp. 476, 670. For a contemporary argument against strict application of universalizability, see Peter Winch, *Ethics and Action* (London: Routledge & Kegan Paul, 1972).

7 W. D. Ross, *The Right and the Good* (Oxford: Clarendon Press, 1930). See also Frankena, *Ethics*.

8 Paul Ramsey raises this concern in *Fabricated Man* (New Haven and London: Yale University Press, 1970).

9 See the discussion in James Rachels, ed., *Understanding Moral Philosophy* (Encino, Calif.: Dickenson Publishing Company, Inc., 1976), pp. 38–9.

10 See Lawrence Kohlberg and R. Kramer, "Continuities and Discontinuities in Childhood and Adult Moral Development," *Human Development* 12 (1969), 93–120. See also Lawrence Kohlberg, "Stages in Moral Development as a Basis for Moral Education," in *Moral Education: Interdisciplinary Approaches,* ed. C. M. Beck, B. S. Crittenden, and E. V. Sullivan (Toronto: Toronto University Press, 1971).

11 Carol Gilligan, "Woman's Place in Man's Life Cycle," *Harvard Educational Review* 49 (1979), 440.

12 See Nancy Chodorow, *The Reproduction of Mothering* (Berkeley, Los Angeles, London: University of California Press, 1978).

13 Luke 16: 24–6.

14 Søren Kierkegaard, *Fear and Trembling*, trans. Walter Lowrie (Princeton: Princeton University Press, 1954), p. 129.

15 For a lovely exposition of this view, see A. S. Neill, *Summerhill* (New York: Hart Publishing Company, 1960).

16 Willard Gaylin, *Caring* (New York: Alfred A. Knopf, 1976), p. 115.

17 Gene Outka, *Agapé: An Ethical Analysis* (New Haven and London: Yale University Press, 1972), pp. 300–5.

18 Immanuel Kant, *The Metaphysics of Morals,* Part II: *The Doctrine of Virtue* (New York: Harper and Row, 1964), pp. 44–5.

Questions for Discussion

1. If you were Rick/Ilsa in *Casablanca*, would you have made the same decision as he/she did at the end of the film? Why or why not? Try to place your answer in the context of an ethical theory.

2. Did Almásy, in *The English Patient*, do the right thing when he traded secrets to the Germans in order to return to Katharine (chapters 27–9)? Compare and contrast his decision with that of Rick in *Casablanca*.

3. Compare and contrast the conceptions of the moral responsibilities of intimates suggested by the actions of Martins and Anna in *The Third Man*. With whom do you agree and why?

4. Given Aristotle's view on friendship, how do you think he would assess Anna and Holly's attitudes and actions towards Harry (*The Third Man*) after they learn the true extent of Harry's racketeering?

5. Describe the conflict faced by Amy in *High Noon*. How does she resolve this conflict? How would you have resolved the conflict? Justify your answer by reference to a moral theory.

6. Can one formulate a coherent defense of pacifism? Does the situation faced by Amy in *High Noon* constitute a decisive objection to her pacifist principles (stated by her in chapter 16)?

7. Why do you think that Helen in *High Noon* refused to help Will Kane? Didn't she have reasons of intimacy to come to his aid? How would Sommers analyze Amy's apparently conflicting principles?

8. Explain how Railton argues that we may be justified in showing greater concern for our intimates on utilitarian grounds. Do you think that adhering to pacifist principles will in the long run maximize intrinsic value? Is Railton committed to a view about what Amy in *High Noon* should do?

9. Did Laszlo know the truth about the relationship between Rick and Ilsa in *Casablanca*? If so, how should he have responded? Should he have let Ilsa leave Rick?

10. Was Louis in *Casablanca* a good or a bad person? What leads you to your conclusion?

11. Was the young wife in *Casablanca* who was willing to sleep with Louis to get an exit visa for her husband and herself (chapter 22) about to do the right thing? Why or why not?

12. Why did Martins shoot Harry Lime when he had him trapped at gunpoint near the end of *The Third Man* (chapters 33–4)? Did he do the right thing? Why or why not?

13   In *The Music Box*, should Ann have remained loyal to her father? Explain Sommers's analysis of the duty of promise-keeping, and explain how she thinks that this duty may be analogous to filial duties. Do you think that Sommers would argue that Ann has filial duties to her father? How would Jeske evaluate the claim that Ann continues to have obligations to her father? Explain.

14   Is there anything that you might find out about your parents that would significantly change your attitude toward them? If you found out that they were guilty of some horrible crime, would you be morally obligated to inform the appropriate authorities?

15   Noddings argues that a consequence of an ethic of caring is that "our obligation is limited and delimited by relation." How does Noddings explain and defend this claim? How far out does she think our circle of obligation extends? Apply Noddings ethic of caring to the dilemma faced by Jack Bauer in the series *24* (Season 1, 7.00−8.00 a.m.)

Part V
Philosophy of Time

Films:
Somewhere in Time
Back to the Future
Planet of the Apes
Frequency
A Sound of Thunder

Introduction

Philosophical questions concerning the nature of time (and in the wake of relativity theory – space/time) have always been among the most intriguing and difficult questions in metaphysics. On the one hand, it seems that we have, and have had since we were very young, a fairly unproblematic understanding of reference to time. We have no difficulty understanding the notion of one thing happening before or after another. We know when we are early or late for an appointment. But it takes only a little philosophical curiosity to raise fundamental issues concerning the nature of time. For example, is our notion of temporal relation (being before, after, at the same time as) more fundamental than other temporal notions (occurring now, yesterday, in 2007)? Can we successfully define, for example, "taking place in 2007," talking only about sequences of events standing in the temporal relations of being before, after, or simultaneous with? How precisely should we understand the relationship between past, present, and future? Commonsense probably takes the view that there "is" a past that makes true such sentences as "Caesar was assassinated." At first blush we can also make true claims about the future. I can say now in 2008 that G. W. Bush will not be president in 2010 and be saying something true. "Is" there a fact about the future that makes true my statement about Bush just as there "is" a fact about the past that makes true my statement about Caesar? The "is" is in scare quotes, of

course, for a reason. In one sense, it seems trivial to point out that neither the past nor the future is *present*. And if they are not present, we should be careful talking about what "is" the case with respect to either the past or the future. Still, many suggest that there is a kind of tenseless "is" that can be used to report all of reality – past, present, and future. Just as there are various objects scattered throughout the entirety of space, so there are various events scattered throughout the entirety of time (see Richard Taylor's "Space and Time" for an overview of these issues). We occupy one part of time now, the way we occupy one part of space now. But the rest of space exists and the rest of time "exists" (where the use of scare quotes highlights the problematic use of the present tense here). On this view, we travel through time the way we travel through space.

If there is a symmetry with respect to past and future, one can find oneself worrying about issues related to freedom (as we shall discuss more in the next unit). It is taken to be a (frequently uttered) truism that one cannot change the past. What has happened has happened and there is no way anyone can do anything now to affect what has already occurred. But (in the musical stylings of Doris Day) it is equally trivial to point out that what will be will be, and if the future is already written, so to speak, how can anyone do anything to affect it? In "The Paradoxes of Time Travel," David Lewis warns us not to be seduced by the fatalist's argument for inability to control the future. He defends, in effect, a version of compatibilism that takes control over the future to be a function of what is co-possible with respect to certain present states of affairs and certain future states of affairs (and he uses a similar strategy to resolve certain paradoxes of time travel that we will discuss in a moment). Crudely, one might argue that even if I get run over by a truck tomorrow, it is true to say that I could have avoided it, because there is nothing in the description of my current states and conditions that is incompatible with my avoiding the accident. Of course, if one includes in descriptions of me now the fact that I and others will do certain things, then trivially *that* description will be incompatible with my not doing them. Similarly, when I go back in time, there will be a description of me at that time that is compatible with my behaving in a number of different ways. Again, there is another description of what I am about to do (and since I'm back in time – a description of what I have already done) which will be, trivially, incompatible with my doing anything else. It is an understatement to suggest that Lewis's attempt to explain the intuition that we have freedom in our travels to the past is controversial.

Perhaps the most intriguing questions concerning the nature of time, questions that have found their way into the plots of many a film, concern the possibility of travel through time, and related questions concerning what one could do were one to achieve such travel. The possibility of time travel has come to the fore with the advancement of scientific theories positing that the length of time lapsed is, in part, a function of the velocity with which we are traveling. So if we travel fast enough from here to some distant point, our sense of the time elapsed will be of a much shorter time than will be measured by conventional time pieces not having traveled at that speed (see *Planet of the Apes*).

In what follows, we'll focus on the possibility of time travel to the past, for it is there that the issues concerning causation come to the fore. The movie *Somewhere in Time* begins with a young playwright celebrating at a reception the opening of his play. A very old woman slowly approaches the playwright, gives him a gold watch, and asks him simply to come back to her (chapter 1). She then leaves the room. A number of years later, in a writing slump, he visits the Grand Hotel on Mackinac Island and comes upon the picture of a stunningly beautiful actress who once played at the hotel theatre near the turn of the century (chapter 3). Strangely haunted by the picture, he investigates and finds out that the woman in the picture is one and the same as the old woman who gave him the watch. While the mechanism of time travel employed is hardly clear, he eventually succeeds in traveling back in time to find the woman. This movie raises no obvious issues concerning changing the past. Indeed, the photograph of the woman that so entranced him was, as it happens, a photograph of her looking at him (chapter 12). It does, however, raise serious issues concerning the causal connections integral to the story. While traveling back in time, the playwright gives the actress the watch – the very watch that he received from the actress late in her life. That watch then has a strange causal history. In terms of "objective" time as we ordinarily conceive it, the watch seems to pop into existence first at the turn of the century (with the playwright's sudden appearance at the hotel). It continues in existence until it is given to the playwright. The playwright, as just noted, also seems to pop into existence at the turn of the century, but the cause of his getting there includes his later acquaintance with the old woman. Given the plot, he can only get back in time if he truly believes he can, and as it turns out, the way he convinces himself that he can time travel is his discovery of his own signature in the turn-of-the-century hotel registry (chapters 7–8). So the fact that he did get back in time at a time $t1$, causes him to believe at a later time $t10$ that he could get back in time, which in turn (partially) causes him to get back in time at $t1$.

The vast majority of philosophers in the history of philosophy just took for granted that causes must precede their effects (or at the very least be cotemporaneous with their effects). Time travel into the past, by its very nature, seems to involve *backward* causation: there is always some mechanism or technique employed in the *present* that causally results in someone's coming into existence in the *past*. If one can make sense of backward causation, then perhaps one can also make sense of the kinds of causal loops that are present in almost all the best-known time travel movies.

David Lewis tries to convince you that you should, in fact, concede the intelligibility (though not, of course, the empirical reality) of these sorts of causal chains. In "Making Things to Have Happened," Roderick M. Chisholm and Richard Taylor argue that *if* one accepts law-based accounts of causation, perhaps one should have no objection to the idea that one can make (cause) things to have happened. Since Hume, a great many philosophers have argued that the heart of causal causation is lawful regularity. Let's say that X is lawfully sufficient for Y when there are laws of nature L such that (X and L) logically entails Y (where neither X nor L alone entails Y). So, for example, heating metal under certain conditions might be *lawfully sufficient* for the metal's expanding in virtue of there being a law (whenever metal is heated under these conditions it expands) which together with the fact that metal was heated under these conditions entails that the metal expands. X is *lawfully necessary* for Y if there are laws of nature L such that (Y and L) entails X (where neither Y nor L alone entails X). So, for example, there being oxygen in my house might be a lawfully necessary condition for my starting a fire in my fireplace if there is a law stating that fire takes place only in the presence of oxygen. One might argue that C is the cause of E when C is either lawfully sufficient for E or is some relevant *part* of a lawfully sufficient condition for E. Others have suggested that causes are, or are parts of, conditions that are both lawfully sufficient and lawfully necessary for Y.

Now if one thinks that such accounts get at the *heart* of causation, then there is no reason to deny that present events can cause past events in the same way that past events can cause present events. The definitions offered above of lawful sufficiency and lawful necessity *entail* that whenever X is lawfully necessary for Y, Y is lawfully sufficient for X. Everyone admits that a past state of affairs can be lawfully necessary for a present state of affairs. It follows, therefore that a present state of affairs can be lawfully sufficient for a past state of affairs. If something I do now is lawfully necessary for something I do later, then that later action is lawfully sufficient for the earlier one. Now one can of course simply *stipulate* that causes must precede their effects. But that might seem like an *ad hoc* stipulation if the heart of causal connections is lawful connection.

The appropriate moral to draw from the above discussion might well be that one shouldn't think that lawful connection is the heart of causal connection. Indeed, Chisholm and Taylor's conclusion was, as we saw, conditional. They probably want you to reject the law-based account of causal connection. And if you do, you have to convince yourself again that you can make sense of backward causation to make sense of time travel (into the past).

There is a related problem that affects our ability to understand completely the possibility of time travel (and the plots of films that center on such possibility). It seems that we need two different concepts of time, or two different dimensions of time, in order to understand what is happening. From the time traveler's perspective, after all, the excursion into the past takes place *after* he has invented his time machine, entered it, and done whatever else was necessary in order to effect the "movement" through time. But in what we might call external (Lewis's term) or objective time, the time traveler's actions in the past obviously take place *prior to* the invention of the time machine and the actions that precipitated the time travel. Issues of backward causation may arise here also. The time traveler *remembers* entering the time machine, for example. But it is plausible to argue that S remembers having done X only if S's having done X is causally responsible for S's state of seeming to remember having done X. Again, it is helpful to have two temporal lines. In one sense of course, S will think of the events of the objective present that he remembers as earlier than the events that constitute his living for a while in a past. In another sense, though, if S really is living in a past, he is doing things that are earlier than the events allowing his traveling through time. Lewis tries to capture these different senses of time by distinguishing "personal" time from "external" time, and he wants to deny that this distinction involves allowing for more than one temporal dimension. It is interesting to ask whether he succeeds in making sufficiently clear the difference.

All of the above is baffling enough, but film (and philosophical thought experiments) inevitably raise questions about what one can do once one travels back in time. In *Back to the Future*, Michael J. Fox's character (Marty McFly) travels back in time and meets his own parents. In doing so, he "changes" the past in various ways. He prevents the event which caused his father and mother to fall in love and he has a limited amount of time to set things right before he (and his brother and sister) disappear – they are, after all, the product of their parents' union. While he manages to preserve his family by getting his father and mother together, he does, in the film, change enough things about the past to bring about a quite different future – his "previously" unsuccessful parents are "now" successful, for example. When one goes back in time, can one change the past, and if one does, can one change the present from which one departed? If one changes the past, is there more than one past? If I warn Caesar about his assassination changing significantly the history of the Western world, are there two pasts (like parallel universes perhaps) – one in which things happened just as I read about them before my time travel; the other, the past in which Caesar goes on well past the Ides of March to conquer the rest of the world? Of course, if there can be parallel pasts, one might as well allow for different but parallel presents and futures each corresponding to changes initiated by time travelers. While the movie *Frequency* doesn't involve time travel per se, it does involve "communication" between someone living in the present and his father living in the past (see, for example, chapter 9). The communication allows the father to "change" what has happened, and, in doing so, to change the future. Once again we seem to have something that looks like backward causation. In *A Sound of Thunder* (loosely based on the Ray Bradbury short story), we are taken to a future in which customers rich enough to afford it can travel back in time to engage in such exotic adventures as the hunt for dinosaurs. The dinosaurs to be shot were carefully researched and their death by gunfire is supposed to occur precisely at the same time as they were to suffer a natural death. The hunters are warned that they must not leave an electronically produced path lest they alter the past and with it the future. Nevertheless, through an accident one of the hunters inadvertently kills an insect – an event which changes the entire evolution of most species of animals (chapters 6–8). Returning to the future, the time travelers discover that there are indeed dramatic changes produced, changes that take place in "waves" (chapter 11). The rest

of the movie involves a concerted effort to return to the past in order to "erase" the change that was made.

David Lewis argues for the intelligibility of time travel, but reaches the conclusion that if I have traveled back to 1900, for example, then I have, in an objective temporal sense, already done whatever I do "after" my time travel. It is impossible that as a result of my time travel something that has already happened in 1900 doesn't happen. Similarly, nothing the dinosaur hunters did having traveled to the past could "change" a past that has already occurred (a past that either did or didn't contain time travelers). To be sure, it would *seem* to me as if I could alter the past once I'm back there. And perhaps we can develop a sense in which that claim is true. But however much it is true to say that I *could* do certain things, intelligible conceptions of time travel entail that I *won't* do those things. And remember our discussion of the future. If there are future facts – if, for example, I will get run down by a truck this afternoon – then it follows there is nothing I *will* do to change my getting run down by the truck. It may not follow from this, however, that there is nothing I *could* have done to avoid getting hit.

Paradoxes of time travel get even worse once the time travelers move to a temporal location that includes an earlier (or later) version of themselves. In *Back to the Future*, Marty McFly returns to the present just in time to see his friend shot by terrorists. He also sees himself looking in horror at this event (chapters 17–18). So where, precisely, is Marty McFly? He seems to occupy two different places at one and the same time. He seems to have two quite different sets of mental properties at one and the same time. If we weren't thinking about the possibility of time travel, we might have endorsed the principle that if X is identical with Y then there can't be anything true of X at time t that isn't true of Y at time t. But the Marty that jumps out of his time-traveling car at t occupies a space that is not the space occupied by the Marty who watched in horror his friend being shot – the Marty who was about to travel back in time. Doesn't this preclude the one Marty from being identical with the other? But doesn't the plot of the film ask us to imagine that they are one and the same?

In our general introduction to this book we stressed the importance of thought experiments for philosophical theories about what is or isn't possible. We suggested that film might give us a particularly vivid way of fleshing out details of the hypothetical situations that test our judgments about what is and isn't possible. But we also warned that one must guard against being seduced by film into thinking that the unintelligible is intelligible. Some films might be a bit like an Escher painting. When one looks at such paintings, one's first reaction is that something possible is depicted. But as one examines the painting more carefully, one begins to see that staircases, for example, disappear into nothingness. There is a two-dimensional picture that initially seems to represent a three-dimensional reality. But on careful inspection, one can't "hook up" that two-dimensional representation with a three-dimensional world. One should, perhaps, think long and hard before one concludes that the "reality" depicted by time travel movies is a genuine intelligible possibility.

38

Making Things to Have Happened

Roderick M. Chisholm and Richard Taylor

It is not our purpose to add to the voluminous arguments[1] purporting to prove, or to refute, the claim that effects might precede their causes, but to show that the commonest type of argument given against that view is inconclusive.

We define the concept of *sufficiency* in terms of an undefined notion of *impossibility* by saying:

"A is sufficient for B" means: (A and ~ B) is impossible,

and we define *necessity* in terms of the same notion by saying:

"A is necessary for B" means: (~ A and B) is impossible,

from which it follows that if A is sufficient for B, then B is necessary for A, and if A is necessary for B, then B is sufficient for A.

The unanalyzed impossibility in terms of which these concepts are defined can be either logical, or what is sometimes oddly called "physical". Thus, a thing's being a cube is sufficient for its having twelve edges, in the sense that it is logically impossible for it to be a cube and have more or less than twelve edges. Similarly, a man's being beheaded is sufficient for his dying, since it is impossible for him to be beheaded and

live, just as it is impossible that petrol-soaked rags brought into contact with fire under certain specifiable conditions should not ignite; but no logical impossibilities are involved in such cases.

We are concerned only with the latter, non-logical sense of impossibility. And for our purposes, the relation of causation can be defined as follows, in terms of sufficiency:

"A causes B" means: A is sufficient for B,

wherein A and B designate conditions that are assumed actually to occur at some time.

Neither A nor B needs to designate a single condition or event, for the cause of any event is almost invariably a *set* of these. Thus, it is elliptical to say of a burning match that striking it caused it to light, for it is not impossible that it should have been struck without lighting – in case it had been wet, for instance. But there is a finite set of conditions among all those that occurred, which was sufficient for its lighting, in the sense of sufficiency defined; for example, some such set as (i) its being dry, (ii) its being struck, (iii) its being of such and such composition, (iv) the pressure on it being such and such, (v) the striking surface being of such and such character ... and so on. And it is this set of conditions which, being sufficient for a certain effect, *causes* that effect.

Roderick M. Chisholm and Richard Taylor, "Making Things to Have Happened." *Analysis* 20, no. 4 (March 1960), pp. 73–8. © 1960 by Analysis. Reprinted with permission from Blackwell Publishing.

Now surely there is nothing in the causal relation, other than this relation of sufficiency. In order to get a match lighted, we need only establish some set of conditions sufficient for its lighting; we do not need, in addition to this, to establish another condition having the "power" or whatnot to "produce" the desired effect. The effect is guaranteed simply by the occurrence of such conditions as are sufficient for it.

As a matter of vocabulary, however, people do not ordinarily call any condition or set of these a "cause" of anything else unless it is also *prior* to it in time. But this seems to be merely a point of vocabulary. Obviously, we could modify our definition by *stipulating* that A must precede B in order to count as a cause of B, thus guaranteeing the priority of causes by definition – just as someone could as easily stipulate that A must *follow* B in order to count as a cause of B. But our point is that if we do not thus secure the principle by stipulation, if we do not add on some such clause as "A precedes B in time" to our definition, then there seems to be no reason for supposing that causes must precede their effects.

We can, to be sure, "make things happen" by producing antecedent conditions sufficient for their happening, thus using causes as "levers" for controlling the future, and there is no doubt that we do tend to think of causes in this way. But, it now turns out, we can apparently in the same sense "make things to have happened" in the past, so this consideration has no significance.

Assume the following situation:

$$C_1 \longrightarrow E \longleftarrow C_2$$
$$T_1 \qquad T_2 \qquad T_3 \qquad T_4 \qquad T_5$$

T_1, T_2, etc., are successive times, T_1 being the earliest. C_1 is a set of conditions sufficient, but not necessary, for an event, E, and E is in turn necessary, but not sufficient, for another set of conditions, C_2. It follows, that C_1 and C_2 are alike sufficient, though neither is necessary, for E, this relation being indicated by the two arrows.

To represent this sort of situation imaginatively but in a much over-simplified way, we might suppose that Smith's drinking poison (C_1) is sufficient for his dying (E), which is in turn necessary for Jones' being elected to office (C_2) – but, we assume, C_1 is not necessary for E, nor is E sufficient for C_2.[2]

Now what reasons can be given for regarding C_1, but not C_2, as being responsible for E? Why, that is, should anyone say that it was Smith's drinking poison that was responsible for his dying, but that Jones' being elected had nothing to do with it, when both events are alike sufficient for that event, i.e., when the occurrence of either of them is enough to ensure Smith's dying? The temptation is to say that it is because C_2 did not occur until *after* E had already happened. But we want now to show how irrelevant that is, by considering the various arguments that might be offered in favour of it.

First argument.   We can, at T_1, bring about the occurrence of C_1, thus ensuring the occurrence of E later on. But we cannot, at T_5, bring about the occurrence of C_2, thus ensuring the prior occurrence of E at T_3 – for T_3 will then be past, and E either will, or will not, have happened, regardless of C_2. To suppose otherwise, would be to suppose that we have some sort of control over what is past.

Reply.   E either does, or does not, happen at T_3. Now if we assume that E does not happen, then it is false that we can bring about the occurrence of C_1 – because E is a necessary (though subsequent) condition of C_1. Only, then, if we assume that E does happen is it true to say that we can bring about C_1.

But similarly, E either does, or does not, happen at T_3. If we assume that E does not happen, then it is indeed false that we can bring about the occurrence of C_2 – because E is a necessary (antecedent) condition of C_2. But if E does happen, then we no longer have any reason for asserting that we cannot, at T_5, bring about the occurrence of C_2.

Now it is tempting to say, that whether E happens or not *depends* on whether C_1 occurs. But it equally depends on whether C_2 occurs – for we can guarantee the occurrence of E by bringing about C_2, just as surely as by bringing about C_1.

As for the thought that by the time T_5 arrives, T_3 will already be past, and E either will or will not have then happened, regardless of C_2, we can equally say that at T_1, T_3 will be as yet future, and E either will or will not then happen, regardless of C_1.

Now it is true that, under the conditions we have assumed, E does not occur "regardless of C_1", for C_1 is obviously responsible for the occurrence of E, that is, is sufficient for it. But it is no less obvious that C_2 is responsible for E – for it, too, is sufficient for it.

If, accordingly, this first argument is thought to prove that no cause can follow its effect, the reply to it seems to show, with as much or as little force, that a cause cannot precede its effect. And this is absurd.

Second argument. We can find a situation in which E has already happened, and then (since E is not sufficient for C_2) we can arrange for C_2 *not* to happen. This shows that C_2 cannot be regarded as being responsible for E – for an event which does not occur, or which can be prevented from occurring, cannot be regarded as causing one that does.

Reply. In any sense in which this second argument is correct, the following appears to be correct too: We can find a situation in which E is going to happen,[3] and then arrange for C_1 not to happen. This indicates that C_1 cannot be regarded as the cause of E – for an event that does not occur, or which can be prevented from occurring, cannot be regarded as causing one that does.

If, accordingly, this second argument is thought to show that no cause can follow its effect, the reply seems equally to show that a cause cannot precede its effect, which is, again, absurd.

Third argument. "Arranging for something not to happen" means doing something, which is sufficient for that event not happening. The second argument therefore means, that we can do something, X, at (say) T_4, such that X is sufficient for the non-occurrence of C_2. And it seems that we *can* thus do something to prevent C_2 – for instance, we can poison Jones, in time to prevent him from being elected.

Reply. Either C_2 will occur at T_5, or it will not. Now if C_2 will occur at T_5, then it is false that we can do X at T_4 – because the non-occurrence of C_2 is a necessary condition for the occurrence of X. Only, then, if C_2 is not going to occur at T_5, can we do X at T_4.

Moreover, in any sense in which we *can* do X at T_4, thus preventing C_2, we can also do something, Y, at (say) T_2, thus postventing C_1 – for instance, we can go and find Smith healthy and free from all poisons. For we can surely say, that C_1 either did occur at T_1, or it did not. If C_1 did occur at T_1, then it is indeed false that we can do Y at T_2. But if C_1 did not then occur, there is no reason to deny that we can do Y.

Hence, it seems that in any sense in which we *can* do X, and thus prevent C_2, we also can do Y, and thus postvent C_1; and, in any sense in which we *cannot* do the latter, we apparently cannot do the former either.

Fourth Argument. Let us suppose that "we can do X" has a hypothetical meaning, something like: we shall do X if we want to, but not unless we want to; and similarly, for "we can do Y". Now in this sense it seems that we surely can do X, at T_4, thus preventing C_2 – for it is presumably true that we shall do it if we want to. But we cannot in a similar fashion ensure that C_1 did not happen, *even* if we want to.

Reply. The reply to this is in part similar to the others. Namely, if we suppose that C_1 has already happened, it is indeed false that we can do Y, for we shall not be able to do Y, even if we want to. But similarly, on the supposition that C_2 is going to happen, it is likewise false that we can do X, for we shall not be able to do X, even if we want to. If, accordingly, we want to do X, presumably we shall – provided C_2 is not already going to happen.

Now one might be tempted to argue that we really could not do Y, because there is now at least one condition, viz., our having not done Y, which renders it impossible that we wanted to do Y, and hence impossible that we should have done it. But clearly, we can give the same kind of reason for saying that we really cannot do X either.

Or one might insist that it is still true that we *can* do X, in the hypothetical sense of "can" defined, even though certain conditions, known or unknown, should render it impossible that we shall want to do X, and hence impossible that we shall in fact do X. But in this same hypothetical sense, we can say that we can have done Y – even granting that it is impossible that we in fact did do Y.

Fifth argument. But our present desires, intentions, decisions, etc., can *influence* our future actions, and thereby influence other things too, whereas our present desires (etc.) cannot influence our past actions, or any past event, these being now beyond our control.

Reply. To say that our present desires (etc.) can *influence* our future actions, evidently means that they can, along with other conditions, be sufficient for those actions.

If, then, our present desires (etc.) could ever be sufficient for our past actions – i.e., if having a certain desire now is, together with other things, enough to ensure our acting in a certain way in the past – then in the sense in which such desires (etc.) influence our future actions, they might influence our past actions as well.

And in fact, the desires (etc.) we now have *are* very often sufficient for our acting in certain ways in the past – namely, in all those cases in which our past actions are necessary conditions for our present desires.

For example, suppose a student wants to go into the law, and this desire is, together with other things, sufficient for his so doing. Suppose further, though, that he would not have that desire, had he not visited courts of law in the past. This means, that his making such visits was necessary for his desiring as he does, and hence, that his subsequent desires are sufficient for his having made those visits.

In the sense in which his desire "influences" his subsequent action, then – viz., is, together with other things, sufficient for that action – so also does it "influence" his past actions.

Sixth argument. But things future – viz., certain actions of ours, or arrangements for various things to happen or not to happen – are sometimes up to us, in the sense that it is up to us *whether* they happen or not. Things past, however, are no longer up to us, there being no longer anything we can do about their happening, or their not happening.

Comment. This thought *seems* to embody something that is true. But if it does, then it would seem that the expression "it is up to us" conveys some idea that cannot be analyzed in terms of conditions necessary or sufficient for each other. It is exceedingly difficult to see what that idea might be.

Notes

1 The general question whether effects can precede their causes has been discussed from various viewpoints and sometimes with highly imaginative examples in the following papers: M. Dummett and A. Flew, "Can an Effect Precede its Cause?" (symposium), *Arist. Soc.*, suppl. vol. 28 (1954); M. Black, "Why Cannot an Effect Precede its Cause?" *Analysis*, vol. 16 (1956); A. Flew, "Effects Before Their Causes? Addenda and Corrigenda", *Analysis*, vol. 16 (1956); M. Scriven, "Randomness and the Causal Order", *Analysis*, vol. 17 (1956); A. J. Ayer, "Why Cannot Cause Succeed Effect?" pp. 170–5 of *The Problem of Knowledge*, Penguin Books, 1956; D. F. Pears, "The Priority or Causes", *Analysis*, vol. 17 (1957); A. Flew, "Causal Disorder Again", *Analysis*, vol. 17 (1957).

2 This example is grossly over-simplified in view of what was said before. A complete description would require us to say that C_1 is, together with such other conditions as exist between T_1 and T_3, sufficient (though not necessary) for E, but that these, without C_1, are not sufficient for E, and that C_2 is, together with such other conditions as exist between T_3 and T_5, sufficient (though not necessary) for E, but again that these, without C_2, are not sufficient for E.

3 The question, how we would *know* that E was going to happen, is of course irrelevant.

39

Space and Time

Richard Taylor

Few things have seemed more metaphysically puzzling than space and time. Each of these two terms seems to refer to something, yet it is impossible to find, in any ordinary way, what it is they refer to. If, as seems true, every real being must exist in space, or in time, or perhaps in both together, then what shall we say of space and time themselves? That they are not real beings? But how could we say that without implying the unreality of everything that exists within them?

Time, especially, has always been regarded by many philosophers as a dark subject of speculation, enigmatic and even incomprehensible. Part of this mysteriousness of time has resulted from thinking of it as something that *moves*, as when we speak, as all persons do, of the passage of time. Time seems to be presupposed whenever we speak of anything moving, since nothing can move or undergo any change whatever except over a brief or long period of time. So how, then, can time itself move?

It is partly out of rebellion against this notion of temporal passage, and all the difficulties this entails, that many metaphysicians have declared time to be unreal, to be some sort of illusion. Indeed, it is almost characteristic of metaphysicians to make this claim. Against the idea of a moving and hence paradoxical time they have set the idea of *eternity*, not as something that moves

on and on endlessly, but rather as a kind of timelessness, wherein there is no changing, decaying, or dying, and wherein what is real is immutably so.

Similarities Between Spatial and Temporal Concepts

Before trying to fathom and unravel some of the more difficult problems of space and time and the differences between them, it will be useful to note their similarities. Some of these can be seen quite readily by noting that many of the same terms can be used and easily understood as expressing either spatial or temporal relationships.

The idea of being at a *place*, for example, can express either a spatial or a temporal idea, or both. If you speak of something as existing at Ivy, Virginia, for instance, you name its spatial place, and if you speak of it as existing on June 12, 1962, you name its place in time. By combining these you give, quite simply, its location in space and time. A corollary to this is the notion of a *distance* or an *interval*, which is easily used in either a spatial or a temporal sense. New York and Boston are spatially distant from each other, Plato and Kant are temporally so, because one can speak intelligibly of a long interval of time between

From Richard Taylor, *Metaphysics*, 4th edn. (Englewood Cliffs, NJ: Prentice Hall, 1992), pp. 68–74, 77–87. © 1992 by Prentice Hall, Inc. Reprinted by permission of Pearson Education, Inc., Upper Saddle River, NJ.

these two. An allied notion is that of *being present*, which is, significantly, often used to express either the spatial concept of being *here* or the temporal concept of being *now*, or both. Again, the concept of *length* or *being extended* has a use in both contexts, though this is often overlooked. The expression "a length of time" has, in fact, a common use, and there is no more difficulty in understanding the idea of something lasting through a certain length of time than the idea of its extending through a certain length of space. The notion of length, in turn, leads to that of *parts*, which can be either spatial or temporal. Distinctions between the spatial parts of things are commonplace, but we sometimes also speak of the parts of a melody, or of a person's life. In fact, anything having temporal length, or duration in time, can be divided into temporal parts. The spatial parts of a thing are sometimes very similar to each other, as in the case of a brick wall, but so also are the temporal parts of something often quite similar to each other – for instance, those of a gravestone, which is much the same at one time as at another. Finally, it should be noted that the concept of a *physical object* involves both space and time, since any such object has, for instance, both kinds of length or extension and both kinds of parts. Some objects are spatially very small, like dust particles, and others are temporally so, like a flash of lightning; others are both, and some are neither.

The Comparison of Spatial and Temporal Relationships

If one describes things in terms of such concepts as we have just illustrated he finds, often to his surprise, that the differences between their spatial and temporal relations are not as great as he might have supposed. It is intellectually stimulating and edifying to the understanding to see just how far such comparisons can sometimes be carried. A few examples will illustrate the point.

It will be noted that in formulating these comparisons we shall for the most part eschew the terms *space* and *time* and speak instead of *places* and *times*, and of *spatial* and *temporal relations*. This will help avoid the common error of thinking of space and time as strange, huge, and invisible substances but will still enable us to express

whatever we wish to say on these subjects. Thus instead of describing two objects as "a mile apart in space," which suggests that there is a huge but invisible vessel called "space" in which these objects are contained, we can say instead that they are spatially separated by an interval of a mile, the word *interval* here quite properly suggesting not some sort of filament that holds the two things apart but rather a relationship between them. Similar modes of description can be used in speaking of time, such that we shall say how various things are temporally related to one another instead of speaking of certain events as "occurring in time." When we speak of particular *times* we shall be referring not to absolute moments in something called "time," but rather to the relations of certain parts of a clock to one another – for instance, the spatial relations of its "hands" to the numbers on its "face."

Some Comparative Examples

It is often claimed that no object can be in two places at once, though it can occupy two or more times at one place, and some persons imagine that this expresses a very great and basic difference between the spatial and temporal relations of objects.

There are two ways in which an object can occupy two different times at only one place. It might simply remain where it is through an interval of time, or it might be removed from its place and later returned. Now it does at first seem as though nothing corresponding to these situations can ever happen the other way around; that is, that no object can be in two places at one time, and in particular that it cannot be returned to a time. When one tries to imagine situations that might be so described, he almost unavoidably finds himself thinking of two objects instead of one.

What must first be noted, however, is that an object can be in one place at two times only if it also occupies all the time in between, whether at that same place or another, and it must accordingly have some temporal length. Otherwise, we find that we are talking about two objects and not one. But with a similar provision, an object surely can be in two places at one time – by occupying the space between them as well.

Someone who is standing with one foot in the doorway and the other outside is occupying two places at once, for instance. Of course it is tempting here to object that only a *part* of the person is in either place; he is not both entirely inside and entirely outside. But when this has been said, it must be remembered that it is a different *temporal* part of an object that, at a given place, occupies each of two or more times. Thus a person might just stay where he is for a while, and be in the same place at two different times – but it is not the same temporal part of the person that is at those two times. We have to remember that as things are more or less extended in space and have spatial boundaries, they are also extended in time and have temporal boundaries, defining their beginnings and endings. The intervals between such boundaries, of either kind, can be divided up into parts, both spatial and temporal. The comparison so far is, then, quite complete.

Moving Forth and Back in Space and Time

What about an object that moves from its place and then returns to it? This is easy enough to conceive, but can we think of anything similar to this with respect to a thing's temporal relations? Can something, for example, move from its time and return to it? Can anything, indeed, move in time at all?

The situation analogous to that of an object that moves from its place and later returns involves some particular details of description, but it is perfectly possible. An object can, accordingly, move forth and back "in time," just as it can "in space," provided one sees exactly what this means and sets forth descriptions in terms of the relationships involved.

To see this, we need only to give an exact description of an object that moves from its spatial location and then returns to it, which is easy enough, and then rewrite that description – substituting spatial terms for temporal terms, and vice versa. Our question, whether anything can move from its place in time and return to it, then becomes nothing but this question: Does our second description apply to anything that ever happens? It is important to see that this *is* what the question comes to, and not, at that point, lapse

into imaginative but incoherent fables of science fiction.

Consider first, then, an object, O, which moves from its place and later returns to it. An exact description of this set of events is this:

1. O is at place$_1$ at time$_1$, and also at place$_1$ at time$_2$; it endures from time$_1$ through time$_2$, but is *then* (*i.e.*, at some time within that temporal interval) at places other than place$_1$.

Now it can be seen that any object O whose behavior fits that description is one that moves from its place and returns to it, and one that, therefore, can be described as "moving forth and back in space."

Now let us rewrite that description, exchanging all spatial and temporal terms for each other, so as to have times where before we had places and vice versa. Doing this, we get the following description:

2. O is at time$_1$ at place$_1$ and also at time$_1$ at place$_2$; it extends from place$_1$ through place$_2$ but is *there* (*i.e.*, at some place within that spatial interval) at times other than time$_1$.

Before proceeding another step it must be noted that this is exactly the description we are looking for; that is, descriptions 1 and 2 should be carefully compared to see that they are the same, except that spatial and temporal concepts and relations have been switched around.

Does the second description, then, apply to anything that ever happens? That is, does anything ever behave in such a way as this? It is not hard to see that it does, and that an object can, accordingly, move forth and back in time just as well as it can in space. One will be inclined to reject this suggestion *only* if he departs from the description actually before him and begins reveling in incoherent fables, a temptation almost irresistible to most persons unaccustomed to thinking philosophically.

Consider, for example, something fairly well known, such as an earthquake. Suppose that at time$_1$ it occurs (simultaneously) in two nearby towns, which we may refer to as place$_1$ and place$_2$, and that it occurs everyplace between these two towns, but at one of those intermediate places at a time other than time$_1$. Such a set of events fits exactly our description 2. The earthquake, therefore, is something that (over an interval of space) moves forth and back in time; for this means nothing more than that it does fit that description.

Now some would want to insist here that more than one object is involved in this example, or even that an earthquake is no proper object at all. But it is an object in every significant way – it has a location in space and time, has interesting properties, such as the property of being destructive, and might even have a name, as hurricanes, for example, usually do. Nor is it to the point to suggest that, in the example given, more than one such object is involved. The people in the different towns could say, rightly, that they suffered from the same earthquake. Moreover, we can and ordinarily do say that moving about in space does not destroy the identity of a thing; no one would say, for instance, that if a chair is moved from one side of the room to the other and then back again it thereby becomes a different chair. And so, likewise, there is no reason for saying that moving about in time, in the manner suggested, destroys the identity of a thing. In the case of the chair, a temporal continuity is retained between its different temporal parts; it at no time, in the temporal interval in which it is moved, ceases to exist altogether. Similarly, the earthquake retains a spatial continuity between its different spatial parts; it at no place, in the spatial interval in which it moves, ceases to exist altogether. The analogies, then, seem quite complete.

Time Travel

A common device of imaginative story tellers is to have their characters move to a time long past or, even more imaginatively, to a time distantly future. Typically, someone steps into a time machine, much as one would step into a boat, and then, soon thereafter, finds himself surrounded by things and events that existed long ago or, in the case of a trip to the future, things that are still waiting to happen. Here the assumed similarity to a great "river of time" is obvious, for one can thus move up or down a river.

Such stories cannot, however, be understood as describing movement back or forth in time.

The incoherence of such accounts is exposed in saying that, shortly thereafter – *i.e., at a later time* – someone finds himself living *at an earlier time*. To imagine "returning" to an earlier time is merely to imagine the recurrence of the events of that time. More precisely, it is to imagine everything *except oneself* just as it was then. One can, perhaps, imagine the world as it was long ago, imagine one's mother as a young woman in the surroundings then familiar to her, but it does not make sense to imagine oneself as a witness to all this, observing her as she matures, bears her children (oneself among them), and raises her family. Such words convey no coherent description.

Time and Change

People have always thought of space and time as differing most markedly with respect to the way in which they are involved in the mutability of things. That is, time has always been thought of as an essential ingredient to motion and change, to the manner in which things arise and perish, flourish and decay, whereas there seems to be nothing quite comparable to this with respect to space. Change and time thus seem inseparable, whereas no such notion seems presupposed in the conception of space.

This way of looking at things is no more than a reflection of certain prejudices, however. Ordinarily when one thinks of motion and change he is thinking of temporal processes. Similarly, arising and perishing are thought of as events in time, and the descriptions of them are therefore appropriately tensed. Such ways of thinking and speaking do not, however, preclude the possibility of exactly analogous relationships in space, and when one attempts a description of such spatial change, he finds that it is not very difficult.

Ordinarily, to say that something *moves* means only that it occupies one place at one time and another place at another. But it obviously comes to exactly the same thing to say that it occupies one time at one place and another time at another. This kind of motion, then, which is referred to in Aristotelian philosophy as "local motion," is neither more nor less temporal than spatial; it is precisely both.

There is a more general sense of "change," however, according to which something is said to have a more or less interesting history. Something changes in this sense, in other words, in case it acquires and loses various properties and relationships over an interval of time – in case its temporal parts are dissimilar. But why may we not say, analogously, that a thing may acquire and lose various properties and relationships over an interval of space – or in other words, have spatial parts that are dissimilar? A thing would change *temporally*, in the sense we are considering, in case it was, for example, blue at one time and red at another. But then something, such as a wire, might be blue at one end and red at the other, and perhaps various other colors between these two places. This would accordingly be an example of *spatial* change. This sense of "change" is not, moreover, strange or unusual. It would make sense, for instance, to say of a wire, which was found to be red in one town and blue in another, that *somewhere* (not sometime) between those two places it changes color, and such change, like temporal change, might be gradual or abrupt, or in other words, occur over a long or brief interval.

The Fixity of Spatial or Temporal Positions

Another way in which temporal and spatial relationships are widely thought to differ is expressed in the dictum that things can change their spatial positions but not their temporal ones, these being, once given, fixed eternally. Thus, something that is north of another can be moved around to the south of it, but something that is future to another cannot be "moved" around to its past. This is partly what is meant by speaking of time as irreversible, and it seems to have no parallel in space.

This way of looking at things, however, is again no more than a reflection of familiar habits of thought and speech, and it really amounts to very little once one sees beyond these. The claim, for example, that things cannot change their positions in time amounts to no more than the trivial claim that something cannot be in two times at once (at one time). It is thus comparable to the equally trivial claim that something cannot be in two places at one place. Similarly, the claim that two things, that are so related that the one is future

to the other, are *always* so related is of course true, but again it is trivial. It is exactly comparable to a claim that two things that are related in such a way that one is north of the other are *everywhere* so related. The expressions "always" and "everywhere" in such statements add absolutely nothing to what is said in them. My son's birth belongs to a time future to my own birth, but it adds nothing to this to say that these events are "always" so related. Similarly, my son now happens to be several hundred miles east of me, but it adds nothing to this to say we are now "everywhere" so related.

[. . .]

The Relativity of Time and Space

Most people think of time as a great river. This gives rise to much confusion, the commonest being, as we have seen, the idea of getting into a "time machine" and "going back" or perhaps even "going forth" in time, as one might get into a boat and go up or down a river.

Thus time is thought of as something that flows, like a river, at a constant rate and in one direction only. A river wears down the things in its path, and things similarly age and decay over time. A river has a distant and obscure source, and eventually flows into a vast ocean. Philosophers and theologians have similarly speculated on the beginning of time itself, and on the vast and unflowing eternity in which it ends.

Space, on the other hand, is popularly thought of as resembling not a river but a great and motionless vessel within which everything is spread out and contained. Thus we think of objects as moving through space, much as fish move about in a vast lake.

The fundamental error in these popular conceptions is thinking of time and space as *things* or, in Kantian terms, as "real beings." Space and time are not things. The words derive their meaning from certain relationships that all objects have to each other. Examples of common *spatial* relationships, for example, are those of being next to, being distant from, approaching, receding, surrounding, being inside of or outside of, and so on. Similarly, familiar *temporal* relationships are those of being simultaneous with, being earlier or later than, being younger or older than, being brief or persisting, and so on.

Time and Motion

The concept of time is inseparable from the concept of change. When one thinks of "the passage of time" one is likely to think of sand flowing in an hour glass, the lengthening shadow of a sun dial, or of aging. And it is, of course, from the regularly changing relationships of the earth, moon, and sun that our basic temporal concepts arise. A *day* is the "amount of time" required for one rotation of the earth. But that is misleadingly expressed. We should say, rather, that "one day" refers to the temporal distance between adjacent sunrises. The term "year" similarly refers to the temporal distance between, for example, adjacent winter solstices. And the idea of a month derives from the regular but ever changing relationship between earth and moon.

These three concepts – day, year, and month – are not purely conventional, for they rest upon unalterable natural cycles. Thus we could not, for example, divide a year into one hundred days, the way we have divided days into twenty-four hours rather than, say, twenty. Clocks could be designed to complete their regular cycles twenty times per day, rather than twenty-four, and this would not generate any real problems of time measurement. But a year cannot be thus arbitrarily divided up.

All temporal relationships are set against the background, not of some great river of time, but rather, the orderly and repetitive configurations of earth, sun, and moon. To enable us to refer to events, and when they occur, and how they are related to others, we arbitrarily designate one such set of configurations as a point of departure. Thus, "year one" refers to that set of configurations of sun, earth, and moon that coincide with some more or less dramatic event, such as the birth of some religious figure. Then, given that framework, *any* event, large or small, can be located within it, and the events then related to each other, as being before or after, and the extent of their temporal separation can be measured. Thus we can locate great and complex events, such as the rise and fall of nations, or small and simple ones, such as the winning of a race, where

a fraction of a second becomes crucial. But in all such cases we are relating events to the successive configurations of earth, sun, and moon, or, more generally, to the earth in relation to the heavens; nothing more.

Particular Times

Inasmuch as time, considered as an endless, invisible, and intangible thing perpetually flowing upon us, has no real being, the same must be true of particular times, even though philosophers and others often allude to times as if pointing to identifiable things.

The corresponding point can perhaps be more readily seen with respect to individual places. Thus, if you allude to particular places, by such expressions as "Times Square," "the finish line," "where we met," and so on, you find that you are in fact only referring to physical objects, which are located not by the places they somehow occupy but by their spatial relationships to other objects. Spatial locations are, accordingly, purely relative. Thus one might toss his hat into the back seat of his car, spend the day driving around, and then say that the hat was right there, in the same place, the whole time. The statement is true, or false, depending on what other objects are being indirectly referred to as reference frames.

It is the same with times. Thus, such expressions as "the time of Socrates' birth," "the moment the race began," "the Elizabethan era," and so on – all of which appear to refer to particular times, of greater or lesser duration – really refer only to things and events in relation to other things and events. "The moment the race began," for example, does not refer to some bit of time, but to some such set of events as the firing of a gun, the state of a clock, and, ultimately, the temporal relationships of these to earth and sun. Thus time is, like space, relative.

Temporal Direction

We think of time as having a fixed direction, like an arrow that cannot be turned around or, again, a river that cannot be reversed. The future is something necessarily lying ahead of us, and the past, behind us.

The ascription of temporal direction rests, however, not on any metaphysical feature of time, but on the irreversibility of certain processes, that is, changes in objects. Some changes have no such fixed sequence. Thus one can design a clock that runs backwards. Ice can melt, then refreeze, and melt again. You can walk to the store, then walk home again, even walking backwards if you have the patience. Other changes, however, have a fixed and unalterable direction. Thus a fried egg cannot become unfried and restored to its shell. Light emanates from a candle flame, but the reverse process is impossible. An acorn grows to an oak, but never the reverse. Other examples of such irreversibility come easily to mind. The general description of any such process is that it contains a set of states, namely, A, B, C . . . etc., which are such that, as a matter of physical law, A must precede B, B must precede C, and so on, the reverse sequence being impossible. Thus, the alleged "direction of time" turns out to be a feature only of some, but not all, temporal processes, that is, relations between states of things. If every process were reversible, then there would be nothing to suggest any inherent direction of time.

Temporal Passage

One thing concerning time that has always been the greatest stumbling block to comparing it with space is its *passage* or *flow*, or what amounts to the same thing, the characteristic all things seem to have of continuously moving along through time. Thus, we speak of future things as *drawing nearer*, of then *becoming* present and, having passed into the present, of *receding* endlessly into an ever-growing past. These are all expressions of change or movement. They clearly imply that something is moving, though certainly not in the ordinary manner in which things move. In fact, something needs only to be in time, or in other words, to exist as an object, in order to be moving in the manner suggested; for concerning any such object we can say that, until it exists, it draws closer and closer to existing; that while it exists it becomes older; and after it ceases to exist it recedes ever farther into the past.

This kind of motion or passage, which seems to be such a basic and even necessary characteristic of time, has profoundly bewildered philosophers ever since St. Augustine tried, without much success, to make sense of it in his *Confessions*. It becomes so strange and loaded with absurdities, as soon as one tries to think rationally about it, that some thinkers have simply concluded that it is an illusion and that, accordingly, time itself must be unreal. Plato, taking this view, called time nothing but a moving image of eternity, the suggestion being that what is only an image has no genuine reality, but that eternity does. Eternity is the realm of reality in which there is no change, becoming, or decay. It has been almost characteristic of metaphysics to take this view. Eternity is the temporal dimension of the world as it would be seen by an eternal and changeless being such as God. Nothing arises or perishes, as thus apprehended; it simply *is*. There is here no becoming or changing, no growing older. Concerning the universe and all it contains, one can say that it exists. One cannot in addition say that it is passing through time, or that time is passing over it.

For example, one can say, concerning some more or less interesting thing, such as your birth, that there is such an event. And one can say concerning another more or less interesting thing, such as your death, that there is also such an event as that. Further, one can say that the first of these is *earlier* than the other, and that there are other events in the world – such as the birth of your father – to which it is subsequent; and that there are other events with which it is simultaneous. And so it is with everything that ever exists or happens. The entire universe is spread out in a changeless space and a changeless time, and everything in it has a place, defined by its spatial relationships to other things, and a time, defined by its temporal relationships to other things. Things move in space, in the sense that something can be at one place at one time and at another place at another time, but there is no sense in which space itself can be described as moving. Similarly, as we have seen, things move in time, in the sense that something can be at one time at one place and at another time at another place, but there is no sense in which time itself can be described as moving. Or at least, that is the view of things that a metaphysical mind is apt to prefer.

Still, it cannot be denied that things in time *seem* to pass into, through, and out of existence. That can be our datum or starting point, and if metaphysics declares this to be an illusion, then it is up to metaphysics to show it is. Until the illusory character of this apprehension has been demonstrated, then we can say, concerning anything whatever that ever exists, that until it exists it draws ever closer to existing; that while it exists it grows older; and that after it ceases to exist it recedes ever farther into the past. Or at least, so it certainly seems.

Conscious and reflective beings like us find the passage of time inescapable. No metaphysical theories can make this passage seem less real to us who dwell in time and who look forward and back in it. Past things have a sense of distance quite unlike things that are present, and the recession of things past is something that can almost be felt. We sometimes want to grasp for them, to seize them, and hold them a bit longer, but this in vain. Human beings have both the inherent determination to exist and the intelligence or understanding to realize that their tenure of existence is limited. One's passage through time is for oneself, then, an appalling fact. That lifeless things should deteriorate and perish makes no difference anywhere. These things have no will to life and no dread of its passage and cessation. The fact that their duration is finite has no more significance than that their bulk is such. If the world turned lifelessly around, carrying only its atmosphere and lifeless things upon it, its passage through time would be quite without significance, and it would not matter whether it was now turning for the millionth or the thousand millionth time. But a person is aware that his life is something that he *passes through*, and that its end is something that, whether near or remote, is nonetheless surely *approaching*. Whether it is his thousandth or twenty thousandth sunrise that he is seeing makes an overwhelming difference, for it marks the extent of his pilgrimage along a path upon which he can neither pause nor turn back, and that has only one possible destination, which is the cessation of his own being. It marks, in fact, how much is gone, and how much is still left, of his own ebbing existence. Nor is it here the mere prospect of his debility that appalls, for a man would be only partially comforted by the realization that the vigor of his youth could be held a bit longer. It is the fact of *passage* itself, with or without the vigor of youth, that concerns one. Someone awaiting certain execution draws no comfort from the fact that he need suffer no decay before death. It is the approach of the latter by itself, and the total calamity of it, that voids his hope. It is perhaps worth noting, however, that every one of us is approaching his end, no less certainly and inevitably than one who has had its date fixed for him.

Pure Becoming

Let us use the expression "pure becoming" to designate the passage through time to which all things seem to be subjected, merely by virtue of their being in time. It is aptly called *pure* becoming because any other kind of change or becoming that anything might undergo *presupposes* this kind of change, whereas this pure becoming presupposes no other change at all. Thus, in order for anything to become red, or square, or larger, or weaker, or whatnot, it must pass through a certain amount of time, which is equivalent to saying that it must *become older*. The fact that something becomes older, however, or that it acquires a greater age than it had does not entail that it undergoes any other change whatever.

The idea of a thing's becoming older is not always, to be sure, thought of in this metaphysical sense. When we describe something as becoming older we often have in mind certain definite and observable changes. For instance, if we say of a man that he is becoming older, we are apt to be referring to the diminution of his strength or vigor, and so on. Aging is, in this sense, simply a physiological concept, and as it is used in this way we can speak without absurdity of someone's aging more or less rapidly, or even of his becoming younger.

By *pure becoming*, however, we have in mind becoming older simply in the sense of acquiring a greater age, whether that increase of age is attended by any other changes or not. In this sense a thing can become older without undergoing any other change whatever, for it can simply increase in age from one day to the next. This, then, seems to be a kind of becoming or passing through time that can be asserted of anything whatever that exists in time, for it is a consequence simply of its being in time. A thing can be as stable and unchanging as we care to suppose, and yet this appears to be one change that nothing can elude. Even if something should acquire the attributes of newness, and thus elude the process of aging in that sense, it would still have to become older to do so. If a decaying flower, for instance, resumed the fresh form of a bud, it would in one sense appear to become younger but it would nonetheless become older, for otherwise no meaning could be given to the idea of its *resuming* that form. We could say of such a flower on any given day, whatever might be its form and properties, that it is a day older than it was yesterday, that in the meantime it has *become* older, however new and young it may seem. And this, of course, would mark a change – namely, a change in its age, which it had in time undergone.

Now, for anything to be passing through time or becoming older it must, of course, exist. Nonentities do not become older or pass through time, for they are not even *in* time; nor do real things that once existed but have since ceased, or other real things that will at some time exist but that do not exist yet. Diogenes' cup, for instance, became both old and rusty, but both changes ceased with the cessation of that cup's existence. Yet even things that have ceased to exist, and others that will exist in the future but do not exist yet, undergo a *relational* kind of change that is simply a corollary of pure becoming or passage through time. That is, we can speak of Diogenes' cup as *receding* ever farther into the past. It is more remote from us in time today than it was yesterday, and this is a relational change it is undergoing. Similarly, the birth of my first grandchild, assuming there will be one, is something that is *drawing closer*, and this is a relational change that something that will, but does not yet, exist, is already undergoing. I can look forward to it now, but someday I shall only be able to look back upon it; and this is a change that it will meanwhile have undergone and is even now undergoing, in relation to me. Nor is this merely a change in the manner in which I choose to view it, for it is no matter of my choice at all. Just as I cannot now look forward in anticipation to using Diogenes' cup, because this has forever after – for all future time – ceased to be, so also I cannot now look back in memory to the birth of my first grandchild, because this has forever before – for all past time – not yet come to be.

The Strangeness of This Idea

This kind of passage or change is surely very odd, so odd that anyone who thinks about it is apt to feel impelled either to deny outright that it even exists, which amounts to denying the datum with which we began, or else to find alternative ways of expressing it. The idea of pure becoming or temporal passage will seem even more strange, however, in the light of the following considerations.

In the first place, we must note that pure becoming is not only an unobservable change but is compatible with, and in fact entailed by, any change whatever that is observed. If, for instance, we see that something, such as a leaf, is green and then becomes red, or red and then becomes green, we must conclude that it also becomes older, for nothing can become anything at all without becoming older in the process. The conception of something's becoming older, then, is a purely *a priori* notion, a consequence of its simply being in time. Second, any event is a change, and it is therefore quite odd to think of events as themselves changing. Yet events are in time and have duration; hence, while they last, they become older, and when they have ceased they begin an endless recession into the past, like anything else. And finally, the continual recession of things past, and the advance upon us of things future, is a strange kind of passage for the reason that no *rate* of passage can possibly be assigned to it without making nonsense. We cannot, for instance, sensibly say that Diogenes' cup is receding into the past at the rate of one day every twenty-four hours, or even at the rate of one day for every complete rotation of the earth; but what else can one say?

Confronted with such considerations as these, it is tempting to dismiss the pure becoming or temporal passage of things as an illusion, to say that nothing ever really does change in this sense. If a metaphysician wants to make a case for this, he has abundant materials with which to construct his arguments. This amounts, however, to denying the datum with which we began. Moreover, in case the idea of the passage or flow of time is essential to the very conception of time itself, as it may well be, then to deny that there is any such passage would amount to denying that anything is even in time at all. Ever so many metaphysicians have found this conclusion an agreeable one, but it is hardly in accordance with one of the most basic convictions of mankind. However puzzling it may be to metaphysics, it is very difficult for anyone really to convince himself of the falseness of the idea that the end of his life, for example, whether it be near or remote, is something that is approaching, that it will, alas, become present, and that it will then begin receding into the past. Such a statement is readily understood by everyone and seems quite certainly to express a fact of some sort. If a prisoner who is awaiting execution is told that the hour of his death is approaching and already near, he realizes that he has learned something of great importance to himself. He knows that there is little left of his life, and that what little is left is diminishing with every passing moment. His terror at this thought would hardly be relieved by his having it pointed out to him by a metaphysician that this kind of change is very strange and even absurd. However strange and mysterious the passage of time might be, it is sometimes nonetheless appalling.

Time and a River

While temporal passage is a difficult philosophical concept, it should not be compared with the flow of a river. A river flows at a certain rate – for example, two miles per hour – but, as we have noted, no rate can be assigned to the passage of time. To say that time passes at a "rate" of one day at a time is no more meaningful than saying it passes one year at a time, nor can any meaning be given here to the words "at a time." Similarly, to speak of "one day every twenty-four hours" is merely to signify that a day can be thus divided into hours, just as a foot can be divided into inches. This is not of philosophical interest.

Again, the flow of a river can be stopped, or sometimes accelerated, or retarded, by dams, for instance; but no meaning can be given to time stopping, speeding up, or slowing. When people speak of time "standing still" what they actually imagine is everything *but* time standing still. They imagine a total cessation of all change – for a certain brief or long *period of time*. Similarly, when one tries to form an idea of time moving more or less rapidly, he finds himself imagin-

ing something other than time increasing or decreasing its rate of change. If, for example, a man were to pass from birth to adolescence, maturity, old age, and death all in a single year, then this would not mean that time had, for him, been greatly accelerated. It would mean, rather, that his life processes had been accelerated. All the stages of his life are imagined to occur within the fixed time of one standard year.

The Elusive Present

The words "time" and "space," we have noted, are not names of things, and hence do not stand for strange beings that flow, expand, contract, or do anything at all. Instead, then, of speaking of time and space, we should speak of temporal and spatial relationships between things. And the temporal relationships between things and events, it should now be noted, do not change. If a given event occurs one hour before another, then that always was and always will be the temporal relationship the two events have to each other. Viewing the matter this way, then the whole history of the world, together with its entire future, can be regarded as fixed and changeless, for the relationship which any event whatever has to every other event that ever occurs, whether past, present, or future, is quite unalterable. Thus your birth and your death, two events that are of momentous importance to you, are eternally separated by a certain fixed interval of time, which is the length of your life, and this never changes.

The pastness or futurity of an event, however, is not something that is fixed and unchanging. We are especially aware of this with respect to all those things we view as being *present*. They seem to be continuously slipping away. We feel this more and more acutely as we get older, for what is left of our lives seems to be constantly shrinking, just as what has already been lived seems to be constantly growing. Perhaps this is why old people dwell so much on the past, but give little thought to the future. The former has become rich and full, while the latter seems to be rapidly, and depressingly, dwindling to nothingness.

The philosophical problem of temporal passage, or what has been called "pure becoming," can be expressed by saying that, when a given set of events or items of history have been completely described in terms of which ones come before and which ones come after some other event or set of events, we still do not know which, if any, are past and which future. For example, consider the set of lunar eclipses visible from a certain place over a period of one hundred years. Call these A, B, C . . . etc., with the understanding that A occurs before B, that B occurs before C, and so on, and let the temporal distances, or "amounts of time," between them be specified. Now we still do not know, from such a description, which of these events, if any, have already occurred, and which, if any, are still in the future. These properties, moreover, seem to be changing ones, for if any of these events happens to be a future one, then it will eventually cease to be future, briefly become present, and then, it would seem, commence its endless recession into the past. And this seems inconsistent with the conception of time endorsed by most philosophers, to the effect that all statements involving time can be reduced to statements describing the temporal relationships of events to each other.

One way of trying to get around this difficulty is to understand "the present" as referring not to some fleeting moment, but rather to a certain changeless date, and then treat the events under consideration as occurring either before or after that date. Thus, the statement that a lunar eclipse occurs on July 3, 1989, will turn out to be equivalent to saying that it is future, on every date prior to then, and that it is past on every date thereafter.

This proposed solution does not work, however, for even though the date of the event is understood, one still does not know whether that event is occurring now, is going to occur, or has already occurred, unless he *also* happens to know which date happens to correspond with the present moment. And that is something that changes. The date itself is something that is at one time future, then becomes present, and shortly thereafter slips into the past, and we thus still have on our hands the same problem with which we began.

Suppose, then, we try relating such a set of events, not to some fleeting present moment, but to the very act of describing or alluding to them, which is of course nothing but an additional event. Thus, we can understand the description

"the eclipse that is occurring now," to be a reference to whatever eclipse happens to coincide with the utterance of that very description. And this, of course, amounts to nothing more than asserting the simultaneity of two events. To say that a given pair of events occur simultaneously implies nothing about any mysterious kind of temporal passage.

This proposal contains the same difficulty as the preceding one, however, for we can now ask whether the utterance alluded to is one that is occurring *now*, or whether it is one that is past, perhaps long past. The mere assertion of the coincidence of an eclipse with someone's description of it tells us nothing about when the eclipse occurs, unless we know when, in relation to the fleeting present, that description occurs.

So finally, approaching the problem from still another direction, let us suppose that the idea of the *present* is not really a temporal concept at all, but rather, a psychological one, referring, not to some elusive moment of time, but to what William James and others have called "the specious present." Thus, in speaking of an event as happening *now*, one simply relates the event in question to his awareness of it.

But here, not surprisingly, the same problem recurs, for one can now ask, concerning the state of awareness alluded to, whether it is one's *present* awareness, or perhaps some past awareness that is now merely being recalled. And with that it can be seen that we have made no progress at all with respect to getting rid of the concept of the present moment and its elusive character.

Thus the passage of time seems to remain as an irreducible mystery – not mysterious in the sense of being unknown, for nothing could be more familiar, but mysterious in the metaphysical sense that it cannot be described in a way that is not an invitation to absurdity. The world would certainly be less philosophically puzzling if all temporal relationships could, like spatial ones, be reduced to relationships between objects. The world could then be thought of as consisting of infinitely many things and events simply spread out in space and time. But the seemingly irreducible mystery of temporal passage, or the fleetingness of the present moment, is a persisting obstacle to such simplicity, and time remains hardly less puzzling than when St. Augustine tried, in vain, to comprehend it.

40

The Paradoxes of Time Travel

David Lewis

Time travel, I maintain, is possible. The paradoxes of time travel are oddities, not impossibilities. They prove only this much, which few would have doubted: that a possible world where time travel took place would be a most strange world, different in fundamental ways from the world we think is ours.

I shall be concerned here with the sort of time travel that is recounted in science fiction. Not all science fiction writers are clear-headed, to be sure, and inconsistent time travel stories have often been written. But some writers have thought the problems through with great care, and their stories are perfectly consistent.[1]

If I can defend the consistency of some science fiction stories of time travel, then I suppose parallel defenses might be given of some controversial physical hypotheses, such as the hypothesis that time is circular or the hypothesis that there are particles that travel faster than light. But I shall not explore these parallels here.

What is time travel? Inevitably, it involves a discrepancy between time and time. Any traveler departs and then arrives at his destination; the time elapsed from departure to arrival (positive, or perhaps zero) is the duration of the journey. But if he is a time traveler, the separation in time between departure and arrival does not equal the duration of his journey. He departs; he travels for

an hour, let us say; then he arrives. The time he reaches is not the time one hour after his departure. It is later, if he has traveled toward the future; earlier, if he has traveled toward the past. If he has traveled far toward the past, it is earlier even than his departure. How can it be that the same two events, his departure and his arrival, are separated by two unequal amounts of time?

It is tempting to reply that there must be two independent time dimensions; that for time travel to be possible, time must be not a line but a plane.[2] Then a pair of events may have two unequal separations if they are separated more in one of the time dimensions than in the other. The lives of common people occupy straight diagonal lines across the plane of time, sloping at a rate of exactly one hour of time$_1$ per hour of time$_2$. The life of the time traveler occupies a bent path, of varying slope.

On closer inspection, however, this account seems not to give us time travel as we know it from the stories. When the traveler revisits the days of his childhood, will his playmates be there to meet him? No; he has not reached the part of the plane of time where they are. He is no longer separated from them along one of the two dimensions of time, but he is still separated from them along the other. I do not say that two-dimensional time is impossible, or that there is

David Lewis, "The Paradoxes of Time Travel." *American Philosophical Quarterly* 13, no. 2 (April 1976), pp. 145–52.

no way to square it with the usual conception of what time travel would be like. Nevertheless I shall say no more about two-dimensional time. Let us set it aside, and see how time travel is possible even in one-dimensional time.

The world – the time traveler's world, or ours – is a four-dimensional manifold of events. Time is one dimension of the four, like the spatial dimensions except that the prevailing laws of nature discriminate between time and the others – or rather, perhaps, between various timelike dimensions and various spacelike dimensions. (Time remains one-dimensional, since no two timelike dimensions are orthogonal.) Enduring things are timelike streaks: wholes composed of temporal parts, or *stages*, located at various times and places. Change is qualitative difference between different stages – different temporal parts – of some enduring thing, just as a "change" in scenery from east to west is a qualitative difference between the eastern and western spatial parts of the landscape. If this paper should change your mind about the possibility of time travel, there will be a difference of opinion between two different temporal parts of you, the stage that started reading and the subsequent stage that finishes.

If change is qualitative difference between temporal parts of something, then what doesn't have temporal parts can't change. For instance, numbers can't change; nor can the events of any moment of time, since they cannot be subdivided into dissimilar temporal parts. (We have set aside the case of two-dimensional time, and hence the possibility that an event might be momentary along one time dimension but divisible along the other.) It is essential to distinguish change from "Cambridge change," which can befall anything. Even a number can "change" from being to not being the rate of exchange between pounds and dollars. Even a momentary event can "change" from being a year ago to being a year and a day ago, or from being forgotten to being remembered. But these are not genuine changes. Not just any old reversal in truth value of a time-sensitive sentence about something makes a change in the thing itself.

A time traveler, like anyone else, is a streak through the manifold of space-time, a whole composed of stages located at various times and places. But he is not a streak like other streaks.

If he travels toward the past he is a zig-zag streak, doubling back on himself. If he travels toward the future, he is a stretched-out streak. And if he travels either way instantaneously, so that there are no intermediate stages between the stage that departs and the stage that arrives and his journey has zero duration, then he is a broken streak.

I asked how it could be that the same two events were separated by two unequal amounts of time, and I set aside the reply that time might have two independent dimensions. Instead I reply by distinguishing time itself, *external time* as I shall also call it, from the *personal time* of a particular time traveler: roughly, that which is measured by his wristwatch. His journey takes an hour of his personal time, let us say; his wristwatch reads an hour later at arrival than at departure. But the arrival is more than an hour after the departure in external time, if he travels toward the future; or the arrival is before the departure in external time (or less than an hour after), if he travels toward the past.

That is only rough. I do not wish to define personal time operationally, making wristwatches infallible by definition. That which is measured by my own wristwatch often disagrees with external time, yet I am no time traveler; what my misregulated wristwatch measures is neither time itself nor my personal time. Instead of an operational definition, we need a functional definition of personal time: it is that which occupies a certain role in the pattern of events that comprise the time traveler's life. If you take the stages of a common person, they manifest certain regularities with respect to external time. Properties change continuously as you go along, for the most part, and in familiar ways. First come infantile stages. Last come senile ones. Memories accumulate. Food digests. Hair grows. Wristwatch hands move. If you take the stages of a time traveler instead, they do not manifest the common regularities with respect to external time. But there is one way to assign coordinates to the time traveler's stages, and one way only (apart from the arbitrary choice of a zero point), so that the regularities that hold with respect to this assignment match those that commonly hold with respect to external time. With respect to the correct assignment properties change continuously as you go along, for the most part, and in familiar ways. First come infantile stages. Last come senile ones. Memories accumulate. Food digests. Hair grows. Wristwatch hands move. The assignment of coordinates that yields this match is the time traveler's personal time. It isn't really time, but it plays the role in his life that time plays in the life of a common person. It's enough like time so that we can – with due caution – transplant our temporal vocabulary to it in discussing his affairs. We can say without contradiction, as the time traveler prepares to set out, "Soon he will be in the past." We mean that a stage of him is slightly later in his personal time, but much earlier in external time, than the stage of him that is present as we say the sentence.

We may assign locations in the time traveler's personal time not only to his stages themselves but also to the events that go on around him. Soon Caesar will die, long ago; that is, a stage slightly later in the time traveler's personal time than his present stage, but long ago in external time, is simultaneous with Caesar's death. We could even extend the assignment of personal time to events that are not part of the time traveler's life, and not simultaneous with any of his stages. If his funeral in ancient Egypt is separated from his death by three days of external time and his death is separated from his birth by three score years and ten of his personal time, then we may add the two intervals and say that his funeral follows his birth by three score years and ten and three days of *extended personal time*. Likewise a bystander might truly say, three years after the last departure of another famous time traveler, that "he may even now – if I may use the phrase – be wandering on some plesiosaurus-haunted oolitic coral reef, or beside the lonely saline seas of the Triassic Age."[3] If the time traveler does wander on an oolitic coral reef three years after his departure in his personal time, then it is no mistake to say with respect to his extended personal time that the wandering is taking place "even now".

We may liken intervals of external time to distances as the crow flies, and intervals of personal time to distances along a winding path. The time traveler's life is like a mountain railway. The place two miles due east of here may also be nine miles down the line, in the westbound direction. Clearly we are not dealing here with two independent dimensions. Just as distance along the railway is not a fourth spatial dimension, so a time traveler's personal time is not a second dimension of time.

How far down the line some place is depends on its location in three-dimensional space, and likewise the locations of events in personal time depend on their locations in one-dimensional external time.

Five miles down the line from here is a place where the line goes under a trestle; two miles further is a place where the line goes over a trestle; these places are one and the same. The trestle by which the line crosses over itself has two different locations along the line, five miles down from here and also seven. In the same way, an event in a time traveler's life may have more than one location in his personal time. If he doubles back toward the past, but not too far, he may be able to talk to himself. The conversation involves two of his stages, separated in his personal time but simultaneous in external time. The location of the conversation in personal time should be the location of the stage involved in it. But there are two such stages; to share the locations of both, the conversation must be assigned two different locations in personal time.

The more we extend the assignment of personal time outwards from the time traveler's stages to the surrounding events, the more will such events acquire multiple locations. It may happen also, as we have already seen, that events that are not simultaneous in external time will be assigned the same location in personal time – or rather, that at least one of the locations of one will be the same as at least one of the locations of the other. So extension must not be carried too far, lest the location of events in extended personal time lose its utility as a means of keeping track of their roles in the time traveler's history.

A time traveler who talks to himself, on the telephone perhaps, looks for all the world like two different people talking to each other. It isn't quite right to say that the whole of him is in two places at once, since neither of the two stages involved in the conversation is the whole of him, or even the whole of the part of him that is located at the (external) time of the conversation. What's true is that he, unlike the rest of us, has two different complete stages located at the same time at different places. What reason have I, then, to regard him as one person and not two? What unites his stages, including the simultaneous ones, into a single person? The problem of personal identity is especially acute if he is the sort of time traveler whose journeys are instantaneous, a broken streak consisting of several unconnected segments. Then the natural way to regard him as more than one person is to take each segment as a different person. No one of them is a time traveler, and the peculiarity of the situation comes to this: all but one of these several people vanish into thin air, all but another one appear out of thin air, and there are remarkable resemblances between one at his appearance and another at his vanishing. Why isn't that at least as good a description as the one I gave, on which the several segments are all parts of one time traveler?

I answer that what unites the stages (or segments) of a time traveler is the same sort of mental, or mostly mental, continuity and connectedness that unites anyone else. The only difference is that whereas a common person is connected and continuous with respect to external time, the time traveler is connected and continuous only with respect to his own personal time. Taking the stages in order, mental (and bodily) change is mostly gradual rather than sudden, and at no point is there sudden change in too many different respects all at once. (We can include position in external time among the respects we keep track of, if we like. It may change discontinuously with respect to personal time if not too much else changes discontinuously along with it.) Moreover, there is not too much change altogether. Plenty of traits and traces last a lifetime. Finally, the connectedness and the continuity are not accidental. They are explicable; and further, they are explained by the fact that the properties of each stage depend causally on those of the stages just before in personal time, the dependence being such as tends to keep things the same.[4]

To see the purpose of my final requirement of causal continuity, let us see how it excludes a case of counterfeit time travel. Fred was created out of thin air, as if in the midst of life; he lived a while, then died. He was created by a demon, and the demon had chosen at random what Fred was to be like at the moment of his creation. Much later someone else, Sam, came to resemble Fred as he was when first created. At the very moment when the resemblance became perfect, the demon destroyed Sam. Fred and Sam together are very much like a single person: a time traveler whose personal time starts at Sam's birth, goes on

to Sam's destruction and Fred's creation, and goes on from there to Fred's death. Taken in this order, the stages of Fred-*cum*-Sam have the proper connectedness and continuity. But they lack causal continuity, so Fred-*cum*-Sam is not one person and not a time traveler. Perhaps it was pure coincidence that Fred at his creation and Sam at his destruction were exactly alike; then the connectedness and continuity of Fred-*cum*-Sam across the crucial point are accidental. Perhaps instead the demon remembered what Fred was like, guided Sam toward perfect resemblance, watched his progress, and destroyed him at the right moment. Then the connectedness and continuity of Fred-*cum*-Sam has a causal explanation, but of the wrong sort. Either way, Fred's first stages do not depend causally for their properties on Sam's last stages. So the case of Fred and Sam is rightly disqualified as a case of personal identity and as a case of time travel.

We might expect that when a time traveler visits the past there will be reversals of causation. You may punch his face before he leaves, causing his eye to blacken centuries ago. Indeed, travel into the past necessarily involves reversed causation. For time travel requires personal identity – he who arrives must be the same person who departed. That requires causal continuity, in which causation runs from earlier to later stages in the order of personal time. But the orders of personal and external time disagree at some point, and there we have causation that runs from later to earlier stages in the order of external time. Elsewhere I have given an analysis of causation in terms of chains of counterfactual dependence, and I took care that my analysis would not rule out causal reversal *a priori*.[5] I think I can argue (but not here) that under my analysis the direction of counterfactual dependence and causation is governed by the direction of other *de facto* asymmetries of time. If so, then reversed causation and time travel are not excluded altogether, but can occur only where there are local exceptions to these asymmetries. As I said at the outset, the time traveler's world would be a most strange one.

Stranger still, if there are local – but only local – causal reversals, then there may also be causal loops: closed causal chains in which some of the causal links are normal in direction and others are reversed. (Perhaps there must be loops if there is reversal; I am not sure.) Each event on the loop has a causal explanation, being caused by events elsewhere on the loop. That is not to say that the loop as a whole is caused or explicable. It may not be. Its inexplicability is especially remarkable if it is made up of the sort of causal processes that transmit information. Recall the time traveler who talked to himself. He talked to himself about time travel, and in the course of the conversation his older self told his younger self how to build a time machine. That information was available in no other way. His older self knew how because his younger self had been told and the information had been preserved by the causal processes that constitute recording, storage, and retrieval of memory traces. His younger self knew, after the conversation, because his older self had known and the information had been preserved by the causal processes that constitute telling. But where did the information come from in the first place? Why did the whole affair happen? There is simply no answer. The parts of the loop are explicable, the whole of it is not. Strange! But not impossible, and not too different from inexplicabilities we are already inured to. Almost everyone agrees that God, or the Big Bang, or the entire infinite past of the universe, or the decay of a tritium atom, is uncaused and inexplicable. Then if these are possible, why not also the inexplicable causal loops that arise in time travel?

I have committed a circularity in order not to talk about too much at once, and this is a good place to set it right. In explaining personal time, I presupposed that we were entitled to regard certain stages as comprising a single person. Then in explaining what united the stages into a single person, I presupposed that we were given a personal time order for them. The proper way to proceed is to define personhood and personal time simultaneously, as follows. Suppose given a pair of an aggregate of person-stages, regarded as a candidate for personhood, and an assignment of coordinates to those stages, regarded as a candidate for his personal time. Iff the stages satisfy the conditions given in my circular explanation with respect to the assignment of coordinates, then both candidates succeed: the stages do comprise a person and the assignment is his personal time.

I have argued so far that what goes on in a time travel story may be a possible pattern of events in four-dimensional space-time with no extra time dimension; that it may be correct to regard the scattered stages of the alleged time traveler as comprising a single person; and that we may legitimately assign to those stages and their surroundings a personal time order that disagrees sometimes with their order in external time. Some might concede all this, but protest that the impossibility of time travel is revealed after all when we ask not what the time traveler *does*, but what he *could do*. Could a time traveler change the past? It seems not: the events of a past moment could no more change than numbers could. Yet it seems that he would be as able as anyone to do things that would change the past if he did them. If a time traveler visiting the past both could and couldn't do something that would change it, then there cannot possibly be such a time traveler.

Consider Tim. He detests his grandfather, whose success in the munitions trade built the family fortune that paid for Tim's time machine. Tim would like nothing so much as to kill Grandfather, but alas he is too late. Grandfather died in his bed in 1957, while Tim was a young boy. But when Tim has built his time machine and traveled to 1920, suddenly he realizes that he is not too late after all. He buys a rifle; he spends long hours in target practice; he shadows Grandfather to learn the route of his daily walk to the munitions works; he rents a room along the route; and there he lurks, one winter day in 1921, rifle loaded, hate in his heart, as Grandfather walks closer, closer, . . .

Tim can kill Grandfather. He has what it takes. Conditions are perfect in every way: the best rifle money could buy, Grandfather an easy target only twenty yards away, not a breeze, door securely locked against intruders, Tim a good shot to begin with and now at the peak of training, and so on. What's to stop him? The forces of logic will not stay his hand! No powerful chaperone stands by to defend the past from interference. (To imagine such a chaperone, as some authors do, is a boring evasion, not needed to make Tim's story consistent.) In short, Tim is as much able to kill Grandfather as anyone ever is to kill anyone. Suppose that down the street another sniper, Tom, lurks waiting for another victim, Grandfather's partner. Tom is not a time traveler, but otherwise he is just like Tim: same make of rifle, same murderous intent, same everything. We can even suppose that Tom, like Tim, believes himself to be a time traveler. Someone has gone to a lot of trouble to deceive Tom into thinking so. There's no doubt that Tom can kill his victim; and Tim has everything going for him that Tom does. By any ordinary standards of ability, Tim can kill Grandfather.

Tim cannot kill Grandfather. Grandfather lived, so to kill him would be to change the past. But the events of a past moment are not subdivisible into temporal parts and therefore cannot change. Either the events of 1921 timelessly do include Tim's killing of Grandfather, or else they timelessly don't. We may be tempted to speak of the "original" 1921 that lies in Tim's personal past, many years before his birth, in which Grandfather lived; and of the "new" 1921 in which Tim now finds himself waiting in ambush to kill Grandfather. But if we do speak so, we merely confer two names on one thing. The events of 1921 are doubly located in Tim's (extended) personal time, like the trestle on the railway, but the "original" 1921 and the "new" 1921 are one and the same. If Tim did not kill Grandfather in the "original" 1921, then if he does kill Grandfather in the "new" 1921, he must both kill and not kill Grandfather in 1921 – in the one and only 1921, which is both the "new" and the "original" 1921. It is logically impossible that Tim should change the past by killing Grandfather in 1921. So Tim cannot kill Grandfather.

Not that past moments are special; no more can anyone change the present or the future. Present and future momentary events no more have temporal parts than past ones do. You cannot change a present or future event from what it was originally to what it is after you change it. What you *can* do is to change the present or the future from the unactualized way they would have been without some action of yours to the way they actually are. But that is not an actual change: not a difference between two successive actualities. And Tim can certainly do as much; he changes the past from the unactualized way it would have been without him to the one and only way it actually is. To "change" the past in this way, Tim need not do anything momentous; it is enough just to be there, however unobtrusively.

You know, of course, roughly how the story of Tim must go on if it is to be consistent: he

somehow fails. Since Tim didn't kill Grandfather in the "original" 1921, consistency demands that neither does he kill Grandfather in the "new" 1921. Why not? For some commonplace reason. Perhaps some noise distracts him at the last moment, perhaps he misses despite all his target practice, perhaps his nerve fails, perhaps he even feels a pang of unaccustomed mercy. His failure by no means proves that he was not really able to kill Grandfather. We often try and fail to do what we are able to do. Success at some tasks requires not only ability but also luck, and lack of luck is not a temporary lack of ability. Suppose our other sniper, Tom, fails to kill Grandfather's partner for the same reason, whatever it is, that Tim fails to kill Grandfather. It does not follow that Tom was unable to. No more does it follow in Tim's case that he was unable to do what he did not succeed in doing.

We have this seeming contradiction: "*Tim doesn't, but can, because he has what it takes*" versus "*Tim doesn't, and can't, because it's logically impossible to change the past.*" I reply that there is no contradiction. Both conclusions are true, and for the reasons given. They are compatible because "can" is equivocal.

To say that something can happen means that its happening is compossible with certain facts. *Which* facts? That is determined, but sometimes not determined well enough, by context. An ape can't speak a human language – say, Finnish – but I can. Facts about the anatomy and operation of the ape's larynx and nervous system are not compossible with his speaking Finnish. The corresponding facts about my larynx and nervous system are compossible with my speaking Finnish. But don't take me along to Helsinki as your interpreter: I can't speak Finnish. My speaking Finnish is compossible with the facts considered so far, but not with further facts about my lack of training. What I can do, relative to one set of facts, I cannot do, relative to another, more inclusive, set. Whenever the context leaves it open which facts are to count as relevant, it is possible to equivocate about whether I can speak Finnish. It is likewise possible to equivocate about whether it is possible for me to speak Finnish, or whether I am able to, or whether I have the ability or capacity or power or potentiality to. Our many words for much the same thing are little help since they do not seem to correspond to different fixed delineations of the relevant facts.

Tim's killing Grandfather that day in 1921 is compossible with a fairly rich set of facts: the facts about his rifle, his skill and training, the unobstructed line of fire, the locked door and the absence of any chaperone to defend the past, and so on. Indeed it is compossible with all the facts of the sorts we would ordinarily count as relevant is saying what someone can do. It is compossible with all the facts corresponding to those we deem relevant in Tom's case. Relative to these facts, Tim can kill Grandfather. But his killing Grandfather is not compossible with another, more inclusive set of facts. There is the simple fact that Grandfather was not killed. Also there are various other facts about Grandfather's doings after 1921 and their effects: Grandfather begat Father in 1922 and Father begat Tim in 1949. Relative to these facts, Tim cannot kill Grandfather. He can and he can't, but under different delineations of the relevant facts. You can reasonably choose the narrower delineation, and say that he can; or the wider delineation, and say that he can't. But choose. What you mustn't do is waver, say in the same breath that he both can and can't, and then claim that this contradiction proves that time travel is impossible.

Exactly the same goes for Tom's parallel failure. For Tom to kill Grandfather's partner also is compossible with all facts of the sorts we ordinarily count as relevant, but not compossible with a larger set including, for instance, the fact that the intended victim lived until 1934. In Tom's case we are not puzzled. We say without hesitation that he can do it, because we see at once that the facts that are not compossible with his success are facts about the future of the time in question and therefore not the sort of facts we count as relevant in saying what Tom can do.

In Tim's case it is harder to keep track of which facts are relevant. We are accustomed to exclude facts about the future of the time in question, but to include some facts about its past. Our standards do not apply unequivocally to the crucial facts in this special case: Tim's failure, Grandfather's survival, and his subsequent doings. If we have foremost in mind that they lie in the external future of that moment in 1921 when Tim is almost ready to shoot, then we exclude them just as we exclude the parallel facts in Tom's case. But if we have foremost in mind that they precede that moment in Tim's extended personal time, then we tend to include them. To make the latter be foremost in your mind, I chose to tell Tim's story in the order of his personal time, rather than in the order of external time. The fact of Grandfather's survival until 1957 had already been told before I got to the part of the story about Tim lurking in ambush to kill him in 1921. We must decide, if we can, whether to treat these personally past and externally future facts as if they were straightforwardly past or as if they were straightforwardly future.

Fatalists – the best of them – are philosophers who take facts we count as irrelevant in saying what someone can do, disguise them somehow as facts of a different sort that we count as relevant, and thereby argue that we can do less than we think – indeed, that there is nothing at all that we don't do but can. I am not going to vote Republican next fall. The fatalist argues that, strange to say, I not only won't but can't; for my voting Republican is not compossible with the fact that it was true already in the year 1548 that I was not going to vote Republican 428 years later. My rejoinder is that this is a fact, sure enough; however, it is an irrelevant fact about the future masquerading as a relevant fact about the past, and so should be left out of account in saying what, in any ordinary sense, I can do. We are unlikely to be fooled by the fatalist's methods of disguise in this case, or other ordinary cases. But in cases of time travel, precognition, or the like, we're on less familiar ground, so it may take less of a disguise to fool us. Also, new methods of disguise are available, thanks to the device of personal time.

Here's another bit of fatalist trickery. Tim, as he lurks, already knows that he will fail. At least he has the wherewithal to know it if he thinks, he knows it implicitly. For he remembers that Grandfather was alive when he was a boy, he knows that those who are killed are thereafter not alive, he knows (let us suppose) that he is a time traveler who has reached the same 1921 that lies in his personal past, and he ought to understand – as we do – why a time traveler cannot change the past. What is known cannot be false. So his success is not only not compossible with facts that belong to the external future and his personal past, but also is not compossible with the present fact of his knowledge that he will fail. I reply that the fact of his foreknowledge, at the moment while he waits to shoot, is not a fact entirely about that moment. It may be divided into two parts. There is the fact that he then believes (perhaps only implicitly) that he will fail; and there is the further fact that his belief is correct, and correct not at all by accident, and hence qualifies as an item of knowledge. It is only the latter fact that is not compossible with his success, but it is only the former that is entirely about the moment in question. In calling Tim's state at that moment knowledge, not just belief, facts about personally earlier but externally later moments were smuggled into consideration.

I have argued that Tim's case and Tom's are alike, except that in Tim's case we are more tempted than usual – and with reason – to opt for a semi-fatalist mode of speech. But perhaps they differ in another way. In Tom's case, we can expect a perfectly consistent answer to the counterfactual question: what if Tom had killed Grandfather's partner? Tim's case is more difficult. If Tim had killed Grandfather, it seems offhand that contradictions would have been true. The killing both would and wouldn't have occurred. No Grandfather, no Father; no Father, no Tim; no Tim, no killing. And for good measure: no Grandfather, no family fortune; no fortune, no time machine; no time machine, no killing. So the supposition that Tim killed Grandfather seems impossible in more than the semi-fatalistic sense already granted.

If you suppose Tim to kill Grandfather and hold all the rest of his story fixed, of course you get a contradiction. But likewise if you suppose Tom to kill Grandfather's partner and hold the rest of his story fixed – including the part that told of his failure – you get a contradiction. If you make *any* counterfactual supposition and hold all else fixed you get a contradiction. The thing to do is rather to make the counterfactual supposition and hold all else as close to fixed as you consistently can. That procedure will yield perfectly consistent answers to the question: what if Tim had not killed Grandfather? In that case, some of the story I told would not have been true. Perhaps Tim might have been the time-traveling grandson of someone else. Perhaps he might have been the grandson of a man killed in 1921 and miraculously resurrected. Perhaps he might have been not a time traveler at all, but rather someone created out of nothing in 1920 equipped with false memories of a personal past that never was. It is hard to say what is the least revision of Tim's story to make it true that Tim kills Grandfather, but certainly the contradictory story in which the killing both does and doesn't occur is not the least revision. Hence it is false (according to the unrevised story) that if Tim had killed Grandfather then contradictions would have been true.

What difference would it make if Tim travels in branching time? Suppose that at the possible world of Tim's story the space-time manifold branches; the branches are separated not in time, and not in space, but in some other way. Tim travels not only in time but also from one branch to another. In one branch Tim is absent from the events of 1921; Grandfather lives; Tim is born, grows up, and vanishes in his time machine. The other branch diverges from the first when Tim turns up in 1920; there Tim kills Grandfather and Grandfather leaves no descendants and no fortune; the events of the two branches differ more and more from that time on. Certainly this is a consistent story; it is a story in which Grandfather both is and isn't killed in 1921 (in the different branches); and it is a story in which Tim, by killing Grandfather, succeeds in preventing his own birth (in one of the branches). But it is not a story in which Tim's killing of Grandfather both does occur and doesn't: it simply does, though it is located in one branch and not the other. And it is not a story in which Tim changes the past. 1921 and later years contain the events of both branches, coexisting somehow without interaction. It remains true at all the personal times of Tim's life, even after the killing, that Grandfather lives in one branch and dies in the other.

Notes

1 I have particularly in mind two of the time travel stories of Robert A. Heinlein: "By His Bootstraps" in R. A. Heinlein, *The Menace from Earth* (Hicksville, NY, 1959), and "—All You Zombies—." in R. A. Heinlein, *The Unpleasant Profession of Jonathan Hoag* (Hicksville, NY, 1959).

2 Accounts of time travel in two-dimensional time are found in Jack W. Meiland, "A Two-Dimensional Passage Model of Time for Time Travel,"

Philosophical Studies, vol. 26 (1974), pp. 153–73; and in the initial chapters of Isaac Asimov, *The End of Eternity* (Garden City, NY, 1955). Asimov's denouement, however, seems to require some different conception of time travel.

3   H. G. Wells, *The Time Machine, An Invention* (London, 1895), epilogue. The passage is criticized as contradictory in Donald C. Williams, "The Myth of Passage," *The Journal of Philosophy*, vol. 48 (1951), p. 463.

4   I discuss the relation between personal identity and mental connectedness and continuity at greater length in "Survival and Identity" in *The Identities of Persons*, ed. Amélie Rorty (Berkeley, 1976).

5   "Causation," *The Journal of Philosophy*, vol. 70 (1973), pp. 556–67; the analysis relies on the analysis of counterfactuals given in my *Counterfactuals* (Oxford, 1973).

Questions for Discussion

1   David Lewis suggests that in order to make sense of time travel, we need to make a distinction between personal time and external time. Is the distinction intelligible? Illustrate with respect to the plot of at least one time travel movie.

2   Is the concept of backward causation intelligible? Does the intelligibility of time travel presuppose the intelligibility of backward causation?

3   If one could go back in time, could one change the past and, with it, the future? If one could, what became of the old past (or the old future)? Discuss with reference to Lewis's article and the plots of *Back to the Future* and *A Sound of Thunder*.

4   Is the history of the watch in *Somewhere in Time* a history of which one can make sense? What is the moment at which it first exists? Does its beginning to exist have a cause? Can there be such causal loops?

5   In *Planet of the Apes*, the astronauts landed in earth's distant future. They were puzzled as to how the apes could have evolved in the way that they did. In one of the sequels to the original movie, Cornelius and Zira travel to Earth's past. It turns out that they initiate the evolutionary process by having an intelligent offspring who leads the apes in revolt. It also turns out that they are their own ancestors. Is this any more problematic than the history of the watch in *Somewhere in Time*?

Part VI

Free Will, Foreknowledge, and Determinism

Films:

Minority Report
The Boys From Brazil
A Clockwork Orange
The Omen
Compulsion
Law and Order ("black rage" defense): Season 5, Episode 69414, *Rage* (2/01/95)

Introduction

Just seconds ago, I typed the words "free will, foreknowledge, and determinism" as the heading on this page. As I look back on my typing of that string of words, I naturally think that I might have typed some other string of words, or even have refrained from typing at all – I had the option of going to buy a Diet Coke instead, as I was thinking of doing. But is my sense that I could have done otherwise merely an illusion? Perhaps I had no genuine choice but to write the words that I wrote, and maybe, in addition, I had no genuine choice but to believe, at the time of writing, that I did in fact have options.

But, given our strong sense that we do have genuine options in most of our actions (including our mental actions), why should we deny that I could have done something other than type those five words in bold italics? One motivation for such a denial involves a commitment to *determinism*, the thesis that every event has a cause, where a cause is a preceding or concurrent event that necessitates the occurrence of the effect. Consider a rock dropped from my hand out of my office window. What will happen to the rock? Well, obviously, it will fall to the ground (barring any physical barriers on its current trajectory). And, many believe, given physical laws, the rock *must* fall to the ground: physical laws in conjunction with the history of the rock, the earth, etc., up until the moment when I release the rock, entail that the rock will follow a particular path to the ground, which it will hit at some

determined time after the moment that I release it from my hand. If this is true for trajectories of rocks dropping from windows, isn't it true for any event that has causal antecedents, i.e. for any event whatsoever? If every event has a cause, as the determinist claims, then, given the presence of the cause, causal laws guarantee the effect. So each state of the world determines the immediately succeeding state, and ultimately, therefore, *all* future states.

If determinism is true, then, it might seem that our actions are causally determined and our beliefs about options are merely illusions, themselves causally determined. From the first moment of the existence of the universe, its entire future course, including all my actions and thoughts, was irrevocably fixed. *Hard determinists* accept that causation is incompatible with human freedom, and, given that all events have causes, they deny that human beings are free. So *hard determinism* (see John Hospers, "Meaning and Free Will") involves a commitment to determinism *plus* the claim that determinism is *incompatible* with freedom. A hard determinist will insist that the causal determinants of human behavior – our genetic inheritance, our environment – make it the case that our future course of action is set for us and there is nothing that we can do to alter it. In the film *The Boys from Brazil* Mengele takes for granted these sorts of determinist claims and sets out to create new Hitlers by recreating the biological and social factors that yielded the original Hitler. It is interesting to ask whether the film's climax (chapters 28–30) is meant to suggest that Mengele's assumptions were mistaken.

Many of us, philosophers and non-philosophers alike, have difficulty accepting these claims of the hard determinist. In addition to our unshakeable sense that we have genuine options in thought and action (including genuine choice as to whether we accept hard determinism), many of our social practices, in particular our moral practices (and legal practices meant to reflect those moral practices), seem to require that persons have genuine options in action, that they are in fact free. (In *Compulsion*, defense attorney Clarence Darrow attempts to get his clients, Leopold and Loeb, acquitted by claiming that social factors determined that they kill the young boy with whose death they are charged.) The film *Minority Report* suggests how strongly we rebel against denials of genuine freedom. In the future envisioned in the film, the state has identified some persons who can "see" the future, thereby revealing to the state which persons will, in the future, commit crimes. The state then acts preventively, arresting and incarcerating these future criminals before they can actually break the law. After all, why in the world should we wait until a murder has occurred to act? Arrest the "murderer" now and protect the innocent "victim."

But, we cannot help but wonder how these supposed clairvoyants *know* that Joe Schmoe would kill someone in the future if he were not prevented from doing so? In order for the clairvoyants to have such knowledge, it must be the case that it is true now that Joe will commit the murder in the future unless he is put in prison. But if it is true that Joe will commit the murder barring incarceration, then it seems that Joe could not do other than commit the murder in the absence of state intervention – Joe is not free, because there is already a fact about what he would do left to his own devices. But, then, why do we persist in believing it *unfair* to arrest Joe until he has actually committed a crime? And, if Joe cannot do otherwise than kill in the absence of intervention, then how can we hold him morally responsible at all? Responsibility seems to require that one could have done otherwise – after all, we do not blame someone who has a seizure and, during the seizure, hits a bystander. We do not hold the seizure victim responsible because the seizure

victim had no options; but, if determinism is true, or, for that matter, if what we are going to do under certain conditions is already settled, aren't we all, all of the time, in the same situation as the seizure victim? The only difference is that we are also in the grips of a delusion that we have options. In the film *A Clockwork Orange* Alex is a violent thug who is subjected to a conditioning process meant to cause him to be averse to criminal activity (chapters 19–24). In the film, protestors object to this kind of conditioning because of its effects on Alex: it seems to remove his ability to make genuine choices. But would such treatment be objectionable if none of us ever has genuine choices in the first place?

There is another argument superficially similar to the above. This argument, however, relies only on the fact that there are truths about the future and if it is already true that someone will do X at some future time, then, trivially, it is already true that nothing he does or will do will alter that fact. (It is precisely this sort of worry that Aristotle appears to have in mind when he argues, in the selection from *De Interpretatione*, that only *some* claims about the future are either true or false.) In the film *The Omen* (chapters 15 and 30) Thorn and Jennings discover that future deaths and the mode of dying are predicted by photographs. Jennings, for example, discovers a photograph of himself that shows him being decapitated. Sure enough, in a somewhat gruesome scene (chapter 30) a pane of glass takes his head off. On the assumption that the images on the photograph are the result of future events, one might wonder whether there was anything Jennings could possibly do to avoid his fate. The issue raised here is familiar to many who have struggled to reconcile freedom with belief in a God like the Judeo-Christian God. God is, supposedly, omniscient, and his knowledge extends over all time: the past, the present, and the future. God knows what you and I will do tomorrow, the next day, the next year, etc. But, if God knows that I will steal money from Richard tomorrow, then it is true now that I will steal Richard's money tomorrow. So how can I be free to refrain from stealing the money? It seems that I have no genuine options. But then how can God hold me responsible for doing what I could not have refrained from doing? This is known as the problem of free will and foreknowledge (discussed in our selection by J. R. Lucas, addressing what he calls "theological determinism"): how can I have free will if God knows what I am going to do in the future? Theologians and philosophers of religion continue to struggle in their attempts to reconcile human freedom with God's knowledge of the future. You might recall from our introduction to the unit on time that David Lewis is convinced that one can reconcile freedom with truths about the future, and we'll discuss more below the kind of argument he advances.

If we cannot accept that we lack freedom, one option is to accept *libertarianism*. Libertarians deny the determinist thesis that all events have causes that necessitate their effects. Some libertarians insist that the human will – our capacity for choosing and initiating actions – lies outside the causal nexus in which the physical world is caught. So, no matter what has preceded my sitting down in front of a blank computer screen, I can type certain words, I can type different words, or I can type nothing at all. I even have the option of plotting and carrying out a killing spree. I, as an agent, can intervene in the world, and I am free to type or to refrain from typing – my decision and consequent action are not determined by the history of the world up until that time.

If the libertarian is insisting that we are free because, like quantum particles, we are not governed by *universal* law, the view seems at best problematic. The analogy with quantum theory would suggest that our actions are in some sense random – merely probabilistic. To be sure, even the quantum world is governed by laws. But a "law" governing the half-life of a radioactive element is a statistical claim that simply averages out the life spans of elements of that kind. In this sense, even the actions of a person with Tourette's syndrome might be "governed" by law. One form that this syndrome can take is the involuntary utterance of various words or phrases such as expletives. There might well be a certain predictable frequency with which these outbursts occur. But would anyone feel any more free if they came to the conclusion that all actions are like the statistically predictable outbursts of a Tourette's victim? Normally, I think that my decisions are in some sense a product of my character, of what I am. As I sit here right now, is it at all likely

that instead of continuing to type and to think about freedom, I will go to a gun store, steal a gun, and then go on a killing spree at the local McDonald's? I want to say that of course it is not – my character and prior history make it the case that I will not, in fact, engage in a killing spree. So are my character and prior history not causally relevant in any way to my being willing to sit and continue typing rather than acquiring a weapon and going on a killing spree? If I "found myself" suddenly behaving in a bizarre manner unrelated to my prior choices, wouldn't I be more likely to think of myself as having lost my freedom, my control over my actions?

To avoid this objection, one sort of libertarian appeals to what is known as *agent causation*. The libertarian we described above claimed that the activity of the human will is undetermined by the previous course of events in the world. The libertarian who appeals to agent causation, on the other hand, admits that in some sense our choices are caused – they are caused by the agent where the agent's exercise of power is not *determined* by prior *events* (including even my prior choices). Through the choices I make, I determine what I do, and am appropriately held responsible for those actions.

It is an understatement to suggest that the idea of agent causation is not completely clear. This agent who chooses exists for a period of time without making the choice. Doesn't something need to change "in the agent" before a decision gets made? Is the agent like a ticking time bomb that can go off with a decision at any point in time where the decision occurring at one time rather than another has no explanation other than "that's when he decided?" Of course, the proponent of agent causation will accuse critics of simply presupposing the view that only events can be causes. But the critics are more often than not happy to concede that, indeed, they have no idea what agent causation is supposed to be.

David Hume recognized the difficulties inherent in both hard determinism and various forms of libertarianism. He offered a *compatibilist* option. According to Hume, and other compatibilists, our actions, like other events in the physical world, have causes, but that fact does not entail that human beings are unfree. According to Hume, we need to get clear on what causation is and on what freedom is in order to see that causation and freedom are compatible with one another. For Hume, causation is just a matter of constant conjunction: whenever an A is observed, a B has been observed following A. Sufficient regularity in the conjunction of an A with a (temporally succeeding) B constitutes what it is for A to cause B. Other compatibilists adopt the general approach described below but may disagree with Hume's so-called regularity theory of law and causation.

It seems obvious to Hume that human actions are caused: there is a lawful connection between motives/character traits and certain actions. Someone who wants to write an introduction to a unit on free will and determinism, and who cares about other human beings, is not the kind of person whom we observe rushing out to go on a killing spree. We make predictions about human behavior based on what we know about people's characters and desires, and our predictions often turn out to be correct.

If what we mean by "free" is "uncaused," then we are not, Hume says, free. But as we discussed above, uncaused action would seem to be arbitrary, random action, hardly the kind of action that we think of as the action of a morally responsible agent. However, Hume claims, an agent is able to do otherwise as long as she would in fact have done otherwise if she had chosen to do so: as long as one's actions have the right kind of causes – desires and motives of the agent herself – the agent's action was a free action, and the agent is responsible, because her actions are the causal result of her character and choices. Bertrand Russell once said that we can do as we please, but we can't please as we please. Hume can be thought of as suggesting that doing as we please is enough to make us free.

Hume's account has the virtue of accepting the claim that actions are caused and of reconciling that claim with human freedom. However, Hume's account seems to leave human freedom on a par with feline and canine freedom. Consider a cat's action of scratching an expensively upholstered wing chair. We do not regard her as responsible for her action in the way that we would hold you responsible if you came into a home and slashed the chair with a razor blade. But isn't the cat as free as you are, on Hume's account? Just as you would have done otherwise if you had chosen to do otherwise, so the cat would have done otherwise – scratch the big comfy chair, eat some kibbles, snooze on its owner's lap – if she had chosen to do otherwise. The actions of cats and dogs, it seems, are just as much a product of their desires as are human actions, so if the desires of a cat had been different, the cat's actions would have been different. So cats and dogs are responsible, free agents, just as humans are?

Harry G. Frankfurt says, no, they are not. According to Frankfurt, Hume has given us an account of freedom of action, not of freedom of the will. While it may be the case that a cat would have done otherwise if she had chosen to do otherwise, the cat was not able to choose to do otherwise: her will – her effective (action-causing) desire – is not something that she has the ability to alter. The cat is what Frankfurt calls a "wanton" – she lacks second-order desires, desires that take first-order desires as their objects, where first-order desires take actions as their objects. So the cat cannot be said to have the will that she wants to have because she has no desires concerning her will. Many human beings, on the other hand, have second-order desires, and their wills either conform or fail to conform to those second-order desires. Contra Russell, Frankfurt thinks that we as humans can please as we please. Frankfurt claims that an agent has freedom of the will and is, thus, responsible, if she could have willed otherwise, i.e. if she would have had a different will if she had wanted a different will. Of course, a natural question to ask is, why stop with second-order desires? What if I am causally determined to have the second-order desires that I in fact have? Why don't I have to choose my desire to have a desire in order to be genuinely free?

These questions about the nature of freedom and responsibility become much more than theoretical when we consider issues in the criminal law. In our culture, we exempt non-human animals from criminal responsibility for their actions (although we may hold owners culpable for the actions of their pets). We also exempt very young children, because we do not think that they can have the requisite kind of control over and understanding of the nature of their actions. What sorts of factors, either internal or external, can render an adult human being less than fully responsible for his or her actions?

One common thought securely embedded in Anglo-American jurisprudence is that certain kinds of mental illness can undermine criminal responsibility (see the still-governing "M'Naghten Rules," and The American Law Institute's "The Insanity Defense"). For example, if someone was hearing voices in their head telling them to kill, we often judge them insane and therefore not responsible for their actions. But is this justified? Do delusions render someone unable to do otherwise in situations where, but for the delusions, she would have had that ability? Do delusions lessen one's ability to do otherwise? Or do the delusions simply give the insane person reasons to act that the sane do not have? It is more than a little difficult to come up with plausible principles that distinguish the sane from the insane in such a way that the distinction parallels a distinction we want to make between the legally culpable and the legally excused. In "What Is So Special About Mental Illness?" Joel Feinberg explores at some length the question of whether and why mental illness should be taken as exculpatory, showing how complex the issue really is.

On a more mundane level, we commonsensically recognize a category of actions taken under a kind of duress that renders them in a sense unfree and not subject to appropriate blame or punishment. If you are accosted by a man with a gun and told to hand over your wallet or die, your decision to hand over your wallet is in a perfectly clear sense coerced. It was not something you freely did. No sane person will absolve the thief from wrongdoing on the ground that you freely chose to hand over your wallet. A host of controversial issues arise, however, in trying to characterize in a principled way external "forces" that interfere with freedom. Can Nazi concentration guards claim that they didn't act freely in helping to execute Jews because they faced possible punishment for refusing to carry out orders? Can a person raised in poverty claim that she had no choice but to turn to a life of crime?

The *Law and Order* episode raises these sorts of questions about whether cultural factors can undermine individual responsibility. The defense attorney in the episode claims that his black client was raised in a culture that induced anger and rage in him at the actions of the white people who oppressed him. The right trigger released that rage and rendered him unable to refrain from killing a white person. Can such cultural factors render an individual unfree?

41

From *De Interpretatione*

Aristotle

8

A [statement] is one affirmation or one denial if it signifies [something which is] about [a subject which is] one, whether the [subject] is a universal taken universally, or not. Such statements are 'every man is white' and 'not every man is white', 'men are white' and 'men are not white', 'no man is white' and 'some men are white', provided that the word 'white' has one meaning. If in a statement the name posited has two meanings which cannot make up something which is one, then the statement is not one affirmation or one denial. For example, if one were to posit the name 'coat' as meaning a horse and also a man in 'coats are white', this statement would not be one affirmation; nor [would the corresponding denial be] one denial; for the affirmation would not differ from the statement 'men and horses are white', and this itself would not differ from the two statements 'horses are white' and 'men are white'. Accordingly, if these [two statements] signify many [objects] and are many, it is clear that the first [statement], too, signifies many [objects], or else nothing at all (for an individual man is not a horse). So in contradictory statements of this sort, too, it is not necessary for one of the statements to be true and the other false.

9

In the case of that which exists or has occurred, it is necessary for the corresponding affirmation or its denial to be true, or to be false. And in the case of two contradictories with a universal subject universally taken, or with an individual subject, it is always necessary for one of them to be true and the other false, as we stated; but if the subject is a universal without being universally taken, there is no such necessity, and we stated this fact too. Concerning future particulars, on the other hand, the situation is not similar.

First, if every affirmation and every denial is either true or false, then it is necessary for every object, too, either to be or not to be. Accordingly, if one man says that something will be the case while another man denies this, then clearly it is necessary for just one of them to be speaking truly if an affirmation or a denial is either true or false, for in such cases both will not exist at the same time. For if it were true to say that a thing is white (or not white), it would be necessary for the thing to be white (or not white), and if it is white (or not white), then it would be true to affirm that it is (or to deny it); and if the thing is not as stated, the statement is false, and if the statement is false, the thing is not as stated.

From *Aristotle's Categories and Propositions (De Interpretatione)*, trans. H. G. Apostle (Des Moines, IA: Peripatetic Press, 1980), pp. 34–7. © 1980 by H. G. Apostle. Reprinted by permission of Peripatetic Press.

Accordingly, either the affirmation or the denial must be true, or must be false.

If so, [it would appear that] nothing occurs by chance or in either of two ways; nor will it so occur in the future or fail to so occur, but everything [will occur, or will fail to occur,] of necessity and not in either of two ways. For either he who affirms a future event will speak truly or he who denies it; otherwise the event would be just as likely to occur as not to occur, for that which may occur in either of two ways does not occur or will not occur in one way more than in the other.

Again, if a thing is white now, it was true to say earlier that it would be white; so concerning an event which has taken place, it was always true to say 'it is' or 'it will be'. And if it was always true to say 'it is' or 'it will be', the event was not of such a nature as not to be or not to come to be; and if it was not of such a nature as not to occur, it was impossible for it not to occur; and if was impossible for it not to occur, it was necessary for it to occur. So [it appears that] all future events will occur of necessity. Hence nothing will come to be in either of two ways or by chance, for if it will occur by chance, it will not occur of necessity.

Further, one cannot [truly] say of an event that neither the affirmation nor the denial is true, i.e., that the event will neither occur nor fail to occur. Otherwise, if the affirmation is false, the denial [will] not [be] true, and if the denial is false, it turns out that the affirmation [will] not [be] true. In addition, if it is true to say [of a thing] that it is white and large, both [these attributes] will have to belong [to the thing], and if [it is true to say that] they will belong [to the thing] tomorrow, then they will [have to] belong to it tomorrow. But if an event will neither occur nor fail to occur tomorrow, there would be no happening [tomorrow] in either of two ways, e.g., a sea fight would neither have to occur nor have to fail to occur tomorrow.

These and other such absurdities would indeed result, if of every affirmation and its denial, whether with a universal subject taken universally or with an individual subject, it were necessary for one of the opposites to be true and the other false, and if, of things in the process of becoming, that which would be or which would come to be could not be in either of two ways but of

necessity only one of them, in which case there would be no need to deliberate or take *action* with the expectation that, if we act in a certain way, a certain result will come about, but if we do not, it will not come about. For nothing prevents one man from saying now that a certain event will occur ten thousand years hence, and another from saying that the event will not occur; and so that alternative [occurrence or non-occurrence], of which it was at one time true to state that it will come to be, would of necessity come to be [at a later time]. Further, neither would it make any difference whether some men make the contradictory statements or not, for it is clear that things would be such even if neither the affirmation nor the denial were stated; for events would, or would not, occur not because we have affirmed or denied them, and [they would occur, or not occur,] no less if we had said so ten thousand years earlier rather than any other period of time. So if at all times things were such that [a definite] one of two contradictory statements [about the future] would be true, then what that statement says would of necessity come to be, and each [future] occurrence would always be such as to come to be of necessity. For that of which someone stated truly that it will be would not be of such a nature as to fail to occur, and of [such] an occurrence it was always true to say [earlier] that it will be.

Now these things are impossible; for we observe that principles of things which will occur arise both from deliberations and from *actions*, and that, in general, objects which do not exist always in *actuality* have alike the potentiality of existing and of not existing; and objects which may be or may not be may also come to be or may not come to be. It is clear, too, that there are many objects which have such [a nature]. For example, this coat has the potentiality of being cut to pieces [at a certain time later] but may wear out before being so cut. Similarly, it has the potentiality of not being so cut; for if it did not have this potentiality, it could not have the potentiality of wearing out before. Such is also the case with the other kinds of generations which are said to possess such potentiality. It is evident, then, that it is not of necessity that all things exist or are in the process of coming to be; in some cases a thing may come to be in either of two ways, in which case the affirmation of each alternative is no more true than the denial of it, whereas in other cases one of the two alternatives is more likely to occur and in most cases it does occur, but the less likely alternative may still come to be [*actually*].

Now when a thing exists, it does so of necessity, and when a nonbeing does not exist, it is of necessity that it does not exist; but it is not of necessity that every existing thing exists or that every nonbeing does not exist. For it is not the same for a thing to exist of necessity when it exists and for that thing to exist of necessity without qualification, and similarly with nonbeing. The same remarks apply to any two contradictories also. Thus everything of necessity either is or is not, and everything of necessity will either be or not be; but one cannot [always truly] state that a definite one of the two alternatives is or will be of necessity. I mean, for example, that a sea fight will of necessity either take place tomorrow or not; but a sea fight will not necessarily take place tomorrow, nor will it necessarily fail to take place either, though it will of necessity either take place tomorrow or fail to take place. So since statements are true in a way which is similar to the corresponding facts, it is clear that if objects are such that they may turn out in either of two ways or may admit contraries, the two contradictory statements corresponding to them are of necessity related in a similar manner. And such indeed is the case with objects which do not always exist or which are not always nonexistent. For though one of the two contradictories concerning these objects must be true (or false), it is not [definitely] the affirmation, nor [definitely] the denial, that will be true but either one of them; and one of them may be more likely to be true, but not already true (or already false) at the time [when a man states it]. Clearly, then, it is not necessary in the case of every affirmation and its opposite denial [concerning future particulars] that one of them be [definitely] true and the other [definitely] false; for the situation with objects which do not exist but have the potentiality of existing and of not existing is not like that of existing things, but as we have stated.

42

Of Liberty and Necessity

David Hume

We come now to explain the *direct* passions, or the impressions, which arise immediately from good or evil, from pain or pleasure. Of this kind are, *desire and aversion, grief and joy, hope and fear*.

Of all the immediate effects of pain and pleasure, there is none more remarkable than the WILL; and tho', properly speaking, it be not comprehended among the passions, yet as the full understanding of its nature and properties, is necessary to the explanation of them, we shall here make it the subject of our enquiry. I desire it may be observ'd, that by the *will*, I mean nothing but *the internal impression we feel and are conscious of, when we knowingly give rise to any new motion of our body, or new perception of our mind*. This impression, like the preceding ones of pride and humility, love and hatred, 'tis impossible to define, and needless to describe any farther; for which reason we shall cut off all those definitions and distinctions, with which philosophers are wont to perplex rather than clear up this question; and entering at first upon the subject, shall examine that long disputed question concerning *liberty and necessity*; which occurs so naturally in treating of the will.

'Tis universally acknowledg'd, that the operations of external bodies are necessary, and that in the communication of their motion, in their attraction, and mutual cohesion, there are not the least traces of indifference or liberty. Every object is determin'd by an absolute fate to a certain degree and direction of its motion, and can no more depart from that precise line, in which it moves, than it can convert itself into an angel, or spirit, or any superior substance. The actions, therefore, of matter are to be regarded as instances of necessary actions; and whatever is in this respect on the same footing with matter, must be acknowledg'd to be necessary. That we may know whether this be the case with the actions of the mind, we shall begin with examining matter, and considering on what the idea of a necessity in its operations are founded, and why we conclude one body or action to be the infallible cause of another.

It has been observ'd already, that in no single instance the ultimate connexion of any objects is discoverable, either by our senses or reason, and that we can never penetrate so far into the essence and construction of bodies, as to perceive the principle, on which their mutual influence depends. 'Tis their constant union alone, with which we are acquainted; and 'tis from the constant union the necessity arises. If objects had not an uniform and regular conjunction with each other, we shou'd never arrive at any idea of cause and effect; and even after all, the necessity, which enters into that idea, is nothing but a

David Hume, "Of Liberty and Necessity," from David Hume, *A Treatise on Human Nature*, ed. L.A. Selby-Bigge (Oxford: Clarendon Press, 1896).

determination of the mind to pass from one object to its usual attendant, and infer the existence of one from that of the other. Here then are two particulars, which we are to consider as essential to necessity, *viz.* the constant *union* and the *inference* of the mind; and wherever we discover these we must acknowledge a necessity. As the actions of matter have no necessity, but what is deriv'd from these circumstances, and it is not by any insight into the essence of bodies we discover their connexion, the absence of this insight, while the union and inference remain, will never, in any case, remove the necessity. 'Tis the observation of the union, which produces the inference; for which reason it might be thought sufficient, if we prove a constant union in the actions of the mind, in order to establish the inference, along with the necessity of these actions. But that I may bestow a greater force on my reasoning, I shall examine these particulars apart, and shall first prove from experience, that our actions have a constant union with our motives, tempers, and circumstances, before I consider the inferences we draw from it.

To this end a very slight and general view of the common course of human affairs will be sufficient. There is no light, in which we can take them, that does not confirm this principle. Whether we consider mankind according to the difference of sexes, ages, governments, conditions, or methods of education; the same uniformity and regular operation of natural principles are discernible. Like causes still produce like effects; in the same manner as in the mutual action of the elements and powers of nature [. . .]

Are the changes of our body from infancy to old age more regular and certain than those of our mind and conduct? And wou'd a man be more ridiculous, who wou'd expect that an infant of four years old will raise a weight of three hundred pound, than one, who from a person of the same age, wou'd look for a philosophical reasoning, or a prudent and well-concerted action?

We must certainly allow, that the cohesion of the parts of matter arises from natural and necessary principles, whatever difficulty we may find in explaining them: And for a like reason we must allow, that human society is founded on like principles; and our reason in the latter case, is better than even that in the former; because we not only observe, that men *always* seek society, but can also explain the principles, on which this universal propensity is founded. For is it more certain, that two flat pieces of marble will unite together, than that two young savages of different sexes will copulate? Do the children arise from this copulation more uniformly, than does the parents care for their safety and preservation? [. . .]

The skin, pores, muscles, and nerves of a day-labourer are different from those of a man of quality: So are his sentiments, actions and manners. The different stations of life influence the whole fabric, external and internal; and these different stations arise necessarily, because uniformly, from the necessary and uniform principles of human nature. Men cannot live without society, and cannot be associated without government. Government makes a distinction of property, and establishes the different ranks of men. This produces industry, traffic, manufactures, law-suits, war, leagues, alliances, voyages, travels, cities, fleets, ports, and all those other actions and objects, which cause such a diversity, and at the same time maintain such an uniformity in human life.

Shou'd a traveller, returning from a far country, tell us, that he had seen a climate in the fiftieth degree of northern latitude, where all the fruits ripen and come to perfection in the winter, and decay in the summer, after the same manner as in *England* they are produc'd and decay in the contrary seasons, he wou'd find few so credulous as to believe him. I am apt to think a travellar wou'd meet with as little credit, who shou'd inform us of people exactly of the same character with those in *Plato's* republic on the one hand, or those in *Hobbes's Leviathan* on the other. There is a general course of nature in human actions, as well as in the operations of the sun and the climate. There are also characters peculiar to different nations and particular persons, as well as common to mankind. The knowledge of these characters is founded on the observation of an uniformity in the actions, that flow from them; and this uniformity forms the very essence of necessity.

I can imagine only one way of eluding this argument, which is by denying that uniformity of human actions, on which it is founded. As long as actions have a constant union and connexion with the situation and temper of the agent, however we may in words refuse to acknowledge the necessity, we really allow the thing. Now some may, perhaps, find a pretext to deny this regular union and connexion. For what is more capricious than human actions? What more inconstant than the desires of man? And what creature departs more widely, not only from right reason, but from his own character and disposition? An hour, a moment is sufficient to make him change from one extreme to another, and overturn what cost the greatest pain and labour to establish. Necessity is regular and certain. Human conduct is irregular and uncertain. The one, therefore, proceeds not from the other.

To this I reply, that in judging of the actions of men we must proceed upon the same maxims, as when we reason concerning external objects. When any phænomena are constantly and invariably conjoin'd together, they acquire such a connexion in the imagination, that it passes from one to the other, without any doubt or hesitation. But below this there are many inferior degrees of evidence and probability, nor does one single contrariety of experiment entirely destroy all our reasoning. The mind ballances the contrary experiments, and deducting the inferior from the superior, proceeds with that degree of assurance or evidence, which remains. Even when these contrary experiments are entirely equal, we remove not the notion of causes and necessity; but supposing that the usual contrariety proceeds from the operation of contrary and conceal'd causes, we conclude, that the chance or indifference lies only in our judgment on account of our imperfect knowledge, not in the things themselves, which are in every case equally necessary, tho' to appearance not equally constant or certain. No union can be more constant and certain, than that of some actions with some motives and characters; and if in other cases the union is uncertain, 'tis no more than what happens in the operations of body, nor can we conclude any thing from the one irregularity, which will not follow equally from the other.

'Tis commonly allow'd that mad-men have no liberty. But were we to judge by their actions, these have less regularity and constancy than the actions of wise-men, and consequently are farther remov'd from necessity. Our way of thinking in this particular is, therefore, absolutely inconsistent; but is a natural consequence of these confus'd ideas and undefin'd terms, which we so commonly make use of in our reasonings, especially on the present subject.

We must now shew, that as the *union* betwixt motives and actions has the same constancy, as that in any natural operations, so its influence on the understanding is also the same, in *determining* us to infer the existence of one from that of another. If this shall appear, there is no known circumstance, that enters into the connexion and production of the actions of matter, that is not to be found in all the operations of the mind; and consequently we cannot, without a manifest absurdity, attribute necessity to the one, and refuse it to the other.

There is no philosopher, whose judgment is so riveted to this fantastical system of liberty, as not to acknowledge the force of *moral evidence*, and both in speculation and practice proceed upon it, as upon a reasonable foundation. Now moral evidence is nothing but a conclusion concerning the actions of men, deriv'd from the consideration of their motives, temper and situation. Thus when we see certain characters or figures describ'd upon paper, we infer that the person, who produc'd them, wou'd affirm such facts, the death of *Caesar*, the success of *Augustus*, the cruelty of *Nero*; and remembering many other concurrent testimonies we conclude, that those facts were once really existant, and that so many men, without any interest, wou'd never conspire to deceive us; especially since they must, in the attempt, expose themselves to the derision of all their contemporaries, when these facts were asserted to be recent and universally known. The same kind of reasoning runs thro' politics, war, commerce, economy, and indeed mixes itself so entirely in human life, that 'tis impossible to act or subsist a moment without having recourse to it. A prince, who imposes a tax upon his subjects, expects their compliance. A general, who conducts an army, makes account of a certain degree of courage. A merchant looks for fidelity and skill in his factor or supercargo. A man, who gives orders for his dinner, doubts not of the obedience of his servants. In short, as nothing more nearly interests us than our own actions and those of others, the greatest part of our reasonings is employ'd in judgments concerning them. Now I assert, that whoever reasons after this manner, does *ipso facto* believe the actions of the will to arise from necessity, and that he knows not what he means, when he denies it.

All those objects, of which we call the one *cause* and the other *effect*, consider'd in themselves, are as distinct and separate from each other, as any two things in nature, nor can we ever, by the most accurate survey of them, infer the existence of the one from that of the other. 'Tis only from experience and the observation of their constant union, that we are able to form this inference; and even after all, the inference is nothing but the effects of custom on the imagination. We must not here be content with saying, that the idea of cause and effect arises from objects constantly united; but must affirm, that 'tis the very same with the idea of these objects, and that the *necessary connexion* is not discover'd by a conclusion of the understanding, but is merely a perception of the mind. Wherever, therefore, we observe the same union, and wherever the union operates in the same manner upon the belief and opinion, we have the idea of causes and necessity, tho' perhaps we may avoid those expressions. Motion in one body in all past instances, that have fallen under our observation, is follow'd upon impulse by motion in another. 'Tis impossible for the mind to penetrate farther. From this constant union it *forms* the idea of cause and effect, and by its influence *feels* the necessity. As there is the same constancy, and the same influence in what we call moral evidence, I ask no more. What remains can only be a dispute of words.

And indeed, when we consider how aptly *natural* and *moral* evidence cement together, and form only one chain of argument betwixt them, we shall make no scruple to allow, that they are of the same nature, and deriv'd from the same principles. A prisoner, who has neither money nor interest, discovers the impossibility of his escape, as well from the obstinacy of the gaoler, as from the walls and bars with which he is surrounded; and in all attempts for his freedom chuses rather to work upon the stone and iron of the one, than upon the inflexible nature of the other. The same prisoner, when conducted to the scaffold, foresees his death as certainly from the constancy and fidelity of his guards as from the operation of the ax or wheel. His mind runs along a certain train of ideas: The refusal of the soldiers to consent to his escape, the action of the executioner; the separation of the head and body; bleeding, convulsive motions, and death. Here is a connected chain of natural causes and voluntary actions; but the mind feels no difference betwixt them in passing from one link to another; nor is less certain of the future event than if it were connected with the present impressions of the memory and senses by a train of causes cemented together by what we are pleas'd to call a *physical necessity*. The same experienc'd union has the same effect on the mind, whether the united objects be motives, volitions and actions; or figure and motion. We may change the names of things; but their nature and their operation on the understanding never change.

I dare be positive no one will ever endeavour to refute these reasonings otherwise than by altering my definitions, and assigning a different meaning to the terms of *cause, and effect, and necessity, and liberty, and chance*. According to my definitions, necessity makes an essential part of causation; and consequently liberty, by removing necessity, removes also causes, and is the very same thing with chance. As chance is commonly thought to imply a contradiction, and is at least directly contrary to experience, there are always the same arguments against liberty or free-will. If any one alters the definitions, I cannot pretend to argue with him, 'till I know the meaning he assigns to these terms.

43

Meaning and Free Will

John Hospers

It has become customary in philosophy to treat the free-will issue as "simply a matter of words," as "a mere verbal dispute." And indeed one can hardly deny that the question of whether or not human beings or human actions are to be called free depends on the meaning we give to the term "free." But once this is granted, a number of interesting problems arises which are not usually given due consideration in connection with this issue – problems partly of a general semantic nature, and partly associated with the word "free" in particular.

I

If we say, "It all depends on what you mean by the word 'free,'" we might first proceed to inquire of various persons what they meant by the word. But if we did this, we would soon find, not so much that different persons used the term in different ways – this would be easy, for then we would classify it as an ambiguous word and simply list the various senses of it – but that they had no clear idea in mind at all, that they could not say what they did mean by it. Most people, confronted by the question "What do you mean by 'free' when you say that we are free?" could

only sputter, "I mean – well, I mean that we're free, that's all!"

This brings us at once to a problem of a general nature which we may well pause over before coming to our specific issue. It is a commonplace of semantics that meanings are not intrinsic to words or sentences, but that they are *given* meaning by the users of language. Meanings, that is to say, are not inherent but conferred. To use Schlick's happy analogy, which cannot be repeated too often, the meaning of a sentence is not like a nut, which we have to crack to get at the meat (meaning) inside,[1] the meaning is not inside at all, but conferred from without, and the same symbol could acquire a different meaning simply by reason of a different fiat, a different act of conferring. Thus, we come to say in some specific dispute, it's not quite accurate to say that it's a question of what the words mean, rather it's a question of what we mean by the words.

It is true that this approach succeeds in solving many problems which would remain puzzling without an awareness of this fact. To take a non-philosophical example first, when someone says, "She didn't marry him because of his money," instead of asking ourselves "What does this statement mean?" we should ask ourselves, "What did the speaker mean to assert? Did he

John Hospers, "Meaning and Free Will." *Philosophy and Phenomenological Research* 10, no. 3 (March 1950), pp. 307–30.
© 1950 by Philosophy and Phenomenological Research. Reprinted with permission from Blackwell Publishing.

mean (intend) to say that she did marry him but not on account of his money, or that she didn't marry him and the reason for her failure to marry him was the fact that he had money?" Ultimately we must always get back to what the speaker intended, not to what the statement in itself "means." To ask what the statement in itself "means" would be like asking "How is 'm-i-n-u-t-e' pronounced?" failing to recognize that the answer depends on whether the word is intended as a noun referring to sixty seconds of time or as an adjective characterizing anything that is extremely small.

Thus we ask ourselves whether the standard A-proposition "All S's are P's" means "*If* there are S's, then all of them are P's" or "There *are* S's and *all* of them are P's." Or again, we ask, "Does 'Lions are fierce' mean 'All lions are fierce' or only 'Some lions are fierce,' and if the former, is the meaning of this rendered by 'If there are lions, then all of them are fierce'?" etc. For a definite answer to such questions we would have to go back to the person who uttered the original sentence and ask him, "See here, when you said that all S's are P's, did you intend as part of what you were asserting, that there *are* S's, or were you leaving that an open question?" etc.

And the old puzzle about the barber who shaves everyone who doesn't shave himself should, on this analysis, be easily resolved if we ask the person who presents the puzzle to us, "Did you, or did you not, when you made the assertion, intend to include the barber himself among those persons whom the barber shaves?" The seeming paradox is due to the unclarified nature of the question. The question is unclear, at least as regards the barber himself, and it is up to the speaker to make clearer what his original formulation has left unclear, by specifically including or excluding the barber from the group of those who are shaved by the barber.

The moral of all this, of course, is that sentences in themselves do not possess meaning; it is misleading to speak of "the meaning of sentences" at all; meaning being conferred in every case by the speaker, the sentence's meaning is only like the light of the moon: without the sun to give it light, it would possess none. And for an analysis of the light we must go to the sun.

Yet this very fact is puzzling. If the question "What did you mean by sentence S?" is the same as the question "What did you have in mind when you uttered sentence S?" or perhaps "What did you intend to convey by sentence S?" it is all too often the case that sentence S covers a whole nest of confusions and unclarities, and that the speaker had nothing definite in mind at all when he uttered sentence S; and when asked what it is that he wanted to convey, he can only repeat the sentence or give it a slightly new emphasis, or substitute another sentence at least as unclear as the first one.

Thus we seem to have lost as much ground as we have gained. By showing how misleading it is to ask "What does sentence S mean?" (because different people may give different meanings to the same set of words), we have been aided in resolving such questions as "What is the meaning of 'She didn't marry him because of his money'?" It helps us because the speaker almost certainly intended one or another of the alternatives. But it is the cases where the speaker is mute that puzzle us. When he had nothing definite in mind at all, what are we to say of the meaning? If it is not to be located in the sentence, and we must refer the meaning to the speaker, where are we to locate the meaning when the speaker fails us?

(One might allege that we can indeed talk about "the meaning of the sentence," not forgetting of course that meaning is conferred and not inherent. We can speak of Jones's statement as meaning so-and-so if and only if Jones, when he uttered the statement, meant that so-and-so by it. This, of course, only puts our difficulty in another form: we must now ask what the sentence means when Jones can't say what it was he meant by it. Nevertheless it is often convenient to speak of "the meaning of sentences," in this derived sense.)

Philosophers often make hard-and-fast distinctions between meaningful and meaningless sentences; and the examples they use generally prejudice the issue in the direction of making such hard-and-fast distinctions seem reasonable. They cite nonsense-syllables, groups of words without nouns and verbs, perhaps self-contradictory sentences, and other verbal absurdities as "meaningless"; on the other hand, "two plus Two is four" and "Cats catch mice" are examples of "meaningful" sentences. But the twilight-zone between these two territories, it seems to me, covers a great part of our actual daily discourse. When someone says that music expresses emotions, I am inclined to agree; I would hesitate to call his sentence meaningless; yet I am at a loss to know what the speaker means (nor do requests for explication usually yield any result), and I would not know exactly what I meant if I asserted it myself. Would I mean that music evokes emotions, at least in some listeners? then of course it is true. Would I mean that the composer had emotions when he wrote the work? then of course it is true also. That he wrote his composition in such a way as to arouse, or try to arouse, certain kinds of emotions in his listeners? then it is probably true as well. Or perhaps I would mean something different still. It is hard to say. I have used sentences like this all my life, and felt that people had very little trouble in understanding me; yet I do not know. Can we say that the sentence has meaning over and above what I and other persons who use it give it? Surely not. But if it means merely what we give it, then it is the nature of our gift that is in doubt.

Shall we call such sentences meaningful or meaningless? If we hesitate to say, it is only because the meaning of these terms is itself not clear, i.e., we are not clear about what we mean when we use them – all our definitions and explanations to the contrary notwithstanding. We are not even clear about the meaning of the word "clear" when we say that the speaker's intent is not clear; and no one, so far as I know, has ever analyzed this metaphorical word satisfactorily. Nor are we definite about the use of the word "definite" when we say that the speaker "had nothing definite in mind." Such is our language – and the state of those who use it.

Most of the statements made, e.g., by students in philosophy courses are of this nature. "Philosophy provides a pure undeviating basis for all of human existence." "Music is a logical setting forth of emotional relationships." "Art has no meaning and is therefore deliberately irrational." Or from Jacques Maritain: "Truth in art lies in its logic; the logic of the structure of living thought, the intimate geometry of nature." What are we to say of such assertions? None of them are meaningless in the way that "Pirots carulize elatically" is called meaningless, yet to what extent are we to label them as meaningful, or to indicate the meaning-in-mind of the speakers?

Such sentences after all occur with the greatest frequency, and we have all uttered thousands of them ourselves; and while we are in the business of branding sentences as meaningful or meaningless, we had better pay some attention to these.

Perhaps all we can do is to arrange successive "analyses of meaning" as to "degree of clarity" (in spite of the *unclarity* of this metaphor). When someone says "She is dependent on her father," we would not be likely to call his sentence meaningless; but if we are given additional information, such as "She's not financially dependent on her father, but emotionally," we would have a better idea of its meaning, i.e., of what the speaker meant to assert; and we would have a still better one if we were told, "She tries to imitate her father, she can't make a decision when he isn't present, she must always have his advice even on the most trivial issues," etc. Now we have a much clearer idea of what it was that the speaker wanted to convey; but we could in turn make it clearer too.

What is so disconcerting about all this is that no matter how "clear" we make the formulation, or how "clear" a meaning the speaker had in mind when he made his utterance, it always seems possible to clarify it further, whereupon we arrive at something that the speaker surely did *not* have in mind. In the more rigorous branches of philosophy, for example, there is a tendency to reduce statements to the "If p then q" form. "Only black cats bring bad luck" is rendered as "If a cat brings bad luck then it is a black cat"; and similarly "I won't stay unless he goes" becomes "If he does not go, I won't stay." But having tracked down "the meaning" this far, we can track it down still further: "Does 'If p then q' mean simply 'It is not the case that p and not q' or does it mean more?" etc.; and no speaker outside of technical philosophy is likely ever to have "had in mind" any of the interpretations of the hypothetical proposition which are rendered as "its meaning" or "its true meaning." There seems to be no limit to the possible process of refinement. And surely no one will say that until we have reached the limit of this process of analysis upon a given statement, that statement is to be branded as meaningless; few if any statements would then emerge as meaningful. But at what point in this process of gradual "clarification" is one to draw the line? We are involved here, surely, in the "slippery slope" difficulty: we don't want to stop at the top of the hill, but once we start sliding down it we can't stop short of the bottom.

More disconcerting still, perhaps, is the fact that there is no universal agreement on the direction which the "line of increasing clarity" shall take. If we said that "Unless p, then q" means "If not p, then q" and someone said "Why not say that 'If not p, then q' means 'Unless p, q,' taking the latter as the ultimate in clarity of meaning?" "A thought exists in my mind" means "I am thinking a thought"; but why not reverse the procedure and render the latter in terms of the former? Who is, in every case, to say which meaning is "clearer"? And how are we to know what method to employ to get at a "clearer meaning?" When the sculptor Henry Moore says that he likes sea-shells because they express the hard, hollow structure of the world, how is such an assertion (leaving aside the question of its meaningfulness) to be clarified? By analyzing the "meaning" of each individual word? by going to the museum where his sea-shell sculptures are exhibited? by reading his biography, or perhaps the biography of the earth itself? What does one even mean by referring to "his meaning?"

To many of these questions we shall fortunately not require an answer in coming to grips with the topic of this paper. However, one thing is surely evident: if we are interested not in conferring some arbitrary meaning on the word "free," but want to get at some analysis which, as we say, "really tells us what people in ordinary life mean when they use the word," then it is a genuine obstacle to discover that people as a whole cannot explicate their meaning because they have no "clear and distinct idea" in their minds at all in employing words such as this.

Now, it is true that even in employing ordinary words like "cat" people do not "have in mind" the dictionary meaning of "cat" as a domesticated carnivorous quadruped of a certain specifiable variety; nor do they have in their minds an image of all the creatures they would classify as cats; nor do they have any definite non-imaged criterion-in-mind which would enable them to choose and label as "cat" or "non-cat" all possible instances of creatures that might fall under their surveillance – one can easily imagine creatures cat-like in some respects but not in others in which

one would be hard put to it to classify. And if one asks whether such a person "really knows" what the word "cat" means unless he can do all these things, one is surely asking for a "clearer" meaning of the phrase "knowing the meaning of." Yet if there is no common criterion-in-mind, how can one proceed to analyze the meaning of the word "as ordinarily employed by English-speaking people?"

One might say that what the person "really means" is not "what he had consciously in mind at the time of utterance" but rather "what he had in the back of his mind"; and this figure of speech might be interpreted to mean "what he *would* have had in the foreground of his mind, i.e., what he *would* consciously have intended in the use of the word, if he had been prodded a bit and some Socratic method used on him." Of course, in this event his meaning must generally remain something problematic, since most people do not have Socratic method used on them, and their "real meaning" – what they would assent to be a correct analysis of what they meant, or "really had in mind all the time" – must remain a deep dark mystery.

We may then try to extract "what he really had in mind when he used the word" by observing the context in which he uses it, the kind of situation in which he employs it, and the kind of situation in which he does not, to see what is common to all the cases in which he uses it *and* peculiar to those cases. Thus we see "what he really means by 'cat'" by observing the objects to which he applies the word and noting to which objects he declines such application. (Perhaps it would be more accurate to say that we use the phrase "what he really means by 'cat'" in such a way as to be equivalent to "the characteristics common to all things he calls 'cat' and peculiar to them.")

I think that this is generally a much better procedure than simply to ask the person what he means. What he says he means is often contradicted by his verbal behavior, i.e., his actual usage of the word in practice. A good motto is, "If you want to know what a person means by a word or sentence, don't ask him – watch him use it for a while; see when he applies the word and when he doesn't."

This method will not always work. It does not apply, for example, to the question of the meaning of the if-then relation, or the meaning of "cause," or any of those cases where the range of application (denotation) of the term is the same regardless of what its analysis is: two people may agree on all instances of causality and acausality and yet disagree violently on what, philosophically speaking, causality is. (This phenomenon is most likely to occur in philosophical analysis, but is not limited to this field: two persons might examine every animal in the world and agree perfectly on which ones are elephants and which ones are not, and yet disagree on what the criteria are for the inclusion of these particular animals in the class "elephants" – one person, for example, might call "elephant" any animal that draws water up its nose and squirts it into its mouth, while the other, with a different connotation, may yet agree entirely on the denotations.)

Still, this method may help us in analyzing "the meaning" of a term such as "free." If we know in what situations people are willing to use the word and in what situations they are not, shall we not have a much better idea what they "mean" by it?

But the moment we have embarked on this enterprise we shall find that not all persons are in agreement in the criteria thus revealed. There are certain fundamental similarities in the way people use the word, but certainly no identity. (This is especially true in a field which we are not considering, namely "political freedom," where some persons would consider human beings free in a "free enterprise" system, for example, while others would not.) Hence, philosophers who want to use the term "free" precisely without doing any great violence to "the sort of thing that most people most of the time mean when they use the word" – or perhaps what they could be interpreted to mean, judging by their verbal behavior – have suggested varying but overlapping criteria. The following section is concerned with this point.

II

Perhaps the most obvious conception of freedom is this: an act is free if and only if it is a voluntary act. A response that occurs spontaneously, not as a result of your willing it, such as a reflex action, is not a free act. I do not know that this view is ever held in its pure form, but it is the basis for other ones. As it stands, of course, it is ambiguous: does "voluntary" entail "premeditated?" are acts we perform semi-automatically through habit to be called free acts? To what extent is a conscious decision to act required for the act to be classified as voluntary? What of sudden outbursts of feeling? They are hardly premeditated or decided upon, yet they may have their origin in the presence or absence of habit-patterns due to self-discipline which may have been consciously decided upon. Clearly the view needs to be refined.

Now, however we may come to define "voluntary," it is perfectly possible to maintain that all voluntary acts are free acts and vice versa; after all, it is a matter of what meaning we are giving to the word "free" and we can give it this meaning if we choose. But it soon becomes apparent that this is not the meaning which most of us *want* to give it: for there *are* classes of actions which we want to refrain from calling "free" even though they are voluntary (not that we have this denial in mind when we use the word "free" – still, it is significant that we do not use the word in some situations in which the act in question is nevertheless voluntary).

When a man tells a state secret under torture, he does choose voluntarily between telling and enduring more torture; and when he submits to a bandit's command at the point of a gun, he voluntarily chooses to submit rather than to be shot. And still such actions would not generally be called free; it is clear that they are performed under compulsion. Voluntary acts performed under compulsion would not be called free; and the cruder view is to this extent amended.

For some persons, this is as far as we need to go. Schlick, for example, says that the free-will issue is the scandal of philosophy and nothing but so much wasted ink and paper, because the whole controversy is nothing but an inexcusable confusion between compulsion and universal causality.[2] The free act is the uncompelled act, says Schlick, and controversies about causality and determinism have nothing to do with the case. When one asks whether an act done of necessity is free, the question is ambiguous: if "of necessity" means "by compulsion," then the answer is no; if, on the other hand, "of necessity" is a way of referring to "causal uniformity" in nature – the sense in which we may misleadingly speak of the laws of nature as "necessary" simply because there are no exceptions to them – then the answer is clearly yes; every act is an instance of some causal law (uniformity) or other, but this has nothing to do with its being free in the sense of uncompelled.

For Schlick, this is the end of the matter. Any attempt to discuss the matter further simply betrays a failure to perceive the clarifying distinctions that Schlick has made.

> Freedom means the opposite of compulsion; a man is *free* if he does not act under *compulsion*, and he is compelled or unfree when he is hindered from without in the realization of his natural desires. Hence he is unfree when he is locked up, or chained, or when someone forces him at the point of a gun to do what otherwise he would not do. This is quite clear, and everyone will admit that the everyday or legal notion of the lack of freedom is thus correctly interpreted, and that a man will be considered quite free . . . if no such external compulsion is exerted upon him.[3]

This all seems clear enough. And yet if we ask whether it ends the matter, whether it states what we "really mean" by "free," many of us will feel qualms. We remember statements about human beings being pawns of their environment, victims of conditions beyond their control, the result of causal influences stemming from parents, etc., and we think, "Still, are we really free?" We do not want to say that the uniformity of nature itself binds us or renders us unfree; yet is there not something in what generations of wise men have said about man being fettered? Is there not something too facile, too sleight-of-hand, in Schlick's cutting of the Gordian knot?

It will be noticed that we have slipped from talking about acts as being free into talking about human beings as free. Both locutions are employed, I would say about 50-50. Sometimes an attempt is made to legislate definitely between the two: Stebbing, for instance, says that one must never call acts free, but only the doers of the acts.[4]

Let us pause over this for a moment. If it is we and not our acts that are to be called free, the most obvious reflection to make is that we are free to do some things and not free to do other things; we are free to lift our hands but not free to lift

the moon. We cannot simply call ourselves free or unfree *in toto*; we must say at best that we are free in respect of certain actions only. G. E. Moore states the criterion as follows: we are free to do an act if we can do it *if* we want to; that which we can do if we want to is what we are free to do.[5] Some things certain people are free to do while others are not: most of us are free to move our legs, but paralytics are not; some of us are free to concentrate on philosophical reading matter for three hours at a stretch while others are not. In general, we could relate the two approaches by saying that a *person* is free *in respect of* a given action if he can do it if he wants to, and in this case his *act* is free.

Moore himself, however, has reservations that Schlick has not. He adds that there *is* a sense of "free" which fulfills the criterion he has just set forth; but that there may be *another* sense in which man cannot be said to be free in all the situations in which he could rightly be said to be so in the first sense.

And surely it is not necessary for me to multiply examples of the sort of thing we mean. In practice most of us would not call free many persons who behave voluntarily and even with calculation aforethought, and under no compulsion either of any obvious sort. A metropolitan newspaper headlines an article with the words "Boy Killer Is Doomed Long before He Is Born,"[6] and then goes on to describe how a twelve-year-old boy has just been sentenced to thirty years in Sing Sing for the murder of a girl; his family background includes records of drunkenness, divorce, social maladjustment, epilepsy, and paresis. He early displays a tendency to sadistic activity to hide an underlying masochism and "prove that he's a man"; being coddled by his mother only worsens this tendency, until, spurned by a girl in his attempt on her, he kills her – not simply in a fit of anger, but calculatingly, deliberately. Is he free in respect of his criminal act, or for that matter in most of the acts of his life? Surely to ask this question is to answer it in the negative. Perhaps I have taken an extreme case; but it is only to show the superficiality of the Schlick analysis the more clearly. Though not everyone has criminotic tendencies, everyone has been moulded by influences which in large measure at least determine his present behavior; he is literally the product of these influences, stemming from periods prior to his "years of discretion," giving him a host of character traits that he cannot change now even if he would. So obviously does what a man is depend upon how a man comes to be, that it is small wonder that philosophers and sages have considered man far indeed from being the master of his fate. It is not as if man's will were standing high and serene above the flux of events that have moulded him; it is itself caught up in this flux, itself carried along on the current. An act is free when it is determined by the man's character, say moralists; but when there was nothing the man could do to shape his character, and even the degree of will power available to him in shaping his habits and disciplining himself to overcome the influence of his early environment is a factor over which he has no control, what are we to say of this kind of "freedom?" Is it not rather like the freedom of the machine to stamp labels on cans when it has been devised for just that purpose? Some machines can do so more efficiently than others, but only because they have been better constructed.

It is not my purpose here to establish this thesis in general, but only in one specific respect which has received comparatively little attention, namely, the field referred to by psychiatrists as that of unconscious motivation. In what follows I shall restrict my attention to it because it illustrates as clearly as anything the points I wish to make.

Let me try to summarize very briefly the psychoanalytic doctrine on this point.[7] The conscious life of the human being, including the conscious decisions and volitions, is merely a mouthpiece for the unconscious – not directly for the enactment of unconscious drives, but of the compromise between unconscious drives and unconscious reproaches. There is a Big Three behind the scenes which the automaton called the conscious personality carries out: the id, an "eternal gimme," presents its wish and demands its immediate satisfaction; the super-ego says no to the wish immediately upon presentation, and the unconscious ego, the mediator between the two, tries to keep peace by means of compromise.[8]

To go into examples of the functioning of these three "bosses" would be endless; psychoanalytic case books supply hundreds of them. The important point for us to see in the present context is that it is the unconscious that determines what the conscious impulse and the conscious action shall be. Hamlet, for example, had a strong Oedipus wish, which was violently counteracted by super-ego reproaches; these early wishes were vividly revived in an unusual adult situation in which his uncle usurped the coveted position from Hamlet's father and won his mother besides. This situation evoked strong strictures on the part of Hamlet's super-ego, and it was this that was responsible for his notorious delay in killing his uncle. A dozen times Hamlet could have killed Claudius easily; but every time Hamlet "decided" not to: a free choice, moralists would say – but no, listen to the super-ego: "What you feel such hatred toward your uncle for, what you are plotting to kill him for, is precisely the crime which you yourself desire to commit: to kill your father and replace him in the affections of your mother. Your fate and your uncle's are bound up together." This paralyzes Hamlet into inaction. Consciously all he knows is that he is unable to act; this conscious inability he rationalizes, giving a different excuse each time.[9]

We have always been conscious of the fact that we are not masters of our fate in every respect – that there are many things which we cannot do, that nature is more powerful than we are, that we cannot disobey laws without danger of reprisals, etc. Lately we have become more conscious, too, though novelists and dramatists have always been fairly conscious of it, that we are not free with respect to the emotions that we feel – whom we love or hate, what types we admire, and the like. More lately still we have been reminded that there are unconscious motivations for our basic attractions and repulsions, our compulsive actions or inabilities to act. But what is not welcome news is that our very acts of volition, and the entire train of deliberations leading up to them, are but facades for the expression of unconscious wishes, or rather, unconscious compromises and defenses.

A man is faced by a choice: shall he kill another person or not? Moralists would say, here is a free choice – the result of deliberation, an action consciously entered into. And yet, though the agent himself does not know it, and has no awareness of the forces that are at work within him, his choice is already determined for him: his conscious will is only an instrument, a slave, in the hands of a deep unconscious motivation which determines his action. If he has a great deal of what the analyst calls "free-floating guilt," he will not; but if the guilt is such as to demand immediate absorption in the form of self-damaging behavior, this accumulated guilt will have to be discharged in some criminal action. The man himself does not know what the inner clockwork is; he is like the hands on the clock, thinking they move freely over the face of the clock.

A woman has married and divorced several husbands. Now she is faced with a choice for the next marriage: shall she marry Mr A, or Mr B, or nobody at all? She may take considerable time to "decide" this question, and her decision may appear as a final triumph of her free will. Let us assume that A is a normal, well-adjusted, kind, and generous man, while B is a leech, an impostor, one who will become entangled constantly in quarrels with her. If she belongs to a certain classifiable psychological type, she will inevitably choose B, and she will do so even if her previous husbands have resembled B, so that one would think that she "had learned from experience." Consciously, she will of course "give the matter due consideration," etc., etc. To the psychoanalyst all this is irrelevant chaff in the wind – only a camouflage for the inner workings about which she knows nothing consciously. If she is of a certain kind of masochistic strain, as exhibited in her previous set of symptoms, she *must* choose B: her superego, always out to maximize the torment in the situation, seeing what dazzling possibilities for self-damaging behavior are promised by the choice of B, compels her to make the choice she does, and even to conceal the real basis of the choice behind an elaborate facade of rationalizations.

A man is addicted to gambling. In the service of his addiction he loses all his money, spends what belongs to his wife, even sells his property and neglects his children. For a time perhaps he stops; then, inevitably, he takes it up again, although he himself may think he chose to. The man does not know that he is a victim rather than an agent; or, if he sometimes senses that he is in the throes of something-he-knows-not-what, he will have no inkling of its character and will soon relapse into the illusion that he (his conscious self) is freely deciding the course of his own actions. What he does not know, of course, is that he is still taking out on his mother the original lesion to his infantile narcissism, getting back at her for her fancied refusal of his infantile wishes – and this by rejecting everything identified with her, namely education, discipline, logic, common sense, training. At the roulette wheel, almost alone among adult activities, chance – the opposite of all these things – rules supreme; and his addiction represents his continued and emphatic reiteration of his rejection of Mother and all she represents to his unconscious.

This pseudo-aggression of his is of course masochistic in its effects. In the long run he always loses; he can never quit while he is winning. And far from playing in order to win, rather one can say that his losing is a *sine qua non* of his psychic equilibrium (as it was for example with Dostoyevsky): guilt demands punishment, and in the ego's "deal" with the super-ego the super-ego has granted satisfaction of infantile wishes in return for the self-damaging conditions obtaining. Winning would upset the neurotic equilibrium.[10]

A man has wash-compulsion. He must be constantly washing his hands – he uses up perhaps 400 towels a day. Asked why he does this, he says, "I need to, my hands are dirty"; and if it is pointed out to him that they are not really dirty, he says "They feel dirty anyway, I feel better when I wash them." So once again he washes them. He "freely decides" every time; he feels that he must wash them, he deliberates for a moment perhaps, but always ends by washing them. What he does not see, of course, is the invisible wires inside him pulling him inevitably to do the thing he does: the infantile id-wish concerns preoccupation with dirt, the super-ego charges him with this, and the terrified ego must respond, "No, I don't like dirt, see how clean I like to be, look how I wash my hands!"

Let us see what further "free acts" the same patient engages in (this is an actual case history): he is taken to a concentration camp, and given the worst of treatment by the Nazi guards. In the camp he no longer chooses to be clean, does not even try to be – on the contrary, his choice is now to wallow in filth as much as he can. All he is aware of now is a disinclination to be clean, and every time he must choose he chooses not to be. Behind the scenes, however, another drama is being enacted: the super-ego, perceiving that enough torment is being administered from the outside, can afford to cease pressing its charges in this quarter – the outside world is doing the torturing now, so the super-ego is relieved of the responsibility. Thus the ego is relieved of the agony of constantly making terrified replies in the form of washing to prove that the super-ego is wrong. The defense no longer being needed, the person slides back into what is his natural predilection anyway, for filth. This becomes too much even for the Nazi guards: they take hold of him one day, saying "We'll teach you how to be clean!" drag him into the snow, and pour bucket after bucket of icy water over him until he freezes to death. Such is the end-result of an original id-wish, caught in the machinations of a destroying super-ego.

Let us take, finally, a less colorful, more every-day example. A student at a university, possess-ing wealth, charm, and all that is usually considered essential to popularity, begins to develop the following personality-pattern: although well taught in the graces of social con-versation, he always makes a *faux pas* some-where, and always in the worst possible situation; to his friends he makes cutting remarks which hurt deeply – and always apparently aimed in such a way as to hurt the most: a remark that would not hurt A but would hurt B he invariably makes to B rather than to A, and so on. None of this is conscious. Ordinarily he is considerate of people, but he contrives always (unconsciously) to impose on just those friends who would resent it most, and at just the times when he should know that he should not impose: at 3 o'clock in the morning, without forewarning, he phones a friend in a near-by city demanding to stay at his apartment for the weekend; naturally the friend is offended, but the person himself is not aware that he has provoked the grievance ("common sense" suffers a temporary eclipse when the neurotic pattern sets in, and one's intelligence, far from being of help in such a situation, is used in the interest of the neurosis), and when the friend is cool to him the next time they meet, he won-ders why and feels unjustly treated. Aggressive behavior on his part invites resentment and aggression in turn, but all that he consciously sees is others' behavior toward him – and he considers himself the innocent victim of an unjustified "persecution."

Each of these choices is, from the moralist's point of view, free: he chose to phone his friend at 3 a.m.; he chose to make the cutting remark that he did, etc. What he does not know is that an ineradicable masochistic pattern has set in. His unconscious is far more shrewd and clever than is his conscious intellect; it sees with uncanny accuracy just what kind of behavior will damage him most, and unerringly forces him into that behavior. Consciously, the student "doesn't know why he did it" – he gives different "reasons" at different times, but they are all, once again, rationalizations cloaking the unconscious mech-anism which propels him willy-nilly into actions that his "common sense" eschews.

The more of this sort of thing you see, the more you can see what the psychoanalyst means when he talks about "the illusion of free-will." And the more of a psychiatrist you become, the more you are overcome with a sense of what an illusion this precious free-will really is. In some kinds of cases most of us can see it already: it takes no psychi-atrist to look at the epileptic and sigh with sadness at the thought that soon this person before you will be as one possessed, not the same thought-ful intelligent person you knew. But people are not aware of this in other contexts, for example when they express surprise at how a person whom they have been so good to could treat them so badly. Let us suppose that you help a person financially or morally or in some other way, so that he is in your debt; suppose further that he is one of the many neurotics who unconsciously identify kindness with weakness and aggression with strength, then he will unconsciously take your kindness to him as weakness and use it as the occasion for enacting some aggression against you. He can't help it, he may regret it himself later; still, he will be driven to do it. If we gain a little knowledge of psychiatry, we can look at him with pity, that a person otherwise so worthy should be so unreliable – but we will exercise realism too and be aware that there are some types of people that you cannot be good to in "free" acts of their conscious volition, they will use your own goodness against you.

Sometimes the persons themselves will become dimly aware that "something behind the scenes" is determining their behavior. The divorcee will sometimes view herself with detachment, as if she were some machine (and indeed the psychoanalyst does call her a "repeating-machine"): "I know I'm caught in a net, that I'll fall in love with this guy and marry him and the whole ridiculous merry-go-round will start all over again."

We talk about free will, and we say, yes, the person is free to do so-and-so if he can do so *if* he wants to – and we forget that his wanting to is itself caught up in the stream of determinism, that unconscious forces drive him into the wanting or not wanting to do the thing in question. The idea of the puppet whose motions are manipulated from behind by invisible wires, or better still, by springs inside, is no mere figure of speech. The analogy is a telling one at almost every point.

And the pity of it is that it all started so early, before we knew what was happening. The personality-structure is inelastic after the age of five, and comparatively so in most cases after the age of three. Whether one acquires a neurosis or not is determined by that age – and just as involuntarily as if it had been a curse of God. If, for example, a masochistic pattern was set up, under pressure of hyper-narcissism combined with real or fancied infantile deprivation, then the masochistic snowball was on its course downhill long before we or anybody else know what was happening, and long before anyone could do anything about it. To speak of human beings as "puppets" in such a context is no mere metaphor, but a stark rendering of a literal fact: only the psychiatrist knows what puppets people really are; and it is no wonder that the protestations of philosophers that "the act which is the result of a volition, a deliberation, a conscious decision, is free" leave these persons, to speak mildly, somewhat cold.

But, one may object, all the states thus far described have been abnormal, neurotic ones. The well-adjusted (normal) person at least is free.

Leaving aside the question of how clearly and on what grounds one can distinguish the neurotic from the normal, let me use an illustration of a proclivity that everyone would call normal, namely, the decision of a man to support his wife and possibly a family, and consider briefly its genesis.[11]

Every baby comes into the world with a full-fledged case of megalomania – interested only in himself, naively assuming that he is the center of the universe and that others are present only to fulfill his wishes, and furious when his own wants are not satisfied immediately no matter for

what reason. Gratitude, even for all the time and worry and care expended on him by the mother, is an emotion entirely foreign to the infant, and as he grows older it is inculcated in him only with the greatest difficulty; his natural tendency is to assume that everything that happens to him is due to himself, except for denials and frustrations, which are due to the "cruel, denying" outer world, in particular the mother; and that he owes nothing to anyone, is dependent on no one. This omnipotence-complex, or illusion of non-dependence, has been called the "autarchic fiction." Such a conception of the world is actually fostered in the child by the conduct of adults, who automatically attempt to fulfill the infant's every wish concerning nourishment, sleep, and attention. The child misconceives causality and sees in these wish-fulfillments not the results of maternal kindness and love, but simply the result of his own omnipotence.

This fiction of omnipotence is gradually destroyed by experience, and its destruction is probably the deepest disappointment of the early years of life. First of all, the infant discovers that he is the victim of organic urges and necessities: hunger, defecation, urination. More important, he discovers that the maternal breast, which he has not previously distinguished from his own body (he has not needed to, since it was available when he wanted it), is not a part of himself after all, but of another creature upon whom he is dependent. He is forced to recognize this, e.g., when he wants nourishment and it is at the moment not present; even a small delay is most damaging to the "autarchic fiction." Most painful of all is the experience of weaning, probably the greatest tragedy in every baby's life, when his dependence is most cruelly emphasized; it is a frustrating experience because what he wants is no longer there at all; and if he has been able to some extent to preserve the illusion of non-dependence heretofore, he is not able to do so now – it is plain that the source of his nourishment is not dependent on him, but he on it. The shattering of the autarchic fiction is a great disillusionment to every child, a tremendous blow to his ego which he will, in one way or another, spend the rest of his life trying to repair. How does he do this?

First of all, his reaction to frustration is anger and fury; and he responds by kicking, biting,

etc., the only ways he knows. But he is motoric-
ally helpless, and these measures are ineffective,
and only serve to emphasize his dependence the
more. Moreover, against such responses of the
child the parental reaction is one of prohibition,
generally accompanied by physical force of some
kind. Generally the child soon learns that this form
of rebellion is profitless, and brings him more
harm than good. He wants to respond to frustration with violent aggression, and at the same
time learns that he will be punished for such
aggression, and that in any case the latter is ineffectual. What face-saving solution does he find?
Since he must "face facts," since he must in any
case "conform" if he is to have any peace at all,
he tries to make it seem as if he himself is the
source of the commands and prohibitions: the
external prohibitive force is *internalized* – and here
we have the origin of conscience. By making the
prohibitive agency seem to come from within
himself, the child can "save face" – as if saying,
"The prohibition comes from within me, not
from outside, so I'm not subservient to external
rule, I'm only obeying rules I've set up myself,"
thus to some extent saving the autarchic fiction,
and at the same time avoiding unpleasant consequences directed against himself by complying
with parental commands.

Moreover, the boy[12] has unconsciously never
forgiven the mother for his dependence on her
in early life, for nourishment and all other things.
It has upset his illusion of non-dependence. These
feelings have been repressed and are not remembered; but they are acted out in later life in many
ways – e.g., in the constant deprecation man
has for woman's duties such as cooking and
housework of all sorts ("All she does is stay
home and get together a few meals, and she
calls that work"), and especially in the man's
identification with the mother in his sex experiences with women. By identifying with someone
one cancels out in effect the person with whom
he identifies – replacing that person, unconsciously denying his existence, and the man,
identifying with his early mother, playing the
active role in "giving" to his wife as his mother
has "given" to him, is in effect the denial of his
mother's existence, a fact which is narcissistically
embarrassing to his ego because it is chiefly
responsible for shattering his autarchic fiction.
In supporting his wife, he can unconsciously

deny that his mother gave to him, and that he
was dependent on her giving. Why is it that the
husband plays the provider, and wants his wife
to be dependent on no one else, although twenty
years before he was nothing but a parasitic baby?
This is a face-saving device on his part: he can act
out the reasoning "See, I'm not the parasitic baby,
on the contrary I'm the provider, the giver." His
playing the provider is a constant face-saving
device, to deny his early dependence which is so
embarrassing to his ego. It is no wonder that men
generally dislike to be reminded of their babyhood,
when they were dependent on woman.

Thus we have here a perfectly normal adult
reaction which is unconsciously motivated. The
man "chooses" to support a family – and his
choice is as unconsciously motivated as anything
could be. (I have described here only the "normal" state of affairs, uncomplicated by the well-
nigh infinite number of variations that occur in
actual practice.)

Now, what of the notion of responsibility?
What happens to it on our analysis?

Let us begin with an example, not a fictitious
one. A woman and her two-year-old baby are
riding on a train to Montreal in mid-winter. The
child is ill. The woman wants badly to get to
her destination. She is, unknown to herself, the
victim of a neurotic conflict whose nature is
irrelevant here except for the fact that it forces her
to behave aggressively toward the child, partly to
spite her husband whom she despises and who
loves the child, but chiefly to ward off super-ego
charges of masochistic attachment. Consciously
she loves the child, and when she says this she says
it sincerely, but she must behave aggressively
toward it nevertheless, just as many children
love their mothers but are nasty to them most
of the time in neurotic pseudo-aggression. The
child becomes more ill as the train approaches
Montreal; the heating system of the train is not
working, and the conductor advises the woman
to get off the train at the next town and get the
child to a hospital at once. The woman says no,
she must get to Montreal. Shortly afterward, as
the child's condition worsens, and the mother does
all she can to keep it alive, without, however, leaving the train, for she declares that it is absolutely
necessary that she reach her destination. But
before she gets there the child is dead. After that,
of course, the mother grieves, blames herself,

weeps hysterically, and joins the church to gain surcease from the guilt that constantly overwhelms her when she thinks of how her aggressive behavior has killed her child.

Was she responsible for her deed? In ordinary life, after making a mistake, we say, "Chalk it up to experience." Here we say, "Chalk it up to the neurosis." No, she is not responsible. She could not help it if her neurosis forced her to act this way – she didn't even know what was going on behind the scenes, she merely acted out the part assigned to her. This is far more true than is generally realized: criminal actions in general are not actions for which their agents are responsible; the agents are passive, not active – they are victims of a neurotic conflict. Their very hyper-activity is unconsciously determined.

To say this is, of course, not to say that we should not punish criminals. Clearly, for our own protection, we must remove them from our midst so that they can no longer molest and endanger organized society. And, of course, if we use the word "responsible" in such a way that justly to hold someone responsible for a deed is by definition identical with being justified in punishing him, then we can and do hold people responsible. But this is like the sense of "free" in which free acts are voluntary ones. It does not go deep enough. In a deeper sense we cannot hold the person responsible: we may hold his neurosis responsible, but he is not responsible for his neurosis, particularly since the age at which its onset was inevitable was an age before he could even speak.

The neurosis is responsible – but isn't the neurosis a part of *him*? We have been speaking all the time as if the person and his unconscious were two separate beings; but isn't he one personality, including conscious and unconscious departments together?

I do not wish to deny this. But it hardly helps us here; for what people want when they talk about freedom, and what they hold to when they champion it, is the idea that the *conscious* will is the master of their destiny. "I am the master of my fate, I am the captain of my soul" – and they surely mean their conscious selves, the self that they can recognize and search and introspect. Between an unconscious that willy-nilly determines your actions, and an external force which pushes you, there is little if anything to choose. The

unconscious is just *as if* it were an outside force; and indeed, psychiatrists will assert that the inner Hitler can torment you far more than any external Hitler can. Thus the kind of freedom that people want, the only kind they will settle for, is precisely the kind that psychiatry says that they cannot have.

Heretofore it was pretty generally thought that, while we could not rightly blame a person for the color of his eyes or the morality of his parents, or even for what he did at the age of three, or to a large extent what impulses he had and whom he fell in love with, one *could* do so for other of his adult activities, particularly the acts he performed voluntarily and with premeditation. Later this attitude was shaken. Many voluntary acts came to be recognized, at least in some circles, as compelled by the unconscious. Some philosophers recognized this too – Ayer[13] talks about the kleptomaniac being unfree, and about a person being unfree when another person exerts a habitual ascendancy over his personality. But this is as far as he goes. The usual examples, such as the kleptomaniac and the schizophrenic, apparently satisfy most philosophers, and with these exceptions removed, the rest of mankind is permitted to wander in the vast and alluring fields of freedom and responsibility. So far, the inroads upon freedom left the vast majority of humanity untouched; they began to hit home when psychiatrists began to realize, though philosophers did not, that the domination of the conscious by the unconscious extended, not merely to a few exceptional individuals, but to all human beings, that the "big three behind the scenes" are not respecters of persons, and dominate us all, even including that *sanctum sanctorum* of freedom, our conscious will. To be sure, the domination in the case of "normal" individuals is somewhat more benevolent than the tyranny and despotism exercised in neurotic cases, and therefore the former have evoked less comment; but the principle remains in all cases the same: the unconscious is the master of every fate and the captain of every soul.

We speak of a machine turning out good products most of the time but every once in a while it turns out a "lemon." We do not, of course, hold the product responsible for this, but the machine, and via the machine, its maker. Is it silly to extend to inanimate objects the idea of responsibility? Of course. But is it any less silly to employ the notion in speaking of human creatures? Are not the two kinds of cases analogous in countless important ways? Occasionally a child turns out badly too, even when his environment and training are the same as that of his brothers and sisters who turn out "all right." He is the "bad penny." His acts of rebellion against parental discipline in adult life (such as the case of the gambler, already cited) are traceable to early experiences of real or fancied denial of infantile wishes. Sometimes the denial has been real, though many denials are absolutely necessary if the child is to grow up to observe the common decencies of civilized life; sometimes, if the child has an unusual quantity of narcissism, every event that occurs is interpreted by him as a denial of his wishes, and nothing a parent could do, even granting every humanly possible wish, would help. In any event, the later neurosis can be attributed to this. Can the person himself be held responsible? Hardly. If he engages in activities which are a menace to society, he must be put into prison, of course, but responsibility is another matter. The time when the events occurred which rendered his neurotic behavior inevitable was a time long before he was capable of thought and decision. As an adult, he is a victim of a world he never made – only this world is inside him.

What about the children who turn out "all right"? All we can say is that "it's just lucky for them" that what happened to their unfortunate brother didn't happen to them; *through no virtue of their own* they are not doomed to the life of unconscious guilt, expiation, conscious depression, terrified ego-gestures for the appeasement of a tyrannical super-ego that he is. The machine turned them out with a minimum of damage. But if the brother cannot be blamed for his evils, neither can they be praised for their good. It will take society a long time to come round to this attitude. We do not blame people for the color of their eyes, but we have not attained the same attitude toward their socially significant activities.

We all agree that machines turn out "lemons", we all agree that nature turns out misfits in the realm of biology – the blind, the crippled, the diseased; but we hesitate to include the realm of the personality, for here, it seems, is the last retreat of our dignity as human beings. Our ego can endure anything but this; this island at least must remain above the encroaching flood. But may not precisely the same analysis be made here also? Nature turns out psychological "lemons" too, in far greater quantities than any other kind; and indeed all of us are "lemons" in some respect or other, the difference being one of degree. Some of us are lucky enough not to have a gambling-neurosis or criminotic tendencies or masochistic mother-attachment or overdimensional repetition-compulsion to make our lives miserable, but most of our actions, those usually considered the most important, are unconsciously dominated just the same. And, if a neurosis may be likened to a curse of God, let those of us, the elect, who are enabled to enjoy a measure of life's happiness without the hell-fire of neurotic guilt, take this, not as our own achievement, but simply for what it is – a gift of God.

Let us, however, quit metaphysics and put the situation schematically in the form of a deductive argument.

1. An occurrence over which we had no control is something we cannot be held responsible for.
2. Events E, occurring during our babyhood, were events over which we had no control.
3. Therefore events E were events which we cannot be held responsible for.
4. But if there is something we cannot be held responsible for, neither can we be held responsible for something that inevitably results from it.
5. Events E have as inevitable consequence Neurosis N, which in turn has as inevitable consequence Behavior B.
6. Since N is the inevitable consequence of E and B is the inevitable consequence of N, B is the inevitable consequence of E.
7. Hence, not being responsible for E, we cannot be responsible for B.

In Samuel Butler's Utopian satire *Erewhon* there occurs the following passage, in which a judge is passing sentence on a prisoner:

> It is all very well for you to say that you came of unhealthy parents, and had a severe accident in your childhood which permanently undermined your constitution; excuses such as these are the

ordinary refuge of the criminal; but they cannot for one moment be listened to by the ear of justice. I am not here to enter upon curious metaphysical questions as to the origin of this or that – questions to which there would be no end were their introduction once tolerated, and which would result in throwing the only guilt on the tissues of the primordial cell, or on the elementary gases. There is no question of how you came to be wicked, but only this – namely, are you wicked or not? This has been decided in the affirmative, neither can I hesitate for a single moment to say that it has been decided justly. You are a bad and dangerous person, and stand branded in the eyes of your fellow countrymen with one of the most heinous known offenses.[14]

As moralists read this passage, they may perhaps nod with approval. But the joke is on them. The sting comes when we realize what the crime is for which the prisoner is being sentenced: namely, consumption. The defendant is reminded that during the previous year he was sentenced for aggravated bronchitis, and is warned that he should profit from experience in the future. Butler is employing here his familiar method of presenting some human tendency (in this case, holding people responsible for what isn't their fault) to a ridiculous extreme and thereby reducing it to absurdity. How soon will mankind appreciate the keen edge of Butler's bitter irony? How long will they continue to read such a passage, but fail to smile, or yet to wince?

III

Our discussion thus far has developed into a kind of double-headed monster. We started to talk about analysis of meaning, and we have ended by taking a journey into the realm of the unconscious. Can we unite the two heads into one, or at least make them look at each other?

I think the second possibility is not a remote one. Surely we have shown that the "meaning of a word" is not the same as "what we had in mind in using the word," and the word "free" is a concrete illustration of this. The psychoanalytic examples we have adduced have (if one was not acquainted with them before) added, so to speak, a new dimension to the term "free." In our ordinary use of this word we probably had

nothing in mind as concrete as the sort of thing brought to light in our examples; but now that we have, we hesitate to label many actions as free which previously we had so labeled without hesitation. And we would, I think, call people "free" in far fewer respects than we would have previously.

Can human beings, in the light of psychiatric knowledge, be called "free" in any respect at all?

We must remember that every term that can be significantly used must have a significant opposite. If the opposite cannot significantly be asserted, neither can its original. If the term "unfree" can be significantly used, so can the term "free." Even though there may be no actual denotation of a term naming an opposite, one must know what it would be like – what it would mean to speak of it; even though there are no white crows, it must be significant, as indeed it is, to speak of them. Now is the case of freedom like that of the white crows that don't exist but can be significantly spoken of, or like the black crows that do exist and can be significantly spoken of as well?

Unless "freedom" is taken to mean the same as "lack of cause" and a principle of universal causality is taken for granted, I think the latter must be the case.

If we asked the psychoanalysts for their opinion on this, they would doubtless reply somewhat as follows. They would say that they were not accustomed to using the term "free" at all, but that if they had to suggest a criterion for distinguishing the free from the unfree, they would say that a person's freedom occurs in inverse proportion to his neuroticism; the more he is compelled in his behavior by a *malevolent* unconscious, the less free he is. We speak of degrees of freedom – and the psychologically normal and well-adjusted individual is comparatively the freest, even though most of his behavior is determined by his unconscious.

But suppose it is the determination of his behavior by his unconscious, no matter what kind, that we balk at? We may then say that a man is free only to the extent that his behavior is *not* unconsciously motivated at all. If this be our criterion, most of our behavior could not be called free: everything, including both impulses and volitions, having to do with our basic attitudes toward life, the general tenor of our tastes, whether we become philosophers or artists or business men, our whole affective life including our preferences for blondes or brunettes, active or passive, older or younger, has its inevitable basis in the unconscious. Only those comparatively vanilla-flavored aspects of life – such as our behavior toward people who don't really matter to us – are exempted from this rule.

These, I think, are the two principal criteria for distinguishing freedom from the lack of it which we might set up on the basis of psychoanalytic knowledge. Conceivably we might set up others. In every case, of course, it remains trivially true that "it all depends on how we choose to use the word." The facts are what they are, regardless of how we choose to label them. But if we choose to label facts in a way which is out of accordance with people's deep-seated and traditional methods of labeling them, as we would be doing if we labeled "free" human actions which we know as much about as we now do through modern psychiatry, then we shall only be manipulating words to mislead our fellow creatures.

Notes

1   Moritz Schlick, "Meaning and Verification," *Philosophical Review*, vol. XLV (1936), p. 348.
2   Moritz Schlick, *The Problems of Ethics*, trans. David Rynin (New York, 1939) chapter VII.
3   *Ibid.*, p. 150.
4   L. Susan Stebbing, *Philosophy and the Physicists* (London, 1937), p. 242.
5   G. E. Moore, *Ethics* (London, 1912), p. 205.
6   *New York Post*, Tuesday, May 18, 1948, p. 4.
7   I am aware that the theory presented below is not accepted by all practicing psychoanalysts. Many non-Freudians would disagree with the conclusions presented below. But I do not believe that this fact affects my argument, as long as the concept of unconscious motivation is accepted. I am aware, too, that much of the language employed in the following descriptions is animistic and metaphorical; but as long as I am presenting a view I would prefer to "go the whole hog" and present it in its strongest possible light. The theory can in any case be made clearest by the use of such language, just as atomic theory can often be made clearest to students with the use of models.
8   This view is very clearly developed in Edmund Bergler, *Divorce Won't Help* (New York, 1948), especially chapter I.
9   See *The Basic Writings of Sigmund Freud* (Modern Library Edition), p. 310. (In *The Interpretation of Dreams*.) Cf. also the essay by Ernest Jones, "A Psycho-analytical Study of Hamlet."
10 See Edmund Bergler's article on the pathological gambler in *Diseases of the Nervous System* (1943). Also "Suppositions about the Mechanism of Criminosis," *Journal of Criminal Psychopathology* (1944) and "Clinical Contributions to the Psychogenesis of Alcohol Addiction," *Quarterly Journal of Studies on Alcohol*, 5: 434 (1944).
11 Edmund Bergler, *The Battle of the Conscience* (Washington, DC, 1948), chapter I.
12 The girl's development after this point is somewhat different. Society demands more aggressiveness of the adult male, hence there are more super-ego strictures on tendencies toward passivity in the male; accordingly his defenses must be stronger.
13 A. J. Ayer, "Freedom and Necessity," *Polemic* (September–October 1946), pp. 40–3.
14 Samuel Butler, *Erewhon* (Modern Library edition), p. 107.

44

Determinism

J. R. Lucas

General Arguments For and Against Determinism

The chief general arguments for determinism turn on ideas, often confused, of explicability. Provided we take reasonable care to distinguish the different senses of 'explanation', 'cause' and 'causal', we see that the arguments do not really hold at all.

Historians are sometimes determinists, because they confuse partial and complete explanations. They are committed to explaining historical events, and explanation, they feel, involves determination. If a historian can explain why an event took place, he is explaining why it must have taken place. For he is explaining why the event in question took place, and not any other. And if no other event could have taken place, then the event that did take place must have taken place, and determinism is true. An explanation which does not have deterministic implications is less than complete, and therefore less than satisfactory. The only libertarian history is incomplete history. Only the idle or incompetent historian can avoid aspiring to be a determinist.

Historical determinism takes many forms. The Marxist claims that economic factors alone determine the course of history, and are themselves governed by the definite laws of dialectical materialism. Even those historians who reject the crudities of Marxism are liable to the feeling that some set of factors, not necessarily economic, determines the course of history, and that the decisions of the individual play no real part. It may be just a feeling of impotence and the recalcitrance of human affairs. "I pondered," said William Morris ". . . how men fight and lose the battle, and the thing they fought for comes about in spite of their defeat, and when it comes turns out to be not what they meant, and other men have to fight for what they meant under another name": often this feeling is cast in metaphysical form, and a theory of historical determinism propounded.

The argument turns on the nature of historical explanation. It assumes that a satisfactory explanation must not only show why the event in question took place, but why no other event could have taken place. But actual explanations offered by historians seldom do this. Often they are not of the "Why necessarily" form, but of the "How possibly".[1] Even those explanations which explain why, do not reveal a necessity that precludes freedom. In explaining why a man did something we may give, or reconstruct, his reasons. But reasons are seldom all one way. Usually there are arguments on both sides, some for the proposed action, some against: if not, the action hardly needs explaining. Where there are

J. R. Lucas, "Determinism," from *The Freedom of the Will* (Oxford: Oxford University Press, 1970), pp. 51–66. © 1970 by Oxford University Press. Reprinted with permission from Blackwell Publishing.

arguments on both sides, we can explain the man's decision by recounting the arguments on that side: but if he had decided against the action, we could have then explained his decision to the contrary, by recounting the arguments on the other side. Either way we could have given an explanation. In each case the explanation would have explained why the alternative action was not undertaken. But in neither case would it have shown that the agent had to act the way he did, and was unable to act otherwise. We give his reasons in each case, and his reasons show why he should have acted as he did; but not that, in the relevant sense of 'could', he could not have acted otherwise. Historical explicability fails to yield determinism, because a characteristic historical explanation is not a complete one, and the reasons adduced are not outside the agent's control. It is up to him whether he regards them as cogent, or some factor on the other side as decisive. We may ask the further question, why did such and such a person regard such and such reasons as good ones; but that is a different question and one that historians do not normally seek to answer. It is difficult enough to tell us how things happened and show us the reasons why people acted as they did, without presuming to prove that nothing could have happened otherwise than it did.

Besides confusing partial with complete explanations, people often confuse explanations of different types. Many thinkers affirm a principle of universal causation, that Every Event has a Cause. If we take the word 'cause' to mean 'causal cause' (i.e. regularity cause) as seems reasonable, then granted certain conditions, the principle is a determinist one. But when pressed to justify the principle of universal causation, its proponents interpret it to mean that every event has an explanation. This is a different principle, and a much easier one to maintain. If the word 'cause' means simply 'explanation', then it may well be true that every event has a cause, but it carries no determinist implications: if it means cause in the strict regularity sense, then it is far from self-evident that every event has a cause.

The argument is particularly seductive when applied to human actions. For it is characteristic of actions that the agent can say why he did them. If we think of our actions, we can usually remember why we did them, and assign as "causes" (i.e. partial explanations) some antecedent condition;

and then interpret these causes as causal causes, as parts of complete regularity explanations. Blanshard[2] tells of Sir Francis Galton, who "kept account in a notebook of occasions on which he made important choices with a full measures of [the] feeling of freedom; then shortly after each choice he turned his eye backward in search of constraints[3] that might have been acting on him stealthily. He found it so easy to bring such constraining factors to light that he surrendered to the determinist view." "You are too much preoccupied," he tells the reader ". . . to give any attention to the causes of which your choice may be an effect. But that is no reason for thinking that if you did preoccupy yourself you would not find them at work."

Many besides Sir Francis Galton have been convinced of the truth of determinism by this line of reasoning. But once we distinguish different types of explanation, the spring of the argument is broken. From the fact that an action is explicable, it does not follow that it is determined, in the sense in which we are using the word 'determined'. I refuse an invitation. You ask me to think why I refused. On reflection I say that it was because the last time I went to a party, I found it very boring. The boringness of the previous party was, if you like, the cause of my refusing now. But it did not necessitate a refusal on my part. I could perfectly well have accepted – I might have decided it was my duty to put up with being bored for the sake of sociability. I had a reason for refusing, but my refusing was not inevitable, ineluctable, necessitated or determined.

Some philosophers, however, do use the word 'determined' in a wider sense, in which it is more or less equivalent to 'explained'. So far as ordinary usage goes, it is perfectly permissible: we do speak of a man's decision being "determined by the need to preserve his reputation". Blanshard instances a musician composing a piece or a logician making a deduction.[4] But although we use these locutions in common parlance, it only generates confusion to use them in philosophy. For the reasons which "determine" a composer to add a particular bar to his composition are parts of some sort of rational explanation, not a regularity one; they do not enable us to make predictions in advance, but only to see how right it was *ex post facto*. It is the mark of creative genius that it is original and unpredictable; although after it has manifested itself, its *rationale* is manifest also. There is no question of denying the artist's freedom, or of explaining away his stroke of genius as not being his but the inevitable result of circumstance. To explain his achievement is to explain it as *his*. Therefore it is not the sort of determinism with which we need to be concerned. The only relevance it has to the freedom of the will is that it provides one *route* whereby philosophers are led from possibly true and certainly innocuous premises to dangerously false and disastrous conclusions. It is easy to accept "determinism" in some dilute sense, in which all that is being claimed is that there is some reason for every action, and then believe that one is committed to determinism in a strong sense, in which all our actions are causally determined by conditions outside our control because occurring before our birth. Having agreed that there is a *rationale* to everything, we allow that each thing is rationally necessary – morally necessary, artistically necessary, aesthetically necessary – and then drop the adverb that qualifies the systematically ambiguous term 'necessary' and assume that they are all necessary, pure and simple, that is to say, physically necessary. But the shift is illegitimate. Our starting-point was the principle that every event has an explanation; which is not the same as, and does not imply, the contention that every event has a regularity explanation.

The shift from the wide, unspecified, sense of 'explanation' to the narrow causal one is made less glaring and more plausible in virtue of three considerations. First, there is a corresponding shift between *methodological* and *ontological* interpretations of the principle of universal causation. Second, the argument is often made to proceed through the negative concepts 'random' or 'chance'. Third, an explicit metaphysical doctrine that regularity explanations are the only real explanations is sometimes invoked. "Nothing," according to Leucippus,[5] "occurs by chance, but there is a reason and a necessity for everything."[6] He seems to be talking ontologically about the nature of things, how things are. But the appeal to reason is more methodological – how we are to think of the world, and how conduct our enquiries – in tone. Chrysippus[7] is more explicitly ontological. He says

Everything that happens is followed by something else which depends on it by causal necessity. Likewise, everything that happens is preceded by something with which it is causally connected. For nothing exists or has come into being in the cosmos without a cause. There is nothing in it that is completely divorced from all that went before. The Universe will be disrupted and disintegrate into pieces and cease to be a unity functioning as a single system, if any uncaused movement is introduced into it. Such a movement will be introduced, unless everything that exists and happens has a previous cause from which it of necessity follows. In their view, the lack of cause resembles a *creatio ex nihilo* and is just as possible.[8]

It would be unreasonable to criticize severely the confusion between ontological and methodological interpretations of the Principle of Universal Causation: indeed the distinction, as we shall see, is a difficult one to sustain absolutely. We are all inclined to construe our fundamental principles as being ones about Reality. Many modern scientists would feel that Chrysippus expressed exactly what they felt. If pressed, we should allow that the principle that Every Event has a Cause may be taken as an ontological principle, about the nature of things; but then we should be very much on our guard against unconsciously supposing that since 'every event has a cause (i.e. an explanation)' is a statement about Reality, about the nature of things, therefore the cause must be a thingly cause (i.e. an explanation in terms of things, a regularity explanation). Subject to an important qualification,[9] I shall argue that we can say 'Every event has an explanation', and this is a statement about the universe. But the explanations are not all causal or regularity ones, and carry no determinist implications.

With the advent of quantum mechanics, the Leucippus fallacy has been revived, so that even if the human body is subject to quantum indeterminism, it still may be argued that it does not give the libertarian what he wants. Undetermined actions are random actions. But a man's random actions are not those we can usefully ask him his reasons for undertaking, or hold him responsible for. "A genuinely uncaused action could hardly be said to be an action of the agent at all;" says Nowell-Smith[10] "for in referring the action to an agent we are referring it to a cause." ". . . if one of our actions happened by 'pure chance' in the sense in which, according to modern physics, the change of state of a particular radium atom happens by pure chance, then this action would not be one for which we could be held *responsible*."[11]

Professor Ayer has argued the point repeatedly[12]

> For [the moralist] is anxious to show that men are capable of acting freely in order to infer that they can be morally responsible for what they do. But if it is a matter of pure chance that a man should act in one way rather than another, he may be free but he can hardly be responsible. And indeed when a man's actions seem to us quite unpredictable, when, as we say, there is no knowing what he will do, we do not look on him as a moral agent. We look upon him, rather, as a lunatic.

and then, again,[13]

> Either it is an accident that I choose to act as I do or it is not. If it is an accident, then it is merely a matter of chance that I did not act otherwise; and if it is merely a matter of chance that I did not choose otherwise, it is surely irrational to hold me morally responsible for choosing as I did. But if it is not an accident that I choose to do one thing rather than another, then presumably there is some causal explanation of my choice: and in that case we are led back to determinism.

Professor Smart's argument is more like Chrysippus'.[14] He gives two definitions

> D1. I shall state the view that there is "unbroken causal continuity" in the universe as follows. It is in principle possible to make a sufficiently precise determination of the state of a sufficiently wide region of the universe at time t_0, and sufficient laws of nature are in principle ascertainable to enable a superhuman calculator to be able to predict any event occurring within that region at an already given time t^1.

> D2. I shall define the view that "pure chance" reigns to some extent within the universe as follows. There are some events that even a superhuman calculator could not predict, however precise his knowledge of however wide a region of the universe at some previous time.

Smart then claims that his opponent must allow that an agent is not morally responsible for an action that comes about by "pure chance".[15] Since the two definitions are jointly exhaustive, it follows that all actions for which we can be held responsible are determined. We can briefly represent his argument thus. All, or almost all, actions can be explained. Often the spectator can give one or two explanations, and the agent nearly always can give his reasons. On the few occasions where a person acts for apparently no reason at all, we stigmatize his action as random, and wonder whether it should really be called *his* action, or even *an action*. Certainly we do not want to say that all our moral actions are random, and therefore, Smart argues, they must be determined.

All these arguments turn on an equivocation in the use of the terms 'random' or 'uncaused', or the phrase 'by pure chance'. These concepts are *negative* concepts. 'Random' means *in*explicable. But since the concepts of explanation, cause and prediction are themselves equivocal, the concepts 'random', 'uncaused' and 'by pure chance' are so too. The randomness of quantum mechanics is opposed to *physical* explanation.[16] It says nothing about whether there is any *human* or *rational* explanation to be offered. An action not altogether caused by antecedent physical conditions is in one sense uncaused, but not in the same sense as an action uncaused by the agent, which therefore is really not an action of his at all. There is a simple fallacy implicit in describing actions as genuinely uncaused, absolutely random or occurring by pure chance; for uncausedness, randomness and chance, are not qualities, which are either present or absent, and if present are always the same. They are, instead, chameleon words, which take their colour from their context, and cannot be transferred from one context to another, and still carry the same significance. We can reconstruct Leucippus' argument thus

> Everything has *an* explanation ($\lambda\delta\gamma\sigma$)
> ∴ Nothing is inexplicable
> ∴ Nothing occurs at random ($\mu\acute{a}\tau\eta\nu$)[17]
> ∴ Nothing is inexplicable in Hempel's sense,

or

> Nothing occurs for which there is no explanation

∴ Everything has a regularity explanation

∴ There is a (regularity) necessity for everything

and the fallacy is obvious.

The argument from explicability is usually a muddle. Occasionally, however, it is advanced respectably, on the explicit claim that all explanation must be, really, regularity explanation. Although, as we have seen in our discussion of Hempel's analysis of explanation, we cannot say that explanations as we know them in ordinary life are all regularity explanations, it can be maintained as an explicit metaphysical thesis that they must be. Materialists believe it. They regard things as the fundamental entities, and therefore regard thing-like explanation as the fundamental category of explanation. They are wrong, as I hope to show, to believe in things rather than in persons, but they are respectably wrong. Equally respectable, although equally wrong, are those followers of Hume, who hold that all valid reasoning must be either deductive or inductive. If that were true, it would follow that explanations, other than purely formal ones, must be regularity explanations, and then the disjunction 'Either random or (causally) explicable' would be exhaustive, and the argument for determinism valid. But there is no reason to believe that all reputable non-tautological arguments are inductive, but rather the reverse. For if there were any such reason, we should ask whether it was itself deductive or inductive. If it was deductive, from premises that were entirely analytic, then it would be an argument about the meaning of the words 'valid' and 'cogent' 'reason' and 'argument'. It would be laying down how they were to be used. But such a *fiat* would commit the Naturalistic Fallacy. We could always go on to ask whether we ought to accept valid reasons or be guided by cogent arguments, and whether we ought not to accept invalid ones or be guided by non-cogent ones. If on the other hand it was an inductive argument or was based on synthetic premises, then it is vulnerable to counter-examples. Many arguments have been urged by many people which are not on the face of it either invalid or deductive or inductive. In order to establish the truth of the thesis, each *prima facie* counter-example must be examined and shown to fall, first appearances notwithstanding, into one of the three categories. But this is not done.

The thesis is used as a legislative (or, more politely, regulative) principle, to rule out reasons and arguments as invalid, without benefit of trial. Therefore the arguments for the thesis are not inductive either. Either, then, there are no valid reasons for accepting it at all – in which case there are also no valid reasons for accepting its determinist consequences – or there are valid reasons. But if there are, since they are neither deductive nor inductive, but nonetheless are valid, the thesis is false. For there are then valid reasons that are neither deductive nor inductive: which is what was denied.[18] With this more generous notion of reasoning and reasons goes a more generous notion of explaining and explanations, and hence the possibility of actions being undetermined causally without their being altogether inexplicable and random.

We may argue more positively for construing 'explanation' generously. For only so can *every* thing be explained. It is a weakness of any metaphysical scheme which selects one type of explanation (*e.g.* a regularity explanation) as *the* fundamental type of explanation, that even a complete explanation of that type cannot explain everything. It is always possible, as every child knows, to ask a further 'Why?' at the end of every explanation. And even if we have expanded an explanation to be a complete explanation, it is still possible to put the whole explanation in question. Given a purely deductive explanation, we may ask why the rules of inference should be what they are, and when given a meta-logical justification, ask for a further justification of that: the tortoise can always out-query Achilles. Given a causal explanation we can ask two questions: why the laws of nature should be what they are; and why the initial conditions should have been what they were: and the materialist has no answer. Many other events he, and not only he, must dismiss as coincidences, concomitances of phenomena, fortunate perhaps, but entirely fortuitous. A chance meeting of a friend is a coincidence: although there is an explanation of each person's being in a particular place at a particular time, there is no explanation of the event under the description of the two friends meeting each other. The origin of life, under that description, is similarly inexplicable by the materialist. His complete explanation is a complete explanation only of events described in his terms. Completeness is secured in part by ruling awkward questions unaskable. If, *per contra*, we want always to be able to ask questions and not rule out any as being inherently unanswerable – I am not sure it is a reasonable request, but it seems to be what the principle of Universal Causation comes to, taken as a methodological principle – then we cannot fix on any one pattern of explanation as being the paradigm. When we have completed one type of explanation we must be ready to switch to another type, in order to answer questions which still arise, but can no longer be answered on the lines of the original explanation. If there is always to be a 'because', the 'becauses' must be of all sorts of types. The wider the universality of our principle of universal explicability, the wider the range of possible explanations.

It is sometimes argued that every event must have a cause, because only so can we manipulate events. The argument fails; because, when it comes to other people, we neither think that we can, nor that we ought to be able to, manipulate them. All that the argument from manipulability shows is that things must be fairly reliable and persons sometimes reasonable. Life would be impossible, as Nowell-Smith argues,[19] if the fish I have just decided to eat "is liable to turn into a stone or to disintegrate in mid-air or to behave in any other utterly unpredictable manner". But to exclude this radical unpredictability is not to embrace complete inevitability. For practical purposes, we do not require strongly quantified universal laws, that under certain conditions a specific event will absolutely always happen, but only weakly quantified universal laws, that the event will usually happen.[20] Indeed, so far as our actual knowledge of material objects goes, we reckon ourselves lucky when we can go even as far as that. So far as other people are concerned, it is enough that we can sometimes influence them, either by argument and reason, or by virtue of our having under our control some factor which would be for them a reason for acting in the way we wish. You want my car. You offer me money for it. Being offered money is a perfectly good reason for my selling you my car. But it does not make it inevitable that I should sell it. I am perfectly free not to.

The argument from manipulation does not support determinism. Indeed, it argues against it, and shows that the whole notion of cause does

not imply the truth of determinism, but, on the contrary, presupposes its falsity. For the notion of cause is based not, as Hume thought, on our *observing* constant conjunctions of events, but on our being able *to make things happen*. I can, if I want to, bring about a certain result, and afterwards, if I do so, say "I did it", or, more grandly, "I caused it". I discover that I can achieve some of my ends only by accomplishing certain means first, whereupon the end ensues. Construing 'cause' as a transitive relation, I say "I caused the means and the means caused the end and that is how I caused the end". In this way we obtain the third-personal use of 'cause'. It is a back-formation from the first-personal use which is the primary one and gave the original sense. The conceptual environment in which 'I cause', 'I do' and 'I make things happen' flourish is our normal untutored one in which men are the initiators of chains of events and I can cause things without myself having been caused: and although the third personal use is now much the more extensive, it is unlikely that even the third-personal meaning would survive being transplanted into a conceptual environment in which the root meaning could not survive.

This turns out to be the case. Even when reformulated so as to fit the third-personal use only, the notion of cause still requires that of the freedom of the will. Constant conjunction by itself does not rule out the possibility of pre-arranged harmony or of both events being consequences of some third event rather than being directly related to each other. Two college clocks always chime, the one shortly after the other; it may be that they are electrically connected, but other explanations are possible. The decisive test would be for the observer to introduce an arbitrary alteration in the earlier-chiming clock, and see whether this has any effect on the other. More generally, we discover causal relations not by merely observing passively but by experimenting as well. We have to be agents, not just spectators. And the reason is this: we believe that as free agents we can introduce an arbitrary disturbance into the universe and thus destroy any pre-arranged harmony: under the transformations that our arbitary interventions produce, only real regularities will be preserved, and coincidental and pre-arranged ones will be destroyed. This argument is valid if we really are free agents. Unless we are, the argument is invalid, because we still have not ruled out the possibility of the agent's intervention and the occurrence of the second event both being consequences of some earlier determining factor. We just do not know, supposing the determinist thesis is to be true, what are the causal antecedents of my "deciding" to introduce an "arbitrary" alteration in the universe. It might be that the only occasions on which an experimenter could or would do this were occasions in which the occurrences of the second event were already going to be disturbed. Thus in this case, as in others, man can only have a true view of the universe and the laws of nature by excepting himself from their sway, and considering himself over against the universe, not as part of it, but independent of it, and not subject to its laws.[21]

A second general argument against determinism stems not from intervention in natural phenomena but communication with other sentient beings.[22] Communication is not manipulation. When I tell somebody something, I am not making him believe it or do anything: I am giving him a reason which he is free to accept or reject. It is a presupposition of communication that each party believes the other to have been, or to be, able to act otherwise. A linguistic utterance is one which the speaker could have not uttered, and which the hearer believes he need not have uttered, and which is intended, and known to be intended, to be taken in a particular way, but to which the response is not, and is not supposed to be, automatic. There are important differences between our responses to linguistic utterances and conditioned reflexes. Conversation is not a series of parade-ground commands.

Types of Determinism

Four sorts of determinism have at various times been put forward, and have been felt to threaten the freedom of the will and human responsibility, besides the historical determinism we have already touched upon.[23] They are: logical determinism, theological determinism, psychological determinism, and physical determinism. There are many variants of each type. They all, in different ways, satisfy the three conditions for being frightening. Different types of arguments are

adduced in support of each type, and different counter-arguments are needed to rebut them.

Logical determinism maintains that the future is already fixed as unalterably as the past. It is already written in the book of destiny: it is already formed in the womb of the past. Various arguments are put forward for this, often turning on the timelessness of truth. The predictions are infallible, because logically necessary. They are based on factors already obtaining at present, and therefore exclude the possibility of a subsequent change of mind, and in some cases – long-range predictions – exclude the possibility of any factor under the agent's control being relevant. And the predictions are completely specific.

Theological determinism argues that since God is omniscient, He knows everything, the future included. Since He is God, His knowledge is infallible. Since He is a personal God, temporal epithets must be capable of being ascribed to Him, and in particular, we must say that what He knows, He knows now. Therefore, as with logical determinism, the possibility of change of mind is always excluded, and, in the long run, of any human contribution to the course of events. And divine knowledge is not only infallible, but perfect and completely specific.

Psychological determinism maintains that there are certain psychological laws, which we are beginning to discover, enabling us to predict, usually on the basis of his experiences in early infancy, how a man will respond to different situations throughout his later life. It is suggested that we should, one day, have as much confidence in the laws of psychology as we do in the laws of physics. The basis of the predictions is always intended to be limited so as to exclude the innocuous predictions we make every day. And the claim is that the predictions could be specific enough to constitute a real threat to freedom.

Physical determinism is based on there being physical laws of nature, many of which have actually been discovered, and of whose truth we can reasonably hope to be quite certain, together with the claim that all other features of the world are dependent on physical factors. Given a complete physical description of the world at any one time, we can calculate its complete physical description at any other time, and then given the complete physical description at that other time, we can calculate also what all its other, non-physical, features must be. Hence on the basis of the physical factors at one time, which because they are physical exclude all personal factors, we can, at one remove, calculate what a person's future actions must, infallibly, be. And so again we have a threat to freedom.

Notes

1   See W. H. Dray, *Laws and Explanation in History*, Oxford, 1957, ch. VI; or W. H. Dray, "Explanatory Narrative in History", *The Philosophical Quarterly*, 4, 1954, pp. 15–27.

2   Brand Blanshard, "The Case for Determinism", in Sidney Hook, ed., *Determinism and Freedom in the Age of Modern Science*, New York, 1961, p. 21.

3   Blanshard uses 'constraints' and 'causes' interchangeably. See next quotation, which comes immediately before this one in his text.

4   *Op. cit.*, pp. 26–30.

5   fl. c. 440 BC.

6   In G. S. Kirk and J. E. Raven, *The Presocratic Philosophers*, Cambridge, 1957, no. 568; and in H. Diehls, *Fragmente der Vorsokratiker*, 6th ed. by W. Kranz, Berlin, 1951, 67B2; for a useful account see S. Sambursky, *The Physical World of the Greeks*, tr. Merton Dagut, London, 1956 and 1963, pp. 158–76.

7   Lived c. 280–207 BC.

8   *Apud* Alexander of Aphrodisias *De Fato* 22; in J. von Arnim, *Stoicorum Veterum Fragmenta*, Leipzig, 1903, II, 945.

9   See below.

10 P. H. Nowell-Smith, "Freewill and Moral Responsibility", *Mind*, LVI, 1947, p. 47.

11 J. J. C. Smart, "Free-Will, Praise and Blame", *Mind*, LXX, 1961, p. 296; compare Frederick Vivian, *Human Freedom and Responsibility*,

London, 1964, pp. 117–18. A. C. MacIntyre, "Determinism", *Mind*, LXVI, 1957, p. 30; M. C. Bradley, *Mind*, LXVIII, 1959, p. 522; John Plamenatz, "Responsibility, Blame and Punishment", in Peter Laslett and W. G. Runciman, eds., *Philosophy, Politics and Society*, 3rd series, Oxford, 1967, pp. 178–9.

12 A. J. Ayer, "Freedom and Necessity", *Polemic*, 5, 1946, p. 38; reprinted in A. J. Ayer, *Philosophical Essays*, p. 275. Compare R. E. Hobart, "Free Will as Involving Determinism", *Mind*, XLIII, 1934, p. 5. For later versions of Ayer's argument see A. J. Ayer, *The Concept of a Person*, London, 1963, p. 254; for a general criticism, see C. A. Campbell. *On Selfhood and Godhood*, London, 1957, lecture IX, Section 10, pp. 175–6.

13 *Op. cit., Polemic*, p. 39, *Philosophical Essays*, p. 275.

14 J. J. C. Smart, "Free Will, Praise and Blame", *Mind*, LXX, 1961, pp. 293–8.

15 *Op. cit.*, p. 296.

16 [. . .] For a fuller discussion of randomness and explanation, see J. R. Lucas, *The Concept of Probability*, Oxford, 1970, ch. VII, pp. 112–18.

17 The Greek word has also the senses idly, fruitlessly, in vain; i.e. it is opposed to what is teleologically explicable as well as to what is causally explicable.

18 Some philosophers have objected to this argument on the grounds of its being self-referential. [. . .]

19 P. H. Nowell-Smith, "Freewill and Moral Responsibility", *Mind*, LVII, 1948, p. 47.

20 Compare Jonathan Bennett, "The Status of Determinism", *British Journal for the Philosophy of Science*, XIV, 1963–4, pp. 106–19.

21 See also, Isaiah Berlin, *Historical Inevitability*, Oxford, 1954, pp. 32–3; reprinted in *Four Essays on Liberty*, Oxford, 1969, pp. 70–1.

22 See more fully, Frederick J. Crosson and Kenneth M. Sayre, eds., *Philosophy and Cybernetics*, London, 1967, pp. 28–9.

23 See pp. 533–4.

45

Freedom of the Will and the Concept of a Person

Harry G. Frankfurt

What philosophers have lately come to accept as analysis of the concept of a person is not actually analysis of *that* concept at all. Strawson, whose usage represents the current standard, identifies the concept of a person as "the concept of a type of entity such that *both* predicates ascribing states of consciousness *and* predicates ascribing corporeal characteristics . . . are equally applicable to a single individual of that single type."[1] But there are many entities besides persons that have both mental and physical properties. As it happens – though it seems extraordinary that this should be so – there is no common English word for the type of entity Strawson has in mind, a type that includes not only human beings but animals of various lesser species as well. Still, this hardly justifies the misappropriation of a valuable philosophical term.

Whether the members of some animal species are persons is surely not to be settled merely by determining whether it is correct to apply to them, in addition to predicates ascribing corporeal characteristics, predicates that ascribe states of consciousness. It does violence to our language to endorse the application of the term 'person' to those numerous creatures which do have both psychological and material properties but which are manifestly not persons in any normal sense of the word. This misuse of language is doubtless innocent of any theoretical error. But although the offense is "merely verbal," it does significant harm. For it gratuitously diminishes our philosophical vocabulary, and it increases the likelihood that we will overlook the important area of inquiry with which the term 'person' is most naturally associated. It might have been expected that no problem would be of more central and persistent concern to philosophers than that of understanding what we ourselves essentially are. Yet this problem is so generally neglected that it has been possible to make off with its very name almost without being noticed and, evidently, without evoking any widespread feeling of loss.

There is a sense in which the word 'person' is merely the singular form of 'people' and in which both terms connote no more than membership in a certain biological species. In those senses of the word which are of greater philosophical interest, however, the criteria for being a person do not serve primarily to distinguish the members of our own species from the members of other species. Rather, they are designed to capture those attributes which are the subject of our most humane concern with ourselves and the source of what we regard as most important and most problematical in our lives. Now these attributes would be of equal significance to us even if they were not in fact peculiar and common to the

Harry G. Frankfurt, "Freedom of the Will and the Concept of a Person." *The Journal of Philosophy* 68, no. 1 (January 1971), pp. 5–20. © 1971 by The Journal of Philosophy, Inc. Reprinted with permission from the author and The Journal of Philosophy.

members of our own species. What interests us most in the human condition would not interest us less if it were also a feature of the condition of other creatures as well.

Our concept of ourselves as persons is not to be understood, therefore, as a concept of attributes that are necessarily species-specific. It is conceptually possible that members of novel or even of familiar nonhuman species should be persons; and it is also conceptually possible that some members of the human species are not persons. We do in fact assume, on the other hand, that no member of another species is a person. Accordingly, there is a presumption that what is essential to persons is a set of characteristics that we generally suppose – whether rightly or wrongly – to be uniquely human.

It is my view that one essential difference between persons and other creatures is to be found in the structure of a person's will. Human beings are not alone in having desires and motives, or in making choices. They share these things with the members of certain other species, some of whom even appear to engage in deliberation and to make decisions based upon prior thought. It seems to be peculiarly characteristic of humans, however, that they are able to form what I shall call "second-order desires" or "desires of the second order."

Besides wanting and choosing and being moved *to do* this or that, men may also want to have (or not to have) certain desires and motives. They are capable of wanting to be different, in their preferences and purposes, from what they are. Many animals appear to have the capacity for what I shall call "first-order desires" or "desires of the first order," which are simply desires to do or not to do one thing or another. No animal other than man, however, appears to have the capacity for reflective self-evaluation that is manifested in the formation of second-order desires.[2]

I

The concept designated by the verb 'to want' is extraordinarily elusive. A statement of the form "*A* wants to *X*" – taken by itself, apart from a context that serves to amplify or to specify its meaning – conveys remarkably little information. Such a statement may be consistent, for

example, with each of the following statements: (a) the prospect of doing *X* elicits no sensation or introspectible emotional response in *A*; (b) *A* is unaware that he wants to *X*; (c) *A* believes that he does not want to *X*; (d) *A* wants to refrain from *X*-ing; (e) *A* wants to *Y* and believes that it is impossible for him both to *Y* and to *X*; (f) *A* does not "really" want to *X*; (g) *A* would rather die than *X*; and so on. It is therefore hardly sufficient to formulate the distinction between first-order and second-order desires, as I have done, by suggesting merely that someone has a first-order desire when he wants to do or not to do such-and-such, and that he has a second-order desire when he wants to have or not to have a certain desire of the first order.

As I shall understand them, statements of the form "*A* wants to *X*" cover a rather broad range of possibilities.[3] They may be true even when statements like (a) through (g) are true: when *A* is unaware of any feelings concerning *X*-ing, when he is unaware that he wants to *X*, when he deceives himself about what he wants and believes falsely that he does not want to *X*, when he also has other desires that conflict with his desire to *X*, or when he is ambivalent. The desires in question may be conscious or unconscious, they need not be univocal, and *A* may be mistaken about them. There is a further source of uncertainty with regard to statements that identify someone's desires, however, and here it is important for my purposes to be less permissive.

Consider first those statements of the form "*A* wants to *X*" which identify first-order desires – that is, statements in which the term 'to *X*' refers to an action. A statement of this kind does not, by itself, indicate the relative strength of *A*'s desire to *X*. It does not make it clear whether this desire is at all likely to play a decisive role in what *A* actually does or tries to do. For it may correctly be said that *A* wants to *X* even when his desire to *X* is only one among his desires and when it is far from being paramount among them. Thus, it may be true that *A* wants to *X* when he strongly prefers to do something else instead; and it may be true that he wants to *X* despite the fact that, when he acts, it is not the desire to *X* that motivates him to do what he does. On the other hand, someone who states that *A* wants to *X* may mean to convey that it is this desire that is motivating or moving *A* to do what he is actually doing or that A will in fact be moved by this desire (unless he changes his mind) when he acts.

It is only when it is used in the second of these ways that, given the special usage of 'will' that I propose to adopt, the statement identifies A's will. To identify an agent's will is either to identify the desire (or desires) by which he is motivated in some action he performs or to identify the desire (or desires) by which he will or would be motivated when or if he acts. An agent's will, then, is identical with one or more of his first-order desires. But the notion of the will, as I am employing it, is not coextensive with the notion of first-order desires. It is not the notion of something that merely inclines an agent in some degree to act in a certain way. Rather, it is the notion of an *effective* desire – one that moves (or will or would move) a person all the way to action. Thus the notion of the will is not coextensive with the notion of what an agent intends to do. For even though someone may have a settled intention to do X, he may nonetheless do something else instead of doing X because, despite his intention, his desire to do X proves to be weaker or less effective than some conflicting desire.

Now consider those statements of the form "A wants to X" which identify second-order desires – that is, statements in which the term 'to X' refers to a desire of the first order. There are also two kinds of situation in which it may be true that A wants to want to X. In the first place, it might be true of A that he wants to have a desire to X despite the fact that he has a univocal desire, altogether free of conflict and ambivalence, to refrain from X-ing. Someone might want to have a certain desire, in other words, but univocally want that desire to be unsatisfied.

Suppose that a physician engaged in psychotherapy with narcotics addicts believes that his ability to help his patients would be enhanced if he understood better what it is like for them to desire the drug to which they are addicted. Suppose that he is led in this way to want to have a desire for the drug. If it is a genuine desire that he wants, then what he wants is not merely to feel the sensations that addicts characteristically feel when they are gripped by their desires for the drug. What the physician wants, insofar as he wants to have a desire, is to be inclined or moved to some extent to take the drug.

It is entirely possible, however, that, although he wants to be moved by a desire to take the drug, he does not want this desire to be effective. He may not want it to move him all the way to action. He need not be interested in finding out what it is like to take the drug. And insofar as he now wants only to *want* to take it, and not to *take* it, there is nothing in what he now wants that would be satisfied by the drug itself. He may now have, in fact, an altogether univocal desire *not* to take the drug; and he may prudently arrange to make it impossible for him to satisfy the desire he would have if his desire to want the drug should in time be satisfied.

It would thus be incorrect to infer, from the fact that the physician now wants to desire to take the drug, that he already does desire to take it. His second-order desire to be moved to take the drug does not entail that he has a first-order desire to take it. If the drug were now to be administered to him, this might satisfy no desire that is implicit in his desire to want to take it. While he wants to want to take the drug, he may have *no* desire to take it; it may be that *all* he wants is to taste the desire for it. That is, his desire to have a certain desire that he does not have may not be a desire that his will should be at all different than it is.

Someone who wants only in this truncated way to want to X stands at the margin of preciosity, and the fact that he wants to want to X is not pertinent to the identification of his will. There is, however, a second kind of situation that may be described by 'A wants to want to X'; and when the statement is used to describe a situation of this second kind, then it does pertain to what A wants his will to be. In such cases the statement means that A wants the desire to X to be the desire that moves him effectively to act. It is not merely that he wants the desire to X to be among the desires by which, to one degree or another, he is moved or inclined to act. He wants this desire to be effective – that is, to provide the motive in what he actually does. Now when the statement that A wants to want to X is used in this way, it does entail that A already has a desire to X. It could not be true both that A wants the desire to X to move him into action and that he does not want to X. It is only if he does want to X that he can coherently want the desire to X not merely to be one of his desires but, more decisively, to be his will.[4]

Suppose a man wants to be motivated in what he does by the desire to concentrate on his work. It is necessarily true, if this supposition is correct, that he already wants to concentrate on his work. This desire is now among his desires. But the question of whether or not his second-order desire is fulfilled does not turn merely on whether the desire he wants is one of his desires. It turns on whether this desire is, as he wants it to be, his effective desire or will. If, when the chips are down, it is his desire to concentrate on his work that moves him to do what he does, then what he wants at that time is indeed (in the relevant sense) what he wants to want. If it is some other desire that actually moves him when he acts, on the other hand, then what he wants at that time is not (in the relevant sense) what he wants to want. This will be so despite the fact that the desire to concentrate on his work continues to be among his desires.

II

Someone has a desire of the second order either when he wants simply to have a certain desire or when he wants a certain desire to be his will. In situations of the latter kind, I shall call his second-order desires "second-order volitions" or "volitions of the second order." Now it is having second-order volitions, and not having second-order desires generally, that I regard as essential to being a person. It is logically possible, however unlikely, that there should be an agent with second-order desires but with no volitions of the second order. Such a creature, in my view, would not be a person. I shall use the term 'wanton' to refer to agents who have first-order desires but who are not persons because, whether or not they have desires of the second order, they have no second-order volitions.[5]

The essential characteristic of a wanton is that he does not care about his will. His desires move him to do certain things, without its being true of him either that he wants to be moved by those desires or that he prefers to be moved by other desires. The class of wantons includes all non-human animals that have desires and all very young children. Perhaps it also includes some adult human beings as well. In any case, adult humans may be more or less wanton; they may

act wantonly, in response to first-order desires concerning which they have no volitions of the second order, more or less frequently.

The fact that a wanton has no second-order volitions does not mean that each of his first-order desires is translated heedlessly and at once into action. He may have no opportunity to act in accordance with some of his desires. Moreover, the translation of his desires into action may be delayed or precluded either by conflicting desires of the first order or by the intervention of deliberation. For a wanton may possess and employ rational faculties of a high order. Nothing in the concept of a wanton implies that he cannot reason or that he cannot deliberate concerning how to do what he wants to do. What distinguishes the rational wanton from other rational agents is that he is not concerned with the desirability of his desires themselves. He ignores the question of what his will is to be. Not only does he pursue whatever course of action he is most strongly inclined to pursue, but he does not care which of his inclinations is the strongest.

Thus a rational creature, who reflects upon the suitability to his desires of one course of action or another, may nonetheless be a wanton. In maintaining that the essence of being a person lies not in reason but in will, I am far from suggesting that a creature without reason may be a person. For it is only in virtue of his rational capacities that a person is capable of becoming critically aware of his own will and of forming volitions of the second order. The structure of a person's will presupposes, accordingly, that he is a rational being.

The distinction between a person and a wanton may be illustrated by the difference between two narcotics addicts. Let us suppose that the physiological condition accounting for the addiction is the same in both men, and that both succumb inevitably to their periodic desires for the drug to which they are addicted. One of the addicts hates his addiction and always struggles desperately, although to no avail, against its thrust. He tries everything that he thinks might enable him to overcome his desires for the drug. But these desires are too powerful for him to withstand, and invariably, in the end, they conquer him. He is an unwilling addict, helplessly violated by his own desires.

The unwilling addict has conflicting first-order desires: he wants to take the drug, and he also wants to refrain from taking it. In addition to these first-order desires, however, he has a volition of the second order. He is not a neutral with regard to the conflict between his desire to take the drug and his desire to refrain from taking it. It is the latter desire, and not the former, that he wants to constitute his will; it is the latter desire, rather than the former, that he wants to be effective and to provide the purpose that he will seek to realize in what he actually does.

The other addict is a wanton. His actions reflect the economy of his first-order desires, without his being concerned whether the desires that move him to act are desires by which he wants to be moved to act. If he encounters problems in obtaining the drug or in administering it to himself, his responses to his urges to take it may involve deliberation. But it never occurs to him to consider whether he wants the relations among his desires to result in his having the will he has. The wanton addict may be an animal, and thus incapable of being concerned about his will. In any event he is, in respect of his wanton lack of concern, no different from an animal.

The second of these addicts may suffer a first-order conflict similar to the first-order conflict suffered by the first. Whether he is human or not, the wanton may (perhaps due to conditioning) both want to take the drug and want to refrain from taking it. Unlike the unwilling addict, however, he does not prefer that one of his conflicting desires should be paramount over the other; he does not prefer that one first-order desire rather than the other should constitute his will. It would be misleading to say that he is neutral as to the conflict between his desires, since this would suggest that he regards them as equally acceptable. Since he has no identity apart from his first-order desires, it is true neither that he prefers one to the other nor that he prefers not to take sides.

It makes a difference to the unwilling addict, who is a person, which of his conflicting first-order desires wins out. Both desires are his, to be sure; and whether he finally takes the drug or finally succeeds in refraining from taking it, he acts to satisfy what is in a literal sense his own desire. In either case he does something he himself wants to do, and he does it not because of some external influence whose aim happens to coincide with his own but because of his desire to do it. The unwilling addict identifies himself, however,

through the formation of a second-order volition, with one rather than with the other of his conflicting first-order desires. He makes one of them more truly his own and, in so doing, he withdraws himself from the other. It is in virtue of this identification and withdrawal, accomplished through the formation of a second-order volition, that the unwilling addict may meaningfully make the analytically puzzling statements that the force moving him to take the drug is a force other than his own, and that it is not of his own free will but rather against his will that this force moves him to take it.

The wanton addict cannot or does not care which of his conflicting first-order desires wins out. His lack of concern is not due to his inability to find a convincing basis for preference. It is due either to his lack of the capacity for reflection or to his mindless indifference to the enterprise of evaluating his own desires and motives.[6] There is only one issue in the struggle to which his first-order conflict may lead: whether the one or the other of his conflicting desires is the stronger. Since he is moved by both desires, he will not be altogether satisfied by what he does no matter which of them is effective. But it makes no difference *to him* whether his craving or his aversion gets the upper hand. He has no stake in the conflict between them and so, unlike the unwilling addict, he can neither win nor lose the struggle in which he is engaged. When a *person* acts, the desire by which he is moved is either the will he wants or a will he wants to be without. When a *wanton* acts, it is neither.

III

There is a very close relationship between the capacity for forming second-order volitions and another capacity that is essential to persons – one that has often been considered a distinguishing mark of the human condition. It is only because a person has volitions of the second order that he is capable both of enjoying and of lacking freedom of the will. The concept of a person is not only, then, the concept of a type of entity that has both first-order desires and volitions of the second order. It can also be construed as the concept of a type of entity for whom the freedom of its will may be a problem. This concept excludes all wantons, both infrahuman and human, since they fail to satisfy an essential condition for the enjoyment of freedom of the will. And it excludes those suprahuman beings, if any, whose wills are necessarily free.

Just what kind of freedom is the freedom of the will? This question calls for an identification of the special area of human experience to which the concept of freedom of the will, as distinct from the concepts of other sorts of freedom, is particularly germane. In dealing with it, my aim will be primarily to locate the problem with which a person is most immediately concerned when he is concerned with the freedom of his will.

According to one familiar philosophical tradition, being free is fundamentally a matter of doing what one wants to do. Now the notion of an agent who does what he wants to do is by no means an altogether clear one: both the doing and the wanting, and the appropriate relation between them as well, require elucidation. But although its focus needs to be sharpened and its formulation refined, I believe that this notion does capture at least part of what is implicit in the idea of an agent who *acts* freely. It misses entirely, however, the peculiar content of the quite different idea of an agent whose *will* is free.

We do not suppose that animals enjoy freedom of the will, although we recognize that an animal may be free to run in whatever direction it wants. Thus, having the freedom to do what one wants to do is not a sufficient condition of having a free will. It is not a necessary condition either. For to deprive someone of his freedom of action is not necessarily to undermine the freedom of his will. When an agent is aware that there are certain things he is not free to do, this doubtless affects his desires and limits the range of choices he can make. But suppose that someone, without being aware of it, has in fact lost or been deprived of his freedom of action. Even though he is no longer free to do what he wants to do, his will may remain as free as it was before. Despite the fact that he is not free to translate his desires into actions or to act according to the determinations of his will, he may still form those desires and make those determinations as freely as if his freedom of action had not been impaired.

When we ask whether a person's will is free we are not asking whether he is in a position to translate his first-order desires into actions. That is the question of whether he is free to do as he pleases. The question of the freedom of his will does not concern the relation between what he does and what he wants to do. Rather, it concerns his desires themselves. But what question about them is it?

It seems to me both natural and useful to construe the question of whether a person's will is free in close analogy to the question of whether an agent enjoys freedom of action. Now freedom of action is (roughly, at least) the freedom to do what one wants to do. Analogously, then, the statement that a person enjoys freedom of the will means (also roughly) that he is free to want what he wants to want. More precisely, it means that he is free to will what he wants to will, or to have the will he wants. Just as the question about the freedom of an agent's action has to do with whether it is the action he wants to perform, so the question about the freedom of his will has to do with whether it is the will he wants to have.

It is in securing the conformity of his will to his second-order volitions, then, that a person exercises freedom of the will. And it is in the discrepancy between his will and his second-order volitions, or in his awareness that their coincidence is not his own doing but only a happy chance, that a person who does not have this freedom feels its lack. The unwilling addict's will is not free. This is shown by the fact that it is not the will he wants. It is also true, though in a different way, that the will of the wanton addict is not free. The wanton addict neither has the will he wants nor has a will that differs from the will he wants. Since he has no volitions of the second order, the freedom of his will cannot be a problem for him. He lacks it, so to speak, by default.

People are generally far more complicated than my sketchy account of the structure of a person's will may suggest. There is as much opportunity for ambivalence, conflict, and self-deception with regard to desires of the second order, for example, as there is with regard to first-order desires. If there is an unresolved conflict among someone's second-order desires, then he is in danger of having no second-order volition; for unless this conflict is resolved, he has no preference concerning which of his first-order desires is to be his will. This condition, if it is so severe that it prevents him from identifying himself in a sufficiently decisive way with *any* of his conflicting first-order desires, destroys him as a person. For it either tends to paralyze his will and to keep him from acting at all, or it tends to remove him from his will so that his will operates without his participation. In both cases he becomes, like the unwilling addict though in a different way, a helpless bystander to the forces that move him.

Another complexity is that a person may have, especially if his second-order desires are in conflict, desires and volitions of a higher order than the second. There is no theoretical limit to the length of the series of desires of higher and higher orders; nothing except common sense and, perhaps, a saving fatigue prevents an individual from obsessively refusing to identify himself with any of his desires until he forms a desire of the next higher order. The tendency to generate such a series of acts of forming desires, which would be a case of humanization run wild, also leads toward the destruction of a person.

It is possible, however, to terminate such a series of acts without cutting it off arbitrarily. When a person identifies himself *decisively* with one of his first-order desires, this commitment "resounds" throughout the potentially endless array of higher orders. Consider a person who, without reservation or conflict, wants to be motivated by the desire to concentrate on his work. The fact that his second-order volition to be moved by this desire is a decisive one means that there is no room for questions concerning the pertinence of desires or volitions of higher orders. Suppose the person is asked whether he wants to want to want to concentrate on his work. He can properly insist that this question concerning a third-order desire does not arise. It would be a mistake to claim that, because he has not considered whether he wants the second-order volition he has formed, he is indifferent to the question of whether it is with this volition or with some other that he wants his will to accord. The decisiveness of the commitment he has made means that he has decided that no further question about his second-order volition, at any higher order, remains to be asked. It is relatively unimportant whether we explain this by saying that this commitment implicitly generates an endless series of confirming desires of higher orders, or by saying that the commitment is tantamount to a dissolution of the pointedness of all questions concerning higher orders of desire.

Examples such as the one concerning the unwilling addict may suggest that volitions of the second order, or of higher orders, must be formed deliberately and that a person characteristically struggles to ensure that they are satisfied. But the conformity of a person's will to his higher-order volitions may be far more thoughtless and spontaneous than this. Some people are naturally moved by kindness when they want to be kind, and by nastiness when they want to be nasty, without any explicit forethought and without any need for energetic self-control. Others are moved by nastiness when they want to be kind and by kindness when they intend to be nasty, equally without forethought and without active resistance to these violations of their higher-order desires. The enjoyment of freedom comes easily to some. Others must struggle to achieve it.

IV

My theory concerning the freedom of the will accounts easily for our disinclination to allow that this freedom is enjoyed by the members of any species inferior to our own. It also satisfies another condition that must be met by any such theory, by making it apparent why the freedom of the will should be regarded as desirable. The enjoyment of a free will means the satisfaction of certain desires – desires of the second or of higher orders – whereas its absence means their frustration. The satisfactions at stake are those which accrue to a person of whom it may be said that his will is his own. The corresponding frustrations are those suffered by a person of whom it may be said that he is estranged from himself, or that he finds himself a helpless or a passive bystander to the forces that move him.

A person who is free to do what he wants to do may yet not be in a position to have the will he wants. Suppose, however, that he enjoys both freedom of action and freedom of the will. Then he is not only free to do what he wants to do; he is also free to want what he wants to want. It seems to me that he has, in that case, all the freedom it is possible to desire or to conceive. There are other good things in life, and he may not possess some of them. But there is nothing in the way of freedom that he lacks.

It is far from clear that certain other theories of the freedom of the will meet these elementary but essential conditions: that it be understandable why we desire this freedom and why we refuse to ascribe it to animals. Consider, for example, Roderick Chisholm's quaint version of the doctrine that human freedom entails an absence of causal determination.[7] Whenever a person performs a free action, according to Chisholm, it's a miracle. The motion of a person's hand, when the person moves it, is the outcome of a series of physical causes; but some event in this series, "and presumably one of those that took place within the brain, was caused by the agent and not by any other events" (18). A free agent has, therefore, "a prerogative which some would attribute only to God: each of us, when we act, is a prime mover unmoved" (23).

This account fails to provide any basis for doubting that animals of subhuman species enjoy the freedom it defines. Chisholm says nothing that makes it seem less likely that a rabbit performs a miracle when it moves its leg than that a man does so when he moves his hand. But why, in any case, should anyone *care* whether he can interrupt the natural order of causes in the way Chisholm describes? Chisholm offers no reason for believing that there is a discernible difference between the experience of a man who miraculously initiates a series of causes when he moves his hand and a man who moves his hand without any such breach of the normal causal sequence. There appears to be no concrete basis for preferring to be involved in the one state of affairs rather than in the other.[8]

It is generally supposed that, in addition to satisfying the two conditions I have mentioned, a satisfactory theory of the freedom of the will necessarily provides an analysis of one of the conditions of moral responsibility. The most common recent approach to the problem of understanding the freedom of the will has been, indeed, to inquire what is entailed by the assumption that someone is morally responsible for what he has done. In my view, however, the relation between moral responsibility and the freedom of the will has been very widely misunderstood. It is not true that a person is morally responsible for what he has done only if his will was free when he did it. He may be morally responsible for having done it even though his will was not free at all.

A person's will is free only if he is free to have the will he wants. This means that, with regard to any of his first-order desires, he is free either to make that desire his will or to make some other first-order desire his will instead. Whatever his will, then, the will of the person whose will is free could have been otherwise; he could have done otherwise than to constitute his will as he did. It is a vexed question just how 'he could have done otherwise' is to be understood in contexts such as this one. But although this question is important to the theory of freedom, it has no bearing on the theory of moral responsibility. For the assumption that a person is morally responsible for what he has done does not entail that the person was in a position to have whatever will he wanted.

This assumption *does* entail that the person did what he did freely, or that he did it of his own free will. It is a mistake, however, to believe that someone acts freely only when he is free to do whatever he wants or that he acts of his own free will only if his will is free. Suppose that a person has done what he wanted to do, that he did it because he wanted to do it, and that the will by which he was moved when he did it was his will because it was the will he wanted. Then he did it freely and of his own free will. Even supposing that he could have done otherwise, he would not have done otherwise; and even supposing that he could have had a different will, he would not have wanted his will to differ from what it was. Moreover, since the will that moved him when he acted was his will because he wanted it to be, he cannot claim that his will was forced upon him or that he was a passive bystander to its constitution. Under these conditions, it is quite irrelevant to the evaluation of his moral responsibility to inquire whether the alternatives that he opted against were actually available to him.[9]

In illustration, consider a third kind of addict. Suppose that his addiction has the same physiological basis and the same irresistible thrust as the addictions of the unwilling and wanton addicts, but that he is altogether delighted with his condition. He is a willing addict, who would not have things any other way. If the grip of his addiction should somehow weaken, he would do whatever he could to reinstate it; if his desire for the drug should begin to fade, he would take steps to renew its intensity.

The willing addict's will is not free, for his desire to take the drug will be effective regardless of whether or not he wants this desire to constitute his will. But when he takes the drug, he takes it freely and of his own free will. I am inclined to understand his situation as involving the overdetermination of his first-order desire to take the drug. This desire is his effective desire because he is physiologically addicted. But it is his effective desire also because he wants it to be. His will is outside his control, but, by his second-order desire that his desire for the drug should be effective, he has made this will his own. Given that it is therefore not only because of his addiction that his desire for the drug is effective, he may be morally responsible for taking the drug.

My conception of the freedom of the will appears to be neutral with regard to the problem of determinism. It seems conceivable that it should be causally determined that a person is free to want what he wants to want. If this is conceivable, then it might be causally determined that a person enjoys a free will. There is no more than an innocuous appearance of paradox in the proposition that it is determined, ineluctably and by forces beyond their control, that certain people have free wills and that others do not. There is no incoherence in the proposition that some agency other than a person's own is responsible (even *morally* responsible) for the fact that he enjoys or fails to enjoy freedom of the will. It is possible that a person should be morally responsible for what he does of his own free will and that some other person should also be morally responsible for his having done it.[10]

On the other hand, it seems conceivable that it should come about by chance that a person is free to have the will he wants. If this is conceivable, then it might be a matter of chance that certain people enjoy freedom of the will and that certain others do not. Perhaps it is also conceivable, as a number of philosophers believe, for states of affairs to come about in a way other than by chance or as the outcome of a sequence of natural causes. If it is indeed conceivable for the relevant states of affairs to come about in some third way, then it is also possible that a person should in that third way come to enjoy the freedom of the will.

Notes

1 P. F. Strawson, *Individuals* (London: Methuen, 1959), pp. 101–2. Ayer's usage of 'person' is similar: "it is characteristic of persons in this sense that besides having various physical properties . . . they are also credited with various forms of consciousness" (A. J. Ayer, *The Concept of a Person* (New York: St Martin's, 1963), p. 82). What concerns Strawson and Ayer is the problem of understanding the relation between mind and body, rather than the quite different problem of understanding what it is to be a creature that not only has a mind and a body but is also a person.

2 For the sake of simplicity, I shall deal only with what someone wants or desires, neglecting related phenomena such as choices and decisions. I propose to use the verbs 'to want' and 'to desire' interchangeably, although they are by no means perfect synonyms. My motive in forsaking the established nuances of these words arises from the fact that the verb 'to want', which suits my purposes better so far as its meaning is concerned, does not lend itself so readily to the formation of nouns as does the verb 'to desire'. It is perhaps acceptable, albeit graceless, to speak in the plural of someone's "wants." But to speak in the singular of someone's "want" would be an abomination.

3 What I say in this paragraph applies not only to cases in which 'to X' refers to a possible action or inaction. It also applies to cases in which 'to X' refers to a first-order desire and in which the statement that 'A wants to X' is therefore a shortened version of a statement – "A wants to want to X" – that identifies a desire of the second order.

4 It is not so clear that the entailment relation described here holds in certain kinds of cases, which I think may fairly be regarded as nonstandard, where the essential difference between the standard and the nonstandard cases lies in the kind of description by which the first-order desire in question is identified. Thus, suppose that A admires B so fulsomely that, even though he does not know what B wants to do, he wants to be effectively moved by whatever desire effectively moves B; without knowing what B's will is, in other words, A wants his own will to be the same. It certainly does not follow that A already has, among his desires, a desire like the one that constitutes B's will. I shall not pursue here the questions of whether there are genuine counterexamples to the claim made in the text or of how, if there are, that claim should be altered.

5 Creatures with second-order desires but no second-order volitions differ significantly from brute animals, and, for some purposes, it would be

desirable to regard them as persons. My usage, which withholds the designation 'person' from them, is thus somewhat arbitrary. I adopt it largely because it facilitates the formulation of some of the points I wish to make. Hereafter, whenever I consider statements of the form "*A* wants to want to *X*," I shall have in mind statements identifying second-order volitions and not statements identifying second-order desires that are not second-order volitions.

6   In speaking of the evaluation of his own desires and motives as being characteristic of a person, I do not mean to suggest that a person's second-order volitions necessarily manifest a *moral* stance on his part toward his first-order desires. It may not be from the point of view of morality that the person evaluates his first-order desires. Moreover, a person may be capricious and irresponsible in forming his second-order volitions and give no serious consideration to what is at stake. Second-order volitions express evaluations only in the sense that they are preferences. There is no essential restriction on the kind of basis, if any, upon which they are formed.

7   "Freedom and Action," in K. Lehrer, ed., *Freedom and Determinism* (New York: Random House, 1966), pp. 11–44.

8   I am not suggesting that the alleged difference between these two states of affairs is unverifiable.

On the contrary, physiologists might well be able to show that Chisholm's conditions for a free action are not satisfied, by establishing that there is no relevant brain event for which a sufficient physical cause cannot be found.

9   For another discussion of the considerations that cast doubt on the principle that a person is morally responsible for what he has done only if he could have done otherwise, see my "Alternate Possibilities and Moral Responsibility," *Journal of Philosophy*, LXVI, 23 (Dec. 4, 1969): 829–39.

10   There is a difference between being *fully* responsible and being *solely* responsible. Suppose that the willing addict has been made an addict by the deliberate and calculated work of another. Then it may be that both the addict and this other person are fully responsible for the addict's taking the drug, while neither of them is solely responsible for it. That there is a distinction between full moral responsibility and sole moral responsibility is apparent in the following example. A certain light can be turned on or off by flicking either of two switches, and each of these switches is simultaneously flicked to the "on" position by a different person, neither of whom is aware of the other. Neither person is solely responsible for the light's going on, nor do they share the responsibility in the sense that each is partially responsible; rather, each of them is fully responsible.

46

The M'Naghten Rules (1843)

(Q.I.) "What is the law respecting alleged crimes committed by persons afflicted with insane delusion in respect of one or more particular subjects or persons: as for instance, where, at the time of the commission of the alleged crime, the accused knew he was acting contrary to law, but did the act complained of with a view, under the influence of insane delusion, of redressing or revenging some supposed grievance or injury, or of producing some supposed public benefit?"

(A.I.) "Assuming that your lordships' inquiries are confined to those persons who labor under such partial delusions only, and are not in other respects insane, we are of opinion that notwithstanding the accused did the act complained of with a view, under the influence of insane delusion, of redressing or avenging some supposed grievance or injury, or of producing some public benefit, he is nevertheless punishable, according to the nature of the crime committed, if he knew at the time of committing such crime that he was acting contrary to law, by which expression we understand your lordships to mean the law of the land."

(Q.II.) "What are the proper questions to be submitted to the jury where a person alleged to be afflicted with insane delusion respecting one or more particular subjects or persons is charged with the commission of a crime (murder, for example), and insanity is set up as a defence?"

(Q.III.) "In what terms ought the question to be left to the jury as to the prisoner's state of mind at the time when the act was committed?"

(A.II and A.III.) "As these two questions appear to us to be more conveniently answered together, we submit our opinion to be that the jury ought to be told in all cases that every man is presumed to be sane, and to possess a sufficient degree of reason to be responsible for his crimes, until the contrary be proved to their satisfaction; and that to establish a defence on the ground of insanity it must be clearly proved that, at the time of committing the act, the accused was labouring under such a defect of reason, from disease of the mind, as not to know the nature and quality of the act he was doing, or, if he did know it, that he did not know he was doing what was wrong. The mode of putting the latter part of the question to the jury on these occasions has generally been whether the accused at the time of doing the act knew the difference between right and wrong: which mode, though rarely, if ever, leading to any mistake with the jury, is not, as we conceive, so accurate when put generally and in the abstract as when put with reference to the party's knowledge of right and wrong, in respect to the very act with which he is charged. If the

The M'Naghten Rules, House of Lords, 1843.

question were to be put as to the knowledge of the accused solely and exclusively with reference to the law of the land, it might tend to confound the jury, by inducing them to believe that an actual knowledge of the law of the land was essential in order to lead to conviction: whereas, the law is administered upon the principle that everyone must be taken conclusively to know it, without proof that he does know it. If the accused was conscious that the act was one that he ought not to do, and if that act was at the same time contrary to the law of the land, he is punishable; and the usual course, therefore, has been to leave the question to the jury, whether the accused had a sufficient degree of reason to know that he was doing an act that was wrong; and this course we think is correct, accompanied with such observations and explanations as the circumstances of each particular case may require."

(Q.IV.) "If a person under an insane delusion as to existing facts commits an offence in consequence thereof, is he thereby excused?"

(A.IV.) "The answer must, of course, depend on the nature of the delusion; but making the same assumption as we did before, namely, that he labors under such partial delusion only, and is not in other respects insane, we think he must be considered in the same situation as to responsibility as if the facts with respect to which the delusion exists were real. For example, if under the influence of his delusion he supposes another man to be in the act of attempting to take away his life, and he kills that man, as he supposes in self-defence, he would be exempt from punishment. If his delusion was that the deceased had inflicted a serious injury to his character and fortune, and he killed him in revenge for such supposed injury, he would be liable to punishment."

47

The Insanity Defense (1956)

Article 4. Responsibility

Section 4.01. Mental disease or defect
excluding responsibility

(1) A person is not responsible for criminal conduct if at the time of such conduct as a result of mental disease or defect he lacks substantial capacity either to appreciate the criminality of his conduct or to conform his conduct to the requirements of law.
(2) The terms "mental disease or defect" do not include an abnormality manifested only by repeated criminal or otherwise antisocial conduct.

Alternative formulations of paragraph (1).

(a) A person is not responsible for criminal conduct if at the time of such conduct as a result of mental disease or defect his capacity either to appreciate the criminality of his conduct or to conform his conduct to the requirements of law is so substantially impaired that he cannot justly be held responsible.
(b) A person is not responsible for criminal conduct if at the time of such conduct as a result of mental disease or defect he lacks substantial capacity to appreciate the criminality of his conduct or is in such state that the prospect of conviction and punishment cannot constitute a significant restraining influence upon him.

Comments §4.01. Article 4.
Responsibility

Section 4.01. Mental disease or defect
excluding responsibility

The problem of defining the criteria of irresponsibility

1. No problem in the drafting of a penal code presents larger intrinsic difficulty than that of determining when individuals whose conduct would otherwise be criminal ought to be exculpated on the ground that they were suffering from mental disease or defect when they acted as they did. What is involved specifically is the drawing of a line between the use of public agencies and public force to condemn the offender by conviction, with resultant sanctions in which there is inescapably a punitive ingredient (however constructive we may attempt to make the process of correction) and modes of disposition in which that ingredient is absent, even though restraint may be involved. To put the matter

The Insanity Defense, The American Law Institute, 1956.

differently, the problem is to discriminate between the cases where a punitive-correctional disposition is appropriate and those in which a medical-custodial disposition is the only kind the law should allow.

2. The traditional M'Naghten rule resolves the problem solely in regard to the capacity of the individual to know what he was doing and to know that it was wrong. Absent these minimal elements of rationality, condemnation and punishment are obviously both unjust and futile. They are unjust because the individual could not, by hypothesis, have employed reason to restrain the act; he did not and he could not know the facts essential to bring reason into play. On the same ground, they are futile. A madman who believes that he is squeezing lemons when he chokes his wife or thinks that homicide is the command of God is plainly beyond reach of the restraining influence of law; he needs restraint but condemnation is entirely meaningless and ineffective. Thus the attacks on the M'Naghten rule as an inept definition of insanity or as an arbitrary definition in terms of special symptoms are entirely misconceived. The *rationale* of the position is that these are cases in which reason cannot operate and in which it is totally impossible for individuals to be deterred. Moreover, the category defined by the rule is so extreme that to the ordinary man the exculpation of the persons it encompasses bespeaks no weakness in the law. He does not identify such persons and himself; they are a world apart.

Jurisdictions in which the M'Naghten test has been expanded to include the case where mental disease produces an "irresistible impulse" proceed on the same *rationale*. They recognize, however, that cognitive factors are not the only ones that preclude inhibition; that even though cognition still obtains, mental disorder may produce a total incapacity for self-control. The same result is sometimes reached under M'Naghten proper, in the view, strongly put forth by Stephen, that "knowledge" requires more than the capacity to verbalize right answers to a question, it implies capacity to function in the light of knowledge. Stephen, *History of English Criminal Law*, Vol. 2, p. 171. [...] In modern psychiatric terms, the "fundamental difference between verbal or purely intellectual knowledge and the mysterious other kind of knowledge is familiar to every clinical

psychiatrist; it is the difference between knowledge divorced from affect and knowledge so fused with affect that it becomes a human reality." Zilboorg, "Misconceptions of Legal Insanity," 9 *Am. J. Orthopsychiatry*, pp. 540, 552. [...]

3. The draft accepts the view that any effort to exclude the nondeterrables from strictly penal sanctions must take account of the impairment of volitional capacity no less than of impairment of cognition; and that this result should be achieved directly in the formulation of the test, rather than left to mitigation in the application of M'Naghten. It also accepts the criticism of the "irresistible impulse" formulation as inept in so far as it may be impliedly restricted to sudden, spontaneous acts as distinguished from insane propulsions that are accompanied by brooding or reflection. [...]

Both the main formulation recommended and alternative (a) deem the proper question on this branch of the inquiry to be whether the defendant is without capacity to conform his conduct to the requirements of law. [...]

Alternative (b) states the issue differently. Instead of asking whether the defendant had capacity to conform his conduct to the requirements of law, it asks whether, in consequence of mental disease or defect, the threat of punishment could not exercise a significant restraining influence upon him. To some extent, of course, these are the same inquiries. To the extent that they diverge, the latter asks a narrower and harder question, involving the assessment of capacity to respond to a single influence, the threat of punishment. Both Dr Guttmacher and Dr Overholser considered the assessment of responsiveness to this one influence too difficult for psychiatric judgment. Hence, though the issue framed by the alternative may well be thought to state the question that is most precisely relevant for legal purposes, the Reporter and the Council deemed the inquiry impolitic upon this ground. In so far as nondeterrability is the determination that is sought, it must be reached by probing general capacity to conform to the requirements of law. The validity of this conclusion is submitted, however, to the judgment of the Institute.

4. One further problem must be faced. In addressing itself to impairment of the cognitive capacity, M'Naghten demands that impairment be complete: the actor must *not* know. So, too,

the irresistible impulse criterion presupposes a complete impairment of capacity for self-control. The extremity of these conceptions is, we think, the point that poses largest difficulty to psychiatrists when called upon to aid in their administration. The schizophrenic, for example, is disoriented from reality; the disorientation is extreme; but it is rarely total. Most psychotics will respond to a command of someone in authority within the mental hospital; they thus have some capacity to conform to a norm. But this is very different from the question whether they have the capacity to conform to requirements that are not thus immediately symbolized by an attendant or policeman at the elbow. Nothing makes the inquiry into responsibility more unreal for the psychiatrist than limitation of the issue to some ultimate extreme of total incapacity, when clinical experience reveals only a graded scale with marks along the way. . . .

We think this difficulty can and must be met. The law must recognize that when there is no black and white it must content itself with different shades of gray. The draft, accordingly, does not demand *complete* impairment of capacity. It asks instead for *substantial* impairment. This is all, we think, that candid witnesses, called on to infer the nature of the situation at a time that they did not observe, can ever confidently say, even when they know that a disorder was extreme.

If substantial impairment of capacity is to suffice, there remains the question whether this alone should be the test or whether the criterion should state the principle that measures how substantial it must be. To identify the degree of impairment with precision is, of course, impossible both verbally and logically. The recommended formulation is content to rest upon the term *substantial* to support the weight of judgment; if capacity is greatly impaired, that presumably should be sufficient. Alternative (a) proposes to submit the issue squarely to the jury's sense of justice, asking expressly whether the capacity of the defendant "was so substantially impaired that he cannot justly be held responsible." Some members of the Council deemed it unwise to present questions of justice to the jury, preferring a submission that in form, at least, confines the inquiry to fact. The proponents of the alternative contend that since the jury normally will feel that it is only just to exculpate if the disorder was

extreme, that otherwise conviction is demanded, it is safer to invoke the jury's sense of justice than to rest entirely on the single word *substantial*, imputing no specific measure of degree. The issue is an important one and it is submitted for consideration by the Institute.

5. The draft rejects the formulation warmly supported by psychiatrists and recently adopted by the Court of Appeals for the District of Columbia in *Durham v. United States*, 214, F. 2d 862 (1954), namely, "that an accused is not criminally responsible if his unlawful act was the product of mental disease or defect." [. . .]

The difficulty with this formulation inheres in the ambiguity of "product." If interpreted to lead to irresponsibility unless the defendant would have engaged in the criminal conduct even if he had not suffered from the disease or defect, it is too broad: an answer that he would have done so can be given very rarely; this is intrinsic to the concept of the singleness of personality and unity of mental processes that psychiatry regards as fundamental. If interpreted to call for a standard of causality less relaxed than but-for cause, there are but two alternatives to be considered: (1) a mode of causality involving total incapacity or (2) a mode of causality which involves substantial incapacity. See Wechsler, "The Criteria of Criminal Responsibility," 22 *U. of Chi. L. Rev.* (1955), p. 367. But if either of these causal concepts is intended, the formulation ought to set it forth.

The draft also rejects the proposal of the majority of the recent Royal Commission on Capital Punishment, namely, "to leave to the jury to determine whether at the time of the act the accused was suffering from disease of the mind (or mental deficiency) to such a degree that he ought not to be held responsible." *Report* (1953), par. 333, p. 116. While we agree, as we have indicated, that mental disease or defect involves gradations of degree that should be recognized, we think the legal standard ought to focus on the *consequences* of disease or defect that have a bearing on the justice of conviction and of punishment. The Royal Commission proposal fails in this respect.

6. Paragraph (2) of section 4.01 is designed to exclude from the concept of "mental disease or defect" the case of so-called "psychopathic personality." The reason for the exclusion is

that, as the Royal Commission put it, psycho-pathy "is a statistical abnormality; that is to say, the psychopath differs from a normal person only quantitatively or in degree, not qualitatively; and the diagnosis of psychopathic personality does not carry with it any explanation of the causes of the abnormality." While it may not be feasible to formulate a definition of "disease," there is much to be said for excluding a condition that is manifested only by the behavior phenomena that must, by hypothesis, be the result of disease for irresponsibility to be established. Although British psychiatrists have agreed, on the whole, that psychopathy should not be called "disease," there is considerable difference of opinion on the point in the United States. Yet it does not seem useful to contemplate the litigation of what is essentially a matter of terminology; nor is it right to have the legal result rest upon the resolution of a dispute of this kind.

48

What Is So Special About Mental Illness?

Joel Feinberg

Professor Dershowitz has very effectively put psychiatry in its proper place.[1] As far as the law and public policy are concerned, a psychiatrist is an expert on the diagnosis and treatment of mental illness. His testimony becomes relevant to questions of responsibility only when mental illness itself is relevant to such questions, and that is only when it deprives a person of the capacity to conform his conduct to the requirements of law. Mental illness should not itself be an independent ground of exculpation, but only a sign that one of the traditional standard grounds – compulsion, ignorance of fact, or excusable ignorance of law – may apply. Mental illness, then, while often relevant to questions of responsibility, is no more significant – and significant in no different way – than other sources of compulsion and misapprehension.

Now although I am almost completely convinced that this is the correct account of the matter, I am nevertheless going to air my few lingering doubts as if they were potent objections, just to see what will happen to them. I shall suggest, then, in what follows, that mental illness has an independent significance for questions of responsibility not fully accounted for by reference to its power to deprive one of the capacity to be law-abiding.

I

At the outset we must distinguish two questions about the relation of mental illness to criminal punishment. (There are two parallel questions about the bearing of mental illness on civil commitment.)

1. How are mentally sick persons to be distinguished from normal persons?
2. When should we accept mental illness as an excuse?

The first appears to be a medical question that requires the expertise of the psychiatrist to answer; the second appears to be an essentially controversial question of public policy that cannot be answered by referring to the special expertise of any particular group.

Some psychiatrists may wish to deny this rigid separation between the two questions. They might hold it self-evident that sick people are not to be treated as responsible people; hence the criteria of illness are themselves criteria of nonresponsibility. But, obviously, this won't do. First of all, the fact of illness itself, even greatly incapacitating illness, does not automatically lead us to withhold ascription of responsibility, or

Joel Feinberg, "What Is So Special About Mental Illness?" from *Doing and Deserving* (Princeton: Princeton University Press, 1970), pp. 272–92. © 1970 by Joel Feinberg. Reprinted by kind permission of Betty Feinberg.

else we would treat *physical* illness as an automatic excuse. But in fact we would not change our judgments of Bonnie and Clyde one jot if we discovered that they both had had 103-degree fevers during one of their bank robberies, or of Al Capone if we learned that he had ordered one of his gangland assassinations while suffering from an advanced case of chicken pox. Secondly, there are various crimes that can be committed by persons suffering from mental illnesses that can have no relevant bearing on their motivation. We may take exhibitionism to be an excuse for indecent exposure, or pedophilia for child molestation, but neither would be a plausible defense to the charge of income-tax evasion or price-fixing conspiracy. These examples show, I think, that the mere fact of mental illness, no more than the mere fact of physical illness, automatically excuses. We need some further criterion, then, for distinguishing cases of mental illness that do excuse from those that do not, and this further question is not an exclusively psychiatric one. What we want to know is this: what is it about mental illness that makes it an excuse when it is an excuse?

So much, I think, is clear. But now there are two types of moves open to us. The first is preferred by most legal writers, and it is the one to which I am most favorably disposed. According to this view, there is nothing very special about mental disease as such. Mental illness is only one of numerous possible causes of *incapacity*, and it is incapacity – or, more precisely, the incapability to conform to law – that is incompatible with responsibility. Ultimately, there is only one kind of consideration that should lead us to exempt a person from responsibility for his wrongful deeds, and that is that he *couldn't help it*. Sometimes a mental illness compels a man to do wrong, or at least makes it unreasonably difficult for him to abstain, and in these cases we say that, because he was ill, he couldn't help what he did and, therefore, is not to be held responsible for his deviant conduct. But in other cases, as we have seen, mental illness no more compels a given wrongful act than the chicken pox does, or may be totally irrelevant to the explanation of the wrongdoing, in that the wrongdoer would have done his wrong even if he had been perfectly healthy. What counts, then, for questions of responsibility is whether the accused could have helped himself, not whether he was mentally well or ill.

Aristotle put much the same point in somewhat different but equally familiar language. A man is responsible, said Aristotle, for all and only those of his actions that are voluntary; to whatever extent we think a given action less than voluntary, to that extent we are inclined to exempt the actor from responsibility for it. There are, according to Aristotle, two primary ways in which an action can fail to be voluntary: it can be the result of *compulsion*, or it can be done in *ignorance*. Thus if a hurricane wind blows you twenty yards across a street, you cannot be said to have crossed the street voluntarily, since you were compelled to do it and given no choice at all in the matter. And if you put arsenic in your wife's coffee honestly but mistakenly believing it to be sugar, you cannot be said to have poisoned her voluntarily, since you acted in genuine ignorance of what you were doing.

Now if we take just a few slight liberties with Aristotle, we can interpret most of the traditionally recognized legal excuses in terms of his categories. Acting under duress or necessity, or in self-defense, or defense of others, or defense of property, and so on, can all be treated as cases of acting under compulsion, whereas ignorance or mistake of fact, ignorance or mistake of law, and perhaps even what used to be called "moral idiocy" or ignorance of the "difference between right and wrong" can all be treated as cases of acting in responsibility-cancelling ignorance. On the view I am considering (a view which has gained much favor among lawyers, and to which Professor Dershowitz, I feel sure, is friendly), the mental illness of an actor is not still a third way in which his actions might fail to be voluntary; rather, it is a factor which may or may not compel him to act in certain ways, or which may or may not delude, or mislead, or misinform him in ways that would lead him to act in ignorance. Indeed, on this view, mental illness ought not even to be an independent category of exculpation on a level with, say, self-defense or mistake of fact. Self-defense and relevant blameless mistakes of fact always excuse, whereas mental illness excuses only when it compels or deludes. We now know of the existence of inner compulsions unsuspected by Aristotle: obsessive ideas, hysterical reactions, neurotic compulsion, phobias, and addictions.

Other mental illnesses characteristically produce delusions and hallucinations. But not all neurotic and psychotic disorders by any means produce compulsive or delusionary symptoms, and even those that do are not always sufficient to explain the criminal conduct of the person suffering from them.

The nineteenth-century judges who formulated the famous M'Naghten Rules were presumably quite sympathetic with the view I have been describing, that there really is nothing very special about mental illness. These rules are not at all concerned with neurotically compulsive behavior – a category which simply was not before their minds at the time. Rather, they were concerned with those dramatic and conspicuous disorders that involve what we call today "paranoid delusions" and "psychotic hallucinations." The interesting thing about the rules is that they treat these aberrations precisely the same as any other innocent "mistakes of fact"; in effect the main point of this part of the M'Naghten Rules is to acknowledge that mistakes of fact resulting from "disease of the mind" really are genuine and innocent and, therefore, have the same exculpatory force as more commonplace errors and false beliefs. The rules state that, "when a man acts under an insane delusion, then he is excused only when it is the case that *if* the facts were as he supposed them his act would be innocent. . . ." Thus if a man suffers the insane delusion that a passerby on the street is an enemy agent about to launch a mortal attack on him and kills him in what he thinks is "self-defense," he is excused, since if the facts were as he falsely supposed them to be, his act would have been innocent. But if (in James Vorenberg's example) he shoots his wife because, in his insane delusion, he thinks her hair has turned gray, he will be convicted, since even if her hair had turned gray, that would not have been an allowable defense. Note that the mental disease that leads to the insane delusion in these instances is given no special significance except insofar as it mediates the application of another kind of defense that can be used by mentally healthy as well as mentally ill defendants.

The M'Naghten Rules do, however, make one important concession to the peculiarity of mental illness. Mentally normal persons, for the most part, are not permitted to plead *ignorance of the law* as a defense, especially for crimes that are *"malum in se."* No normal person, for example, can plead in the state of Arizona that "he didn't know that murder is prohibited in Arizona." *That* kind of ignorance could hardly ever occur in a normal person, and even if it did, it would be negligent rather than innocent ignorance. (One should at least take the trouble to find out whether a state prohibits murder before killing someone in that state!) If a person, however, is so grossly ignorant of what is permitted that he would murder even (as the saying goes) with "a policeman at his elbow," then if his ignorance is attributable to a diseased mind and therefore innocent, he is excused. One can conceive (just barely) of such a case. Imagine a man standing on a street corner chatting with a policeman. A third person saunters up, calmly shoots and kills the man, turns to the astonished policeman and says "Good morning, officer," and starts to walk away. When the policeman apprehends him, then *he* is the astonished one. "Why, what have I done wrong?" he asks in genuine puzzlement.

In accepting this kind of ignorance when it stems from disease as an excuse, the M'Naghten Rules do not really make *much* of a concession to the uniqueness of mental illness. Ignorance of law does not excuse in the normal case because the law imposes a duty on all normal persons to find out what is prohibited at their own peril. When a statute has been duly promulgated, every normal person is presumed to know about it. If any given normal person fails to be informed, his ignorance is the consequence of his own negligence, and he is to blame for it. But when the ignorance is the consequence of illness, it is involuntary or faultless ignorance and may therefore be accepted as an excuse. Again, it is not the mental illness as such which excuses, but rather the ignorance which is its indirect byproduct. The ultimate rationale of the exculpation is that the actor "couldn't help it." We hardly need the separate insanity defense at all if we accept the propositions that mentally ill people may be subject to internal compulsions, that mental illness can cause innocent ignorance, and that both compulsion and innocent ignorance are themselves excuses.

Suppose a mentally ill defendant is acquitted on the ground that his illness has rendered his unlawful conduct involuntary in one of these traditional ways. He may still be a menace to himself or others, even though he is perfectly innocent of any crime. Hence the state reserves to itself or to others the right to initiate civil commitment proceedings. Now whether it follows acquittal or is quite independent of any prior criminal proceedings, civil commitment can have one or both of two different purposes, and for each of these purposes the mere fact of mental illness is not a sufficient condition. The two purposes are (1) forcible detention of a dangerous person to prevent him from committing a crime and (2) compulsory therapeutic confinement of a mentally ill person "for his own good." For the purpose of preventive detention, mental illness is neither a necessary nor a sufficient condition: not necessary because mentally normal persons too can be very dangerous in certain circumstances,[2] and not sufficient because some mentally ill people, unhappy or withdrawn as they may be, are still quite harmless. Hence psychiatric testimony that a person is mentally ill is hardly sufficient to justify detaining him without a further showing of dangerousness. What is needed are very high standards of due process at detention hearings analogous to those governing criminal trials and, as Professor Dershowitz points out, clear and precise legal definitions of "harmfulness" and "danger."

The other possible purpose of civil commitment – compulsory therapy – does of course require mental illness as a necessary condition, and here psychiatric testimony is crucial. But if civil liberty has any appeal to us and if state paternalism is repugnant, we can hardly regard the simple fact of mental illness as sufficient warrant for imposing therapeutic confinement on a person against his will. To force a person to submit to our benevolence is a fearsome and ugly kind of tyranny. The traditional doctrine of *Parens Patriae* to which Professor Dershowitz refers, however, authorizes such coercion only in very special and, I think, unobjectionable circumstances. Some mental illnesses so affect the cognitive processes that a victim is unable to make inferences or decisions – a severe disablement indeed. According to the *Parens Patriae* doctrine, the state has the duty to exercise its "sovereign power of guardianship" over these intellectually defective and disordered persons who are unable to realize their needs on their own. But even on occasions where this doctrine applies, the state

presumes to "decide for a man as . . . he would decide for himself if he were of sound mind."[3] By no means all mentally ill persons, however, suffer from defects of reason. Many or most of them suffer from emotional or volitional disorders that leave their cognitive faculties quite unimpaired. To impose compulsory therapy on such persons would be as objectionably paternalistic as imposing involuntary cures for warts or headaches or tooth decay.

To summarize the view I have been considering: a mere finding of mental illness is not itself a sufficient ground for exempting a person from responsibility for a given action; nor is it a sufficient ground for finding him not to be a responsible or competent person generally, with the loss of civil rights such a finding necessarily entails. At most, in criminal proceedings mental illness may be evidence that one of the traditional grounds for moral exculpation – compulsion or ignorance – applies to the case at hand, and in civil commitment hearings it may be evidence of dangerousness or of cognitive impairment. But it has no independent moral or legal significance in itself either as an excuse or as a ground for commitment.

II

I fully accept this account of the relation of mental illness to civil commitment. Preventive detention of a person who has committed no crime is a desperate move that should be made only when a person's continued liberty would constitute a clear and present danger of substantial harm to others. We should require proof of a very great danger indeed before resorting to such measures if only because people are inclined generally to overestimate threats to safety and to underestimate the social value of individual liberty. Mere evidence of mental illness by itself does not provide such proof. Nor does it by itself provide proof of that mental derangement or incompetence to grant or withhold consent that is required if compulsory therapeutic confinement is to be justified. But, for all of that, I have a lingering doubt that the above account does full justice to the moral significance of mental illness as it bears on blame and punishment. I shall devote the remainder of my remarks to a statement of that doubt.

Let me turn immediately to the kind of case that troubles me. I have in mind cases of criminal conduct which appear to be both voluntary (by the usual Aristotelian tests) and sick. Let me give some examples and then contrast them with normal voluntary criminal acts.

First consider a nonviolent child molester. He is sexually attracted to five- and six-year-old boys and girls. His rational faculties are perfectly normal. He knows that sexual contacts with children are forbidden by the criminal law, and he takes no unnecessary risks of detection. For the most part, he manages to do without sex altogether. When he does molest a child he characteristically feels guilt, if not remorse, afterward. He has no understanding of his own motivation and often regrets that his tastes are so odd.

Next in our rogues' gallery is a repetitive exhibitionist. He has been arrested numerous times for exposing his genitalia in public. He does this not to solicit or threaten, but simply to derive satisfaction from the act itself: exposure for exposure's sake. For some reason he cannot understand, he finds such exposure immensely gratifying. Still, he knows that it is offensive to others, that it is in a way publicly humiliating, that it is prohibited by law, and that the chances of being caught and punished are always very great. These things trouble him much and often, but not always, lead him to restrain himself when the impulse to self-exposure arises.

My third example is drawn from a landmark case in the criminal law, one of the first in which kleptomania was accepted as an excuse: *State v. McCullough*, 114 *Iowa* 532 (1901). The defendant, a high school student, was charged with stealing a school book worth seventy-five cents. It was discovered that stolen property in his possession included "14 silverine watches, 2 old brass watches, 2 old clocks, 24 razors, 21 pairs of cuff buttons, 15 watch chains, 6 pistols, 7 combs, 34 jack knives, 9 bicycle wrenches, 4 padlocks, 7 pair of clippers, 3 bicycle saddles, 1 box of old keys, 4 pairs of scissors, 5 pocket mirrors, 6 mouth organs, rulers, bolts, calipers, oil cans, washers, punches, pulleys, spoons, penholders, ramrods, violin strings, etc." ["etc."!]. One can barely imagine the great price in anxiety this boy must have paid for his vast accumulation of worthless junk.

Finally, consider a well-off man who shoplifts only one kind of item, women's brassieres. He could easily afford to pay for these items and, indeed, often does when there is no other way of getting them, or when he is in danger of being caught. He does not enjoy stealing them and suffers great anxiety in worrying about being found out. Yet his storerooms are overflowing with brassieres. He burgles homes only to steal them; he assaults women only to rip off their brassieres and flee. And if you ask him for an explanation of his bizarre conduct, he will confess himself as puzzled by it as any observer.

Now, for contrast, consider some typical voluntary normal crimes. A respectable middle-aged bank teller, after weighing the risks carefully, embezzles bank funds and runs off to Mexico with his expensive lady friend. A homeowner in desperate need of cash sets his own house on fire to defraud an insurance company. A teenager steals a parked car and drives to a nearby city for a thrill. An angry man consumed with jealousy, or indignation, or vengefulness, or spite commits criminal battery on a person he hates. A revolutionary throws a bomb at the king's carriage during an insurrection. These criminals act from a great variety of unmysterious motives – avarice, gain, lust, hate, ideological zeal; they are all rationally capable of calculating risks; they all act voluntarily.

How do the "sick" criminals in my earlier list differ from these normal ones? We might be tempted to answer that the pedophiliac, the exhibitionist, the kleptomaniac, and the fetishist are all "compulsives" and that their criminal conduct is therefore not entirely voluntary after all; but I believe it is important to understand that this answer is unsatisfactory. There is no *a priori* reason why the desires, impulses, and motives that lead a person to do bizarre things need necessarily be more powerful or compulsive than the desires that lead normal men to do perfectly ordinary things. It is by no means self-evident, for example, that the sex drives of a pedophiliac or an exhibitionist must always be stronger than the sexual desires normal men and women may feel for one another.

There is much obscurity in the notion of the "strength of a desire," but I think several points are clear and relevant to our purposes. The first is that, strictly speaking, no impulse is "irresistible." For every case of giving in to a desire, I would argue, it will be true that, if the person had tried harder, he would have resisted it successfully. The psychological situation is never – or hardly ever – like that of the man who hangs from a windowsill by his fingernails until the sheer physical force of gravity rips his nails off and sends him plummeting to the ground, or like that of the man who dives from a sinking ship in the middle of the ocean and swims until he is exhausted and then drowns. Human endurance puts a severe limit on how long one can stay afloat in an ocean; but there is no comparable limit to our ability to resist temptation. Nevertheless, it does make sense to say that some desires are stronger than others and that some have an intensity and power that are felt as overwhelming. Some desires, in fact, may be so difficult to resist for a given person in a given state at a given time that it would be unreasonable to expect him to resist. A dieting man with a strong sweet tooth may find it difficult to resist eating an ice cream sundae for dessert; but a man who has not eaten for a week will have a much harder time still resisting the desire to eat a loaf of bread, which just happens to belong to his neighbor. Any person in a weakened condition, whether the cause be hunger or depression, fatigue or gripping emotion, will be less able to resist any given anti-social impulse than a person in a normal condition. But, again, there is no reason to suppose that bizarre appetites and odd tastes are always connected with a "weakened condition," so that they are necessarily more difficult to resist than ordinary desires. And thus there is no reason to suppose that so-called sick desires must always be compulsive or unreasonably difficult to resist.

It might seem to follow that there is *no* morally significant difference between normal and mentally ill offenders, that the one class is just as responsible as the other, provided only that their criminal actions are voluntary in the usual sense. But if this is the proper conclusion, then I am at a loss to see what difference there can be between mental illness and plain wickedness. As an ordinary citizen, before I begin to get confused by philosophy, I sometimes permit myself to feel anger and outrage at normal criminals, whereas I cannot help feeling some pity (mixed, perhaps, with repugnance) toward those whose conduct appears bizarre and unnatural. But unless I can find some morally telling difference between the two classes of criminals, then these natural attitudes must be radically reshaped, so that the fetish thief, for example, be thought as wicked as the professional burglar.

There do seem to be some striking differences between the two classes, however, and perhaps some of these can rescue my prephilosophical attitudes. Most of them have to do not with the criminal's intentions, but with his underlying motivation – the basis of the appeal in his immediate goals or objectives. The first such difference is that the sick criminal's motives appear quite *unintelligible* to us. We sometimes express our puzzlement by saying that his crimes have no apparent motive at all. We cannot see any better than the criminal himself "what he gets out of it," and it overburdens our imaginative faculties to put ourselves in his shoes. We understand the avaricious, irascible, or jealous man's motives all too well, and we resent him for them. But where crimes resist explanation in terms of ordinary motives, we hardly know what to resent. Here the old maxim "to understand all is to forgive all" seems to be turned on its ear. It is closer to the truth to say of mentally ill wrongdoers that to forgive is to despair of understanding.

Yet mere unintelligibility of motive is not likely to advance our search for the moral significance of mental illness very far, especially if we take the criterion of unintelligibility in turn to be the frustration of our "imaginative capacities" to put ourselves in the criminal's shoes and understand what he gets out of his crimes. This test of imaginability is far too elastic and variable. On the one hand, it seems too loose, since it permits the classification as unintelligible (or even sick) of *any* particular passion or taste, provided only that it is sufficiently different from those of the person making the judgment. Some nonsmokers cannot understand what smokers get out of their noxious habit, and males can hardly understand what it is like to enjoy bearing children. On the other hand, once we begin tightening up the test of imaginability, there is likely to be no stopping place short of the point at which *all* motives become intelligible to anyone with a moderately good imagination and sense of analogy. The important thing is not that the sick criminal's motives may seem unintelligible, but rather that they are unintelligible in a certain respect or for a certain reason.

We get closer to the heart of the matter, I think, if we say that the mentally ill criminal's motives are unintelligible because they are irrational – not just unreasonable, but *irrational*. All voluntary wrongdoing, of course, is unreasonable. It is always unreasonable conduct to promote one's own good at another's expense, to be cruel, deceitful, or unfair. But in a proper sense of "rational," made familiar by economists and lawyers, wrongdoing, though unreasonable, can be perfectly rational. A wrongdoer might well calculate his own interests, and gains and risks thereto, and decide to advance them at another's expense, without making a single intellectual mistake. A rational motive, in the present sense, is simply a *self-interested* motive, or perhaps an intelligently self-interested one. The motives of mentally ill criminals are not usually very self-interested. The Supreme Court of Iowa, in overturning the conviction of young McCullough, held that the question for the jury should have been: did the accused steal because of a mental disease driving him by "an insane and irresistible impulse" to steal, or did he commit said acts "through excessive greed or avarice?" The Court's alternatives are not exhaustive. Very likely McCullough's impulses were neither irresistible nor "greedy and avaricious." Greed and avarice are forms of selfishness, excessive desires for material goods and riches for oneself. As motives they are preeminently self-interested and "rational." McCullough's sick desires, however, were not for his own good, material or otherwise. He stole objects that could do him no good at all and assumed irrational risks in the process. The desire to steal and hoard these useless trinkets was a genuine enough desire, and it was *his* desire; but it does not follow that it was a desire to promote his own good.

This point too, however, can be overstated. It may well be true that none of the mentally ill crimes we are considering is done from a self-interested motive, but this feature hardly distinguishes them (yet) from a wide variety of voluntary crimes of great blameworthiness committed by perfectly normal criminals. By no means all voluntary crimes by normal criminals are done from the motive of gain. Some are

done to advance or retard a cause, to help a loved one, or to hurt an enemy, often at great cost to the criminal's self-interest. What distinguishes the sick crimes we have been considering is not that they are unself-interested, but rather that they are *not interested at all*. They do not further *any* of the actor's interests, self *or* other-regarding, benevolent or malevolent. The fetishist's shoplifting is not rational and self-serving; he attains no economic objective by it. But neither does it hurt anyone he hates nor help anyone he loves; it neither gains him good will and prestige, nor satisfies his conscience, nor fulfills his ideals. It is, in short, not interested behavior.

But even this distinction does not quite get to the very core of the matter. The fetishist's behavior not only fails to be interested; it fails even to appear interested to him. To be sure, it is designed to fulfill the desire which is its immediate motive; but fulfillment of desire is not necessarily the same thing as abiding satisfaction. He may be gratified or relieved for an instant, but this kind of fulfillment of desire leaves only the taste of ashes in one's mouth. The important point is that his behavior tends to be *contrary to interest, as senseless* almost as the repetitive beating of one's head against an unyielding stone wall. Bishop Butler was one of the first to point out how profoundly misleading it is to call such behavior "self-indulgent" simply because it appears voluntary, fulfills the actor's own desire, and leads to an instant's satisfaction before a torrent of guilt and anxiety. One might as well call the thirsty marooned sailor "self-indulgent" when he drinks deeply of the sea water that will surely dry him out further, as he well knows.

I believe there is a tendency in human nature, quite opposite to the one I have already mentioned, to consider the senselessness of a crime a kind of moral aggravation. That a cruel crime seemed pointless or senseless, a source of no gain to anyone, makes the harm it caused seem in the most absolute sense *unnecessary*, and that rubs salt in our psychic wounds. The harm was *all for nothing*, we lament, as if an intelligible motive would make our wounds any less injurious or the wounder less blameable. What happens, I think, is that the senselessness of a crime, particularly when it seems contrary to the criminal's interest, is profoundly frustrating. We are naturally disposed to be angry at the selfishly cruel, the ruthlessly self-aggrandizing man; but that anger is frustrated when we learn that the criminal, for no reason *he* could understand, was hurting *himself* as well as his victim. That is simply not the way properly self-respecting wicked persons are supposed to behave! But then we become angry at him precisely because we cannot be angry in the usual ways. We blame him now for our own frustration – not only for the harm he has caused, but for his not getting anything out of it. Indignation will always out.

Still, in a calmer reflective moment, punishment of the pitiably odd is likely to seem a kind of "pouring it on." Indeed, we might well say of such people what the more forgiving Epictetus said of all wrongdoers, that they are sufficiently punished simply to be the sorts of persons they are. Their crimes are obviously profitless to themselves and serve no apparent other-regarding interest, either malevolent or benevolent. Thus if the point of punishment is to take the profit out of crime, it is superfluous to impose it upon them.

Not only are the motives of some mentally ill but noncompulsive wrongdoers *senseless*, they are senseless in the special way that permits us to speak of them as *incoherent*. Their motives do not fit together and make a coherent whole because one kind of desire, conspicuous as a sore thumb, keeps getting in the way. These desires serve ill the rest of their important interests, including their overriding interest in personal integration and internal harmony. They "gum up the works," as we would say of machinery, and throw the person out of "proper working order." The reason they do is that, insofar as these desires are fulfilled, barriers are put in the paths of the others. They are inconsistent with the others in that it is impossible for all to be jointly satisfied, even though it is possible that the others could, in principle, be satisfied together. Moreover, the "senseless" desires, because they do not cohere, are likely to seem alien, not fully expressive of their owner's essential character.[4] When a person acts to satisfy them, it is as if he were acting on somebody else's desires. And, indeed, the alien desires may have a distinct kind of unifying character of their own, as if a new person were grafted on to the old one.

The final and perhaps most important feature common to the examples of voluntary crimes by mentally ill persons is the actor's *lack of insight into his own motives*. The normal person, in rehearsing the possibilities open to him, finds some prospects appealing and others repugnant, and he usually (but not always) knows what it is about a given prospect that makes it appealing or repugnant. If robbing a bank appeals to him, the reason may be that the excitement, the romance, or (far more likely) the money attracts him; and if having more money appeals to him, he usually knows *why* it does too. Normal persons, to be sure, can be mistaken. A criminal may think it is the adventure that is attracting him, instead of the money, or vice versa. It is easy enough to be confused about these things. Often enough we can test our understanding of our own motives by experimental methods. I may think that prospect X, which has characteristics a, b, and c, appeals to me solely because of a; but then, to my surprise, prospect Y, which has characteristics a and b, but not c, *repels* me. Hence I conclude that it was not simply the a-ness of X after all that attracted me. Moreover, even a person who is a model of mental health will be often ignorant or mistaken about the *ultimate* basis of appeal in the things that appeal to him.

The mentally ill person, however, will be radically and fundamentally benighted about the source of the appeal in his immediate objectives, and the truth will be hid from his view by an internal iron curtain. He may think that he is constructed in such a way that little children arouse him sexually, and that is the end of the matter, hardly suspecting that it is the playful, exploratory, irresponsible, and non-threatening character of his recollected childhood experiences that moves him; or he may think that "exposure for exposure's sake" is what appeals to him in the idea of public undress, whereas really what appeals to him is the public "affirmation of masculinity, a cry of 'Look, here is proof I am a man.'"[5] The true basis of appeal in the criminal's motivation may be, or become, obvious to an outsider, but his illness keeps him blind to it, often, I think, because this blindness is a necessary condition of the appeal itself. At any rate, his lack of self-awareness is no merely contingent thing, like the ignorance that can be charged to absentmindedness, unperceptiveness, objective ambiguities, or the garden varieties of self-deception. The ignorance is the necessary consequence, perhaps even a constituent, of the mental illness, which, taken as a collection of interconnected symptoms, is an alien condition involuntarily suffered.

III

We come back to our original question, then, in a new guise: why should the incoherent and self-concealed character of the mentally ill man's motives be a ground for special consideration when he has voluntarily committed a crime? Perhaps we should enlarge our conception of *compulsion* so that senseless, misunderstood motives automatically count as compulsive. If Jones's chronic desire to do something harmful is as powerful as, but no more powerful than, normal people's desires to do socially acceptable things, then we might think of Jones's desire as a kind of unfair burden. It is no harder for him to restrain on individual occasions, but he must be restraining it *always*; one slip and he is undone. He is really quite unlucky to have this greater burden and danger. The ordinary person is excused when he is made to do what he does not want to do; but the mentally ill man, the argument might go, is excused because of the compulsive weight of his profitless *wants* themselves.

There may be some justice in this argument, but there is little logic. When we begin to tamper this profoundly with the concept of compulsion, it is likely to come completely apart. If men can be said to be compelled by their own quite resistible desires, then what is there left to contrast compulsion with?

A more plausible move is to enlarge our conception of what it is to act "in ignorance" – the other category in the Aristotelian formula. The kleptomaniac and the fetishist have no conception of what it is that drives them to their bizarre actions. As we have seen, their conduct may well seem as puzzling to themselves as to any observer. So there is a sense in which they do not know, or realize, what it is they are really doing, and perhaps we should make this ignorance a ground for exculpation; but if we do, we shall be

in danger of providing a defense for almost all criminals, normal and ill alike. The bank robber, who is deceived into thinking that it is the adventure that appeals to him when it really is the money, has this excuse available to him, as well as the bully who thinks he inflicts beatings in self-defense when it really is the sight of blood that appeals to him. Lack of insight by itself, then, can hardly be a workable extension of the ignorance defense in courts of law.

It is plain, I think, why the penal law requires rather strict interpretations of compulsion and ignorance. One of its major aims is to deter wrongdoers by providing them with a motive, namely, fear of punishment, which they would not otherwise have for refraining from crime. In close cases involving competent calculators, this new motive might be sufficient to tip the motivational scales toward self-restraint. Mentally ill but rationally competent offenders of the sort I have been discussing, provided only that they *can* restrain themselves, are eminently suited for responsibility because the fear of punishment might make some difference in their behavior. But if they truly cannot help what they do, then the fear of punishment is totally useless and might as well not be induced in them in the first place.

Thus, from the point of view of what punishment can achieve for others, it is a perfectly appropriate mode of treatment for rationally competent, noncompulsive, mentally ill persons. But from the point of view of what can be achieved for the offender himself, I still think it is altogether inappropriate. Some of the aims of an enlightened criminal law, after all, do concern the offender himself. Sometimes punishment is supposed to "reform" him by intimidation. This no doubt works once in a while for normally prudent and self-interested offenders. For others, greater claims still are made for punishment, which is expected to achieve not merely effective intimidation but also moral regeneration of the offender. But if we treat the mentally ill criminal in precisely the same way as we treat the normal one, we can only bring him to the point of hopeless despair. The prisoner, still devoid of insight into his own motives, will naturally come to wonder how his so-called illness differs from plain wickedness. His bizarre desires will be taken as simply "given," as evil impulses with no point and no reward, simply "there," an integral and irreducible part of himself; and there is no one more pitiably incorrigible than the man convinced of his own intrinsic wickedness and simply resigned to it.

I agree with Professor Dershowitz that it is outrageous to impose compulsory therapeutic treatment on an unwilling, mentally competent subject. I submit, however, that punishment imposed on the mentally ill, even though it might produce a small social gain in deterrence, is an equally odious measure. I admit that, insofar as the sick offender has voluntarily committed a crime he could have avoided, the state has a perfect right to deprive him of his liberty for a limited period; but, instead of using that time to have him break up rocks with the convicted embezzlers and burglars, we should be making every sympathetic effort to enable him to understand himself, in the hope that self-revelation will permit him to become a responsible citizen.[6] There is no easy way to avoid the problems that come from the institutional mixture of compulsion and therapy. I am afraid I must leave them for my legal and psychiatric friends. My aim in this paper has been the very limited one of showing that mental illness, even without compulsion and general cognitive impairment, is a good deal more pertinent to our moral concerns than the mumps or chicken pox.

Notes

1 Alan M. Dershowitz, "The Psychiatrist's Power in Civil Commitment: A Knife that Cuts Both Ways." An abridged version of this talk was published in *Psychology Today*, 2/9 (Feb. 1969), 43–7.

2 Consider Professor Dershowitz's example of Dallas Williams, "who at age thirty-nine had spent half his life in jail for seven convictions of assault with a deadly weapon and one conviction of manslaughter. Just before his scheduled release from jail, the government petitioned for his civil commitment. Two psychiatrists testified that although 'at the present time [he] shows no evidence of active mental illness . . . his is potentially dangerous to others and if released is likely to repeat his patterns of criminal behavior, and might commit homicide.' The judge, in denying the government's petition and ordering Williams' release, observed that: 'the courts have no legal basis for ordering confinement on mere apprehension of future unlawful acts. They must wait until another crime is committed or the person is found insane.' Within months of his release, Williams lived up to the prediction of the psychiatrists and shot two men to death in an unprovoked attack." *Ibid.*, 44.

3 Note on "Civil Restraint, Mental Illness, and the Right to Treatment," *Yale Law Review*, 77/1 (1967), 87.

4 Hence the point of the ancient metaphor of "possession."

5 Paul H. Gebhard et al., *Report on Sex Offenders* (New York: Harper & Row, and Paul B. Hoeber, 1965), 399.

6 I.e., he is clutchable, but not necessarily punishable.

Questions for Discussion

1 Is the plot of *Minority Report* consistent with genuine human freedom? Compare and contrast how a hard determinist, a libertarian, and a compatibilist would answer that question.

2 If in *Minority Report*, the pre-cogs are able to know which people would commit crimes in the future (if not apprehended in advance), would it make sense to hold them responsible for what they would have done? Would people, in such circumstances, be deserving of punishment?

3 What assumptions about the causal determinants of human behavior was Mengele making in his attempt to make junior Hitlers in *The Boys from Brazil*? Do you think that his assumptions are correct? Were the assumptions falsified by the actions of the boy in the climactic scenes (chapters 28–30)?

4 Suppose that Mengele was correct about the determination of human action in *The Boys from Brazil*. Would Hume regard the junior Hitlers (or any other person, for that matter) as free and therefore as responsible? Do you agree with Hume?

5 In *A Clockwork Orange* protestors complained that the kind of conditioning that Alex underwent is morally objectionable because it deprives people of freedom. Do you think that the conditioning rendered Alex unfree in some important sense? How would a libertarian, a hard determinist, or a compatibilist assess that claim?

6 Compare and contrast the defense strategies used in *Compulsion* and in *Law and Order*. If those defenses are valid, what wider implications do they have for human responsibility and moral agency?

7 Do you believe that any of the defendants in either *Compulsion* or *Law and Order* were mentally ill? Why or why not? If they were, does this make them less responsible or even not responsible? Does it make them less free or even unfree?

8 In *The Omen*, the photographer's photographs contain images that supposedly foretell how the individual pictured will die. If the photographs genuinely foretell someone's death, is it futile for the photographer, for example, to attempt to prevent his own death? Is there any difference between living in a world in which photographs foretell death and living in a world in which there are now truths about what one will do and how one will die?

Part VII

Philosophy of Religion

Films:
Jason and the Argonauts
Star Trek V: The Final Frontier
Dogma
YouTube: Mr Deity and the Evil

Introduction

The question of whether there is a God, and, if there is, what that God is like, is one that has occupied center stage since the inception of philosophical thought. While the most fundamental metaphysical question in philosophy of religion concerns God's existence, that question, of course, immediately raises the epistemological questions of how one could know, or justifiably believe either that there is or isn't such a being.

Blaise Pascal seems to suggest that we needn't worry all that much about epistemological questions in order to reach the conclusion that we should believe in the existence of God. In "The Wager," he offers, in effect, a pragmatic reason for believing in the existence of God. On one standard interpretation, a pragmatic reason for having a belief is a reason constituted by some relevant goal or end that would or might be achieved by having the belief. So, for example, if believing that I'll get well increases the chances that I will, that might give me a reason for doing what I can to bring about that belief. Similarly, Pascal argues that given a reasonable person's goals or ends, that person will do what he or she can to bring about belief in God. We take fire insurance out on our homes because we realize that however unlikely it is that our house burns down, the enormous cost to us of that occurring requires us to protect our well-being with an insurance policy that protects us against what would be an otherwise devastating loss. If we take fire insurance out on our homes, surely we should take eternal damnation insurance out on

our souls. It may be unlikely that there is a God who will punish atheists, but it surely isn't worth taking the chance of suffering for eternity or forgoing eternal bliss, particularly given that it isn't so very onerous to believe (Pascal thinks one will actually gain important side benefits even if one believes falsely). The classic response to Pascal's argument involves pointing out that there are other possible Gods besides the one who will reward those theists in the Judeo-Christian tradition. If there is a God, for example, who particularly resents those nagging theists constantly petitioning him for favors, the atheist might have the last laugh on all those theists who were bound and determined to avoid the torments of hell. It looks as if it might not be all that easy for Pascal to avoid epistemological questions concerning at least the comparative likelihood of hypotheses about the nature of God (a question raised by the films we discuss below).

Turning to epistemological questions (questions about reasons for believing, which, if good, make likely the truth of what is believed), there are three classical arguments for the existence of a God. One is the Cosmological or "First Cause" argument (see the selection by William L. Rowe). Its least charitable version is as follows:

(1) Everything must have a cause.
(2) Either there are causal chains that extend infinitely into the past or there is a first cause (of the sort that theists identify with God).

(3)   Causal chains cannot extend infinitely into the past.

Therefore,

(4)   There was a first cause – God.

It can hardly escape the attention of anyone that the conclusion of the argument seems to ignore its first premise. If everything needs a cause that why wouldn't this God who is posited as the "first" cause, also need a cause?

A more charitable version of the argument makes a distinction between kinds of things that need, or even could have causes, and kinds of things that don't need, and perhaps couldn't have causes:

(1)   Everything that comes into existence (that has a beginning) must have a cause.
(2)   Causal chains whose links are events that have beginnings cannot extend infinitely into the past.
(3)   If (1) and (2), then there must be a "first" cause understood as something that is eternal, that has no beginning, even though it sets in motion (creates) causal chains.

Therefore,

(4)   There is an eternal first cause – God.

The revised cosmological argument is itself hardly uncontroversial. Many wonder why we should assume that everything requires a cause. Others would deny that there is anything problematic about a causal chain extending infinitely into the past. And still others question the intelligibility of something eternal causing something to begin. On this last question, a great deal hinges on the interpretation of "eternal." Some theists want God to be *outside* of time itself. And some of those theists want God to be something that doesn't *change*. On certain plausible views about causal connection it is unclear how an unchanging being outside of time can cause things to happen within time.

It's interesting to note that the argument for a "first" cause seems to leave open, formally at least, the precise nature of that cause. Many contemporary theists who are broadly in the Judeo-Christian tradition seem to take for granted that if there is a God, that God would have to be perfect – omnipotent, omniscient, and omnibenevolent, and the kind of being worthy of worship. But even if there were an entity or being that was eternal, perhaps outside of time (if that makes sense), causally responsible for everything else that exists, why should we assume that such a being would be perfect? Why should we even assume that such an entity would have a conscious mind? The second question might seem to be addressed by another prominent argument for the existence of God, the argument from design, but the first question may remain:

(1)   The natural world seems to exhibit a wondrous and intricate design – organisms, for example, have parts that work together in complicated ways to help the organisms function effectively in a wide range of environments (much the way the parts of human artifacts are designed to work together to achieve a goal or end).
(2)   The best explanation of (1) is that the natural world has a designer.

Therefore,

(3)   The natural world has a designer – God.

As presented the argument is highly compressed. One would like to know a great deal more about how one evaluates competing explanations for a given phenomenon. Even if we suppose that we have clear criteria for choosing among alternative explanations, the argument from design is, of course, highly controversial. Many would argue that natural selection explains perfectly well all the appearance of "design." Others wonder why the God that is posited as designer would Himself not exhibit all the marks of a designed entity, thus generating a regress of designers. Hume raises many of the above objections to both the cosmological argument and the argument from design, and he also wonders why we should assume that even if there is a designer that designer would be perfect.

Indeed, of the three most famous arguments for the existence of God, only the ontological argument seems specifically designed to establish the existence of a *perfect* being. It is also an argument that strikes most students (and many professional philosophers) as decidedly odd. A version of the argument goes as follows:

(1) God is *by definition* perfect. (Alternatively, on some versions: The very concept or idea of God is the concept or idea of a perfect being; or, a perfect being exists "in the mind.")

(2) A perfect being is a being greater than which cannot be conceived.

(3) A being that necessarily exists is a being that is greater than a being that just happens to exist.

(4) If (1), (2), and (3), then God necessarily exists.

(5) If God necessarily exists, then God exists. Therefore,

(6) God exists.

Needless to say, many philosophers find the argument more than a bit problematic. The critical premise is probably the first. Compare the claim about God's perfection to other claims that are true by definition, the claim that bachelors are unmarried, for example. From the fact that it is true by definition that bachelors are unmarried, it doesn't follow that there *are* any bachelors. From the fact that we have the concept of a bachelor, it doesn't follow that there are any bachelors. From the fact that bachelors exist "in the mind," it doesn't follow that there are any bachelors. The more perspicuous statement of the proposition that seems to be necessary is the following:

If there are any bachelors *then* they are unmarried.

But the analogous interpretation of premise (1) in the ontological argument would be:

(1*) *If* there is a God *then* that God is perfect.

The additional premises the argument needs, the critic says, should also all be rendered as conditionals:

(2*) *If* there is a perfect being *then* that being necessarily exists.

(3*) *If* there is a being that necessarily exists, *then* that being exists.

But one won't get from conditional premises of this sort anything but a conditional conclusion. One won't get the conclusion that God exists.

One might instead treat the expression "God" as it appears in premise (1) as a disguised definite description. Bertrand Russell argued that almost all ordinary proper names are equivalent in meaning to definite descriptions (descriptions that begin with the definite article, e.g. "*the* tallest person in the NBA"). He advanced this view in part because he wanted to allow that we can meaningfully use a name that fails to refer, e.g. "Santa Claus left me presents." We can't view the meaning of the name "Santa Claus" as the person referred to and still think that we have succeeded in making an assertion, albeit a false assertion, about Santa Claus leaving presents. On Russell's view, a statement of the form "The F is G" means something like "There exists one and only one thing that is F and that thing is G." If we treat "God" as having a meaning captured by a definite description, say, "the perfect being who is causally responsible for all finite reality," then the first premise of the ontological argument becomes:

(1**) There *exists* one and only one thing that is perfect and that thing is perfect!

According to the atheist, the proponent of an ontological argument with (1**) as a premise has just begged the question as to whether there is or isn't a God.

Whether or not one can defend a version of the ontological argument, one can see that it does at least speak to the question of whether the God posited in the conclusion is perfect. As we saw earlier, neither the cosmological argument nor the argument from design seems to address head on the question of why God needs to be considered perfect. In *Jason and the Argonauts* we are presented with not one, but the full array of ancient Greek Gods. They are clearly more powerful than human beings and have the ability to interfere successfully with the various projects we have. In *Dogma*, the fallen angels have a decidedly jaded view of the character of a God whom they view as unforgiving and vindictive (chapters 2–3 and 6). Furthermore, that God seems hardly omniscient or omnipotent. Would or should the existence of the "God" or "Gods" portrayed in these films fill the role of the being whose existence is asserted in the conclusions of the cosmological argument and the argument from design?

There might be an added bonus for a theist who asserts only the existence of a less than perfect God. One of the most powerful arguments against the existence of God points to the problem of evil. One can get a feel for the problem (albeit through a somewhat irreverent skit) in *Mr Deity and the Evil*. God's assistant Larry is running through the various evils that "Mr Deity" will allow. Mr Deity's decisions puzzle even his faithful assistant and are bound to puzzle most of us. More formally, the argument from evil against the existence of a perfect God goes something like this:

(1) If a perfect (omnipotent, omniscient, omnibenevolent) God exists, then there would be no evil.
(2) There is evil.
Therefore,
(3) A perfect God does not exist.

To be sure, there are possible replies to the argument. One familiar response to evil is the classic "God works in mysterious ways." Expanded, the comment presumably challenges our ability to fathom the reasons a being so very different from us might have to bring about or allow what we take to be evil. Another classic response to the problem of evil involves the free will defense. Even God cannot be expected to do the impossible. God created us with the ability to make free choices because a creature with freedom of this sort is better than one without such freedom. But the necessary price for allowing us this freedom is that we can use it badly. Much of the evil that exists can be laid at the feet of people who have exercised their freedom to choose evil. It's not clear that an imaginative enough God couldn't allow relevant freedom of choice and somehow insure that bad consequences don't flow from bad decisions. But even if we grant the free will defense, there is the obvious problem of natural evil. Earthquakes, cancer, hurricanes, and the like seem to have nothing to do with the decisions of people, but wreak havoc on the well-being of men, women, and children. Alvin Plantinga has suggested that we can't assume that humans are the only conscious beings that God created and that natural disasters might be the result of free choices made by creatures with quite different powers (the fallen angels of *Dogma*, perhaps).

Another intriguing response to the problem of evil suggests that once God creates a less than perfect world (something that would be required given the alleged impossibility of having more than one perfect being), it was *impossible* for God to create the best possible world. It is then foolish to complain about the world He *did* create. Consider an analogy. Suppose a God-like being grants you the power to give your best friend whatever amount of money you specify in the next five seconds. You come up with $1,000,000,000. Your friend, if churlish, could complain that there are infinitely many larger amounts that you could have named. But, of course, for *any* amount you named *that* was true. God, the argument goes, was in the same position with respect to the creation of a world and you would be as churlish as your friend to complain about the world you got.

The problem of evil presents at least a serious challenge to the theist who argues for the existence of a perfect God. If God is less than perfect, however, there is no problem of evil. A God who is neither all-good, all-knowing, or all-powerful might simply be unable to prevent evil, or have no particular *interest* in preventing it. If a God or Gods like those portrayed in *Jason and the Argonauts* exist, they might find the spectacle of humans in conflict somewhat entertaining. Indeed, that might explain nicely why we were created – perhaps we are a soap opera on a grand scale to keep the Gods amused.

There is, though, a conceptual price one pays for allowing that "God" can be less than perfect. In particular, it is no longer clear just exactly what *makes* a being a God. Suppose, for example, that the earth and the seeds of life on it were created by very powerful aliens from another planet. Would that make those beings Gods? One might argue that nothing much hinges on the meaning of a word, but if one conceptually ties being a God to being the kind of entity deserving of worship and praise – the kind of being radically distinct from anything one could encounter as a powerful alien on another planet – one might be again driven to define that God as perfect. These questions come to the fore in *Star Trek V*. In the film, the *Enterprise* is hijacked by a cult leader on a search for God. Toward the end of the movie, it actually looks for a while as if they succeeded in their quest. They do, indeed, find a very powerful being on a distant planet (chapters 11–14). It turns out that the being had a bit of a temper and they quickly decide it is anything but a God. But if one doesn't require of Gods that they be perfect, it is not all that clear *why* the being they discovered wasn't still a plausible candidate for a deity. The God of the Old Testament, after all, had a bit of a temper as well.

49

The Wager

Blaise Pascal

Infinity, nothingness.

———

Our soul is cast into the body, where it finds number, time, dimensions; it reasons about these things and calls them nature, necessity, and can believe nothing else.

———

Unity added to infinity does not increase infinity at all, any more than a foot added to an infinite length. The finite is annihilated in the presence of the infinite and becomes pure nothingness. So it is with our mind before God, with our justice before divine justice. Yet the disproportion between our justice and God's justice is not as great as that between unity and infinity.

———

God's justice must be as vast as his mercy. Now, his justice toward the damned is less vast and should be less shocking to us than his mercy toward the chosen.

———

We know that there is an infinite, but do not know its nature, just as we know it to be false that numbers are finite. It is therefore true that there is an infinite in number, but we do not know what it is. It is false that it is even, false that it is odd, for the addition of a unit does not change its nature. Yet it is a number, and every number is odd or even. (It is true that this is understood of every finite number.)

So, we may well know that there is a God without knowing what he is.

Is there no substantial truth, seeing that there are so many true things that are not truth itself?

———

We know then the existence and nature of the finite, because we also are finite and have extension.

We know the existence of the infinite and do not know its nature, because it has extension like us, but not limits like us.

But we do not know either the existence or the nature of God, because he has neither extension nor limits.

———

But by faith we know his existence. In glory we shall know his nature.

Now, I have already shown that we can know the existence of a thing without knowing its nature.

Let us now speak according to our natural lights.

If there is a God, he is infinitely incomprehensible, since, having neither parts nor limits, he bears no relation to us. We are therefore incapable of knowing either what he is or whether he is. This

From Blaise Pascal, *Pensées*, ed. and trans. Roger Ariew (Indianapolis: Hackett Publishing Co, 2005), pp. 211–15. ©

being so, who will dare undertake to resolve the question? Not we, who bear no relation to him.

Who then will blame Christians for not being able to give rational grounds for their belief, they who profess a religion for which they cannot give rational grounds?

They declare, in proclaiming it to the world, that it is a folly – *stultitiam*[1] – and then you complain that they do not prove it! If they proved it, they would not be keeping their word. It is by lacking proofs that they are not lacking sense. "Yes, but although this excuses those who offer their religion in this way and removes the blame of putting it forward without rational grounds, it does not excuse those who accept it."

Let us then examine this point and say: either God is or he is not. But to which side shall we incline? Reason can determine nothing here. There is an infinite chaos that separates us. At the extremity of this infinite distance, a game is being played in which heads or tails will turn up. How will you wager? You have no rational grounds for choosing either way or for rejecting either alternative.

Do not, then, blame as wrong those who have made a choice, for you know nothing of the matter! "No, but I will blame them for having made, not this choice, but a choice. For although the player who chooses heads is no more at fault than the other one, they are both in the wrong. The right thing is not to wager at all."

Yes; but you must wager. It is not optional. You are committed. Which will you choose, then? Let us see. Since you must choose, let us see what is the less profitable option. You have two things to lose, the true and the good; and two things to stake, your reason and your will, your knowledge and your beatitude; and your nature has two things to avoid, error and wretchedness. Since you must necessarily choose, your reason is no more offended by choosing one rather than the other. This settles one point. But your beatitude? Let us weigh the gain and the loss in calling heads that God exists. Let us assess the two cases. If you win, you win everything; if you lose, you lose nothing. Wager, then, without hesitation that he exists! "This is wonderful. Yes, I must wager. But perhaps I am wagering too much." Let us see: since there is an equal chance of winning and losing, if there were two lives to win for one, you could still wager. But if there were three lives to win,

you would have to play (since you must necessarily play), and it would be foolish, when you are forced to play, not to risk your life to win three at a game in which there is an equal chance of losing and winning. But there is an eternity of life and happiness. This being so, if there were an infinity of chances, and only one in your favor, it would still be right to wager one life in order to win two; and, being obliged to play, you would be making the wrong choice if you refused to stake one life against three in a game in which, out of an infinity of chances, there is only one in your favor, if there were an infinite life of infinite happiness to be won. But here there is an infinite life of infinite happiness to be won, there is one chance of winning against a finite number of chances of losing, and what you are staking is finite. All bets are off wherever there is an infinity and wherever there is not an infinite number of chances of losing against the chance of winning. There is no time to hesitate; you must give everything. And thus, when you are forced to play, you must be renouncing reason to preserve life, instead of risking it for an infinite gain, which is as likely to happen as is a loss amounting to nothing.

It is no use saying that it is uncertain whether you will win, that it is certain you are taking a risk, and that the infinite distance between the *certainty* of what you are risking and the *uncertainty* of what you stand to gain makes the finite good you are certainly staking equal to the infinite good that is uncertain. It is not so. All players take a certain risk for an uncertain gain; and yet they take a certain finite risk for an uncertain finite gain without sinning against reason. It is not true that there is an infinite distance between the certain risk and the uncertain gain. Indeed, there is an infinity between the certainty of winning and the certainty of losing. But the uncertainty of winning is proportional to the certainty of the risk, in proportion to the chances of winning and losing. Hence, if there are as many chances on one side as on the other, you are playing for even odds, and then the certainty of what you are risking is equal to the uncertainty of what you may win – so far is it from being infinitely distant. Thus our proposition is infinitely powerful, when the stakes are finite in a game where the chances of winning and losing are even, and the infinite is to be won.

This is conclusive and if people are capable of any truth, this is it.

"I confess it, I admit it. But, still . . . Is there no means of seeing what is in the cards?" Yes, Scripture and the rest, etc. "Yes, but my hands are tied and my mouth is shut; I am forced to wager, and am not free. I have not been released and I am made in such a way that I cannot believe. What, then, would you have me do?" That is true. But at least realize that your inability to believe comes from your passions, since reason brings you to this and yet you cannot believe. Work, then, on convincing yourself, not by adding more proofs of God's existence, but by diminishing your passions. You would like to find faith and do not know the way? You would like to be cured of unbelief and ask for the remedies? Learn from those who were bound like you, and who now wager all they have. These are people who know the way you wish to follow, and who are cured of the illness of which you wish to be cured. Follow the way by which they began: they acted as if they believed, took holy water, had masses said, etc. This will make you believe naturally and mechanically.[2] "But this is what I am afraid of." And why? What do you have to lose? But to show you that this is the way, this diminishes the passions, which are your great obstacles, etc.

"Oh! This discourse moves me, charms me, etc." If this discourse pleases you and seems cogent, know that it is made by a man who has knelt, both before and after it, in prayer to that being, infinite and without parts, before whom he submits all he has, so that he might bring your being to submit all you have for your own good and for his glory, and that thus strength may be reconciled with this lowliness.

End of This Discourse

Now, what harm will come to you by taking this side? You will be faithful, honest, humble, grateful, generous, a sincere, true friend. Certainly you will not be taken by unhealthy pleasures, by glory and by luxury, but will you not have others?

I tell you that as a result you will gain in this life, and that, at each step you take on this road, you will see such a great certainty of gain and so much nothingness in what you risk, that you will at last recognize that you have wagered for something certain and infinite, for which you have given nothing.

——

We owe a great debt to those who point out faults. For they mortify us. They teach us that we have been despised. They do not prevent our being so in the future, for we have many other faults for which we may be despised. They prepare for us the exercise of correction and freedom from a fault.

——

Custom is our nature. He who is accustomed to faith believes it, can no longer fear hell, and cannot believe anything else. He who is accustomed to believe that the king is terrible, etc. Who doubts, then, that our soul, being accustomed to see number, space, and motion, believes that and nothing else?

——

Do you believe it to be impossible that God is infinite, without parts? Yes. I wish, therefore, to show you an image of God and his immensity, an infinite and indivisible thing: it is a point moving everywhere with infinite speed.

For it is one in all places and completely whole in every location.

Let this effect of nature, which previously seemed impossible to you, allow you to understand that there may be others you still do not know. Do not draw the conclusion from your experiment that there remains nothing for you to learn, but rather that there remains an infinity for you to learn.

It is false that we are worthy of the love of others; it is unfair that we should want it. If we were born reasonable and indifferent, knowing ourselves and others, we would not give this inclination to our will. However, we are born with it. Therefore we are born unfair. For all tends to self; this is contrary to all order. We must tend to the general, and the tendency to self is the beginning of all disorder, in war, politics, economy, and man's particular body.

The will is therefore depraved. If the members of natural and civil communities tend toward the good of the body, the communities themselves ought to look to another, more general body of which they are members. We should, therefore, tend to the general. We are, therefore, born unfair and depraved.

No religion but our own has taught that man is born in sin. No sect of philosophers has said this. Therefore none has told the truth.

No sect or religion has always existed on earth, save for the Christian religion.

The Christian religion alone makes man altogether *lovable* and *happy*. In polite society we cannot be both lovable and happy.

It is the heart that experiences God, and not reason. Here, then, is faith: God felt by the heart, not by reason.

Notes

1   Paul, I Corinthians 1:18.
2   Pascal's word is *abêtira* – literally, will make you more like the beasts. Man is in part a beast or machine, and one needs to allow that part its proper function: that is, one needs to act dispassionately or mechanically.

50

The Ontological Argument

Anselm

That God Truly Exists

Therefore, Lord, you who grant understanding to faith, grant that, insofar as you know it is useful for me, I may understand that you exist as we believe you exist, and that you are what we believe you to be. Now we believe that you are something than which nothing greater can be thought. So can it be that no such being exists, since "The fool has said in his heart, 'There is no God'"? (Psalm 14:1; 53:1) But when this same fool hears me say "something than which nothing greater can be thought," he surely understands what he hears; and what he understands exists in his understanding,[1] even if he does not understand that it exists [in reality]. For it is one thing for an object to exist in the understanding and quite another to understand that the object exists [in reality]. When a painter, for example, thinks out in advance what he is going to paint, he has it in his understanding, but he does not yet understand that it exists, since he has not yet painted it. But once he has painted it, he both has it in his understanding and understands that it exists because he has now painted it. So even the fool must admit that something than which nothing greater can be thought exists at least in his understanding, since he understands this when he hears it, and whatever is understood exists in the understanding. And surely that than which a greater cannot be thought cannot exist only in the understanding. For if it exists only in the understanding, it can be thought to exist in reality as well, which is greater. So if that than which a greater cannot be thought exists only in the understanding, then that than which a greater cannot be thought is that than which a greater *can* be thought. But that is clearly impossible. Therefore, there is no doubt that something than which a greater cannot be thought exists both in the understanding and in reality.

That He Cannot Be Thought Not to Exist

This [being] exists so truly that it cannot be thought not to exist. For it is possible to think that something exists that cannot be thought not to exist, and such a being is greater than one that can be thought not to exist. Therefore, if that than which a greater cannot be thought can be thought not to exist, then that than which a greater cannot be thought is *not* that than which a greater cannot be thought; and this is a contradiction. So that than which a greater cannot

Anselm, "The Ontological Argument," from *Proslogion: With the Replies of Gaunilo and Anselm*, trans. Thomas Williams (Indianapolis: Hackett Publishing Co., 2001), pp. 7–9. Translation © 2001 by Hackett Publishing Company, Inc. Reprinted by permission of Hackett Publishing Company, Inc. All rights reserved.

be thought exists so truly that it cannot be thought not to exist.

And this is you, O Lord our God. You exist so truly, O Lord my God, that you cannot be thought not to exist. And rightly so, for if some mind could think something better than you, a creature would rise above the Creator and sit in judgment upon him, which is completely absurd. Indeed, everything that exists, except for you alone, can be thought not to exist. So you alone among all things have existence most truly, and therefore most greatly. Whatever else exists has existence less truly, and therefore less greatly. So then why did "the fool say in his heart, 'There is no God,'" when it is so evident to the rational mind that you of all beings exist most greatly? Why indeed, except because he is stupid and a fool?

How the Fool Said in his Heart What Cannot be Thought

But how has he said in his heart what he could not think? Or how could he not think what he said in his heart, since to say in one's heart is the same as to think? But if he really – or rather, *since* he really – thought this, because he said it in his heart, and did not say it in his heart, because he could not think it, there must be more than one way in which something is 'said in one's heart' or 'thought'. In one sense of the word, to think

a thing is to think the word that signifies that thing. But in another sense, it is to understand what exactly the thing is. God can be thought not to exist in the first sense, but not at all in the second sense. No one who understands what God is can think that God does not exist, although he may say these words in his heart with no signification at all, or with some peculiar signification. For God is that than which a greater cannot be thought. Whoever understands this properly, understands that this being exists in such a way that he cannot, even in thought, fail to exist. So whoever understands that God exists in this way cannot think that he does not exist.

Thanks be to you, my good Lord, thanks be to you. For what I once believed through your grace, I now understand through your illumination, so that even if I did not want to *believe* that you exist, I could not fail to *understand* that you exist.

Note

1 The word here translated "understanding" is "*intellectus.*" The text would perhaps read better if I translated it as "intellect," but this would obscure the fact that it is from the same root as the verb "*intelligere,*" "to understand." Some of what Anselm says makes a bit more sense if this fact is constantly borne in mind.

51

The Cosmological and Design Arguments

William L. Rowe

The Traditional Cosmological Argument

[...]

Arguments for the existence of God are commonly divided into *a posteriori* arguments and *a priori* arguments. An *a posteriori* argument depends on a principle or premise that can be known only by means of our experience of the world. An *a priori* argument, on the other hand, purports to rest on principles all of which can be known independently of our experience of the world, by just reflecting on and understanding them. Of the three major arguments for the existence of God – the Cosmological, the Design, and the Ontological – only the last is entirely *a priori*. In the Cosmological Argument one starts from some simple fact about the world, such as that it contains things which are caused to exist by other things. In the Design Argument a somewhat more complicated fact about the world serves as a starting point, the fact that the world exhibits order and design. In the Ontological Argument, however, one begins simply with a concept of God. [...]

[...]

The first part of the eighteenth-century form of the Cosmological Argument seeks to establish the existence of a self-existent being. The second part of the argument attempts to prove that the self-existent being is the theistic God – that is, has the features which we have noted to be basic elements in the theistic idea of God. We shall consider mainly the first part of the argument, for it is against the first part that philosophers from Hume to Bertrand Russell have advanced very important objections.

In stating the first part of the Cosmological Argument we shall make use of two important concepts: the concept of a *dependent being* and the concept of a *self-existent being*. By a *dependent being* we mean *a being whose existence is accounted for by the causal activity of other things*. Recalling Anselm's division into the three cases – "explained by another," "explained by nothing," and "explained by itself" – it's clear that a dependent being is a being whose existence is explained by another. By a *self-existent being* we mean *a being whose existence is accounted for by its own nature*. This idea, as we saw in the preceding chapter, is an essential element in the theistic concept of God. Again, in terms of Anselm's three cases, a self-existent being is a being whose existence is

From William L. Rowe, *Philosophy of Religion: An Introduction*, 4th edn. (Belmont, CA: Wadsworth Thomas Learning, 2007), pp. 19, 21–6, 36, 54–66, 68. © 2007 by Wadsworth, a part of Cengage Learning, Inc. Reproduced by permission. www.cengage.com/permissions.

explained by itself. Armed with these two concepts, the concept of a dependent being and the concept of a self-existent being, we can now state the first part of the Cosmological Argument.

1. Every being (that exists or ever did exist) is either a dependent being or a self-existent being.
2. Not every being can be a dependent being. Therefore,
3. There exists a self-existent being.

Deductive validity

Before we look critically at each of the premises of this argument, we should note that this argument is, to use an expression from the logician's vocabulary, *deductively valid*. To find out whether an argument is deductively valid, we need only ask the question: If its premises were true, would its conclusion have to be true? It the answer is yes, the argument is deductively valid. If the answer is no, the argument is deductively invalid. Notice that the question of the validity of an argument is entirely different from the question of whether its premises are in fact true. The following argument is made up entirely of false statements, but it is deductively valid.

1. Babe Ruth is the president of the United States.
2. The president of the United States is from Indiana. Therefore,
3. Babe Ruth is from Indiana.

The argument is deductively valid because even though its premises are false, if they were true its conclusion would have to be true. Even God, Aquinas would say, cannot bring it about that the premises of this argument are true and yet its conclusion is false, for God's power extends only to what is possible, and it is an absolute impossibility that Babe Ruth be the president, the president be from Indiana, and yet Babe Ruth not be from Indiana.

The Cosmological Argument (that is, its first part) is a deductively valid argument. If its premises are or were true, its conclusion would have to be true. It's clear from our example about Babe Ruth, however, that the fact that an

argument is deductively valid is insufficient to establish the truth of its conclusion. What else is required? Clearly that we know, or have rational grounds for believing, that the premises are true. If we know that the Cosmological Argument is deductively valid, and can establish that its premises are true, we shall thereby have proved that its conclusion is true. Are, then, the premises of the Cosmological Argument true? To this more difficult question we must now turn.

PSR and the first premise

At first glance the first premise might appear to be an obvious or even trivial truth. But it is neither obvious nor trivial. And if it appears to be obvious or trivial, we must be confusing the idea of a self-existent being with the idea of a being that is not a dependent being. Clearly, it is true that any being is either a dependent being (explained by other things) or it is not a dependent being (not explained by other things). But what our premise says is that any being is either a dependent being (explained by other things) or it is a self-existent being (explained by itself). Consider again Anselm's three cases:

1. explained by another
2. explained by nothing
3. explained by itself

What our first premise asserts is that each being that exists (or ever did exist) is either of sort *a* or of sort *c*. It denies that any being is of sort *b*. And it is this denial that makes the first premise both significant and controversial. The obvious truth we must not confuse it with is the truth that any being is either of sort *a* or not of sort *a*. While this is true, it is neither very significant nor controversial.

Earlier we saw that Anselm accepted as a basic principle that whatever exists has an explanation of its existence. Since this basic principle denies that any thing of sort *b* exists or ever did exist, it's clear that Anselm would believe the first premise of our Cosmological Argument. The eighteenth-century proponents of the argument also were convinced of the truth of the basic principle we attributed to Anselm. And because they were convinced of its truth, they readily accepted the first premise of the Cosmological

Argument. But by the eighteenth century, Anselm's basic principle had been more fully elaborated and had received a name, the *Principle of Sufficient Reason*. Since this principle (PSR, as we shall call it) plays such an important role in justifying the premises of the Cosmological Argument, it will help us to consider it for a moment before we continue our inquiry into the truth or falsity of the premises of the Cosmological Argument.

PSR, as it was expressed by both Leibniz and Clarke, is a very general principle and is best understood as having two parts. In its first part it is simply a restatement of Anselm's principle that there must be an explanation of the *existence* of any being whatever. Thus if we come upon a man in a room, PSR implies that there must be an explanation of the fact that that particular man exists. A moment's reflection, however, reveals that there are many facts about the man other than the mere fact that he exists. There is the fact that the man in question is in the room he's in rather than somewhere else, the fact that he is in good health, and the fact that he is at the moment thinking of Paris rather than, say, London. Now the purpose of the second part of PSR is to require an explanation of these facts as well. We may state PSR, therefore, as the principle that *there must be an explanation (a) of the existence of any being and (b) of any positive fact whatever*. We are now in a position to study the role this very important principle plays in the Cosmological Argument.

Since the proponent of the Cosmological Argument accepts PSR in both its parts, it is clear that he will appeal to its first part, PSRa, as justification for the first premise of the Cosmological Argument. Of course, we can and should inquire into the deeper question of whether the proponent of the argument is rationally justified in accepting PSR itself. But we shall put this question aside for the moment. What we need to see first is whether he is correct in thinking that *if* PSR is true then both of the premises of the Cosmological Argument are true. And what we have just seen is that if only the first part of PSR – that is, PSRa – is true, the first premise of the Cosmological Argument will be true. But what of the second premise of the argument? For what reasons does the proponent think that it must be true?

The second premise

According to the second premise, not every being that exists can be a dependent being – that is, can have the explanation of its existence in some other being or beings. Presumably, the proponent of the argument thinks there is something fundamentally wrong with the idea that every being that exists is dependent, that each existing being was caused by some other being which in turn was caused by some other being, and so on. But just what does he think is wrong with it? To help us in understanding his thinking, let's simplify things by supposing that there exists only one thing now, A_1, a living thing perhaps, that was brought into existence by something else, A_2, which perished shortly after it brought A_1 into existence. Suppose further that A_2 was brought into existence in similar fashion some time ago by A_3, and A_3 by A_4, and so forth back into the past. Each of these beings is a *dependent* being; it owes its existence to the preceding thing in the series. Now if nothing else ever existed but these beings, then what the second premise says would not be true. For if every being that exists or ever did exist is an A and was produced by a preceding A, then every being that exists or ever did exist would be dependent and, accordingly, premise two of the Cosmological Argument would be false. If the proponent of the Cosmological Argument is correct, then, there must be something wrong with the idea that every being that exists or did exist is an A and that they form a causal series: A_1 caused by A_2, A_2 caused by A_3, A_3 caused by A_4, ... A_n caused by A_{n+1}. How does the proponent of the Cosmological Argument propose to show us that there is something wrong with this view?

A popular but mistaken idea of how the proponent tries to show that something is wrong with this view, the view that every being might be dependent, is that he uses the following argument to reject it.

1. There must be a *first* being to start any causal series.
2. If every being were dependent there would be no *first* being to start the causal series.

Therefore,

3. Not every being can be a dependent being.

Although this argument is deductively valid, and its second premise is true, its first premise overlooks the distinct possibility that a causal series might be *infinite*, with no first member at all. Thus if we go back to our series of *A* beings, where each *A* is dependent, having been produced by the preceding *A* in the causal series, it's clear that if the series existed it would have no first member; for every *A* in the series there would be a preceding *A* which produced it, *ad infinitum*. The first premise of the argument just given assumes that a causal series must stop with a first member somewhere in the distant past. But there seems to be no good reason for making that assumption.

The eighteenth-century proponents of the Cosmological Argument recognized that the causal series of dependent beings could be infinite, without a first member to start the series. They rejected the idea that every being that is or ever was is dependent not because there would then be no first member to the series of dependent beings, but because there would then be no explanation for the fact that there are and have always been dependent beings. To see their reasoning let's return to our simplification of the supposition that the only things that exist or ever did exist are dependent beings. In our simplification of that supposition only one of the dependent beings exists at a time, each one perishing as it produces the next in the series. Perhaps the first thing to note about this supposition is that there is no individual *A* in the causal series of dependent beings whose existence is unexplained – A_1 is explained by A_2, A_2 by A_3, and A_n by A_{n+1}. So the first part of PSR, PSRa, appears to be satisfied. There is no particular being whose existence lacks an explanation. What, then, is it that lacks an explanation, if every particular *A* in the causal series of dependent beings has an explanation? It is the *series itself* that lacks an explanation. Or, as I've chosen to express it, *the fact that there are and have always been dependent beings*. For suppose we ask why it is that there are and have always been *A*s in existence. It won't do to say that *A*s have always been producing other *A*s – we can't explain why there have always been *A*s by saying there always have been *A*s. Nor, on the supposition that only *A*s have ever existed, can we explain the fact that there have always been *A*s by appealing to some-

thing other than an *A* – for no such thing would have existed. Thus the supposition that the only things that exist or ever existed are dependent things leaves us with a fact for which there can be no explanation – namely, the fact that there are dependent beings rather than not.

Questioning the justification of the second premise

Critics of the Cosmological Argument have raised several important objections against the claim that if every being is dependent the series or collection of those beings would have no explanation. Our understanding of the Cosmological Argument, as well as of its strengths and weaknesses, will be deepened by a careful consideration of these criticisms.

The first criticism is that the proponent of the Cosmological Argument makes the mistake of treating the collection or series of dependent beings as though it were itself a dependent being, and, therefore, requires an explanation of its existence. But, so the objection goes, the collection of dependent beings is not itself a dependent being any more than a collection of stamps is itself a stamp.

A second criticism is that the proponent makes the mistake of inferring that because each member of the collection of dependent beings has a cause, the collection itself must have a cause. But, as Russell noted, such reasoning is as fallacious as to infer that the human race (that is, the collection of human beings) must have a mother because each member of the collection (each human being) has a mother.

A third criticism is that the proponent of the argument fails to realize that for there to be an explanation of a collection of things is nothing more than for there to be an explanation of each of the things making up the collection. Since in the infinite collection (or series) of dependent beings, each being in the collection does have an explanation – by virtue of having been caused by some preceding member of the collection – the explanation of the collection, so the criticism goes, has already been given. As Hume remarked, "Did I show you the particular causes of each individual in a collection of twenty particles of matter, I should think it very unreasonable, should you afterwards ask me, what was the cause of the whole twenty. This is sufficiently explained in explaining the cause of the parts."[1]

Finally, even if the proponent of the Cosmological Argument can satisfactorily answer these objections, he must face one last objection to his ingenious attempt to justify premise two of the Cosmological Argument. For someone may agree that if nothing exists but an infinite collection of dependent beings, the infinite collection will have no explanation of its existence, and still refuse to conclude from this that there is something wrong with the idea that every being is a dependent being. Why, he might ask, should we think that everything has to have an explanation? What's wrong with admitting that the fact that there are and have always been dependent beings is a *brute fact*, a fact having no explanation whatever? Why does everything have to have an explanation anyway? We must now see what can be said in response to these several objections.

[. . .]

The Design Argument (Old and New)

The old Design Argument has as its starting point our sense of wonder not that things exist, but that so many things that exist in our universe exhibit order and design. Beginning from this sense of wonder, the argument endeavors to convince us that whatever produced the universe must be an intelligent being. Perhaps the best-known statement of the argument is given in David Hume's *Dialogues Concerning Natural Religion*:

Look round the world: contemplate the whole and every part of it: You will find it to be nothing but one great machine, subdivided into an infinite number of lesser machines, which again admit of subdivisions to a degree beyond what human senses and faculties can trace and explain. All these various machines, and even their most minute parts, are adjusted to each other with an accuracy which ravishes into admiration all men who have ever contemplated them. The curious adapting of means to ends, throughout all nature, resembles exactly, though it much exceeds, the productions of human contrivance; of human design, thought, wisdom, and intelligence. Since therefore the effects resemble each other, we are led to infer, by all the rules of analogy, that the causes also resemble; and that the Author of Nature is somewhat similar to the mind of man, though possessed of much larger faculties, proportioned to the grandeur of the work which he has executed. By this argument *a posteriori*, and by this argument alone, do we prove at once the existence of a Deity, and his similarity to human mind and intelligence.[2]

Argument by analogy

There is an *analogy*, this passage tells us, between many things in nature and things produced by human beings – for example, machines. Since we know that machines (watches, cameras, typewriters, automobiles, and so forth) have been produced by intelligent beings, and since many things in nature so closely resemble machines, we are justified "by all the rules of analogy" in concluding that whatever produced those things in nature is an intelligent being. The Design Argument, then, as expressed in this passage, is an *argument from analogy*, and for our purposes may be set forth as follows:

1. Machines are produced by intelligent design.
2. The universe resembles a machine.

Therefore,

3. Probably the universe was produced by intelligent design.

The critical questions we must consider in assessing the old Design Argument spring mainly from the fact that it employs *analogical reasoning*. To better understand such reasoning, let's consider the following example in which it is used. Suppose you are working in a chemical laboratory and somehow manage to produce a new chemical compound. It occurs to you that this chemical might have some very beneficial results if you were to swallow a bit of it. On the other hand, since its properties are not well understood, it also occurs to you that the chemical might harm you considerably. Being both cautious and curious, you seek some way of finding out whether the chemical will benefit you or harm you, short of actually swallowing some of it. It occurs to you that you might surreptitiously place some in the food of your dinner guests that evening and simply sit back and observe what happens. It they all die within an hour of ingesting the chemical, you then have exceptionally strong evidence that the chemical would harm you. For obvious reasons, however, you feel it improper to try out an unknown chemical on other human beings, particularly your dinner guests. Instead, you expose some monkeys or rats to the chemical and conclude from its effect on them what its likely effect on you will be.

Reflecting on this example will help us understand both what analogical reasoning is and why we sometimes must employ it in trying to discover something about ourselves and our world. If you had given the chemical to a number of human beings, say your dinner guests, then from the effect of the chemical on them you could have inferred its effect on you. Such reasoning would not have been analogical since your dinner guests are exactly like you; they belong to the same natural class to which you belong, the class of human beings. As it was, you could not engage in such straightforward reasoning because the immediate natural class – the class of human beings – to which you belong could not be examined in connection with the chemical. You then did the next best thing: you picked a natural class, the class of monkeys, to which you don't belong, but whose members you *resemble* in certain ways. You resemble monkeys in having a nervous system, being warm-blooded, and in numerous other respects.

Moreover, the ways in which you resemble monkeys are *relevant* to finding out the likely effect of the chemical on you. Creatures that have a central nervous system, are warm-blooded, and are otherwise similar, tend to have similar responses to chemical substances. So although the analogical reasoning you end up employing is somewhat weaker than the straightforward reasoning you would have used if you could have tried out the chemical on human beings, it is, nevertheless, good reasoning and provides you with evidence concerning the likely effect of the chemical on you.

The Design Argument endeavors to answer the question of whether our universe results from intelligent design. If we had observed the origin of many universes other than our universe and also observed that all or most of them resulted from intelligent design, we then could have reasoned in a straightforward fashion that

our universe likely arose from intelligent design. This would not have been analogical reasoning since we would have reasoned from things (other universes) that are exactly the same as the subject of our investigation, our universe. But since we have no knowledge or experience of universes other than our own, we must employ analogical reasoning; we must start with things that resemble, but are not the same as, our universe and infer that because these other things arose from intelligent design, it is likely that our universe arose from intelligent design. Such an argument, being an analogical argument based on resemblance of different things, is bound to be weaker than a straightforward argument from things exactly the same (that is, other universes), but it is clearly the best we can do if we are seeking knowledge about whatever it is that produced our universe. Of course, the strength of the argument will depend on the features in terms of which these other things resemble our universe and on the relevance of these features to the question of whether our universe arose from intelligent design. We must now pursue these larger questions. We must ask two questions: (1) What are the features in terms of which our universe is said to resemble a machine? (2) Are these features relevant to the question of whether the universe arose from intelligent design?

The Universe as machine

In what way or ways is the universe like a machine? The eighteenth-century English theologian, William Paley, one of the major exponents of the Design Argument, compared the universe to a watch and claimed that every manifestation of design which exists in a watch also exists in the works of nature. And, in the passage quoted earlier from Hume's *Dialogues Concerning Natural Religion*, we are reminded that there is "a curious adaptation of means to ends" throughout all nature. Apparently, then, the way in which the universe is supposed to resemble a machine is that parts of nature are seen to be related to one another in the *same way* as parts of a machine are related to one another. If we can get a clearer picture of just how the parts of machines are related to one another, we can then see whether the proponents of the Design Argument are correct in thinking that there are many things in nature whose parts are related to one another in exactly the same way.

If we examine a pocket watch that is in good working order, we will note rather quickly that its parts are so connected that when one part moves, other parts are caused to move as well – gears, for example, are so arranged that the movement of one causes another to move. This is a common feature of machines with moving parts, and it is also a feature to be found within the universe. Our solar system, for example, is composed of parts – the sun, the planets, and their moons – which move, and in their moving cause, by gravitational force, other parts to move. While all this is true, however, it is not the full story of how the parts of machines are related to one another. For if we look again at our watch, we discover not only that its parts are so arranged that they work together, but that under proper conditions they work together to serve a certain *purpose*. The parts of a watch are so arranged that under proper conditions they work together to enable us to tell the time of day. So too with the parts of other machines – automobiles, cameras, or typewriters. The parts of these machines are all so related to one another that under proper conditions they work together to serve some purpose.

Let's capture this interesting feature of machines by introducing the idea of a *teleological system*. A teleological system, we shall say, is any system of parts in which the parts are so arranged that under proper conditions they work together to serve a certain purpose. Most machines are clearly teleological systems. Moreover, a somewhat complex machine may well have parts that are themselves teleological systems. An automobile, for example, is a teleological system; its parts are so arranged that under proper conditions, they work together to enable someone to be transported quickly from one place to another. But various parts of an automobile are also teleological systems. The carburetor, for example, is a system of parts so arranged to provide the proper mixture of fuel and air for combustion.

What the proponents of the Design Argument claim as the basis for the analogy between the universe and machines is that in the world of nature, we find many things, and parts of things, that are teleological systems. The human eye, for example, is clearly a teleological system. Its parts exhibit an intricate order and are so arranged that under proper conditions they work together for the purpose of enabling a person to see. Other organs in humans and animals are undoubtedly also teleological systems, each serving some reasonably clear purpose. Indeed, it seems reasonable to believe that the plants and animals which compose a great part of the world of nature are teleological systems. As the twentieth-century philosopher C. D. Broad has remarked:

> The most superficial knowledge of organisms does make it look as if they were very complex systems designed to preserve themselves in face of varying and threatening external conditions and to reproduce their kind. And, on the whole, the more fully we investigate a living organism in detail the more fully does what we discover fit in with this hypothesis. One might mention, e.g., the various small and apparently unimportant glands in the human body whose secretions are found to exercise a profound influence over its growth and well-being. Or again we might mention the production in the blood of antitoxins when the body is attacked by organisms likely to injure it.[3]

We can now see, I think, the force with which this argument strikes the imagination of its supporters. Once we understand what a watch is, how it works and for what purpose, it would be utterly absurd to suppose that its origin is due to some accident rather than to intelligent design. But if we look carefully at many things in nature – plants and animals, for example – we discover that their parts exhibit an orderly arrangement fitted to a purpose (survival of the organism and the reproduction of its kind) that, if anything, exceeds the purposeful arrangement of parts in the watch. How absurd, then, to suppose that the world of nature arose from accident rather than intelligent design. Something of the force of this argument on the human imagination is conveyed in the following observation by the seventeenth-century philosopher Henry More:

> For why have we three joints in our legs and arms, as also in our fingers, but that it was much better than having two or four? And why are our fore-teeth sharp like chisels to cut, but our inward teeth broad to grind (instead of) the

fore-teeth broad and the other sharp? But we might have made a hard shift to have lived through in that worser condition. Again, why are the teeth so luckily placed, or rather, why are there not teeth in other bones as well as in the jaw-bones? for they might have been as capable as these. But the reason is nothing is done foolishly or in vain; that is, there is a divine Providence that orders all things.[4]

We have been trying to answer the first of two critical questions directed at the Design Argument: What are the features in terms of which our universe is said to resemble machines? What we have seen is that in the world of nature, there are many things (plants and animals, for example) that appear to share with machines the interesting and important feature of being *teleological systems.* Before we turn to our second critical question, however, we need to recognize exactly what we have acknowledged about our universe if we accept the claim that plants and animals, no less than machines, are teleological systems.

It is one thing to believe that the universe contains many *parts* which are teleological systems, and quite another thing to believe that the *universe itself* is a teleological system. Nothing we have considered thus far would show that the universe itself is a teleological system. To show that, we would have to claim that the universe itself has a purpose and that its parts are so arranged that they work together toward the realization of that purpose. But can we, by just looking at the small fragment of our universe available to us, hope to discern the purpose of the universe itself? It seems clear that we cannot. If we know that God created the universe and also why he created it, we might reasonably infer that the universe itself is a teleological system. But since the Design Argument is an argument for the existence of God, it cannot presuppose his existence and purposes without assuming what it is trying to prove. At best, then, what we can say is that the universe contains many parts (other than objects made by human beings, like machines) that are teleological systems. And this means that we aren't justified in saying that the *universe itself* is like a machine. What we are perhaps justified in saying is that the universe contains many natural parts (that is, parts that are not made by human beings) that resemble machines; they resemble machines

because, like machines, they are teleological systems. Accepting this limitation, we can revise our statement of the Design Argument as follows:

1. Machines are produced by intelligent design.
2. Many natural parts of the universe resemble machines.

Therefore,

3. Probably the universe (or at least many of its natural parts) was produced by intelligent design.

Evidence of intelligent design

The second critical question we must raise concerning the Design Argument is whether the feature in terms of which many natural parts of the universe resemble machines is *relevant* to the question of whether the universe (or many of its natural parts) arose from intelligent design. To this question it is clear that the answer is *yes*. We know that intelligent design accounts for the fact that machines are teleological systems. We then discover that the world of nature is populated with many teleological systems. What more plausible account can we give of their origin than to suppose that they too arose from intelligent design? And since it's clear that no human being could have been the intelligent designer of the universe (or its natural parts which are teleological systems), it seems reasonable to suppose that some suprahuman being intelligently designed the universe as a whole, or at least many of its parts.

Although intelligent design is a plausible hypothesis by which to account for the many teleological systems in the world of nature, is it the only hypothesis available to us? Until Charles Darwin (1809–1882) and the theory of evolution, it is doubtful that anyone had a naturalistic explanation of teleological systems in nature that could seriously compete with the hypothesis of intelligent design. But since the development of the theory of evolution, the Design Argument has lost some of its persuasive force, for we now possess a fairly well-developed naturalistic hypothesis by which the teleological systems in nature can be explained, a hypothesis that makes no mention of intelligent design. Briefly put, the Darwinian theory of natural selection purports to explain why nature contains so many organisms whose various parts are so well fitted to their survival. According to this theory, animals and plants undergo variations or changes that are inherited by their descendants. Some variations provide organisms with an advantage over the rest of the population in the constant struggle for life. Since plants and animals produce more offspring than the environment will support, those in which favorable variations occur tend to survive in greater numbers than those in which unfavorable variations occur. Thus, it happens that over great periods of time there slowly emerge large populations of highly developed organisms whose parts are so peculiarly fitted to their survival.

During the late twentieth century and the early twenty-first century a debate has occurred over the ability of the Darwinian theory of natural selection to adequately explain the complex living organisms that populate our planet. Although the science of biology appears to be firmly rooted in Darwinian evolutionary theory, the theory itself continues to be criticized by some biologists who argue that natural selection without intelligent design is inadequate to account for the complexity of living things that populate our planet. For example, the biologist Michael J. Behe argues that Darwin's principle of natural selection cannot account for the fact that many biological systems are "irreducibly complex" at the molecular level.[5] Behe offers a mousetrap as an example of something that is irreducibly complex. Mousetraps have several interconnected parts (spring, base, hammer, catch, and holding bar), and all of these are necessary for carrying out the purpose of the mousetrap – catching mice. An irreducibly complex biological system is a system that, like a mousetrap, simply cannot function unless all its parts are present and properly connected. Since Darwinian evolution proceeds by successive slight modifications of functioning systems, modifications that happen to be adaptive to changes in the environment, the claim is that it is enormously difficult, if not impossible, to see how irreducibly complex systems at the molecular level could come about on the Darwinian theory. If the position advocated by Behe should turn out to be correct, it would be a significant objection to the ability of Darwinian natural selection to account for complex systems at the molecular level. Of course,

it is a long step from Behe's data to the conclusion that an adequate explanation of irreducible complex biological systems at the molecular level requires the existence of an omnipotent, omniscient, perfectly good being who has directly created these irreducibly complex systems. Indeed, neither Behe nor William Dempski,[6] another important proponent of intelligent design, explicitly claims that the intelligent design argument is evidence for the existence of the theistic God. Dempski is officially silent on the identity of the designer, and Michael Behe allows that the designer might be part of the natural world.[7] At the present time there is some scholarly debate over whether Darwinian natural selection can adequately account for irreducibly complex biological systems at the molecular level. It is fair to say, however, that the majority of biologists take the view that there is no sufficient reason to think that it cannot.

Kenneth R. Miller, Professor of Biology at Brown University and a theist, agrees with Behe that if Darwinism cannot account for the apparent irreducible complexity at the level of the living cell then it is doomed. He notes, however, that although cell biology did not exist in Darwin's day, Darwin took care to endeavor to explain how his theory could account for an irreducibly complex system when he provided an evolutionary explanation for Paley's example of the human eye.[8] In Miller's view, Behe's argument from irreducible complexity is just one more failed attempt to find something occurring on our planet that science is supposedly unable to explain.

As a theist, Miller regards the universe as God's creation. Indeed, he argues that given the big bang theory of the origin of the universe, it makes good sense to suppose that our universe was caused to exist by a supernatural being. But he claims that Darwinian theory can account for the slow emergence over time of intricate teleological systems, including plants, the lower animals, and human beings. For Miller, only the origin of our universe can reasonably be claimed to be an act of creation and intelligent design. Indeed, unlike Behe, he is very cautious about claiming that there are events occurring on our planet that are inexplicable apart from some immediate, direct activity of God. For all too often something that occurs on earth that is claimed to be due solely to the direct intervention of God is shown in due course to be the causal product of purely natural forces. It is the origin of the universe itself, a universe whose constants are such as to permit human life to emerge on this rather insignificant planet, that Miller believes to be directly caused by God. Since it is one thing to argue that God is required to explain the intricate teleological systems we observe on the earth, and quite another thing to argue that God is required to explain why there is a universe whose constants are such as to permit the occurrence of a planet with conditions making life possible, it is best to treat the latter as a separate argument – the new Design Argument. We will examine that argument later in the chapter, after considering Hume's criticisms of the old Design Argument.

Whether the Darwinian theory of natural selection is true or false, it must be admitted that it stands in competition with the intelligent-designer hypothesis as a possible explanation of the fact that the world of nature contains so many highly developed teleological systems. The implication of this for the Design Argument is that it no longer has the persuasive force it once enjoyed. Although it undoubtedly provides us with some grounds for thinking that many parts of the world of nature arose from intelligent design, we now have reason to question the *strength* of the inference from teleological systems in nature to an intelligent designer, for in the theory of natural selection we possess a competing hypothesis by which to explain those teleological systems.

Hume's criticisms of the Design Argument

Although Hume's *Dialogues Concerning Natural Religion* was written before the advent of the Darwinian theory, it has long been recognized as the classical attack on the Design Argument. For our purposes, Hume's criticisms can be divided into two groups: criticisms of the claim that the universe is like a machine, and criticisms of the claim that the Design Argument provides us with adequate grounds for belief in the theistic God. We can best conclude our study of the old Design Argument by considering some of Hume's main objections.

Hume points out first that the vastness of the universe weakens the claim that it resembles a machine or some other human creation such as a house or a ship. Secondly, he notes that although design and order exist in the part of the universe we inhabit, for all we know there are vast reaches of the universe in which absolute chaos reigns. And, finally, although admitting that intelligent design is observed to be a cause in the production of things within the small fragment of the universe we can observe, he argues that it is an unreasonable leap to conclude that intelligent design is the productive force throughout the entire universe. "A very small part of this great system, during a very short time, is very imperfectly discovered to us; and do we thence pronounce decisively concerning the origin of the whole?"[9]

These objections are aimed at the second premise of our original formulation of the Design Argument, the premise that the universe as a whole resembles a machine. The objections, however, do not affect so directly our revised version of the argument in which the second premise reads, "Many natural parts of the universe resemble machines." In the revised version no claim is made about the universe as a whole or about those parts of the universe that we are unable to observe. Hence, since it is the revised version that now concerns us, we may safely put aside the first group of Hume's criticisms.

The second group of criticisms is directed not at the argument as we have formulated it, but at any attempt to construe the argument as providing adequate grounds for theistic belief – for believing that there exists a supremely perfect being who created the universe. And on this score, there can be little doubt that Hume is right. From inspecting the universe, we may perhaps conclude that it arose from intelligent design, but beyond that point the Design Argument is unable to go; it provides us with no rational grounds for thinking that whatever produced the universe is *perfect, one,* or *spiritual.* We can't infer that what produced the universe is supremely wise or good because, for all we know, the universe is a very imperfect production, more like an Edsel or a Corvair than a Rolls Royce. And even if the world in its vastness were known to be a very fine piece of work, still, for all we know, this world might be the last in a series of worlds, many of which are botched and bungled creations, before the Deity finally managed to learn the art of world making.

It is part of theistic belief that there is a single being who produced the world, but since we know that many machines, buildings, automobiles, and other devices result from the combined efforts of many designers, the universe, for all we know, might be the product of the work of many minor deities, each possessed of limited intelligence and skill.

It is part of theistic belief that the Deity is incorporeal (lacking a body), a purely spiritual being. But, again, if we infer from the similarity between the world of nature and a machine to a similarity of their causes, then, since in the case of machines we know of no cause (human being) that is incorporeal, we have no grounds to infer that whatever produced the world is an incorporeal being.

Hume sums up this second group of objections by noting that anyone who limits his grounds for religious belief to the Design Argument "is able perhaps to assert, or conjecture, that the universe, sometime, arose from something like design: but beyond that position he cannot ascertain one single circumstance; and is left afterwards to fix every point of his theology by the utmost license of fancy and hypothesis."[10]

The implication of Hume's second set of criticisms is clear. Theism cannot be established by means of the Design Argument alone. Many theists would accept this implication. They would contend, however, that the several major arguments for the existence of God, *taken together*, do provide rational grounds for believing in the theistic God. So the second set of criticisms advanced by Hume, although clearly showing the limitations of the Design Argument, do not touch the more general claim that the traditional arguments for God, taken together, provide rational grounds for theism.

The new Design Argument

The new Design Argument emerged during the twentieth century, fueled by scientific discoveries and theories concerning both the origin of our universe and the conditions that had to prevail in it from the very beginning if life as we know it was to have any chance at all of occurring in the universe as it developed. Unlike the proponents of the argument Darwin and Hume criticized, the proponents of the new argument do not start from

the existence of living things (plants and animals) and seek an explanation of the fact that they are such intricate teleological systems. They may even concede that Darwin has an explanation of that. Rather, the proponents of the new Design Argument ask what conditions must be present in the universe if it is to be *possible* for living things to come into existence at all. And they claim that given the most promising account of the origin of the universe available in modern science – the big bang theory – the chances of the universe developing in such a way that life is possible are incredibly small, much less than one chance in a million. So, think of it this way. There were millions of different ways in which the universe could have developed out of the big bang. And in only one of those ways would the universe come to have the features necessary for the emergence and continuing existence of life as we know it. One popular example of one of the enormous number of conditions that had to be just so if the emergence of life was to be even possible concerns the rate of expansion of the universe from the initial big bang. If the rate of expansion had been ever so slightly faster, it would not have been possible for galaxies, stars, and planets to have been formed, with the result that life as we know it would have no chance of coming into existence. Alternatively, as Stephen Hawking tells us: "If the rate of the universe's expansion one second after the 'big bang' had been smaller by even one part in a hundred thousand million million, the universe would have recollapsed into a hot fireball."[11] When we realize that the rate of expansion is only one of many different conditions that had to be just right for life to be possible in the universe, the hypothesis of an intelligent designer/creator who fine-tuned the initial state of the universe seems a much more likely explanation of the fact that our universe is suitable for life than an appeal to mere chance.

It must be acknowledged, I believe, that this argument for an intelligent designer of the initial conditions has some merit. However, it would be a mistake, as we've learned from Hume, to conclude anything more than that the argument provides some support for the existence of intelligent design as having a role in the beginning of the universe. There may have been many designers cooperating together; the designer, if there be just one, might have finally gotten the rate of expansion just right after botching many other attempts; the intelligent designer might have since then lost any interest he once had in the welfare of the living things in the universe. In short, even if this argument is successful, it leaves the question of whether the intelligent designer of our universe is the theistic God still up in the air. (As we noted above in discussing the old Design Argument, theists may well agree with this point, contending instead that each of the arguments for the existence of God may provide support for different features of the theistic idea of God.)

There is, however, one objection to the argument that merits consideration. What if there were millions of other big bangs taking place? What if our universe (the universe that started with the big bang referred to by our scientific theories) is only one of millions that have occurred which, since they don't contain conditions required for life, are unknown. If so, then it would not be unlikely that one of these big bangs would have the initial conditions enabling it to develop in such a way that life can occur in it. Taking a fair deck of cards, it is extremely unlikely that drawing five cards at random will result in a royal flush. But if there are thousands upon thousands of fair decks of cards from each of which five cards are drawn at random it will be very propable indeed that one of those drawings will be a royal flush. Perhaps that is the situation with our big-bang universe, in which case it would not be surprising that some big-bang universe contains life. And since we are living beings, we must then be a part of that unsurprising universe.[12]

We earlier considered the objections of biologist Kenneth R. Miller to Michael Behe's criticisms of Darwinian natural selection as an explanation of the irreducibly complex biological systems found on our planet. As a Christian, Miller believes that God is the creator of the universe in which, as is happens, there is a small planet with the conditions suitable for the emergence of living, intelligent beings. Against his view we've considered an objection favored by nontheists. For, as we've seen, if there were millions upon millions of big bangs resulting in millions upon millions of universes, it would not be unlikely that one of them would happen to contain constants that permit human life to come into existence. Miller, of course, is aware of this alternative possibility. It must be admitted, however, that since we

can make observations only of our own universe, evidence cannot be obtained to determine whether the multiple universe hypothesis is correct. Miller, not unreasonably, concludes that since evidence for the multiple universe hypothesis is unattainable, one is intellectually justified in seriously considering the traditional alternative: that our universe, rather than occurring by chance, has been created by God.[13] It should be noted, however, that any supernatural being with absolute power and sufficient knowledge would also be able to create our universe. It need not require, for example, a being who is morally perfect. Nevertheless, since we lack evidence for the multiple universe hypothesis, the alternative of a supernatural creator remains a genuine possibility.

Notes

1 David Hume, *Dialogues Concerning Natural Religion*, pt. IX, ed. H. D. Aiken (New York: Hafner Publishing Company, 1948), pp. 59–60.
2 Hume, *Dialogues*, pt. II, p. 17.
3 C. D. Broad, *The Mind and Its Place in Nature* (London: Routledge & Kegan Paul Ltd., 1925), p. 83.
4 Quoted by J. J. C. Smart in "The Existence of God" in *New Essays in Philosophical Theology*, ed. Antony Flew and Alasdair MacIntyre (London: SCM Press Ltd., 1955), p. 43.
5 Michael J. Behe, *Darwin's Black Box: The Biochemical Challenge to Evolution* (New York: The Free Press, 1996), p. 54.
6 William A. Dempski, *No Free Lunch: Why Specified Complexity Cannot Be Purchased Without Intelligence* (Lanham, MD: Roman and Littlefield, 2002).
7 Michael J. Behe, "The Modern Design Hypothesis: Breaking Rules," in *God and Design: The Teleological Argument and Modern Science*, ed. Neil A. Manson (New York: Routledge, 2003), pp. 277–91.
8 Kenneth R. Miller, *Finding Darwin's God* (New York: HarperCollins Publishers Inc., 1999), p. 135.
9 Hume, *Dialogues*, pt. II, pp. 22–3.
10 Hume, *Dialogues*, pt. V, p. 40.
11 Stephen Hawking, *A Brief History of Time* (New York: Bantam Books, 1988), p. 123.
12 For a fuller account of this objection see Peter van Inwagen, *Megaphysics* (San Francisco: Westview Press, 1993), pp. 132–48.
13 Kenneth R. Miller, *Finding Darwin's God*, pp. 230–2.

52

Evil and Omnipotence

(all power/all mighty)

J. L. Mackie

The traditional arguments for the existence of God have been fairly thoroughly criticised by philosophers. But the theologian can, if he wishes, accept this criticism. He can admit that no rational proof of God's existence is possible. And he can still retain all that is essential to his position, by holding that God's existence is known in some other, non-rational way. I think, however, that a more telling criticism can be made by way of the traditional problem of evil. Here it can be shown, not that religious beliefs lack rational support, but that they are positively irrational, that the several parts of the essential theological doctrine are inconsistent with one another, so that the theologian can maintain his position as a whole only by a much more extreme rejection of reason than in the former case. He must now be prepared to believe, not merely what cannot be proved, but what can be *disproved* from other beliefs that he also holds.

The problem of evil, in the sense in which I shall be using the phrase, is a problem only for someone who believes that there is a God who is both omnipotent and wholly good. And it is a logical problem, the problem of clarifying and reconciling a number of beliefs: it is not a scientific problem that might be solved by further observations, or a practical problem that might be solved by a decision or an action. These points

are obvious; I mention them only because they are sometimes ignored by theologians, who sometimes parry a statement of the problem with such remarks as "Well, can you solve the problem yourself?" or "This is a mystery which may be revealed to us later" or "Evil is something to be faced and overcome, not to be merely discussed".

In its simplest form the problem is this: God is omnipotent; God is wholly good; and yet evil exists. There seems to be some contradiction between these three propositions, so that if any two of them were true the third would be false. But at the same time all three are essential parts of most theological positions: the theologian, it seems, at once *must* adhere and *cannot consistently* adhere to all three. (The problem does not arise only for theists, but I shall discuss it in the form in which it presents itself for ordinary theism.)

However, the contradiction does not arise immediately; to show it we need some additional premises, or perhaps some quasi-logical rules connecting the terms 'good', 'evil', and 'omnipotent'. These additional principles are that good is opposed to evil, in such a way that a good thing always eliminates evil as far as it can, and that there are no limits to what an omnipotent thing can do. From these it follows that a good omnipotent thing eliminates evil completely, and then the

J. L. Mackie, "Evil and Omnipotence." *Mind* 64, no. 254 (April 1955), pp. 200–12. © 1955 by the Mind Association. Reprinted with permission from Oxford Unviersity Press.

propositions that a good omnipotent thing exists, and that evil exists, are incompatible.

A. Adequate Solutions

Now once the problem, is fully stated it is clear that it can be solved, in the sense that the problem will not arise if one gives up at least one of the propositions that constitute it. If you are prepared to say that God is not wholly good, or not quite omnipotent, or that evil does not exist, or that good is not opposed to the kind of evil that exists, or that there are limits to what an omnipotent thing can do, then the problem of evil will not arise for you.

There are, then, quite a number of adequate solutions of the problem of evil, and some of these have been adopted, or almost adopted, by various thinkers. For example, a few have been prepared to deny God's omnipotence, and rather more have been prepared to keep the term 'omnipotence' but severely to restrict its meaning, recording quite a number of things that an omnipotent being cannot do. Some have said that evil is an illusion, perhaps because they held that the whole world of temporal, changing things is an illusion, and that what we call evil belongs only to this world, or perhaps because they held that although temporal things *are* much as we see them, those that we call evil are not really evil. Some have said that what we call evil is merely the privation of good, that evil in a positive sense, evil that would really be opposed to good, does not exist. Many have agreed with Pope that disorder is harmony not understood, and that partial evil is universal good. Whether any of these views is *true* is, of course, another question. But each of them gives an adequate solution of the problem of evil in the sense that if you accept it this problem does not arise for you, though you may, of course, have *other* problems to face.

But often enough these adequate solutions are only *almost* adopted. The thinkers who restrict God's power, but keep the term 'omnipotence', may reasonably be suspected of thinking, in other contexts, that his power is really unlimited. Those who say that evil is an illusion may also be thinking, inconsistently, that this illusion is itself an evil. Those who say that "evil" is merely privation of good may also be thinking, inconsistently,

that privation of good is an evil. (The fallacy here is akin to some forms of the "naturalistic fallacy" in ethics, where some think, for example, that "good" is just what contributes to evolutionary progress, and that evolutionary progress is itself good.) If Pope meant what he said in the first line of his couplet, that "disorder" is only harmony not understood, the "partial evil" of the second line must, for consistency, mean "that which, taken in isolation, falsely appears to be evil", but it would more naturally mean "that which, in isolation, really is evil". The second line, in fact, hesitates between two views, that "partial evil" isn't really evil, since only the universal quality is real, and that "partial evil" is really an evil, but only a little one.

In addition, therefore, to adequate solutions, we must recognise unsatisfactory inconsistent solutions, in which there is only a half-hearted or temporary rejection of one of the propositions which together constitute the problem. In these, one of the constituent propositions is explicitly rejected, but it is covertly re-asserted or assumed elsewhere in the system.

B. Fallacious Solutions *(based on a mistaken belief)*

Besides these half-hearted solutions, which explicitly reject but implicitly assert one of the constituent propositions, there are definitely fallacious solutions which explicitly maintain all the constituent propositions, but implicitly reject at least one of them in the course of the argument that explains away the problem of evil.

There are, in fact, many so-called solutions which purport to remove the contradiction without abandoning any of its constituent propositions. These must be fallacious, as we can see from the very statement of the problem, but it is not so easy to see in each case precisely where the fallacy lies. I suggest that in all cases the fallacy has the general form suggested above: in order to solve the problem one (or perhaps more) of its constituent propositions is given up, but in such a way that it appears to have been retained, and can therefore be asserted without qualification in other contexts. Sometimes there is a further complication: the supposed solution moves to and fro between, say, two of the constituent propositions, at one point asserting the first of these but covertly abandoning the second, at another point asserting the second but covertly abandoning the first. These fallacious solutions often turn upon some equivocation with the words 'good' and 'evil', or upon some vagueness about the way in which good and evil are opposed to one another, or about how much is meant by 'omnipotence'. I propose to examine some of these so-called solutions, and to exhibit their fallacies in detail. Incidentally, I shall also be considering whether an adequate solution could be reached by a minor modification of one or more of the constituent propositions, which would, however, still satisfy all the essential requirements of ordinary theism.

Discusses counter parts but not ultimate outcome.

1. "Good cannot exist without evil" or "Evil is necessary as a counterpart to good"

It is sometimes suggested that evil is necessary as a counterpart to good, that if there were no evil there could be no good either, and that this solves the problem of evil. It is true that it points to an answer to the question "Why should there be evil?" But it does so only by qualifying some of the propositions that constitute the problem.

First, it sets a limit to what God can do, saying that God *cannot* create good without simultaneously creating evil, and this means either that God is not omnipotent or that there are *some* limits to what an omnipotent thing can do. It may be replied that these limits are always presupposed, that omnipotence has never meant the power to do what is logically impossible, and on the present view the existence of good without evil would be a logical impossibility. This interpretation of omnipotence may, indeed, be accepted as a modification of our original account which does not reject anything that is essential to theism, and I shall in general assume it in the subsequent discussion. It is, perhaps, the most common theistic view, but I think that some theists at least have maintained that God can do what is logically impossible. Many theists, at any rate, have held that logic itself is created or laid down by God, that logic is the way in which God arbitrarily chooses to think. (This is, of course, parallel to the ethical view that morally right actions are those which God arbitrarily chooses to command, and the two views encounter similar difficulties.) And *this* account of logic is clearly inconsistent

with the view that God is bound by logical necessities – unless it is possible for an omnipotent being to bind himself, an issue which we shall consider later, when we come to the Paradox of Omnipotence. This solution of the problem of evil cannot, therefore, be consistently adopted along with the view that logic is itself created by God.

But, secondly, this solution denies that evil is opposed to good in our original sense. If good and evil are counterparts, a good thing will not "eliminate evil as far as it can". Indeed, this view suggests that good and evil are not strictly qualities of things at all. Perhaps the suggestion is that good and evil are related in much the same way as great and small. Certainly, when the term 'great' is used relatively as a condensation of 'greater than so-and-so', and 'small' is used correspondingly, greatness and smallness are counterparts and cannot exist without each other. But in this sense greatness is not a quality, not an intrinsic feature of anything; and it would be absurd to think of a movement in favour of greatness and against smallness in this sense. Such a movement would be self-defeating, since relative greatness can be promoted only by a simultaneous promotion of relative smallness. I feel sure that no theists would be content to regard God's goodness as analogous to this – as if what he supports were not the *good* but the *better*, and as if he had the paradoxical aim that all things should be better than other things.

This point is obscured by the fact that 'great' and 'small' seem to have an absolute as well as a relative sense. I cannot discuss here whether there is absolute magnitude or not, but if there is, there could be an absolute sense for 'great', it could mean of at least a certain size, and it would make sense to speak of all things getting bigger, of a universe that was expanding all over, and therefore it would make sense to speak of promoting greatness. But in *this* sense great and small are not logically necessary counterparts: either quality could exist without the other. There would be no logical impossibility in everything's being small or in everything's being great.

Neither in the absolute nor in the relative sense, then, of 'great' and 'small' do these terms provide an analogy of the sort that would be needed to support this solution of the problem of evil. In neither case are greatness and smallness *both* necessary counterparts *and* mutually opposed forces or possible objects for support and attack.

It may be replied that good and evil are necessary counterparts in the same way as any quality and its logical opposite: redness can occur, it is suggested, only if non-redness also occurs. But unless evil is merely the privation of good, they are not logical opposites, and some further argument would be needed to show that they are counterparts in the same way as genuine logical opposites. Let us assume that this could be given. There is still doubt of the correctness of the metaphysical principle that a quality must have a real opposite: I suggest that it is not really impossible that everything should be, say, red, that the truth is merely that if everything were red we should not notice redness, and so we should have no word 'red'; we observe and give names to qualities only if they have real opposites. If so, the principle that a term must have an opposite would belong only to our language or to our thought, and would not be an ontological principle, and, correspondingly, the rule that good cannot exist without evil would not state a logical necessity of a sort that God would just have to put up with. God might have made everything good, though *we* should not have noticed it if he had.

But, finally, even if we concede that this *is* an ontological principle, it will provide a solution for the problem of evil only if one is prepared to say, "Evil exists, but only just enough evil to serve as the counterpart of good". I doubt whether any theist will accept this. After all, the *ontological* requirement that non-redness should occur would be satisfied even if all the universe, except for a minute speck, were red, and, if there were a corresponding requirement for evil as a counterpart to good, a minute dose of evil would presumably do. But theists are not usually willing to say, in all contexts, that all the evil that occurs is a minute and necessary dose.

2.   "Evil is necessary as a means to good"

It is sometimes suggested that evil is necessary for good not as a counterpart but as a means. In its simple form this has little plausibility as a solution of the problem of evil, since it obviously implies a severe restriction of God's power. It would be a *causal* law that you cannot have a certain end without a certain means, so that if

God has to introduce evil as a means to good, he must be subject to at least some causal laws. This certainly conflicts with what a theist normally means by omnipotence. This view of God as limited by causal laws also conflicts with the view that causal laws are themselves made by God, which is more widely held than the corresponding view about the laws of logic. This conflict would, indeed, be resolved if it were possible for an omnipotent being to bind himself, and this possibility has still to be considered. Unless a favourable answer can be given to this question, the suggestion that evil is necessary as a means to good solves the problem of evil only by denying one of its constituent propositions, either that God is omnipotent or that 'omnipotent' means what it says.

3.   "The universe is better with some evil in it than it could be if there were no evil"

Much more important is a solution which at first seems to be a mere variant of the previous one, that evil may contribute to the goodness of a whole in which it is found, so that the universe as a whole is better as it is, with some evil in it, than it would be if there were no evil. This solution may be developed in either of two ways. It may be supported by an aesthetic analogy, by the fact that contrasts heighten beauty, that in a musical work, for example, there may occur discords which somehow add to the beauty of the work as a whole. Alternatively, it may be worked out in connexion with the notion of progress, that the best possible organisation of the universe will not be static, but progressive, that the gradual overcoming of evil by good is really a finer thing than would be the eternal unchallenged supremacy of good.

In either case, this solution usually starts from the assumption that the evil whose existence gives rise to the problem of evil is primarily what is called physical evil, that is to say, pain. In Hume's rather half-hearted presentation of the problem of evil, the evils that he stresses are pain and disease, and those who reply to him argue that the existence of pain and disease makes possible the existence of sympathy, benevolence, heroism, and the gradually successful struggle of doctors and reformers to overcome these evils. In fact, theists often seize the opportunity to accuse those who stress the problem of evil of taking a low, materialistic view of good and evil, equating these with pleasure and pain, and of ignoring the more spiritual goods which can arise in the struggle against evils.

But let us see exactly what is being done here. Let us call pain and misery 'first order evil' or 'evil (1)'. What contrasts with this, namely, pleasure and happiness, will be called 'first order good' or 'good (1)'. Distinct from this is 'second order good' or 'good (2)' which somehow emerges in a complex situation in which evil (1) is a necessary component – logically, not merely causally, necessary. (Exactly *how* it emerges does not matter: in the crudest version of this solution good (2) is simply the heightening of happiness by the contrast with misery, in other versions it includes sympathy with suffering, heroism in facing danger, and the gradual decrease of first order evil and increase of first order good.) It is also being assumed that second order good is more important than first order good or evil, in particular that it more than outweighs the first order evil it involves.

Now this is a particularly subtle attempt to solve the problem of evil. It defends God's goodness and omnipotence on the ground that (on a sufficiently long view) this is the best of all logically possible worlds, because it includes the important second order goods, and yet it admits that real evils, namely first order evils, exist. But does it still hold that good and evil are opposed? Not, clearly, in the sense that we set out originally: good does not tend to eliminate evil in general. Instead, we have a modified, a more complex pattern. First order good (*e.g.* happiness) *contrasts with* first order evil (*e.g.* misery): these two are opposed in a fairly mechanical way; some second order goods (*e.g.* benevolence) try to maximise first order good and minimise first order evil; but God's goodness is not this, it is rather the will to maximise *second* order good. We might, therefore, call God's goodness an example of a third order goodness, or good (3). While this account is different from our original one, it might well be held to be an improvement on it, to give a more accurate description of the way in which good is opposed to evil, and to be consistent with the essential theist position.

There might, however, be several objections to this solution.

First, some might argue that such qualities as benevolence – and *a fortiori* the third order goodness which promotes benevolence – have a merely derivative value, that they are not higher sorts of good, but merely means to good (1), that is, to happiness, so that it would be absurd for God to keep misery in existence in order to make possible the virtues of benevolence, heroism, etc. The theist who adopts the present solution must, of course, deny this, but he can do so with some plausibility, so I should not press this objection.

Secondly, it follows from this solution that God is not in our sense benevolent or sympathetic: he is not concerned to minimise evil (1), but only to promote good (2); and this might be a disturbing conclusion for some theists.

But, thirdly, the fatal objection is this. Our analysis shows clearly the possibility of the existence of a *second* order evil, an evil (2) contrasting with good (2) as evil (1) contrasts with good (1). This would include malevolence, cruelty, callousness, cowardice, and states in which good (1) is decreasing and evil (1) increasing. And just as good (2) is held to be the important kind of good, the kind that God is concerned to promote, so evil (2) will, by analogy, be the important kind of evil, the kind which God, if he were wholly good and omnipotent, would eliminate. And yet evil (2) plainly exists, and indeed most theists (in other contexts) stress its existence more than that of evil (1). We should, therefore, state the problem of evil in terms of second order evil, and against this form of the problem the present solution is useless.

An attempt might be made to use this solution again, at a higher level, to explain the occurrence of evil (2): indeed the next main solution that we shall examine does just this, with the help of some new notions. Without any fresh notions, such a solution would have little plausibility: for example, we could hardly say that the really important good was a good (3), such as the increase of benevolence in proportion to cruelty, which logically required for its occurrence the occurrence of some second order evil. But even if evil (2) could be explained in this way, it is fairly clear that there would be third order evils contrasting with this third order good: and we should be well on the way to an infinite regress, where the solution of a problem of evil, stated in terms of evil (n), indicated the existence of an evil ($n + 1$), and a further problem to be solved.

4. "Evil is due to human freewill"

Perhaps the most important proposed solution of the problem of evil is that evil is not to be ascribed to God at all, but to the independent actions of human beings, supposed to have been endowed by God with freedom of the will. This solution may be combined with the preceding one: first order evil (e.g. pain) may be justified as a logically necessary component in second order good (e.g. sympathy) while second order evil (e.g. cruelty) is not justified, but is so ascribed to human beings that God cannot be held responsible for it. This combination evades my third criticism of the preceding solution.

The freewill solution also involves the preceding solution at a higher level. To explain why a wholly good God gave men freewill although it would lead to some important evils, it must be argued that it is better on the whole that men should act freely, and sometimes err, than that they should be innocent automata, acting rightly in a wholly determined way. Freedom, that is to say, is now treated as a third order good, and as being more valuable than second order goods (such as sympathy and heroism) would be if they were deterministically produced, and it is being assumed that second order evils, such as cruelty, are logically necessary accompaniments of freedom, just as pain is a logically necessary precondition of sympathy.

I think that this solution is unsatisfactory primarily because of the incoherence of the notion of freedom of the will: but I cannot discuss this topic adequately here, although some of my criticisms will touch upon it.

First I should query the assumption that second order evils are logically necessary accompaniments of freedom. I should ask this: if God has made men such that in their free choices they sometimes prefer what is good and sometimes what is evil, why could he not have made men such that they always freely choose the good? If there is no logical impossibility in a man's freely choosing the good on one, or on several, occasions, there cannot be a logical impossibility in his freely choosing the good on every occasion. God was not, then, faced with a choice between

making innocent automata and making beings who, in acting freely, would sometimes go wrong: there was open to him the obviously better possibility of making beings who would act freely but always go right. Clearly, his failure to avail himself of this possibility is inconsistent with his being both omnipotent and wholly good.

If it is replied that this objection is absurd, that the making of some wrong choices is logically necessary for freedom, it would seem that 'freedom' must here mean complete randomness or indeterminacy, including randomness with regard to the alternatives good and evil, in other words that men's choices and consequent actions can be "free" only if they are not determined by their characters. Only on this assumption can God escape the responsibility for men's actions; for if he made them as they are, but did not determine their wrong choices, this can only be because the wrong choices are not determined by men as they are. But then if freedom is randomness, how can it be a characteristic of will? And, still more, how can it be the most important good? What value or merit would there be in free choices if these were random actions which were not determined by the nature of the agent?

I conclude that to make this solution plausible two different senses of 'freedom' must be confused, one sense which will justify the view that freedom is a third order good, more valuable than other goods would be without it, and another sense, sheer randomness, to prevent us from ascribing to God a decision to make men such that they sometimes go wrong when he might have made them such that they would always freely go right.

This criticism is sufficient to dispose of this solution. But besides this there is a fundamental difficulty in the notion of an omnipotent God creating men with free will, for if men's wills are really free this must mean that even God cannot control them, that is, that God is no longer omnipotent. It may be objected that God's gift of freedom to men does not mean that he *cannot* control their wills, but that he always *refrains* from controlling their wills. But why, we may ask, should God refrain from controlling evil wills? Why should he not leave men free to will rightly, but intervene when he sees them beginning to will wrongly? If God could do this, but does not, and if he is wholly good, the only explanation could be that even a wrong free act of will is not really evil, that its freedom is a value which outweighs its wrongness, so that there would be a loss of value if God took away the wrongness and the freedom together. But this is utterly opposed to what theists say about sin in other contexts. The present solution of the problem of evil, then, can be maintained only in the form that God has made men so free that he *cannot* control their wills.

This leads us to what I call the Paradox of Omnipotence: can an omnipotent being make things which he cannot subsequently control? Or, what is practically equivalent to this, can an omnipotent being make rules which then bind himself? (These are practically equivalent because any such rules could be regarded as setting certain things beyond his control, and *vice versa*.) The second of these formulations is relevant to the suggestions that we have already met, that an omnipotent God creates the rules of logic or causal laws, and is then bound by them.

It is clear that this is a paradox: the questions cannot be answered satisfactorily either in the affirmative or in the negative. If we answer "Yes", it follows that if God actually makes things which he cannot control, or makes rules which bind himself, he is not omnipotent once he has made them: there are *then* things which he cannot do. But if we answer "No", we are immediately asserting that there are things which he cannot do, that is to say that he is already not omnipotent.

It cannot be replied that the question which sets this paradox is not a proper question. It would make perfectly good sense to say that a human mechanic has made a machine which he cannot control: if there is any difficulty about the question it lies in the notion of omnipotence itself.

This, incidentally, shows that although we have approached this paradox from the free will theory, it is equally a problem for a theological determinist. No one thinks that machines have free will, yet they may well be beyond the control of their makers. The determinist might reply that anyone who makes anything determines its ways of acting, and so determines its subsequent behaviour: even the human mechanic does this by his *choice* of materials and structure for his machine, though he does not know all about either of these: the mechanic thus determines,

though he may not foresee, his machine's actions. And since God is omniscient, and since his creation of things is total, he both determines and foresees the ways in which his creatures will act. We may grant this, but it is beside the point. The question is not whether God *originally* determined the future actions of his creatures, but whether he can *subsequently* control their actions, or whether he was able in his original creation to put things beyond his subsequent control. Even on determinist principles the answers "Yes" and "No" are equally irreconcilable with God's omnipotence.

Before suggesting a solution of this paradox, I would point out that there is a parallel Paradox of Sovereignty. Can a legal sovereign make a law restricting its own future legislative power? For example, could the British parliament make a law forbidding any future parliament to socialise banking, and also forbidding the future repeal of this law itself? Or could the British parliament, which was legally sovereign in Australia in, say, 1899, pass a valid law, or series of laws, which made it no longer sovereign in 1933? Again, neither the affirmative nor the negative answer is really satisfactory. If we were to answer "Yes", we should be admitting the validity of a law which, if it were actually made, would mean that parliament was no longer sovereign. If we were to answer "No", we should be admitting that there is a law, not logically absurd, which parliament cannot validly make, that is, that parliament is not now a legal sovereign. This paradox can be solved in the following way. We should distinguish between first order laws, that is laws governing the actions of individuals and bodies other than the legislature, and second order laws, that is laws about laws, laws governing the actions of the legislature itself. Correspondingly, we should distinguish two orders of sovereignty, first order sovereignty (sovereignty (1)) which is unlimited authority to make first order laws, and second order sovereignty (sovereignty (2)) which is unlimited authority to make second order laws. If we say that parliament is sovereign we might mean that any parliament at any time has sovereignty (1), or we might mean that parliament has both sovereignty (1) and sovereignty (2) at present, but we cannot without contradiction mean both that the present parliament has sovereignty (2) and that every parliament at every time has sovereignty (1), for if the present parliament has sovereignty (2) it may use it to take away the sovereignty (1) of later parliaments. What the paradox shows is that we cannot ascribe to any continuing institution legal sovereignty in an inclusive sense.

The analogy between omnipotence and sovereignty shows that the paradox of omnipotence can be solved in a similar way. We must distinguish between first order omnipotence (omnipotence (1)), that is unlimited power to act, and second order omnipotence (omnipotence (2)), that is unlimited power to determine what powers to act things shall have. Then we could consistently say that God all the time has omnipotence (1), but if so no beings at any time have powers to act independently of God. Or we could say that God at one time had omnipotence (2), and used it to assign independent powers to act to certain things, so that God thereafter did not have omnipotence (1). But what the paradox shows is that we cannot consistently ascribe to any continuing being omnipotence in an inclusive sense.

An alternative solution of this paradox would be simply to deny that God is a continuing being, that any times can be assigned to his actions at all. But on this assumption (which also has difficulties of its own) no meaning can be given to the assertion that God made men with wills so free that he could not control them. The paradox of omnipotence can be avoided by putting God outside time, but the freewill solution of the problem of evil cannot be saved in this way, and equally it remains impossible to hold that an omnipotent God *binds himself* by causal or logical laws.

Conclusion

Of the proposed solutions of the problem of evil which we have examined, none has stood up to criticism. There may be other solutions which require examination, but this study strongly suggests that there is no valid solution of the problem which does not modify at least one of the constituent propositions in a way which would seriously affect the essential core of the theistic position.

Quite apart from the problem of evil, the paradox of omnipotence has shown that God's omnipotence must in any case be restricted in one way or another, that unqualified omnipotence cannot be ascribed to any being that continues through time. And if God and his actions are not in time, can omnipotence, or power of any sort, be meaningfully ascribed to him?

53

Why I Am Not A Christian

Bertrand Russell

As your Chairman has told you, the subject about which I am going to speak to you tonight is "Why I Am Not A Christian." Perhaps it would be as well, first of all, to try to make out what one means by the word "Christian." It is used in these days in a very loose sense by a great many people. Some people mean no more by it than a person who attempts to live a good life. In that sense I suppose there would be Christians in all sects and creeds; but I do not think that that is the proper sense of the word, if only because it would imply that all the people who are not Christians – all the Buddhists, Confucians, Mohammedans, and so on – are not trying to live a good life. I do not mean by a Christian any person who tries to live decently according to his lights. I think that you must have a certain amount of definite belief before you have a right to call yourself a Christian. The word does not have quite such a full-blooded meaning now as it had in the times of St. Augustine and St. Thomas Aquinas. In those days, if a man said that he was a Christian it was known what he meant. You accepted a whole collection of creeds which were set out with great precision, and every single syllable of those creeds you believed with the whole strength of your convictions.

What is a Christian?

Nowadays it is not quite that. We have to be a little more vague in our meaning of Christianity. I think, however, that there are two different items which are quite essential to anybody calling himself a Christian. The first is one of a dogmatic nature – namely, that you must believe in God and in immortality. If you do not believe in those two things, I do not think that you can properly call yourself a Christian. Then, further than that, as the name implies, you must have some kind of belief about Christ. The Mohammedans, for instance, also believe in God and in immortality, and yet they would not call themselves Christians. I think you must have at the very lowest the belief that Christ was, if not divine, at least the best and the wisest of men. If you are not going to believe that much about Christ, I do not think that you have any right to call yourself a Christian. Of course there is another sense which you find in *Whitaker's Almanack* and in geography books, where the population of the world is said to be divided into Christians, Mohammedans, Buddhists, fetish worshippers, and so on; and in that sense we are all Christians. The geography books count us all in, but that is

Bertrand Russell, "Why I Am Not A Christian," from *Bertrand Russell on God and Religion*, ed. Al Seckel (Buffalo, NY: Prometheus Books, 1986), pp. 57–71. © 1957, 1985 by George Allen & Unwin Ltd. All rights reserved. Reprinted with the permission of Simon & Schuster Adult Publishing Group, Taylor & Francis Books UK, and The Bertrand Russell Peace Foundation Ltd, from "Why I Am Not A Christian", by Bertrand Russell.

a purely geographical sense, which I suppose we can ignore. Therefore I take it that when I tell you why I am not a Christian I have to tell you two different things: first, why I do not believe in God and in immortality; and, secondly, why I do not think that Christ was the best and the wisest of men, although I grant him a very high degree of moral goodness.

But for the successful efforts of unbelievers in the past, I could not take so elastic a definition of Christianity as that. As I said before, in olden days it had a much more full-blooded sense. For instance, it included the belief in hell. Belief in eternal hell fire was an essential item of Christian belief until pretty recent times. In this country, as you know, it ceased to be an essential item because of a decision of the Privy Council, and from that decision the Archbishop of Canterbury and the Archbishop of York dissented; but in this country our religion is settled by Act of Parliament, and therefore the Privy Council was able to override their Graces, and hell was no longer necessary to a Christian. Consequently I shall not insist that a Christian must believe in hell.

The Existence of God

To come to this question of the existence of God, it is a large and serious question, and if I were to attempt to deal with it in any adequate manner I should have to keep you here until Kingdom Come, so that you will have to excuse me if I deal with it in a somewhat summary fashion. You know, of course, that the Catholic Church has laid it down as a dogma that the existence of God can be proved by the unaided reason. That is a somewhat curious dogma, but it is one of their dogmas. They had to introduce it because at one time the Freethinkers adopted the habit of saying that there were such and such arguments which mere reason might urge against the existence of God, but of course they knew as a matter of faith that God did exist. The arguments and the reasons were set out at great length, and the Catholic Church felt that they must stop it. Therefore they laid it down that the existence of God can be proved by the unaided reason, and they had to set up what they considered were arguments to prove it. There are, of course, a number of them, but I shall take only a few.

The first cause argument

Perhaps the simplest and easiest to understand is the argument of the First Cause. It is maintained that everything we see in this world has a cause, and as you go back in the chain of causes further and further you must come to a First Cause, and to that First Cause you give the name God. That argument, I suppose, does not carry very much weight nowadays, because, in the first place, cause is not quite what it used to be. The philosophers and the men of science have got going on cause, and it has not anything like the vitality that it used to have; but, apart from that, you can see that the argument that there must be a First Cause is one that cannot have any validity. I may say that when I was a young man, and was debating these questions very seriously in my mind, I for a long time accepted the argument of the First Cause, until one day, at the age of eighteen, I read John Stuart Mill's *Autobiography*, and I there found this sentence: "My father taught me that the question, Who made me? cannot be answered, since it immediately suggests the further question, Who made God?" That very simple sentence showed me, as I still think, the fallacy in the argument of the First Cause. If everything must have a cause, then God must have a cause. If there can be anything without a cause, it may just as well be the world as God, so that there cannot be any validity in that argument. It is exactly of the same nature as the Indian's view, that the world rested upon an elephant and the elephant rested upon a tortoise; and when they said, "How about the tortoise?" the Indian said, "Suppose we change the subject." The argument is really no better than that. There is no reason why the world could not have come into being without a cause; nor, on the other hand, is there any reason why it should not have always existed. There is no reason to suppose that the world had a beginning at all. The idea that things must have a beginning is really due to the poverty of our imagination. Therefore, perhaps, I need not waste any more time upon the argument about the First Cause.

The natural law argument

Then there is a very common argument from natural law. That was a favorite argument all through the eighteenth century, especially under the influence of Sir Isaac Newton and his cosmogony. People observed the planets going round the sun according to the law of gravitation, and they thought that God had given a behest to these planets to move in that particular fashion, and that was why they did so. That was, of course, a convenient and simple explanation that saved them the trouble of looking any further for explanations of the law of gravitation. Nowadays we explain the law of gravitation in a somewhat complicated fashion that Einstein has introduced. I do not propose to give you a lecture on the law of gravitation, as interpreted by Einstein, because that again would take some time; at any rate, you no longer have the sort of natural law that you had in the Newtonian system, where, for some reason that nobody could understand, nature behaved in a uniform fashion. We now find that a great many things that we thought were natural laws are really human conventions. You know that even in the remotest depths of stellar space there are still three feet to a yard. That is, no doubt, a very remarkable fact, but you would hardly call it a law of nature. And a great many things that have been regarded as laws of nature are of that kind. On the other hand, where you can get down to any knowledge of what atoms actually do, you find that they are much less subject to law than people thought, and that the laws at which you arrive are statistical averages of just the sort that would emerge from chance. There is, as we all know, a law that if you throw dice you will get double sixes only about once in thirty-six times, and we do not regard that as evidence that the fall of the dice is regulated by design; on the contrary, if the double sixes came every time we should think that there was design. The laws of nature are of that sort as regards a great many of them. They are statistical averages such as would emerge from the laws of chance; and that makes this whole business of natural law much less impressive than it formerly was. Quite apart from that, which represents the momentary state of science that may change tomorrow, the whole idea that natural laws imply a lawgiver is due to a confusion between natural and human laws. Human laws are behests commanding you to behave in a certain way, in which way you may choose to behave, or you may choose not to behave; but natural laws are a description of

how things do in fact behave, and, being a mere description of what they in fact do, you cannot argue that there must be somebody who told them to do that, because even supposing that there were you are then faced with the question, Why did God issue just those natural laws and no others? If you say that he did it simply from his own good pleasure, and without any reason, you then find that there is something which is not subject to law, and so your train of natural law is interrupted. If you say, as more orthodox theologians do, that in all the laws which God issued he had a reason for giving those laws rather than others – the reason, of course, being to create the best universe, although you would never think it to look at it – if there was a reason for the laws which God gave, then God himself was subject to law, and therefore you do not get any advantage by introducing God as an intermediary. You have really a law outside and anterior to the divine edicts, and God does not serve your purpose, because he is not the ultimate lawgiver. In short, this whole argument about natural law no longer has anything like the strength that it used to have. I am travelling on in time in my review of the arguments. The arguments that are used for the existence of God change their character as time goes on. They were at first hard intellectual arguments embodying certain quite definite fallacies. As we come to modern times they become less respectable intellectually and more and more affected by a kind of moralizing vagueness.

The argument from design

The next step in this process brings us to the argument from design. You all know the argument from design: everything in the world is made just so that we can manage to live in the world, and if the world was ever so little different we could not manage to live in it. That is the argument from design. It sometimes takes rather a curious form; for instance, it is argued that rabbits have white tails in order to be easy to shoot. I do not know how rabbits would view that application. It is an easy argument to parody. You all know Voltaire's remark, that obviously the nose was designed to be such as to fit spectacles. That sort of parody has turned out to be not nearly so wide of the mark as it might have seemed in the eighteenth century, because since the time of Darwin we understand much better why living creatures are adapted to their environment. It is not that their environment was made to be suitable to them, but that they grew to be suitable to it, and that is the basis of adaptation. There is no evidence of design about it.

When you come to look into this argument from design, it is a most astonishing thing that people can believe that this world, with all the things that are in it, with all its defects, should be the best that omnipotence and omniscience has been able to produce in millions of years. I really cannot believe it. Do you think that, if you were granted omnipotence and omniscience and millions of years in which to perfect your world, you could produce nothing better than the Ku Klux Klan, the Fascisti, and Mr. Winston Churchill?[1] Really I am not much impressed with the people who say: "Look at me: I am such a splendid product that there must have been design in the universe." I am not very much impressed by the splendor of those people. Therefore I think that this argument of design is really a very poor argument indeed. Moreover, if you accept the ordinary laws of science, you have to suppose that human life and life in general on this planet will die out in due course: it is merely a flash in the pan; it is a stage in the decay of the solar system; at a certain stage of decay you get the sort of conditions of temperature and so forth which are suitable to protoplasm, and there is life for a short time in the life of the whole solar system. You see in the moon the sort of thing to which the earth is tending – something dead, cold, and lifeless.

I am told that that sort of view is depressing, and people will sometimes tell you that if they believed that they would not be able to go on living. Do not believe it; it is all nonsense. Nobody really worries much about what is going to happen millions of years hence. Even if they think they are worrying much about that, they are really deceiving themselves. They are worried about something much more mundane, or it may merely be a bad digestion; but nobody is really seriously rendered unhappy by the thought of something that is going to happen to this world millions and millions of years hence. Therefore, although it is of course a gloomy view to suppose that life will die out – at least I suppose we may say so, although sometimes when I contemplate the things that people do with their lives I think

it is almost a consolation – it is not such as to render life miserable. It merely makes you turn your attention to other things.

The moral arguments for deity

Now we reach one stage further in what I shall call the intellectual descent that the Theists have made in their argumentations, and we come to what are called the moral arguments for the existence of God. You all know, of course, that there used to be in the old days three intellectual arguments for the existence of God, all of which were disposed of by Immanuel Kant in the *Critique of Pure Reason*; but no sooner had he disposed of those arguments than he invented a new one, a moral argument, and that quite convinced him. He was like many people: in intellectual matters he was skeptical, but in moral matters he believed implicitly in the maxims that he had imbibed at his mother's knee. That illustrates what the psychoanalysts so much emphasize – the immensely stronger hold upon us that our very early associations have than those of later times.

Kant, as I say, invented a new moral argument for the existence of God, and that in varying forms was extremely popular during the nineteenth century. It has all sorts of forms. One form is to say that there would be no right or wrong unless God existed. I am not for the moment concerned with whether there is a difference between right and wrong, or whether there is not: that is another question. The point I am concerned with is that, if you are quite sure there is a difference between right and wrong, you are then in this situation: Is that difference due to God's fiat or is it not? If it is due to God's fiat, then for God himself there is no difference between right and wrong, and it is no longer a significant statement to say that God is good. If you are going to say, as theologians do, that God is good, you must then say that right and wrong have some meaning which is independent of God's fiat, because God's fiats are good and not bad independently of the mere fact that he made them. If you are going to say that, you will then have to say that it is not only through God that right and wrong come into being, but that they are in their essence logically anterior to God. You could, of course, if you liked, say that there was a superior deity who gave orders to the God who made this world, or you could take up the line that some of the gnostics took up – a line which I often thought was a very plausible one – that as a matter of fact this world that we know was made by the devil at a moment when God was not looking. There is a good deal to be said for that, and I am not concerned to refute it.

The argument for the remedying of injustice

Then there is another very curious form of moral argument, which is this: they say that the existence of God is required in order to bring justice into the world. In the part of this universe that we know there is great injustice, and often the good suffer, and often the wicked prosper, and one hardly knows which of those is the more annoying; but if you are going to have justice in the universe as a whole you have to suppose a future life to redress the balance of life here on earth, and so they say that there must be a God, and there must be heaven and hell in order that in the long run there may be justice. That is a very curious argument. If you looked at the matter from a scientific point of view, you would say: "After all, I know only this world. I do not know about the rest of the universe, but so far as one can argue at all on probabilities one would say that probably this world is a fair sample, and if there is injustice here the odds are that there is injustice elsewhere also." Supposing you got a crate of oranges that you opened, and you found all the top layer of oranges bad, you would not argue: "The underneath ones must be good, so as to redress the balance." You would say: "Probably the whole lot is a bad consignment"; and that is really what a scientific person would argue about the universe. He would say: "Here we find in this world a great deal of injustice, and so far as that goes that is a reason for supposing that justice does not rule in the world; and therefore so far as it goes it affords a moral argument against a deity and not in favor of one." Of course I know that the sort of intellectual arguments that I have been talking to you about are not what really moves people. What really moves people to believe in God is not any intellectual argument at all. Most people believe in God because they have been taught from early infancy to do it, and that is the main reason.

Then I think that the next most powerful reason is the wish for safety, a sort of feeling that there is a big brother who will look after you. That plays a very profound part in influencing people's desire for a belief in God.

The Character of Christ

I now want to say a few words upon a topic which I often think is not quite sufficiently dealt with by Rationalists, and that is the question whether Christ was the best and the wisest of men. It is generally taken for granted that we should all agree that that was so. I do not myself. I think that there are a good many points upon which I agree with Christ a great deal more than the professing Christians do. I do not know that I could go with him all the way, but I could go with him much further than most professing Christians can. You will remember that he said: "Resist not evil, but whosoever shall smite thee on thy right cheek, turn to him the other also." That is not a new precept or a new principle. It was used by Lâo-Tse and Buddha some 500 or 600 years before Christ, but it is not a principle which as a matter of fact Christians accept. I have no doubt that the present Prime Minister, for instance, is a most sincere Christian, but I should not advise any of you to go and smite him on one cheek. I think that you might find that he thought this text was intended in a figurative sense.

Then there is another point which I consider is excellent. You will remember that Christ said: "Judge not lest ye be judged." That principle I do not think you would find was popular in the law courts of Christian countries. I have known in my time quite a number of judges who were very earnest Christians, and they none of them felt that they were acting contrary to Christian principles in what they did. Then Christ says: "Give to him that asketh of thee, and from him that would borrow of thee turn not thou away." That is a very good principle. Your Chairman has reminded you that we are not here to talk politics, but I cannot help observing that the last General Election was fought on the question of how desirable it was to turn away from him that would borrow of thee, so that one must assume that the Liberals and Conservatives of this country are composed of people who do not agree with the teaching of

Christ, because they certainly did very emphatically turn away on that occasion.

Then there is one other maxim of Christ which I think has a great deal in it, but I do not find that it is very popular among some of our Christian friends. He says: "If thou wilt be perfect, go and sell that which thou hast, and give to the poor." That is a very excellent maxim, but, as I say, it is not much practiced. All these, I think, are good maxims, although they are a little difficult to live up to. I do not profess to live up to them myself; but then, after all, I am not by way of doing so, and it is not quite the same thing as for a Christian.

Defects in Christ's Teaching

Having granted the excellence of these maxims, I come to certain points in which I do not believe that one can grant either the superlative wisdom or the superlative goodness of Christ as depicted in the Gospels; and here I may say that one is not concerned with the historical question. Historically it is quite doubtful whether Christ ever existed at all, and if he did we do not know anything about him, so that I am not concerned with the historical question, which is a very difficult one. I am concerned with Christ as he appears in the Gospels, taking the Gospel narrative as it stands, and there one does find some things that do not seem to be very wise. For one thing, he certainly thought that his second coming would occur in clouds of glory before the death of all the people who were living at that time. There are a great many texts that prove that. He says, for instance: "Ye shall not have gone over the cities of Israel till the Son of Man be come." Then he says: "There are some standing here which shall not taste death till the Son of Man come into his kingdom"; and there are a lot of places where it is quite clear that he believed that his second coming would happen during the lifetime of many then living. That was the belief of his earlier followers, and it was the basis of a good deal of his moral teaching. When he said, "Take no thought for the morrow," and things of that sort, it was very largely because he thought that the second coming was going to be very soon, and that all ordinary mundane affairs did not count. I have, as a matter of fact, known some Christians who did believe that the second coming was imminent. I knew a parson who frightened his congregation terribly by telling them that the second coming was very imminent indeed, but they were much consoled when they found that he was planting trees in his garden. The early Christians did really believe it, and they did abstain from such things as planting trees in their gardens, because they did accept from Christ the belief that the second coming was imminent. In that respect clearly he was not so wise as some other people have been, and he was certainly not superlatively wise.

The Moral Problem

Then you came to moral questions. There is one very serious defect to my mind in Christ's moral character, and that is that he believed in hell. I do not myself feel that any person who is really profoundly humane can believe in everlasting punishment. Christ certainly as depicted in the Gospels did believe in everlasting punishment, and one does find repeatedly a vindictive fury against those people who would not listen to his preaching – an attitude which is not uncommon with preachers, but which does somewhat detract from superlative excellence. You do not, for instance, find that attitude in Socrates. You find him quite bland and urbane towards the people who would not listen to him; and it is, to my mind, far more worthy of a sage to take that line than to take the line of indignation. You probably all remember the sort of things that Socrates was saying when he was dying, and the sort of things that he generally did say to people who did not agree with him.

You will find that in the Gospels Christ said: "Ye serpents, ye generation of vipers, how can ye escape the damnation of hell." That was said to people who did not like his preaching. It is not really to my mind quite the best tone, and there are a great many of these things about hell. There is, of course, the familiar text about the sin against the Holy Ghost: "Whosoever speaketh against the Holy Ghost it shall not be forgiven him neither in this world nor in the world to come." That text has caused an unspeakable amount of misery in the world, for all sorts of people have imagined that they have committed the sin against the Holy Ghost, and thought that it would not be forgiven them either in this world or in the world to come. I really do not think that a person with a proper degree of kindliness in his nature would have put fears and terrors of that sort into the world.

Then Christ says: "The Son of Man shall send forth his angels, and they shall gather out of his kingdom all things that offend, and them which do iniquity, and shall cast them into a furnace of fire; there shall be wailing and gnashing of teeth"; and he goes on about the wailing and gnashing of teeth. It comes in one verse after another, and it is quite manifest to the reader that there is a certain pleasure in contemplating wailing and gnashing of teeth, or else it would not occur so often. Then you all, of course, remember about the sheep and the goats; how at the second coming he is going to divide the sheep from the goats, and he is going to say to the goats: "Depart from me, ye cursed, into everlasting fire." He continues: "And these shall go away into everlasting fire." Then he says again: "If thy hand offend thee, cut it off; it is better for thee to enter into life maimed, than having two hands to go into hell, into the fire that never shall be quenched; where their worm dieth not and the fire is not quenched." He repeats that again and again also. I must say that I think all this doctrine, that hell fire is a punishment for sin, is a doctrine of cruelty. It is a doctrine that put cruelty into the world and gave the world generations of cruel torture; and the Christ of the Gospels, if you could take him as his chroniclers represent him, would certainly have to be considered partly responsible for that.

There are other things of less importance. There is the instance of the Gadarene swine, where it certainly was not very kind to the pigs to put the devils into them and make them rush down the hill to the sea. You must remember that he was omnipotent, and he could have made the devils simply go away; but he chooses to send them into the pigs. Then there is the curious story of the fig-tree, which always rather puzzled me. You remember what happened about the fig-tree. "He was hungry; and seeing a fig-tree afar off having leaves; he came if haply he might find anything thereon; and when he came to it he found nothing but leaves, for the time of figs was not yet. And Jesus answered and said unto it: 'No man eat fruit of thee hereafter for ever' . . . and Peter . . . saith unto him: 'Master, behold the fig-tree which thou cursedst is withered away.'" That is a very curious story, because it was not the right time of year for figs, and you really could not blame the tree. I cannot myself feel that either in the matter of wisdom or in the matter of virtue Christ stands quite as high as some other people known to history. I think I should put Buddha and Socrates above him in those respects.

The Emotional Factor

As I said before, I do not think that the real reason why people accept religion is anything to do with argumentation. They accept religion on emotional grounds. One is often told that it is a very wrong thing to attack religion, because religion makes men virtuous. So I am told; I have not noticed it. You know, of course, the parody of that argument in Samuel Butler's book, *Erewhon Revisited*. You will remember that in *Erewhon* there is a certain Higgs who arrives in a remote country, and after spending some time there he escapes from that country in a balloon. Twenty years later he comes back to that country and finds a new religion, in which he is worshipped under the name of the "Sun Child"; and it is said that he ascended into heaven. He finds that the Feast of the Ascension is about to be celebrated, and he hears Professors Hanky and Panky say to each other that they never set eyes on the man Higgs, and they hope they never will; but they are the high priests of the religion of the Sun Child. He is very indignant, and he comes up to them, and he says: "I am going to expose all this humbug and tell the people of Erewhon that it was only I, the man Higgs, and I went up in a balloon." He was told: "You must not do that, because all the morals of this country are bound round his myth, and if they once know that you did not ascend into heaven they will all become wicked"; and so he is persuaded of that, and he goes away quite quietly.

That is the idea – that we should all be wicked if we did not hold to the Christian religion. It seems to me that the people who have held to it have been for the most part extremely wicked. You find this curious fact, that the more intense has been the religion of any period and the more profound has been the dogmatic belief, the greater has been the cruelty and the worse has been the state of affiars. In the so-called ages of faith, when men really did believe the Christian religion in all its completeness, there was the Inquisition, with its tortures; there were millions of unfortunate women burnt as witches; and there was every kind of cruelty practiced upon all sorts of people in the name of religion.

You find as you look round the world that every single bit of progress in humane feeling, every improvement in the criminal law, every step towards the diminution of war, every step towards better treatment of the colored races, or every mitigation of slavery, every moral progress that there has been in the world, has been consistently opposed by the organized Churches of the world. I say quite deliberately that the Christian religion, as organized in its Churches, has been and still is the principal enemy of moral progress in the world.

How the Churches Have Retarded Progress

You may think that I am going too far when I say that that is still so. I do not think that I am. Take one fact. You will bear with me if I mention it. It is not a pleasant fact, but the Churches compel one to mention facts that are not pleasant. Supposing that in this world that we live in today an inexperienced girl is married to a syphilitic man, in that case the Catholic Church says: "This is an indissoluble sacrament. You must stay together for life," and no steps of any sort must be taken by that women to prevent herself from giving birth to syphilitic children. That is what the Catholic Church says. I say that that is fiendish cruelty, and nobody whose natural sympathies have not been warped by dogma, or whose moral nature was not absolutely dead to all sense of suffering, could maintain that it is right and proper that that state of things should continue.

That is only an example. There are a great many ways in which at the present moment the Church, by its insistence upon what it chooses to call morality, inflicts upon all sorts of people undeserved and unnecessary suffering. And of course, as we know, it is in its major part an opponent still of progress and of improvement in all the ways that diminish suffering in the world, because it has chosen to label as morality a certain narrow set of rules of conduct which have nothing to do with human happiness; and when you say that this or that ought to be done because it would make for human happiness, they think that has nothing to do with the matter at all. "What has human happiness to do with morals? The object of morals is not to make people happy. It is to fit them for heaven." It certainly seems to unfit them for this world.

Fear for the Foundation of Religion

Religion is based, I think, primarily and mainly upon fear. It is partly the terror of the unknown, and partly, as I have said, the wish to feel that you have a kind of elder brother who will stand by you in all your troubles and disputes. Fear is the basis of the whole thing – fear of the mysterious, fear of defeat, fear of death. Fear is the parent of cruelty, and therefore it is no wonder if cruelty and religion have gone hand-in-hand. It is because fear is at the basis of those two things. In this world we can now begin a little to understand things, and a little to master them by the help of science, which has forced its way step by step against the Christian religion, against the Churches, and against the opposition of all the old precepts. Science can help us to get over this craven fear in which mankind has lived for so many generations. Science can teach us, and I think our own hearts can teach us, no longer to look round for imaginary supports, no longer to invent allies in the sky, but rather to look to our own efforts here below to make this world a fit place to live in, instead of the sort of place that the Churches in all these centuries have made it.

What We Must Do

We want to stand upon our own feet and look fair and square at the world – its good facts, its bad facts, its beauties, and its ugliness; see the world as it is, and be not afraid of it. Conquer the world by intelligence, and not merely by being slavishly subdued by the terror that comes from it. The whole conception of God is a conception derived from the ancient Oriental despotisms. It is a conception quite unworthy of free men. When you hear people in church debasing themselves and saying that they are miserable sinners, and all the rest of it, it seems contemptible and not worthy of self-respecting human beings. We ought to stand up and look the world frankly in the face. We ought to make the best we can of the world, and if it is not so good as we wish, after all it will still be better than what these others have made of it in all these ages. A good world needs knowledge, kindliness, and courage; it does not need a regretful hankering after the past, or a fettering of the free intelligence by the words uttered long ago by ignorant men. It needs a fearless outlook and a free intelligence. It needs hope for the future, not looking back all the time towards a past that is dead, which we trust will be far surpassed by the future that our intelligence can create.

Note

1   Russell removed Winston Churchill's name from all later editions of this essay.

Questions for Discussion

1 Could one accept the argument from design and think of the designer(s) as like the Gods portrayed in *Jason and the Argonauts*? Is there any reason to choose a hypothesis that posits a single designer over one that posits several different designers? Perhaps there was a contest between designers (with the verdict on the winning entry still out).

2 On the assumption that the fallen angels portrayed in *Dogma* were genuinely repentant (a dubious assumption perhaps), should a perfect being forgive them and let them back into heaven? Can one even make a rational judgment about what a perfect being would or should do?

3 Can one reconcile the plot of *Dogma* with the hypothesis that God is perfect?

4 Was there a decisive indication in *Star Trek V* that the powerful being they discovered was not the God for whom they were searching? What further evidence might they have discovered that would have confirmed that they had indeed found God?

5 If you were God, could you think of a way of allowing humans free will while insuring that no evil to innocents occurs?

6 If you were God, would you conclude that free will was so valuable that it was worth insuring even at the expense of great suffering?

7 If you were God and were creating a world from scratch, how would you have made the world different? Could you succeed in creating a world so good that there couldn't be a better one?

8 Could the Gods of *Jason and the Argonauts* have interfered more with the outcome of the quest, while still allowing humans genuine freedom? How much interference with an individual's life is compatible with that individual's being free? Does the society within which we live, and the natural world in which we live, allow us a robust sort of freedom?

9 Can one rationally take out the sort of insurance that Pascal suggests? Would the attempt to follow Pascal's advice have been successful in achieving the obvious goal if the God or Gods depicted in *Jason and the Argonauts* or *Dogma* exist? What would your chances of success be if God were really like Mr Deity?

10 Many people presuppose that the existence of God is relevant to how they ought to act. What must be true of God for this to be the case?

11 In chapter 18 and chapter 28 of *Dogma*, Rufus and Serendipity claim that it is preferable to have an idea of God rather than a belief in God. Have you any idea what they are talking about?

12 How would you respond to the suggestion made in the movie *Dogma* that a perfect being would forgive Loci and Bartleby if they were truly repentant?